THE VALMIKI RAMAYANA 1

Translated by Bibek Debroy

PENGUIN BOOKS
An imprint of Penguin Random House

PENGUIN BOOKS

USA | Canada | UK | Ireland | Australia
New Zealand | India | South Africa | China

Penguin Books is part of the Penguin Random House group of companies whose addresses can be found at global.penguinrandomhouse.com

Published by Penguin Random House India Pvt. Ltd
7th Floor, Infinity Tower C, DLF Cyber City,
Gurgaon 122 002, Haryana, India

First published in Penguin Books by Penguin Random House India 2017

10 9 8 7 6 5 4

ISBN 9780143428046

Typeset in Sabon by Manipal Digital Systems, Manipal
Printed at Replika Press Pvt. Ltd, India

www.penguin.co.in

PENGUIN BOOKS

THE VALMIKI RAMAYANA VOLUME 1

Bibek Debroy is a renowned economist, scholar and translator. He has worked in universities, research institutes, industry and for the government. He has widely published books, papers and articles on economics. As a translator, he is best known for his magnificent rendition of the Mahabharata in ten volumes, and additionally the *Harivamsha*, published to wide acclaim by Penguin Classics. He is also the author of *Sarama and Her Children*, which splices his interest in Hinduism with his love for dogs.

PRAISE FOR *THE MAHABHARATA*

'The modernization of language is visible, it's easier on the mind, through expressions that are somewhat familiar. The detailing of the story is intact, the varying tempo maintained, with no deviations from the original. The short introduction reflects a brilliant mind. For those who passionately love the Mahabharata and want to explore it to its depths, Debroy's translation offers great promise . . .'—*Hindustan Times*

'[Debroy] has really carved out a niche for himself in crafting and presenting a translation of the Mahabharata . . . The book takes us on a great journey with admirable ease'—*Indian Express*

'The first thing that appeals to one is the simplicity with which Debroy has been able to express himself and infuse the right kind of meanings . . . Considering that Sanskrit is not the simplest of languages to translate a text from, Debroy exhibits his deep understanding and appreciation of the medium'—*The Hindu*

'Debroy's lucid and nuanced retelling of the original makes the masterpiece even more enjoyably accessible'—*Open*

'The quality of translation is excellent. The lucid language makes it a pleasure to read the various stories, digressions and parables'—*Tribune*

'Extremely well-organized, and has a substantial and helpful Introduction, plot summaries and notes. The volume is a beautiful example of a well thought-out layout which makes for much easier reading'—*Book Review*

'The dispassionate vision [Debroy] brings to this endeavour will surely earn him merit in the three worlds'—*Mail Today*

'Debroy's is not the only English translation available in the market, but where he scores and others fail is that his is the closest rendering of the original text in modern English without unduly complicating the readers' understanding of the epic'—*Business Standard*

'The brilliance of Ved Vyasa comes through, ably translated by Bibek Debroy'—*Hindustan Times*

For Professor Shailendra Raj Mehta

Contents

Acknowledgements

This journey, with Penguin, started more than a decade ago. It is a journey of translating Sanskrit texts into English, in unabridged form. It commenced with the Bhagavad Gita in 2006, followed by the Mahabharata (2010 to 2014) and the Harivamsha (2016). It continues with the Valmiki Ramayana and will be followed by the Puranas. To the best of my knowledge, the great translator, Manmatha Nath Dutt (1855–1912), is the only other person who has accomplished the 'double' of unabridged translations of both the Valmiki Ramayana and the Mahabharata in English. In this journey with Penguin, special thanks to Meru Gokhale, Ambar Sahil Chatterjee and Paloma Dutta. All three have made this journey easier to traverse.

My wife, Suparna Banerjee (Debroy), has not only been *patni*, she has been *grihini* and *sahadharmini* too. Had she not provided an enabling and conducive environment, juggling professional commitments and carving out the time required for translating would have been impossible. यः तया सह स स्वर्गो निरयो यस्त्वया विना (2.27.16).

This translation is based on the Critical Edition brought out (between 1951 and 1975) by the Oriental Institute, now part of Maharaja Sayajirao University, Baroda. When I started work on translating the Mahabharata in 2009, there was a thought, however hazy, of attempting the Valmiki Ramayana too. Therefore, one had to acquire the seven published volumes of the Critical Edition. Those who have tried this acquisition will testify this is no mean task. Multiple channels and multiple efforts failed. The Oriental Institute is not known for its marketing and distribution successes.

The context changed in 2015, because I joined the government. By then, I had still not been able to get copies of the Critical Edition. What with joining the government, which made finding time difficult, and an inability to get the text, I remarked to my wife that destiny willed otherwise. A few months later, on a flight, I found myself seated next to Shailendra Mehta, economist, scholar, friend, and currently president, director and distinguished professor at MICA, Ahmedabad. 'What next, after the Mahabharata?' asked Shailendra and I described my frustration. A few weeks down the line, Shailendra Mehta walked into my office, lugging a trolley bag, with all seven volumes in them. 'All yours,' he said. What destiny willed was clear enough. The dedication of this three volume set to Shailendra is a paltry attempt to say thank you.

'What next, after the Valmiki Ramayana?' Life moves on to the Puranas, beginning with the Bhagavata Purana. At one point, the Mahabharata translation seemed like a mammoth task, stretching to infinity. With the major Puranas collectively amounting to four times the size of the Mahabharata, they are more monumental than the mammoth. But as always, if it so wills, destiny finds a way.

Introduction

The Ramayana and the Mahabharata are known as *itihasas*. The word itihasa means 'it was indeed like that'. Therefore, the word is best rendered as legend or history, and not as myth. This does not mean everything occurred exactly as described. In a process of telling and retelling and oral transmission, embellishments are inevitable. However, the use of the word itihasa suggests a core element of truth. There were two great dynasties—*surya vamsha* and *chandra vamsha*.[1] The first proper king of the surya vamsha was Ikshvaku and the Ramayana is a chronicle of the solar dynasty, or at least a part of its history. Similarly, the first king of the chandra vamsha was Ila and the Mahabharata is a chronicle of the lunar dynasty. The Puranas also describe the histories of the solar and lunar dynasties. Though there are some inconsistencies across genealogies given in different Puranas, the surya vamsha timeline has three broad segments: (1) from Ikshvaku to Rama; (2) from Kusha to Brihadbala; and (3) from Brihadbala to Sumitra. In that stretch from Ikshvaku to Rama, there were famous kings like Bharata (not to be confused with Rama's brother), Kakutstha, Prithu, Yuvanashva, Mandhata, Trishanku, Harishchandra, Sagara, Dilipa, Bhagiratha, Ambarisha, Raghu, Aja and Dasharatha. These ancestors explain why Rama is referred to as Kakutstha, Raghava or Dasharathi.

Rama had two sons—Lava and Kusha. Ikshvaku and his descendants ruled over the kingdom of Kosala, part of today's Uttar Pradesh. The Kosala kingdom lasted for a long time, with

[1] The solar and the lunar dynasty, respectively.

the capital sometimes in Ayodhya and sometimes in Shravasti. When Rama ruled, the capital was in Ayodhya. After Rama, Lava ruled over south Kosala and Kusha ruled over north Kosala. Lava's capital was in Shravasti, while Kusha's capital was in Kushavati. We don't know what happened to Lava thereafter, though he is believed to have established Lavapuri, today's Lahore. The second segment of the surya vamsha timeline, from Kusha to Brihadbala, doesn't have any famous kings. Brihadbala was the last Kosala king. In the Kurukshetra War, he fought on the side of the Kouravas and was killed by Abhimanyu. The third segment of the surya vamsha timeline, from Brihadbala to Sumitra, seems contrived and concocted. Sumitra is described as the last king of the Ikshvaku lineage, defeated by Mahapadma Nanda in 362 BCE. Sumitra wasn't killed. He fled to Rohtas, in today's Bihar.

The Ramayana isn't about these subsequent segments of the timeline. Though there are references to other kings from that Ikshvaku to Rama stretch, it isn't about all of that segment either. Its focus is on Rama. It is difficult to date the poet Kalidasa. It could be anytime from the first century CE to the fifth century CE. Kalidasa wrote a *mahakavya*[2] known as *Raghuvamsha*. As the name of this mahakavya suggests, it is about Raghu's lineage, from Dilipa to Agnivarna, and includes Rama. But it isn't exclusively about Rama. Ramayana is almost exclusively about Rama. That's the reason it is known as रामायण = राम + अयण. अयन means travel or progress. Thus, Ramayana means Rama's progress. There is a minor catch though. अयन means travel or progress and अयण is a meaningless word. The word used in Ramayana is अयण, not अयन. This transformation occurs because of a rule of Sanskrit grammar known as internal *sandhi*. That is the reason रामायन becomes रामायण.

Who is Rama? The word राम means someone who is lovely, charming and delightful. There are Jain and Buddhist versions (*Dasharatha Jataka*) of the Rama account and they differ in significant details from the Ramayana story. For instance, in Jain accounts, Ravana is killed by Lakshmana. In *Dasharatha Jataka*,

[2] Epic.

Sita is Rama's sister. In Ramayana and Purana accounts, Rama is Vishnu's seventh *avatara*.[3] Usually, ten avataras are named for Vishnu, though sometimes, a larger number is also given. When the figure is ten, the avataras are *matsya*,[4] *kurma*,[5] *varaha*,[6] *narasimha*,[7] *vamana*,[8] Parashurama, Rama, Krishna, Buddha and Kalki (Kalki is yet to come). In the cycle of creation and destruction, *yugas*[9] follow each other and one progressively goes down *krita yuga* (alternatively *satya yuga*), *treta yuga*, *dvapara yuga* and *kali yuga*, before the cycle starts again. In the list of ten avataras, matysa, kurma, varaha and narasimha are from the present krita yuga; Vamana, Parashurama and Rama are from the present treta yuga; Krishna is from dvapara yuga; and Buddha and Kalki are from kali yuga. Rama was towards the end of treta yuga. (In the 'Uttara Kanda', dvapara yuga has started.) Just as Krishna's departure marked the transition from dvapara yuga to kali yuga, Rama's departure marked the transition from treta yuga to dvapara yuga.

When did these events occur? It is impossible to answer this question satisfactorily, despite continuous efforts being made to find an answer. At one level, it is an irrelevant question too. There is a difference between an incident happening and it being recorded. In that day and age, recording meant composition and oral transmission, with embellishments added. There was noise associated with transmission and distribution. It is impossible to unbundle the various layers in the text, composed at different points in time. Valmiki is described as Rama's contemporary, just as Vedavyasa was a contemporary of the Kouravas and the Pandavas. But that doesn't mean today's Valmiki Ramayana text is exactly what Valmiki composed, or that today's Mahabharata text

[3] Incarnation, or descent.
[4] Fish.
[5] Turtle.
[6] Boar.
[7] Half-man, half-lion.
[8] Dwarf.
[9] Eras.

is exactly what Krishna Dvaipayana Vedavyasa composed. Therein lies the problem with several approaches to dating.

The first and favoured method of dating is undoubtedly the astronomical one, based on positions of *nakshatra*s and *graha*s,[10] or using information about events like eclipses. However, because layers of the text were composed at different points in time, compounded by precession of the equinoxes, this leads to widely divergent dates for an event like Rama's birth, ranging from 7323 BCE to 1331 BCE. Second, one can work with genealogies, notwithstanding problems of inconsistencies across them. One will then obtain a range of something like 2350 BCE to 1500 BCE. Third, one can work with linguistics and the evolution of language, comparing that of the Ramayana to other texts. Fourth, one can work with the archaeological evidence, such as the pottery discovered in sites known to be associated with the Ramayana. Even then, there will be a wide range of dates, from something like 2600 BCE to 1100 BCE. Fifth, one can consider geography, geology, changes in the course of rivers. Finally, there are traditional views about the length of a *manvantara*[11] or yuga. Given the present state of knowledge, it is impossible to impart precision to any dating of the incidents in the Ramayana. Scholars have grappled with the problem in the past and will continue to do so in the future. This may be an important question. But from the point of view of the present translation, it is an irrelevant one.

The present translation is about the Ramayana text. But what is the Ramayana text? After a famous essay written by A.K. Ramanujan in 1987 (published in 1991), people often mention 300 Ramayanas. It is impossible to fix the number, 300 or otherwise, since it is not possible to count satisfactorily—or even define—what is a new rendering of the Ramayana story, as opposed to a simple retelling, with or without reinterpretation. Contemporary versions, not always in written form, are continuously being rendered. There are versions of the Ramayana story in East Asia (China, Japan),

[10] Constellations/stars and planets.

[11] Lifespan of a Manu.

South-East Asia (many countries like Thailand, Indonesia and Malaysia), South Asia (Nepal, Sri Lanka) and West Asia (Iran). As mentioned earlier, there are Buddhist and Jain versions. Every state and every language in India seems to have some version of the Rama story. Our impressions about the Rama story are often based on such regional versions, such as, the sixteenth-century *Ramcharitmanas* by Goswami Tulsidas. (Many of these were written between the twelfth and seventeenth centuries CE.) Those depictions can, and will, vary with what is in this translation. This translation is about the Sanskrit Ramayana. But even there, more than one text of the Sanskrit Ramayana exists—Valmiki Ramayana, Yoga Vasishtha Ramayana, Ananda Ramayana and Adbhuta Ramayana. In addition, there are versions of the Ramayana story in the Mahabharata and in the Puranas. With the exception of the Ramayana story in the Mahabharata, the Valmiki Ramayana is clearly the oldest among these. This is a translation of the Valmiki Ramayana and yes, there are differences between depictions in the Valmiki Ramayana and other Sanskrit renderings of the Rama story.

If one cannot date the incidents of the Ramayana, can one at least conclusively date when the Valmiki Ramayana was written? Because of the many layers and subsequent interpolations, there is no satisfactory resolution to this problem either. The Valmiki Ramayana has around 24,000 *shloka*s, a shloka being a verse. The Mahabharata is believed to have 100,000 shlokas, so the Valmiki Ramayana is about one-fourth the size of the Mahabharata. These 24,000 shlokas are distributed across seven *kanda*s—'Bala Kanda' (Book about Youth), 'Ayodhya Kanda' (Book about Ayodhya), 'Aranya Kanda' (Book of the Forest), Kishkindha Kanda (Book about Kishkindha), 'Sundara Kanda' (Book of Beauty), 'Yuddha Kanda' (Book about the War) and 'Uttara Kanda' (Book about the Sequel). Kanda refers to a major section or segment and is sometimes translated into English as Canto. 'Canto' sounds archaic, 'Book' is so much better. This does not mean the kanda-wise classification always existed. For all one knows, initially, there were simply chapters. In this text itself, there is a reference to the Valmiki Ramayana possessing 500 *sarga*s. The

word sarga also means Book, but given the number 500, is more like a chapter. (For the record, the text has more than 600 chapters.) Most scholars agree 'Uttara Kanda' was written much later. If one reads the 'Uttara Kanda', that belief is instantly endorsed. The 'Uttara Kanda' doesn't belong. This isn't only because of the content, which is invariably mentioned. It is also because of the texture of the text, the quality of the poetry. It is vastly inferior. To a lesser extent, one can also advance similar arguments for the 'Bala Kanda'. Therefore, the earlier portions were probably composed around 500 BCE. The later sections, like the 'Uttara Kanda', and parts of the 'Bala Kanda', were probably composed around 500 CE. It isn't the case that all later sections are in 'Uttara Kanda'.

There is a mix of earlier and later sections across all kandas. The word kanda also means trunk or branch of a tree. The Mahabharata is also classified into such major sections or Books. However, in the Mahabharata, these major sections are known as *parvas*. The word parva also means branch. However, parva suggests a smaller branch, one that is more flexible. Kanda suggests one that is more solid, less flexible. There may have been slight variations in shlokas across different versions of the Sanskrit Mahabharata, but fundamentally the Sanskrit Mahabharata is a single text. The original text expanded, like a holdall, to include everything. Those different versions have been 'unified' in a Critical Edition published by the Bhandarkar Oriental Research Institute, Poona (Pune). In the case of the Valmiki Ramayana, with its kanda-kind of classification, the evolution seems to have been different. If someone was unhappy with what Valmiki had depicted, he simply composed another Ramayana. In Sanskrit, mention has already been made of the Yoga Vasishtha Ramayana, Ananda Ramayana and Adbhuta Ramayana. This continued to happen with vernacular versions.

This translation is of the Valmiki Ramayana. It is necessary to stress this point. Both the Ramayana and the Mahabharata are so popular that one is familiar with people, stories and incidents. That doesn't necessarily mean those people, stories and incidents occur in the Valmiki Ramayana in the way we are familiar with them. Just as the Bhandarkar Oriental Research Institute produced a Critical

Edition of the Mahabharata, between 1951 and 1975, the Oriental Institute, Baroda, produced a Critical Edition of the Valmiki Ramayana. This translation is based on that Critical Edition, published sequentially between 1958 and 1975. Producing a Critical Edition meant sifting through a large number of manuscripts of the Valmiki Ramayana. The editors had around 2000 manuscripts to work with. Not all of these were equally reliable. Therefore, in practice, they worked with fifty to hundred manuscripts, the specific number depending on the kanda in question. It is not that there were significant differences across the manuscripts and broadly, there was a Southern Recension (version) and a Northern one, the latter sub-divided into a North-Western and a North-Eastern one. The earliest of these written manuscripts dates to the eleventh century CE. In passing, the language may have been Sanskrit, but the script wasn't always Devanagari. There were scripts like Sharada, Mewari, Maithili, Bengali, Telugu, Kannada, Nandinagari, Grantha and Malayalam. Since this translation is based on the Baroda Critical Edition, it is necessary to make another obvious point. Even within the Sanskrit Valmiki Ramayana, not everything we are familiar with is included in the Critical text. For instance, the configuration of nakshatras and planets at the time of Rama's birth is not part of the Critical text. Nor is the bulk of one of the most beautiful sections of the Valmiki Ramayana, Mandodari's lamentation. Those are shlokas that have been excised. That's also the case with a shloka that's often quoted as an illustration of Lakshmana's conduct. नाहं जानामि केयूरं नाहं जानामि कुण्डलं। नूपुरं तु अभिजानामि नित्यं पादाभिवन्दनात॥ This is a statement by Lakshmana to the effect that he cannot recognize the ornament on Sita's head or her earrings. Since he has always served at her feet, he can only recognize her anklets. This too has been excised. There are instances where such excision has led to a break in continuity and inconsistency and we have pointed them out in the footnotes.

There are two numbers associated with every chapter. The first number refers to the kanda, while the second number, within brackets, refers to the number of the chapter (sarga) within that kanda. Thus, Chapter 1(33) will mean the thirty-third chapter in

'Bala Kanda'. The table below shows the number of chapters and shlokas we have in the Critical Edition. The Critical text has 606 chapters, 106 more than the 500 sargas mentioned in the text itself. And there are 18,670 shlokas. If one considers chapters and shlokas from non-Critical versions, irrespective of which version it is, there are almost 650 chapters and just over 24,000 shlokas. Compared to such non-Critical versions, very few chapters have been excised from 'Bala', 'Ayodhya', 'Aranya', 'Kishkindha' or 'Sundara' kandas. The excision is primarily from 'Yuddha' and 'Uttara' kandas. The excision of shlokas is uniformly spread throughout the kandas, though most excision, relatively speaking, is from the 'Ayodhya', 'Yuddha' and 'Uttara' kandas.

Name of kanda	*Number of chapters*	*Number of shlokas*
Bala Kanda	76	1941
Ayodhya Kanda	111	3160
Aranya Kanda	71	2060
Kishkindha Kanda	66	1898
Sundara Kanda	66	2487
Yuddha Kanda	116	4435
Uttara Kanda	100	2689
Total	606	18,670

Valmiki is the first poet, *adi kavi*. By the time of classical Sanskrit literature, some prerequisites were defined for a work to attain the status of mahakavya. Kalidasa, Bharavi, Magha, Shri Harsha and Bhatti composed such works. Though these notions and definitions came later, the Valmiki Ramayana displays every characteristic of a mahakavya and is longer than any of these subsequent works. The story of how it came about is known to most people who are familiar with the Ramayana. The sage Valmiki had gone, with his disciple Bharadvaja, to bathe in the waters of the River Tamasa. There was a couple of *krouncha*[12] birds there, in the act of making

[12] Curlew.

love. Along came a hunter[13] and killed the male bird. As the female bird grieved, Valmiki was driven by compassion and the first shloka emerged from his lips. Since it was composed in an act of sorrow—*shoka*—this kind of composition came to be known as shloka. So the Ramayana tells us. Incidentally, this first shloka doesn't occur in the first chapter. It isn't the first shloka of the Valmiki Ramayana. The incident and the shloka occur in the second chapter. More specifically, it is the fourteenth shloka in the second chapter and is as follows. मा निषाद प्रतिष्ठां त्वमगमः शाश्वतीः समाः। यत्क्रौंचमिथुनादेकमवधी काममोहितम् ॥ 'O nishada! This couple of curlews was in the throes of passion and you killed one of them. Therefore, you will possess ill repute for an eternal number of years.'

Till a certain period of history, all Sanskrit works were in poetry or verse, not in prose. The Vedangas are limbs or auxiliaries and the six Vedangas are *shiksha*,[14] *chhanda*,[15] *vyakarana*,[16] *nirukta*,[17] *jyotisha*[18] and *kalpa*.[19] These are needed to understand not just the Vedas, but also Sanskrit works. Chhanda is one of these. Chhanda can be translated as metre and means something that is pleasing and delightful. Chhanda *shastra* is the study of metres or prosody. Sanskrit poetry wasn't about what we tend to identify as poetry today, the act of rhyming. Chhanda begins with the concept of *akshara*, akin to, but not exactly identical with, the English concept of syllable, that is, part of a word with a single vowel sound. Other than possessing a single vowel sound, an akshara must not begin with a vowel. Aksharas can be *hrasva* or *laghu*—light or L—and *guru*—heavy or G. Simply stated, with a short vowel, the akshara is L and with a long vowel, the akshara is G. There are some additional conditions, but we needn't get into those. Every verse consists of four *pada*s, the word pada meaning one quarter. Depending on how

[13] *Nishada*.
[14] Articulation and pronunciation.
[15] Prosody.
[16] Grammar.
[17] Etymology.
[18] Astronomy.
[19] Rituals.

many aksharas there are in a pada and the distribution of those aksharas into L and G, there were a variety of metres. Depending on the subject and the mood, the poet consciously chose a metre. Analysing in this way, there were more than 1300 different metres. One of the most popular was *anushtubh*. This figures prominently in the Valmiki Ramayana, the Mahabharata and the Puranas. The anushtubh structure meant eight aksharas in each pada, with a total of thirty-two aksharas. In addition, for anushtubh, in every pada, the fifth akshara would have to be L and the sixth akshara would have to be G. In classical Sanskrit literature, conditions were also applied to the seventh akshara, but such refinements came later. For that first verse, the decomposition runs as follows: (1) L L L G L G L G; (2) L G L G L G L G; (3) L L G G L G G L; (4) G G L L L G G L. (1) *ma ni sha da pra tish tham*; (2) *tva ma ga mah shash vati sa mah*; (3) *yat kroun cha mi thu na de ka*; (4) *ma va dhi ka ma mo hi tam*. It is not that Valmiki only used anushtubh. There are actually sixteen different metres in the Valmiki Ramayana.

It is impossible to capture the beauty of chhanda in an English translation. One can attempt to do a translation in verse, but it will fail to convey the beauty. If the original text is poetry, one starts with an initial question. Should one attempt a translation in verse or in prose? This translation is based on the premise that the translation should be as close as possible to the original Sanskrit text. One should not take liberties with the text. This translation is therefore almost a word-to-word rendering. If one sits down with the original Sanskrit, there will be almost a perfect match. In the process, deliberately so, the English is not as smooth as it might have been, had one taken more liberties, and this is a conscious decision. Had one attempted a translation in verse, one would perforce have had to take more liberties. Hence, the choice of prose is also a deliberate decision. As composers, there is quite a contrast between Valmiki and Vedavyasa. Vedavyasa focuses on people and incidents. Rarely does the Mahabharata attempt to describe nature, even if those sections are on geography. In contrast, Valmiki's descriptions of nature are lyrical and superlative, similar to Kalidasa. A translation can never hope to transmit that flavour. There is no substitute to

reading the original Sanskrit, more so for the Valmiki Ramayana than for the Mahabharata.

Which occurred earlier, the incidents of the Ramayana or the Mahabharata? Which was composed earlier, the Ramayana or the Mahabharata? The Ramayana incidents occurred in treta yuga, the Mahabharata incidents in dvapara yuga. Rama was an earlier avatara, Krishna a later one. Hence, the obvious deduction is that the Ramayana incidents predated those of the Mahabharata—an inference also bolstered by the genealogy and astrological arguments mentioned earlier. However, and not just for the sake of being perverse, consider the following. Geographically, the incidents of the Mahabharata mostly occur along an east–west axis, along either side of what used to be called Uttarapath, the northern road, more familiar as Grand Trunk Road or National Highway (NH) 1 and 2. The incidents of the Ramayana often occur along a north–south axis, along what used to be called Dakshinapath, the southern road. Sanjeev Sanyal[20] has made the point that while Uttarapath remained stable over time, the Dakshinapath during Rama's time was different from the subsequent Dakshinapath, with the latter more like today's NH 44. To return to the point, the geographical terrain of the Mahabharata was restricted to the northern parts of the country, with the south rarely mentioned. The Aryan invasion theory has been discredited because of a multitude of reasons, but myths and perceptions that have lasted for decades are difficult to dispel. However, regardless of the Aryan invasion theory, the Ramayana reveals a familiarity with the geography of the southern parts of the country that the Mahabharata does not. The fighting in the Mahabharata, in the Kurukshetra War, is cruder and less refined. In the Ramayana, bears and apes may have fought using trees and boulders, but humans did not. A human did not tear apart another human's chest and drink blood. The urbanization depicted in the Ramayana is rarely found in the Mahabharata. We have cited these counter-arguments to make a simple point. Which incident

[20] *Land of the Seven Rivers: A Brief History of India's Geography*, Sanjeev Sanyal, Penguin, 2012.

occurred earlier and which text was composed earlier are distinct questions. They should not be confused. Even if the Ramayana incidents occurred before the incidents of the Mahabharata, that doesn't automatically mean the Ramayana was composed before the Mahabharata. The Rama story occurs in the Mahabharata, known as the 'Ramopakhyana' section. There is no such reference to the Mahabharata incidents in the Ramayana. This is the main reason for arguing that the Ramayana was composed before the Mahabharata.

The relationship between the 'Ramopakhyana' and the Valmiki Ramayana is also of scholarly interest. Which was earlier? Did one borrow from the other, or did both have a common origin? That need not concern us. What should be stressed is the obvious—the Valmiki Ramayana wasn't composed at a single point in time and there is a difference between the original composition and the present text, as given to us say in the Critical Edition. If bears and apes fought with the help of trees and boulders, and Angada suddenly kills someone with a weapon, that part is probably a later composition, with the composer having deviated from the original template. If a verse is in anushtubh, but deviates from the L–G pattern, this may have been a conscious decision, but in all probability, reflects the inferior skills of a subsequent poet. If we take the Critical text as it stands, while there are no direct references to the incidents of the Mahabharata, there are plenty of indirect allusions. There are shlokas reminiscent of the Bhagavatgita. When Bharata comes to Rama to inform him about Dasharatha's death, Rama asks him about the welfare of the kingdom, reminiscent of similar questions asked by Narada to Yudhishthira. In the Valmiki Ramayana, there are references to kings of the lunar dynasty (Yayati) and incidents (Ilvala and Vatapi) that are only described in the Mahabharata. The evidence may be circumstantial and speculative, but it is the following. It is as if the later composers knew about the Mahabharata incidents and the text, but consciously avoided any direct references.

Why is another translation of the Valmiki Ramayana needed? Surely, there are plenty floating around. That's not quite true. Indeed, there are several translations of the Valmiki Ramayana,

including some recent ones, but they are abridged. In any act of abridgement, some sections are omitted or summarized. Abridged translations, no matter how good they are, are not quite a substitute for unabridged translations, which bring in the nuances too. To the best of my knowledge, the list of unabridged translations of the Valmiki Ramayana is the following: (1) Ralph T.H. Griffith;[21] (2) Manmatha Nath Dutt;[22] (3) Hari Prasad Shastri;[23] (4) Desiraju Hanumanta Rao and K.M.K. Murthy;[24] and (5) Robert P. Goldman.[25] Given the timelines, the Goldman translation is the only one based on the Critical Edition. Having translated the Mahabharata,[26] it was natural to translate the Valmiki Ramayana. The intention was to do a translation that was popular in style. That meant a conscious decision to avoid the use of diacritical marks, as would have been the case had one used IAST (International Alphabet of Sanskrit Transliteration). If diacritical marks are not going to be used, there may be problems rendering names, proper and geographic. We have sought to make the English renderings as phonetic as is possible. Thus, we use 'Goutama' to refer to the sage of that name—although others have often referred to him elsewhere as 'Gautama'. We have chosen Goutama on the logic that if Gomati is not Gamati, why should Goutama be rendered as Gautama? There remains the question of what one does with vowel sounds. How does one differentiate the short sound from the long? Should Rama be written as Raama and Sita as Seeta? That seemed to be too artificial and contrary to popular usage. On rare occasions, this does

[21] *The Ramayana of Valmiki, translated into English verse,* Ralph T.H. Griffith, E.Z. Lazarus and Company, London, 1895.

[22] *Valmiki Ramayana,* Manmatha Nath Dutt, R.K. Bhatia, Calcutta, 1891–92. Manmatha Nath Dutt (Shastri) was one of India's greatest translators (in English). He also translated the Mahabharata and several Puranas.

[23] *The Ramayana of Valmiki,* Hari Prasad Shastri, Shanti Sadan, London, 1952.

[24] This is net based, on the site http://www.valmikiramayan.net/ and leaves out 'Uttara Kanda'.

[25] *The Ramayana of Valmiki: An Epic of Ancient India,* Robert P. Goldman, Princeton University Press, 1984 to 2016.

[26] *The Mahabharata,* Bibek Debroy, Penguin (India), 10 volumes, 2010–2014, boxed set 2015.

cause a problem, with a danger of confusion between the ape Taara and his daughter Taaraa, Vali's wife. Such occasions are however rare and we have explained them. However, there are also instances where we have deviated from popular usage. Hanumat is a case in point, where Hanuman seemed to be too contrary to grammatical principles. There are some words that defy translation, *dharma* is an example. Hence, we have not even tried to translate such words. The Goldman translation is academic in style. This translation's style is more popular. Therefore, there is no attempt to overburden the reader with extensive notes. However, a straight translation may not be self-explanatory. Hence, we have put in footnotes, just enough to explain, without stretching the translation.

As with the Mahabharata, the Valmiki Ramayana is a text about dharma. Dharma means several different things—the dharma of the four *varna*s and the four *ashrama*s, the classes and stages of life; the governance template of *raja dharma*, the duty of kings; principles of good conduct, *sadachara*; and the pursuit of objectives of human existence, *purushartha*—dharma, *artha* and *kama*. As with the Mahabharata, the Valmiki Ramayana is a *smriti* text. It has a human origin and composer, it is not a *shruti* text. Smriti texts are society and context specific. We should not try to judge and evaluate individuals and actions on the basis of today's value judgements. In addition, if the span of composition was one thousand years, from 500 BCE to 500 CE, those value judgements also change. The later composers and interpreters may have had problems with what the earlier composers authored. A case in point is when Sita is being abducted by Ravana. At a certain point in time, men and women universally wore an upper garment and a lower one. When she is being abducted through the sky, Sita casts aside and throws down not just her ornaments, but her upper garment too. As this translation will illustrate, this caused problems for subsequent composers and interpreters.

To return to the notion of dharma—transcending all those collective templates of dharma—there is one that is individual in nature. Regardless of those collective templates, an individual has to decide what the right course of action is and there is no universal answer as to what is right and what is wrong. There are always

contrary pulls of dharma, with two notions of dharma pulling in different directions. It is not immediately obvious which is superior. Given the trade-offs, an individual makes a choice and suffers the consequences. Why is there an impression that these individual conflicts of dharma are more manifest in the Mahabharata than in the Ramayana?

The answer probably lies in the nature of these two texts. What is the difference between a novel and a long story, even when both have multiple protagonists? The difference between a novel and a long story is probably not one of length. A novel seeks to present the views of all protagonists. Thus, the Mahabharata is a bit like a novel, in so far as that trait is concerned. A long story does not seek to look at incidents and actions from the point of view of every protagonist. It is concerned with the perspective of one primary character, to the exclusion of others.

If this distinction is accepted, the Valmiki Ramayana has the characteristics of a long story. It is Ramayana. Therefore, it is primarily from Rama's point of view. We aren't told what Bharata or Lakshmana thought, or for that matter, Urmila, Mandavi or Shrutakirti. There is little that is from Sita's point of view too. That leads to the impression that the Mahabharata contains more about individual conflicts of dharma. For the Valmiki Ramayana, from Rama's point of view, the conflicts of dharma aren't innumerable. On that exile to the forest, why did he take Sita and Lakshmana along with him? Was Shurpanakha's disfigurement warranted? Why did he unfairly kill Vali? Why did he make Sita go through tests of purity, not once, but twice? Why did he unfairly kill Shambuka? Why did he banish Lakshmana? At one level, one can argue these are decisions by a personified divinity and therefore, mere humans cannot comprehend and judge the motives. At another level, the unhappiness with Rama's decisions led to the composition of alternative versions of the Ramayana. Note that Sita's questions about dharma remained unanswered. If you are going to the forest as an ascetic, why have you got weapons with you? If the *rakshasas*[27]

[27] Demons.

are causing injuries to hermits, punishing the rakshasas is Bharata's job, now that he is the king. Why are you dabbling in this? Note also Rama's justification at the time of Sita's first test. It wasn't about what others would think, that justification came later. The initial harsh words reflected his own questions about Sita's purity. Thus, Rama's conflicts over dharma also exist. It is just that in the Valmiki Ramayana, it is about one individual alone.

In conclusion, this translation is an attempt to get readers interested in reading the unabridged Valmiki Ramayana. Having read abridged versions, and there is no competition with those, to appreciate the nuances better, one should read the unabridged. And, to appreciate the beauty of the poetry, one should then be motivated to read the text in Sanskrit. A translation is only a bridge and an unsatisfactory one at that.

CHAPTER ONE

Bala Kanda

Sarga (1): 79 shlokas
Sarga (2): 41 shlokas
Sarga (3): 29 shlokas
Sarga (4): 27 shlokas
Sarga (5): 23 shlokas
Sarga (6): 24 shlokas
Sarga (7): 17 shlokas
Sarga (8): 23 shlokas
Sarga (9): 32 shlokas
Sarga (10): 29 shlokas
Sarga (11): 21 shlokas
Sarga (12): 34 shlokas
Sarga (13): 46 shlokas
Sarga (14): 21 shlokas
Sarga (15): 28 shlokas
Sarga (16): 20 shlokas
Sarga (17): 39 shlokas
Sarga (18): 20 shlokas
Sarga (19): 25 shlokas
Sarga (20): 19 shlokas
Sarga (21): 19 shlokas
Sarga (22): 19 shlokas
Sarga (23): 30 shlokas
Sarga (24): 19 shlokas
Sarga (25): 22 shlokas
Sarga (26): 25 shlokas
Sarga (27): 18 shlokas
Sarga (28): 20 shlokas
Sarga (29): 23 shlokas
Sarga (30): 23 shlokas
Sarga (31): 22 shlokas
Sarga (32): 26 shlokas
Sarga (33): 20 shlokas
Sarga (34): 21 shlokas
Sarga (35): 26 shlokas
Sarga (36): 31 shlokas
Sarga (37): 24 shlokas
Sarga (38): 26 shlokas
Sarga (39): 28 shlokas
Sarga (40): 26 shlokas
Sarga (41): 24 shlokas
Sarga (42): 24 shlokas
Sarga (43): 20 shlokas
Sarga (44): 27 shlokas
Sarga (45): 22 shlokas
Sarga (46): 22 shlokas
Sarga (47): 32 shlokas
Sarga (48): 22 shlokas
Sarga (49): 25 shlokas
Sarga (50): 28 shlokas
Sarga (51): 23 shlokas
Sarga (52): 24 shlokas

Sarga (53): 23 shlokas
Sarga (54): 28 shlokas
Sarga (55): 24 shlokas
Sarga (56): 20 shlokas
Sarga (57): 23 shlokas
Sarga (58): 23 shlokas
Sarga (59): 33 shlokas
Sarga (60): 22 shlokas
Sarga (61): 27 shlokas
Sarga (62): 26 shlokas
Sarga (63): 15 shlokas
Sarga (64): 30 shlokas
Sarga (65): 27 shlokas
Sarga (66): 27 shlokas
Sarga (67): 19 shlokas
Sarga (68): 18 shlokas
Sarga (69): 32 shlokas
Sarga (70): 24 shlokas
Sarga (71): 24 shlokas
Sarga (72): 27 shlokas
Sarga (73): 22 shlokas
Sarga (74): 28 shlokas
Sarga (75): 23 shlokas
Sarga (76): 18 shlokas

Chapter 1(1)

Narada[1] was a bull among sages, devoted to austerities and self-studying. He was an ascetic and supreme among those who were eloquent. Valmiki asked him, 'Right now, who in this world is valorous and possesses all the qualities? Who knows about *dharma*[2] and about what has been done? Who is truthful in his words and firm in his vows? Who also possesses good conduct and is engaged in the welfare of all creatures? Who is also learned and capable? Who alone is the handsome one? Who has control over his own self and has conquered anger? Who is radiant and devoid of jealousy? When his anger is aroused in a battle, whom are even the gods scared of? I wish to hear about all this. My curiosity is great. O great sage! You are the person who is capable of knowing about this kind of man. Narada knew about the three worlds.[3] On hearing these words, he was delighted.

[1] Narada was a son born to Brahma through Brahma's mental powers.

[2] We will not translate the word dharma, because there is no satisfactory word that captures all of its nuances —duty, good behaviour, morality, ethics, governance (for kings) and the metaphysical or the spiritual. The nuance depends on the context.

[3] Heaven, earth and the nether regions. Alternatively, heaven, earth and the region between heaven and earth.

He invited Valmiki to listen and said, 'O sage! The many qualities you have recounted are extremely rare. Using my intelligence, I will tell you about such a man. I have heard about him.[4] He was born in the lineage of Ikshvaku[5] and he is known to people as Rama. He is self-controlled in his soul and immensely valorous. He is radiant, possesses fortitude and is capable of controlling.[6] He is intelligent and follows good policy. He is eloquent and handsome. He is a destroyer of enemies. He possesses broad shoulders and mighty arms. His neck is like a conch shell and his cheekbones stand out. His chest is broad and his bow is huge. He is a subjugator of enemies and his collarbones are hidden. His arms stretch down to his knees and he possesses an excellent head and a beautiful forehead. His tread is superb. He is medium in size and his limbs are well proportioned. He is pleasant in complexion and powerful. His chest is muscled and his eyes are large. He is prosperous and possesses all the auspicious qualities. He knows about dharma. He is firm in adhering to the truth and is devoted to the welfare of the subjects. He is famous and full of learning. He is pure, controlled and has restrained himself. He is a protector of the world of the living and is also a protector of dharma. He knows the truth about the Vedas and Vedangas and is skilled in *dhanurveda*.[7] He knows the truth about all the sacred texts. He is resplendent and has knowledge of the *smriti* texts.[8] He is virtuous and is loved by all the people. He can discriminate and is not distressed in his soul. Just as all rivers head towards the ocean, all virtuous people approach him. He is noble[9] and impartial towards everyone. He alone is the

[4] From Brahma. Narada recounts the core story of the Ramayana, in brief.

[5] The first king of the solar (*surya*) dynasty.

[6] This second reference to control is with reference to the senses and vices.

[7] The Vedas are Rig Veda, Sama Veda, Yajur Veda and Atharva Veda. The six Vedangas are *shiksha* (articulation and pronunciation), *chhanda* (prosody), *vyakarana* (grammar), *nirukta* (etymology), *jyotisha* (astronomy) and *kalpa* (rituals). Dhanurveda is the science of war or fighting.

[8] This can also be translated as possessing an excellent memory. However, the sacred texts are of two types—shruti and smriti. The texts mentioned earlier, as ones that Rama knows, are shruti texts. Therefore, it seems natural to interpret this as smriti texts.

[9] The word used is *arya*.

handsome one. The one who extends Kousalya's[10] lineage thus possesses all the qualities. In his gravity, he is like the ocean. In his patience, he is like the Himalayas. He is like Vishnu in valour.[11] He is as handsome as the moon. In his rage, he is like the fire of destruction.[12] In generosity, he is like the lord of riches.[13] Yet again, he is like Dharma[14] in truthfulness. Rama possesses such qualities and truth is his valour. He is the eldest and possesses the best of qualities. He is Dasharatha's beloved son. In his affection, the lord of the earth wished to instate him as the heir apparent.[15] His wife, Kaikeyee, saw that arrangements were being made for the consecration.[16] The queen asked for the boons that she had been granted earlier—that Rama be exiled and Bharata be anointed. The king was bound by the sanctity of his words and by the noose of dharma. Dasharatha banished his beloved son, Rama. To follow the instruction in his father's words and to do what would bring pleasure to Kaikeyee, the brave one honoured the pledge and left for the forest. When he left, his beloved brother, Lakshmana, the extender of Sumitra's joy and full of affection and humility, followed him. Rama's wife, Sita, is supreme among women and possesses all the auspicious qualities. She also followed him, like Rohini follows the moon.[17] For some distance, the citizens and his father, Dasharatha, also followed him and then took leave of his son in Shringaverapura, on the banks of the Ganga.[18] They went from one forest to another forest and crossed rivers that were full of large

[10] Rama's mother.

[11] This sentence is used to argue that the idea of Rama as Vishnu's incarnation is a later one.

[12] The fire that comes at the time of the destruction of a *yuga* (era).

[13] Kubera.

[14] The god of dharma.

[15] Dasharatha wanted to make Rama the crown prince.

[16] Dasharatha had three wives—Kousalya, Kaikeyee and Sumitra. Dasharatha had granted two boons to Kaikeyee earlier, boons she was going to redeem when the time was right. Bharata was Kaikeyee's son. Lakshmana and Shatrughna were Sumitra's sons.

[17] The twenty-seven *nakshatras* are married to the moon god, though the moon god loves Rohini (Aldebaran) more. The nakshatras are not quite stars, they can also be constellations.

[18] Shringaverapura is in Uttar Pradesh, near Allahabad.

quantities of water. Finally, they arrived in Chitrakuta, under Bharadvaja's control.[19] In that beautiful forest, the three of them constructed a beautiful abode and dwelt there happily, like the gods and the *gandharva*s.[20] When Rama left for Chitrakuta, lamenting with sorrow on account of his son, King Dasharatha went to heaven. When he died, the *brahmana*s, with Vasishtha at the forefront, wished to instate Bharata as the king, but the immensely strong one did not desire the kingdom. The brave one went to the forest and falling at Rama's feet, sought his favours.[21] Bharata's elder brother repeatedly asked Bharata to return and for the sake of the kingdom, gave him his sandals. With his desire unsatisfied, he touched Rama's feet. Wishing to wait for Rama's return, he began to rule the kingdom from Nandigrama.[22] Rama discerned that he might return there again and so might citizens and other people. Single-minded, he entered Dandaka.[23] He slew the *rakshasa*[24] Viradha and saw Sharabhanga.[25] He met Suteekshna, Agastya and his brother.[26] Following Agastya's words, he received Indra's bow and arrow, a sword and two inexhaustible quivers and was extremely pleased.[27] Rama dwelt in that forest. With the other forest dwellers, all the sages approached him, so that the *asura*s and rakshasas could be slain. While he dwelt there, a rakshasa lady named Shurpanakha, who resided in Janasthana and could assume any form at will, was disfigured.[28] Goaded by Shurpanakha's words, all the rakshasas

[19] It is difficult to pin down Chitrakuta now—it could have been in Uttar Pradesh, Madhya Pradesh or Chhattisgarh. Bharadvaja was a sage.

[20] Semi-divine species, companions of Kubera, celestial musicians.

[21] Bharata wanted Rama to return and become king, but Rama refused. Thereupon, Bharata returned with Rama's sandals, which would be placed on the throne.

[22] A village near Ayodhya.

[23] Rama was single-minded that his exile should not be disturbed. Etymologically, the forest of Dandaka, or Dandakaranya, has a sense of punishment, that is, it is a place to which one was exiled or banished. Today, Dandakaranya straddles several central Indian states.

[24] Demon.

[25] A sage. Suteekshna is another sage.

[26] Agastya's brother.

[27] He obtained these weapons from Agastya, Indra having given them to Agastya.

[28] Lakshmana severed her nose and ears. Janasthana is a place in Dandakaranya. The place where Shurpanakha's nose (and ears) were severed is identified as Nashika.

attacked—Khara, Trishira and the rakshasa Dushana. In the ensuing battle, Rama slew them and their followers. He killed fourteen thousand rakshasas. On hearing that his kinsmen had been killed, Ravana became senseless with rage. He summoned and sought the help of the rakshasa named Maricha. Maricha tried to restrain Ravana several times. "O Ravana! You will not be pardoned if you oppose someone as powerful as him." Ravana, goaded by destiny, did not pay any heed to these words. With Maricha, he went to his[29] hermitage. The two princes were drawn far away by the one versed in *maya*.[30] Having slain the vulture Jatayu, he[31] abducted Rama's wife. On hearing about the vulture being killed and on hearing about Maithilee, Raghava was tormented by sorrow.[32] He lamented, his senses distracted. In that state of grief, he cremated the vulture, Jatayu. While he was searching for Sita in the forest, he saw a rakshasa. His name was Kabandha. He was malformed and terrible to see. The mighty-armed one killed him. While he[33] ascended upwards towards heaven, he told him about Shabaree, who was a follower of dharma. "O Raghava! This ascetic lady is full of dharma. Go to her." The immensely energetic one, the slayer of enemies, went to Shabaree. Shabaree worshipped Dasharatha's son in the proper way. On the shores of the Pampa, he met the ape, Hanumat.[34] On Hanumat's words, he met Sugriva. The immensely strong Rama told Sugriva everything that had happened. In affection and full of grief, the king of the apes told Rama everything about the enmity.[35] The ape also told him about Vali's strength. Rama promised that he would kill Vali. However, Sugriva always suspected the extent of

[29] Rama's.

[30] Maya is the power of illusion. Maricha used these powers to adopt the form of a deer and draw Rama and Lakshmana away.

[31] Ravana.

[32] Maithilee is Sita, daughter of the king of Mithila, Janaka. The kingdom was Videha, the capital was Mithila. Sita is thus also known as Vaidehi. Raghu was one of Rama's ancestors. Hence, Rama is referred to as Raghava.

[33] Kabandha.

[34] Hanumat is Hanuman, Hanumat being the correct way of translating the name. The lake Pampa is near Hampi, in Karnataka.

[35] The enmity between Vali and Sugriva.

Raghava's valour. Dundubhi's gigantic skeleton was there.[36] To establish credibility, Raghava used the big toe on his foot to fling this ten *yojana*s away.[37] Yet again, with one single and large arrow, he pierced seven *sala* trees.[38] To generate confidence, he also dispatched a mountain to the nether regions. After this, the giant ape was assured and delighted in his mind. He went with Rama to Kishkindha[39] and to the mouth of the cave. Sugriva, supreme among apes and golden brown in complexion, started to roar there. On hearing this loud roar, the lord of the apes[40] emerged. Following Sugriva's words, he killed Vali in the encounter. Raghava returned the kingdom to Sugriva and instated him there. The bull among apes summoned all the apes. To search for Janaka's daughter, he sent them in all the directions. The strong Hanumat heard the words of the vulture, Sampati.[41] He leapt over the salty ocean that extended for one hundred yojanas. He reached the city of Lanka, ruled by Ravana. He saw Sita meditating in the forest of Ashoka. To establish Vaidehi's confidence, he gave her the sign[42] he had been given. He comforted her and broke down the gate. He killed five foremost commanders and seven sons of ministers. Having crushed the brave Aksha, he allowed himself to be captured. Because of a boon received from the grandfather,[43] he knew that he was capable of freeing himself from any weapon. However, the brave one wished to tolerate the rakshasas and those who had captured him. With the exception of Maithilee Sita, he burnt down the city of Lanka. To bring pleasure to Rama and to give him the news, the giant ape then returned. Having reached, he circumambulated the great-souled Rama. The one whose soul is immeasurable reported the truth about how he had seen Sita. With Sugriva, he[44] went to the shores

[36] A gigantic demon in the form of a buffalo, killed by Vali.

[37] A yojana is a measure of distance, between 8 and 9 miles.

[38] A large tree, *Shorea robusta*.

[39] The kingdom of the apes.

[40] Vali.

[41] Jatayu's elder brother.

[42] Rama's ring.

[43] Brahma.

[44] Rama.

of the great ocean. He agitated the ocean with arrows that were like the rays of the sun. The ocean, the lord of the rivers, showed himself. On the words of the ocean, he[45] asked Nala to construct a bridge. Using this, he went to the city of Lanka and killed Ravana in a battle. He instated Vibhishana, Indra among rakshasas, in the kingdom of Lanka. Because of the great-souled Raghava's deeds, the mobile and immobile objects in the three worlds and the gods and the sages were satisfied. Supremely content, all the gods worshipped him. Having accomplished his task, Rama was delighted and devoid of anxiety. Having obtained a boon from the gods, he revived all the slain apes. Ascending Pushpaka,[46] he left for Nandigrama. In Nandigrama, with his brothers, the unblemished one removed his matted hair. Rama got Sita back and also got back his kingdom. The people are joyous and delighted. Those who are scrupulous in following dharma are nurtured. There is recovery from disease. There are no famines and everything is devoid of fear. No man has to witness the death of his son. Women are not ignoble and never become widows. They are devoted to their husbands. There is no fear from the wind. Creatures never get submerged in water. There is no fear from fire. It is exactly as it was in *krita yuga*.[47] He performs one hundred horse sacrifices and gives away a lot of gold. Following the appropriate ordinances, he gives away crores of cattle to the learned. Raghava will establish one hundred royal lineages that possess all the qualities. In this world, he will engage the four *varna*s[48] in their own respective tasks. Rama will thus honour the kingdom for eleven thousand years and then go to Brahma's world.

'This is a sacred account and destroys all sins. It is auspicious and in conformity with the Vedas. If a person reads about this

[45] Rama.

[46] A celestial vehicle, *vimana*. This belonged originally to Kubera, but was seized by Ravana.

[47] There are four yugas—*satya* (krita), *treta*, *dvapara* and *kali*. Everything worsens as one moves from krita yuga to kali yuga. Though the incidents of the Ramayana occur in treta yuga, it seems as if it is krita yuga.

[48] Brahmanas, *kshatriyas*, *vaishyas* and *shudras*.

conduct, he is cleansed of all sins. A man who reads the account of the Ramayana has a long life, with his sons, grandsons and followers. After death, he obtains greatness in heaven. A brahmana who reads this becomes eloquent in speech, a kshatriya obtains lordship over land, a merchant[49] obtains the fruits of trading and a shudra person obtains greatness.'

Chapter 1(2)

Hearing Narada's words, who was accomplished in speech, the great sage,[50] with dharma in his soul, worshipped him, accompanied by his disciple. Having been worshipped in the proper way, the celestial sage, Narada, took his leave and departed through the sky[51] to the world of the gods. After some time had passed,[52] the sage went to the banks of the Tamasa, not very far from the Jahnavee.[53] The great sage reached the banks of the Tamasa. With his disciple standing next to him, he saw that this *tirtha* was free from all mud.[54] He said, 'O Bharadvaja![55] Look. This tirtha is free from all mud. It is beautiful and the waters are pleasing, like the mind of a virtuous man. O son![56] Place the water pot here and give my garment made of bark. I will immerse myself in this supreme tirtha of Tamasa.' Bharadvaja was thus addressed by the great-souled Valmiki. Controlled and attentive towards his preceptor, he gave the sage the garment made of bark. The one who had controlled

[49] That is, a vaishya.

[50] Valmiki.

[51] Alternatively, left for heaven.

[52] The text uses the word *muhurta*. It is a measure of time. More specifically, it is a span of forty-eight minutes.

[53] Jahnavee is the Ganga and Tamasa is a tributary that flows through Madhya Pradesh and Uttar Pradesh. Valmiki's hermitage was on the banks of the Tamasa.

[54] A tirtha is a sacred place of pilgrimage with water where one can have a bath.

[55] Valmiki's disciple.

[56] The word used is *tata*. Though it means son, it is affectionately used for anyone who is younger or junior.

his senses received the garment made of bark from his disciple. He advanced, glancing in every direction at the great forest.

Near the spot, the illustrious one saw a couple of curlews[57] wandering around, attached to each other. The sound they made was beautiful. There was a *nishada*[58] who bore evil intent towards those who resided there. While he looked on,[59] he killed the male one from that couple. Limbs covered with blood, it trembled on the ground. On seeing it slain, the wife lamented in piteous tones. The sage had dharma in his soul. He saw that the bird had been brought down by the hunter and was moved by compassion. Full of compassion and on seeing the female curlew that was weeping, the brahmana recognized this as *adharma*. He spoke these words. 'O nishada! This couple of curlews was in the throes of passion and you killed one of them. Therefore, you will possess ill repute for an eternal number of years.'[60] Having said this, a thought arose in his heart. 'Overcome by sorrow on account of the bird, what is this that I have uttered?' The intelligent and immensely wise one reflected on this. Having made up his mind, the bull among sages spoke these words to his disciple. 'While I was overcome by grief, these words emerged. They have rhythm and metre and are arranged in *pada*s with an equal number of *akshara*s. This and nothing else will be a shloka.'[61] The sage spoke these supreme words to his disciple and he accepted them cheerfully. The preceptor was also content. Following the prescribed rites, the sage performed his ablutions in that tirtha. He returned, thinking about the purport of what had transpired. Bharadvaja, the humble and learned disciple, followed his preceptor at the rear, having filled the water pot.

[57] The *krouncha* bird.

[58] The nishadas were hunters who dwelt in mountains and forests.

[59] Valmiki looked on.

[60] This celebrated verse (shloka) is regarded as the beginning of Sanskrit poetry.

[61] There is an implied pun on the etymology of the word shloka, from *shoka* (sorrow). Sanskrit poetry has different kinds of metres. This particular one is known as *anushtubh*. An akshara is not quite a syllable, but syllable is a good enough approximation. Pada means a quarter and an anushtubh shloka possesses four padas, with eight syllables in each pada. That celebrated verse has these attributes.

The one who knew about dharma entered the hermitage with his disciple. Seating himself, he conversed about other things, but continued to meditate on what had happened. The lord Brahma, the creator of the worlds, himself arrived there. The immensely energetic one, with four faces, arrived there to see the bull among sages. Seeing him, the self-controlled Valmiki was at a loss for words. Supremely astounded, he quickly arose and joined his hands in salutation. He worshipped the god and honoured him with *padya*, *arghya* and a seat.[62] Having prostrated himself in the proper way, he asked him about his welfare. Worshipped in this wonderful way, the illustrious one seated himself. He instructed the great sage, Valmiki, to also be seated. In the presence of the grandfather of the worlds himself, Valmiki sat down, his mind still meditating on what had happened. 'His intelligence clouded by a sense of enmity, that evil-souled one[63] created a hardship. Without any valid reason, he killed a curlew that sang in such beautiful tones.' He was again overcome by sorrow on account of the curlew. Full of sorrow, in his mind, he again chanted the shloka. Brahma smiled at the bull among sages and said, 'You have composed a structured shloka. There is no need to think about this. O brahmana! The metre and the speech arose from me. O supreme among sages! This was so that you could recount Rama's conduct in its entirety. In this world, the intelligent Rama possesses all the qualities and has dharma in his soul. He possesses fortitude and you have heard about his conduct from Narada, everything that the intelligent Rama did, openly and in secret, with Sumitra's son, and all that concerns the rakshasas. You know about Vaidehi's conduct, whether it has been revealed or is a secret. All that is unknown will also become known to you. In the *kavya*[64] you compose, not a single word will be false and there will be nothing that will not happen. In structured and beautiful shlokas, compose the auspicious account of Rama's conduct. As long as there are mountains and as long as there are rivers on this

[62] These are objects always offered to a guest—padya (water to wash the feet), *achamaniya* (water to wash the mouth/face), arghya (a gift) and *asana* (a seat).

[63] The hunter.

[64] A long poem.

earth, till such a time, this Ramayana account will circulate in the worlds.[65] As long as Rama's account, composed by you, circulates, till that time, you will reside in the upper regions, the nether regions and even in my world.' Having spoken these words, the illustrious Brahma vanished. With his disciple, the sage, Valmiki, was struck by great wonder. All the disciples again chanted the shloka.

Cheerful and extremely surprised, they chanted it repeatedly. It was chanted by the great sage in four padas, with an equal number of aksharas in each. Because of repeated recitation and because it emerged from sorrow, it came to be known as a shloka.[66] Thus, intelligence came to Valmiki and thinking about it in his mind, he composed the entire Ramayana kavya. He decided that this is what he should do. In beautiful padas, the broad-minded and illustrious one composed the account of the illustrious Rama's conduct, with an equal number of aksharas in hundreds of shlokas. The generous and intelligent sage composed a kavya that brought him fame.

Chapter 1(3)

Having heard everything about the intelligent one's[67] conduct, which was in conformity with dharma, the one with dharma in his soul again sought out all that was known about this. Following dharma, the sage touched water,[68] joined his hands in salutation and stood on a mat of *darbha*[69] grass, facing the east. He sought out a chart for progress.[70] The birth of the extremely brave Rama, who showed his favours towards everyone, was loved by the worlds, his perseverance, amiability and devotion to the truth; the many

[65] Literally, *Ramayana* means Rama's progress (*ayana*).

[66] There is the implication that something becomes a shloka when it is recited by others, not just the composer.

[67] Rama's. Having heard from Narada.

[68] Water is touched before an auspicious act.

[69] Sacred grass. It is not clear whether he stood, or seated himself.

[70] What follows is a description of what is in the Ramayana. The sentence is incomplete (without a subject and a verb), not unusual in Sanskrit.

other wonderful deeds with Vishvamitra as an aide, the shattering of the bow and the marriage with Janakee; the dispute between Rama and Rama[71] and the qualities of Dasharatha's son, Rama's consecration and Kaikeyee's evil intentions; the obstacle created for the consecration and Rama's exile, the miserable lamentations of the king[72] and his departure for the world hereafter; the sorrow of the ordinary subjects and the separation from the ordinary subjects, the conversation with the king of the nishadas[73] and the charioteer's return; the crossing of the Ganga and the meeting with Bharadvaja, having obtained Bharadvaja's permission, their sight of Chitrakuta; the construction of an abode and Bharata's arrival there to seek Rama's favours, the performance of the water rites for the father; the consecration of the sandals and the residence in Nandigrama, the departure for Dandakaranya and the meeting with Suteekshna; Anasuya's problem and the granting of an ointment for the body, the conversation with Shurpanakha and her disfigurement; the slaying of Khara and Trishira and Ravana's rise,[74] the slaying of Maricha and Vaidehi's abduction; Raghava's lamentations and the slaying of the king of the vultures, the sighting of Kabandha and the sighting of Pampa; the sighting of Shabaree and the sighting of Hanumat, the lamentations of the great-souled Raghava in Pampa; the departure for Rishyamuka and the meeting with Sugriva, the generation of friendship between the two and the conflict between Bali and Sugriva; the crushing of Bali and the bestowal on Sugriva,[75] Tara's lamentations and the agreement to reside there until the monsoon nights were over; the rage of the Raghava lion[76] and the gathering of the army, the departure in various directions and a description of the earth; the gift of the ring and the sighting of the bear's den, their fasting to death[77] and their sighting of Sampati;

[71] Parashurama.
[72] Dasharatha.
[73] Guha.
[74] A consequent rise in Ravana's wrath.
[75] The kingship of the apes.
[76] At Sugriva's delay.
[77] Because the apes had not been able to find Sita.

the ascent of the mountain and the leap across the ocean, the solitary entry into Lanka in the night[78] and thinking about what should be done; the visit to the liquor room and an examination of the fortifications, the visit to Ashoka forest and the sighting of Sita; the giving of the sign[79] and Sita's address, the censure of the rakshasa ladies and Trijata's nightmare; Sita's gift of the jewel and the destruction of the trees, the driving away of the rakshasa ladies and the slaying of the guards; the capture of the son of Vayu,[80] his roaring and the burning down of Lanka, the seizure of the honey on the leap back; the presentation of the jewel and the assurance of Raghava, the meeting with the ocean and Nala's construction of the bridge; the crossing of the ocean and the siege of Lanka in the night, the meeting with Vibhishana and the recounting of the method of killing;[81] the slaying of Kumbhakarna and the crushing of Meghanada, Ravana's destruction and the regain of Sita in that city of enemies; the instatement of Vibhishana and the sighting of Pushpaka, the departure for Ayodhya and the meeting with Bharata; and the disbandment of all the soldiers and arrangements for Rama's crowning, the delight brought to his own kingdom and Vaidehi's exile. In this kavya, the illustrious *rishi* Valmiki described everything that happened as long as Rama was on earth and all that would occur in the future, thereafter.[82]

Chapter 1(4)

When Rama obtained his kingdom, the illustrious rishi Valmiki, in control of his soul, composed the entire account of his conduct, in wonderful padas. The immensely wise one recounted what had happened and what would transpire in the future,

[78] By Hanumat.
[79] The ring.
[80] The wind god; Hanumat was Vayu's son.
[81] Vibhishana explained how Ravana could be killed.
[82] After Rama had left earth.

thereafter. Having composed it, the lord thought about who would recount the tale. While the great sage was thinking about this in his mind, in the garb of sages, Kusha and Lava came and touched his feet. The illustrious princes, Kusha and Lava, knew about dharma. He saw that the two brothers, residents of the hermitage, possessed melodious voices. He saw that these two intelligent ones were accomplished in the Vedas. Since this only served to extend the Vedas, the lord gave this to them, the entire Ramayana kavya and Sita's greatness of character. The sage who was devoted in his vows told them about Poulastya's[83] death. This is to be read and sung in pleasant tones, categorized into three scales and seven notes.[84] It possesses rhythm that can be adjusted to the tunes of stringed instruments. This kavya is sung in *hasya*, *shringara*, *karunya*, *roudra*, *veera*, *bhayanaka*, *beebhatsa* and other *rasas*.[85] They[86] possessed the knowledge of the gandharvas[87] and were accomplished in pausing and pitching their voices. Those two brothers had melodious voices and looked like gandharvas. They possessed beauty and the auspicious signs. They were sweet in speech. Having emerged from Rama's body, they were like two mirror images of him. The kavya was a supreme account and devoted to dharma, those two princes learnt it in its entirety, reciting it in the proper way, without any blemishes. Those two great-souled and immensely fortunate ones were seen to possess all the qualities and knew about the truth. Controlled, and as instructed, they sang this in assemblies of sages, brahmanas and the virtuous. On one occasion, they were seated in a gathering of sages, cleansed in their souls. They sung the kavya in their presence. On hearing this, all the sages had tears in their eyes.

[83] Ravana's.

[84] *Svara* (note) can be in seven tones—*shadja*, *rishabha*, *gandhara*, *madhyama*, *panchama*, *dhaivat* and *nishada*, commonly known as sa-re-ga-ma-pa-dha-ni. The three scales are *udatta* (high), *anudatta* (low) and *svarita* (accented).

[85] There are nine rasas (emotions) in aesthetics—shringara (romance), hasya (comedy), karunya (compassion), roudra (ferocity), beebhatsa (disgusting), bhayanaka (horrible), veera (heroic), *adbhuta* (wonderful) and *shanta* (peaceful). However, other rasas are also sometimes mentioned.

[86] Kusha and Lava.

[87] Singing, dancing and music.

They were filled with great wonder and uttered words of praise. All the sages, devoted to dharma, were delighted. They praised the singing of Kusha and Lava, who deserved to be praised. 'Wonderful! This song, in particular the shlokas, are melodious. Although all this happened a long time ago, it is as if we have witnessed it now. Those two immersed themselves in it and sung it in accordance with the sentiments. Accomplished in a wealth of svaras, they sang together, melodiously and with affection.' The great sages, who could pride themselves on their austerities, praised those two in this way. They sang in beautiful tones, full of deep meaning and affection. Delighted, a sage who was there gave them a water pot. Delighted, another extremely illustrious sage gave them garments of bark. The account composed by the sage,[88] arranged in successive sections, was extraordinary and would be a foundation for poets who would come in the future.

Those two singers were praised everywhere. On one occasion, while they were thus singing on the royal road, Bharata's elder brother[89] saw them. Rama, the slayer of enemies, honoured the two brothers, Kusha and Lava, who deserved to be praised, and brought them to his own abode. The lord, the scorcher of enemies, seated himself on a golden and divine throne. His advisers and brothers were seated around him. Rama saw those two handsome ones, with *veenas*,[90] and spoke to Lakshmana, Shatrughna and Bharata. 'They are as radiant as the gods. Let this account be heard from them. It is structured into wonderful and meaningful padas. Let it be properly sung by these two, who possess melodious voices. These two sages, Kusha and Lava, bear all the marks of kings, but are great ascetics. Listen to the great account they speak about. It brings prosperity even to me.' Those two were accomplished in the different techniques and modes of singing. Urged by Rama, they sang. And in that assembly, Rama was also gradually immersed in their narration.

[88] Valmiki.

[89] Rama.

[90] Stringed musical instrument.

Chapter 1(5)

Beginning with Prajapati,[91] several victorious and unrivalled kings have ruled over this entire earth. There was one named Sagara, who dug up the ocean.[92] When he advanced, his sixty thousand sons surrounded him. This was the lineage of the Ikshvakus, one of great-souled kings. It has been heard that the great Ramayana account originates in this lineage. From the beginning to the end, everything will be recounted. It is full of dharma, *kama* and *artha*[93] and must be heard without any censure.

There was the great kingdom[94] of Kosala, prosperous and happy. It possessed a lot of wealth and grain and was located on the banks of the Sarayu. The city of Ayodhya,[95] famous in the worlds, was situated there. Manu, Indra among men, himself constructed that city. That great city was twelve yojanas long and three yojanas wide. It was beautiful and spread out, divided by highways. The beautiful and large royal roads were laid out well. They were always sprinkled with water and flowers were strewn on them. The king there was Dasharatha, an extender of the great kingdom. He made that city his abode, like the king of the gods in heaven. There were gates and arches and the interiors of the buildings were laid out well. There were machines and implements of war everywhere, constructed by all manner of artisans. There were bards and minstrels everywhere. That handsome city was infinite in splendour. There were tall walls with standards, surmounted by hundreds of *shataghni*s.[96] Everywhere, that city was also full of large numbers of dancers and actors. There were mango groves and a giant wall formed a girdle around the city. There were moats

[91] Implying Manu.

[92] The king's name is Sagara and the ocean is named *saagara* after him.

[93] These are regarded as the three objectives (*trivarga*) of human existence. Kama is the pursuit of the senses and artha is the pursuit of wealth. The goal of *moksha* (emancipation) transcends these three.

[94] The text uses the word *janapada*.

[95] The capital of Kosala.

[96] A shataghni is a weapon that can kill one hundred at one stroke.

that were difficult to cross. Thus, the fortification was impossible for others to breach. It was populated by horses, elephants, cattle, camels and donkeys. Large numbers of vassal kings came from the frontiers to offer tribute. Merchants and residents of many countries came there. The palaces were embedded with jewels and were as beautiful as mountains. There were secret residences[97] and the place was like Indra's Amaravati.[98] The city was full of large numbers of beautiful women and was wonderfully laid out, like an *ashtapada* board.[99] It was encrusted with gems everywhere and the mansions were like celestial vehicles. The houses were densely constructed on level ground and there was no space between them. There were stores of *shali* rice[100] and the water was like the juice of sugar cane. There were drums, percussion instruments,[101] veenas and cymbals. They were sounded loudly, signifying that this was the best city on earth. Through their austerities, *siddhas*[102] obtain celestial vehicles in heaven. With extremely well-laid-out residences and populated by the best among men, this city was like one of those. The archers there were skilled and dexterous of hand. But they did not use their arrows to pierce someone who was alonc, someone who was without heirs, or someone who was running away. Nor did they aim by sound alone.[103] Intoxicated lions, tigers and wild boars roared and roamed around in the forests. They killed these with their sharp weapons and even through the sheer strength of their arms. The place was full of thousands of such *maharathas*.[104] The city that was King Dasharatha's residence was like this. It was populated by those with qualities, those who offered oblations into the fire. There

[97] For women.

[98] Indra's capital.

[99] Ashtapada was a game, probably a precursor to chess.

[100] A fine rice.

[101] We have translated *mridanga* in this way and *dundubhi* as drum.

[102] Successful sages.

[103] *Shabdavedhyam*, shooting at a target on the basis of sound, rather than sight. Unlike the others, which are principles of fair fighting, this prohibition might have been because of Dasharatha's experience and curse, recounted later.

[104] Great warrior, more specifically, a maharatha is someone who can single-handedly fight ten thousand warriors.

were the best among brahmanas, accomplished in the Vedas and the Vedangas. There were thousands of great-souled ones, devoted to the truth. All of them were like sages and some were the equals of the great sages.

Chapter 1(6)

King Dasharatha resided in that city of Ayodhya and collected those who knew about the Vedas around him. He was far-sighted and immensely energetic and loved by the residents of the city and the countryside. He was a great warrior from the Ikshvaku lineage who performed sacrifices. He controlled himself and was devoted to dharma. He was a *rajarshi* who was the equal of a *maharshi*.[105] He was famous in the three worlds. He was powerful and slew his enemies. He possessed friends and had conquered his senses. He accumulated wealth and other kinds of riches. He was like Shakra and Vaishravana.[106] Like the immensely energetic Manu, he protected the world. He ruled over the earth. Adhering to the truth, he pursued the three objectives.[107] He ruled over that best of cities, like Indra in Amaravati. There were extremely learned people in that best of cities, happy and with dharma in their souls. The men were satisfied with the riches they had obtained themselves. They were truthful in speech and not avaricious. In that supreme of cities, there was no one who had not accumulated some amount of riches. There was no household without riches in the form of cattle, horses, wealth and grain. There was no man who was lustful, ignoble or cruel. One was incapable of seeing an ignorant person or a non-believer in Ayodhya. All the men and women were extremely controlled and devoted to dharma. They were joyful and good in conduct, like unblemished maharshis. There was no one without an earring, without a headdress, without a garland and

[105] A maharshi is a great sage. A rajarshi is a royal sage.

[106] Respectively, Indra and Kubera.

[107] Dharma, artha and kama.

without some means of finding pleasure. There was no one who did not have a bath, nor anyone who did not smear the body with unguents and fragrances. There was no one who did not have the best of food. There was no one who was not generous, no one who did not decorate the body with ornaments. No one could be seen without ornaments on the hands, nor one who was heartless. There was no one who did not light the sacrificial fire. There were thousands of brahmanas who performed sacrifices. There was no one in Ayodhya who was without a means of subsistence, nor anyone of mixed varna. The brahmanas had conquered their senses and were always engaged in their own tasks. They were devoted to donating and studying. They were controlled and received gifts. There was no one who was a non-believer, no one who was a liar, nor anyone who was not extremely learned. There was no one who was jealous or incapable. There was no one who was not learned. There was no one who was distressed or disturbed in mind, no one who was miserable. There was no man or woman who was poor or ugly. In Ayodhya, one was incapable of seeing a person who was not devoted to the king. All the four varnas worshipped gods and guests. All the men possessed long lifespans and were devoted to dharma and the truth. The kshatriyas placed brahmanas ahead of them and the vaishyas followed the kshatriyas. The shudras were devoted to their own dharma and served the other three varnas. That city was guarded extremely well by that lord of the Ikshvaku lineage, just like the intelligent Manu, Indra among men, in ancient times. The accomplished warriors were intolerant and were like the touch of fire. They had completed all their training and were like lions in caves. There were the best of horses, born in the kingdoms of Kamboja and Bahlika. It was full of other horses born in mountainous regions and riverine tracts.[108] They were like Indra's horse. The place was full of extremely strong and crazy elephants that were like mountains, born in the Vindhya mountains and the Himalayas. These elephants were descended from Anjana

[108] Instead of mountainous region, Vanayu might also refer to the name of a specific country, such as Arabia. Riverine tract might mean the region of the five rivers, especially the area around the Sindhu.

and Vamana.[109] The city's elephants were *bhadra-mandra*, *bhadra-mriga* and *mriga-mandra*.[110] The city was always full of crazy elephants that were like mountains. Making true its name, the city extended for another two yojanas beyond.[111] With firm gates and ramparts, it was true to its name. With colourful houses, it was auspicious and beautiful. There were thousands of men in the city of Ayodhya. Like Shakra, the king ruled it.

Chapter 1(7)

There were eight brave and illustrious advisers. They were pure and devoted and were always engaged in the king's tasks—Dhrishti, Jayanta, Vijaya, Siddhartha, Arthasadhaka, Ashoka, Mantrapala—and Sumantra was the eighth. There were two officiating priests, supreme among rishis—Vasishtha and Vamadeva. There were other ministers too. They were prosperous and great-souled, learned in the sacred texts and firm in their valour. They were controlled and the performers of deeds, acting just as they said they would. They possessed energy, forgiveness and fame. They smiled before they spoke. Because of anger, desire or wealth, they never spoke false words. There was nothing that was unknown to them, in their own kingdom, or in that of others, whether it had been done, was being done, or was being thought of. This was ensured through spies. They were skilled in administration and their affections had been tested.[112] At the right time, the appropriate punishment was imposed, even on

[109] The Critical Edition excises half a shloka, where Iravata and Mahapadma are also mentioned. Eight elephants stand in the eight directions and their names are Airavata, Pundarika, Vamana, Kumuda, Anjana, Pushpadanta, Sarvabhouma and Suprateeka. All that is meant is that Ayodhya's elephants had divine ancestry.

[110] There were four classes of elephants, classified according to complexion, tusk and belly—*bhadra, mandra, mriga* and *mishra*. The first three are mentioned here, Ayodhya's elephants interbred from these three classes.

[111] Ayodhya means something that cannot be assailed. The sense is that the fortifications extended for another two yojanas, beyond the city's perimeter.

[112] By the king, so that they did not yield to nepotism and other relationships.

their own sons. They were devoted to accumulating the treasury and the army. They caused no violence to even men who were unfriendly, as long as they were blameless. They were brave and always full of enterprise, devoted to the science of governing. They were pure and always protected those who resided in the kingdom. In an attempt to fill up the treasury, they did not cause violence to brahmanas and kshatriyas. After examining a man's strengths and weaknesses, they imposed extremely stiff punishments. Pure and single-minded, all of them governed together. In the city or in the kingdom, there was no man who was a liar. There was no man who was wicked, addicted to another person's wife. Everything in the kingdom was peaceful and the city was also like that. All of them[113] were well attired and well decorated, excellent in conduct. For the sake of the king, their eyes of good policy were always open. They obtained their good qualities from their preceptors and were renowned for their valour. Because of their intelligence and decisions, they were famous in foreign countries too. These were the qualities that the advisers possessed. With their aid, the unblemished King Dasharatha ruled the earth. Using spies, he kept an eye on what happened. He delighted the subjects through dharma. There was no one who was his superior or equal. Nor did he have any enemies. Those ministers were devoted to providing advice that brought welfare. They were devoted, accomplished and skilled, and surrounded him. The king thus gained radiance. He was like the rising sun, illuminating with its blazing rays.

Chapter 1(8)

He knew about dharma, was great-souled and was powerful. However, he did not have a son who would extend the lineage and he was tormented because of the lack of a son. While he reflected on this, a thought occurred to the great-souled one. 'For the sake of a son, why don't I perform a horse sacrifice?' The intelligent

[113] The ministers.

one made up his mind to undertake such a sacrifice and consulted with all his pure ministers. The king told Sumantra, supreme among ministers, 'Quickly summon the priests and all my seniors.'

Having heard this, the *suta*,[114] Sumantra, spoke to the king in secret. 'I have heard an ancient account that was instructed by the officiating priests. O king! In an assembly of sages, the illustrious Sanatkumara had earlier recounted this tale about how you would obtain sons.[115] Kashyapa has a son who is famous by the name of Vibhandaka. He will have a son who will be renowned by the name of Rishyashringa.[116] That sage will always be reared in the forest and will always roam around in the forest. That Indra among brahmanas will not know anyone else and will always follow his father. That great-souled one will observe both kinds of *brahmacharya*.[117] O king! He will be famous in the world and will always be spoken about by brahmanas. The illustrious one will tend to the sacrificial fire and his father. The time will come for him to be brought here. At that time, there will also be an extremely strong, powerful and famous king named Romapada in Anga. Because of a transgression committed by the king, there will be an extremely terrible period of drought. It will be so terrible that all the creatures will face fear. Because of the onset of the drought, the king will be overcome by grief. He will summon brahmanas and those who are aged in learning and address them. "All of you know the sacred texts of dharma and also know about the nature of the worlds. Instruct me about the rituals and about the atonement I should perform." The brahmanas, learned in

[114] The sutas were charioteers and bards, but were sometimes, advisers to kings.

[115] Sanatkumara, Sanaka, Sanatana and Sanandana were four sages who were created through Brahma's mental powers.

[116] This is being foretold as something that will happen in the future. Literally, Rishyashringa means the rishi who possesses horns. Since *shringa* also means peak, this can also be interpreted as a lofty sage.

[117] The word brahmacharya is usually translated as celibacy, but that's a simplification. Brahmacharya means conduct along the path of the *brahman*. In the four stages (*ashramas*) of life, brahmacharya is the first, followed by *garhasthya, vanaprastha* and *sannyasa*, in that order. Brahmacharya is the stage when one is a student and follows celibacy. Hence, this is the first kind of ashrama. On attaining the stage of a householder (garhasthya), brahmacharya is not interpreted as celibacy. Instead, it means intercourse at prescribed times and for prescribed purposes. This is the second kind of brahmacharya.

the Vedas, will tell the king, "O king! Vibhandaka's son provides all the means. Bring him here. O king! Bring Rishyashringa and honour him extremely well. Control yourself, follow the rituals and bestow your daughter, Shanta, on him." Hearing their words, the king will begin to think. Through what means will I be able to bring the valiant one here? Having consulted with his ministers, the king will make up his mind. With the requisite honours, he will dispatch his priests and advisers. On hearing the king's words, they will be distressed and will lower their faces. "O king! We entreat you. We are scared of the rishi[118] and cannot go there. Having thought about it, we will tell you of a means whereby he can be brought here. We will be able to bring the brahmana here and no taint will result." Hence, the lord of Anga will employ a courtesan to bring the rishi's son there. The god[119] will shower down and he will bestow Shanta on him. This son-in-law, Rishyashringa, will also ensure sons for you.[120] I have told you everything that Sanatkumara had said.'

At this, Dasharatha was delighted and replied, 'How can Rishyashringa be brought here? You should tell me in detail.'

Chapter 1(9)

Urged by the king, Sumantra replied in these words. 'With your ministers, hear about how Rishyashringa can be brought here. The advisers and priests told Romapada, "We have thought of a means so that there is no harm. Devoted to austerities and studying, Rishyashringa wanders around in the forest. He is inexperienced about women, worldly matters and pleasure. Excessive addiction to the senses causes turbulence in the minds of men. We must make efforts to bring him to the city quickly. Let beautiful and ornamented

[118] Vibhandaka.

[119] The rain god.

[120] There is another aspect to the expression son-in-law. According to some accounts, before he had sons, through Kousalya, Dasharatha had a daughter named Shanta, who became King Romapada's adopted daughter.

courtesans go there. Let them honour and seduce him in many kinds of ways and bring him here." On hearing this, the king agreed to what the priests had said. Accordingly, the priests and ministers made the arrangements. Hearing the instruction, the best among courtesans entered that great forest. They stationed themselves close to the hermitage and made efforts to show themselves. The rishi's patient son always resided in the hermitage. He was always content with his father and never ventured outside the hermitage. Since his birth, the ascetic had never seen anyone else, woman, man, or any other being, from either the city or the countryside. Wandering around as he willed, on an occasion, he arrived at that spot.[121] Vibhandaka's son arrived there and saw the courtesans. The women were splendidly attired and were singing in melodious voices. All of them approached the rishi's son and spoke these words. "O brahmana! Who are you? Why do you conduct yourself like this? We wish to know this. You are roaming around alone in this desolate and terrible forest? Tell us." In that forest, those women possessed desirable forms and these were forms he had not seen earlier. Affection was generated in him and he desired to tell them about his father and himself. "My father is Vibhandaka and I am his son. I am known as Rishyashringa because of an act that happened on earth.[122] O beautiful ones! Our hermitage is not far from here. I wish to honour all of you there, following the prescribed rites." Hearing the words of the rishi's son, all of them desired to see the hermitage and all of them went there with him. When they had gone there, the rishi's son worshipped them. "Here are arghya, padya, roots and fruits for you." All of them eagerly accepted this worship. However, they were scared of the rishi and made up their minds to depart quickly. "O brahmana! Take these best of fruits from us. May you be fortunate. Accept them and eat them, without any delay." Full of delight, all of them embraced him. They gave him many kinds of wonderful sweetmeats to eat. The energetic one

[121] Where the courtesans were.

[122] There are different stories about Rishyashringa's birth, such as he being the son of Vibhandaka and Urvashi. In some, not all, of these accounts, he is born from a doe, which explains the horns. Vibhandaka was descended from the sage Kashyapa.

ate them, taking them to be fruits. Having always resided in the forest, he had never tasted anything like this before. They told the brahmana that they had their vows to tend to and took his leave. The women were terrified of the father and desired to leave the spot. When they had all left, the brahmana who was Kashyapa's descendant was miserable and did not feel well. His heart was in a whirl. After some time, the valiant one went to the spot where the delightful and ornamented courtesans could be seen. On seeing the brahmana arrive, they were delighted in their minds. All of them surrounded him and spoke these words. "O amiable one! Come to our hermitage. There will be special and wonderful rituals there." He heard all their words, pleasing to the heart. He made up his mind to go and the women took him away. When the great-souled brahmana was thus brought,[123] the god suddenly showered down and delighted the world. When the brahmana arrived in his kingdom with the rains, the king[124] advanced to worship the sage, bowing his head down on the ground. Controlled, as is proper, he offered him arghya. He sought the favour of that Indra among brahmanas, in particular from the anger the brahmana[125] would be overwhelmed with. He made him enter the inner quarters and following the prescribed rites, bestowed his daughter Shanta on him. The king obtained peace of mind.[126] In this way, the immensely energetic Rishyashringa resided there, with his wife, Shanta, worshipped extremely well and with all his desires satisfied.'

Chapter 1(10)

'O Indra among kings![127] Listen yet again to my beneficial words. This is what the intelligent one, foremost among

[123] To Anga.

[124] Romapada.

[125] Meaning Vibhandaka.

[126] Since peace is *shanti,* there is a bit of a pun.

[127] Sumantra is still speaking.

gods,[128] had said. "A king named Dasharatha will be born in the lineage of Ikshvaku. He will be extremely devoted to dharma. He will be handsome and truthful to his vows. That king will be friendly with the king of Anga. He will have an extremely fortunate daughter named Shanta.[129] Anga's[130] son will be a king who will be spoken of as Romapada. The immensely illustrious King Dasharatha will go to him and say, 'O one with dharma in your soul! I am without a son. For the sake of my sacrifice, grant me Shanta's husband. For the sake of a son and for the sake of the lineage, he will preside over the sacrifice.' The king who will be controlled will hear these words and think about them in his mind, about granting Shanta's husband for the sake of obtaining a son. He will grant him, and devoid of anxiety, the king[131] will receive the brahmana. Delighted in his mind, he will make arrangements for the sacrifice. Desiring to perform the sacrifice, King Dasharatha, knowledgeable about dharma, will join his hands in salutation and request Rishyashringa, foremost among brahmanas. For the sake of the sacrifice, for the sake of sons and for the sake of heaven, the lord of men and the lord of the earth will have his desires satisfied by that foremost among brahmanas. He will have four sons, infinite in valour. They will establish lineages and will be famous in all the worlds." This is what the illustrious lord Sanatkumara, foremost among gods, told in an account in an ancient time, during *deva yuga*.[132] O great king! Let that tiger among men be honoured well and brought here. You should yourself go, with your army and mounts.'

Having heard the suta's words and having obtained Vasishtha's permission, he[133] left for where that brahmana was, with the residents of his inner quarters and his advisers. They gradually passed over forests and rivers. They entered the country where that bull among

[128] Sanatkumara.

[129] The text leaves this vague enough for the 'he' to be interpreted as either Dasharatha or Romapada.

[130] This Anga means Romapada's father.

[131] Dasharatha.

[132] Obviously, another name for krita yuga.

[133] Dasharatha.

sages was. He approached that best among brahmanas, seated near Romapada. He saw the rishi's son, who blazed like a fire. On seeing the king, the king[134] followed the proper rites and worshipped him, especially because of their friendship. He was delighted in his mind. Romapada told the intelligent rishi's son and about their friendship and relationship and he also worshipped him.[135] Honoured extremely well in this way, the bull among men spent some time there. After having spent seven or eight days there, the king told the king, 'O king! O lord of the earth! Let your daughter, Shanta, and her husband come to my city. There is the task of a great sacrifice to be performed.' Hearing this, the intelligent king agreed to the idea of their travelling there and spoke these words. 'O brahmana! Go there with your wife.' The rishi's son agreed with what the king had said. Having taken the king's permission, he left with his wife. The valiant Dasharatha and Romapada were delighted. They joined their hands in salutation and affectionately embraced each other. Having taken leave of his well-wisher,[136] the descendant of the Raghu lineage departed. He sent along swift messengers ahead, to inform the citizens. 'Swiftly make arrangements for the city to be decorated in every possible way.' The citizens were delighted to hear that the king was arriving. They made all the arrangements, as the king's messengers had conveyed. Placing the bull among brahmanas ahead of him and to the sound of the blaring of conch shells and the beating of drums, the king entered the ornamented city. On seeing the brahmana, everyone in the city was delighted. When the Indra among men,[137] with deeds to rival those of Indra, entered, he was honoured extremely well. He made him[138] enter the inner quarters and following the sacred texts, worshipped him. Having brought him there, he thought that his task had already been accomplished. All those in the inner quarters saw that the large-eyed Shanta had arrived there, with her husband. They were filled with joy. She was

[134] Dasharatha and Romapada respectively.

[135] Rishyashringa also worshipped Dasharatha.

[136] Romapada.

[137] Dasharatha.

[138] Rishyashringa.

honoured by them, especially by the king. With the brahmana, she happily resided there for a while.

Chapter 1(11)

After several days had passed, the extremely pleasant season of spring presented itself and the king made up his mind to undertake the sacrifice. He bowed his head down before the brahmana,[139] whose complexion was like that of the gods, and sought his favours. For the sake of sons and the lineage, he requested him to be the officiating priest at the sacrifice. Honoured extremely well, he agreed to the king's words. 'Let the requisite objects be brought and let the horse be released.'[140] The king spoke the following words to Sumantra, supreme among ministers. 'O Sumantra! Quickly invite officiating priests who are knowledgeable about the *brahman*.'[141] Sumantra, swift in his valour, departed quickly. He brought all the brahmanas who were accomplished in the Vedas—Suyajna, Vamadeva, Javali, Kashyapa, the priest Vasishtha and other supreme brahmanas. King Dasharatha, with dharma in his soul, worshipped them. He gently spoke these words, full of dharma and artha. 'My mind is not at peace. There is no happiness without a son. That is the reason I have made up my mind to undertake a horse sacrifice. I wish to perform that sacrifice in accordance with the rites laid down in the sacred texts. Through the powers of the rishi's son,[142] I hope to accomplish my desire.' All the brahmanas, with Vasishtha at the forefront, praised the undecaying words that had emerged from the king's mouth and honoured the

[139] Rishyashringa.

[140] Spoken by Rishyashringa. In a horse sacrifice, a horse is released, left free to wander around. When the horse wanders into another king's kingdom, that king seizes the horse and provokes a battle, or accepts vassalage. When the triumphant horse eventually returns, it is sacrificed.

[141] The brahman or *paramatman* is the supreme soul. Though Rishyashringa was the chief officiating priest, there were other officiating priests too.

[142] Rishyashringa.

king back. With Rishyashringa at the forefront, they told the king, 'Let all the necessary objects be brought and let the horse be released. By all means, you will obtain four infinitely valorous sons. Because your mind has turned towards dharma, those sons will arrive.' On hearing the words that the brahmanas had spoken, the king was delighted. Filled with joy because of those auspicious words, the king told the advisers, 'Obeying the words of the preceptors, let all the necessary objects be brought quickly. Let the horse be released, guarded adequately and followed by preceptors. Let the sacrificial arena be marked out on the northern banks of the Sarayu. Following the ordinances laid down in the sacred texts, let peace prosper. This is the supreme sacrifice. If all the kings are capable of performing this sacrifice without any hindrances, they do not suffer from any hardships. The learned *brahma-rakshasas*[143] always seek out weaknesses. If the ordinances are not observed, the performer of a sacrifice is always destroyed. Therefore, let the sacrifice be completed in accordance with the prescribed ordinances. All of you are capable of acting in accordance with the ordinances.' All the ministers agreed to this and honoured him back. They followed the king's words, exactly as they had been instructed. All the brahmanas also granted permission to that bull among kings, who knew about dharma, and returned to wherever they had come from. When the brahmanas had departed, the lord of men also allowed the ministers to leave. The immensely radiant one entered his own abode.

Chapter 1(12)

After an entire year had passed, it was spring again.[144] Following the rites, he[145] greeted Vasishtha and worshipped him. To obtain sons, he spoke these humble words to that supreme among brahmanas. 'O brahmana! O bull among sages! Please perform

[143] Brahmanas who become rakshasas after death.

[144] The horse returned after wandering around for a year.

[145] Dasharatha.

the sacrifice properly. Let impediments not be caused to any part of the sacrifice. You are extremely affectionate towards me and you are my supreme preceptor. The sacrifice that I am about to undertake is a burden and you are capable of bearing that load.' The supreme among brahmanas agreed to what the king had said and replied, 'I will do everything that you have asked.' He accordingly instructed all the aged brahmanas who were familiar with sacrificial rites, accomplished architects, those who were aged and extremely devoted to dharma, artisans who could see everything through until completion, carpenters, those who dug, astrologers, craftsmen, actors, dancers and extremely learned men acquainted with the unsullied sacred texts, 'Following the king's command, engage yourselves in tasks connected with the sacrifice. Quickly bring several thousand bricks. For the kings, construct many structures that possess all the qualities. You must build hundreds of auspicious residences for the brahmanas. They must be properly stocked with many kinds of food and drink. For the residents of the city and the countryside, there must be many beautiful abodes that are stocked with diverse kinds of food and all the objects of desire. Food must be given properly and with honour, not indifferently. All the varnas must be worshipped, respected well and given this. Nothing must be offered with disrespect, or with sentiments of desire and anger. Men and artisans who are eagerly engaged in tasks connected with the sacrifice must be specially worshipped, in the due order. If no one is disrespected, then they will perform their tasks properly. All of you act in this way, pleasantly and with affection.' Vasishtha summoned all of them and told them this and they promised that they would all act in this way, with nothing being ignored.

Vasishtha summoned Sumantra and spoke these words. 'Invite all the kings on earth who are devoted to dharma and thousands of brahmanas, kshatriyas, vaishyas and shudras. Respectfully summon men from all the countries and the brave Janaka, lord of Mithila, for whom truth is his valour. He is devoted to all the sacred texts and devoted to the Vedas. Honour that immensely fortunate one well and bring him here yourself. It is because I know about the earlier alliance that I am mentioning him first.[146] Then there is the gentle king of Kashi, always pleasant in speech. His conduct is like that of a god. Bring him yourself. The aged king of Kekaya is extremely devoted to dharma. He is the father-in-law of this lion among kings. Bring him, together with his son. The illustrious and immensely fortunate Romapada, lord of Anga, is a friend to this lion among kings. Honour him well and bring him here. Bring all the kings from the east, Sindhu, Souvira and the kings from the southern regions. Bring all the other virtuous and pleasant kings on earth. Bring all of them swiftly, with their followers and relatives.' Hearing Vasishtha's words, Sumantra quickly instructed men to act in accordance with the king's auspicious words. Following the sage's instructions, Sumantra, with dharma in his soul, himself departed quickly to invite the kings.

Everyone came and informed the intelligent Vasishtha that the designated tasks had been completed. All of them told him that the objects needed for the sacrifice had been brought. Delighted, the foremost among brahmanas again told all of them, 'Even in jest, nothing should be given with any mark of disrespect. There is no doubt that if something is given without respect, the giver is destroyed.' After some days and nights, the kings started to arrive. They brought many kinds of gems for King Dasharatha. Extremely joyful, Vasishtha told the king, 'O tiger among men! Following your command, the kings have arrived. As each one deserved, I have honoured those best among kings. O king! Disciplining themselves, the men have made arrangements for the sacrifice. So that the sacrifice can be performed, you should now go to the sacrificial ground. In every direction, it has been stocked with all the objects of desire.' Following the words of Vasishtha and Rishyashringa, on an auspicious day and nakshatra, the lord of the earth left. With Vasishtha leading the way and placing Rishyashringa at the forefront, the supreme among brahmanas started the process for the sacrifice.

[146] This probably means earlier friendship. At a stretch, this might also mean that Vasishtha knew about the future matrimonial alliance.

Chapter 1(13)

After an entire year was over, the horse returned. The king's sacrifice started on the northern bank of the Sarayu. Placing Rishyashringa at the forefront, the bulls among brahmanas started the rites for the great horse sacrifice of the extremely great-souled king. Learned in the Vedas, the officiating priests performed the required rites. In due order, they followed the ordinances and policies of the sacred texts. The brahmanas followed the sacred texts in observing the *pravargya* and *upasad* rites.[147] In accordance with the sacred texts, they performed all the other tasks. Delighted, all the bulls among the sages worshipped and, following the rites, performed all the rituals that have to be performed in the morning. In no way was there any deviation in any of these. The brahmana[148] checked that everything was properly performed. No one who was exhausted or hungry could be seen there. There was no ignorant brahmana present, nor one without hundreds of followers. The brahmanas incessantly ate. The ascetics ate. The mendicants ate. The aged, the diseased, women and children incessantly ate and were still not satisfied. Many urgings of 'give', 'give food and different kinds of garments' were heard there. Many heaps of food could be seen, as large as mountains and every day, they were cooked in the proper way. The brahmanas praised the tasty food that had been prepared in the proper way. 'I am content. We are fortunate.' These are the words Raghava[149] heard. Ornamented men served the brahmanas. They were aided by others wearing polished and bejewelled earrings. In gaps between the rituals, the brahmanas indulged in many kinds of debates. Wishing to defeat each other, those patient and extremely eloquent ones spoke to each other. From one day to another day, those accomplished brahmanas performed all the rites, urged on by the sacred texts. There was no one there who did not know the six Vedangas. There

[147] Specific rites connected with a *soma* sacrifice.
[148] Rishyashringa.
[149] Dasharatha.

was no one without vows, or without learning. As an assistant priest, the king had no brahmana who was not skilled.

When the time came to erect the sacrificial posts, there were six each made out of *bilva*, *khadira* and *parnina*. There was one constructed from *shleshmataka* and two from *devadaru*, these two being laid out like two outstretched arms.[150] All of these were erected by those who were learned about the sacred texts and about sacrifices. To bring beauty to the sacrifice, these were ornamented and embellished in gold. In accordance with the ordinances, all of these were firmly laid out by accomplished artisans. Each possessed eight smooth sides. They were covered with garments and decorated with flowers and fragrances. They were radiant, like the *saptarshi*s in heaven.[151] Bricks were properly measured and laid out and brahmanas knowledgeable about *shulba* rites readied the place for the fire.[152] Eighteen bricks were laid out on three sides[153] and it looked like Garuda[154] with golden feathers. As instructed by the sacred texts, animals, serpents, birds, horses and aquatic creatures were tethered to sacrificial stakes, as offerings to the gods. Following the sacred texts, the officiating priests sacrificed these. Three hundred animals were tethered to sacrificial stakes, including King Dasharatha's supreme horse. In great joy, Kousalya worshipped the horse and used three swords to kill it.[155] With a peaceful mind and wishing to obtain dharma, Kousalya then spent a single night with that

[150] In a horse sacrifice, stretching from the north to the south, twenty-one sacrificial posts are laid out. The horse is tied to the main one and this is made out of the *rajjudala* (shleshmataka) tree. Two posts made out of devadaru are to the north and south of this. There are six posts each from bilva, khadira and *palasha* (parnina).

[151] The saptarshis are the seven great sages. The list varies, but the standard one is Marichi, Atri, Angira, Pulastya, Pulaha, Kratu and Vasishtha. In the sky, the saptarshis are identified with the constellation of Ursa Major (Great Bear).

[152] Shulba rites are those connected with the construction of the altar for the sacrifice. The associated sacred texts are known as *Shulba Sutras*.

[153] In the shape of a triangle.

[154] The king of the birds, Vishnu's mount.

[155] Or three strokes of the sword.

horse. The *hotri*s, *adhvaryu*s and *udgatri*s[156] united the *mahishi*, *parivritti* and *vavata* with the horse.[157] The extremely controlled officiating priests, controlled in their senses, extracted the horse's entrails, and following the sacred texts, offered this as oblation into the fire. At the appropriate time, following the rituals and desiring to cleanse himself of sins, the lord of men inhaled the fragrance of the smoke from the entrails. Sixteen brahmanas who were officiating priests observed the rituals and offered all the limbs of the horse into the fire. In other sacrifices, oblations are offered using the branch of a *plaksha* tree.[158] However, in the case of a horse sacrifice, the sacrifice is conducted with a single reed. According to the *Kalpa Sutra*s and the *Brahmana* texts,[159] the horse sacrifice numbers three days. The first day after that has been thought of as *chatushtoma*, the second has been counted as *uktha* and the third is known as *atiratra*.[160] Thereafter, other great sacrifices like *jyotishtoma*, *ayushtoma*, atiratra, *abhijit*, *vishvajit* and *aptoryama* were performed. The king, the extender of his own lineage, gave away the eastern direction to the hotri, the western direction to the adhvaryu, the southern direction to the brahmana and the northern direction to the udgatri as *dakshina*.[161] In ancient times, Svayambhu had performed a great horse sacrifice. Having properly completed the sacrifice, the king,

156 There were four classes of priests, though the classification varied over time. The hotri is the chief priest and is accomplished in the Rig Veda. The adhvaryu is the assistant priest and is accomplished in the Yajur Veda, though later, the udgatri came to be identified with the Sama Veda. In addition, there was the brahmana or *purohita*.

157 Mahishi is the chief queen, the one who has been consecrated. Parivritti or *parivrikti* is a queen who was earlier favoured, but is now neglected. Vavata is a favourite wife. *Palagali* is mentioned as the most inferior wife, a king being entitled to four wives. Sometimes, mahishi is said to be the kshatriya wife, vavata is said to be the vaishya wife and parivritti is said to be the shudra wife. In this case, the former meaning is appropriate.

158 The holy fig tree.

159 *Kalpa Sutras* are sacred texts that describe rituals, *Brahmanas* are sacred texts, not to be confused with the varna of brahmana.

160 These are days on which soma sacrifices are offered, chatushtoma also being known as *agnishtoma*.

161 Sacrificial fee. These were donated symbolically.

bull among men and extender of sacrifices, donated the earth to the officiating priests. With the king cleansed of all his sins, all the officiating priests told him, 'You alone are capable of protecting the entire earth. We have nothing to do with the earth. We are incapable of ruling it. O lord of the earth! We are always engaged in studying. Instead, give us something that has an equivalent value.' The king gave them one million cows, ten crore gold coins and forty crore silver coins. Collectively, all the officiating priests gave those riches to the sage Rishyashringa and the intelligent Vasishtha. Each of those supreme among brahmanas received his proper share. All of them were supremely delighted and said that they were satisfied. Having performed that supreme sacrifice, which destroyed sins and conveyed one to heaven, the king was delighted. It was a sacrifice that was extremely difficult for kings to perform. King Dasharatha then told Rishyashringa, 'O one who is excellent in his vows! You should act so that my lineage is extended.' The supreme among brahmanas told the king that it would indeed be that way. 'O king! You will have four sons who will extend your lineage.'

Chapter 1(14)

The intelligent one[162] reflected for some time on what he should say. Having regained his senses, the one who knew about the Vedas told the king, 'So that you can have sons and daughters, I will perform a sacrifice.[163] I will observe the ordinances and *mantra*s decreed by *Atharvashirasa*[164] and they will be successful.' He then performed the sacrifice that generates sons and daughters. Chanting mantras and following the indicated rites, the energetic one offered

[162] Rishyashringa.

[163] The horse sacrifice has only removed the sins. A specific ceremony now has to be performed, to obtain offspring.

[164] While this clearly refers to the Atharva Veda, many *Atharvashirasa* texts are of much later vintage.

oblations into the fire. As is appropriate, the gods, the gandharvas, the siddhas[165] and the supreme rishis assembled there to receive their shares.

In the proper way, the gods who had gathered in that assembly spoke these great words to Brahma, the creator of the worlds. 'O illustrious one! Through your favours, the rakshasa named Ravana is using his valour to obstruct us in every possible way. We are incapable of subjugating him. O illustrious one! In ancient times, because of your affection, you granted him a boon. Since then, we have had to respect him in every way and have had to tolerate him. The evil-minded one shows his enmity against all those who rise up and oppresses the three worlds. As he wills, he torments Shakra, the king of the gods. He is invincible and confused because of the boon he has received. He acts against the rishis, the *yaksha*s,[166] the gandharvas, the asuras and the brahmanas. The sun god cannot torment him. The wind god cannot blow against his flanks. On seeing him, the god of the ocean, with his turbulent waves, cannot make him tremble. There is great fear from that rakshasa, who is terrible to look at. O illustrious one! You should think of a means to bring about this death.' He[167] was thus addressed by all the gods. He thought for a while and said, 'The means of countering that evil-souled one and slaying him has been decided. He had asked that gandharvas, yakshas, gods, *danava*s[168] and rakshasas should be incapable of slaying him and I had agreed to his desire. Because of his disrespect towards them, the rakshasa had not mentioned humans. Therefore, a man will bring about his death. His death cannot occur in any other way.' On hearing the agreeable words Brahma spoke, all the gods and maharshis were delighted. At that time, the immensely radiant Vishnu arrived there. He approached Brahma, who was still meditating. All the gods bowed down before him and said, 'O Vishnu! For the sake of the welfare of the worlds, we wish

[165] Term used for successful sages who have become semi-divine.

[166] Yakshas are semi-divine species, described as companions of Kubera, the lord of riches.

[167] Brahma.

[168] Demons.

to invoke you. The lord King Dasharatha is the king of Ayodhya. He knows about dharma and is talked about. His energy is like that of a maharshi. His three wives are virtuous, prosperous and famous.[169] O Vishnu! Divide yourself into four parts and become their sons. You will be born as men. The gods find him to be invincible. He is a like a growing thorn that the worlds face. Defeat Ravana in a battle. The rakshasa Ravana is stupid. However, because his valour has been ignited, he obstructs gods, the gandharvas, the siddhas and the supreme rishis. The terrible Ravana is fierce in his energy. His enmity and intolerance towards the lord of the gods has increased. He is like a thorn to the virtuous ascetics and makes them scream.[170] Save the ascetics from that great fear.'

Chapter 1(15)

Narayana Vishnu was thus engaged by the supreme gods, though he knew all this. He spoke these gentle words to the gods. 'O gods! What is the means to bring about the death of the lord of the rakshasas? How will I slay the one who is a like a thorn to the rishis?' Thus addressed, all the gods replied to the undecaying Vishnu. 'Assume a human form and slay Ravana in a battle. O destroyer of enemies! Over a long period of time, he has tormented himself through fierce austerities. Brahma, the creator of the worlds and worshipped by the worlds, was satisfied at this. Content, the lord granted a boon to that rakshasa. With the exception of humans, he will not face fear from any other creature. Because of disrespect, in those ancient times, he ignored humans at the time of the boon. O scorcher of enemies! Therefore, it is evident that his death can only come about through men.' The compassionate Vishnu heard the words spoken by the gods. The idea of choosing King Dasharatha as his father appealed to him. The king was without a son and at that

[169] It is possible to identify Kousalya with virtue, Sumitra with prosperity and fame with Kaikeyee.

[170] There is a pun. The word *rava* means to scream or shriek.

time, the immensely radiant destroyer of enemies was performing a sacrifice with a desire to obtain sons.

A great being manifested himself from the sacrificial fire. He was immensely valorous and immensely strong, infinitely radiant. He was dark and attired in red garments. His face was red and his voice was like the rumbling of a drum. His eyes were tawny. However, his body, with an excellent beard and hair, was pleasant. He possessed all the auspicious signs and he was adorned with celestial ornaments. He was as tall as the peak of a mountain and his valour was like that of a proud tiger. His form was like that of the sun, blazing like the flames of a fire. He held a vessel made of molten gold, covered with a lid made out of silver. It looked as agreeable as a beloved wife and was full of celestial *payasam*.[171] He held it himself in his extended hands and it seemed to be like some maya. On seeing King Dasharatha, he spoke these words. 'O king! Know me to be a being who has been sent here by Prajapati.' The king joined his hands in salutation and addressed the supreme one. 'O illustrious one! Welcome. What can I do for you?' The being sent by Prajapati again spoke these words. 'O king! You have worshipped the gods and have now obtained this. O tiger among men! This payasam has been made by the gods and gives rise to progeny. It is blessed and increases good health. Accept it. Give it to your deserving wives and make them eat it. O king! Through them, you will obtain the sons you performed the sacrifice for.' The king was delighted. He bowed his head down and accepted the golden vessel given by the gods, filled with food that the gods ate. He worshipped that extraordinary being, so agreeable to behold. He was filled with great delight and circumambulated him. Dasharatha obtained the payasam, prepared by the gods. He was overcome by great delight, like a poor person who has obtained riches. Having accomplished his task, the supremely radiant being, extraordinary in form, instantly vanished.

The inner quarters seemed to be bathed in rays of delight, like the pleasant autumn sky when it is enveloped by the moon's

[171] A dish made out sweetened milk and rice.

beams. He entered the inner quarters and told Kousalya, 'For the sake of obtaining a son, accept this payasam. The king gave half of the payasam to Kousalya. The king gave half of what remained to Sumitra. For the sake of obtaining a son, he gave half of what remained to Kaikeyee. Having thought about it, the lord of the earth again gave what remained of the payasam, which was like *amrita*,[172] to Sumitra.[173] In this way, the king gave separate shares of the payasam to his wives. The supreme wives of the king obtained the payasam and all of them thought this was a great honour. Their hearts were full of joy.

Chapter 1(16)

After Vishnu had become the son of the great-souled king, the illustrious Svayambhu[174] spoke these words to all the gods. 'The valiant Vishnu is devoted to the truth and all of you are his well-wishers. Assume forms that you desire and create powerful aides for him. Let these be accomplished in maya and bravery, with a speed that is like that of the wind. Let them know about policy and possess intelligence. Let them be like Vishnu in valour. Let them be indestructible and let them know about all the means. Let their bodies be divine. Let them know about all weapons, like those who subsist on amrita. Let them be born from the bodies of the best among *apsaras* and gandharva women.[175] Let them be born through yaksha, *pannaga, riksha* and *vidyadhara* maidens.[176] Let them be born from the limbs and bodies of *kinnara* and *vanara*

[172] Nectar or ambrosia.

[173] Thus, Kousalya obtained ½, Kaikeyee obtained ⅛, Sumitra obtained ¼+⅛= ⅜.

[174] The one who created himself, Brahma.

[175] Apsaras are celestial dancers, while gandharvas are celestial musicians. Both are semi-divine.

[176] Pannagas or *nagas* are semi-divine. We have translated them as serpents. Nagas are not snakes (*sarpas*). Unlike sarpas, nagas have special powers and can assume any form at will. They also have specific habitats, such as in the nether regions. Rikshas are bears. Vidyadharas are semi-divine, occupying the region between heaven and earth.

ladies.[177] Create sons who are your equals in valour. Create them in the form of apes.' Thus addressed by the illustrious one, they agreed to adhere to his instructions. They gave birth to sons who were like apes in form. The great-souled rishis, the siddhas, the vidyadharas, the serpents and *charanas*[178] created brave sons who roamed around in the forest. They created many thousand, who would rise up to slay Dashagriva.[179] They were brave and valiant, immeasurable in strength. They could assume any form at will. Those immensely strong ones possessed bodies that were like elephants and mountains. They swiftly took birth as rikshas, vanaras and *gopuchchhas*.[180] Each god had a different kind of form, attire and valour and the sons who were separately born mirrored these from the father. Some born from golangula women were superior in valour. There were others born to riksha, vanara and kinnara women. All of them fought with rocks. All of them used trees as weapons. All of them fought with nails and teeth. All of them were knowledgeable about all kinds of weapons. They were capable of dislodging the greatest of mountains. They could shatter and uproot large trees. With their speed, they were capable of agitating the ocean, the lord of the rivers. They were capable of shattering the ground with their feats. They could leap over the great ocean. They were capable of seizing the clouds in the sky. They could capture crazy elephants when these roamed around in the forest. With the sound of their roars, they could make birds fall down. Such were the apes that were born and they could assume any form at will. The number of such great-souled ones was in millions. Brave ones were born as leaders of troops of apes. There were thousands who departed, to dwell on the slopes of Mount Rikshavat. There were many others who resided in other mountains and groves. Sugriva

[177] Kinnara, also known as *kimpurusha,* is a semi-divine species, described as Kubera's companions. Vanaras are apes, at least we have translated it in that way. There is no consensus on the identification of vanaras. Etymologically, the word means those who roam around in the forests.

[178] Celestial bards.

[179] Ravana.

[180] With a tail like that of a cow, langur. Also known as *golangula.*

was the son of Surya and Vali was the son of Shakra. All the lords among apes served these two brothers. Their bodies were like large masses of clouds. The leaders among the herds of vanaras were immensely strong. They arrived on earth, assuming terrible forms. They assembled so as to help Rama.

Chapter 1(17)

When the great-souled one's horse sacrifice was over, the gods accepted their respective shares and returned to wherever they had come from. With the consecration and rituals over, the king entered the city with his servants, soldiers and mounts, and accompanied by his wives. The king honoured the other kings, in accordance with what they deserved. Bowing down before that bull among sages,[181] they joyfully returned to their own countries. When the kings had departed, placing the supreme brahmanas at the forefront, the prosperous King Dasharatha again entered his own city. Honoured well, Rishyashringa left, with Shanta. Having taken his leave, the intelligent king[182] also left with his followers.

Born as a portion of Vishnu, Kousalya gave birth to the immensely fortunate Rama, the extender of the Ikshvaku lineage and one who possessed all the divine signs.[183] With the infinitely energetic son, Kousalya was radiant. She was like Aditi, after having given birth to the supreme god, the one with the *vajra* in his hands.[184] Kaikeyee gave birth to Bharata, for whom truth was his valour. He was like a fourth portion of Vishnu himself and possessed all the qualities. Sumitra gave birth to the sons Lakshmana and Shatrughna. All of them were brave and skilled in all the weapons.

[181] Vasishtha.

[182] Romapada.

[183] The Critical text excises the shloka which gives the positions of the nakshatras at the time of Rama's birth.

[184] Aditi, Kashyapa's wife, is the mother of the gods, who are known as the Adityas. Indra is the wielder of the vajra.

They were born as Vishnu's portions. The king's four great-souled sons were born separately. They possessed all the qualities and were as resplendent as Proshthapada.[185] When eleven days were over, the ceremony for giving names was undertaken. The eldest was the great-souled Rama. Kaikeyee's son was Bharata. Sumitra's sons were Lakshmana and Shatrughna. Extremely delighted, Vasishtha gave them their names. He also performed the rites connected with birth and all the other sacraments. The eldest one, Rama, was like a standard and brought great pleasure to his father. He appeared to all creatures as if he was the revered Svayambhu. All of them knew about the Vedas. All of them were brave and devoted to the welfare of creatures. All of them were learned and all of them possessed all the qualities. Among them, Rama, with truth as his valour, was immensely energetic. Since childhood, Lakshmana, the extender of prosperity, was extremely pleasant.[186] He was always devoted to his eldest brother, Rama, one who brought delight to the worlds. With body and soul, he always did what brought Rama pleasure. Lakshmana possessed prosperity. Though his body was different, his breath of life was like Rama's. Without him, Purushottama[187] was unable to go to sleep. Without him, he[188] would not eat any delicious food that was brought to him. When Raghava[189] rode a horse and went out on a hunt, he[190] wielded a bow and protected him from the rear. Shatrughna, Lakshmana's younger brother, was thus attached to Bharata. He was always dearer than his[191] own life and remained devoted to him. Dasharatha loved these four

[185] Proshthapada is a nakshatra. More accurately, it is a collective name for two nakshatras, Purva Bhadrapada and Uttara Bhadrapada. These are stars in the constellation Pegasus, which partly consists of a quadrilateral, with four stars at four vertices. The four stars are probably being compared with the four sons.

[186] Lakshmana's name is derived in that way, someone who has Lakshmi in him, or makes Lakshmi prosper. Rama means someone who causes delight. Bharata is someone who bears a burden and Shatrughna is someone who destroys the enemy.

[187] Rama.

[188] Rama.

[189] Rama.

[190] Lakshmana.

[191] Bharata's.

extremely fortunate sons. He was extremely delighted with them, like the grandfather[192] with the gods. All of them possessed learning. All of them possessed all the qualities. They possessed humility and were renowned. They knew everything and were far-sighted.

With his priests and relatives, the great-souled King Dasharatha started to think about their marriages. In an assembly of his ministers, the great-souled one reflected on this. At that time, the immensely energetic and great sage, Vishvamitra, arrived there. He told the gatekeeper that he wished to meet the king. 'Quickly tell him that Koushika, Gadhi's son, has arrived.' Hearing this and frightened in their minds,[193] they were urged by these words and rushed towards the king's residence. They went to the king's abode and told the king who was descended from the Ikshvaku lineage that rishi Vishvamitra had arrived. Hearing these words, he was delighted. He controlled himself and, with his priests, headed for the place, like Vasava[194] towards Brahma. The ascetic, firm in his vows, was radiant. On seeing him, with a cheerful face, the king offered him arghya. Following the rituals instructed in the sacred texts, he accepted arghya from the king and asked about the king's welfare. When Vasishtha arrived, the immensely fortunate one asked about the welfare of that bull among sages and also that of the other rishis. Worshipped and cheerful in their minds, all of them entered the king's residence. Each sat down on the seat he deserved. The extremely generous king was delighted in his mind. He cheerfully worshipped the great sage, Vishvamitra, and said, 'Your arrival here is like the receipt of amrita, like rain in a place that is without water, like a barren wife giving birth and like getting back riches that have been destroyed. O great sage! I think that your arrival here signifies joy like that. Welcome. I am delighted. What can I do for you? What is your great desire? O brahmana! O one who follows dharma! You are a worthy recipient and it is good fortune that you have come here. Today, my birth has been rendered successful and it is as if I have indeed lived a successful

[192] Brahma.

[193] Vishvamitra was known for his rage.

[194] Indra.

life. You were earlier known as a rajarshi and blazed in radiance because of your austerities. You then became a brahmana rishi.[195] You should be worshipped by me in several ways. O brahmana! Your arrival here is supremely sacred and wonderful. O lord! Merely by looking at you, it is as if I have visited an auspicious spot. Please tell me what you desire and the reasons for your coming here. If I can ensure the fruition of your desires, I will be greatly blessed. O Koushika! You are like a god to me. Unless I do not deserve to be told, you should tell me about the task that needs to be performed and I will accomplish it completely.' The supreme rishi heard these words, which were pleasant to hear about and brought happiness to the heart. They were uttered with humility by someone who possessed all the qualities and was famous for his qualities. He was greatly delighted.

Chapter 1(18)

On hearing the wonderful words of that lion among kings, expounded in detail, the immensely energetic Vishvamitra's body hair stood up and he said, 'O tiger among kings! It is befitting that you, and no one else on earth, should speak these words. You have been born in a great lineage and have been instructed by Vasishtha. I will tell you what is in my heart and you can decide on your course of action accordingly. O tiger among kings! You are true to your pledges. Act in accordance with that. O bull among men! To become successful, I am now engaged in some rituals. Two rakshasas are causing obstacles along that path and they can assume any form at will. I am nearing the completion of my vows. However, those two rakshasas, Maricha and Subahu, are valiant and well trained. They shower down torrents of flesh and blood on the sacrificial altar. With the advent of this obstruction, the completion of the rituals is uncertain. Though I had exerted myself, I have lost

[195] Born as a kshatriya, because of his austerities, Vishvamitra became a brahmana.

all interest and have left that place. O king! My intelligence should not be excited and fall prey to anger. When one is practising rituals of that kind, one should not come under the influence of rage. O tiger among kings! Rama is your own son and truth is his valour. He is brave and the eldest. The sidelocks of his hair are like a crow's wings.[196] Give him to me. He will be protected by me and is also celestial in his own energy. He is capable of countering the rakshasas and destroying them. There is no doubt that I will also confer many kinds of objects on him and they will be beneficial. Through those, he will obtain fame in the three worlds. Those two are incapable of standing before Rama in any way. No man other than Raghava[197] is capable of killing them. Intoxicated by their valour, those two wicked ones have been bound by the noose of destiny. O tiger among kings! They are incapable of withstanding the great-souled Rama. O king! Just because he is your son, you should not display excessive affection. I am assuring you. Know that those two rakshasas are as good as slain. I know the great-souled Rama. Truth is his valour. The immensely energetic Vasishtha knows this and so do all the ascetics who are stationed here. O Indra among kings! If you desire to obtain dharma and constant and supreme fame on earth, you should give Rama to me. O Kakutstha![198] If your ministers grant you permission and so do the others, with Vasishtha at the forefront, grant him to me and let go of Rama. Without any attachment towards him, you should grant me your desired son, the lotus-eyed Rama. The sacrifice will only last for ten nights. O Raghava! Act so that the designated time for my sacrifice is not in vain. You should not have any unnecessary sorrow in your mind. Act so that there is good fortune.' The one with dharma in his soul spoke these words, which were full of dharma. Then the great sage, the immensely energetic Vishvamitra, stopped speaking. The lord of men heard these words and they shattered his heart and mind. He was distressed in his mind and, suffering from great fear, was dislodged from his throne.

196 A mark of beauty, *kaka* (crow) *paksha* (wing).

197 Rama.

198 Kakutstha was an ancestor. Hence, both Dasharatha and Rama are addressed as his descendants.

Chapter 1(19)

Hearing the words spoken by Vishvamitra, for some time, the tiger among kings lost his senses. Having regained his senses, he said, 'My lotus-eyed Rama is still less than sixteen years of age.[199] I do not see him as being capable of fighting against the rakshasas. Here is an entire *akshouhini* and I am its lord and commander.[200] Surrounded by them, I will go there and fight against those who roam around in the night.[201] These servants are brave and valiant and accomplished in the use of weapons. They are capable of fighting against large numbers of rakshasas. You should not take Rama. In the forefront of the battle, I will protect you with a bow in my hand. As long as I have life, I will fight against those who roam around in the night. Thus protected well, you will face no obstructions in the completion of your vows. I will go there. You should not take Rama. He is a child. He has not completed his education. He does not know about strengths and weaknesses.[202] He does not possess the strength of weapons. Nor is he accomplished in fighting. There is no doubt that the rakshasas will resort to deceitful methods of fighting and he cannot counter that. O brahmana! O tiger among sages! Separated from Rama, I am not interested in remaining alive, not even for an instant. You should not take Rama. O brahmana! O one who is excellent in his vows! However, if you do wish to take Raghava, take me with him, with the four kinds of forces.[203] O Koushika! Sixty thousand years have passed since my birth. He has been born after a lot of misery. You should not take Rama. I am extremely affectionate towards my four sons. According to dharma, the eldest is the most important. You should not take Rama. What valour do those rakshasas possess? Whose sons are they? O bull

[199] For several purposes, sixteen is a threshold and all that is known is that Rama was younger than that.

[200] An akshouhini is an army, consisting of 21,870 chariots, 21,870 elephants, 65,610 horse riders and 1,09,350 foot soldiers.

[201] That is, rakshasas.

[202] Of the enemy.

[203] Chariots, elephants, cavalry and infantry.

among sages! What is their size and who protects them? How will Rama be able to act against those rakshasas? O brahmana! They will fight in deceitful ways and I alone possess the strength to counter them. O illustrious one! Instruct me everything, about how I can fight against them in the battle. Those rakshasas are full of valour and base themselves on evil sentiments.'

Hearing his words, Vishvamitra replied, 'There is a rakshasa named Ravana, born in Poulastya's lineage. Thanks to a boon obtained from Brahma, he oppresses and obstructs the three worlds. He is immensely strong and immensely valorous. He is surrounded by a large number of rakshasas. It has been heard that the immensely valorous Ravana, lord of the rakshasas, is the brother of Vaishravana[204] himself and the son of the sage Vishravasa. The immensely strong one does not cause obstructions to sacrifices himself. He urges two immensely strong rakshasas named Maricha and Subahu and they cause obstructions to sacrifices.'

The king was thus addressed by the sage and told the sage, 'In an encounter, I am myself incapable of standing before that evil-souled one. O one who knows about dharma! You should show your favours towards me and towards my young son.[205] We are limited in fortune. You are our god and our preceptor. The gods, danavas, gandharvas, yakshas and pannagas are incapable of standing before Ravana in an encounter. What can humans do? In an encounter, that brave rakshasa sucks away the valour of his adversaries. O best among sages! I am incapable of fighting against him and his army, even with my soldiers and even if I am with my sons. My son is said to be an equal of the immortals. But he does not know about fighting. O brahmana! My son is but a child. Grant him to me. In addition, those two are the descendants of Sunda and Upasunda[206] and are like Death in a battle. They may obstruct sacrifices, but I will not give you my son. Maricha and Subahu are full of valour and

[204] Kubera.

[205] And not ask either of us to fight against Ravana.

[206] Famous demons. Deceived by Vishnu, they ended up fighting against each other and killing each other.

are extremely well trained. In an extremely terrible battle, I will fight against one or the other of those two.'

Chapter 1(20)

Koushika heard what he had said, his words were full of affection. Filled with anger, he answered the king in these words. 'You have been born in Raghava's lineage and will bring destruction to the line. Having pledged earlier, you now wish to deviate from your promise. O king! Pardon me. I will go to wherever I came from. O Kakutstha! Having taken a false pledge, may you be happy with your relatives.' The intelligent Vishvamitra was thus filled with rage and the entire earth trembled. The gods were terrified. The great and patient rishi, Vasishtha, excellent in his vows, discerned that the form of the entire universe was scared. He addressed the king in these words. 'You have been born in the Ikshvaku lineage and are like another Dharma[207] yourself. You possess fortitude and are excellent in your vows, and prosperous. You should not abandon dharma. Raghava[208] is famous in the three worlds as one who has dharma in his soul. Follow your own dharma and do not resort to adharma. O Raghava! If a person has taken a pledge and then transgresses it, he destroys the fruits of all the sacrifices he has performed earlier. Therefore, let Rama go. Whether he is accomplished in the use of weapons or unaccomplished in the use of weapons, the rakshasas cannot harm him. He will be protected by Kushika's son, like amrita by the fire.[209] He[210] is supreme among valiant ones and is the personified form of Dharma. In intelligence and strength of austerities, there is no one in this world who is superior to him. He is the only one in the three worlds of mobile and immobile objects who knows about all the weapons. There is no

[207] The god of dharma.
[208] An oblique way of referring to Dasharatha himself.
[209] Amrita is protected by a circle of fire that surrounds it.
[210] Vishvamitra.

other man who knows about these, or for that matter, gods, rishis, asuras, rakshasas, gandharvas, the best among yakshas, kinnaras and the giant serpents. Krishashva's sons were supremely devoted to dharma and while he ruled his kingdom, in ancient times, he gave all these weapons to Koushika.[211] Krishashva's sons were the sons of Prajapati's[212] daughters. They[213] were not similar in form. They were immensely valorous, resplendent and brought victory. The slender-waisted Jaya and Suprabha were Daksha's daughters. They generated hundreds of thousands of supremely radiant weapons. In ancient times, Jaya gave birth to five hundred supreme sons. They were capable of adopting many different forms and were designed to slay the soldiers of the asuras.[214] Then again, Suprabha gave birth to another five hundred sons. They were strong, impossible to withstand and invincible, designed to destroy.[215] Kushika's son knows about these weapons. He knows about dharma and is capable of also creating many other weapons that have not been known earlier. Vishvamitra is immensely energetic and a great ascetic. Such is his valour. O king! You should not harbour any doubts about Rama going.'

Chapter 1(21)

When he was thus addressed by Vasishtha, with a cheerful face, King Dasharatha summoned his sons, Rama and Lakshmana. Their mothers, their father, Dasharatha, and Vasishtha and the other priests pronounced benedictions and chanted auspicious mantras. Extremely delighted in his mind, King Dasharatha

[211] That is, Krishashva gave these weapons. Krishashva is described as a famous king. He is also described as one of the original Prajapatis (guardians or rulers of the world) who married Daksha's daughters.

[212] Daksha's.

[213] The sons.

[214] The sons were weapons.

[215] These sons were also weapons.

inhaled the fragrances of the heads of his beloved sons and handed them over to Kushika's son. A fragrant breeze, pleasant to the touch, began to blow, when it was seen that the lotus-eyed Rama approached Vishvamitra. The drums of the gods were sounded and a great shower of flowers rained down. Those great-souled ones departed to the sounds of conch shells and drums. Vishvamitra was at the front and the immensely illustrious Rama, with sidelocks like a crow's wing and wielding a bow, followed him. He was followed by Sumitra's son. With quivers and bows in their hands, they illuminated the ten directions. They were with the great-souled Vishvamitra, thus resembling a three-headed serpent. It was as if the two Ashvins followed the grandfather,[216] protecting him.

After having travelled for half a yojana, they reached the southern banks of the Sarayu and Vishvamitra addressed Rama in these sweet words. 'O son! Accept some water and do not allow any more time to pass. With the respective set of mantras, accept Bala and Atibala.[217] As a result of these, there will be no exhaustion, no fever and no destruction of form. Even if you are asleep or distracted, the *nairritas*[218] will not be able to assail you. There will be no one on earth who will be your equal in valour or in the strength of your arms. O Rama! There will be no one in the three worlds who will be your equal. O unblemished one! In this world, there will be no one who will be your equal in fortune, generosity, wisdom, intelligence, determination and ability to respond. The mothers of Bala and Atibala are the sources of all learning and having obtained these two kinds of knowledge, there will be no one who will be your equal. O Rama! O best among men! You will not suffer from hunger and thirst. O Raghava! Along the way, study Bala and Atibala. Having studied these two kinds of knowledge, one obtains unsurpassed fame on earth. These two kinds of knowledge are full

[216] Brahma.

[217] Water has to be touched and ablutions performed before any auspicious act. Bala and Atibala are the divine weapons. Divine weapons are invoked through the use of mantras.

[218] Demons.

of energy and were generated from the grandfather's daughters.[219] O Kakutstha! Because you are full of dharma, you are worthy of receiving these. There is no doubt that you will also reap all the objects of desire that have many qualities, the treasure that is only the outcome of many kinds of austerities.' At this, with a cheerful face, Rama touched water and purified himself. He then accepted the knowledge from the maharshi with the cleansed soul. Suffused with that knowledge, Rama became radiant in his great valour. Kushika's son, who was like a preceptor, was ready to engage them in various tasks. In great happiness, the three of them spent the night on the banks of the Sarayu.

Chapter 1(22)

When night was over, Vishvamitra addressed Kakutstha, who was lying down on a bed of leaves. 'O excellent son of Kousalya! O Rama! It is dawn. O tiger among men! Arise and perform rites for the gods.' The two princes heard the words of the extremely generous rishi. They bathed and performed ablutions in the water. Those two brave ones chanted supreme mantras. Having performed their ablutions, those two extremely valorous ones cheerfully bowed down before Vishvamitra, store of austerities, and made arrangements for departure. Those two extremely valorous ones departed and saw the sacred confluence of the Sarayu with the divine river that has three flows.[220] The sacred hermitages of fierce and energetic rishis were there, those who had tormented themselves through supreme austerities for many thousand years. On seeing that sacred hermitage,[221] the two descendants of Raghava were greatly delighted. They spoke these words to the great-souled Vishvamitra. 'Whose sacred hermitage is this and which man resides here? O illustrious one! We are

[219] In an extended sense, since Daksha was born from Brahma.

[220] The Ganga has three flows, in heaven, on earth and in the nether regions.

[221] In the singular.

overcome by great curiosity and wish to know this.' On hearing their words, the bull among sages laughed. He said, 'O Rama! I will tell you whom this hermitage belonged to earlier. Listen. Kandarpa[222] used to have a body earlier. The learned ones also speak of him as Kama. Sthanu[223] was controlled in his rituals and performed austerities here. Having married, the lord of the gods left, accompanied by large numbers of Maruts. At that time, the great-souled one was afflicted by the one with evil intelligence[224] and uttered the sound of *humkara*.[225] O descendant of the Raghu lineage! All the limbs and body of that evil-minded one were burnt down and destroyed by Rudra's eyes. The great-souled one scorched him and destroyed his body. Because of the great god's rage, Kama was rendered without a body. O Raghava! That is the reason he came to be known as Ananga.[226] The place where he released his handsome body came to be known as the land of Anga. His ancient hermitage came to be frequented by sages who were his disciples.[227] Since they were supremely devoted to dharma, there is no evil in this place. O Rama! O one who is auspicious to behold! We will spend the night here. Tomorrow, we will again proceed along this sacred river.' While they were conversing, the sages, who were far-sighted because of their austerities, realized that they were there. They were greatly delighted and arrived happily. They offered arghya and padya to the guest who was Kushika's son. After this, they also tended to Rama and Lakshmana as guests. Having been honoured well, they cheerfully resided in Kamashrama[228] and delighted themselves in all kinds of conversation.

[222] The god of love, also known as Kama, Ananga or Madana. He was burnt down by Shiva's rage and ceased to have a body.

[223] Shiva.

[224] Kandarpa.

[225] Humkara means to utter the sound 'hum', a sound believed to possess special powers.

[226] The one without a body (*anga*).

[227] Shiva's hermitage, the sages were Shiva's followers.

[228] The hermitage (ashrama) associated with Kama.

Chapter 1(23)

When the morning sparkled, the two scorchers of enemies performed their ablutions. Placing Vishvamitra at the forefront, they arrived at the banks of the river. All those great-souled sages, rigid in their vows, also went there. They prepared an excellent boat and spoke to Vishvamitra. 'Placing the princes in the front, ascend this boat without any delay, so that you can proceed along your path without any hindrances.' Honouring those rishis, Vishvamitra agreed. Taking those two with him, he went to the river that was heading towards the ocean. When they were in the middle of the river, Rama asked the bull among sages, 'What is this tumultuous sound that seems to be shattering the waters?' Raghava's words were full of curiosity. On hearing them, the one with dharma in his soul told him about the reason for the sound. 'O Rama! O tiger among men! In Mount Kailasa, Brahma created a lake through the powers of his mind and that is the reason the lake is known as Manasa.[229] The sacred Sarayu originates from that lake, from the lake created by Brahma. Emerging from that lake, it flows past Ayodhya. That tumultuous sound results when it unites with Jahnavee,[230] from the friction caused by the two flows of water. O Rama! Control yourself and bow down.' Those two were extremely devoted to dharma and bowed down. At that time, they approached the southern bank and dexterous in their valour, alighted.

Those two supreme sons of the king saw a forest that was terrible in form. Having alighted, the descendant of the Ikshvaku lineage asked the bull among sages about this. 'This forest is impenetrable and resounds with the sound of crickets. It is populated by ferocious predatory creatures and the noise of horrible birds can be heard. There are many kinds of predatory birds that shriek in fierce tones. It is populated by lions, tigers, wild boars and elephants. It is full of *dhava*, *ashva*, *karna*, *kakubha*, bilva, *tinduka*, *patala* and *badari*

[229] From *mana* (mind).

[230] Ganga.

trees.[231] What a terrible forest this is!' The immensely energetic and great sage, Vishvamitra, replied, 'O son! O Kakutstha! Listen to the reason why this forest is so terrible. O supreme among men! Earlier, this habitation used to be extremely prosperous. Two countries created by the gods, named Malada and Karusha, used to be here.[232] In ancient times, the one with the one thousand eyes killed Vritra and the sin of having killed a brahmana penetrated him.[233] The gods and the rishis, stores of austerities, therefore bathed Indra. When they bathed him with pots of water, the filth was released. The filth was released on the ground, the muck was released on the ground.[234] When these were released from his body, the great Indra was delighted. Cleansed of the filth and muck, Indra became pure. Greatly delighted, the lord granted those two countries a supreme boon. "Malada and Karusha have borne the filth that was released from my body. Therefore, these two countries will be prosperous and will be famous in the world." When the chastiser of Paka[235] spoke in this way, the gods praised him, on seeing that the intelligent Shakra had honoured the countries in this way. O destroyer of enemies! For a long time, those two countries, Malada and Karusha, were happy and prosperous places, full of wealth and grain. After some time, a female yaksha was born and she could assume any form at will. She possessed the strength of one thousand elephants. O fortunate one! Her name is Tataka and she is the intelligent Sunda's wife. Her son is the rakshasa Maricha, who is like Shakra in his valour. O Raghava! The evil-acting Tataka has incessantly destroyed these two countries, Malada and Karusha. She obstructs the path here and dwells half a yojana away. Using the strength of your arms, slay that evil-acting one. On my instructions, remove this region of its thorn. O Rama! Uproot this terrible female yaksha who is

[231] Dhava is the axle-wood tree, ashva can't be identified, karna is the Indian laburnum, kakubha is the Arjuna tree, bilva is wood apple, tinduka is ebony, patala is *Bignonia suaveolens* and badari is the jujube tree.

[232] Malada and Karusha are in the Baghelkhand-Mirzapur-Shahabad region.

[233] The one with the one thousand eyes is Indra. Vritra was the son of a brahmana.

[234] *Mala* means filth or dirt, hence Malada. Karusha is not that easy to derive, though *karisha* means dung.

[235] Indra, Indra having killed a demon named Paka.

so difficult to withstand, so that she is incapable of destroying this region in this way. I have told you everything about how this forest came to be terrible. The female yaksha does not refrain and still continues to destroy everything.'

Chapter 1(24)

Hearing the words of the immeasurable sage, the tiger among men replied in auspicious words. 'O bull among sages! It has been heard that the yakshas are limited in valour. How can this weak one[236] bear the strength of a thousand elephants?' Vishvamitra spoke these words. 'Hear how she came to bear great strength. This weak one bears valour and strength because of a boon that was bestowed on her. Earlier, there was a great and valiant yaksha named Suketu. He was without offspring. Therefore, he followed auspicious conduct and tormented himself through great austerities. O Rama! Thus, the grandfather[237] was extremely pleased with that lord among yakshas and bestowed a gem of a daughter on him. Her name was Tataka. The grandfather also bestowed the strength of one thousand elephants on her. The immensely illustrious Brahma did not give that yaksha a son.[238] Having been born, she grew up and possessed beauty and youth. He[239] bestowed the illustrious one on Sunda, Jambha's son, as a wife. After some time, the female yaksha gave birth to a son. He was invincible and his name was Maricha. However, because of a curse, he became a rakshasa. O Rama! When Sunda was slain by Agastya, the supreme rishi, Tataka and her son wished to take revenge. He[240] cursed Maricha that he

[236] The word used is *abala,* meaning weak one, or woman. Yakshas are limited in valour and a female yaksha must be even more so.

[237] Brahma.

[238] Anticipating that a strong daughter would be less dangerous than a strong son.

[239] Suketu.

[240] Agastya.

would become a rakshasa.[241] In great rage, Agastya also cursed Tataka. "You will give up this form and assume a terrible form. O great yaksha! You will become a maneater. You will become deformed, with a distorted visage." Thus cursed, Tataka became intolerant and senseless with anger. Agastya roamed around in this sacred region and she started to destroy it. O Raghava! This female yaksha is extremely terrible and wicked in conduct. She is evil in her valour. For the welfare of cattle and brahmanas, slay her. O descendant of the Raghu lineage! She is so enveloped in the curse that in the three worlds, no man except you is capable of standing up to her. O supreme among men! You should not be revolted at the prospect of killing a woman. O son of a king! This is what must be done for the welfare of the four varnas. This is eternal dharma for someone who has been entrusted with the burden of a kingdom. O Kakutstha! Slay the source of adharma. There is no dharma in her. O king! We have heard that, in ancient times, Shakra destroyed Manthara, Virochana's daughter, when she desired to devastate the earth. O Rama! Bhrigu's wife and Kavya's[242] mother was firm in her vows. However, when she desired to remove Indra from the worlds, Vishnu crushed her. O prince! The great-souled ones have performed many such tasks. Those supreme beings have slain women who were devoted to adharma.'

Chapter 1(25)

On hearing the sage's words, the son of the supreme among men, lost all despondency. Raghava, firm in his vows, joined his hands in salutation and replied, 'On my father's instructions, to honour my father's words and to follow Koushika's words, I will dispel all doubt and undertake this task. In the midst of my superiors, my father, the great-souled Dasharatha, commanded me

[241] The Critical text excises a shloka where Tataka and Maricha attack Agastya.

[242] Kavya is Shukra or Shukracharya.

in Ayodhya and his command cannot be disregarded. I have heard my father's words and the instructions of one who knows about the brahman.[243] Without a doubt, I will undertake the supreme task of killing Tataka. For the welfare of cattle and brahmanas, for the happiness of the country and to follow your immeasurable words, I will engage myself in this task.' Having said this, the destroyer of enemies grasped the middle of his bow with his fist. He twanged his bow and filled the directions with this terrible sound. Tataka, the resident of the forest, was terrified at this sound. Tataka was confounded by this sound, but was also enraged. Senseless with rage, the *rakshasi*[244] determined where that sound had come from. Having heard the sound, she swiftly dashed towards the direction from where it had emerged. Raghava saw that enraged one, malformed, distorted in visage and extremely gigantic in size. He spoke to Lakshmana. 'Behold Lakshmana! This female yaksha possesses a fierce and terrible body. On seeing her, the hearts of cowards will be shattered. Behold her. She is invincible and possesses the strength of maya. I will now make her withdraw by severing her ears and the tip of her nose. Since she is protected by her nature of being a woman, I do not wish to kill her. It is my view that one should only destroy her valour and her speed.' When Rama said this, Tataka became senseless with rage. Raising her arms, she roared and rushed towards Rama. She descended with great force and valour, like a bolt of thunder. However, he pierced her body and she fell down, dead. Her form was terrible. On seeing that she had been slain, the lord of the gods uttered words of praise. The gods worshipped Kakutstha. Extremely delighted, the thousand-eyed Purandara[245] spoke these words. Extremely happy, all the gods also spoke to Vishvamitra. 'O sage! O Koushika! O fortunate one! Indra, and all the large numbers of Maruts, are satisfied at this task. Display your affection towards Raghava. The sons of Prajapati and Krishashva have truth for their valour. They possess the strength of austerities. O brahmana! Offer them to Raghava. O brahmana!

[243] Vishvamitra.

[244] Female rakshasa.

[245] Indra, the destroyer of cities.

He is a worthy recipient and is steadfast in following you. This is your task. This son of a king will perform a great task for the gods.' All the gods said this. After worshipping Vishvamitra, delighted, they returned to wherever they had come from. Evening had set in. The supreme among sages was happy and content at Tataka having been killed. He inhaled the fragrance of Rama's head and spoke these words. 'O Rama! O one with an auspicious face! We will spend the night here. Tomorrow, when it is morning, we will go to my hermitage.'

Chapter 1(26)

The immensely illustrious Vishvamitra spent the night there. He smiled at Raghava and spoke these sweet words. 'O fortunate one! O prince! O greatly illustrious one! I am satisfied with you. I am extremely delighted and will give you all the weapons. With these, you will be able to pacify, subjugate and defeat large numbers of gods, asuras, gandharvas, serpents and enemies. O fortunate one! I will bestow all those divine weapons on you. O Raghava! I will give you the extremely divine *dandachakra*.[246] O brave one! I will give you *dharmachakra* and *kalachakra*.[247] I will give you Vishnu's fierce chakra and Indra's chakra too. O best among men! I will give you the vajra weapon and Shiva's supreme trident. O Raghava! I will give you the *brahmashira* and *aishika* weapons. O mighty-armed one! I will give you Brahma's supreme weapon. O Kakutstha! I will give you both the Modaki and Shikhari clubs. O tiger among men! O son of a king! O Rama! I will give you the blazing weapons, Dharma's noose and Death's noose. I will give you the supreme weapon that is Varuna's net. O descendant of the Raghu lineage! I will give you two vajra weapons, one that dries up and one that wets. I will give you the Painaka weapon and the Narayana weapon. I will

[246] *Chakra* which acts like a staff of chastisement.

[247] Respectively, chakra which ensures dharma and chakra which drives time/destiny.

give you Agni's beloved weapon, the one that is named Shikhara. O Raghava! I will give you Vayu's weapon, known as Prathama. I will give you the weapon Hayashira and the weapon Krouncha. O Kakutstha! I will give you two spears, Kapala and Kankana, and the terrible mace, Kankala. I will give you everything that the asuras wield. I will give you the great weapon of the vidyadharas, named Nandana. O mighty-armed one! O son of supreme among men! I will give you a jewel among swords. I will give the beloved weapon of the gandharvas, known by the name of Manava. O Raghava! I will give you Prasvapana, Prashamana, Soura, Darpana, Shoshana, Santapana and Vilapana.[248] I will give you Kandarpa's[249] beloved and invincible weapon, Madana. I will give you the weapon loved by the *pishachas*,[250] named Mohana.[251] O tiger among men! O prince! O greatly illustrious one! Accept these. O tiger among men! O prince! O mighty-armed one! There are Tamasa, the immensely strong Soumana, Samvarta, the invincible Mousala, the weapon known as Satya, the supreme weapon that wields maya, the terrible weapon named Tejaprabha that saps away the energy of others, Soma's weapon Shishira, Tvashtra's weapon Sudamana, Bhaga's Daruna and Manu's Shiteshu. O Rama! O mighty-armed one! These are extremely strong and are capable of assuming any form at will. O prince! Swiftly accept these extremely pervasive ones.' Then, the supreme among sages purified himself and stood, facing the east. Extremely delighted, he gave Rama those supreme mantras.[252] The intelligent sage, Vishvamitra, chanted the mantras and all those extremely revered weapons presented themselves before Raghava. All of them joined their hands in salutation and joyfully addressed Rama. 'O greatly generous one! O Raghava! We are your servants.' Kakutstha extended his hands and accepted them. He urged them,

[248] Prasvapana puts to sleep, Prashamana pacifies, Shoshana dries up, Santapana scorches and Vilapana causes lamentations. Soura is a weapon identified with the sun. Darpana causes vanity.

[249] Kandarpa, or Kama or Madana, is the god of love.

[250] Malevolent beings.

[251] Something that confounds and intoxicates.

[252] Divine weapons were invoked, released and withdrawn through the use of mantras.

'May you remain in my mind.' Rama was delighted and worshipped the immensely energetic and great sage, Vishvamitra. He got ready to leave.

Chapter 1(27)

Kakutstha purified himself. He accepted the weapons with a cheerful face. Ready to go, he spoke to Vishvamitra. 'O illustrious ones! I have accepted weapons that are difficult for even the gods to withstand. O bull among sages! I also wish to know about how these weapons can be countered.' Thus addressed by Kakutstha, the great sage, Vishvamitra, full of patience, excellent in his vows and pure, instructed him about countering and withdrawing. 'O Raghava! O fortunate one! O Raghava! These radiant ones are known as Bhrishashva's[253] sons and can assume any form at will. You are a worthy recipient. Accept them—Satyavanta, Satyakirti, Dhrishta, Rabhasa, the one named Pratiharatara, Paranmukha, Avanmukha, Laksha, Alaksha, Vishama, Dridanabha, Sunabha, Dashaksha, Shatavaktra, Dashashirsha, Shatodara, Padmanabha, Mahanabha, Dundunabha, Sunabha,[254] Jyotisha, Krishana, Nairashya, Vimala, Yougandhara, Haridra, Daitya-pramathana, Pitrya, Soumanasa, Vidhutama, Makara, Karavirakara, Dhana, Dhanya, Kamarupa, Kamaruchi, Mohama, Avarana, Jrimbhaka, Sarvanabha, Santana and Varanou.' Cheerful in his mind, Kakutstha accepted the pleasant and embodied forms of those radiant and divine ones. Having manifested themselves before Rama, they joined their hands in salutation and addressed him in sweet voices. 'O tiger among men! We are here. Instruct us about what we can do for you.' The descendant of the Raghu lineage replied, 'Remain in my mind, so that you can assist me when the opportune moment presents itself. Till then, as you wish, leave.' They agreed to what Kakutstha had

[253] This should probably read Krishashva.

[254] Sunabha is mentioned twice.

said. They circumambulated Rama and taking his leave, went away to wherever they had come from.

Having got to know about them, as they proceeded, Raghava addressed the great sage, Vishvamitra, in soft and gentle words. 'What is that, located not far from the mountain? This clump of trees is as radiant as a cloud. I am supremely curious. It is beautiful and a sight to see. It is full of many kinds of animals. It is ornamented with birds that possess melodious tones. O best among sages! We have clearly emerged from the desolate forest that makes the body hair stand up. We are headed towards a region that is agreeable. O illustrious one! Tell me everything. Whose hermitage is this? Is this the place where those wicked ones of evil conduct, the slayers of brahmanas, come?'

Chapter 1(28)

When the immeasurable one asked about the grove, the greatly energetic Vishvamitra started to explain. 'O Rama! Earlier, this used to be the hermitage of the great-souled Vamana. This was famous as Siddhashrama, because the great ascetic obtained success here.[255] At this time, King Bali, Virochana's son, conquered the large numbers of gods, with Indra and the arrays of Maruts. The famous one ruled over the kingdom of the three worlds. Bali performed a sacrifice. With Agni at the forefront, the gods approached Vishnu himself in this hermitage.[256] They said, "O Vishnu! Bali, Virochana's son, is undertaking a supreme sacrifice. Our own sacrifice, which will accomplish all our tasks, is yet incomplete. Whichever supplicant arrives before him, from whatever direction he may come, he[257] gives all of them everything, regardless of what they ask for. For the welfare of

[255] To become a siddha is to obtain success in one's austerities/meditations.

[256] This makes it clear that Vishnu observed austerities in this hermitage, prior to assuming his vamana (dwarf) incarnation.

[257] Bali.

the gods, resort to your maya and present yourself before him. O Vishnu! Assume the form of a vamana and perform this supremely beneficial act. Through your favours, this spot will assume the name of Siddhashrama. O lord of the gods! O illustrious one! Arise and accomplish this task." At this, the greatly energetic Vishnu generated himself through Aditi.[258] He assumed the form of a dwarf and presented himself before Virochana's son. He asked for three strides and respectfully received the gift.[259] Engaged in the welfare of all creatures, the soul of the worlds, encompassed all the worlds. He controlled Bali's energy and again gave the three worlds back to the great Indra. The greatly energetic one again brought them under Shakra's subjugation. This hermitage was inhabited by him earlier, in his vamana form, and is the destroyer of all exhaustion. Because of my devotion, I enjoy it now. The rakshasas, the creators of obstructions, arrive at this hermitage. O tiger among men! This is where the ones of evil conduct will be killed by you. O Rama! We will now head for the supreme Siddhashrama. O son![260] This hermitage belongs to you, just as it does to me.'

On seeing him, all the sages who were residents of Siddhashrama quickly presented themselves before Vishvamitra and worshipped him. As he deserved, they worshipped the intelligent Vishvamitra. They then performed the rites for the two princes, who were the guests. The princes, the scorchers of enemies, rested for a short while. The descendants of the Raghu lineage then joined their hands in salutation and addressed the bull among sages. 'O fortunate one! O bull among sages! Please consecrate yourself today. Let this Siddhashrama bring about success and may your words come true.' The immensely energetic and great sage, Vishvamitra, was addressed in this way. He controlled himself, controlled his senses and consecrated himself.[261] Having slept in the night, when it

[258] Kashyapa's wife, the mother of the gods.

[259] Vishnu asked for the region that could be covered in three strides. He covered the earth with one stride, heaven with another and the nether regions (alternatively, Bali's head) with the third, so that Bali was driven down to the nether regions.

[260] The word used is tata.

[261] Consecration is *diksha*, a preparatory to the main rite.

was morning, the princes arose. They controlled themselves and worshipped Vishvamitra.

Chapter 1(29)

The two princes, destroyers of enemies, knew about the time and the place. Conscious of what should be said at the right time and the right place, they spoke these words to Koushika. 'O illustrious one! O brahmana! We wish to hear when those dwellers of the night present themselves. When must this place be protected? Let the moment not pass.' Hastening to fight, the two Kakutsthas spoke in this way. All the sages were pleased and praised the two princes. 'O Raghavas! From today, you will have to protect this spot for six nights. Having consecrated himself, the sage[262] is observing a vow of silence.' Having heard their words, the two illustrious princes dispensed with sleep for six days and six nights and protected the hermitage. The brave ones were supreme archers and roamed around. Those two destroyers of enemies protected the supreme sage, Vishvamitra.

Time passed and the sixth day arrived. Rama told Soumitri,[263] 'Be attentive and alert.' Having said this, Rama quickly readied himself for the fight. The priests and assistant priests kindled the fire on the sacrificial altar. As is proper, mantras were uttered and the sacrifice proceeded. At that time, a great and terrible sound was heard in the sky. It was as if clouds had enveloped the sky during the monsoon. Resorting to maya, the rakshasas attacked. There were Maricha and Subahu and their followers. They arrived, fierce in form, and showered down torrents of blood. The lotus-eyed one saw that they were violently descending. Glancing towards Lakshmana, Rama said, 'O Lakshmana! Behold these rakshasas. They are evil in conduct and eat raw flesh. I will use the Manava

[262] Vishvamitra.

[263] Sumitra's son, Lakshmana.

weapon to drive them away, like clouds dispelled by the wind.' The Manava weapon was extremely powerful and supremely resplendent. Supremely angry, Raghava hurled this at Maricha's chest. He was struck by that supreme weapon, Manava, and hurled one hundred yojanas away, amidst the waves of the ocean. He was whirled around and became unconscious, oppressed by the strength of Shiteshu.[264] On seeing that Maricha had been repulsed, Rama told Lakshmana, 'O Lakshmana! Behold. Shiteshu and Manava are suffused with dharma. They have confounded him and carried him away, but have not deprived him of his life. However, I do wish to slay these abhorred ones, who are evil in conduct.[265] The rakshasas are wicked in conduct. They destroy sacrifices and subsist on blood.' The descendant of the Raghu lineage affixed the extremely great Agneya weapon and hurled it at Subahu's chest. Thus pierced, he fell down on the ground. The immensely illustrious one seized the Vayavya weapon and killed the remaining ones. The extremely powerful Raghava brought delight to the sages. The descendant of the Raghu lineage slew all the rakshasas who sought to destroy the sacrifice. He was worshipped by the rishis, as the victorious Indra was in earlier times. When the sacrifice was completed, the great sage, Vishvamitra, saw that the directions were free of all difficulties. He told Kakutstha, 'O mighty-armed one! I have become successful and you have accomplished your preceptor's words. O Rama! O immensely illustrious one! You have made the name of Siddhashrama come true.'

Chapter 1(30)

Having been successful, the brave Rama and Lakshmana rejoiced in their heart of hearts. Cheerfully, they spent the night there. When night turned into morning, they performed

[264] The Manava and Shiteshu weapons are probably being used partly synonymously.

[265] The other rakshasas.

their morning ablutions. They then approached Vishvamitra, who was with the other rishis. They greeted that best among sages, who was like a blazing fire. Gentle in speech, those generous ones spoke these sweet words to him. 'O tiger among sages! We, your servants, are present before you. Instruct us about what is beneficial. Command us what we must do.' When they spoke in this way, all the maharshis, with Vishvamitra at the forefront, spoke these words to Rama. 'O best among men! Janaka of Mithila is devoted to dharma and will undertake a supreme sacrifice. We will go there. O tiger among men! You should also come with us. There is an extraordinary gem of a bow there and you should see that. It is fierce and is immeasurable in strength. It is supremely radiant in a battle. O best among men! In an assembly, the gods gave it to him earlier.[266] The gods, the gandharvas, the asuras and the rakshasas are incapable of raising it, not to speak of men. Many kings wished to test the energy of that bow. However, those supremely strong princes were incapable of raising it. O tiger among men! That bow belongs to the great-souled lord of Mithila. O Kakutstha! You will be able to see it and witness the extraordinary sacrifice. O tiger among men! The bow possesses an excellent grip. The lord of Mithila had sought this supreme bow as the fruit of a sacrifice from all the gods.' Having said this, the supreme among sages[267] prepared to leave with the large number of rishis and Kakutstha, having taken his leave of the gods of the forest. 'I have become successful in Siddhashrama. May I be safe in the course of my journey. I will leave for the Himalaya mountains, located on the northern banks of the Jahnavee.' Having circumambulated the supreme Siddhashrama, he got ready to leave for the northern direction. The supreme among sages departed, accompanied by his followers. One hundred carts followed the one who knew about the brahman. The birds and animals that resided in Siddhashrama also followed the great-souled and great sage, Vishvamitra.

[266] Gave it to Janaka.
[267] Vishvamitra.

When the sun stretched out,[268] the large number of sages had proceeded some distance. They controlled themselves and rested on the banks of the Shona river. When the sun set, they bathed and kindled a fire. They seated themselves in front of the infinitely energetic Vishvamitra. Rama and Soumitri worshipped the sages. They too seated themselves in front of the intelligent Vishvamitra. The infinitely energetic Rama was full of curiosity. He asked the great sage, Vishamitra, tiger among sages. 'O illustrious one! What is this place, prosperous with forests? O fortunate one! I wish to hear. You should tell me the truth about this.' Thus urged by Rama's words, in the midst of the rishis, the great ascetic, excellent in his vows, told him everything about that region.

Chapter 1(31)

'There was a great ascetic named Kusha, descended from the great Brahma. Through the princess of Vidarbha, he had four sons who were exactly like him—Kushamba, Kushanabha, Adhurtarajas and Vasu. They were radiant and great in enterprise, interested in observing the dharma of kshatriyas. The sons were devoted to dharma and truthful in speech. Kusha told them, "O sons! Rule properly, so that you may obtain all the fruits of dharma." Having heard Kusha's words, those best among men, revered in the worlds, sought to create four cities. The immensely energetic Kushamba constructed the city of Koushambi.[269] Kushanabha, with dharma in his soul, constructed the city of Mahodaya. O Rama! King Adhurtarajas constructed Dharmaranya and King Vasu constructed Girivraja,[270] supreme among cities. O Rama! This is the dominion of the great-souled Vasu, known as Vasumati. In every direction, five great mountains can be seen. This beautiful river,

[268] Was ready to set.

[269] Identified with Kannauj, or the village of Kosam, on the banks of the Yamuna and near Allahabad.

[270] Identified with Rajagriha or Rajgir.

Sumagadhi,[271] flows towards the famous land of Magadha. In the midst of those five great mountains, it is as radiant as a garland. O Rama! Sumagadhi[272] flows eastwards through the great-souled Vasu's land. O Rama! The area is garlanded by excellent fields that yield a lot of grain. O descendant of the Raghu lineage! Through Ghritachi,[273] the great-souled royal sage, Kushanabha, with dharma in his soul, had one hundred supreme daughters. They were young and beautiful. Once, ornamented, they went to a grove and were like one hundred flashes of lightning during the monsoon. O Raghava! They sang, danced and played on musical instruments. Adorned in excellent ornaments, they were in a paroxysm of delight. Their limbs were beautiful and their beauty was unmatched on earth. They went to that grove and were like stars amidst clouds. Having seen them, Vayu, who pervades everything, told them, "I desire all of you. Become my wives. Abandon your human forms and obtain long lifespans instead." They heard the words of Vayu, unsullied in his deeds. However, those one hundred maidens laughed at his words and replied, "O supreme among gods! You roam around inside all creatures. All of us know about your powers. But why are you slighting us? O supreme among gods! All of us are Kushanabha's daughters and are capable of dislodging you from your status. It is just that we want to preserve our store of austerities. O evil-minded one! Our father is truthful in speech. The time will never come when we will cross our father, transgress dharma and resort to *svayamvara*.[274] Our father is our lord. He is our supreme divinity. Our husband will be the one to whom our father bestows us." Hearing their words, Vayu was greatly enraged. The illustrious lord entered their bodies and disfigured their limbs. Mangled by Vayu, those maidens entered the king's residence. On seeing that they had been mangled, the king was terrified and spoke these words. "O daughters! How did this happen? Who has shown

[271] A name for the Shona.

[272] The text says Magadhi, but we have used Sumagadhi to avoid confusion.

[273] The name of an apsara.

[274] When a maiden chooses her own husband.

disrespect towards dharma? Who has made your bodies crooked? Why are you trembling and not saying anything?"'

Chapter 1(32)

'Hearing the words of the intelligent Kushanabha, the one hundred daughters touched his feet with their heads and said, "O king! Vayu pervades everything and desired to dishonour us. He did not pay heed to dharma and resorted to an inauspicious path. We told the fortunate one that we are not independent and are devoted to our father's words. He should ask our father and our father will decide whether we should be bestowed on him or not. However, addicted to evil, he did not accept our words. Vayu has severely afflicted us." All of them told him this. The king, supremely devoted to dharma, heard their words. The extremely energetic one replied to those one hundred supreme maidens. "O daughters! Forgiveness is the trait of the forgiving and you have observed that great duty. You have remembered my lineage and all of you have united in acting in this way. Whether it is a woman or a man, forgiveness is the true ornament. It is extremely difficult to be forgiving, especially when the gods are involved. O daughters! This is particularly true of the kind of forgiveness you have exhibited. Forgiveness is generosity. Forgiveness represents sacrifices. O daughters! Forgiveness is truth. Forgiveness is fame. Forgiveness is dharma. The universe is established on forgiveness." O Kakutstha! The king, who was like the gods in his valour, gave his daughters permission to leave. He knew about good policy and consulted his ministers about who they should be bestowed on. What would be the time and the place for the bestowal? Which groom would be their equal?

'At that time, there was a great sage named Chuli. He held up his seed and was auspicious in conduct. He had attained the brahman. While the rishi was engaged in austerities, a gandharva lady served him. The fortunate one's name was Somada and she was Urmila's daughter. Devoted to serving him, she prostrated herself before him. She was devoted to dharma. After she had spent some time there, her preceptor was satisfied with her. O descendant of the Raghu lineage! When the time was right, he told her, "O fortunate one! I am satisfied with you. What can I do to please you?" Knowing that the sage was satisfied, the gandharva lady spoke to him in sweet words. She was accomplished in speech and was conversant with the use of words. Supremely delighted, she replied, "O great ascetic! The brahman is in you and pervaded by the brahman, prosperity is manifest in you. I desire a son who is devoted to dharma, one who is united with the brahman and with austerities. O fortunate one! I do not have a husband. I am no one's wife. I have come here because you are suffused with the brahman. You should grant me a son." Pleased with her, the brahmana rishi gave her a supreme son. This son was born through Chuli's mental powers and was famous as Brahmadatta. King Brahmadatta resided in the supremely prosperous city of Kampilya,[275] like the king of the gods in heaven.

'O Kakutstha! King Kushanabha, extremely devoted to dharma, made up his mind that he would bestow his one hundred daughters on Brahmadatta. The immensely energetic king invited Brahmadatta. Extremely happy in his mind, he bestowed the one hundred daughters on him. O descendant of the Raghu lineage! In due order, King Brahmadatta, who was like the lord of the gods, accepted their hands. As soon as he touched them with his hands, their deformations disappeared and they became devoid of anxiety. The one hundred maidens were united with supreme beauty. On seeing that they had become free of Vayu, King Kushanabha was supremely delighted and rejoiced repeatedly. When the marriage was over, the king sent King Brahmadatta on his way, with his wives and with large numbers of priests. Somada was also extremely happy at seeing the act that her son had accomplished. As is proper, the gandharva lady found delight in her daughters-in-law.'

[275] Described as the capital of Panchala, specifically, South Panchala. Identified with Kampil, in Farrukhabad district of Uttar Pradesh.

Chapter 1(33)

'O Raghava! After the marriage was over, Brahmadatta departed. Since he was without a son, King Kushanabha thought of performing a sacrifice so that he might have a son. While the sacrifice was going on, Kusha, Brahma's son, was extremely happy and spoke these words.[276] "O son! There will be a son who will be extremely devoted to dharma, like you. His name will be Gadhi and he will obtain eternal fame in this world. O Rama! Kusha spoke in this way to King Kushanabha. He then went up into the sky and entered Brahma's eternal abode. After some time, the intelligent Kushanabha had a son named Gadhi, who was supremely devoted to dharma. O Kakutstha! Gadhi, supremely devoted to dharma, is my father. O descendant of the Raghu lineage! I have been born in Kusha's lineage and am Koushika. O Raghava! Earlier, I had a sister who was excellent in her vows. Her name was Satyavati and she was bestowed on Richika. Following her husband, she went to heaven in her own physical body. The extremely generous one started to flow as the great river Koushiki.[277] She is divine, with sacred waters. She is beautiful and flows through the Himalayas. For the welfare of the worlds, my sister flowed as a river. That is the reason I always dwell happily on the slopes of the Himalayas. O descendant of the Raghu lineage! This is because of the affection I bear towards my sister, Koushiki. Satyavati is sacred and is established in true dharma. The immensely fortunate one is devoted to her husband and is Koushiki, supreme among rivers. O Rama! Because of my vows, I left her and came to Siddhashrama. Because of your energy, I have obtained success. O Rama! This is my origin and I have recounted my lineage and about this region. O mighty-armed one! That is what you had asked me about. O Kakutstha! Half the night has passed in telling you about my account. O fortunate one! We should sleep now. We have come half the way and let there be no hindrances. O descendant of the Raghu lineage! Everything is quiet

[276] To Kushanabha.
[277] The river Koshi.

and the birds and animals are resting. The darkness of the night has pervaded all the directions. Evening has slowly crept away and the sky is covered with nakshatras and planets that look like eyes. Their radiance illuminates everything. The moon, the dispeller of darkness from the worlds, has arisen, with its cool beams. O lord! With its radiance, it gladdens the worlds and the minds of creatures. Here and there, the creatures of the night are roaming around. There are large numbers of yakshas and rakshasas. They are terrible and feed on raw flesh.'

Having spoken in this way, the immensely energetic and great sage ceased. All the other sages praised him and worshipped him. Rama and Soumitri were somewhat astounded. They also praised the tiger among sages and went to sleep.

Chapter 1(34)

With the maharshis, Vishvamitra spent the rest of the night on the banks of the Shona. When night turned into an excellent morning, he said, 'O Rama! The night has turned into an excellent morning and the first *sandhya* has commenced.[278] Arise. O fortunate one! Arise. You should get ready for departure.' On hearing his words, he[279] performed the morning ablutions. He prepared to leave and replied in these words. 'The Shona possesses auspicious waters. It is full of sandbanks and can be crossed. O brahmana! What mode should we use to cross over it?'[280] Thus addressed by Rama, Vishvamitra said, 'I instruct that we should follow the path that the maharshis have travelled along.'[281] After having travelled some distance, for half a day, they saw Jahnavee, best among rivers, frequented by the sages. On seeing the sacred waters, populated by swans and cranes, all the sages, together with the two Raghavas,

[278] Sandhya is any conjunction of day and night. Hence, it is dawn, as well as dusk.
[279] Rama.
[280] That is, boats are not necessary. Should one use a boat or should one walk across?
[281] That is, walking across.

were delighted. They set up residence along the banks. They bathed there. As is proper, they offered water to the ancestors and the gods. They rendered offerings into the *agnihotra* fire and those oblations were like amrita. Pure and cheerful in their minds, they resided on the banks of the Jahnavee. In every direction, they surrounded the great-souled Vishvamitra.

Delighted in his mind, Rama spoke to Vishvamitra. 'O illustrious one! I wish to hear about the Ganga, the river with the three flows. How does she flow through the three worlds and reach the lord of the male and female rivers?'[282] Urged by Rama's words, Vishvamitra, the great sage, started to describe the birth and progress of Ganga. 'The Himalayas, Indra among mountains, is a great store of minerals. O Rama! He had two daughters and their beauty was unmatched on earth. O Rama! Their mother was the slender-waisted daughter of Mount Meru. Her name was Mena. That beautiful one was the beloved wife of the Himalayas. Her daughter Ganga was the elder daughter of the Himalayas. O Raghava! There was a second daughter and her name was Uma. All the gods wished that the elder daughter should accomplish a task for the gods. They asked the Indra among mountains and she became a river with three flows. Following dharma, the Himalayas donated his daughter, for the sake of purifying the worlds. For the welfare of the three worlds, Ganga started to flow as she willed. For the benefit of the three worlds, those who desired the welfare of the three worlds[283] accepted Ganga and returned, successful at their inner wishes having been met. O descendant of the Raghu lineage! The mountain had another daughter. That store of austerities resorted to fierce vows and asceticism. That daughter of the supreme among mountains engaged in terrible austerities. The unmatched Uma, revered in the worlds, was bestowed on Rudra. These daughters of the king of mountains are worshipped by the worlds. O Raghava! Ganga is best among rivers and Uma is a goddess. I have told you everything about the river that has

[282] The ocean is the lord of the rivers.

[283] The gods.

three flows. O son![284] The one with the best of flows first flowed in the sky.'

Chapter 1(35)

When the sage said these words, the brave Rama and Lakshmana applauded the account and spoke to the bull among sages. 'O brahmana! You have recited a supreme account that is full of dharma. You should tell us about the elder daughter of the king of the mountains in detail. You are capable of recounting divine and human origins in detail. What is the reason why the purifier of the worlds has three flows? Why is Ganga, the one with the three flows, known as the best among rivers? O one who knows about dharma! What are the tasks that she has performed in the three worlds?'

When the two Kakutsthas addressed him in this way, in the midst of all the rishis, Vishvamitra, the store of austerities, narrated the entire account. 'O Rama! In ancient times, the great ascetic, Shitikantha,[285] married. Having seen the goddess,[286] he desired to have intercourse with her. One hundred divine years passed for the god Shitikantha.[287] O Rama! O scorcher of enemies! However, he still did not have a son. At this, with the grandfather at the forefront, all the gods were anxious. "When an offspring is born, who will be able to sustain him?"[288] All the gods went and prostrated themselves before him. They said, "O Mahadeva! O god of the gods! O one who is engaged in the welfare of the worlds! The gods have prostrated themselves before you. You should show them your favours. O supreme among the gods! The world will not be able to sustain your energy. Resort to the

[284] The word used is tata.

[285] The one with the blue throat, Shiva.

[286] Uma.

[287] 360 human years equal one divine year.

[288] Because the offspring would be extremely energetic.

austerities of the brahman. Unite with the goddess in that kind of austerity.[289] For the welfare of the three worlds, withdraw your semen and energy. Protect all these worlds. You should not destroy the worlds." Maheshvara, the lord of all the worlds, heard the words of the gods. He agreed to this. He again told all of them, "I will restrain my semen and my energy within Uma. The gods and the earth will be secure. However, the part of my energy that has already been stirred cannot be restrained. O supreme among the gods! Tell me who is going to sustain this." Thus addressed, the gods replied to the one who has a bull on his banner.[290] "The earth will bear the energy that has already been dislodged." Thus addressed, the lord of the gods released it on the surface of the ground. The earth, with its mountains and groves, was pervaded by this energy. At this, the gods again spoke to the fire god. "Aided by Vayu, enter Rudra's great energy." It again pervaded Agni and created Mount Shveta. There was a celestial clump of reeds that was like the fire and the sun in complexion. Created from Agni, the greatly energetic Kartikeya was born there. The gods, with the large number of rishis, were greatly delighted and wholeheartedly worshipped Uma and Shiva. O Rama! However, the daughter of the mountain[291] was enraged and her eyes turned red with anger. Full of intolerance, she cursed the gods and told them, "I desired to have intercourse for the sake of a son, but you restrained me. Because of that, you will never be able to obtain offspring through your own wives. From today, your wives will remain infertile." Having spoken in this way to all the gods, she also cursed the earth. "O earth! You will never possess one single form and will always be the wife to many. You will be tainted through my rage and will never know any affection towards your sons. O extremely evil-minded one! You obtained my son, though you never wished for him." The lord of the gods saw that all the gods were ashamed. He prepared to leave for the direction that is protected by Varuna.[292]

[289] That is, do not have physical offspring.
[290] Shiva has a bull on his banner.
[291] Uma.
[292] Varuna rules over the western direction.

He went to the slopes of the northern mountains[293] and performed austerities there. Through the powers of Maheshvara and the goddess, a summit was created there, in the Himalayas. O Rama! I have told you in detail about the daughter of the mountain. With Lakshmana, now hear about the origin of the Ganga.'

Chapter 1(36)

'In ancient times, the gods performed austerities in this way.[294] At that time, the gods, with large numbers of rishis, went to the grandfather, desiring a general. All the gods, with Indra and Agni at the forefront, bowed down before the illustrious grandfather and spoke these auspicious words. "O illustrious one! In earlier times, you gave us a general.[295] However, with Uma, he is now resorting to supreme austerities and is scorching himself. Desiring the welfare of the worlds, you must decide on what should be done now. O one who knows about what must be done! You are our supreme refuge and must decide on a course of action." The grandfather of all the worlds heard the words of the gods. He comforted the gods and spoke these sweet words to them. "The mountain's daughter has said that you will not have offspring through your wives. There is no doubt that her unsullied words will come true. However, through Ganga, who flows in the sky, Agni can have a son and that destroyer of enemies will be the general of the gods.[296] The eldest daughter of the Indra among mountains will welcome this son. There is no doubt that this will also find great sanction with Uma." O descendant of the Raghu lineage! On hearing his words, all the gods thought that they had obtained success. They bowed down and worshipped the grandfather. O Rama! All the gods went to Mount Kailasa, which is decorated with minerals. There, they urged

[293] Obviously the Himalayas.
[294] This is still Vishvamitra speaking.
[295] Referring to Shiva.
[296] Since Ganga is not married to Agni, the curse will not be violated.

Agni to produce a son. "O god! O fire god! Accomplish the task of the gods. The great energy has so far been contained in Ganga, the daughter of the mountain. Release that energy." Pavaka[297] gave his pledge to the gods and approached Ganga. "O goddess! To bring pleasure to the gods, please bear this in your womb." Hearing these words, she assumed a divine form. On seeing her great form, he[298] spread throughout her person. Pavaka spread throughout the goddess and sprinkled her.[299] O descendant of the Raghu lineage! All of Ganga's flows became full. At this, Ganga spoke to the priest of the gods.[300] "O god! Your energy is extremely potent and I am incapable of bearing it. I am being scorched by the fire and my senses are distressed." All the gods and the fire god spoke to Ganga. "Deposit the embryo on the foothills of the Himalayas." O unblemished one! Hearing Agni's words, Ganga released that radiant embryo in torrents of great energy. Wherever that flow, with the complexion of molten gold, was released in the Himalayas, the sacred ground became sparkling and golden. From the friction between the gods,[301] copper and iron ore were also generated. The residue that was left became tin and lead. It is from this that the earth obtained many kinds of minerals. As soon as that embryo was flung down, the sparkling energy created a golden grove everywhere in that mountain. O Raghava! O tiger among men! Since then, with a complexion like that of the fire, gold has been known as Jatarupa.[302]

'When the son was born, Indra, with the large number of Maruts, engaged the Krittikas to provide milk for him.[303] As soon as he was born, they[304] took an excellent pledge. "He is our son." Having decided this, all of them gave him milk. Because of this, all

[297] The one who purifies, one of Agni's names.

[298] Agni.

[299] With the seed.

[300] Agni is being described as the priest of the gods.

[301] Shiva and Agni.

[302] Literally, something that obtains form from birth.

[303] There are various stories about Kartikeya's birth. For example, he was found in a clump of reeds and reared by the Krittikas (the Pleiades).

[304] The Krittikas.

the gods said, "This son will be known as Kartikeya and there is no doubt that he will be famous in the three worlds." The embryo that had been dislodged from the womb was exceedingly beautiful and blazed like the fire. On hearing these words, they[305] bathed it. O Kakutstha! The immensely fortunate Kartikeya was like the fire. Since he had been secreted from the womb, the gods called him Skanda.[306] Excellent milk began to ooze out from the breasts of the six Krittikas and assuming six faces, he fed on this. Having fed on this milk, he grew up to be a boy in a single day. Because of the lord's valour, the soldiers of the *daityas*[307] found him to be invincible. With Agni at the forefront, the large number of gods assembled and consecrated the unblemished and radiant one as the general of the soldiers of the gods. O Rama! I have thus told you about Ganga in detail and about the blessed and sacred account of Kumara's birth.'

Chapter 1(37)

In a sweet voice, Koushika told Rama about that account. He again addressed the following words to Kakutstha. 'There was a brave king who was earlier the lord of Ayodhya. His name was Sagara and he possessed dharma in his soul. However, since he did not have any offspring, he desired offspring. In her beauty, Arishtanemi's daughter was unmatched on earth. She was known as Sumati and she was Sagara's second wife.[308] With those two wives, the king went to the Himalayas, to the mountain known as Bhriguprasravana.[309] There, he tormented himself through austerities. After the sage

[305] The Krittikas.

[306] From *skanna*, which means to be secreted out.

[307] Demons who are descendants of Diti.

[308] In a shloka excised from the Critical Edition, we are told that the first wife's name was Keshini.

[309] This is also known as Bhrigutunga and is identified as a mountain in Nepal, on the banks of the Gandaki.

Bhrigu, supreme among those who uphold the truth, had been worshipped with austerities for one hundred years, he gave a boon to Sagara. "O unblemished one! You will obtain extremely great offspring. O bull among men! You will obtain unsurpassed fame in this world. O son![310] One of your wives will give birth to a son who will extend the lineage. The other will give birth to sixty thousand sons." Having shown his favours to the king's wives, this is what he told that tiger among men. Extremely delighted, they joined their hands in salutation and said, "O brahmana! Who will have a single son and who will give birth to many? O brahmana! We wish to learn this. May your words come true." Having heard their words, Bhrigu, extremely devoted to dharma, spoke these supreme words. "This will be decided by you, independently. Who wants a son who will extend the lineage? Who wants many sons who are extremely strong, famous and great in endeavour? Who wants which boon?" O descendant of the Raghu lineage! O Rama! Hearing the sage's words, in the presence of the king, Keshini desired a son who would extend the lineage. Sumati, Suparna's[311] sister, wished for sixty thousand sons who would be great in endeavour and famous. O descendant of the Raghu lineage! With his wives, the king bowed his head down before the rishi, circumambulated him and returned to his own city. After some time had passed, the elder wife, Keshini, gave birth to a son. This son of Sagara came to be known by the name of Asamanja. O tiger among men! Sumati gave birth to a gourd. When this gourd was shattered, sixty thousand sons emerged. Nursemaids nurtured them in pots filled with *ghee* and reared them there. After a long period of time, they became youths. After another long period of time, these sixty thousand of Sagara's sons became handsome adults. O best among men! O descendant of the Raghu lineage! The eldest of Sagara's sons[312] used to grab children and hurl them into the waters of the Sarayu. Having hurled them there, seeing them drown, he always used to laugh. Since he was engaged in injuring the citizens, his father

[310] The word used is tata.

[311] Garuda's name is Suparna.

[312] Asamanja.

banished him from the city. However, Asamanja had a valiant son named Amshumat. He was respected by all the worlds and spoke pleasantly to everyone. O best among men! After a long period of time, Sagara reflected and made up his mind about performing a sacrifice. Having thus made up his mind, the king, who knew about the Vedas, told his preceptors to begin the rites for undertaking a sacrifice.'

Chapter 1(38)

Hearing Vishvamitra's words, the descendant of the Raghu lineage was supremely delighted. When the account was over, he spoke to the sage, who blazed like the fire. 'O fortunate one! I wish to hear about this account in detail. O brahmana! How did my ancestor complete the sacrifice?'

Vishvamitra seemed to smile at Kakutstha and said, 'O Rama! Hear in detail about the great-souled Sagara. Shankara's father-in-law is the supreme mountain, known as Himalayas. He approaches Mount Vindhya and the two glance at each other. O supreme among men! O best among men! The land that extends between them is a region that is praised for performing sacrifices. O Kakutstha! O son![313] Following Sagara's words, maharatha Amshumat, the firm archer, tended to the horse.[314] On the auspicious day when the sacrificer was going to undertake the sacrifice, Vasava assumed the form of a female rakshasa and stole the sacrificial horse. O Kakutstha! When the great-souled sacrificer's horse was stolen, all the large number of preceptors spoke to the sacrificer. "This is the auspicious time. Quickly fetch the sacrificial horse. O Kakutstha! Slay the thief and bring the horse. If there is a lacuna in the sacrifice, all of us will face something inauspicious. O king! Therefore, act so

[313] The word used is tata.

[314] In a horse sacrifice, a horse is left free to roam around. Kings who allow the horse unimpeded access agree to pay tribute to the king who is undertaking the horse sacrifice. Those unwilling to do so, seize the horse and a battle ensues.

that there is no weakness in the sacrifice." Hearing the words of the preceptors in that assembly, the king spoke these words to his sixty thousand sons. "O sons! O bulls among men! I do not perceive any means for rakshasas to make an entry. Extremely fortunate ones have sanctified this great sacrifice with mantras. O sons! Therefore, go and search. May you be safe. Go to everywhere on earth, right up to the garland of the ocean. O sons! Each of you search for the expanse of one yojana. Until you see the horse, dig up the earth. On my command, seek out the horse and the thief. I have been consecrated with my grandson.[315] O fortunate ones! Until I see the horse, I will remain here with all the preceptors." Thus addressed, the extremely strong princes were cheerful in their minds. O Rama! Urged by their father's words, they penetrated the surface of the earth. O tiger among men! With arms that were like the touch of the vajra, they dug it up. They used extremely terrible ploughs and spears that were like the vajra. O descendant of the Raghu lineage! Thus shattered, the earth began to shriek. O Raghava! The serpents and the asuras were slaughtered and so were rakshasas and other invincible beings. There was a tumultuous roar. O descendant of the Raghu lineage! Those brave ones penetrated the earth for sixty thousand yojanas, right up to the excellent *rasatala*.[316] O tiger among kings! Jambudvipa[317] is girded by mountains and those princes dug it up everywhere. At this, all the gods, gandharvas, asuras and serpents were terrified in their minds and went to the grandfather. With distressed faces, they sought the favours of the great-souled one. Extremely scared, they spoke these words to the grandfather. "O illustrious one! Everywhere, Sagara's sons are digging up the earth. Many great-souled aquatic creatures are being killed. 'The one who has stolen the horse is destroying our sacrifice.' Thinking this, Sagara's sons are slaughtering all the creatures.'"

[315] Amshumat. Therefore, they cannot search for the horse.

[316] Generally, the nether regions. There are actually seven nether regions—*atala, vitala, sutala, rasatala, talatala, mahatala* and *patala*.

[317] Jambudvipa is one of the seven continents (*dvipa*) that surround Mount Meru and Bharatavarsha is in Jambudvipa. Jambudvipa is named after *jambu* (*jamun*) trees that grow there.

Chapter 1(39)

'The gods were extremely terrified and confounded by the strength of those destroyers. The illustrious grandfather replied to them. "The entire earth is owned by the intelligent Vasudeva and he eternally holds up the earth. He has assumed the form of Kapila. A long time ago, the shattering of the earth was foreseen and so was the destruction of the sons of Sagara, who will not live for a long time." Hearing the grandfather's words, the thirty-three gods, the scorchers of enemies, were extremely happy and returned to wherever they had come from.[318]

'When Sagara's great-souled sons shattered the earth, a great sound was heard, like that of thunder. Having penetrated the earth, they circled it everywhere. All of Sagara's sons then went to their father and spoke these words. "We have travelled through the entire earth and destroyed all the creatures—gods, danavas, rakshasas, pishachas, serpents and kinnaras. However, we have not been able to see the horse, or the thief who stole the horse. O fortunate one! What will we do now? It is necessary to reflect on this." O descendant of the Raghu lineage! Hearing the words of his sons, Sagara, supreme among kings, was overcome by rage and spoke these words. "O fortunate ones! Dig the earth again and penetrate the surface of the earth. Search out the horse and the thief. Return only when you are successful." Hearing the words of their father, the great-souled Sagara, the sixty thousand sons rushed to rasatala. They dug there and saw the *dishagaja* Virupaksha.[319] He was like a mountain and held up the earth. O descendant of the Raghu lineage! The great elephant, Virupaksha, held up the entire earth, with its mountains, on his head. O Kakutstha! When the great elephant is tired and wishes

[318] The thirty-three gods are the eight Vasus, the eleven Rudras, the twelve Adityas and the two Ashvins. Sometimes, instead of the two Ashvins, Indra and Prajapati are included.

[319] Four (sometimes eight) elephants are believed to hold up the four (or eight) directions. They are known as *diggajas* or dishagajas, from *gaja* (elephant) and *dig/disha* (direction). The names differ. Virupaksha holds up the eastern direction.

to rest, it moves its head and earthquakes result. O Rama! They circumambulated the great elephant, the guardian of the direction. Having showed it honours, they penetrated the earth and went to rasatala. They penetrated the eastern direction and again penetrated the southern direction. They saw a great elephant in the southern direction too. This was the great-souled Mahapadma and he was like an extremely gigantic mountain, holding up the earth on his head. They were extremely astonished. Having circumambulated him, Sagara's great-souled sixty thousand sons penetrated the western direction. In the western direction too, those extremely strong ones saw the dishagaja Soumanasa, who was like a gigantic mountain. They circumambulated him and asked him about his welfare. They continued to dig and reached the northern direction.[320] O best among the Raghu lineage! In the northern direction, they saw Bhadra, holding up the earth. He was as white as snow and his form was auspicious. All of them touched him and circumambulated him. Those sixty thousand sons then penetrated the surface of the earth. Sagara's sons then went to the famous north-east direction. In great rage, Sagara's sons dug up the entire earth. They saw Kapila, the eternal Vasudeva, there. The horse was also wandering around there, not very far from the god.[321] Taking him to be the one who had destroyed the sacrifice, their eyes dilated with rage. Asking him to wait, they angrily dashed towards him. "You are the one who has stolen our horse and destroyed the sacrifice. O evil-minded one! You should know that we, the sons of Sagara, have arrived." O descendant of the Raghu lineage! Hearing their words, Kapila was overcome by great anger and uttered the sound of humkara. O Kakutstha! The immeasurable and great-souled Kapila reduced all of Sagara's sons to ashes.'

[320] The text states, the Somavati direction. Soma is another name for Kubera and Kubera is the guardian of the north. Soma is also a name for the moon and the moon's direction is the north.

[321] To destroy Sagara's sons, Indra hid the horse there.

Chapter 1(40)

'O descendant of the Raghu lineage! When King Sagara saw that his sons had been gone for a long time, he spoke to his grandson,[322] who was radiant in his own energy. "You are brave and accomplished in learning. In energy, you are an equal of your ancestors.[323] Go and search for your fathers[324] and for the person who has stolen the horse. There are great and valiant beings in the bowels of the earth. To repulse their attacks, take your sword and your bow. Honour the ones that deserve honour and slay the ones who cause obstructions. Return when you have ensured the success of the sacrifice, or cross over to the other side."[325] Amshumat was thus properly addressed by the great-souled Sagara. He grasped his bow and sword and departed, dexterous in his valour. He proceeded along the path that had been dug up in the earth by his great-souled fathers. O best among men! He proceeded, urged on by the king's words. He saw the immensely energetic dishagaja, worshipped by the daityas, danavas, pishachas, birds and serpents. He circumambulated him and asked him about their welfare. He asked him about his fathers and about the person who had stolen the horse. On hearing this, the dishagaja was pleased and replied in these words. "O Amshumat! O son of Asamanja! You will be successful and will swiftly return, with the horse." As is proper, in due order, he then asked all the other dishagajas. Hearing his words, all the guardians of the directions,[326] who were accomplished in speech, honoured and urged him with words and said, "You will return with the horse." Hearing their words, he proceeded, dexterous in his valour. He reached the spot where his fathers, Sagara's sons, had been reduced to ashes. At this, Asamanja's son was overcome by grief. Extremely miserable and severely afflicted that they had been killed, he wept. He saw the sacrificial horse wandering around, not very far away. Full of sorrow

[322] Amshumat.
[323] That is, the uncles.
[324] By extension, meaning the uncles.
[325] Die in the process.
[326] The dishagajas.

and misery, the tiger among men saw it. To perform the water rites for the princes, the immensely energetic one searched for water, but could not find a store of water. Casting his trained eye around, he saw the lord of the birds.[327] O Rama! Suparna was like the wind and was the maternal uncle of his fathers.[328] Vinata's extremely strong son spoke these words to him. "O tiger among men! Do not sorrow. This slaughter has been sanctioned by the worlds. The immeasurable Kapila has burnt down these extremely strong ones. O wise one! Therefore, you should not offer them water through the normal water rites. O bull among men! Ganga is the eldest daughter of the Himalayas. That purifier of the worlds will purify these mounds of ashes. When the ashes of these sixty thousand sons are sprinkled by the waters of the Ganga, beloved by the worlds, they will be conveyed to the world of heaven. O immensely fortunate one! O bull among men! Seizing the horse, leave this spot. O brave one! Return, so that your grandfather's sacrifice can be carried out." Hearing Suparna's words, the valiant and immensely illustrious Amshumat quickly seized the horse and returned. O descendant of the Raghu lineage! He went to the king who had been consecrated and reported what had happened. He also recounted Suparna's words. Hearing Amshumat's terrible words, the king performed the sacrifice, following the rites and observing the rituals. Having completed the desired sacrifice, the king returned to his own city. However, the king could not make up his mind about how Ganga was to be brought. Even after a long period of time, the king could not arrive at a decision. Having ruled the kingdom for thirty thousand years, he went to heaven.'

Chapter 1(41)

'O Rama! When Sagara departed, following the rule of time, the ordinary people wished to make Amshumat, who was

[327] Garuda.

[328] Garuda was Sumati's brother and Vinata's son.

extremely devoted to dharma, the king. O descendant of the Raghu lineage! Amshumat was an extremely great king. He had a great son, who was famous by the name of Dileepa. O descendant of the Raghu lineage! Having handed over the kingdom to Dileepa, he[329] went to a beautiful summit in the Himalayas. There, he tormented himself through extremely terrible austerities.[330] The extremely illustrious king performed austerities in the hermitage for thirty-two thousand years. The store of austerities then went to heaven. The immensely energetic Dileepa heard about the slaughter of his grandfathers. Though he was afflicted by grief, he could not make up his mind about what should be done. "How will Ganga be brought down? How will water rites be performed for them? How will they be saved?" These were the profound thoughts he pondered about. With his mind immersed in dharma, he always thought about this. He had a son named Bhageeratha, who was supremely devoted to dharma. The immensely energetic Dileepa performed many desired sacrifices. The king ruled over the kingdom for thirty thousand years. However, the king could not make up his mind about how they should be saved. O tiger among men! Following the dharma of time, the king succumbed to disease. Because of the deeds that he had himself performed, the king went to Indra's world, after the bull among men had instated his son, Bhageeratha, in the kingdom.

'O descendant of the Raghu lineage! Bhageeratha was a royal sage who was devoted to dharma. The immensely energetic one was without offspring. He didn't possess any sons and desired sons. O descendant of the Raghu lineage! For a long period of time, the king performed austerities in Gokarna.[331] He conquered his senses. He raised up his hands and ate only once, at the end of the month. He observed the vow of the five fires.[332] He engaged in these fierce austerities for one thousand years. The illustrious Brahma, the lord and god of all subjects, was extremely pleased. Accompanied by a large number of gods, the grandfather appeared before the

[329] Amshumat.

[330] So as to bring Ganga down.

[331] Gomukha, near Gangotri.

[332] To meditate amidst four fires on four sides, with the sun above one's head.

great-souled Bhageeratha, who was tormenting himself through austerities, and said, "O Bhageeratha! O immensely fortunate one! O lord of men! I am pleased with you. You have tormented yourself with excellent austerities. O one who is great in vows! Accept a boon." The immensely energetic and immensely fortunate Bhageeratha joined his hands in salutation and spoke to the grandfather of all the worlds. "O illustrious one! If you are pleased with me and if my austerities have borne fruit, let all of Sagara's sons obtain water through me. With their ashes sprinkled with the water of the Ganga, let all my great-souled great grandfathers find their ultimate objective in heaven. O god! Grant me offspring. There is no one in our lineage, in this lineage of the Ikshvakus. This is the next boon that I ask for." Having been thus addressed, the grandfather of all the worlds replied in auspicious and sweet words, which were full of sweet syllables, to the king. "O Bhageeratha! O maharatha! This desire of yours is great. O fortunate one! O extender of the lineage of the Ikshvakus! It shall be this way. Ganga, who flows through the Himalayas, is the eldest daughter of the Himalayas. O king! The earth is incapable of withstanding the descent of the Ganga. O king! Hara[333] has been given the task of bearing her burden. O brave one! With the exception of the wielder of the trident, I do not see anyone else who can take on that burden." Speaking in this way to the king, the creator of the worlds addressed Ganga. With the large number of gods, the god then went to heaven.'

Chapter 1(42)

'O Rama! When the god of the gods[334] had departed, he[335] pressed down on the earth with his big toe and stood there, performing austerities for one year. When one year had passed, Pashupati, Uma's consort, worshipped by all the worlds, spoke to the king. "O best

[333] Shiva.

[334] Brahma.

[335] Bhageeratha. He performed austerities in that way, standing on his toe.

among men! I am pleased with you. I will do what is agreeable to you. I will bear the daughter of the king of the mountains on my head. O Rama! The eldest daughter of the Himalayas is worshipped by all the worlds. She assumed an extremely great form, with a force that is difficult to withstand. She descended from the sky, on Shiva's auspicious head. Having been released from there, she was confused by that mass of matted hair. The goddess roamed around there for a large number of years. O descendant of the Raghu lineage! Hara was extremely delighted at this and eventually released Ganga in the direction of Vindusara.[336] The gods, the rishis, the gandharvas, the yakshas and the large number of siddhas witnessed the progress of Ganga from the sky to that spot. The gods were stationed on celestial vehicles that were like cities, yoked to the best of horses and elephants. These mounts staggered at the sight. The supreme descent of Ganga on the earth was extraordinary. All the infinitely energetic gods who had assembled witnessed this. As they were surprised, the ornaments fell down from the bodies of these infinitely energetic gods and it was as if one hundred suns glittered amidst the clouds in the sky. Large numbers of porpoises, serpents and fish were agitated. It was as if flashes of lightning were streaked throughout the sky. Thousands of flows of foam from the water were splashed around. It was as if a flock of swans was stretched out against clouds in the autumn sky. In some places, the flow coursed speedily. In other places, it meandered along curves. In some places, the flow was humble and slow. In other places, it proceeded faster and faster. In some places, water dashed against water and rose up in torrents. It rose up in an instant and then fell down on the earth again. Dislodged once,[337] it was dislodged once again from Shankara's head on to the surface of the earth. Devoid of all taints, the sparkling water roamed freely. The large number of rishis, gandharvas and the residents of earth touched the sacred water released from Bhava's[338] body. There were those who were cursed and had fallen down from the sky to earth. They were sprinkled with this water and cleansed of all sin. With their sins cleansed by the water,

[336] A lake near Gangotri.

[337] From the sky.

[338] Shiva's name.

they regained their radiant forms. They again headed towards the sky and regained their own respective worlds. Cheerfully, the world sprinkled itself with that resplendent water. Cleansed of sin, everyone was delighted. Bhageeratha, the royal sage, was on a celestial chariot. As the immensely energetic one proceeded in front, Ganga followed him at the rear. O Rama! The gods, the rishis, all the daityas, danavas and rakshasas, the best of gandharvas and yakshas, kinnaras and giant serpents and all the apsaras followed Bhageeratha's chariot. All the aquatic creatures also cheerfully followed Ganga. Wherever King Bhageeratha went, the illustrious Ganga, best among rivers and the cleanser of all sins, followed.'

Chapter 1(43)

'The king went to the ocean and penetrated the surface of the ground where the mounds of ashes were, followed by Ganga. O Rama! The ashes were sprinkled with the waters of the Ganga. Brahma, the lord of all the worlds, spoke these words to the king. "O tiger among men! Sagara's sixty thousand great-souled sons have been saved and will go to heaven, like gods. O king! As long as there is water in this ocean on earth, till then, Sagara's sons will reside in heaven, like gods. This Ganga will be known as your eldest daughter. Because of your deeds, she will be famous on earth through your name. The divine Ganga, with three flows, will be known as Bhageerathee. Since she has three flows, she will be known as Tripathaga.[339] O lord of men! Perform the water rites for all your ancestors here. O king! You will thus accomplish your pledge. O king! Your ancestors were exceedingly illustrious. However, even though they were supremely devoted to dharma, they could not achieve what you have. O son![340] In that way, Amshumat was infinitely energetic in this world. However,

[339] The one with three courses.

[340] The word used is tata.

even he could not accomplish the pledge of bringing Ganga down. Your father, Dileepa, was immensely fortunate and infinite in his energy. He was a royal sage, but like a maharshi in his qualities. Though he was established in the dharma of kshatriyas, he was like me in austerities. O unblemished one! Even he was unable to accomplish his desire of bringing Ganga down. O bull among men! However, you have been able to accomplish your pledge. You will obtain supreme worlds and fame and will be greatly revered. O destroyer of enemies! You have accomplished the task of bringing Ganga down. Because of this, you have obtained a great deal of dharma. O supreme among men! O tiger among men! You will always be able to bathe yourself in these waters and purify yourself, thus obtaining sacred fruits. Now go and perform the water rites for all your ancestors. O king! May you be fortunate. I will now go to my own world and so should you." The lord of the gods, the grandfather of all the worlds, spoke in this way. After this, the immensely illustrious one went away to the world of the gods, which is where he had come from. The royal sage, Bhageeratha, performed the excellent water rites for the immensely illustrious sons of Sagara, as is proper, and following the due order. Having purified himself by bathing in the water, the king entered his own city. O best among men! O Raghava! For the sake of prosperity, he ruled his own kingdom well and the people were delighted to get their king back. He was devoid of sorrow and devoid of anxiety. He was prosperous and wealthy. O Rama! I have thus told you about Ganga in detail. O fortunate one! May you be safe. The time for sandhya has passed. This account of Ganga's descent, recounted by me, is blessed and brings fame, long life, heaven and sons.'

Chapter 1(44)

On hearing Vishvamitra's words, Rama and Lakshmana were overcome by great wonder. Rama told Vishvamitra, 'O brahmana! The account recited by you, about Ganga's sacred descent and the filling up of the ocean, is wonderful. With Soumitri, I spent the entire night thinking about the auspicious account that you had told us.' When a sparkling morning dawned, after having performed the morning ablutions, Raghava, the destroyer of enemies, spoke these words to Vishvamitra, the great sage. 'While we heard this supreme account, the illustrious night has passed. O great ascetic! It is as if the entire night passed in a single instant, as we reflected on everything that you have told us. We now have to cross this best of rivers, the sacred river with the three flows. O illustrious one! On knowing that you have come, the rishis, the performers of auspicious deeds, have swiftly come here and have brought boats with comfortable spreads.' On hearing Raghava's words, the great-souled one,[341] made arrangements for crossing over, with Raghava and with the large number of rishis. Having reached the northern bank, they worshipped all the rishis. They saw the city of Vishala,[342] situated on the banks of the Ganga. With Raghava, the supreme among sages quickly proceeded towards the beautiful city of Vishala, which was as divine as heaven.

The immensely wise Rama joined his hands in salutation and asked Vishvamitra, the great sage, about the supreme city of Vishala. 'O great sage! To which royal lineage does Vishala belong? O fortunate one! I am supremely curious and wish to hear about this.' Hearing Rama's words, the bull among sages started to recount the ancient tale about Vishala. 'O Rama! Listen to what I have heard. This is an auspicious account about Shakra. O Raghava! Hear the truth about what happened in this region. O Rama! Earlier, in krita yuga, there were the extremely strong sons of Diti. Aditi had immensely fortunate and brave sons who were extremely devoted to dharma.[343] O tiger among men! Those great-souled

[341] Vishvamitra.

[342] Vaishali, in Bihar.

[343] Diti and Aditi were the daughters of Daksha and married the sage Kashyapa. Diti's sons were the daityas, loosely, the demons. Aditi's sons were the *adityas*, the gods. Diti was older, so the daityas were elder brothers of the gods. Daksha had another daughter named Danu, also married to Kashyapa. Danavas are her sons. However, daityas, danavas and asuras (the counter to *suras* or gods) are words often used synonymously.

ones began to think about how they might be immortal, about how they might be without old age and without disease. O Rama! Reflecting on this, those learned ones arrived at a conclusion. They would churn the ocean and obtain juices from this.[344] Having made up their minds to churn, they made Vasuki the rope to be used for churning. With Mount Mandara as the churning road, those infinitely energetic ones started to churn. Dhanvantari[345] arose and so did the extremely radiant apsaras.[346] O best among men! Since those supreme women were generated when the juices of the water were churned, they came to be known as apsaras. Sixty crores of such immensely radiant apsaras arose. O Kakutstha! The number of their attendants was infinite. None of the gods or the danavas wished to accept them. Since they were not accepted, they came to be known as general women.[347] O descendant of the Raghu lineage! The immensely fortunate Varuni,[348] Varuna's daughter, arose and began to search for the path that she should follow. O Rama! Diti's sons did not accept her, Varuna's daughter. O brave one! Aditi's sons accepted that unblemished one. Thereby, the daityas came to be asuras and Aditi's sons became suras.[349] Having accepted Varuni, the suras were delighted and rejoiced. O best among men! Uchchaishrava, best among horses, arose, and so did the jewel Koustubha. O Rama! So did the supreme amrita and there was a great destruction of the lineage because of that. The sons of Aditi devastated the sons of Diti. The brave sons of Aditi slaughtered Diti's sons in that great, terrible and fierce battle that raged between the daityas and the adityas. When Diti's sons were slain, Purandara obtained the kingdom. Delighted, he ruled over the worlds, with large numbers of rishis and charanas.'

[344] The juices mean amrita, the nectar that confers immortality.

[345] The physician of the gods. The Critical Edition excises shlokas about poison emerging and Shiva drinking the poison.

[346] Etymologically, apsara means someone created from the water.

[347] That is, apsaras were never married to anyone.

[348] The goddess of liquor.

[349] Sura means liquor and the gods became suras because they accepted Varuni. Rejecting Varuni, the daityas became asuras, those without liquor.

Chapter 1(45)

'When her sons were killed, Diti was extremely miserable. O Rama! She went to her husband Kashyapa, the son of Marichi, and said, "O illustrious! Your immensely strong sons[350] have killed my sons. Through a long period of austerities, I wish to obtain a son who will kill Shakra. I will observe austerities and you should grant me such a conception. I seek your permission to obtain a son who will be Indra's slayer." Hearing her words, the immensely energetic Kashyapa, Marichi's son, replied to Diti, who was supremely afflicted by grief. "O fortunate one! O store of austerities! This will indeed be the case if you remain pure. You will give birth to a son who will kill Shakra in an encounter. However, you will have to remain pure for the entire duration of one thousand years. Through me, you will then give birth to a son who will destroy the three worlds. Having said this, the immensely energetic one touched her with his hand and embraced her. Saying, "May you be safe," he left for his own austerities. O best among men! When he had departed, Diti was greatly delighted. She went to Kushaplavana[351] and tormented herself through extremely terrible austerities. O best among men! While she observed these austerities, the thousand-eyed one,[352] full of supreme qualities, tended to her. The thousand-eyed one supplied her with whatever she desired—fire, *kusha* grass, kindling, water, fruits, roots and everything else. To remove her exhaustion, he massaged her body. Through the entire period, Shakra tended to Diti. O descendant of the Raghu lineage! Only ten years were left for the thousand years to be completed. Extremely happy, Diti told the one with the one thousand eyes, "O supreme among valiant ones! Only ten years are left for my austerities to be complete. O fortunate one! When those are over, you will be able to see your brother. O son! It is for your sake that I will rear him as someone who wishes for victory. O

[350] The gods.

[351] A hermitage to the east of Vishala.

[352] Indra.

son! He will conquer the three worlds and you will be able to enjoy them with him, without any anxiety." As Diti spoke in this way, the sun reached the midpoint of the sky. The goddess went to sleep, with her feet placed where her head should have been.[353] Since her feet were where her head should have been, Shakra saw that she had become impure. He was delighted to see that her head was where her feet should have been and laughed. O Rama! Through that weakness, Purandara entered her body. The supremely brave one split her embryo into seven parts. He shattered the embryo with a vajra that possessed one hundred joints. O Rama! Diti woke up at the sound of the weeping and lamenting. Shakra addressed the embryo, "Do not cry! Do not cry!" However, having been shattered by the immensely energetic Vasava, it continued to cry. Diti exclaimed, "Do not kill it. Do not kill it." To show respect to his mother's[354] words, Shakra fell out of the body. Still holding the vajra, Shakra joined his hands in salutation and told Diti, "O goddess! You are impure. You slept with your head in the direction that your feet should have been in. I got the chance to strike at the one who would kill Shakra in an encounter. O goddess! I shattered it into seven fragments. You should pardon this act."'

Chapter 1(46)

'When the embryo was shattered into seven fragments, Diti was extremely miserable. She entreated the invincible and thousand-eyed one in these words. "The embryo has been shattered into seven fragments because of my crime. O lord of the

[353] Indra didn't really want to help and serve her. He didn't want the son to be born and was in close attendance to spot for a weakness in Diti. Obviously, Diti shouldn't have slept in the afternoon. In addition, when sleeping, the head should be in a certain direction, usually east or south, and the feet should face the opposite direction. In her carelessness, Diti did the opposite.

[354] Stepmother.

gods! O slayer of Bala![355] No sin attaches to you because of this. Though my embryo has been destroyed, I wish that you should do something agreeable for me. Let the seven times seven Maruts become guardians of different places.[356] Let these seven sons of mine roam around in the firmament, on the shoulders of the wind. Let these sons of mine be divine in form and let them be famous as Maruts. Let one of them roam around in Brahma's world and another in Indra's world. Let the third and immensely illustrious one be known as the wind that blows through the firmament. O best among the gods! Let the fourth follow your command and roam around in the directions. Let the name Maruts be given by you and let them be known as this." Hearing her words, the thousand-eyed Purandara joined his hands in salutation. Bala's slayer spoke the following words to Diti. "There is no doubt that everything will occur exactly as you have spoken. O fortunate one! Your sons will roam around in the form of gods." This is what mother and son decided in that hermitage. O Rama! Having become successful, we have heard that they[357] proceeded to heaven. O Kakutstha! In ancient times, this is the country where the great Indra used to reside. This is where Diti obtained success in her austerities and he tended to her.

'O tiger among men! Ikshvaku had a son who was supremely devoted to dharma. His mother was Alambusha and he was famous as Vishala.[358] In this spot, he is the one who constructed the city of Vishala. O Rama! Vishala's son was the immensely strong Hemachandra. After this, Hemachandra's son was the famous Suchandra. O Rama! Suchandra's son was famous by the name of Dhumrashva. Dhumrashva had a son named Srinjaya.

[355] Indra killed a demon named Bala.

[356] The Maruts are wind gods and the word is derived from do not (*ma*) cry (*ruda*). The Maruts are Indra's companions. They are usually said to be seven in number. But sometimes, each of the seven is divided into another seven, so that there are forty-nine Maruts. The Maruts are rarely named individually. One possible listing of the seven Maruts is Avaha, Pravaha, Samvaha, Udvaha, Vivaha, Parivaha and Varavaha.

[357] Diti and Indra.

[358] The son was named Vishaala (Vishala), while the city was named Vishaalaa. This Ikshvaku is clearly different from the Ikshvaku of Ayodhya.

Srinjaya's son was the handsome and powerful Sahadeva. Kushashva was Sahadeva's son and he was extremely devoted to dharma. Kushashva had a greatly energetic and powerful son, Somadatta. Somadatta's son was known as Kakutstha. His son is greatly famous and invincible. That immensely energetic one is named Sumati and he is the one who now resides in this city. Through Ikshvaku's favours, all the kings of Vishala are great-souled, valiant and extremely devoted to dharma. They have long lives. O Rama! We will happily spend the night here. O best among men! Tomorrow, when it is morning, we should see Janaka.' The immensely energetic and greatly illustrious Sumati heard that Vishvamitra had come. On hearing this, the best among men came out to welcome him. With his priests and relatives, he worshipped him in excellent ways. Asking about his welfare, he joined his hands in salutation and told Vishvamitra, 'O sage! I am blessed that you have shown me your favours by coming to my kingdom. I have now seen you. There is no one who is more fortunate than I am.'

Chapter 1(47)

Having met, they asked about each other's welfare. After the conversation was over, Sumati addressed the great sage in these words. 'O fortunate one! These two young ones are like the gods in their valour. These brave ones possess the strides of elephants and lions. They are like tigers and bulls. Their eyes are large, like the petals of lotuses. They hold swords, quivers and bows. They are about to become adults and are as handsome as the Ashvins. They are like immortals from the world of the gods, who have followed their will and come down to earth. Why have they come here? O sage! What is the reason? Whose sons are they? They are ornaments for this kingdom, like the moon and the sun in the sky. The proportions of their limbs and signs are just like each other's, identical. What is the reason why these best of men have traversed this difficult path?[359] These brave ones wield the best of weapons. I wish to hear the truth about this.' Hearing his words, Vishvamitra told him about what had happened—the residence in Siddhashrama and the slaughter of the rakshasas. Hearing Vishvamitra's words, the king was greatly delighted. Dasharatha's sons had arrived there, as great guests. He worshipped them in the proper way and tended to the two extremely strong ones. The two Raghavas were honoured extremely well by Sumati. After having spent a night there, they left for Mithila.

On seeing Janaka's sacred city, all the sages had words of commendation and praise for Mithila and worshipped it. Raghava saw that there was a hermitage in a grove near Mithila. 'This looks like a beautiful hermitage. Why has it been abandoned by the sages? O illustrious one! I wish to hear about it. Whose hermitage was it earlier?' Hearing the words spoken by Raghava, the immensely energetic and great sage, Vishvamitra, eloquent in the use of words, replied. 'O Raghava! I will tell you with pleasure. Hear the truth about whose hermitage this was and which great-souled one cursed it in rage. O best among men! Earlier, it belonged to the great-souled Goutama. This hermitage was divine and it was worshipped even by the gods. Earlier, he practised austerities here, together with Ahalya. O prince! The immensely illustrious one spent innumerable years here. Discerning that there was an opportunity,[360] the thousand-eyed one, Shachi's husband,[361] assumed the garb of a sage. He came to Ahalya and addressed her in these words. "O one who is well proportioned! Those who seek pleasure[362] do not wait for the time of conception to arrive. O slender-waisted one! I desire to have intercourse with you." O descendant of the Raghu lineage! She knew that it was the one with the one thousand eyes in the garb of a sage. However, because of her curiosity, the evil-minded one acceded to what the king of the gods wanted. Satisfied in her heart of hearts, she

[359] They could have used other means to come there.

[360] Goutama was away.

[361] Shachi is Indra's wife.

[362] As opposed to those who seek progeny.

told the best of the gods, "O best among the gods! I have been satiated. O lord! However, leave this spot quickly. O lord of the gods! O one who shows honours! Always protect me and your own self." Indra laughed at these words and told Ahalya, "O one with the excellent hips! I am also satiated. I will go back to where I have come from." After the act of intercourse, he emerged from the cottage. O Rama! He was terrified and scared that Goutama might return. He saw that the great sage, Goutama, was entering. He was full of the strength of austerities and the gods and danavas found him impossible to withstand. He blazed like the fire and was wet with water from various tirthas. The bull among sages arrived there, after collecting kindling and kusha grass. On seeing him, the lord of the gods was terrified. His face bore the marks of distress. Seeing the one with the one thousand eyes, attired in the garb of a sage, the sage, full of good conduct, became angry. He spoke these words to the one with evil conduct. "O evil-minded one! You have assumed my form[363] and have done this. Since you have done what should not have been done, you will become infertile." The great-souled sage, Goutama, said this in rage and instantly, the testicles of the thousand-eyed one fell down on the ground. Having cursed Shakra, he also cursed his wife. "You will reside here for many thousands of years. Subsisting on air and without food, you will torment yourself through austerities. You will sleep on ashes. You will live in this hermitage, unseen by all creatures. When the invincible Rama, Dasharatha's son, arrives in this terrible forest, you will be purified. O one who is evil in conduct! When he becomes your guest, you will lose your avarice and confusion. You will then regain your own form and find delight with me." The extremely energetic Goutama spoke in this way to the one who was evil in conduct. He abandoned this hermitage, once frequented by siddhas and charanas. The great ascetic performed austerities on a beautiful summit in the Himalayas.'

[363] The earlier shlokas didn't make it clear that Indra hadn't assumed the form of any sage. He had specifically assumed Goutama's form.

Chapter 1(48)

'Having been rendered infertile, with Agni at the forefront and with a distressed face, Shakra spoke to the gods and large numbers of rishis and charanas. "I have caused an obstruction in the austerities of the great-souled Goutama and have ignited his rage, but I have accomplished a task for the gods.[364] In his rage, he has rendered me infertile and has banished her. Because he released that great curse, I have been able to rob him of his store of austerities.[365] I have helped the cause of the gods. O best among the gods! O large numbers of rishis! O charanas! Therefore, all of you should strive to render me potent again." Hearing Shatakratu's words, the gods, with all the Maruts and with Agni at the forefront, went to the ancestors[366] and spoke these words. "This ram has testicles and Shakra has lost his testicles. Quickly take away the testicles from this ram and give them to Shakra. To cause you delight, if humans offer you rams without testicles, even then, you will grant them supreme satisfaction."[367] Hearing Agni's words, the assembled ancestors severed the ram's testicles and gave them to the thousand-eyed one. O Kakutstha! Since then, the assembled ancestors enjoy rams without testicles and discard the testicles if those are offered.[368] O Raghava! Since then, Indra possesses the testicles of a ram. This is as a result of the power of austerities of the great-souled Goutama. O immensely energetic one! Therefore, enter the hermitage of the performer of auspicious deeds.[369] Save the immensely fortunate Ahalya, who has the form of a goddess.'

[364] This requires explanation. Austerities confer power. Sometimes, austerities and consequent powers can be used to dislodge Indra from his status. Therefore, Indra always sought to prevent anyone from successfully completing austerities.

[365] Any curse takes away from the store of austerities/merit accumulated by the one who is doing the cursing.

[366] The *pitris*, usually translated as manes. These are the original ancestors, born through Brahma's mental powers. They are not gods. They are also the souls of dead human ancestors.

[367] Henceforth, ancestors can be offered castrated rams.

[368] If a ram with testicles is offered, they ignore the testicles.

[369] Goutama.

Hearing Vishvamitra's words, with Vishvamitra at the forefront, Raghava entered the hermitage, accompanied by Lakshmana. He saw the immensely fortunate one, radiant in complexion because of her austerities. He approached the one who could not be seen by the worlds, not even by gods and asuras. She had been carefully crafted by the creator, using divine maya. Her limbs were covered in smoke and she was like the blazing flames of a fire. She was like a cloud covered in snowy mist, with a radiance like that of the full moon. She was unapproachable, with the complexion of the blazing sun, amidst a store of water. Because of Goutama's words, she had been rendered invisible to the three worlds, until she had seen Rama. The two Raghavas approached her and touched her feet. Remembering Goutama's words, she received them. Extremely controlled, she treated them as guests and offered padya and arghya. Following the prescribed rites, Kakutstha accepted this hospitality. A great shower of flowers descended from above and the drums of the gods were sounded. There was a large assembly of gandharvas and apsaras. The gods worshipped Ahalya and uttered words of praise. She had followed Goutama's instructions and had purified her limbs through the strength of austerities. The immensely energetic Goutama was happy with Ahalya. Following the prescribed ordinances, the great ascetic worshipped Rama. Rama also worshipped the great sage, Goutama, in excellent ways. Having met him in the proper way, he then moved on to Mithila.

Chapter 1(49)

With Vishvamitra at the forefront and with Soumitri, Rama then travelled towards the north-east and arrived at the sacrificial arena. With Lakshmana, Rama spoke to the tiger among sages. 'The sacrifice of the great-souled Janaka is auspicious and prosperous. O immensely fortunate one! There are many thousand brahmanas who have come here. There are the residents of many countries and are accomplished in studying the Vedas. The residences of the rishis can be seen and there are hundreds of carts. O brahmana! We should identify a proper spot for us to dwell.' Hearing Rama's words, Vishvamitra, the great sage, instructed that an abode should be constructed in an uninhabited spot that had water.

Hearing that Vishvamitra, the best among sages, had arrived, the great king came, with his unblemished priest, Shatananda, at the forefront. With arghya, the great-souled officiating priests also arrived. Following dharma, they offered this and water sanctified with mantras to Vishvamitra. The great-souled one accepted Janaka's worship. He asked about the king's welfare and about whether all was well with the sacrifice. As is proper, the sage cheerfully asked about the priests and the preceptors and about all those who had arrived. The king joined his hands in salutation and spoke to the best among sages. 'O illustrious one! With all the excellent sages, please be seated.' Hearing Janaka's words, the great sage sat down. With his officiating priest[370] at the forefront, and with his ministers, so did the king. On seeing that everyone had properly sat down on seats in different directions, the king spoke to Vishvamitra. 'Today, the gods have ensured that my sacrifice will be successful. O illustrious one! Now that I have seen you, I will obtain the fruits of the sacrifice. I am blessed. I am favoured. O bull among sages! O brahmana! With all the sages, you have come to this sacrificial arena. O brahmana rishi! The learned ones have said that only twelve days remain for the sacrifice to be concluded. O Koushika! You should remain here, to see the gods receive their shares.' With a cheerful face, the king addressed the tiger among sages in this way.

Controlling himself, he joined his hands in salutation and asked, 'O fortunate one! These two young ones are like the gods in their valour. These brave ones possess the strides of elephants and lions. They are like tigers and bulls. They have large eyes that are like the petals of lotuses. They hold swords, quivers and bows. They are like the Ashvins in beauty and are about to become adults. They

[370] Shatananda.

are like immortals from the world of the gods, who have voluntarily come down to earth. O sage! Why have they come here on foot? What is the reason? Whose sons are they? O great sage! These brave ones wield the best of weapons. Whose sons are they? They are ornaments for this country, like the moon and the sun in the sky. They are identical to each other, in the proportion of their limbs and in their bodily signs. These brave ones possess sidelocks that are like the wings of a crow. I wish to hear the truth about this.' Hearing the words of Janaka, the great-souled one told him that these two were Dasharatha's great-souled sons. He also recounted the residence in Siddhashrama, the slaughter of the rakshasas, their subsequent sight of Vishala, the meeting with Ahalya, Goutama's arrival and their decision to come there, to examine the great bow. Vishvamitra, the great sage, told all this to the great-souled and immensely energetic Janaka. He then stopped.

Chapter 1(50)

Hearing the words of the intelligent Vishvamitra, the body hair of the immensely energetic and great sage, Shatananda, stood up. He was Goutama's eldest son and was extremely radiant because of his austerities. Having seen Rama, he was supremely astounded. Those two princes were happily seated, with their heads bowed. On seeing them, Shatananda spoke to Vishvamitra, best among sages. 'O tiger among sages! After having performed austerities for a long period of time, my illustrious mother[371] showed herself to these two princes. Using forest fare, my illustrious mother worshipped the immensely energetic Rama, who deserves to be worshipped by all creatures that have bodies. You have told Rama about the ancient account, whereby my mother was treated badly by that immensely energetic god.[372] O Koushika! O fortunate

[371] Ahalya was Shatananda's mother.

[372] Indra.

one! O best among sages! After having met Rama, my mother has been united with my senior.[373] O descendant of Kushika! My senior has been worshipped by Rama. The immensely energetic and great-souled one has now arrived here and deserves to be worshipped. O descendant of Kushika! Before coming here, did Rama honour my father with a peaceful and controlled state of mind?' The great sage, Vishvamitra, was accomplished in the use of words and eloquent in speech. Hearing Shatananda's words, he replied, 'O best among sages! I have not neglected anything that I could have done. The sage has been united with his wife, just as Bhargava was with Renuka.'[374]

Hearing the words of the intelligent Vishvamitra, the immensely energetic Shatananda spoke these words to Rama. 'O best among men! Welcome. O Raghava! It is good fortune that you have come here, with Vishvamitra, the unvanquished maharshi, leading the way. The brahmana rishi is infinite in his splendour and austerities and has accomplished unthinkable deeds. The immensely energetic Vishvamitra has to be recognized as the supreme destination. O Rama! The truth is that there is no one on earth who is more blessed than he is. You have been protected by Kushika's son, who tormented himself through great austerities. Listen. I will tell you about the great-souled Koushika, about his strength and his conduct. Listen attentively. For a long time, this destroyer of enemies used to be a king, with dharma in his soul. He knew about dharma and was accomplished in learning. He was devoted to the welfare of the subjects. There was a king named Kusha and he was Prajapati's son. Kusha's son was the powerful Kushanabha, who was extremely devoted to dharma. Kushanabha's son was the famous Gadhi. The immensely energetic and great sage, Vishvamitra, is Gadhi's son. The immensely energetic Vishvamitra ruled over the earth. He was a king and ruled the kingdom for many thousand years. On one occasion, the immensely energetic

[373] His father, Goutama.

[374] Goutama has been united with Ahalya. Bhargava means a descendant of the Bhrigu lineage. Here, Bhargava means Jamadagni, Parashurama's father. Jamadagni's wife was Renuka. On Jamadagni's instructions, Parashurama beheaded Renuka. However, subsequently, Renuka was reunited with Jamadagni.

one arrayed an army. Surrounded by an akshouhini, he roamed around the earth. The king progressively travelled through cities, kingdoms, rivers and mountains and arrived at a hermitage. This was Vasishtha's hermitage and there were trees with many kinds of flowers and fruit there. There were diverse kinds of animals and the place was frequented by siddhas and charanas. It was adorned by gods, danavas and gandharvas and those who were in the form of kinnaras. It was populated by peaceful deer and large numbers of birds dwelt there. It was full of a large number of brahmana rishis and inhabited by *devarshi*s.[375] There were siddhas who practised austerities and those great-souled ones were like the fire. There was prosperity everywhere and there were great-souled ones who were like Brahma. Some lived on water, others survived on air. There were others who subsisted on dry leaves. There were self-controlled ones who lives on fruits and roots. They had conquered anger and had conquered their senses. There were *valakhilya* rishis,[376] devoted to chanting and the offering of oblations. Vasishtha's hermitage was like Brahma's world. The immensely strong Vishvamitra, best among victorious ones, saw that.'

Chapter 1(51)

'Seeing this, the immensely strong Vishvamitra was greatly delighted. In humility, the brave one bowed down before Vasishtha, supreme among those who meditate. The great-souled Vasishtha said, "Welcome." The illustrious Vasishtha requested him to take a seat. When the intelligent Vishvamitra had seated himself, as is proper, the supreme among sages offered him roots and fruits. The supreme among kings accepted the honour Vasishtha showed him. The immensely energetic Vishvamitra asked him about the well-being of austerities, the agnihotra, his disciples

[375] Divine sages.

[376] 60,000 sages who were the sizes of thumbs. They preceded the sun's chariot.

and the trees. Vasishtha told the supreme among kings that all was well, everywhere. King Vishvamitra was seated comfortably. The great ascetic, Vasishtha, Brahma's son[377] and best among those who meditate, then asked, "O king! Is everything well with you? Do you take delight in dharma? O king! O one who follows dharma! Are you upright in ruling over your subjects? Are your servants well trained? Do they adhere to your commands? O slayer of enemies! Have you defeated all your enemies? O scorcher of enemies! O tiger among men! O unblemished one! Is everything well about your army, treasury, friends and your sons and grandsons?" The king told Vasishtha that all was well, everywhere. The immensely energetic Vishvamitra behaved in a humble way towards Vasishtha. Devoted to dharma, they spent a long period of time in conversing about auspicious accounts. They were supremely delighted and behaved affectionately towards each other. O descendant of the Raghu lineage! When the conversation was over, the illustrious Vasishtha smiled and spoke these words to Vishvamitra. "O greatly strong one! I wish to show my hospitality towards you and your army. O immeasurable one! Accept the honours that you deserve. I wish to behave properly towards you. Please accept what I am about to render. O king! You are the best of guests and I will make efforts to show you worship." When Vasishtha spoke in this way, the immensely intelligent King Vishvamitra replied, "You have already shown me hospitality. You have given me honours through your words. O illustrious one! I have received the fruits and roots that can be obtained in the hermitage. O illustrious one! I have received padya and achamaniya and I have seen you. O immensely wise one! You have worshipped me well in every possible way of worship. I bow down before you. I will depart now. Please look on me with eyes of affection."[378] The king spoke in this way. However, Vasishtha, with dharma in his soul, invited him again and repeatedly entreated him. At this, Gadhi's son agreed and replied to Vasishtha, "O illustrious one! O supreme sage! Then, so be it—whatever

[377] Through Brahma's mental powers.

[378] Vishvamitra was conscious that a hermitage couldn't have offered proper hospitality to a king and his army.

brings you pleasure." Thus addressed, the immensely energetic Vasishtha, supreme among those who meditate, was delighted. The one who was cleansed of sin summoned his speckled cow. "O Shabala![379] Come here quickly and listen to my words. I wish to make all the arrangements to treat this royal sage and his army. Make all the arrangements for an extremely expensive banquet. Let every desirable food be brought, characterized by the six kinds of flavour.[380] O divine one! O one who yields every object of desire! For my sake, shower all of this down. Let the food be succulent. Let there be drink. Let there be *lehya* and *choshya*.[381] O Shabala! Swiftly create a store of every kind of food."'

Chapter 1(52)

'O slayer of enemies! Vasishtha spoke to Shabala in this way. The cow that can be milked for every object of desire brought everything that had been wished for. There were sugar cane, honey, parched grain, *maireya*, the best of *asava*,[382] expensive kinds of drink and diverse kinds of food to eat. There were heaps of hot food, piled as high as mountains. There were sweetmeats, liquids and flows of curds. There were many kinds of succulent juices, with the six kinds of flavours. The vessels were full with thousands of products made out of cane. All the people there were satisfied. They ate well and were cheerful. O Rama! Vasishtha made Vishvamitra's army content. The royal sage, Vishvamitra, rejoiced at having been fed so well. Those who were in the king's inner quarters[383] and the brahmanas and the priests were also fed well.

[379] *Shabala* means speckled or spotted. This was a *kamadhenu*, a cow that could yield every object of desire.

[380] Caustic, acidic, sweet, salty, bitter and alkaline.

[381] The four types of food are those that are chewed (*charvya*), sucked (*choshya* or *chushya*), licked (*lehya*) and drunk (*peya*).

[382] Both maireya and asava are kinds of liquor. Specifically, maireya is made from molasses or grain and asava is made through a process of distillation, not mere fermentation.

[383] The royal ladies.

The advisers, ministers and servants were also honoured in this way. Filled with great delight, he[384] spoke to Vasishtha. "O brahmana! You deserve to be worshipped. Yet, you have honoured us well and worshipped us. O one who is eloquent in speech! Hear my words now. Give me Shabala in exchange for one hundred thousand cows. O illustrious one! She is a jewel and a king is the one who should accumulate jewels. O brahmana! Give me Shabala. According to dharma, she belongs to me." The illustrious Vasishtha, supreme among sages, was addressed in this way. The one with dharma in his soul replied to Vishvamitra, the lord of the earth. "O king! In exchange for one hundred thousand cows, one billion cows, or large amounts of silver, I am incapable of giving you Shabala. O destroyer of enemies! I should not abandon her, nor should she be separated from me. Shabala is eternally inseparable from me, like deeds are from one's own self. She is the one who provides *havya*, *kavya*,[385] the means of sustaining my life and undertaking agnihotra and the source of sacrificial offerings and oblations. She is the source of utterances of *svaha* and *vashatkara*[386] and different kinds of learning. O royal sage! There is no doubt that all of these are obtained because of her. In truth, she represents everything for me and she always satisfies me. O king! There are many kinds of reasons why I cannot give you Shabala." Vasishtha was eloquent in speech and spoke these words. However, Vishvamitra became exceedingly angry and said, "I will give you fourteen thousand elephants that have golden harnesses and are decorated with golden necklaces and golden goads. I will give you eight hundred golden chariots that are ornamented with tinkling bells, each yoked to four white horses. O one who is excellent in vows! I will give you eleven thousand extremely energetic horses, born in noble lineages from the best of countries. I will give you ten million adult cows, classified into different complexions. Give me this single cow, Shabala." When the

[384] Vishvamitra.

[385] Offerings to gods are havya, offerings to ancestors are kavya.

[386] Vashatkara is the exclamation '*vashat*' made at the time of offering an oblation. *Svadha* is said at the time of offering oblations to the ancestors and svaha is said at the time of offering oblations to the gods.

intelligent Vishvamitra spoke in this way, the illustrious one replied, "O king! Under no circumstances will I give you Shabala. She alone is my gem. She alone represents my treasure. She is everything to me. She is truly my life. When sacrifices are performed at the time of the new moon and the full moon, she is the one who supplies the dakshina. O king! She is the one who ensures the performance of many kinds of rites. O king! There is no doubt that all my rites have her as the foundation. There is no need to speak any more. I will not give the one who can be milked for every object of desire."'

Chapter 1(53)

'The sage Vasishtha refused to give up the kamadhenu. O Rama! Vishvamitra then started to drag Shabala away. O Rama! As Shabala was dragged away by the great-souled king, she was miserable. Afflicted by grief and thinking about this, she wept. "Why have I been abandoned by extremely great-souled Vasishtha? I am distressed and extremely miserable, being thus seized by the servants of the king. What injury have I done to the maharshi with the cleansed soul? I have committed no crime. I am devoted to him and love him. Why is the one who is devoted to dharma abandoning me?" She thought in this way and sighed repeatedly. With great speed, she dashed towards the supremely energetic Vasishtha. O destroyer of enemies! She flung away the hundreds of servants. With the speed of the wind, she rushed towards the feet of the great-souled one. She wept and lamented. Stationed before Vasishtha, in a voice that was like the rumbling of the clouds, Shabala said, "O illustrious one! O son of Brahma! Why am I being abandoned by you? How is it that the servants of the king are dragging me away from your presence?" The brahmana rishi was thus addressed by the one whose heart was grief-stricken. She was grieving and was like his own sister. He said, "O Shabala! I am not abandoning you, nor have you caused me any injury. The immensely strong king is dragging you away from me by force. I do not possess the strength that is equal to his. In particular, he is a king. A king is powerful. The kshatriyas are like the lords of the earth. This akshouhini is full of horses and chariots. There are many elephants and standards. His strength is superior to mine." The brahmana rishi was infinite in his splendour. Thus addressed by Vasishtha, the one who knew about the use of words, humbly replied in these words. "It has been said that the strength of kshatriyas is not superior in power to that of brahmanas. Brahmanas possess the divine strength of the brahman. They are superior to kshatriyas. Your strength is immeasurable. He is not stronger than you. Vishvamitra may be immensely valiant. However, your energy is impossible to withstand. You possess the power of the brahman. Invoke your great energy in me. I will destroy the insolence and strength of that evil-souled one." O Rama! The greatly illustrious Vasishtha then said, "Create an army that will overcome the army of the enemy." O king! With her bellow, she created Pahlavas in hundreds. While Vishvamitra looked on, they destroyed his entire army. The king became extremely angry and his eyes dilated with rage. Using superior and inferior weapons, he destroyed the Pahlavas. On seeing that the hundreds of Pahlavas were afflicted by Vishvamitra, she again created a mixed and terrible force consisting of Shakas and Yavanas. The earth was completely covered by this mixed army of Shakas and Yavanas. They were brave and exceedingly valiant. They blazed like golden filaments in a flower. They wielded long swords and javelins. Their golden complexion seemed to envelop the sky. Like a blazing fire, they burnt down his[387] entire army. At this, the immensely energetic Vishvamitra released his weapons.'

Chapter 1(54)

'Vasishtha saw that they were being devastated, confounded by Vishvamitra's weapons. He invoked the powers of *yoga*

[387] Vishvamitra's.

and urged the kamadhenu to create more forces. Through her bellowing, she created Kambojas who were like the sun in their complexion. The Pahlavas, wielding weapons in their hands, were generated from her udders, the Yavanas from the region around her vagina, the Shakas from the region around her rectum and the *mlechchhas*[388] from her body hair. There were also Haritas and Kiratakas. O descendant of the Raghu lineage! In an instant, they devastated Vishvamitra's army of soldiers, the infantry, the elephants, the cavalry and the chariots. On seeing that the soldiers had been destroyed by the great-souled Vasishtha, one hundred of Vishvamitra's sons attacked Vasishtha, supreme among those who meditate. They wielded many kinds of weapons. With his humkara, the great rishi burnt all of them down. In an instant, the great-souled Vasishtha reduced Vishvamitra's sons to ashes, with their horses, chariots and foot soldiers. The extremely illustrious Vishvamitra saw that the army of his sons was destroyed. He was ashamed and immersed in thought. It[389] was like an ocean without force, like a defanged serpent and like a sun without colour, having just lost its radiance. With his sons slain, he was distressed, like a bird that has lost its wings. His insolence was destroyed, his enterprise was destroyed and he didn't know what to do.

'Engaging the single son who was left to rule over the kingdom and the earth, following the dharma of kshatriyas, he resorted to the forest. He went to the slopes of the Himalayas, frequented by kinnaras and serpents. To obtain the favours of Mahadeva, the great ascetic tormented himself through austerities. After a long period of time, the lord of the gods, the granter of boons who has the bull on his banner, showed himself to Vishvamitra, the great sage. "O king! Why are you engaged in these austerities? Tell me what you desire. I am the one who grants boons. What boon do you wish for? Let it be known." Thus addressed by the god, the great ascetic, Vishvamitra, prostrated himself and spoke these words to Mahadeva. "O Mahadeva! O unblemished one! If you

[388] Barbarians, non-Aryans, those who did not speak Sanskrit.

[389] The army.

are satisfied with me, bestow on me dhanurveda and its various limbs and the Upanishads with their different limbs and mysteries. O unblemished one! Let all the weapons that are known to gods, danavas, maharshis, gandharvas, yakshas and rakshasas manifest themselves before me. O god of the gods! Through your favours, may I obtain what I desire." Saying that he agreed to this, the lord of the gods went away to heaven. The immensely strong royal sage, Vishvamitra, obtained these weapons. He was filled with great insolence. He was full of pride. His valour increased, like that of the ocean on the day of the full moon. He thought that the supreme rishi, Vasishtha, was already dead. The king went to the hermitage and released these weapons. He burnt down the entire hermitage with the energy of these weapons. On seeing that the place was devastated because of the weapons released by the intelligent Vishvamitra, all the sages were terrified and fled in hundreds of directions. Vasishtha's disciples and the birds and animals were frightened. Scared, they fled in thousands of directions. The great-souled Vasishtha's hermitage became deserted. In an instant, it became as silent as a cremation ground. Vasishtha repeatedly said, "Do not be frightened. I will destroy Gadhi's son, like the sun dispels the mist." The immensely energetic Vasishtha, supreme among those who meditate, said this. Angrily, he spoke these words to Vishvamitra. "I have nurtured this hermitage for a long time and you have destroyed it. You are foolish and evil in conduct. Therefore, you will no longer survive." Saying this, in great rage, he quickly raised his staff. It was like the fire of destruction, devoid of smoke, and was just like the other staff.'[390]

Chapter 1(55)

'The immensely strong Vasishtha spoke in this way to Vishvamitra. Asking him to wait, he raised the Agneya

390 A reference to Yama's rod or staff.

weapon.[391] In anger, the illustrious Vasishtha spoke these words. "O worthless kshatriya! Stay there and show me whatever strength you possess. O son of Gadhi! I will destroy your insolence and your weapons. What is the strength of kshatriyas when it faces the great strength of brahmanas? O worst of kshatriyas! Behold my divine strength, one that comes from being a brahmana." With the supreme Agneya weapon, invoked on the brahmana's rod, he pacified the weapon of Gadhi's son, like a flood of water douses a fire. In rage, Gadhi's descendant hurled *varuna*, roudra, *aindra*, *pashupata* and aishika weapons and *manava*, *mohana*, *gandharva*, *svapana*, *jrimbhana*, *mohana*, *santapana* and *vilapana*.[392] There were *shoshana* and *darana* and the vajra weapon, which is extremely difficult to withstand. There was Brahma's noose, Kala's[393] noose and Varuna's noose. There was the beloved weapon *pinaka*,[394] the weapon that dries up, the weapon that wets and the weapon that is like thunder. There were the weapons *danda*, *paishacha* and *krouncha*.[395] There were the chakras of Dharma, Kala and Vishnu. There were the weapons *vayavya*, *mathana* and *hayashira*.[396] He hurled two spears known as *kankala* and *musala*. There was the extremely great weapon of the Vidyadharas and Kala's terrible weapon. There was the terrible trident and *kapala* and *kankana*.[397] O descendant of the Raghu lineage! He hurled all these different weapons. Vasishtha is supreme among those who meditate and

[391] The rod was invoked with this weapon.

[392] Varuna, roudra, aindra and pashupata are divine weapons respectively associated with Varuna, Rudra, Indra and Shiva. Aishika is a weapon invoked on a blade of grass. Manava means a human weapon, mohana causes confusion, gandharva is associated with the gandharvas, svapana puts to sleep, jrimbhana causes yawning, santapana scorches and vilapana causes lamentations. The Critical text uses the word mohana twice. Non-Critical versions have *madana* in place of the second mohana, meaning a weapon that causes intoxication. Shoshana dries up and darana shatters.

[393] Time or Destiny.

[394] Shiva's bow or trident.

[395] Danda punishes and paishacha is associated with pishachas. In this context, krouncha probably means a weapon tinged with poison.

[396] Vayavya is associated with Vayu, it is a weapon that uses the wind to blow away. Mathana churns and hayashira is a weapon that is in the form of a horse's head.

[397] Kapala is a skull and kankana is something that twirls.

what transpired was extraordinary. The son of a brahmana used his staff to devour all of these. When all these were pacified, in anger, Gadhi's descendant invoked *brahmastra*.[398] On seeing that weapon, on seeing that brahmastra had been invoked, all the gods, with Agni at the forefront, the divine rishis, the gandharvas, the giant serpents and all the three worlds were terrified. However, even that extremely terrible brahmastra was devoured by the brahmana's energy. O Raghava! Vasishtha devoured everything through the brahmana's staff. The great-souled Vasishtha devoured brahmastra and assumed an extremely terrible and fierce form that confounded the three worlds. From the great-souled Vasishtha's body hair, flames seemed to emerge and those fiery rays seemed to be tinged with smoke. The brahmana's staff flamed as it was held in his hand. It was like the fire of destruction, devoid of smoke, and was like Yama's rod. The large number of sages praised Vasishtha, supreme among those who meditate. "O brahmana! Your strength is invincible and so is the energy you bear and ignite. O brahmana! You have countered the great ascetic, Vishvamitra. O supreme among those who meditate! Show your favours. Let the distress of the worlds be dispelled." Thus addressed, the immensely strong and great ascetic was calmed. Countered, Vishvamitra sighed and spoke these words. "Shame on the strength of kshatriyas. The strength of a brahmana's energy is indeed the strength that is most powerful. A single staff of a brahmana has destroyed all my weapons. On examining the matter, my mind and senses are pleased. I will resort to great austerities so that I can become a brahmana."'

•

Chapter 1(56)

'His heart was tormented,[399] remembering the subjugation he had been subjected to. Because of the enmity with the

[398] Brahma's weapon.
[399] Vishvamitra's.

great-souled one,[400] he sighed repeatedly. O Raghava! With his wife, he headed for the southern direction. Vishvamitra, the great ascetic, subjected himself to supreme austerities. He followed self-control, practising those supreme austerities and subsisting on fruits and roots. He had sons who were devoted to truth and dharma—Havishpanda, Madhushpanda, Dridhanetra and Maharatha. After a full one thousand years, Brahma, grandfather of the worlds, spoke these sweet words to Vishvamitra, the store of austerities. "O son of Kushika! Through your austerities, you have conquered the worlds meant for rajarshis. Because of your austerities, we will know you as a rajarshi." Having said this, with the other gods, the immensely energetic Brahma, the supreme lord of the worlds, went to heaven and to Brahma's world. Hearing this, Vishvamitra was somewhat ashamed and crestfallen. Full of great misery and intolerance, he said, "Despite my having practised great austerities, all the gods and the large number of rishis have only come to know me as a rajarshi. I think all my austerities have been fruitless." O Kakutstha! Having made up his mind in this way, the supreme-souled and great ascetic undertook supreme austerities again. At that time, there was the famous Trishanku, a descendant of the lineage of the Ikshvakus. He was truthful in speech and had conquered his senses. O Raghava! His mind turned towards undertaking a sacrifice whereby, in his own physical body, he could go to the supreme destination of the gods.[401] Having thought of this, he invited Vasishtha.[402] However, the great-souled Vasishtha expressed his inability. Having been refused by Vasishtha, he left for the southern direction, where Vasishtha's sons had been tormenting themselves through austerities for a long time. Trishanku saw one hundred of Vasishtha's supremely radiant, extremely energetic and illustrious sons, tormenting themselves. He approached all those great-souled sons of his preceptor.[403] He first greeted them, somewhat ashamed and with a downcast face. He joined his hands in salutation and addressed all those greatly

[400] Vasishtha.

[401] That is, heaven.

[402] To be the officiating priest at the sacrifice.

[403] Vasishtha.

energetic ones. "I have come here to seek refuge with you. You are the ones who grant refuge and I am one who seeks refuge. O fortunate ones! I have been refused by the great-souled Vasishtha. I wish to perform a great sacrifice and you should grant me your permission. I have bowed down before all the sons of my preceptor, seeking their favours. O brahmanas! You have based yourselves in austerities and I bow down my head and worship you. I desire that you self-controlled ones should ensure the success of my sacrifice, so that I can reach the world of the gods in my own physical body. O stores of austerities! Refused by Vasishtha, I do not see any other refuge anywhere, with the exception of all the sons of my preceptor. For all those who belong to the Ikshvaku lineage, priests are the supreme destination. Therefore, thereafter,[404] all of you are like gods to me."'

Chapter 1(57)

'O Rama! On hearing Trishanku's words, the one hundred sons of the rishi were enraged. They addressed the king in these words. "O evil-minded one! You have been refused by your preceptor, who is truthful in speech. How can you cross him and approach a different branch?[405] In every situation, priests are the supreme destination for those of the Ikshvaku lineage. We are incapable of negating the words of the one who is truthful in speech. The illustrious rishi, Vasishtha, has conveyed his inability. How can you then think of inviting us to undertake such a sacrifice? O best among men! You are foolish. You should go back to your own city. O king! In the three worlds, that illustrious person[406] is the only one who can undertake such a sacrifice." Hearing their words, the king's eyes dilated in rage. He again addressed them in these words. "I have been refused by my preceptor and by the sons

[404] After Vasishtha's refusal.

[405] Vasishtha is being compared to a tree.

[406] Vasishtha.

of my preceptor. O stores of austerities! May you be fortunate. I will find another destination." Hearing those terrible words, the sons of the rishi became extremely angry. They cursed him, "You will become a *chandala*."[407] Saying this, those great-souled ones entered their own respective hermitages. When the night was over, the king became a chandala. He was dark and was attired in dark-blue garments. His form was harsh and his hair stood up, like a standard. He was smeared in paste and adorned with garlands from funeral pyres. His ornaments were made out of iron. Seeing this, all the ministers abandoned the person who now had the form of a chandala. O Rama! The citizens who followed him also fled. O Kakutstha! Alone, the king went to the supreme-souled Vishvamitra, the store of austerities who was scorching himself, day and night. O Rama! Vishvamitra saw that the king had been unsuccessful. Seeing his form of a chandala, the sage was overcome by compassion. Overcome by compassion, the extremely energetic one, supremely devoted to dharma, spoke these words to the king, who was terrible in form. "May you be fortunate. O prince! O immensely strong one! What task has brought you here? O brave one! The lord of Ayodhya has been cursed and has attained the state of a chandala." He was addressed in these words by one who was eloquent in speech. Hearing these words, the king, who had become a chandala, joined his hands in salutation and said, "I have been rebuffed by my preceptor and by the sons of my preceptor. I have not accomplished my wish and am now confronted by this catastrophe. O one who is amiable to behold! I desire to go to heaven in my own physical body. I have performed one hundred sacrifices, but have not obtained that fruit. I have never uttered a lie in the past, nor will I ever utter a falsehood. O amiable one! Following the dharma of kshatriyas, I vouch that this is the reason for this catastrophe. Curse me if it is otherwise. I have performed many kinds of sacrifices. I have followed dharma and ruled over the subjects. I have satisfied my great-souled preceptors with my good conduct. I sought and desired

[407] Chandala has different nuances and a chandala is not necessarily a shudra. A chandala is also of mixed parentage, with a shudra father and a brahmana mother. More generally, chandalas are outcastes, while shudras are within the caste fold.

to perform a sacrifice in accordance with dharma. O bull among sages! However, my preceptors are not content at this. I think that destiny is supreme and human endeavour is futile. Destiny cannot be crossed. In every way, destiny is the supreme refuge. That is the reason I am supremely afflicted and seek your favours. O fortunate one! My deeds have been countered by destiny. You should do what needs to be done. There is no other destination for me. There is no other refuge for me. You should counter destiny through your human endeavour."'

Chapter 1(58)

'Full of compassion, Kushika's descendant spoke these sweet words to the king, who presented himself in the form of a chandala. "O son![408] O descendant of the Ikshvaku lineage! Welcome. I know that you are extremely devoted to dharma. O bull among sages! Do not be scared. I will be your refuge. I will invite all the maharshis who are auspicious in their deeds, so that they can assist in the sacrifice. O king! You will perform the sacrifice that was foiled. You will go to heaven in your own physical body, in your original form, as well as in the form obtained because of the curse of your preceptors. O lord of men! I think that heaven is as good as in your hands. You have approached and sought refuge with Koushika, who is the one who grants refuge." Having said this, the immensely energetic and immensely wise one instructed his sons, who were supremely devoted to dharma, to make all the arrangements for the sacrifice. He summoned all his disciples and spoke these words to them. "O sons! Following my instructions, bring all the rishis and their disciples. Bring their well-wishers and the extremely learned assistant priests. If anyone ignores these words, or inflamed by the strength of their words, speaks anything against them, and also everything that is left unsaid, let all that be

[408] The word used is tata.

reported to me." Hearing these words and following his command, they left in different directions. All those who knew about the brahman started to assemble from different countries. The disciples returned to the sage, who blazed in his energy, and reported all the words spoken by those who knew about the brahman. "On hearing your words, all the brahmanas have arrived from different countries, or are coming. However, Mahodaya[409] ignored them. Also, all those one hundred sons of Vasishtha dilated their eyes in rage. O bull among sages! You should hear everything that they said. 'A kshatriya[410] is the officiating priest for a chandala who is undertaking a sacrifice. In such an assembly, how can the gods and the rishis partake of the oblations? Having enjoyed the food of a chandala, how will the great-souled brahmanas go to heaven, even if they are protected by Vishvamitra?' O tiger among sages! Their eyes dilated with rage, all the sons of Vasishtha, together with Mahodaya, uttered these harsh words." Hearing all their words, the eyes of that bull among sages dilated with rage. He angrily said, "I am established in my fierce austerities. All those evil-souled ones who revile an unblemished one like me will be reduced to ashes. There is no doubt about this. Right now, the noose of time will convey them to Yama's eternal abode. For seven hundred births, all of them will be those who feed on corpses. They will be known as *mushtikas*.[411] They will be shunned and will always feed on the flesh of dogs. They will roam around in the worlds, deformed and disfigured. The evil-minded Mahodaya has abused someone as unblemished as me. He will be abhorred by all the worlds and will become a nishada. He will always be engaged in taking the lives of others and will always be cruel. Because of my rage, he will face this catastrophe for a long period of time." The great ascetic, Vishvamitra, spoke these words. After this, in the midst of the rishis, the immensely energetic and great sage stopped.'

[409] The name of a priest.

[410] Vishvamitra.

[411] A variety of chandala. Vasishtha's sons became this.

Chapter 1(59)

'In the midst of the sages, through the strength of his austerities, the immensely energetic Vishvamitra said that he would slay Mahodaya and the sons of Vasishtha. He said, "This heir of the Ikshvaku lineage is known by the name of Trishanku. He is generous and is devoted to dharma. He has sought refuge with me. He wishes to conquer the world of the gods in his own physical body. With me, all of you undertake this sacrifice, so that he can go the world of the gods in his own physical body." All those maharshis knew about dharma. Hearing his words, all of them consulted with each other and spoke words that were full of dharma. "The sage who is an heir of the Kushika lineage is extremely prone to anger. There is no doubt that we must completely act in accordance with his words. The illustrious one is like the fire. He will curse us in his rage. Therefore, let us undertake this sacrifice, so that the heir of the Ikshvaku lineage can go to heaven in his own physical body, thanks to Vishvamitra's energy." Thus, all of them engaged themselves in undertaking that sacrifice. Having spoken those words, all the maharshis initiated the rites. The immensely energetic Vishvamitra became the officiating priest for the sacrifice. The officiating priests, accomplished in the use of mantras, chanted mantras. Following the prescribed ordinances, they performed all the rituals. After a long period of time, Vishvamitra, the great ascetic, invited all the gods to accept their shares in the sacrifice. However, all the gods did not arrive to accept their shares in the sacrifice. At this, Vishvamitra, the great sage, was infused with rage. He angrily raised a sacrificial ladle and spoke to Trishanku. "O lord of men! Behold the strength of the austerities I have earned for myself. Through my own energy, I will convey you to heaven in your physical body. It is extremely difficult to go to heaven in one's own physical body. O lord of men! Go there. O king! Even if I have earned a little bit of merit through my own austerities, through that energy, go to heaven in your own physical body." O Kakutstha! When the sage spoke in this way, while the sages looked on, the lord of men went to heaven in his own physical body.

'When he saw that Trishanku had soared to the world of the gods, with all the other large number of gods, the chastiser of Paka addressed him in these words. "O Trishanku! Leave this place. You have not done anything to make heaven your abode. O foolish one! You have been cursed by your preceptor. Fall down to earth, with your head facing downwards." Thus addressed by the great Indra, Trishanku started to fall down again. He screamed out to Vishvamitra, the store of austerities, "Save me." Hearing his loud wails, Koushika became extremely angry and said, "Stay there. Stay there." He was like another Prajapati.[412] In the midst of the sages, along the southern direction, the energetic one created another group of saptarshis.[413] Senseless with rage, in the midst of the sages, the extremely illustrious one then started to create garlands of nakshatras, located in the southern direction. Tainted by his rage, he created generations of nakshatras. "I will create another world with an Indra, or perhaps it doesn't need an Indra." In his anger, he started to create another set of gods. The large number of rishis and the bulls among the gods were extremely terrified at this. They entreated the great-souled Vishvamitra in these words. "O immensely fortunate one! This king is blemished because of the curse imposed by his preceptor. O store of austerities! He does not deserve to go to heaven in his own physical body." Hearing the words of the gods, Koushika, bull among sages, spoke these extremely great words to all the gods. "O fortunate ones! I have promised King Trishanku that he will ascend there in his own physical body. I am not interested in ensuring the falsity of that pledge. In his own physical body, let Trishanku enjoy heaven for eternity. Let all my fixed nakshatras also be there. As long as the worlds exist, let all of them remain there. For my sake, all of you gods should agree to this." Thus addressed, all the gods replied to the bull among sages. "O fortunate one! It shall be that way and all of them will remain there. Many of them will be there, but will be outside

[412] Meaning Brahma.

[413] Ursa Major.

Vaishvanara's path.[414] O best among sages! Trishanku will also be there, amidst the radiance of the blazing nakshatras, like an immortal, but with his head hanging downwards." In the midst of the rishis, worshipped by all the gods, the immensely energetic Vishvamitra, with dharma in his soul, agreed to what the gods had said. O supreme among men! After this, at the conclusion of the sacrifice, all the gods and the great-souled sages, stores of austerities, returned to wherever they had come from.'

Chapter 1(60)

'O tiger among men! The immensely energetic Vishvamitra saw that the rishis had left. He spoke to all the residents of the forest. "A great obstruction has now arisen in the southern direction.[415] We will head for another direction and perform austerities there. O great-souled ones! There is the extensive region of Pushkara in the western direction. We will happily practise austerities in the supreme hermitages there." Having said this, the immensely energetic, invincible and great sage performed fierce austerities in Pushkara. He subsisted on roots and fruit. At that time, there was a king who was the lord of Ayodhya. He was famous as Ambareesha and he started to perform a sacrifice. However, Indra seized the animal the sacrificer had earmarked. When the animal was destroyed, the brahmanas spoke to the king. "O king! Because of your carelessness, the animal has been seized and destroyed. If objects belonging to the king are left unprotected and are destroyed, the sin devolves on the king. O bull among men! A great rite of atonement must be performed. Let a man or an animal be quickly brought, so that the ritual can continue." O bull among men! Hearing the words of the preceptors, the immensely intelligent king offered thousands of

[414] Vaishvanara has several meanings. The sense is that these new creations will be in a parallel galaxy/universe.

[415] Because of Trishanku's ascent to heaven there.

cows in exchange, so that he might obtain an animal. The lord of the earth searched in countries, habitations, cities, forests and even in sacred hermitages. O descendant of the Raghu lineage! O son![416] He saw Richika seated in Bhrigutunda, with his son and his wife. The infinitely radiant rajarshi bowed his head down and worshipped the immensely energetic brahmana rishi, who blazed in the radiance of his austerities. In every possible way, he asked about Richika's welfare and then spoke these words. "O immensely fortunate one! O descendant of the Bhrigu lineage! If you give me your son in exchange for one hundred thousand cows, I will obtain a sacrificial animal and will be successful. I have visited all the countries, but have not obtained an appropriate sacrificial animal. In exchange for that price, you should grant me one of your sons."[417] Thus addressed, the immensely energetic Richika replied in these words. "O best among men! I will never sell my eldest son." Hearing those words, the ascetic mother of those great-souled ones spoke to Ambareesha, tiger among men. "O king! Know that the youngest son is my beloved.[418] O best among men! It is often the case that the eldest is loved by fathers and the youngest by mothers. Therefore, I am protecting the youngest." O Rama! When the sage spoke those words and the sage's wife spoke similar words, the son in the middle, Shunahshepa,[419] himself said, "My father has said that the eldest cannot be sold and my mother has said the same about the youngest. O king! I therefore think that the son in the middle can be sold. Take me." O descendant of the Raghu lineage! Extremely happy, the lord of men gave one hundred thousand cows, accepted Shunahshepa and left. Rajarshi Ambareesha swiftly ascended his chariot. The immensely energetic and greatly illustrious one left quickly with Shunahshepa.'

[416] The word used is tata.

[417] So far, only a single son has been mentioned.

[418] The Critical text uses the word *shunaka,* though non-Critical versions don't always have this word. We have translated this as youngest son. But shunaka actually means young dog or puppy.

[419] Shunahshepa should be translated as dog's penis, though it can also be translated as dog's tail.

Chapter 1(61)

'O best among men! O descendant of the Raghu lineage! Having taken Shunahshepa, when it was noon, the immensely illustrious king rested in Pushkara. While he was resting, the immensely illustrious Shunahshepa also came to the excellent Pushkara and saw Vishvamitra. He showed distress in his face. He was miserable because of thirst and exhaustion. He fell down on the sage's lap and spoke these words. "I do not have a mother, nor a father. Where are my kin and relatives? O amiable one! O bull among sages! Following dharma, you should save me. O best among sages! You alone are the protector, the preserver of everything. Let the king be successful, but let me also have an undecaying and long life. Let me torment myself through the best of austerities and obtain the world of heaven. Using your intelligence become a protector to one who is without a protector. O one with dharma in his soul! Like a father, you should save me from all difficulty." Hearing his words, Vishvamitra, the great ascetic, comforted him in various ways. He spoke these words to his sons. "Fathers give birth to sons for the sake of welfare and benefit in the world hereafter. That time has come to pass. This child, the son of a sage, desires refuge with me. O sons! We should bring him pleasure by ensuring his life. All of you are the performers of excellent deeds. All of you are devoted to dharma. Satisfy Agni by offering one of your own selves, like a sacrificial animal, to the Indra among kings. Then Shunahshepa will have a protector and there will be no obstructions to the sacrifice. The gods will be satisfied and I will also adhere to my pledge." O best among men! On hearing the sage's words, Madhushyanda and the other sons were insolent. They dismissively said, "O lord! How can you abandon your own sons and protect the son of another? We perceive this as something that should not be done, it is like an act of eating dog meat." When he heard the words of his sons, the eyes of that bull among sages became red with rage. He said, "You have foolishly uttered these words and have thereby censured dharma. You have transgressed me in words that are terrible. They make the body hair stand up. Like the sons of Vasishtha, all of you will be reborn as those who subsist on dog meat. For a full one thousand years, you will roam around on the earth in that way." Having cursed his sons in that way, the supreme sage then sought to protect the afflicted Shunahshepa and ensure his welfare. "When you are tied to the Vaishnava sacrificial altar with sacred bonds and adorned with red garlands and paste, address these eloquent words to Agni. O son of a sage! At Ambareesha's sacrifice, chant these two divine hymns and you will obtain success." Controlled in his mind, Shunahshepa accepted those two chants. He quickly went to Ambareesha and said, "O lion among kings! O great spirit! Let us quickly go to the assembly. O Indra among kings! Let your consecration take place." On hearing the words of the rishi's son, the king was eager and happy. Without deviating, he swiftly went to the sacrificial arena. With the permission of the assistant priests, he dressed the sacrificial animal[420] in red garments, marked him out with auspicious signs and tied him to the altar. When he had been tied there, the sage's son pleased the two gods, Indra and Indra's younger brother[421] with those two chants. The thousand-eyed one was pleased at that secret chanting. O Raghava! He granted a long life to Shunahshepa. O best among men! O Rama! The king completed his sacrifice and through the favours of the thousand-eyed one, obtained a multitude of fruits. O best among men! The great ascetic, Vishvamitra, with dharma in his soul, performed austerities in Pushkara for another one thousand years.'

Chapter 1(62)

'One thousand years were over. After the vow was over, the great sage bathed and all the gods assembled to grant him the fruits he desired from the austerities. The greatly energetic Brahma spoke these extremely agreeable words to him. "O fortunate

[420] Shunahshepa.
[421] Vishnu.

one! Through your own auspicious deeds, you have now become a rishi." Having said this, the lord of the gods again returned to heaven. The immensely energetic Vishvamitra performed great austerities again. O best among men! After a long period of time, the supreme apsara, Menaka, arrived and started to bathe in Pushkara. Kushika's greatly energetic son saw Menaka. She was unmatched in her beauty and was like a flash of lightning in a cloud. On seeing her, the sage came under the subjugation of Kandarpa and spoke these words. "O apsara! Welcome. Reside here, in my hermitage. O fortunate one! Show me your favours. I am extremely confounded by Madana." Thus addressed, the beautiful one started to dwell there. Vishvamitra was confronted with a great obstruction in his austerities. O Raghava! O amiable one! While she happily dwelt there, in Vishvamitra's hermitage, ten years passed. After this time had passed, the great sage, Vishvamitra, became ashamed. He was overcome by sorrow and started to think. O descendant of the Raghu lineage! The sage had intolerant thoughts. "All the gods have done this, to rob me of my great austerities. Ten years have passed, like only a day and a night. Because I was overcome by desire and confusion, this obstruction has presented itself." The supreme among sages sighed. He sorrowed with repentance. He saw that the apsara was terrified and trembling, her hands joined in salutation.[422] Using sweet words, Kushika's son asked Menaka to leave. O Rama! Vishvamitra then went to the northern mountains.[423] Wishing to conquer desire, the immensely illustrious one turned to devotion. On the banks of the Koushiki, he tormented himself through extremely difficult austerities. O Rama! In the northern mountains, he practised terrible austerities for one thousand years and the gods were scared. All the large number of rishis and gods assembled and consulted, deciding that Kushika's son should be successful in obtaining the appellation of "maharshi". Hearing the words of the gods, the grandfather of all the worlds spoke these sweet words to Vishvamitra, the store of austerities. "O son! O

[422] In case she was cursed.

[423] Presumably the Himalayas.

maharshi! Welcome. I am satisfied by your fierce austerities. O Koushika! I grant you the title of maharshi." Hearing Brahma's words, Vishvamitra, the store of austerities, bowed down, joining his hands in salutation. He replied to the grandfather, "O illustrious one! If I have accumulated unsurpassed merit through my own auspicious deeds, if I have conquered my senses, you should address me as *brahmarshi*."[424] Brahma told him, "O tiger among sages! You have still not conquered your senses and need to strive more." Saying this, he returned to heaven. The gods also departed. The great sage, Vishvamitra, stood with his hands raised up, without any support. Subsisting only on air, he performed austerities. During the summer, he observed the five fires. During the monsoon, the open sky was his shelter. During the winter, during night and day, the store of austerities slept in the water. In this way, he performed fierce austerities for one thousand years. While Vishvamitra, the great sage, tormented himself in this way, Vasava and the other gods were extremely frightened. With the large number of Maruts, Shakra spoke words that were beneficial to him, but not beneficial to Koushika, or to the apsara Rambha.'

Chapter 1(63)

'"O Rambha! You have to perform an extremely great task for the gods. You have to seduce Koushika, confounding him with desire." O Rama! Thus addressed, the apsara spoke to the intelligent and thousand-eyed one. She joined her hands in salutation and replied to the lord of the gods. "O lord of the gods! The great sage, Vishvamitra, is terrible. O god! There is no doubt that he will unleash his terrible rage on me. O god! I am frightened on that account and you should show me your favours." The thousand-eyed one replied to the one who was trembling, her hands joined in salutation. "O Rambha! Do not be

[424] A sage with knowledge of the supreme being (brahman).

scared and act according to my instructions. I will become a cuckoo that sings in beautiful and agreeable tones in the trees during the spring. With Kandarpa, I will be at your side. Assume an extremely radiant form that is beautiful in many ways. O Rambha! Create conflict in that rishi and ascetic, Koushika." Hearing these words, she assumed a form that was supreme in beauty. The sweet-smiling and beautiful one tempted Vishvamitra. He heard the melodious tones of the cuckoo singing and with a gladdened heart, he glanced towards her. However, on hearing the unmatched tones of the song and on seeing Rambha, the sage was suspicious. The bull among sages discerned that this was the work of the thousand-eyed one. Overcome with rage, Kushika's son cursed Rambha. "O Rambha! I have been trying to conquer desire and anger, but you have tempted me. O unfortunate one! For ten thousand years, you will become a rock. O Rambha! You have been tainted by my rage. An extremely energetic brahmana, full of the strength of austerities, will eventually save you."[425] Vishvamitra, the extremely energetic and great sage, spoke in this way. However, because he was incapable of controlling his anger, he also repented. Because of that great curse, Rambha became a rock. On hearing these words, Kandarpa fled from the maharshi. Having succumbed to rage, the immensely energetic one was divested of his store of austerities. O Rama! Having not been able to conquer his senses, he could not find any peace in his mind.'

Chapter 1(64)

'O Rama! The great sage abandoned the direction of the Himalayas. He resorted to the eastern direction and practised extremely terrible austerities. He observed a supreme vow and did not speak for one thousand years. O Rama! He performed extremely difficult and unmatched austerities. For one thousand

[425] Meaning Vasishtha.

years, the great sage was like a block of wood. Though confronted with many kinds of obstructions, anger did not enter his heart. The gods, the gandharvas, the serpents, the asuras and the rakshasas were confounded by his energy. His austerities dulled their own radiance. Since this was like a taint, all of them addressed the grandfather. "We have sought to tempt the great sage, Vishvamitra, in many kinds of ways. But because of his austerities, he has not allowed his rage to increase. Not even a subtle sign of weakness can be seen in him. If he is not granted what is in his mind, through his austerities, he will destroy the three worlds and all their mobile and immobile objects. All the directions are anxious and nothing can be seen. All the oceans are turbulent and the mountains are being shattered. The earth is trembling and an extremely tumultuous wind is raging. O god! O illustrious one! The immensely radiant one has a form like that of Agni. The great sage should be shown favours, before he makes up his mind to destroy everything. In earlier times, the fire of destruction destroyed everything in the three worlds. Even if he desires the kingdom of the gods, it is our view that he should be granted that." All the gods, with the grandfather at the forefront, approached the great-souled Vishvamitra and addressed him in these sweet words. "O brahmarshi! Welcome. We are extremely satisfied with your austerities. O Koushika! Through your fierce austerities, you have obtained the status of a brahmana. O brahmana! With the large number of Maruts, I grant you a long life. O fortunate one! O amiable one! May you be fortunate! You can now return to wherever you came from." Hearing the grandfather's words and those of all the residents of heaven, the great sage was delighted. He bowed down before them and said, "Since I have obtained the status of a brahmana and have also received a long life, may *oum*,[426] vashatkara and the Vedas reveal themselves to me. O gods! Vasishtha is Brahma's son. May he also acknowledge me as the best among those who possess the knowledge of the kshatriyas and the knowledge of the brahmanas. O bulls among the gods! Depart only after you have accomplished this supreme desire of mine." The

[426] The sacred akshara, also written as *om* or *aum*.

gods showed him their favours. Vasishtha, supreme among those who meditate, also arrived, made his friendship and said, "You are a brahmarshi. Since you are now a brahmarshi, there is no doubt that everything will now manifest itself before you." After this was said, all the gods went away to wherever they had come from. Vishvamitra, with dharma in his soul, obtained the supreme status of being a brahmana. He worshipped brahmarshi Vasishtha, supreme among those who meditate. Having obtained his wish, he based himself on austerities and roamed around the entire earth. O Rama! This is how the great-souled one obtained the status of being a brahmana. O Rama! He is the best among sages. He is the embodiment of austerities. He is always devoted to supreme dharma and valour.'

In the presence of Rama and Lakshmana, Janaka heard Shatananda's words. He joined his hands in salutation and spoke these words to Kushika's son. 'O bull among sages! O one who follows dharma! I am blessed that you have shown me your favours and have come to this sacrifice with Kakutstha. O brahmana! O great sage! Your mere sight has purified me. By beholding you, I have obtained many kinds of qualities. O brahmana! I, and the immensely energetic and great-souled Rama, have heard the detailed recital of your great austerities. The assistant priests in this assembly have also heard about your many qualities. Your austerities are immeasurable. Your strength is immeasurable. O Kushika's son! Your qualities are always immeasurable. O lord! Creatures are never satisfied at hearing about your extraordinary account. O best among sages! However, the solar disc is elongated[427] and it is time for the rituals. O immensely energetic one! Tomorrow morning, I will see you again. O best among ascetics! Welcome. You should grant me permission to leave now.' The best among sages was thus addressed by the lord of Videha and Mithila, who circumambulated him, together with his priests and relatives. Worshipped by the maharshis, with Rama and Lakshmana, Vishvamitra, with dharma in his soul, left for his own residence.

[427] It is evening.

Chapter 1(65)

When it was sparkling morning, the king performed the morning rituals and invited the great-souled Vishvamitra and Raghava. Following the ordinances laid down in the sacred texts, he worshipped the great-souled one[428] and the two great-souled Raghavas. He then spoke these words. 'O illustrious one! O unblemished one! Welcome. What can I do for you? O illustrious one! Command me. I am ready to be commanded by you.' The one with dharma in his soul was thus addressed by the great-souled Janaka. The sage, eloquent in the use of words, replied in these words to the valiant one. 'These two are the sons of Dasharatha. They are kshatriyas and are famous in the worlds. They wish to see the supreme bow that is in your possession. O fortunate one! If they can see the bow, the wishes of these two princes will be satisfied. Having seen the bow, as they wish, they can then return.'

Thus addressed, Janaka replied to the great sage. 'Hear about the bow and about why it is kept here. There was a king famous by the name of Devarata and he was the sixth in line from Nimi.[429] The illustrious and great-souled one[430] left it in his hands in trust. Earlier, at the time of the destruction of Daksha's sacrifice, the valiant Rudra angrily raised the bow and playfully spoke to the gods. "O gods! I desired a share of the sacrifice, but you did not think of a share for me. Therefore, I will sever your heads with this extremely revered bow." O bull among sages! At this, all the gods were distressed. They sought the favours of the lord of the gods and Bhava was pleased. Happy, he bestowed his favours on those great-souled ones. O lord! After this, the great-souled god of the gods handed over this gem of a bow in trust to our ancestor. Later, I was ploughing and purifying my field. From the field, my upraised plough brought up the one who has become famous by the

[428] Vishvamitra.

[429] Nimi was the king who established the dynasty in Mithila. He was Janaka's ancestor.

[430] Shiva.

name of Sita.[431] Having been raised from the surface of the ground, she was reared as my daughter. She was not born from a womb and this maiden will be bestowed as *viryashulka*.[432] Having been raised from the surface of the ground, she has grown up as my daughter. O bull among sages! These kings have come to seek her hand. O illustrious one! I have not bestowed my daughter on any of the kings who have come. I will bestow my daughter through the mode of viryashulka. O bull among sages! That is the reason all these kings have assembled here. They have arrived in Mithila to test their valour. Their valour will be tested by their ability to raise the bow. However, none of them have been able to grasp the bow or raise it. O great sage! I got to know that those valiant ones possess little valour. O store of austerities! Listen. I therefore refused all those kings. O bull among sages! At this, the kings were extremely enraged. Since their valour was being doubted, all of them laid siege to Mithila. O bull among sages! They thought that they had been slighted. Therefore, prey to great rage, they oppressed the city of Mithila. After an entire year passed everything began to suffer and the supplies were exhausted. O best among sages! That is the reason I became extremely miserable. After this, I pleased the large number of gods through my austerities. Extremely pleased, the gods gave me armies with four kinds of forces.[433] Through these, those evil-acting and cowardly kings, who doubted my valour, were routed, killed and driven away in different directions, together with their advisers. O tiger among sages! O one excellent in vows! I will show that extremely radiant bow to Rama and Lakshmana too. O sage! If Rama is capable of stringing that bow, I will bestow my daughter Sita, who was not born from a womb, on Dasharatha's son.'

[431] The word *sita* means the furrow caused by a plough.

[432] Viryashulka is not the same as a svayamvara. Svayamvara is a ceremony where the maiden herself (*svayam*) chooses her husband (*vara*) from assembled suitors. Viryashulka is when the maiden is offered to the suitor who shows the most valour (*virya*), *shulka* meaning price.

[433] Chariots, elephants, horses and foot soldiers.

Chapter 1(66)

Having heard Janaka's words, the great sage, Vishvamitra, told the king, 'Show Rama the bow.' At this, King Janaka instructed his advisers, 'Bring the divine bow, decorated with fragrances and garlands, here.' Commanded by Janaka, the advisers entered the city. Following the king's command, they emerged, placing the bow at the front. There were five thousand tall and great-souled men. Together, they somehow managed to tug it along on a casket with eight wheels. Having brought the iron casket with the bow, the ministers informed the king, who was like a god. 'O king! This is the supreme bow that is worshipped by all the kings. O lord of Mithila! O Indra among kings! This is what you wished to be shown.' Hearing their words, the king joined his hands in salutation and addressed the great-souled Vishvamitra and Rama and Lakshmana. 'O brahmana! This is the supreme bow, worshipped by those of the Janaka lineage. Extremely valiant kings have not been able to use it to take aim. Nor have the large numbers of gods, asuras, rakshasas, gandharvas, the best of yakshas, kinnaras, or the giant serpents. How can men raise the bow, string it, affix an arrow and take aim with it? O bull among sages! O immensely fortunate one! The best among bows has been brought so that it can be shown to the two princes.' Vishvamitra, with dharma in his soul, heard Janaka's words. He told Raghava, 'O Rama! O son! Behold the bow.'

Hearing the maharshi's words, Rama opened the casket where the bow was kept. He saw the bow and said, 'O brahmana! I wish to touch this supreme bow with my hands. I want to try to raise it and take aim with it.' The king and the sage said, 'Go ahead.' Hearing the sage's words, he playfully grasped the bow at the middle. While many thousands of men looked on, the descendant of the Raghu lineage, with dharma in his soul, playfully strung the bow. The valiant one, immensely illustrious and best among men, strung the bowstring and took aim. The bow snapped at the middle. A great sound arose, like the roar of a storm. It was as if there was an extremely giant earthquake that made the mountains shatter. Confounded by that sound, all the men, with the exception of the supreme among sages, the king and the two Raghavas, fell down unconscious. When the men regained their senses, having got his composure back, the king joined his hands in salutation and spoke these words to the bull among sages, who was eloquent with words. 'O illustrious one! I have witnessed the valour of Rama, Dasharatha's son. This is extremely wonderful and unthinkable. This is something that has not even been talked about. If Sita gets Rama, Dasharatha's son, as her husband, my daughter will bring fame to the lineage of the Janakas. O Koushika! My truthful pledge is that she will be bestowed as viryashulka. My daughter Sita is worth many of my lives and it is my view that she should be given to Rama. O brahmana! With your permission, let my ministers quickly go. O Koushika! O fortunate one! Let them go to Ayodhya on chariots. With diligent words, let them bring the king[434] to my city. Let them tell him everything and about the bestowal through viryashulka. They will also tell the king that the two Kakutsthas are under the protection of the sage.[435] With affectionate words, they will bring the king extremely swiftly.' When Koushika agreed to this, the king addressed his ministers. The one with dharma in his soul commanded them and sent them to Ayodhya.

Chapter 1(67)

Following Janaka's instructions, the messengers used mounts that did not get exhausted. Resting for three nights along the way, they entered the city of Ayodhya. Following the instructions of the king, they entered the royal residence and saw the aged King Dasharatha, who was like a god. All the messengers showed their reverence by joining their hands in salutation. Controlled, they

[434] Dasharatha.

[435] Vishvamitra.

spoke words with sweet syllables to the king. 'O one who follows the agnihotra rites! King Janaka of Mithila asks about your welfare and that of your preceptors and priests. O great king! Repeatedly using sweet words that are full of affection, Janaka also asks about the welfare of your servants. The lord of Videha and Mithila first eagerly asks about your welfare. With Koushika's permission, he then addresses you in the following words. "My former pledge is known, that I will offer my daughter as viryashulka. Those intolerant kings were seen to be devoid of valour and were refused. O king! With Vishvamitra at the forefront, your brave sons[436] have come and have won my daughter. O great king! In a great assembly of people, the great-souled Rama has shattered the divine bow in the middle. As viryashulka, I must bestow Sita on the great-souled one. That is my pledge and I desire that you should grant me your permission. O great king! O fortunate one! With the priest[437] at the forefront, you should quickly come with your preceptors and see the two Raghavas. O Indra among kings! You should display your affection towards me. You will also be delighted at seeing both your sons." These are the sweet words that the lord of Videha has spoken. This has Vishvamitra's permission and Shatananda holds the same view.' On hearing the words of the messengers, the king was greatly delighted. He addressed Vasishtha, Vamadeva and the other ministers. 'The one who extends Kousalya's delight has been protected by Kushika's son. With his brother, Lakshmana, he now resides in Videha. The great-souled Janaka has witnessed Kakutstha's valour. He wishes to bestow his daughter on Raghava. If all of you find the great-souled Janaka's intentions desirable, let us quickly go to that city, without wasting any time on reflection.' The ministers, and all the maharshis, agreed to this. Extremely happy, the king told his ministers, 'We will leave tomorrow.' Honoured well, the king's[438] ministers, all of whom possessed all the desired qualities, happily spent the night there.

[436] Though Rama is meant, the plural is being used as a mark of respect.
[437] Vasishtha.
[438] Janaka's.

Chapter 1(68)

When the night was over, with his preceptors and his relatives, King Dasharatha happily spoke to Sumantra. 'Let all the superintendents of treasuries collect large quantities of riches. Prepared well, let them advance in front, with many kinds of jewels. Following my instructions, let excellent carriages be yoked at the same time and let an army with the four kinds of forces quickly advance.[439] Vasishtha, Vamadeva, Jabali, Kashyapa, Markandeya and Katyayana—let these brahmanas with long lives advance in the front. Let my chariot be yoked. The messengers are asking me to speed up and not delay.' Following the king's words, half of the army, consisting of the four kinds of forces, proceeded with the king and the rishis. The other half followed at the rear. After travelling for four days along the road, they reached the extremities of Videha. On hearing this, the prosperous King Janaka arranged for all the honours to be shown. On meeting King Janaka, the aged King Dasharatha was delighted. The king[440] was also supremely delighted. Happy, the best of men spoke to the best of men.[441] 'O great king! O Raghava! Welcome. It is good fortune that you have come here. You will obtain happiness through your two sons, who have triumphed because of their valour. It is good fortune that the greatly energetic and illustrious rishi, Vasishtha, has come here with all the other supreme brahmanas, like Shatakratu with the gods. It is good fortune that all obstructions have been conquered. It is good fortune that my lineage has been honoured. I will have this matrimonial alliance with the Raghavas, who are great-souled and the best among those who are brave. O Indra among kings! You should begin the arrangements tomorrow morning. O best among kings! After the conclusion of the sacrifice, with the permission of the rishis, the marriage ceremony will be held.' In

[439] Instead of the four kinds of forces that characterize an army, since this is a marriage, the four can also be understood as riches, gold, equipment and vehicles.

[440] Janaka.

[441] Janaka and Dasharatha respectively.

the midst of the rishis, the lord of men[442] heard his words. The one who was best among those who are eloquent with words replied to the lord of the earth.[443] 'The nature of a gift is determined by the donor. This is what I have heard in earlier times. O one who knows about dharma! We will do exactly what you have said.' He[444] was devoted to dharma and famous. He was truthful in speech. On hearing his words, the lord of Videha was greatly astounded. All the sages were greatly delighted at having met each other.[445] They spent the night happily. The king was greatly delighted at having spoken to his sons, the two Raghavas. Honoured extremely well by Janaka, he resided there. The greatly energetic Janaka, who knew the truth about the rituals, followed dharma and performed them. Having performed sacrifices for his two daughters, he spent the night there.[446]

Chapter 1(69)

When it was morning, Janaka had the rituals performed by the maharshis. The one who was eloquent with the use of words then spoke these words to the priest, Shatananda. 'My greatly energetic younger brother is extremely devoted to dharma. He is famous by the name of Kushadhvaja and lives in an auspicious city that has moats all around it. This sacred city of Samkashya seems to drink the waters of the river Ikshumati.[447] This city is like

[442] Dasharatha.

[443] Janaka.

[444] Dasharatha.

[445] Those on Janaka's side and those on Dasharatha's side.

[446] This causes a problem of translation. The word can be translated as two sons or two daughters. It makes perfect sense if one is talking about Dasharatha. However, one is talking about Janaka. Therefore, it has to be two daughters, though we have not yet been told anything about Janaka having a second daughter.

[447] Literally, Ikshumati means a river whose water tastes like sugar cane juice. Elsewhere, it is said that Ikshumati flowed near Kurukshetra and Ikshumati has also been identified with the river Sarasvati.

Pushpaka vimana.[448] I wish to see him and it is my view that he should arrange for this sacrifice. With me, that extremely energetic one will be delighted to participate in this.' On the instructions of the king, who was a tiger among men, like Vishnu following Indra's command, messengers on swift steeds were dispatched. On the king's command, Kushadhvaja arrived. He saw the great-souled Janaka, who was devoted to dharma. He greeted Shatananda and the king who was devoted to dharma. He ascended a supremely divine seat that befitted kings. Those two infinitely energetic brothers seated themselves. The brave ones then sent for Sudamana, best among ministers. 'O lord of ministers! Quickly go to the infinitely resplendent descendant of Ikshvaku. Invite the invincible one here, with his sons and his ministers.' He went to the place meant for guests and saw the extender of the lineage of Raghu. Bowing his head down and greeting him, he said, 'O brave one! O lord of Ayodhya! The lord of Mithila and Videha is waiting to see you, with his preceptors and priests.' Hearing the words of the best among ministers, the king, with the large number of rishis and his relatives, went to the place where Janaka was. With his ministers, his preceptors and his relatives, the king, best among those who are eloquent with words, spoke these words to the lord of Videha. 'O great king! It is known to you that the illustrious rishi, Vasishtha, is like a god to the lineage of the Ikshvakus and can speak on our behalf about our conduct. With the permission of Vishvamitra, and that of all the maharshis, Vasishtha, with dharma in his soul, will speak about my ancestry.'

When Dasharatha was silent, the illustrious rishi, Vasishtha, eloquent in the use of words, spoke these words to the lord of Videha and his priest. 'Brahma's powers are not manifest. He is eternal, everlasting and without decay. He had a son named Marichi[449] and Marichi's son was Kashyapa. Vivasvan[450] was Kashyapa's son and Manu is said to be Vivasvan's son. Manu was the first Prajapati

[448] A vimana is a celestial vehicle. Pushpaka belonged to Kubera and was later seized by Ravana.

[449] Through Brahma's mental powers.

[450] The sun.

and Ikshvaku was Manu's son. Know that Ikshvaku was the first king of Ayodhya. Ikshavku had a prosperous son, Vikukshi. The greatly energetic Vikukshi's son was the powerful Bana. The greatly energetic Bana's son was the powerful Anaranya. Anaranya had a son named Prithu and Prithu's son was Trishanku. Trishanku had an immensely illustrious son named Dhundumara. Dhundumara's son was the immensely energetic maharatha, Yuvanashva. Yuvanashva's son was the handsome King Mandhata. Mandhata's son was the handsome Susandhi. Susandhi had two sons—Dhruvasandhi and Prasenjit. Dhruvasandhi had an illustrious son named Bharata. The immensely energetic Bharata had a son named Asita. Since he was born with poison, he came to be known as Sagara.[451] Sagara had a son named Asamanja and Asamanja's son was Amshumat. Dileepa was Amshumat's son and Dileepa's son was Bhageeratha. Bhageeratha's son was Kakutstha and Kakutstha's son was Raghu. Raghu had an energetic son named Pravriddha, but he grew up to be an eater of human flesh. He thus became Kalmashapada and his son was Shankana.[452] Sudarshana was Shankana's son and Sudarshana's son was Agnivarna. Agnivarna's son was Sheeghraga and Sheeghraga's son was Maru. Maru's son was Prashushruka and Ambareesha was born through Prashushruka. Ambareesha's son was Nahusha, lord of the earth. Yayati was Nahusha's son and Yayati's son was Nabhaga. Nabhaga's son was Aja and Aja's son is Dasharatha. The brothers, Rama and Lakshmana, are Dasharatha's sons. Right from the beginning, this lineage of kings is pure and is extremely devoted to dharma. There are brave ones who have been born in the lineage of Ikshvaku and they are truthful in speech. O king! Your daughters should be bestowed on Rama and Lakshmana. O best among men! They are equal[453] and bestowal must always be on equals.'

[451] The Critical Edition excises some shlokas and this breaks the continuity. While Sagara was still in his mother's womb, his stepmother tried to unsuccessfully poison him. Hence, he was *sa* (with) *gara* (poison).

[452] Vasishtha cursed Pravriddha that he would be an eater of human flesh. Pravriddha wished to curse Vasishtha in turn and held some sanctified water in his hand. However, he was dissuaded by his wife, Madayanti. The sanctified water fell on his feet. He was thus known as Kalmashapada, because his feet (pada) had a blemish (*kalmasha*).

[453] In lineage.

Chapter 1(70)

Thus addressed, Janaka joined his hands in salutation and replied, 'O fortunate one! You should now hear the supreme account of our lineage. O best among sages! At the time of bestowal, a person born in a noble lineage should recount everything about his lineage. O great sage! Listen. There was a king named Nimi who was famous in the three worlds because of his own deeds. With dharma in his soul, he was supreme. He was greatest among spirited ones. His son was named Mithi and Mithi's son was Janaka.[454] This was the first one by the name Janaka and Udavasu was Janaka's son. Nandivardhana was born from Janaka and he had dharma in his soul. Nandivardhana's son was known by the name of Suketu. Suketu's son was the extremely strong Devarata, who had dharma in his soul. It has been heard that rajarshi Brihadratha was born from Devarata. Brihadratha's son was the extremely brave, intelligent and powerful Mahaveera. Sudhriti, with truth as his valour, was Mahaveera's son. Sudhriti's son was Dhrishtaketu, who was extremely devoted to dharma and had dharma in his soul. Dhrishtaketu's son was the famous rajarshi Haryashava. Haryashava's son was Maru and Maru's son was Prativandhaka. Prativandhaka's son was King Kirtiratha, who had dharma in his soul. Kirtiratha's son is known as Devamidha. Devamidha's son was Vibudha and Vibudha's son was Maheedhraka. Maheedhraka's son was the extremely strong King Keertirata. Rajarshi Keertirata gave birth to Maharoma. Maharoma's son was Svarnaroma, who had dharma in his soul. Rajarshi Svarnaroma's son was Hrasvaroma, who was great-souled and knew about dharma. He had two sons. I am the elder and my younger brother is the brave Kushadhvaja. Since I am elder, the king, my father, instated me in the kingdom. Having entrusted the task of looking after Kushadhvaja on me, he went to the forest. When my aged father went to heaven, I have followed dharma in bearing this burden and have affectionately reared my brother Kushadhvaja, who is like a god. After some time,

[454] This was an earlier Janaka.

the brave King Sudhanva came from the city of Samkashya and laid siege to Mithila. He asked me to give him Shiva's supreme bow. He also said, "Bestow on me your lotus-eyed daughter, Sita." O brahmana rishi! When I did not give him these, he fought with me. In the battle, I killed Sudhanva, who had acted against me. O best among sages! When King Sudhanva was slain, I instated my brave brother, Kushadhvaja, in Samkashya. O great sage! I am the elder and he is younger to me. O bull among sages! Extremely delighted, I will give you these two fortunate daughters-in-law, Sita for Rama and Urmila for Lakshmana. My daughter Sita is like a daughter of the gods and is offered as viryashulka and Urmila is the second. O descendant of the Raghu lineage![455] There is no doubt that extremely cheerfully, I will bestow these two daughters-in-law. I state this in three ways.[456] O king! Let the *godana* ritual be performed for Rama and Lakshmana.[457] O fortunate one! Let rites for the ancestors be performed next. After that, let the marriage ceremony be undertaken. O lord! The nakshatra Magha is in the ascendant now and three days from now, it will be Uttaraphalguni.[458] O king! Arrange for the ceremony then. So that Rama and Lakshmana enjoy happiness, let donations be made.'

Chapter 1(71)

When the lord of Videha spoke in this way, the great sage, Vishvamitra, together with Vasishtha, spoke these words to the brave king. 'O bull among men! These two lineages are unthinkable and immeasurable. There is no other lineage that is a

[455] This is directed at Dasharatha.

[456] Through thoughts, words and deeds.

[457] Though godana literally means the donation of a cow, it has a symbolic connotation here. Since Rama and Lakshmana enter the householder (garhasthya) stage, they go through a sacrament (*samskara*).

[458] Some nakshatras are regarded as auspicious for marriage, but that list includes both Magha and Uttaraphalguni.

match for the Ikshvakus and the Videhas. O king! These marriages are among those who are equal in dharma, equal in beauty and equal in prosperity—Rama and Lakshmana, and Sita and Urmila. O best among men! I have something to say. Listen to me. Your younger brother, King Kushadhvaja, knows about dharma. O king! He has two daughters who are devoted to dharma and their beauty is unmatched on earth. Bestow them as wives on Prince Bharata and the intelligent Shatrughna. O king! For the sake of those two great-souled ones, we will accept these daughters. In their beauty and youth, all of Dasharatha's sons are like the guardians of the worlds and are like the gods in valour. O Indra among kings! Let these two excellent lineages, auspicious in deeds, yours and that of the Ikshvakus, be closely tied to each other through an alliance.' Having heard Vishvamitra's words, which were in agreement with Vasishtha's views, Janaka joined his hands in salutation and addressed those bulls among sages. 'As you have commanded, I also think this alliance is between two lineages that are equal. O fortunate ones! Let it be that way. Let Kushadhvaja's daughters tend to Shatrughna and Bharata as their wives. O great sage! Let the four princesses accept the hands of the four extremely strong princes on the same day. O brahmana! The learned ones have praised a marriage on the day of Uttaraphalguni, when Bhaga is the presiding lord.'[459] Having spoken in this way, the amiable one arose and joined his hands in salutation. King Janaka spoke these words to those two supreme sages. 'You have performed a supreme act of dharma for me. I will always be your disciple. O bulls among sages! Seat yourselves on these excellent seats. In the way they are ruled, there is no difference between my kingdom and Dasharatha's city of Ayodhya. You should therefore act so that everything is properly undertaken.'

When the lord of Videha said this, King Dasharatha, descendant of the Raghu lineage, cheerfully replied to King Janaka in these words. 'O lords of Mithila! You two brothers are immeasurable

[459] The presiding deity of Uttaraphalguni (Denebola) is Bhaga, the god of marital bliss and prosperity. In fairness, there is scope for interpretation here, with the word *uttara* also being interpreted as the latter part of the day.

in your qualities. You have honoured the rishis in this assembly of kings. O fortunate one! May everything be well with you. I will now go to my own abode and undertake the funeral rites for the ancestors.' Having said this, King Dasharatha took his leave of the two kings, placing those two Indras among sages at the forefront. The immensely illustrious one swiftly departed. Having gone to his abode, the king followed the ordinances and performed the funeral rites. When it was morning, he arose and performed the excellent rite of godana. The king donated one hundred thousand cows to brahmanas. Following dharma, the king donated these in the names of each of his sons. The horns of these cows were encrusted with gold. They were donated with their calves and with brass vessels for milking them. The bull among men gave away four hundred thousand cows.[460] The descendant of the Raghu lineage gave away many other kinds of riches to brahmanas. Devoted to his sons, he undertook godana in the names of his sons. Having undertaken godana in the names of his sons, the king was as radiant as the agreeable Prajapati,[461] surrounded by the guardians of the worlds.

Chapter 1(72)

On the day when the king performed the excellent godana rite, on that very same day, the brave Yudhajit arrived. He was the son of the king of Kekaya and Bharata's own maternal uncle. Having met the king, he asked about his welfare in these words. 'Affectionately, the king of Kekaya has inquired about your welfare. You will also be interested in the welfare of those who are there and as of now, they are well. O Indra among kings! O descendant of the Raghu lineage! The king wished to see my sister's son[462] and that is the reason I was sent to Ayodhya. I heard in Ayodhya that

[460] For each son, one hundred thousand cows were donated.

[461] Brahma.

[462] Bharata.

you had left for the marriage, with your sons.[463] O king! That is the reason I have come here to Mithila, to meet you. To see my sister's son, I have quickly come here.' King Dasharatha saw that his beloved guest had arrived. On seeing this, he honoured the one who deserved honours with great worship.

When the night was over, with his great-souled sons, and placing the rishis at the forefront, he arrived at the sacrificial arena. At the appropriate hour, when all the auspicious signs for victory were present, adorned in ornaments, Rama and his brothers performed the sacred rites. They placed Vasishtha and the other maharshis ahead of them. The illustrious Vasishtha addressed the lord of Videha. 'O king! King Dasharatha has performed all the auspicious rites. With his sons, the supreme one among the best among men now desires a donor. All forms of prosperity result when the receiver accepts from the donor. Following your own dharma, now perform the excellent wedding rites.' He was addressed in these words by the great-souled Vasishtha. The extremely generous and immensely energetic one, supremely devoted to dharma, replied in these words. 'Who is preventing entry?[464] Whose instructions are you waiting for? This is your own house. What are you thinking about? This kingdom is like your own. O best among sages! Having performed the auspicious rites, my daughters have arrived at the sacrificial altar. They are like the flames of a blazing fire. I have prepared everything and am waiting for you at the sacrificial altar. There are no obstructions. What is the king waiting for?' Hearing Janaka's words, with his sons and with the large number of rishis, Dasharatha entered. King Janaka spoke to the one who extended Kousalya's delight. 'This is my daughter Sita and she will perform every act of dharma with you. O fortunate one! If you also desire her, accept her hand with your hand. O Lakshmana! O fortunate one! Come here. I have earmarked Urmila for you. If you also desire her, accept her hand. You should not waste any time in thinking.' Having spoken to him, Janaka addressed

[463] Bharata and Shatrughna.

[464] These are ceremonial and rhetorical questions, not meant to be answered.

Bharata. 'O descendant of the Raghu lineage! Accept Mandavi's hand with your hand.' Lord Janaka, with dharma in his soul, also spoke to Shatrughna. 'O mighty-armed one! Accept Shrutakeerti's hand with your hand. All of you are agreeable. O Kakutsthas! With your wives, all of you will be excellent in the observance of vows. You should not waste time in thinking.' Hearing Janaka's words and with Vasishtha's sanction, the four accepted the hands of those four with their hands. With their wives, those excellent ones, born in Raghu's lineage, progressively circumambulated the fire, the sacrificial altar, the king[465] and the rishis. They acted as they had been asked to. Following the ordinances, the marriages were concluded. A great shower of radiant flowers rained down from the sky. Divine drums were sounded and there were the sounds of singing and musical instruments. Large numbers of apsaras danced and gandharvas sang in melodious tones. At the marriages of the best among the Raghus, this was the wonderful spectacle. While this was going on, trumpets were sounded. With their wives, those greatly energetic ones circumambulated the fire thrice. After this, with their wives, the descendants of the Raghu lineage went to the residences meant for guests. While the large number of rishis looked on, the king[466] followed them, with his relatives.

Chapter 1(73)

When night was over, taking his leave of the kings, Vishvamitra, the great sage, left for the northern mountains. After Vishvamitra had left, the king[467] took his leave of the lord of Videha and Mithila. King Dasharatha swiftly left for his own city. The king of Videha gave his daughters many kinds of riches. The lord of Mithila gave them hundreds of thousands of cows, the best of

[465] Janaka.

[466] Dasharatha.

[467] Dasharatha.

blankets, crores of silken garments, elephants, horses, chariots and foot soldiers. The father also gave his daughters excellent male and female servants, adorned in ornaments that seemed divine. There were gold, silver, pearls and coral. Extremely happy, he gave his daughters these supreme riches. Having given these many kinds of riches, the king took the king's permission.[468] The lord of Mithila entered his own residence in Mithila.

With his great-souled sons, the king and lord of Ayodhya proceeded. All the rishis were at the forefront and he was followed by his forces. The tiger among men proceeded, with the large number of rishis and the Raghavas. At this time, in every direction, a terrible sound of birds was heard. On earth too, all the animals circled leftwards.[469] On seeing this, the tiger among kings asked Vasishtha, 'The birds are distracted and behaving in a terrible way. The animals are also circling leftwards. Why is this? My heart is trembling and my mind is distressed.' Hearing Dasharatha's words, the great rishi replied sweetly. 'Hear what these portend. A terrible and divine fear presents itself and this is being voiced from the mouths of the birds. The animals will be pacified and this torment will pass.' While they were conversing, a wind began to rage. It made the earth tremble and brought down the auspicious trees. The sun was enveloped in darkness and none of the directions could be discerned. Everything was covered in ashes and the army was confounded. Vasishtha and the other sages and the king and his sons remained stationed there. Though all of them were in their senses, they seemed to be unconscious. The army was shrouded in that terrible darkness and the ashes. At that time, a form was seen. He was terrible in appearance, with circles of matted hair. He was as unassailable as Kailasa and he was extremely difficult to withstand, like the fire of destruction. He seemed to blaze in his energy and ordinary people found it impossible to look at him. A battleaxe was slung on his shoulder and he wielded a bow that was like a flash of lightning. He held the best of arrows, like Hara at the time

[468] Janaka and Dasharatha respectively.

[469] The left is regarded as inauspicious.

of the destruction of Tripura.[470] They saw him, terrible in form, like a blazing fire. Vasishtha and the best among brahmanas were devoted to meditations and oblations. All those assembled sages began to discuss among themselves. 'He became intolerant because of his father's death and destroyed the kshatriyas.[471] Having killed the kshatriyas earlier, his intolerance and fever were dispelled. Is he again interested in destroying the kshatriyas?' Having said this, they offered arghya to Bhargava, who was terrible to behold. The rishis addressed him in these sweet words. 'O Rama![472] O Rama!' Having accepted the honours from the powerful rishi,[473] the Rama who was Jamadagni's son spoke to the Rama who was Dasharatha's son.

Chapter 1(74)

'O Rama! O Dasharatha's son! O brave one! I have heard about your extraordinary valour. I have heard everything about how you shattered the bow. That shattering of the bow is wonderful and unthinkable. On hearing this, I have come here, with another auspicious bow. This is the great bow received from Jamadagni and it is terrible in form. String it and affix a bow. Show me your own strength. I will witness your strength in your ability to string this bow. If you can do this, you can pride yourself on being valiant and I will then grant you a duel.' Hearing these words, King Dasharatha's face became downcast. Distressed, he joined his hands in salutation and said, 'O brahmana! Your anger against the immensely illustrious kshatriyas has been pacified. My sons are children. You should grant them freedom from fear. You have been

[470] The demons had a city named Tripura and Shiva (Hara) destroyed this with a single arrow.

[471] Parashurama destroyed the kshatriyas twenty-one times, because Kartavirya Arjuna (a kshatriya) killed his father, Jamadagni. Jamadagni was descended from Bhrigu. Hence, Parashurama is called Bhargava.

[472] Meaning Parashurama. Parashurama means the Rama with the battleaxe (*parashu*).

[473] Vasishtha.

born in the lineage of the Bhargavas. You are engaged in studying and are devoted to your vows. You promised the one with the one thousand eyes that you would cast aside your weapons. Devoted to dharma, you then gave the earth away to Kashyapa. Having given him that, you went to the forest, becoming like a standard to Mount Mahendra. O great sage! Have you decided to destroy all of us? While all of us are alive, it is not possible for you to kill Rama alone.' While he was speaking in this way, Jamadagni's powerful son ignored Dasharatha's words and spoke to Rama instead. 'There are two supreme bows. They are divine and famous in the worlds. They are firm and excellent and have been crafted well by Vishvakarma. O best among men! O Kakutstha! The gods gave one of these to Tryambaka, when he wished to fight and destroy Tripura. This is the one that has been shattered by you. The best among the gods gave the second invincible one to Vishnu. O Kakutstha! This is innately equal to Rudra's bow. Once, all the gods reflected on the strengths and weaknesses of Shitikantha and Vishnu and asked the grandfather. The grandfather, supreme among those who are truthful, ascertained that the gods wished to engender a conflict. There was a great encounter between Shitikantha and Vishnu, as they sought to defeat each other. This made the body hair stand up. Through his[474] yawn and humkara, Shiva's terrible and excellent bow was countered. The three-eyed Mahadeva was rendered motionless. The gods, with large numbers of rishis and charanas, assembled. They sought pacification and those two supreme among gods desisted. On seeing that Vishnu's powerful yawn had rendered Shiva's bow powerless, the gods, and the large number of rishis, deduced that Vishnu was superior. The immensely illustrious Rudra was enraged and gave his bow, with the arrow still held in his hand, to rajarshi Devarata from Videha. O Rama! This is Vishnu's excellent bow, capable of vanquishing the cities of enemies. Vishnu gave it to Richika Bhargava, to be held in trust. The immensely energetic Richika gave this divine bow to his great-souled son Jamadagni, who cannot be countered in his deeds and who was my father. My

[474] Vishnu's.

father, full of the strength of austerities, cast aside his weapons and was killed by Arjuna,[475] whose intelligence was inferior. I heard about the extremely terrible and unrivalled account of my father's death. Because of the anger that resulted, I exterminated a large number of kshatriyas. O Rama! Having obtained the entire earth, I handed it over to the great-souled Kashyapa, as an auspicious act of dakshina at the end of a sacrifice. Having given it away, full of the strength of austerities, I made my abode on Mount Mahendra. Having heard about the shattering of the bow, I have quickly come here. O Rama! This supreme and great Vaishnava bow has come to me through my father and grandfather. Placing the dharma of kshatriyas at the forefront, wield it. String it and affix an arrow to this bow, which is the conqueror of enemy cities. O Kakutstha! If you are capable of doing this, I will thereafter grant you a duel.'

Chapter 1(75)

Hearing the words of Jamadagni's son, showing respect to his father, Rama, Dasharatha's son, addressed him in these words. 'O Bhargava! I have heard about the deeds that you have accomplished. O brahmana! I also applaud what you did to repay the debt to your father. O Bhargava! In following the dharma of kshatriyas, you deem me to be inferior in valour and incapable. You slight my energy. Therefore, witness my valour now.' Raghava's hands were dexterous in their valour. Having said this, he angrily seized Bhargava's supreme weapon and an arrow. Rama strung the bow and affixed an arrow to it. Rama then angrily spoke these words to Rama who was Jamadagni's son. 'You are a brahmana and deserve to be worshipped. There is also Vishvamitra to consider.[476] O Rama! Therefore, I am incapable of releasing this arrow, which can take away your life. O Rama! You can swiftly

[475] Kartavirya Arjuna.

[476] Jamadagni was married to Satyavati, Vishvamitra's sister.

travel wherever you want. You have also conquered and obtained unmatched worlds through the strength of your austerities. Of these two, I will destroy whichever one you wish. This is a Vaishnava bow and a divine arrow that can destroy the cities of enemies affixed to it. This destroys strength and insolence and its valour is inviolate.' Placing the grandfather at the forefront, large numbers of rishis and gods assembled to see Rama and the supreme weapon. There were gandharvas, apsaras, siddhas, charanas, kinnaras, yakshas, rakshasas and serpents, desiring to witness this great and extraordinary wonder. As Rama wielded that supreme bow, the worlds seemed to be senseless. Rama, who was Jamadagni's son, became devoid of his valour and glanced at Rama. Devoid of his energy and devoid of his valour, Jamadagni's son was benumbed.

Extremely gently and softly, he spoke to the lotus-eyed Rama. 'Earlier, I gave the earth to Kashyapa. Kashyapa told me, "Do not reside in my dominion." Following the words of my preceptor, I do not dwell on the earth at nights. O Kakutstha! This is the pledge I made to Kashyapa. O brave one! O Raghava! Therefore, you should not destroy my mobility. With the speed of thought, I will go to the supreme Mount Mahendra. O Rama! Through my austerities, I have conquered unmatched worlds. Do not waste time in thinking. With this supreme arrow, destroy those worlds. I know you to be the destroyer of Madhu, the one without decay.[477] You are the lord of the gods. I know this from your touch on the bow. O scorcher of enemies! May you be well. This large number of gods has assembled and is looking at you. Your deeds are unmatched and you cannot be countered in a fight. O Kakutstha! I should not be ashamed at this. You are the protector of the three worlds and I have been countered by someone like you. O Rama! O one excellent in vows! Release the unmatched arrow. When the arrow has been released, I will go to the supreme Mount Mahendra.' Jamadagni's son spoke in this way to Rama. The handsome Rama, Dasharatha's son, released the supreme arrow. The darkness was dispelled and all the directions could be seen. The gods and all the rishis praised Rama and the

[477] Vishnu, who killed a demon named Madhu.

upraised weapon. Rama who was Jamadagni's son praised the Rama who was Dasharatha's son. Having circumambulated him, the lord,[478] who no longer possessed any worlds, went away.

Chapter 1(76)

When Rama had departed, Rama who was Dasharatha's son became serene of soul. He handed over the bow and the arrow to the immeasurable Varuna. Rama worshipped Vasishtha and the other best of rishis. Seeing that his father was still distracted, Rama, the descendant of the Raghu lineage said, 'Jamadagni's son has departed. Protected by you, let the army with the four kinds of forces proceed towards Ayodhya.' Hearing Rama's words, King Dasharatha embraced his son with his arms and inhaled the fragrance of Raghava's head. On hearing that Rama had departed, the king was delighted. He urged the soldiers to quickly leave for the city. There were beautiful flags and standards. Sounds could be heard from the trumpets. The charming royal roads were sprinkled with water and flowers were strewn on them. Citizens sounded auspicious musical instruments at the gate of the royal palace. As the king entered, the place was adorned and full with a large number of people.

With other royal women, Kousalya, Sumitra and the slender-waisted Kaikeyee engaged themselves in welcoming the daughters-in-law. The immensely fortunate Sita, the illustrious Urmila and Kushadhvaja's two daughters were received by the royal ladies. Everyone was smeared with auspicious paste and adorned in silken garments. All of them quickly went to the abodes meant for the gods and performed worship there. All the princesses[479] worshipped those who should be honoured. All of them found pleasure with their husbands. They had obtained wives and weapons. They had

[478] Parashurama.

[479] Sita, Urmila, Mandavi and Shrutakeerti.

obtained riches and well-wishers. Those bulls among men engaged themselves in tending to their father.

Rama, with truth as his valour, obtained great fame in this world. Because of his superior qualities, he was like Svayambhu to all creatures. With Sita, Rama found pleasure for many seasons. The spirited one was devoted to her and her heart was also always devoted to him. Her father had bestowed her as a wife and she became Rama's beloved. His delight and qualities were enhanced by her qualities. Her husband's heartfelt devotion to her doubled because of this. Whatever was in the innermost portions of their hearts became manifest to each other. Maithilee Sita, Janaka's daughter, was special and was like the gods in her beauty. She was as beautiful as Shri.[480] The beautiful and supreme princess was united with the delightful son of a rajarshi. Rama was extremely radiant, like someone who is extremely desired. He was like the god Vishnu, the lord of the immortals, united with Shri.

This ends Bala Kanda.

[480] Lakshmi.

CHAPTER TWO

Ayodhya Kanda

Sarga (1): 37 shlokas
Sarga (2): 34 shlokas
Sarga (3): 32 shlokas
Sarga (4): 45 shlokas
Sarga (5): 24 shlokas
Sarga (6): 28 shlokas
Sarga (7): 31 shlokas
Sarga (8): 27 shlokas
Sarga (9): 47 shlokas
Sarga (10): 41 shlokas
Sarga (11): 15 shlokas
Sarga (12): 24 shlokas
Sarga (13): 28 shlokas
Sarga (14): 27 shlokas
Sarga (15): 14 shlokas
Sarga (16): 61 shlokas
Sarga (17): 33 shlokas
Sarga (18): 40 shlokas
Sarga (19): 22 shlokas
Sarga (20): 36 shlokas
Sarga (21): 25 shlokas
Sarga (22): 20 shlokas
Sarga (23): 34 shlokas
Sarga (24): 19 shlokas
Sarga (25): 15 shlokas
Sarga (26): 22 shlokas
Sarga (27): 33 shlokas
Sarga (28): 20 shlokas
Sarga (29): 27 shlokas
Sarga (30): 24 shlokas
Sarga (31): 37 shlokas
Sarga (32): 22 shlokas
Sarga (33): 19 shlokas
Sarga (34): 36 shlokas
Sarga (35): 38 shlokas
Sarga (36): 17 shlokas
Sarga (37): 28 shlokas
Sarga (38): 20 shlokas
Sarga (39): 16 shlokas
Sarga (40): 30 shlokas
Sarga (41): 33 shlokas
Sarga (42): 26 shlokas
Sarga (43): 15 shlokas
Sarga (44): 27 shlokas
Sarga (45): 24 shlokas
Sarga (46): 79 shlokas
Sarga (47): 33 shlokas
Sarga (48): 36 shlokas
Sarga (49): 15 shlokas
Sarga (50): 22 shlokas
Sarga (51): 30 shlokas
Sarga (52): 26 shlokas

Sarga (53): 26 shlokas
Sarga (54): 20 shlokas
Sarga (55): 21 shlokas
Sarga (56): 17 shlokas
Sarga (57): 39 shlokas
Sarga (58): 57 shlokas
Sarga (59): 14 shlokas
Sarga (60): 19 shlokas
Sarga (61): 25 shlokas
Sarga (62): 15 shlokas
Sarga (63): 18 shlokas
Sarga (64): 24 shlokas
Sarga (65): 28 shlokas
Sarga (66): 45 shlokas
Sarga (67): 15 ṣhlokas
Sarga (68): 29 shlokas
Sarga (69): 34 shlokas
Sarga (70): 23 shlokas
Sarga (71): 25 shlokas
Sarga (72): 25 shlokas
Sarga (73): 17 shlokas
Sarga (74): 21 shlokas
Sarga (75): 14 shlokas
Sarga (76): 30 shlokas
Sarga (77): 23 shlokas
Sarga (78): 17 shlokas
Sarga (79): 21 shlokas
Sarga (80): 25 shlokas
Sarga (81): 23 shlokas
Sarga (82): 27 shlokas
Sarga (83): 22 shlokas
Sarga (84): 22 shlokas
Sarga (85): 77 shlokas
Sarga (86): 36 shlokas
Sarga (87): 27 shlokas
Sarga (88): 27 shlokas
Sarga (89): 19 shlokas
Sarga (90): 25 shlokas
Sarga (91): 17 shlokas
Sarga (92): 15 shlokas
Sarga (93): 41 shlokas
Sarga (94): 59 shlokas
Sarga (95): 47 shlokas
Sarga (96): 29 shlokas
Sarga (97): 24 shlokas
Sarga (98): 71 shlokas
Sarga (99): 19 shlokas
Sarga (100): 17 shlokas
Sarga (101): 31 shlokas
Sarga (102): 31 shlokas
Sarga (103): 32 shlokas
Sarga (104): 25 shlokas
Sarga (105): 24 shlokas
Sarga (106): 24 shlokas
Sarga (107): 22 shlokas
Sarga (108): 26 shlokas
Sarga (109): 28 shlokas
Sarga (110): 52 shlokas
Sarga (111): 20 shlokas

Chapter 2(1)

After some time, King Dasharatha, descendant of the Raghu lineage, spoke to his son Bharata, who was Kaikeyee's son.

'O son! Yudhajit is the brave son of the king of Kekaya. Your maternal uncle came to take you there and has been residing here.'[1] Hearing Dasharatha's words, Bharata, Kaikeyee's son, made arrangements to leave, along with Shatrughna. The brave one, best among men, took his leave of his father, Rama, the performer of unblemished deeds and his mother, and left with Shatrughna. Yudhajit was delighted. Taking Bharata and Shatrughna, the brave one entered his own city and his father rejoiced. With his brother, he[2] was treated with great honour. Like a son, he was affectionately reared by his uncle, who was a lord of horses. They resided there and enjoyed all the objects of desire. However, the brave brothers remembered their aged father, King Dasharatha. The immensely energetic king also remembered the two sons who were away, Bharata and Shatrughna, who were like the great Indra and Varuna. He loved those four bulls among men equally, as if they were four arms growing out of his own body.

Among them, the greatly energetic Rama brought great delight to his father. Endowed with superior qualities, he was like Svayambhu[3] to creatures. When Bharata had gone, Rama and the immensely strong Lakshmana tended to their father, who was like a god. Placing his father's instructions at the forefront, Rama, with dharma in his soul, performed all the agreeable and pleasant tasks required by the citizens. Supremely attentive, he tended to all the tasks required by their mothers. All the time, he took care of all the tasks required by the preceptors. In this way, because of Rama's good conduct, Dasharatha, the learned brahmanas and all the residents of the kingdom were delighted. He was also peaceful in his soul and spoke gently. He did not respond to harsh and loud words spoken by others. He was content with whatever good deed was done to him. Even if a hundred acts of injury were committed against him, he did not remember them. Whenever he found time while practising with weapons, he always conversed with those who were aged, whether they were aged in conduct or wisdom, and with virtuous people. His birth was fortunate. He was

[1] He stayed on because of the marriage.

[2] Bharata.

[3] Brahma.

virtuous and not distressed. He was truthful and upright. He was instructed by aged brahmanas who were conversant with dharma and artha. He knew about dharma, artha and kama.[4] He possessed memory and innate intelligence. He was skilled and accomplished in prevalent customs. He knew about the sacred texts and about how they should be followed. He understood differences among people. He was accomplished in policy and knew about whom to reward and whom to punish. He knew about earning revenue and was accomplished in the techniques of expenditure. He obtained instructions about the best collections of sacred texts and about the ancillary texts. He knew that artha should not be accumulated through adharma. He was not lazy when pursuing pleasure. He was acquainted with details about artisanship and the fine arts. He knew how to control and ride elephants and horses. He was best among those who knew about dhanurveda. The world revered him as an *atiratha*.[5] He was accomplished in commanding armies and could strike while advancing. The prince exhibited the best of qualities while dealing with the subjects. He was revered in the three worlds and his qualities of forgiveness was like those of the earth. He was like Brihaspati[6] in his wisdom and like Shachi's consort[7] in his valour. He was thus loved by all the subjects and brought joy to his father. Rama was radiant in his qualities, like the sun with its rays. He followed all the vows and his valour was unassailable. The earth desired him as her protector, as if he was a guardian of the world. Rama was endowed with many such supreme qualities.

On seeing this, Dasharatha, scorcher of enemies, started to think. A great reason for delight began to circulate in his heart. 'When will I see my son instated as the heir? His prosperity in this world is growing and he is compassionate towards all creatures.

[4] Dharma, artha and kama are the three objectives (purushartha) of human existence. Artha is the pursuit of material prosperity, kama is the pursuit of sensual pleasure, it being best not to translate dharma. Sometimes, moksha (emancipation) is added as a fourth objective.

[5] Dhanurveda is the science of war. An atiratha is a great warrior, greater than a maharatha.

[6] The preceptor of the gods.

[7] Indra.

Like Parjanya[8] showering down, he is loved more than me in this world. He is like Yama and Shakra in his valour and like Brihaspati in his wisdom. He is like the earth in patience and is superior to me in qualities. Will I see my son instated over this entire earth? As I age, will I behold this and then ascend to heaven?' The great king saw that he was endowed with all these qualities. With his advisers, he determined that he would be made the heir apparent. He summoned all the foremost kings on earth and all those who resided in different cities and habitations. All of them seated themselves in different seats earmarked by the king. Attentive, all those kings seated themselves and looked towards the king.[9] All the revered and humble kings and men from cities and habitations seated themselves. Surrounded by them, he looked like the one with one thousand eyes, surrounded by the immortals.

Chapter 2(2)

The lord of men invited all the courtiers. He spoke these unmatched, beneficial and agreeable words. His voice was deep, like the rumbling of a drum. The king's voice was great, like the rumbling of the clouds. 'Kings from the Ikshvaku lineage have ruled here earlier. I wish that this entire earth, which deserves happiness, should be full of welfare. I have acted in accordance with and followed the path of my ancestors. To the best of my capacity, I have attentively protected the subjects. In ensuring the welfare of the world, this entire body of mine has decayed and has become pale from the shadow of the umbrella.[10] I have obtained a lifespan lasting for many thousand years. Since the body has decayed, I desire to rest. Regal power is extremely difficult to bear and can only be sustained by a person who has conquered his senses. I am exhausted from bearing the extremely heavy burden of dharma that

[8] The god of rain.
[9] Dasharatha.
[10] A white umbrella is held aloft a king's head.

holds up the world. Engaging my son in the welfare of the subjects, I desire to rest, after taking the permission of all the bulls among brahmanas who are nearby. My eldest son, Rama, the conqueror of enemy cities, possesses all the qualities. He is Purandara's equal in valour. He is supreme among those who uphold dharma. He is like the moon, in conjunction with Pushya nakshatra. I will cheerfully anoint that bull among men as the heir apparent. As a protector, Lakshmana's prosperous elder brother is like the protector of the three worlds. He will be the supreme protector. By entrusting this entire earth to such a son now, I will do what is beneficial and ensure that it suffers from no hardships.' Delighted, the kings loudly welcomed the words of the king, like peacocks crying in delight when they see a giant cloud showering down. All of them got to know the desire and sentiments of the aged King Dasharatha, who was accomplished in dharma and artha. 'O king! Having lived for many thousand years, you are aged. O king! Therefore, consecrate Rama as the heir apparent.' Hearing their words, the king got to know what was agreeable to their minds. He had not known this earlier and wished to test them. He spoke these words. 'I follow dharma and rule over this earth. Why do you then wish to see my son instated as the heir apparent?'

All the inhabitants of the city and the countryside replied to the great-souled one. 'O king! Your son possesses many auspicious qualities. Rama has truth for his valour. Invested with divine qualities, he is like Shakra. O lord of the earth! He is superior to all those in the Ikshvaku lineage. Rama is devoted to truth and dharma and is a virtuous man in this world. He knows about dharma and never wavers from the truth. He is good in conduct and suffers from no jealousy. He is patient and comforting. He speaks gently and is grateful. He has conquered his senses. He is mild and his mind is not fickle. He is always good in behaviour and does not suffer from envy. Towards all creatures, he is pleasant in speech. Raghava is truthful in speech. He worships the aged brahmanas who are extremely learned. His deeds and fame are infinite and are increasing. He is accomplished in all the weapons of gods, asuras and humans. With Soumitri, when he advances into a battle for the sake of a village or a city, he does not return without being victorious. When he returns from a battle, whether it is on an elephant or a chariot, he always asks about the welfare of the citizens and their relatives. Progressively, he asks about everything, their sons, their sacrificial fires, their wives, their servants and their disciples, like a father asking about his own biological sons. He attentively asks us whether our disciples are tending to our needs. This is what Rama, tiger among men, always asks us. He is extremely miserable when people suffer from hardships. In all festivals, he is as satisfied as a father. He is truthful and a great archer. He has conquered his senses and serves the aged. It is good fortune that Raghava has been born to you as an excellent son. It is good fortune that you have a son with such qualities, like Kashyapa was to Marichi. Rama's soul is known. All the people in the kingdom and in this supreme city, all the people who are inside and outside the city and the countryside, women, aged and young—morning and night, all of them attentively desire strength, freedom from disease and a long life for him. They bow down before all the gods, wishing fame for Rama. Through prayers to the gods they worship and through your favours, we will obtain prosperity. O king! We will see your son Rama, with the complexion of a dark lotus, the destroyer of enemies everywhere, instated as the heir apparent. Your son is like the god of the gods. He is engaged in the welfare of the worlds. O one who grants boons! For the sake of welfare, you should swiftly and cheerfully instate the one who is generous in qualities.'

Chapter 2(3)

The king joined his hands, which were like lotuses, in salutation. He accepted their words. Having accepted them, he spoke these agreeable and beneficial words to them. 'I am extremely delighted and my power has become unmatched, now that you desire that my beloved eldest son should be instated as the heir apparent.'

The king worshipped the brahmanas Vasishtha and Vamadeva and told them, 'Listen. This is the prosperous and sacred month of Chaitra.[11] The groves are full of blossoming flowers. Let all the arrangements be made for Rama to become the heir apparent.' Delighted and full of joy, those two bulls among brahmanas told the lord of the earth, 'Everything has been arranged as you had instructed.' The radiant king spoke these words to Sumantra. 'Bring Rama, cleansed in his soul, here quickly.' Sumantra pledged to do what the king had asked him to. He brought Rama, supreme among charioteers, there in a chariot. King Dasharatha seated himself. He was surrounded by kings from the east, the west, the north and the south. There were mlechchhas and aryas and others who resided in forests and extremities of mountains.[12] All of them seated themselves there, like the gods around Vasava. The royal sage was in their midst, like Vasava among the Maruts. From the palace, he saw that his son had arrived on a chariot. He[13] was like a king of the gandharvas. He was famous in this world because of his manliness. He was long-armed and great in spirit. His stride was like that of a crazy elephant. Rama's face was pleasant to behold, like the moon. His beauty, generosity and qualities stole the sight and hearts of men. Like rain, he gladdened subjects who had been tormented by the summer. The king was not satisfied from looking at him.

Raghava descended from the supreme chariot. Hands joined in salutation, he approached his father, Sumantra following at the rear. To see the king, along with the charioteer, Raghava, bull among men, climbed up to the palace, which was like the summit of Kailasa. Having approached his father, he joined his hands in salutation. He worshipped at his father's feet and recited his own name.[14] On seeing him bow down, join his hands in salutation and stand near him, the king embraced his beloved son. The king

[11] March–April.

[12] Arya means a noble one and is used for those who speak Sanskrit.

[13] Rama.

[14] This is a customary form of greeting. It is not as if Dasharatha did not know who Rama was.

gave Rama a beautiful and supreme seat. It was tall and beautiful, adorned with gems and gold. Having ascended that supreme seat, Raghava dazzled with his own resplendence, like the sparkling and rising sun atop Meru. His radiance made the assembly shine, like the resplendence of the moon amidst planets and nakshatras in a clear autumn sky. On seeing his beloved son, the king was delighted, just as one is happy to see one's ornamented person reflected in a mirror. The king, supreme among those who have sons, smiled and spoke these words to his son, like Kashyapa to Indra of the gods.[15] 'You have been born to my eldest wife and are a son who is just like me. O Rama! You have been born with the best of qualities and are the most beloved of my sons. You have delighted the subjects with your qualities. Therefore, at the conjunction of Pushya, you will be instated as the heir apparent. Your nature is extremely humble. You possess the qualities. O son! Though you possess the qualities, out of affection for you, I will tell you something for your welfare. Be even more humble. Always conquer your senses. Cast aside any distractions that arise because of desire and anger. Use direct and indirect means of examination to keep all the advisers and ordinary people happy. If you protect the earth in that way, the ordinary people will be satisfied and devoted. Your friends will rejoice, like the immortals having obtained amrita. O son! Therefore, act towards them as towards one's own self."

On hearing this, Rama's well-wishers, who wished to do him well, quickly went to Kousalya and told her what had happened. Kousalya, supreme among women, gave her friends gold, cattle and many kinds of jewels. Raghava honoured the king and ascended his chariot. Worshipped by large numbers of people, he went to his radiant house. Having heard, the citizens had obtained what they had wished for. They worshipped the king. Obtaining the king's permission, they went to their own houses and joyfully offered worship to the gods.

[15] The gods, including Indra, are Kashyapa's sons.

Chapter 2(4)

When the citizens had left, the king, who was firm in taking decisions that needed to be taken, consulted with his ministers. 'There is a conjunction of Pushya tomorrow. My son, lord Rama, with eyes that are as coppery red as a red lotus, will be instated as heir apparent tomorrow.' After this, King Dasharatha entered the inner quarters of his residence and again instructed the charioteer that Rama should be brought. Obeying these words, the charioteer swiftly left for Rama's residence again, so as to bring Rama. The gatekeepers informed Rama that he had arrived again. On hearing that he had come, Rama was worried. Having allowed him to enter, Rama addressed him in these words. 'Tell me completely the reason for your arrival.' Thus addressed, the charioteer replied, 'The king wishes to see you. On hearing this, you have to decide whether to go or stay.' Hearing the charioteer's words, Rama swiftly left for the king's residence, so as to see the king. On hearing that Rama had arrived, King Dasharatha instructed that he should enter the house. He wished to speak some agreeable and supreme words. The handsome Raghava entered his father's residence. On seeing his father from a distance, he joined his hands in salutation and prostrated himself. The king raised the one who was prostrate and embraced him. He offered him a beautiful seat and again spoke, 'O Rama! I am aged and have lived for a long time. I have enjoyed all the desired objects of pleasure. I have performed hundreds of sacrifices at which I have offered food and copious quantities of dakshina. I have had the desired offspring and you are unmatched on earth. O supreme among men! I have donated and studied, as I wished. O brave one! I have felt the desired happiness. I have repaid the debts due to gods, rishis, ancestors, brahmanas and towards my own self. No other task remains, but for you to be consecrated. Therefore, I am engaging you in undertaking what needs to be done. Now, all the ordinary people desire that you should be the king. O son! Therefore, I wish to instate you as the heir apparent. O Rama! In my sleep, I see many kinds of terrible portents. Showers of giant meteors descend from the sky and they make a loud noise. Those who know about portents tell me that terrible planets, the sun, Angaraka and Rahu, are approaching the nakshatra.[16] Whenever such evil portents present themselves, the king dies, or confronts a terrible catastrophe. O Raghava! Therefore, before my senses are confounded, you need to be instated. The intelligence of living beings is fickle. Today, the moon is in Punarvasu, which comes before Pushya. Those who think about the portents have said that the conjunction of Pushya is tomorrow. Your consecration will be during the conjunction of Pushya. My mind is urging me to hurry. O scorcher of enemies! I wish to instate you as the heir apparent tomorrow. Therefore, control your soul and observe the vows. Fast with your wife and sleep on the ground, on a mat made of darbha grass. Your well-wishers will attentively protect you from all directions. Whenever a task presents itself, there are many kinds of obstructions. Bharata is not in this city and is far away. It is my view that this is the right time for you to be consecrated. It is indeed true that your brother, Bharata, is virtuous. He has dharma in his soul and follows his elder brother. He is compassionate and has conquered his senses. However, it is my view that the minds of men are fickle. O Raghava! Even those who are virtuous and always devoted to dharma may act impetuously.' Having thus told him about the consecration the following day, he gave Rama permission to leave. Worshipping his father, he left for his own house.

After this, he left for his mother's residence, in the inner quarters. He saw his mother worshipping there, clad in silken garments. He saw her silently meditating in the abode meant for the gods, worshipping Shri.[17] On hearing the agreeable news about

[16] Angaraka is another name for Mangala (Mars). Though the text leaves it implicit, the nakshatra presumably means Dasharatha's natal nakshatra. There is an anomaly that caught Rama unawares too. Dasharatha decided that Rama should be made the heir apparent. He subsequently decided that it needed to be done instantly, though Bharata was still away in his maternal uncle's kingdom. A charioteer was sent to fetch Rama. We have kept this as charioteer (suta), though most translations interpret this as Sumantra. Since that equation is not obvious, we retained charioteer.

[17] Lakshmi, the goddess of wealth and prosperity.

Rama's consecration, Sumitra and Lakshmana arrived there, even before Sita was brought. At that time, Kousalya's eyes were closed and she was meditating. Sumitra was seated there, along with Sita and Lakshmana. On hearing that her son would be instated at the time of Pushya's conjunction, she was engaged in *pranayama*[18] and meditating on the supreme being, Janardana. While she was engaged in these vows, he approached and greeted her. Rama spoke these words to her, causing her joy. 'O mother! My father has engaged me in the task of protecting the subjects. Following my father's command, my consecration will be tomorrow. With me, Sita must fast throughout the night. My father, along with his preceptors, have told me this. Let all the auspicious rites, for me and Vaidehi, be performed in preparation for the consecration tomorrow.' Kousalya had desired this for a long time. Hearing this, her eyes filled with tears of joy and she spoke these words to Rama. 'O Rama! May you live for a long time and let those who cause obstructions in your path be destroyed. Let my kin and that of Sumitra's find delight at your prosperity. O son! You were born to me at the time of an auspicious nakshatra. That is the reason you have surpassed your father, Dasharatha, in your qualities. My austerities before the lotus-eyed being[19] are inviolate. O son! Hence, the prosperity of this kingdom of the Ikshvakus will find a refuge in you.' His brother was humbly seated nearby, hands joined in salutation. Hearing his mother's words, he glanced towards him, smiled and spoke these words. 'O Lakshmana! You will rule over this earth with me. You are like my second self and this prosperity will also find a refuge in you. O Soumitri! Enjoy all the desired objects of pleasure and the fruits of this kingdom. I wish to remain alive and desire this kingdom for your sake.' Having addressed Lakshmana in these words, Rama greeted his two mothers and took their permission. With Sita, he left for his own residence.

[18] Yoga has eight elements—*yama* (restraint), *niyama* (rituals), asana (posture), pranayama (control of the breath), *pratyahara* (withdrawal), *dharana* (retention), *dhyana* (meditation) and *samadhi* (liberation). That's the reason the expression *ashtanga* (eight-formed) yoga is used.

[19] Vishnu.

Chapter 2(5)

After instructing Rama, the king summoned his priest, Vasishtha, and told him about the consecration the next day. 'O store of austerities! Go to Kakutstha and make him fast. For the sake of prosperity, fame and the kingdom, make him observe the rites, together with his wife.' The one who was supreme among those who knew about the Vedas agreed to what the king had said. The illustrious Vasishtha himself went to Rama's residence. He reached Rama's residence, with the pale radiance of a thick cloud. The supreme among sages passed through the three chambers on his chariot.[20] Showing respect, Rama quickly came forward to greet the rishi. He emerged from his residence to show honours to the one to whom honours were due. He swiftly approached the learned one's chariot and himself grasped him and helped him descend from the chariot. On seeing Rama, the one who brought pleasure, the priest spoke these words, bringing him joy and delight. 'O Rama! Your father is pleased with you and you will become the heir apparent. With Sita, you must fast today. When it is morning, the king will anoint you as the heir apparent. Your father, Dasharatha, is pleased with you, as Nahusha was with Yayati.'[21] Having said this, the sage made Rama, together with Vaidehi, observe the vows of fasting, accompanied by the associated mantras. Rama worshipped the royal preceptor. Having taken Kakutstha's leave, he[22] left Rama's residence. Seated there, Rama spoke pleasant words to his well-wishers and was congratulated by them. Taking their permission, he entered his own house. Rama's residence was radiant, full of delighted men and women. It was like a lake populated by herds of crazy elephants and blooming lotuses.

Vasishtha emerged from Rama's residence, which was like the royal palace. He saw that the roads were full of people. In every direction, Ayodhya's royal roads were crowded with large numbers

[20] The sense is that ordinary people would have got down from the chariot at the outer gate and proceeded through the three chambers on foot.

[21] Nahusha was Yayati's father.

[22] Vasishtha.

of people. Large numbers of curious people created a melee. As those large crowds met, there were sounds of joy. The royal roads were resplendent and seemed to roar like the ocean. All the roads, flanked by garlands of trees, were sprinkled with water.[23] Flags were raised in all the houses in the city of Ayodhya. All the people who resided in Ayodhya, women, children and disabled, wished that the sun would rise, so that Rama's desired consecration could take place. People were anxious to witness that great festival in Ayodhya, which would be like an adornment for the subjects and would increase the delight of people. Those crowds and large masses of people along the royal roads created obstructions, like a *vyuha*.[24] Slowly, the priest reached the royal residence. He ascended up to the palace, which was like the summit of a mountain, tinged by a white cloud. He went and met the king, like Brihaspati meeting Shakra. On seeing that he had come, the king got down from his throne. He asked him and was told that all the rituals had been observed. Taking his preceptor's permission and that of the large number of people, the king left them and entered his inner quarters, like a lion entering a cave in a mountain. That best of residences was full of a large number of women. The residence was like the great Indra's abode. As the king entered the beautiful residence, it seemed to become even more resplendent, like the moon in the firmament, surrounded by a large number of stars.

Chapter 2(6)

When the priest had left, Rama controlled his mind and bathed. With his large-eyed wife, he approached Narayana.[25] As is recommended in the ordinances, he placed the vessel of oblations on his head. He then rendered these oblations into the blazing fire, as offerings to the great god. For his own good, he then partook of

[23] These were avenues, lined with trees.

[24] A vyuha is a battle formation.

[25] Figuratively.

the remainder of the oblations. Meditating on the god Narayana, he lay down on a mat of kusha grass. Vaidehi was controlled in her speech and controlled in her mind. With her, the son of the supreme among men slept in Vishnu's beautiful shrine.[26] He awoke when one *yama* of the night was still left.[27] He arranged that all the decorations should be made in his house. He heard the pleasant words of sutas, *magadha*s and *vandi*s.[28] Seated, and controlled in his mind, he meditated on the chants for the morning sandhya. He bowed his head down and praised Madhusudana. Attired in clean and silken garments, he made brahmanas utter words of praise. Those sacred chants were deep and sweet. Ayodhya was filled with the sounds of trumpets being sounded. With Vaidehi, Raghava had fasted.

On hearing this, all the people who resided in Ayodhya rejoiced. All the residents of the city had heard that Rama would be consecrated. On seeing that night had turned into morning, they again arranged for excellent decorations—on the summits of temples that looked like peaks with clouds around them, at crossroads, along roads, in sanctuaries and in mansions, in the shops of traders, filled with many expensive objects, in the handsome houses of prosperous families, in all the assembly halls and all the visible parts of trees. Colourful flags and pennants were raised. Large numbers of dancers danced. Singers sang. Words that were pleasant to the mind and the eyes were heard. On the occasion of Rama's consecration, people conversed with each other. As Rama's consecration approached, they did this in squares and houses. Large numbers of children were playing at the entrances to the houses. They too spoke to each other about Rama's consecration. On the occasion of Rama's consecration, the citizens made the royal roads

[26] There was such a shrine inside the palace. This image is now believed to be in Srirangam.

[27] A yama is a period of three hours. Since it is made up of three yamas, the night is known as *triyama*.

[28] A suta is a bard, a magadha is a minstrel and a vandi is one who sings words of praise. Vandis probably did not compose anything themselves, while sutas and magadhas did, the former focusing on stories and the latter on rendering these into songs.

look splendid. They sprinkled flowers there and burnt incense and fragrances. Just in case night wasn't over, they had arranged for means of illumination, placing lamps in all the trees that lined all the roads. All the residents of the city decorated the city in this way. All of them desired Rama's consecration. Large numbers of them gathered in the squares and the assembly halls. They spoke to each other there, praising the king. 'This king, the delight of the Ikshvaku lineage, is great-souled. He knows himself to be aged. Therefore, for the sake of the kingdom, he wishes to anoint Rama in the kingdom. Rama, who is favoured by all of us, will become the lord of the earth. He can see what is inside and outside people and will be our protector for a long period of time. His mind is not insolent. He is learned and has dharma in his soul. He is devoted to his brothers. Raghava is as gentle towards us as he is towards his brothers. Let the unblemished King Dasharatha, with dharma in his soul, live for a long time. It is through his favours that we have been able to witness Rama's consecration.' These were the kinds of words that could be heard among the citizens. The people who came from different directions, and those who were from the countryside, heard them. People came to the city from different directions to witness Rama's consecration. On the occasion of Rama's consecration, the city was filled with people from the countryside. Large numbers of people moved around and a sound could be heard, like the roar of the ocean when it is time for the full moon. The city resembled Indra's residence. In a desire to witness the spectacle, people arrived from the countryside. In every direction, there was a loud roar, like that of the ocean, filled with aquatic creatures.

Chapter 2(7)

Kaikeyee had a maid who lived with her. She had come to her from the household of her kin.[29] Roaming around as she willed,

[29] From her father's household.

she climbed up to the palace, which looked like the moon. From the palace, Manthara looked at Ayodhya, with all the royal roads sprinkled with water and strewn with lotuses and lilies. The entire place was decorated with expensive flags and standards. It was full of people who had washed their heads and anointed themselves with sandalwood paste. On seeing a nursemaid nearby, Manthara asked her, 'Why is Rama's mother filled with supreme delight? Despite being attached to riches herself, why is she giving away riches to the people? Why are the people extremely joyous? Tell me. Has the king done something to cause such delight?' The nursemaid was extremely happy and seemed to be bursting with joy. Rejoicing, she told Kubja[30] about Raghava's great prosperity. 'Raghava has conquered anger and tomorrow, when it is the conjunction of Pushya, King Dasharatha will instate the faultless Rama as the heir apparent.' On hearing the nursemaid's words, Kubja was filled with anger.

She quickly descended from the palace that was like the summit of Kailasa. Manthara, evil in her thoughts, was consumed by rage. Kaikeyee was lying down. She went to her and spoke these words. 'O foolish one! Arise. You confront a great fear and are going to be submerged in a flood of calamity. Why are you sleeping? Why don't you yourself realize what is going to happen? You pride yourself as someone who is fortunate,[31] but harm is going to be caused to your fortune. Fortune is fickle, like the flow of a river during the summer.' Kaikeyee heard these angry and harsh words spoken by Kubja, whose thoughts were evil. Overcome by great misery, Kaikeyee spoke these words to Kubja. 'O Manthara! Why are you not at peace? One can see that your face is distressed and that you are extremely miserable.' Manthara heard Kaikeyee's words, expressed in sweet syllables. Accomplished in the use of words, she spoke words that were full of rage. Desiring her[32] welfare, Manthara spoke words that enhanced her unhappiness. She sought

[30] *Kubja* means humpbacked and this is how Manthara is described. However, kubja also means a class of housemaids and Manthara need not have been humpbacked.

[31] Because Dasharatha loved her more.

[32] Kaikeyee's.

to create dissension between the miserable one and Raghava. 'O extremely great queen! You are no longer at peace and a miserable catastrophe confronts you. King Dasharatha will instate Rama as the heir apparent. I am submerged in fathomless fear and am full of grief and misery. I am being scorched, as if by a fire. I have come here for the sake of your welfare. O Kaikeyee! My misery has become greater because of your misery. There is no doubt that my prosperity lies in your prosperity. You have been born in a lineage of kings and are queen to a lord of the earth. O queen! How can you not realize that there is a ferocity in the dharma of kings? Your husband speaks about dharma, but is deceitful. Though he speaks gently, he is terrible. Because you are pure in your sentiments, you do not know that you are being gravely cheated by him. He approaches you and unites with you. He comforts you with futile words. Wherever there is a prospect of prosperity, your husband passes that on to Kousalya. The evil-souled one has sent Bharata away to your relatives. With the obstruction out of the way, at the opportune time, he will establish Rama in the kingdom. Like a mother, you desire his welfare. However, in the garb of a husband, he is your enemy. O foolish one! You have nourished a venomous serpent in your lap. King Dasharatha has acted towards you and your own son just as a snake or an ignored enemy does. O child! Though you always deserve happiness, he has comforted you with wicked and false words. With Rama established in the kingdom, you and your relatives will be destroyed. O Kaikeyee! The time has come. To ensure your own welfare, act quickly. O one who is amazing to behold! Save your son and your own self.'

Hearing Manthara's words, the one with the beautiful face arose from her bed. She gave a beautiful ornament to Kubja. Having given that ornament to Kubja, Kaikeyee, supreme among women, again spoke these cheerful words to Manthara. 'O Manthara! What you have told me brings me great delight. You have recounted something agreeable. What can I do for you next? I do not see any difference between Rama and Bharata. Therefore, I am content that the king is instating Rama in the kingdom. Thus, you deserve to be given something again. These supreme words bring happiness. They are agreeable and cause pleasure. You cannot possibly say anything that is more agreeable than this. Ask for a boon and I will grant it to you next.'

Chapter 2(8)

Full of jealousy, Manthara cast aside that ornament. Overcome with anger and rage, she spoke these words. 'O foolish one! Why are you filled with delight? You are immersed in an ocean of grief, but are incapable of comprehending it yourself. Kousalya is indeed fortunate that her son will be consecrated. Tomorrow, at the conjunction of Pushya, the supreme among brahmanas will confer greatness on him by making him the heir apparent. With his enemies destroyed, he will obtain great delight and fame. Like a maid, you will have to join your hands in salutation and present yourself before Kousalya. Rama's women[33] will certainly be filled with great joy. However, your daughters-in-law will be unhappy at Bharata's destruction.' On seeing that Manthara spoke these extremely unpleasant words, Queen Kaikeyee praised Rama's qualities. 'He knows about dharma. His preceptors have trained him in being controlled. He is grateful. He is truthful in words and pure. Rama is the king's eldest son. He deserves to be the heir apparent. He will have a long life. Like a father, he will protect his brothers and servants. O Kubja! On hearing about Rama's consecration, why are you tormented? After Rama has ruled for one hundred years, it is certain that Bharata, bull among men, will obtain the kingdom of his father and grandfathers. O Manthara! A beneficial occasion has presented itself now. Why are you tormented? Does he not tend to me more than he does to Kousalya?' Hearing Kaikeyee's words, Manthara was extremely miserable. Her sighs were long and warm. She addressed Kaikeyee in these words. 'You do not see the catastrophe. Because of your stupidity, you do not realize

[33] His wife and mother.

it yourself. You are going to be submerged in an ocean of grief that is full of misery and hardship. If Raghava becomes the king, his son will succeed him. O Kaikeyee! Bharata will be excised from the royal lineage. O beautiful one! All of a king's sons do not inherit the kingdom. If all of them are instated in this way, there will be great anarchy. O Kaikeyee! Therefore, kings pass on the various elements of the kingdom to the eldest son. O one with the unblemished limbs! They are instated, even though others may be superior in qualities. This son of yours will be completely shattered and dislodged from this royal lineage. O devoted one! He will be miserable and without a protector. I have come here for your sake, but you do not understand me. When your co-wife becomes prosperous, you desire to give me something. Shorn of thorns, when Rama obtains this kingdom, it is certain that he will banish Bharata to some other country, or perhaps remove him from this world. Even when Bharata was a child, you sent him to his maternal uncle's house. Affection is generated through proximity, even if it is towards an immobile object.[34] Rama is protected by Soumitri and Raghava protects Lakshmana. Their fraternal love is as famous in the worlds as that of the two Ashvins. Therefore, Rama will not perform any wicked deed towards Lakshmana. However, there is no doubt that Rama will act in a wicked way towards Bharata. Therefore, it is best that your son should go to the forest from the royal residence.[35] This appeals to me and it will bring great benefit to you. Even if Bharata were to obtain his father's kingdom through dharma, that would be better for your relatives.[36] That child[37] deserves happiness and he is Rama's natural enemy. With one's own prosperity destroyed, how can one live under the subjugation of another person who has obtained prosperity? Like a lion chasing a herd of elephants in the forest, Rama is enveloping Bharata and you should save him. Earlier, because of your good fortune and

[34] Thus, Dasharatha never developed affection towards Bharata.

[35] From his uncle's royal residence.

[36] Bharata going to the forest.

[37] Bharata.

pride, you slighted Rama's mother.[38] Why will your co-wife not pursue that enmity? When Rama obtains the earth, it is certain that Bharata will be destroyed. Therefore, think of a means to obtain the kingdom for your son and of a reason to exile the enemy.'

Chapter 2(9)

Thus addressed, Kaikeyee's face blazed with anger. With a long and warm sigh, she spoke these words to Manthara. 'Right now, I will quickly dispatch Rama to the forest. I will swiftly instate Bharata as the heir apparent. O Manthara! Now think of a means whereby Bharata, and not Rama, gets the kingdom.' Manthara, wicked in her thoughts, was addressed in this way by the queen. Desiring to cause injury and violence to Rama, she spoke to Kaikeyee. 'O Kaikeyee! I will tell you. Listen to me. This is the means whereby your son, Bharata, alone can obtain the kingdom.' On hearing Manthara's words, Kaikeyee arose a bit from her well-laid-out bed and said, 'O Manthara! Tell me the method and the reason. How can Bharata obtain the kingdom and never Rama?' Manthara, wicked in her thoughts, was addressed in this way by the queen. Desiring to cause injury and violence to Rama, Kubja spoke these words. 'There was a battle between the gods and the asuras. The rajarshi, your husband, went to help the king of the gods and took you along with him. O queen! He advanced in a southern direction, towards Dandaka.[39] He went to the city of Vaijayanta, where Timidhvaja was. He was famous by the name of Shambara.[40] That great asura was conversant with one hundred different kinds of maya.[41] In the battle, he fought with

[38] The details are not known.

[39] The forest of Dandaka, known as Dandakaranya. The word *dandaka* means that people were exiled there, as punishment (*danda*).

[40] Timidhvaja was one of Shambara's names. Timidhvaja means one who had a whale on his standard.

[41] The power of illusion.

Shakra and vanquished the army of the gods. King Dasharatha fought in that great battle. O queen! When he lost his senses in the battle, you removed him from the spot. Your husband was mangled by weapons and you saved him from that spot. O one with the beautiful face! Satisfied with you, he gave you two boons. O queen! Your husband offered to grant you two boons. However, you told the great-souled one that you would ask for the boons when the time came and he agreed. O queen! I did not know about this. But on an earlier occasion, you yourself told me. Ask for those two boons from your husband—Bharata's consecration and Rama's exile for a period of fourteen years. O Ashvapati's daughter! Go and enter the chamber earmarked for you to exhibit anger. Without any spreads, lie down on the bare ground, attired in dirty garments. Do not arise and do not say anything to him. There is no doubt that your husband always loves you. For your sake, the great king will even enter a fire. He is incapable of being angry with you. He cannot even glance at you in rage. To bring pleasure to you, the king will even give up his own life. The great king will be incapable of transgressing your words. O one who is foolish in nature! Comprehend your own good fortune and strength. King Dasharatha will offer you many kinds of gems, pearls, gold and jewels. But let your mind not be fruitlessly attracted to these. At the time of the battle between the gods and the asuras, Dasharatha gave you two boons. O immensely fortunate one! Remind him of those and do not get diverted from your own prosperity. Raghava will himself make you rise and give you those boons. When the great king is steady, seek those two boons from him. Rama must be exiled to the forest for fourteen years and the bull among kings must make Bharata the king of this earth. Having exiled Rama in this way, he will not obtain peace. However, with the enemies destroyed, Bharata will become the king. By the time Rama returns from the forest, your son will have obtained enough time to create a foundation for himself. He will have accumulated men and well-wishers on his own side. I think the time has come for you to prepare yourself and cast aside fear. Persuade him to withdraw from his intention of consecrating Rama.'

What was undesirable appeared to Kaikeyee as something that was desirable. She happily responded to Manthara in these words. 'O Kubja! You speak about what is best. So far, I have not understood what is best. In using the intelligence to determine what should be done, you are the best among all kubjas on earth. You are the one who has always been engaged in my welfare and have sought what brings me benefit. O Kubja! In determining what the king desires, my intelligence is not equal to yours. There are many kubjas who are badly placed. They are extremely wicked and crooked.[42] However, you are beautiful to behold, like a lotus bent by the wind. Your chest is proportionate, right up to your lofty shoulder. Below that, the stomach stretches out, with a shy navel. Adorned with a golden belt, your hips make a sound. Your thighs are extremely plump and your feet are long. O Manthara! O one attired in silken garments! As you walk before me on your long thighs, you are as radiant as a swan. Your tall hump is as large as the front of a chariot. The intelligence of kshatriyas and of maya reside in you. O Kubja! When Bharata has been consecrated and Raghava has gone to the forest, I will adorn you with a golden garland. O beautiful one! When I am happy and obtain what I desire, I will decorate your hump with that well-crafted ornament made out of molten gold. I will adorn your face with auspicious and colourful marks that are made out of molten gold. O Kubja! I will have auspicious ornaments constructed for you. Adorned in beautiful garments, you will walk around like a god. Your unmatched face will be like the face of the moon. Priding yourself above your enemies, you will walk around, chief among the best. O Kubja! Adorned in all kinds of ornaments, the kubjas will always serve at your feet, just as they do at mine.

Kaikeyee was still lying down on a sparkling bed, like the flame of a fire on a sacrificial altar. Praised in this way, she replied to her.[43] 'O fortunate one! There is no point to constructing a dam when the water has left. Arise. Act so as to show the king what

[42] This still doesn't make it obvious that the crookedness is physical, though the succeeding shlokas do suggest this.

[43] Manthara replied to Kaikeyee.

is beneficial.' The large-eyed one was proud of her good fortune. Thus urged, the queen went with Manthara to the chamber where she showed her anger. The beautiful one took off the necklace that had hundreds and thousands of pearls and also many other beautiful and expensive ornaments. Kaikeyee was like a golden rod. Succumbing to the words of Kubja, she lay down on the ground and told Manthara, 'O Kubja! Let it be known to the king that unless Raghava goes to the forest and Bharata obtains the earth, I will die here.' She spoke these extremely terrible words. The beautiful one cast aside all the ornaments. Like a kinnara lady who has fallen down, she lay down on the bare and uncovered ground. Having cast aside the garlands and ornaments, her face was only enveloped in anger. Despite being the wife of a king, she was distracted. She was like a star in the sky, enveloped in darkness.

Chapter 2(10)

Having instructed that the arrangements should be made for Raghava's consecration, the great and powerful king entered the inner quarters to tell the one who should be loved about the good news. She was lying down on the ground there, in a state that did not befit her. On seeing her in this state, the lord of the earth was tormented by grief. He was aged, but his wife was young. She was dearer to him than his own life. She should be sinless, but her resolution was wicked. He saw her lying down on the ground. She was like a female elephant in the forest, struck by a poisoned arrow in the course of a hunt. He touched her, like a giant elephant touching that female elephant in the forest. Scared and bereft of his senses, he engulfed her in his arms. Desiring the lotus-eyed woman, he spoke these words. 'I do not know why there is this anger in you. O queen! Who has accused you or insulted you? O fortunate one! Your lying down in the dust causes me grief. O fortunate one! Why are you lying down on the ground, as if you are unconscious? You are the one who disturbs the senses, yet your senses seem to have been possessed by a demon. There are plenty of accomplished and praised physicians. O beautiful one! Tell me what ails you and they will cure you. Whom do you desire something agreeable to be done to? Whom do you desire something disagreeable to be done to? To whom shall I do something agreeable and to whom shall I do something extremely disagreeable? Will I kill someone who should not be killed? Whom will I kill and whom will I free? Who shall be made poor? Who shall be made rich? Who shall be given riches? Whose riches will be taken away? I, and all those who are subservient to me, are under your control. I am not interested in countering any of your wishes. Even if it concerns my own life, tell me what you wish for. The earth belongs to me, wherever the wheel of the chariot goes.'

Addressed and comforted in this way, she desired to say what was disagreeable. She readied herself to make her husband suffer. 'O king! No one has insulted me. No one has shown me disrespect. There is something that I desire and it can be accomplished by you. When you know what I wish for, do it, if you so desire. After you give me your pledge, I will tell you what I wish for.' The king was completely under the control of his beloved wife and was addressed in this way. The greatly energetic one smiled a little and told Kaikeyee, 'O proud one! With the exception of Rama, tiger among men, do you not know that there is no other human I love more than you? O fortunate one! My heart is sinking, energize it through your touch. O Kaikeyee! Discerning this, tell me what virtuous act have you thought of? You know about your own strength. Therefore, you should not harbour any suspicions. I will do what causes you pleasure. I take a pledge on all my good deeds.' Delighted at his words, she told him about the desire that was in her mind, extremely terrible, like the news of a sudden death. 'With Indra at the forefront, let the thirty gods progressively hear about the boons you have pledged to bestow on me. Let the moon, the sun, the sky, the planets, the night, the day, the directions, the universe, the earth, gandharvas, rakshasas, the roamers of the night, the living beings in houses, the gods in houses and all the creatures hear the words you have spoken. He does not waver from the truth.

He is extremely energetic and knows about dharma. He is extremely controlled. He is granting me a boon. Let the gods hear about it.' The queen seized the great archer, who was ready to grant boons, but had promised excessively, confounded by desire. Thereafter, she spoke these words. 'O lord! O great king! You had granted me two boons earlier. I am asking you to grant those to me now. Listen to my words. All the arrangements have been made for Raghava's consecration. I desire that these arrangements should be used for Bharata's consecration. Rama will become an ascetic and will reside in Dandakaranya for fourteen years. He will sport matted hair and will be attired in rags and bark. Bereft of any thorns, Bharata must be made the heir apparent. Right now, I wish to see Raghava leave for the forest.'

The great king heard Kaikeyee's terrible words. He was distressed and lost his senses, like a deer which has seen a tiger. Bereft of his senses, he sank down on the bare ground and sighed deeply. In rage, the king uttered the word, 'Shame!' With his senses overtaken by sorrow, he again fell unconscious. After a long period of time, the king regained his senses, but was extremely miserable. He spoke angrily to Kaikeyee, as if he was going to burn her down with his sight. 'O cruel one! O one who is wicked in conduct! O one who destroys the lineage! What wicked act has Rama done towards you? What evil have I done? Raghava's conduct towards you has always been like that towards a mother. That being the case, why are you engaged in causing this injury to him? You entered my own house with a view to bring about my destruction. I did not know that the daughter of a king was actually a snake with virulent poison. All the living beings on earth extol Rama's qualities. What crime have I committed that I have to cast aside my beloved son? I can abandon Kousalya, Sumitra, my prosperity and my own life. But as long as I am alive, how can I cast aside Rama, who is devoted to his father? On seeing my eldest son, I am overcome by great delight. If I do not see Rama, my consciousness is destroyed. The world can exist without a sun and crops without water. However, without Rama, there cannot be life in my body. O one who has made up her mind about something wicked! Enough is enough, cast this resolution aside. I will even touch your feet with my head, be pacified.' The lord of the earth lamented like one without a protector. Suffering exceedingly in his heart, he fell down before the extended feet of his wife, the queen, and seized them. He embraced them, like one who was afflicted.

Chapter 2(11)

The great king did not deserve to lie down in this fashion. He was like Yayati, dislodged from the world of the gods after his store of good merits had been exhausted. Kaikeyee was in the form of something unpleasant, wishing to attain an undesirable objective. She was without fear and was causing fear instead. The beautiful one asked for the boons yet again. 'O great king! You pride yourself on speaking the truth and being firm in your vows. Why do you then wish to refuse the boon I asked for?' Thus addressed by Kaikeyee, for a while, King Dasharatha's anger made him lose his senses. He then replied, 'O ignoble one! You are my enemy. When Rama, bull among men, leaves for the forest and I am dead, you will accomplish your desire. May you be happy. If I tell the truth about banishing Rama to the forest in an attempt to cause pleasure to Kaikeyee, this will not be regarded as the truth. It is certain that my infinite ill fame in this world will destroy me.' His senses distracted, he lamented in this way. The sun set and night presented itself. Though it was adorned with the lunar disc, the night seemed to be afflicted. To the lamenting king, the night seemed to be dark. The aged King Dasharatha sighed long and warm sighs. With his eyes directed towards the sky, he lamented in his misery. 'I join my hands in salutation. I do not wish for a morning. Or pass swiftly.[44] I am shameless, since I am beholding Kaikeyee, who has brought about this great calamity.' After having said this, the king joined his hands in salutation and addressed Kaikeyee in these words. 'O Kaikeyee!

[44] Dasharatha is addressing the night.

Show me your favours. I am virtuous in conduct, but am distressed. I am devoted to you, but my lifespan is over. O queen! O fortunate one! You should show me your favours, especially because I am a king. O one with the beautiful hips! Everything that I have said has indeed been addressed to nothingness. O virtuous one! O child! You are kind-hearted. Show me your favours.' The king's coppery red eyes were full of tears and his sentiments were pure. However, she was wicked in her sentiments. Having heard the wonderful and piteous lamentations of her husband, the cruel one did not heed his words. At this, the king fell senseless again. His beloved one was not content and spoke against his words. On seeing that his son would be exiled, he was miserable and, bereft of his senses, fell down on the ground.

Chapter 2(12)

Afflicted by sorrow on account of his son and bereft of his senses, he fell down on the ground and writhed there. Glancing towards the descendant of the Ikshvaku lineage, the wicked one said, 'What is this wickedness you are displaying by lying down on the ground? Having heard my words, you gave me your pledge. You should remain within the sanctioned bounds. People who know about dharma say that truth is the supreme dharma. I have adhered to the truth and have urged you to follow dharma. O king! Having given a pledge to a hawk, King Shaibya gave the bird a part of his own body and obtained a supreme end.[45] In that fashion, without faltering, the energetic Alarka offered his own eyes when he was asked by a brahmana accomplished in the Vedas.[46] Devoted to truth, the lord of the rivers[47] does not budge from his pledge to the

[45] King Shibi/Shaibya granted protection to a dove that was being chased by a hawk. When the hawk asked for its natural prey, King Shibi sliced off an equivalent portion of flesh from his own body and offered it to the hawk.

[46] King Alarka offered his eyes to a blind brahmana.

[47] The ocean.

slightest extent. Adhering to his pledge and the truth, he does not transgress the shoreline. O noble one! If you do not adhere to the pledge you have given me and act accordingly, I will be abandoned. In front of you, I will cast aside my life.' The king was thus addressed by Kaikeyee, who had no hesitation at all. He was incapable of freeing himself from the bond, like Bali was deprived by Indra.[48] His heart was disturbed and his face was pale. He was like a bull trembling in the yoke, caught between two wheels.[49] The king's eyes were clouded, as if he was unable to see. With great difficulty, he used his fortitude to calm himself and spoke to Kaikeyee. 'O wicked one! Before the fire and with the use of mantras, I accepted your hand. I abandon you and the son born to me through you.'[50] At this, Kaikeyee, wicked in her conduct, again spoke to the king. She was eloquent in the use of words and became senseless with rage. She spoke these harsh words. 'O king! Why are you uttering words that are like destructive poison? Without any hesitation, you should summon your son, Rama, here. Instate my son in the kingdom and make Rama a resident of the forest. Eliminate my enemies and do what needs to be done.' The king was like an excellent horse, fiercely struck by the whip. Thus goaded, he repeatedly spoke to Kaikeyee. 'I am tied down by the noose of dharma. My senses have been destroyed. I wish to see my eldest and beloved son Rama, who is devoted to dharma.'

Hearing the king's words, Kaikeyee herself told the suta, 'Go and fetch Rama here.' Miserable about his son and with his eyes red with sorrow, the prosperous king of the Ikshvaku lineage, devoted to dharma, also spoke to the suta. Sumantra heard the piteous words and saw that the king was distressed. He joined his hands in salutation and withdrew some distance away. Because of his distress, the great king was unable to say anything. Kaikeyee, who knew about the consultation, spoke to Sumantra. 'O Sumantra!

[48] In his dwarf (vamana) incarnation, Vishnu sought the three worlds from Bali and the generous Bali gave them.

[49] Of adhering to his pledge and love for Rama.

[50] The Critical Edition excises shlokas and this breaks the continuity. By abandoning, the king meant depriving Bharata of the right to offer funeral oblations to Dasharatha.

I wish to see the handsome Rama. Fetch him here quickly.' With delight in his heart, he paid heed to these auspicious words. Thus urged, Sumantra hurried. The one who knew about dharma thought it was evident that Rama was being brought for the consecration. Having made up his mind in this way, the suta was filled with great delight. The greatly energetic one departed, wishing to see Raghava. As he suddenly emerged, near the gate, he saw many kings who had assembled. He also saw many prosperous citizens. They too had arrived near the gate and were stationed there.

Chapter 2(13)

Brahmanas, accomplished in the Vedas, had resided there during the night. With the royal priests, they also arrived at the spot. There were advisers, commanders of armies and the foremost citizens. Delighted at the prospect of Raghava's consecration, they assembled there. On the day of Pushya's conjunction, when a sparkling sun arose, the Indras among brahmanas had thought of Rama's consecration. There were golden pots of water and the auspicious seat was ornamented. The chariot was covered with shining tiger skin. Water was brought from the sacred conjunction of the Ganga and the Yamuna and also from other auspicious rivers, lakes, wells, ponds and rivulets. Water was brought from rivers that flowed eastwards, upwards, diagonally, those that merged together and from those that merged with the ocean from every direction. Honey, curds, clarified butter, parched grain, darbha grass, flowers and milk were gathered. Golden and silver pots were filled with parched grain and milk. They were filled with excellent water and shone with lotuses and lilies. An excellent whisk made of yak hair was kept ready for Rama. Pale, it spread out like the moon's beams and was decorated with jewels. There was a white umbrella, shaped like the lunar disc. It was beautiful and radiant and was kept ready for the consecration. A white bull was kept ready and a white horse was stationed there. A handsome elephant was also there, ready to be mounted. There were eight auspicious maidens, adorned in every kind of ornament. There were all kinds of musical instruments and minstrels. All this had been collected for a consecration in the kingdom of the Ikshvakus. All this had been arranged for the prince's consecration. Following the king's words, the kings had assembled. Unable to see him, they asked, 'Who will inform the king?[51] We do not see the king and the sun has arisen. Arrangements have been made for the intelligent Rama to be consecrated as the heir apparent.' Sumantra, who was respected by the king, spoke these words to the kings from various countries who were conversing among themselves. 'I will convey your words and ask the long-lived king, who must have awoken, about his welfare and the reason for his not coming.'

Having said this, the one who knew about the ancient accounts, entered the inner quarters. He pronounced words of benediction and praised Raghava.[52] 'The illustrious night has passed and the auspicious day has presented itself. O tiger among kings! Arise and do what must be done next. O king! Brahmanas, commanders of armies and merchants have arrived.' He was thus praised by the suta Sumantra, who was accomplished in counselling. The king arose and spoke these words. 'I am not asleep. Quickly bring Raghava[53] here.' King Dasharatha again told the suta this. Hearing the king's words, he bowed his head down and honoured him. Thinking about the great joy that would follow, he left the king's residence. Happy, he proceeded along the royal road that was decorated with flags and standards. The suta heard words being spoken about Rama's consecration. Sumantra saw Rama's beautiful residence, which was as radiant as Kailasa and as resplendent as Shakra's residence. There were large doors and it was adorned with hundreds of balconies. The top was golden and the gates were decorated with jewels and coral. It was as radiant as autumn clouds and was like a cave in Meru. That gigantic place was decorated with the best of wreaths and garlands. While the assembled men and the assembled kings

[51] About their arrival.
[52] Dasharatha.
[53] Rama.

looked on, the charioteer advanced on a chariot yoked to horses. Having reached the extremely expensive and extremely large residence, the charioteer was delighted and his body hair stood up. That excellent residence was like the summit of a mountain, like an immobile cloud and like a large vimana. With no one barring the way, the charioteer entered, like a *makara*[54] entering an ocean filled with a large number of jewels.

Chapter 2(14)

Passing through that crowd of people, he approached the door to the inner quarters. The one who knew about ancient accounts entered the chamber. There were young guards with polished earrings, wielding shining spears and bows, devoted, attentive and not distracted in their duties. There were aged and ornamented ones, dressed in ochre garments and holding canes. He saw these self-controlled supervisors stationed there at the doors. They were engaged in doing what brought Rama pleasure and saw him arrive. He said, 'Go and quickly tell Rama and his wife that the suta wishes to enter, to convey his father's command.' Wishing to bring him pleasure, Raghava instructed that he should be brought in. Seated on an ornamented seat, he[55] looked like Vaishravana.[56] The suta saw him on that golden couch, covered with an excellent spread. The scorcher of enemies was smeared with sacred and fragrant sandalwood paste that had the complexion of the blood of a boar. With a whisk made of yak hair in her hand, Sita stood by his side. He was like the moon, with Chitra nakshatra by the side. Blazing in his own energy, he seemed to scorch like the sun. The minstrel was accomplished in humility. Humbly, he worshipped the granter of boons. Joining his hands in salutation, he asked about the welfare of the one who was reclining on the couch. Sumantra, who was

[54] A mythical aquatic creature, which can be loosely translated as shark or crocodile.
[55] Rama.
[56] Kubera.

respected by the king, spoke these words to the prince. 'O prince! O Kousalya's excellent son! Your father and Queen Kaikeyee wish to see you. Go there quickly.'

Thus addressed, the immensely radiant lion among men was delighted. Honouring him, he spoke to Sita. 'O queen! The king and the queen have summoned me to their presence. They have certainly thought of something connected with the consecration. It is evident that the extremely generous one with the maddening eyes[57] must intend to do something for me and has accordingly urged the king. A messenger befitting the assembly there has arrived. It is certain that the king will anoint me as the heir apparent today. I must quickly leave this place and go and see the king. You stay happily in this household and find your pleasure.' The black-eyed Sita honoured her husband. Thinking of auspicious things, she followed him up to the door. He greeted all those who had assembled there and ascended the supreme chariot, which was like a fire. Its radiance was golden and it stole the eyes. Supreme horses that were like baby elephants were yoked to it. It was as swift as the thousand-eyed Indra's chariot, yoked to tawny horses. Raghava, blazing in his prosperity, departed swiftly. Its clatter was like the roaring of clouds in the sky. As it emerged from the residence, its beauty was like that of the moon emerging from clouds. Raghava's younger brother, Lakshmana, ascended the chariot at the rear. He held a whisk and an umbrella in his hands and protected his brother. As the crowds of people emerged in every direction, a tumultuous roar arose. Raghava heard the conversation of the people who had assembled there. All the citizens of the city cheerfully spoke many things about his own prospective rule. 'Through the king's favours, Raghava is advancing towards great prosperity today. He will make all our dreams of prosperity come true, once he becomes our ruler. If he rules over this kingdom for a long time, the people will have everything to gain.' He proceeded amidst the noise created by the horses and elephants. Sutas and magadhas pronounced benedictions ahead of him. The best of musicians praised his greatness and he

[57] A reference to Kaikeyee.

proceeded like Vaishravana. The squares were full of large crowds of people and female elephants, male elephants, chariots and horses. There were shops with a lot of jewels and many commodities. As he went along, Rama saw the beautiful and large road.

Chapter 2(15)

With his joyful well-wishers, Rama ascended the chariot. He saw the beautiful city, populated by crowds of people. Painted white, the houses were like clouds. Rama proceeded along the royal road, amidst incense from *agaru*.[58] The excellent royal road was adorned and was free of obstructions. There were many kinds of merchandise and diverse kinds of food. He heard the benedictions pronounced by many well-wishers and proceeded, honouring all the men as they deserved. 'Follow the conduct of your grandfathers and great-grandfathers. Get consecrated today. Rule according to the path they traversed. We were nurtured by his father and by his earlier ancestors. Once Rama becomes the king, all of us will reside even more happily. We have had enough of enjoying objects of pleasure and we have had enough of pursuing the supreme objective, now that we see Rama leave, to become established in the kingdom. There is nothing that will be more agreeable to us than that the infinitely energetic Rama should become consecrated in the kingdom.' The well-wishers uttered these and other auspicious words, honouring his own self. Hearing these, Rama proceeded along the royal road. No one could turn his sight away from that supreme among men. No man was capable of crossing Raghava. He had dharma in his soul and exhibited compassion towards all the four varnas and towards those who were aged. Therefore, they were devoted to him. He reached the royal palace, which was like the great Indra's residence. The prince entered his father's abode, which blazed in prosperity. Dasharatha's son passed through all

[58] Paste from the agallochum tree.

the chambers. Taken his leave of all the people, with a pure heart, he entered the inner quarters. All the people were delighted. The king's son entered and approached his father. They waited for him to emerge again, just as the lord of the rivers waits for the moon to rise.

Chapter 2(16)

Rama saw his father seated on an auspicious seat. His face was distressed. He was with Kaikeyee, who was tending to him. Humbly, he first worshipped at his father's feet. Extremely controlled, he next worshipped at Kaikeyee's feet. With tears in his eyes, the miserable king only uttered the word 'Rama'. He was incapable of glancing at him, or saying anything more. He had never seen such a fearful form of the king earlier. Therefore, Rama was overcome with fear, like when one touches a snake with one's feet. The great king sighed, his senses miserable. He was afflicted by sorrow and torment. His mind was disturbed and grief-stricken. He was like an ocean that cannot be agitated, turbulent because of a garland of waves. He was like the sun during an eclipse, or like a rishi who has uttered a lie. On seeing the unthinkable, his father enveloped in sorrow, he was also agitated, like the ocean on the day of the full moon. Engaged in ensuring the welfare of his father, Rama began to think. 'Why has the king not greeted me back today? At other times, even when he is enraged, my father is pacified on seeing me. However, today, he seems exhausted on seeing me.' Rama became miserable and afflicted by sorrow. Greeting Kaikeyee, Rama spoke these words. 'Have I ignorantly committed a crime that my father is angry with me? Tell me and pacify him. His face is distressed and he is miserable. He is not speaking to me. Is something troubling him physically or mentally, making him suffer? It is rare to be happy always. Has something happened to Prince Bharata, handsome to behold, or the great-spirited Shatrughna? Has something inauspicious befallen my mothers? If the king is angry, I do not wish to remain alive even for an instant, causing dissatisfaction to the great king and not following my father's words. A great-souled man perceives him[59] as a divinity from whom he himself has emerged. That being evident, how can one act otherwise? I trust that in your rage, you have not uttered any harsh words, as a result of which, my father has been slighted and his mind is disturbed. O queen! I am asking you. Tell me the truth. Why is the lord of men suffering from an affliction that has not happened earlier? If the king's words lead to that, I will leap into the fire. I will consume fierce poison, or submerge myself in the ocean. The king is engaged in my welfare and I am devoted to my preceptor, my father. O queen! Therefore, tell me the king's words and what he desires. I promise to do that. Rama does not speak in two contrary ways.'

He was truthful in speech and upright. The ignoble Kaikeyee spoke these extremely terrible words to Rama. 'O Raghava! Earlier, in a battle between the gods and the asuras, your father was hurt by darts. When I protected him in that great battle, he granted me two boons. O Raghava! On that basis, I have asked the king for Bharata's consecration and for you to leave for Dandakaranya today. O best among men! If you desire that you and your father should stick to the pledge of truth, then hear my words. Adhere to your father's instructions and to what he has pledged. You must go to the forest for fourteen years. You will have to reside in Dandakaranya for fourteen years. You will have to forget about the consecration and wear bark and rags. Bharata will rule this earth, full of many jewels and with horses, chariots and elephants, from the city of Kosala.'[60] Rama, the slayer of enemies, heard these disagreeable words, which were like death. However, he was not distressed and spoke to Kaikeyee. 'It shall be that way. I shall depart from this residence to there, the forest. To ensure that the king's pledge is satisfied, I will wear bark and rags. But I wish to know why the invincible and great king, the scorcher of enemies, is unhappy with me. O queen! You should not be angry. You should be extremely happy. In front of you, I am telling you

[59] The father.

[60] Meaning the capital of Kosala, Ayodhya.

that I will go the forest in bark and rags. I am grateful to the king. How can I not be engaged in the welfare of my preceptor, my father? Engaged by him, I will faithfully do what is agreeable to him. But something unpleasant is tormenting my mind and heart. Why has the king not told me about Bharata's consecration himself? Without being urged, I would have cheerfully given my brother, Bharata, Sita, the kingdom, the desired riches and even my own life. To ensure what brings you pleasure and to accomplish the pledge, why did my father, Indra among men, not urge me himself? Therefore, you should comfort him. Why is the lord of the earth sprinkling the earth with tears from his eyes and releasing these inauspicious tears? On the instructions of the king, let messengers on fleet-footed steeds go to Bharata's maternal uncle's household and fetch him here. I will hasten to leave for Dandakaranya, unthinkingly following my father's words. I will reside there for fourteen years.'

On hearing Rama's words, Kaikeyee was delighted. Believing them, she asked Raghava to hurry about his departure. 'Let it be that way. Let messengers on fleet-footed steeds leave for Bharata's maternal uncle's house and let those men bring him back. Since you are so anxious, I think it is inappropriate that you should tarry. O Rama! Therefore, you should quickly leave for the forest. It is because of his shame that the king has not addressed you himself. O best among men! This rage is nothing and it will pass. O Rama! Until you leave for the forest and depart from this city, you father will not bathe, or eat anything.' The king was overcome by sorrow. He cried 'shame' and sighed. Losing his senses, he fell down on the golden couch. Urged by Kaikeyee, Rama raised the king. Like a horse goaded by a whip, he hastened to leave for the forest. Those words were terrible, disagreeable and ignoble. Having heard them, devoid of distress, Rama addressed Kaikeyee in these words. 'O queen! I am not attached to artha. I am not interested in the ways of the world. Know me to be the equal of a rishi, only interested in being established in dharma. I will do whatever I am capable of doing to ensure pleasure, even if it amounts to giving up my own life. There is nothing greater than acting in accordance with dharma, in the form of serving one's father or complying with his words. Even though he has not told me, I will follow your words and dwell alone in the forest for fourteen years. O Kaikeyee! Since you have told the king and not me,[61] it is evident that you suspect my qualities and take me to be inferior to my lord. After taking my mother's leave and persuading Sita, today itself, I will leave for the great forest of Dandaka. Bharata will rule the kingdom and tend to our father. This is eternal dharma and it is your task to ensure this.'

On hearing Rama's words, his father was struck with extreme grief. In a voice that choked with tears, he wept loudly. Rama worshipped at the feet of his unconscious father. The immensely radiant one also fell down at the feet of the ignoble Kaikeyee. Rama circumambulated his father and Kaikeyee. He emerged from the inner quarters and saw the well-wishers. Lakshmana, the extender of Sumitra's delight, was extremely angry. With eyes full of tears, he followed at the rear. Rama circumambulated the vessel meant for the consecration. Glancing here and there, but without being disturbed, he slowly left. The destruction of the kingdom did not affect his great prosperity, like the onset of the night cannot touch the one with the cool rays.[62] He was pleasant and was loved by the people. Having cast aside the earth, he wished to leave for the forest. He was beyond worldly pursuits and no mental disturbance could be discerned. He controlled his senses and subdued the sorrow in his mind. To inform his mother about the disagreeable tidings, he entered his own house. He entered the house, which was filled with great joy. On seeing them, he did not tell them about the calamity that had struck. Suspecting the misery of his well-wishers, Rama did not exhibit the least bit of disturbance.

Chapter 2(17)

Rama was extremely hurt and sighed like an elephant. However, he controlled himself and with his brother, went to his mother's

[61] About Kaikeyee's wishes.

[62] The moon.

inner quarters. He saw the extremely revered and aged man seated there, at the door to the house. He was stationed there, with many others.[63] He entered the first chamber and saw the second chamber. Aged brahmanas who were accomplished in the Vedas and honoured by the king were there. Bowing down before those aged ones, Rama saw the third chamber. Aged women and girls were engaged in guarding the door to that. As he entered the house, the joy of the women was enhanced. They quickly informed Rama's mother about the agreeable news.[64] Queen Kousalya had spent the night in a self-controlled way. In the morning, for the welfare of her son, she was worshipping Vishnu. She was cheerful and attired in silken garments. She was always devoted to her vows. To the sound of auspicious mantras, she was then offering oblations into the fire. Rama entered the auspicious inner quarters of his mother. He saw his mother there, offering oblations into the fire. Having seen that her son, whom she had not seen for a long time and who enhanced the delight of his mother, had arrived, she was happy, like a mare on seeing its colt. Kousalya, affectionate towards her son, spoke these agreeable and beneficial words to the invincible Raghava, her own son. 'May you obtain the lifespans of the aged who are devoted to dharma and of great-souled rajarshis. May you obtain fame and ensure the dharma of your lineage. O Raghava! Behold. Your father, the king, is devoted to the pledge of truth. Today, the one with dharma in his soul, will consecrate you as the heir apparent.'

Advancing a bit towards his mother, Raghava joined his hands in salutation. He was naturally humble and bowed down more, out of respect for her. 'O queen! It is certain that you do not know that a great calamity has presented itself. This will cause sorrow to you, Vaidehi and Lakshmana. I will have to live alone in the forest for fourteen years. Like a sage, I will have to forsake meat and live on honey, roots and fruits. The great king will make Bharata the heir apparent. As for me, like an ascetic, I will be exiled to Dandakaranya.' She did not deserve unhappiness.[65] On

[63] As guards.
[64] That he had come.
[65] The Critical Edition excises a shloka where Kousalya falls down, senseless.

seeing that his mother had fallen down like a plantain tree and was unconscious, Rama raised her. He raised the distressed one, who had fallen down like an overburdened horse. Her limbs were covered with dust. He touched her with his hands. Rama seated the one who was afflicted by grief, though she deserved happiness. While Lakshmana heard, she addressed the tiger among men. 'O Raghava! Had I not had a son, I would not have been this miserable. My sorrow is greater, since I see that I will now be without a son. Had I been barren, I would have had only one sorrow in my mind. O son! There would have been no torment but for the fact that I don't have a son. While my husband possessed his manliness, I did not experience any benefit or happiness earlier. O Rama! All my hopes were vested in my son. I have heard many disagreeable words that shatter the heart. Though I am superior to them, I have heard them from my inferior co-wives. What can bring greater grief to a woman than that? Despite you being near me, I have been slighted in this fashion. O son! On top of that, when you leave, it is certain that death is better for me. When they see Kaikeyee's son, people who serve me and follow me now will no longer speak to me. O Raghava! Seventeen years have passed since your birth. That time has elapsed, while I have expectantly waited for my sorrows to be over. I have observed many fasts and exhausting yogas. In vain have I nurtured you in my misery. My sorrows are insurmountable. Since my heart has not been shattered, like the banks of a new river overflowing with new water during the monsoon, I think that it is still. It is certain that there is no death for me. Yama's abode has no space for me. The Destroyer[66] doesn't want to carry me off either, like a weeping deer carried by a lion. Since my still heart is not pierced and shattered, it is certainly made of iron. This sorrow is ingrained in my body and it is certain that I will not die before my time. Because of this sorrow, my vows, donations and control have clearly been futile. For the sake of offspring, I tormented myself through austerities. That too has been futile, like seeds sown in barren soil. I am afflicted by great distress. Without you, I will

[66] Yama.

be like a cow without its calf. Had one been able to obtain an untimely death through one's own wishes, I would have departed now and obtained the world hereafter.' She was extremely unhappy and angry. As Raghava looked on, she lamented a lot. Amidst that great hardship, she spoke in this way to her son, like a kinnara lady who had been tied.

Chapter 2(18)

Kousalya, Rama's mother, was lamenting. Distressed, Lakshmana addressed her in words that were appropriate for the occasion. 'O noble lady! The prospect of Raghava abandoning the prosperous kingdom and going to the forest, because one is succumbing to the words of a woman, does not appeal to me. The aged king acts in a contrary way because he has been goaded by sensual pleasures. What can one say to a person excited by Manmatha? I do not see any taint in Raghava, or any sin that he has committed, that he should be exiled from the kingdom to the forest. In this world, I have not seen any man, whether he is an enemy or whether he has been banished, who points out any sin in him. He is like a god—upright, controlled and kind towards enemies. Looking towards dharma, who can unnecessarily cast aside such a son? The words of the king suggest that he has again become a child. Remembering the conduct of kings, how can one's heart act in such a way towards a son? Before any other man gets to know about what has happened, with my help, make this kingdom your own.[67] O Raghava! With a bow, I will protect you at your side, stationed like Yama. Who is capable of surpassing me? O bull among men! If anyone acts disagreeably against you, I will use sharp arrows to make Ayodhya devoid of all its men, those who are on Bharata's side and those who wish him well. I will slay all of them. It is indeed the mild who get vanquished.

[67] This is addressed to Rama.

O subjugator of enemies! Exhibiting great enmity towards you and me, who has the strength to give Bharata the prosperity? O queen! In truth, my sentiments are devoted to my brother. I truthfully pledge this on my bow and on whatever I have donated at sacrifices. O queen! Know that if Rama enters a blazing fire or the forest, before him, I will destroy myself there. Like a sun that rises, I will use my valour to dispel the darkness of your sorrow. O queen! Behold my valour. Let Raghava also witness it.' Hearing the great-souled Lakshmana's words, Kousalya completely abandoned her weeping and grief. She told Rama, 'O son! You have heard the words your brother, Lakshmana, has spoken. If it pleases you, you should next act in accordance with this. You have heard the words of adharma spoken to me by my co-wife. Leaving me in this tormented and grieving state, you should not go away from here. O one who knows about dharma! O one who acts according to dharma! If you wish to follow dharma, remain here and tend to me. Perform a supreme act of dharma. O son! Dwelling in his own house in a controlled way, Kashyapa served his mother. Thereby performing supreme austerities, he went to heaven. The king should be worshipped because of the respect he wields. But I am also like that. I am not giving you permission. You should not go to the forest. Separated from you, what will I do with my life or with happiness? It is better for me to be with you, even if I have to survive on grass. I am afflicted by misery. If you abandon me and go to the forest, without eating, I will give up my life. I will be incapable of remaining alive. I will then myself obtain the hell that is famous in the worlds, like the one obtained by the ocean, the lord of the rivers, on killing a brahmana.'[68] Distressed, his mother, Kousalya, lamented in this way.

With dharma in his soul, Rama addressed her in words that were in conformity with dharma. 'I do not possess the strength to act contrary to my father's words. I bow down my head and seek your favours. I wish to go to the forest. The learned rishi

[68] Suicide is a crime. The brahmana in question is Vritra. Indra acquired a sin from killing a brahmana and part of that sin was distributed to the ocean, the remainder was distributed among the earth, trees and women.

Kandu knew about dharma and followed his vows. Even then, obeying his father's words, he killed a cow. Earlier, in our lineage, following their father Sagara's instructions, his sons dug up the earth and faced a great destruction. In the forest, Rama,[69] Jamadagni's son, acted in accordance with his father's words and used his battleaxe to kill his mother, Renuka. Indeed, I am not the only one who is acting in accordance with his father's command. I am only following the path that has been agreed upon earlier. That is the way I must act. There is no other mode on earth. There is no ill fame from acting in accordance with a father's words.' Having spoken to his mother in this way, he next addressed Lakshmana. 'O Lakshmana! I know about your supreme affection for me. However, you do not understand the meaning of truth and tranquility. Dharma is supreme in the world. Truth is established in dharma. Our father's supreme words are also laced with dharma. O brave one! If one is established in dharma, if one has given one's word to a father, a mother, or a brahmana, one must not violate it. I am incapable of violating what my father has asked me to do. O brave one! Kaikeyee has urged me in this way because of my father's words. Therefore, cast aside this ignoble attitude of resorting to the dharma of kshatriyas. Follow dharma, not ferocity. Follow my inclination.' Lakshmana's elder brother spoke to his brother in this affectionate way. Joining his hands in salutation and bowing his head down, he again spoke to Kousalya. 'O Queen! Grant me permission to go to the forest. I am requesting you, on my life. Perform the benedictions. After accomplishing my pledge, I will again return to the city from the forest. My fame is only because of the kingdom. I cannot turn my back on this great glory. O queen! Following the dharma of those on earth, no one lives for a long time. Grant me the boon today.' The bull among men sought his mother's favours. Because of his prowess, he wished to go to Dandaka. He used the foresight of his heart to comfort his younger brother and circumambulated his mother.

[69] Parashurama.

Chapter 2(19)

He[70] was like an Indra among elephants, miserable, distressed and extremely angry.[71] With his eyes dilated in rage, he seemed to be sighing. Rama resorted to the fortitude that was in his own inner self. He addressed his beloved brother, Soumitri, who wished him well. 'O Soumitri! You collected various objects for the consecration. Now that there will be no consecration, collect similar objects.[72] My mother's mind was tormented on account of my consecration. Act so that she does not harbour any suspicions.[73] O Soumitri! Not for an instant, can I tolerate misery and suspicion being generated in her mind, nor can I ignore it. Consciously or unconsciously, I cannot recall a single occasion when I have done anything disagreeable towards my mother or father. My father has always been truthful, unwavering from the truth. Truth is his valour. He is scared of what will happen in the world hereafter.[74] May he be fearless. If we do not refrain from this act,[75] his mind will be tormented that truth has not been followed and I will also be tormented. O Lakshmana! Therefore, refrain from this rite of consecration. Let me again say that I wish to leave for the forest. O son of a king! If I leave for the forest today, she[76] will be successful and will no longer have any anxiety about her son, Bharata's, consecration. If I attire myself in rags and bark and sporting matted hair, leave for the forest, Kaikeyee will be happy in her mind. I should not cause grief to the one who has given me intelligence and training and instructed me about great control of the mind.[77] I must leave quickly. O Soumitri! It remains to be seen whether Yama

[70] Lakshmana.

[71] Towards Kaikeyee.

[72] This can be interpreted in two ways—collect objects for departure to the forest or collect objects for Bharata's consecration. The latter is probably right.

[73] The mother means Kaikeyee, who may still have suspicions about Rama actually leaving for the forest.

[74] In case he doesn't keep his pledge.

[75] Of consecration.

[76] Kaikeyee.

[77] A reference to Dasharatha.

will grant me the kingdom once I return from my exile. But for destiny and the sanction of the gods, how could Kaikeyee's powers and my affliction have happened? O amiable one! You know that I have never exhibited any difference between my mothers, nor have I ever differentiated between their sons. However, to prevent my consecration and ensure my exile, she has used wicked words and fierce speech. This couldn't have occurred without the sanction of the gods. That lady is a princess and possesses the requisite qualities. Yet, in her husband's presence, she addressed me like an ordinary woman and caused me grief. Whatever is unthinkable is destiny and no being can transgress it. It is evident that this conflict between her and me has been caused by this. O Soumitri! Which man can fight against destiny? It is evident that nothing can be done, except to accept it. Happiness, unhappiness, fear, anger, gain, loss, what happens, what does not happen—all of these are indeed the work of destiny. I suffer no torment on account of the consecration not happening. Therefore, listen to me and still any torment. Quickly stop all the rites that have been arranged for the consecration. O Lakshmana! Let my younger mother[78] not harbour any suspicion about my standing in the way of the kingdom. She has spoken those undesirable words because of destiny. You know the power of destiny.'

Chapter 2(20)

As Rama spoke again, Lakshmana lowered his head and heard, his mind filled with both misery and delight. The bull among men had his brows furrowed in a frown. Like an angry and large snake inside its hole, he sighed. With that frown, he was extremely difficult to behold. His angry visage was like that of a wrathful lion. He waved his forearm around, like an elephant waving its trunk around, when it bends its body and lowers its neck. With the upper

[78] Kaikeyee.

portions of his eyes he glanced sideways at his brother and said, 'There is a great deal of respect in you for what doesn't warrant it. In connection with dharma, you do not suspect that there are people who are wicked. O bull among kshatriyas! O valiant leader! How can a person like you be scared of destiny, which is powerless? Like a miserable person, why are you praising destiny, which is powerless? Why do you not harbour any suspicion about those two wicked ones?[79] O one who knows about dharma! Why do you not comprehend that there are those who deceive in the name of dharma? People will hate the idea of starting a consecration for someone else. O lord of the earth! I hate the fact that your intelligence is pulled in two opposite directions and that you are confused about the subject of dharma. You are of the view that this is the power of destiny. I do not like the idea that you are ignoring them[80] because of this. Impotent ones who lack valour follow destiny. Brave ones with self-respect do not serve destiny. A man who is capable of countering destiny through his manliness is not helpless and does not suffer from lassitude on account of destiny. Today, the difference between destiny and a man's manliness will be witnessed. The distinction between a man and his destiny will become manifest. Today, people will see that destiny has been crushed by my manliness. The destiny that has destroyed your instatement in the kingdom will itself be destroyed. Just as one uses a fierce goad on a crazy and rampaging elephant, I will use my manliness to counter and repel this destiny. Today, all the guardians of the worlds and all the three worlds will not be able to prevent Rama's consecration, not to speak of our father. O king! Those who futilely support the prospect of your exile in the forest will themselves have to dwell in the forest for fourteen years. I will thus shatter her[81] hopes and those of our father. For the sake of her son, she is seeking to create an obstruction to your consecration. The power of my fierce manliness will cause misery to those who seek to counter my strength, far more than the strength of destiny. O noble one! After having ruled over the subjects for

[79] Dasharatha and Kaikeyee.

[80] Dasharatha and Kaikeyee.

[81] Kaikeyee's.

more than one thousand years, you will leave for the forest and leave the kingdom for your sons. Residing in the forest has been recommended as proper conduct by former royal sages, but after having ruled over the subjects like sons and then handing them over to one's own sons. O one with dharma in his soul! O Rama! It is possible that you do not wish for the kingdom because you doubt that you will yourself be able to take care of it attentively as a king and will therefore not enjoy the worlds meant for the valiant. O brave one! Know that I will protect your kingdom, like the shoreline holds back the ocean. With all the auspicious objects, be consecrated. Because of my strength, I alone am sufficient to counter the kings.[82] These arms are not meant to be decorations and this bow is not an ornament. This sword is not intended for buckling and these arrows are not meant to be immobile. All these four[83] are meant for subduing enemies. I am not excessively affectionate towards someone I regard as an enemy. This sword is sharp at the edges and is as radiant as a flash of lightning. While I wield it, I do not respect any enemy, not even the wielder of the vajra. Elephants, horses, men, arms, thighs and heads will be severed by the sword and will be strewn on the earth, which will become desolate and impenetrable. Today, they will be shattered like mountains, struck by this sharp and blazing sword. Elephants will fall down on the ground, like clouds tinged with lightning. When I wear finger guards made out of the skin of lizards and wield my bow and arrow, which man, who prides himself on being a man, will be able to stand before me? I will use my arrows to strike at the inner organs of horses and elephants. Even if many strive against me, I alone am enough to take on many. O lord! Today, the power of my weapons will establish your prowess, remove the lordship from the king[84] and confer the lordship on you. O Rama! You should act. Your arms are meant for sporting sandalwood paste, wearing armlets, ensuring prosperity and protecting your well-wishers. Repulse the agents who seek to create obstructions towards your consecration.

[82] Those who oppose the consecration.

[83] Arms, bow, arrows and sword.

[84] Dasharatha.

Tell me. Which ill-wisher deserves to be deprived of his life, fame and well-wishers by me? I am your servant. Instruct me about how this earth can be brought under your subjugation.' The extender of the Raghava lineage[85] repeatedly wiped away Lakshmana's tears and comforted him. He said, 'I stand by my father's pledge. O amiable one! Listen to me. This is the path of virtue.'

Chapter 2(21)

Kousalya saw that he was firm about following his father's command. Her voice choking with tears, she spoke words that were full of dharma. 'He[86] has never faced unhappiness earlier. He has dharma in his soul. He is pleasant in speech towards all creatures. He has been born from me and Dasharatha. How can he survive on *unchha*?[87] The dependents and servants will enjoy pleasant food. How will their protector survive on roots and fruits in the forest? On hearing that the qualified and beloved Raghava has been exiled by the king, who will believe this? Who will not be frightened? Separated from him, my misery will be like that of a great, unmatched and colourful fire which burns down dry kindling during the winter. How can a cow not follow her wandering calf? O son! Wherever you go, I will follow you.' The bull among men heard the words spoken by his mother, who was extremely miserable.

Having heard, Rama addressed his mother in these words. 'Kaikeyee has deceived the king. When I leave for the forest and he is also abandoned by you, it is certain that he will not remain alive. Only a cruel woman is capable of forsaking her husband and such a thought is reprehensible. You should not do this. Kakutstha, my father, is the lord of the earth. As long as he is alive, you should serve him. That is eternal dharma.' Kousalya, beautiful in appearance,

[85] Rama.

[86] Rama.

[87] There are grains left after a crop has been harvested, or after grain has been milled. If one subsists on these leftovers, that is known as *unchhavritti*.

was addressed by Rama in this way. Extremely pleased, she spoke to Rama, the performer of unblemished deeds, and agreed. Rama, supreme among the upholders of dharma, again spoke these words to his mother, who sorrowed greatly. 'It is my duty and yours to follow the instructions of my father. He is the king and master. He is the best among preceptors. Among all masters, he is the supreme lord. After wandering around in the great forest for fourteen years, I will be extremely happy to abide by your words.' She was thus addressed by her beloved son. Kousalya, extremely afflicted and devoted to her son, replied, her face overflowing with tears. 'I am incapable of residing in the midst of my co-wives. O Kakutstha! Looking towards your father, if you have made up your mind to leave for the forest, take me also with you, like a wild deer.' She wept as she said this. Rama told the one who was lamenting, 'As long as the husband is alive, he is a woman's master and god. Today, as our master, the king exercises his powers over you and me. Bharata has dharma in his soul and speaks pleasantly to all creatures. Always devoted to dharma, he will follow you. When I leave, the king will be afflicted by grief over his son. Be attentive towards him, so that he does not suffer from the slightest bit of exhaustion. Even if a supreme woman is devoted to vows and fasting, if she does not follow her husband, she comes to an evil end. She must serve her husband and be engaged in bringing him pleasure. Since ancient times, this dharma has been witnessed in the world and has been spoken about in the Vedas, shrutis and smritis.[88] O queen! For my sake, worship brahmanas who are excellent in their vows. Expectantly looking forward to my return, spend the time in this way. If the supreme upholder of dharma is still alive, when I return, you will obtain the supreme object of your desire.' In this way, Rama spoke to the one whose eyes were full of tears. Kousalya was afflicted by grief on account of her son. She addressed Rama in these words. 'O son! O lord! Go without any disturbance. May you always be fortunate.' The queen saw that

[88] Shrutis are sacred texts that have been revealed, they have no author. Smritis are sacred texts that have authors. They have been heard and memorized, and thus passed down the generations.

Rama had made up his mind to leave for the forest. Supreme in her intelligence, she addressed Rama in auspicious words, wishing to ensure that benedictions were pronounced.

Chapter 2(22)

Rama's spirited mother cast aside her grief. To perform the auspicious rites, she purified herself and touched water. 'May the Sadhyas, Vishvadevas, Maruts and maharshis be favourable. May Dhatri, Vidhatri, Pusha, Bhaga and Aryama be favourable.[89] May the seasons, fortnights, months, years, nights, days and muhurtas always look favourably on you. O son! May the smritis, resolution, dharma, the illustrious god Skanda, Soma and Brihaspati protect you in every way. May the saptarshis and Narada protect you in every direction. While you intelligently wander around in the great forest in the garb of a sage, may the nakshatras, all the planets and gods also do this. As long as you are in that desolate forest, may monkeys, scorpions, gnats, mosquitoes, reptiles and insects not frequent those groves. O son! May giant elephants, lions, tigers, bears, those with fangs, and fierce and horned buffaloes not exhibit hostility towards you. O son! Worshipped by me, may spirited and fierce creatures that survive on human flesh not cause you injury. May your paths be auspicious. May your valour meet with success. O Rama! O son! Depart auspiciously, with all your prosperity. May those in the firmament and also those on earth be auspicious towards you. May all the gods and those who cause you impediments also be auspicious. As long as you reside in the forest, may the lord of all the worlds,[90] Brahma the creator, the preserver,[91] the rishis and all the remaining gods protect you.' The

[89] Dhatri and Vidhatri are often used synonymously. Dhatri has the sense of creator, while Vidhatri can be translated as ordainer. Pusha, Bhaga and Aryama are three of the twelve Adityas, the sons of Aditi. They can be regarded as different aspects of the sun god.

[90] Probably meaning Shiva.

[91] Vishnu.

illustrious and large-eyed one uttered these and other benedictions, with garlands and fragrances, worshipping the large number of gods. 'When Vritra was destroyed, the one with the one thousand eyes was worshipped by all the gods with auspicious portents. May those auspicious portents also occur for you. In ancient times, when Suparna[92] went in search of amrita, Vinata prayed for auspicious portents. May those auspicious portents occur for you.' To ensure success and protect him, Kousalya invoked mantras on the sacred herb *vishalyakarani*.[93] The illustrious one invoked the fragrance on his forehead and embraced him. She said, 'O son! O Rama! Go cheerfully and be successful. O son! I will see you return to Ayodhya, without disease and successful in every way. You will be happy and will reside in this palace then. Worshipped by me, the large number of gods, Shiva and the others, the maharshis, demons, giant asuras, serpents and the directions will wish for your welfare, when you spend a long time in the forest.' Her eyes full of tears, she thus completed the rites of benedictions in the decreed way. She circumambulated Raghava and repeatedly embraced him. Having thus been circumambulated by the queen, he repeatedly pressed his mother's feet. The immensely illustrious Raghava then went to Sita's abode, blazing in his own prosperity.

Chapter 2(23)

Having bowed down before Kousalya, Rama was ready to leave for the forest. He was firmly established on the path of dharma and his mother had performed the rites of benediction. Surrounded by men, the prince entered the royal road. Because of his qualities and conduct, he crushed the hearts of the people. The ascetic Vaidehi had still not heard anything. Her heart was still set on his instatement as the heir apparent. Happy in

[92] Garuda. Garuda's mother was Vinata.

[93] Literally, something that removes arrows/weapons. The interpretation is that she fastened an amulet on him, with vishalyakarani in it.

her mind, she gratefully performed all the rites for the gods. Knowledgeable about the dharma of kings, she waited for the prince. Rama entered his own residence, which was decorated well. It was full of cheerful people. Humbly, he lowered his face a little.

On seeing that her husband was trembling, Sita stood up. She saw that he was tormented by grief and that his senses were distracted with thoughts. She saw that he was pale in face and sweating, as if he couldn't stand it. Tormented by sorrow, she asked, 'O lord! What has happened? O Raghava! Barhaspata Pushya is full of prosperity today.[94] That is indeed what the wise brahmanas have pronounced. Why are you distressed in your mind? Your beautiful face is covered. It does not shine like an umbrella with one hundred ribs, white like the foam in water. When fanned by a whisk, your lotus-eyed face is as radiant as the moon or a swan. But your face is not being fanned today. O bull among men! Delighted, the vandis, sutas and magadhas aren't singing praises today. Nor are they pronouncing the auspicious benedictions. After you have sprinkled your head,[95] nor are the brahmanas, accomplished in the Vedas, following the decreed rites and smearing your head with honey and curds. The ordinary people, all the ornamented leaders of the *shreni*s[96] and the inhabitants of the city and the countryside do not wish to follow you. The best *pushyaratha*[97] is yoked to four swift steeds with golden reins. Why is it not proceeding in front of you? O brave one! The handsome elephant is worshipped because it possesses the auspicious signs. It has the complexion of a dark cloud or a mountain. Why can't it be seen, proceeding before you? O handsome one! O brave one! Ahead of you, I do not see it bearing the golden and colourful throne. When arrangements have been made for the consecration, why is the complexion of your

[94] Brihaspati is the lord of Pushya nakshatra.

[95] Meaning, washed your hair.

[96] A shreni is like a guild, it is an association of traders or artisans who follow the same line of business. The word means a rank or line.

[97] A pushyaratha is a special chariot, ornamented and decorated, used not for fighting, but for pleasure.

face like this? This has never happened before. Why can no joy be discerned?'

She lamented in this way. The descendant of the Raghu lineage replied, 'O Sita! My father is exiling me to the forest. O one who knows about dharma! O one who follows dharma! You have been born in a great lineage! O Janakee! In due order, listen to what has befallen me. My father, King Dasharatha, is pledged to the truth. In earlier times, pleased in his mind, he granted two great boons to Kaikeyee. Now, the king has made arrangements for my consecration. Subduing him because of dharma, she has now held him to that pledge. I will have to dwell in Dandaka for fourteen years and my father will make Bharata the heir apparent. Before leaving for the desolate forest, I have come here to see you. When you are in Bharata's presence, you must never praise me. A prosperous person can never tolerate another one being praised. Therefore, in front of Bharata, you must never praise my qualities. You need not serve him in any special way. However, when you are near him, be kindly disposed. O spirited one! Observing the pledge given by my senior, I will leave for the forest today. Be steady. O fortunate one! O unblemished one! When I have left for the forest, frequented by sages, you can observe vows and fasting. You can wake at the appropriate time and following the ordinances, worship the gods. Worship my father, Dasharatha, lord of men. My mother, Kousalya, is aged and afflicted by grief. Placing dharma at the forefront, you should indeed show her respect. All my other mothers have always deserved worship. In their love, affection and fondness, all my mothers have been equal. In particular, I love Lakshmana and Shatrughna more than my own life. You should look on them as brothers or sons. Never do anything that is disagreeable to Bharata. He is the king and the lord, for the country and for the family. Kings are pleased when they are worshipped with good conduct and served carefully. If this is not done, they are enraged. If their own sons cause injury, kings cast them aside and accept other capable people. O beloved one! O beautiful one! I will leave for the great forest. Reside here. Never do anything injurious. Act in accordance with my words.'

Chapter 2(24)

Vaidehi, who deserved to be loved and was pleasant in speech, was addressed in this way. However, because of her love, she became angry and addressed her husband in this way. 'O noble son! A father, a mother, a brother, a son and a daughter-in-law enjoy the fruits of their own auspicious deeds. They reap their own respective fortunes. O bull among men! However, the wife alone reaps her husband's fortune. Therefore, I have also been instructed to reside in the forest. In this world and in the next, for a woman, the husband is alone the refuge—not a father, not a son, not her own self, not a mother and not a friend. O Raghava! If you leave for the impenetrable forest today, I will proceed in front of you, trampling down kusha grass and thorns. Like water cast aside after a drink, abandon all jealousy and anger. O brave one! Have faith. There is no wickedness in me. In every situation, the shadow of a husband's feet is superior to being on the top of a palace or travelling in a celestial vehicle. My mother[98] and my father taught me about various situations. There is no need to tell me now about how to conduct myself. Without thinking about the three worlds and thinking only of my vow towards my husband, I will happily dwell in the forest, like residing in my father's residence. I will serve you always, devoted to the vow of brahmacharya. O brave one! I will reside with you in the forest that smells of honey. O Rama! In the forest, you are capable of protecting other people. O one who grants honours! Why not me? There is no doubt that I will always subsist on fruits and roots. I will dwell with you and not cause you any hardship. O intelligent lord! Fearless with you, I wish to see everything—rivers, mountains, lakes and groves. There will be beautiful and superb blossoming lotuses, populated by swans and ducks. O brave one! With you, I desire to happily see these. O large-eyed one! With you, I will be greatly delighted and find pleasure. I will be with you for a hundred thousand years. O Raghava! O tiger among men! Without you, even if I get to reside in heaven, that will

[98] Obviously, this refers to a stepmother.

not please me. I will go to the forest, which is extremely difficult to penetrate, full of many animals, monkeys and elephants. Clinging to your feet, I will live in the forest, as if it is my father's residence. Without any other thoughts, my mind is devoted to you. Without you, it is certain that I will be dead. Do what is virtuous. Grant me my wish and take me with you. Because of me, there will be no burden on you.' The one who was devoted to dharma spoke in this way. Not wishing to take her, the best among men said several things to restrain Sita and spoke about the difficulties of residing in the forest.

Chapter 2(25)

Sita, who knew about dharma and was devoted to dharma, spoke in this way. To restrain her, the one who knew about dharma spoke these words. 'O Sita! You have been born in a great lineage. You are always devoted to dharma. Perform your own dharma here. That will bring pleasure to my mind. O Sita! O delicate one! I am telling you what you should do. There are many difficulties in the forest. Listen to what I say. O Sita! Abandon this intention of residing in the forest. It has been said that there are many hardships associated with dwelling in the desolate forest. Indeed, it is with your welfare in mind that I spoke those words of advice. I know that the forest is always fraught with misery, there is never any joy there. There are the sounds of waterfalls generated in the mountains and the roars of lions that reside in mountainous caverns. These are unpleasant to hear. Therefore, the forest has hardships. When one is exhausted at night, one has to sleep on the bare ground, on a bed of fallen leaves that one has made oneself. Therefore, the forest has great misery. O Maithilee! Depending on one's strength, one has to fast. One has to bear the burden of matted hair and wear garments made of bark. Strong winds, darkness and hunger are always there. There are many kinds of great fear. Therefore, the forest has greater misery. O beautiful one! There are many reptiles, diverse in form. These proudly roam around on the ground. Therefore, the forest has greater misery. There are snakes that make their abode in the rivers. These roam crookedly in the rivers and remaining there, make the rivers difficult to cross. Therefore, the forest has greater misery. There are flying insects, scorpions, insects, gnats and mosquitoes. O delicate one! These always cause annoyance. Therefore, in every way, the forest has greater misery. O beautiful one! There are trees with thorns and kusha grass and reeds. In every direction, these pervade the forest with their branches. Therefore, the forest has greater misery. Thus, enough about leaving for the forest. You will find the forest unbearable. Thinking about it, I see that the forest possesses many hardships.' The great-souled Rama couldn't consent to taking her to the forest. However, Sita did not accept these words. Extremely miserable, she told him the following.

Chapter 2(26)

Hearing Rama's words, Sita was miserable. Her face overflowing with tears, she softly spoke these words. 'You have spoken about the hardships of living in the forest. Since your affection is more important, know that these are actually qualities. My seniors have instructed me that I should go with you.[99] O Rama! Separated from you, I will give up my life on earth. O Raghava! As long as I am near you, not even Shakra, the lord of the gods, is capable of oppressing me with his energy. A woman without a husband is incapable of remaining alive. O Rama! I have been taught by you about this being desirable. O immensely wise one! In earlier times, when I was in my father's house, I tell you truthfully that I heard from brahmanas that I was indeed going to live in the forest. O immensely strong one! In that house, I heard the words of the brahmanas that I possessed these

[99] At the time of marriage, not specifically about going to the forest.

signs. Therefore, I have always been ready to live in the forest. That destiny of living in the forest must indeed be fulfilled by me. O beloved one! I must go there with you. It cannot be otherwise. Destiny will come true and I will go with you. The time has come for the brahmana's[100] words to come true. Indeed, I know that there are many kinds of hardships associated with residing in the forest. O brave one! However, those are certainly faced by men with uncleansed souls. As a maiden in my father's house, I heard about living in the forest. In my mother's presence, a female mendicant, with virtuous conduct, told me this. O lord! Earlier, in many kinds of ways, I have given you pleasure. Therefore, with you, I wish to leave for the forest. O fortunate one! O Raghava! I am waiting for the time when I can go with you. The idea of being brave and dwelling in the forest appeals to me. Because of my pure soul and love, I will be without any taints. I will follow my husband. My husband is my divinity. Even if I die, I will be fortunate in remaining with you. O immensely wise one! In this connection, the sacred words of the illustrious brahmanas have been heard. "In this world, if a woman's father gives her away with sanctified water, her own dharma is to be with her husband, even after death." You desire this woman. She is excellent in conduct and is devoted to her husband. That being the case, why don't you wish to take me with you? I am faithful and devoted to my husband. I am distressed. I share equally in your happiness and unhappiness. O Kakutstha! Since I share equally in your joy and misery, you should take me with you. I am miserable. If you do not wish to take me to the forest, I will resort to poison, fire or water, and thereby cause my death.' She wished to go, in this and many other ways. However, the mighty-armed one did not agree to take her to the desolate forest. Thus addressed, Maithilee was overcome with thoughts. Warm tears issued from her eyes and she seemed to be bathed in these. Vaidehi was full of rage and immersed in thought. The self-controlled Kakutstha restrained her and comforted her in many ways.

[100] The text uses the word in the singular.

Chapter 2(27)

Maithilee, Janaka's daughter, was comforted by Rama about living in the forest. She spoke to her husband. Greatly agitated, Sita reproached the broad-chested Raghava in words full of love and pride. 'What will my father, the lord of Videha and Mithila think of himself? O Rama! He has obtained a son-in-law who is a woman in the guise of a man. In their ignorance, the people utter a falsehood about Rama's strength scorching like the rays of the sun. There is no great energy in you. Why are you distressed? What fear assails you? I have no other refuge. Why do you wish to forsake me? O brave one! Know me to be as devoted to you as Savitree, who followed Satyavan, Dyumatsena's son.[101] O unblemished one! With the exception of you, I do not wish to see anyone else, not even in my mind. I am not like others, who cause ill repute to their lineages. O Raghava! I will go with you. I am your own wife. Since I was a maiden, I have dwelt with you. O Rama! You now wish to give me away to others, as if I am a public dancer. Without taking me with you, you should not leave for the forest. Whether it is austerities, the forest or heaven, it should only be with you. I will follow behind you, whether you are sporting or sleeping. Along the road, I will not suffer from any exhaustion there. When I am on the path with you, kusha, reeds, cane, grass and thorns of trees will touch me. However, they will be like the touch of cotton or deer skin. Great storms will rise and will envelop me in dust. However, I will take pleasure in this, as if it is a supreme gift of sandalwood powder. While in the forest, at the extremities of the forest, I will lie down on green grass. Can lying down on a bed covered with spreads provide greater happiness than that? You will give me leaves, roots and fruits that you have collected yourself. Whether it is little or a lot, that will be like amrita to me. I will not remember the abodes of my mother and my father. I will enjoy the seasonal flowers and fruit. Having gone there, I will not see anything disagreeable. There

[101] Savitree was Satyavan's wife. When Satyavan died, she followed him to Yama's world, prayed to Yama and brought her husband back to life.

will not be any sorrow on my account. I will not be a great burden to bear. Being with you is heaven. Being without you is hell. O Rama! Knowing about my great love, go with me. I am anxious. Even after this, if you don't take me with you, I will drink poison. I will not come under the subjugation of the enemy. Therefore, I do not wish to live in misery. O beloved! If I am neglected by you, death is superior. Alone, I am incapable of tolerating this misery and grief for an instant, not to speak of fourteen years.' In this way, tormented, she lamented piteously in many ways. She embraced her husband and wept loudly. She was like a female elephant, pierced with the poisoned arrows of many words. Like a piece of kindling emitting a fire, she released tears that had been held back for a long time. As a result of her torment, tears flowed from her eyes. They were like crystal, like drops of water on lotuses.

In her misery, she seemed to be unconscious. Rama embraced her in his arms. Comforting her, he spoke these words. 'O queen! When you are in grief, even heaven does not appeal to me. Like Svayambhu, I do not have the slightest fear from any direction. O one with the beautiful face! I am capable of protecting you. However, without knowing all your intentions, I would not have liked to take you to the forest, to dwell there. O Maithilee! You have been created for the purpose of living in the forest with me. You are like my own deeds and I am incapable of abandoning you. O one with thighs like an elephant's trunk. In ancient times, virtuous ones observed dharma. You will follow me today, like Suvarchala[102] follows Surya. O one with excellent hips! Being obedient to the father and the mother is dharma. Therefore, transgressing their command, I am not interested in remaining alive. Established in the path of truth and dharma, my father has commanded me. I wish to act accordingly. That is eternal dharma. O timid one! Follow me. Be the one with whom I follow dharma.[103] Give jewels to brahmanas and food to mendicants. Grant them assurance. But be quick and do not delay.' Knowing that her husband was favourably inclined

[102] Surya's wife.

[103] The text uses the word *sahadharmachari*. The wife is *sahadharmini*, one with whom one follows dharma.

to the idea of her going, the queen was delighted. She quickly made arrangements for the donations. She was completely delighted in her mind. Hearing what her husband had said, the illustrious and beautiful lady made arrangements for giving away riches and jewels. The spirited one was one who upheld dharma.

Chapter 2(28)

The immensely energetic Rama spoke to Lakshmana, who was in front of him. The brave one joined his hands in salutation. He was waiting there, desiring to proceed in front. 'O Soumitri! If you leave for the forest with me today, who will take care of Kousalya and the illustrious Sumitra? The immensely energetic king is bound by the noose of desire, as if Parjanya[104] is showering down desire on earth. After obtaining this kingdom, King Ashvapati's daughter[105] will not act properly and will cause grief to her co-wives.' Lakshmana was thus addressed by Rama, who knew about the use of words. The one who was accomplished in words replied in a gentle voice to Rama. 'O brave one! Because of your energy, Bharata will endeavour to worship Kousalya and Sumitra. There is no doubt about this. Because of the arrangements made, the noble Kousalya was given one thousand villages and those one thousand are enough to ensure her means of subsistence.[106] Wielding a bow, arrows, a spade and a basket, I will advance ahead of you, clearing and showing you the path. I will always collect roots and fruits and all the other food available in the forest, suitable for ascetics. You and Vaidehi will enjoy yourselves along the slopes of mountains. Whether you are awake or asleep, I will do everything.'

Rama was greatly delighted at these words and replied, 'O Soumitri! Go and take your leave from all your well-wishers. At

[104] The god of rain.

[105] Kaikeyee.

[106] When he married Kaikeyee, Dasharatha granted the income from one thousand villages to Kousalya.

Janaka's great sacrifice, the great-souled Varuna himself gave the king divine bows that are terrible to see. There are divine and impenetrable armour and quivers with inexhaustible stocks of arrows. There are two swords decorated with gold. They sparkle like the sun. All of those have been carefully kept in our preceptor's[107] residence. O Lakshmana! Collect those and return quickly.' Having made his mind up to reside in the forest, he[108] took his leave from the well-wishers. He took the permission of the preceptor of the Ikshvakus and took those supreme weapons. They were divine, maintained well and decorated with garlands. Soumitri, tiger among kings, showed Rama all those weapons. When Lakshmana returned, the self-controlled Rama cheerfully told him, 'O Lakshmana! O amiable one! You have returned at the time I wished for. O scorcher of enemies! With you, I desire to give away all my wealth to brahmanas and ascetics and to preceptors who are excellent brahmanas, residing here, firm in their devotion. I also wish to give to all those who are dependent on me for survival. Bring the noble Suyajna, Vasishtha's son, here. Also quickly bring the best among brahmanas. I wish to honour all the other excellent brahmanas and then leave for the forest.'

Chapter 2(29)

His brother's command was auspicious and agreeable. Listening to this, he quickly went to Suyajna's residence. Lakshmana worshipped the brahmana, who lived in a house of fire,[109] and spoke to him. 'O friend! Come to the house of someone who is going to perform an extremely difficult task.' Having performed the sandhya rites, with Soumitri, he quickly went to Rama's large, prosperous and beautiful residence, populated by people. On seeing that the one

[107] Vasishtha.

[108] Lakshmana.

[109] This probably means that Suyajna performed austerities with fires around him on all four sides.

who knew about the Vedas had arrived, with Sita, Raghava joined his hands in salutation and honouring Suyajna, circumambulated the fire. Kakutstha offered him the best of sparkling earrings and armlets made out of molten gold, gems strung together on threads, bracelets to be worn on the upper arm and bracelets to be worn around the wrist. There were many other jewels too. He honoured them back. Urged by Sita, Rama spoke to Suyajna. 'O friend! O amiable one! For your wife, Sita now wishes to give a necklace, a golden thread and a girdle. Please accept them. Vaidehi desires to give you a couch strewn with the best of spreads and decorated with many kinds of jewels. My maternal uncle gave me an elephant named Shatrunjaya. O bull among brahmanas! I wish to give you that and one thousand other elephants.' Thus addressed by Rama, Suyajna accepted these and pronounced auspicious benedictions on Rama, Lakshmana and Sita.

Collected, Rama, who was pleasant in speech, spoke to his beloved brother Soumitri, like Brahma to the lord of the gods. 'O Soumitri! Both Agastya and Koushika are excellent brahmanas. Summon them and worship them with jewels, like pouring water on crops. There is a devoted preceptor who serves Kousalya and pronounces his benedictions on her. He knows about the Vedas and the rules that are in conformity with *Taittiriya*.[110] O Soumitri! Give that brahmana vehicles, female servants and silken garments, until he is content. The noble Chitraratha has been a charioteer and adviser for a very long time. Satisfy him with extremely expensive jewels, garments and wealth. Give him one thousand bullocks for carrying grain and two hundred bulls for ploughing. O Soumitri! Give him one thousand cows for sustenance.' At this, as addressed, Lakshmana, tiger among men, himself gave away those riches, like Kubera, to the best of brahmanas who had been named. He[111] gave away many kinds of objects to each person who was dependent on him. With tears choking his voice, he spoke to the dependents who were present there. 'Until my return, Lakshmana's house and my

[110] The *Taittiriya Upanishad,* associated with the Yajur Veda.
[111] Rama.

house should never be empty. In turn, each of you must ensure this.' Thus addressed, all those dependents were extremely unhappy. He instructed the treasurer, 'Bring my riches here.' At this, all the dependents brought the riches there. With Lakshmana, the tiger among men distributed those riches to brahmanas, children, the aged and those who were destitute.

There was a brahmana named Trijata. He was born in Gargya's lineage and was tawny in complexion. Till the fifth chamber, no one ever obstructed his path.[112] Trijata approached the prince and spoke these words. 'O immensely illustrious prince! I am poor and have many sons. Look at me. I always earn a subsistence through unchhavritti.' As if in jest, Rama replied, 'I have not given away even one thousand cows so far. Fling your staff. You will get as many as that expanse.' Anxious, he[113] girded his lower garment around his waist and flung the staff with as much strength and force as he could muster. Rama comforted Gargya's descendant and said, 'You should not be angry. I said this only in jest.' The great sage, Trijata, was delighted. He and his wife accepted a herd of cows. He pronounced benedictions for the extension of the great-souled one's fame, strength, joy and happiness.

Chapter 2(30)

With Vaidehi, the two Raghavas gave away a lot of riches to brahmanas. With Sita, they then went to see their father. They took those blazing weapons, which were so difficult to look at. Sita adorned them with heaps of garlands. The mansions in the palace were like the tips of celestial vehicles. However, the prosperous and handsome people who ascended them seemed to be indifferent. The roads were full of many anxious people and it was

[112] In visiting royalty, one had to pass through successive gates and chambers, with guards at each gate. Usually, the third chamber is regarded as an exclusive preserve. This is superior to the third chamber.

[113] Trijata.

impossible to walk. Therefore, they climbed up to the palaces and distressed, glanced at Raghava. Those people saw Rama on foot, having cast aside his umbrella. With their senses distraught because of their sorrow, they uttered many kinds of words. 'He used to be followed by a large army with the four limbs.[114] He is now alone with Sita, followed by Lakshmana. He possessed riches. Though he knew about the essence of desire, he is the one who granted objects of desire. Because he revered dharma, he did not desire to make his father's words come false. The people who are on the royal road today can see Sita. Earlier, even creatures that flew through the sky were unable to see her. Sita applied unguents to her body and used red sandalwood paste. Rains, heat and cold will quickly render her pale. Truly, a spirit that has entered Dasharatha has spoken today. The king should not have exiled his beloved son. Even if a son is devoid of qualities, how can he be exiled, not to speak of a person who has conquered the world through his qualities? There are six qualities that adorn Raghava, best among men—non-injury, compassion, learning, good conduct, self-control and tranquility. The entire world is afflicted because this lord of the world is afflicted, just as a tree with flowers and fruit suffers when its foundation is destroyed. Like Lakshmana is following him, with our wives and our relatives, we will quickly go wherever Raghava is going. Abandoning the groves, fields and houses, we will follow Rama, who observes dharma, and endure the same kind of happiness and unhappiness. Treasures dug up,[115] desolate courtyards bereft of grains and riches, the best objects removed in every way, enveloped by dust and abandoned by the gods—let Kaikeyee enjoy those houses discarded by us. Since Raghava is going there, let the forest become a city. Since we are abandoning it, let the city become a forest. Since we have abandoned it, let fanged creatures in holes and animals and birds from the mountains inhabit this place. As long as we were here, they had abandoned it.' The large number of people uttered such diverse words. Though

[114] Chariots, elephants, horses and infantry.

[115] Meaning that the hidden treasures have been dug up and are no longer there.

he heard them, Rama's mind was not disturbed. Though he saw that the people were distressed, his mind was not disturbed and he seemed to be smiling. Wishing to follow his father's instructions in the proper way, Rama went to see his father. The great-souled Rama, the son of the descendant of Ikshvaku, saw that the suta Sumantra was in front of him, miserable at the prospect of his leaving for the forest. He waited, so that he could be announced to his great-souled father. He was devoted to dharma and to obey his father's command, had made up his mind to go to the forest. On seeing Sumantra, Raghava told him, 'Tell the king that I have come.'

Chapter 2(31)

Sent by Rama, the suta entered quickly and saw the king, whose senses were tormented. He was sighing. The immensely wise one saw that his senses were greatly afflicted. He was grieving over Rama. With hands joined in salutation, the suta approached. 'Your son, tiger among men, is waiting at the door. He has given away all his riches to brahmanas and the dependents. O fortunate one! Let Rama, for whom truth is his valour, see you. Having taken his leave of all the well-wishers, he wishes to see you now. O lord of the earth! He will leave for the great forest. See him. He is surrounded by all the royal qualities, like the sun with its rays.' That Indra among men[116] was truthful in speech. He had dharma in his soul. He was like the ocean in his gravity. He was like the sky in cleanliness and replied, 'O Sumantra! Bring all my wives who are present. I wish to see Raghava when I am surrounded by all my wives.' He passed through to the inner quarters and addressed the women in these words. 'O noble ones! The king has summoned you. You should go there without delay.' Sumantra addressed all those women and told them about the king's command. Knowing about the king's

[116] Dasharatha.

command, they went to their husband's residence. Three hundred and fifty women, with coppery red eyes and firm in their vows, surrounded Kousalya and went there slowly. When the wives had arrived, the king glanced at them. The king told the suta Sumantra, 'Bring my son here.'

Quickly, the suta brought Rama, Lakshmana and Maithilee and went to where the king was. From a distance, the king saw his son arriving, hands joined in salutation. Surrounded by the miserable women, he swiftly arose from his seat. On seeing Rama, the king speedily advanced towards him. However, before reaching him, afflicted by sorrow, he fell down on the ground, senseless. Rama and maharatha Lakshmana saw that the king had fallen down, afflicted by sorrow and grief. Mixed with the sound of the tinkling of ornaments, the wails of thousands of women suddenly arose from the palace, 'Alas, Rama! Alas!' With Sita, the weeping Rama and Lakshmana raised him with their arms and laid him down on a bed. Soon, the king regained his senses, though he was still submerged in an ocean of grief. Joining his hands in salutation, Rama told him, 'For all of us, you are the lord. O great king! I seek your leave. I am leaving for Dandakaranya. Look on me with kindly eyes. Permit Lakshmana and Sita to follow me to the forest. Despite being restrained by many kinds of reasons, they do not wish to remain here. O one who grants honours! Abandon grief and grant all of us permission, like Prajapati did to his sons.'[117] Rama waited anxiously for the king's permission to reside in the forest. The king glanced towards Raghava and replied, 'O Raghava! Because I had granted boons to Kaikeyee, I was confused. Imprison me and become the king of Ayodhya today.' The king addressed Rama, who was supreme among the upholders of dharma, in this way. The one who was eloquent in the use of words joined his hands in salutation and replied to his father. 'O king! May you be the lord of the earth for one thousand years. I will reside in the forest. I must

[117] Four sages who were created through Brahma's (Prajapati's) mental powers—Sanatkumara, Sanaka, Sanatana and Sanandana. They took Brahma's permission to go to the forest and practise austerities.

not act so as to make you false.' 'O son![118] For your benefit, advance fearlessly along the auspicious path, without any distractions, until you return. O son! However, it is night now, when one should never leave. Do not go today. Spend this night with your mother and me, so that we can see you. Having satisfied yourself with all the objects of desire, leave at the appropriate time tomorrow.' Hearing the words spoken by their miserable father, Rama, and his brother Lakshmana, were distressed. He[119] spoke these words. 'Even if we obtain these objects with qualities today, who will give them to us tomorrow? Therefore, without these objects of desire, I wish to leave this place. I have abandoned the earth and this kingdom, full of people, wealth and grain. May it be given to Bharata. Abandon this grief. Don't let your eyes overflow with tears. The ocean, the lord of the rivers, cannot be assailed and is not agitated. I do not wish for the kingdom, happiness, Maithilee, or you. O bull among men! Without any falsehood, I desire the truth. Forsaken by me, this city, kingdom and the entire earth should be given to Bharata. I will follow your instructions. I will go to the forest and dwell there for a long time. Forsaken by me, let this entire earth, with its mountains, boulders, cities, groves and frontiers, be given to Bharata, so that he can justly rule over it. Let it be the way you have pledged. O king! My mind does not hanker after great objects of desire or what brings pleasure to my own self. As is instructed by the virtuous, I will follow your command. O unblemished one! Do not be miserable on my account. O unblemished one! Therefore, right now, I do not desire the undecaying kingdom, happiness or Maithilee. When I am associated with falsehood, I do not wish to remain alive. I desire that the pledge of truth should come true. We will eat fruits and roots in the forest. We will see the mountains, rivers and lakes. We will enter the forest, with its wonderful trees. May you be happy. Let us withdraw.'[120]

[118] The Critical Edition excises some shlokas and this breaks the continuity. This is Dasharatha replying.

[119] Rama.

[120] The word used is *nivritti,* which therefore has the implied sense of withdrawal from the senses and objects of pleasure.

Chapter 2(32)

The descendant of the Ikshvaku lineage[121] was afflicted because of the pledge he had himself given. Shedding tears, he sighed repeatedly and spoke to Sumantra. 'O suta! Let an army with the four kinds of forces be prepared. Let it be given all the jewels, so that it can quickly follow Raghava. Let the prince's army be extensive. Let it be adorned with courtesans who are good in conduct and extremely rich merchants. Engage all those dependents whose valour he takes delight in and give them many kinds of gifts. Once he kills deer and elephants, tastes honey from the forest and sees many rivers, he will not remember the kingdom. Let my store of grain and store of riches follow Rama, as he goes to reside in the desolate forest. He will then reside happily in the forest. He will be able to summon the rishis and perform sacrifices in auspicious spots, giving away the appropriate dakshina. The mighty-armed Bharata will rule over Ayodhya. However, let all the objects of desire be arranged for the prosperous Rama.'

When Kakutstha spoke in this way, Kaikeyee was overcome by fear. Her mouth went dry and her voice also choked. Pale and frightened, Kaikeyee spoke these words. 'All the virtuous people will leave the kingdom and it will be like a vessel from which the liquor has been drunk. It will be empty, bereft of all essence. Bharata will not accept it.' Kaikeyee discarded her shame and spoke these extremely terrible words. King Dasharatha spoke these words to the large-eyed one. 'Having imposed this unfortunate burden on me, why do you strike me when I am bearing the burden?' Kaikeyee became doubly angry and addressed the king. 'It is in your lineage that Sagara cast away his eldest son, known as Asamanja. He[122] should also leave in that way.' Thus addressed, King Dasharatha said, 'Shame.' All the people were ashamed, but she did not perceive this. There was an aged adviser who was virtuous and was greatly revered by the king. His name was Siddhartha and he addressed Kaikeyee. 'Asamanja

[121] Dasharatha.
[122] Rama.

seized children playing in the streets and flung them into the waters of the Sarayu. The evil-minded one took pleasure in this. On seeing this, all the citizens were angry and told the king, "O extender of the kingdom! You have to choose between us and Asamanja." At this, the king asked them, "What are you scared of?" Thus asked by the king, the ordinary people spoke these words. "When our sons are playing, the foolish one, confounded in his sense, seizes those children and flings them into the Sarayu. He obtains infinite delight from this." Hearing the words of the ordinary people, the king wished to bring pleasure to them and cast aside his inauspicious son. This is what King Sagara, extremely devoted to dharma, did. What wicked act has Rama perpetrated that he should be restrained?' The king heard Siddhartha's words. In a tired voice and afflicted by sorrow, he addressed Kaikeyee in these words. 'I will now follow Rama, forsaking the kingdom, happiness and riches. With King Bharata, you can happily enjoy the kingdom for a long period of time.'

Chapter 2(33)

Rama knew about humility. On hearing the adviser's words, he humbly addressed Dasharatha in these words. 'O king! I have cast aside objects of pleasure, to dwell in the forest on forest fare. When I have cast everything aside, why should anyone follow me? If a person has given away the best of elephants, why will he turn his mind to the harness alone? If one has cast aside the best of elephants, why will he have affection only for the rope? O best among virtuous ones! O lord of the earth! In that way, what will I do with flags and all those who will follow me? Let tattered rags be brought for me. I am going to reside in the forest for fourteen years. As I leave, let a spade and a basket be brought for me.' At this, Kaikeyee herself brought tattered rags for Raghava. Despite the assembly, she wasn't ashamed and said, 'Wear these.' The tiger among men accepted those two[123]

[123] One as an upper garment, the second as a lower.

tattered rags from Kaikeyee. Casting aside his fine garments, he wore the garb of an ascetic. In front of his father, Lakshmana also cast aside his excellent clothes and covered himself in an ascetic's attire. Sita, attired in silken clothes, was alarmed, like a deer that sees a snare, on seeing the tattered rags that were meant to be worn by her. She was ashamed and distressed in her mind. She spoke to her husband, who was like a king of the gandharvas. 'How do sages, who reside in the forest, wear these rags?' She held one piece against her neck and the other in her hand. Janaka's daughter did not know how to wear these and was ashamed. Rama, supreme among those who uphold dharma, quickly came to her. He himself fastened the rags over Sita's silken garments.

She was attired in those tattered rags. Though she had a protector, she was like one without a protector. All the people were angry and said, 'Shame on Dasharatha.' The descendant of the Ikshvaku lineage[124] emitted warm sighs and addressed his wife. 'O Kaikeyee! Sita does not deserve to go, wearing kusha grass and rags. O wicked one! Exiling Rama should be sufficient for you. Why do you again wish to perform this wicked and cruel act?' Rama, about to leave for the forest, addressed his father, whose head was lowered down, though he was seated, in these words. 'My illustrious mother, Kousalya, is devoted to dharma. O king! She is aged. But her conduct isn't inferior and she won't censure you. O one who grants boons! Without me, she will be immersed in an ocean of grief. She has not confronted such a hardship earlier. You should respect her. O king who is like the great Indra! She has great affection for her son. When I am in the forest, she will be afflicted by grief. You should ensure that my mother remains alive and does not leave for Yama's eternal abode.'

Chapter 2(34)

The king was bereft of his senses. With his wives, he heard Rama's words and saw that he was attired in a sage's garments.

[124] Dasharatha.

Tormented by grief, he was incapable of looking towards Raghava. Distressed in his mind, he was incapable of glancing towards him, or replying. However, though miserable, the great king regained his senses in a moment. The mighty-armed one thought of Rama and lamented. 'I think that in the past, I must have separated several from their children. I must have caused injury to creatures. That is the reason I am now confronted with this. Until the time arrives, life is not separated from the body. Despite being afflicted by Kaikeyee, I am not faced with death. I see my son stationed before me and he is like a fire. However, abandoning his delicate garments, my son is clad in the garb of an ascetic. Indeed, it is because of Kaikeyee's deeds alone that all these people are suffering. Driven by selfish motives, she has brought about this act of deceit.' These are the words he spoke, his eyes overflowing with tears. Afflicted by grief, he was incapable of saying anything other than 'Rama!' After an instant, the great king regained his senses. His eyes overflowing with tears, he addressed Sumantra in these words. 'Arrange a chariot that can be driven and yoke it to excellent steeds. Take this extremely fortunate one from here, beyond the boundaries of the habitation. I think that these are the fruits being reaped by someone with qualities, by virtue of his qualities. A brave and virtuous person is being exiled to the forest by his father and his mother.'

Following the king's command, Sumantra, swift in his valour, yoked an ornamented chariot with horses and brought it there. The suta prepared a chariot decorated in gold for the prince. He joined his hands in salutation and reported that it had been yoked to excellent steeds. The king knew about what should be done at the right time and place and was also clear about everything auspicious. He quickly summoned the person who was in charge of accumulating riches and said, 'Remembering the number of years that has to be spent, quickly bring extremely expensive garments and excellent ornaments for Vaidehi.' Thus addressed by the Indra among men, he went to the treasury. He quickly brought everything and offered it to Sita. Vaidehi, born in a noble lineage and beautiful in her limbs, was about to leave for the forest. She adorned her limbs with those wonderful ornaments. Adorned in those excellent ornaments, Vaidehi made the residence look radiant. She was like the sun with rays, arising at the right time and illuminating the sky with its resplendence. Her mother-in-law engulfed her in her arms. Maithilee never did anything that was inferior. She inhaled the fragrance of her head[125] and spoke these words. 'In this world, even though they are respected and loved, false women cease to honour their husbands when they face hardships. Do not disrespect my son, who is being exiled. Though he possesses riches, he is poor now. However, he is still your divinity.' Sita understood the words spoken, full of dharma and artha. She joined her hands in salutation and addressed her mother-in-law, who stood in front of her. 'O noble one! I will do everything that you had instructed me. I know how I should conduct myself towards my husband. I had heard this earlier too. O noble one! You should not equate me with wicked women. I am not capable of deviating from dharma, just as the moon cannot be separated from its radiance. Without chords, the veena doesn't make a sound. Without wheels, a chariot does not move. Even if she has one hundred sons, a woman doesn't obtain happiness without her husband. A father gives a limited amount. What a mother and a son give are also limited. What a husband gives is unlimited. Who does not worship a husband? O noble one! I have been instructed by the best, those who are supreme upholders of dharma. How can I disrespect him? To a woman, the husband is a divinity.' Sita's words penetrated Kousalya's heart and on hearing them, the one who was pure of heart, suddenly released tears, because they were a source of both misery and joy.

Rama was supreme in knowledge of dharma. Amidst all his mothers, he joined his hands in salutation and approached his own mother, who was most revered of all. He spoke these words. 'O mother! You should not be sad. Look towards my father. The period of dwelling in the forest will soon be over. The period of fourteen years will pass, as if you were sleeping. You will see me return here, surrounded by well-wishers. He spoke these words to his mother and they conveyed deep meaning. He then glanced at

[125] Kousalya and Sita respectively.

his three hundred and fifty mothers.[126] In a similar way, joining his hands in salutation, Dasharatha's son then spoke similar words, full of dharma and artha, to those distressed mothers too. 'While I resided here with you, if I said anything harsh, or if I did anything in ignorance, please pardon me. Now I seek my leave from all of you.' As Raghava spoke in this way, the sounds of lamentations arose from the king's wives, like those of curlews wailing. In former times, Dasharatha's residence used to resound with the sound of tambourines and drums, like the roar of thundering clouds. Because of the hardship, there was now the sound of extremely miserable wails and lamentations.

Chapter 2(35)

The miserable Rama, Sita and Lakshmana joined their hands in salutation. They bowed down before the king and circumambulated him. Having taken his leave, Raghava, who knew about dharma, with Sita, bowed down before his mother, who was confounded by grief. Lakshmana followed his brother and bowed down before Kousalya. He next touched the feet of his mother, Sumitra. He worshipped his mother, who was weeping. For the sake of the mighty-armed one's welfare, she inhaled the fragrance of Lakshmana's head and addressed Soumitri. 'Because you are devoted to your well-wisher,[127] I have permitted you to reside in the forest. O son! Do not fail to take care of Rama, your brother who is leaving for the forest. O unblemished one! Whether it is prosperity or adversity, he is your refuge. In this world, that is the dharma of the virtuous, being obedient to an elder. This is the eternal appropriate behaviour for this lineage—donations, consecration for sacrifices and giving up one's body in battles. Know Rama to be like Dasharatha. Know Janaka's

[126] The stepmothers.

[127] Meaning Rama.

daughter to be like me. Know the forest to be Ayodhya. O son! Depart cheerfully.'

Knowledgeable about humility, Sumantra joined his hands in salutation and humbly spoke to Kakutstha, like Matali[128] to Vasava. 'O fortunate one! O immensely illustrious one! Ascend the chariot. O Rama! I will quickly take you to whichever place you tell me to. You will have to reside in the forest for fourteen years, as has been instructed by the queen. That period has commenced.' That chariot was like the sun. Having ornamented herself, the beautiful-hipped Sita ascended it with a cheerful mind. The brothers also ascended, with weapons and armour that they laid down on the firm leather seat of the chariot. On seeing that Sita, the third one, had also ascended, Sumantra urged the respected horses, which were as fleet as the speed of the wind. For many nights, Raghava departed for the great forest. It was as if the city's strength had been sapped, as if people had lost their senses. The city used to emit a great sound—because it was full of crazy, intoxicated and respected elephants and because of the neighing of the horses and the tinkling of their ornaments. That city was greatly afflicted.

Children and aged rushed towards Rama, like a person who is suffering in the summer rushes towards water. Their long and anxious faces could be seen at the rear and towards the sides. All of them were extremely miserable and their faces were overflowing with tears. They said, 'O suta! Hold back the reins of the horses and proceed slowly. We wish to see Rama's face, which will become extremely difficult for us to behold. There is no doubt that Rama's mother's heart is indeed made of iron. It has not got shattered despite her son, who is like a god, leaving for the forest. Vaidehi is doing what should be done and is following her husband like a shadow. She is devoted to dharma and does not abandon it, like Meru does not forsake the radiance of the sun. O Lakshmana! You are always pleasant in speech. Since you serve your brother, who is like a god, you have become successful in your objective. This is a great success and is a great accomplishment. Since you are following him, this is

[128] Indra's charioteer.

a path to heaven.' Incapable of restraining their tears, they spoke in this way.

The king was miserable in his mind and was surrounded by the grieving women. Saying that he wished to see his son, he emerged from his house. Ahead of him, the great sound of lamenting women could be heard. This was like the wailing of female elephants, when a large male elephant has been tied up. The father, King Kakutstha, used to be handsome. But he seemed shrunken, like the full moon when it has been enveloped in an eclipse. When the men saw that the king was distressed and extremely miserable, a tumultuous sound arose from Rama's rear. Some said, 'Alas, Rama!' Others said, 'Alas, Rama's mother!' All those in the prosperous inner quarters started to weep and lament. As he glanced back, Rama saw his father and mother, following along the path, distressed and not in control of their senses. He was bound in the noose of dharma and could not look at them directly. They deserved happiness and did not deserve this unhappiness. Though they deserved vehicles, they were on foot. On seeing this, he instructed the charioteer to drive swiftly. The tiger among men caught the miserable sight of his father and mother and could not bear it, like an elephant struck by a goad. The weeping Kousalya ran after the chariot, wailing, 'Alas, Rama! Rama! Alas, Sita! Alas, Lakshmana!' His mother seemed to be dancing and he could not stand the sight. The king said, 'Wait.' Raghava said, 'Go. Go.' Sumantra was caught between the two, as if in the midst of a whirlpool. Rama told him, 'It is wicked to witness their grief for a long period of time. When the king berates you later, you can say that you did not hear him.'[129] Hearing Rama's words, the charioteer acted in accordance with them. He took his leave of the people and urged the horses to proceed even faster.

Circumambulating Rama mentally,[130] the king's attendants returned. However, the men were incapable of controlling the flow of their tears. The advisers addressed the great king Dasharatha in these words. 'If one wishes for a person to return, one should

[129] Sumantra was caught in two minds about whom to obey. This is a rare instance of Rama asking someone to lie.

[130] Obviously, they couldn't do it physically.

not follow him for a long distance.' The king heard their words, which were full of all the qualities. His body was perspiring and his form was dejected. With his wives, the miserable king stood there, looking towards his son.

Chapter 2(36)

Having joined his hands in salutation, the tiger among men departed. Great sounds of sorrow and lamentation arose from the inner quarters. 'Where is our protector going, like an ascetic, leaving the people weak and without a protector? He was our refuge and destination. Even when he was accused, he was never angry. He cast aside all kinds of rage. He pacified all those who were angry, sharing in their sorrow. Where is he going? The immensely energetic and great-souled one's mother is Kousalya and he respected us the way he respected her. Where is he going? Urged and afflicted by Kaikeyee, the king sent him to the forest. He is the saviour of the people and the world. Where is he going? Alas! The king is bereft of his senses. Rama's vow is dharma and truth. He is loved by all living beings on earth. Yet, he has been exiled for living in the forest.' All the queens were afflicted by grief. They wept and lamented loudly, like cows separated from their calves. On hearing those terrible sounds of sorrow that arose from the inner quarters, the great king was tormented by sorrow on account of his son and became extremely miserable. Despite the sun having set, no agnihotra oblations were offered. The cattle were neglected and not given their food. The cows and calves were not given water to drink. Trishanku, Brihaspati and Budha assumed a red tinge throughout.[131] All the planets assumed a terrible form and were in conjunction with the moon. The nakshatras lost their lustre. The planets lost their energy. Vishakha nakshatra was enveloped

[131] Brihaspati is Jupiter and Budha is Mercury. In this context, Trishanku means the Trishanku nakshatra, identified as the Southern Cross.

in smoke and no longer shone in the firmament. All the people in the city were suddenly overcome by distress. Their minds turned away from eating or finding pleasure. The faces of people along the royal roads overflowed with tears. Everyone was full of sorrow. Not a single happy person could be discerned. The wind that blew was no longer cool. The moon was no longer pleasant to behold. The sun did not heat the world any more. Everything on earth was in disarray. Women no longer asked about their sons, husbands and brothers. Thinking about Rama alone, they abandoned each other. All of Rama's well-wishers were bereft of their senses. They suffered from that great burden of sorrow and did not leave their beds. Deprived of the great-souled one, Ayodhya was like the earth with its mountains, abandoned by Purandara. Oppressed by that terrible burden of fear, it seemed to quake. There was a road among the large number of elephants, warriors and horses.

Chapter 2(37)

When he departed, as long as the dust raised could be seen, the best of the Ikshvaku lineage[132] could not withdraw his gaze. His beloved son was extremely devoted to dharma and as long as the king wished to see him, the dust arose from the earth so that he could see his son. When the king could no longer see the dust raised by Rama, he became distressed and miserable and fell down on the ground. On the right, the lady Kousalya raised him in her arms. On the left flank, the lady Kaikeyee, who loved Bharata, raised him. The king was accomplished in policy, dharma and humility. However, afflicted in his senses, the king glanced towards Kaikeyee and said, 'O Kaikeyee! You are wicked in conduct. Do not touch my limbs. I do not wish to see you. You are not my wife, or my relative. I do not depend on you. I do not belong to you and you do not belong to me. For you, artha alone is supreme. Since you have discarded dharma,

[132] Dasharatha. The dust raised by Rama's chariot.

I discard you. I accepted your hand and circumambulated the fire. I am giving all of that up, in this world and in the next. If Bharata is delighted at having obtained this undecaying kingdom, if he gives anything to me in the form of funeral oblations, let those not reach me.'[133] The lord of men was covered in dust and Queen Kousalya, afflicted by grief, made him return.[134] The one with dharma in his soul thought about his ascetic son. He was tormented, as if he had wilfully slain a brahmana, or touched the fire with his hand. Distressed, he turned repeatedly towards the path followed by the chariot. The king was no longer radiant, like the one with rays[135] at the time of an eclipse. Remembering his beloved son, he lamented in grief and affliction. Discerning that his son had reached the boundaries of the city, he said, 'My son has been borne by the best of mounts. That is the reason marks of hooves can be seen along the road, but the great-souled one cannot be seen. It is certain that he will have to find a refuge at the foot of a tree today. He will have to lie down with its trunk, or a rock, as a pillow. The unfortunate one will wake on the ground, covered in dust. He will sigh like a bull elephant, surrounded by she elephants, does in a stream. It is certain that those who roam around in the forest will see a long-armed man, when Rama awakes and leaves. Though he is the protector of the world, he is like one without a protector. O Kaikeyee! May your wishes be fulfilled. May you reside in the kingdom like a widow. Without that tiger among men, I am not interested in remaining alive.' The king was surrounded by a crowd of people and lamented in this way. He entered that supreme city, like one who has bathed after an unfortunate event.[136]

The crossroads and houses were deserted. The shops and temples were covered. Exhausted, weak, miserable and afflicted, not too many people could be seen along the wide roads. Thinking of Rama, he looked at the entire city. Lamenting, the king entered

[133] That is, Dasharatha does not want Bharata to perform funeral oblations for him.

[134] To the city.

[135] The sun.

[136] Meaning death and the bath that one takes before entering the house after a funeral ceremony.

his residence, like the sun disappearing amidst clouds. It was like a large lake that was no longer agitated, since Suparna[137] had emptied it of all the serpents. Without Rama, Vaidehi and Lakshmana, that is what the residence looked like. 'Convey me quickly to the residence of Kousalya, Rama's mother.' This is what the king told the gatekeepers. Having entered Kousalya's residence, he lay himself down on a bed, but his mind was agitated. The great and valiant king looked around. He lamented in a loud voice, 'Alas, Raghava! You have left me. The best among men who survive this period and see Rama, and embrace him on his return, are happy. O Kousalya! O virtuous one! I am unable to see you. Touch me with your hand. My eyesight has followed Rama and has not returned.' The queen saw that though the Indra among men was lying down on the couch, he was thinking of Rama. She became even more distressed and sat down. Because of the hardship, she too sighed and lamented.

Chapter 2(38)

The king was lying down, afflicted by grief. On seeing this, Kousalya, who was also grief-stricken because of her son, addressed the lord of the earth. 'Having released her poison on Raghava, tiger among men, Kaikeyee will roam around like a fork-tongued female serpent that has cast of its skin. The immensely fortunate one has satisfied her wish of banishing Rama. Self-controlled, she will now terrify me, like a wicked snake in a house. It would have been better had a boon been granted of my son dwelling in the house as a servant who roams around in the city, like a beggar looking for alms. As she desired, Kaikeyee has brought Rama down from his position. She is like a person who offers oblations into the fire on an auspicious occasion, but offers the indicated shares to rakshasas instead. The brave one possesses the

137 Garuda.

stride of a king of elephants. He is a mighty-armed archer. He must certainly have entered the forest with his wife and with Lakshmana. Because of Kaikeyees's instruction and yours, in the forest, he will face hardships that he has not faced before. When he finishes his dwelling in the forest, what state will he be in? Devoid of riches, those young ones have been exiled and will be deprived of the fruits their ages warrant. Miserable, how will they live there, surviving on fruits and roots? When will that auspicious time, when I will see Raghava, with his wife and brother, and when my sorrows will be destroyed, arrive? When will Ayodhya hear that the brave ones have returned? When will the city be illustrious, with standards and garlands, full of happy people? When will we see those two tigers and men return from the forest? When will the city be happy and delighted, like the ocean at the time of the full moon? When will the brave and mighty-armed one enter the city of Ayodhya, placing Sita at the front of the chariot, like a bull behaving towards a cow? When will my sons, scorchers of enemies,[138] enter and proceed along the royal road, with thousands of people showering them with parched grain? When will they, with cheerful minds, happily circumambulate the city, offering fruits to maidens and brahmanas? When will the one who knows about dharma, as radiant as an immortal, return, with mature intelligence and age, and nourish me for three years?[139] O brave one! It is certain that I must have committed a cruel act earlier.[140] When calves wished to suck at milk, I must have sliced off the teats of mother cows. I am like a cow with a calf, rendered calf-less by a lion. O tiger among men! I am like a cow with a tender calf, forcibly rendered calf-less by Kaikeyee. He is ornamented with all the qualities and is accomplished in all the sacred texts. I only have one son. Without the son, I do not desire to remain alive. I cannot discern any capacity to remain alive. I am unable to see my beloved son, who is mighty-armed and immensely strong. My body is being scorched by grief, from the heat of a fire that has arisen. It

[138] In the dual, including Lakshmana.

[139] The imagery is of rains, specifically, three consecutive years of good rainfall.

[140] In an earlier life.

is as if the illustrious sun is scorching this earth with the radiance of its blazing rays during the summer.'

Chapter 2(39)

Kousalya, supreme among women, lamented in this way. Established in dharma, Sumitra addressed her in words that were full of dharma. 'O noble one! Your son is supreme among men and possesses all the virtuous qualities. Why are you lamenting? Why are you weeping piteously? O noble one! Your immensely strong son has forsaken the kingdom and has left. The great-souled one has performed a virtuous act and has made his father's words come true. If one acts properly and virtuously, one obtains eternal fruits, even after death. Rama has been established in the best of dharma and one should never sorrow over him. The unblemished Lakshmana follows excellent conduct and is devoted to him. His compassion towards all creatures will bring benefit to the great-souled one.[141] Vaidehi is used to happiness and will know misery during her residence in the forest. However, she has followed your son, who has dharma in his soul. The radiance of the lord's deeds will flutter like a flag in the world. He possesses self-control and the vow of truth. After this, what can your son not obtain? Knowing about Rama's evident purity and supreme greatness, the sun will not be able to scorch his body with its rays. Auspicious breezes, appropriate for all seasons, will be released from the groves. Whether it is hot or cold, these cheerful winds will serve Raghava. When he lies down in the night to sleep, the cool beams of the moon will touch him and gladden him, like a father's embrace. On seeing that he had slain the Indra among danavas, Timidhvaja's son,[142] in a battle, the greatly energetic brahmana gave him divine weapons. The bull among men will obtain prosperity, together with

[141] Lakshmana's conduct will bring benefits to Rama.

[142] Timidhvaja is Shambara, whom Dasharatha fought against. Shambara's son is Subahu, killed by Rama. The brahmana who gave the weapons is Vishvamitra.

Vaidehi, who came out of the earth. With these three,[143] Rama will be consecrated as king. On seeing him leave this place, people shed tears of sorrow. You will soon see tears of joy emerge from their eyes. On seeing the well-wishers honour your son, you will soon release tears of joy, like an array of clouds during the monsoon. Your son, the granter of boons, will quickly return to Ayodhya. He will knead your feet with his thick, but gentle, hands.' Hearing these words of Lakshmana's mother, Rama's mother, the wife of the king, instantly made all sorrow disappear from her body, like an autumn cloud vanishes with only a little bit of water.[144]

Chapter 2(40)

There were men who were devoted to the great-souled Rama, for whom, truth was his valour. When he left to live in the forest, they followed him. The king and his army returned. However, the groups of well-wishers did not return and followed Rama's chariot. He possessed all the qualities. Therefore, when he lived in Ayodhya, he was loved by those immensely illustrious men, as if he was the full moon. Despite being entreated to the contrary, Kakutstha rendered his father's pledge true and took to the forest. They glanced at him affectionately, as if they were drinking him in with their eyes. Affectionately, Rama addressed those subjects, as if they were his own offspring. 'O residents of Ayodhya! You have shown me affection and great respect. For the sake of bringing me pleasure, display this particularly towards Bharata. His character is fortunate and he extends Kaikeyee's delight. He will do whatever is appropriate, for benefit and pleasure. He may be young in age, but he is aged in wisdom. He is mild, but has the qualities of valour. He is worthy to be your lord and will dispel your fears. He possesses the qualities of being a king and has been identified as the heir apparent.

143 The earth, Sita and prosperity.

144 Probably meaning that an autumn cloud rains little.

In addition, we must abide by virtue and follow the commands of our master.[145] As I leave for the forest, ensure that the great king does not suffer. If you wish to bring me pleasure, this is what you should do.' The more Rama abided by the principles of dharma, the more the ordinary people desired him as their lord. They were distressed, overflowing with tears. The people who resided in the city were tied to Rama because of his qualities, and to Soumitri.

There were brahmanas who were aged in three ways—learning, age and energy. Their heads trembled because of their age.[146] From a distance, they cried out, 'O swift steeds that are bearing Rama! O fast horses born in noble lineages! If you desire the welfare of your lord, return and do not proceed to the destination. Your lord deserves to be brought back to the city. He does not deserve to be taken to the forest.' The aged brahmanas suffered and lamented in this way. On seeing that they were lamenting, Rama quickly descended from his chariot. With Sita and Lakshmana, Rama, headed for the forest, walking on foot and keeping pace with them.[147] Rama's character was affectionate and because of compassion, he was incapable of looking at the brahmanas who were on foot. Therefore, he abandoned the chariot. On seeing that Rama was still proceeding, the brahmanas were scared in their minds. Suffering greatly, they addressed Rama in these words. 'Just as you follow brahmanas, all the brahmanas are following you. These brahmanas are following you, carrying their sacred fires on their shoulders. Behold our white umbrellas from *vajapeya* sacrifices, held aloft.[148] They are following at the rear, like swans at the end of the monsoon. You do not have an umbrella and are tormented by the rays.[149] We will offer you shade from umbrellas obtained at vajapeya sacrifices. Our intelligence has always followed the mantras of the Vedas. O child! For your sake, we are now following you as you leave for

[145] Dasharatha.

[146] Because of their age, they couldn't follow.

[147] The brahmanas.

[148] Brahmanas who officiate at vajapeya sacrifices are given white umbrellas, normally the exclusive right of kings.

[149] Of the sun.

the forest. The Vedas are our supreme treasure and they are stored in our hearts. Our wives will be protected by their good characters and will reside in our homes. There is no need to think again about our course of action. We have taken the excellent decision of going with you. Since you are considering dharma, who is capable of not adhering to dharma? Our grey hair is like the white feathers on swans. We wish that you should return. Because our heads touched the ground, they are covered with dust from the earth.[150] O child! The brahmanas who have come here have commenced many sacrifices and their completion is conditional on your return. Both inanimate objects and animate creatures are devoted to you. They desire your affection. You should show them your affection. These trees seem to be weeping, raised by the force of the wind. Since they are unable to follow you, they are forcibly tugging at their roots. The birds are also beseeching you. They are perched in one spot on the trees, not trying to gather food. You are compassionate towards all creatures.' In this fashion, the brahmanas lamented, wanting his return. At this time, the river Tamasa was seen, as if it was also restraining Raghava.

Chapter 2(41)

Raghava reached the beautiful banks of the Tamasa. He looked towards Sita and Soumitri and spoke these words. 'O Soumtri! Today is the first night of our residing in the forest. O fortunate one! You should not be anxious about dwelling in the forest. Behold. In every direction, the empty forest seems to be crying. Seeking shelter, the animals and birds are returning to their own abodes. The city of Ayodhya, my father's capital, and all the women and men there, will no doubt grieve about our departure. Bharata has dharma in his soul. He will no doubt comfort my father and mother with words that are full of dharma, artha and kama. O Lakshmana! Repeatedly

[150] When the brahmanas prostrated themselves and begged him to return.

thinking about the fact that Bharata does not cause injury, I am not sorrowing over my father and mother. O tiger among men! You have done your duty by following me. Otherwise, for Vaidehi's protection, I would have had to search for help. O Soumitri! Tonight, I will only subsist on water. Though there are many kinds of forest fare, this is what appeals to me.'

Having addressed Soumitri in this way, Raghava spoke to Sumantra. 'O amiable one! Tend attentively to the horses.' With the sun having set, Sumantra tethered the horses close by and gave them sufficient grass. On seeing that the evening was auspicious and that night had presented itself, with Soumitri, the suta prepared a bed for Rama to lie down on. On the banks of the Tamasa, a bed was prepared with the leaves of trees. With Soumitri's help, Rama and his wife entered that place. On seeing that his brother was asleep with his wife, Lakshmana told the suta about Rama's manifold qualities. Soumitri remained awake the entire night on the banks of the Tamasa, recounting Rama's qualities to the suta. The sun arose.

Not very far from the banks of the Tamasa, there were many herds of cows. With the ordinary people, Rama had spent the night there. Having awoken, the immensely energetic Rama saw those ordinary people and spoke to his brother Lakshmana, who possessed auspicious signs. 'O Soumitri! Look. Ignoring their homes, these people are looking towards us. O Lakshmana! See. They are sleeping near the roots of trees. These citizens are making efforts to make us return.[151] They will give up their lives, but will not give up their determination. In the limited time that we have while they are still asleep, let us ascend the chariot and leave, along a path that is devoid of fear. These residents from the capital city of the Ikshvakus, who are devoted to me, must not sleep near the roots of trees again. Because of two princes, these citizens have brought this suffering on themselves and must be freed from it. This misery is for us and the residents of the city must not be made to suffer.' Rama was stationed like Dharma[152] himself and Lakshmana told

[151] The citizens of Ayodhya who were still with them.

[152] The god of dharma.

him, 'O immensely wise one! This idea appeals to me. Ascend the chariot quickly.'

The charioteer swiftly yoked the excellent horses to the chariot. He joined his hands in salutation and told Rama that the yoking had been done. To confuse the citizens, Rama addressed the suta in these words. 'O charioteer! Mount the chariot and drive it towards the north. After swiftly driving for some time, bring the chariot back. Do this carefully, so that the citizens do not know where I am.' Hearing Rama's words, the charioteer drove the chariot around in a circle. Retracing the steps, he informed Rama that the chariot had returned. With all the accompanying objects, Raghava ascended the chariot. They quickly crossed the river Tamasa, which was full of whirlpools. The mighty-armed and prosperous one reached a large and auspicious road that was free from all obstructions and had no reason to scare even those who were afraid.

When night was over and it was morning, the citizens saw that Raghava wasn't there. Devoid of their senses and grief-stricken, they couldn't move. Their eyes overflowing with tears of grief, they cast their eyes here and there. However, they couldn't see Rama and were miserable. For some time, they followed the path. But unable to discern the tracks, they were filled with great sorrow. The chariot's tracks had vanished. Those spirited ones returned, exclaiming, 'What will we do? We have been struck by destiny.' Exhausted, senseless and full of distress, all of them returned to the city of Ayodhya along the path they had followed while coming there.

Chapter 2(42)

The residents of the city gave up their attempt to follow Rama. They were dispirited and were ready to give up their lives. They reached their own respective houses and were surrounded by their sons and wives. All of them wept and their faces were covered with tears. No one was happy. No one was delighted. No trader displayed his wares. No merchandise glittered. No one who was responsible for a house cooked. No one was delighted at great riches, once lost, having been regained. No mother was joyous that the first son had been born. When the husbands returned home, there was weeping in every house. Afflicted by grief, like striking elephants with goads, they[153] struck them with words. 'What work do they have at home? What will they do with wives and riches? If they cannot see Raghava, what happiness will they obtain from sons? There is only one virtuous man in this world, Lakshmana. With Sita, he has followed Kakutstha Rama, so as to serve him. The rivers and lotus ponds must have earned good merits with their deeds, since Kakutstha will enter their auspicious waters and bathe there. The forests with charming groves, lands with great rivers and peaked mountains will beautify themselves for Kakutstha. Whenever Rama goes to a grove or a mountain, like a beloved guest who has arrived, it cannot but worship him. There are colourful blossoming trees that bear many kinds of flowers. The mountains will speak of Rama's arrival and the best of flowers and fruits will be shown to him, even if it is not the right season. Diverse colourful waterfalls will be displayed to him. On the summits of mountains, trees will cause delight to Raghava. Where Rama is, there is no fear. There is no defeat there. Dasharatha's son is brave and mighty-armed. Raghava is in front of us. He has not gone a long distance away. The shadow of the feet of such a great-souled lord constitutes happiness. He is the protector of the people. He is the supreme destination. We will tend to Sita, while you serve Raghava.' Thus, afflicted by grief, the women of the city told their husbands. 'In the forest, Raghava will ensure yoga and *kshema* for us.[154] Sita will ensure yoga and kshema for the womenfolk. Who will be happy in this place, populated by anxious people? Unless senseless, who will wish to dwell in such an unpleasant place? If this kingdom belongs to Kaikeyee, it will be full of adharma and

[153] The wives.

[154] Yoga has several meanings. In this context, it means getting objectives that one aspires for, but doesn't yet possess. In contrast, kshema means protecting and preserving what one already possesses.

we will be without a protector. There is no purpose to remaining alive. What is the point of sons? What is the point of riches? Who else will Kaikeyee, the defiler of the lineage, cast aside for the sake of riches? Her husband and son have abandoned her. We will not reside as servants in Kaikeyee's kingdom. We swear on our living sons that we will not do this as long as we are alive. Without any pity, she has banished the son of the king. She is wicked in conduct and has followed adharma. Having obtained it in this way, who can live happily? With Rama having been exiled, the lord of the earth will not remain alive. It is evident that after Dasharatha is dead, only lamentations will remain. Your[155] merits have been exhausted and you face a great catastrophe. Stir up some poison and drink it. Either follow Raghava, or follow the path of the ignorant. It is by resorting to deceit that Rama, his wife, and Lakshmana have been banished. We have been handed over to Bharata, like animals to an executioner.' In the city, the women who lived in the city lamented in this fashion. They wept, tormented by grief, as if they faced the fear of death. The women were afflicted on account of Rama, as if their sons or brothers had been exiled. Grief-stricken, they lamented, and senseless, wept. For them, he was superior to their own sons.

Chapter 2(43)

Remembering his father's command, when night descended, Rama, tiger among men, travelled a great distance away. He travelled in this way throughout that auspicious night. He travelled beyond the boundaries of the kingdom and worshipped the morning sandhya. He proceeded swiftly on those excellent horses, which were like arrows, and passed by villages. He saw that their boundaries had flowering groves. He heard the words of the men who lived in those villages. 'Shame on King Dasharatha, who succumbed to

[155] Addressing the men.

desire. Alas! The wicked and cruel Kaikeyee has now been bound down by sin. Having fiercely transgressed norms, she has engaged in a fierce act. She has exiled such a son and prince, who is devoted to dharma. With her senses clouded by rage, she has dispatched the immensely wise one to residence in the forest.' He heard such words from the men who dwelt in those villages.

The brave lord of Kosala went beyond the boundaries of Kosala. There was a river named Vedashruti there, the bearer of auspicious waters. Having travelled towards the north, he next advanced towards the direction occupied by Agastya.[156] After travelling for a long period of time, he reached the river Gomatee, with cool waters. Its banks were ornamented with large numbers of cattle and it was headed towards the ocean. With those swift horses, Raghava crossed the Gomatee. He also crossed the river Syandika, resounding with the calls of peacocks and swans. In ancient times, this land had been given to the Ikshvakus by King Manu. Rama showed Vaidehi the boundaries of this prosperous kingdom. The handsome bull among men then glanced towards the charioteer and addressed him in a voice that was like that of a swan in love. 'When will I again return to the flowering forests on the banks of the Sarayu? When will I unite with my mother and my father and roam around on hunts? I do not excessively crave for hunting in the forests along the banks of the Sarayu. I love that place, unmatched in the world, and revered by rajarshis.' The descendant of the Ikshvaku lineage addressed the suta in these sweet words and spoke other desired words that were full of meaning. He continued to advance.

Chapter 2(44)

Lakshmana's mighty-armed elder brother crossed the beautiful and extensive land of Kosala and reached Shringaverapura.

[156] Agastya's direction is the south. Rama crossed Tamasa and headed north. When he reached Vedashruti (which is difficult to identify), he turned south.

There Raghava saw the auspicious Ganga of the three flows, with divine and auspicious waters that were free of moss, populated by sacred rishis. There were the sounds of swans and cranes, the crying of *chakravaka* birds. Dolphins, crocodiles and serpents resided there. The maharatha saw waves and eddies and told the suta Sumantra, 'Let us reside here today. There is an extremely large *inguda* tree[157] not far from this river, with many flowers and branches. O charioteer! We will reside here.' Lakshmana and Sumantra said that they agreed with what Raghava had said and tied the horses to the inguda tree. Rama, the descendant of the Ikshvaku lineage, approached that beautiful tree. With his wife and with Lakshmana, he descended from the chariot. Sumantra also descended and released the supreme horses. He presented himself before Rama, at the foot of the tree, and joined his hands in salutation.

There was a king named Guha. He was Rama's friend and Rama loved him like his own self. He was born as a powerful nishada and was famous as an architect.[158] He heard that Rama, tiger among men, had arrived in his dominion. Therefore, surrounded by elders, advisers and kin, he arrived there. From a distance, Rama saw that the king of the nishadas was arriving. With Soumitri, he went forward to receive Guha. Guha was distressed.[159] He embraced Raghava and said, 'O Rama! For you, this place is just like Ayodhya. What can I do for you?' He brought the best quality of rice and other objects. He swiftly offered arghya and spoke these words. 'O mighty-armed one! Welcome. This entire earth is yours. All of us are your servants and you are our lord. Rule our kingdom. *Bhakshya*, *bhojya*, peya and lehya have been presented.[160] There are the best of beds and fodder for the horses.' When Guha spoke in this way, Raghava replied to him. 'We are delighted and you have honoured us in every

[157] *Balanites roxburghii.*

[158] Architect or builder is the natural translation, but this can also be translated as king.

[159] Because of Rama's exile.

[160] The four types of food are those that are chewed (charvya), sucked (choshya or chushya), licked (lehya) and drunk (peya). Bhakshya is the same as charvya and bhojya is the same as choshya.

possible way. To display your affection, you have arrived here on foot.' He engulfed him in his thick and auspicious arms and added these words. 'O Guha! It is good fortune that I see that you and your relatives are healthy. Is everything well with your kingdom, friends and riches? I know everything about your affection, which is why you have arranged all this. However, I should not accept them. Know that I am certain to abide by the dharma of an ascetic who lives in the forest. I will wear kusha grass, rags and bark. I will eat fruits and roots. I do not wish for anything other than fodder for the horses. If you do only this much, I will be greatly honoured. These horses are extremely well trained and are loved by my father, King Dasharatha. I will be honoured if this is done.' Guha instructed the men present, 'Let food and water be given to the horses. Give it quickly.'

He[161] only wore an upper garment made of bark. He worshipped the western sandhya. For food, he only had water that Lakshmana had brought himself. As he lay down on the ground with his wife, Lakshmana washed his feet and stood near a tree there. Guha conversed with the suta and Lakshmana. Without being distracted, the archer[162] remained awake and guarded Rama. The intelligent, illustrious and great-souled son of Dasharatha slept in this way. He had never faced unhappiness and deserved happiness. The long night passed in this way.

Chapter 2(45)

Lakshmana was tormented. On account of his brother, he remained awake. Also grief-stricken, Guha humbly addressed Raghava[163] in these words. 'O father![164] This comfortable bed has

[161] Rama.

[162] This could mean Guha, but Lakshmana is more likely.

[163] Lakshmana.

[164] The word used is tata. While this does mean father or son, it is affectionately used for anyone who is senior or junior. While there are no indications as to whether Guha would address Lakshmana as a senior or a junior, senior seems more likely.

been constructed for you. O prince! Cheerfully, lie down and relax on it. All these people are used to hardships. You are used to ease. For the sake of protecting Kakutstha, we will remain awake during the night. There is nothing on earth that is as dear to me as Rama. I am telling you this truthfully. If this is not true, you can curse me. Through his favour, I hope to attain extremely great fame in this world. I will not only obtain artha, but will also obtain great dharma. My beloved friend, Rama, is lying down with Sita. With all my kin, I will protect him with the bow in my hand. Though I always roam around in the forest, there is nothing that is unknown to me. We are capable of repulsing a great army that consists of the four kinds of forces.'

At this, Lakshmana replied, 'O unblemished one! You look towards dharma and protected by you, all of us have nothing to fear here. When Dasharatha's son is lying down on the ground with Sita, as long as I am alive, how is it possible for me to lie down happily? All the gods and asuras are incapable of standing before him in a battle. Look at him, sleeping happily on the grass with Sita. Through mantras, austerities and many other kinds of efforts, Dasharatha obtained this son, with such qualities. With him exiled, the king will not live for a long time. It is certain that the earth will soon become a widow.[165] Having wept extremely loudly, the women must be exhausted. O son![166] I think the sounds must have ceased in the king's abode. I am not certain that Kousalya, the king and my mother will survive the night. However, looking towards Shatrughna, my mother may remain alive. But it will be misery if Kousalya, the mother of a brave son, dies. The king brought happiness to this world and that place is full of devoted people. With the catastrophe that results,[167] the city will perish. His extremely fond desire to see Rama instated as heir apparent in the kingdom has not been accomplished. With that not accomplished, my father will be destroyed. When that time presents itself, those who are around my father will be successful

[165] Figuratively, since the king is the lord of the earth.
[166] The word used is tata.
[167] Were the king to die.

in their objectives and will perform all the funeral rites for the lord of the earth. The crossroads are beautiful and the large roads have been laid out well. There are mansions and palaces, adorned with the best of courtesans. Obstructions are created by chariots, horses and elephants. There is the sound of trumpets blaring. There are all the fortunate signs and the place is populated by happy and well-nourished people. There are gardens for pleasure, maintained by the communities. Everything in my father's capital is full of happiness. After completing the pledge of truth and the period of exile in the forest faithfully, will we return to Ayodhya together?' Afflicted by grief, the great-souled one lamented in this way. As the prince stood there, the night passed. For the sake of the subjects, the son of the Indra among men spoke these true words, out of affection for his senior.[168] Overcome by the calamity, Guha released warm tears, like an elephant suffering from fever and afflicted by pain.

Chapter 2(46)

When night was over, the broad-chested and immensely illustrious Rama spoke to Soumitri Lakshmana, who possessed all the auspicious qualities. 'The illustrious night has passed and it is time for the sun to rise. O son![169] This extremely dark bird, the cuckoo, is calling. The sounds of peacocks crying in the forest can be heard. O amiable one! We will cross the swift-flowing Jahnavee, which heads towards the ocean.' Standing in front of Rama, Soumitri, the extender of the delight of his friends, heard his brother's words and summoned Guha and the suta. Those two archers, the two Raghavas, girded swords with ornamented handles around their loins and prepared to swiftly head towards the Ganga, with Sita.

[168] Probably meaning Dasharatha, but could mean Rama too.
[169] The word used is tata.

The suta, conversant with dharma, humbly arrived before Rama. He joined his hands in salutation and asked, 'What will I do?' He was addressed in these words. 'Return. This is all that I required. Abandoning the vehicle, we will now proceed to the great forest on foot.' On seeing that he had been thus instructed, the charioteer was distressed. Sumantra addressed the descendant of the Ikshvaku lineage, the tiger among men, in these words. 'No man in the world has ever had to go through anything like this—like an ordinary person, you will have to live in the forest with your brother and your wife. I do not think that there are any fruits from brahmacharya or self-study, or from mildness or uprightness, since this kind of a hardship has befallen you. O Raghava! O brave one! By residing in the forest with Vaidehi and your brother, you will obtain ends obtained by one who has conquered the three worlds. O Rama! Since you have been deceived, we have also been destroyed. Having come under the subjugation of the wicked Kaikeyee, we will have our share of misery.' To the charioteer, Sumantra, Rama was like his own soul. He spoke in this way and wept for a long time. Afflicted by grief, from a distance, he looked on. When the weeping was over, the suta touched water and purified himself. Rama repeatedly spoke these sweet words to him. 'For the lineage of the Ikshvakus, a well-wisher like you cannot be discerned. Act so that King Dasharatha does not grieve over me. The lord of the earth is aged and his senses are afflicted by grief. He suffers from the burden of desire. That is the reason I am telling you this. Whatever the great-souled lord of the earth commands you to do, in an attempt to bring pleasure to Kaikeyee, do that without any hesitation. Lords of men rule their kingdoms with this objective in mind, that whatever tasks their minds desire should be carried out without impediments. O Sumantra! Act so that the great king does not suffer from sorrow that his commands are in vain. The king is noble and aged and has conquered his senses. He faces a sorrow that he has not confronted earlier. For my sake, bow down before him and address him in these words. "I, Lakshmana and Maithilee are not grieving that we have been dislodged from Ayodhya and have to reside in the forest. After fourteen years have passed, we will quickly return and you will again see me, Lakshmana and Sita." O Sumantra! Speak to the king and my mother in this way. Repeatedly tell Kaikeyee and the other queens this. Bow down before Kousalya's feet and tell her I am well. Say this about Sita, me and the noble Lakshmana. Tell the great king that he should swiftly summon Bharata. As the king wishes, once Bharata has arrived, let him be consecrated. Embrace Bharata and get him consecrated as the heir apparent. Let the grief and torment on our account not overcome you. Bharata should be told that, without any distinction, he should behave towards the mothers as he would towards the king. Sumitra is no different from Kaikeyee. In particular, this is also true of my mother, Queen Kousalya.' Sumantra was thus sent back by Rama and he was full of sorrow.

Hearing all these words, he spoke affectionately to Kakutstha. 'If I speak fearlessly and without due courtesies, that is because of my affection. I am devoted to you. Therefore, you should pardon any misdemeanour in my words. How can I return to a city where you are not present? O son![170] Without you, I will suffer the separation from a son. The people lamented when they saw my chariot with Rama astride it. On seeing a chariot without Rama, the city will be shattered. On seeing the empty chariot, the city will be submerged in grief. It will be as if the charioteer alone is left when a hero and all his soldiers have been slain in a battle. Even when you reside far away, you are always topmost in their minds. It is certain that today, thinking of you, the subjects have starved. The citizens uttered cries of distress when you were exiled. On seeing my chariot, those cries will be multiplied a hundredfold. Can I tell the queen the following? "I have conveyed your son to his maternal uncle's house. Do not unnecessarily sorrow over him." I cannot speak such words, since they are false. How can I speak truthful words, since they are exceedingly unpleasant? I have engaged these mounts to carry you and your relatives. How can I tell these excellent steeds to bear a chariot that doesn't have you? If you ask me to leave you

[170] The word used is tata. Because of the affection, son seems more appropriate than father.

here, as soon as I am abandoned by you, with the chariot, I will hurl myself into a fire. O Raghava! When you proceed to the forest, there are creatures that will cause obstructions in your austerities. Using this chariot, I will repulse them. It is on your account that I have obtained pleasure from driving this chariot. I hope that I will obtain happiness from residing in the forest with you. Show me your favours. In the forest, I desire to remain near you. I wish to hear your agreeable words that you want me to remain near you. Residing in the forest, I will bow down my head and serve you. In every way, I am ready to give up Ayodhya, and even the world of the gods. Without you, I am incapable of entering Ayodhya, just as a person who performs evil deeds is incapable of entering the great Indra's capital. O brave one! Residing in the forest, if these horses serve you, they will attain the supreme objective. My heart's desire is that once the period of residing in the forest is over, I will again convey you back to the city in this chariot. With you, the fourteen years in the forest will pass like an instant. Without you, it will seem like a hundred times longer. You are devoted to your servants and I am a servant who has been like a son to you. I am a servant who has remained within the bounds of devotion. Therefore, you should not abandon one who has been thus established.' Distressed, he repeatedly entreated in many kinds of ways. Compassionate towards servants, Rama addressed Sumantra in these words. 'I know of your supreme devotion and I know that you are devoted towards me, your master. Listen to the reason why I want you to leave this place and proceed to the city. On seeing you return to the city, my younger mother, Kaikeyee, will be reassured that Rama has indeed left for the forest. The queen will be content that I have left for dwelling in the forest. She will not suspect the king, who is devoted to dharma, of having uttered a falsehood. This is my first intention, that my younger mother should be prosperous and protected, on account of her son, Bharata, having obtained the kingdom. To bring pleasure to me and the king, go to the city with the chariot. As you have been instructed, respectively tell them about what has transpired.' Addressing the suta in these words, he repeatedly comforted him.

Without any lassitude, Rama then addressed Guha in words that were full of reason. 'Please bring me the sap of a *nyagrodha* tree.[171] Before proceeding further, I want to wear matted hair.' Guha quickly brought the sap for the prince and Rama used it to make his and Lakshmana's hair matted. They wore garments made of bark and their hair was matted. Those two brothers, Rama and Lakshmana, were as resplendent as rishis. With Lakshmana, Rama adopted the path followed by a hermit, ready for the vows. He addressed his aide Guha, 'O Guha! It has been held that a kingdom is extremely difficult to protect. Without any distraction, protect its army, treasury, forts and habitations.' The delight of the Ikshvaku lineage took his leave of Guha. Without any anxiety, he quickly left, with his wife and with Lakshmana.

The descendant of the Ikshvaku lineage saw the boat on the banks of the river.[172] Desiring to cross the swift-flowing Ganga, he told Lakshmana, 'O tiger among men! Hold the boat steady, so that the spirited Sita can climb on to it. You get into it later.' Hearing his brother's command, which he never ignored, he made Maithilee ascend first and climbed on to it later. After this, Lakshmana's energetic elder brother himself climbed in. Guha, the lord of the nishadas, urged his kin.[173] Taking his leave of Sumantra, his forces and Guha, Rama resorted to the boat and instructed the boatmen. The well-trained helmsmen of the boat were thus instructed and swiftly using oars, forcefully conveyed it across those auspicious waters. On reaching the middle of the Bhageerathee, the unblemished Vaidehi joined her hands in salutation and addressed the river. 'This is the son of the intelligent and great King Dasharatha. O Ganga! Protected by you, he is observing what he has been commanded to. Having spent a full fourteen years in the desolate forest, with his brother and me, he will return again. O goddess! O extremely fortunate one! O Ganga! Happy on returning safely and prosperous with all my desires fulfilled, I will worship you. O goddess with

[171] The Indian fig tree.

[172] The Critical Edition has excised some shlokas towards the beginning of this chapter, telling us that Guha had readied the boat.

[173] To ferry them across.

the three flows! You are seen in Brahma's world. You are also seen in this world as the wife of the lord of the waters.[174] O goddess! I bow down before you. O beautiful one! I praise you. When the tiger among men returns safely and gets the kingdom back, to give you pleasure, I will give away one hundred thousand cows, food and delicate garments to brahmanas.' The unblemished and accomplished Sita addressed Ganga in this way. They swiftly reached the southern bank.

On reaching the bank, the bull among men descended from the boat. With his brother and Vaidehi, the scorcher of enemies proceeded. The mighty-armed one spoke to the one who extended Sumitra's joy. 'O Soumitri! Advance in front and let Sita follow you. I will follow at the rear and protect you and Sita. From now on, Sita will experience the hardships of dwelling in the forest.' As Rama swiftly reached the other bank of the Ganga, Sumantra steadily continued to glance at him. But because of the great distance, grieving and distressed, he released tears.

They slew four large animals there—varaha, *rishya*, *prishata* and *maharuru*.[175] Hungry, they quickly ate the parts that could be eaten. They then went to a tree and took refuge there.

Chapter 2(47)

Rama, best among those who cause delight, reached the tree and worshipped the western sandhya.[176] He spoke to Lakshmana. 'This is our first night, away from a habitation and without Sumantra. However, you should not be anxious. From tonight, we must attentively remain awake at night. O Lakshmana!

[174] The ocean.

[175] Rama and Lakshmana slew a varaha (this can mean boar or ram), rishya (antelope), prishata (spotted antelope) and maharuru (another kind of antelope). The word *mriga* means deer, but also means animal. They probably killed four kinds of deer. But it can also mean that they killed three kinds of deer and a boar.

[176] Evening.

Sita's comfort and security depend on us. O Soumitri! Let us spend the night, in whatever way we can. Let us cover the ground with whatever we collect ourselves and lie down there.' Though he was used to expensive beds, Rama lay down on the ground and addressed Soumitri in these auspicious words. 'O Lakshmana! It is certain that the great king is sleeping in misery. With her desires satisfied, Kaikeyee should be content. On seeing that Bharata has arrived, Queen Kaikeyee, for the sake of the kingdom, will not take away the great king's life. He is aged and without a protector and he has been separated from me. Overcome by desire and under Kaikeyee's subjugation, what will he do? On seeing the hardship the king has suffered on account of the distraction in his senses, it is my view that kama can be superior to artha and dharma. O Lakshmana! Which man, however ignorant he is, will voluntarily, for the sake of a woman, abandon a son like me? Kaikeyee's son, Bharata, is happy with his wife. Like a supreme king, he will alone happily enjoy Kosala. He will alone be foremost in the kingdom. My father is aged and I have resorted to the forest. Like King Dasharatha, if a person follows kama and abandons artha and dharma, he is swiftly reduced to such a state. O amiable one! It seems to be that Kaikeyee arrived to bring about Dasharatha's end, my exile and Bharata's obtaining of the kingdom. Perhaps Kaikeyee is now intoxicated by her good fortune and pride and on my account, is causing difficulties for Kousalya and Sumitra. On my account, let not Queen Sumitra live in misery. O Lakshmana! Tomorrow, leave this place and go to Ayodhya. I will go to Dandaka with Sita alone. Kousalya has no protector. Be her protector. Kaikeyee is inferior in conduct and acts with enmity towards others. O one who knows about dharma! Hand my mother over to Bharata. O Soumitri! In another life, my mother must have separated women from their sons, and that is the reason this has now happened. Kousalya has nourished me for a long time and reared me with difficulty. Shame on me! When it is time to reap the fruits, she has been separated from me. O Soumitri! Let no woman give birth to a son like me, who brings infinite sorrow to his mother. It is my view that the *sarika* bird displays greater affection, since it listens to the words, "O *shuka*!

Bite the feet of my enemy."[177] O scorcher of enemies! She is grieving and is unfortunate. Her son cannot help her. On my account, it is as if she is without a son. Separated from me, my mother, Kousalya, is limited in good fortune. Immersed in an ocean of grief, she is lying down in misery and affliction. O Lakshmana! When I am enraged, with my arrows, I can single-handedly save Ayodhya and even the entire earth. However, one must certainly not exhibit valour without reason. O unblemished one! O Lakshmana! I am terrified of adharma and the world hereafter. Therefore, I do not want myself to be consecrated now.' In that desolate spot, Rama lamented piteously in many other ways. His face overflowing with tears, he sat silently.

Rama lamented and was like a fire whose flames had gone out, or an ocean without any force. Lakshmana comforted him. 'O Rama! O supreme among those who fight! With you having left, it is certain that the city of Ayodhya is without any radiance now, like the moon when the night has passed. O Rama! It is not appropriate that you should be tormented in this way. O bull among men! You are making Sita and me also grieve. O Raghava! Without you, Sita and I will not be alive for even an instant, like fish taken out of water. O scorcher of enemies! Without you, I do not wish to see our father, Shatrughna or Sumitra, or even go to heaven now.' Lakshmana's words were excellent and after listening to all of them, Raghava, scorcher of enemies, accepted the idea of following dharma and living in the forest for an extremely long period of time.

Chapter 2(48)

Having spent the auspicious night under that large tree, when the sparkling sun arose, they left that spot. They entered that extremely large forest and headed for the region where Bhageerathee

[177] A sarika bird is a kind of thrush, *Turdus salica,* a talking bird kept as a pet. Kousalya had a sarika bird as a pet. But a shuka is a parrot, though the two words are being used synonymously. A female parrot is sometimes referred to as a sarika.

Ganga and Yamuna have a confluence. Those illustrious ones saw many beautiful countries and tracts of land that they had never seen before. Advancing comfortably, Rama saw many trees. When day had passed, he told Soumitri, 'O Soumitri! Behold. Smoke is rising from near Prayaga.[178] I think this illustrious fire is a sign that the sage[179] is close. We have certainly reached the confluence of the Ganga and the Yamuna. That is the reason the sound of water dashing against water can be heard. Many trees can be seen in Bharadvaja's hermitage. Those who make their living from the forest are splitting wood.' When the sun was long and it was evening, the two archers cheerfully reached the confluence of the Ganga and the Yamuna and the sage's abode. When Rama reached the hermitage, the animals and birds were frightened. After spending a short while along the path, they reached Bharadvaja. On reaching the hermitage, those two brave ones, with Sita following them, wished to see the sage, but halted some distance away.

The immensely illustrious one was offering agnihotra oblations into the fire. Rama, with Soumitri and Sita, joined his hands in salutation and worshipped him. Lakshmana's elder brother introduced himself. 'O illustrious one! We are Rama and Lakshmana, Dasharatha's sons. This is my fortunate wife Vaidehi, Janaka's daughter. The unblemished one has followed me to the desolate forest to perform austerities. When my father banished me, my beloved younger brother, Soumitri, was firm in his vows that he would follow me. O illustrious one! Commanded by our father, we have entered the forest to perform austerities. We will follow dharma there, living on roots and fruits.' Hearing the words of the intelligent prince, the one with dharma in his soul, offered him a cow, arghya and water.[180] The sage was seated, with animals and birds

[178] The confluence of Ganga and Yamuna, today's Allahabad.

[179] Bharadvaja.

[180] The text uses the word *ga*, Bharadvaja offered Rama ga. This is interpreted in translations as *madhuparka*, a mixture of milk and honey offered to a guest. However, a cow was also offered to a guest as a gift. Ga means cow and there is no reason why Bharadvaja shouldn't have symbolically offered a cow. The madhuparka interpretation is possible, but is unnecessary.

around him. When Rama arrived, the sage honoured and welcomed him. Having accepted these honours, Raghava seated himself and Bharadvaja addressed him in words that were full of dharma. 'O Kakutstha! It has indeed been a long time since you came here and I saw you. I have heard about your being exiled without reason. This region of the confluence of the two great rivers is secluded. It is sacred and beautiful. Dwell here happily.' Addressed by Bharadvaja in these words, Raghava, engaged in the welfare of everyone, replied in these auspicious words. 'O illustrious one! Inhabitants of the city and the countryside live near this spot. Wishing to see me and Vaidehi, those people will come here. That is the reason the idea of living here does not appeal to me. O illustrious one! Think of some lonely and excellent hermitage, so that Vaidehi, Janaka's daughter who deserves every kind of happiness, can find pleasure there.' On hearing these auspicious words, the great sage, Bharadvaja, addressed Raghava in words that were full of meaning. 'O son![181] You can reside in a mountain that is ten *krosha*s from this place.[182] That spot is sacred, pleasant to see everywhere and frequented by maharshis. It is populated by golangulas, apes and bears. The place is like Gandhamadana and is known by the name of Chitrakuta. As long as a man can see the summit of Chitrakuta, he performs auspicious deeds and the mind does not turn towards sin. Many rishis have spent hundreds of autumns there, performed austerities and ascended to heaven, to obtain the company of Kapalashiras.[183] I think that this lonely spot will be a happy place for you to reside in. O Rama! Otherwise, for the duration of your abode in the forest, live here with me.' Bharadvaja thus offered all the objects of desire for Rama, his beloved guest. With his wife and his brother, the one who knew about dharma accepted them.

When Rama approached the maharshi in Prayaga, the auspicious night arrived and they conversed about wonderful

[181] The word used is tata.

[182] This has a bearing on Chitrakuta and where it was, Madhya Pradesh or Uttar Pradesh. One krosha is two miles and ten kroshas make it twenty miles from Prayaga. However, the definition of krosha was not standardized.

[183] Shiva.

accounts. When night was over and it was morning, the tiger among men approached Bharadvaja.[184] He spoke to the sage, who blazed in his energy. 'O illustrious one! O one who is truthful in conduct! We have spent the night in your hermitage. Now grant us permission to find our abode.' With the night over, Bharadvaja said, 'Go to Chitrakuta, which possesses plenty of honey, roots and fruits. O Raghava! Around the extremities of the forest there, you will see herds of elephants and herds of deer roaming around. The auspicious ground there resounds with the cheerful notes of water hens and cuckoos. There are many kinds of crazy deer and elephants. Dwell there, in an extremely beautiful hermitage.'

Chapter 2(49)

When the night was over, the two princes, scorchers of enemies, greeted the maharshi and left for that mountain. When they left, the great sage glanced towards them, like a father towards his sons, and addressed them in these words. 'From here, you will reach the Kalindi,[185] swift in its flow. Prepare a raft and cross the river Amshumati[186] there. After that, approach the giant nyagrodha tree, enveloped in green. This dark-green tree is surrounded by many trees and is frequented by siddhas. After having advanced hardly a krosha from that spot, you will see a blue grove. O Rama! It is full of beautiful palasha and badari trees, and bamboo leans over the Yamuna. That is the path towards Chitrakuta and there are many occasions when I have gone along it. It is beautiful and mild and is free from forest conflagrations.' After indicating the path, the maharshi returned.

[184] Inexplicably, the Critical Edition excises a shloka which mentions their sleeping happily during the night. Hence, there is a break in continuity.

[185] The Yamuna.

[186] Another name for the Yamuna. Yamuna was the daughter of the sun god and Amshumati means Amshumat's (the sun god's) daughter.

When the sage returned, Rama told Lakshmana, 'O Soumitri! Since the sage has shown us his compassion, we must have performed auspicious deeds.' The two spirited tigers among men consulted each other. Placing Sita ahead of them, they headed for the river Kalindi. Fastening timber together, they fashioned a large raft. Severing reeds,[187] Lakshmana created a comfortable seat for Sita. His beloved was as unthinkable as Shri and was a trifle ashamed. Rama, Dasharatha's son, helped her climb on to the raft. Using the raft, they crossed the swift-flowing Amshumati, garlanded by waves. They crossed the river Yamuna, with many trees standing along the banks. Once they crossed the Yamuna, they abandoned the raft. They reached the dark-blue nyagrodha, enveloped in a cool and green canopy. Sita approached the tree. She joined her hands in salutation and said, 'Let us again see Kousalya and the illustrious Sumitra.' After having proceeded hardly one krosha, the two brothers, Rama and Lakshmana, killed many deer that could be killed[188] and ate in the grove alongside the Yamuna. They roamed around in that auspicious forest, full of herds of elephants and apes and resounding with the cries of peacocks. They reached some flat terrain along the river and without showing any sorrow, readied an abode.[189]

Chapter 2(50)

When the night was over, the descendant of the Raghu lineage gently awoke Lakshmana, who was sleeping without any interruptions. 'O Soumitri! Hear the beautiful sounds of the forest echo. O scorcher of enemies! The time for our departure has arrived.' His brother, Lakshmana, was asleep and was awakened at the right time. Because of the exhaustion along the path, he was

[187] Because the Critical Edition excises the relevant shloka, reeds is left implicit. Lakshmana severed reeds and branches.

[188] Some animals were not permitted to be killed.

[189] For the night.

prone to laziness, but abandoned the thought of sleep. Having awoken, all of them touched the sacred waters of the river. They followed the path towards Chitrakuta, as indicated by the rishi. At the right time, Rama, together with Soumitri, spoke these words to the lotus-eyed Sita. 'O Vaidehi! The *kimshuka* trees are blazing in every direction.[190] Behold. At the end of the winter, with their own blossoms, they have formed garlands. Behold the flowering *bhallatakas*,[191] plucked by men. They are bending down, because of the fruit and leaves. We are capable of surviving here. O Lakshmana! Behold. There are honeycombs in each tree, long and as large as a *drona*,[192] and bees collect honey from these. A *chataka* bird is crying and a peacock is crying back in response. This beautiful spot in the forest is strewn with flowers. Look at Mount Chitrakuta, with a tall and imposing summit. It echoes with the sound of birds and herds of elephants wander around.' On foot, with Sita, they advanced and reached the beautiful Mount Chitrakuta.

On reaching the mountain, frequented by hordes of many kinds of birds, 'We will dwell in this beautiful and peaceful spot.[193] O Lakshmana! Bring firm and beautiful wood. O amiable one! Construct a residence here. My mind finds delight at the prospect of living here.' Hearing his words, Soumitri collected many kinds of trees. The scorcher of enemies made a hut out of leaves. He[194] was attentive in serving him and he[195] addressed him in these words. 'O Soumitri! Bring the meat of an antelope and we will perform a sacrifice in this hut.' The powerful Lakshmana slew a black antelope, of the kind that could be killed. Soumitri flung this into the kindled fire. When he discerned that it was cooked and cleansed of all blood, Lakshmana addressed Raghava, tiger among men. 'This has been cooked and is dark in all its limbs, so that is truly a black antelope. O one who is like a god! You are accomplished. Worship

[190] Because of the red blossoms.
[191] Cashew nut.
[192] Drona has different meanings. Here, it is a measure of capacity.
[193] In English, the sentence is without a subject, but it is Rama speaking.
[194] Lakshmana.
[195] Rama.

the gods now.' Rama possessed the qualities of being conversant with techniques of chanting. He controlled himself and bathed. To pacify all kinds of sin, Rama offered that supreme sacrifice.

The abode was beautiful, covered with leaves from trees. It had been constructed well, in a place that was free from winds. Together, they entered it, like the congregation of gods entering the assembly hall Sudharma.[196] That supreme forest was full of many kinds of animals and birds. The trees had clumps of wonderful flowers. There were the sounds of predatory beasts. Extremely happy and in conquest of their senses, they wandered around there. They reached the extremely beautiful region of Chitrakuta and the river Malyavati,[197] which was a great place of pilgrimage. Cheerfully, collections of birds and animals called there. They forgot any misery that was due to their having been banished from the city.

Chapter 2(51)

When Rama crossed over to the southern bank, extremely miserable and afflicted, Guha conversed with Sumantra for a very long time and finally returned to his own house. Having been permitted to leave,[198] Sumantra yoked the supreme steeds and grieving severely, proceeded towards the city of Ayodhya. He saw fragrant groves, rivers, lakes, villages and cities and extremely swiftly, passed through them. On the evening of the third day, the charioteer reached Ayodhya and saw that it was bereft of joy. Extremely distressed in his mind, he saw that it was silent, as if it was deserted. Immersed in waves of sorrow, Sumantra thought, 'Have the elephants, horses, people, kings and the city been consumed in a fire of grief, tormented and miserable on account of Rama?' Thinking in this way, the suta entered quickly. On seeing Sumantra arrive, hundreds and thousands of men rushed towards

[196] Sudharma is the assembly hall of the gods.
[197] This river is also known as Mandakinee.
[198] By Rama, not by Guha.

the suta and asked, 'Where is Rama?' He told them, 'I left him on the banks of the Ganga. The great-souled Raghava, devoted to dharma, then asked me to withdraw and return.' Hearing that they had crossed, the faces of the people filled with tears. They sighed and shrieked, 'Shame! Alas, Rama!' standing around in groups. He heard them say, 'We do not see Raghava here. It is certain that we will be destroyed. At the time of donations, sacrifices, weddings and grand assemblies, we will never again see Rama, who is devoted to dharma. Knowing what the people were capable of and what would bring them benefit and happiness, Rama protected the city, like a father.' As he drove along the roads between the shops, through the windows, he heard the lamentations of women, extremely tormented and miserable on account of Rama.

As he passed through the royal road, Sumantra covered his face. He reached the house where King Dasharatha was. He quickly descended from the chariot and entered the king's residence. He passed through seven chambers that were full of large crowds of people. Dasharatha's wives were scattered here and there in the palace. On account of Rama, they were tormented by grief and he could hear them converse softly. 'The suta departed with Rama and has returned here without Rama. How will he reply to the grieving Kousalya? I think it is extremely difficult to live in this way. It is certainly not easy. Despite her son having left, Kousalya remains alive.' The king's wives uttered words that were full of truth. Hearing these, he quickly entered the residence, which seemed to be blazing in its sorrow. He entered the eighth chamber and saw the distressed and grief-stricken king there, in that white house, pale because of sorrow on account of his son. The Indra among men was seated and Sumantra approached and greeted him, reporting exactly the words that Rama had uttered. With his senses in a whirl, the king heard silently. Overcome by grief on account of Rama, he lost his senses and fell down on the ground. When the lord of the earth lost his senses, it was as if the inner quarters were struck. When the king fell down on the ground, they[199] raised their arms up and shrieked.

[199] The residents.

With Sumitra, Kousalya raised her husband, who had fallen down. She then addressed him in these words. 'O immensely fortunate one! This messenger has accomplished an extremely difficult deed. He has arrived after living in the forest. Why are you not replying to him? O Raghava![200] Having acted inappropriately, today you are embarrassed. Do a good act and get up. There can be no help from sorrow. O king! Who do you fear that you are not asking the charioteer about Rama? Kaikeyee is not present here. You can reply without any fear.' Kousalya yielded to grief and addressed the great king in this way. She spoke in the midst of her tears and suddenly fell down on the ground. On seeing that Kousalya had fallen down on the ground, all the women glanced at their husband[201] and wailed. They wept loudly. An uproar arose from inside the inner quarters. All the women, in every direction, cried, and so did the aged and young men. Yet again, the city was disturbed.

Chapter 2(52)

When the king regained his senses and his composure, he summoned the suta near him, so that he could hear about Rama's conduct. The aged one was extremely tormented, like an elephant that had just been caught.[202] As he reflected, he sighed, like an elephant that was ill. The suta's limbs were covered with dust. When he approached, the king, who was supremely afflicted, cheerless in his face and with eyes full of tears, spoke to him. 'How will the one with dharma in his soul reside at the foot of a tree? O suta! Raghava is used to great comfort. What will he eat? How will the son of a king lie down on the bare ground, as if he is without a protector? When he advanced, foot soldiers, chariots and elephants used to follow him. Having resorted to a desolate forest, how will Rama live there? Predatory beasts wander around there. The

[200] That is, Dasharatha.

[201] Dasharatha.

[202] Implying a wild elephant.

place is populated by black snakes. With Vaidehi, how have the princes entered the forest? O Sumantra! The ascetic Sita is delicate. With her, how have the princes descended from the chariot and proceeded on foot? O suta! Since you have seen my sons enter the extremities of the forest, like the two Ashvins entering Mandara, you have indeed been successful in your objective. What were the words that Rama uttered? What were the words that Lakshmana uttered? O Sumantra! On reaching the forest, what did Maithilee say? O suta! Recount where Rama seated himself. Where did he lie down? What did he eat?'

When the Indra among men urged him thus, the suta answered the king in a trembling voice and in words that choked with tears. 'O great king! Raghava continued to observe dharma. He joined his hands in salutation, lowered his head and bowed down and said,[203] "O suta! Convey my words to my father, who is one who knows about his own soul. The great-souled one is a person, before whom, one must lower one's head down at his feet. O suta! Convey my words to all those in the inner quarters and without any partiality, ask them about their welfare. Honour those who deserve it. Honour my mother, Kousalya, and ask about her welfare. Revere the feet of the king and the queen, as you would to a god. Ask about Bharata's welfare and also convey my words to him. Tell him to follow the conduct of being fair towards all the mothers. The mighty-armed descendant of the Ikshvaku lineage should be told that he must be instated as the heir apparent, so as to protect my father, who is still instated in the kingdom." O great king! This is what the immensely illustrious Rama, with coppery red eyes like a lotus, said, shedding tears profusely. However, Lakshmana was extremely angry. He sighed and addressed me in these words. "What is the crime that has led to the prince being exiled? Whether the act of banishing Rama was done on account of greed, or whether it was done because a boon had been granted, it was in every respect, something that should not have been done. I do not discern any reason behind

[203] This message is meant to be relayed by Sumantra to Dasharatha and the respect is also being shown to Dasharatha.

the abandonment of Rama. Whether this was undertaken without thinking about it, or whether it was done because of lack of intelligence, there will be resentment and rage at Raghava being exiled. I do not discern any traits of a father in the great king. For me, Raghava is the brother, lord, relative and father. He is engaged in the welfare of all beings. He is loved by all the worlds. Why will all the worlds be delighted at this act of abandoning him?" O great king! The ascetic Janakee sighed. Forgetting her own self, as if her intelligence had been overtaken by a demon, she stood there. The illustrious princess has not faced such a hardship ever earlier. She wept in misery and was incapable of saying anything to me. With her mouth parched, she glanced towards her husband. On seeing me leave, she suddenly started to cry. Tears also flowed down Rama's face and he joined his hands in salutation. He stood there, obtaining support from Lakshmana's arms. The ascetic Sita also wept, as she glanced at the royal chariot and at me.'

Chapter 2(53)

'When Rama left for the forest, my horses shed warm tears and refused to return along the path. I controlled my misery and joined my hands in salutation before the two princes. I then ascended the chariot. In the hope that I might again hear Rama's words addressed to me, I remained with Guha for many days.[204] O great king! Your kingdom has also been affected by this hardship. Without yielding flowers, shoots or buds, the trees have withered away. Creatures are not moving and predatory beasts have stopped roaming around. Overcome by sorrow on account of Rama, no sounds emerge from the forest. O Indra among kings! Lotuses have drawn in their petals and the water is muddied. The lilies in the lakes have become warm. Fish and waterbirds have disappeared. Aquatic flowers and blossoms on the land are no longer radiant

[204] This contradicts what has been said earlier.

and have very little fragrance left. The fruits are no longer as they used to be. As I entered Ayodhya, no one greeted me. Having not seen Rama, the men sighed repeatedly. When the chariot returned, suffering because they couldn't see Rama, women lamented from mansions, buildings and palaces. Their large and sparkling eyes were filled with flows of tears. They glanced towards each other and it was evident that the women suffered more.[205] I do not discern any difference in the sorrow exhibited by those who are not friends, those who are friends and those who are neutral. Men are unhappy. Elephants and horses are distressed. They are jaded and screaming in affliction, or they are sighing silently. O great king! Miserable at Rama having been exiled, Ayodhya seems to me to be like Kousalya, separated from her son.'

On hearing the suta's words, the king became even more miserable. Shedding tears, he told the suta, 'I was persuaded by Kaikeyee, whose sentiments were driven by wickedness. I went along with her, without consulting the accomplished and the aged. I did not seek the views of well-wishers, advisers, ministers and those who know about the sacred texts. Urged by a woman, I was confused and did this suddenly. It is certain that this great catastrophe has come about because of destiny. O suta! As it desires, it will bring about the destruction of this lineage. O suta! If I have done any good deed towards you, quickly take me to Rama. The breath of life is about to leave me. If there is anyone who still listens to my command, let Raghava be brought back. Without Rama, I am incapable of remaining alive even for an instant. Or perhaps the mighty-armed one has gone a long distance away. In that event, make me ascend the chariot and quickly show me Rama. Where is the great archer with the rounded teeth? Where is Lakshmana's elder brother? If I can see him, with Sita, I will manage to remain alive. If I do not see the mighty-armed Rama, red-eyed and wearing bejewelled earrings, I will go to Yama's eternal abode. What can be a greater misery than attaining this state, where I cannot see Raghava, the descendant of the Ikshvaku lineage? Alas, Rama! Alas, Rama's younger brother!

[205] Than the men.

Alas, the ascetic Vaidehi! You do not know that I am without a protector and am about to die in misery. O queen![206] It is difficult for me to remain alive. It is unseemly that I cannot see Raghava now, nor can I see Lakshmana.' The immensely illustrious king lamented in this way. He became senseless and suddenly fell down on his couch. Lamenting in this way, the king became unconscious. The queen heard his words and her grief was doubled on account of Rama. Rama's mother was frightened yet again.

Chapter 2(54)

Kousalya seemed to be possessed by a spirit and trembled repeatedly. As if lifeless on the ground, she spoke to the suta. 'Take me to the place where Kakutstha and Sita are, where Lakshmana is. Without them, I am not interested in remaining alive, not even for an instant. Retrace the chariot immediately and take me to Dandaka. If I do not follow them, I will go to Yama's eternal abode.' Her words choked with tears and she spoke softly. The suta joined his hands in salutation and addressed the queen. 'Abandon sorrow, delusion and any fright that gives rise to misery. Cast aside all torment, so that Raghava can reside in the forest. In the forest, Lakshmana will serve at Rama's feet. He knows about dharma and has conquered his senses. He is serving the cause of the world hereafter. Even though she is in a desolate forest, it is as if Sita is dwelling at home. She is not scared. Because her mind is devoted to Rama, she is at peace. Not even the most subtle kind of grief can be discerned in her. It seems to me that Vaidehi is used to living in exile. In earlier times, she used to visit groves in the city and find delight there. Despite it being a desolate forest, Sita finds a similar delight there. Her face is like the young moon and Sita finds pleasure like a child. Since her soul is immersed in Rama, even in

[206] This is addressed to Kousalya. Since the Critical Edition has excised some shlokas, there is a break in continuity.

that desolate forest, she finds delight. Her heart is in him. She lives for his sake. Had she been in Ayodhya, without Rama, it would have been like a forest to her. Along the path, on seeing villages and towns, the courses of rivers and many kinds of trees, Vaidehi asked about them. Vaidehi's radiance is like the beams of the moon and has not suffered from travelling, from the force of the wind, from fear, or from the heat. Her radiance is like the full moon, she is like a lotus.[207] The generous Vaidehi's face has not trembled. She is deprived of the red *alakta* juice and can no longer apply the alakta juice.[208] Even then, her feet are as radiant as the buds of lotuses. The beautiful one walks as if in sport, with her playful anklets tinkling. Because of her affection for him, even now, Vaidehi adorns herself in ornaments. Resorting to the forest, when she sees an elephant, a lion or a tiger, she resorts to Rama's arms and is not terrified. They do not grieve and you and the lord of men shouldn't grieve either. Such conduct will eternally be established in this world. They have cast aside grief and their minds are cheerful. They have properly established themselves along the path followed by maharshis. They reside in the forest and survive on wild fruit. They are following the auspicious pledge given to their father.' In this way, the suta spoke eloquently. However, though she was restrained, the queen was grief-stricken over her son and her lamentation did not cease. She exclaimed, 'O beloved son! O Raghava!'

Chapter 2(55)

Rama was supreme among those who caused delight and supremely devoted to dharma. Thus, he left for the forest. However, Kousalya was herself afflicted. She wept and addressed her husband in these words. 'Your great fame is renowned in the three worlds. Raghava is compassionate, generous and pleasant

[207] The text uses the word *shatapatra*. This means something with one hundred petals, that is, a lotus.

[208] Alakta is a red juice obtained from resin and is used to colour the soles of the feet.

in speech. O best among supreme men! Your two sons and Sita have been reared in happiness. Miserable, how will they be able to withstand the misery in the forest? She is young, *shyama*,[209] delicate and used to happiness. How will Maithilee be able to withstand the heat and the cold? With her beautiful teeth, the large-eyed Sita has eaten auspicious broth. How will she be able to partake food cooked from wild rice? The auspicious and unblemished one has heard the sounds of singing and musical instruments. How will she be able to hear the inauspicious sounds of predatory beasts and lions? The mighty-armed one[210] is like the great Indra's standard. How will the immensely strong one lie down, using his own arm as a pillow? His complexion is like that of a lotus. The tips of his hair are excellent. His excellent breath has the fragrance of lotuses. When will I see the lotus-eyed Rama's face? There is no doubt that my heart possesses the essence of a diamond. Despite my being unable to see him, it has not shattered into a thousand fragments. Even if Raghava returns in the fifteenth year, it is not evident that Bharata will give up the kingdom and the treasury. O lord of the earth! The kingdom will thus have been enjoyed by a younger brother. Why will an elder and superior brother not refuse to accept such a kingdom? A tiger does not wish to eat food that has been brought and tasted by another. In that fashion, a tiger among men will not accept something that has been enjoyed by another. Once they have been used at a sacrifice, oblations, clarified butter, cakes, kusha and altars made of khadira wood[211] are not again used for another sacrifice. Enjoyed by another, this kingdom will be like liquor that has lost its essence. It is like a soma plant that has already been used in a sacrifice and indeed, Rama will not accept it. Raghava will not commit such an act of dishonour, just as a powerful tiger does not tolerate anyone touching the hair on its tail. The bull among men possesses the strength of a lion. He has

[209] We have deliberately not translated shyama. Usually, this means dark. But shyama also means a woman who has not had children and it is this second meaning that is intended here.

[210] Rama.

[211] A kind of tree.

been destroyed by his own father, like a fish devouring its young. The dharma followed by *dvijas*[212] has always been instructed as the dharma of the sacred texts. Having banished your son, how have you been devoted to that dharma? A husband is a woman's first refuge, a son is the second refuge. O king! A kin is the third refuge and in this world, there isn't a fourth one. Among those, you do not exist for me and Rama has resorted to the forest. I do not wish to go to the forest. Therefore, I have been destroyed in every way. This kingdom and the country have been destroyed by you. You have destroyed yourself and your ministers. I and my son have been destroyed. The citizens have been destroyed. Only your son and wife[213] are happy.' She used such terrible words. Having heard them, the king was confounded and miserable. Remembering his misdeed yet again, the king was immersed in grief.

Chapter 2(56)

In grief, Rama's mother angrily said this. Hearing these harsh words, the king was miserable and started to think. He thought about the terrible misdeed he had perpetrated earlier.[214] Ignorantly, he had struck, depending on sound alone. The lord's mind was distracted by this and by sorrow on account of Rama. Addressed by Kousalya, the king was afflicted by these two different kinds of sorrow. He said, 'O Kousalya! I have joined my hands in supplication. Show me your favours. You have always been affectionate and non-violent towards others. O queen! Whether he possesses qualities or does not possess qualities, one must remember the dharma that a husband is like a divinity himself. You have witnessed the superior and the inferior in this world, but have always been supremely devoted to

[212] Dvija means twice-born, a reference to the sacred thread ceremony, a kind of second birth. Though dvija often means brahmana, the three superior varnas were all entitled to sacred thread ceremonies and were therefore dvijas.

[213] Bharata and Kaikeyee respectively.

[214] This will be explained subsequently.

dharma. Whether you are miserable or extremely miserable, you should not have spoken these disagreeable words to me.'

Hearing the piteous words of the king, uttered in misery, Kousalya shed tears, like fresh water[215] flowing down a drain. She cupped her hands in the form a lotus and held the king's head, weeping as she did this. She was terrified and scared and she spoke so fast that the syllables were indistinct. 'I am bowing down my head and seeking your favours. I am lying down on the ground in front of you. O king! I am afflicted and am requesting you, though I do not deserve to be pardoned. O brave one! In both the worlds, there is no intelligent woman who has thus been lauded by her husband. O one who knows about dharma! I know about dharma. I know you to be truthful in speech. Afflicted on account of grief over my son, what have I said to you? Sorrow destroys patience. Sorrow destroys learning. Sorrow destroys everything. There is no enemy like sorrow. One is capable of withstanding a blow that is struck by the hands of an enemy. However, if it is sorrow, even if it is very subtle, that is impossible to tolerate. Five nights have passed since Rama left for residing in the forest. However, since my joy has been destroyed by grief, it seems like five years to me. Thinking of him, the sorrow of my heart is enhanced. It is like the great water of the ocean, enhanced by the force of rivers.' As Kousalya spoke these auspicious words, the sun's rays turned mild and night arrived. The king was cheered by Queen Kousalya's words. Though overcome by sorrow, he came under the subjugation of sleep.

Chapter 2(57)

King Dasharatha was senseless with sorrow. However, he regained his senses in an instant and started to think. He was Vasava's equal. But because of Rama and Lakshmana's exile, he faced a calamity, like the sun darkened by the asura.[216]

[215] From a shower.
[216] Rahu, responsible for an eclipse.

On the sixth night after Rama had left for the forest, in the middle of the night, King Dasharatha remembered the wicked deed that he had done. Afflicted by grief on account of his son, he addressed Kousalya in these words. 'O fortunate one! According to whether he performs an auspicious act or an inauspicious act, the doer reaps the consequences of any deed that he has done. A person who commences a deed without considering whether it is grave or trivial, the fruits of the deed and its taints, is said to be a child. Some look at flowers and, desiring fruits, cut down mango trees and nurture palasha trees.[217] They sorrow when the fruits are obtained. I have also cut down a grove of mango trees and nurtured palasha. Being evil-minded, I have forsaken the fruit that is Rama and am grieving later. O Kousalya! When I was young, I became proficient with the bow and could strike at the sound.[218] As a young man, I was known as *shabdabhedi*.[219] That is when I perpetrated a wicked deed. O queen! Because of what I myself did, I am now faced with this misery. It is as if I consumed poison through childish confusion. In my ignorance, I have reaped this fruit of being a shabdabhedi. O queen! I was the heir apparent then and was not married to you. The monsoon season arrived and it increased my desire.[220] Having drunk all the juices from the earth, the sun, the one who pervades the earth with its rays, had entered the terrible southern direction, frequented by those others.[221] The heat suddenly disappeared and cool clouds could be seen. All the frogs, antelopes[222] and peacocks were filled with joy. Water continued to pour down on water that had already showered down. Inhabited by maddened antelopes, the mountains were submerged in torrents of water. This was an

[217] Palasha trees have lovely flowers and no fruit, it being the reverse for mangoes.

[218] Without visually seeing the target.

[219] One who can strike at the sound.

[220] To go on a hunt.

[221] Though not explicitly stated, this seems to imply that the sun had moved to *dakshinayana*, the southern solstice. In today's terms, this would mean the month of July. Dakshinayana is associated with the *pitris*, the ancestors. With this interpretation, 'others' would mean the ancestors. However, the south is also regarded as inauspicious, associated with death, ghosts and spirits. 'Others' might also mean that.

[222] *Saranga*, this can also mean a type of bird.

extremely pleasant period. I resolved to have some exercise. With a bow and arrows and on a chariot, I followed the course of the Sarayu river. I was in control of my senses and wished to kill a buffalo, elephant or any other predatory beast that would come to the river in the night.[223] In the darkness, I heard the sound of a pot being filled with water. Since I wasn't able to see, I thought that it was the sound of an elephant trumpeting. Therefore, I affixed a blazing arrow that was like virulent poison. I released the sharp arrow that was like virulent poison. I heard a human voice scream "Alas! Alas!" as the person fell down. It was evident that these sounds were uttered by a resident of the forest, who said, "How did a weapon strike down an ascetic? In the night, I came to the river to collect some water. Who has struck me with this arrow? What have I done to anyone? I am a rishi who has cast aside the staff.[224] I dwell in the forest on forest fare. Who has recommended the use of a weapon to slay a person like me? I wear a mass of matted hair. My garments are made of bark and deer skin. What purpose will be served by killing me? What injury have I caused to anyone? This is a pointless act that is full of ill intent. No one will say that this act is virtuous. It is like transgressing the preceptor's bed.[225] I am not grieving because my own life has come to an end. Since I will die, I am sorrowing about my mother and my father. For a long time, this aged couple has been nurtured by me. After my death, how will they sustain themselves? It is as if I and my aged mother and father have been slain by that single arrow. Who is the extremely foolish person who has killed all of us?" Always desirous of dharma, I heard those piteous words. Since I was distressed, the bow and arrows fell down from my hands on the ground. Distressed in spirit and miserable in my mind, I went to that spot. On the banks of the Sarayu, I saw the ascetic who had been struck by the arrow. I stood there, terrified, with my senses distracted. He glanced at me with his eyes, as if he would burn me down through his energy. He then spoke these cruel words. "O king! While I resided here, what injury have I caused to

[223] To drink water.

[224] The staff used for chastisement or punishment.

[225] Having intercourse with the preceptor's wife.

you? I wished to collect water for my seniors and you have struck me down. Indeed, a single arrow has been enough to strike at my vital organs. But it has also slain my aged and blind mother and father. They are weak, blind and thirsty and are waiting for me. Bearing their thirst and difficulties, they have been waiting for me for a long time. There may indeed be ascetics who have obtained the fruits of their yoga and learning. But my father does not know that I have fallen down and am lying down on the ground here.[226] He does not know. He is weak and incapacitated. What will he do? He is like a tree that is unable to save another tree that is being cut down. O Raghava! Go there quickly and tell my father, so that he does not angrily burn you down, like a forest by a fire. O king! This path will take you to my father's hermitage. If you go and seek his favours, he will not curse you in his anger. O king! Take out this stake of the sharp arrow from my body. It is tormenting me, just as even gentle flows of water can stir an unstable riverbank. O king! I am not a brahmana. Do not be distressed on that account.[227] O lord of habitations! My mother is a shudra and my father is a vaishya." Since the arrow had struck at his vital organs, he spoke these words with difficulty. As he was losing his senses, I drew out the arrow. His body was drenched with water and he lamented at this calamity. With his inner organs struck by the arrow, he sighed repeatedly. O fortunate one! Extremely miserable, I lay him down in the Sarayu and looked at him.'

Chapter 2(58)

'I had committed a great crime in my ignorance and my senses were afflicted. I used my intelligence to think about what could best be done under the circumstances. I brought the pot and filled it with auspicious water. Following the indicated path, I reached the

[226] Since my father has not obtained fruits that lead to such insight.

[227] Killing a brahmana would have been a terrible crime.

hermitage. There I saw the two weak, blind and aged ones, without anyone to support them now. I saw the parents there, like birds whose wings had been severed. They were seated there, without anything to do, and were conversing among themselves. Since they had lost hope because of me,[228] they were miserable, immobile and without a protector. On hearing my footsteps, the hermit spoke these words. "O son! Why did you take such a long time? Quickly give me a drink. O son! That is the reason you had gone. Why did you tarry to play in the water? Your mother is anxious. Quickly enter the hermitage. O son! If your mother or I have done anything unreasonable towards you, you should not have secreted that in your mind. O son! You should have behaved like an ascetic. You are the refuge for those who have no refuge. You are the eyes for those who have no eyes. Our lives depend on you. Why are you not saying anything?" When the hermit spoke these words, I was terrified and glanced towards him. Like one who was scared, I spoke indistinctly, in words that were not properly formed.[229] Then I invoked my mental strength and imparted strength to my speech. I told him the fearful news of the catastrophe that had befallen his son. "I am a kshatriya named Dasharatha. I am not your great-souled son. Through my own deeds, I have caused this misery that is condemned by virtuous people. O illustrious one! With a bow in my hand, I arrived at the banks of the Sarayu. I wished to kill an elephant or a predatory beast that would come to drink water. I heard the sound of a pot being filled with water. Taking this to be an elephant, I struck with my arrow. Upon going to the banks of the river, I saw an ascetic lying down lifeless on the ground, the arrow having shattered his heart. O illustrious one! Wishing to kill an elephant, I aimed in the direction of the sound in the water. Thus released, the iron arrow slew your son. O illustrious one! I

[228] Of their son returning. A considerable amount of time has elapsed. Dasharatha struck the young ascetic in the middle of the night. In non-Critical versions, Dasharatha waits out the night before he discovers the young ascetic in the morning. The Critical text excises these shlokas, so that the discovery seems to be immediate. These incidents are actually happening next morning.

[229] Literally, in words that lacked the appropriate consonants.

approached him and he lamented and grieved about the two of you, since you are blind. When I took out the arrow, he went to heaven. In my ignorance, I violently killed your son. O hermit! Show me your favours and tell me what should be done about his remains."

'Hearing these cruel words, he was afflicted by grief and sighed. I stood before him, with my hands joined in salutation. The immensely energetic one said, "O king! If you had not yourself told me about this inauspicious act, as a consequence, your head would have shattered into a hundred thousand fragments. O king! If a kshatriya knowingly kills a person who has resorted to vanaprastha, he is dislodged from his state, even if the perpetrator happens to be the wielder of the vajra himself.[230] You are still alive because you did not do this knowingly. Had it been otherwise, not only would you have been destroyed today, but so would have been the lineage of the Raghavas.[231] O king! Take me to the spot that you have spoken about. We now wish to take a last look at our son, whose limbs are covered with blood and whose garment of deer skin has got dishevelled. He is lying down unconscious on the ground and has come under the subjugation of Dharmaraja."[232] I took those two extremely miserable ones to the spot and made the hermit and his wife touch their son. Those two ascetics approached and touched the fallen body of their son. The father said, "O son! O one devoted to dharma! I love you, but behold your mother. O delicate son! Why are you not embracing us? Why don't you say something? In the second half of the night,[233] whose words will I hear, so that they touch the heart? Who will recite sweet words from the sacred texts or from something else? Who will make us perform the sandhya worship? Who will bathe us and make us offer oblations into the fire? O son! When I am afflicted by sorrow and grief, who will sit beside me and assure me? As if I am a beloved guest, who will bring me roots and fruits? Who will feed me? I cannot do anything. I cannot act on my own. I am without my guide. Your ascetic mother

[230] Indra.
[231] A conscious act would have destroyed the entire lineage.
[232] The lord of dharma, Yama.
[233] This suggests that it is still night.

is blind and aged. O son! She desires her son and is in a pitiable state. Who will sustain her? O son! Stay here. Do not leave for Yama's abode. Depart tomorrow, with your mother and me. In the forest, both of us are grieving and miserable. We are without a protector. Without you, we will quickly leave for Yama's eternal abode. On seeing Vaivasvata,[234] I will address him in these words. 'O Dharmaraja! Pardon him. Let him nurture his parents.' O son! You did not commit a sin. This perpetrator of wicked deeds has killed you. Because this is true, quickly go to the worlds reserved for those who fight with weapons. That is where brave ones who do not retreat from the field of battle and face the front go, when they are slain. O son! Go to that supreme destination. O son! Attain the destination obtained by Sagara, Shaibya, Dileepa, Janamejaya, Nahusha and Dhundumara.[235] There are destinations obtained by those who devote themselves to studying and austerities, those who donate land, offer oblations into the fire and observe the vow of having a single wife. Go there and to destinations obtained by those who repay debts to their preceptors by gifting them thousands of cows. O son! Go to the destinations obtained by those who cast aside their bodies.[236] A person who has been born in this lineage will not obtain an inauspicious end." In this fashion, he lamented piteously. With his wife, he then performed the water rites. Because of his own deeds, the hermit's son manifested himself in a divine form. He assured his parents for a while and spoke these words. "Because I served both of you, I have obtained this exalted state. You will also quickly come to where I am." Having said this, in control of his senses, the hermit's son quickly ascended to heaven in a radiant and divine vimana.

'I stood there, with my hands joined in salutation. Having performed the water rites with his wife, the immensely energetic ascetic addressed me. "O king! Using a single arrow and killing my

[234] Yama.

[235] There could have been a different Janamejaya. But otherwise, Janamejaya does not belong in this list. Nor for that matter does Shaibya.

[236] Such as through *prayopavesa*, voluntary fasting to death, adopted by someone who has no worldly desires left.

son, you have rendered me without a son. Kill me now. I have no sorrow in dying. In your ignorance, you have killed my virtuous son. Therefore, I am cursing you that you will suffer from an extremely terrible grief. On account of my son, you have presented me with this calamity and misery. O king! Therefore, you will also die grieving over your son."[237] O fortunate one! I face that generous person's words now. They have come true. Though I am still alive, I am grieving on account of my son. Can I immediately see Rama or touch him now? O queen! Having done this to Raghava, there is no one like me. I cannot see him with my eyes and my memory is fading. O Kousalya! Vaivasvata's messengers are hurrying towards me. What can be more miserable than my life ending in this way? I am unable to see Rama, who knows about dharma and for whom truth is his valour. He is handsome, with auspicious earrings. Those who will be able to see Rama's face again in the fifteenth year are gods, not humans. His eyes are like lotus petals. He possesses excellent brows and excellent teeth. His nose is beautiful. Those who will be able to see Rama, with a face like that of the lord of the stars,[238] are blessed. His face is like the autumn moon and like a blooming lotus. Those who are able to see my fragrant lord are blessed. After the period of exile in the forest is over, he will return to Ayodhya again, like Shukra[239] returning to its path. Those who see Rama then will be happy. I have brought this sorrow on myself. I am without a protector and senseless. I am like the bank of a river, being destroyed by the water. Alas, Raghava! O mighty-armed one! Alas! O one who destroys my discomfort!'

As he sorrowed in this way, King Dasharatha's life ended. The lord of men spoke in this miserable fashion. He was afflicted because his beloved son had been exiled. At midnight, severely suffering from grief, the one who was generous in appearance gave up his life.[240]

[237] The Critical text excises shlokas where the aged parents immolate themselves in a fire.

[238] The moon.

[239] Venus.

[240] The Critical text excises part of a shloka, telling us that Kousalya and Sumitra were present then. Because of what we are told in the next chapter, Dasharatha seems to have died alone, in the sense that Kousalya and Sumitra were deep in slumber.

Chapter 2(59)

Night passed and the next day arrived. The bards presented themselves at the king's residence. Those who were accomplished in the auspicious rites presented themselves. As used to be the practice, women and the best of eunuchs also arrived. They brought golden pots, filled with water mixed with yellow sandalwood paste. At the right time, as was the practice, those who were skilled in bathing brought these.[241] There were other women, most of whom were maidens. They brought auspicious objects, food and decorations. There were women who were authorized to approach the place where the Indra of Kosala slept.[242] They approached and sought to wake up their lord. They trembled when they thought that the king was no longer alive. They trembled like blades of grass facing a flood. Trembling in this way, those women looked at the king. They became certain that the calamity they had suspected was true. Those beautiful women began to wail in loud and miserable voices. They were like female elephants in a forest, when the leader of the herd has been dislodged. At the sound of this shrieking, Kousalya and Sumitra suddenly regained their senses and woke up from their sleep. Kousalya and Sumitra looked at the king and touched him. Lamenting 'Alas, lord!' they fell down on the ground. The daughter of the Indra of Kosala writhed around on the ground. Covered with dust, she was no longer radiant and was like a star that had been dislodged from the sky. The entire place was filled with a crowd of anxious and terrified people. As the miserable relatives lamented, there were sounds of wailing everywhere. All joy instantly vanished and despondency and misery were seen everywhere. This is what happened when the god among men met his end. Knowing that the illustrious bull among kings had passed away, his wives surrounded him. They were extremely miserable

[241] To bathe the king.

[242] This reference to Dasharatha as the Indra of Kosala is odd. Perhaps Kousalya's Indra is meant.

and wailed in piteous tones. As if without a protector, they clung to each other's arms.

Chapter 2(60)

He was like a fire that had been pacified, like an ocean without water, like the sun robbed of its radiance. On seeing that the lord of the earth had left for heaven, Kousalya's eyes filled with tears and she was afflicted by many kinds of grief. Taking the king's head on her lap, she spoke to Kaikeyee. 'O Kaikeyee! You have accomplished your desire. Without any thorns, enjoy the kingdom alone, abandoning the king. O cruel one! O one evil in conduct! Abandoning me, Rama has departed and my husband has left for heaven. Dislodged from the path, I am without any sense of purpose. I have no interest in remaining alive. Abandoning a husband who was himself like a divinity, which woman would wish to remain alive, with the sole exception of Kaikeyee, who has cast aside dharma? Like a person who eats what should not be eaten, a greedy individual does not understand a sin. Because of Kubja, Kaikeyee has destroyed the lineage of the Raghavas. She forced the king to do what should not be done and exiled Rama and his wife. Hearing this, Janaka will lament, just as I am. Though he is alive, the lotus-eyed Rama has been destroyed and so has the ascetic Sita, the daughter of the king of Videha. She does not deserve unhappiness and will be miserable at the difficulties in the forest. In the night, animals and birds will shriek in terrible tones. On hearing these, it is certain that she will be frightened and seek refuge with Raghava. He is aged and has no sons. Thinking of Vaidehi, it is certain that he will be immersed in grief and will give up his life.'

The ascetic Kousalya embraced him and lamented in this way, extremely miserable. The attendants removed her from the spot. The advisers immersed the king in a vessel of oil and thereafter did everything else that needed to be done for the king. Without a son being present, the ministers did not wish to perform the king's last rites. Knowing everything about what needed to be done, they therefore preserved the king's body in this way. The advisers laid down the king in a vessel of oil. Knowing that he was dead, the women lamented. They threw up their arms and were in a pitiable state, their eyes and faces overflowing with tears. Tormented by grief, they wept and wailed piteously. The city of Ayodhya was deprived of the great-souled king and was like a night without stars, or like a woman abandoned by her husband. The eyes of people were full of tears and women from noble lineages lamented. The crossroads and houses were empty and were no longer resplendent, as they used to be earlier. It was as if the firmament, bereft of the sun, had lost its lustre and the night was bereft of its large number of nakshatras. Without the great-souled one, the city lost its radiance. The roads and crossroads were crowded with people whose voices choked with tears.[243] Crowds of men and women gathered and condemned Bharata's mother. When the god among men died, the city was afflicted and could not find any peace.

Chapter 2(61)

When night was over and the sun arose, there was an assembly of the king's officers and brahmanas. There were Markandeya, Moudgalya, Vamadeva, Kashyapa, Katyayana, Goutama and the immensely famous Jabali. One by one, these brahmanas and the advisers faced Vasishtha, best among royal priests, and spoke to him. 'The night of misery has passed and it has been like one hundred years. Overcome by sorrow on account of his son, the king has died. The great king has gone to heaven and Rama has resorted to the forest. The energetic Lakshmana has also departed with Rama. Bharata and Shatrughna, scorchers of enemies, are in Kekaya. They are in the beautiful city and royal palace, in their maternal uncle's abode. Someone from the lineage of the Ikshvakus should now

[243] However, it has just been said that the crossroads were empty.

be made the king. In the absence of a king, the kingdom will be destroyed. If there is no king in a habitation, clouds garlanded with lightning will not loudly thunder in the sky and Parjanya will not shower down water from the sky on earth. If there is no king in a habitation, even a fistful of seeds does not sprout. If there is no king, a son does not remain under a father's control, nor a wife under her husband's. In the absence of a king, there is no wealth. In the absence of a king, there is no wife either. There is yet another misfortune too. If there is no king, how can there be truth? If there is no king in a habitation, men do not construct assemblies, beautiful groves and cheerful and auspicious houses. In the absence of a king, brahmanas do not engage in sacrifices and generous rites. Nor are brahmanas devoted to their vows. If there is no king in a habitation, large numbers of actors and dancers do not gather at assemblies and festivals and thereby enhance the prosperity of the kingdom. If there is no king in a habitation, disputes do not come to a satisfactory resolution. Those who love tales and are accomplished in reciting the accounts do not delight hearers with their stories. If there is no king in a habitation, men do not leave for the forest in swift-moving vehicles, desiring to find pleasure there with women. If there is no king in a habitation, prosperous people are not protected properly and cannot sleep with their doors open, nor can those who earn a living from agriculture and animal husbandry. If there is no king in a habitation, merchants cannot safely travel long distances, carrying with them large quantities of merchandise. There are controlled sages who roam around alone at will, thinking only of the *atman*, and making a home for the night wherever evening falls. If there is no king in a habitation, they cannot do this. If there is no king in a habitation, yoga and kshema are not ensured. Without a king, soldiers cannot defeat the enemy in a battle. A kingdom without a king is like a river without water, a forest without grass and cows without a cowherd. If there is no king in a habitation, there is nothing like one's own property. Then, like fish, men devour each other. Without any fear, non-believers violate the ordinances, thinking that their inclinations will no longer be chastised by the king's rod. Alas! Without a king, it will be impossible to differentiate between anything in this world and separate the virtuous from the wicked. When the great king was alive, we never transgressed your words, like the ocean does not cross the shoreline. O noble brahmana! Look at us around you. Without a king, the kingdom will become a forest. You can yourself consecrate a young and generous descendant of the Ikshvaku lineage as the king.'

Chapter 2(62)

Hearing their words, Vasishtha replied to the large number of friends, advisers and all the brahmanas in these words. 'Bharata, together with his brother Shatrughna, is happily residing in the city of his maternal uncle, in the royal palace. Using swift steeds, let messengers quickly go there and bring the two brave brothers here. What else do we need to think about?' All of them told Vasishtha, 'Let them go.' Hearing what they said, Vasishtha spoke these words. 'Siddhartha, Vijaya, Jayanta, Ashoka and Nandana—come here. Listen to me. I will tell all of you about everything that needs to be done. Using horses that can travel fast, go to the city and the royal palace. Abandon all sorrow and convey my instructions to Bharata. "The priest and all the ministers have asked about your welfare. Depart quickly. There is an extremely urgent work that you have to undertake here." Do not tell him about Rama's exile and do not tell him that his father is dead. Do not tell him about the catastrophe that confronts the Raghava lineage. Quickly collect the best of garments and ornaments from the treasury, so that they can be given to the king and to Bharata. Then leave.'

Taking Vasishtha's permission, the messengers left quickly. They crossed the river at Hastinapura and headed in a western direction. In the midst of Kurujangala,[244] they reached the Panchala

[244] The area around Kurukshetra.

kingdom. They quickly crossed the divine Sharadanda river,[245] filled with sparkling water and populated by many birds, and proceeded through a region populated by people. They approached the divine *nikula* tree, also known as *satyopayachana*.[246] Passing beyond it, they entered the city of Kulinga. From there they reached Abhikala and the extensive region of Tejobhibhavana. Through the midst of the Bahlika region, they reached Mount Sudama. They saw Vishnupada, Vipasha and Shalmali. Because of the difficult journey that had been undertaken, the mounts and the messengers were exhausted. However, swiftly and safely, they reached the supreme city of Girivraja.[247] To do what would bring pleasure to their lord,[248] to protect the lineage and to bring welfare to the lineage of their lord,[249] the messengers obeyed their instructions quickly and respectfully. They reached the city in the night.

Chapter 2(63)

On the same night that the messengers entered the city, Bharata had an unpleasant dream during the night. He had that unpleasant dream when night was about to turn into dawn.[250] Because of this, the son of the king of kings was extremely tormented. His friends, pleasant in speech, got to know that he was tormented. To dispel this and to comfort him, they arranged for stories to be told in an assembly. Some played on peaceful musical instruments, others arranged for the production of plays. There were many kinds of jokes that were cracked. The friends,

245 Literally, a river that had many clumps of reeds. Identification of these geographical places is difficult and a lot has been speculatively written on these. We are deliberately avoiding any such references, because they are inherently speculative.

246 Because prayers made before the tree came true.

247 The capital of Kekaya.

248 Vasishtha.

249 Now meaning Dasharatha.

250 It is believed that dreams seen at dawn turn out to be true.

pleasant in speech, sought to bring pleasure to the great-souled Bharata through these joyous gatherings. However, Raghava did not rejoice.

When he was surrounded by his friends, his most beloved friend asked Bharata, 'O friend! Why are you not happy, even when you are served by your well-wishers?' Thus addressed by the well-wisher, Bharata replied, 'Listen to the reason why I am overcome by this despondency. I saw my father in my sleep. He was faded and his hair was dishevelled. From the summit of a mountain, he fell down in a lake that was filled with filth and cow dung. I saw him float away in that lake filled with cow dung. He seemed to drink oil from his cupped hands and laughed repeatedly. With his head facing downwards, he repeatedly fed on sesamum seeds. With his limbs covered in oil, he then immersed himself in oil. In the dream, I saw the ocean turn dry and the moon fall down on the ground. Suddenly, the blazing fire seemed to be extinguished. The earth was shattered and many kinds of trees dried up. I saw mountains being whirled around, enveloped in smoke. I saw the king seated on an iron seat, attired in black garments. Women dressed in black and brown seemed to be laughing at him. The one with dharma in his soul was decorated in red garlands and paste. In a chariot drawn by asses, he seemed to be hurrying towards the southern direction.[251] This is the terrible sight I saw in the night, as if I, Rama, the king or Lakshmana will die. In a dream, if a man sees a vehicle that is drawn by asses, in a short period of time, the smoke from a funeral pyre will be seen above him. That is the reason for my distress, the reason why I am unable to honour you properly. My throat is parched and my mind is not at peace. Since I cannot comprehend the reason, I am hating myself. Having had this bad dream in different forms, the like of which I have not seen earlier, my mind is disturbed. A great fear has arisen in my heart. I have been thinking about the unthinkable sight of the king.'

[251] The direction of death.

Chapter 2(64)

As Bharata was speaking about his dream, the messengers, with their exhausted mounts, crossed over the impenetrable moats and entered the beautiful royal palace in the city. They met the king and was honoured by the prince.[252] Having touched the king's feet, they addressed Bharata in these words. 'The priest and all the ministers have asked about your welfare. You should leave quickly. There is an extremely urgent task that you have to undertake. O son of a king! This complete collection of thirty crores is to be given to the king, your maternal uncle.' Bharata was devoted to his well-wishers and accepted all this. Having honoured them with all the objects of desire, he told the messengers, 'I hope that my father, King Dasharatha, is well. I also hope that the great-souled Rama and Lakshmana are healthy. Is Rama's intelligent mother, Kousalya, healthy? The noble one knows about dharma and is devoted to dharma. She possesses the insight of dharma. Is the mother in the middle, Sumitra who knows about dharma and is the mother of the brave Lakshmana and Shatrughna, healthy? My mother, Kaikeyee, always pursues her own desires. She is wrathful and prone to anger, though she prides herself on her wisdom. What has she said?' The messengers were thus addressed by the great-souled Bharata. They respectfully replied to Bharata in the following words. 'O tiger among men! Everyone that you have asked about is well.' Thus addressed, Bharata told the messengers, 'I will take the great king's permission and tell him that the messengers are urging me to hurry.'

Bharata, the son of a king, told the messengers this. Having urged the messengers in these words, he told his maternal uncle, 'O king! The messengers have urged me to go to my father's residence. Whenever you remember me, I will come here again.' Having been thus addressed by Bharata, the king, his maternal uncle, inhaled the fragrance of Raghava's head and addressed him in these auspicious

[252] Yudhajit, the son of Ashvapati, the king of Kekaya. However, the way the sentence is structured, 'prince' could also mean Bharata.

words. 'O son![253] Go, you have my permission. Kaikeyee has a good son like you. O scorcher of enemies! Tell your mother and father that I have asked about their welfare. O son! Ask about the welfare of the priest, the other excellent brahmanas and your two brothers who are great archers, Rama and Lakshmana.' The king of Kekaya generously offered Bharata gifts of excellent elephants, colourful blankets and deer skin, riches, two thousand gold coins and sixteen hundred horses. The king of Kekaya honoured Kaikeyee's son by offering all these riches. Ashvapati also provided beloved and trusted advisers who possessed all the qualities, so that they could follow Bharata on the fast return journey. There were handsome Airavata elephants from the Indrashira region.[254] There were well-trained and swift mules. His maternal uncle gave him all these riches. As a gift, he also gave him extremely large dogs that had been bred in the inner quarters of the palace. These were powerful, with the valour of tigers, and could use their teeth in fighting. Having taken the leave of his maternal grandfather, his maternal uncle, Yudhajit, Bharata, with Shatrughna, ascended the chariot and got ready to leave. There was a circle of more than one hundred chariots, yoked to camels, cattle, horses and mules. There were also servants who would follow Bharata. The great-souled Bharata was protected by this large force. He was also accompanied by advisers who were as noble as him. Possessing no enemies, he also took Shatrughna with him. They left the residence, like the Siddhas leaving Indra's world.

Chapter 2(65)

From the royal palace, the valiant one headed in an eastern direction. He crossed the wide Hladini river, which flowed in

[253] The word used is tata.

[254] While Airavata is the name of Indra's elephant, there were different species of elephants and Airavata was also one of these. Indrashira was a mountainous area in Kekaya. Kekaya was famous for its animals, elephants and horses included.

an eastern direction.[255] The handsome descendant of the Ikshvaku lineage crossed the Shatadru river. Having crossed the Eladhana river, he reached the region of Aparaparpata. At the places known as Agneya and Shalyakartana, he used rocks to cross over. Truthful in his objective and pure, the handsome one looked at the rocks that were being borne along in the flow. He crossed over a giant mountain and headed for the grove of Chaitraratha. There was the forceful flow of the river named Kulinga. This was surrounded by mountains and gladdened the heart. He reached the banks of the Yamuna and made his forces rest there. Their limbs were cooled and the exhausted horses were comforted. They bathed and drank and collected water for use. The prince traversed a gigantic forest that was rarely visited and rarely inhabited. The fortunate one crossed it on well-trained mounts, like the wind coursing through the sky. He reached Jambuprastha, located on the southern parts of the Torana region. Dasharatha's son reached the beautiful village of Varutha. Having set up camp in the beautiful forest and dwelt there, they headed eastwards. They reached a grove in Ujjihana, full of *priyaka* trees. Having reached there, the horses were tethered to the sala and priyaka trees. Having given the forces permission to rest there, Bharata left swiftly. He spent some time in Sarvatirtha and crossed the Uttanaka river. Using the horses, he crossed many other mountainous rivers. Astride an elephant, he crossed Kutika. The tiger among men crossed the Kapeevati at Louhitya. He crossed the Sthanumatee at Ekasala and the Gomatee river at Vinata. He reached a grove of sala trees in the city of Kalinga. Though the mounts were extremely exhausted, Bharata proceeded swiftly. Through the night, he swiftly traversed through the forest. When the sun was about to rise, he saw the city of Ayodhya, built by King Manu. Having spent seven nights on the road, the tiger among men saw that city.

From the chariot, he saw Ayodhya in front of him and told the charioteer, 'O charioteer! Ayodhya can be seen at a distance, like

[255] As will become apparent, this route from Rajagriha to Ayodhya doesn't seem to be quite the same as the route from Ayodhya to Rajagriha followed by the messengers. In addition, it is difficult to understand what some of the expressions mean.

a mass of white clay. It is illustrious and filled with sacred groves, though it cannot be seen clearly from here. Because of sacrifices performed, it possesses all the qualities and it is full of brahmanas who are accomplished in the Vedas. It also has a large number of aged people, protected by the best of royal sages.[256] Earlier, a large and tumultuous sound used to be heard from Ayodhya in every direction, spoken by the men and women. However, I do not hear that today. In the evening, in every direction, the gardens would be full of sporting men who would run around. However, it seems to me to be otherwise today.[257] Abandoned by those who seek pleasures, the gardens seem desolate now. O charioteer! To me, the city seems to be like a forest. Vehicles cannot be seen there, nor can the neighing of horses be heard. Earlier, the best among men used to constantly enter and leave. I see many kinds of evil signs and inauspicious portents. That is the reason my mind is distressed.'

With the exhausted mounts, he entered through the Vaijayanta gate.[258] With pronouncements of victory uttered by gatekeepers who stood up, he entered with his followers. With an anxious heart, he greeted the many people at the gate. Raghava told Ashvapati's exhausted charioteer, 'Earlier, we have heard about what happens when kings are destroyed. O charioteer! I see all those signs here. I see anxious people, men and women, in the city—distressed, eyes full of tears, miserable, deep in thought and extremely afflicted.' Distressed in his mind, Bharata spoke these words to the charioteer. Witnessing all these inauspicious signs, he proceeded towards the royal palace. He saw the city, which used to be like Indra's city. The tops of the gates and houses and the roads were deserted. The red gates and the machines on the gates were covered with dust. He saw many such things that were disagreeable to the mind, those that had never been seen in the city earlier. He was unhappy and distressed in his mind, with his head lowered down. He thus entered his great-souled father's residence.

[256] Dasharatha.

[257] Though it was morning when Bharata reached.

[258] Gate that signifies victory.

Chapter 2(66)

He did not see his father there, in his father's residence. To see his mother, Bharata went to his mother's residence. Kaikeyee saw that her son, who had been away, had arrived. Delighted in her mind, she leapt up from her golden seat. The one with dharma in his soul entered his own house, which was devoid of all signs of prosperity. On seeing his mother, Bharata touched her auspicious feet. She embraced the illustrious one and inhaled the fragrance of his head. Placing Bharata on her lap, she started to question him. 'How many nights have passed since you left the Aryaka's residence?[259] Having swiftly come on a chariot, are you not exhausted? Is Aryaka well? How is Yudhajit, your maternal uncle? O son! Was your residence there happy? Tell me everything.' Kaikeyee asked these questions to her beloved son of the king. The lotus-eyed Bharata told his mother everything that he had been asked. 'This is the seventh night since I left Aryaka's residence. My mother's father is well and so is Yudhajit, my maternal uncle. The king, the scorcher of enemies, gave me riches and jewels as gifts. However, my companions became exhausted along the way and I arrived ahead of them. I came quickly because the messengers conveyed the king's message. O mother! You should answer what I wish to ask you. This gold-decorated bed, used for lying down, is empty. The people of the Ikshvaku lineage do not seem to be happy to me. The king is usually here, in my mother's residence. I do not see him here now. I came here to meet him. I wish to touch my father's feet. Tell me what I am asking you. I see. Perhaps he is there in my eldest mother, Kousalya's, residence.'

At this, Kaikeyee told him the terrible and disagreeable news, as if she was recounting something pleasant. She told him what she knew, but he did not, about how she was confounded by her greed for the kingdom. 'Your father has confronted the end that is attained by all living creatures.' Bharata followed dharma and was born in a noble and auspicious lineage. Hearing these words, afflicted by great grief on account of his father, he suddenly fell down on the ground.

[259] Ashvapati's father.

He was extremely miserable on account of his father's death and was senseless with grief. His senses awhirl and distracted, the immensely energetic one lamented. 'In earlier times, this extremely beautiful bed of my father's used to be radiant. Deprived of the intelligent one, that is the reason it does not shine any longer.' She saw that the one who was like a god was afflicted and had fallen down on the ground. She raised the afflicted one and addressed him in these words. 'Arise! O immensely illustrious prince! Why are you lying down? Arise! Those like you, revered in the assemblies of men, do not grieve in this way.' Writhing around on the ground, he wept for a long time. Afflicted by many kinds of grief, he replied to his mother. 'I thought that the king was going to consecrate Rama, or that he had decided to perform a sacrifice. Having thought in this way, I cheerfully undertook this journey. Everything has turned out to be the opposite and my mind is shattered. I do not see my father, who was always engaged in my welfare. O mother! Before I returned, what disease did my father die of? Tell me that quickly. My elder, Rama, whose deeds are unblemished, is like a father now. A noble one who follows dharma knows this. I will grasp his feet. He is my refuge now. O noble lady! For my father, truth was his valour. What did he say? I want to myself hear his last and virtuous words.'

Thus asked, Kaikeyee told him words that were in conformity with the truth. 'The king lamented, uttering the names of Rama, Sita and Lakshmana. Thus did the great-souled one, supreme among all refuges, go to the world hereafter. These were the last words spoken by your father. He was like a giant elephant in a noose, entangled in the dharma of time. "Men who see Rama, Sita and the mighty-armed Lakshmana return again will accomplish their objective."' Hearing this second piece of unpleasant news, he was distressed again. With a miserable face, he again asked his mother, 'Where is the extender of Kousalya's delight, the one with dharma in his soul, now? Where have my brother, Lakshmana, and Sita gone with him?' Thus asked, his mother started to tell him everything that had happened. This was unpleasant news, though she thought it was pleasant. 'O son! The prince has attired himself in bark and has gone to the great forest. With Vaidehi and Lakshmana following him, he has gone to Dandaka.' Hearing this, Bharata was terrified, because he suspected this might have had something to do with his brother's character and would therefore reflect on his lineage's greatness. He asked, 'Has Rama seized the riches of a brahmana? Has he caused injury to a rich or poor person, or to an innocent one? Has the prince sought after another person's wife? Has he been exiled to Dandakaranya because of foeticide?' At this, the fickle mother narrated the truth about what she had exactly done, because of her feminine sentiments. 'Rama has not seized any brahmana's riches. He has not caused injury to a rich or poor person, or to one who is innocent. Nor has Rama cast a glance at another person's wife. O son! I heard about Rama being consecrated as the heir apparent. I immediately asked your father for the kingdom and for Rama's exile. Following standards of conduct he set for himself, your father acted accordingly. He sent Rama, Soumitri and Sita away. The king could no longer see his beloved and immensely illustrious son. He died on account of sorrow over his son. O one who knows about dharma! You can rightfully claim the kingship now. All that I did was done for your sake. O son! Following the ordinances, quickly meet the ones who know about the rites—the Indras among brahmanas, led by Vasishtha. At the right time, without any distress in your heart, consecrate yourself as the king over this earth.'

Chapter 2(67)

He heard the account about his father and about his brothers being banished. Bharata was tormented by grief and spoke these words. 'As I am grieving, what use is this devastated kingdom to me now? I am deprived of my father and of my brother, who is like a father. Like applying salt on a wound, you have imposed a sorrow on another sorrow. You have made my father die and have turned Rama into an ascetic. You have brought about the destruction of the lineage, as if a night of destruction has arrived. My father did not know that he had embraced a burning piece of coal. You are my mother. But overcome by sorrow on account of their sons, Kousalya and Sumitra will find it extremely difficult to reside with you. The noble one[260] had dharma in his soul and displayed supreme conduct towards you, treating you like his own mother. He knew about how one should behave with seniors. In that way, my eldest mother, Kousalya, possesses foresight. Resorting to dharma, she behaved with you as if with one's own sister. You have made her son don garments of rags and bark and leave for residing in the forest. Despite this wickedness, you are not sorrowing. You do not realize the evil you have caused to that illustrious one. You have exiled him, with bark as attire. Do you see any reason for this? I do not think you know how much I desire Raghava. Otherwise, for the sake of the kingdom, you would not have brought about this great and unnecessary calamity. In the absence of the strength brought about by those tigers among men, Rama and Lakshmana, why will I be interested in protecting the kingdom? He[261] is powerful and extremely strong and the great king always found succour in him. The one with dharma in his soul was like the forest around Meru, sustaining Meru. This great burden has been thrust upon me. How can I bear this load? It requires energy. I do not possess the insolence to attempt this burden. On account of your son, you are greedy. Even if I were to possess the capacity brought about through yoga, intelligence and strength, I will not allow you to accomplish your objective. I will bring back my brother, who is loved by his relatives, from the forest.' The great-souled Bharata spoke in this way and added a multitude of other pleasant words. Though he was afflicted by grief, like a lion in a mountainous cavern, he roared.

Chapter 2(68)

Bharata censured his mother in this way. Overcome by great rage, he again spoke these words. 'O Kaikeyee! O cruel one!

[260] Rama.

[261] Rama.

O one who is wicked in conduct! Go away from this kingdom. You have abandoned dharma. When I am dead, weep over me. What harm has the king, or Rama, who is extremely devoted to dharma, done to you? Because of what you have done, his death and the exile have occurred simultaneously. Because you have brought about the destruction of this lineage, it is as if you have committed foeticide. O Kaikeyee! Go to hell. You will not obtain the world obtained by your husband. You have perpetrated an extremely terrible deed like this. Having abandoned someone who is loved by all the worlds, you have created a great fear in me too. My father is dead and Rama has resorted to the forest because of you. For me, you have brought about ill fame in the world of the living. O cruel one! O one who is greedy for the kingdom! In the form of a mother, you are my enemy. I will not speak to you. O evil in conduct! You have killed your husband. O defiler of the lineage! Because of you, Kousalya, Sumitra and my other mothers are immersed in great misery. The intelligent king, Ashvapati, is devoted to dharma. You are not his daughter. You have been born as a rakshasa lady, to destroy your father's lineage. Rama was always devoted to the truth and abided by dharma. Because of you, he has left for the forest and, grieving, my father has gone to heaven. Your grievous sin has been to deprive me of my father. O one hated by all the worlds! You have also made my brothers abandon me. Kousalya is devoted to dharma. Having turned your mind towards wickedness, you have deprived her. Having done this, you will now obtain worlds destined for those who go to hell. O cruel one! Did you not comprehend that Rama, my elder brother and Kousalya's son, is like a father to me? He is a refuge for all his relatives. The son is born from the limbs and the heart. That is the reason a son is most loved by a mother. All the other relatives come after that. Surabhee[262] is revered by the gods and knows about dharma. There was an occasion when she lost her senses on seeing her two sons bear heavy burdens on earth. She saw that her two

[262] The mother of cows and the cow of the gods.

sons were exhausted on earth, having borne the burden for half a day. Afflicted on account of her sons, she wept, her eyes overflowing with tears. The great-souled king of the gods was travelling below her and those fine and fragrant drops fell on his body. Indra, the wielder of the vajra, saw that the illustrious one was tormented by grief. Anxious, the king of the gods joined his hands in salutation and spoke these words. "I hope no great fear has been caused to you by us. O one who wishes everyone's welfare! What has given rise to this sorrow? Tell me." Thus addressed by the intelligent king of the gods, Surabhee, eloquent in the use of words, replied in these patient words, "O lord of the immortals! May anything that causes you evil be pacified. I am immersed in grief because my two sons are facing a hardship. They are distressed and weak, because they have been scorched by the rays of the sun. O lord of the gods! Dragging the plough, the two bulls are being killed. They have been born from my body. They are suffering and are afflicted by the burden. I am tormented on seeing them. There is nothing as beloved as a son." The cow which provides all the objects of desire sorrowed, even though she possessed a thousand sons. Without Rama, how will Kousalya sustain herself? The virtuous one has a single son and because of what you have done, she has been separated from her son. Therefore, you will always suffer from grief, in this world and in the world hereafter. I will do everything that needs to be done for my father and compensate my brother by enhancing his fame. There is no doubt about this. I will bring back Kousalya's immensely radiant son. I will myself go to the forest that is frequented by the hermits.' Like an elephant in the forest, which has been prodded by a javelin or a goad, he fell down angrily on the ground and sighed like a serpent. His eyes were red and his clothing was dishevelled. All his ornaments were thrown around. The king's son, scorcher of enemies, fell down on the ground, like the standard of Shachi's consort, once the festival is over.[263]

[263] Shachi's consort is Indra. As long as the festival is observed, Indra's standard is raised. Thereafter, it is flung away.

Chapter 2(69)

Hearing the words spoken by the great-souled Bharata and recognizing the voice, Kousalya spoke to Sumitra. 'Bharata, the son of Kaikeyee, the perpetrator of cruel deeds, has arrived. I wish to see the far-sighted Bharata.' She was trembling and she wasn't in control of her senses. Pale and dressed in faded garments, she told Sumitra this and left for where Bharata was. Meanwhile, together with Shatrughna, Bharata, Rama's younger brother, also left for Kousalya's residence. Bharata and Shatrughna saw the miserable Kousalya. Afflicted with grief, she had lost her senses and fallen down along the way. They embraced her. Kousalya, extremely miserable, addressed Bharata. 'You desired this kingdom and you have obtained the kingdom, bereft of thorns. Thanks to Kaikeyee, the performer of cruel deeds, you have quickly obtained it. My son, dressed in rags, has left, to reside in the forest. What merit did the evil-sighted Kaikeyee see in this? Kaikeyee should quickly grant me permission to leave for the place where my extremely illustrious son, Hiranyanabha,[264] is. Or perhaps I can cheerfully leave on my own, with Sumitra following me. With the agnihotra fire in front, I will go to wherever Raghava is. But perhaps that is what you yourself desire now. You should convey me there, where my ascetic son, tiger among men, is tormenting himself through austerities. This extensive kingdom, with its store of grain, riches, elephants, horses and chariots, has been handed over to you.'

When she lamented in this way, Bharata joined his hands in salutation. Kousalya was suffering from many kinds of grief and he spoke to her. 'O noble lady! Why are you reprimanding me? I am ignorant and innocent of any sin. You know that my affection for Raghava is great. The noble one is devoted to the truth and is best among virtuous ones. May the intelligence of anyone who ensured his departure never turn to the sacred texts. May the servants of any such wicked person release urine in the direction of the sun. May the

[264] The one with the golden navel, Vishnu's name. It is odd that Kousalya should use this expression.

person who ensured his departure kill a sleeping cow with his foot. A servant who causes great injury and performs a great misdeed is imposed a punishment by his master. May the person who ensured the adharma of his departure endure that punishment. May the person who ensured his departure suffer from the sin committed by an individual who causes injury to a king who protects his subjects like his own sons. A king who extracts more than one-sixth of taxes makes his subjects suffer and commits adharma. May the person who ensured his departure suffer from that sin. An individual who promises ascetics dakshina at sacrifices and deviates from the pledge commits a sin. May the person who ensured his departure suffer from that sin. In a tumultuous battle where weapons are used, there are rules for fighting with elephants, horses and chariots and any deviation is not dharma. May the person who ensured his departure suffer from that sin. An evil-souled person destroys the extremely subtle meaning of the sacred texts, taught by intelligent instructors. May the person who ensured his departure suffer from that sin. Without offering it first to seniors, there are those who pointlessly eat the shunned food of payasam, *krisara* and goat meat.[265] May the person who ensured his departure suffer from that sin. It is a sin to eat alone in one's house, when one is surrounded by sons, wives and servants. May the person who ensured his departure suffer from that sin. It is a sin to kill a king, a woman, a child or an aged person, just as it is a sin to abandon a servant. May that kind of sin visit the person. Sleeping during both the sandhyas has been thought of as a sin. May the person who ensured his departure suffer from that sin. It is a sin to indulge in arson. It is a sin to transgress a preceptor's bed. It is a sin to cause injury to a friend. May the person suffer from that sin. It is a sin not to serve the gods, the ancestors, the mother and the father. May the person suffer from that sin. It has been recounted that there are worlds for the virtuous and for those who perform virtuous deeds. May the person who ensured his departure be swiftly dislodged from those.' Kousalya had been deprived of her

[265] Krisara is a dish made out of sesamum and grain. The point is that shares must first be offered to gods and other seniors. Otherwise, it is abhorred food and any sacrificial food, not offered first to the gods, is a pointless sacrifice.

husband and her son. While comforting her in this way, the king's son was also overcome by grief and fell down.

Bharata had just taken extremely difficult pledges. Having taken those pledges, he had become unconscious. Kousalya spoke these words to the one who was tormented by grief. 'O son! My sorrow has become greater. Through the pledges that you have taken, you are making me suffer even more. It is good fortune that, like Lakshmana, your soul is devoted to dharma. O son! You have sworn on the truth and you will obtain worlds meant for the virtuous.' Afflicted by grief, the great-souled one[266] lamented in this way. His mind was agitated. He was confused and racked by tides of grief. He lamented and lost his senses. With his intelligence devastated, he fell down on the ground. He repeatedly emitted long sighs. The night passed in the midst of such misery.

Chapter 2(70)

In this way, Bharata, Kaikeyee's son, was tormented by grief. Vasishtha, foremost among rishis and best among eloquent ones, spoke to him. 'O fortunate one! O immensely illustrious prince! Enough of this sorrow. The time has come to perform the last rites for the lord of men.' Hearing Vasishtha's words, Bharata prostrated himself. The one who knew about dharma performed all the funeral rites. The body of the king was raised from the vessel of oil. The face was yellow in complexion, as if he was asleep. The body was first laid down on the best of beds, decorated with many kinds of jewels. At this, Dasharatha's son lamented in great misery. 'O king! When I was away and had not returned from my trip, why did you send off Rama, who knows about dharma, and the immensely strong Lakshmana on exile? O great king! Abandoning these grieving people, where will you go? They have also been deprived of Rama, the performer of unblemished deeds and lion among men. O king!

[266] Bharata.

Who will now think of yoga and kshema for this city? O father! You have gone and Rama has left for the forest. O king! Without you, the earth is a widow and does not shine any more. The city seems to me to be like the night without the moon.' Distressed in his mind, Bharata lamented in this way.

The great rishi, Vasishtha, again addressed him in these words. 'Funeral and other rites need to be performed for the king. O mighty-armed one! Without any distraction or reflection, perform those rites.' Bharata worshipped Vasishtha and agreed to his words. He quickly welcomed all the officiating priests, priests and preceptors. Following the indicated ordinances, the officiating priests and assistants initially kindled the fire for the king outside the fire chamber. The king's senseless body was then placed on a palanquin and borne by distracted attendants whose voices choked with tears. Ahead of the king, people advanced along the road, scattering silver, gold and many kinds of garments. The funeral pyre was prepared with wood from *sarala*, *padmaka* and devadaru trees and sprinkled with the essence of sandalwood and aloe. Many other kinds of fragrances were flung there and the officiating priests placed the king in the midst of all these. The officiating priests poured oblations into the fire and chanted. Following the sacred texts, those accomplished in the Sama Veda chanted Sama hymns.

As each one deserved, the women mounted palanquins and vehicles. Surrounded by the elders, they left the city and reached the place. The king was on the funeral pyre and the officiating priests circumambulated him anticlockwise. With Kousalya at the forefront, the women were tormented by grief. Like the sound of female curlews, the wails of the women could be heard. At the time, thousands of them lamented in piteous tones. On the banks of the Sarayu, those beautiful women descended from their vehicles and distressed, repeatedly wept and lamented. With the royal women, the ministers and the priests, Bharata performed the water rites. Eyes full of tears, they entered the city. In misery, they spent ten days on the ground.[267]

[267] That is, they slept on the floor for ten days.

Chapter 2(71)

After ten days had passed, the son of the king purified himself. On the twelfth day, he performed the *shraddha* ceremony. He gave brahmanas large quantities of jewels, riches, food, many white goats, hundreds of cows, female servants, male servants and extremely expensive houses. As part of the funeral rites, the king's son gave these to brahmanas.

On the morning of the thirteenth day, the mighty-armed Bharata went for cleansing.[268] He became senseless with sorrow and lamented. The words choked in his throat. Extremely miserable, at the foot of the funeral pyre, he addressed his father in these words. 'O father! I entrusted your care to my brother, Raghava. But you exiled him to the forest. Abandoned by you, I am alone now. O father! Mother Kousalya's refuge was her son. But you exiled him to the forest. O king! Forsaking her, where have you gone now?' He saw the red ashes and the burnt circle of skin and bones. He grieved that his father had given up his body. He was miserable on seeing the remnants and fell down on the ground. It was as if Shakra's standard had been raised, but fell down because the machines to work the standard failed. All the advisers, pure in their vows, approached. It was like the rishis rushing to Yayati when the time for his death arrived.

Shatrughna also saw that Bharata was overcome with sorrow. Remembering the king, he also lost his senses and fell down on the ground. It was as if he[269] went mad. He lamented in great misery. He remembered all the many qualities that his father had possessed. 'We are being agitated and have been immersed in this ocean of grief. This is because of Manthara's terrible influence and Kaikeyee is like a crocodile swimming in the two boons. O father! As a child, you have always tended to the delicate Bharata. He is lamenting. Abandoning him, where have you gone? You have always given us

[268] This doesn't convey the sense. He went to clean the cremation ground and collect the remaining bones.

[269] Shatrughna.

everything that we desired—food, drink, garments and ornaments. Why don't you do that now? As a king, you knew about dharma and were great-souled. Without you, the earth should be shattered. Why is it not being shattered? Our father has gone to heaven and Rama has resorted to the forest. What is the point of remaining alive? I should enter the fire. I am without a brother. I am without a father. Ayodhya, ruled by the Ikshvakus, is empty. Why should I return there? I should enter a hermitage.'

Hearing their lamentations and witnessing their distress, all their followers were again immersed in great grief. Both Shatrughna and Bharata were exhausted and distressed. They writhed around on the ground, like insensate bulls whose horns had been broken. Vasishtha was the priest of their father. Like a physician who restores to normalcy, he raised Bharata and addressed him in these words. 'Without exception, there are three kinds of opposite sentiments all living creatures have to face.[270] Since this is inevitable, you should not behave like this.' Sumantra knew about the truth. He raised Shatrughna and comforted him, telling him about the origin and destruction of all creatures. Those two illustrious tigers among men were raised. They were as radiant as Indra's standard, having suffered through rains and the heat. Their eyes were still red and their speech was miserable. But they wiped away their tears. The advisers urged them to hurry with the remaining rites.

Chapter 2(72)

Bharata was tormented by grief and wished to undertake the journey.[271] Shatrughna, Lakshmana's younger brother, addressed him in these words. 'The spirited Rama is the refuge of all creatures. What can be a greater grief to us than that he has been exiled to the forest by a woman? Lakshmana is so named

[270] Birth and death, joy and misery and heat and cold.
[271] To meet Rama.

because he possesses strength and valour.[272] Why did he not free Rama and restrain our father? Even before the act had happened, on considering good and bad policy and on seeing that the king had resorted to a wrong path, having come under the subjugation of a woman, he should have restrained him.' While Shatrughna, Lakshmana's younger brother, was speaking in this way, Kubja appeared at the eastern gate, adorned in every kind of ornament. She was radiant in royal garments and was smeared with the essence of sandalwood. Attired in colourful girdles, she looked like a female monkey, bound with ropes. She was the perpetrator of an extremely wicked deed. On seeing her, the doorkeepers seized the cruel Kubja. Delivering her to Shatrughna, they said, 'It is because of what she did that Rama has left for the forest and your father has given up his life. This is the wicked and cruel one. Do what you want with her.'

Shatrughna, firm in his vows, was extremely miserable. He instructed all those in the inner quarters in these words. 'This perpetrator of cruel deeds has led to this great calamity and owes a debt to my brothers and my father. Let her reap the fruits of her action.' Kubja was surrounded by her friends. Having said this, he powerfully seized her, so that the residence echoed with her cries. Hearing Shatrughna's angry words, all her friends became extremely miserable and fled in different directions. All those friends came to the following conclusion. 'The way he is advancing, he will destroy all of us. The illustrious Koushalya knows about dharma and is generous and compassionate. Let us seek refuge with her. It is certain that she is our only refuge.' The eyes of Shatrughna, tormentor of enemies, were coppery red with rage. He dragged the shrieking Kubja along the ground. As Manthara was dragged along the ground, her many colourful ornaments were strewn around on the floor. When those ornaments were strewn around, the radiant royal palace was as resplendent as the autumn sky.[273] The powerful one, bull among men, seized her in his rage. He reprimanded Kaikeyee in harsh words. Kaikeyee was extremely miserable and pained at

[272] The word *lakshmana* means mark or sign.

[273] The ornaments looked like stars.

these harsh words. Terrified of Shatrughna, she sought refuge with her own son. On seeing her and the angry Shatrughna, Bharata said, 'Among all living beings, women should never be killed. She should be pardoned. Kaikeyee is wicked and evil in conduct. However, Rama is devoted to dharma and will be angry if I were to kill my mother. But for this, I would have killed her. Raghava has dharma in his soul. If he gets to know that this Kubja has been killed, it is certain that he will not speak to you or to me.' Hearing Bharata's words, Shatrughna, Lakshmana's younger brother, controlled his rage and released Manthara. Manthara fell down at Kaikeyee's feet. Suffering greatly, she lamented piteously and sighed. Flung away by Shatrughna, Kubja was senseless and grief-stricken, like a female curlew that had been captured. On seeing her, Bharata's mother gently comforted her.

Chapter 2(73)

It was the morning of the fourteenth day. Those entrusted with the task of anointing a king assembled and addressed Bharata in these words. 'Dasharatha, senior to all our seniors, has gone to heaven. Rama, the eldest, has been exiled and so has the immensely strong Lakshmana. O greatly illustrious king! You should be our king now. Without a leader, it is fortunate that the kingdom has not suffered from a calamity so far. O Raghava! O son of a king! With everything required for a consecration, your own relatives and the citizens are awaiting you. O Bharata! Accept this great kingdom of your father and grandfathers. O bull among men! Consecrate yourself and save us.'

Bharata circumambulated all the vessels kept for the consecration. Firm in his vows, he replied to all those people. 'In our lineage, it has always been proper that the kingdom should be vested with the eldest. O those who are accomplished! You should not speak to me in this way. My brother, Rama, is elder to me and he will be the lord of the earth. I will reside in the forest for fourteen years. Let a large and extremely strong army, with the four kinds of forces, be yoked. I will bring my elder brother, Raghava, back from the forest. Placing all these objects required for the coronation in front of me, for Rama's sake, I will go to the forest. With these objects, I will consecrate that tiger among men there. I will bring Rama back, like bringing back the sacrificial fire.[274] I will not allow the one who pretends to be by mother to be successful. I will reside in the impenetrable forest and Rama will be the king. Let artisans create a path through flat and uneven terrain. Let those who know about impenetrable paths protect us along the way.' For Rama's sake, the son of the king spoke in this way. All the people replied in these supreme and excellent words. 'Since you have spoken in this way, let Padma always be with you, in the form of Shri.[275] You have desired to give away the earth to your elder, the son of the king.' They heard those supreme words spoken by the son of the king. Because of their delight, tears of joy fell down from their noble eyes. Hearing those words, the advisers and the counsellors were delighted and abandoned their misery. They said, 'O supreme among men! Following your instructions, devoted men and large numbers of artisans will be engaged to construct the road.'

Chapter 2(74)

Those who knew about land and the regions, those accomplished with strings,[276] brave ones engaged in their own tasks, diggers, those who worked with machines, labourers, architects, men accomplished about machines, carpenters, road builders, those who would cut down trees, those who would dig wells, those who would do plaster work, those who would work with bamboo and those

[274] The image is of a sacrifice performed outside a city, the sacrificial fire then brought back to the city.

[275] Lakshmi, also known as Shri, the goddess of wealth and prosperity. Since Lakshmi is seated on a lotus, she is also known as Padma.

[276] For levelling the ground.

who were capable, departed, placing the supervisors at the front. That large crowd of men departed joyously and was as radiant as the great force of the ocean at the time of the full moon. They were accomplished in building roads and each engaged himself in his own appointed task, with his own respective implement. They thus advanced. Those people cleared away creepers, lantanas, shrubs, trees and rocks. Cutting down many kinds of trees, they created a path. Some planted trees in spots where there were no trees. Others used axes, hatchets and sickles to cut down thickets. Other strong ones, stronger than the others, removed clumps of *veerana* grass. Here and there, they levelled the impenetrable parts. Some filled up wells and pits with earth. Some levelled the spots that sloped downwards. Bridges were built where they could be constructed. Throughout the region, the men crushed and shattered obstructions that stood along the way. In a short while, many canals and wells were built. There were many such and some of them looked like oceans. In spots where there was no water, many excellent wells were dug and decorated with platforms around them. The surface of the road was plastered and lined with blossoming trees, on which, intoxicated birds chirped. The road was decorated with flags. The road was decorated with many kinds of flowers and sprinkled with water mixed with the fragrance of sandalwood. Constructed for those many soldiers, the road was as radiant as a road to heaven. The supervisors were men who had been instructed for the purpose. In a beautiful spot that had many kinds of succulent fruit, they constructed a residence for the great-souled Bharata. Adorned with many kinds of ornaments, this itself looked like an ornament. Those who knew about such things determined an auspicious nakshatra and at that time, camps were set up for the great-souled Bharata. Each of these was surrounded by moats and walls of earth. Each of these possessed excellent roads and looked like sapphires. There were garlands of mansions and walls and fortifications were erected around them. Each had excellent and large roads, decorated with flags. The tops of the mansions were like vimanas and extended up into the sky. As they rose up, they were as resplendent as Shakra's city. With many trees and groves, the road approached the Jahnavee, which was full of cool and sparkling water and populated by giant fish. The clear and sparkling night is radiant with the moon and a large number of stars. Constructed progressively and auspiciously by the artisans, the beautiful royal road was as resplendent as that.

Chapter 2(75)

There were bards and minstrels, eloquent in the use of words. On that *nandimukha* night,[277] they praised Bharata with auspicious words of praise. There was a drum that was used to sound the progress of the yamas. This was struck with a golden drumstick. Hundreds of conch shells, with loud and soft notes, were blown. The sky was filled with the extremely large sound of trumpets. Bharata was already tormented by sorrow and this increased his grief. Awoken by the sound, Bharata instructed that it should cease. He said 'I am not the king.' He next told Shatrughna, 'O Shatrughna! Look at the great injury Kaikeyee has caused to the world. King Dasharatha has left, releasing this grief on me. This royal prosperity, with dharma as its foundation, belongs to the great-souled king who followed dharma. It is now being tossed around, like a boat without a steersman in the water.' On seeing Bharata senseless, lamenting in this way, all the women wept piteously, in loud tones.

When they were lamenting in this way, the immensely illustrious Vasishtha, who knew about the dharma of kings, entered the assembly hall of the lord of the Ikshvakus. It was beautiful, decorated with molten gold, gems and jewels and was like Sudharma.[278] The one with dharma in his soul entered with his followers. The one who knew all the Vedas seated himself on a golden seat that was strewn with spreads. He then instructed the messengers, 'Without being distracted, quickly summon the brahmanas, kshatriyas,

[277] Nandimukha has different meanings. Here, it simply means joyous night. The word is also used for a special shraddha ceremony.

[278] The assembly hall of the gods.

warriors, advisers and leaders of the armies. We have to perform an extremely urgent task.' A large and tumultuous sound was generated, as chariots, horses, elephants and people started to assemble. Bharata arrived, like Shatakratu of the immortals, and all the subjects greeted him, as if he was Dasharatha. Adorned by Dashratha's son, the assembly hall was like a lake with tranquil waters, filled with water, gems, conch shells, gravel, whales and serpents, just as, in earlier times, it used to be with Dasharatha.

Chapter 2(76)

The well-designed assembly hall was full of noble people and was like the night, adorned by the full moon. Bharata, full of understanding, saw it. The noble ones were seated on their own respective seats and he saw it, dazzling like a night of the full moon after the end of the monsoon. The priest, knowledgeable about dharma, looked at all the royal and ordinary people and addressed Bharata in these gentle words. 'O son![279] Having followed dharma, King Dasharatha has gone to heaven. He has given you this prosperous earth, full of riches and grain. Rama is virtuous and upholds the truth. Remembering dharma, he did not cast aside his father's command, just as a rising moon does not cast aside the moonlight. Bereft of thorns, your father and your brother have given you this kingdom. Enjoy it. With the delighted advisers, quickly arrange for the coronation. Let those from the north, from the west, from the south, those without kingdoms[280] and those from the boundaries of the ocean bring you crores of jewels.'

Hearing these words, Bharata, knowledgeable about dharma, was filled with sorrow. He mentally thought of Rama and desired to ensure dharma. In a voice overcome with tears and in a tone like that of a swan, in the midst of the assembly, the youth reprimanded

[279] The word used is tata.

[280] The word used is *kevala*. It is not obvious that this refers to those from the east. Literally, the word would mean isolated countries.

the priest. 'I have followed brahmacharya and having acquired learning, have bathed.[281] I am intelligent and endeavour to pursue dharma. How can someone like me steal someone else's kingdom? How can someone born from Dasharatha steal a kingdom? Both I and the kingdom belong to Rama. You should speak in accordance with dharma. He is elder and superior, possessing dharma in his soul. He is the equal of Dileepa and Nahusha.[282] As did Dasharatha, Kakutstha should receive the kingdom. If I commit this crime, I will act like an ignoble person and will not go to heaven. In this world, I will become the defiler of the lineage of the Ikshvakus. I do not take delight in the wicked act perpetrated by my mother. From here, I am joining my hands in salutation and bowing down before the one who is in the impenetrable forest. He is supreme among bipeds and I will follow King Rama. Raghava deserves the kingdom of the three worlds.' Hearing those words, in conformity with dharma, all the courtiers shed tears of joy, their minds immersed in Rama. 'If I am incapable of bringing back the noble one from the forest, I will reside in the forest, as the noble Lakshmana is doing. I will use every means, even force, to bring him back. I will present the noble one before this assembly of virtuous people who possess all the qualities.' With dharma in his soul and affectionate towards his brother, Bharata spoke in this fashion. Sumantra, skilled in counsels, was nearby and he addressed him in these words. 'O Sumantra! Arise. Follow my command and go quickly. Summon the forces and ask them to leave swiftly.' Thus addressed by the great-souled Bharata, Sumantra cheerfully instructed that everything should be done as he[283] had desired. The ordinary soldiers and the commanders of the forces were delighted on learning about the journey to bring back Raghava. Knowing this, in every house, the wives of all the warriors were also filled with joy and urged their husbands to hurry. The commanders of the forces urged all the forces—horses, bullock carts, chariots that were as fleet as thought and warriors. Bharata saw that the army was ready. In the

[281] The ritual bath at the end of a period of studies.

[282] While Dileepa is from the solar dynasty, Nahusha is from the lunar dynasty.

[283] Bharata.

presence of his preceptor,[284] he spoke to Sumantra, who was by his side. 'Swiftly prepare my chariot.' Happy, he accepted Bharata's instructions. He yoked the chariot to excellent steeds and brought it, ready to leave. Raghava[285] was powerful and firm in adherence to the truth. He spoke what was appropriate. He was firm and truth was his valour. The illustrious one wanted to go to the great forest to seek the favours of his elder. Bharata said, 'O Sumantra! Arise quickly and go. Tell the leaders of the forces to yoke the army. For the welfare of the world, I desire to seek Rama's favours and bring him back from the forest.' The son of the suta was thus directly instructed by Bharata to accomplish his desire. He instructed all the leaders of the ordinary soldiers, the commanders of the armies and the well-wishers. Every family arose and started yoking chariots to camels, mules, elephants and well-bred horses—royalty, vaishyas, *vrishala*s and brahmanas.[286]

Chapter 2(77)

When it was morning, Bharata arose and wishing to see Rama, ascended an excellent chariot and swiftly departed. All the ministers and priests ascended chariots that were like the sun's chariot, yoked to horses, and proceeded ahead of him. There were nine thousand elephants that had been prepared in the proper way. They followed Bharata, the delight of the Ikshvaku lineage, on his journey. There were six thousand chariots with archers armed with many kinds of weapons. They followed illustrious Prince Bharata on his journey. There were one hundred thousand horses and riders. They followed illustrious Prince Bharata Raghava on his journey. Kaikeyee, Sumitra and the illustrious Kousalya left on a radiant

[284] Vasishtha.

[285] Bharata.

[286] Vrishala means shudra, but also outcast in general. Royalty obviously represents kshatriyas.

vehicle, delighted at the prospect of bringing Rama back.[287] Cheerful in their minds at the prospect of seeing Rama and Lakshmana, that noble assembly left, conversing about his[288] wonderful exploits. 'He is mighty-armed and as dark as a cloud. He is firm in his spirit and firm in his vows. When will we see Rama, the dispeller of the world's misery? As soon as we see him, Raghava will dispel our grief, just as the rising sun dispels darkness from all the worlds.' Delighted, they addressed each other in these auspicious words. The citizens embraced each other and proceeded. There were others there who were respected, merchants and ordinary people. All of them also left, delighted at the prospect of seeing Rama. There were some who worked with gems, those who fashioned beautiful pots, those who were carpenters, those who made weapons, those who worked with peacock feathers, those who used saws, those who fashioned ornaments, those who pierced gems, those who worked with tusks, those who worked with plaster, those who made their living through fragrances, famous goldsmiths, those who wove woollen blankets, those who bathed and attired people, physicians, incense makers, those who distilled liquor, washermen, tailors, leaders of villages and habitations, dancers, fishermen and their women. All of them proceeded. There were self-controlled brahmanas, learned in the Vedas and respected for their conduct. Astride thousands of bullock carts, they followed Bharata. They were attired in pure and excellent garments, anointing themselves with red sandalwood paste. All of them swiftly followed Bharata, on many kinds of vehicles. Delighted and comforted, the soldiers followed Bharata, Kaikeyee's son.

The army was thus stationed there. On seeing the army following him and Ganga, full of auspicious waters, ahead of him, Bharata, accomplished in the use of words, spoke to all his advisers.[289] 'It is my desire that the entire army should set up camp. They are exhausted. We will cross this great river tomorrow. I desire to descend into the waters of the river and offer the funeral water

[287] Kaikeyee seems to have repented.

[288] Rama's.

[289] Some time had been spent on the journey.

rites to the king who has left for heaven.' Hearing his words, the self-controlled advisers agreed. They arranged for separate camps for everyone, in accordance with each one's wishes. They carefully set up camp on the banks of the great river, Ganga. With all the equipment, the army looked beautiful. The great-souled Bharata resided there, thinking about how he would bring Rama back.

Chapter 2(78)

The banks of the river Ganga were full of flags. On seeing these, the king of the nishadas[290] spoke urgently to his kin. 'From here, this giant army is seen to have the appearance of an ocean. Though I have been thinking about this in my mind, I cannot see an end to this. There is a giant *kovidara* standard on a chariot.[291] Perhaps he will bind our fishermen or slay us. Dasharatha's son, Rama, has been banished from the kingdom by his father. Perhaps Bharata, Kaikeyee's son, has advanced so as to kill him. Rama, Dasharatha's son, is my lord and my friend too. To accomplish his desires, armour yourselves and remain on this bank of the Ganga. Let all our servants station themselves along the river Ganga. Let the army subsist on meat, roots and fruit and protect the river. Let there be five hundred boats, each with one thousand fishermen. Let them remain ready.' These were his instructions. 'If Bharata is kindly disposed towards Rama, only then will he be allowed to safely cross the Ganga now.' Having said this, Guha, the lord of the nishadas, took fish, meat and honey as offerings and approached Bharata. The powerful son of the suta[292] saw him approach and the humble one spoke to Bharata with humility. 'This lord is surrounded by one thousand of his kin. He is knowledgeable about the Dandaka forest and has also been your brother's friend for a long time. O Kakutstha! Therefore, let Guha, lord of the nishadas, see you. There

[290] Guha.
[291] Bharata's standard was made out of kovidara (a kind of orchid tree).
[292] Sumantra.

is no doubt that he will know where Rama and Lakshmana are.' Hearing the auspicious words spoken by Sumantra, Bharata replied, 'Let Guha see me quickly.' Having obtained permission, Guha was delighted. Surrounded by his kin, he humbly approached Bharata and spoke these words. 'This region is like a pleasure garden and we are your subjects. We are presenting ourselves before you. Reside in this family of your servants. These roots and fruit have been collected by the nishadas. There is fresh and dried meat and large amounts of inferior and superior forest fare. I hope your army will eat and spend the night here. After accepting these diverse objects of desire, you can leave tomorrow with your soldiers.'

Chapter 2(79)

Thus addressed by Guha, the lord of the nishadas, the immensely wise Bharata replied in words that were full of purport and meaning. 'O friend of my senior! An army like this is extremely large. Your desire to extend hospitality to them is indeed great.' Having spoken these excellent words to Guha, the immensely energetic and prosperous Bharata again addressed the lord of the nishadas in these words. 'O Guha! Which route should I follow to reach Bharadvaja's hermitage? This difficult region is impenetrable and the waters of the Ganga are difficult to cross.' Hearing the words of the intelligent prince, Guha, who was used to travelling in impenetrable regions, joined his hands in salutation and spoke these words. 'O immensely illustrious prince! These self-controlled servants, who are archers, will follow you. I will also follow you. I hope you are not going because you harbour ill intentions towards Rama, unblemished in deeds. This large army leads me to suspect that.' Bharata was as clear as the sky.[293] Thus addressed, he spoke to Guha in gentle words. 'Let there never be such a time. You should not have suspected me. Raghava is my elder brother and is like a

[293] His mind was as clear as the sky.

father to me. Kakutstha is residing in the forest and I am going to make him return. O Guha! You should not think otherwise. I tell you this truthfully.' Hearing the words spoken by Bharata, his face became joyful and delighted, he again addressed Bharata in these words. 'You are blessed. On the surface of the earth, I do not see anyone like you. Though you did not strive for it, you obtained this kingdom and you wish to cast it aside. Your deeds will indeed be recounted in this world for an eternity, since you wish to bring Rama back from the calamity he is in.' While Guha was addressing Bharata in this way, the sun lost its radiance and night arrived.

Tended to by Guha, the handsome one[294] made the army set up camp and with Shatrughna, lay down on a bed. As he thought about Rama, who did not deserve this kind of misery, the great-souled Bharata grieved. He only looked towards dharma. At the time of a forest conflagration, a fire can be hidden inside a hollow tree. Like that, an inner fire burnt and tormented Raghava.[295] Generated by this fire of grief, perspiration exuded from all over his body, just as the rays of the sun scorch snow on the Himalayas and make them flow. His thoughts were like mountainous caverns. His sighs were like dark minerals. His misery was like clumps of trees. His sorrow and exhaustion were like summits. His swooning was like that of beasts. His torment was like herbs and bamboo. Kaikeyee's son was assailed by great grief that was like a mountain. Thereafter, the noble Bharata composed himself and with his relative,[296] went and met Guha. Bharata was low in spirits, but Guha again assured Bharata about his elder brother.

Chapter 2(80)

Then Guha, who was familiar with impenetrable regions, told the immeasurable Bharata about the good conduct of the

[294] Bharata.

[295] Bharata.

[296] Shatrughna.

great-souled Lakshmana. 'I spoke to Lakshmana, the possessor of qualities. Extremely attentive to protecting his brother, he remained awake, wielding an excellent bow and arrows. "O father![297] This comfortable bed has been prepared for you. O descendant of the Raghava lineage! Lie down here, comfortably and happily. You are used to comfort and all of us are used to hardships. O one with dharma in your soul! It is appropriate for us to remain awake and protect him. There is no one on earth whom I love more than Rama. Do not be anxious. In your presence, I am telling you that this is not a falsehood. Through his favours, I desire to obtain great fame in this world. I wish to obtain great dharma, not only mere artha. Rama, my beloved friend, is lying down with Sita. With my kin, and with bows and arrows in our hands, we will protect him. There is no one who wanders around in this forest who is unknown to me. In a battle, we are capable of withstanding an army with the four kinds of forces." Thus did I speak to the great-souled Lakshmana. However, he only looked towards dharma and entreated all of us. "With Sita, Dasharatha's son is lying down on bare ground. How is it possible for me to get sleep, life or happiness? All the gods and asuras are incapable of withstanding him in a battle. O Guha! Behold. With Sita, he is lying down on a bed of grass. He alone, among Dasharatha's sons, possesses his[298] qualities and he was obtained after great austerities and many kinds of exertions. Having banished him, the king will not live for a long time. It is certain that the earth will soon become a widow. It is certain that the women in the royal palace will utter great shrieks now and exhausted thereafter, there will be silence there. I am not hopeful that Kousalya, the king and my mother will survive through this night. Perhaps my mother will look towards Shatrughna and remain alive. However, Kousalya, the mother of a brave son, will be destroyed. My father will not be able to accomplish his heart's desire of getting Rama consecrated in the kingdom and, countered and unsuccessful, will be destroyed. When the time of my father's

[297] The word used is tata. Guha would presumably address Lakshmana as a senior.

[298] Dasharatha's.

death presents itself tomorrow, all those who have been successful in their objective will perform the funeral rites for the king. The crossroads are beautiful, the wide roads are laid out well.[299] There are mansions and palaces, decorated with all the jewels. There are hordes of elephants, horses and chariots. There are the sounds of trumpets blaring. It is full of all the signs of welfare and populated by happy and healthy people. It is full of gardens for pleasure and there are assemblies and festivals. They roam around happily in the capital that was my father's. When he[300] has accomplished his pledge of truth and the period is over, together with him, will we, happy and well, enter that place?" Thus did the extremely great-souled prince lament, standing there. The night passed. When the sparkling sun rose in the morning, they matted their hair. On these banks of the Bhageerathee, I happily conveyed them across. Both of them sported matted hair and were attired in garments made out of the barks of trees. They were extremely strong, like two leaders of herds of elephants. Those two scorchers of enemies wielded supreme arrows, bows and swords. They glanced back at me and left with Sita.'

Chapter 2(81)

Hearing those extremely unpleasant words from Guha, Bharata started to think about the unpleasant words that he had heard. He was delicate and great in spirit. He was mighty-armed and possessed the shoulders of a lion. He was young and handsome, with large eyes like lotus petals. He sighed for a while and after some time, became extremely distressed. He suddenly fell down, like an elephant that has been struck in the heart with a goad. Shatrughna was standing nearby. On seeing the state the unconscious Bharata was in, he was afflicted by grief, and embracing him in his arms,

[299] This is a description of Ayodhya.

[300] Rama.

began to lament loudly. All Bharata's mothers were lean from fasting. They were distressed and miserable on account of their husband. They rushed towards him, when he fell down on the ground. They surrounded him and wept. Distressed in her mind, Kousalya bent down and embraced him. Distressed by grief, she was affectionate towards him, as if towards her own child. Weeping, she asked Bharata, 'O son! Are you suffering from any disease in your body? This royal lineage is now dependent on your remaining alive. O son! Now that Rama has left with his brother, my survival is contingent on seeing that you are alive. King Dasharatha has died and you alone are our protector now. O son! I hope you have not heard anything unpleasant about Lakshmana, or about my only son, who left for the forest with his wife.'

The immensely illustrious one[301] regained his composure in an instant. Though he still seemed to be weeping, he comforted Kousalya and addressed Guha in these words. 'Where did my brother, Sita and Lakshmana spend the night? O Guha! Where did they make their beds for lying down? What did they eat? Tell me.' Asked by Bharata, Guha, the lord of the nishadas engaged in ensuring the welfare of his guests, reported the arrangements he had made for Rama. 'There were superior and inferior kinds of food and many kinds of fruit. For Rama's consumption, I brought many such. Rama, for whom truth is his valour, refused all these. Remembering the dharma of kshatriyas, he did not accept any of these.[302] O king! The great-souled one entreated us in this way. "O friend! We must not accept. We must always give." With Sita, the immensely illustrious Raghava fasted and drank the water that had been brought by Lakshmana. Lakshmana drank the water that was left. After that, the three of them observed silence and controlling themselves, observed the sandhya rites. After this, for Raghava's sake, Soumitri quickly brought kusha grass himself and prepared an auspicious bed. With Sita, Rama lay down on that bed. Washing their feet with water, Lakshmana withdrew. On this grass at the

[301] Bharata.

[302] A kshatriya should kill or collect his own food, not accept it from others as a gift.

foot of this inguda tree,[303] Rama and Sita lay down and spent the night. Lakshmana, scorcher of enemies, wore armour made of lizard skin on his palms and fingers. He tied a quiver full of arrows on his back. He strung a giant bow. Throughout the night, he stood there, circling them. With an excellent bow and arrows, I also stood there with Lakshmana. So were my kin, without distraction and with bows in their hands. Like the great Indra, he[304] protected him.'

Chapter 2(82)

With his advisers, Bharata heard this entire accurate account. He arrived at the foot of the inguda tree and saw the spot where Rama had lain down. The great-souled one told all his mothers, 'This is where he lay down in the night, with his body pressing down on the ground. He was born in an immensely fortunate lineage from the intelligent and immensely fortunate Dasharatha. Rama does not deserve to sleep on the ground. The tiger among men used to lie down on a bed spread with the best collection of covers. How could he lie down on the bare ground, covered with hairy antelope skin? There was a palace, with tops like vimanas, with constant fortifications. The floor was decorated with gold and silver and there were the best of carpets. There were wonderful collections of flowers and fragrances of sandalwood and aloe. It[305] was like a white cloud in complexion, resounding with the sounds of a large number of parrots. There were the sounds of singing and musical instruments, the tinkling of the best of ornaments. He always woke to the sound of drums. At that right time, the scorcher of enemies awoke to the sounds of praise and ballads sung by many bards, minstrels and raconteurs. I no longer have faith in truth being manifested in this world. My mind is indeed confounded. It is my view that all this is nothing but a

[303] Inguda is a medicinal tree.

[304] Lakshmana.

[305] The palace.

dream. It is certain that there is no divinity who is greater than destiny, since a person like Rama, Dasharatha's son, had to lie down on the bare ground. The beautiful Sita is the daughter of the king of Videha and Dasharatha's beloved daughter-in-law. She too had to lie down on the ground. My brother made his bed on this hard ground and as he tossed around in his sleep, the grass bears the marks of being crushed by his limbs. Since, here and there, specks of gold can be seen, I think that Sita must have slept on this bed without taking her ornaments off. Since strands of silk have got attached to the grass, it is clearly evident that Sita's upper garment must have got entangled. I think that the young and ascetic lady must have been happy lying down with her husband. Though she is delicate, Maithilee cannot have experienced any sorrow. He was born in a lineage of emperors. He is the one who brings happiness to all the worlds. He is loved by all the worlds. He has cast aside his beloved and supreme kingdom. Raghava is handsome, with red eyes and the complexion of a blue lotus. He deserves happiness, not unhappiness. How could he lie down on the ground? Since she has followed her husband to the forest, Vaidehi has indeed been successful in her objective. Without that great-souled one, there is no doubt that all of us have suffered. The earth seems empty to me, without anyone to steer it. Dasharatha has gone to heaven and Rama has resorted to the forest. Even though he resides in the forest, this earth is protected by the strength of his arms and no one can covet it. The capital is unprotected. The ramparts are empty of guards and there is no one to control the horses and elephants. The gates of the city have been thrown open. It is evident that the soldiers are distressed. Everything is exposed, as if during a catastrophe. However, regarding it as poisoned food, even the enemies do not wish to taste it. From today, I will lie down on the ground, or on grass. I will subsist on fruits and roots. I will always don matted hair and bark. For his sake, I will happily reside for the rest of the time in the forest.[306] Thus, the pledge will

[306] Instead of Rama, Bharata will dwell in the forest.

not be rendered false, though he will be freed from it. Instead of his brother,[307] Shatrughna will dwell in the forest with me. With Lakshmana, let the noble one rule over Ayodhya. The brahmanas will crown Kakutstha in Ayodhya. May the gods make this wish of mine come true. Bowing down my head, I will seek his favours and entreat him in many ways. He should not disregard me. However, if he does not accept it, for a long time, I will live in the forest with Raghava.'

Chapter 2(83)

Having reached the banks of the Ganga, Raghava Bharata spent the night there. Waking at the right time, he told Shatrughna, 'O Shatrughna! Awake. Why are you still asleep? Quickly bring the fortunate Guha, lord of the nishadas, here, so that the army can cross.' Urged by his brother, Shatrughna replied in these words. 'I am awake. I am not asleep. I have been thinking about the noble one.'[308] While those two lions among men were conversing with each other, Guha arrived. Joining his hands in salutation, he spoke to Bharata. 'O Kakutstha! Did you happily spend the night on the banks of the river? Are you well, with all your soldiers?' Hearing Guha's words, which were uttered with affection, Bharata, devoted to Rama, addressed him in these words. 'O king! Honoured by you, we have happily spent the night. Let servants with many boats ferry us across the river.'

Hearing Bharata's instructions, Guha hurried. He entered the city and spoke to his relatives. 'Arise. Awake. May you always be fortunate. Fetch boats, so that the army can be ferried across.' Thus addressed and obeying the commands of their king, they quickly arose. From every direction, they collected five hundred boats. Some were marked with the *svastika* sign. Some were excellent, with large

[307] Lakshmana.

[308] Rama.

bells. They were adorned with flags and sails were unfurled. To the sounds of praises, Guha brought an excellent boat that was marked with the svastika sign and was spread with a white blanket. Bharata, the immensely strong Shatrughna, Kousalya, Sumitra and the other royal women climbed on to this. However, even before this, the priests, the preceptors and the brahmanas climbed on. The royal women followed and so did the carts with provisions. The sky was filled with the sounds of camps being burnt,[309] people descending to the boats and of vessels being carried. The boats with flags were steered by the servants. Bearing the people who had ascended, they travelled swiftly. Some were filled with women. Others carried horses. Some carried wagons filled with great wealth, yoked to mounts. When they reached the other bank, the people descended. The servants and kin brought those boats back, as if they were colourful toy boats.[310] The elephants bore flags with signs of victory and were urged by drivers of elephants. As they swam across with their flags, they looked like mountains. While some climbed on to boats, others crossed over to the other bank on rafts. Some swam across with the use of pots and pitchers, others used their arms. The fishermen helped the sacred army cross the Ganga. At the time of *maitra* muhurta, they reached the excellent forest of Prayaga.[311] The great-souled Bharata comforted the army and as each one willed, made them set up camp. Surrounded by the officiating priests, he left to meet rishi Bharadvaja.

Chapter 2(84)

From a distance that was one krosha away, the bull among men saw Bharadvaja's hermitage. Asking the entire army to remain

[309] Camps of soldiers were burnt so that there were no signs for the enemy to follow.

[310] Empty of loads, they moved as quickly as toy boats.

[311] A muhurta is a measure of time, equal to forty-eight minutes. Some muhurtas are good, others bad, maitra being a good one. The precise timing of maitra muhurta varies from day to day, but is roughly one-and-a-half hours after sunrise.

there, he proceeded with his ministers. He knew about dharma. Therefore, he cast aside his weapons and garments and proceeded on foot. He attired himself in silken garments and placed the priest[312] ahead of him. When he could see Bharadvaja, Raghava asked the ministers to remain and went alone, following the priest. On seeing Vasishtha, Bharadvaja, the great ascetic, quickly got up from his set and asked his disciples to offer arghya. Having met Vasishtha, he recognized Bharata to be Dasharatha's immensely energetic son and greeted him. The one who knew about dharma offered him arghya and padya. He then gave him fruits and one by one, asked him about the welfare of everyone in the family. He asked about the army, treasury, friends and ministers of Ayodhya. However, knowing that Dasharatha was dead, he did not ask about the king. Vasishtha and Bharata also asked about his physical welfare, the sacrificial fires, trees, disciples, animals and birds.

Bharadvaja, the great ascetic, said that everything was well. Because he was tied to Raghava[313] with bonds of affection, he then addressed Bharata in the following words. 'You are the ruler of the kingdom. Why have you come here? Tell me everything about this. Otherwise, my mind harbours a doubt. He is the slayer of enemies and being born from Kousalya, is the extender of her joy. With his brother and his wife, he has been exiled to the forest for a long period of time. He is immensely illustrious in this world. However, because he was commanded by a woman, his father instructed him to reside in the forest for fourteen years. He committed no crime. Do you wish to cause harm to him, so that you can enjoy the kingdom, bereft of thorns, with your younger brother?' Thus addressed by Bharadvaja, tears of sorrow began to flow from Bharata's eyes. He replied in an indistinct voice, 'If an illustrious one like you thinks in this fashion, I am devastated. I cannot even think of such wickedness. Do not accuse me in this way. I do not approve of what my mother did while I was away. I am not happy with her, nor do I accept her instructions. I have come to seek the

[312] Vasishtha.
[313] Rama.

favours of that tiger among men, worship his feet and take him back to Ayodhya. Knowing my intentions, you should show me your favours. O illustrious one! Tell me where Rama, the lord of the earth, is now.' Satisfied, Bharadvaja addressed Bharata in these words. 'O tiger among men! You have been born in the Raghava lineage. It is appropriate that you should possess good conduct towards your seniors, self-control and an inclination to follow virtuous people. I knew what was in your mind, but I wanted to be absolutely certain. I asked you so that your fame might increase even more. I know where Rama, knowledgeable about dharma, dwells, with Sita and with Lakshmana. Your brother is on the great mountain of Chitrakuta. With your ministers, reside here today. You can go to that region tomorrow. O one who is extremely wise! O one who knows about kama and artha. Act in accordance with what I want.' With his intentions clear, Bharata, generous in his outlook, agreed to this. The son of a king made up his mind to reside in that great hermitage during the night.

Chapter 2(85)

When Bharata, Kaikeyee's son, made up his mind to reside there, the sage made all the arrangements to offer hospitality to the guest. Bharata said, 'You have already offered me padya and arghya and provided the guest with whatever forest fare is available.' Bharadvaja smiled and replied to Bharata, 'I know that you are kindly disposed and are content with whatever little is available. O bull among men! But I wish to feed your soldiers. Affectionate towards me, you should allow me to do this. Why did you leave your army at a distance and then come here? O bull among men! Why did you not come here with your army?' Bharata joined his hands in salutation and replied to the store of austerities. 'O illustrious one! I did not come with my soldiers because I was scared of you. O illustrious one! The best of horses, men and excellent and crazy elephants are following me, covering an extensive area. They might cause damage to the trees, water, ground and cottages in the hermitage. That is the reason I came alone.' When the supreme rishi commanded that the army should be brought there, Bharata instructed that the soldiers should be brought.

He[314] entered the place where the sacrificial fire was kept. He drank water and touched it. After this, he invited Vishvakarma[315] to arrange for hospitality towards the guests. 'I invite Vishvakarma. I invite Tvashtra too. I wish to extend hospitality. Let arrangements be made for this purpose. Let all the rivers that flow towards the east, those that flow towards the west, those that flow on earth and those that flow in the firmament come here now, from every direction. Let some have flows of maireya, let others have flows of other kinds of sura.[316] Let others flow with cool water that is like sugar cane juice. From every direction, I invoke the gods, the gandharvas, Vishvavasu, Haha, Huhu,[317] the apsaras, goddesses and female gandharvas. I invoke Ghritachee, Vishvachee, Mishrakeshee and Alambusa, those who tend to Shakra and those beautiful ones who tend to Brahma. Let all of them arrive with Tumburu and all the equipment.[318] Kubera has a divine and eternal garden in a forest in the Kuru region.[319] Let it manifest itself here, with the leaves taking the form of garments and ornaments and the fruits taking the form of celestial women. Let the illustrious Soma arrange for excellent food and many and diverse kinds of bhakshya, bhojya, choshya and lehya. Let the trees give rise to wonderful garlands. Let there be sura and other things to drink. Let there be many kinds of

[314] Bharadvaja.

[315] The architect of the gods. Tvashtra/Tvashtri is sometimes equated with Vishvakarma and is the carpenter of the gods. Tvashtra is also one of the sun's manifestations.

[316] Maireya is made from molasses or grain, while sura is a general term for liquor.

[317] Vishvavasu is the king of the gandharvas, Haha and Huhu are the names of specific gandharvas. Gandharvas are semi-divine species and celestial musicians, often described as Kubera's companions. Apsaras are also semi-divine and celestial dancers. Ghritachee, Vishvachee, Mishrakeshee and Alambusa are the names of specific apsaras.

[318] Tumburu is the name of a gandharva, sometimes described as a teacher of singing and dancing. But since equipment is mentioned, one should mention *tambura/tanpura,* the stringed musical instrument, though neither tambura nor tanpura is a Sanskrit word.

[319] This means northern Kuru.

meat.' The sage, with infinite energy acquired through meditation and austerities, pronounced these invocations in a trained voice. As he joined his hands in salutation, faced the east and meditated in his mind, one by one, all those divinities arrived. A pleasant and auspicious breeze that delighted the soul and removed the sweat began to blow from the Malaya and Dardura mountains. From the firmament, clouds started to shower down flowers. In every direction, the sounds of the drums of the gods could be heard. As that excellent breeze blew, large numbers of apsaras started to dance. The tones of the veenas of the gods and the gandharvas could be heard. The gentle, harmonious and rhythmic sound penetrated the earth, the firmament and the ears of living beings. Those divine sounds brought happiness to the eyes of men and Bharata's soldiers saw what Vishvakarma had arranged. There was a flat region that was five yojanas in every direction. It was covered by many layers of grass and assumed the complexion of blue lapis lazuli. There were trees there—bilva, *kapittha*, *panasa*, *beejapuraka*, *amalaka* and *chuta* laden with fruit.[320] The divine forest arrived from the northern Kuru region. A divine river, with many trees along its banks, also arrived. There were square and dazzling residences, with stables and lodgings for elephants. There were mansions and palaces with radiant turrets. With excellent gates, the royal residence was like a white cloud. This was festooned with white garlands and divine fragrances wafted through it. There was a square and extensive courtyard, with couches, seats and vehicles. It was filled with all kinds of divine drinks and divine food and garments. Every kind of food was prepared and placed in clean and sparkling vessels. All the seats were properly arranged and excellent beds were spread with handsome covers.

With the maharshi's permission, mighty-armed Bharata, Kaikeyee's son, entered the residence that was filled with jewels. All the ministers and priests followed him. On seeing that excellent residence, they were filled with joy. There was a divine

[320] Bilva is wood apple and a tree sacred to Shiva, kapittha is also a variety of wood apple, panasa is jackfruit, beejapuraka is a citrus tree, amalaka is myrobalan and chuta is mango.

royal throne there, with a whisk and an umbrella. Like a king, Bharata circumambulated it with his ministers. However, he only worshipped and honoured the seat as if Rama was seated there.[321] With the whisk made of hair in his hand, he sat down on a seat meant for an adviser. In due order, all the ministers and priests seated themselves. After this, the commander and the platoon leaders seated themselves. In a short while, on Bharadvaja's instructions, a river began to flow towards Bharata, with payasam as its mud. Through Brahma's favours, divine and beautiful residences appeared on both banks of this, plastered with white clay. In an instant, on Brahma's instructions, twenty thousand women arrived, adorned in celestial ornaments. On Kubera's instructions, another twenty thousand women arrived, beautifully adorned in gold, jewels, pearls and coral. Twenty thousand apsaras arrived from Nandana.[322] If a man was embraced by any of these, he would be seen to turn mad. Narada, Tumburu, Gopa, Prarvata and Suryavarchasa—these kings of gandharvas started to sing in front of Bharata. On Bharadvaja's command, Alambusa, Mishrakeshee, Pundareeka and Vamana started to dance before Bharata. On Bharadvaja's command, divine garlands from the grove of Chaitraratha were seen at Prayaga. Through the energetic Bharadvaja's command, bilva trees assumed the form of drummers, *bibheetaka* trees[323] assumed the form of those who played on cymbals and *ashvattha* trees assumed the form of dancers. Sarala, *tala*, *tilaka* and *naktamalaka* trees were delighted and arrived there in the form of kubjas and vamanas.[324] On Bharadvaja's command, *shimshapa*, amalaka, jambu and other creepers from groves assumed the form of women[325] and said, 'O those who drink! Drink this liquor. O those who are hungry! Eat the payasam. The meat is fresh. Eat as you will.' Seven or eight women

[321] He did not occupy the royal throne.

[322] Indra's pleasure garden.

[323] A type of myrobalan.

[324] Sarala is a species of pine, tala is a palm tree, tilaka is a tree with beautiful flowers and naktamalaka is a tree that flowers in the night. Kubja means hunchbacked and vamana means dwarf. However, these two words are probably being respectively used in the sense of female and male servants.

[325] Shimshapa is the ashoka tree and jambu is the rose apple tree.

massaged each man with oil and bathed him on the beautiful banks of the river. The women with beautiful eyes cleansed them and one after another, wiped them. Those beautiful women made them drink. Horses, elephants, mules, camels, Surabhee's offspring[326] and other mounts were fed sugar cane and roasted grain mixed with honey, urged on by the extremely strong warriors of the Ikshvaku lineage. A horse keeper no longer recognized his horse. An elephant keeper no longer recognized his elephant. The entire army was crazy, intoxicated and delighted. All the objects of desire were satisfied. The bodies were smeared with red sandalwood paste. Surrounded by large numbers of apsaras, the soldiers said, 'We will certainly not go to Ayodhya. We will not go to Dandaka. Let Bharata be well. Let Rama also be happy.' Having been tended to in this way, the foot soldiers and the riders and keepers of elephants and horses no longer recognized their leaders and told them that. Happy, the thousands of men who had followed Bharata said, 'This is heaven.' They had eaten the food that was like amrita. However, when they looked at this divine food, they felt like eating again. In every direction, servants, slaves, young women and soldiers were all greatly content, attired in new garments. Elephants, donkeys, camels, bullocks, horses, animals and birds were fed exceedingly well and one's share did not eat into another one's share. There was no one there who was in soiled garments, hungry or jaded. No man could be seen with his hair covered in dust. There was the meat of goats and wild boar, in delicious sauces. There was fragrant and tasty soup, cooked well in the juice of fruits. In every direction, there were heaps of white rice, decorated with flowers that were like flags. Amazed, the men saw thousands of vessels made out of rare metals. There were wells along the flanks of the forest and their mud was turned into payasam. The trees exuded honey and turned into cows that yielded all the objects of desire. The ponds were filled with maireya, while some were filled with venison and the meat of wild cocks and peacocks, cooked in hot vessels. There were thousands of vessels made out of molten gold and well-cleaned

[326] Bulls, Surabhee is the mother of cattle.

plates, pots and shallow dishes filled with curds, shining, fragrant and with the complexion of kapittha fruit. There were lakes filled with curds mixed with spices, others being filled with white curds. Still others were filled with payasam and heaps of sugar. As they went down to the river, the men saw ointments, powders, unguents and other objects used for bathing. There were twigs for cleaning the teeth, as white as the moon. White sandalwood paste was kept in caskets. There were polished mirrors and piles of clothing. There were thousands of pairs of footwear and sandals. There were collyrium, combs, brushes, umbrellas and bows. There were colourful beds and couches to comfort the inner organs. The ponds for drinking were full of donkeys, camels, elephants and horses. There were lakes that these could descend and bathe in, filled with lotuses and lilies. For feeding the animals, stores of gentle grass were seen in every direction, blue in complexion, like lapis lazuli. The men were astounded to see the hospitality the maharshi had arranged for Bharata. It was extraordinary and like a dream. They sported themselves there, like the gods in Nandana.

As they found pleasure in Bharadvaja's hermitage, the night passed. Having taken Bharadvaja's permission, the rivers, the gandharvas and all the beautiful women went away to wherever they had come from. The men were crazy and intoxicated with liquor, smeared with divine sandalwood paste and aloe. Many kinds of excellent and celestial garlands were strewn around, crushed by the men.

Chapter 2(86)

Bharata was extended hospitality by Bharadvaja. Having spent the night there, with his retinue, he desired to leave. The rishi saw that the tiger among men had arrived, hands joined in salutation. Having offered oblations into the agnihotra fire, Bharadvaja addressed Bharata. 'O unblemished one! Have you spent the night happily, having arrived in our region? Have your people received hospitality? Tell me.' The rishi, excellent in his energy, had emerged from his hermitage. Thus addressed, Bharata joined his hands in salutation and bowed down before him. 'O illustrious one! I, and all the soldiers and mounts, have spent the time happily. Thanks to you, the advisers and the soldiers have been satisfied with every object of desire. We have eaten well. We obtained an excellent abode. All our exhaustion and hardship has been dispelled. Having obtained everything, all our servants have also spent the time happily. O illustrious one! O supreme rishi! I seek your permission to leave and approach my brother now. Please cast a friendly eye towards me. O one who knows about dharma! Where is the hermitage of the great-souled one who is devoted to dharma? Tell me which path I should follow and how far it is from this spot.' Bharata, desirous of seeing his brother, asked this and the immensely energetic Bharadvaja, great in austerities, replied. 'O Bharata! Three-and-a-half yojanas from here, there is a desolate forest.[327] Mount Chitrakuta is there, with beautiful caverns and groves. If you approach the northern flank, there is the river Mandakinee, shrouded by blossoming trees and beautiful and flowering groves. Mount Chitrakuta is beyond that river. O son![328] It is certain that they are dwelling there, in a cottage made of leaves and twigs. O lord of the army! Make the army full of elephants, horses and chariots follow the southern path, or go left and then south. O immensely fortunate one! You will then be able to directly see Raghava.'

The women of the king of kings[329] deserved to be in carriages. However, hearing about the path, they got down from their carriages and surrounded the brahmana. Kousalya was wan, distressed and trembling. With Queen Sumitra, she seized the sage's feet with her hands. Kaikeyee's objectives had not been accomplished and she had been censured by all the worlds. Ashamed, she too seized his feet. She then circumambulated the illustrious and great sage and distressed in her mind, stood near Bharata. Bharadvaja, firm in

[327] This makes it twenty-eight to thirty-two miles.
[328] The word used is tata.
[329] Dasharatha.

his vows, told Bharata, 'O Raghava! I wish to know the special characteristics of your mothers.' Thus addressed by Bharadvaja, Bharata, who was devoted to dharma and accomplished in the use of words, joined his hands in salutation and replied, 'O illustrious one! This one is distressed and miserable, afflicted through fasting. She is my father's chief queen. You can see that she is like a goddess. Rama is a tiger among men, with a valorous stride like that of a lion. Kousalya gave birth to him, just as Aditi did to Dhata.[330] There is the one who is distressed in her mind and clings to her[331] left arm. She is like the branch of a *karnikara* tree,[332] with dried flowers, standing at the end of a forest. This queen's sons are the two brave princes Lakshmana and Shatrughna, for whom truth is their valour and whose complexion is like that of the gods.[333] This is the one because of whom the lives of the two tigers among men have been destroyed and, deprived of his sons, King Dasharatha has gone to heaven. This is Kaikeyee, who desired prosperity and is ignoble, though noble in appearance. Know her to be my cruel mother, wicked in her determination. I discern that she is the root cause behind my great hardship.'

The tiger among men said this, in a voice choking with tears. With his eyes coppery red, he sighed like an irate serpent. The immensely intelligent maharshi Bharadvaja replied to Bharata in words that were full of meaning. 'O Bharata! Understand that you should not ascribe any wickedness to Kaikeyee. Rama's exile will lead to the generation of happiness.'[334] Content, Bharata honoured him and circumambulated him. He instructed that the soldiers should be yoked. Divine chariots decorated with gold were yoked to steeds. Desiring to leave, many kinds of people ascended these.

[330] The words Dhata (Dhatri) and Vidhata (Vidhatri) are used synonymously, but have slightly different nuances. Vidhata is more like creator, while Dhata is more like presever. Hence, Dhata can be interpreted as Vishnu.

[331] Kousalya's.

[332] The Indian laburnum.

[333] Referring to Sumitra.

[334] The Critical Edition excises a shloka that expands on this, mentioning the purification of gods, danavas and rishis. With or without that shloka, Bharadvaja's statement can only mean the rishi had some inkling about the future course of events.

There were female and male elephants with golden harnesses and flags. They left, trumpeting like clouds at the end of the summer. Many other vehicles, large, small and expensive, departed. The foot soldiers walked on foot. Desiring to see Rama, the women, with Kousalya at the forefront, happily left on their excellent vehicles. The handsome Bharata and his companions left on an auspicious palanquin that had been kept ready and was as radiant as the young moon. Full of elephants, horses and chariots, that great army left in this way, enveloping the southern direction like a gigantic cloud that had arisen. They passed through the forest that was full of animals and birds. The elephants, horses and warriors were delighted, but they terrified the large number of animals and birds. As it penetrated that great forest, Bharata's army was resplendent.

Chapter 2(87)

As that large army with its flags marched, the residents of the forest, the maddened leaders of the herds[335] were frightened and fled, with their herds. In every direction, along forest paths, mountains and rivers, large numbers of bear, spotted dear and *ruru* antelopes could be seen. Dasharatha's son, with dharma in his soul, happily marched. He was surrounded by a roaring army with the four kinds of forces. The great-souled Bharata's army was like the waves of the ocean and covered the earth, like clouds cover the sky before showers. Because of the waves of speedy horses and extremely swift elephants, for a long period of time, the earth could not be seen. Having travelled a great distance, the mounts were extremely exhausted.

The handsome Bharata spoke to Vasishtha, supreme among ministers. 'Matching the appearance of this place with what I had heard, it is evident that we have reached the region Bharadvaja spoke

[335] Of animals.

about. This is Mount Chitrakuta and that river is Mandakinee. From a distance, the forest has the complexion of a blue cloud. This beautiful spot at the foot of Mount Chitrakuta is now being trampled by my elephants, which are themselves like elephants. These trees on the summit of the mountain are showering down flowers, just as at the end of the summer, dark and dense clouds shower down water on the earth. O Shatrughna! Behold the spot on the mountain, frequented by kinnaras. In every direction, it is now covered by horses, like makaras in the ocean. These herds of deer are swift in food. They are being driven away, like a mass of clouds driven away by the wind in the autumn sky. These trees are crested with fragrant flowers and have clumps of fruit that have the complexion of clouds, like men from the south.[336] This forest, terrible in form, used to be silent. Filled with people, it now seems like Ayodhya to me. The dust raised by the hooves covers the sky, but is swiftly carried away by the wind, thus causing me pleasure. O Shatrughna! Behold. The chariots are yoked to horses and controlled by the best among charioteers. They are swiftly entering the forest. Look at these beautiful peacocks and birds. Terrified, they are entering their nests in the mountain. To me, this region appears to be extremely pleasant. It is evident that this is the residence of ascetics and the path to heaven. In the forest, there are many male spotted deer, with female deer. Their beautiful forms can be seen, as if they are decorated with flowers. Let the virtuous soldiers explore the forest to see where the two tigers among men, Rama and Lakshmana, can be seen.'

Hearing Bharata's words, the brave men, with weapons in their hands, entered the forest and saw some smoke. On seeing the smoke in front of them, they came and told Bharata, 'There cannot be a fire without men. It is evident that the two Raghavas are there. If the two princes, tigers among men and scorchers of enemies, are not there, it is evident that other ascetics who are like Rama must be there.' Hearing their words, which were in conformity with what the virtuous would say, Bharata, the destroyer of the forces of the enemy, spoke to all the soldiers. 'Remain here. You

[336] Implying darkness in complexion.

should not proceed further ahead. I will go alone, with Sumantra and the preceptor.'[337] Thus addressed, in every direction, they spread themselves out there. Bharata looked towards the smoke and proceeded ahead. Bharata's army could see the smoke in front, but remained there. Knowing that they would soon meet their beloved Rama, they were delighted.

Chapter 2(88)

Dasharatha's son, who loved mountains and forests and was like an immortal, had lived near that mountain for a long period of time. He wished to please his own mind and bring pleasure to Vaidehi. He showed his wife the beauty of Chitrakuta, like Purandara to Shachi. 'O fortunate one! On seeing this beautiful forest, my mind is no longer distressed at being dislodged from the kingdom or from the absence of the well-wishers. O fortunate one! Behold this mountain, populated by many kinds of birds. Decorated with minerals, the summits rise up into the sky. Some places are like silver, others have the complexion of wounds.[338] Some places are yellow in hue, others possess the complexion of excellent jewels. Some have the complexion of topaz, crystal and *ketaka*.[339] Others possess the radiance of *jyotirasa*.[340] Decorated by minerals, this spot in this Indra among mountains is dazzling. The place is surrounded by large numbers of many kinds of deer, elephants, hyenas and bears. This spot in the mountain is radiant with many kinds of birds that aren't injurious. There are mangoes, jamuns, *lodhras*,[341] *priyalas*,[342] jackfruit, dhavas,[343] *ankola* trees,

[337] Vasishtha.
[338] They are red.
[339] Flowering plant.
[340] A kind of gem.
[341] The lotus bark tree.
[342] The chironji tree, also known as *piyala*.
[343] The axle-wood tree.

bhavyas,[344] *tinishas*,[345] bilvas, tindukas, bamboos, *kashmiras*,[346] *arishtas*,[347] *varanas*,[348] *madhukas*,[349] tilakas,[350] badaris, amalakas, *neepas*,[351] cane, *dhanvana* trees and pomegranates. They are laden with flowers. They are laden with fruit. They provide shade and the spot is beautiful. This place on the mountain is covered with such beautiful flowers. O fortunate one! Behold these spirited kinnara couples, roaming around on the slopes of the mountain, delighted and in the throes of desire. They have slung their swords and their excellent garments from the branches. Behold the beautiful spots where the vidyadharas are sporting with their women. Here and there on the mountain, shining waterfalls are emerging, like musth exuding from crazy elephants. A breeze bearing the fragrances of many flowers wafts through the caverns, pleasing to the nose. Which man will not be delighted? O unblemished one! If I have to reside here, with you and Lakshmana, for many autumns, I will not suffer from any sorrow. It is beautiful with many kinds of flower and fruit. Large numbers of birds populate it. O beautiful one! I am indeed enraptured by this wonderful summit. I have obtained two kinds of fruit through residing in this forest—I have followed dharma in repaying my father's debt and I have brought Bharata pleasure. O Vaidehi! Are you happy that you are in Chitrakuta with me? Look at these many kinds of things that bring pleasure to the mind, words and the body. The kings and rajarshis, my great grandfathers, have said that for objectives after death, one must reside in the forest, since it is like amrita. In every direction, hundreds of large boulders of this mountain are shining. There are many with many colours—blue, yellow, white and red. In the night, on this Indra among mountains, the radiance of thousands of herbs can be seen, shining with their own resplendence, like the tips of flames from a

[344] The starfruit tree.
[345] The Indian rosewood.
[346] The Indian rubber plant.
[347] Medicinal plant.
[348] The sacred garlic pear tree.
[349] The honey tree.
[350] The bleeding heart plant.
[351] The *kadamba* tree.

fire. Some parts have the complexion of mansions. Others possess the complexion of groves. O beautiful one! In other parts of this mountain, a single boulder shines. Chitrakuta seems to have arisen after shattering the earth. In every direction, Chitrakuta's summit is seen to be auspicious. Behold. Coloured and fragrant white lotuses and leaves of birch provide excellent covers, while mats of kusha grass act as beds for those who wish to indulge in desire. O lady! Behold. Garlands of lotuses can be seen, crushed and cast aside by those who have indulged in desire. There are many kinds of fruits too. With many kinds of roots, fruit and water, Mount Chitrakuta is superior to Vasvoukasara, Nalini and Uttara Kuru.[352] O lady! O Sita! With you and Lakshmana, I will roam around here for some time. I will obtain delight from extending the dharma of the lineage. I will engage in supreme rituals and follow the path of the virtuous.'

Chapter 2(89)

Maithilee and the lord of Kosala emerged from the mountain and saw the auspicious and beautiful waters of the river Mandakinee. The lotus-eyed Rama spoke to the daughter of the king of Videha, who possessed a face that was as beautiful as the moon and lovely thighs. 'Behold the wonderful and beautiful banks of the river Mandakinee, frequented by swans and cranes and with flowers leaning down over it. There are many kinds of trees, with flowers and fruit, which grow along the banks. In every direction, it is resplendent, like Rajaraja's Nalini.[353] Herds of deer are drinking now and dirtying the water. The beautiful descents into the water are creating great pleasure in me. O beloved one! At the right time, rishis who wear matted hair and have upper garments made up of bark and antelope skin immerse themselves in the river Mandakinee. O large-eyed one! There are other sages, rigid in their vows. They follow the

[352] Vasvoukasara is another name for Alaka, Kubera's capital. Nalini is the name of Kubera's lake. The Uttara Kuru region is beautiful.

[353] Rajaraja is one of Kubera's names.

rituals, raise up their arms and worship the sun god. On both sides of the river, the crests of trees are stirred by the wind and make leaves and flowers shower down, creating the impression that the mountain is dancing. In some places, the water sparkles like a jewel. In others, there are sand banks. Behold the river Mandakinee. In some places, it is full of siddhas. Behold the heaps of flowers that are shaken down by the wind. Behold the others that are floating away in the water. There are birds, the red ducks,[354] with extremely melodious voices. O fortunate one! They are ascending,[355] uttering auspicious tones. O beautiful one! I think that this sight of Chitrakuta and Mandakinee and the sight of you are better than residing in a city. The siddhas have cleansed themselves of sin and possess austerities, self-control and restraint. They always stir the waters. You should also have a bath with me. O Sita! Immerse yourself in this Mandakinee, it is like a friend to you. O beautiful one! Immerse yourself amidst the red and white lotuses. O lady! Think of the predatory beasts as citizens, this mountain as Ayodhya and this river as Sarayu. Lakshmana has dharma in his soul and his mind is devoted to commands. O Vaidehi! You are also kindly disposed towards me and this causes me delight. I bathe thrice a day. I subsist on honey, roots and fruit. With you, I don't desire Ayodhya or the kingdom now. These beautiful waters are agitated by herds of elephants. Elephants, lions and apes drink it. Blossoming flowers adorn the ground. Who is there who will not overcome his exhaustion and be happy here?' Rama spoke many other appropriate words about the river. Chitrakuta possessed the complexion of collyrium used on the eyes. With his beloved, the extender of the Raghu lineage roamed around in that beautiful spot.

Chapter 2(90)

While they were there, Bharata's soldiers approached. The noise and dust created by them rose up and touched the sky.

[354] The ruddy shelduck.

[355] The banks.

At that moment, terrified by the great noise that was created, the crazy leaders of herds were afflicted and, with their herds, fled in different directions. Raghava heard the clamour that was created by the soldiers. He saw that all the herds were running away. Having seen them run away and having heard the noise, Rama spoke to Soumitri Lakshmana, who blazed in his energy. 'O Lakshmana! Alas! Sumitra has given birth to a good son like you. A tumultuous sound can be heard, like the terrible and deep thunder of a cloud. Is a king or a prince roaming around in the forest in search of a hunt, or is it some predatory beast? O Soumitri! You should find out. You should quickly find out everything about this.'

Lakshmana swiftly ascended a flowering sala tree. He glanced towards all the directions and looked at the eastern direction. He saw a giant army in the northern direction. It had a large number of chariots, horses and elephants and well-trained infantry. There were many horses and elephants. The chariots were adorned with flags. He told Rama about the army and spoke these words. 'O noble one! Extinguish the fire and let Sita find refuge in a cave. Ready your bow, arrows and armour.' At this, Rama, tiger among men, replied to Lakshmana. 'O Soumitri! Look at the signs. Whose army do you think this is?' Lakshmana was like an enraged fire, wishing to burn down the soldiers. Thus addressed, he replied to Rama in these words. 'It is evident that having accomplished the objective of obtaining the kingdom and having been crowned, Bharata, Kaikeyee's son, is coming here to kill us. An extremely large and dazzling tree can be seen. On a chariot, a standard with a kovidara, raising up its shining trunk, can be seen.[356] As they will, horse riders are prancing around astride their horses. There are resplendent and delighted riders astride the elephants. O brave one! Let us seize our bows and ascend the mountain. Or let us remain here, armoured and with weapons upraised. In a battle, perhaps the kovidara standard will come under our control. O Raghava! Perhaps we will see Bharata, because of whom we—you, Sita and I—have faced this great hardship. O Raghava! You have been dislodged from the eternal kingdom because of him. O brave one! That enemy Bharata is approaching. He should be slain

[356] Bharata's standard.

by me. O Raghava! I do not see any sin attached to slaying Bharata. If one abandons a person who has caused an injury earlier, no adharma has been said to be attached to that. When he has been killed, you will rule over the entire earth. Kaikeyee desires the kingdom. In the encounter today, she will see her son slain by me, like a tree by an elephant, and will be extremely miserable. I will also slay Kaikeyee, with all her followers and relatives. Today, I will free the earth from this great taint. O one who grants honours! Because of the slight, my rage has been ignited and I will destroy the soldiers of the enemy, like a fire amidst dry wood. Today, I will mangle the bodies of the enemy with sharp arrows and make the forest of Chitrakuta overflow with the consequent blood. The hearts of elephants and horses will be shattered with arrows. Predatory beasts will drag them away and the bodies of the men who are killed by me. In this great forest, I will repay my debt to my bow and arrows. There is no doubt that I will slay Bharata, with his soldiers.'

Chapter 2(91)

Soumitri Lakshmana was enraged and senseless with anger. Rama pacified him and spoke these words. 'In this case, where is the need for a bow, sword or shield? The great archer and immensely wise Bharata is coming himself. Bharata wishes to see us and this is the right time for him to come here. Even in his thoughts, he has never acted injuriously towards us. Earlier, has Bharata ever acted disagreeably towards you? Why are you scared in this way and why are you suspecting Bharata today? Indeed, Bharata should not hear these cruel and disagreeable words from you. If you speak disagreeably about Bharata, it is as if you have spoken disagreeably about me. O Soumitri! Even if there is a hardship, how can sons slay their father? How can a brother slay a brother whom one loves like his own life? If you have spoken these words for the sake of the kingdom, when I see Bharata, I will ask him to give the kingdom to you. O Lakshmana! In truth, if I tell Bharata to give you the kingdom, he will reply in words of assent.' He was thus addressed by his brother, who was engaged in his welfare and followed dharma and good conduct. In shame, Lakshmana seemed to shrink into his own body. On seeing that Lakshmana was ashamed, Raghava said, 'I think that the mighty-armed one[357] has come here to see us. This Vaidehi has been used to great happiness. Perhaps he has thought of taking her home from residence in the forest. O brave one! Two excellent horses, beautiful and born of noble lineages, can be seen. They are swift and like the wind in their speed. Ahead of the army, an extremely large elephant is walking. His name is Shatrunjaya and he belongs to our intelligent and aged father.' Lakshmana, who was victorious in assemblies, got down from the top of the sala tree. He joined his hands in salutation and stood by Rama's side.

Bharata had instructed that the soldiers should not cause any destruction. Therefore, they set up their camps all around the mountain. The army of the Ikshvakus, full of elephants, horses and chariots, covered the area around the mountain, to the extent of one-and-a-half yojanas. Bharata placed dharma at the forefront and gave up any sense of pride. His army was properly instructed to remain in Chitrakuta in this way. The one who knew about good policy found pleasure in seeking the favours of the descendant of the Raghu lineage.

Chapter 2(92)

The lord[358] made arrangements for the army to be camped. Supreme among those who walked on foot, he then sought to approach Kakutstha, who was following his senior,[359] on foot. Once the soldiers had been camped, as they had been instructed, Bharata humbly addressed his brother, Shatrughna, in these words. 'O amiable one! With groups of men and trackers to aid them, you should quickly search the forest on all sides of this forest. I will not

[357] Meaning Dasharatha.

[358] Bharata.

[359] Rama was following the instructions of Dasharatha.

obtain peace until I see Rama, the immensely strong Lakshmana and the immensely fortunate Vaidehi. I will not obtain peace until I see the auspicious face of my brother, which is like the moon and which has eyes like lotuses. I will not obtain peace until I place the feet, marked with all the signs, of my brother, the king, on my head. I will not obtain peace until his head is sprinkled with water for crowning him in this kingdom of our father and grandfather. He is the one who deserves the kingdom. The immensely fortunate Vaidehi, Janaka's daughter, has been successful in her objective. She is the one who follows her husband on this earth, right up to the frontiers of the ocean. Mount Chitrakuta is like the king of the mountains.[360] Since Kakutstha is residing here, like Kubera in Nandana,[361] it is extremely fortunate. This impenetrable forest is populated by predatory beasts. Since the immensely energetic Rama, supreme among those who wield weapons, resides here, it has been successful in its objective.'

Having said this, the immensely energetic Bharata, bull among men, energetically entered that great forest on foot. The summit of the mountain was dense with many different species of trees, with flowers blossoming at the top. The supreme among eloquent ones proceeded through them. On Mount Chitrakuta, he climbed up a flowering sala tree and saw the smoke from Rama's hermitage, curling up like an upraised standard. On seeing this, the handsome Bharata and his relatives were delighted, like those who have been able to cross a body of water. Having instructed the army to again set up camp, the great-souled one quickly proceeded, with Guha, towards Rama's hermitage on Mount Chitrakuta.

Chapter 2(93)

Bharata instructed the soldiers to be camped. Having shown Shatrughna,[362] he left, eager to see his brother. He asked rishi

[360] The Himalayas.

[361] Kubera's pleasure garden.

[362] The signs of Rama's hermitage.

Vasishtha to quickly bring the mothers. Devoted to his seniors, he then quickly went on ahead. Sumantra was as anxious to see Rama as Bharata was. Therefore, he also followed Shatrughna at a distance. The place was full of the abodes of ascetics. As Bharata proceeded, he saw a handsome cottage. This was his brother's, constructed with leaves. In front of the cottage, Bharata saw that wood had been splintered and flowers had been gathered. Because of the cold, he also saw in the forest huge heaps of the dung of deer and buffaloes.[363] As he proceeded, the mighty-armed and radiant Bharata cheerfully spoke to Shatrughna and all the advisers. 'I think that we have reached the spot Bharadvaja spoke about. I think that the river Mandakinee cannot be far from here. These barks must have been tied by Lakshmana. These are signs to mark the path, in case one wishes to return at odd times.[364] The slopes of the mountain are marked with the tusks of spirited elephants, as they roamed around and trumpeted at each other. In the forest, ascetics always desire to light fires.[365] The smoke can be seen, trailing black plumes. I am delighted that I will see the noble tiger among men here, devoted to attending to his seniors. Raghava is like a maharshi.' After having proceeded for some time along Chitrakuta, Raghava[366] reached Mandakinee and spoke these words to those people. 'The Indra of men, the tiger among men, seated himself on the ground in *virasana* in this desolate spot.[367] Shame on my birth and life. It is on account of me that the immensely radiant lord of the world has faced this hardship. Having given up all the objects of desire, Raghava is residing in the forest.'

On seeing that large, sacred and beautiful hut made out of leaves in that forest, Dasharatha's son lamented in this way. It was large and covered with many delicate leaves from sala, tala and *ashvakarna*[368] trees. It looked like a sacrificial altar covered with kusha grass. There

[363] Gathered so that these could be burnt to ward off the cold.

[364] Such as at night. The barks were tied to trees.

[365] To keep away wild animals.

[366] Bharata.

[367] Literally, posture of a hero. A seated position used by ascetics.

[368] Similar to sala.

were many heavy bows that were like Shakra's weapons. These were immensely heavy, capable of obstructing the enemy. They were ornamented and overlaid with gold. There were arrows in the quivers. These were terrible, like the rays of the sun. They were adorned with blazing tips, like serpents in Bhogavati.[369] The place was adorned with two swords that were in sheaths of silver. It was also adorned with two colourful shields that were dotted with gold. Colourful finger guards made of lizard skin hung there, decorated with gold. A large number of enemies were incapable of assailing the spot, like deer attacking the cave of a lion. A large sacrificial altar sloped down towards the north-east and it blazed like the fire. In Rama's sacred residence, Bharata saw this. After looking at this for an instant, Bharata saw his senior, Rama, seated there in the cottage, wearing a circle of matted hair. He was attired in black antelope skin and garments made out of bark. He saw the fearless Rama seated there, like a fire. His shoulders were like those of a lion. He was mighty-armed and lotus-eyed. He followed dharma and was the lord of the earth, right up to the frontiers of the ocean. On the ground covered with darbha grass, the mighty-armed one was seated there, like the eternal Brahma, and with Sita and Lakshmana.

On seeing him, the handsome Bharata was overcome with grief and confusion. Bharata, Kaikeyee's son, with dharma in his soul, rushed forward. On seeing him, he started to lament in an afflicted tone, his voice choking with tears. He was incapable of remaining patient and spoke these words. 'The ordinary people worshipped my brother in an assembly. Wild animals now attend to him in the forest. Earlier, the one who follows dharma possessed many thousands of garments. He has now covered himself in deer skin. Earlier, he decorated himself with many colourful flowers. How can that Raghava now bear this mass of matted hair? He observed the prescribed sacrifices and accumulated a store of dharma. He is now following a path of dharma that involves oppression of the body. His limbs used to be smeared with expensive sandalwood paste. How can this noble one's limbs now be smeared with filth? Rama

[369] The capital of the nagas in the nether regions.

was used to happiness and it is because of me that he is facing this hardship. Shame on my life. Because of my cruelty, I am condemned by the world.' Distressed, he lamented in this way. His face was like a lotus and it began to perspire. Bharata wept and fell down at Rama's feet. Bharata, the immensely strong prince, was tormented by grief. Having said, 'O noble one,' he was so miserable that he was unable to say anything further. His voice choked with tears and he glanced towards the illustrious Rama. He could only loudly say 'O noble one' and was incapable of saying anything more. Weeping, Shatrughna also worshipped at Rama's feet. Rama also shed tears and embraced both of them. In the forest, Sumantra and Guha saw those sons of the king, like the sun and the moon in the sky, together with Venus and Jupiter. Those princes met in that great forest, like the leaders of herds of elephants. All the residents of the forest saw them and forgetting all their happiness, started to shed tears.

Chapter 2(94)

Rama Raghava controlled himself. He embraced Bharata and inhaled the fragrance of his head. Placing him on his lap, he asked about him. 'O son![370] Where is our father, since you have come to the forest? As long as he is alive, you should not come to the forest. O Bharata! From a distance, for a long time, I saw you come to this forest, with a mournful face. O son! Why have you come to the forest? Is King Dasharatha, devoted to the truth, well?[371] Having turned his mind towards dharma, he is the performer of royal and horse sacrifices. O son! Are you properly honouring the immensely radiant and learned brahmana, who is always devoted to dharma and is the preceptor of the lineage of the Ikshvakus?[372] O

[370] The word used is tata.

[371] There is an inconsistency in this section. Having asked about Dasharatha, Rama doesn't wait for the answer. But the succeeding questions seem to suggest that Rama knows that Bharata is the ruler now. In any event, this section doesn't seem to belong.

[372] This is a reference to Vasishtha.

son! Are Kousalya and Sumitra, the mother of offspring, happy? Does the noble Queen Kaikeyee rejoice? Is the priest who possesses humility and is extremely learned revered by you?[373] He has been born in a noble lineage, possesses insight and is without envy. I hope intelligent and upright ones who know about the rituals light the sacrificial fire at the right time and always inform you that oblations have been offered into the fire at the right time. O son! I hope you show respect to the preceptor Sudhanva. He is supreme among those who know about arrows and weapons and is accomplished in *arthashastra*.[374] O son! I hope you have appointed as ministers noble ones who know about the signs, those who are brave, learned and have conquered the senses, those who are like your own self. O Raghava! The foundation of a king's victory lies in good counsel, from well-trained advisers who are accomplished in the sacred texts and can maintain secrets. I hope you have not come under the subjugation of sleep. I hope you wake up at the right time. During the second half of the night, I hope you think about the appropriateness of policies. I hope you do not seek counsel from a single person, nor do you seek counsel from too many. I hope your secret counsels with ministers do not spread throughout the kingdom. O Raghava! I hope you determine whether an objective has minimum cost and maximum gain and having decided, act swiftly, without delays. I hope other kings get to know about all the acts you have successfully completed and also those you have commenced, but not those that are yet to begin. O son! I hope your debates and discussions, within your own self, or secretly with your advisers, are not divulged to others. I hope you prefer a single learned person over one thousand foolish ones. To accomplish an objective, a learned person can bring about great gain. Even if a king engages one thousand foolish people, their help will not bring about any benefit. A single intelligent, brave, accomplished and skilled adviser can bring about great prosperity to a king, or to one

[373] The name isn't mentioned. This could be a reference to Vasishtha, but is more likely to be a reference to Vasishtha's son, since Vasishtha has already been mentioned. Vasishtha's son was named Suyajna.

[374] Loosely, political economy, or the science of creating wealth.

who aspires to be a king. I hope the best servants are engaged in superior tasks, medium ones in medium tasks and the inferior ones in inferior tasks. For your tasks, I hope you engage advisers who have learned lineages, with unsullied fathers and grandfathers, those who are the best among the best. I hope those who perform sacrifices do not regard you as an outcast, one who accepts terrible gifts and one whose desires are like those of a woman. If a person does not kill a physician who is unskilled, a servant who is engaged in reviling and a brave person who desires prosperity, he is himself destroyed.[375] I hope the commander-in-chief appointed is someone who is happy, brave, wise, intelligent, pure, noble in birth, devoted and accomplished. I hope powerful and foremost warriors skilled in fighting, whose bravery has been witnessed earlier, are honoured and respected by you. I hope you give the appropriate food and wages to the soldiers when the time arrives, without any delays. It has been said that if the right time passes, salaried servants, even if they are devoted, are angry at their master and censure him, thus leading to an extremely great calamity. I hope all those who are foremost in their lineages are devoted to you. Are they self-controlled? For your sake, are they ready to lay down their lives? O Bharata! As ambassador in any specific habitation, I hope you have appointed a person who is learned, accomplished and talented, speaking what should be spoken. In every tirtha, do you employ three spies, who do not know about each other's existence, to find out the eighteen functionaries of the enemy and the fifteen on your own side?[376] O slayer of enemies! There are those who are exiled, but always return to cause injury. Taking them to be weak, I hope

[375] The king destroys himself in the process. A brave person who desires prosperity might seek to become the king himself.

[376] The eighteen officers of the enemy are the prime minister, the royal priest, the crown prince, the commander in chief, the chief warder, the treasurer of the palace, the superintendent of jails, the treasurer of the kingdom, the herald, the public prosecutor, the judge, the assessor of taxes, the one who disburses salaries to soldiers, the one who disburses salaries to workers, the superintendent of public works, the protector of the borders, the magistrate and the supervisor of forests and waterbodies. On one's own side, the prime minister, the royal priest and the crown prince are exempted from scrutiny, thus yielding fifteen.

you do not ignore them. O son! I hope you do not serve brahmanas who are excessively addicted to worldly pursuits. Those who are foolish, but pride themselves to be learned, are skilled at causing harm. Though the foremost among sacred texts exist and though intelligent ones look on, those who are evil in intelligence continue to prattle about futile things. O son! Earlier, Ayodhya was inhabited by our brave ancestors. With its firm gates and full of elephants, horses and chariots, it is true to its name.[377] Brahmanas, kshatriyas and vaishyas are always engaged in their own tasks. There are thousands of advisers who have conquered their senses and are great in enterprise. Surrounded by many kinds of palaces, it is full of learned people. I hope it is happy and prosperous and that you protect it. In the habitations of people, I hope hundreds of altars are properly laid out. I hope the temples are adorned with stores of drinking water and lakes. I hope assemblies and festivals are decorated with happy men and women. I hope pens for the animals are laid out well and they are not subjected to violence. I hope the agricultural land is excellent and free of predatory beasts. O Raghava! I hope the habitations are prosperous and happy places of residence. O son! I hope that people who earn a living from agriculture and animal husbandry are cherished by you and are indeed happy. I hope that everything is being done for protecting them, maintaining them and tending to their needs. Following dharma, the king must protect all those who reside inside his kingdom. I hope you comfort the women and protect them well. I hope you do not trust them and tell them secrets. I hope the places frequented by elephants are protected and elephants are not tormented. O prince! Do you wake in the forenoon and having woken, always ornament and show yourself to the people along the great highways? I hope all the forts are stocked with riches, grain, weapons and water and full of machines, artisans and archers. I hope the revenue is a lot and that the expenditure is limited. O Raghava! I hope the treasury does not reach those who are undeserving. I hope your expenditure is meant for the gods, for

[377] Ayodhya means something that cannot be attacked or fought against.

ancestors, for brahmanas, for guests, for warriors and for those who are in the nature of friends. I hope a noble and virtuous person, pure in soul, when accused of an act of theft, is not killed out of avarice, without having been questioned by those who are accomplished in the sacred texts. O bull among men! I hope that a thief when seen, caught and sufficiently questioned at the time of the act, is not freed because of a desire for riches. O Raghava! I hope that when there is a dispute between a rich and a poor person, your extremely learned advisers resolve it impartially, without differentiating because of the relative prosperity. O Raghava! If a person rules wilfully, out of pleasure alone, the tears that fall from the eyes of one who is falsely accused, kill that person's sons and animals. O Raghava! I hope that through gifts, thoughts and words, you please three categories of people—the aged, the children and the foremost among those who are learned. I hope you bow down before seniors, the aged, ascetics, gods, guests, *chaityas*[378] and all the brahmanas who have become successful in their objectives. I hope you do not obstruct the observance of dharma through the pursuit of artha, or the observance of artha through the pursuit of dharma, or the pursuit of either through excessive attachment to kama. O supreme among victorious ones! O Bharata! O one who knows about the apportioning of time! I hope you devote your time equally to artha, dharma and kama. O immensely wise one! I hope that brahmanas who are accomplished about the purport of all the sacred texts and inhabitants of the city and the countryside hope for your happiness. I hope you abandon the fourteen kinds of sins for kings—non-belief, falsehood, anger, distraction, procrastination, disregard for the learned, laziness, pursuit of the five senses, single-minded devotion to artha, seeking counsel of those who don't know the objectives, failure to start projects that have been decided, failure to protect secrets, failure to observe auspicious signs and a readiness to rise from one's seat for everyone. O Raghava! I hope you do not eat tastily prepared food alone. I hope you also give shares to friends who so desire.'

[378] The word chaitya has several meanings—sacrificial shed, temple, altar, sanctuary and a tree that grows along the road.

Chapter 2(95)

Hearing Rama's words, Bharata replied, 'How can someone like me violate the canons of dharma and perform the dharma of kings? O bull among men! The eternal dharma has always been followed by us. O king! As long as an elder son is present, the younger can never be a king. O Raghava! Therefore, with me, go to prosperous Ayodhya. For the lineage and for our sake, crown yourself. A king is said to be a man. However, if his conduct is in conformity with dharma and artha, he is said to be superhuman. For me, such a person is revered like a divinity. While I was in Kekaya and while you resorted to the forest, the king who performed sacrifices[379] and was revered by the virtuous has gone to heaven. O tiger among men! Arise and perform the water rites for our father. I and Shatrughna have already performed the water rites earlier. O Raghava! In the world of the ancestors, it has been said that what is given by the beloved becomes inexhaustible and you are our father's beloved.'

Hearing those piteous words uttered by Bharata, conveying news about the death of his father, Raghava lost his senses. The disagreeable words spoken by Bharata were like words with a vajra in them. Rama, scorcher of enemies, stretched out his arms and fell down on the ground, like a tree with blossoms at the top, when it is severed by an axe in the forest. Rama, the lord of the universe, fell down in this way, like an exhausted elephant sleeping on a bank that has now been washed away. His brothers, great archers, were afflicted by grief and surrounded him from all sides, weeping. So did Vaidehi and they sprinkled him with water. When he regained consciousness, tears began to flow from Kakutstha's eyes and he spoke many piteous words of lamentation. 'My birth is in vain. What task can I perform for the great-souled one? He has died on account of sorrow over me and I have been unable to perform the last rites for him. Alas! O Bharata! O unblemished one! Since you and Shatrughna have been able to perform all the funeral rites, you

[379] Dasharatha.

are indeed successful. Without its leader and without that Indra among men, Ayodhya is in a deranged state. When the period of exile in the forest is over, I am not interested in returning there. O scorcher of enemies! Since our father has gone to the other world, when the period of exile in the forest is over, who will instruct me in Ayodhya? In earlier times, on witnessing my good conduct, my father used to comfort me and address me in words that were pleasant to hear. Where will I hear such words now?' Having addressed Bharata in this way, Raghava sought out his wife, whose face was like the full moon. Tormented with grief, he spoke to her. 'O Sita! Your father-in-law is dead. O Lakshmana! You are without a father. Bharata has brought the sorrowful tiding that the lord of the earth has gone to heaven.' Rama comforted Janaka's daughter, who was weeping.

Lakshmana was miserable and he addressed him in these words of grief. 'Bring the pulp of an inguda tree. Bring bark for an upper garment. I will go and perform the water rites for our great-souled father. Let Sita walk in front. Follow her at the rear. I will follow thereafter in this extremely terrible procession.' The immensely intelligent Sumantra was always devoted to them and knew about the soul. He was firm in his devotion to the mild, self-controlled and composed Rama. He comforted Raghava and holding him by the hand, made him descend into the auspicious river Mandakinee. With blossoming trees, river Mandakinee was always beautiful. Faced with the catastrophe, the illustrious one reached this excellent tirtha.[380] This auspicious tirtha was free of mud and the waters flowed fast. He[381] said, 'O king! Accept this water that is being offered to you.' The lord of the earth cupped his hands and filled them with water. He faced the southern direction and weeping, spoke these words. 'O tiger among kings! This sparkling water is eternal. As soon as I offer it to you, may it reach you in the world of the ancestors.' Ascending the banks of the Mandakinee again, the energetic Raghava, with his brothers, offered funeral cakes to

[380] Tirtha is a ford, a sacred place of pilgrimage.

[381] Rama.

their father. The pulp of inguda and badari were mixed and laid out on darbha grass by Rama. Grieving and weeping, he spoke these words. 'O great king! Be pleased and eat this. This is what we also eat. What is food for a man is also food for the gods.'[382] Following the same path, the tiger among men then ascended from the banks of the river and reached the beautiful summit of the mountain.

The lord of the universe reached the cottage made out of leaves. He embraced Bharata and Lakshmana in his arms. The sounds of the brothers and Vaidehi weeping could be heard and echoed in the mountain, like the roaring of lions. Hearing this tumultuous sound, Bharata's soldiers were alarmed. They said, 'It is certain that Bharata has met Rama and this great sound is because they are sorrowing over their dead father.' All of them abandoned their camps and headed in the direction of the sound. Their single intention was to rush towards the spot. Some men went on horses. Some went on elephants. Some went on ornamented chariots. Those who were young proceeded on foot. All the people suddenly rushed towards the hermitage, desiring to see Rama. Though he had been away only for a short period, it was as if he had been away for a long period of time. They rushed, eager to witness the meeting of the brothers. They resorted to different kinds of mounts and vehicles, with hooves and with wheels. As the earth was struck by many different kinds of vehicles, with hooves and axles, a tumultuous sound arose, like clouds dashing against each other in the sky. There were male elephants surrounded by female elephants[383] and they were terrified at this. Releasing the scent of their musth, they left for another forest. Large numbers of boars, wolves, lions, buffaloes, bears, apes, tigers, *gokarnas*, *gavayas* and spotted deer were frightened.[384] Red ducks, waterfowl, swans, *karandas*,[385] herons, male cuckoos and curlews lost their senses and fled in different directions. The sky

[382] This explains why forest fare is being offered, instead of properly prepared funeral cakes.

[383] Wild ones.

[384] Gokarna means cow-eared and is a kind of antelope. Gavaya is the *gayal*, it is the wild variety of domesticated cattle.

[385] Kind of duck.

was filled with birds frightened by the sound. The earth was filled with men and both looked beautiful at the time.

The men had tears in their eyes and were extremely miserable. On seeing them, the one who knew about dharma[386] embraced them, like their own father and mother. He embraced some of the men. Some other men worshipped him. The son of the king met them all, including his friends and relatives and treated each one according to what was deserved. The sounds of the great-souled ones weeping filled the earth and the sky and the sound echoed in the mountain caverns and all the directions, as if the beating of drums could be heard.

Chapter 2(96)

Vasishtha placed Dasharatha's wives at the forefront and desiring to see Rama, approached the spot. The king's wives gently approached Mandakinee and saw the tirtha frequented by Rama and Lakshmana. Kousalya's eyes were full of tears and her mouth was dry. Distressed, she spoke to Sumitra and the other royal women. 'The performers of unblemished deeds have been banished from the kingdom and this is the tirtha towards the east of the forest that those unfortunate ones, deprived of protectors, frequent. O Sumitra! This is the spot from where, without any distraction, Soumitri, your son, himself draws water for my son.' On the ground, laid out on darbha grass, the large-eyed one saw the pulp of inguda offered to his father, with the tip pointing to the south. She saw what the unfortunate Rama had laid out on the ground for his father. On seeing this, Queen Kousalya spoke to all of Dasharatha's women. 'Look at this. Following the prescribed rites, Raghava[387] has offered this to his great-souled father, Raghava,[388] the protector of the lineage of the Ikshvakus. The great-souled king was the equal

[386] Rama.

[387] Rama.

[388] Dasharatha.

of a god. Given the objects of pleasure that he enjoyed, I do not think that this is appropriate food. On earth, he was the equal of the great Indra and was the lord of the earth, ruling over the four quarters of the earth. How can he eat this pulp of inguda? I cannot see a greater misery in this world than that the prosperous Rama has to offer a pulp of inguda to his father. I have seen the pulp of inguda that Rama has offered to his father. At the misery of this, why does my heart not shatter into one thousand fragments?'

She was afflicted and her co-wives comforted her. They went and saw Rama in his hermitage, like an immortal who has been dislodged from heaven. On seeing that Rama had given up all the objects of pleasure, his mothers were afflicted. Afflicted by grief, they shed tears and lamented loudly. Rama, tiger among men and devoted to the truth, arose and seized the auspicious feet of all his mothers. Those large-eyed ones used their hands, pleasant to the touch, and their gentle and auspicious fingers and palms to wipe the dust off Rama's back. On seeing that all the mothers were miserable, immediately after Rama, Soumitri gently worshipped all the mothers. Lakshmana was born from Dasharatha and bore the auspicious signs. All the women acted towards him just as they had acted towards Rama. Miserable and with tears in her eyes, Sita also seized the feet of her mothers-in-law and stood before them. She was afflicted by grief and lean from residing in the forest. Kousalya embraced the miserable one, like a mother does to a daughter, and spoke these words. 'This is the daughter of the king of Videha. This is Dasharatha's daughter-in-law. This is Rama's wife. What misery has led to her being in this desolate forest? O Vaidehi! I can see your face. It is like a lotus scorched by the heat. It is like a water lily that has faded. It is like gold defiled by dust. It is like the moon shrouded in clouds. The grief is tormenting my mind like a fire and it is as if the hardship has acted like kindling that generates the fire.'

While the miserable mothers were speaking in this way, Raghava, Bharata's elder brother, approached Vasishtha and seized his feet. Extremely great in his energy, the priest was Agni's equal. Raghava, the lord of men, seized his feet, like Indra does to Brihaspati, and sat down beside him. After they were seated, Bharata, who knew about dharma and followed dharma, approached and sat down below his elder brother, with the advisers, the foremost citizens, the soldiers and other people. The valiant Raghava was seated in the garb of an ascetic and blazed in his prosperity. On seeing him, Bharata joined his hands in salutation, like the great Indra bowing down before Prajapati.[389] After having worshipped and honoured him, what virtuous words would Bharata speak to Raghava? All the noble people were supremely curious to know the truth about this. Raghava was devoted to the truth, Lakshmana was extremely generous and Bharata was devoted to dharma. Surrounded by their well-wishers, these three were like the three fires surrounded by assistant priests.[390]

Chapter 2(97)

Rama comforted his brother, who was devoted to his seniors. With Lakshmana, he questioned his brother. 'I wish to hear the reason behind your coming to this place, with matted hair and attired in bark and antelope skin. Why have you come to this region, with black antelope skin and matted hair? Why have you abandoned the kingdom? You should tell me everything.'

When the great-souled Kakutstha addressed him in this way, Kaikeyi's son forcibly controlled his sorrow. He joined his hands in salutation and said, 'O noble one! Father abandoned you and performed an extremely difficult deed. Overcome by sorrow on account of his son, the mighty-armed one went to heaven. O scorcher of enemies! He was urged by a woman, my mother, Kaikeyee. She performed an extremely wicked act that brought her ill fame. Desiring the fruit of the kingdom, she has become a

[389] Brahma.

[390] The three sacrificial fires are *ahavaniya, garhapatya* and *dakshinatya* (the fire that burns in a southern direction). Garhapatya is the fire that burns in households. Ahavaniya has various meanings, the simplest being the monthly sacrificial rites offered to the ancestors on the day of the new moon.

widow and is afflicted by grief. My mother will descend into an extremely terrible hell. Though I am her son, I am your servant and you should show me your favours. Like Maghavan,[391] consecrate yourself in the kingdom today. These ordinary people and all the widowed mothers have come before you. You should show them your favours. O one who grants honours! Following the norm of progression[392] and dharma, you yourself are the one who should be united with the kingdom. Satisfy the desires of your well-wishers. Like the autumn sky when there is a sparkling moon, this entire widowed earth will obtain you as a husband. With these advisers, I am bowing my head down and beseeching you. I am your brother, disciple and servant and you should show me your favours. O tiger among men! This entire circle of advisers was always revered by our father and you should not contradict what they want.' Kaikeyee's mighty-armed son said this, his voice choking with tears. Bharata repeatedly touched Rama's feet with his head. He was like a maddened elephant and sighed repeatedly.

Rama embraced his brother, Bharata, and said, 'You have been born in a noble lineage. You possess spirit and energy and are good in conduct. For the sake of the kingdom, how can you commit a wicked act, like an ordinary person? O slayer of enemies! I do not see the slightest bit of taint in you. Like a child, you should not censure your mother. O one who knows about dharma! O supreme among those who uphold dharma! The honour and respect a father receives in this world is exactly the same as the honour that a mother receives. O Raghava! These two, mother and father, who are devoted to dharma in conduct, asked me to leave for the forest. How could one have acted contrary to this? You should receive the kingdom of Ayodhya and be revered by the people. With bark as a garment, I need to reside in Dandakaranya. In the presence of people, this is the division that the great king had ordained and instructed. The immensely energetic Dasharatha has now gone to heaven. The king, with dharma in his soul, is the preceptor of the

[391] Indra.

[392] Primogeniture.

worlds and of ours too and this is the norm he set. You should enjoy the share that our father has given. O amiable one! I will remain in Dandakaranya for fourteen years. Enjoy the share that our great-souled father has given to you. Our great-souled father is like the lord of the gods. He is respected in the world of men. I think what he told me is supremely beneficial for me, not an undecaying lordship over all the worlds.'

Chapter 2(98)

While the lions among men were still grieving, surrounded by a large number of their well-wishers, the night of misery passed. When night turned into a wonderful morning, surrounded by their well-wishers, the brothers meditated and offered oblations in Mandakinee, then approaching Rama. They sat in silence and no one uttered a word. In the midst of the well-wishers, Bharata then spoke these words to Rama. 'Having given this kingdom to me, my mother has now been pacified. I am giving the kingdom back to you, bereft of thorns. Enjoy it. When a dam has been breached by the great force of water that the advent of the monsoon brings, it is difficult to mend it. Like that, this giant dominion of the kingdom cannot be ruled by anyone other than you. O lord of the earth! The speed of a horse cannot be replicated by a donkey, nor that of Tarkshya[393] by an ordinary bird. I do not have the capacity to mimic your speed. A person on whom others depend for a living always lives well. O Rama! A person who depends on others for a living lives badly. A tree planted and tended to by a man may become a gigantic tree with a firm trunk, which always has flowers, but does not show any fruit. However, a dwarf finds it difficult to climb it. No pleasure is obtained by the person who planted it for a reason.[394] O mighty-armed one! You should understand the reason

[393] Garuda.

[394] Because it does not yield any fruit.

behind this simile. You are the bull and lord among us. Instruct us, your servants. O great king! O scorcher of enemies! May all the classes look upon you established in front of them in the kingdom, scorching like the sun. O Kakutstha! Let crazy elephants follow you and trumpet. When you reach the inner quarters, let all the self-controlled women rejoice.' When they heard Bharata's words, beseeching Rama, the many people from the city thought that he spoke virtuous words.

Seeing that the illustrious Bharata was extremely miserable and was lamenting in this way, Rama, self-restrained and in control of his soul, comforted him. 'A man is not the master and cannot act according to his own desires. From here to there, he is dragged around by the one who brings an end to all action.[395] Everything that is stored up is destroyed. Anything that goes up, ends in a fall. Union ends in separation. Life ends in death. A ripened fruit has no other fear other than that of falling down. In that way, a man who is born, has no other fear other than that of death. A house built on a firm foundation is eventually dilapidated and destroyed. Like that, a man comes under the subjugation of old age and death and is destroyed. In this world, as day and night pass, the lifespan of every living being is diminished, just as during summer, the sun's rays quickly do the same to water. You should sorrow over your own self. Why are you sorrowing over another?[396] Whether you are in one place or whether you roam around, your lifespan will be diminished. Death roams around with us. Death is seated with us. Even if one travels a long distance away, death returns with us. Wrinkles appear on the body. The hair on the head turns grey. A man decays because of old age. How can he regain his old powers? Men are delighted when the sun arises and are delighted when the sun sets. They do not comprehend that their own lifespans decrease. They are delighted when they see the onset of a season, as if something new and newer has arrived. However, the change of the seasons heralds the destruction of the lifespans of

[395] The text uses the word *kritanta,* meaning fate, destiny, death.

[396] Dasharatha.

living creatures. In the great ocean, a piece of wood rubs against another piece of wood. Having come together for a time, they drift apart again. Wives, sons, relatives and riches are like that. They come together, but their separation is also certain. No living being can transgress its destiny. Therefore, there should be no capacity to grieve over death. When a caravan passes, someone who is standing along the road says, "I will also follow you at the rear." In that way, we must certainly follow the path taken by our fathers and grandfathers earlier. That being the case, since there is no violation to this, why should one sorrow? Age rushes on and like a flow, does not return. The atman should be engaged in something that brings happiness. It has been said that subjects deserve happiness. The lord of the earth, our father, had dharma in his soul. He performed all the sacrifices and gave away copious quantities of dakshina. Having cleansed his sins, he has gone to heaven. He maintained the servants and protected the subjects properly. Having followed dharma in accumulating artha, our father has gone to heaven. He performed many kinds of rites and sacrifices. He enjoyed all the objects of pleasure. Having spent an excellent life, the lord of the earth has gone to heaven. Our father has cast aside a decayed human body. He has obtained divine prosperity and roams around in Brahma's world. Someone who is as wise as you should not grieve in this fashion. Someone like you and someone like me are learned and possess superior intelligence. All those who are patient and intelligent in all situations should abandon these many kinds of sorrow, lamentations and weeping. Therefore, be steady. Do not grieve. Go and reside in that city. O supreme among eloquent ones! That is what our self-controlled father engaged you to do. I have also been thus engaged by that performer of auspicious deeds. I will act in accordance with our noble father's instructions. O scorcher of enemies! It is not proper for me to cast aside his instructions. He was our relative and our father and you must always also respect his wishes.' Rama, devoted to dharma, spoke these words that were full of meaning and stopped.

Bharata replied in wonderful words that were full of dharma. 'O scorcher of enemies! Where in this world is there a person like you? You are not distressed at misery, nor are you delighted at joy. You are revered by the aged and you ask them when there is a doubt. If a person has obtained the intelligence to look upon death and life equally, and existence and non-existence equally, why should he be tormented? He does not deserve to grieve even when he confronts an adversity. Your spirit is like that of the immortals. You are great in soul and devoted to the truth. O Raghava! You know everything. You see everything. You are intelligent. You possess such qualities and know about existence and non-existence. You do not deserve to suffer from the most terrible of miseries. While I was away, for my sake, my mother performed a wicked deed. It was inferior and injurious, but you should show me your favours. I am tied by the bond of dharma.[397] That apart, she is my mother. I should kill her and chastise her with this terrible punishment. She is the perpetrator of a wicked deed and deserves to be punished. But I have been born from Dasharatha, whose deeds were noble and pure. Knowing about dharma, how can I perform an act of adharma, even though I might desire to commit that act? He was my senior. He performed rites and was aged. He was the king. He was my father. He is now dead and one should not condemn a father. In an assembly, he was like a divinity. How could a person who knew about dharma and artha have performed such a sinful act? He knew about dharma and followed dharma, but acted in this way to bring pleasure to a woman. There is an ancient saying that at the time of destruction, creatures are confounded. Having done what he did, in the eyes of the world, the king has made that saying come true. Our father knew the meaning of virtue. Yet, he transgressed it because of anger,[398] confusion or rashness. Therefore, correct that transgression. It is the view of the world that if a son thinks it virtuous to counter a father's transgression, such a son is regarded as a true son, not one who acts in a contrary way. You should be a son like that, do not be one who assents to a wicked act committed by our father. The act that he perpetrated is condemned by the patient people of this world. Save

[397] Of not killing a woman.

[398] Kaikeyee's anger.

all of us—Kaikeyee, me, our father, the well-wishers, our relatives and all the inhabitants of the city and the countryside. What is this forest? Where is the duty of a kshatriya? What is this matted hair? What about ruling? You should not act in this contrary way. If you wish to follow dharma by accepting a hardship, then accept the hardship of ruling the four varnas in accordance with dharma. Among the four ashramas, garhasthya is the best ashrama.[399] This has been said by those who know about dharma. O one who knows about dharma! How can you give that up? Compared to you, I am a child in learning, status and birth. When you are there, how can I rule over the earth? I am inferior to you in intelligence. I am like a child in qualities. I am inferior in status. Without you, I have no interest in remaining alive. O one who knows about dharma! With your relatives and without any distraction and thorns, follow your own dharma and rule over this entire kingdom of our father. With all the ordinary subjects, let the officiating priests with Vasishtha and those who know about the mantras crown you here with the appropriate mantras. After having been crowned, you can leave with us and go and rule Ayodhya. You will quickly conquer the worlds, like Vasava with the Maruts.[400] You will repay the three debts[401] and properly punish all those who commit wicked deeds. You will satisfy the well-wishers with all the objects of desire. And you will also instruct me. O noble one! The well-wishers will rejoice today at your coronation. Today, the evildoers will be terrified and will flee in the ten directions. O bull among men! Wipe away the outrage that my mother has caused. Today, protect our father from the sin he has committed. With my head bowed down, I am beseeching you. Show compassion towards me. To relatives and all creatures, you are like Maheshvara.[402] Or, if you turn your back

[399] The four ashramas are brahmacharya, garhasthya, vanaprastha and sannyasa. Stated simply, brahmacharya is the state of being a celibate student, garhasthya is the state of being a householder, vanaprastha is when one resorts to the forest and sannyasa is the state of being an ascetic.

[400] The Maruts are wind gods who are companions of Indra (Vasava).

[401] The three debts are owed to gods, ancestors and sages.

[402] The great lord, also a name for Shiva.

towards me and leave this place for the forest, I will also follow you wherever you may go.'

Bharata bowed his head down and sought the favours of Rama, the lord of the earth. However, the spirited one had no intention of returning. He was established in the word given by his father. On witnessing that extraordinary perseverance in Raghava, the people were delighted and miserable at the same time. They were miserable because he was not going to Ayodhya. However, on seeing that he would stick to his pledge, they were also delighted. Bharata prostrated himself before Rama. The officiating priests, the aged leaders of the people and the weeping and senseless mothers praised Bharata's words and also added their entreaties to his.

Chapter 2(99)

Lakshmana's elder brother, handsome and extremely revered amidst his kin, again responded to Bharata, who had spoken. 'The words that you have spoken are deserving of a son from Kaikeyee and Dasharatha, excellent among kings. O brother! In ancient times, when our father married your mother, he promised your maternal grandfather this excellent kingdom as a bride price. In a battle between the gods and the asuras, the lord, the king, was extremely delighted with your mother. The king offered her two boons. With that pledge having been made, your illustrious and beautiful mother sought those two boons from that best of men. O tiger among men! Thus urged by her, the king gave her those boons—the kingdom for you and my exile. O bull among men! Because that boon was given, I have been instructed by our father to reside in the forest for fourteen years. Without any violation of the truthful pledge that our father had given, I have thus come to this desolate forest, followed by Lakshmana and Sita. You should also ensure that our father, Indra among kings, was truthful in his speech. You should swiftly crown yourself. O Bharata! For my sake, release the lord, the king, from his debt. O one who knows about dharma! Save our father and delight your mother. O son![403] The sacred texts recount a chant by the illustrious Gaya. This is when he performed a sacrifice to repay the debt to his ancestors in Gaya.[404] 'A son is said to be putra because he saves his ancestors from the hell known as *pum*.[405] One who repays debts to his ancestors is a true son. It is desired that there should be many sons who possess all the qualities and are extremely learned. Among all those, there will be at least one who will go to Gaya.' O delight of the king! This is what all the rajarshis felt. O best among men! O lord! Therefore, save your father from the hell. O Bharata! Go to Ayodhya and delight the ordinary subjects. O brave one! Go with Shatrughna and all the brahmanas. O king! With Vaidehi and Lakshmana, without any delay, I will enter Dandakaranya. O Bharata! Become the king of men yourself. In the forest, I will be the king of the animals. Now cheerfully go to the most excellent of cities. I will also cheerfully enter Dandaka. O Bharata! Let the umbrella cast a cool shadow over your head and protect you from the rays of the sun. For me, there are the plentiful trees in the forest to cast a shadow. I will happily seek refuge under them. Shatrughna is accomplished and intelligent and will be your aide. Soumitri is known to be my foremost friend. We four are excellent sons for that Indra among men. O Bharata! We will resort to the path of the truth. Do not grieve.'

Chapter 2(100)

Rama knew about dharma and addressed Bharata in these excellent words. However, a brahmana named Jabali spoke these words that were against dharma.[406] 'O Raghava! Excellent,

[403] The word used is tata.

[404] The place known as Gaya.

[405] The hell is known as pum. *Pumnama* means 'known as pum'. One who saves (*trayate*) from pum is *putra*.

[406] Jabali is an exponent of the *lokayata* school. While there are nuances as to what this school believed in, the emphasis is on the material world and not on the metaphysical and the world hereafter.

but do not turn your intelligence towards a futile end. O noble one! Your intelligence should be like that of an ascetic, but you are behaving like an ordinary man. Who is related to what man? What can ever be obtained by anyone? A creature is born alone and is also destroyed alone. O Rama! If a man clings to anyone as a mother or a father, he should be known as a person who is mad. No one ever belongs to another person. Having entered a village, a man resides for a while in a certain place. However, on the very next day, he abandons that residence and moves on elsewhere. For men, a father, a mother, a house and riches are like that. O Kakutstha! They are just like a residence. Virtuous people do not find delight in these. O supreme among men! You should not forsake your father's kingdom and dwell in this desolate place that is full of great misery and full of many thorns. Crown yourself in prosperous Ayodhya. The city is waiting for you, with a single braid of hair.[407] O son of a king! Enjoy the extremely expensive royal objects of pleasure. Pleasure yourself in Ayodhya, like Shakra in heaven. Dasharatha is nothing to you and you are nothing to him. He was a different king and you are another. Therefore, do what I am telling you. That king has gone wherever he was supposed to go. That is the nature of everyone who is mortal. You are concerned with this in vain. I sorrow over all those who are excessively devoted to artha and dharma. They suffer in this world and are destroyed after death. There are people who say that the eighth day is for the divinity who was a father.[408] Look at the wastage of food. What will a dead person eat? If in the course of a shraddha, food is meant to reach another body and be enjoyed by it, then let it be given to those who are setting out on a journey. At least they will have food for the road. Perform sacrifices, give donations, consecrate yourself for a sacrifice, torment yourself through austerities, renounce—intelligent people wrote these injunctions down in texts so as to persuade people to give. O immensely intelligent one! Therefore,

[407] There is the image of a woman, *ekavenidhara,* wearing a single braid of hair. This is done by a mourning woman, when the husband is away or dead.

[408] The word used is *ashtaka* (eighth). This is a special kind of funeral ceremony (shraddha) performed on the eighth day of the bright lunar fortnight (*shukla paksha*), where food is offered to the deceased ancestors.

arrive at the conclusion that nothing exists beyond this world. Resort to whatever is directly in front of you. Turn your back on whatever is not manifest. Place at the forefront the intelligence of the virtuous, that which has been demonstrated by all the worlds. Placated by Bharata, accept the kingdom.'

Chapter 2(101)

Rama, supreme among those who have truth in their souls, heard Jabali's words. Without any disturbance to his own intelligence, he spoke these excellent words. 'You have spoken these words with a view to ensuring my pleasure. Though it seems to be a possible course of action, it is actually impossible. Though it seems to be sanctioned food, it is actually food that should not be eaten. If a man is full of evil conduct and violates pledges, he does not receive respect from the virtuous and destroys perceptions about his character. Conduct makes it evident whether a person is noble or ignoble, brave or vain, pure or impure. If I am ignoble but appear noble, devoid of purity but appear pure, bereft of signs but seem to possess signs, practise bad conduct in the garb of good conduct, practise adharma dressed up as dharma, create confusion in this world, abandon everything auspicious and forsake rites and rituals, will any man who can distinguish between what should be done and what should not be done show me great respect in this world? I will be censured by the world as someone who is wicked in conduct. If I follow bad policies, how can I expect good conduct from anyone? If I deviate from pledges, how will I obtain heaven? The entire world will then conduct itself as it wills. Whatever is the conduct followed by kings, that is indeed the conduct followed by the subjects. Truth and non-violence are the eternal conduct of kings. Therefore, there must be truth in the soul of the kingdom. The world is established in truth. The rishis and the gods also revere truth. A person who speaks truth in this world obtains what is supreme after death. A man who practises falsehood is feared like a snake. In this world, truth is supreme dharma. It is said to be the foundation for heaven. Truth is the lord of this world. Padma[409] is established in truth. Truth is the foundation of everything. There is no objective that is superior to truth. Donations, sacrifices, oblations, tormenting through austerities and the Vedas—all these are established in truth. Therefore, there is nothing superior to truth. A single person can rule over the world.[410] A single person can protect the lineage. A single person can immerse it in hell. A single person can obtain greatness in heaven. For what purpose should I not follow the instructions of my father? I am true to pledges. He was truthful and he made a pledge in accordance with the truth. My senior has taken a pledge of truth. Because of greed, confusion, or ignorance of darkness, I will not shatter that bridge of truth. The gods and the ancestors will not accept the offerings of those who are fickle and unstable in their intelligence and deviate from the truth. This is what we have heard. I can myself see that the dharma of truth pervades the atman. This burden of the truth has been accepted by virtuous people and has been respected as an objective. I forsake the dharma of kshatriyas. It is adharma in the name of dharma. It is practised by the greedy, the violent, the inferior and the performers of evil deeds. After having been thought of by the mind, the body performs wicked deeds and the tongue utters a falsehood. All three are forms of sin. The earth, deeds, fame, prosperity and heaven desire and seek a man who serves the truth. You have used words of reason to persuade me to do seemingly beneficial things. However, what you have presented as superior is actually ignoble. I gave a pledge to my senior to reside in the forest. How can I abandon the pledge given to my senior and act in accordance with Bharata's words? The pledge and promise I made in the presence of my senior is inviolate. That is when Queen Kaikeyee was delighted in her mind. I will reside in the forest. I will control myself and eat pure food. With auspicious roots, flowers and fruits, I will render offerings to the gods and ancestors. In this world, I will satisfy my five senses and embark on this journey. Able to discriminate between what should be done and what should not be done, I will do this faithfully and without deceit. Having obtained this earth, an arena for action, I will undertake auspicious deeds.

[409] Lakshmi, the goddess of wealth, who is seated on a lotus (*padma*).

[410] All of these are a function of adherence to the truth.

Agni, Vayu and Soma will receive their shares in the fruits of these acts. Having performed one hundred sacrifices, the lord of the gods went to heaven. Having practised fierce austerities, the maharshis obtained heaven. The virtuous have said that truth, dharma, valour, compassion towards beings, agreeable speech and worship to brahmanas, gods and guests are the paths to heaven. Those who are devoted to dharma, associating with virtuous men, those who are spirited and possess the foremost quality of generosity, those who are non-violent and those who are devoid of taints in this world are worshipped as the foremost among sages.'

Chapter 2(102)

Discerning that Rama was angry, Vasishtha replied, 'Even Jabali knows about the comings and goings of this world. He spoke these words with a view to making you return. O lord of the world! Hear from me about the creation of this world. Everything was submerged in water and the earth was created from this. Svayambhu Brahma was created, together with all the gods. Assuming the form of a boar, he raised up the earth.[411] With sons who were created from his own self, he created this universe and everything in it. The eternal, everlasting and undecaying Brahma was created from space. Marichi was born from him[412] and Marichi's son was Kashyapa. Vivasvat was born from Kashyapa. Manu is known as Vivasvat's son. He was the first Prajapati and Ikshvaku was Manu's son. This prosperous earth was first given by Manu to him. Know that Ikshvaku was the first king of Ayodhya.[413] Ikshvaku's son was the handsome Kukshi, who was famous. Kukshi gave birth to a brave son named Vikukshi. Vikukshi had an immensely energetic and powerful son named Bana. Bana's son was the mighty-armed and immensely illustrious Anaranya. When

[411] From the water. The implied identification is with Brahma, though Vishnu assumed the varaha (boar) incarnation.

[412] Marichi was one of the sons born through Brahma's mental powers.

[413] There are some inconsistencies with the genealogy given in 'Bala Kanda'.

the supremely virtuous and great king Anaranya ruled, there was no lack of rain and no famine. There were no thieves. Anaranya gave birth to the mighty-armed King Prithu. From Prithu was born the great king, Trishanku. The brave one spoke the truth and went to heaven in his own physical body. Trishanku's son was the immensely illustrious Dhundumara. Dhundumara gave birth to the immensely energetic Yuvanashva. Yuvanashva had a handsome son named Mandhata. The immensely energetic Susandhi was born from Mandhata. Susandhi had two sons—Dhruvasandhi and Prasenjit. The illustrious Bharata, the slayer of enemies, was born from Dhruvasandhi. Asita was born from the mighty-armed Bharata. Kings who were his enemies were also born—the Haihayas, the Talajanghas and the brave Shashabindus. Having set up counter-battle formations in an encounter, the king was exiled. He[414] became a devoted sage on a beautiful and excellent mountain. It has been heard that his two wives became pregnant. Bhargava Chyavana had resorted to the Himalayas. Kalindee[415] approached and worshipped that rishi. She desired a boon from the brahmana that a son might be born to her. The queen returned home and gave birth to a son. However, desiring to destroy the foetus, her co-wife gave her poison. Because he was born with poison, he came to be known as Sagara. On the day of the full moon and in the course of a sacrifice, it was King Sagara who dug up the ocean, thus terrifying the subjects through this force. We have heard that a son named Asamanja was born to Sagara. Because he was engaged in wicked deeds, his father spared his life, but exiled him. Asamanja had a valiant son named Amshuman. Dileepa was Amshuman's son and Dileepa's son was Bhageeratha. Bhageeratha's son was Kakutstha and the Kakutsthas are named after him. Kakutstha had a son named Raghu and the Raghavas are descended from him. Raghu's energetic son was Pravriddha. However, he is famous on earth as Purushadaka, Kalmashapada and Soudasa. Kalmashapada had a son who was famous as Shankhana. However, though he was

[414] Asita.

[415] One of Asita's wives.

valiant, he and his soldiers were destroyed. Shankhana's son was the brave and handsome Sudarshana. Sudarshana's son was Agnivarna and Agnivarna's son was Sheeghraga. Sheeghraga's son was Maru and Maru's son was Prashushruka. Prashushruka's son was the immensely radiant Ambareesha. Ambareesha's son was Nahusha, for whom, truth was his valour. Nahusha had a son named Nabhaga and he was supremely devoted to dharma. Nabhaga had two sons named Aja and Suvrata. Aja's son was King Dasharatha, who possessed dharma in his soul. O Rama! You are his eldest and famous heir. O king of the universe! Considering this, accept your own kingdom. In the entire lineage of the Ikshvakus, it is only the eldest who becomes the king, not a younger one when the elder is alive. The eldest is consecrated as the king. O one with dharma in your soul! This is the eternal practice in the lineage of the Raghavas. You should not forsake this now. Rule the earth with its great store of jewels and this extensive kingdom, as your immensely illustrious father did.'

Chapter 2(103)

Vasishtha, the royal priest, told Rama this. Then, he again spoke words that were full of dharma. 'O Raghava! O Kakutstha! When a man is born, he has three teachers—the preceptor, the father and the mother. O bull among men! The parents only give birth to the being. Since the preceptor gives wisdom, he is known as a true teacher. O scorcher of enemies! I was your father's preceptor and am yours too. Act in accordance with my words and do not violate the path of the virtuous. O son![416] The courtiers and classes have assembled. For their sake, follow dharma. Do not violate the path of the virtuous. Do not cross your mothers. They are aged and devoted to dharma. Act in accordance with their words. Do not violate the path of the virtuous. O Raghava! Bharata's words have entreated you. O one who possesses valour and the dharma

[416] The word used is tata.

of truth! Do not cross yourself.' The preceptor, who was seated, himself addressed him in these sweet words.

Raghava, bull among men, replied to Vasishtha. 'It is not very easy to perform good deeds towards the mother and the father so as to compensate for the good deeds that they always undertake towards a son. To the best of their capacities, they bathe him and give him clothing, they always speak to him in pleasant words and rear him. My father, King Dasharatha, gave birth to me. His instructions to me cannot be rendered false.' The extremely generous Bharata was seated near him. When Rama spoke in this way, he became extremely distressed and addressed the suta.[417] 'O charioteer! Quickly spread out some kusha grass on this ground. Until the noble one shows his favours, I will commit *praya*.[418] Until he returns, I will be like a brahmana who lies down before a cottage, without food, without light and without riches.'[419] Distressed in his mind, he then looked towards Rama and looked towards Sumantra. He himself began to spread out kusha grass on the ground there. At this, the immensely energetic Rama, supreme among rajarshis, said, 'O Bharata! O son![420] Why are you engaged in this act of praya? This is the single-minded objective for a brahmana. The rite of praya is not recommended for someone who has sprinkled his hair[421] with the objective of saving men. O tiger among men! Arise. Give up this terrible vow. O Raghava! Quickly go to Ayodhya, supreme among cities.' Bharata remained seated. He looked all around, at the inhabitants of the city and the countryside, and asked, 'Why aren't you saying anything?' The great-souled soldiers and the inhabitants of the city and the countryside said, 'O Kakutstha![422] We know that Raghava[423] has

[417] Sumantra.

[418] The practice in question is prayopavesa. While this does mean voluntary fasting to death, it is adopted by someone who has no worldly desires left.

[419] This doesn't mean the brahmana is poor. He has simply given everything away, including his wealth.

[420] The word used is tata.

[421] That is, has crowned himself as a king.

[422] Bharata.

[423] Rama.

said the right thing. This immensely fortunate one firmly adheres to the words given by his father. Therefore, we are incapable of asking him to return quickly.'[424] Hearing their words, Rama spoke these words. 'Listen to the words of the well-wishers who possess the insight of dharma. O Raghava! Listen to their words about what is proper and what is not proper. O mighty-armed one! Arise and do not touch the water.'[425] Arising, Bharata touched water and spoke these words. 'O courtiers, ministers and classes! Listen. I do not desire my father's kingdom or the words of my mother. Nor do I know Raghava, who is noble and supremely devoted to dharma. If it is mandatory that one must follow one's father's instructions and dwell in the forest for fourteen years, then I will reside there.' Rama, with dharma in his soul, was astounded at these true words spoken by his brother. He looked at the people from the city and the countryside and said, 'While he was alive, if my father undertook an act of sale or purchase,[426] then I or Bharata are incapable of transgressing it. As my representative, I do not wish to send someone to reside in the forest. A good deed is to adhere to what Kaikeyee urged my father to do. I know that Bharata is self-controlled and devoted to performing tasks for his seniors. He always looks at what is beneficial. The great-souled one is devoted to the truth. When I return again from the forest, with my brother, who possesses dharma in his conduct, I will become an excellent king on earth. Let me act in accordance with the words spoken by the king and Kaikeyee. Let us free our father, the king, from any act of falsehood.'

Chapter 2(104)

All the assembled maharshis were astounded on witnessing this meeting, which made the body hair stand up, between

[424] That is, before the period of exile is over.

[425] Water is touched before taking a vow.

[426] A reference to a contract of sale.

these two brothers who were unmatched in energy. Large numbers of invisible rishis, siddhas and supreme rishis praised the two brothers, the great-souled Kakutsthas. 'We love the conversation that we have heard between these two. They know about dharma and have dharma as their valour. A person who has two sons like these is blessed.' The large number of rishis desired to ensure that Dashagriva was quickly killed. They approached Bharata, tiger among kings, and addressed him in these words. 'O immensely wise one! You have been born in a noble lineage. You are great in conduct and immensely illustrious. If you have respect towards your father, accept Rama's words. Now that Dasharatha has gone to heaven, we always desire to see Rama freed from the debt he owes to his father and the debt to Kaikeyee.' Having said this, all the gandharvas, the maharshis and the rajarshis returned to their own respective destinations. Delighted at these auspicious words, Rama, auspicious in form, worshipped the rishis with a gladdened face.

Bharata's body was trembling. He joined his hands in salutation and in a choking voice, again addressed Raghava in these words. 'O Kakutstha! Look towards the dharma of kings and the dharma revered by our lineage. You should do what I and your mother desire. I am not interested in protecting and ruling this large kingdom alone. In that way, I will not be able to delight the inhabitants of the city and the countryside and others who are devoted. Our kin, warriors, friends and well-wishers are waiting for you, like farmers for rain. O immensely wise one! When you return, establish this kingdom. O Kakutstha! You are capable of ruling over the world.' Having said this, Bharata, who was pleasant in speech, fell down at his brother Rama's feet and earnestly beseeched him. Rama's eyes were like those of a lotus. He was dark. He raised his brother up on his lap and in a voice like that of a maddened swan, himself addressed him in these words. 'You have obtained the intelligence, that which was innate and that which has been taught. O son! You are extremely competent to protect the earth. In all acts, consult and use the intelligence of advisers, well-wishers and ministers. Perform great deeds. Radiance may desert the moon, snow may desert the Himalayas and the ocean may breach the shoreline, but I am incapable of crossing my father's pledge. O son! Your mother acted in this way because of greed and avarice and on your account. You should not harbour this in your mind. Behave towards her as a mother.'

Thus addressed by Kousalya's son, who was like the sun in his energy and as handsome as the moon during *pratipada*,[427] Bharata replied, 'O noble one! These sandals are decorated with gold. Wear them on your feet. It is from these that the entire world will obtain yoga and kshema.' Thus addressed, the tiger among men wore the sandals on his foot. The immensely energetic one then handed them over to the great-souled Bharata. The powerful Bharata, who knew about dharma, worshipped those ornamented sandals. He circumambulated Raghava and placed them on the head of an excellent elephant. The extender of the lineage of Raghava[428] was as firm in his own dharma as the Himalaya mountains. In due order, he honoured the people, the seniors, the ordinary subjects and his younger brothers, and took their leave. The voices of the mothers choked with tears and because of their grief, they were incapable of saying anything. Rama worshipped all his mothers and weeping, entered his own cottage.

Chapter 2(105)

Bharata placed those sandals on his head and with Shatrughna, cheerfully ascended the chariot. Vasishtha, Vamadeva, Jabali, firm in his vows and all the ministers who were revered because of their intelligence proceeded ahead. After circumambulating the great mountain of Chitrakuta, they advanced eastwards, along the beautiful river Mandakinee. Seeing thousands of many beautiful kinds of minerals, with his soldiers, Bharata proceeded along its

[427] Pratipada means the first quarter from the start, so this is the first quarter of shukla paksha.

[428] Rama.

flank.[429] Not very far from Chitrakuta, Bharata saw the hermitage where the sage Bharadvaja had made his abode. On reaching the hermitage, the extender of the lineage descended from his chariot and worshipped at the feet of the intelligent Bharadvaja. Delighted, Bharadvaja addressed Bharata in these words. 'O son![430] Have you been successful in your intention of meeting Rama?' Bharata was thus addressed by the intelligent Bharadvaja. Bharata, devoted to dharma, replied to Bharadvaja. The seniors and I beseeched him. However, firm in his valour and extremely happy, Raghava spoke the following words to Vasishtha. 'I will truthfully abide by my father's pledge. I have given word to my father about fourteen years.' When the immensely wise one, Raghava, who is eloquent in the use of words, addressed him in this way, Vasishtha, who is also eloquent in the use of words, replied in these great words. 'Cheerfully give these sandals that are ornamented with gold.[431] O immensely wise one! They will ensure yoga and kshema in Ayodhya.' Thus addressed by Vasishtha, Raghava stood up and faced the east. For the sake of the kingdom, he gave me the sandals embellished with gold. Having accepted the auspicious sandals, I took the permission of the extremely great-souled Rama and am leaving for Ayodhya.' Hearing the words of the great-souled Bharata, the sage Bharadvaja addressed him in words that were even more beneficial. 'O tiger among men! It is not surprising that you should be supreme among those who are good in conduct. Nobility is natural in you, just as water naturally proceeds downwards. With a son like you, who possesses dharma in his soul and is devoted to dharma, your mighty-armed father, Dasharatha, has become immortal.' Hearing the words of the great-souled rishi, he[432] joined his hands in salutation and touching his feet, took leave of him. Having repeatedly circumambulated Bharadvaja, with his ministers, the prosperous Bharata departed for Ayodhya.

[429] The flank of the mountain.

[430] The word used is tata.

[431] This makes it unclear whether the idea was originally Vasishtha's or Bharata's. Perhaps the idea was Bharata's, but Bharata gave the credit to Vasishtha.

[432] Bharata.

The extensive army of vehicles, carriages, horses and elephants followed Bharata on his return journey. They crossed the divine river Yamuna, garlanded with waves. All of them again saw the river Ganga, with auspicious waters. With his relatives, he crossed the river that was full of beautiful water. With his soldiers, he saw the beautiful region of Shringaverapura. From Shringaverapura, he saw Ayodhya. Tormented by grief, Bharata told the charioteer in a sorrowful voice, 'O charioteer! Behold. Ayodhya seems devastated and is not radiant. It seems to have no form and is miserable. It is distressed.'

Chapter 2(106)

The immensely illustrious Lord Bharata quickly entered Ayodhya astride a chariot that made a gentle and deep sound. Cats and owls roamed around. The men and elephants crouched down. The place seemed to be covered in darkness. It was indistinct, as if during the night. Rohini alone is the beloved wife, blazing in her radiance and prosperity.[433] It was as if the planet Rahu had arisen and was oppressing her. It was like a thin mountain stream with limited and agitated waters, the birds scorched by the summer and small and large fish and crocodiles destroyed. It was like a golden fire that rises up when oblations are offered into it, bereft of smoke, but with the flames extinguished after the oblations have been devoured. It was like an army devastated in a great battle, armour, chariots and standards shattered, elephants and horses suffering and the best of warriors dead. It was like an ocean that had risen up with foam and sound, but the water and the waves now rendered quiet and silent by a wave that has arisen. It was like a silent sacrificial altar when the time for offering oblations is over and the place has been cleared of all the sacrificial objects

[433] The nakshatras are the wives of the moon, but the moon loves Rohini more than the others.

and officiating priests. It was like the anxious wife of a bull, which is standing miserable in the middle of a pen and does not graze on new grass, because it has been abandoned by the bull. It was like a resplendent, blazing and excellent necklace made of coral and fresh pearls, now devoid of lustre because the collection of good gems had been taken away. It was like a star dislodged from the firmament because its store of merit had got exhausted, thus violently descending on the earth and losing its radiance. It was like a creeper from the forest, laden with flowers during the spring and with maddened bees hovering around it, now withered and consumed in a forest blaze. All the movement stopped on the roads. The shops and stores were closed. It was like the sky, completely covered with clouds and with the moon and the stars shrouded. It was like a dirty drinking house in the open ground, when the excellent liquor was exhausted, the best of vessels strewn around and all the drinkers having left. It was like a place with drinking water that was now devastated, the flat ground below strewn with empty and shattered vessels for drinking, the store of water having been exhausted. It was like bow that was once large and stretched, strung with a spirited bowstring, now lying down on the ground because it had been severed with arrows. It was like a horse that was violently urged by a rider in a battle, but turned out to be a weak and young female horse and thus had its decorations and harness flung away.[434] It was like the radiance of the sun, enveloped by dark monsoon clouds when the sun enters a dense cluster of clouds.

The handsome Bharata, Dasharatha's son, was astride his chariot. Borne by the best of chariots, he addressed the charioteer in these words. 'Earlier, the sounds of singing and the noise of musical instruments could be heard from Ayodhya. Why can't that deep music be heard today? The maddening fragrance of *varuni*,[435] the scent of garlands and the fragrance of incense and aloe are no longer wafting around everywhere. There used to be the excellent sound

[434] Killed by the enemy in the battle.

[435] Liquor.

of carriages, the gentle sound of horses neighing, the trumpeting of crazy elephants and the loud roar of chariots. Earlier, before Rama was exiled, such sounds were heard. The large roads in Ayodhya are no longer radiant with the young attired in beautiful garments and men straight in their strides.' Conversing thus in many ways, he entered his father's residence. Without that Indra among men, it was like a cave without a lion.

Chapter 2(107)

Firm in his vows, Bharata took his mothers to Ayodhya. Tormented by grief, he then addressed his seniors. 'I am now taking my leave of all of you. I will go to Nandigrama. Without Raghava, I will bear all the hardships there. The king has gone to heaven and my senior has resorted to the forest. For the sake of the kingdom, I will await Rama. The immensely illustrious one is the king.' Hearing the auspicious words of the great-souled Bharata, all the ministers and the priest Vasishtha said, 'O Bharata! The words that you have spoken are praiseworthy. These words show your affection for your brother and are deserving of you. You are always affectionate towards your relative and are established in love for your brother. O noble one! Which man will not approve of the path that you have resorted to?' He heard the agreeable and desired words of his ministers. He addressed the charioteer in these words. 'Yoke my chariot.' With a cheerful face, taking leave of all the mothers, the handsome one ascended the chariot with Shatrughna. Extremely happy, Shatrughna and Bharata quickly ascended the chariot and left, surrounded by the ministers and priests. The brahmanas, with the priest Vasishtha at the forefront, led the way. All of them headed east, in the direction where Nandigrama was. Though not asked, the army, full of elephants, horses and chariots, followed Bharata and so did all the residents of the city. Bharata, devoted to his brother and with dharma in his soul, was astride the chariot. With the sandals atop his head, he quickly went to Nandigrama.

Bharata quickly entered Nandigrama. Swiftly descending from his chariot, he addressed his seniors. 'My brother has himself given me this kingdom as a trust. These sandals, ornamented with gold, will bring yoga and kshema. I will rule it until Raghava returns. I will myself quickly put them back on Raghava's feet. I will see Rama's feet, with the sandals on them. When Raghava returns, I will thus give the burden back to him. Having given the kingdom back to my senior, I will serve him the way one should serve a senior. These excellent sandals are marks of trust and I will give them back to Raghava, with the kingdom of Ayodhya. I will thus be cleansed of my sins. Kakutstha will be crowned and the people will be delighted. My joy and the kingdom's fame will multiply fourfold.' The immensely illustrious Bharata lamented in this way. Though distressed, with his ministers, he ruled the kingdom from Nandigrama. The lord donned bark and had matted hair. He was in the garb of a hermit. With his soldiers, the brave Bharata resided in Nandigrama. Bharata, devoted to his brother, desired Rama's return. Devoted to his pledge, he carried out his brother's words. He crowned those sandals in Nandigrama. Bharata ruled the kingdom in the name of the sandals.

Chapter 2(108)

When Bharata left, Rama continued to reside in the hermitage. He noticed that the ascetics were anxious and disturbed. However, earlier, the ascetics who dwelt in hermitages in Chitrakuta, under Rama's protection, were not seen to display any signs of anxiety. Rama could discern their fear from their eyes and frowns. They conversed with each other, secretly and softly. Noticing their anxiety, Rama was himself worried. He joined his hands in salutation and spoke to the rishi who was the leader of the group. 'O illustrious one! I had not noticed this kind of behaviour earlier. I see an agitation, as if something is disturbing the ascetics. Has my younger brother committed an act causing offence? Has Lakshmana looked at the rishis in a way that is not deserving of his own self? Has Sita not followed the conduct that is deserving of women? She serves me well. Has she not served you?' The aged rishi was aged in austerities and he also suffered from old age. Trembling, he replied to Rama, who was compassionate towards all beings. 'O son![436] Vaidehi is benevolent in her spirit and in her conduct, always does what is beneficial, especially for ascetics. It is because of you that this hardship has come upon the ascetics. They anxiously and secretly converse about the depredations of the rakshasas. Ravana has a younger brother and he is a rakshasa named Khara. He oppresses all the ascetics who have made their residences in Janasthana.[437] He is insolent and desires victory. He is cruel and devours human flesh. O son! He is proud and wicked and cannot tolerate you. O son! Ever since you came to this hermitage, the rakhsasas have acted against the ascetics. They exhibit many terrible, gruesome and cruel forms. Some forms are so ugly that those forms are unpleasant to see. They fling filth and impure objects on the ascetics. There are ignoble ones who remain in front and quickly kill others.[438] Unseen, they hide themselves in those hermitages. They are evil in intelligence and find delight in destroying the ascetics there. When the time for rendering oblations presents itself, they throw away the sacrificial vessels and ladles, sprinkle water on the fire and break the pots. Since the hermitage has been infiltrated by those evil-souled ones, the rishis have decided to leave and have urged me to go to some other region today. O Rama! Before the wicked ones cause some physical harm to the ascetics and display such inclinations, they wish to abandon this hermitage. Not far from this forest, there is an ancient and colourful hermitage with an abundance of roots and fruits. With my companions, I will again find a refuge there. O son! Before Khara does something against you too, if your intelligence is so inclined, go with us to that place. O Raghava! You are with your wife and you will always be anxious. Though you are capable, a

[436] The word used is tata.

[437] Janasthana is another name for the Dandakaranya region. Sometimes, Janasthana is also described as the capital of Dandakaranya.

[438] That is, kill other ascetics.

residence here now is fraught with hardship.' When he had spoken in this way, since the ascetics were so very anxious, Prince Rama was unable to restrain them with his reply. Having explained his reasons, the leader of the group greeted Raghava and sought his leave. With his group, he then left the hermitage. Rama understood why the large number of rishis wanted to leave the region and he greeted the rishi who was the leader of the group and accompanied them for a while. They were happy that their reasons had been understood. He then took their leave and returned to his own sacred residence.

Chapter 2(109)

Raghava thought about the departure of the ascetics and could think of many reasons why it was no longer desirable to live in that place. 'This is where Bharata met me, with the mothers and the citizens. That memory remains with me and I always sorrow over it. The great-souled one's army set up camp here and the dung from the horses and the elephants has caused a great deal of devastation here. Therefore, we should go somewhere else.' This is what Raghava thought and left, with Vaidehi and Lakshmana.

He reached the hermitage of the immensely illustrious Atri and worshipped him. The illustrious one welcomed him like a son. He personally instructed that all the arrangements should be made for treating the guests well. He honoured Soumitri and the immensely fortunate Sita. He summoned his aged wife and welcomed her too. The one who knew about dharma and was engaged in the welfare of all beings spoke to her. Anasuya was an immensely fortunate ascetic lady who followed dharma. The excellent rishi told her, 'Welcome Vaidehi.' He told Rama about the ascetic lady who was devoted to dharma. 'The world incessantly suffered from ten years of drought and she is the one who created roots and fruits and made the Jahnavee flow then. She performed fierce austerities and was ornamented with all the rituals. She performed great austerities for ten thousand years. O son![439] Through her vows, Anasuya removed all the impediments. O unblemished one! To accomplish the task of the gods, she converted ten nights into one night.[440] She is like a mother to you. This aged and illustrious one is never angry and all creatures bow down before her. Let Vaidehi approach her. When the rishi said this, Raghava agreed. He spoke these excellent words to Sita, who knew about dharma. 'O princess! You have heard what the sage has said. For the sake of your own welfare, quickly approach the ascetic lady. Because of her deeds, Anasuya has obtained fame in the world. You should swiftly approach the ascetic lady.'

Raghava always sought Sita's welfare. On hearing this, Maithilee circumambulated Atri's wife, who knew about dharma. She was aged and weak and her body was marked with wrinkles. Because of old age, her hair had turned grey. Her limbs always trembled, like a plantain tree in the wind. Sita attentively worshipped the immensely fortunate Anasuya, who was devoted to her husband, and told her her own name. Vaidehi worshipped the unblemished ascetic lady. Cupping her hands in salutation, she cheerfully asked about her welfare. The one who followed dharma saw the immensely fortunate Sita. Comforting her, she happily said, 'It is good fortune that you look towards dharma. O Sita! O beautiful one! It is good fortune that you have given up your relatives, honours and prosperity and have followed Rama in his exile to the forest. For a woman who loves her husband, regardless of whether he resides in a city or a forest and irrespective of whether he is wicked and vile, the great worlds result. For a noble woman, the husband is the supreme divinity, even if he is evil in conduct, addicted to desire and bereft of riches. O Vaidehi! When I think about it, I do not see a relative who is superior to an appropriate husband. He is like the undecaying result of austerities. Wicked

[439] The word used is tata.

[440] The story is that the sage Mandavya cursed Shandeeli, a lady sage and a friend of Anasuya's that she would become a widow within ten nights. Anasuya responded with her own curse that there would be no dawn. To remedy the situation, and thus accomplish the task of the gods, Anasuya subsequently transformed ten nights into one night and Shandeeli did not become a widow.

women who make their hearts drive their desire and those who lord it over their husbands do not understand what is a good quality and what is a sin. O Maithilee! Indeed, women who act in this undesirable way of controlling[441] obtain ill fame and are dislodged from dharma. However, women like you, who possess the quality, regardless of prosperity or adversity in this world, roam around in heaven, like the performers of auspicious deeds.'

Chapter 2(110)

Vaidehi was thus addressed by Anasuya, who was without jealousy.[442] She worshipped her in gentle words and said, 'It is not extraordinary that a noble one like you should address me in this way. I also know that the husband is the preceptor for a woman. O noble one! Even if my husband is without a means of subsistence, I should show no hesitation in obeying him. What more can one say for someone who is praised for his qualities, compassion, conquest of the senses, firmness in devotion and for one who has dharma in his soul, following his mother and loved by his father? Whatever conduct the immensely strong Rama exhibits towards Kousalya is identical to the conduct he exhibits towards all the other women of the king. He knows about dharma and is devoid of false pride. Even if the affectionate king has looked towards a woman with a favourable glance, the brave one treats her like a mother. When I left for the desolate forest that conveys fear, my mother-in-law told me something great and it is firmly lodged in my heart. I also bear the words my mother used to instruct me in earlier times, when my hand was given in marriage, with the fire as a witness. "O one who follows dharma! Your words will render everything new. Serving a husband represents austerities for a woman. Nothing else has been recommended. Having

[441] Their husbands.

[442] The name Anasuya means someone without jealousy (*asuya*).

served her husband, Savitree obtained greatness in heaven.[443] If you follow that kind of conduct of serving your husband, you will obtain heaven. The goddess Rohini is supreme among all the women in the sky and the moon is not seen without her, not even for an instant. Such supreme women are firm in their devotion to their husbands. Through their own auspicious deeds, they have obtained greatness in the world of the gods."' Hearing Sita's words, Anasuya was delighted. She happily inhaled the fragrance of Maithilee's head and said, 'O Sita! O one who is pure in vows! Because I have tormented myself through many rituals, great austerities exist in me. Using that strength, I wish to confer a boon on you. O Maithilee! Your words are appropriate and right and I am pleased. Tell me. What can I do for you?' Sita told the one who possessed the store of austerities, 'I have already obtained success.'[444]

Thus addressed, the one who knew about dharma became happier still. She said, 'O Sita! I will do something that will make you successful and happy. O Vaidehi! Here are some divine and excellent garlands, garments, ornaments, unguents for the limbs and extremely expensive pastes. O Sita! I am giving these to you so that your body can be ornamented. You deserve them. Even when they have been used, they will remain fresh. O Janaka's daughter! With these pastes and unguents smeared on your limbs, you will be beautiful with your husband, like Shri with the undecaying Vishnu.' Maithilee accepted the garments, pastes, unguents, ornaments and garlands that had been given as a supreme gift of love. Having accepted those gifts of love, the illustrious Sita joined her hands in salutation and patiently sat down near the store of austerities.

When Sita was seated, Anasuya, firm in her vows, started to question her, conversing about the pleasant things that had once happened. 'O Sita! I have heard the story that you were obtained by the illustrious Raghava in an act of svayamvara. O Maithilee! I wish to hear that account in detail. You should tell me everything, exactly as you felt it.' Thus addressed, Sita said, 'Listen to the

[443] Savitree's husband, Satyavan, died. Savitree followed the dead body to Yama's abode and obtained the boon of bringing her husband back to life.

[444] She didn't want a boon.

account.' She told the one who followed dharma the story. 'The brave lord of Mithila was Janaka and he followed dharma. Devoted to the dharma of kshatriyas, he ruled over the earth properly. With a plough in his hand, he was tilling a plot of land. It is said that I split the earth and arose as the king's daughter. King Janaka was engaged in scattering seeds from his fist and was astounded to see me, all my limbs covered in dust. Affectionately, he placed me on his own lap. Since then, lovingly, he has referred to me as his daughter. It is said that an invisible human voice was heard from heaven. "O king! Following dharma, she will be your daughter." My father, the lord of Mithila with dharma in his soul, was delighted at this. After having obtained me, the lord of men obtained great prosperity. The performer of auspicious deeds gave me to the eldest queen, like something obtained from a sacrifice. She gently reared me, with maternal affection. My father saw that I had attained the age when I should be united with a husband. He was overcome by thoughts, like one without riches when his wealth has been destroyed. Even if a daughter's father is Shakra's equal on earth, in this world, he is reviled by those who are his equal and inferior.[445] The king saw that such condemnation was not far away. He was immersed in an ocean of thoughts, like a person without a boat who is unable to cross over to the other shore. He knew that I was not born from a womb and was unable to find an answer to his thoughts. Where was an equal or similar king who would be my husband? After thinking incessantly about this, he arrived at a determination. The intelligent one decided that he would marry his daughter off through a svayamvara. In a great sacrifice, the great-souled Varuna was delighted with him and had given him a supreme bow and two quivers with an inexhaustible supply of arrows.[446] It was so heavy that even if men made efforts, they were unable to move it. Even in their dreams, the lords of men were unable to bend it. My father, truthful in speech, invited the kings first. When they assembled, he told the Indras among men that the bow would have to be raised.

[445] If the daughter is not married.

[446] In some versions, this bow and the quivers were received from Shiva.

"If a man raises this bow and strings it, I will bestow my daughter on him as a wife. There is no doubt about this." That excellent bow was as heavy as a mountain. The kings were incapable of raising it. They worshipped it and went away. After a long period of time, the immensely radiant Raghava came to witness a sacrifice, together with Vishvamitra. Rama, for whom truth is his valour, was with his brother Lakshmana. Vishvamitra, with dharma in his soul, was honoured exceedingly well by my father and told my father, "These two Raghavas, Rama and Lakshmana, are the sons of Dasharatha and they wish to see the bow." When the brahmana said this, the bow was brought there. In a mere instant, the valiant one bent the bow. The valiant one then quickly strung the bow and stretched it. Because of the force of the stretching, the bow snapped in the middle into two parts. The resultant sound was terrible, as if a bolt of thunder had descended. My father, fixed to the truth, fetched an excellent vessel of water and immediately bestowed me on Rama, with that vessel. Though bestowed, Raghava did not accept me then, not until the views of his father, the lord who was the king of Ayodhya, had been ascertained. My father, the aged King Dasharatha was invited and my father bestowed me on Rama, who knows about his atman. My younger sister is the virtuous Urmila, lovely to behold. My father himself bestowed her on Lakshmana as a wife. In this way, I was bestowed on Rama in that svayamvara. Following dharma, I am devoted to my husband. He is supreme among valiant ones.'

Chapter 2(111)

Anasuya, who knew about dharma, heard this great account. She inhaled the fragrance of Maithilee's head and embraced her in her arms. 'You have recounted it in distinct, colourful and sweet syllables and sentences. I have heard everything about the story of the svayamvara. O one who is pleasant in speech! I am delighted and happy to hear about this account. The sun has set and the auspicious and beautiful night has arrived. The chirping of birds can be heard. During the day, they travelled long distances in search of food. Now that it is evening, they are back in their nests, desiring to sleep. The sages are wet from their ablutions, having eaten fruits. They are returning together, their garments of bark wet with water. Following the prescribed ordinances, the rishis are offering oblations into the agnihotra fire. Raised by the wind, the smoke can be seen, red like a pigeon's neck. In every direction, though they possess limited leaves, the trees seem dense. In this region, where the senses are restrained, the directions are never visible. The animals that roam around in the night are travelling everywhere. The deer of the hermitage are sleeping around the sacrificial altar. O Sita! The night has arrived, adorned with nakshatras. The moon can be seen to have arisen in the sky, surrounded by moonlight. I grant you permission. Go and follow Rama now. I am satisfied with the pleasant conversation with you. O Maithilee! In front of me, adorn yourself with these ornaments. O child! I will be delighted when you become beautiful with these divine ornaments.' Sita adorned herself with those ornaments and was like a daughter of the gods. She bowed her head down and prostrated herself and left to meet Rama.

The supreme among eloquent ones saw the ornamented Sita. Raghava rejoiced at what the lady ascetic had given as a gift of affection. Sita Maithilee showed Rama everything that was given as a gift of affection by the lady ascetic—the garments, the ornaments and the garlands. Rama and maharatha Lakshmana were delighted on seeing that Maithilee had been honoured in this excellent way, extremely difficult for a human to obtain. The descendant of the Raghu lineage, with a face like the moon, was delighted and spent the auspicious night there, worshipped by the ascetics and the siddhas.

When the night was over, the two tigers among men asked the ascetics, who had offered oblations into the fire and dwelt in the forest. The ascetics who resided in the forest and followed dharma told them about parts of the forest that teemed with rakshasas. 'This is the path that the maharshis follow to fetch fruits from the forest. O Raghava! It is proper that you should follow this. There is this other one through this impenetrable forest.'[447] The scorcher of enemies joined his hands in salutation before the ascetics, and the brahmanas pronounced words of benediction over them. With Lakshmana and his wife, Raghava entered the forest, like the sun entering a mass of clouds.

This ends Ayodhya Kanda.

[447] Though not stated very clearly, there seems to have been a choice of two paths through Dandakaranya.

PENGUIN BOOKS

THE VALMIKI RAMAYANA VOLUME 2

Bibek Debroy is a renowned economist, scholar and translator. He has worked in universities, research institutes, industry and for the government. He has widely published books, papers and articles on economics. As a translator, he is best known for his magnificent rendition of the Mahabharata in ten volumes, and additionally the *Harivamsha*, published to wide acclaim by Penguin Classics. He is also the author of *Sarama and Her Children*, which splices his interest in Hinduism with his love for dogs.

PRAISE FOR *THE MAHABHARATA*

'The modernization of language is visible, it's easier on the mind, through expressions that are somewhat familiar. The detailing of the story is intact, the varying tempo maintained, with no deviations from the original. The short introduction reflects a brilliant mind. For those who passionately love the Mahabharata and want to explore it to its depths, Debroy's translation offers great promise . . .'—*Hindustan Times*

'[Debroy] has really carved out a niche for himself in crafting and presenting a translation of the Mahabharata . . . The book takes us on a great journey with admirable ease'—*Indian Express*

'The first thing that appeals to one is the simplicity with which Debroy has been able to express himself and infuse the right kind of meanings . . . Considering that Sanskrit is not the simplest of languages to translate a text from, Debroy exhibits his deep understanding and appreciation of the medium'—*The Hindu*

'Debroy's lucid and nuanced retelling of the original makes the masterpiece even more enjoyably accessible'—*Open*

'The quality of translation is excellent. The lucid language makes it a pleasure to read the various stories, digressions and parables'—*Tribune*

'Extremely well-organized, and has a substantial and helpful Introduction, plot summaries and notes. The volume is a beautiful example of a well thought-out layout which makes for much easier reading'—*Book Review*

'The dispassionate vision [Debroy] brings to this endeavour will surely earn him merit in the three worlds'—*Mail Today*

'Debroy's is not the only English translation available in the market, but where he scores and others fail is that his is the closest rendering of the original text in modern English without unduly complicating the readers' understanding of the epic'—*Business Standard*

'The brilliance of Ved Vyasa comes through, ably translated by Bibek Debroy'—*Hindustan Times*

THE VALMIKI RAMAYANA 2

Translated by Bibek Debroy

PENGUIN BOOKS
An imprint of Penguin Random House

PENGUIN BOOKS

USA | Canada | UK | Ireland | Australia
New Zealand | India | South Africa | China

Penguin Books is part of the Penguin Random House group of companies
whose addresses can be found at global.penguinrandomhouse.com

Published by Penguin Random House India Pvt. Ltd
7th Floor, Infinity Tower C, DLF Cyber City,
Gurgaon 122 002, Haryana, India

First published in Penguin Books by Penguin Random House India 2017

10 9 8 7 6 5 4

ISBN 9780143428053

Typeset in Sabon by Manipal Digital Systems, Manipal
Printed at Replika Press Pvt. Ltd, India

www.penguin.co.in

For Professor Shailendra Raj Mehta

Contents

Acknowledgements

This journey, with Penguin, started more than a decade ago. It is a journey of translating Sanskrit texts into English, in unabridged form. It commenced with the Bhagavad Gita in 2006, followed by the Mahabharata (2010 to 2014) and the Harivamsha (2016). It continues with the Valmiki Ramayana and will be followed by the Puranas. To the best of my knowledge, the great translator, Manmatha Nath Dutt (1855–1912), is the only other person who has accomplished the 'double' of unabridged translations of both the Valmiki Ramayana and the Mahabharata in English. In this journey with Penguin, special thanks to Meru Gokhale, Ambar Sahil Chatterjee and Paloma Dutta. All three have made this journey easier to traverse.

My wife, Suparna Banerjee (Debroy), has not only been *patni*, she has been *grihini* and *sahadharmini* too. Had she not provided an enabling and conducive environment, juggling professional commitments and carving out the time required for translating would have been impossible. यः तया सह स स्वर्गो निरयो यस्त्वया विना (2.27.16).

This translation is based on the Critical Edition brought out (between 1951 and 1975) by the Oriental Institute, now part of Maharaja Sayajirao University, Baroda. When I started work on translating the Mahabharata in 2009, there was a thought, however hazy, of attempting the Valmiki Ramayana too. Therefore, one had to acquire the seven published volumes of the Critical Edition. Those who have tried this acquisition will testify this is no mean task. Multiple channels and multiple efforts failed. The Oriental Institute is not known for its marketing and distribution successes.

The context changed in 2015, because I joined the government. By then, I had still not been able to get copies of the Critical Edition. What with joining the government, which made finding time difficult, and an inability to get the text, I remarked to my wife that destiny willed otherwise. A few months later, on a flight, I found myself seated next to Shailendra Mehta, economist, scholar, friend, and currently president, director and distinguished professor at MICA, Ahmedabad. 'What next, after the Mahabharata?' asked Shailendra and I described my frustration. A few weeks down the line, Shailendra Mehta walked into my office, lugging a trolley bag, with all seven volumes in them. 'All yours,' he said. What destiny willed was clear enough. The dedication of this three volume set to Shailendra is a paltry attempt to say thank you.

'What next, after the Valmiki Ramayana?' Life moves on to the Puranas, beginning with the Bhagavata Purana. At one point, the Mahabharata translation seemed like a mammoth task, stretching to infinity. With the major Puranas collectively amounting to four times the size of the Mahabharata, they are more monumental than the mammoth. But as always, if it so wills, destiny finds a way.

Introduction

The Ramayana and the Mahabharata are known as *itihasas*. The word itihasa means 'it was indeed like that'. Therefore, the word is best rendered as legend or history, and not as myth. This does not mean everything occurred exactly as described. In a process of telling and retelling and oral transmission, embellishments are inevitable. However, the use of the word itihasa suggests a core element of truth. There were two great dynasties—*surya vamsha* and *chandra vamsha*.[1] The first proper king of the surya vamsha was Ikshvaku and the Ramayana is a chronicle of the solar dynasty, or at least a part of its history. Similarly, the first king of the chandra vamsha was Ila and the Mahabharata is a chronicle of the lunar dynasty. The Puranas also describe the histories of the solar and lunar dynasties. Though there are some inconsistencies across genealogies given in different Puranas, the surya vamsha timeline has three broad segments: (1) from Ikshvaku to Rama; (2) from Kusha to Brihadbala; and (3) from Brihadbala to Sumitra. In that stretch from Ikshvaku to Rama, there were famous kings like Bharata (not to be confused with Rama's brother), Kakutstha, Prithu, Yuvanashva, Mandhata, Trishanku, Harishchandra, Sagara, Dilipa, Bhagiratha, Ambarisha, Raghu, Aja and Dasharatha. These ancestors explain why Rama is referred to as Kakutstha, Raghava or Dasharathi.

Rama had two sons—Lava and Kusha. Ikshvaku and his descendants ruled over the kingdom of Kosala, part of today's Uttar Pradesh. The Kosala kingdom lasted for a long time, with

[1] The solar and the lunar dynasty, respectively.

the capital sometimes in Ayodhya and sometimes in Shravasti. When Rama ruled, the capital was in Ayodhya. After Rama, Lava ruled over south Kosala and Kusha ruled over north Kosala. Lava's capital was in Shravasti, while Kusha's capital was in Kushavati. We don't know what happened to Lava thereafter, though he is believed to have established Lavapuri, today's Lahore. The second segment of the surya vamsha timeline, from Kusha to Brihadbala, doesn't have any famous kings. Brihadbala was the last Kosala king. In the Kurukshetra War, he fought on the side of the Kouravas and was killed by Abhimanyu. The third segment of the surya vamsha timeline, from Brihadbala to Sumitra, seems contrived and concocted. Sumitra is described as the last king of the Ikshvaku lineage, defeated by Mahapadma Nanda in 362 BCE. Sumitra wasn't killed. He fled to Rohtas, in today's Bihar.

The Ramayana isn't about these subsequent segments of the timeline. Though there are references to other kings from that Ikshvaku to Rama stretch, it isn't about all of that segment either. Its focus is on Rama. It is difficult to date the poet Kalidasa. It could be anytime from the first century CE to the fifth century CE. Kalidasa wrote a *mahakavya*[2] known as *Raghuvamsha*. As the name of this mahakavya suggests, it is about Raghu's lineage, from Dilipa to Agnivarna, and includes Rama. But it isn't exclusively about Rama. Ramayana is almost exclusively about Rama. That's the reason it is known as रामायण = राम + अयण. अयन means travel or progress. Thus, Ramayana means Rama's progress. There is a minor catch though. अयन means travel or progress and अयण is a meaningless word. The word used in Ramayana is अयण, not अयन. This transformation occurs because of a rule of Sanskrit grammar known as internal *sandhi*. That is the reason रामायन becomes रामायण.

Who is Rama? The word राम means someone who is lovely, charming and delightful. There are Jain and Buddhist versions (*Dasharatha Jataka*) of the Rama account and they differ in significant details from the Ramayana story. For instance, in Jain accounts, Ravana is killed by Lakshmana. In *Dasharatha Jataka*,

[2] Epic.

Sita is Rama's sister. In Ramayana and Purana accounts, Rama is Vishnu's seventh *avatara*.[3] Usually, ten avataras are named for Vishnu, though sometimes, a larger number is also given. When the figure is ten, the avataras are *matsya*,[4] *kurma*,[5] *varaha*,[6] *narasimha*,[7] *vamana*,[8] Parashurama, Rama, Krishna, Buddha and Kalki (Kalki is yet to come). In the cycle of creation and destruction, *yugas*[9] follow each other and one progressively goes down *krita yuga* (alternatively *satya yuga*), *treta yuga*, *dvapara yuga* and *kali yuga*, before the cycle starts again. In the list of ten avataras, matysa, kurma, varaha and narasimha are from the present krita yuga; Vamana, Parashurama and Rama are from the present treta yuga; Krishna is from dvapara yuga; and Buddha and Kalki are from kali yuga. Rama was towards the end of treta yuga. (In the 'Uttara Kanda', dvapara yuga has started.) Just as Krishna's departure marked the transition from dvapara yuga to kali yuga, Rama's departure marked the transition from treta yuga to dvapara yuga.

When did these events occur? It is impossible to answer this question satisfactorily, despite continuous efforts being made to find an answer. At one level, it is an irrelevant question too. There is a difference between an incident happening and it being recorded. In that day and age, recording meant composition and oral transmission, with embellishments added. There was noise associated with transmission and distribution. It is impossible to unbundle the various layers in the text, composed at different points in time. Valmiki is described as Rama's contemporary, just as Vedavyasa was a contemporary of the Kouravas and the Pandavas. But that doesn't mean today's Valmiki Ramayana text is exactly what Valmiki composed, or that today's Mahabharata text

[3] Incarnation, or descent.
[4] Fish.
[5] Turtle.
[6] Boar.
[7] Half-man, half-lion.
[8] Dwarf.
[9] Eras.

is exactly what Krishna Dvaipayana Vedavyasa composed. Therein lies the problem with several approaches to dating.

The first and favoured method of dating is undoubtedly the astronomical one, based on positions of *nakshatras* and *grahas*,[10] or using information about events like eclipses. However, because layers of the text were composed at different points in time, compounded by precession of the equinoxes, this leads to widely divergent dates for an event like Rama's birth, ranging from 7323 BCE to 1331 BCE. Second, one can work with genealogies, notwithstanding problems of inconsistencies across them. One will then obtain a range of something like 2350 BCE to 1500 BCE. Third, one can work with linguistics and the evolution of language, comparing that of the Ramayana to other texts. Fourth, one can work with the archaeological evidence, such as the pottery discovered in sites known to be associated with the Ramayana. Even then, there will be a wide range of dates, from something like 2600 BCE to 1100 BCE. Fifth, one can consider geography, geology, changes in the course of rivers. Finally, there are traditional views about the length of a *manvantara*[11] or yuga. Given the present state of knowledge, it is impossible to impart precision to any dating of the incidents in the Ramayana. Scholars have grappled with the problem in the past and will continue to do so in the future. This may be an important question. But from the point of view of the present translation, it is an irrelevant one.

The present translation is about the Ramayana text. But what is the Ramayana text? After a famous essay written by A.K. Ramanujan in 1987 (published in 1991), people often mention 300 Ramayanas. It is impossible to fix the number, 300 or otherwise, since it is not possible to count satisfactorily—or even define—what is a new rendering of the Ramayana story, as opposed to a simple retelling, with or without reinterpretation. Contemporary versions, not always in written form, are continuously being rendered. There are versions of the Ramayana story in East Asia (China, Japan),

[10] Constellations/stars and planets.

[11] Lifespan of a Manu.

South-East Asia (many countries like Thailand, Indonesia and Malaysia), South Asia (Nepal, Sri Lanka) and West Asia (Iran). As mentioned earlier, there are Buddhist and Jain versions. Every state and every language in India seems to have some version of the Rama story. Our impressions about the Rama story are often based on such regional versions, such as, the sixteenth-century *Ramcharitmanas* by Goswami Tulsidas. (Many of these were written between the twelfth and seventeenth centuries CE.) Those depictions can, and will, vary with what is in this translation. This translation is about the Sanskrit Ramayana. But even there, more than one text of the Sanskrit Ramayana exists—Valmiki Ramayana, Yoga Vasishtha Ramayana, Ananda Ramayana and Adbhuta Ramayana. In addition, there are versions of the Ramayana story in the Mahabharata and in the Puranas. With the exception of the Ramayana story in the Mahabharata, the Valmiki Ramayana is clearly the oldest among these. This is a translation of the Valmiki Ramayana and yes, there are differences between depictions in the Valmiki Ramayana and other Sanskrit renderings of the Rama story.

If one cannot date the incidents of the Ramayana, can one at least conclusively date when the Valmiki Ramayana was written? Because of the many layers and subsequent interpolations, there is no satisfactory resolution to this problem either. The Valmiki Ramayana has around 24,000 *shloka*s, a shloka being a verse. The Mahabharata is believed to have 100,000 shlokas, so the Valmiki Ramayana is about one-fourth the size of the Mahabharata. These 24,000 shlokas are distributed across seven *kanda*s—'Bala Kanda' (Book about Youth), 'Ayodhya Kanda' (Book about Ayodhya), 'Aranya Kanda' (Book of the Forest), Kishkindha Kanda (Book about Kishkindha), 'Sundara Kanda' (Book of Beauty), 'Yuddha Kanda' (Book about the War) and 'Uttara Kanda' (Book about the Sequel). Kanda refers to a major section or segment and is sometimes translated into English as Canto. 'Canto' sounds archaic, 'Book' is so much better. This does not mean the kanda-wise classification always existed. For all one knows, initially, there were simply chapters. In this text itself, there is a reference to the Valmiki Ramayana possessing 500 *sarga*s. The

word sarga also means Book, but given the number 500, is more like a chapter. (For the record, the text has more than 600 chapters.) Most scholars agree 'Uttara Kanda' was written much later. If one reads the 'Uttara Kanda', that belief is instantly endorsed. The 'Uttara Kanda' doesn't belong. This isn't only because of the content, which is invariably mentioned. It is also because of the texture of the text, the quality of the poetry. It is vastly inferior. To a lesser extent, one can also advance similar arguments for the 'Bala Kanda'. Therefore, the earlier portions were probably composed around 500 BCE. The later sections, like the 'Uttara Kanda', and parts of the 'Bala Kanda', were probably composed around 500 CE. It isn't the case that all later sections are in 'Uttara Kanda'.

There is a mix of earlier and later sections across all kandas. The word kanda also means trunk or branch of a tree. The Mahabharata is also classified into such major sections or Books. However, in the Mahabharata, these major sections are known as *parva*s. The word parva also means branch. However, parva suggests a smaller branch, one that is more flexible. Kanda suggests one that is more solid, less flexible. There may have been slight variations in shlokas across different versions of the Sanskrit Mahabharata, but fundamentally the Sanskrit Mahabharata is a single text. The original text expanded, like a holdall, to include everything. Those different versions have been 'unified' in a Critical Edition published by the Bhandarkar Oriental Research Institute, Poona (Pune). In the case of the Valmiki Ramayana, with its kanda-kind of classification, the evolution seems to have been different. If someone was unhappy with what Valmiki had depicted, he simply composed another Ramayana. In Sanskrit, mention has already been made of the Yoga Vasishtha Ramayana, Ananda Ramayana and Adbhuta Ramayana. This continued to happen with vernacular versions.

This translation is of the Valmiki Ramayana. It is necessary to stress this point. Both the Ramayana and the Mahabharata are so popular that one is familiar with people, stories and incidents. That doesn't necessarily mean those people, stories and incidents occur in the Valmiki Ramayana in the way we are familiar with them. Just as the Bhandarkar Oriental Research Institute produced a Critical

Edition of the Mahabharata, between 1951 and 1975, the Oriental Institute, Baroda, produced a Critical Edition of the Valmiki Ramayana. This translation is based on that Critical Edition, published sequentially between 1958 and 1975. Producing a Critical Edition meant sifting through a large number of manuscripts of the Valmiki Ramayana. The editors had around 2000 manuscripts to work with. Not all of these were equally reliable. Therefore, in practice, they worked with fifty to hundred manuscripts, the specific number depending on the kanda in question. It is not that there were significant differences across the manuscripts and broadly, there was a Southern Recension (version) and a Northern one, the latter sub-divided into a North-Western and a North-Eastern one. The earliest of these written manuscripts dates to the eleventh century CE. In passing, the language may have been Sanskrit, but the script wasn't always Devanagari. There were scripts like Sharada, Mewari, Maithili, Bengali, Telugu, Kannada, Nandinagari, Grantha and Malayalam. Since this translation is based on the Baroda Critical Edition, it is necessary to make another obvious point. Even within the Sanskrit Valmiki Ramayana, not everything we are familiar with is included in the Critical text. For instance, the configuration of nakshatras and planets at the time of Rama's birth is not part of the Critical text. Nor is the bulk of one of the most beautiful sections of the Valmiki Ramayana, Mandodari's lamentation. Those are shlokas that have been excised. That's also the case with a shloka that's often quoted as an illustration of Lakshmana's conduct. नाहं जानामि केयूरं नाहं जानामि कुण्डलं। नूपुरं तु अभिजानामि नित्यं पादाभिवन्दनात॥ This is a statement by Lakshmana to the effect that he cannot recognize the ornament on Sita's head or her earrings. Since he has always served at her feet, he can only recognize her anklets. This too has been excised. There are instances where such excision has led to a break in continuity and inconsistency and we have pointed them out in the footnotes.

There are two numbers associated with every chapter. The first number refers to the kanda, while the second number, within brackets, refers to the number of the chapter (sarga) within that kanda. Thus, Chapter 1(33) will mean the thirty-third chapter in

'Bala Kanda'. The table below shows the number of chapters and shlokas we have in the Critical Edition. The Critical text has 606 chapters, 106 more than the 500 sargas mentioned in the text itself. And there are 18,670 shlokas. If one considers chapters and shlokas from non-Critical versions, irrespective of which version it is, there are almost 650 chapters and just over 24,000 shlokas. Compared to such non-Critical versions, very few chapters have been excised from 'Bala', 'Ayodhya', 'Aranya', 'Kishkindha' or 'Sundara' kandas. The excision is primarily from 'Yuddha' and 'Uttara' kandas. The excision of shlokas is uniformly spread throughout the kandas, though most excision, relatively speaking, is from the 'Ayodhya', 'Yuddha' and 'Uttara' kandas.

Name of kanda	*Number of chapters*	*Number of shlokas*
Bala Kanda	76	1941
Ayodhya Kanda	111	3160
Aranya Kanda	71	2060
Kishkindha Kanda	66	1898
Sundara Kanda	66	2487
Yuddha Kanda	116	4435
Uttara Kanda	100	2689
Total	606	18,670

Valmiki is the first poet, *adi kavi*. By the time of classical Sanskrit literature, some prerequisites were defined for a work to attain the status of mahakavya. Kalidasa, Bharavi, Magha, Shri Harsha and Bhatti composed such works. Though these notions and definitions came later, the Valmiki Ramayana displays every characteristic of a mahakavya and is longer than any of these subsequent works. The story of how it came about is known to most people who are familiar with the Ramayana. The sage Valmiki had gone, with his disciple Bharadvaja, to bathe in the waters of the River Tamasa. There was a couple of *krouncha*[12] birds there, in the act of making

[12] Curlew.

love. Along came a hunter[13] and killed the male bird. As the female bird grieved, Valmiki was driven by compassion and the first shloka emerged from his lips. Since it was composed in an act of sorrow—*shoka*—this kind of composition came to be known as shloka. So the Ramayana tells us. Incidentally, this first shloka doesn't occur in the first chapter. It isn't the first shloka of the Valmiki Ramayana. The incident and the shloka occur in the second chapter. More specifically, it is the fourteenth shloka in the second chapter and is as follows. मा निषाद प्रतिष्ठां त्वमगमः शाश्वतीः समाः। यत्क्रौंचमिथुनादेकमवधी काममोहितम्॥ 'O nishada! This couple of curlews was in the throes of passion and you killed one of them. Therefore, you will possess ill repute for an eternal number of years.'

Till a certain period of history, all Sanskrit works were in poetry or verse, not in prose. The Vedangas are limbs or auxiliaries and the six Vedangas are *shiksha*,[14] *chhanda*,[15] *vyakarana*,[16] *nirukta*,[17] *jyotisha*[18] and *kalpa*.[19] These are needed to understand not just the Vedas, but also Sanskrit works. Chhanda is one of these. Chhanda can be translated as metre and means something that is pleasing and delightful. Chhanda *shastra* is the study of metres or prosody. Sanskrit poetry wasn't about what we tend to identify as poetry today, the act of rhyming. Chhanda begins with the concept of *akshara*, akin to, but not exactly identical with, the English concept of syllable, that is, part of a word with a single vowel sound. Other than possessing a single vowel sound, an akshara must not begin with a vowel. Aksharas can be *hrasva* or *laghu*—light or L—and *guru*—heavy or G. Simply stated, with a short vowel, the akshara is L and with a long vowel, the akshara is G. There are some additional conditions, but we needn't get into those. Every verse consists of four *pada*s, the word pada meaning one quarter. Depending on how

[13] *Nishada*.
[14] Articulation and pronunciation.
[15] Prosody.
[16] Grammar.
[17] Etymology.
[18] Astronomy.
[19] Rituals.

many aksharas there are in a pada and the distribution of those aksharas into L and G, there were a variety of metres. Depending on the subject and the mood, the poet consciously chose a metre. Analysing in this way, there were more than 1300 different metres. One of the most popular was *anushtubh*. This figures prominently in the Valmiki Ramayana, the Mahabharata and the Puranas. The anushtubh structure meant eight aksharas in each pada, with a total of thirty-two aksharas. In addition, for anushtubh, in every pada, the fifth akshara would have to be L and the sixth akshara would have to be G. In classical Sanskrit literature, conditions were also applied to the seventh akshara, but such refinements came later. For that first verse, the decomposition runs as follows: (1) L L L G L G L G; (2) L G L G L G L G; (3) L L G G L G G L; (4) G G L L L G G L. (1) *ma ni sha da pra tish tham*; (2) *tva ma ga mah shash vati sa mah*; (3) *yat kroun cha mi thu na de ka*; (4) *ma va dhi ka ma mo hi tam*. It is not that Valmiki only used anushtubh. There are actually sixteen different metres in the Valmiki Ramayana.

It is impossible to capture the beauty of chhanda in an English translation. One can attempt to do a translation in verse, but it will fail to convey the beauty. If the original text is poetry, one starts with an initial question. Should one attempt a translation in verse or in prose? This translation is based on the premise that the translation should be as close as possible to the original Sanskrit text. One should not take liberties with the text. This translation is therefore almost a word-to-word rendering. If one sits down with the original Sanskrit, there will be almost a perfect match. In the process, deliberately so, the English is not as smooth as it might have been, had one taken more liberties, and this is a conscious decision. Had one attempted a translation in verse, one would perforce have had to take more liberties. Hence, the choice of prose is also a deliberate decision. As composers, there is quite a contrast between Valmiki and Vedavyasa. Vedavyasa focuses on people and incidents. Rarely does the Mahabharata attempt to describe nature, even if those sections are on geography. In contrast, Valmiki's descriptions of nature are lyrical and superlative, similar to Kalidasa. A translation can never hope to transmit that flavour. There is no substitute to

reading the original Sanskrit, more so for the Valmiki Ramayana than for the Mahabharata.

Which occurred earlier, the incidents of the Ramayana or the Mahabharata? Which was composed earlier, the Ramayana or the Mahabharata? The Ramayana incidents occurred in treta yuga, the Mahabharata incidents in dvapara yuga. Rama was an earlier avatara, Krishna a later one. Hence, the obvious deduction is that the Ramayana incidents predated those of the Mahabharata—an inference also bolstered by the genealogy and astrological arguments mentioned earlier. However, and not just for the sake of being perverse, consider the following. Geographically, the incidents of the Mahabharata mostly occur along an east–west axis, along either side of what used to be called Uttarapath, the northern road, more familiar as Grand Trunk Road or National Highway (NH) 1 and 2. The incidents of the Ramayana often occur along a north–south axis, along what used to be called Dakshinapath, the southern road. Sanjeev Sanyal[20] has made the point that while Uttarapath remained stable over time, the Dakshinapath during Rama's time was different from the subsequent Dakshinapath, with the latter more like today's NH 44. To return to the point, the geographical terrain of the Mahabharata was restricted to the northern parts of the country, with the south rarely mentioned. The Aryan invasion theory has been discredited because of a multitude of reasons, but myths and perceptions that have lasted for decades are difficult to dispel. However, regardless of the Aryan invasion theory, the Ramayana reveals a familiarity with the geography of the southern parts of the country that the Mahabharata does not. The fighting in the Mahabharata, in the Kurukshetra War, is cruder and less refined. In the Ramayana, bears and apes may have fought using trees and boulders, but humans did not. A human did not tear apart another human's chest and drink blood. The urbanization depicted in the Ramayana is rarely found in the Mahabharata. We have cited these counter-arguments to make a simple point. Which incident

[20] *Land of the Seven Rivers: A Brief History of India's Geography*, Sanjeev Sanyal, Penguin, 2012.

occurred earlier and which text was composed earlier are distinct questions. They should not be confused. Even if the Ramayana incidents occurred before the incidents of the Mahabharata, that doesn't automatically mean the Ramayana was composed before the Mahabharata. The Rama story occurs in the Mahabharata, known as the 'Ramopakhyana' section. There is no such reference to the Mahabharata incidents in the Ramayana. This is the main reason for arguing that the Ramayana was composed before the Mahabharata.

The relationship between the 'Ramopakhyana' and the Valmiki Ramayana is also of scholarly interest. Which was earlier? Did one borrow from the other, or did both have a common origin? That need not concern us. What should be stressed is the obvious—the Valmiki Ramayana wasn't composed at a single point in time and there is a difference between the original composition and the present text, as given to us say in the Critical Edition. If bears and apes fought with the help of trees and boulders, and Angada suddenly kills someone with a weapon, that part is probably a later composition, with the composer having deviated from the original template. If a verse is in anushtubh, but deviates from the L–G pattern, this may have been a conscious decision, but in all probability, reflects the inferior skills of a subsequent poet. If we take the Critical text as it stands, while there are no direct references to the incidents of the Mahabharata, there are plenty of indirect allusions. There are shlokas reminiscent of the Bhagavatgita. When Bharata comes to Rama to inform him about Dasharatha's death, Rama asks him about the welfare of the kingdom, reminiscent of similar questions asked by Narada to Yudhishthira. In the Valmiki Ramayana, there are references to kings of the lunar dynasty (Yayati) and incidents (Ilvala and Vatapi) that are only described in the Mahabharata. The evidence may be circumstantial and speculative, but it is the following. It is as if the later composers knew about the Mahabharata incidents and the text, but consciously avoided any direct references.

Why is another translation of the Valmiki Ramayana needed? Surely, there are plenty floating around. That's not quite true. Indeed, there are several translations of the Valmiki Ramayana,

including some recent ones, but they are abridged. In any act of abridgement, some sections are omitted or summarized. Abridged translations, no matter how good they are, are not quite a substitute for unabridged translations, which bring in the nuances too. To the best of my knowledge, the list of unabridged translations of the Valmiki Ramayana is the following: (1) Ralph T.H. Griffith;[21] (2) Manmatha Nath Dutt;[22] (3) Hari Prasad Shastri;[23] (4) Desiraju Hanumanta Rao and K.M.K. Murthy;[24] and (5) Robert P. Goldman.[25] Given the timelines, the Goldman translation is the only one based on the Critical Edition. Having translated the Mahabharata,[26] it was natural to translate the Valmiki Ramayana. The intention was to do a translation that was popular in style. That meant a conscious decision to avoid the use of diacritical marks, as would have been the case had one used IAST (International Alphabet of Sanskrit Transliteration). If diacritical marks are not going to be used, there may be problems rendering names, proper and geographic. We have sought to make the English renderings as phonetic as is possible. Thus, we use 'Goutama' to refer to the sage of that name—although others have often referred to him elsewhere as 'Gautama'. We have chosen Goutama on the logic that if Gomati is not Gamati, why should Goutama be rendered as Gautama? There remains the question of what one does with vowel sounds. How does one differentiate the short sound from the long? Should Rama be written as Raama and Sita as Seeta? That seemed to be too artificial and contrary to popular usage. On rare occasions, this does

[21] *The Ramayana of Valmiki, translated into English verse,* Ralph T.H. Griffith, E.Z. Lazarus and Company, London, 1895.

[22] *Valmiki Ramayana,* Manmatha Nath Dutt, R.K. Bhatia, Calcutta, 1891–92. Manmatha Nath Dutt (Shastri) was one of India's greatest translators (in English). He also translated the Mahabharata and several Puranas.

[23] *The Ramayana of Valmiki,* Hari Prasad Shastri, Shanti Sadan, London, 1952.

[24] This is net based, on the site http://www.valmikiramayan.net/ and leaves out 'Uttara Kanda'.

[25] *The Ramayana of Valmiki: An Epic of Ancient India,* Robert P. Goldman, Princeton University Press, 1984 to 2016.

[26] *The Mahabharata,* Bibek Debroy, Penguin (India), 10 volumes, 2010–2014, boxed set 2015.

cause a problem, with a danger of confusion between the ape Taara and his daughter Taaraa, Vali's wife. Such occasions are however rare and we have explained them. However, there are also instances where we have deviated from popular usage. Hanumat is a case in point, where Hanuman seemed to be too contrary to grammatical principles. There are some words that defy translation, *dharma* is an example. Hence, we have not even tried to translate such words. The Goldman translation is academic in style. This translation's style is more popular. Therefore, there is no attempt to overburden the reader with extensive notes. However, a straight translation may not be self-explanatory. Hence, we have put in footnotes, just enough to explain, without stretching the translation.

As with the Mahabharata, the Valmiki Ramayana is a text about dharma. Dharma means several different things—the dharma of the four *varna*s and the four *ashrama*s, the classes and stages of life; the governance template of *raja dharma*, the duty of kings; principles of good conduct, *sadachara*; and the pursuit of objectives of human existence, *purushartha*—dharma, *artha* and *kama*. As with the Mahabharata, the Valmiki Ramayana is a *smriti* text. It has a human origin and composer, it is not a *shruti* text. Smriti texts are society and context specific. We should not try to judge and evaluate individuals and actions on the basis of today's value judgements. In addition, if the span of composition was one thousand years, from 500 BCE to 500 CE, those value judgements also change. The later composers and interpreters may have had problems with what the earlier composers authored. A case in point is when Sita is being abducted by Ravana. At a certain point in time, men and women universally wore an upper garment and a lower one. When she is being abducted through the sky, Sita casts aside and throws down not just her ornaments, but her upper garment too. As this translation will illustrate, this caused problems for subsequent composers and interpreters.

To return to the notion of dharma—transcending all those collective templates of dharma—there is one that is individual in nature. Regardless of those collective templates, an individual has to decide what the right course of action is and there is no universal answer as to what is right and what is wrong. There are always

contrary pulls of dharma, with two notions of dharma pulling in different directions. It is not immediately obvious which is superior. Given the trade-offs, an individual makes a choice and suffers the consequences. Why is there an impression that these individual conflicts of dharma are more manifest in the Mahabharata than in the Ramayana?

The answer probably lies in the nature of these two texts. What is the difference between a novel and a long story, even when both have multiple protagonists? The difference between a novel and a long story is probably not one of length. A novel seeks to present the views of all protagonists. Thus, the Mahabharata is a bit like a novel, in so far as that trait is concerned. A long story does not seek to look at incidents and actions from the point of view of every protagonist. It is concerned with the perspective of one primary character, to the exclusion of others.

If this distinction is accepted, the Valmiki Ramayana has the characteristics of a long story. It is Ramayana. Therefore, it is primarily from Rama's point of view. We aren't told what Bharata or Lakshmana thought, or for that matter, Urmila, Mandavi or Shrutakirti. There is little that is from Sita's point of view too. That leads to the impression that the Mahabharata contains more about individual conflicts of dharma. For the Valmiki Ramayana, from Rama's point of view, the conflicts of dharma aren't innumerable. On that exile to the forest, why did he take Sita and Lakshmana along with him? Was Shurpanakha's disfigurement warranted? Why did he unfairly kill Vali? Why did he make Sita go through tests of purity, not once, but twice? Why did he unfairly kill Shambuka? Why did he banish Lakshmana? At one level, one can argue these are decisions by a personified divinity and therefore, mere humans cannot comprehend and judge the motives. At another level, the unhappiness with Rama's decisions led to the composition of alternative versions of the Ramayana. Note that Sita's questions about dharma remained unanswered. If you are going to the forest as an ascetic, why have you got weapons with you? If the *rakshasas*[27]

[27] Demons.

are causing injuries to hermits, punishing the rakshasas is Bharata's job, now that he is the king. Why are you dabbling in this? Note also Rama's justification at the time of Sita's first test. It wasn't about what others would think, that justification came later. The initial harsh words reflected his own questions about Sita's purity. Thus, Rama's conflicts over dharma also exist. It is just that in the Valmiki Ramayana, it is about one individual alone.

In conclusion, this translation is an attempt to get readers interested in reading the unabridged Valmiki Ramayana. Having read abridged versions, and there is no competition with those, to appreciate the nuances better, one should read the unabridged. And, to appreciate the beauty of the poetry, one should then be motivated to read the text in Sanskrit. A translation is only a bridge and an unsatisfactory one at that.

CHAPTER THREE

Aranya Kanda

Sarga (1): 22 shlokas
Sarga (2): 24 shlokas
Sarga (3): 27 shlokas
Sarga (4): 36 shlokas
Sarga (5): 21 shlokas
Sarga (6): 22 shlokas
Sarga (7): 19 shlokas
Sarga (8): 29 shlokas
Sarga (9): 21 shlokas
Sarga (10): 92 shlokas
Sarga (11): 34 shlokas
Sarga (12): 25 shlokas
Sarga (13): 36 shlokas
Sarga (14): 29 shlokas
Sarga (15): 39 shlokas
Sarga (16): 25 shlokas
Sarga (17): 26 shlokas
Sarga (18): 21 shlokas
Sarga (19): 25 shlokas
Sarga (20): 18 shlokas
Sarga (21): 26 shlokas
Sarga (22): 34 shlokas
Sarga (23): 27 shlokas
Sarga (24): 28 shlokas
Sarga (25): 24 shlokas
Sarga (26): 20 shlokas
Sarga (27): 30 shlokas
Sarga (28): 28 shlokas
Sarga (29): 35 shlokas
Sarga (30): 22 shlokas
Sarga (31): 23 shlokas
Sarga (32): 24 shlokas
Sarga (33): 38 shlokas
Sarga (34): 22 shlokas
Sarga (35): 23 shlokas
Sarga (36): 28 shlokas
Sarga (37): 20 shlokas
Sarga (38): 21 shlokas
Sarga (39): 20 shlokas
Sarga (40): 32 shlokas
Sarga (41): 49 shlokas
Sarga (42): 21 shlokas
Sarga (43): 37 shlokas
Sarga (44): 36 shlokas
Sarga (45): 45 shlokas
Sarga (46): 23 shlokas
Sarga (47): 36 shlokas
Sarga (48): 27 shlokas
Sarga (49): 40 shlokas
Sarga (50): 42 shlokas

Sarga (51): 25 shlokas
Sarga (52): 29 shlokas
Sarga (53): 35 shlokas
Sarga (54): 32 shlokas
Sarga (55): 20 shlokas
Sarga (56): 20 shlokas
Sarga (57): 25 shlokas
Sarga (58): 35 shlokas
Sarga (59): 29 shlokas
Sarga (60): 52 shlokas
Sarga (61): 16 shlokas
Sarga (62): 20 shlokas
Sarga (63): 26 shlokas
Sarga (64): 36 shlokas
Sarga (65): 31 shlokas
Sarga (66): 15 shlokas
Sarga (67): 31 shlokas
Sarga (68): 22 shlokas
Sarga (69): 36 shlokas
Sarga (70): 27 shlokas
Sarga (71): 26 shlokas

Chapter 3(1)

Rama, in control of his *atman*, entered the impenetrable and great forest of Dandakaranya[1] and saw a circle of hermitages of the ascetics. *Kusha* grass and bark were strewn around and the place was pervaded by all the signs of the *brahman*. It blazed and was difficult to look at, like the solar disc in the sky. The region was always the refuge of all creatures. Large numbers of *apsara*s always worshipped it and danced around there. There were large altars for sacrificial fires and ladles, vessels, deer skin and kusha grass. There were large trees and auspicious trees in the forest, laden with succulent fruit.

[1] This is the right place to mention the story of Dandakaranya. Ikshvaku's youngest son was Danda. Since he was wicked, his father exiled him. Danda went to the region around the Vindhya mountains and built a kingdom there, with a capital in Madhumanta. Danda consorted with the demons there and became the disciple of Shukracharya, the preceptor of the demons. However, he molested Shukracharya's daughter and was cursed by him. Madhumanta was destroyed and the area came to be known as Dandaka, *danda* also being punishment. The southern part of Dandakaranya, to the south of Madhumanta, was known as Janasthana. While Madhumanta was cursed, the southern part was exempted from the curse. Therefore, people began to reside in Janasthana, though Madhumanta was deserted. Ravana made Khara the ruler of Janasthana. When Rama entered Dandakaranya, with a desire that Rama should destroy the demons, the sages continually urged him towards the south, towards Janasthana. In the process, an area that was once under the Ikshvaku empire would again be brought under it.

Homage was rendered through sacrificial offerings and oblations. The place echoed with sounds of the brahman. Wild flowers were everywhere. There were female elephants with male elephants. It was populated by aged sages who possessed the radiance of the sun and the fire. They were self-controlled and were attired in bark and antelope skin, surviving on fruits and roots. The region was adorned by these sacred and supreme *rishi*s, who were restrained in what they ate. Resounding with the sound of the brahman, it was as remarkable as Brahma's abode. It was ornamented by those immensely fortunate *brahmana*s who knew about the brahman. The handsome Raghava saw that circle of hermitages of the ascetics. The immensely energetic one advanced, taking off the string from his great bow.

The *maharshi*s possessed divine insight. They were delighted to see that Rama and the illustrious Sita were approaching. The followers of *dharma* saw him,[2] like a rising moon. Firm in their vows, they received them, with all the auspicious rites. The residents of the forest were astounded on seeing Rama's form. He was handsome, powerful, prosperous and graceful and attired well. All the residents of the forest did not blink and were surprised to see Vaidehi, Lakshmana and Rama. All those immensely fortunate ones were engaged in the welfare of all beings and received the guest, Raghava, in their huts made out of leaves. Those immensely fortunate ones were like the fire. Following the indicated rites, the followers of dharma honoured Rama and received him properly, offering him water. All those in the hermitages knew about dharma. They offered the great-souled one roots, flowers and fruits from the forest. Joining their hands in salutation, they said, 'The king ensures adherence to dharma among the people. He is the immensely illustrious refuge. He is revered and worshipped. He wields the staff of chastisement and is a senior. O Raghava! He is a fourth part of Indra and protects the subjects.[3] Therefore, the king is worshipped by the people and enjoys the best among objects of pleasure. We reside in your kingdom and you are the one who will protect us.

[2] Rama.

[3] The king was created with one fourth of the parts from each of the guardians of the world, Indra being one of these guardians.

Whether you are in the city or whether you are in the forest, you are the king and the lord of the people. O king! We have cast aside our own staffs of chastisement. We have conquered anger and we have conquered our senses. We, stores of austerities, must always be protected by you, like a foetus inside a womb.' Having said this, they worshipped Raghava and Lakshmana with fruits, roots, flowers and many other kinds of forest fare. There were other successful ascetics, who were like the fire. Following the proper and appropriate rites, they worshipped him, like the lord of the gods.

Chapter 3(2)

Rama was thus treated to hospitality. When the sun arose, he took leave of all the sages and entered the forest. It was full of a large number of animals and frequented by tigers and wolves. There were devastated trees, creepers and bushes and waterbodies that were terrible to behold. The birds did not chirp, but the sound of crickets could be heard. Followed by Lakshmana, Rama saw that the centre of the forest was like that. In the middle of the forest, surrounded by many such terrible animals, Kakutstha saw one who lived off human flesh. He was like the summit of a mountain and uttered a loud noise. His eyes were deep and his mouth was huge and horrible. His stomach was also horrible. He was gruesome, malformed, tall, hideous and horrible to behold. He was attired in a tiger skin that was wet with fat and smeared with blood. All creatures found him to be dreadful, like the Destroyer with a gaping mouth.[4] His iron spear had impaled on it three lions, four tigers, two wolves, ten spotted deer and the fat-smeared, tusked and gigantic head of an elephant. He roared in a loud voice. On seeing Rama, Lakshmana and Maithilee Sita, he became enraged and rushed towards them, like the Destroyer towards beings. As he roared loudly, the earth seemed to quake. He grasped Vaidehi in

[4] Yama.

his lap, went some distance away, and told them, 'You wear matted hair and are attired in bark. With your wife, you will not live for a long time. You have entered Dandakaranya with arrows, bows and swords in your hands.[5] What kind of an ascetic are you, since you are residing here with a woman? You are wicked and following *adharma*. You have defiled the status of a sage? With my weapons, I roam around in this impenetrable forest and am a *rakshasa*[6] named Viradha. I always devour the flesh of rishis. This beautiful woman will be my wife. The two of you are wicked. I will drink your blood in an encounter.' The insolent and evil-souled Viradha said this.

On hearing these proud words, Janaka's daughter was terrified. In her anxiety, Sita trembled, like a plantain tree in a storm. On seeing that the auspicious Sita was in Viradha's lap, with a dry mouth, Raghava addressed Lakshmana in these words. 'O amiable one! Look at the one who created herself from King Janaka.[7] She is my wife, auspicious in conduct. But she is in Viradha's lap. This illustrious princess was reared in a great deal of happiness. O Lakshmana! Kaikeyee had a cherished boon. Exactly as she had intended, the objective has swiftly befallen us today. She is a far-sighted person and was not content with obtaining the kingdom for her son. Though I am engaged in the welfare of all creatures, I was dispatched to the forest. My mother, the one in the middle,[8] has achieved her desire today. O Soumitri! Vaidehi being touched by another is a greater misery for me than my father banishing me or the loss of my own kingdom.' In a grieving voice that choked with tears, Kakutstha said this. Enraged, like a sighing serpent, Lakshmana said, 'You should not be like one without a protector. You are the protector of all creatures and are Vasava's equal. O Kakutstha! When I am serving you, why are you tormented? In my rage, I will now slay the rakshasa with my arrow. Viradha's life is over and the earth will drink his blood. I was angry with Bharata when he desired the kingdom. I will release that rage

[5] Pointing out the anomaly of ascetics (dressed in bark) wielding weapons and apparently finding pleasure with a wife.

[6] Demon.

[7] Since she was born from the earth and was not a biological daughter.

[8] This is an inconsistency, since Sumitra is the one in the middle.

on Viradha now, like the wielder of the *vajra* releasing the vajra on a mountain. This speedy and long arrow will receive a greater force from the strength of my arms. It will descend on his large chest and take away life from his body, which will then whirl around and fall down on the ground.'

Chapter 3(3)

At this, Viradha spoke again, making the forest echo with his words. 'You should ask yourself. Who are you and where are you going? Tell me.' The rakshasa's face blazed like the fire and Rama told him about himself and the Ikshvaku lineage, since the extremely energetic one kept asking. 'Know that we follow the conduct of *kshatriya*s, though we are roaming around in the forest now. However, we wish to know about you too. You roam around in Dandaka. Who are you?' Viradha replied to Rama, for whom, truth was his valour. 'O king! O Raghava! I will tell you. Listen. I am the son of Java and my mother is Shatahrada. All the rakshasas on earth refer to me as Viradha. Having performed austerities, I received the favours of Brahma. In this world, I would not be slain by any weapon, nor would it be able to penetrate me or slice through me. Cast aside this woman. Forget about her and go wherever you came from. Unless you run away, you will swiftly be robbed of your lives.' The rakshasa's eyes were red with rage. Viradha was wicked in intelligence and his body was malformed. Rama answered him. 'O inferior one! Shame on you. In the pursuit of something that is inferior, it is certain that you are looking for your death. Remain steadfast in the encounter. You will not be able to escape with your life.'

Rama strung his bow and affixed extremely sharp arrows to it. To slay the rakshasa, he aimed swiftly. From the excellent bow that had been strung, he released seven gold-shafted arrows that were extremely swift, like Suparna[9] or the wind. Tufted with peacock

[9] Garuda.

feathers and like fire, they penetrated Viradha's body and smeared with blood, fell down on the ground. He roared extremely loudly and raised a spear that was like Shakra's standard. Having seized it, he dazzled, like the Destroyer with a gaping mouth. That spear was like the vajra and blazed in the sky, like a fire. Rama, supreme among those who wielded weapons, severed it with two of his arrows. Soumitri severed the left arm of that terrible one. Rama swiftly severed the rakshasa's right arm. With his arms severed, the rakshasa quickly fainted and fell down on the ground like a cloud, resembling a mountain shattered by the vajra. Viradha uttered these words to Kakutstha, bull among men. 'O son![10] I know you to be Kousalya's excellent son and I also know the immensely fortunate Vaidehi and the immensely illustrious Lakshmana. I assumed this rakshasa body because of an extremely terrible curse. I am a *gandharva*[11] named Tumburu and was cursed by Vaishravana.[12] When I sought his favours, the immensely illustrious one[13] said, "Dasharatha's son, Rama, will kill you in an encounter and you will then obtain your natural form and go to heaven." Because I was attracted to Rambha,[14] I was not present when I should have been and King Vaishravana had angrily addressed me in this way. Through your favours, I have now been freed from that terrible curse and will go to my own abode. O scorcher of enemies! May you fare well. O son! The powerful Sharabhanga, with dharma in his soul, resides one-and-a-half *yojanas*[15] from here and that maharshi is as resplendent as the sun. Quickly go to him and he will tell you what is best for you. O Rama! Fling me into a pit and go safely. This is the eternal dharma for rakshasas who have lost their lives.[16] Those who are flung into pits obtain the eternal worlds.' Viradha, afflicted by arrows, spoke to Kakutstha in this way. The mighty-armed one

[10] The word used is *tata*. Though it means son, it is affectionately used for anyone who is younger or junior.

[11] Semi-divine species, companions of Kubera, celestial musicians.

[12] Kubera.

[13] Kubera.

[14] An apsara.

[15] A yojana is a measure of distance, between 8 and 9 miles.

[16] That is, rakshasas were buried.

gave up his body and reached heaven. The one with ears like cones emitted a loud roar from his throat. As Viradha was flung into a pit, he roared in a terrible tone. Having slain the rakshasa, the ones with the colourful and golden bows rescued Maithilee. Delighted, like the moon and the sun stationed in the firmament, they continued to travel through the great forest.

Chapter 3(4)

Having slain that fiercely strong rakshasa, Viradha, in the forest, the valiant one embraced Sita and comforted her. Rama spoke to his brother, Lakshmana, who blazed in his energy. 'This forest is impenetrable and difficult and we are not used to roaming around in the forest. We should quickly go to Sharabhanga, the store of austerities.' Raghava went towards Sharabhanga's hermitage, who possessed divine powers through his austerities and was in control of his atman. Near Sharabhanga's hermitage, he saw a great and wonderful sight. He saw the lord of the gods astride a chariot that did not touch the ground. His form was resplendent, like the complexion of the sun and the fire. The god dazzled in blazing ornaments and garments. He was worshipped by many divinities and great-souled ones. The chariot was yoked to tawny steeds and travelled through the sky. He could be seen from a distance, like a young and rising sun, like excellent and white clouds, or like the lunar disc. There was a white umbrella, colourfully decorated with garlands. Two excellent women held two superb and extremely expensive whisks above his head and fanned him. The god was in the sky and gandharvas, immortals, *siddhas*[17] and many supreme rishis praised him with their eloquent hymns.

On seeing Shatakratu, Rama told Lakshmana, 'We have earlier heard about Shakra Puruhuta's horses. These divine and

[17] Successful sages.

tawny ones that are in the sky must certainly belong to him. O tiger among men! There are hundreds and hundreds of young ones stationed around the chariot, sporting earrings and with swords in their hands. All of them are wearing blazing necklaces around their chests. O Soumitri! Their forms are blazing and they seem to be twenty-five years old. For the gods, the age always remains constant and these tigers among men are seen to be handsome. O Lakshmana! For a while, remain here with Vaidehi. Let me clearly find out who is the dazzling one on the chariot.' He asked Soumitri to remain there. Kakutstha then advanced towards Sharabhanga's hermitage. Shachi's consort saw that Rama was approaching. Having taken Sharabhanga's permission, he told the gods, 'This Rama is coming here. You should nudge him towards his vow.[18] Until then, he should not speak to me, or see me.[19] When he is victorious and successful, I will soon show myself to him. He has to perform an extremely great task and it is a task that anyone else will find extremely difficult.' Therefore, the wielder of the vajra[20] worshipped the ascetic and took his leave. Using the chariot that was yoked to horses, the destroyer of enemies went to heaven. The one with the one thousand eyes left.

Sharabhanga was seated near the *agnihotra* fire and Raghava approached him, with his companions.[21] Rama, Sita and Lakshmana touched his feet. Having obtained his permission, they sat down. They were also invited to stay there. Raghava asked about Shakra's arrival and Sharabhanga told Raghava everything about this. 'O Rama! That granter of boons wishes to take me to Brahma's world. Through my fierce austerities I have obtained that which is extremely difficult for those with uncleansed souls to get. O tiger among men! I knew that you were not very far away now. I will

[18] Of killing the rakshasas.

[19] This requires explanation. When soliciting a boon about who could kill him, Ravana forgot to mention humans and therefore, Ravana could only be killed by a human. Until this happened, if Indra spoke to Rama, Rama's divine nature would have been revealed and he wouldn't have been able to kill Ravana. This was to be avoided.

[20] Indra.

[21] Lakshmana and Sita. Once Indra had departed, they joined him.

not go to Brahma's world without first seeing my beloved guest. Having met, I will go to heaven, frequented by the gods. O tiger among men! I have obtained the auspicious and eternal world of Brahma and others in the vault of heaven. Accept them from me.' Raghava, tiger among men and accomplished in all the sacred texts, addressed the rishi Sharabhanga in these words. 'O great sage! I will also obtain all the worlds. I only wish that you indicate a residence for me in this forest.' He was thus addressed by Raghava, who was like Shakra in his strength. The immensely wise Sharabhanga again spoke these words. 'In this auspicious region meant for ascetics, go to Suteekshna. In this beautiful forest, he will tell you where you should reside.[22] O tiger among men! O son![23] That is your path. However, remain for a moment and see me give up my body, just as a snake casts off old skin.' With clarified butter, the one who knew about mantras ignited a fire. The immensely energetic Sharabhanga entered the fire. The fire consumed the great-souled one's body hair, hair, old skin, bones, flesh and blood. From the fire, a young and radiant Sharabhanga emerged and he was like the fire himself. He passed over the worlds where great-souled rishis offered oblations into the fire, and the world of the gods and went to Brahma's world. Going to the world meant for the performers of auspicious deeds, the bull among brahmanas saw the grandfather[24] and his companions. The grandfather also saw the brahmana and, happy and delighted, welcomed him.

Chapter 3(5)

When Sharabhanga went to heaven, a group of sages assembled and approached Kakutstha Rama, blazing in his

[22] With Sharabhanga dead, Rama could have resided there. But Sharabhanga directs him to Suteekshna and Suteekshna directs him to Agastya. This is part of the plan to make Rama head southwards.

[23] The word used is tata.

[24] Brahma.

energy. There were *vaikhanasa*s,[25] *valakhilya*s,[26] *samprakshala*s,[27] *marichipa*s,[28] *ashmakutta*s,[29] many sages who subsisted on leaves, *dantaulukhalina*s,[30] others who were *unmajjaka*s,[31] sages who subsisted on water, others who subsisted on air, those who made their abodes under the open sky, those who slept on the bare ground, self-controlled ones who lived on high ground, those who were attired in wet garments, those who always meditated and performed austerities and those who tormented themselves with the five fires.[32] All of them possessed the radiance of the brahman and were firm in their devotion to *yoga*. Those ascetics came to Rama in Sharabhanga's hermitage. Those who knew about dharma approached Rama, supreme among the upholders of dharma. The large number of self-controlled sages spoke to the one who was supremely knowledgeable about dharma. 'You are a *maharatha*[33] on earth and belong to the Ikshvaku lineage. You are the foremost of protectors, like Maghavan among the gods. Your fame and valour is known in the three worlds. You are also invested with the truthful vow given to your father and all types of dharma. O great-souled one! O one who knows about dharma! O one who is devoted to dharma! O protector! We have approached you for a purpose and you should pardon us for this. O son![34] Great adharma befalls a king who receives a sixth part[35] as taxes, but does not protect the subjects like his sons.

[25] Sages believed to have been born from Brahma's nails.

[26] Sages believed to have been born from Brahma's hair. There are 60,000 such sages and they are the sizes of thumbs. They precede the sun's chariot.

[27] Sages believed to have been born from the water used to wash Brahma's feet.

[28] Those who subsist on the rays of the sun and the moon. There may also be some connection with the sage Marichi, who was born through Brahma's mental powers.

[29] Those who eat raw grain after it has been ground on stone.

[30] Those who use their teeth as mortars, that is, they eat raw grain that has not been ground.

[31] Those who perform austerities by submerging themselves in water.

[32] Those who performed austerities with four fires around them and the sun overhead.

[33] Great warrior, more specifically, a maharatha is someone who can single-handedly fight ten thousand warriors.

[34] The word used is tata.

[35] Of production.

He must protect their lives like his own life, like his own desires and like his own son. He must always be engaged in protecting those who reside within his kingdom. O Rama! Such a person obtains everlasting fame for many years. He attains Brahma's abode and achieves greatness there. Sages survive on roots and fruits and follow supreme dharma. A king who follows dharma and protects his subjects obtains a one-fourth share in their merits.[36] There are many great brahmanas who have resorted to *vanaprastha*.[37] O Rama! You are the protector. However, despite that, they are being fiercely slain by the rakshasas. Come and behold the bodies of the sages with cleansed souls. In this forest, there are many of them, who have been killed in many ways by the fierce rakshasas. This great carnage is going on among the abodes along the river Pampa, along Mandakinee and in the residences in Chitrakuta. We cannot tolerate this injury caused to the ascetics. In this forest, these are the horrible deeds being perpetrated by the rakshasas, who are terrible in their acts. You are the one who offers refuge. Therefore, in search of protection, we have come to you. O Rama! Protect us and slay the ones who roam during the night.' Kakutstha heard this from the ascetics who were performing austerities. The one with dharma in his soul told all the ascetics, 'You should not speak to me in this way. O ascetics! Command me. Roaming around as I willed, I have come here to accomplish your objective. I will thereby obtain great fruits from residing in the forest. In a battle, I wish to slay the rakshasas, the enemies of the ascetics.' With Lakshmana, the one whose soul was firm in its devotion to dharma granted this assurance to the stores of austerities. With the stores of austerities and with the one who was noble in conduct,[38] the brave one advanced towards Suteekshna.

[36] Of the merits obtained by the sages, though this is true of all subjects in general.

[37] In the four stages (*ashramas*) of life, *brahmacharya* is the first, followed by *garhasthya*, vanaprastha and *sannyasa*, in that order. Vanaprastha is when one resorts to the forest.

[38] Obviously meaning Sita.

Chapter 3(6)

With his brother and with Sita, Rama, the scorcher of enemies, went to Suteekshna's hermitage on foot, accompanied by the brahmanas. He travelled a long distance and crossed rivers with a lot of water. He saw a mountain that was as large as a tall cloud. With Sita, the two Raghavas, supreme among the Ikshvaku lineage, entered a forest that was always full of many kinds of trees. They entered that terrible forest, with trees laden with many flowers and fruits. In a lonely spot, they saw the hermitage, decorated with garlands of rags.[39] The ascetic was seated there, sporting matted hair and dirty lotuses that grow in the mud. Following the prescribed rites, Rama spoke to Suteekshna, store of austerities. 'O illustrious one! I am Rama and I have come here to meet you. O one who knows about dharma! O maharshi! O one for whom truth is his valour! Therefore, speak to me.' He looked at the brave Rama, supreme among those who uphold dharma and embraced him in his arms. He said, 'O brave one! O Rama! O supreme among those who uphold dharma! You are indeed welcome. With you suddenly having come to this hermitage, it is as if I have obtained a protector. O immensely illustrious one! O brave one! I have been waiting for you. Until you arrived, I could not cast aside my body on this earth and ascend to the world of the gods. I had heard that you have been dislodged from the kingdom and have reached Chitrakuta. O Kakutstha! Shatakratu, the king of the gods, came here and told me that because of my auspicious deeds, I have won all the worlds, cherished by the gods and the rishis. I have conquered them through my austerities. Through my favours, with your wife and with Lakshmana, find pleasure there.' Because of his fierce austerities, the maharshi, truthful in speech, blazed. Rama, in control of his soul, replied, like Vasava to Brahma. 'O great sage! I will myself obtain those worlds. I wish that you indicate a place where I can live in this forest. You are accomplished in every way and are engaged in the welfare of all beings. The great-souled Sharabhanga, descended from Goutama, told me this.'

[39] The word used is *cheera,* meaning bark or rags worn by ascetics as garments.

The maharshi, famous in the worlds, was addressed by Rama in this way. Overcome by great happiness, he replied in these sweet words. 'O Rama! This hermitage possesses all the qualities and you will find pleasure here. Large numbers of rishis wander around here and there are always roots and fruits. However, large numbers of excellent deer come to this hermitage. They are without fear. Having tempted us and wandered around, they return.' Having heard the words of the maharshi, Lakshmana's patient elder brother stretched his bow, with an arrow affixed to it, and said, 'O extremely fortunate one! When those large numbers of deer arrive, I will slay them with extremely sharp arrows that are as radiant as the vajra. However, because of your compassion, there may be no greater misery for you than this. Therefore, it is not befitting that I should dwell in this hermitage for a long time.' Rama spoke to the granter of boons in this way and meanwhile, evening arrived. Having worshipped the western *sandhya*,[40] he[41] fashioned an abode there. When evening was over, the great-souled Suteekshna saw that night had arrived. He himself treated them hospitably and gave the two bulls among men auspicious food that ascetics could eat.

Chapter 3(7)

With Soumitri, Rama was honoured by Suteekshna and spent the night there. He awoke when it was morning. At the right time, Raghava awoke with Sita and performed his ablutions in cool water that was fragrant with the smell of lotuses. At the appropriate time, in the refuge of the ascetics in the forest, Rama, Lakshmaṇa and Vaidehi followed the rites and rendered offerings to the fire and the gods. Cleansed of sin, they saw that the sun had arisen. They went to Suteekshna and gently spoke these words. 'O illustrious one! We have been honoured by a revered one like you and have slept happily.

[40] Sandhya is any conjunction of day and night. Hence, it is dawn, as well as dusk.
[41] Rama.

Since the sages are hurrying us, we seek your permission to leave. We wish to quickly see the entire circle of hermitages, where the rishis, auspicious in their conduct, reside in Dandakaranya. We desire your permission so that we can leave with these bulls among sages. They are self-controlled and always devoted to dharma and austerities, like fires with flames. When the sun becomes too hot, it will be impossible to tolerate the scorching, like an ignoble person obtaining prosperity through undesirable means. We desire to leave before that.' With Soumitri and Sita, Raghava worshipped at the sage's feet and said this. When they touched his feet, the bull among sages raised them. Embracing them tightly, he affectionately addressed them in these words. 'O Rama! May you proceed safely along your path, with Soumitri and with this Sita, who is with you and follows you like a shadow. O brave one! Behold the beautiful hermitages of those who dwell in Dandakaranya. These ascetics have cleansed their souls through austerities. There are forests where fruits, roots and flowers grow well. There are extensive herds of deer and calm flocks of birds. There are clumps of blooming lotuses in placid waters. *Karandava*s[42] are spread out in the lakes and ponds. You will see beautiful waterfalls in the mountains. There are pleasant groves filled with the calls of peacocks. O child! Go. O Soumitri! You also go. However, when you have seen all this, come back to my hermitage again.' Thus addressed, Kakutstha, with Lakshmana, agreed. They circumambulated the sage and got ready to leave. The large-eyed Sita gave the brothers auspicious quivers, bows and sparkling swords. They girded those auspicious quivers and the bows that made loud sounds. Rama and Lakshmana emerged from the hermitage and left.

Chapter 3(8)

Having obtained Suteekshna's permission, the descendant of the Raghu lineage departed. Vaidehi addressed her husband

[42] Type of duck.

in gentle words. 'This dharma is extremely subtle and great and has been brought about by destiny.[43] It is possible to withdraw from a hardship that can come about through desire. There are three kinds of hardships that can come about through desire. False utterances are the most severe of these. However, there are two others that are also serious—intercourse with someone else's wife and fierceness without enmity. O Raghava! You have never uttered false words in the past, nor will you in the future. The desire for someone else's wife is destructive of dharma. How can you ever have that?[44] O mighty-armed one! Since you have conquered your senses, I know that you are capable of countering all of these. O one who is handsome to behold! I know all the senses are under your control. The third is the one of fiercely causing injury to the lives of others. That enmity may be due to confusion and it has presented itself before us. O brave one! You have given a pledge to the residents of Dandakaranya, for the sake of protecting the rishis, that you will slay the rakshasas in an encounter. It has been heard that this is the reason you are leaving for the Dandaka forest[45] with your brother, wielding a bow and arrows. On seeing that you are leaving in this way, my mind is full of worries. Thinking about what you will do, I am convinced that nothing beneficial will come out of this. O brave one! This departure towards Dandaka does not appeal to me. I will tell you the reasons. Listen to what I have to say. You will go to the forest with your brother, holding a bow and arrows in your hand. On seeing all those who roam around in the forest, you will exhaust your arrows on them. For kshatriyas on earth, a bow is like kindling offered into a fire. If it is near at hand, their energy and strength are greatly ignited. O mighty-armed one! In earlier times, there was an ascetic. He was pure and truthful in speech. Birds and animals used to frequent that auspicious forest. Indra, Shachi's consort, wished to create

[43] The dharma of kshatriyas to kill rakshasas. However, the rakshasas are being killed without any valid reason. They have caused no injury to Rama, Lakshmana and Sita.

[44] The only possibility that remains is fierceness without enmity.

[45] The southern parts of Dandaka.

an impediment for the ascetic.[46] He adopted the form of a warrior and went to the hermitage, with a sword in his hand. He left that excellent sword in the hermitage. Following the prescribed rites,[47] he left it with the virtuous ascetic. Having obtained the weapon in trust, he[48] thereafter sought to protect himself. Wishing to protect himself, he would hold it while roaming around in the forest. Wherever he went, even if it was to collect roots and fruits, because he desired to protect himself, he would not go without the sword. Always carrying the weapon around, gradually, the store of austerities abandoned his own intelligence and determination about ascetic pursuits and assumed a fierce trait. Because of attachment to the weapon, the confused sage became addicted to fierce pursuits and was dragged into adharma. He went to hell. I am not trying to teach. Because of affection and the great respect I hold for you, I am reminding you. You should never permit the act of picking up the bow and turn your mind towards causing enmity and slaying the rakshasas who have found a refuge in Dandaka. O brave one! In this world, it is not desirable to kill someone who has committed no crime. For kshatriyas and brave ones who have turned their minds to dwelling in the forest, the bow must only be taken up to protect those who are afflicted. What is this weapon? What is this forest? Who is a kshatriya? What are austerities? For us, all these are contradictory. The dharma of the country is what must be respected. O noble one! Association with weapons taints the intelligence. Follow the dharma of kshatriyas when you return to Ayodhya again. Let my affection for my father-in-law and mothers-in-law be eternal. Since you have given up the kingdom, become like a sage. *Artha* flows from dharma. Happiness results from dharma. Everything is obtained through dharma. Dharma is the essence of this universe. Those who are accomplished in dharma make attempts to control themselves and restrain their souls. Happiness cannot be obtained through the pursuit of

[46] Austerities lead to powers and Indra was always worried that ascetics would acquire powers and dislodge him. Therefore, he created impediments.

[47] For leaving something in trust. He would pick up the sword later.

[48] The ascetic.

happiness. O amiable one! Always follow pure intelligence and observe austerities in the forest. You know everything about the truth of the three worlds. I have told you this because of the fickleness of feminine nature. Who is capable of telling you about dharma? Use your intelligence to discuss this with your younger brother. Without any delay, do what pleases you.'

Chapter 3(9)

Full of devotion, Vaidehi addressed these words to her husband. Established in dharma, Rama heard this and then replied to Maithilee. 'O queen! As is appropriate for you, you have spoken gentle and beneficial words. O one who knows about dharma! O Janaka's daughter! This befits your lineage. O queen! In response to your words, I can say no more than the following. "As long as a kshatriya wields a bow, the word affliction should not be heard." The sages who reside in Dandakaranya are firm in their vows and are afflicted. O Sita! Taking me to be a refuge, they have themselves sought refuge with me. They are devoted to dharma. They reside in the forest and survive on roots and fruits. They are terrified of the rakshasas, the perpetrators of cruel deeds, and cannot find any happiness. The terrible rakshasas subsist on human flesh and are devouring them. The sages who live in Dandakaranya are being eaten. The excellent brahmanas came to me and told me this. I heard the words that descended from their mouths. Having worshipped at their feet, I spoke those words to them. Show me your favours. This is a source of great shame to me, that the brahmanas should present themselves before me in that way. I asked that assembly of brahmanas, "What should I do?" All of them, eloquent in speech, addressed me in these words. "There are many rakshasas in Dandakaranya and they can assume any form at will. O Rama! They are oppressing us. Therefore, you should protect us. O unblemished one! At the time of offering oblations and on other auspicious occasions, those invincible rakshasas, who survive on human flesh, oppress us. The sages and ascetics are thus oppressed by the rakshasas. In searching for a solution, we found you to be our supreme refuge. Through the strength of our austerities, we are capable of slaying those who roam around in the night. But we do not wish to diminish the store of austerities, earned over a long period of time. O Raghava! Austerities are always extremely difficult to perform and there are many impediments. Therefore, even when we are eaten by the rakshasas, we do not pronounce curses. The residents of Dandakaranya are thus oppressed by the rakshasas. With your brother, protect us. You are our protector in this forest." O Janaka's daughter! Hearing the words of the rishis of Dandakaranya, I gave them my word that I would protect them in every way. Having pledged to protect them, as long as I am alive, I am incapable of not following the pledge that I have given to the sages. I have always sought benefit in adherence to the truth. O Sita! I am capable of giving up my life, you, or Lakshmana, but not abandoning a pledge that I have given, especially one given to brahmanas. It is certainly my task to protect the rishis. O Vaidehi! I have given a pledge. What more remains to be said? Out of affection and love, you have spoken those words to me. O Sita! I am satisfied with you. Those who desire harm do not seek to instruct. O beautiful one! You have been true to yourself and your lineage.' The great-souled one spoke these words to the beloved Sita, the princess of Mithila. With Lakshmana and with the bow, Rama left for the beautiful hermitages in the forest.

Chapter 3(10)

Rama walked in front. The extremely beautiful Sita was in the middle. With a bow in his hand, Lakshmana followed at the rear. As they advanced with Sita, they saw many kinds of forests, level ground around the mountains and many beautiful rivers. Cranes and *chakravaka*s wandered around the riverbanks. There were lakes with lotuses and many kinds of aquatic birds. There were herds of antelopes, crazy and horned buffaloes and boars and elephants that treated trees like enemies. After they had travelled a long distance along the way, the sun became elongated. They saw a beautiful lake that was one yojana in expanse. It was full of red and white lotuses and ornamented with herds of elephants. There were cranes, swans, *kadambas*[49] and other aquatic birds. In the sparkling water of that beautiful lake, the sounds of singing and the playing of musical instruments could be heard, but no one could be seen. Because of their curiosity, Rama and maharatha Lakshmana asked the sage named Dharmabhrita. Raghava, with dharma in his soul, asked the sage, 'O great sage! All these wonderful sounds can be heard. A curiosity has been generated. You should tell us about the auspicious account.'

He started to tell them about the powers of the lake. 'O Rama! This perennial lake, named Panchapsara[50] has been constructed by the sage Mandakarni through his austerities. The great sage, Mandakarni, tormented himself through fierce austerities for ten thousand years, lying down in the water and surviving only on air. All the gods, with Agni at the forefront, came together. Having assembled together, they addressed each other in these words. "The sage desires to obtain one of our positions." All the gods instructed five foremost apsaras, with forms as radiant as the lightning, to cause impediments to his austerities. The sage possessed insight about this world and the next. However, to accomplish the task of the gods, the apsaras brought him under the subjugation of desire. Those five apsaras became the wives of the sage. Inside the lake, he built an invisible house for them. The five apsaras dwell there happily. They pleasure themselves with the sage, who became young because of his austerities and yoga. As they sport, the sounds of the musical instruments can be heard. The beautiful sounds of singing can be heard, mingling with the tinkling of ornaments.' Hearing the words of the one with the cleansed soul, Raghava and his immensely illustrious brother said that this was indeed wonderful.

[49] Kind of goose.

[50] Literally, five apsaras.

As they conversed, they saw a circle of hermitages. There were many kinds of trees, and kusha grass and bark were strewn around. With Vaidehi and Lakshmana, Raghava Kakutstha entered that beautiful circle of hermitages. Honoured by the maharshis, they happily resided there, progressively going from the hermitage of one ascetic to that of another. When the cycle was over, the one who knew about all the great weapons went back to one he had dwelt with earlier. He resided for ten months in one place and for one year in another. He resided for four months in one place and five months in another. There were some places where he resided for more than one month and others where he resided for more than one-and-a-half months. In some places, Raghava happily dwelt for three months and for eight months in others. As he happily dwelt in the hermitages of the sages, through their favours, ten years passed. With Sita, Raghava, who knew about dharma, took their leave. The handsome one again went to Suteekshna's hermitage. When he arrived at the hermitage, he was honoured by the sages. Rama, destroyer of enemies, resided there for some time too.

Once, at this hermitage, Suteekshna was seated and Kakutstha humbly addressed the great sage. 'O illustrious one! I have always heard accounts that Agastya, supreme among sages, resides in this forest. Because of the vastness of the forest, I do not know where that spot is. Where is the sacred hermitage of that intelligent maharshi? With my younger brother and with Sita, I wish to obtain the favours of that illustrious one, by going and worshipping the sage Agastya. This great desire is circling around in my heart, that I should myself be able to serve that supreme sage.' Suteekshna heard the words of Rama, who possessed dharma in his soul. Delighted, the sage replied to Dasharatha's son. 'I also wished to speak to you and Lakshmana about this. O Raghava! With Sita, go to Agastya. It is good fortune that you have yourself spoken to me about this. O child! I will tell you where Agastya, the great sage, is. O son![51] If you go four yojanas from this hermitage, towards the south, you will find the great and beautiful hermitage of Agastya's brother. It

[51] The word used is tata.

is located on flat ground within the forest and is ornamented with groves of *pippala* trees.[52] There are many kinds of beautiful flowers and fruit and the sounds of many kinds of birds. In the sparkling and auspicious waters, there are diverse kinds of lotuses. The place is full of swans and karandavas and decorated with chakravakas. O Rama! Spend one night there and leave next morning towards the southern direction, alongside that forest region. Agastya's hermitage is one yojana from there. This is a beautiful part of the forest, with many trees. With you, Vaidehi and Lakshmana will find pleasure there. That beautiful part of the forest is full of many kinds of trees. O immensely illustrious one! If your mind has turned towards seeing Agastya, the great sage, you should make up your mind to leave today itself.'

Having heard the words of the sage, with his brother, Rama worshipped the sage. With his younger brother and Sita, he left to see Agastya. Along the path, they saw many wonderful forests and mountains that were like clouds, lakes and rivers that flowed along the path. As they cheerfully proceeded along the path indicated by Suteekshna, in supreme delight, he addressed Lakshmana in these words. 'This must indeed be the hermitage of the great-souled sage, Agastya's brother,[53] the performer of auspicious deeds. It can be seen. In this forest, along the path, thousands of trees can be discerned, bent down with the burden of fruits and flowers. Suddenly, the bitter smell of ripe pippala fruit has arisen from the forest and is being borne by the wind. Heaps of wood have been kept here and there. Along the path, cut *darbha* grass can be seen, as radiant as lapis lazuli. In the middle of the forest, from the hermitage, a crest of smoke can be seen to arise from the fire, dark like the top of a cloud. Having had their baths in the fords, the brahmanas wish to collect offerings of flowers themselves.[54] O amiable one! I have heard Suteekshna's words. This must certainly be the hermitage of Agastya's brother.

[52] The sacred fig tree.

[53] Agastya's brother's name was Sudarshana, but the name is not mentioned here.

[54] It is preferable that flowers meant for worshipping are collected by the worshipper himself. If obtained from someone else, half of the merit goes to the person who originally gathered the flowers and only half goes to the worshipper.

His brother,[55] auspicious in his deeds, is the refuge of this direction. In a desire to ensure the welfare of the worlds, he quickly controlled death. Once upon a time, there were the cruel brothers, Vatapi and Ilvala.[56] Together, those two great *asura*s used to kill brahmanas. The cruel Ilvala would assume the form of a brahmana and with polished words, would invite brahmanas to a funeral ceremony.[57] Following the rites prescribed for a funeral ceremony, he would cook his brother, who would assume the form of a ram, and feed this to the brahmanas. Once the brahmanas had eaten, Ilvala would shout in a loud voice, "O Vatapi! Come out." Hearing his brother's words, Vatapi would roar like a ram and emerge, tearing through and mangling the bodies of the brahmanas. Subsisting on human flesh and assuming whatever form they willed, they always destroyed and killed thousands of brahmanas.[58] The gods prayed to maharshi Agastya and in a funeral ceremony, he ate the great asura.[59] Ilvala said that the ceremony was over and giving him[60] water to wash his hands, asked his brother to come out. The slayer of brahmanas spoke in this way to his brother. The intelligent Agastya, supreme among sages, laughed and said, "I have digested the rakshasa and he no longer possesses the strength to come out. In the form of a ram, your brother has gone to Yama's abode." On hearing the words that his brother had indeed been killed, the one who roamed in the night was enraged and started to attack the sage. He attacked the Indra among brahmanas. However, blazing in his energy, the sage burnt him down with the fire in his sight and he came by his death. Because of his compassion, the brahmana performed this extremely difficult deed. Adorned with lakes and groves, this is his brother's hermitage.' As Rama was conversing in this way with Soumitri, the sun set and

[55] Meaning Agastya.

[56] Vatapi was Viprachitti's son and Hiranyakashipu's nephew.

[57] The text uses the phrase *samskritam vadan*. This means—with polished words. It can also mean—speaking Sanskrit. The latter seems unlikely, since the word Sanskrit (which means polished) was used for the language much later. Earlier, the language was simply referred to as *bhasha*.

[58] They ate the flesh of the brahmanas who had been killed.

[59] Ilvala invited Agastya to a funeral ceremony and Agastya digested Vatapi.

[60] Agastya.

evening arrived. With his brother, he followed the prescribed rites and worshipped the western sandhya. He entered the hermitage and greeted the rishi. The sage welcomed Raghava in the proper way. He spent a night there and subsisted on roots and fruits. When night was over and the solar disc became sparkling, Raghava took his leave from Agastya's brother. 'O illustrious one! We worship you. We have happily spent the night here. We seek your leave to see your senior, your elder brother. When the permission to leave was granted, the descendant of the Raghu lineage departed.

He followed the indicated path and saw the forests. There was wild grain and *sala*, jackfruit, *ashoka*, *tinisha*, *dhava*, young *bilva*, bilva, *madhuka* and *tinduka* trees. They had blossoms and flowering creepers on their tops. Rama saw hundreds of such beautiful trees there. They had been crushed by the trunks of elephants and were adorned with apes. Flocks of hundreds of maddened birds chirped. The brave Lakshmana, the extender of prosperity, was following at the rear and was nearby. The lotus-eyed Rama spoke to him. 'The trees possess gentle leaves. The animals and birds are quiet. The hermitage of the maharshi with the cleansed soul can't be far away. Because of his own deeds, Agastya is famous in this world. His hermitage can be seen and it destroys the tiredness of those who are exhausted. The forest is enveloped in smoke.[61] The place is clean, with garlands of bark. The herds of deer are quiet. Nor are the birds calling. For the welfare of the worlds, he swiftly controlled death. That performer of auspicious deeds is a refuge and he cleaned the southern direction. This is his sacred hermitage. Because of his powers, the rakshasas are terrified and are not seen to frequent the southern direction. Ever since the performer of auspicious deeds came to the southern direction, those who roam in the night have become pacified and have stopped all enmity.[62] The southern direction is named after that illustrious and accomplished one.[63] He is famous in the three worlds and the perpetrators of

[61] From sacrificial fires.

[62] Probably enmity among themselves.

[63] There is a pun. The south is known as *dakshina* and the word *daksha*/dakshina means someone who is accomplished.

cruel deeds found him difficult to assail. The excellent mountain, Vindhya, always obstructed the sun's path. It is because of his command that the mountain did not increase.[64] The one with the long lifespan is famous in the worlds because of his deeds. Agastya's beautiful hermitage is served by gentle deer. The virtuous one is worshipped in the world and is always engaged in the welfare of the righteous. When we approach him, he will do what is best for us. We will worship the great sage, Agastya, here. O amiable one! O lord! I will spend the rest of the exile in the forest here. The gods, the gandharvas, the siddhas and the supreme rishis always worship Agastya, who is restrained in diet, here. No one who lives here is a liar, cruel, deceitful, violent or addicted to desire. The sage ensures that. The gods, the *yakshas*,[65] the serpents and the birds dwell here together, restrained in diet and worshipping dharma. The supreme rishis cast aside their bodies here. Having become siddhas, without bodies, those great-souled ones go to heaven on celestial vehicles that are like the sun. The gods confer the status of being a yaksha, immortality and many kinds of kingdoms to the auspicious creatures who worship here. We have arrived at the sacred hermitage. O Soumitri! You enter first and tell the rishi that I have come with Sita.'[66]

Chapter 3(11)

Lakshmana, Raghava's younger brother, entered the sacred hermitage. He approached Agastya's disciple and spoke these

[64] Mount Meru was the tallest mountain and Mount Vindhya was jealous. Vindhya grew taller and obstructed the sun's path. Agastya interceded and asked Vindhya to lower itself, so that he and his wife (Lopamudra) could travel southwards. Once he returned from the south, Vindhya could increase its height again. However, Agastya never returned from the south. The name Agastya is derived from mountain (*aga*), stay (*stha*).

[65] Yakshas are semi-divine species, described as companions of Kubera, the lord of riches.

[66] This is a departure from their practice of entering a hermitage together and is worth noting.

words. 'There was a king named Dasharatha. His eldest son, the powerful Rama, has come here with his wife, Sita, and wishes to see the sage. My name is Lakshmana. I am his brother and am engaged in the welfare of my elder brother. If you have heard of us, you know that I am devoted and faithful to him. We have entered this terrible forest on the instructions of our father. All of us wish to see the illustrious one. Please tell him.' Hearing Lakshmana's words, the store of austerities agreed. He entered the place where the sacrificial fire was kept to pass on the information. He quickly entered the place where the unassailable one, foremost among sages, was engaged in austerities. Joining his hands in salutation, he conveyed the news about Rama's arrival. 'Dasharatha's two sons, Rama and Lakshmana have entered the sacred hermitage. His wife, Sita, is also with him. The destroyers of enemies have come here to see you and serve you. You should instruct us about what needs to be done next.' He heard from his disciple about Rama and Lakshmana's arrival and also about the extremely fortunate Vaidehi. He spoke these words. 'It is good fortune that Rama has come here to see me, after a long time. My mind was hoping for his arrival here, to meet me. Go and receive Rama, his wife and Lakshmana properly. Make them enter and come here. Why have they not entered already?' The great-souled sage, who knew about dharma, spoke in this way. The disciple joined his hands in salutation, honoured him and agreed to what he had said. Concerned,[67] the disciple emerged and told Lakshmana, 'Where is Rama? He should himself enter and see the sage.' With the disciple, Lakshmana went to the entrance to the hermitage and pointed out Kakutstha and Sita, Janaka's daughter, to him. The disciple honoured him and repeated Agastya's words. He welcomed them hospitably, following the proper rites, and made the deserving ones enter. Rama entered, with Sita and Lakshmana, and saw the hermitage, which was full of truculent deer.

They progressively passed through Brahma's place, Agni's place, Vishnu's place, the great Indra's place, Vivasvat's[68] place,

[67] Probably because he had not ushered them in immediately.
[68] The sun god.

Soma's place, Bhaga's place, Kubera's place, Dhatri–Vidhatri's place and Vayu's place.[69] Surrounded by his disciples, the sage emerged. In front of him, Rama saw the sage, blazing in his energy. The brave one[70] spoke these words to Lakshmana, the extender of prosperity. 'O Lakshmana! The illustrious rishi, Agastya, is emerging. I can recognize him from his eminence and store of austerities.' Having said this, the mighty-armed scorcher of enemies prostrated himself and seized the feet of Agastya, resplendent like the sun. Honouring him, Rama, with dharma in his soul, joined his hands in salutation. Rama, Lakshmana and Vaidehi Sita stood there. He[71] received Kakutstha and offered him a seat and water. Having asked about his welfare, he asked him to be seated. He rendered oblations into the fire and honoured the guest with *arghya*.[72] Following the dharma of those who are in vanaprastha, he offered them food.[73] The bull among sages, who knew about dharma, sat down first. Rama, who knew about dharma, sat down and joined his hands in salutation. He[74] said, 'O Kakutstha! If an ascetic acts contrary to this,[75] in the world hereafter, he will be treated as one who indulged in perjury and will be made to eat his own flesh. You are a king of all the worlds and a maharatha. You follow dharma. You must be worshipped and revered and you have come here as my beloved guest.' Having said this, he honoured Raghava with fruits, roots and all the other objects of desire. He then added, 'This is a great and divine bow, decorated with gold and diamonds. O tiger among men! This belonged to Vishnu[76] and was constructed by Vishvakarma. These excellent arrows are invincible and are like the sun. They were

[69] To this list of ten, non-Critical versions add the names of other gods too, such as Varuna, Vasu, Garuda, Kartikeya, Dharma and so on.

[70] Rama.

[71] Agastya.

[72] These are objects always offered to a guest—*padya* (water to wash the feet), *achamaniya* (water to wash the mouth/face), arghya (a gift) and *asana* (a seat).

[73] The food offered was appropriate for vanaprastha.

[74] Agastya.

[75] The practice of honouring a guest.

[76] The text says Vaishnava. Strictly speaking, this means associated with Vishnu.

given by Brahma. The great Indra gave me two quivers with an inexhaustible supply of arrows. They are filled with sharp arrows that blaze like a raging fire. There is this large sheath made of silver, with a sword decorated with gold.[77] O Rama! In ancient times, Vishnu used this bow to slay the great asuras in a battle and brought back blazing prosperity to the residents of heaven. O one who deserves honours! For the sake of victory, accept this bow, the two quivers, the arrows and the sword, just as the wielder of the vajra accepted the vajra.' Having said this, the immensely energetic illustrious Agastya gave all those supreme weapons to Rama and spoke again.

Chapter 3(12)

'O Rama! I am delighted. May you be fortunate. O Lakshmana! I am satisfied with you. You have come here with Sita to show me respect. You are exhausted from your journey. You are suffering from great exhaustion and sweating. Your anxiety[78] is evident, especially for Maithilee, Janaka's daughter. She is delicate and has not suffered from such exhaustion earlier. Out of love for her husband, she has accepted this hardship in the forest. O Rama! Act so that Sita can find some pleasure. She has performed the extremely difficult task of following you to the forest. O descendant of the Raghu lineage! Since creation, the natural trait of women is to be devoted in times of prosperity and to forsake in times of adversity. They are as fickle as lightning and as sharp as a weapon. Women are quick to follow,[79] like Garuda or the wind. This wife of yours is free from such taints. She is as praiseworthy as the goddess Arundhati.[80] O destroyer of enemies! O Rama! Whichever

[77] By implication, also given by Indra.

[78] The word used is *utkantha*, which means anxiety. However, it is possible to translate the word utkantha as above the neck, that is, they were sweating above their necks.

[79] Those in prosperity.

[80] Vasishtha's wife.

region you reside in, with Soumitri and Vaidehi, that part will be ornamented.' The sage spoke in this way.

The self-controlled Raghava joined his hands in salutation and addressed these gentle words to the rishi who blazed like a fire. 'O bull among sages! I am blessed that you have shown me your favours. I am content that I have received the boon of a brother and a wife with such qualities. Please tell me about a region that has water and many groves, so that we can construct a hermitage there and always reside happily.' Having heard what Rama had said, the best among sages replied. The one with dharma in his soul thought for a while. Then he patiently spoke these penetrating words. 'O son![81] Two yojanas from here, there is a spot with a lot of roots, fruits and water. There are a lot of deer there and the beautiful region is famous as Panchavatee. Go there and construct a sacred hermitage with Soumitri. Find pleasure there and follow exactly the instructions you received from your father. O unblemished one! I know everything about you, because of the power of my austerities and because of my affection towards Dasharatha. Through my austerities, I also know the desire in your heart. You wish to live here in this hermitage with me. However, I am asking you to go to Panchavatee.[82] That part of the forest is beautiful and Maithilee will enjoy herself there. O Raghava! That part is praiseworthy and is not very far from here. It is near the Godavari and Maithilee will enjoy herself there. There are plenty of roots and fruits and numerous birds of diverse kinds. O mighty-armed one! It is isolated, but is also sacred and beautiful. O Rama! You are good in conduct and are capable of protecting. If you reside there, you will be able to protect the ascetics who are there. O brave one! You can see this great forest of madhuka trees. Go northwards past this until you reach a *nyagrodha* tree.[83] Ascend the mountain that is not very far from there. The perennial flowering grove there is known as Panchavatee.' When Agastya said this, together with Soumitri, Rama honoured

[81] The word used is tata.

[82] Agastya doesn't want Rama to live in his hermitage because he wants the destruction of the rakshasas.

[83] The Indian fig tree.

him and sought the permission of the rishi who was truthful in speech. Having obtained his permission, they worshipped at his feet. With Sita, they left for the hermitage of Panchavatee. The two sons of the king seized their bows. Undaunted in battle, they girded their quivers. Controlling themselves, as instructed by the maharshi, they left for Panchavatee.

Chapter 3(13)

As they proceeded towards Panchavatee, the descendant of the Raghu lineage came across an eagle that was giant in form and terrible in valour. In the forest, the immensely fortunate Rama and Lakshmana saw him. Thinking that the bird was a rakshasa, they asked, 'Who are you?' As if he was delighted, he replied in sweet and amiable words. 'O child! Know me to be your father's friend.' Realizing that he was his father's friend, Raghava worshipped him. Composed, he asked him about his name and his lineage. Hearing Rama's words, the bird told him about his own lineage and also about the origin of all beings.

'O Raghava! O mighty-armed one! Listen. In earlier times, there were the Prajapatis.[84] From the beginning, hear about all of them. Kardama was the first and Vikrita came after him. There were Shepa, Samshraya and the valiant Bahuputra.[85] There were Sthanu, Marichi, Atri, the immensely strong Kratu, Pulastya, Angira, Pracheta and Pulaha. O Raghava! After them, there were Daksha, Vivasvat and Arishtanemi. The immensely energetic Kashyapa was the last among them. O Rama! We have heard that the immensely illustrious Prajapati Daksha had sixty famous daughters. Kashyapa accepted eight of them and they possessed excellent waists—Aditi, Diti, Danu, Kalaka, Tamra, Krodhavasha, Manu and Anala. Delighted, Kashyapa spoke

[84] Literally, lords of beings. They were the creators of beings. The number of Prajapatis varies from text to text, though the usual number is ten. We are given a list of seventeen here, unless Bahuputra is an adjective. Then the number becomes sixteen.

[85] This can also mean that Samshraya had many sons.

to those maidens. "You will give me sons who are like me and can be the lords of the three worlds." O Rama! O mighty-armed one! Aditi, Diti, Danu and Kalaka agreed to this, but the remaining ones paid no heed. O scorcher of enemies! Aditi gave birth to the thirty-three gods—the Adityas, the Vasus, the Rudras and the Ashvins.[86] O son![87] Diti gave birth to illustrious sons, the *daitya*s.[88] Earlier, the entire earth, with its forests and oceans, belonged to them. O destroyer of enemies! Danu gave birth to a son named Ashvagreeva. Kalaka gave birth to Naraka and Kalaka.[89] Tamra gave birth to five daughters who are famous in the worlds—Krounchee, Bhasee, Shyenee, Dhritarashtree and Shukee.[90] Krounchee gave birth to owls and Bhasee gave birth to vultures. Shyenee gave birth to extremely energetic eagles and hawks. Dhritarashtree gave birth to swans and all the aquatic birds. Know that the beautiful one[91] gave birth to fortunate chakravakas. Know that Shukee gave birth to Nata and Nata's daughter was Vinata. O Rama! Know that Krodhavasha had ten daughters from her own self[92]—Mrigee, Mrigamanda, Haree, Bhadramada, Matangee, Shardulee, Shveta, Surabhee, Surasa and Kadruka. O supreme among the best of men! Mrigee's offspring are all the deer and Mrigamanda's are bears, *srimara*s[93] and yaks. Bhadramada gave birth to a daughter named Iravatee. Her son is the gigantic elephant Airavata, the protector of the world. Haree's offspring were lions, tawny apes, the monkeys that look like ascetics and *golangula*s.[94] Shardulee's sons were tigers. O bull among men! Matangee's offspring were elephants. O Kakutstha! Shveta gave birth to sons who are the white *dishagaja*s.[95] O Rama!

[86] Twelve Adityas, eight Vasus, eleven Rudras and two Ashvins.

[87] The word used is tata.

[88] Demons who are descendants of Diti.

[89] The mother is Kaalakaa and the son is Kaalaka.

[90] Tamra didn't agree to have sons.

[91] It is unclear whether this is a reference to Dhritarashtree or Shukee, probably the former.

[92] That is, Krodhavasha didn't have sons either.

[93] Kind of animal that is found in marshy places, similar to deer.

[94] With a tail like that of a cow, langur.

[95] Four (sometimes eight) elephants are believed to hold up the four (or eight) directions.

Surabhee gave birth to two daughters—the fortunate Rohini and the illustrious Gandharvee. Rohini gave birth to cows and Gandharvee's sons were the horses. Surasa gave birth to *naga*s and Kadru[96] to *pannaga*s.[97] O bull among men! Through the great-souled Kashyapa, Manu gave birth to humans—brahmanas, kshatriyas, *vaishya*s and *shudra*s. It has been heard that the brahmanas were born from the mouth, the kshatriyas from the chest, the vaishyas from the thighs and the shudras from the feet. All the trees with auspicious fruit were born from Anala. Vinata was Shukee's granddaughter and Surasa and Kadru were sisters. Kadru gave birth to the thousand-headed serpent who holds up the earth.[98] Vinata had two sons—Garuda and Aruna.[99] I have been born from Aruna and Sampati is my elder brother. Know me to be Jatayu and I am descended from Shyenee. If you so wish, I can help you find a residence. O son![100] I can also protect Sita when you and Lakshmana go out.'

Raghava honoured Jatayu. Delighted, he embraced him and lowered his head. He had heard Jatayu repeatedly say that he had been his father's friend. He took Sita Maithilee with him and that extremely strong bird. With Lakshmana, he went to Panchavatee to burn down his enemies, like a fire to insects.

Chapter 3(14)

They went to Panchavatee, which was full of many predatory beasts and herds of deer. Rama spoke to his brother Lakshmana, who blazed in his energy. 'We have come to the place that the

[96] The same as Kadruka.

[97] Throughout the translation, we have generally used serpents for nagas and snakes for *sarpas*. Nagas are not quite snakes. They are semi-divine, can assume human forms and live in specific regions. All these traits are uncharacteristic of snakes. The word naga is usually used as a synonym for pannaga. But a distinction is being drawn here. With that distinction, a naga is a many-hooded serpent, while a pannaga is an ordinary one.

[98] Ananta, also known as Shesha.

[99] Aruna is the sun's charioteer.

[100] The word used is tata.

maharshi told us about. O amiable one! With groves in blossom, this is the region of Panchavatee. You are accomplished. Cast your eye around everywhere in this forest. In which spot can we construct an excellent hermitage? O Lakshmana! Look for a spot that is near a waterbody, where Vaidehi, you and I can find pleasure. The forest must be agreeable and the water must be agreeable. It must be a spot where flowers, kusha grass and water are nearby.' Thus addressed by Rama, Lakshmana joined his hands in salutation. In Sita's presence, he spoke these words to Kakutstha. 'O Kakutstha! I will be dependent on you for one hundred years. You yourself tell me the agreeable spot where I should construct it.' The immensely radiant one was extremely pleased at Lakshmana's words. He sought out an agreeable spot that possessed all the qualities. Rama measured out the agreeable spot where the hermitage could be constructed. Holding Soumitri's hand in his hand, he said, 'This spot is flat and beautiful. It is surrounded by trees in bloom. O amiable one! You should construct an auspicious hermitage here. Not far away, one can see a beautiful lake that is full of lotuses. The lotuses have a fragrant scent and bear the complexion of the sun. This is exactly as the sage Agastya, cleansed in his soul, had recounted. This Godavari is surrounded by beautiful and blossoming trees. It is full of and adorned with swans, karandavas and chakravakas. There are herds of deer, not too far away and not too close. Peacocks are calling in agreeable tones. The slopes have many caves. O amiable one! Beautiful mountains can be seen, covered with flowering trees. In this place and in that place ores of gold, silver and copper can be seen. They are as radiant as windows, or excellent *bhakti* on elephants.[101] There are sala, *tala*, *tamala*,[102] *kharjura*[103] and *panasa*[104] trees. The place is decorated with wild grain, *tinisha* and *punnaga*.[105] There are mango trees,

[101] The word used is *gavaksha*. This literally translates as the eye of a cow, but means a window. Bhakti means ceremonial and auspicious marks made on the body of an elephant.

[102] Tree with dark bark.

[103] Date palm.

[104] Jackfruit.

[105] This can mean either nutmeg or a white lotus. Nutmeg fits better here.

ashokas,[106] *tilakas*,[107] *champakas*[108] and *ketakas*.[109] Flowering creepers and vines have covered the trees from all sides. There is sandalwood, *syandana*,[110] *neepa*,[111] jackfruit, *lokucha*,[112] dhava,[113] *ashvakarna*,[114] *khadira*,[115] *shami*,[116] *kimshuka*[117] and *patala*.[118] This auspicious spot is delightful and is full of many animals and bird. O Soumitri! With this bird, let us reside here.'

Lakshmana, the slayer of enemy heroes, was thus addressed by Rama. Without any delay, the extremely strong one started to fashion a hermitage for his brother. He levelled out the earth there and constructed an extremely large cottage made out of leaves. It was adorned well with excellent pillars that were made out of hollow bamboo cane from long bamboos. The handsome Lakshmana then went to the river Godavari. Having bathed, he collected lotuses and fruits and returned. Following the prescribed rites, he rendered offerings of flowers for pacification. He then showed Rama the auspicious hermitage that he had constructed. With Sita, Raghava saw the hermitage that the amiable one had constructed. He was overcome with great delight at this cottage made out of leaves. Extremely happy, he embraced Lakshmana in his arms. He addressed him in these extremely gentle and profound words. 'O lord! I am delighted at this great task that you have performed. That is the reason why I have embraced you. O Lakshmana! You know about sentiments. You are grateful.

[106] Tree with red flowers.

[107] Tree with beautiful flowers.

[108] The champaka tree.

[109] The crew pine.

[110] The sandana tree.

[111] Kind of ashoka tree.

[112] Kind of breadfruit tree.

[113] Dhava is the axle-wood tree.

[114] Another name for the sala tree, literally like the ear of a horse. Here ashvakarna is the name of the tree. Elsewhere, *ashva* and *karna* are sometimes referred to as separate trees.

[115] Kind of tree.

[116] Name of a large tree.

[117] Tree with red blossoms.

[118] The trumpet flower.

You know about dharma. You possess dharma in your soul. Through you, my father has obtained a son and lives through him.' Raghava, the extender of prosperity, spoke to Lakshmana in this way. Delighted and happy, he dwelt in the region that had many kinds of fruits. The one with dharma in his soul comfortably resided there for some time, with Sita and Lakshmana, like the immortals in the world of heaven.

Chapter 3(15)

The great-souled Raghava dwelt there happily. *Sharat* season was over and the pleasant *hemanta* presented itself.[119] On one occasion, when night became morning, the descendant of the Raghu lineage went to the beautiful river Godavari, with Sita, to have a bath. His valiant brother, Soumitri, followed him at the rear, with a pot in his hand. He[120] said, 'O beloved one! O one who is pleasant in speech! This is the time when everything is decorated and radiant, suggesting that the year is going to be auspicious.[121] The dew is harsh on people. The earth is full of grain. The water is no longer agreeable and the fire is extremely agreeable. At the time of the new solstice,[122] virtuous ones who worship and render offerings to

[119] The cold season is hemanta, between autumn and winter. Winter proper is *shishira.* Hemanta is the months of Margashirsha (also known as Agrahayana) and Pousha. Margashirsha is roughly mid-November to mid-December, while Pousha is mid-December to mid-January. Sharat is the months of Ashvina (mid-September to mid-October) and Kartika (mid-October to mid-November).

[120] Lakshmana.

[121] This naturally suggests that at the time, the year began in November or December. At the time, the month could have ended with the day of the new moon or the day of the full moon. If it is the former, the new year probably began with the first day of *shukla paksha* in Pousha. If it is the latter, the new year probably began with the first day of *krishna paksha* in Margashirsha.

[122] This solstice means the winter solstice (say December). *Uttarayana* is the movement of the sun to the north of the equator, the period from the winter to the summer solstice (say June). *Dakshinayana* is the movement of the sun to the south of the equator, the period from the summer solstice to the winter solstice.

gods and ancestors, appropriate to the solstice,[123] are cleansed of all sins. The desires of the countryside are met because the cows are full of milk. Kings wander around, setting out on journeys, wishing to be victorious and earn wealth. Having steadily served Yama's direction,[124] the sun still doesn't radiate towards the north, like a woman without a mark on her forehead.[125] The Himalayas are naturally a store of snow. However, since the sun is still far away, it is evident that they have been appropriately named. Those mountains are full of snow. However, at midday, the movement of the sun brings joy and its touch is pleasant and agreeable. The shadow and water are unpleasant. Because of dew, the sun is mild. Because of the wind, the cold is bitter. Devastated by ice, the forest is deserted. That is what days are like now. One can no longer sleep under the open sky. Pushya nakshatra brings a brownish-grey mist. The night[126] is now such that each yama seems to be cold and longer. Though the sun has passed over into a period of good fortune, the solar disc is covered with mist.[127] The moon can no longer be seen, like a mirror rendered blind by the breath. Because of the mist, the moonlight is faded and the day of the full moon is not radiant, like Sita who seems to have become dark because of the heat and no longer seems to be that beautiful. Nature is cold to the touch and is now pierced by the ice. The west wind is blowing and at this time, it seems to be twice as cold. The forest is covered with dew and so are the barley and the wheat. But now that the sun has arisen, it is beautiful and curlews and cranes are calling. The dazzling paddy is bent down slightly, the heads full of rice. The complexion is golden

[123] The sacrifice in question is known as *agrayana,* observed either on the day of the new moon or the day of the full moon.

[124] Yama's direction is the south.

[125] The sky is being compared to a woman's forehead. In the morning, when the sun shines properly, the rising sun will be like the mark on a woman's forehead. But since it is still the cold season, this hasn't yet happened.

[126] *Triyama.* A *yama* consists of three hours. Night is called triyama because it lasts for nine hours.

[127] We have taken some liberties with the text. Otherwise, the meaning is not clear. The text uses the word *samkranta,* meaning 'passed over'. This may well be a reference to *makara samkranti,* a harvest festival celebrated on the day after the winter solstice.

and the form is like that of date flowers. As the sun rises in the distance, it seems to be like the moon. Though the rays radiate, they are enveloped in mist and snow. Even though its[128] energy cannot be felt in the morning, the touch is pleasant at midday. The redness is pale, but the heat makes the earth beautiful. The grass is somewhat wet with the fall of dew. The forests are beautiful and the young sun's heat is permeating the earth. The forest region is enveloped in darkness, shrouded in dew and mist. Bereft of flowers, it seems to be sleeping. The water is covered in mist and the cranes can be discerned only because they are calling. The sand along the banks is wet because of the ice. That is what the river looks like now. The sun is mild because of the fall of snow. The water is generally tasty, but cannot be touched now because of the cold. The lotuses in the lakes are no longer radiant. Their leaves have become old with age. The stalks and filaments have withered away. What is left of the stalks has been destroyed by the snow. O tiger among men! This is the time when Bharata is overcome by sorrow. Out of devotion towards you, the one with dharma in his soul will be observing austerities in the city. He has cast aside the kingdom, his pride and many kinds of objects of pleasure. He is restrained in diet, like an ascetic, and sleeps while lying down on the ground. This is the time of the day when he will certainly wake to perform his ablutions. Surrounded by the ordinary people, he will always go to the river Sarayu. He has been reared in a great deal of happiness. The delicate one will be afflicted by the cold. When night is over, how can he possibly bathe in the Sarayu? He is lotus-eyed and dark. He is handsome and great, with a flat stomach. He knows about dharma and is truthful in speech. His humility is unrestrained and he has conquered his senses. He is pleasant in speech and sweet. The destroyer of enemies is mighty-armed. The noble one has given up all the objects of pleasure in every way and has sought refuge with you. Your brother, the great-souled Bharata, has conquered heaven. Though you are in the forest, he is following you in your austerities. "Human beings do not follow their fathers, but follow their mothers

[128] The sun's.

instead." This is a saying that is famous in the world, but Bharata has acted contrary to this. Kaikeyee's husband was Dasharatha and Bharata is her virtuous son. How can a mother like that be so cruel in her foresight?'

Out of affection, Lakshmana was speaking these words to the one who followed dharma. However, Raghava could not tolerate this censure of their mother and said, 'O son![129] Your medium mother[130] must never be censured. You can continue to speak about the lord of the Ikshvaku lineage[131] and Bharata. My mind is firm in its vow of dwelling in the forest. However, tormented and out of affection, Bharata has committed a childish act.'[132] While he lamented in this way, they reached the river Godavari. With his younger brother and with Sita, Kakutstha performed his ablutions. They worshipped the ancestors and the gods with water. Controlling themselves, they prayed to the rising sun and the gods. Having performed his ablutions, Rama was radiant. With Lakshmana, Sita was the second. Having performed her ablutions, the princess was like the daughter of the mountain,[133] with the illustrious Rudra Isha and Nandi.[134]

Chapter 3(16)

With Sita and Soumitri, Rama had his bath and returned to his own hermitage from the banks of the Godavari. Having returned to the hermitage with Lakshmana, Raghava went to the cottage and performed the morning ablutions. Rama was seated in that cottage made of leaves with Sita. The mighty-armed one

[129] The word used is tata.

[130] We have already commented on Kaikeyee being the medium.

[131] Dasharatha.

[132] Of refusing the kingdom.

[133] Parvati.

[134] Sita is being compared with Parvati, Rama with Shiva and Lakshmana with Nandi.

was like the moon, with the nakshatra Chitra. With his brother, Lakshmana, he talked about various things.

While Rama was seated and attentively speaking in this way, a *rakshasi*[135] roamed around as she willed and arrived at the spot. Her name was Shurpanakha and she was the rakshasa Dashagriva's sister. She approached Rama and saw someone who resembled a god. The mighty-armed one's chest was like that of a lion and his eyes were like the petals of a lotus. He was delicate and great in spirit, with all the signs of being a king. Rama was dark, like a blue lotus. His radiance was like Kandarpa.[136] On seeing someone who was like Indra, the rakshasi was flooded with desire. The one with the disagreeable face faced Rama, the one with the agreeable face. The one with a giant stomach faced the slender-waisted one, the one with malformed eyes faced the one with large eyes, the one with copper-coloured hair faced the one with excellent hair, the one with an ugly form faced the one with a handsome form, the one with a horrible voice faced the one with a pleasant voice, the hideous and ugly one faced the young one, the one who was harsh in speech faced the one who was sweet in speech, the one who was extremely wicked in conduct faced the one who was good in conduct, the ugly one faced the handsome one. With her body thus suffused, the rakshasi spoke to Rama. 'You are in the form of an ascetic, with matted hair. But you wield bow and arrows and are with your wife. Why have you come to a region that is frequented by rakshasas?' Thus addressed by the rakshasi Shurpanakha, the scorcher of enemies, who was upright in his intelligence, started to tell her everything. 'There was a king named Dasharatha and he was like a god in his valour. I am his eldest son. People have heard of me under the name of Rama. This is my younger brother, Lakshmana, who follows me. This is my wife Vaidehi, famous as Sita. To follow dharma and desiring dharma, I followed the instructions of my mother and the king, my father, and came here, to reside in the forest. I wish to know about your account. Who

135 Rakshasa lady.

136 Kama, the god of love.

are you and whom do you belong to? Why have you come here? Tell me the truth about this.' Hearing these words, the rakshasi was afflicted by desire. 'O Rama! I will tell you the truth. Hear my words. My name is Shurpanakha. I am a rakshasi who can assume any form at will. I roam around alone in this forest and create fear in all beings. The rakshasa Ravana is my brother and he is the lord of the rakshasas. So is[137] the extremely strong Kumbhakarna, who sleeps all the time. So is Vibhishana. Though he acts like a rakshasa, he possesses dharma in his soul. Khara and Dushana, famous for their valour in battle, are my brothers. I can surpass all of them. O Rama! O Purushottama![138] As soon as I first saw you and approached you, I was overcome by the thought that you should be my husband. Be my husband for a long time. What will you do with Sita? She is malformed and disagreeable and is not your equal.[139] I am your equal. Look upon me in the form of a wife. This one is vile and malformed. She is terrible in appearance and has a flat stomach. I will devour this woman and your brother. After that, as you desire, you can roam around with me in Dandakaranya, on the summits of mountains and the many kinds of forests.' The one with intoxicated eyes laughed and told Kakutstha this. Addressed in these words, the one who was eloquent in the use of words started to reply.

Chapter 3(17)

Shurpanakha was in the throngs of desire. Rama smiled first. Then, as he willed, he addressed her in gentle words. 'I am married and this is my beloved wife. Therefore, for women like you, it will be extremely distressing to have a co-wife. This younger brother of mine is good in conduct and handsome and pleasant.

[137] That is, the ones who are hereafter mentioned are also brothers.

[138] Literally, excellent man. But we have retained Purushottama, as it is also one of Vishnu's names.

[139] Non-Critical versions have shlokas where Shurpanakha assumes a beautiful form.

The valiant one's name is Lakshmana and he doesn't have a wife.[140] He is without a wife and desires one.[141] He is young and handsome. Given your beauty, he is the right husband for you. O large-eyed one! Seek my brother as your husband. O beautiful one! Without a co-wife, you will then be like Meru, with the radiance of the sun.'[142]

Addressed by Rama in this way, the rakshasi was overcome by desire. She instantly abandoned Rama and spoke to Lakshmana. 'I am lovely. I am beautiful and can be your wife. With me, happily roam around, everywhere in Dandakaranya.' Soumitri was thus addressed by the rakshasi. Lakshmana, accomplished in the use of words, smiled and addressed Shurpanakha in words that were full of reason. 'Why do you desire to be a wife and a servant to someone who is a servant? O one with the complexion of a lotus! I am my noble brother's servant. He is the prosperous one! O one with the unblemished complexion! O lotus-eyed one! You will accomplish your objective if you become the noble one's younger wife. O one with the distended stomach! She is malformed, wicked, cruel and aged. He will abandon such a wife and serve you.[143] O one who is beautiful in complexion! Who will abandon someone who is supreme in beauty? O beautiful one! The one who is accomplished will know what it means to be a human woman.' The hideous one, with the distended stomach, heard what Lakshmana said. She did not know

[140] The word used for Lakshmana is *akritadara* and there has been a lot of speculation about the use of this word. On the face of it, this means unmarried and is therefore a lie, lies being justified under certain circumstances. However, the word akritadara is also capable of being interpreted as someone who has not brought his wife with him, but has left her behind.

[141] This entire section is full of puns that are impossible to translate. Each statement has a double meaning. Rama has one meaning in mind, but Shurpanakha interprets it in a different sense. Rama says, he has been without a wife for a long time, Shurpanakha takes it to mean that he has never had a wife. Rama says, he desires his wife, Shurpanakha takes it to mean that he desires a wife. Rama says, he has not seen his wife for a long time, Shurpanakha takes it to mean that he is handsome. Rama says, he can never be your husband, Shurpanakha takes it to mean that he can be your husband.

[142] Lakshmana being the radiance of the sun.

[143] Lakshmana's words are also full of innuendo, impossible to translate. Shurpanakha takes this to mean that Rama will abandon Sita and serve her. The alternative meaning is that Rama will abandon Shurpanakha and serve Sita.

about jesting and took those words to be the truth. Rama, scorcher of enemies and invincible, was seated in the cottage made out of leaves with Sita. The one who was overcome by desire addressed him. 'She is malformed and wicked. She is ugly and possesses a flat stomach. By clinging on and not abandoning this old and decayed wife, you are not exhibiting a great deal of respect for me. While you look on, I will now devour this human female. Without a co-wife, I will happily roam around with you.' The one with eyes like a burnt-out torch said this. Extremely angry, she then dashed towards the deer-eyed one, like a giant meteor towards Rohini. She descended like the noose of death. However, the extremely strong Rama, became enraged and restrained her. He told Lakshmana, 'O Soumitri! One should never jest with a cruel and ignoble woman. O amiable one! Behold Vaidehi. She is barely able to remain alive. This one is malformed and wicked. She is extremely intoxicated and possesses a distended stomach. O tiger among men! You should disfigure this rakshasi.'

Lakshmana was thus addressed and became wrathful. While Rama looked on, the immensely strong one unsheathed his sword and sliced off her ears and nose.[144] With her ears and nose severed, she screamed in a loud voice. The terrible Shurpanakha rushed away to the forest, where she had come from. The extremely terrible rakshasi was disfigured and blood began to flow. She roared in many kinds of tones, like a cloud that is about to rain down. The one who was hideous to see started to exude many flows of blood. She roared. Clasping her arms, she entered the great forest.[145] The disfigured one went to Janasthana, where Khara was surrounded by a large number of rakshasas. She reached her fiercely energetic brother and fell down on the ground, like a bolt of thunder from the sky. Senseless with fear and with blood flowing, Khara's sister told him everything about how she had been disfigured and about Raghava's arrival in the forest with his wife and Lakshmana.

[144] It is believed that the city of Nashika (Nasika) got its name from this incident.

[145] This probably means that she used her arms to cover her ears and nose.

Chapter 3(18)

She fell down there, disfigured and exuding blood. On seeing her, the rakshasa Khara raged with anger and told her, 'You possess strength and valour. You can go wherever you want. You can assume any form at will. You are Death's equal. Who has reduced you to this state? Which god, gandharva, creature or great-souled rishi possesses the great energy to disfigure you in this way? I do not see anyone in the world who can cause displeasure to me in this way, with the exception of the thousand-eyed great Indra, the chastiser of Paka. Today, I will use my arrows, which can take away lives, to take away life from his body, just as a swan drinks milk from water.[146] I will slay him in a battle and mangle his inner organs with arrows. Whose red blood, mixed with froth, will the earth drink? When I cheerfully slay him in a battle, whose flesh will predatory birds gather around and tear apart and eat? When I make the miserable one suffer in a great battle, the gods, the gandharvas, the *pishachas*[147] and the rakshasas will not be able to save him. You should gradually regain your senses and tell me. Which rash person has vanquished your valour in the forest?'

She heard her brother's words, which were especially laced with rage. Choking with tears, Shurpanakha addressed him in these words. 'They are young and handsome. They are delicate, but immensely strong. Their eyes are as large as lotuses. Their garments are made out of bark and antelope skin. They are like the king of the gandharvas and possess the signs of being kings. I am not interested in debating whether they are gods, *danavas*[148] or humans. There, I saw a woman in between them. She was slender-waisted. She was young and beautiful and was adorned in all kinds of ornaments. I have been reduced to this state because of them, primarily because of the woman. It is as if I do not have a protector. She is deceitful in conduct. When those two are killed, I will remain in the forefront of

[146] When milk is mixed with water, a swan has the reputation of being able to drink the milk, while leaving the water untouched.

[147] Malevolent beings.

[148] Demons.

the battle and drink their blood, together with that of the one who is wicked in conduct.[149] O father![150] My first wish is that you should accomplish this. I wish to drink their blood in a battle.'

When she said this, Khara became angry. He instructed fourteen extremely strong rakshasas who were like Death. 'There are two men with weapons, though their garments are made of bark and antelope skin. With a woman, they have entered this terrible Dandakaranya. They are wicked in conduct and you will return only after you have killed them and this sister of mine has drunk their blood. O rakshasas! Without delay, let my sister's wish be accomplished. Crush them with your own energies.' Those fourteen rakshasas were commanded in this way. They left with her, like dense clouds blown by the wind.

Chapter 3(19)

The terrible Shurpanakha went to Raghava's hermitage. She showed the rakshasas the two brothers and Sita. They saw the immensely strong Rama seated in that cottage made of leaves, with Sita and served by Lakshmana. The handsome Raghava saw them and the rakshasi arriving. Rama spoke to his brother Lakshmana, blazing in energy. 'O Soumitri! Immediately remain close to Sita. I will kill the ones who are following in her[151] footsteps.' Rama, who knew about his soul, spoke in this way. Hearing Rama's words, Lakshmana honoured them and signified his assent.

Raghava strung the great bow that was decorated with gold. The one with dharma in his soul addressed the rakshasas. 'We are Dasharatha's sons, the brothers Rama and Lakshmana. With Sita, we have entered this impenetrable Dandaka forest. We are self-controlled and survive on fruits and roots. We follow the dharma of

[149] Meaning Sita.

[150] The word used is tata. However, we don't know whether Khara was younger or older.

[151] Shurpanakha's.

ascetics. We dwell in Dandakaranya. Why do you wish to cause us injury? I have been engaged by the rishis and have come here with a bow and arrows. In a great encounter, I will kill evil-souled ones like you who cause injuries. If you are satisfied with this, remain here and do not retreat. O ones who roam around in the night! If you value your lives on this earth, you should return.' Hearing his words, the fourteen rakshasas, the slayers of brahmanas and with spears in their hands, became extremely angry. They were terrible and their eyes were red with rage. The ends of their eyes turned red. Though the valiant Rama spoke pleasantly, they spoke harshly and disagreeably, not having witnessed his valour. 'You have made our lord, the extremely great-souled Khara, angry. We will slay you in a battle today and rob you of your lives. Who has the strength to single-handedly withstand many in the field of battle? Since you are standing in front of me, why mention your prowess in a battle?[152] We will release clubs, spears and battleaxes from our arms. You will lose your life, your valour and the bow that you are holding in your hand.' Saying this, the fourteen rakshasas became angry. They raised their sharp weapons and rushed towards Rama. They hurled their spears towards the invincible Raghava. Using fourteen arrows that were decorated with gold, Kakutstha sliced down those fourteen spears. After this, the immensely energetic one became extremely angry and picked up fourteen iron arrows that had been sharpened on stone and were as dazzling as the sun. He seized his bow, stretched it and aimed towards the rakshasas. Raghava released the arrows, like Shatakratu releasing the vajra. Those arrows were gold-tufted and decorated with gold. They blazed through the sky like giant meteors and were as radiant as the sun. With great force, they struck the chests of the rakshasas. Covered with blood, they fell down on the ground, as if shattered by a bolt of thunder. With their hearts shattered, they were like trees severed at the roots. They fell down, bathed in blood and disfigured, robbed of their lives.

On seeing that they had fallen down on the ground, the rakshasi became senseless with rage. Having regained her senses, she emitted

[152] That is, demonstrate it, instead of talking about it.

a terrible roar. Shrieking loudly, Shurpanakha again went to Khara, the blood on her having dried somewhat. Afflicted, she again fell down there, like a juicy creeper. On seeing that the rakshasas had been brought down in the battle, Shurpanakha rushed there again. Khara's sister informed him that all the rakshasas had been killed.

Chapter 3(20)

Khara saw Shurpanakha fall down before him. Though she had come as a calamity,[153] it was evident she desired something. He angrily addressed her. 'I have just commanded brave and flesh-eating rakshasas to accomplish your objective. Why are you weeping again? They are faithful and devoted to me, always engaged in my welfare. Even if they are struck, they cannot be killed. There is no doubt about their not acting in accordance with my words. I wish to hear the reason why you have come here again. Why are you shrieking 'Alas, protector'? Why are you writhing around on the ground, like a snake? Why are you lamenting that you do not have a protector? Indeed, there is a protector in me. Arise. Do not be frightened. Arise. Cast aside this lassitude.' The invincible Khara said this and comforted her.

She wiped away the tears from her eyes and spoke to her brother, Khara. 'You sent fourteen brave and terrible rakshasas to bring me pleasure and slay Raghava and Lakshmana. They were intolerant and wielded spears and battleaxes in their hands. However, Rama has killed all of them in an encounter, using arrows that penetrated the inner organs. I saw those immensely strong ones fall down on the ground in an instant. Witnessing Rama's great deed, I am filled with great fright. O one who roams around in the night! I am scared, anxious and distressed. I can see terror everywhere and have again come to you for refuge. I am submerged in a great ocean of grief, with misery in the form of crocodiles. There is great terror in the

[153] The harbinger of destruction for the rakshasas.

form of garlands of waves. Why don't you save me? They have been slain and have been made to fall down on the ground by Rama's sharp arrows. Those flesh-eating rakshasas have been reduced to this state because of me. O one who roams around in the night! If you have compassion for me and for those rakshasas and if you possess strength and energy, kill Rama, who has made an abode in Dandakaranya and is a thorn for the rakshasas. If you do not slay the enemy Rama today, since I have been ashamed, I will cast aside my life in front of you. Using my intelligence, I can see that you are incapable of standing before Rama in an encounter, when he wields his bow in a great battle. You are proud of your valour, but you are not brave. The bravery that is ascribed to you is false, since you are incapable of killing Rama and Lakshmana, who are mere humans. Quickly abandon Janasthana with your relatives. Lacking spirit and limited in valour, why should those like you reside here? Rama's energy will quickly overcome and destroy you. Rama, Dasharatha's son, is full of energy. I possess an immensely valorous brother, yet I have been disfigured.'

Chapter 3(21)

Shurpanakha taunted the brave Khara in this way. In the midst of the rakshasas, Khara spoke these harsher words. 'Because of the insult that has been inflicted on you, my rage is infinite. I am incapable of bearing it and am like the turbulent salty ocean. I do not reckon Rama as valiant. Humans have limited spans of life. Because of the wicked things that he himself has done, he will be slain and be robbed of his life today. Control your tears and cast aside your fear. With his brother, I will convey Rama to Yama's abode. O rakshasi! He will be slain with a battleaxe today. When Rama, weak in life, lies down on the ground, you can drink his warm blood.' She was delighted to hear the words that issued out of Khara's mouth. In her foolishness, she again praised her brother, supreme among rakshasas. Though she had used harsh words earlier, she praised him again.

Khara addressed his general, named Dushana. 'Instruct fourteen thousand terrible and forceful rakshasas, those whose minds are devoted to me and those who do not retreat from the field of battle. Let them be like dark clouds in complexion, horrible and the perpetrators of cruel deeds. Let them be strong, foremost among those with energy, those who take delight in causing violence to creatures. Let them be as proud as tigers, with large mouths and great in energy. O amiable one! Instruct those rakshasas and arm them with all kinds of weapons. O amiable one! Swiftly equip my chariot with bows, arrows, colourful swords and many kinds of sharp spears. To slay the insolent Rama, accomplished in battle, I wish to advance ahead of the great-souled Poulastyas.'[154] Thus addressed, Dushana arranged a great chariot that had the complexion of the sun. Once it had been yoked to well-trained and speckled horses, he informed that this had been done. It was like the summit of Meru and was decorated with molten gold. The wheels and bumpers were made out of gold and the pole[155] was made out of lapis lazuli. The auspicious signs and decorations were made out of gold and were in the form of fish, flowers, trees, the sun, the moon, flocks of birds and stars. It was filled with standards and swords and ornamented with the best of bells. The intolerant Khara ascended the chariot, yoked to well-trained horses. On seeing that he was astride the chariot, those rakshasas, terrible in valour, surrounded him and the immensely strong Dushana.

All the rakshasas saw Khara, the great archer, march out, with his chariot, shield, weapons and standards and spoke about it. The terrible rakshasa soldiers also emerged, with shields, weapons and standards. They emerged from Janasthana with great speed, emitting a loud roar. They held clubs, swords, spears, extremely sharp battleaxes, broad swords and blazing javelins in their hands. Terrible to behold, they seized spikes, fearful maces, extremely long bows, bludgeons, clubs and vajras. There were fourteen thousand extremely terrible rakshasas. Following Khara's wishes, they

[154] These rakshasas were descended from the sage Pulastya.

[155] *Kubara,* the pole for attaching the yoke.

emerged from Janasthana. On seeing that those rakshasas, terrible to behold, were rushing forward, Khara's chariot held back and followed at some distance. The harnesses of those speckled horses were decorated with gold. Ascertaining Khara's intentions, the charioteer urged them on. Khara was the slayer of enemies. When his chariot was urged on swiftly, it filled the directions and the sub-directions with its roar. Khara's intolerance waxed. To slay the enemy, he advanced hurriedly, like the Destroyer. He roared again and urged the charioteer in a harsh voice. The immensely strong one was like a cloud about to shower down rocks.

Chapter 3(22)

As the inauspicious and terrible army departed, a large and tumultuous cloud, in the shape of a red ass, showered down blood.[156] Though the immensely swift horses yoked to the chariot[157] were proceeding, as they willed, along the flat terrain of the royal road where flowers had been strewn, this made them fall down. A disc that was in the shape of a circle of fire seized the sun and surrounded it, dark in the centre and red at the edges. The standard was raised on a golden pole. An extremely terrible and large vulture came and sat atop this. Many kinds of animals and birds that feed on flesh, with harsh voices, approached Janasthana and surrounded it, shrieking in many kinds of unmelodious tones. Facing the blazing directions, jackals howled in loud tones and these terrible and loud sounds were inauspicious for the demons.[158] Terrible clouds that were like shattered elephants,[159] and were full of blood instead of water, made the sky no longer look like the sky. There was a horrible darkness that made the body hair stand up. The directions and the sub-directions could no longer be clearly distinguished. The

[156] These are evil omens.
[157] Khara's chariot.
[158] The word used is *yatudhana*. A yatudhana is an evil spirit or demon.
[159] Elephants in musth.

sandhya was without radiance and had the complexion of blood flowing from wounds. Facing Khara, animals and birds shrieked in fierce voices. In a battle, jackals always signify the inauspicious and the horrible. They howled in front of the army and their mouths seemed to blaze with flames. Clubs that resembled headless torsos could be seen near the sun. Though it was not the right time, the giant planet, Svarbhanu,[160] seized the sun. As swift winds started to blow, the sun lost its radiance. Though it wasn't night, stars could be seen, and they were like fireflies in radiance. In the lakes, fish and aquatic birds stood still and the lotuses dried up. At that time, the trees were without flowers and fruits. Though there was no wind, dust and red clouds arose. Mynahs[161] chirped. Meteors that were terrible to see fell down with a roar. The earth, and the mountains and forests, started to quake. Astride his chariot, the intelligent Khara was roaring. However, his left arm trembled and his voice turned harsh. While he glanced around in every direction, his eyes filled with tears. His head started to ache. However, because of his confusion, he did not retreat.

There were these ominous portents and they made the body hair stand up. But Khara laughed and spoke to all the rakshasas. 'All these great and terrible portents have arisen and they are terrible to behold. However, because of my valour and strength, unlike a weak person, I do not think about them. Using my sharp arrows, I can bring down stars from the firmament. When enraged, with death as my dharma, I can take on Death.[162] I am not interested in retreating without using my sharp arrows to kill Raghava, who has been agitated by his strength, or his brother, Lakshmana. My sister will satisfy her desire and I will drink their blood. It is because of Rama and Lakshmana that the catastrophe has resulted. Earlier, I have not faced defeat in any battle. I do not utter a falsehood and that is evident to all of you. Even if the king of the gods is angry

[160] Svarbhanu is another name for Rahu. An eclipse occurs when Rahu swallows the sun (or the moon).

[161] *Sharika*, the bird *Turdus salica*.

[162] The god of death.

and advances in a battle astride Airavata[163] and with the vajra in his hand, I can kill him, not to speak of mere humans.' That large army of rakshasas heard him roar in this way. Entangled in the noose of death, they obtained great delight from this.

Desiring to witness the battle, the great-souled ones, rishis, gods, gandharvas, siddhas and *charanas*,[164] assembled. Those performers of auspicious deeds assembled and spoke to each other. 'May cattle, brahmanas and those who are revered by the worlds be fortunate. In the battle, let Raghava be victorious over the descendants of Pulastya who roam around in the night, like the one with the *chakra* in his hand[165] acted in an encounter against all the bulls among the asuras.' Those supreme rishis said many other things, having seen that the army consisted of rakshasas who had exhausted their lifespans.

Ahead of the soldiers, Khara speedily emerged on his chariot. On seeing the rakshasa, many other rakshasas also emerged—Shyenagami, Prithugriva, Yajnashatru, Vihamgama, Durjaya, Karaviraksha, Parusha, Kalakarmuka, Meghamali, Mahamali, Sarpasya and Rudhirashana. Immensely valorous, these twelve advanced, around Khara. Mahakapala, Sthulaksha, Pramathi and Trishira—these four were ahead of the soldiers, following Dushana at the rear. Desiring a battle, they were terrible in force. The brave rakshasa soldiers were extremely fierce. They suddenly advanced against the two princes, like a garland of evil planets towards the moon and the sun.

Chapter 3(23)

Khara, terrible in his valour, advanced towards the hermitage. With his brother, Rama also saw those portents, the extremely inauspicious and terrible omens that made the body hair stand up and signified misfortune to beings. On seeing these, he addressed

[163] Indra's elephant.

[164] Celestial bards.

[165] Vishnu.

Lakshmana in these words. 'O mighty-armed one! Behold. These great portents have arisen and they signify the end of all creatures. However, they will destroy all the rakshasas. The clouds are circling around in the sky, showering down blood and thundering in a harsh tone. Red donkeys are braying harshly. All my arrows are delighted at the prospect of a battle and seem to be smoking. O Lakshmana! The bow with the golden handle seems to be itching. The birds that roam around in the forest are calling, suggesting that fear lies ahead. There is a doubt about remaining alive. There is no doubt that there will be a great encounter. My arm is repeatedly twitching. O brave one! Our victory and the defeat of the enemy are imminent. It is manifest that your face has turned extremely radiant. O Lakshmana! When the faces of those who are headed for battle turn pale, that signifies their lifespans have become exhausted. But a learned man who desires welfare must take precautionary measures when he suspects a calamity. Therefore, take arrows and a bow in your hand. Take Vaidehi and find refuge in a cave that is covered with trees within the mountain. O child! Even if you wish to act contrary to my desires, pledge on my feet that you will leave without any delay.'[166]

Thus addressed by Rama, with Sita, Lakshmana took his bow and arrows and sought refuge inside an impenetrable cave. When Lakshmana listened and entered the cave with Sita, as he had been asked to, Rama donned his armour. In dazzling armour that was like the fire, Rama was resplendent, like a great fire that has arisen in the darkness. The valiant one seized his arrows and raised his great bow, twanging the bowstring with a sound that filled the directions. The gods, the gandharvas, the siddhas, the charanas and the *guhyakas*[167] were terrified and spoke to each other. 'There are fourteen thousand rakshasas who are terrible in their deeds. Rama, with dharma in his soul, is alone. What will the encounter be like?'

[166] Because Rama is capable of taking on the rakshasas alone. Safety may not have been the only reason for sending Sita away. Sita was against the idea of killing rakshasas. Perhaps Rama did not want her to witness the destruction.

[167] Semi-divine species, companions of Kubera, similar to yakshas.

The army of the yatudhanas[168] could be seen in every direction, with a deep and terrible roar, full of shields, weapons and standards. They roared like lions and growled at each other. They stretched their bows and jumped around a lot. The sounds of their roaring mingled with the beating of drums and that tumultuous sound filled the forest. The carnivorous beasts who resided in the forest were frightened at this sound. They fled towards the parts that were silent and did not look back. That extremely powerful army rushed against Rama, wielding many kinds of weapons and looking like the unfathomable ocean. Rama, skilled in war, cast his eye in every direction and saw that Khara's soldiers were advancing for the battle. He stretched his terrible bow and took arrows out of his quiver. He was overcome by great rage and wished to destroy all the rakshasas. Enraged,[169] he was like the blazing fire of destruction and was impossible to look at. On seeing him filled with energy, the divinities of the forest were distressed. Rama's wrathful form was like that of the wielder of the *pinaka*, when he was ready to slay Daksha at the time of the sacrifice.[170]

Chapter 3(24)

Khara reached the hermitage in advance of his troops and saw Rama, the slayer of enemies, there, holding the bow in his hand. On seeing him, Khara raised his strung bow, which made a harsh noise. Raising it, he urged his charioteer to drive towards Rama. At Khara's command, the charioteer urged the horses towards where the mighty-armed Rama was standing alone, wielding his bow. Seeing that he[171] was descending, all the roamers in the night

[168] Evil demons.

[169] Rama was not normally prone to anger.

[170] The pinaka is Shiva's weapon. It is sometimes described as a bow and sometimes as a spear/trident. Daksha had not invited Shiva to the sacrifice. When Sati/Parvati immolated herself, Shiva destroyed the sacrifice.

[171] Khara.

emitted a loud roar and his advisers surrounded him. Khara's chariot was in the middle of all those yatudhanas. He dazzled, like the red-limbed one[172] arising in the middle of the stars. Rama was invincible and wielded a terrible bow. Angrily, all the roamers in the night showered down many kinds of weapons on him. The angry rakshasas wished to kill Rama in the battle and used iron clubs, spears, javelins, swords and battleaxes. They were immensely large and immensely strong and were like clouds. Wishing to kill Kakutstha Rama in the battle, they attacked him. The large number of rakshasas showered arrows on Rama. It was like gigantic clouds showering down on an Indra among mountains. Raghava was surrounded by a large number of terrible rakshasas. It was like Mahadeva being surrounded on an auspicious occasion by a large number of his companions.

The yatudhanas released weapons on Raghava. However, he received them the way the ocean receives the rivers and countered them with his arrows. Though his body was mangled by those terrible weapons, he was not pained. He was like a giant mountain against the onslaught of many blazing vajras. Raghava was pierced throughout his body and there were wounds. Rama was as radiant as the sun, enveloped by clouds during evening. Seeing that the single one was enveloped by many thousands, the gods, the gandharvas, the siddhas and the supreme rishis were distressed. Rama became extremely angry and stretched his bow out, in the form of a circle. He released hundreds and thousands of sharp arrows. They were impossible to stop and impossible to withstand. In the battle, they were like nooses of Death. As if playing, Rama released arrows tufted with heron feathers. As if playing, Rama released these arrows towards the enemy soldiers. Like nooses of Death, they robbed the rakshasas of their lives. With the energy of the fire, those arrows blazed through the sky and penetrated the bodies of the rakshasas, becoming covered with blood. Innumerable extremely fierce arrows were released from the circle of Rama's bow. They descended and robbed the rakshasas of their lives. In the

[172] Mars.

battle, Rama severed hundreds and thousands of bows, the tops of standards, shields, heads, many hands, ornaments and thighs that were like the trunks of elephants. There were hollow arrows and iron arrows, sharp at the tip and tufted. Thus severed, the roamers in the night wailed in terrible tones. The soldiers were afflicted by sharp arrows that penetrated the inner organs, like a dry forest consumed by a fire. Rama did not give them any peace. Some brave roamers in the night, terrible in strength, became extremely angry and released javelins, spears and battleaxes towards Rama. The mighty-armed Raghava used arrows to counter those weapons. In the encounter, he sliced off their heads and took away their lives. The remaining roamers in the night became distressed. Afflicted by arrows, they rushed towards Khara to find refuge.

Seizing his bow, Dushana comforted all of them. Like an angry Rudra or angry Death, he rushed towards Kakutstha. Fearless because of the refuge Dushana had granted, all of them returned. With sala trees, tala trees and rocks as weapons, they attacked Rama. There was an extraordinary and tumultuous battle that made the body hair stand up. Yet again, there was an extremely terrible engagement between Rama and the rakshasas.

Chapter 3(25)

A shower of trees and rocks rained down, capable of taking one's life away. Raghava, with dharma in his soul, used sharp arrows to receive them. He was like a bull that closes its eyes and receives the rain. With the objective of slaying all the rakshasas, Rama invoked great rage. Immersed in rage, he blazed in his energy. From every direction, he shrouded the soldiers and Dushana with arrows. The commander, Dushana, the destroyer of enemies, became angry. He seized a club that possessed the complexion of the summit of a mountain and this made the body hair stand up. It was encased in golden cloth and had crushed the soldiers of the gods. It was made of iron, with sharp spikes that were covered with the fat of enemies.

Its touch was like that of thunder or the vajra. It could break down the ramparts of enemies. It was like a giant serpent. Dushana, the roamer in the night who performed cruel deeds, seized that club in the battle and attacked Rama. When Dushana descended on him, Raghava used two arrows to severe his two arms, bedecked as they were with ornaments on the hands. Thus severed, that gigantic one fell down in the field of battle. The severed club in the hand lay down in the front, like Shakra's standard when it is brought down. With his arms spread around, Dushana fell down on the ground. He was like a spirited and giant elephant when the two tusks have been severed. On seeing that Dushana had been killed in the battle and had fallen down on the ground, all the creatures praised Kakutstha.

Meanwhile, there were three foremost warriors ahead of the soldiers. They too had come under the subjugation of Death's noose. Angrily, they attacked Rama together. They were Mahakapala, Sthulaksha and the immensely strong Pramathi. The rakshasa Mahakapala held aloft a giant spear. Sthulaksha used a sword and Pramathi a battleaxe. On seeing them descend, Raghava used arrows that were sharp at the tip to receive them, just as one welcomes guests who have arrived. The descendant of the Raghu lineage severed Mahakapala's head. He used a torrent of innumerable arrows to crush Pramathi. He stuffed Sthulaksha's large eyeballs with arrows, and slain, he fell down on the ground, like a large tree with branches. The spirited one[173] then used arrows that were like the fire, decorated with gold and diamonds, to kill the remaining soldiers.[174] The arrows were gold-tufted and were like flames with trails of smoke. He slew the rakshasas with those, like a bolt of thunder brings down a large tree. In the field of battle, Rama used one hundred barbed arrows to kill one hundred rakshasas and one thousand to kill one thousand. Their armour and ornaments were shattered. Their bows and arrows were severed and scattered. Covered with blood, the roamers in the night fell down on the ground. In the battle, they fell down with dishevelled

[173] Rama.

[174] Rather inexplicably, the Critical Edition excises shlokas that specifically mention the slaying of Dushana.

hair, drenched in blood. The entire earth was strewn with them, like a giant altar spread with kusha grass. In a short while, when the rakshasas were slain, the forest was covered with mud from their flesh and blood and looked extremely terrible, like hell. There were fourteen thousand rakshasas who were the performers of horrible deeds. Rama, a human who was on foot, slew all of them alone. Among all those soldiers, the only ones who were left were maharatha Khara, the rakshasa Trishira and Rama, the slayer of enemies.[175] That terrible army was destroyed in the battle by Rama, whose strength was superior. On seeing this, Khara resorted to a giant chariot and rushed towards Rama, like Indra with an upraised vajra.

Chapter 3(26)

Khara advanced towards Rama. However, the commander of the army was the rakshasa Trishira. He approached and spoke these words. 'Refrain from this rashness and engage me to show my valour. You will see that I will bring down the mighty-armed Rama in the battle. I know that I am speaking the truth when I touch my weapon and pledge that I will slay Rama. He deserves to be killed by all the rakshasas. Restrain your eagerness to do battle for a while. Instead, examine whether I will ensure his death in battle, or whether he will ensure mine. If Rama is killed, you can happily go to Janasthana. If I am killed, you can advance and fight Rama.' Khara was thus persuaded by Trishira to test his love of death and said, 'Go and fight.' He[176] advanced towards Raghava.

Trishira was on a chariot that was yoked to radiant horses. He rushed towards Rama, like a mountain with three peaks.[177]

[175] The structure of the sentence is such that Rama is mentioned along with the rakshasa soldiers. However, a few more were left, the ones who carried the news to Ravana. Those were ordinary rakshasas, not the main ones.

[176] Trishira.

[177] Trishira means three heads and Trishira possessed three heads.

He released a torrent of arrows that was like a giant cloud. These created a noise similar to the sound from a drum that is wet with water. Raghava saw that the rakshasa Trishira was approaching. He grasped and twanged his bow and picked up sharp arrows. There was a tumultuous encounter between Rama and Trishira. It was between two extremely strong ones, like that between a lion and an elephant. Trishira struck Rama on the forehead with three arrows. Angry, enraged and intolerant, he said, 'Such is the valour and strength of this brave rakshasa! He wounds me on the forehead with arrows that are like flowers. Also accept the arrows that are released from my bow.' Saying this, he angrily used fourteen arrows that were like virulent serpents and in rage, struck Trishira on his chest. With four swift arrows with drooping tufts, the spirited one brought down his four skilled horses. With eight arrows, he brought down the charioteer from the seat on the chariot. Using another arrow, Rama severed the standard raised aloft. With the chariot destroyed, the roamer in the night descended. Rama pierced his heart with arrows and he was rendered immobile. The one with the immeasurable soul then used three forceful and sharp arrows. Intolerantly, he brought down the three heads of that rakshasa. Afflicted by Rama's arrows, the roamer in the night fell down on the ground, where his heads had fallen down in the battle earlier, spouting blood. When he was killed, the remaining rakshasas were in disarray and sought refuge with Khara. They didn't stay, but fled, like frightened deer before a tiger. On seeing them run away and retreat, Khara became quickly enraged. He himself rushed towards Rama, like Rahu towards the moon.

Chapter 3(27)

On seeing that Dushana had been slain in the battle, together with Trishira, Khara was terrified, having witnessed Rama's valour. The army of the rakshasas was immensely strong and impossible to withstand. However, Rama destroyed them single-handedly, even Dushana and Trishira. Seeing that the army was entirely destroyed, the rakshasa Khara was distressed and attacked Rama, like Namuchi against Vasava.[178] Khara forcefully stretched his bow and angrily released iron arrows that fed on blood and were like virulent serpents towards Rama. He twanged the bowstring in many different ways and displayed his learning with weapons. As he roamed around in the battle on his chariot, Khara shot his arrows along many paths. The maharatha filled all the directions and sub-directions with his arrows. On seeing this, Rama also released arrows that were extremely difficult to withstand from his extremely large bow. They were like flames with sparks and incessantly coursed through the sky, like Parjanya showering down rain. Because of those sharp arrows released by Khara and Rama, everything was shrouded in arrows and not a single bit of the sky remained to be seen. The sun was enveloped in a net of arrows and could not be seen. They angrily fought, seeking to kill each other. In the encounter, he struck Rama, who was like a giant elephant, with hollow arrows, iron arrows and barbed arrows that were sharp at the tip. Astride the chariot, the rakshasa presented himself, with the bow in his hand. He was like Yama, with a noose in his hand, and all the creatures saw him. He was like a lion in his valour and his stride was like that of a brave lion. However, like a lion against an inferior animal,[179] Rama was not agitated on seeing him. Khara was on a large chariot that was as radiant as the sun. Like an insect towards a fire, he approached Rama on that. Khara affixed an arrow and displaying the dexterity of his hands, severed the bow held in the hands of the great-souled Rama. Wrathfully, he again seized seven arrows that were like Shakra's vajra in radiance. With these, in that battle, he struck the armour.[180] In the encounter, Khara struck the infinitely energetic Rama with one thousand arrows and roared extremely loudly. Rama's armour dazzled like the sun. However, struck by the arrows with excellent tufts released by Khara, it was severed and fell down on the ground. Raghava was struck by arrows

[178] Namuchi was a demon killed by Indra.

[179] Which could also be an inferior lion.

[180] Rama's armour.

all over his body and became angry. Rama dazzled in the battle, like a blazing fire without any smoke. Wishing to kill the foe, Rama, the destroyer of enemies, strung another large bow that emitted a deep roar. This was the Vaishnava bow that had been given by the maharshi.[181] Raising that supreme bow, he rushed towards Khara. In that encounter, Rama angrily used gold-feathered arrows with straight tufts to sever Khara's standard. That golden standard was worth seeing and it was fragmented in many ways. It fell down on the ground, like the sun falling down on the instructions of the gods. The angry Khara, who knew about striking the inner organs, struck Rama on the body, like striking an elephant with a goad, with four arrows that pierced the chest. Rama was struck by many arrows that were released from Khara's bow. He was pierced and blood started to flow from his limbs. He became extremely angry. In that supreme encounter, he seized the bow that was the best among bows. From that foremost bow, he released six arrows that were aimed at the target. He struck the head with one arrow and the two arms with two others. He struck his chest with three crescent-shaped arrows. After that, wishing to kill the rakshasa, the immensely energetic one wrathfully used thirteen arrows that were as radiant as the sun and had been whetted on stone. The yoke was severed with one and the four speckled horses with four. In the battle, the sixth was used to sever the head of Khara's charioteer. With three, the valiant one severed the *trivenu*.[182] With two, the immensely strong one shattered the two wheels. With the twelfth, he severed Khara's bow, with an arrow affixed to it. In that encounter, Raghava, Indra's equal, seemed to laugh, as he used a thirteenth that was like the vajra to pierce Khara. Khara's bow was shattered. He was without a chariot. His horses had been slain. His charioteer was dead. He seized a club in his hands and leapt down on the ground. The assembled gods and maharshis witnessed maharatha Rama's deed. Delighted, they joined their hands in salutation and

[181] Agastya.

[182] Trivenu means three bamboo poles. One doesn't know what part of the chariot this is, except that it is clearly a joint.

worshipped him, astride their celestial vehicles on which they had assembled.

Chapter 3(28)

Khara was without a chariot. He stood there, with a club in his hand. Gently initially, and harshly later, the immensely energetic Rama addressed him in these words.[183] 'You possessed a huge army with elephants, horses and chariots. Using these, you committed extremely terrible deeds of obstruction that were censured by all the worlds. Someone who agitates creatures performs cruel and wicked deeds. Even if he is the lord of the three worlds, he will not be able to maintain his position. He is like a fierce and evil snake that has turned up and all the people should kill him. If a person does not understand and commits wicked deeds out of greed or desire, his end will be seen, like that of a lizard that eats hail stones.[184] The ascetics follow dharma and dwell in Dandakaranya. O rakshasa! If you slay those immensely fortunate ones, why will you not reap the fruits? Cruel ones who perform wicked deeds are condemned by the worlds. Even if they obtain prosperity, that does not remain for a long time, like a tree that has decayed at the roots. A performer of wicked deeds will certainly reap the consequences. At the right time, he will come to a terrible end, like seasonal flowers falling down from trees. In this world, a performer of wicked deeds suffers the consequences within a short space of time. O one who walks around in the night! It is like eating food mixed with poison. O one who roams around in the night! I am the king who has come here and my task is to slay those who perform wicked and terrible deeds and desire to cause unpleasantness to the worlds. I will release arrows that are decorated with gold. They are like serpents emerging from termite hills. They

[183] These also answer the questions Sita had posed earlier.

[184] Specifically, a type of lizard. The text refers to this type of lizard by name. It is a red-tailed lizard, called a *brahmani* lizard. The belief is that if this lizard eats hail stones, it dies.

will descend on you and pierce you and shatter you. You have eaten those who followed dharma in Dandakaranya. In the battle today, I will slay you and the soldiers who follow you. The supreme rishis, whom you injured earlier, are astride their celestial vehicles and will see you slain with arrows and conveyed to hell. O worst of your lineage! Strike me as you will. Today, I will bring down your head, like a palm fruit.' Eyes red with rage, Rama spoke in this way.

However, senseless with anger, he laughed and replied to Rama in this way. 'O Dasharatha's son! You have slain some ordinary rakshasas in the battle and are praising yourself, for something that does not deserve any praise. Bulls among men who are valiant and powerful pride themselves on their energy and do not indulge in self-praise. In this world, it is only the worst among kshatriyas, ordinary ones who have not cleansed their souls, who futilely indulge in self-praise. O Rama! That is the way you are praising yourself. When the time for battle presents itself, when the time for death has arrived, which brave one will praise himself? In every way, this self-praise demonstrates your inferiority. This is just like the blade of kusha grass, which, when on fire, seems to be like gold. You have not seen me standing here, wielding a club in my hand. I am like a mountain that does not tremble, with minerals in its core, held aloft by the earth. With the club in my hand, I am sufficient to rob you of your life in the battle, like Yama, with the noose in his hand, takes away the lives of all those in the three worlds. Though I wish to say many more things, I will not tell you anything more. The sun is about to set and that causes an obstruction in the way of the encounter.[185] You have slain fourteen thousand rakshasas. Therefore, I will kill you now and wipe away their tears.'

Saying this, the extremely enraged Khara flung the supreme club, encrusted with ornaments, towards Rama, like a blazing bolt of thunder. That giant and blazing club was released from Khara's hand. Having consumed the trees and the creepers, it approached him. The giant club descended like Death's noose. However, while it was still in the sky, Rama shattered it with many arrows. Shattered

[185] No fighting took place during the night.

and fragmented by those arrows, the club fell down on the ground, like a female serpent is brought down through mantras and herbs.

Chapter 3(29)

Raghava, devoted to dharma, shattered the club with his arrows. Delighted, he addressed the enraged Khara in these words. 'O worst among rakshasas! Is this the entire strength of your army that you can display? Your strength is inferior. You are roaring in vain. The club has been shattered by these arrows and has fallen down on the ground. You spoke and boasted a lot. But your faith has also been destroyed. You said that you would wipe the tears of the rakshasas who had been destroyed. Those words of yours have also turned out to be false. You are an inferior rakshasa. You are lowly in conduct and your behaviour is full of falsehood. I will take away your life, like Garuda took the *amrita* away.[186] I will sever your throat today, mangle it with my arrows. The earth will drink the blood and foam that gushes out. Your limbs will be decorated with dust. You will stretch out your arms and lie down, as if sleeping while embracing a woman who is extremely difficult to obtain. O worst among rakshasas! While you lie down in that sleep, this Dandaka, which is no longer a refuge today, will actually become a refuge. O rakshasa! My arrows will destroy Janasthana, and fearlessly, the sages will roam around everywhere in the forest. With their relatives slain, the rakshasis who are causing terror today will run away. They will be distressed and terrified, their faces covered with tears. As a husband, you have wives who are equal to you in lineage and have revelled in the misery of others. Their lives will be rendered futile today. You are cruel in conduct and inferior. You yourself have always been a thorn to brahmanas. It is because of you that sages have been reluctant to light sacrificial fires and offer oblations into them.'

[186] Garuda took amrita away from heaven.

In the battle, Raghava spoke in this way to the enraged Khara. Censured, Khara became more angry and used harsher words. 'Indeed, though you will be destroyed, you are firm. Though there is reason for fear, you are fearless. You have said what should not be said. Though you do not comprehend it, you have come under the subjugation of death. When men are ensnared in the noose of destiny, their six senses[187] are disabled and they cannot distinguish between what should be done and what should not be done.' Angry and frowning, he spoke to Rama in this way. Not very far away, the roamer in the night then saw a giant sala tree. Looking around here and there for something that could be used as a weapon in the battle, he bit his lips and uprooted it. Having uprooted it with his arms, the immensely strong one roared and hurled it towards Rama, saying, 'You have been killed.' As it descended, the powerful Rama sliced it down with his arrows. To slay Khara in the battle, he invoked a fierce rage. Rama was sweating and the ends of his eyes were red with rage. In that encounter, he pierced Khara with one thousand arrows. From the gaps left by the arrows,[188] froth and blood issued, like water flowing down a waterfall on a mountain.[189] In the battle with Rama, Khara suffered from those arrows. As if intoxicated with the smell of blood, he rushed forward impetuously. He descended angrily, covered with blood. Accomplished in the use of weapons and swift in valour, he stepped back two or three steps.[190] To slay Khara in the battle, Rama picked up an arrow that was like the fire and was only second to Brahma's staff. This was given to him by Maghavan, the intelligent king of the gods.[191] The one with dharma in his soul affixed it and released it towards Khara. Rama stretched his bow and released that great arrow, with a sound like that of a storm. It struck Khara in the chest. Consumed by the fire in the arrow, Khara fell down on the ground. It was as

[187] The five senses and the mind.

[188] The body was covered by arrows and there were gaps left on the body.

[189] Alternatively, the mountain named Prasravana.

[190] Rama is the one who is accomplished in the use of weapons. He stepped back two or three steps so as to strike better.

[191] Through Agastya.

if Andhaka had been burnt down by Rudra in Shvetaranya.[192] Just as Indra killed Vritra with the vajra, Namuchi with foam and Bala with the vajra, Khara was slain and brought down.[193]

At this time, all the *rajarshi*s and supreme rishis assembled. Delighted, they worshipped Rama and spoke these words. 'It was for this reason that the immensely energetic and great Indra, Purandara, the chastiser of Paka, came to Sharabhanga's sacred hermitage once. The maharshis thought of a means to bring you to this region, so that these cruel rakshasas, the perpetrators of wicked deeds, could be killed. O Dasharatha's son! You have accomplished this task for us. The maharshis can now happily roam around in Dandaka and pursue dharma.'

Meanwhile, with Sita, the brave Lakshmana emerged from the cave in the mountain and happily entered the hermitage. Rama was victorious and was worshipped by the maharshis. The brave one entered the hermitage and was honoured by Lakshmana. Vaidehi was delighted to see her husband, the slayer of the enemy and the one who had brought happiness to the maharshis. She embraced him.

Chapter 3(30)

Shurpanakha saw that Rama had single-handedly slain fourteen thousand rakshasas who were the performers of terrible deeds. In the battle, he had also killed Dushana, Khara and Trishira. On seeing this, she again uttered a mighty roar, like the thunder of a cloud full of water. She witnessed Rama's deed, which others would have regarded as extremely difficult. Extremely anxious, she went to Lanka, ruled over by Ravana. Astride the foremost of *vimana*s,[194] she saw the seated Ravana, blazing in his energy. He was with

[192] Literally, *shvetaranya* means 'white forest'. Andhaka was a demon killed by Shiva.

[193] The demon Namuchi had a boon that he could not be killed by anything wet or dry. Therefore, Indra killed with foam from the water.

[194] This was the Pushpaka vimana. However, the text only uses the word vimana and this could simply mean a palace.

his advisers, like Vasava amidst the Maruts. He was seated on a supreme and golden throne that was like the sun. He was like the fire of a sacrificial altar, when oblations of ghee had been poured on to it. He was terrible and could not be vanquished in battle by the gods, the gandharvas and the great-souled rishis. He was like Death with a gaping mouth. He had crushed the gods and the asuras and there were scars left by the vajra. There were scars on his chest, when Airavata had gored him with his sharp tusks. With his twenty arms and ten heads[195] and his accoutrements, he was a sight to behold. The brave one's broad chest bore all the signs of his being a king. His earrings were made out of molten gold and were decorated with shining lapis lazuli. His arms were excellent. His teeth were white and his mouth was large.[196] He was like a mountain. In hundreds of battles with the gods, his body had been marked by Vishnu's chakra.[197] All his limbs had been struck by the weapons of the gods. Like the ocean, he could not be agitated. However, he was swift in his action and himself caused agitation. He was the one who hurled the summits of mountains and crushed the gods. He was the one who destroyed dharma and oppressed the wives of other people. He possessed all the divine weapons and always caused impediments to sacrifices. He went to the city of Bhogavati and defeated Vasuki.[198] He defeated Takshaka and abducted his beloved wife. He went to Mount Kailasa and vanquished Naravahana.[199] He seized his Pushpaka vimana, which can travel anywhere at will. In his rage, the valiant one destroyed the groves of the gods, the divine grove of Chaitraratha and the grove of Nandana, filled with lotuses.[200] His

[195] Literally, ten necks or throats.

[196] The mouth is mentioned in the singular.

[197] This doesn't mean the famous *sudarshana chakra,* used by Vishnu alone. Presumably, other gods used chakras that were similar to the sudarshana chakra.

[198] Bhogavati was the capital city of the nagas and Vasuki was the king of the nagas. Takshaka was a naga and Takshashila is named after him. In the Mahabharata, Takshaka's wife was killed by Arjuna.

[199] Naravahana is Kubera's name. Literally, the word means someone whose mount is a man.

[200] Chaitraratha is the name of Kubera's pleasure garden, while Nandana is the name of Indra's pleasure garden.

arms were like the summits of mountains and with those, he was capable of restraining the two scorchers of enemies, the immensely fortunate sun and the moon, when they were about to rise. In ancient times, in the great forest, he had tormented himself with austerities for ten thousand years. The patient one had then offered his heads to Svayambhu.[201] He had then obtained the boon that he would not suffer fear in any battle with gods, danavas, gandharvas, pishachas, birds and serpents and would not meet his death through them, with the exception of humans.[202] Consecrated by mantras, brahmanas kept oblations of soma in sacrificial vessels and the immensely strong one seized this. When sacrifices were about to be completed, the cruel one stole them.[203] He was wicked in conduct and killed brahmanas. He was incessantly harsh and engaged in causing harm to subjects. Such was Ravana, fearful to all creatures and to all the worlds. The rakshasi saw her cruel and immensely strong brother. He was attired in divine garments, with celestial ornaments. He was decorated with divine garlands. This was the immensely fortunate Indra among rakshasas, the delight of the lineage of Pulastya.

Senseless with fear and delusion, the large-eyed one displayed these to the blazing one and spoke to him. Fearless in action, Shurpanakha, who had been disfigured by the great-souled one, spoke these extremely terrible words.

Chapter 3(31)

Ravana was one who made the worlds wail.[204] He was in the midst of his advisers. Distressed and angry, Shurpanakha

[201] Brahma.

[202] Because he thought so lightly of humans, Ravana forgot to mention humans in the boon he got.

[203] The personifications of those sacrifices.

[204] There is a pun, based on the derivation of the word Ravana. The word *rava* means to wail, so Ravana means someone who causes wailing. There is a different story about how Shiva made Ravana wail, which explains the derivation of the word Ravana. That story will be told later.

addressed him in these harsh words. 'You are intoxicated because of your addiction to desire and objects of pleasure. You do what you will, without any restraints. A terrible fear has arisen and one should know about it. However, you don't realize it. If a king is addicted to carnal desire and conducts himself in accordance with that desire, the subjects do not respect such an avaricious person, but regard him like the fire of a cremation ground. At the right time, if a king does not himself undertake the tasks that need to be done, he will be destroyed, with his kingdom and with those tasks. If a king cannot control himself and spies find it extremely difficult to meet him, men abhor him from a distance, like elephants avoid mud in a river. If a king cannot control himself and does not protect the kingdom, his prosperity will not manifest itself, like a mountain that is submerged in the ocean. Engaging with gods, gandharvas and danavas, you are apparently enhancing your own prosperity. However, you are fickle and do not engage with spies. How can you be a king? O supreme among victorious ones! If kings do not control themselves and don't possess spies, treasuries and proper policies, they are the equals of ordinary people. From the words spoken by spies, from a distance, kings can discern everything about the pursuit of artha. Such kings are far-sighted. I think that you do not interact with your spies and therefore only consult ordinary advisers. Despite your own relatives having been killed in Janasthana, you do not know about it. There were fourteen thousand rakshasas, terrible in their deeds. Rama has single-handedly slain them, along with Khara and Dushana. He has granted safety to the rishis and brought peace to Dandaka. Rama, unblemished in his deeds, has thus oppressed Janasthana. O Ravana! You are avaricious and intoxicated. You are under the control of others. A fear has arisen within your own dominion, but you do not understand this. If a king is fierce, does not give generously, is intoxicated, proud and deceitful, at times of hardship, creatures do not approach him. If a king is extremely vain, impossible to approach, indulging in self-praise and prone to anger, at times of hardship, his own relatives will kill him. If he does not swiftly perform the required tasks, and is scared even though there is no reason to be frightened, he will be dislodged from his kingdom and, in his distress, he will become like an ordinary blade of grass. Dried wood, stones and even dust serve some purpose. But kings who have been dislodged from their positions have no utility. A king who has been dislodged from his kingdom may be capable. However, he serves no purpose, like a garment that has been worn, or a garland that has been crushed. If a king is not distracted, knows everything, has conquered his senses, is grateful and is devoted to dharma, such a king remains for a long time. If the eyes of good policy are awake even when the eyes are sleeping, and if anger and favours manifest themselves, it is only then that a king is worshipped by people. O Ravana! You are evil in intelligence. You are devoid of these qualities. After all, through your spies, you have not been informed about the great destruction of rakshasas that has occurred. You disrespect others. Though you rule over a kingdom, you do not know the truth about the apportioning of time and space.[205] You do not possess the intelligence to distinguish between qualities and sins. The kingdom is in danger. Within a short span of time, you will be brought down.'

She recounted his own taints in this way. Using his own intelligence, the lord of those who roam around in the night reflected on them. Possessing riches, insolence and strength, Ravana thought for a long time.

Chapter 3(32)

In the midst of the advisers, Ravana spoke these harsh words to the angry one. Enraged, Ravana asked her. 'Who is Rama? What is his valour like? What is his appearance? How brave is he? Dandakaranya is extremely difficult to penetrate. Why has he come here? What are the weapons Rama used to slay the rakshasas and kill Khara, Dushana and Trishira in the battle?'

[205] The idea is that a king must apportion out time between dharma, artha and kama, and not spend all of his time on one, at the expense of the others.

Thus addressed by the Indra among rakshasas, the rakshasi became senseless with rage. She started to describe Rama properly. 'His arms are long and his eyes are large. His garments are made out of bark and dark antelope skin. Rama is Dasharatha's son and his beauty is like Kandarpa.[206] He stretches a bow that is decorated with gold and is like Shakra's bow. He shoots blazing iron arrows that are like serpents with virulent poison. In the battle, I could not see when the immensely strong Rama took out those terrible arrows, released them, or stretched his bow.[207] I saw those soldiers slaughtered by the shower of arrows. It was like an excellent crop of grain devastated by Indra's shower of hail stones. There were fourteen thousand rakshasas who were terrible in their valour. A single one on foot slew them with sharp arrows, together with Khara and Dushana, within the space of one-and-a-half *muhurta*s.[208] He granted safety to the rishis and brought peace to Dandaka. Somehow, I alone managed to escape from being vanquished by that great-souled one. Rama, who knows about his soul, hesitated to kill a woman.[209] His brother is immensely energetic and is his equal in qualities and valour. The valiant one is faithful and devoted to him and his name is Lakshmana. He is intolerant and impossible to defeat. He is victorious, brave, intelligent and strong. He is always like Rama's right arm, as is his[210] breath of life, moving around outside. Rama possesses an illustrious and large-eyed wife.[211] The beautiful and slender-waisted one has the name of Sita Vaidehi. Earlier, I have never seen a woman with her kind of beauty on this earth, be it a goddess, or a gandharva,

[206] Kama, Manmatha or Madana, the god of love.

[207] The action was too fast.

[208] Though it is sometimes used in the sense of an instant, a muhurta is a measure of time, equal to forty-eight minutes. The encounter lasted for just over an hour.

[209] Oddly, the Critical Edition excises some shlokas. In one of these, Ravana asks about Shurpanakha's disfigurement, which he was certain to notice. Though Shurpanakha distorted the story to suit herself, the reply doesn't mention the disfigurement either, at least not directly. In passing, non-Critical versions also have an account about a rakshasa named Akampana informing Ravana about the incident before Shurpanakha does.

[210] Rama's.

[211] Literally, wife according to dharma.

yaksha or *kinnara* lady.[212] If Sita becomes the wife of a person and cheerfully embraces him, he truly lives in all the worlds, even more than Purandara. She is good in conduct. Her form is praiseworthy. Her beauty is unmatched on earth. She is the appropriate wife for you and you are the right husband for her. Her hips are wide. Her breasts are full and peaked. I wished to bring that beautiful one here as your wife. Vaidehi's face is like the full moon. If you see her now, you will also have to seek refuge with Manmatha. If you have intentions of accomplishing the objective of obtaining her as your wife, you should act quickly. Stretch out your right foot for the sake of victory.[213] O lord of rakshasas! Do what will bring pleasure to the rakshasas. Slay the cruel Rama who lives in a hermitage. Slay maharatha Lakshmana with your sharp arrows. When her protectors have been slain, you will be able to happily enjoy Sita. O lord of the rakshasas! O Ravana! If my words appeal to you, without any doubts, act in accordance with my words. You have heard that Rama used straight-flying arrows to slay the roamers of the night who had gone to Janasthana. You have also learnt that Khara and Dushana have been killed. You should now arise and do what needs to be done.'

Chapter 3(33)

He heard Shurpanakha's words and they made the body hair stand up. He made up his mind about what should be done. Taking his leave of his advisers, he departed. He thought about the appropriate course of action that should be followed. He weighed the pros and cons and thought about the strengths and weaknesses. He then made up his mind about what should be done. Having decided this, he went to the beautiful quarter[214] where all the vehicles were kept. The lord of the rakshasas secretly went to

[212] Kinnara, also known as *kimpurusha,* is a semi-divine species, described as Kubera's companions.

[213] The left foot is inauspicious.

[214] That is, a garage.

the garage and instructed the charioteer, 'Yoke the chariot.'[215] In a short while, the charioteer, quick in his valour, yoked the excellent and favourite chariot. The golden chariot could travel, as it willed, through the sky. It was adorned with jewels. It was yoked to mules, with faces like pishachas, and with golden harnesses. The lord of the rakshasas, Dhanada's prosperous younger brother,[216] went to the lord of the male and female rivers.[217] Dashanana[218] was fanned with whisks made of white yak hair and a white umbrella was held aloft his head. His ornaments were made out of molten gold and had the complexion of mild lapis lazuli. With ten faces and twenty arms, his garments deserved to be seen. He was the enemy of the gods and the one who killed sages. With ten heads, he was like a king of the mountains. Astride a chariot that could travel at will, the lord of the rakshasas was radiant. It[219] looked like a cloud in the sky, encircled with lightning and with flying cranes.

The valiant one looked at the shoreline of the ocean, with mountains and full of thousands of trees with many kinds of flowers and fruits. In every direction, there were lakes with lotuses, full of auspicious and cool water. There were large hermitages, with decorated sacrificial altars. It was ornamented with coconut trees and plantain trees were like a dam. There were blossoming sala, tala and *tamala*[220] trees. It was ornamented with supreme rishis who were extremely restrained in their diet. There were thousands of nagas, birds, gandharvas and kinnaras. The place was beautiful with siddhas and charanas who had conquered desire. There were *aaja*s, vaikhanasas, *masha*s, valakhilyas and marichipas.[221] There

[215] The reason for Ravana going secretly and not asking someone else to convey the command to the charioteer remains a matter of speculation.

[216] Dhanada is one who bestows riches and is Kubera's name. Ravana was Kubera's younger brother.

[217] The ocean.

[218] Meaning one with ten faces, Ravana's name.

[219] The chariot.

[220] Tree with dark bark.

[221] Aajas are those without birth, so they mean Brahma's mental children; vaikhanasas are hermits; and mashas are difficult to pin down, probably meaning sages who subsist only on beans.

were thousands of apsaras who knew about the techniques of sexual pastimes, wearing divine ornaments and garlands and enveloped in celestial forms. The beautiful wives of the gods frequented the place and loved it. Large numbers of gods and danavas wandered around, desiring amrita.[222] The place was filled with swans, curlews and frogs. There were the sounds of cranes. It was spread over with mild and beautiful lapis lazuli and the ocean's energy. In every direction, there were vimanas, large and white, decorated with divine garlands and filled with the sound of trumpets and singing. They could travel at will and such worlds could be won[223] by those who practised austerities. Dhanada's younger brother saw them,[224] served by gandharvas and apsaras. He saw thousands of gentle forests, filled with roots that exuded the juices of sandalwood. These satisfied the sense of smell. There were the best of forests and groves, filled with aloe. There were fragrant fruits from nutmeg and bay rum trees.[225] There were blossoming tamala trees and clumps of pepper. Large numbers of oysters were drying along the shore. There were conch shells, rocks and heaps of coral. There were gold and silver hills in every direction. There were waterfalls pleasing to the mind and sparkling lakes. The place was filled with riches and grain and gems among women. He also saw cities, with sheds for elephants, horses and chariots. It was level and pleasant in every direction. The breeze was mild to the touch. He saw the shore of the lord of the rivers and it was like heaven.

He saw a nyagrodha tree there.[226] It had the complexion of a cloud and was surrounded by rishis. In every direction, its branches stretched out for a hundred yojanas. The immensely strong Garuda seized the elephant and the extremely large tortoise as food and sat down on its branch to eat them.[227] When the

[222] Amrita emerged from the churning of the ocean.

[223] With such vimanas.

[224] The vimanas.

[225] *Takkola,* meaning the bay rum tree.

[226] These shlokas about Garuda are a bit of a digression.

[227] The story is about a giant elephant and tortoise who were fighting. While they fought, Garuda seized them both and ate them.

supreme among birds suddenly sat down on the branch, covered with many leaves, because of the burden caused by the immensely strong Suparna, it broke. The supreme rishis, the vaikhanasas, the mashas, the valakhilyas, the marichipas, the aajas and the *dhumras*[228] were collectively attached to the branch.[229] Garuda was overcome with compassion for them. With great force, he seized the broken branch that was one hundred yojanas long and the elephant and the tortoise. The one with dharma in his soul used one talon to devour the flesh. The supreme among birds used the branch to destroy the dominion of the *nishadas*.[230] Having been freed, the great sages were infinitely delighted. Their delight was doubled when the intelligent one turned his intelligence towards bringing the amrita and performed an act of valour. He shattered the mesh made of iron and broke into the excellent vault meant for treasures. He penetrated the protected residence of the great Indra and carried the amrita away. Dhanada's younger brother saw the nyagrodha named Subhadra, frequented by large numbers of maharshis and with Suparna's marks on it.

He passed over to the other shore of the ocean, the lord of the rivers. At the end of a beautiful and sacred forest there, he saw a lonely hermitage. He saw the rakshasa named Maricha there, restrained in his food. He was attired in black antelope skin and bark and sported matted hair. In the proper way, Ravana approached the rakshasa. After this, the one who was eloquent in the use of words[231] addressed him in these words.

[228] Sages who subsist on smoke.

[229] They were performing austerities on the branch.

[230] This requires explanation. Garuda seized the elephant in one talon and the tortoise in the other talon. He then settled down on the branch to eat them, noticing the sages in the process. When the branch broke, Garuda took off. While still in flight, he ate the elephant and caught the tortoise with one talon. After the sages escaped, Garuda flung the branch away. This descended on the dominion of the nishadas and destroyed them.

[231] Ravana.

Chapter 3(34)

'O Maricha! O son![232] Listen to the words I am going to speak. I am afflicted. You are the supreme refuge in my state of affliction. You know about Janasthana. My brother, Khara, the mighty-armed Dushana, my sister, Shurpanakha, the immensely energetic rakshasa, Trishira, who survived on human flesh, and many other brave roamers in the night who were successful in their objectives followed by counsel and resided there. Those rakshasas dwelt there. In that great forest, they obstructed the sages who sought to follow dharma. There were fourteen thousand rakshasas who were terrible in their deeds. They were brave and successful in their objectives. They followed Khara's wishes. Those immensely strong ones used to reside in Janasthana now. In a battle, they had a supreme engagement with Rama. In the field of battle, Rama's rage was ignited by this. Though he did not utter anything harsh, he affixed arrows to his bow. There were fourteen thousand rakshasas who were fierce in their energy. A man on foot used sharp arrows to slay them. In the battle, Khara was slain and Dushana was brought down. Trishira was killed and he rendered Dandaka free from fear. With his wife, his father exiled him in his rage and he possesses a limited lifespan. That Rama, the worst among kshatriyas, has killed those soldiers. He is wicked in conduct and harsh. He is fierce, stupid and greedy and has not conquered his senses. He has abandoned dharma and has adharma in his soul. He is engaged in causing injury to creatures. There was no reason for enmity in the forest. Yet, he resorted to his spirited nature and disfigured my sister by slicing off her nose and ears. His wife is Sita and she is like a daughter of the gods. She is in Janasthana. With you as my aide, I will use my valour to bring her away. O immensely strong one. With you by my side as my aide and with my brothers, I will not worry about fighting against the assembled gods in a battle. O rakshasa! Become my aide. You are capable. With your valour and your pride, there is no one who is your equal in a battle. O one who

[232] The word used is tata.

roams around in the night! This is the reason why I have come here and approached you. Listen to me about what you have to do to help me. My words will spell out your task. Assume the form of a golden deer, with colourful silver spots. Roam around in Rama's hermitage, in front of Sita. On seeing you in the form of a deer, there is no doubt that Sita will ask her husband and Lakshmana to seize you. When they are away and Sita is alone, without any impediments, I will cheerfully abduct her, like Rahu robs the moon of its radiance. After that, Rama will be miserable and afflicted because his wife has been abducted. I will strike him if he retaliates and thus accomplish the inner desire of my heart.'

The great-souled Maricha heard this about Rama. His mouth turned dry and he was terrified. He knew about Rama's valour in the great forest. He was scared and miserable in his mind. He joined his hands in salutation and addressed Ravana in the following words, knowing what would be good and what would be bad for his own self.

Chapter 3(35)

The one who was eloquent in the use of words heard the words spoken by the Indra among the rakshasas. The immensely wise Maricha replied to the lord of the rakshasas. 'O king! It is always easy to get men who are pleasant in speech. It is extremely difficult to find a speaker and a listener for disagreeable medication. There is no doubt that you do not know about Rama's great valour and superior qualities. You are fickle and do not engage with your spies. He is like the great Indra and Varuna. O father![233] Will there be safety for all the rakshasas on earth? Or will Rama be enraged and render the world devoid of rakshasas? Has Janaka's daughter been born to bring an end to your life? Is Sita going to be the reason behind a great catastrophe for us? If you completely follow this

[233] The word used is tata.

conduct engendered by desire and she obtains you as her lord, will the city of Lanka, with you and the rakshasas, be destroyed? If an evil-minded king like you engages in conduct that is engendered by desire and follows wicked conduct and evil counsel, he destroys his own self, the people and the kingdom. He has not been abandoned by his father and no disrespect has been shown to him. He is not greedy. He is not wicked in conduct. Nor is he the worst among kshatriyas. The extender of Kousalya's delight is not devoid of the qualities of dharma. He is engaged in the welfare of all creatures and is not violent towards them. His father was truthful in speech and was deceived by Kaikeyee. On seeing this, the one with dharma in his soul agreed to exile in the forest. He wished to do what would bring pleasure to Kaikeyee and to his father, Dasharatha. He abandoned the kingdom and objects of pleasure and entered the Dandaka forest. O father![234] Rama is not harsh. He is not devoid of learning. It is not that he has not conquered his senses. He is not false. He is not bereft of learning. You should not speak in this way. Rama is the personification of dharma. He is virtuous. Truth is his valour. He is the king of all the worlds, like Vasava among the gods. He can protect Vaidehi through his own energy. Like robbing the sun of its radiance,[235] how can you wish to rob him of his resplendence? In a battle, the rays of his arrows are invincible and his bow and arrows are like kindling. When the fire that is Rama blazes suddenly, you should not enter it. The flaming mouth of the bow will gape. The rays of arrows cannot be tolerated. The brave one will wield bow and arrows that will destroy the enemy soldiers. O father! If you desire your own welfare and do not wish to give up your kingdom, your happiness and your life, you should not test Rama. He is like Death. His energy is immeasurable and Janaka's daughter is his wife. When she is under the protection of Rama's bow in the forest, you are incapable of abducting her. He loves the wife more than his own life and she is always devoted to him. The slender-waisted Sita is

[234] The word used is tata.

[235] The word used is *prabha,* referring to the sun's radiance. However, there is another related meaning too. Prabha is the sun's wife.

like the flames of a sacrificial fire into which oblations have been offered. O lord of the rakshasas! Why do you wish to undertake a futile endeavour? Even if he glances at you in a battle, your life will come to an end. Life, happiness and the kingdom are extremely difficult to obtain. Make up your mind and consult with all the advisers and those who follow dharma, with Vibhishana at the forefront. Reflect on the pros and the cons and the strengths and the weaknesses. Determine the truth about your own strength and that of Raghava's. You should make up your mind about what is most beneficial and act accordingly. I do not think that you should embark on this battle and encounter with the son of the king of Kosala.[236] O lord of those who roam around in the night! Listen yet again to these excellent and desirable words.'

Chapter 3(36)

'With my great valour, I was once travelling around this earth. I possessed the strength of thousands of elephants and was like a mountain. I was like a dark blue cloud and wore golden earrings. Wearing a crown and with a club as a weapon, I generated fear in the worlds. I wandered around Dandakaranya, devouring the flesh of rishis. The great sage, Vishvamitra, with dharma in his soul, was terrified of me. He himself went to King Dasharatha and spoke these words. "The right time has come and let this Rama protect me. O lord of men! A terrible fear has arisen on account of Maricha." Thus addressed, King Dasharatha, with dharma in his soul, replied to the immensely fortunate and great sage, Vishvamitra. "Raghava is less than sixteen years old and is unskilled in the use of weapons. If you wish, I and all my soldiers will go with you. O best among sages! As you wish, I will slay your enemy." Thus addressed, the sage spoke to the king. "With the exception of Rama, no other force will

[236] We have earlier remarked that this reference to Dasharatha as the king of Kosala is odd.

be sufficient for that rakshasa. Though he is a child, he is immensely energetic and is capable of restraining him. O scorcher of enemies! May you be fortunate. Let me take Rama and go." Saying this, the sage took the prince. Extremely delighted, Vishvamitra went to his own hermitage and consecrated himself for a sacrifice. Rama was there, twanging his colourful bow. At that time, the handsome one still didn't have a beard on his face. He was dark and with excellent eyes. He was attired in a single garment, with a bow, crested hair and a golden garland. He rendered Dandakaranya beautiful with the radiance of his own energy. At that time, Rama was seen to be like the young moon when it has arisen.

'I was like a cloud, with earrings made out of molten gold. Strong and insolent because of the boon I had obtained,[237] I went to that hermitage. With an upraised weapon, I entered violently. On seeing me, he was not scared and strung his bow. Because of my delusion, I took Raghava to be a child and did not show him any respect. I quickly rushed towards Vishvamitra's sacrificial altar. He released a sharp arrow that was capable of killing the enemy. Struck by it, I was flung one hundred yojanas away, into the ocean. Because of the force of Rama's arrow, I became unstable and my senses were in a whirl. I was then submerged into the deep waters of the ocean. O father! After having regained my senses after a long time, I went to the city of Lanka. I escaped in this way, though my aides were slain. Though Rama was still a child and not skilled in the use of weapons, he was unblemished in his deeds. Therefore, I will restrain you from a clash with Rama. If you do so, there will be a great catastrophe and you will quickly be destroyed. The rakshasas know about sporting and satisfying desire. Their assemblies are engaged in festivities. You will rob them of those and bring about torment and calamity. The city of Lanka has mansions, palaces and ramparts. It is decorated with many jewels. Because of Maithilee, you will witness its destruction. Like fish in a lake where there is a serpent, even if virtuous people do not engage in wicked acts, but consort with those who are wicked, they are destroyed

[237] Boon obtained from Brahma.

because of the sins of others. The rakshasas are smeared with divine sandalwood paste and celestial unguents. They are adorned with divine ornaments. Because of your sins, you will see them slain and fallen down on the ground. You will see the remaining roamers in the night flee in the ten directions, with their wives and without their wives, without a refuge. There is no doubt that you will see the houses in Lanka burn, surrounded by a circle of fire and enveloped in a net of arrows. O king! You have already married one thousand women. O rakshasa! Be devoted to your own wives and save your own lineage. Make efforts to enhance your respect, the prosperity of the kingdom and your own life. If you desire to enjoy these for a long time, do not do anything disagreeable towards Rama. Despite being restrained by your well-wishers, if you still engage in this terrible act of oppressing Sita, your soldiers and relatives will decay. With your life taken away by Rama's arrows, you will go to Yama's eternal abode.'

Chapter 3(37)

'In an encounter with him, I escaped in this way. Now listen to what happened thereafter. Though I had been shamed by him in this way, with two other rakshasas, I entered the Dandaka forest. They were in the forms of animals. I also roamed around in Dandakaranya in the form of a giant animal that fed on flesh. My tongue was ablaze and I had large tusks. I had sharp horns and was immensely strong. O Ravana! I roamed around in that extremely terrible form and oppressed the ascetics, in the agnihotra sacrifices, in *tirtha*s and *chaitya*s[238] and amidst the trees. In Dandakaranya, I killed the ascetics who followed dharma. I drank their blood and ate their flesh. Acting in this cruel way, I ate the flesh of rishis and terrified those who resided in the forest. Intoxicated by the blood,

[238] A tirtha is a sacred place of pilgrimage with water where one can have a bath. The word chaitya has several meanings—sacrificial shed, temple, altar, sanctuary and a tree that grows along the road.

I roamed around in the forest of Dandaka. I thus roamed around in Dandakaranya, abusing dharma. At that time, I approached Rama, who was following the dharma of ascetics, the immensely fortunate Vaidehi and maharatha Lakshmana. He was in the form of an ascetic, restrained in diet and engaged in the welfare of all creatures. Remembering the former enmity and knowing that Rama had come to the forest in the form of an ascetic, I wished to vanquish the extremely strong one. Extremely angry, not capable of discrimination, but remembering the former chastisement, I rushed against him, wishing to kill him, in the form of an animal with sharp horns. He forcefully stretched his bow and released three sharp arrows that could slay the enemy. They were as swift as Suparna[239] and the wind. Those three extremely terrible arrows were like the vajra and fed on blood. They possessed straight tufts and together, they rushed towards us. Earlier, I had known about his valour and the fear he could cause. I deceived him and escaped.[240] But the other two rakshasas were killed. I somehow managed to escape from the arrow released by Rama with my life. I came here, renounced everything and became an ascetic. Attired in bark and black antelope skin, I can see Rama in each and every tree, wielding the bow, like Yama with the noose in his hand. O Ravana! I am scared and can see thousands of Ramas. It seems to me that this entire forest is full of Rama. O lord of the rakshasas! I do not see anything that is without Rama. Rama appears in my dreams and my senses are whirled around. O Ravana! Because of my terror of Rama, all words that begin with the letter "R", like *ratna* and *ratha*,[241] generate fear in me. I know of his powers and you are not his equal in a battle. O Ravana! You can pardon him[242] or fight with Rama. If you wish to see me,[243] you should not mention anything about Rama. I have spoken these words with a view to ensuring the welfare of my relatives. If you do not like what I have spoken, with

[239] Garuda.

[240] Rama's arrow chased Maricha to the shores of the ocean and retreated.

[241] Respectively, gem and chariot.

[242] The slaughter of Khara, Dushana, Trishira and the other rakshasas.

[243] Alive.

your relatives, you will give up your life in a battle. Rama's straight-flying arrows will kill you today.'

Chapter 3(38)

Maricha's words were full of what was beneficial. However, like a person wishing to die does not accept medicines, Ravana did not accept what he said. Maricha spoke words that were like a medicament. However, goaded by destiny, the lord of the rakshasas addressed him in harsh and inappropriate words. 'O Maricha! You have addressed me in inappropriate and futile words. These are extremely pointless words, like seeds sown in a barren spot. With these words, you are incapable of frightening me against taking on Rama in a battle. He is wicked in conduct and foolish. Moreover, he is human. Rama has abandoned his well-wishers, his kingdom, his mother and his father. Hearing the ordinary words of a woman, he went to the forest alone, on foot. He killed Khara in a battle. In your presence, I should certainly abduct Sita, whom he loves more than his own life. O Maricha! This resolution of my heart has been determined. Even if Indra is there, with the gods and the asuras, I am incapable of withdrawing from it. Had I asked you about the pros and cons and about the appropriate and inappropriate means, it would indeed have been your task to determine that and speak to me in this way. A skilled adviser who desires his own prosperity should speak, with hands joined in salutation, only when he has been asked by the king. If one wishes to address disagreeable words, appropriate and beneficial, to a lord of the earth, they should be properly spoken, displaying mildness first. O Maricha! A king who deserves respect does not take delight in disrespectful and insulting words, even if they are uttered for the sake of benefit. Infinitely energetic kings embody the five forms of Agni, Indra, Soma, Yama and Varuna[244] and the respective attributes of fierceness, valour, gentleness,

[244] Respectively identified with the five elements—fire, wind, earth, space and water.

chastisement and suppleness. Therefore, under all circumstances, kings must be respected and worshipped. You have ignored dharma and are only immersed in delusion. I have come to you, but because of the wickedness of your soul, you have spoken in this harsh way to me. O rakshasa! I did not ask you about the pros and the cons, or about what is beneficial for my own self. You should help me in this task. Assume the form of a wonderful golden deer, with silver spots. After having tempted Vaidehi, you can go wherever you wish to. On seeing your golden form, full of *maya*, Maithilee will be filled with wonder. She will tell Rama, "Bring it here quickly." When Kakutstha and Lakshmana have withdrawn, I will cheerfully abduct Vaidehi, like the one with the one thousand eyes taking away Shachi.[245] O rakshasa! After having performed this task, you can go away wherever you want. O Maricha! O one with the excellent vows! I will give you half of my kingdom. O amiable one! Follow the auspicious path of accomplishing this task. I will deprive Raghava and obtain Sita without a battle. Having accomplished the task, with you, I will leave for Lanka. You will accomplish this task, even if I have to force you to do it. A person who acts against his king does not obtain happiness. When you approach him, there may be a doubt about your remaining alive. However, if you act against me, your death now is certain. You must make your intelligence realize that doing this here and that there, is beneficial for you.'

Chapter 3(39)

The roamer in the night heard the contrary command spoken by the king. Maricha addressed these harsh words to the lord of the rakshasas. 'O roamer in the night! Who has instructed you about this wicked deed that leads to your destruction, with your sons, your kingdom and your advisers? O king! Who is the evil-acting one who

[245] Shachi was the daughter of the asura Puloma. Indra killed Puloma and took Shachi away.

does not rejoice in your happiness? Who has urged you towards a means that will convey you to death's door? O roamer in the night! It is sufficiently clear that they are your enemies, desiring a reduction in your valour and your destruction by urging you against someone who is stronger. Who is the inferior one, disastrous in intelligence, who has instructed you in this way? O roamer in the night! He desires that you should be destroyed because of your own deeds. O Ravana! It is evident that your advisers are not restraining you from killing yourself. Even if their status is elevated, they should be restrained in every way. If a king follows desire and conducts himself, resorting to an inappropriate path, virtuous advisers must restrain him in every way. But though you should be restrained, they are not restraining you. O supreme among victorious ones! O roamer in the night! Advisers obtain dharma, artha, kama and fame through the favours of their master. O Ravana! When there is a catastrophe, all those become futile. The calamity a master reaps because of his evil qualities also devolves on inferior people. O supreme among victorious ones! The king is the foundation for dharma and victory. Therefore, in every situation, kings must be protected. O roamer in the night! O rakshasa! It is impossible to protect a kingdom through ferocity, contrariness and lack of humility. There are advisers who worship you and give you ferocious counsel. Like a wicked charioteer, they will swiftly drive you down an uneven road. In this world, there are many virtuous people who follow dharma. However, because of the crimes of others, they are destroyed, with their followers. O Ravana! When the master is contrary and ferocious, the protection and prosperity of the subjects is not enhanced, like sheep who are protected by a jackal. O Ravana! All the rakshasas will certainly be destroyed, since they have a harsh and evil-minded king like you, who has been unable to conquer his senses. Like a coincidence, you are bringing about this terrible calamity.[246] When you are going to

[246] Coincidence doesn't capture the nuance. The word used is *kakataliya, kaka* means a crow and tala means a palm tree. An injured fox sought refuge under a palm tree. A crow came and sat down on the tree, dislodging a ripe palm fruit, which fell on the fox's head, increasing its misery. The fox sitting there, the crow sitting there and the palm fruit falling occur at the same point in time. But one is not responsible for the other. To attribute causation to one is fallacious. This analogy is used extensively in the *nyaya* school of philosophy (*darshana*).

be destroyed, with your soldiers, what is admirable? After I have been slain, Rama will soon kill you. I will act so that the act is done by him. My death will come about through an enemy.[247] Know that as soon as Rama sees me, my death is certain. Know that you and your relatives will also be killed when you abduct Sita. If you go with me to the hermitage and bring Sita, you will not remain. I will not remain, nor will Lanka and the rakshasas remain. O one who roams in the night! I am restraining you because I seek your welfare. Do not be intolerant about these words. When the lifespans of men are over and they are like those who are dead, they do not accept the beneficial words spoken by their well-wishers.'

Chapter 3(40)

The distressed Maricha addressed these harsh words to Ravana. However, scared of the lord of those who roam around in the night, he agreed to go. 'He is the one who wields arrows, a bow and a sword. If he sees me, and doesn't even raise a weapon, my life will be destroyed. But since you are so evil-souled, what am I capable of doing? O father![248] O one who roams around in the night! May you be fortunate. I will go.' The rakshasa[249] was delighted at these words. He embraced him extremely tightly and spoke these words. 'Despite being under my subjugation, you have uttered these rash and obstinate words.[250] You are Maricha now. But formerly, you used to be another roamer in the night.[251] With me, swiftly ascend this chariot, decorated with jewels, that travels through the sky. It is yoked to mules that have faces like pishachas.' Ravana and Maricha ascended the chariot that was like a vimana. They swiftly travelled towards the circle of hermitages. They saw

[247] Rather than suffer death at your hands.

[248] The word used is tata.

[249] Ravana.

[250] The sense seems to be the following. Maricha is under Ravana's protection. Despite this, he has spoken about Rama killing him. That is rash and obstinate.

[251] You are no longer the Maricha you used to be.

all the habitations, forests, mountains, rivers, kingdoms and cities. They reached Dandakaranya, where Raghava's hermitage was, and with Maricha, Ravana, the lord of the rakshasas, saw it. Ravana descended from the chariot that was decorated with gold. Taking Maricha's hand in his, he spoke these words. 'Rama's hermitage can be seen. It is surrounded with plantain trees. O friend! Quickly do what we have come here for.'

Hearing Ravana's words, the rakshasa Maricha assumed the form of a deer and roamed around near the entrance to Rama's hermitage. The tips of his horns had the best of jewels. His face was partly white and partly dark. His mouth was like a red lotus. His ears were like blue lotuses. His neck was elevated and his stomach had the complexion of a blue diamond. His flanks were partly of the hue of madhuka flowers and partly like the filaments of lotuses. His hooves were like lapis lazuli. His body and calves were formed well. The radiant tail was raised up and had the complexion of Indra's weapon.[252] His complexion was pleasant and mild, decorated with many kinds of jewels. In an instant, the rakshasa assumed the form of this extremely beautiful deer. He seemed to make the forest and Rama's hermitage blaze. The rakshasa created this beautiful form that was a sight to behold. To tempt Vaidehi, there were many kinds of wonderful minerals on his body. He went there and roamed around, grazing on the grass that was there in every direction. He was pleasant to see and there were hundreds of colourful silver spots on him. He grazed on grass and the leaves of trees and wandered around. Here and there, he went into the groves of plantain and *karnikara* trees. He resorted to a gentle pace, so that Sita could see him. The large deer was resplendent, with the marks of red lotuses on his back. At ease and cheerfully, he roamed around in Rama's hermitage. That excellent deer wandered around, entering and retreating. He would swiftly enter and withdraw in an instant. He played around and sometimes sat down on the ground. He went to the hermitage's entrance and then joined a herd of deer. Having

[252] The rainbow.

followed that herd of deer, he returned again. The rakshasa had assumed the form of a deer so as to show himself to Sita. He wandered around in wonderful circles and jumped around. All the others who roam around in the forest saw this deer. They approached him, inhaled his smell and fled in the ten directions. Those wild deer recognized him to be a rakshasa, engaged in the killing of deer. However, he disguised those sentiments and did not touch them or eat them.

At that time, Vaidehi, with the beautiful eyes, approached the trees, eager to collect some flowers. The one with the beautiful eyes and beautiful face wandered around, collecting flowers from karnikara, ashoka and mango trees. She did not deserve to live in the forest. The supreme lady saw the deer, covered with jewels and with wonderful pearls and gems decorating his limbs. His teeth and lips were beautiful. The hair on the body seemed to be made out of silver. As she gazed affectionately at him, her eyes dilated in wonder. Rama's beloved saw the deer that was full of maya. He was wandering around there, as if setting the forest on fire. She had not seen anything like this earlier, a deer decorated with jewels. Sita, Janaka's daughter, was filled with great wonder.

Chapter 3(41)

While she was collecting flowers, the one with the beautiful hips saw him. His flanks were decorated in colours of silver and gold. The one with the unblemished limbs and with a golden complexion was delighted. She called out to her husband and to Lakshmana, who was armed. Rama and Lakshmana, tigers among men, were summoned there by Vaidehi. They glanced around that spot and saw the deer. On seeing him, Lakshmana was suspicious and told Rama, 'I think this is the rakshasa Maricha in the form of a deer. O Rama! When kings came to the forest on a hunt, this wicked one, who can assume any form at will, disguised himself and killed them. He is skilled in the use of maya and has used maya to create the form of a deer. O tiger among men! This is like a dazzling city of the gandharvas.[253] O Raghava! A deer with these kinds of wonderful jewels does not exist. O lord of the world! There is no doubt that this is a maya in this world.'

When he spoke in this way to Kakutstha, Sita, the one with the beautiful smiles, restrained him. Her senses confused by the deceit, she cheerfully said, 'O son of a noble person! This delightful deer has stolen my heart. O mighty-armed one! Bring him here. We will play with him. There are many kinds of auspicious deer that can be seen to wander around in this hermitage, like *chamara*s and *srimara*s.[254] There are large numbers of bears, spotted deer, apes and *kinara*s.[255] O mighty-armed one! Those immensely strong ones assume the best of forms and roam around. O king! But I have not seen a deer like this earlier. In energy, mildness and radiance, this is supreme among deer. His limbs have many wonderful hues and he is dotted with gems. Completely at ease, he beautifies and radiates the forest, like the moon. Look at his form. Look at his radiance. He is calling in a beautiful tone. This extraordinary and wonderful deer is stealing my heart. If this deer allows you to capture him alive, that will be extraordinary and will generate great wonder. When our residence in the forest is over and we return to the royal palace again, this deer will be an ornament in the inner quarters. O lord! This divine form of the deer will generate great wonder in Bharata, in the son of the noble one[256] and in my mothers-in-law. O tiger among men! If you are unable to capture this excellent deer alive, its hide will still be beautiful. Even if the spirited one is killed, I wish to be humbly seated on its golden skin, spread with tender darbha grass. It has been said that this kind of ferocity and conduct driven by desire is unseemly in women. But the form of the spirited one has generated great wonder in me. His body hair is golden. His horns are adorned with the best of jewels. His complexion

[253] Which is not real.

[254] Chamara is a yak. Srimara is a kind of small deer. In general it also means an animal that frequents marshy places and has been identified as nilgai.

[255] Kinara is a kind of deer, not to be confused with kinnaras.

[256] Probably meaning Shatrughna.

is like that of the rising sun and is as radiant as the path of the nakshatras.'[257]

Raghava's mind was also filled with wonder. He heard Sita's words and saw the extraordinary deer. Happily, Raghava addressed his brother, Lakshmana, in these words. 'O Lakshmana! Behold what has caused desire and delight in Vaidehi. This is the best among deer and his like does not exist today in the forest, in the region of Nandana, or in the refuge of Chaitraratha. O Soumitri! Where on earth is there a deer that is his equal? The beautiful hair on his body grows up at some places and down in others. With colourful spots of gold, this deer is splendid. Look at him yawn, with his tongue emerging from his mouth like the blazing flame of a fire, as if a cloud is tinged with lightning. His curved mouth has sapphires and his stomach has the complexion of a conch shell. Can you name anyone whose mind will not be tempted by this deer? His form has the complexion of molten gold. There are many kinds of celestial jewels. On seeing him, whose mind will not be filled with wonder? On hunts, kings roam around in the great forest. O Lakshmana! Wielding bows, they kill deer for the sake of their flesh. They exert themselves in the great forest and collect many kinds of minerals, gems, jewels and gold. All those riches make men prosper. O Lakshmana! Everything thought of in the mind enhances Shukra's treasure house.[258] O Lakshmana! If a person desires artha and goes around unhesitatingly collecting that artha, those who know the sacred texts about artha say that this artha is true artha. With me, the slender-waisted Vaidehi will be seated on half of this deer's golden and gem-encrusted hide. It is my view that nothing will be equal to that touch—not *kadali*, not *priyaki*, not *praveni*, not *aviki*.[259] There are only two deer that

[257] The Milky Way.

[258] Shukra possessed the power that if he thought of anything, it was added to his store of treasures. Similarly, everything in the forest is something that kings can aspire to and accumulate.

[259] These are the names of different kinds of deer prized for their skin. Kadali has white stripes on the neck, priyaki has thick brown and black hair and aviki is sheep. Praveni may be a different species of deer, but may also be a composite expression standing for the hide of the buck and the doe.

are so beautiful and divine. There is this one that is wandering around on earth. There is also the divine one that roams around in the sky, following the path of the stars.[260] O Lakshmana! Even if what you have said is correct, that it is the rakshasa's maya, it is my task to kill him. This is the cruel Maricha who is unclean in his soul. He used to wander around in the forest earlier, causing violence to the bulls among the sages. There were many kings, supreme archers, who came here on hunts and he arose against them and killed them. Therefore, this deer should be slain. On an earlier occasion, Vatapi vanquished the ascetics. When he was in the stomachs of the brahmanas, he slew them, like a mare.[261] After some time, because of his great greed, he ate the great sage, Agastya, whose great energy meant that he[262] was the one who came to be eaten. The illustrious one saw that Vatapi desired to rise up and assume his own form. He smiled and told him, "O Vatapi! Using your energy, you indiscriminately vanquished the best of brahmanas in the world of the living. Therefore, I have digested you." O Lakshmana! There will never be another rakshasa like Vatapi. Even if he is always devoted to dharma and has conquered his senses, if he shows me disrespect, he will be slain, just as Vatapi was devastated by Agastya. Remain here. Arm yourself and attentively protect Maithilee. O descendant of the Raghu lineage! Everything that we wish to do is based on her. I will kill or capture this deer. O Soumitri! I will go and quickly bring the deer back. O Lakshmana! Look at Vaidehi and see how she desires the deerskin. The deer's skin is his remarkable feature and he will no longer remain today. Without any distraction in sentiments, remain in the hermitage with Sita. I will slay the spotted deer with a single arrow. O Lakshmana! I will kill him and quickly come back with the hide.[263] O Lakshmana! The extremely

[260] The one in the sky is the constellation of Orion, with *mrigashira* as the head.

[261] Vatapi's story has already been mentioned. It is the belief that when a mare is about to give birth, the offspring is born after tearing apart the mare's womb, thereby killing it.

[262] Vatapi.

[263] Under the assumption that the deer is not captured.

strong and intelligent bird, Jatayu is circling around. Take care of Maithilee without any distraction. In every instant, be suspicious.'

Chapter 3(42)

The descendant of the Raghu lineage instructed his brother in this way. The immensely energetic one girded the sword with a handle made out of molten gold. He grasped the bow with the three arches that marked him out.[264] Fierce in his valour, he fastened the two quivers and proceeded. The deer saw that the Indra among kings was descending and sought to deceive him. Because of his terror, he disappeared and then showed himself again. With girded sword and seizing his bow, he rushed towards wherever he could see his radiant form in front of him. In the great forest, with the bow in his hand, he rushed to wherever he could be seen. Sometimes, he ran away, far from the reach of the arrow and sometimes, he tempted him. Sometimes, he seemed to be scared and leapt up and down, as if in the sky. Sometimes, he was visible in parts of the forest and sometimes, he became invisible. Sometimes, he appeared like scattered clouds around the lunar disc in the autumn. He could be seen in an instant and disappeared in an instant. Showing himself and hiding himself, he dragged Raghava away. Kakutstha was angry, confused and powerless at the same time. After some time, as if greatly exhausted, he sought out some shade amidst the grass. Surrounding himself with other wild animals, he showed himself from a distance. Having seen him, the immensely energetic Rama made up his mind to kill him. The powerful one stretched his bow, firmly and forcefully. He released a blazing and flaming weapon, that had been constructed by Brahma and dazzled like a serpent. That excellent arrow pierced the body of the one who was in the form of a deer. Like the vajra, it penetrated Maricha's heart. Severely afflicted, he leapt up the

[264] Rama's bow was special. It had three arches, instead of the standard two.

distance of a tala tree and fell down. With a little bit of life left in him, he fell down on the ground and roared in a terrible tone. As he died, Maricha cast aside that artificial body. Knowing that his time was near, he exclaimed in a voice that was like Raghava's, 'Alas, Sita! Alas, Lakshmana!' The unmatched arrow penetrated his inner organs. He abandoned the form of a deer and adopted his own form of a rakshasa. As he gave up his life, Maricha assumed that extremely gigantic form. Rama saw that the rakshasa, terrible to see, had fallen down on the ground. His crown was wonderful and he was adorned with all kinds of ornaments. He possessed large teeth and was decorated with golden garlands. The rakshasa was struck by the arrow. In his mind, he[265] remembered Lakshmana's words to Sita.[266] As the rakshasa was dying, he had loudly shrieked, 'Alas, Sita! Alas, Lakshmana!' On hearing this, how would Sita be? What state would the mighty-armed Lakshmana be in? With his body hair standing up, Rama, with dharma in his soul, thought about this. Rama was immersed in a terrible fear and sorrow. When the rakshasa in the form of a deer had been slain, that voice had been heard. Raghava killed another spotted deer and gathered its flesh. He then quickly hurried in the direction of Janasthana.

Chapter 3(43)

Sita heard an afflicted voice in the forest and knew that it was like that of her husband's. She told Lakshmana, 'Go and find out about Raghava. The breath of life is disturbed in my heart. I have heard that terrible sound of someone screaming extremely grievously. Your brother is screaming in the forest and you should save him. Rush to your brother. He is looking towards you as refuge. He may be distressed, under the subjugation of rakshasas,

[265] Rama.

[266] About the maya of a rakshasa.

like a bull amidst lions.' Though he was addressed in this way, he abided by his brother's instructions and did not leave. At this, Janaka's daughter angrily told him, 'O Soumitri! In the disguise of being a friend to your brother, you are his enemy. Even though your brother is in such a state, you are not going towards him. O Lakshmana! Because of me, you desire Rama's destruction. I think you love the idea of his facing a difficulty. You have no affection for your brother. Therefore, you are not considering the immensely radiant one and remain here, nonchalant. Since you remain here with me, do you doubt that he is facing a difficulty? He is the leader who has brought you here. How can it be your duty to remain here?'

Her voice choking with tears of torment, Vaidehi said this. Sita was like a terrified she-deer and Lakshmana told her, 'O queen! In an encounter, Rama is like Vasava. Among gods, men, gandharvas, birds, rakshasas, pishachas, kinnaras, animals and terrible danavas, there is no one who can stand up to him. Rama cannot be killed in a battle. You should not speak in this way. In Raghava's absence, I am not interested in leaving you here in this forest. His strength is invincible and he is stronger than the strongest, even if the three worlds, with the lords and the immortals, arise against him. You should cast aside the torment that is there in your heart. Having slain the supreme among deer, your husband will arrive soon. It is evident that it wasn't his voice, or that of a divinity. The rakshasas are foremost among those who use maya, like a city of the gandharvas.[267] O Vaidehi! You have been left as a trust. The great-souled Rama has left you as a trust. O beautiful lady! I am not interested in leaving you here. O fortunate one! We have performed an act of enmity against those who roam around in the night. O queen! We did that through Khara's death and the destruction of Janasthana. In the great forest, the rakshasas speak in many kinds of voices. O Vaidehi! They find sport in violence. You should not think about this.'

[267] City of the gandharvas is an expression used for something that is illusory and not real.

Addressed by Lakshmana in this way, her eyes turned red with rage. She spoke these harsh words to Lakshmana, who was truthful in speech. 'O ignoble one! O one who lacks compassion! O cruel one! O worst of your lineage! I think that you love me and that is the reason you have spoken in this way. O Lakshmana! Wicked and cruel ones always act in a colourful way towards their rivals and hide their true character. Since you have alone followed Rama into the forest, you are extremely wicked. You have disguised this for my sake, or perhaps you have been engaged by Bharata. Rama is as dark as a blue lotus and his eyes are like lotuses. With such a person as my husband, how can I desire an ordinary person? O Soumitri! There is no doubt that I will give up my life in your presence. Without Rama, I will not remain alive on this earth even for an instant.'

Sita spoke these harsh words that made the body hair stand up. Lakshmana, who had conquered his senses, joined his hands in salutation and addressed Sita. 'I am not interested in giving you a reply. You are like a divinity to me. O Maithilee! It is not surprising that women should use such contrary words. It can be seen in the worlds that this is the innate nature of women. They are separated from dharma. They are fickle. They are fierce. Women cause dissension. All those who roam around in the forest are witnesses to what I have heard. Though I spoke to you in words that were appropriate, you addressed me harshly. Shame on you now. Since you have suspected me in this way, because of the wicked nature of women, you will be ruined. I have only followed the commands of my senior. O one with the beautiful face! May you be fortunate. I will go where Kakutstha is. O large-eyed one! Let all the divinities of the forest collectively protect you. I can see terrible portents manifesting themselves. When I return again with Rama, I hope I can see you.'

Addressed by Lakshmana in this way, Janaka's daughter started to weep. Her voice choking with tears, she replied in these fierce words. 'O Lakshmana! Without Rama, I will bind myself and enter the waters of the Godavari. Or I will fling my body down from a high place. I will consume terrible poison, or I will enter the fire. Other than Raghava, I will never touch another man with my foot.'[268] Sita, full of sorrow, spoke to Lakshmana in this way. Weeping and miserable, she struck her stomach with her hands. Her form was afflicted and distressed. She was crying. Soumitri glanced at the wide-eyed one. He tried to reassure her about her husband and his brother, but Sita did not say anything. Lakshmana then greeted Sita. He joined his hands in salutation and bowed down a little.[269] The one who was in control of his soul glanced several times towards Maithilee and then left towards Rama.

Chapter 3(44)

Raghava's younger brother was angry at these harsh words. Though he was extremely eager to see Rama, there was no hurry for that. However, he left. Dashagriva swiftly seized the opportunity and approached. Adopting the form of a wandering mendicant,[270] he came towards Vaidehi. He was dressed in a soft ochre garment, with a tuft of hair on his hand. He was clad in sandals and held an umbrella. The sacred staff was on his left shoulder and a water pot dangled from the staff. The extremely strong one approached Vaidehi in the forest in the form of a mendicant, when the two brothers were absent. It was like evening being enveloped by a great darkness when the sun and the moon are missing. He saw the young and illustrious princess, as if an extremely terrible planet was looking at Rohini when the moon was not present. On seeing the fierce perpetrator of wicked deeds, the trees of Janasthana stopped swaying and the wind ceased to blow. On seeing the one with the red eyes, the swift-flowing river Godavari was terrified and its flow became less. Dashagriva desired a weakness to get at Rama. Finding the opportunity, Ravana presented himself before

[268] The touching with the foot requires an explanation. This refers to a wedding custom, where the couple touch each other's feet.

[269] Signifying that this was half-hearted.

[270] *Parivrajaka*.

Vaidehi, in the form of a mendicant. When she was sorrowing over her husband, the ignoble one approached Vaidehi in a noble form, like Saturn approaching Chitra.[271] The wicked one assumed a noble form, like a well covered with grass. Stationed there, he glanced at Vaidehi, Rama's illustrious wife. Standing there, Ravana looked at Rama's wife. She was pure and her teeth and lips were beautiful. Her face was like the full moon. She was seated in that cottage made of leaves, tears of sorrow flowing down. The lotus-eyed one was attired in an ochre silken garment. The evil-minded roamer in the night went to Vaidehi.

As soon as he saw her, he was struck by Manmatha's arrows. She was alone. The lord of the rakshasas uttered hymns to the brahman and addressed her in cultured words. She was supreme in the three worlds and was like Shri[272] without the lotus. Ravana praised her radiant form. 'With the golden complexion and radiance and attired in ochre silken garments, who are you? You are like a garland made out of lotus flowers, as radiant as a lake full of lotuses. O one with the beautiful face! O beautiful one! Are you Hri, Shri, Kirti, auspicious Lakshmi, an apsara, Bhuti, Rati, or someone who acts on her own?[273] The tips of your teeth are smooth and white. Your large eyes sparkle and are red at the ends. Your pupils are black. Your hips are broad. Your thighs are thick and like the trunks of elephants. Your beautiful and rounded breasts are rising up, rubbing against each other. The nipples are peaked and lovely. They are like gentle palm fruits. They are decorated with ornaments that have the best of pearls. O one with the beautiful smiles! O one with the beautiful teeth! O one with the beautiful eyes! O temptress! O beautiful one! You have stolen my heart, like water eroding the banks of a river. Your slender waist can be grasped by the hands. O one with the beautiful hair and with breasts that are close together! I have never seen such a beautiful woman on

[271] The nakshatra Chitra.

[272] Lakshmi.

[273] Hri is the personified form of modesty, Kirti of deeds and Bhuti of one who bestows fortune. Rati is Manmatha's wife. 'Acts on her own' delinks her from being associated with a male divinity.

earth earlier, nor among goddesses, gandharva, yaksha or kinnara ladies. In this world, your beauty is overpowering and so are your gentleness and youth. Why are you residing in this desolate spot, agitating my consciousness? O fortunate one! Return, you should not reside here. Terrible rakshasas are here and they can assume any form at will. There are the best of places and beautiful cities and groves. They are prosperous and full of fragrances. That is where you should roam around. O beautiful one! O dark-eyed one! I think that you should have the best of garlands, the best of fragrances, the best of garments and the best of husbands. O one with the beautiful smiles! Who are you? Do you belong to the Rudras, the Maruts or the Vasus! O beautiful one! You look like a goddess to me. The rakshasas dwell here and gandharvas, gods and kinnaras do not come here. How have you come here? Monkeys,[274] lions, leopards, tigers, animals, bears, hyenas and herons exist here. How come you are not terrified of them? There are terrible and spirited elephants, intoxicated by musth. O one with the beautiful face! You are alone in this great forest. Why are you not scared? Who are you? Whom do you belong to? Where have you come from? Why have you come to Dandaka? O fortunate one! You are roaming around alone in this terrible place, frequented by rakshasas.'

The evil-souled Ravana praised Vaidehi in this way. She saw Ravana, who had arrived in the attire of a brahmana. Maithilee honoured him with everything that should be offered to a guest.[275] She first offered him a seat and then invited him with padya. He was amiable in appearance and looked like a siddha. Maithilee saw the one who had arrived in the attire of a brahmana, holding a vessel meant for alms. On seeing his appearance, she saw no reason to suspect anything. Taking him to be a brahmana who had come, she invited him. She said, 'O brahmana! Here is darbha grass, a desired seat for you. Here is padya. Please accept it. Here is excellent forest fare that has been cooked for your sake. Comfortably partake of it.'

[274] The word used is *shakhamriga*. While this is a monkey, it literally means an arboreal animal.

[275] The word used is *atithi*. Atithi doesn't mean any guest, it means a guest who has arrived unannounced, *a-tithi*, without occasion.

Maithilee, the king's wife, invited him wholeheartedly. Ravana looked at her. Dedicated to the cause of his own destruction, he firmly made up his mind to forcibly abduct her.

Her excellently attired husband had gone out on the hunt. She waited for him and Lakshmana. As she looked around that great forest, she only saw greenery and no Rama or Lakshmana.

Chapter 3(45)

Ravana wished to abduct her. However, asked by him, who was in the form of a mendicant, Vaidehi told him about herself. She reflected for an instant. 'He is a brahmana and a guest. If I do not tell him, he will curse me.' Therefore, Sita addressed him in these words. 'I am the daughter of the great-souled Janaka of Mithila. O fortunate one! O supreme among brahmanas! My name is Sita and I am Rama's wife. I spent one year in Raghava's residence.[276] I enjoyed all the desired objects of prosperity and everything that humans crave after. After one year was over, the king consulted an assembly of his ministers and honoured my husband, Rama, by deciding to instate him as the heir apparent. Arrangements were being made for Raghava's consecration. At that time, the noble Kaikeyee sought a boon from her husband. Because of a good deed she had done for my father-in-law earlier, she sought the boon that my husband should be exiled and Bharata should be consecrated. These were the two boons she sought from her husband, the excellent king who was firm in adherence to the truth. "If Rama is consecrated, from today, I will never eat, sleep or drink, until my life comes to an end." This is what Kaikeyee told my father-in-law, the one who deserves honours. She was asked to refrain from seeking something undesirable. But she persisted in seeking that undesirable end. My immensely energetic husband was twenty-five years old

[276] That is, after marriage, they spent one year in Ayodhya. Since Rama was sixteen at the time of marriage, he was seventeen when he was exiled.

then.[277] Rama is famous in the worlds. He possesses the qualities. He is pure and good in conduct. The large-eyed and mighty-armed one is devoted to the welfare of all creatures. When Rama approached his father for the sake of the consecration, Kaikeyee swiftly addressed my husband in these words. "O Raghava! Hear from me what your father has instructed. Without any thorns, this kingdom must be given to Bharata. O Kakutstha! To save your father from uttering a falsehood, you must indeed be exiled to the forest for fourteen years." Rama fearlessly agreed to what Kaikeyee had said. My husband is firm in his vows and acted in accordance with her words. He gives and does not receive. He speaks the truth, not a falsehood. O brahmana! This is Rama's excellent and unwavering vow. His valiant stepbrother is named Lakshmana. That tiger among men doesn't leave an enemy in a battle and is Rama's aide. The brother named Lakshmana follows dharma and is firm in his vows. With the bow in his hand, and with me, he followed him on the exile. Because of what Kaikeyee did, the three of us were dislodged from the kingdom. O best among brahmanas! Resorting to our energy, we are wandering around in this dense forest. You can be comfortable and stay here for some time. My husband will bring everything[278] from the forest. Tell me the truth about your name and your *gotra*.[279] O brahmana! Why are you roaming around in Dandakaranya alone?'

Sita, Rama's wife, spoke in this way. Thereafter, the immensely strong Ravana, lord of rakshasas, replied harshly. 'O Sita! My name is Ravana and I am the lord of large numbers of rakshasas. I am the one who terrifies the worlds and gods, asuras and men. I saw your golden complexion and ochre garments. O unblemished one! I do not find any pleasure in my own wives. I have abducted many excellent women from here and there. O fortunate one! Among all of them, you will be my chief queen. My great city of Lanka is in the midst of the ocean. It is located on the summit of a mountain and is

[277] Across different versions of the Ramayana and even across different versions of the Valmiki Ramayana, this inconsistency in Rama's age is impossible to reconcile. The Critical Edition excises a shloka where Sita says she was eighteen at the time.

[278] Forest fare.

[279] Family name, denoting common lineage.

protected by the ocean. O Sita! With me, you will roam around in the forests there. O beautiful one! Then, you will no longer desire to reside in this forest. O Sita! If you become my wife, five thousand servant maids, adorned with all the ornaments, will tend to you.'

Addressed in this way by Ravana, Janaka's daughter became angry. Ignoring what the rakshasa had said, the one with the unblemished limbs replied. 'My husband is like the great Indra. Like a great mountain, he does not quake. Like the great ocean, he is not agitated. This is the Rama whom I follow. He is mighty-armed and possesses a broad chest. His stride is like that of a valiant lion. He is like a lion and is a lion among men. This is the Rama whom I follow. The brave one's face is like the full moon. The king's son has conquered his senses. The mighty-armed one is extensive in his deeds. This is the Rama whom I follow. You desire me, but I am extremely difficult to obtain. You are like a jackal, desiring a lioness. Like the radiance of the sun, I am incapable of being touched by you. O unfortunate one! O rakshasa! You desire Raghava's beloved wife, as if you have seen many trees made out of gold.[280] You wish to grasp something from the jaws of a hungry lion, the spirited enemy of deer, though that mouth is filled with virulent poison. You wish to seize the excellent Mount Mandara. You wish to consume lethal poison and remain safe. By approaching Raghava's beloved wife, you desire to wipe your eyes with a needle and lick the blade of a razor with your tongue. With a boulder around your neck, you wish to swim across the ocean. Since you wish to oppress Rama's beloved wife, you desire to seize the sun and the moon in both your hands. Since you desire to abduct Rama's beloved wife, who is enveloped in auspicious conduct, you wish to seize a raging fire wrapped in a piece of cloth. Since you wish to approach a wife who is Rama's equal, you desire to walk on the tips of an excellent spear. In the forest, there is a difference between a lion and a jackal. There is a difference between a stream and the ocean. There is a difference between the best of liquor and sour gruel. That is the difference between you and Dasharatha's son. There is a difference

[280] The image of an unrealistic wish.

between gold and lead or iron. There is a difference between water mixed with sandalwood and muddy water. In the forest, there is a difference between an elephant and a wildcat. That is the difference between you and Dasharatha's son. There is a difference between a crow and Vinata's son.[281] There is a difference between a waterbird and a peacock. In the forest, there is a difference between a crane and a vulture. That is the difference between you and Dasharatha's son. He is like the one with the one thousand eyes in his power. Even if you abduct me, you will not be able to digest me, like a fly or a diamond that has been swallowed.[282] With the bow and arrow in his hands, Rama will be stationed and will kill you.' He was wicked in his sentiments. She addressed these words to the extremely wicked one who roamed around in the night. She was distressed and her body trembled, like a delicate plantain tree swaying in the wind. He saw that Sita was trembling. Ravana, who was like Death in his powers, told her about his own self, about his lineage, strength and name. That was the reason for the fear.

Chapter 3(46)

When Sita spoke in this way, Ravana became angry. With his forehead furrowed, he replied in these harsh words. 'O one who is beautiful in complexion! I am Vaishravana's[283] stepbrother. O fortunate one! My name is Ravana and I am the powerful Dashagriva. Just as all beings are scared of Death, the gods, the gandharvas, the pishachas, the birds and the serpents are terrified of me and flee. Vaishravana is my stepbrother. Because of a certain reason, I angrily challenged him to a duel and in that encounter, vanquished him with my valour. Because he was afflicted by his fear of me, Naravahana abandoned his own seat of prosperity and sought

[281] Garuda.

[282] The diamond tears the stomach and the foul fly has to be vomited out.

[283] Kubera's.

refuge on the excellent Kailasa, supreme among mountains.[284] He possessed an auspicious vimana named Pushpaka that could travel anywhere at will. O fortunate one! I obtained this through my valour and use it to travel through the sky. O Maithilee! When they glance at my face, once my rage has been ignited, the gods, with Shakra at the forefront, are terrified and run away. Wherever I am present, the wind is scared to blow. Scared of me, the sun turns his fierce rays into gentle rays. Wherever I am present or roam around, the leaves on the trees do not flutter and the water in the rivers is quiet. My auspicious city of Lanka is on the other shore of the ocean. It is like Indra's Amaravati and is full of terrible rakshasas. It is decorated and protected by white ramparts. The beautiful city has golden chambers and gates of lapis lazuli. The place is full of elephants, horses and chariots and there is the blaring of trumpets. The gardens are ornamented with trees and these are laden with fruits that yield all the objects of desire. O Sita! O princess! Reside there with me. O spirited one! You will no longer remember that you are a human lady. O one who is supreme in complexion! Enjoy human and divine objects of pleasure. You will no longer remember Rama. As a human, his lifespan is over. King Dasharatha instated his beloved son. But the eldest son was limited in valour. That is the reason he left for the forest. O large-eyed one! Rama has been dislodged from his kingdom. Bereft of his senses, he has become an ascetic. Why should you practise austerities with him? I am the lord of all the rakshasas. However, overcome by desire, I have come here myself. You should not refuse a person who has been afflicted by Manmatha's arrows. O timid one! If you refuse me, you will have to repent, like Urvashi did when she struck Pururava with her foot.'[285]

Thus addressed, Vaidehi became angry and her eyes turned red with rage. In that lonely place, she addressed the lord of the rakshasas in these harsh words. 'You wish to perform an inauspicious deed. How can you say that the god Vaishravana, worshipped by all the

[284] The sense is that Ravana won't attack him in Kailasa.

[285] There are many stories about Urvashi and Pururava, but none where Urvashi struck Pururava with her foot. This must therefore be metaphorical, in the sense of Urvashi having spurned Pururava.

gods, is your brother? O Ravana! All the rakshasas will certainly be destroyed. They have a cruel and evil-minded king like you, who has not been able to conquer his senses. After abducting Shachi, Indra's wife, it is possible to remain alive. However, it is impossible to remain alive after abducting me, Rama's wife. Shachi's beauty has no parallel. After oppressing her, even though the wielder of the vajra holds the weapon in his hand, it is possible to remain alive for a long time. O rakshasa! However, after oppressing someone like me, there can be no emancipation, even if one has drunk amrita.'

Chapter 3(47)

Hearing Sita's words, the powerful Dashagriva struck the palm of one hand with the other and assumed an extremely gigantic form. He again addressed Maithilee in severe words. 'I think that in your madness, you have not heard about my valour and prowess. Using my two arms, I can raise the earth up into the sky. I can drink up the ocean. Stationed in a battle, I can slay Death. Using my sharp arrows, I can shatter the sun and fragment the earth. I can assume any form at will. O mad one! Behold the form of the lord who can grant everything.' When Ravana said this, in the light of the torch, his angry eyes turned red and seemed to be tawny at the edges. Ravana abandoned the agreeable form of a mendicant. Vaishravana's younger brother assumed his own form, with a complexion and form that was like that of the Destroyer. His eyes were red. He was radiant, with ornaments made out of molten gold. The one who roamed around in the night assumed a form with ten heads, holding a bow and arrows. The one who was gigantic in form gave up the disguise of a mendicant. Ravana, the lord of the rakshasas, assumed his own form. Attired in red garments, he looked at Maithilee, jewel among women. Her hair was black at the tips. She was attired in ochre garments and wore ornaments. Her complexion was like the sun. Ravana spoke to Maithilee. 'O beautiful one! If you desire a husband who is famous in the three worlds, seek refuge with me. I am a husband who is your equal. Serve me for a long period of time. I will be a husband you can praise. O fortunate one! I will never do anything that you find to be disagreeable. Abandon your human sentiments and turn your mind towards me. Rama has been dislodged from the kingdom and he will not be successful in his objective. His lifespan is limited. O foolish one who prides herself on her learning! What are the qualities that you love? Because of the words of a woman, he has abandoned the kingdom and the people who are his well-wishers. The evil-minded one is residing in the forest, where predatory beasts wander around.'

Maithilee was pleasant in speech and deserved to be addressed in agreeable words. But saying this, Ravana seized Sita, the way Mercury seizes Rohini in the sky. With his left hand, he grasped the lotus-eyed Sita near the hair on her head. With his right hand, he grasped her by her thighs. With his sharp teeth and mighty arms, his complexion was like that of a mountain peak. On seeing him, resembling Death, the divinities of the forest were afflicted by fear and fled. Ravana's great chariot could be seen, golden in parts. It was divine and full of maya. It was yoked to mules and harsh in its clatter. He raised Vaidehi by her lap and placed her on the chariot. The one with a loud voice censured her with harsh words. The illustrious one was seized by Ravana and shrieked loudly. Rama had gone far away into the forest. Struck by grief, Sita wailed, 'Alas, Rama!' She did not desire this, but he was overcome by desire. She was like the wife of an Indra among serpents, as she writhed. Seizing her, Ravana rose up. Through the sky, the Indra among rakshasas abducted her. With her senses awhirl and afflicted, as if she had gone made, she shrieked loudly. 'Alas, Lakshmana! O mighty-armed one! O one who always pleases his senior's mind! You do not know that I am being abducted by a rakshasa who can assume any form at will. O Raghava! Though alive, you have cast aside happiness and prosperity for the sake of dharma. You do not see that I am being abducted through adharma. O scorcher of enemies! This Ravana is insolent and you are the one who subjugates those who are insolent. Why are you not instructing the one who is committing this kind of crime? Indeed, this insolent one will instantly reap the fruits of his deeds. Just as crops take time to ripe, time proceeds in segments. You have lost your senses and have committed this act because of destiny.[286] Rama will inflict a terrible calamity on you and that will bring an end to your life. Kaikeyee and her relatives have certainly accomplished their wishes now. Following dharma, I am the illustrious wife of one who desires dharma. Nevertheless, I am being abducted. I request the blossoming karnikara trees of Janasthana to quickly inform Rama that Sita has been abducted by Ravana. I bow down before the summit of Malyavan and Mount Prasravana and ask them to quickly inform Rama that Sita has been abducted by Ravana. I bow down before the river Godavari, full of swans and cranes, and request that Rama be quickly informed that Sita has been abducted by Ravana. There are divinities in this forest and in the many trees. I bow down before you. Tell my husband about my abduction. There are many living creatures that reside her. I seek refuge with all of them, the large numbers of birds and animals. Tell my husband that the helpless Sita, his beloved, whom he loves more than his life, has been abducted by Ravana. When the mighty-armed and immensely strong one knows that I have been taken away from here, he will use his valour to bring me back, even if that abduction is done by Vaivasvata.[287] O Jatayu! Tell Rama the truth about my abduction. Without leaving anything out, tell Lakshmana everything.'

Chapter 3(48)

Jatayu was asleep. Hearing the sound, he quickly awoke and saw Ravana and Vaidehi. The excellent bird possessed a sharp beak and his complexion was like that of the summit of a mountain. While seated on a tree, the handsome one uttered these auspicious

[286] Addressing Ravana.
[287] Yama.

words. 'O Dashagriva! I am established in the ancient dharma and am devoted to the truth. My name is Jatayu and I am the extremely strong king of the eagles. Rama, Dasharatha's son, is the king of all the worlds and is like the great Indra and Varuna. He is engaged in the welfare of the worlds. He is the protector of the worlds and this is his illustrious wife. This beautiful one is named Sita and she is the one you wish to abduct. If a king is established in dharma, how can he touch another person's wife? O immensely strong one! Specifically, if she is a king's wife, she must be protected. Refrain from this inferior conduct of touching another person's wife. A patient person does not indulge in an act that is condemned by others. Just as one's own wife is protected from being touched, another person's wife must be protected in that way. O Poulastya's descendant! If kings do not follow dharma and do not follow the sacred texts in obtaining artha or kama, virtuous people do not follow them. The king is the supreme foundation for dharma, kama and objects.[288] The king is the source for auspicious dharma or wickedness. O supreme among rakshasas! How can you be wicked in conduct and fickle? That is the way you have obtained prosperity, like a person who is evil in conduct obtaining a vimana. If a person's nature is based on desire, he finds it impossible to cleanse himself. Nobility does not dwell in the residence of an evil-souled person for a long time. The immensely strong Rama, with dharma in his soul, has not caused any harm to your kingdom or your city. Why are you injuring him? Earlier, Khara went to Janasthana for Shurpanakha's sake and transgressed in his deeds. Rama, unblemished in deeds, killed him. Tell me the truth. How was this a transgression on Rama's part? Why are you abducting the wife of someone who is the lord of the world? Swiftly release Vaidehi. Otherwise, his terrible eyesight, which can burn down beings, will consume you, just as Indra's vajra burnt down Vritra. You do not understand that you have tied up a venomous serpent at the end of your garment. The noose of destiny is entangled around your throat, but you do not see it. O amiable one! A man should

[288] That is, artha.

pick up a burden that does not tire him out. The food that is eaten must be digestible and must not cause disease. Why should one undertake an act that does not certainly bring dharma, deeds and fame, but only brings distress to the body? O Ravana! It has been sixty thousand years since my birth. I have been properly instated in the kingdom of my fathers and grandfathers. I am aged and you are young. You have a bow, a chariot, armour and arrows. But you will not be able to take Vaidehi and go without impediment. While I bear witness, you are incapable of abducting Vaidehi forcibly. This is certainly a good enough reason, like protecting the sacred texts of the Vedas. O Ravana! If you are brave, stay for a while and fight. You will be slain and will lie down on the ground, like Khara before you. He has repeatedly slain daityas and danavas in battles. Though he is attired in rags, Rama will soon kill you in an encounter. When the two princes have gone a long distance away, what am I capable of doing? O inferior one! There is no doubt that you are scared of them and that you will quickly destroy me. However, while I am alive, you cannot take away this auspicious one. The lotus-eyed Sita is Rama's beloved wife. As long as I am alive, I must certainly do what is agreeable to the great-souled one, to Rama and to Dasharatha. Stay. O Dashagriva! Stay for a while and see. O Ravana! O one who wanders in the night! As long as I have life, I will hospitably offer you a duel. I will bring you down from your supreme chariot, like a fruit from its stem.'

Chapter 3(49)

Jatayu addressed Ravana in these appropriate words. However, all of his twenty eyes blazed with anger, like fire. Adorned in earrings made of molten gold, his eyes turned red with rage. Intolerant, the Indra among the rakshasas attacked the Indra among the birds. In the great forest, they violently struck each other. They were like two clouds in the sky and a storm seemed to arise. There was an extraordinary clash between the eagle and the rakshasa. It is as if two gigantic and winged Malyavan mountains were fighting each other.[289] The immensely strong one showered down extremely terrible hollow arrows, sharp iron arrows and piercing barbed arrows on the king of the eagles. In the encounter, the eagle Jatayu, the lord of those who use their wings as chariots, received Ravana's nets of arrows and weapons. With his sharp talons and feet, the immensely strong one, supreme among birds, caused many kinds of wounds on his[290] body. Wishing to crush the enemy, Dashagriva angrily seized ten arrows that were as terrible as the staff of Death. Those terrible arrows were sharp, with pointed heads made out of stone. They were straight-flying. The immensely valorous one stretched his bow all the way back and pierced the eagle with these. Seeing Janakee, with tears in her eyes, on the rakshasa's chariot, he[291] paid no heed to these arrows and attacked the rakshasa. With his claws, the immensely energetic one, supreme among birds, shattered the bow, adorned with pearls and gems, while arrows were still affixed to it. Using his wings, the immensely energetic lord of the birds shattered Ravana's armour, which blazed like the fire. In the encounter, the powerful one slew the mules[292] that were swift, with faces like pishachas and covered with divine and golden breastplates. The great chariot could travel anywhere at will and was like the flames of a fire. It possessed a trivenu, steps adorned with jewels and colourful parts. He shattered this too, with its whisks and an umbrella that was like the full moon. His bow was shattered. He was without a chariot. His horses were slain. His charioteer was killed. Grasping Vaidehi on his lap, Ravana fell down on the ground. When they saw that Ravana had fallen down on the ground, with his chariot destroyed, all the creatures praised this act and honoured the king of the eagles.

However, on seeing that the leader of flocks of birds was exhausted, Ravana was delighted. He seized Maithilee and leapt up again. Delighted, with Janaka's daughter on his lap, he was about

[289] It is believed that mountains once possessed wings.

[290] Ravana's.

[291] Jatayu.

[292] Yoked to Ravana's chariot.

to leave. But Jatayu, king of the eagles, also leapt up and spoke these words. 'O Ravana! O one limited in intelligence! Rama's wife is like an arrow that has the touch of the vajra. You are certainly seeking to abduct her for the destruction of the rakshasas. With your friends, relatives, advisers, soldiers and companions, you are like a thirsty person who drinks poison, taking it to be water. You do not possess discrimination and do not know the consequences that will result from this act. You will quickly be destroyed and so will they. You are bound in the noose of destiny. Where will you go to escape? You are like an aquatic creature[293] bound to a hook baited with flesh, for the sake of its destruction. O Ravana! The two invincible Raghavas, Kakutsthas, will not pardon your causing this violation of their hermitage. You have committed the act of a coward, condemned by the worlds. This is the path followed by thieves, not by those who are brave. O Ravana! If you are brave, stay for a while and fight. You will be slain and will lie down on the ground, like your brother, Khara. This act of adharma is for the sake of your own destruction. A man undertakes such an act only for the sake of going to the world hereafter. If there is wickedness associated with an act, which man undertakes it? Not even the illustrious Svayambhu, the lord of the worlds, acts in this way.' With these auspicious words, Jatayu addressed the rakshasa.

With great force, the valiant one then descended on Dashagriva's back. He was like an elephant rider astride a wicked elephant. With his sharp talons, he grasped and pierced him. He pierced him on the back with his talons and beak. With nails, wings and beak as weapons, he tore out his hair. He was thus repeatedly afflicted by the king of the eagles. The rakshasa trembled and his lips quivered in rage. Afflicted and senseless with anger, he grasped Vaidehi on his left flank and struck Jatayu with his palm.[294] When he was thus attacked, Jatayu, lord of the birds and scorcher of enemies, used his beak to sever his ten left arms. Enraged, Dashagriva released Sita. With his fists and feet, he struck the valiant king of the eagles. There

[293] The word used is general and does not necessarily mean a fish.

[294] The right palm.

was a brief clash between those two infinitely valorous ones, the foremost of rakshasas and the supreme among birds. Ravana raised his sword and severed the wings, feet and flanks of the one who was fighting for Rama's sake. The rakshasa, terrible in deeds, violently severed his wings. Slain, the eagle fell down on the ground, with only a little bit of life left in him. Jatayu fell down on the ground, wounded and wet with blood. Seeing the state her friend was in, Vaidehi was distressed and rushed towards him.

The lord of Lanka also saw Jatayu, extensive in his valour, lying down on the ground, like a conflagration that has been pacified. His form was like that of a dark blue cloud, with an extremely white chest. Crushed by Ravana's force, the one who used his wings as a chariot fell down on the ground. Sita, Janaka's daughter, with a face like a moonbeam, wept and embraced him.

Chapter 3(50)

Near Raghava's hermitage, the lord of the rakshasas saw the eagle who had fallen down on the ground, writhing and with only a little bit of life left in him. The king of the eagles had been slain by Ravana. The one with a face like the lord of the stars[295] saw this. Extremely miserable, she lamented. 'Men can certainly detect happiness and unhappiness through portents and signs seen in dreams and through the sights of harsh birds.[296] O Rama! You certainly do not know about the great catastrophe that has befallen you. O Kakutstha! For my sake, birds and animals must certainly be running towards you.[297] O Kakutstha! O Lakshmana! Save me now.' Terrified, the beautiful one screamed in this way, as if they were within range of hearing. She lamented like one without a protector and her garlands and ornaments were dishevelled. Ravana, the lord of the rakshasas, rushed towards Vaidehi. She

[295] The moon is the lord of the stars.

[296] Some birds that call harshly are regarded as evil portents.

[297] To inform you.

was like a creeper that was clinging to a large tree.[298] 'Let go. Let go.' The lord of the rakshasas said this several times. Separated from Rama in the forest, she screamed, 'O Rama! O Rama!' The one whose life had come to an end[299] and who was like Death, seized her by the hair. When Vaidehi was oppressed in this way, all the mobile and immobile objects in the world deviated from their rules[300] and everything was enveloped in a blinding darkness. The prosperous grandfather,[301] possessed divine sight and saw that Sita had been abducted. Extremely delighted, the god said, 'The task has been accomplished.' On seeing that Sita was supremely afflicted in this fashion, the supreme rishis who resided in Dandakaranya were delighted and distressed at the same time. She was weeping, 'O Rama! Alas Rama! O Lakshmana!' Ravana, the lord of the rakshasas, seized her and left through the sky.

She was attired in ochre silk garments. Her limbs had the complexion of ornaments fashioned from molten gold. The princess was as radiant as flashes of lightning in a cloud. As her ochre garments fluttered over him, Ravana looked excessively brilliant, like a blazing mountain on fire. The supremely fortunate one was adorned with lotus petals that were coppery red and fragrant.[302] As Vaidehi was seized, they covered Ravana everywhere. In the sky, her ochre garments had the complexion of gold. In the heat, this was like a coppery-red cloud, lit up by the rays of the sun.[303] In the sky, her sparkling face was in Ravana's lap. Without Rama, it was no longer resplendent, like a lotus without its stalk. Her forehead was excellent. The tips of her hair were excellent. Her sparkling teeth were white and excellent and adorned her clear face, which had the complexion of the stamen of a lotus and was without

[298] She was clinging to Jatayu.

[299] Ravana, because he was going to be destroyed.

[300] The Critical Edition excises shlokas that explain what this means. The wind did not blow, the sun lost its radiance and so on.

[301] Brahma, because the task of destroying Ravana had been accomplished. This sudden shloka breaks the continuity and doesn't seem to belong.

[302] On Sita's hair.

[303] Heat because it was midday. A red cloud is normal in the morning or the evening. But at midday, it is a bad omen.

marks. It looked as if the moon had arisen, penetrating a dark blue cloud.[304] Her face, with a golden complexion, was as pleasant to see as the moon, with an excellent nose and beautiful coppery lips. In the sky, it hung to one side, as she wept. Suffering because of the Indra among the rakshasas, her auspicious face was like the moon arising during the day, shining, but without Rama. Maithilee's complexion was golden and the lord of the rakshasas was blue in his limbs. The one with the golden complexion was like a sapphire encrusted in a golden ornament.[305] Janaka's daughter was fair, with the complexion of a golden lotus. Her ornaments were made out of molten gold. She was as radiant as a flash of lightning when it had entered the cloud that was Ravana. Vaidehi's ornaments made a sound around the lord of the rakshasas. He therefore sparkled, like a dark cloud that was roaring. As Sita was being abducted, a shower of flowers descended from the upper half of her body[306] and fell down on the ground. That shower of flowers fell down. However, because of Ravana's force, they again followed in Dashagriva's trail. Vaishravana's younger brother was shrouded in those flowers. It was as if Meru, the excellent mountain, was surrounded by an excellent garland of nakshatras. Vaidehi's anklets, decorated with gems, were dislodged. Resembling a circle of lightning, they fell down, making a pleasant sound. The lord of the rakshasas was blue in his limbs and she was as red as a coral tree. Vaidehi was as radiant as a golden harness on an elephant.[307] Because of her own radiance, she was like a giant meteor in the sky.[308] Vaishravana's younger brother had entered the sky and had seized Sita. Her ornaments, with the complexion of fire, were scattered on the ground. As they descended, like stars dislodged from the sky, they made a sound. Vaidehi wore a necklace between her breasts, with a radiance like

[304] Sita's face is like the moon, while Ravana is like the cloud.

[305] This requires explanation. Blue sapphire shines when it is in a silver ornament, not when it is encrusted in an ornament made out of gold. The sense is that Sita and Ravana shouldn't have been together.

[306] From her hair and from her garlands.

[307] Ravana is the elephant.

[308] A giant meteor is an evil portent, that is, for Ravana.

that of the lord of the stars. It fell down, like Ganga being dislodged from the sky. The tops of trees, with large numbers of birds on them, were struck by the force of the wind. The branches seemed to stretch out and tell her, 'Do not be scared.' The lotuses in the lakes decayed and fish and other aquatic creatures were frightened. They sorrowed over Maithilee, as if she was their friend. Lions, tigers, deer and other animals gathered from every direction. Because of their anger, they followed Sita's shadow. The waterfalls on the mountains seemed to wail and weep, as the summits stretched out like hands at Sita's abduction. On seeing that Vaidehi was being abducted, the sun was distressed. The handsome one's radiance diminished and the solar disc turned pale. 'Since Rama's wife, Vaidehi, is being abducted by Ravana, there is no dharma. Where will truth come from? There is no uprightness. Where is non-violence?' All the large number of creatures lamented in this way. The fawns were terrified and wept with miserable faces. With anxious eyes, they raised their eyes upwards and looked repeatedly. The bodies of the divinities of the forest trembled. On seeing Sita in this miserable plight, they lamented loudly. She screamed in a sweet voice, 'Alas, Lakshmana! O Rama!' There were many on the ground who looked at Vaidehi. The tips of her hair were dishevelled and the mark on her forehead was smudged.[309] Dashagriva abducted the spirited one for the sake of his own destruction. Maithilee's teeth were beautiful and her smile was excellent. She had been separated from her relatives. She could not see either Rama or Lakshmana. Her face was pale and she suffered from the burden of fear.

Chapter 3(51)

Maithilee, Janaka's daughter, saw that he had leapt up into the sky. She was anxious and greatly distressed and also filled with great fear. Because of the anger and weeping, her eyes

[309] This could be a *tilaka* too and is not necessarily *sindoor*.

turned coppery red. As she was abducted, she wept piteously and addressed the terrible-eyed lord of the rakshasas in these words. 'O Ravana! Despite this inferior act, you are not ashamed. Knowing that I was alone, you have abducted me and are running away. You are indeed evil-souled. Like a coward, you wish to abduct me, while my husband was dragged away by maya in the form of a deer. He who tried to save me has been brought down.[310] O worst of the rakshasas! Your supreme valour has indeed been seen. I have been conquered by you only in a battle known as trust.[311] Having performed such a reprehensible deed, how is it that you are not ashamed? O one inferior in conduct! You have abducted someone else's wife when she was alone. You pride yourself on being brave, but have performed an extremely cruel act of adharma. The men in this world will talk about your wicked deed. Shame on the valour and spirit that you spoke about then. This brings ill fame to the lineage, and the world will condemn this kind of conduct. Since you are speedily running away, what are you capable of doing? Stay for a while and you will no longer remain alive. When you come within the eyesight of those two princes, with your soldiers, you will not be able to remain alive for an instant. You will never be able to bear the touch of their arrows, just as a bird is unable to bear the touch of a fire raging in the forest. O Ravana! It is better that you take the medication that is good for you. It is better that you release me. Because of my oppression, my husband and his brother will be enraged. If you do not release me, you will arrange for your own destruction. Your conduct is such that you desire to abduct me forcibly. Your conduct is inferior and will prove to be futile. I am unable to see my husband, who is like a god. When I am under the subjugation of an enemy, I am not interested in remaining alive for a long period of time. For your own self, it is indeed best that you look towards finding some medication. At the time of death, mortals consume the opposite of what is indicated.[312] All mortals who are about to die do not find medication to be agreeable. I can

[310] Jatayu.

[311] Because she trusted him, and not in a real battle.

[312] Ignoring the medication.

see that the noose of destiny is entwined around your throat. O Dashanana![313] Despite there being a reason for fear, you are not terrified. It is evident that you can see the golden trees.[314] The river Vaitarani is terrible and has flows of blood.[315] O Ravana! You will see the terrible sight of forests with leaves made out of swords.[316] You will see a *shalmali* tree[317] that has flowers made out of molten gold, covered with lapis lazuli. But inside, they are full of sharp and iron thorns. Like a person who has consumed poison, having done this wicked and contemptible deed towards that great-souled one, you will not be able to remain alive for a long period of time. O Ravana! You are bound in a noose of destiny that cannot be repulsed. Where will you go to find safety from my great-souled husband? Even when he was without his brother, in a battle, he killed fourteen thousand rakshasas in an instant. The powerful and brave Raghava is accomplished in the use of all weapons. Since you have wished to abduct his wife, why will he not kill you with his sharp arrows?' Stuck to Ravana's lap, Vaidehi was filled with fear and grief and lamented piteously, uttering these and other harsh words. Severely afflicted, she spoke a lot. At first, the young and beautiful one lamented piteously. Abducted in this wicked way, her body was then filled with lassitude and she writhed.

Chapter 3(52)

Abducted in this fashion, Vaidehi could not see a protector anywhere. However, on the summit of a mountain, she saw five bulls among apes. The beautiful and large-eyed one wrapped her sparkling ornaments, golden in complexion, in her silken upper garment and hurled it amidst them. Maithilee thought that if they

[313] One with ten faces, Ravana.

[314] It is believed that golden trees are seen at the time of death.

[315] Vaitarani is crossed before one reaches Yama's abode.

[316] This is a description of hell.

[317] The silk-cotton tree. Sinners have to embrace this tree.

informed Rama, he might free her. Wrapping the ornaments in the upper garment, she threw it amidst them. Because he was hurrying, Dashagriva did not notice that this act had been done. Those tawny-eyed bulls among apes saw the large-eyed Sita shrieking and did not blink. Crossing the Pampa and seizing the weeping Maithilee, the lord of the rakshasas headed for the city of Lanka. Extremely delighted, Ravana carried his own death, like a person who carries a sharp-fanged and extremely virulent she-snake in his lap. Swiftly travelling through the sky, he crossed over forests, rivers, mountains and lakes, like an arrow that has been shot from a bow. He reached the ocean, the abode of whales and crocodiles, the refuge of the rivers and Varuna's eternal abode. As Vaidehi was being abducted, Varuna's abode was terrified. The waves tossed around and the fish and giant serpents were still. The charanas and the siddhas who were in the sky, then spoke these words. 'This is the end of Dashagriva.'

Ravana grasped the writhing Sita, who was like his own death, in his lap and entered the city of Lanka. He entered the city of Lanka, with well-laid-out large roads. He crossed through many gated chambers and entered the inner quarters. The black-eyed Sita was overcome by sorrow and confusion. Ravana placed her in the place that Maya had built through the maya of the asuras.[318] Dashagriva told a *pishachi*[319] who was terrible in appearance. 'No man or woman will be allowed to see Sita here. On my instructions, give her pearls, jewels, gold, garments and ornaments—whatever she desires. If a person loves her own life,[320] knowingly or unknowingly, she should not speak any disagreeable words to Vaidehi.' Thus addressed, the rakshasi agreed to what the powerful Indra among rakshasas had said.

After emerging from the inner quarters, he thought about what should be done next. He saw eight extremely valiant rakshasas who survived on human flesh. Confused because of the boon he had

[318] This reference occurs again later. Maya was a demon who was skilled in the use of maya. Using this, Maya had constructed a secret place that was hidden from view.

[319] A female pishacha.

[320] The feminine gender is used because all the guards were women.

received,[321] when he saw those extremely valiant ones, he praised their strength and valour and addressed them in these words. 'Seize many weapons and quickly go to the place named Janasthana, the spot that has been destroyed and which used to be Khara's residence earlier. Reside in Janasthana, which is now empty because the rakshasas have been slain. Cast your fear far away and resort to your manliness and strength. Khara and Dushana, extremely brave, used to reside in Janasthana, with many soldiers. However, in a battle, Rama slew them with his arrows. That is the reason an unprecedented anger is overcoming my patience. An extremely great enmity has been generated towards Rama. I wish to get over the enmity that has arisen against the enemy. I will not be able to sleep without killing the enemy in a battle. I will now slay Rama who has killed Khara and Dushana and obtain peace. He is like a poor person who has obtained some riches. While you reside in Janasthana, apparently under Rama's protection, convey to me the truth about his inclinations and about what he does. O ones who roam around in the night! Without any distractions, go. Your task is to always make attempts for Raghava to be killed. From many fields of battle, I know about your strength. That is the reason I have engaged you for Janasthana.' The eight rakshasas heard those agreeable words, deep in import, from Ravana and greeted him. Together, they left Lanka and left for Janasthana, in a form so that they could not be seen. Ravana was extremely delighted at having obtained Sita. Having abducted Maithilee, the confused rakshasa rejoiced and prepared for a great enmity with Rama.

Chapter 3(53)

Ravana commanded the eight terrible and extremely strong rakshasas. Because of the confusion in his intelligence, he thought that he had accomplished what needed to be done. Struck

[321] Ravana had received a boon from Brahma.

by the arrows of Kama, he thought about Vaidehi. To see Sita, he quickly entered the beautiful house. Ravana, the lord of the rakshasas, entered that residence. Amidst the grieving rakshasis, he saw the grieving Sita. Her face was overflowing with tears. She was distressed and overwhelmed by a burden of sorrow. She was like a boat that was sinking in the ocean, struck by the force of the wind. She was like a doe that had been separated from a herd of deer and was surrounded by dogs.[322] She was miserable and her face was downcast. The roamer in the night approached her. She was immersed in grief. She was miserable and helpless.

The lord of the rakshasas forcibly wished to show her his residence, which was like a residence of the gods.[323] There were mansions, palaces and ramparts, filled with thousands of women. There were large numbers of diverse birds. There were many kinds of jewels. There were beautiful pillars pleasant to behold, colourful with diamonds and lapis lazuli and inlaid with work of ivory, gold, crystal and silver. The gates were made out of molten gold and there were the sounds of divine drums. With her, he ascended the wonderful golden steps. There were handsome windows, inlaid with work in ivory and silver. In the palace there, there were rows of seats, covered with nets made out of gold. Everywhere, parts of the floor were covered with wonderful white marble. Dashagriva showed Maithilee his own residence. Sita was overcome with sorrow and Ravana showed her waterfalls and pools filled with many kinds of flowers. He showed Vaidehi all those excellent residences. The evil-souled Ravana then addressed Janaka's daughter in these words. 'There are ten crore of rakshasas and another twenty-two.[324] This is apart from the roamers in the night who are diseased, old and young. O Sita! I am the lord of all those, terrible in their deeds. To accomplish a single one of my tasks, one thousand of them will come forward. Everything that I rule over in this kingdom and my life are established in you. O large-eyed one! You are greater than my own life. O Sita! I have married many thousand women.

[322] Wild dogs.

[323] Therefore, from Maya's chamber, she must have been taken to Ravana's palace.

[324] That is, thirty-two crores of rakshasas. A crore is ten million.

O beloved one! Become my wife and you will be their mistress. These words of mine should appeal to your intelligence. What can be better than this? I am tormented. You should serve me and show me your favours. This Lanka extends for one hundred yojanas and is protected by the ocean. With all the gods and the asuras, even Indra is incapable of assailing it. Among the gods, the yakshas, the gandharvas and the rishis in the worlds, I do not see anyone whose valour is equal to mine. Rama is a human who is limited in energy. He is distressed and has been dislodged from his kingdom. He is an ascetic. His life is over. What will he do? O Sita! Serve me. I am a husband who is your equal. O timid one! Youth is transient. Therefore, find pleasure here with me. O one with the beautiful face! Do not vainly think about seeing Raghava. O Sita! Even if someone wishes to, how will he possess the capability to come here? In the sky, it is impossible to bind the swift-moving wind in a noose. Nor can one grasp the blazing and sparkling flame of a fire. O beautiful one! While my arms protect you, I do not see anyone in the three worlds who is valiant enough to take you away from here. Rule over this extremely large kingdom of Lanka. Wet your hair with the water of consecration and, content, give me pleasure. Earlier, you performed an extremely difficult task of residing in the forest. But that is over now. Reap the fruits of all the good acts of dharma you have performed. O Maithilee! All these garlands possess divine fragrances. These are the best of ornaments. With me, enjoy them. O one with the excellent hips! My brother, Vaishravana, had a vimana named Pushpaka. It is like the sun. Because of my spirit, I worsted him in a battle and conquered it. That vimana is large and beautiful, possessing the speed of thought. O Sita! As you please, sport in it with me. Your sparkling face is like a lotus. You are beautiful to behold. O beautiful one! O one with the beautiful face! When you are afflicted by grief, you do not look radiant. O Vaidehi! Enough of this shame. If you do this, there will be no violation of dharma. O queen! What you are going to do is entirely compatible with noble conduct. Let your gentle feet be kneaded by my heads. Quickly show me your favours. I am your servant and am under your control. I am desolate and have spoken these words because

I have been completely dried up. Otherwise, Ravana never bows his head down before any woman.' Ravana said this to Maithilee, Janaka's daughter. Since he was under the subjugation of Destiny, he thought that she had become his.

Chapter 3(54)

Vaidehi, afflicted by grief, was addressed in this way. But she was not frightened. She placed a blade of grass between her and Ravana and replied.[325] 'King Dasharatha was a bridge of dharma and never wavered. He was known for being devoted to the truth. Raghava is his son. His name is Rama. He has dharma in his soul and he is famous in the three worlds. He is long-armed and large-eyed. That divinity is my husband. He has been born in the Ikshvaku lineage. He possesses the shoulders of a lion and he is immensely radiant. With his brother, Lakshmana, he will rob you of your life. Had you forcibly oppressed me in his presence, like Khara in Janasthana, you would have been slain in battle and would have been lying down. You have spoken about these extremely strong rakshasas who are terrible in form. Raghava will take away all their poison, like Suparna from the serpents. Arrows decorated with gold will be shot from his bowstring and will pierce your body, like waves against the banks of the Ganga. O Ravana! Even if you cannot be slain by the asuras and the gods, you have caused a great enmity and you will not escape from this with your life. The powerful Raghava will bring an end to what is left of your life. You are like an animal that has been tied to a sacrificial stake and therefore, getting life back will be extremely difficult. O rakshasa! If Rama looks at you with eyes blazing with rage, he will burn you down today and you will be instantly vanquished. From the sky, he can make the moon fall down on earth and destroy it. He can dry up the ocean. He is

[325] There has been speculation about this blade of grass existing in a palace. There is also a story about a curse on Ravana. According to this curse, his head would shatter into a thousand fragments if he forced himself on to a woman, without her consent.

the one who will free Sita. Your lifespan is over. Your prosperity is over. Your spirit is over. Your senses are over. Because of what you have done, Lanka will become a widow. No happiness will result from the wicked deed you have perpetrated. You have brought me here from the forest and have separated me from my husband's side. My immensely radiant husband is tinged with divinity. He resorts to valour and is fearless. He dwells alone in Dandaka. In an encounter, he will shower down arrows on your body and thus take away your insolence, strength, valour and rashness. When they are goaded by destiny, the destruction of creatures is seen. When they come under the subjugation of destiny, men are confused in their deeds. O worst among rakshasas! By oppressing me, you have brought that destiny and destruction on to your own self, the rakshasas and those in the inner quarters. There may be a sacrificial altar in the midst of a sacrifice, decorated with ladles and vessels and sanctified by the mantras of brahmanas. A *chandala* cannot step on it.[326] You can bind or oppress my senseless body. O rakshasa! I may not be able to protect this body or my life. However, as long as I am on this earth, I am incapable of tolerating any dishonour.' Angry, Vaidehi spoke these harsh words. After that, Maithilee did not say anything more to Ravana.

He heard Sita's harsh words, which made the body hair stand up. He replied to Sita in words meant to generate fear. 'O Maithilee! O beautiful one! Listen to my words. O one with the beautiful smiles! If you do not accept me within a period of twelve months, then the cooks will slice you into tiny pieces and make breakfast.'[327] Ravana, who made his enemies scream, uttered these harsh words. Angry, he addressed the rakshasis in these words. 'O rakshasis! O ones who

[326] Chandala has different nuances and a chandala is not necessarily a shudra. A chandala is also of mixed parentage, with a shudra father and a brahmana mother. More generally, chandalas are outcastes, while shudras are within the caste fold. Sita is being compared to the sacrificial altar.

[327] There is a reason for this period of twelve months. A king may defeat another king. The vanquished king may have wives who have also now been conquered by the victor. According to the prevailing norms, the vanquished was given one year to fight back. If he didn't succeed during that period, his wives belonged to the victor. The wives were inviolate for twelve months.

are malformed and terrible to behold! O ones who subsist on flesh and blood! You must quickly destroy this one's pride.' Hearing his words, the ones who were malformed and terrible to behold joined their hands in salutation and encircled Maithilee. They were terrible to behold. King Ravana seemed to shatter the earth with his footsteps, making it tremble. He said, 'Convey Maithilee to the grove of ashoka trees. Surround her and secretly guard her there. Use terrible imprecations against Maithilee, followed by words of reassurance. Use every means to bring her under your control, like one does to a wild she-elephant.' The rakshasis were thus commanded by Ravana. They seized Maithilee and went to the grove of ashoka trees. The trees there had many kinds of flowers and fruits. The fruits yielded every object of desire. In every season, the place was full of maddened birds. Maithilee's limbs were overcome by grief. Janaka's daughter was under the subjugation of those rakshasis, like a doe with tigresses. Maithilee did not find any peace there. She was severely intimidated by those with malformed eyes. She remembered her beloved husband and her brother-in-law. She was overcome by fear and sorrow and lost her senses.

Chapter 3(55)

The rakshasa Maricha could assume any form at will and was wandering around in the form of a deer. After having killed him, Rama started to quickly return along the path. He hurried because he wished to see Maithilee. However, behind him, he heard a jackal howl in a hideous voice.[328] He heard that harsh and terrible howl, which made the body hair stand up. He was concerned and worried at the ominous tone of the jackal. 'I think that this howling of the jackal is inauspicious. I hope that Vaidehi is well and that the rakshasas have not eaten her up. Maricha, in the form of the deer, knew what my voice was like and mimicked me. Lakshmana may

[328] An inauspicious sign.

have heard it. If Soumitri has heard it, or if Maithilee has heard it and urged him, he may abandon her and swiftly rush here for my sake. The rakshasas are certainly collectively aspiring to bring about Sita's death. He assumed the form of a golden deer and removed me from the hermitage. When I was taken far away, the rakshasa Maricha was killed by the arrow. However, he spoke the words, "Alas, Lakshmana! I have been slain." Without me, I hope the two of them are safe in the forest. Because of what happened in Janasthana, I have generated an enmity amidst the rakshasas. Many kinds of terrible portents can be seen now.' Having heard the howling of the jackal, Rama thought in this way. He had been led away by the rakshasa in the form of a deer. Worrying, Raghava returned to Janasthana.[329] His mind was distressed and the animals and birds were also distressed. Screaming in terrible voices, they circled the great-souled one on the left. Raghava saw those extremely terrible portents.

He then saw Lakshmana approaching, devoid of his usual radiance. While they were still some distance away, Lakshmana met Rama. A distressed person met another distressed person. A miserable person met another miserable person. He saw Lakshmana arrive, leaving Sita in a desolate forest frequented by rakshasas. The elder brother reprimanded him. The descendant of the Raghu lineage grasped Lakshmana's left hand in his hand. He addressed him in words that were both sweet and harsh, like one who was afflicted.[330] 'Alas, Lakshmana! You have committed a reprehensible deed by abandoning Sita. O amiable one! I hope that she is safe. O brave one! There are rakshasas who wander around in the forest. I have no doubt that she has been killed or devoured by them. Many kinds of inauspicious portents are manifesting themselves before me. O Lakshmana! I hope we get Sita back, hale. This rakshasa assumed the form of a deer, tempting me, and I followed it a long distance away. I killed him with a great deal of effort. However, while dying, he assumed the form of a rakshasa. My mind is

[329] The hermitage in Janasthana.

[330] Harsh because Lakshmana had left Sita alone. Sweet because it was not Lakshmana's fault alone, he having been urged by Sita.

distressed and without joy. My left eye is twitching. O Lakshmana! I am worried that Sita may have been abducted, killed or led astray along the wrong path.'

Chapter 3(56)

Dasharatha's son saw Lakshmana in that desolate spot and was distressed. The one with dharma in his soul asked him why he had come without Vaidehi. 'When I left for Dandakaranya, she followed me. O Lakshmana! Where is that Vaidehi? You have forsaken her and have come here. I was distressed, dislodged from the kingdom, wandering around in Dandaka. She is a companion in my sorrows. Where is that slender-waisted Vaidehi? O brave one! Without her, I am not interested in remaining alive even for an instant. Where is Sita, a companion in my breath of life and the equal of a daughter of the gods? O Lakshmana! Without the gold-complexioned daughter of Janaka, I do not desire lordship over the immortals or on earth. I love Vaidehi more than my own life. Is she alive? O amiable one! I hope this exile of mine is not rendered fruitless. O Soumitri! When Sita is dead and so am I, will Kaikeyee accomplish her desires and be happy? Kaikeyee will be successful with her son, having obtained the kingdom and prosperity. O amiable one! With her son dead, will the ascetic Kousalya have to serve her? We will again return to the hermitage only if Vaidehi is alive. She is excellent in her conduct. O Lakshmana! With her gone, I will give up my life. O Lakshmana! When I go to the hermitage, if Vaidehi does not address me, if Sita does not laugh again, I will destroy myself. O Lakshmana! Tell me whether Vaidehi is alive or not. You have been distracted from the task of guarding her and perhaps the ascetic one has been devoured. She is delicate and young and has never had to face unhappiness. Separated from me, it is evident that Vaidehi will be distressed in her mind and will grieve. That extremely evil-souled and deceitful rakshasa said "Lakshmana!" Because of that, every kind of fear has been generated in me. I suspect that Vaidehi may have heard a voice that resembled mine. She must have been frightened and sent you, and you have quickly come here to see me. By abandoning Sita in the forest, you have caused her a hardship in every way. You have given an opportunity to the cruel rakshasas to act against us. The rakshasas, who survive on flesh, are miserable at Khara having been killed. There is no doubt that those terrible ones have killed Sita. O destroyer of enemies! Alas! In every way, I am submerged in a catastrophe. Having faced this state of uncertainty, what will I do now?' In this way, Raghava thought about the beautiful Sita. With Lakshmana, he quickly hurried towards Janasthana. Afflicted, he reprimanded his younger brother. His face was distressed. He sighed and with hunger, exhaustion and thirst, his mouth dried up. He returned and found that everything was empty. The brave one entered his own hermitage and went to the places where they used to sport and where they used to dwell. He was distressed and his body hair stood up.

Chapter 3(57)

Rama, the descendant of the Raghu lineage, was afflicted by grief and again asked Soumitri, who had moved away from the centre of the hermitage.[331] 'I trusted you and left her in the forest, without me. Why did you abandon Maithilee and come here? O Lakshmana! My mind was truly distressed and I suspected a great evil. That has been reinforced at the sight of you coming here, after abandoning Maithilee. O Lakshmana! My left arm and eye and my heart are twitching ever since I saw you from a distance, on this path and without Sita.'

Soumitri, Lakshmana, with the auspicious signs, was thus addressed and was filled with sorrow. He miserably told Rama, 'I

[331] These shlokas are not juxtaposed properly. Towards the end of the earlier chapter, they have already reached the hermitage. In the course of the conversation in this chapter, Rama and Lakshmana are still on their way towards the hermitage.

did not abandon her and come here because of my own wishes. She was anxious and I had come to you, urged by her. She heard the words, as if they were spoken by your noble self. "Alas, Sita! Alas, Lakshmana! Save me." Maithilee heard these words. Maithilee heard those miserable words. Driven by her affection for you, she was senseless because of her fear. She wept and told me, "Go. Go." In many ways, she urged me to leave. Because of my confidence, I replied to Maithilee in these words. "I do not see any rakshasa who can cause him any fear. There is someone else who is mimicking him. Be reassured. O Sita! He is noble and saves the gods. How can he utter these reprehensible and inferior words, 'Save me'? For some reason, someone is mimicking my brother's voice. That is the reason such distorted words have been uttered, 'Lakshmana, save me.' You should not be distressed, like an ordinary and inferior woman. Enough of this lassitude. Regain your composure and be confident. There is no man in this world who can face Raghava in a battle. No one has been born or will be born, who can defeat him in an encounter." Though I said this, Vaidehi's senses were confused. She shed tears and addressed me in these terrible words. "You are driven by this extremely wicked sentiment that your brother should be destroyed. However, you will not be able to obtain me. You have followed Rama because of a deal with Bharata. Therefore, despite his screaming in this extremely terrible way, you are not going there. You are an enemy in disguise and have followed him because of me. You have desired to find a weakness in Raghava and that is the reason you are not rushing to him." When Vaidehi said this, I became angry. My lips quivering in rage and with reddened eyes, I left the hermitage.'

Rama was confused and tormented. When Soumitri said this, Rama said, 'O amiable one! Nevertheless, you have committed an undesirable act by coming here without her. You know that I am capable of countering the rakshasas. Because of some angry words that Maithilee spoke, you have come away. I am not satisfied that you abandoned Maithilee in this way. Hearing the harsh words of an angry woman, you have come here. Having fallen prey to anger, you did not act in accordance with my instructions in any way. You came away, just because you had been urged by Sita. This rakshasa is lying down, having been slain by my arrows. He is the one who assumed the form of a deer and drew me away from the hermitage. I stretched the bow and playfully affixed an arrow. My arrow struck him. He cast aside that deer's body and became a rakshasa with armlets, lamenting piteously. Struck by the arrow, he uttered words of affliction. He mimicked my voice and it could be heard a long distance away. He uttered those extremely terrible words that led you to abandon Maithilee and come here.'

Chapter 3(58)

Rama's lower left eyelid fluttered and twitched severely. He stumbled and was overcome by lassitude. He repeatedly witnessed inauspicious portents. He kept saying, 'I hope Sita is safe.' Desiring to see Sita, he hurried. On seeing that the residence was deserted, his mind became anxious. Quickly, the descendant of the Raghu lineage rushed around, here and there. He explored every part of the cottage. But he saw that Sita wasn't there in that cottage made of leaves. It was bereft of all beauty, like a lake full of lotuses, devastated during the winter. The trees seemed to weep. The flowers, the animals and the birds were jaded. Everything was devastated and robbed of beauty. The divinities of the forest seemed to have left. The deerskin and kusha grass were strewn around. The seats, made of tender grass, were unkempt. On seeing that the cottage was empty, he lamented repeatedly. 'She may have been abducted, killed, destroyed or devoured. Perhaps the timid one has sought refuge in the forest and has hidden herself. Or she may have gone to gather flowers and fruits and lost her senses. Perhaps she went to a lake or river for water.'

He carefully searched everywhere in the forest for his beloved. The prosperous one's eyes were red with grief and he seemed to be mad. He rushed from tree to tree, amidst the mountains and male and female rivers. Rama lamented and he was submerged in a grief that was like an ocean full of mud. 'O kadamba tree! Have you seen my beloved, the one who loved you? She is the one with the beautiful face. O kadamba! If you know about Sita, tell me. O bilva tree! She is attired in ochre silken garments and she is as gentle as your leaves. Her breasts are like bilva fruit. Tell me if you have seen her. O *arjuna* tree! My beloved loved the arjuna tree. Tell me if you know whether Janaka's slender daughter is alive or dead. O *kakubha* tree! This tree has creepers and foliage and is full of flowers. Her thighs are like the kakubha. It is evident that it knows about Maithilee. O tilaka tree! You are the best among trees, and bees sing around you. She loved you. It is evident that the tilaka knows about her. O ashoka tree! You are the one who dispels sorrow and my senses are overcome by sorrow.[332] Quickly show me my beloved and make your name come true. O tala tree! Her breasts are like ripe palm fruit. If you have any compassion towards me, tell me about the beautiful one. O *jambu* tree! Her complexion is like molten gold.[333] If you have seen my beloved Sita, do not hesitate. Tell me. O deer! Maithilee's eyes are like those of a fawn. Do you know about her? The beautiful one's glances are like those of a deer. Is she with the female deer? O elephant! O supreme among elephants! Her thighs are like an elephant's nose.[334] I think you know about her. Tell me. O tiger! Her face is like the full moon. Do not be frightened. You have nothing to fear. If you have seen my beloved Maithilee, tell me. O beloved! O lotus-eyed one! Why are you running away and not showing yourself? Why are you hiding yourself behind the trees and not answering me? Stay. O beautiful one! Stay. Why aren't you showing me your compassion? Your good conduct is excellent. Why are you ignoring me? O one who is beautiful in complexion! Even if you run away from me, you will be known through your ochre silken garments. Stay. Because of affection towards me, stay. O one with the beautiful smiles! I am in the middle of a great hardship. If she is cruel and continues to ignore me, she will not be like her true self. Therefore, it is evident

[332] There is a pun. *Shoka* means sorrow and *a-shoka* means without sorrow.

[333] There is another pun. Molten gold is *jambunada*.

[334] That is, trunk.

that the child has been devoured by rakshasas who subsist on flesh. My beloved was separated from me and they have divided up her limbs. Her teeth and lips are excellent. Her nose is excellent. She wears sparkling earrings. Her face is like the full moon and when she was devoured, must have lost its radiance. Her complexion is like the champaka flower. Her neck is adorned with ornaments meant for the neck. She is delicate. As the auspicious and beautiful one was being devoured, she must have lamented. Her arms are as gentle as leaves and the hands have bracelets and ornaments. As she was being devoured, they must have trembled and she must have flung them around. Separated from me, the child could have been devoured by rakshasas. Despite possessing many relatives, she was like an abandoned caravan and must have been devoured. Alas, Lakshmana! O mighty-armed one! Have you seen my beloved? Alas, beloved! O fortunate one! Alas, Sita! Where have you gone?' He lamented repeatedly.

Lamenting in this way, Rama rushed from forest to forest. He was engaged in scarching for his beloved. Sometimes, he seemed to be mad. Sometimes, he was confused and rushed around. Sometimes, he used his powers to control himself. He was restless and quickly rushed around—amidst the forests, rivers, mountains, waterfalls and groves. He wandered around that great forest and looked around for Maithilee all around it. Concentrating his hopes, he repeatedly made great efforts to find his beloved in all the different paths.

Chapter 3(59)

Rama, Dasharatha's son, saw that the hermitage was deserted. She was not there in that cottage made of leaves and the seats were scattered around. He looked everywhere and could not see Vaidehi. Rama grasped his[335] beautiful arms and said, 'O

[335] Lakshmana's.

Lakshmana! Where is Vaidehi? Where could she have gone from here? O Soumitri! Who could have abducted her? Who could have devoured my beloved? O Sita! If you have hidden yourself amidst the trees for the sake of laughing at me, enough of this sport. I am extremely miserable. It is time to come to me. O Sita! You used to play with the fawns that trusted you. O amiable one! Without you, they are brooding now, their eyes full of tears. Because of Sita's abduction and because of this great grief, I will die. The great king, my father, will certainly see me in the world hereafter. It is evident that in the world hereafter, my father will tell me, "What happened to the pledge that I engaged you in? The period is not yet over, but you have come to me. Like an ignoble person, you have acted according to your own wishes. You uttered a falsehood to me. Shame on you." I am tormented by grief and helpless. I am distressed. All my wishes have been shattered. Save me from this piteous state, which is like the deeds of a man who is not upright. O beautiful one! O slender-waisted one! Abandoning me, where have you gone? Separated from you, I will give up my life.' Desiring to see Sita, Rama lamented in this way. Unable to see Janaka's daughter, Raghava was extremely miserable and afflicted. Unable to get Sita, Dasharatha's son was suffering, like an elephant sinking into a great pool of mud.

Desiring Rama's supreme welfare, Lakshmana spoke to him. 'O immensely intelligent one! Do not grieve. Make efforts with me. O brave one! This excellent mountain is adorned with many caverns. Maithilee is careless and loves to wander around in the groves and forests. She may have entered the forest, or gone to a lake filled with blooming lotuses. Or she may have gone to a river or pond filled with a large number of fish. Perhaps she wished to scare us and has hidden herself in some grove. O bull among men! Vaidehi may have wished to test you and me. O prosperous one! We should make efforts to search for her. O Kakutstha! If you so think, let us search everywhere in the forest for Janaka's daughter. Turn your mind away from this futile grief.' Full of affection, Lakshmana said this. Rama controlled himself and, with Soumitri, started to search. Dasharatha's two sons searched everywhere for Sita, in the forests, mountains, rivers, lakes, the summit of that mountain, caves and peaks. They searched everywhere, but did not find her. Having searched everywhere on the mountain, Rama told Lakshmana, 'O Soumitri! I do not see Vaidehi here, on this auspicious mountain.' His brother, blazing in his energy, was wandering around Dandakaranya. Tormented by grief, Lakshmana addressed him in these words. 'O immensely wise one! You will get back Maithilee, Janaka's daughter, just as the mighty-armed Vishnu bound up Bali and regained this earth.' Raghava was thus addressed by the brave Lakshmana. His senses were afflicted by grief. Distressed, he replied in these words. 'We have searched everywhere in this forest and in the lakes, with blossoming lotuses, and in this mountain, with its many caverns and waterfalls. O immensely wise one! I do not see Vaidehi, whom I love more than my own life.'[336] Afflicted by Sita's abduction, Rama lamented in this way. Overcome by distress and grief, for a while, he lost his senses. All his limbs faltered. He lost his intelligence and his senses. Afflicted and distressed, he sank down. He sighed for a long time, as if during summer. The lotus-eyed Rama sighed many times. With tears choking his voice, he repeatedly exclaimed, 'Alas, beloved!' Lakshmana, his beloved relative and knowledgeable about dharma, joined his hands in salutation and subserviently, consoled him in many kinds of ways. He paid no heed to the words that emerged from Lakshmana's lips. Unable to see his beloved Sita, he repeatedly lamented.

Chapter 3(60)

Distressed, he addressed Lakshmana in these miserable words. 'O Lakshmana! Let us quickly go to the river Godavari and find out. Perhaps Sita has gone to the Godavari to fetch lotuses.' Addressed by Rama in this fashion, Lakshmana, swift in his valour, again went to the beautiful river Godavari. Having searched the

[336] The text actually says lives, in the plural.

place that was full of tirthas, Lakshmana told Rama, 'I have not been able to find her in the tirthas, nor have I heard her voice. Vaidehi is the one who dispels difficulties. Where can she be? O Rama! I do not know where that slender-waisted one is.' Hearing Lakshmana's words, he was miserable and became confused because of his torment. Rama himself directly went to the river Godavari. Having reached, Rama exclaimed, 'O Sita! Where are you? Just as the creatures had not told Rama about her abduction by the Indra among rakshasas, who deserved to be killed, neither did the river Godavari. All the creatures urged her[337] to tell him about his beloved. However, though she was asked by the grieving Rama, she did not tell him about Sita. She was terrified of the kind of deeds the evil-souled Ravana had perpetrated. Thinking about this, the river did not tell him about Vaidehi. His hope of being able to see Sita near the river was destroyed. Rama, devastated at not being able to see Sita, spoke to Soumitri. 'O Lakshmana! What disagreeable words will I use when I meet Janaka, or Vaidehi's mother, without Vaidehi with me? I was in the forest, deprived of the kingdom, surviving on forest fare. Vaidehi dispelled all those sorrows. Where has she gone now? I am without my kin and my allies. I cannot see the princess. I think that the nights will be long and I will have to remain awake. I will search everywhere in the Mandakinee,[338] Janasthana and Mount Prasravana, in case Sita is found.'

While those two brothers were conversing with each other in this way, they saw a path along which the earth was strewn with flowers. Rama saw that a shower of flowers had fallen down on the ground. Miserable, the brave one addressed Lakshmana in these grieving words. 'O Lakshmana! I recognize the flowers that are here. These are the ones I gave Vaidehi in the grove and she fastened them.'[339] The mighty-armed one said this to Lakshmana, bull among men. He was angry and spoke to the mountain, like a lion addressing inferior animals. 'O mountain! Her complexion is golden. Her limbs are golden. Show me Sita. Otherwise, I will

[337] The Godavari river.

[338] In this context, Mandakinee means Godavari.

[339] In her hair.

destroy all your summits. The fire of my arrows will consume and reduce you to ashes. Without trees and foliage, no one will ever frequent you again. O Lakshmana! If this river does not tell me about Sita, whose face is like that of the moon, now, I will dry it up.' The enraged Rama seemed to burn everything down with his eyes.

Then, on the ground, he saw the giant footprints of the rakshasa, left when he departed. He saw Sita's footprints, overtaken by those of the rakshasa. Terrified in his heart, Rama spoke to his beloved brother. 'O Lakshmana! O Soumitri! Look at the bits of gold strewn around from Vaidehi's ornaments and the many kinds of garlands. O Soumitri! Behold. Everywhere, the surface of the ground is covered with colourful drops of blood from wounds, like beads of molten gold. O Lakshmana! I think rakshasas, who can assume any form at will, have divided her up, shared her and eaten her up. O Soumitri! Two terrible rakshasas may have had a dispute and a fight here over Vaidehi. O amiable one! This giant bow has been shattered and is lying down on the ground. It is adorned with pearls and jewels and is decorated with molten gold. Whom does it belong to? Whose golden armour has been shattered and is lying down on the ground? It resembles the rising sun and is decorated with beads of lapis lazuli. This umbrella has one hundred spokes and is decorated with divine garlands. Its shaft has been fragmented and is lying down on the ground. O amiable one! Whom does it belong to? These mules have faces like pishachas and are covered with golden breastplates. They are terrible in battle and are gigantic in size. Who has slain them in a battle? This standard blazed in battle and is like a radiant fire. It has been shattered and fragmented. Whom does this chariot, used for fighting, belong to? These arrows are decorated with molten gold and are as long as a chariot's wheel. They are strewn around. Who was killed with these arrows and which performer of terrible deeds used them? O amiable one! This is the work of rakshasas who can assume any form at will and are extremely terrible in their hearts. Behold. My enmity has increased a hundredfold and I will bring an end to their lives. The ascetic Sita has been abducted, killed or devoured. When Sita was abducted in the great forest, dharma could not save her. O Lakshmana! Vaidehi has been devoured or abducted. O amiable one! Where are my gods? In this world, who is capable of doing something agreeable for me? O Lakshmana! The brave creator of the worlds, who knew about this piteous account, did not know about this and will be disrespected by all the creatures. I am gentle and am engaged in the welfare of the worlds. I am controlled, though I know about this piteous account. I think it is certain that the lords of the thirty gods take me to be devoid of valour. O Lakshmana! See how the qualities I have obtained have been enveloped in taints.[340] From today, all the creatures and the rakshasas will be destroyed. I will restrain the gentle beams of the moon and the great sun will arise. O Lakshmana! The yakshas, the gandharvas, the pishachas, the rakshasas, the kinnaras and men will not be able to find happiness. O Lakshmana! Behold. My weapons and arrows will envelop the sky. Today, I will render the three worlds such that they will be impossible to travel in. I will block all the planets and obstruct the path of the moon. The radiance of the fire, the Maruts and the sun will be destroyed and withdrawn. The summits of the mountains will be shattered. The waterbodies will be dried up. The trees, creepers and shrubs will be devastated. The ocean will be destroyed. O Soumitri! Until my gods return Sita safely to me, this very instant, they will witness my valour. O Lakshmana! An incessant net of arrows will be released from the string of my bow and the creatures will not be able to rise up into the sky. The animals and birds will be mangled, devastated and confused by my iron arrows. O Lakshmana! Today, the universe will be in turmoil and all the boundaries will be crossed. I will draw my bow back to my ears and release unstoppable arrows in the world of the living. For Maithilee's sake, I will not leave any pishachas or rakshasas. In my intolerance and rage, I will shoot arrows that will travel a long distance. Let the gods witness my strength now. When the three worlds are destroyed by my rage, there will not be any gods, daityas, pishachas or rakshasas left. The torrents of my arrows will

[340] The sense seems to be the following. Rama, being gentle, should not kill the rakshasas unnecessarily. But that has become a fault.

reduce the gods, the danavas, the yakshas and the rakshasas in the worlds into many fragments and they will fall down. Today, my arrows will destroy all the agreements in the worlds. O Lakshmana! All beings can never counter old age, death, time and destiny. In that way, when I am enraged, there is no doubt that I cannot be repulsed. If you do not show me the beautiful and unblemished one, Sita Maithilee, as used to be the case earlier, I will make the world and the mountains whirl, together with the gods, the gandharvas, men and serpents.'

Chapter 3(61)

Rama was afflicted because of Sita's abduction and was about to scorch the worlds, like the fire of final destruction. He glanced at his strung bow and sighed repeatedly. He desired to kill the animals, like the enraged Rudra at the time of Daksha's sacrifice. This sight of Rama being enraged was not something that Lakshmana had ever seen earlier. With his mouth dry, he joined his hands in salutation and spoke these words. 'Earlier, you were gentle and controlled, engaged in the welfare of all beings. You should not fall prey to rage. You should resume your natural self. The prosperity of the moon, the radiance of the sun, the speed of the wind, the forgiveness of the earth—all these always exist in you and you also possess supreme fame. I do not know whom this shattered chariot, used for fighting, belongs to. I do not know whom the weapon and equipment belong to, nor who shattered them and for what reason. This place has been struck by hooves and an axle. It is sprinkled with drops of blood. O son of a king! This is a spot where a terrible clash has taken place. O supreme among eloquent ones! A single person has been killed here, not both. Nor are there signs of the footprints and conduct of a large army. You should not destroy the worlds because of what a single person has done. Calm kings use the rod of chastisement mildly. You have always been the supreme refuge for all creatures. O Raghava! If you destroy them because of your wife, who will think that you are virtuous? The rivers, oceans, mountains, gods, gandharvas and danavas have behaved like virtuous ones who have consecrated themselves for a sacrifice and have not done anything disagreeable towards you. O king! You should search for the one who has abducted Sita. With a bow in my hand, I will be your second, and the supreme rishis will be our aides. We will search the oceans, the mountains, the forests, the many dreadful caverns and all the lakes in the mountains. We will control ourselves and search the worlds of the gods and the gandharvas, until we have found the person who has abducted your wife. O Indra of Kosala! If the lords of the thirty gods do not peacefully return your wife to you, it is only after that, at the right time, that you should do what you have to. O Indra among men! If you do not get Sita back through good conduct, conciliation, humility and good policy, it is only then that you should use torrents of gold-tufted arrows that are like the great Indra's vajra.'

Chapter 3(62)

He[341] was tormented by grief and lamented like one who was without a protector. A great confusion pervaded him and he lost his senses. After a while, Soumitri Lakshmana comforted him. He kneaded Rama's feet and addressed him. 'O Rama! Like the immortals obtained amrita, King Dasharatha obtained you after great austerities and great deeds. He was attached to your qualities. We have heard from Bharata that it was because of separation from you that the king, the lord of the earth, obtained divinity. O Kakutstha! If you are unable to bear the misery that you are facing now, how will one who is inferior, an ordinary one with limited spirits, withstand it? O tiger among men! If in your misery, you wish your energy to destroy the worlds, to whom will afflicted subjects go, searching for refuge? This is the way of the world.

[341] Rama.

Yayati, Nahusha's son, went to Shakra's world and became like him. However, he was touched by bad policy.[342] There is maharshi Vasishtha, our father's priest. In a single day, he had one hundred sons. But they were slain again.[343] This goddess, the mother of the world,[344] is worshipped by the worlds. O one who resorts to the truth! However, even the earth can be seen to quake. These two extremely strong ones, the sun and the moon, are the eyes of the world and everything is established in them. However, even they are invaded by eclipses. O bull among men! The greatest among creatures, the gods and all creatures who bear bodies cannot free themselves from destiny. O tiger among men! It has been heard that the present gods,[345] Shakra and the others, also face the good and the bad. You should not be distressed at this.[346] O unblemished one! O brave one! Even if Vaidehi has been destroyed, even if she has been abducted, unlike an ordinary person, you should not grieve. O Rama! Those who are like you and always see the truth, those who are detached in their wisdom, do not sorrow, even when they face a great hardship. O best among men! You should use your intelligence to think about the truth. When they use their intelligence, immensely wise ones know what is right and what is wrong. The results of deeds are not certain, their good and bad aspects have not been seen.[347] If a deed is in the heart, but has not been performed, its cherished fruits will not materialize. O brave one! Earlier, you have yourself told me about this several times. You are like Brihaspati himself. Who can instruct you? O immensely wise one! Even the gods cannot comprehend your intelligence. Because of your sorrow, your knowledge is asleep and I am trying to wake it. O bull of the Ikshvaku lineage! Your own valour is both divine and human. Even if you cast your eye on an enemy, he will be killed. O bull among

[342] Yayati's story is given in the Mahabharata. He went to the world of the gods and became Indra. However, because of various transgressions, he was dislodged from heaven.

[343] Vishvamitra killed them.

[344] The earth.

[345] Gods change from one *manvantara* (era) to another.

[346] Some of the shlokas in this chapter bear a striking resemblance to the Bhagavadgita.

[347] Because they may occur later, perhaps in the next life.

men! Why should you try to destroy everything? You should find out who the wicked enemy is and uproot him.'

Chapter 3(63)

No sooner had Lakshmana told his elder brother a little bit of those excellent words, Raghava, who could grasp the essence, understood the great gist and accepted it. The mighty-armed one controlled his increasing rage. Holding on to his colourful bow, Rama told Lakshmana, 'O child! What will we do? O Lakshmana! Where will we go? You should now think about what means we will use to find Sita.' Rama was afflicted by torment and Lakshmana spoke to him. 'You should search in Janasthana. It is covered by trees and creepers and populated by many kinds of rakshasas. There are mountains that are difficult to traverse and glades and valleys. There are many kinds of terrible caves, populated by many kinds of animals. There are the abodes of kinnaras and the residences of gandharvas. With me, you should search all these. O bull among men! That is what an intelligent and great-souled person like you should do. They do not tremble because of a calamity, like mountains against the force of the wind.' Thus addressed, with Lakshmana, he roamed around everywhere in the forest. The angry Rama affixed a sharp and terrible arrow to his bow.

He saw the greatly fortunate Jatayu, supreme among birds, lying down, with the complexion of a mountain top, and the ground was wet with the blood from his wounds. His complexion was like the summit of a mountain. On seeing him, Rama told Lakshmana, 'There is no doubt that this is the one who has devoured Sita Vaidehi. It is evident that this rakshasa has been roaming around in the forest in the form of an eagle. Having eaten the large-eyed Sita, he is now resting happily. I will slay him with straight-flying and terrible arrows that blaze at the tips.' Having said this, he affixed the sharp arrow to his bow and advanced towards the eagle. The angry Rama made the earth, right up to the frontiers of the ocean, tremble. Vomiting froth and blood, the miserable bird addressed

Rama, Dasharatha's son, in grieving words. 'O one with a long life! You are searching for a herb in this great forest. But Ravana has abducted both that queen and my life. O Raghava! The queen was without you and Lakshmana. While I looked on, the stronger Ravana abducted her. I tried to rescue Sita and in the encounter, destroyed his chariot and umbrella and also brought Ravana down on the ground here. This is his shattered bow and this is his armour. O Rama! In the encounter, I shattered the chariot that he used to fight. I was exhausted and Ravana severed my wings with his sword. He seized Vaidehi and leapt up into the sky. The rakshasa has already killed me. You should not slay me.' From him, Rama got to know the account about his beloved Sita. He embraced the king of the eagles and, with Lakshmana, wept.

He[348] was taking a single breath with difficulty and sighed repeatedly. On seeing him, the miserable Rama spoke to Soumitri. 'I have been dislodged from the kingdom. I am residing in the forest. Sita has been lost. The bird is dead. Like a fire, this kind of adversity is burning me. The great ocean is full. However, such is the nature of my adversity, that were I to enter it, the lord of the rivers would dry up. In the world, with all its mobile and immobile objects, there is no one as unfortunate as I am. Why have I faced this devastating calamity? This aged king of the eagles is my father's friend. Because of my misfortune, he has been slain and is lying down on the ground.' With Lakshmana, Raghava said this and many other things. As a sign of affection towards his father, he touched Jatayu's body. His wings had been severed and he was wet with blood. Rama embraced the king of the eagles. 'Where is Maithilee, who is like my own life?' Shedding tears, he fell down on the ground.

Chapter 3(64)

Rama looked at the eagle, who had been brought down on the ground in that terrible way. Soumitri was filled with friendship

[348] Jatayu.

for him and he addressed him in these words. 'This bird certainly tried for my sake. The rakshasa killed him in the encounter. He has given up his life, which is extremely difficult to give up. O Lakshmana! His body has been mangled, but a little bit of life still remains. It seems that he is filled with lassitude and has lost his voice. O Jatayu! If you can, please speak again. O fortunate one! Speak about Sita. Speak about how you were killed. Why did Ravana abduct Sita? What have I done against him? Since Ravana abducted my beloved, what crime did he see? O supreme among birds! At that time, how was that beautiful face, which is like the moon? What did Sita say? How was the rakshasa's valour? What was his form? What were his deeds? Where is his residence? O father![349] I am asking you. Tell me.' Distressed in his soul, he glanced towards him and lamented thereafter.

With a quivering voice, Jatayu addressed Rama in these words. 'She was abducted by Ravana, Indra among the rakshasas, through the sky. He resorted to maya and created a great storm, as if it was a bad day. O son![350] I was exhausted and the roamer in the night severed my wings. Seizing Sita Vaidehi, he left in a southern direction. O Raghava! My breath of life is obstructed and my sight is whirling. I can see trees made of gold, with grass on their tops.[351] O Kakutstha! The muhurta when Ravana seized Sita is the muhurta known as Vinda, but he did not realize this.[352] At this time, the owner of riches quickly loses them.[353] He will be swiftly destroyed, like a fish that has swallowed a baited hook. You should not sorrow on account of Janaka's daughter. You will soon sport with Vaidehi, after having killed the rakshasa in a battle.' With some senses still left, the eagle replied to Rama. As he was about to die, blood and

[349] The word used is tata.

[350] The word used is tata.

[351] A portent signifying death.

[352] A muhurta is a period of forty-eight minutes and in a twenty-four-hour period, there are thirty muhurtas. Some are regarded as good or auspicious muhurtas, others as bad and inauspicious. In a standard list of muhurta names used today, Vinda does not figure. Vinda used to be the name of the eleventh muhurta, regarded as bad. These days, it will often be referred to as Vijaya.

[353] If an act is undertaken at that time.

bits of flesh oozed out of his mouth. 'He is the son of Vishrava and the brother of Vaishravana[354] himself.' Having said this, the lord of the birds gave up his life, which is so very difficult to obtain. Rama joined his hands in salutation and said, 'Tell me. Please tell me.' But the eagle's breath of life gave up his body and rose up into the sky. The head fell down on the ground and the legs were outstretched. His body trembled and he fell down on the ground. The eagle's eyes were coppery red. He had lost his life and was like a mountain.

Afflicted by many kinds of grief, the distressed Rama spoke to Soumitri. 'This bird happily lived in Dandakaranya for many years, amidst the rakshasas. He has now been destroyed. After many years, Destiny has taken him upwards. He has been killed and is lying down now. It is impossible to cross destiny. O Lakshmana! Behold. This eagle tried to help me and has been killed. He tried to rescue Sita, but Ravana was stronger. He has given up the great kingdom of the eagles that belonged to his fathers and grandfathers. This lord of birds has released his breath of life for my sake. Virtuous ones, thosc who follow dharma, are indeed seen everywhere. O Soumitri! Brave ones are born even among inferior species. O amiable one! O scorcher of enemies! My grief at Sita's abduction is not as much as that caused by the eagle being destroyed for my sake. The prosperous and famous King Dasharatha should be worshipped by me, but this lord of the birds should also be revered. O Soumitri! Fetch wood. I will kindle a fire. I will cremate the king of the eagles, who has been killed because of me. I will place the lord of the world of the birds on a pyre. O Soumitri! I will cremate the one who has been killed by a terrible rakshasa. There are destinations for those who perform sacrifices. There are destinations for those who light sacrificial fires. There are destinations for those who do not return[355] and for those who donate land. O great-spirited king of the eagles! With the rites of purification performed by me, take my leave and go to those supreme worlds.' Saying this, he placed the lord of the birds on that blazing pyre. Rama, with dharma in his soul, sadly cremated his

[354] Kubera.

[355] Are not born again.

friend. With Soumitri, the valiant Rama then went to the forest. He killed a large gazelle,[356] laid it out on sacred grass and offered it to the bird. The immensely illustrious Rama took out pieces of meat from the flesh of the gazelle, laid it out on green grass and offered it to the bird. When a mortal person goes to the world hereafter, brahmanas chant hymns for his journey to heaven. Quickly, Rama recited these. The two, best among men, then went to the river Godavari. Both of them offered water to the king of the eagles. The king of the eagles had performed an illustrious deed. Having performed an extremely difficult deed, he had been brought down in the battle. With his rites of purification performed by one who was the equal of a maharshi,[357] he went to the auspicious and sacred worlds that were meant for him.

Chapter 3(65)

Having performed the water rites for him, the two Raghavas left. Heading in the western direction, they searched the forest for Sita. With bows, arrows and swords in their hands, they then left for the southern direction. Those two from the Ikshvaku lineage then came upon a path that was not often used. It was shrouded in many lantanas, trees and creepers. It was covered everywhere and was impenetrable, dense and terrible to behold. Having chosen the southern direction, the two immensely strong ones quickly crossed over and traversed this terrible part of the great forest. The two Raghavas went three *kroshas*[358] beyond Janasthana. Those two immensely energetic ones entered the dense Krouncha forest. There were many dense black clouds there and everything seemed to be happy. There were auspicious flowers of many hues. There were large numbers of animals and birds. They looked around that forest, searching for Vaidehi. Afflicted because of Sita's abduction,

[356] *Maharohi.*

[357] Rama.

[358] One krosha is two miles. However, the definition of krosha was not standardized.

they searched here and there. The spirited and immensely energetic Lakshmana was auspicious and good in conduct. He joined his hands in salutation and addressed his brother, blazing in his energy, in these words. 'My left arm is twitching and my mind is anxious. When something like this is felt, it is usually a bad omen. O noble one! Therefore, act in accordance with my beneficial words and be ready. These portents seem to be telling me that some danger is nearby. This bird known as *vanjulaka*[359] is extremely terrible. It is shrieking, as if signifying our victory in a battle.' Those two energetic ones searched everywhere in the forest.

They then heard a tumultuous sound that seemed to shatter the forest. It was as if an extremely strong storm had struck the desolate forest. The sound filled everything up and rose up into the sky. Desiring to know what was causing the sound, Rama and his younger brother seized their swords. They saw an extremely gigantic and broad-chested rakshasa. The two of them approached the rakshasa who was standing in front of them. This was Kabandha.[360] He was large and was without a head or a neck. His mouth was placed in his stomach. His body hair was thick and sharp. He rose up like a giant mountain. He was as terrible as a dark blue cloud. His roar was like that of thunder. There was only a single sharp-sighted and terrible eye on his chest. This was large in size and had tawny eyelashes. He licked his giant mouth, which possessed large teeth. He ate extremely terrible bears, lions, animals and elephants. He stretched out his horrible arms and each of them was one yojana long. With these arms, he seized many kinds of bears, large numbers of birds and animals. He pulled towards him, and hurled away, many herds of animals. When the two brothers turned up there, he stood there, obstructing their path. When they saw him, they had only travelled for one krosha.[361] Kabandha was gigantic, terrible and horrible and he stretched out his arms. He seized the two Raghavas in his two hands,[362] brought his hands together and

[359] Kind of bird.
[360] *Kabandha* means a headless torso.
[361] After entering the Krouncha forest.
[362] One in each hand.

crushed them with force. They wielded swords and firm bows. They were mighty-armed and fierce in their energy. However, when they were dragged in this way, those two immensely strong brothers could do nothing. The mighty-armed Kabandha, supreme among danavas, spoke to them. 'Who are you? You have shoulders like bulls. You wield gigantic swords and bows. You have reached this terrible place and are like food brought to me. Tell me the reason why you have come here. You have come to the place where I was lying in wait, suffering from hunger. You possess arrows, bows and swords, like two bulls with sharp horns. Now that you have come before me, it is impossible for you to remain alive.'

Lakshmana's mouth dried up at the words of the evil-souled Kabandha. But Rama told him, 'O one with truth as his valour! We face this terrible situation and have moved from one catastrophe to a greater catastrophe. Earlier, I couldn't obtain my beloved and we now face a calamity that will bring an end to our lives. O Lakshmana! Among all beings, the valour of destiny is extremely great. O tiger among men! Behold. We are confused because of this hardship. O Lakshmana! Among all creatures, divinity's burden is extremely great.[363] There may be brave and powerful ones who are accomplished in the use of weapons in the field of battle. However, when they are overcome by destiny, they are destroyed, like a dam made out of sand.' The immensely illustrious and powerful Dasharatha's son, who was firm and truthful in his valour, said this. He looked at Soumitri, who was fierce in his valour. He[364] then acted so as to compose his own intelligence.

Chapter 3(66)

Kabandha saw that those two brothers, Rama and Lakshmana, had composed themselves, though they were still writhing

[363] The text actually says, the burden isn't great. Since this can't be right, we have corrected the typo and followed non-Critical versions, which say that the burden is great.

[364] Rama.

around, within the bondage of his hands. He addressed them in these words. 'O bulls among kshatriyas! You can see that I am afflicted by hunger. How can you be so composed? Destiny has instructed that you should be here as my food. You should lose your senses.' Lakshmana was suffering. However, hearing this, he decided that it was time to exhibit valour and spoke these beneficial words that were appropriate for the occasion.[365] 'O senior! Before this worst among rakshasas can quickly devour us, we should swiftly use swords to severe his arms.' The two Raghavas knew about the time and the place. Extremely cheerful, they used their swords to sever his arms at the shoulders. On the right, Rama used force and his unsheathed sword to slice off the right arm and the brave Lakshmana did this with the left. With his arms severed, the mighty-armed one fell down. Roaring like a thunder cloud, he emitted a loud scream that echoed in the sky, the earth and the directions. The arms were severed and he was covered with torrents of blood. On seeing this, the danava was distressed and asked, 'O brave ones! Who are you?'

Hearing what he said, the immensely strong Lakshmana, the possessor of auspicious signs, told Kabandha about Kakutstha. 'This is the descendant of the Ikshvaku lineage. Among people, he is known by the name of Rama. Know me to be his younger brother, Lakshmana. Though he possesses the power of a god, he is residing in this desolate forest. A rakshasa has abducted his wife. We wished to find her and came here. But who are you? Why are you in the forest, in the form of a headless torso? Your legs have been shattered and you cannot move. You possess a blazing mouth in the middle of your stomach.' Thus addressed, Kabandha was extremely delighted, because he remembered Indra's words. He replied to Lakshmana in these words. 'O tigers among men! Welcome. It is good fortune that I have seen you. It is good fortune that you have severed the bonds of my arms. My form turned to this malformed state because of my lack of humility. O tiger among men![366] I will tell you. Listen to the truth.'

365 He spoke to Rama.

366 In the singular.

Chapter 3(67)

'O Rama! O mighty-armed one! O one who is great in strength and valour! Earlier, I possessed an unthinkable form that was famous in the three worlds, like that of Soma, Shakra, Surya or Vayu. In that form, I caused great fright in the worlds. O Rama! I went to the forest and here and there, terrified the rishis. A maharshi named Sthulashira was enraged with me. Thinking of many kinds of wild forms,[367] I used one of those to oppress him. On seeing me, he inflicted this terrible curse on me. "This is a terrible and contemptible form and you will remain in this." When the angry one cursed me in this way, I sought from him a means to end the curse. He addressed me in these words. "Rama will sever your arms and cremate you in the desolate forest. When that happens, you will regain your own large and auspicious form." O Lakshmana! Know me to be Danu's son, blazing in his beauty. Because of Indra's anger, I obtained this form in the field of battle. I performed fierce austerities and satisfied the grandfather.[368] He granted me a long life and I became confused. Now that I have obtained a long life, what can Shakra do to me? Resorting to this kind of intelligence, I oppressed Shakra in a battle. Using his arm, he released the vajra that has one hundred edges. That made my thighs and head penetrate my body. Though I beseeched him, he did not convey me to Yama's abode. He told me, "Let the grandfather's words come true." However, with my thighs, head and mouth shattered, how could I satisfy my hunger? Struck by the vajra, I would have to remain alive for an extremely long period of time. Thus addressed, Shakra thought of arms that were one yojana long for me. He gave me a mouth with sharp teeth in my stomach. I have been roaming around in this forest. Using these long arms, from every direction, I have dragged lions, elephants, animals and tigers and eaten them. Indra told me, "In an encounter, when Rama and Lakshmana sever your arms, you will go to heaven." You are that fortunate Rama. O

[367] He could assume any form at will.
[368] Brahma.

Raghava! In truth, no one else is capable of slaying me. This is what the maharshi had said. O bull among men! O friend! I will use my intelligence to advise and instruct you about what should be done. The two of you must cremate me in a fire.'

Thus addressed, while Lakshmana heard, Raghava, with dharma in his soul, spoke these words to Danu's son. 'My illustrious wife has been abducted by Ravana. With my brother, I have therefore left Janasthana and am wandering around. I only know the rakshasa's name and not his form. We do not know his age, his powers, or where he lives. We are like ones without a protector, roaming around, afflicted by grief. If you show us your compassion, we will also do an equivalent deed for you.[369] We will bring wood that has been shattered by elephants at different times. O brave one! We will construct a huge trench and burn you in it. If you know the truth, do this extremely good deed for us. Tell us about the person who has abducted Sita and where he has taken her.' Danu's son was addressed by Rama in these excellent words. Both he and Raghava were skilled in the use of words and he replied. 'I do not possess divine knowledge. Nor do I know about Maithilee. However, when you cremate me, I will assume my own form and will tell you what I know.[370] O lord! Until I am cremated, I do not possess the capacity to know about the extremely valiant rakshasa who has abducted Sita. O Raghava! As a consequence of the curse, my extensive knowledge has been destroyed. Because of my own deeds, I obtained this present form, condemned by the worlds. I am like the setting sun, when its mounts are exhausted. O Rama! Fling me into the trench, follow the prescribed rites, and cremate me. O descendant of the Raghu lineage! Fling me into the trench and properly cremate me. O brave one! I will then tell you about the person who knows about that rakshasa. O Raghava! You must follow an appropriate course of conduct and strike a friendship with me. Dextrous in his valour, he will be delighted and will think of a means to help you. O Raghava! There is nothing in the three worlds

[369] If you tell us about Ravana, we will cremate you.

[370] The knowledge will return in his own form.

that is unknown to him. Earlier, because of a different reason, he circled all the worlds.'[371]

Chapter 3(68)

Those two brave ones, lords among men, were thus addressed by Kabandha. They went to a crevice in the mountain and prepared to light a fire there. In every direction, Lakshmana lit blazing and giant torches. He also lit the pyre, which blazed everywhere. Kabandha's body was like a large vessel filled with ghee. The fire gently cooked the fat. Soon, a form that was like a fire without smoke emerged from the smoking pyre. The immensely strong one was adorned in divine garlands and sparkling garments and dazzled. In dazzling and sparkling garments and ornaments adorning every limb, he swiftly leapt up from the pyre, delighted. He was astride a resplendent vimana that brings fame to those who are in it, yoked to swans. In his radiance, the extremely energetic one illuminated the ten directions.

Having ascended into the sky, Kabandha addressed Rama in these words. 'O Raghava! Hear the truth about how you will get Sita back. O Rama! In this world, everyone mentions six kinds of policy.[372] Someone who has been touched by an unfortunate situation will have to ally with another who is suffering from misfortune. O Rama! With Lakshmana, you are suffering and are in an unfortunate situation. There is a person who has oppressed your wife and has created this hardship for you. O one who is best among friends! You must certainly find a friend who is in a similar situation. On reflection, I think that without doing this, you will not

[371] A reference to Sugriva, who has still not been named.

[372] These are six kinds of policy (really foreign policy) recommended for a king in different situations, enumerated extensively in Kautilya's *Arthashastra*. They are alliances, hostility, waging war, waiting it out, creating divisions in the enemy and seeking shelter with an equal.

be successful. O Rama! Listen. I will tell you about the ape[373] named Sugriva. His brother, Shakra's son, Vali, angrily restrained him. The excellent mountain of Rishyamuka is on the beautiful shores of the Pampa. Controlling himself, the brave one resides there, with four other apes. O Raghava! Quickly go there now and strike up a friendship with him. Approach him and before a blazing fire, make an alliance of non-violence towards each other. You should not disrespect Sugriva, lord of the apes. The valiant one can assume any form at will. He will be grateful and will find ways to help you. The two of you will be able to perform the task he desires of you now. Whether his wishes are fulfilled or unfulfilled, you must do what needs to be done. He is the son of Riksharaja, born from the sun god.[374] However, Vali acted sinfully towards him and scared, he is roaming around the Pampa. The ape roams around in the forest and has found an abode in Rishyamuka. O Raghava! Quickly take your weapons and make a pledge of friendship with him.[375] That elephant among apes is accomplished and knows about all the places in this world frequented by those who survive on human flesh.[376] O Raghava! O scorcher of enemies! As long as Surya, the one with the thousand rays, radiates heat, there is nothing in the world that is unknown to him. With the apes, he will search the rivers, the large mountains and impenetrable summits and caverns until your wife is found. O Raghava! You are grieving because of separation from Sita. He will dispatch extremely large-sized apes in all the directions to search for her. Whether that unblemished one has been taken to the summit of Mount Meru, or has been taken to the nether regions

[373] We have translated *vanara* as ape, for want of a better word. This is not a happy translation, since vanara means a special kind of *nara* (man).

[374] Vali and Sugriva's father was Riksharaja. But it was customary to have *kshetraja* sons, born through the father's field (the mother), but through a different biological father. Riksharaja was temporarily transformed into a woman. In that feminine form, Vali was born through Indra and Sugriva through Surya.

[375] Other than the obvious meaning of taking the weapons, the language is such that other meanings are also possible—in addition to the fire, swear on your weapons; since this is an act of friendship, cast aside your weapons.

[376] The rakshasas.

and has found a refuge there, that supreme among apes[377] will find your beloved. He will ensure that the rakshasas are killed and she is returned to you.'

Chapter 3(69)

Kabandha knew about the purport of words. He instructed Rama about the way he would get Sita back. He then again addressed him in words that were full of meaning. 'O Rama! Resort to the western direction, along this auspicious path along which beautiful and blossoming trees can be seen—jambu, *priyala*, *panasa*, *plaksha*, nyagrodha, tinduka, *ashvattha*, karnikara, *chuta*[378] and others. Either climb the trees, or use force to make the fruit fall down on the ground. They are like amrita. Having eaten, proceed. Pass over excellent regions, from mountain to mountain and from forest to forest. O brave ones! In this way, go to Lake Pampa. O Rama! It is decorated with sandbanks. The banks are even on all sides, so that one can descend into the water. It is not slippery. There is no moss, nor any pebbles. It is adorned with lotuses and water lilies. O Raghava! There are swans, cranes, curlews and kingfishers. They frequent the waters of the Pampa and call out in gentle tones. Those auspicious birds do not know how to avoid men who seek to hunt them, because they have never seen them. However, you can eat those birds. They are plump, like vessels full of ghee. O Raghava! There are *rohita*s,[379] *vakratunda*s[380] and *nalamina*s.[381] O Rama! The best of fish from the Pampa can be killed with arrows. Without any difficulty, Lakshmana will remove their scales, fins and bones, grill them and give them to you to eat. After you have

[377] The word used for ape is *plavanga*, meaning one who moves by jumping.
[378] Mango.
[379] Red fish, the carp Rohu.
[380] With a curved snout, dolphins.
[381] Kind of fish.

eaten the fish, he will use vessels made of leaves[382] to offer you the auspicious waters of the Pampa, fragrant with the scent of lotuses. It is pleasant, cool and not polluted. Lakshmana will then collect the clean water that sparkles like crystal in a lotus leaf and drink it. The apes who roam in the forest lie down in a large and excellent mountain cavern. O supreme among men! Roaring like bulls, they will come to the Pampa, in search of water, and you will see them in that form. O Rama! Adorned in garlands of flowers collected from the trees, they will come there in the evening. On seeing the auspicious waters of the Pampa, your sorrow will vanish. O Raghava! Your mind will delight there in the many tilakas, *naktamalakas*[383] and blooming blue and red lotuses. O Raghava! No man has ever made garlands out of those flowers, which do not decay or fade. O Kakutstha! Having gone there, you will see a mendicant lady named Shabaree, wandering around. She has lived for a long time. She is always devoted to dharma and is worshipped by all creatures. O Rama! You are like a god and having seen you, she will go to the world of heaven. O Rama! After that, stick to the western bank of the Pampa. O Kakutstha! You will see a hermitage that is hidden extremely well. The elephants are incapable of entering that hermitage. That is because the rishi Matanga has laid out the grove in that fashion. That forest is like a forest of the gods, like Nandana. O Rama! It is full of many birds and you will find delight there. Rishyamuka, with many blossoming trees, is right in front of the Pampa. It is protected by baby elephants and it is extremely difficult to climb it. In earlier times, the generous Brahma had constructed it. O Rama! If a man reaches the summit of that mountain and lies down there, when he wakes up, he obtains all the riches he dreamt of in his sleep. However, if a person who is wicked in deeds and inappropriate in conduct climbs it, rakshasas seize him while he is asleep and strike him. O Rama! The great noise of baby elephants trumpeting and playing can be heard around the Pampa and by the residents of Matanga's hermitage. Supreme

[382] From lotus flowers.

[383] The Indian beech tree.

elephants clash against each other and become wet with flows of blood. They are spirited, with the complexions of clouds. They clash, roam around separately and clash again. Having drunk the sparkling, clean and undecaying waters, the residents of the forest withdraw and collectively enter the forest again. O Rama! There is a large and radiant cave in that mountain. O Kakutstha! A large boulder prevents entry and it is extremely difficult to enter it. Right in front of the eastern entry to the cave, there is a large lake with cool waters. It is beautiful and there are many trees, laden with roots and fruits, there. With four other apes, Sugriva resides there. He can sometimes also be found on the summit of the mountain.'

After this, adorned in a radiant garland with the complexion of the sun, the valiant Kabandha, stationed in the sky, took his leave from the two of them, Rama and Lakshmana. The immensely fortunate Kabandha was stationed in the sky near them and they gave him permission to leave. He told them, 'Leave, so that you may be successful in your objective.' Delighted, Kabandha took their permission and departed. Kabandha obtained his own form, surrounded in prosperity and radiant in all his limbs. Moving further away in the sky, he glanced towards Rama and said, 'Strike that friendship.'

Chapter 3(70)

In the forest, the two of them followed the path to the Pampa that had been indicated by Kabandha. Those two best of princes resorted to the western direction.[384] In the mountain, they saw many small trees that were laden with fruit. Having seen those, Rama and Lakshmana proceeded, so as to see Sugriva. The two descendants of the Raghu lineage found an abode on the slopes of the mountain. The two Raghavas then approached the Pampa's western bank. They reached the western bank of Lake Pampa and saw Shabaree's beautiful

[384] They first headed west and then turned towards the east.

hermitage there. They reached that hermitage, shrouded by many trees. Having seen that beautiful place, they approached Shabaree. On seeing them, the successful one arose and joined her hands in salutation. She touched Rama's feet and that of the intelligent Lakshmana. The mendicant was firm in her vows and Rama addressed her. 'Have you been able to conquer all the impediments? Are your austerities prospering? O one rich in austerities! Have you been able to control your anger and your food? Are you observing the rituals? Is there happiness in your mind? O one who is beautiful in speech! Has your service to your seniors become successful?'

The successful and ascetic lady, who had observed the norms laid down for virtuous ones, was thus asked by Rama. The aged one replied to Rama. 'There were those I served. When you arrived in Chitrakuta, those ones, unmatched in radiance, left for heaven, astride vimanas. Those immensely fortunate maharshis are knowledgeable about dharma. They told me, "Rama will come to this sacred hermitage. With Soumitri, you should receive him as a guest. Once you have seen him, you will go to the supreme and undecaying worlds." O bull among men! O tiger among men! I have collected many kinds of forest fare for you from the banks of the Pampa.' The one with dharma in his soul was thus addressed by Shabaree, who was never deprived from access to knowledge.[385] Raghava told Shabaree, 'I have heard about your powers from Danu's great-souled son.[386] If you so think, I desire to directly see what I have heard about.'[387] These are the words that emerged from Rama's mouth. Hearing these, Shabaree showed the two of them the great forest. 'Behold. It is full of animals and birds and is like a dense cloud. O descendant of the Raghu lineage! This is famous as Matanga's forest. My immensely radiant preceptors, cleansed in their souls, were here. They knew about mantras. In this tirtha, they offered oblations, worshipping with the use of mantras. There is a sacrificial altar to the west and I have kept it clean. With

[385] This implies that Shabaree belonged to a class that did not usually have access to knowledge.

[386] Kabandha.

[387] The hermitage.

trembling hands,[388] they made efforts to render offerings of flowers. O supreme among the Raghu lineage! Behold. The power of their austerities exists even now. The altars are unmatched in their radiance and are illuminating the directions with their resplendence. Because of fasting, they could not make the exertions required to leave this place.[389] Behold! As soon as they thought of it, the seven seas assembled here. After they had their baths, they placed their garments made of bark on these trees. O descendant of the Raghu lineage! Even today, they have not yet dried. You have seen this entire forest. You have heard everything that deserves to be heard. I wish to obtain your permission to cast aside this body. I desire to go near the ones with cleansed souls, the sages whom I have served in this hermitage.'

Raghava, with Lakshmana, heard the words of the one who was devoted to dharma. With delight on his face, he granted her permission to depart. Having obtained Rama's permission, she offered herself as an oblation into the fire. Dazzling like a flaming fire, she went to heaven. Maharshis who perform good deeds find pleasure in a place. Immersing herself in meditation, Shabaree went to that sacred spot.

Chapter 3(71)

Because of her own deeds, Shabaree went to heaven. With his brother Lakshmana, Raghava started to think. The one with dharma in his soul thought about the powers of those great-souled ones. Raghava spoke to Lakshmana, who was single-mindedly devoted to ensuring his welfare. 'O amiable one! I have seen this hermitage and the many wonders performed by those self-controlled ones. It is full of many animals, tigers and birds that are trusting. O Lakshmana! We must properly touch the water of this tirtha,

[388] Because they were old.

[389] To go and bathe in the ocean. The seven seas came to the Pampa.

which has the seven seas in it, and satisfy the ancestors through water rites. This will destroy all that is inauspicious in us and good fortune will present itself. O Lakshmana! My mind will be delighted if we do this now. O tiger among men! My heart is full of auspicious sentiments. Come. Therefore, let us go to the Pampa, which is pleasant to behold. Not very far from there, Mount Rishyamuka can be seen. Sugriva, with dharma in his soul and the son of the one with the rays, resides there with four apes, always terrified because of fear from Vali. I wish to hurry and see Sugriva, bull among apes. O amiable one! The task of finding out where Sita has gone devolves on him.' Thus addressed, Soumitri told Rama, 'Let us quickly go there. My mind is also urging us to hurry.'

The lord of the earth emerged from the hermitage. With the lord Lakshmana, he went to the Pampa. Everywhere, he saw large trees that were laden with flowers. There were plover birds, peacocks, aquatic birds and parrots. Many other birds called out in that great forest. Rama saw many other trees and diverse kinds of lakes. Tormented by desire, he saw that supreme lake.[390] From a distance, Rama approached it, full of water. He bathed in a lake, a lake that was named after Matanga. Rama, Dasharatha's son, was overcome by sorrow. He entered the area of the lake, one that was covered with lotuses. There were tilakas, ashokas, punnagas, *bakulas*,[391] *uddalas*[392] and reeds. They were like obstructions to that beautiful grove and the water, where lotuses brushed against each other. The water was like crystal and the sand was always soft. There were large numbers of fish and turtles and the banks were adorned with trees. The creepers clung to each other, like friends. It was frequented by kinnaras, serpents, yakshas and rakshasas. It was enveloped by many trees and creepers. The store of water was auspicious and cool. There were clumps of fragrant lotuses and lilies, red and white. There were clumps of blue lotuses and with many other colours, it looked like a many-hued painting. There were pink and black lotuses, full of fragrance. It was surrounded

[390] This is not the Pampa. This is a different lake, named after Matanga.

[391] Tree with fragrant flowers.

[392] The Assyrian plum.

by flowering mango trees, and peacocks called. With Soumitri, Rama saw the Pampa. Filled with desire, Dasharatha's spirited son lamented. There were tilakas, citrus trees, banyan trees, white trees, blossoming *karaviras*,[393] flowering punnagas, *malatis*,[394] *kundas*,[395] creepers, *bhandiras*,[396] *nichulas*,[397] ashokas, *saptaparnas*,[398] ketakas and *atimuktakas*.[399] There were many other trees and it[400] looked like an ornamented woman.

The mountain, full of minerals, spoken about earlier, was near its banks. With blossoming and colourful groves, it was famous as the Rishyamuka. Riksharaja's son was the great-souled ape. That immensely valorous one ruled over the place and was famous as Sugriva. He[401] then addressed Lakshmana, with truth as his valour, in these words. 'O bull among men! Go to Sugriva, Indra among apes. We must go a long distance to accomplish the great task.' Looking at the forest, they progressively proceeded and saw the auspicious Pampa and saw those groves. There were flocks of many kinds of birds there.

This ends Aranya Kanda.

[393] Oleander.
[394] Jasmine.
[395] Another variety of jasmine.
[396] The amaranth or flea tree.
[397] The rattan plant.
[398] The Indian devil tree (*Alstonia scholaris*).
[399] The *harimantha* tree.
[400] The lake.
[401] Rama.

CHAPTER FOUR

Kishkindha Kanda

Sarga (1): 49 shlokas
Sarga (2): 28 shlokas
Sarga (3): 25 shlokas
Sarga (4): 26 shlokas
Sarga (5): 18 shlokas
Sarga (6): 23 shlokas
Sarga (7): 23 shlokas
Sarga (8): 45 shlokas
Sarga (9): 24 shlokas
Sarga (10): 29 shlokas
Sarga (11): 52 shlokas
Sarga (12): 38 shlokas
Sarga (13): 27 shlokas
Sarga (14): 21 shlokas
Sarga (16): 27 shlokas
Sarga (17): 45 shlokas
Sarga (18): 57 shlokas
Sarga (19): 28 shlokas
Sarga (20): 25 shlokas
Sarga (21): 16 shlokas
Sarga (22): 26 shlokas
Sarga (23): 30 shlokas
Sarga (24): 44 shlokas
Sarga (25): 38 shlokas
Sarga (26): 23 shlokas
Sarga (27): 46 shlokas
Sarga (28): 32 shlokas
Sarga (29): 52 shlokas
Sarga (30): 43 shlokas
Sarga (31): 22 shlokas
Sarga (32): 27 shlokas
Sarga (33): 19 shlokas
Sarga (34): 23 shlokas
Sarga (35): 20 shlokas
Sarga (36): 37 shlokas
Sarga (37): 34 shlokas
Sarga (38): 37 shlokas
Sarga (40): 47 shlokas
Sarga (41): 52 shlokas
Sarga (42): 62 shlokas
Sarga (43): 16 shlokas
Sarga (44): 15 shlokas
Sarga (45): 17 shlokas
Sarga (46): 14 shlokas
Sarga (47): 22 shlokas
Sarga (48): 22 shlokas
Sarga (49): 32 shlokas
Sarga (50): 19 shlokas
Sarga (51): 19 shlokas
Sarga (52): 33 shlokas

Sarga (53): 21 shlokas
Sarga (54): 20 shlokas
Sarga (55): 21 shlokas
Sarga (56): 19 shlokas
Sarga (57): 34 shlokas
Sarga (58): 29 shlokas
Sarga (59): 21 shlokas
Sarga (60): 16 shlokas
Sarga (61): 15 shlokas
Sarga (62): 15 shlokas
Sarga (63): 23 shlokas
Sarga (64): 35 shlokas
Sarga (65): 36 shlokas
Sarga (66): 44 shlokas

Chapter 4(1)

Rama went to the lake, full of lotuses, lilies and fish. His senses were overcome and with Soumitri, he started to lament. On seeing it, his senses were filled with delight and he started to tremble. Overcome by desire, he addressed Soumitri. 'O Soumitri! Behold. Pampa's[1] grove is auspicious to behold. The trees, with tops like mountains, are radiant. Grief is tormenting me and my senses are suffering because of Bharata's misery and Vaidehi's abduction. The blue-and-yellow grass seems to be even more radiant and it is strewn with flowers from many trees, like a carpet. O Soumitri! The breeze is pleasant and this is the time when Manmatha wanders around. This month is filled with fragrant scents and there are flowers and fruits on the trees. O Soumitri! The forests are laden with flowers. Behold their forms. A shower of flowers has been created, like rain during the monsoon season. There are many groves and trees on the beautiful plains. The force of the wind is making them wave and the flowers are showering down on the ground. The wind that blows is pleasant to the touch, like cool sandalwood. Bees are humming in the fragrant forests. There are lovely flowers on the beautiful slopes of the mountain. Large and radiant trees cling on to the summit of the mountain. In every direction, look at the karnikara trees, with flowers on their tops. They look like men attired in yellow

[1] Pampa has been identified as the area around Hampi (in Karnataka). This is at the confluence of the rivers Tunga and Bhadra (combining to form Tungabhadra) and there is also a lake there. Hence, Pampa is sometimes described as a lake and sometimes as a river.

garments, decorated with ornaments made out of molten gold. O Soumitri! This is the spring, when many kinds of birds call. The separation from Sita is igniting a sorrow in me. I am overcome by sorrow and Manmatha is tormenting me more. The cuckoo is calling happily and seems to be summoning me. O Lakshmana! This *datyuha*[2] is calling out to me from this beautiful mountain waterfall. O Lakshmana! I am already overcome by Manmatha and its call is drying me up further. The male birds are freely moving around in their unblemished flocks. O Soumitri! Delighted, the *bhringaraja*[3] is calling out in a melodious tone. O Soumitri! Sorrow and worry over that fawn-eyed one[4] are tormenting me, like a cruel forest conflagration in the month of Chaitra.[5] Suffused by desire, on the slopes of the mountains, peacocks are surrounded by peahens and this is increasing my desire. O Lakshmana! Behold. On the slopes of the mountains, afflicted by desire, peahens are dancing around their husbands, the peacocks. It is evident that in the forest, no rakshasa has abducted the peacock's beloved. Without her, living in this month of flowers is extremely difficult for me. O Lakshmana! Behold. At the end of the winter, the forests are rich with a burden of flowers. However, these flowers are futile for me. Delighted, the birds are calling out amidst their flocks. They are summoning each other and this is making me mad with desire. It is certain that Sita, under someone else's subjugation, will be grieving like me. My beloved is young,[6] with eyes like the petals of lotuses and is gentle in speech. The breeze bears the fragrance of flowers. Though it is as cold as snow, it is pleasant to the touch. However, thinking of that beautiful one, it seems to me to be like a fire. At that time,[7] this crow perched on a tree and called happily. Though she is not here, the bird is still cawing.[8] There, a bird[9] told us about Vaidehi's abductor. This

[2] The gallinule.

[3] Shrike or thrush.

[4] Sita.

[5] March–April.

[6] The text uses the word *shyama*. The natural meaning of this is dark. However, shyama also means a woman who hasn't been married (or is a virgin).

[7] When she was with me.

[8] Signifying her return.

[9] Jatayu.

bird will lead us to the large-eyed one. O Lakshmana! Behold. In the forest, the birds are calling from the tops of the trees full of flowers, and this enhances desire. O Soumitri! Look at the colourful forests around the Pampa. Like rising suns, there are dazzling lotuses in the water. The sparkling waters have lotuses and blue water lilies. The Pampa, with red lotuses, is full of swans and ducks. At the end of the colourful forest, there are always chakravaka birds there. Herds of elephants and animals come there, desiring the radiant water. O Lakshmana! When I see the petals of lotus buds, I think that they are like Sita's eyes. The pleasant breeze, emanating from amidst the trees, carries pollen from the lotuses. But when it blows, it is like Sita's breath. O Soumitri! Look at the mountain peaks to the south of the Pampa. Full of flowers, the trunks of the karnikara trees are extremely beautiful. There is one that is like a king of mountains over the others. It is decorated with minerals. Driven by the force of the wind, a wonderful dust has been generated there. O Soumitri! Everywhere, the slope of that mountain is full of flowers. The beautiful kimshuka trees are making it blaze and the leaves are hidden behind flowers. There are fragrant flowers along the banks of the Pampa—malati, *mallika*, *shanda* and blossoming karaviras.[10] In the spring, there are blooming *ketaki*s and *sindhuvara*s.[11] Everywhere, there are *madhavi*s and kunda creepers, full of fragrances.[12] There are *chiribilva*s, madhukas, *vanjula*s, bakulas, champakas, tilakas and flowering *nagavriksha*s.[13] There are neepas, *varana*s, flowering *kharjura*s, *ankola*s, *kuranta*s, *churnaka*s and *paribhadraka*s.[14] There are chutas, patalas and flowering *kovidara*s.[15] *Muchukunda*s

[10] Malati is jasmine, mallika is another variety of jasmine, shanda is a group of plants and karavira is the oleander.

[11] Ketaki is the fragrant crew pine, sindhuvara is the five-leaved chaste tree.

[12] Madhavi is a spring flower, kunda is a kind of jasmine.

[13] Chiribilva is a bilva sapling, madhuka is the honey tree, vanjula is a tree that is similar to the ashoka, bakula is a tree with fragrant flowers, champaka is a tree with yellow and fragrant flowers, tilaka is a tree with beautiful flowers and nagavriksha is a flowering tree.

[14] Nipa is another name for the kadamba tree, varana is the garlic pear tree, kharjura is date, ankola cannot be identified, kuranta is the yellow amaranth, churnaka should probably be *purnaka* (a kind of tree) and paribhadraka is the flame tree.

[15] Chuta is mango, patala is the *Bignonia suaveolens* and kovidara is a kind of orchid.

and arjunas can be seen on the slope of the mountain.[16] There are ketakas, *uddalaka*s, *shirisha*s, *shimshapa*s, dhavas, shalmalis, kimshukas, *rakta*s, *kurubaka*s, tinishas, *naktamala*s, *chandana*s and syandanas.[17] O Soumitri! Many diverse kinds of flowers are spread out on the slopes of the mountain and they have made the rocks yellow and red in complexion. O Soumitri! Behold. At the end of the winter, the trees are blooming with flowers. This is the month of flowers and the blossoming flowers seem to be competing against each other. O Soumitri! Behold these cool waters, filled with lotuses. Chakravakas are roaming around and karandavas frequent the place.[18] Is if full of *plava*s and *kruncha*s and the place is frequented by boars and deer.[19] Because of the calling of the birds, the Pampa is even more beautiful. These many kinds of delighted birds are igniting desire in me. I remember the young one,[20] with a face like the moon and eyes like lotuses. Behold. On the slope, there are female spotted deer with male deer. And then, I have been separated from Vaidehi, the one with eyes like a fawn.'

With senses afflicted by grief, he lamented there, on seeing the sacred and beautiful Pampa, the bearer of auspicious waters. The great-souled one quickly looked around all the forests, waterfalls and caves. With Lakshmana, anxious in his mind and afflicted by grief, he kept thinking and proceeded. Together, they advanced towards Rishyamuka, inhabited by the ape Sugriva. On seeing the two immensely energetic ones, Raghava and Lakshmana, approaching, the apes were frightened.

[16] Muchukunda is the cork-leaved bayur tree and arjuna is a tall tree.

[17] Ketaka is a flowering plant (but this may be *kaitaka*, the fragrant crew pine), uddalaka is probably any tree from which honey is gathered, shirisha is a variety of acacia or mimosa, shimshapa is a tree usually associated with cremation grounds, dhava is axle-wood, shalmali is the silk-cotton tree, kimshuka is a tree with red blossoms, rakta is either the Indian globe thistle or the Indian madder, kurubaka is a kind of amaranth tree, tinisha is the Indian rosewood, naktamala or (naktamalaka) is a tree that flowers in the night, chandana is sandalwood and syandana is the *sandana* tree (chariots were made from this).

[18] Chakravaka is the ruddy goose or Brahmany duck and karandava is a type of duck.

[19] Plava is a diving aquatic bird, krouncha is a curlew.

[20] Shyama.

Chapter 4(2)

The two brave and great-souled brothers, Rama and Lakshmana, wielded the best of weapons. On seeing them, Sugriva was uncertain. Anxious in his heart, he looked at all the directions. The bull among apes was incapable of remaining in one fixed place. As he looked at those two extremely strong ones, he was incapable of steadying his mind. The ape was extremely frightened and his mind suffered. The one with dharma in his soul reflected and weighed his strengths and weaknesses. With all his companions, Sugriva was greatly anxious. Extremely anxious when he saw Rama and Lakshmana, Sugriva, the lord of the apes, spoke to his advisers. 'They have certainly been sent to this impenetrable forest by Vali. They are roaming around and coming here, disguising themselves in garments made of bark.' Having seen those two supreme archers, Sugriva, with his advisers, moved away from the summit of the mountain to another excellent peak. As the others in the herd swiftly left, the apes who were the leaders of the herds came and surrounded the best among the apes.[21] Leaping from one mountain to another mountain, they followed different paths and the force made the summits of the mountain tremble. All those extremely strong apes leapt around. In the process, they shattered the flowering trees in that impenetrable mountain. Everywhere on that giant mountain, the supreme apes jumped around. Deer, wildcats and tigers were frightened and fled. Then, all of Sugriva's advisers, best among apes, composed themselves. On that Indra among mountains, all of them joined their hands in salutation and surrounded him.

Sugriva was terrified and afraid, suspecting that Vali was going to cause injury. However, Hanumat, eloquent in the use of words, addressed him in these words. 'O bull among apes! You ran away, your senses anxious because of the cruel Vali. However, I do not see the cruel-looking one here. O amiable one! You are frightened of your evil-acting elder brother. However, the evil-souled

[21] Sugriva.

Vali isn't here and I do not perceive any fear. Alas! O ape! It is evident that you have acted like an ape. You have shown yourself to be fickle and are unable to control your thoughts. You possess intelligence and knowledge. Always act in accordance with the signs. A king who falls prey to lack to intelligence cannot command all the creatures.' Sugriva heard all the auspicious words that Hanumat had spoken. He replied to Hanumat in words that were even more auspicious. 'They are long-armed and large-eyed. They wield bows, arrows and swords. These two are like the sons of gods. On seeing them, who will not be frightened? I suspect that these two supreme men have been engaged by Vali. Kings have many friends.[22] In this case, trust cannot be pardoned. Men should be known as enemies, they are deceitful in conduct. They should not be trusted. Finding a weakness in those who trust, they strike. The intelligent Vali has undertaken many deeds and kings are extensive in their foresight. Even ordinary men know that they are the ones who slay the enemy. O ape! Go there, assuming an ordinary form.[23] Ascertain through their conduct, forms and speech whether our suspicions are true. If they are cheerful in their minds, find out their sentiments through signs. Repeatedly praise them and gain their trust. O bull among apes! When you ask them, stand with your face towards me.[24] Ask those two archers the reason why they have entered the forest. O ape! You will get to know if they are pure in soul, or whether they intend evil policies, from their forms and the conversation.' Marut's son[25] was thus instructed by the king of the apes. He made up his mind to go where Rama and Lakshmana were. He honoured the words of the unassailable, but extremely terrified, ape.[26] The greatly fortunate and immensely strong Hanumat went to where Rama and Lakshmana were.

[22] Meaning Vali.

[23] So that they do not recognize Hanumat.

[24] So that Sugriva can find out what is going on, from Hanumat's facial signs, despite Hanumat being a fair distance away.

[25] Hanumat. Hanumat was the son of Marut (the wind god).

[26] Sugriva.

Chapter 4(3)

Hanumat understood the words of the great-souled Sugriva. From Mount Rishyamuka, he leapt to where the two Raghavas were. Having gone there, the powerful Hanumat, for whom truth was his valour, supreme among apes and eloquent in the use of words, prepared to speak mildly. The ape abandoned his own form and adopted that of a mendicant. He addressed those two brave ones and praised them appropriately. 'You are like royal sages, equal to the gods. You are ascetics, firm in your vows. You are handsome in appearance. Why have you come to this spot? You have frightened large numbers of animals and others who roam around in the forest. You are looking at the trees that grow everywhere, on the banks of the Pampa. O spirited ones! You are making the auspicious waters of this river radiant. You are patient and golden in complexion, but you are attired in bark. Who are you? O brave ones! Your glances are like those of lions. Your valour is more than that of lions. In your large arms, you are wielding bows that are like those of Shakra. Your forms are prosperous and handsome. Your valour is like that of excellent bulls. O bulls among men! Your arms are like the trunks of elephants. You are dazzling. This radiant Indra among mountains has become resplendent because of you. You deserve kingdoms meant for the best among gods. Why have you come to this region? Your eyes are like lotus petals. You are brave. However, you sport masses of matted hair. O brave ones! You are like each other in appearance. Have you come here from the world of the gods? O brave ones! Your chests are broad. You are gods in the form of humans. As you wish, you have come to earth, like the sun and the moon. Your shoulders are like those of lions. You are great in spirit. You are like sacred bulls. Your arms are long and well rounded, they are like clubs. They deserve to be adorned in all kinds of ornaments. Why are you not ornamented? I think that the two of you are capable of protecting the entire earth, with all its oceans and forests and decorated with the Vindhya and the Meru. These colourful and smooth bows are marked with wonderful signs. They are decorated with diamonds and gold and are as radiant as Indra's bow. These quivers, auspicious to see, are filled with sharp arrows that are terrible and are as flaming as serpents, bringing an end to lives. These radiant swords are like snakes released from their skins. They are gigantic in size and are decorated with molten gold. I have spoken to you in this way. Why are you not replying? There is someone named Sugriva and he is the leader of a band of apes. He possesses dharma in his soul. The brave one has been banished by his brother and is miserably roaming around in the world. Sent by the great-souled Sugriva, the king of the best among apes, I have come here. I am an ape named Hanumat. Sugriva, with dharma in his soul, wishes to strike a friendship with the two of you. I should be known as his adviser, the ape who is the son of the wind god. I can go wherever I want and can assume any form I desire. To do what brings pleasure to Sugriva, I have disguised myself as a mendicant and have come here from Rishyamuka.' Hanumat told the brave Rama and Lakshmana this. Accomplished in speech and skilled in the use of words, he did not say anything after this.

Having heard his words, with a cheerful face, the handsome Rama spoke to his brother Lakshmana, who was standing by his side. 'This is an aide of the great-souled Sugriva, Indra among apes. He is the one I desired to meet and this one has come here to me. O Soumitri! You speak to the ape who is Sugriva's ambassador.[27] O scorcher of enemies! You are eloquent in the use of words. Use gentle words that are full of affection.'

Chapter 4(4)

When these words were uttered, Hanumat was delighted. Having heard the sweet words, he thought that Sugriva's intentions would become successful. 'It is possible that the great-

[27] Generally, kings did not speak to ambassadors directly.

souled Sugriva will get his kingdom back. That must be the reason why these two have come here, to do what needs to be done.'[28] Extremely delighted, Hanumat, supreme among apes and eloquent in the use of words, replied to Rama in these words. 'Why have you come to this terrible forest, with groves around the Pampa? With your younger brother, why you have come to this impenetrable region, full of many predatory beasts and animals?'

On hearing these words, Rama urged Lakshmana and he[29] told him about the great-souled Rama, Dasharatha's son. 'The king named Dasharatha was radiant and devoted to dharma. This is his eldest son, known among people by the name of Rama. He is the refuge of all creatures and is devoted to the instructions of his father. Among Dasharatha's sons, he is the eldest and supreme in qualities. He was dislodged from the kingdom and resides in the forest with me. I have come here with him. The immensely fortunate one's wife, Sita, is devoted to him and followed him. The immensely radiant one is like the sun, with a resplendence like that at the end of the day. I am his younger brother and my qualities are such that I am like a servant to this grateful and learned one. I am known by the name of Lakshmana. He deserves happiness and great prosperity. His mind is devoted to the welfare of all beings. However, deprived of his prosperity, he has now resorted to residing in the forest. He is separated from his wife, who has been abducted by a rakshasa who can assume any form at will. We do not know the rakshasa who has abducted his wife. Shri's son, named Danu, was cursed that he would become a rakshasa.[30] He told us that Sugriva, lord of the apes, would be capable of telling us this. "The immensely valiant one will know who abducted

[28] These are Hanumat's thoughts. There is a break in continuity. Lakshmana was supposed to speak to Hanumat. Those sections exist in non-Critical versions, but have been excised in the Critical Edition.

[29] Lakshmana.

[30] This means Kabandha. Kabandha was Diti's son, Danu and Diti being sisters. Both Danu and Diti were married to the sage Kashyapa. Diti's offspring were daityas and Danu's offspring were danavas. The interchange between Danu and Diti is understandable. But Kabandha/Danu cannot be Shri's son. *Shri* also means prosperity. What may originally have been meant is that Kabandha was cursed, thereby being deprived of prosperity.

your wife." Saying this, in a radiant form, Danu happily went to heaven. I have truthfully told you everything that you asked me about. Rama and I are therefore seeking refuge with Sugriva. Earlier, he[31] donated riches and obtained unmatched fame. He used to be the protector of the worlds, but desires that Sugriva should be his protector. Rama is overcome by grief. Afflicted by sorrow, he seeks a refuge. With all the other leaders of the herds, Sugriva should show him his favours.' Shedding piteous tears, Soumitri said this.

Hanumat, accomplished in the use of words, spoke these words in reply. 'You are full of intelligence. You have conquered anger. You have conquered your senses. It is good fortune that you have come here to see the Indra among apes. He has also been dislodged from his kingdom, because of Vali's enmity. Severely deprived by his brother, and with his wife abducted, he is in this forest, terrified. The son of the sun will help you. With Sugriva, we will also help in finding out where Sita has gone.' In gentle and sweet words, Hanumat said this and told Raghava, 'Let us go to Sugriva.' When Hanumat said this, Lakshmana, with dharma in his soul, honoured him in the proper way and told Raghava, 'This ape, the son of the wind god, has spoken to us in a cheerful way. He has come here because something needs to be done. Let us do that and also become successful. The complexion of his face is happy and it is evident that he is speaking cheerfully. The brave Hanumat, Marut's son, is not uttering a falsehood.'

The extremely wise Hanumat, Marut's son, then grasped the two brave Raghavas and took them to the king of the apes.[32] The extremely famous and supreme ape was delighted that he had accomplished his task. Great in his valour and auspicious in his intelligence, he went to that supreme mountain with Rama and Lakshmana.

[31] Rama.

[32] The Critical Edition has excised a shloka where Hanumat abandoned the form of a mendicant, assumed the form of an ape and placed Rama and Lakshmana on his back.

Chapter 4(5)

From Rishyamuka, Hanumat went to Mount Malaya and told the king of the apes about the two brave Raghavas.[33] 'Rama, immensely wise and firm in his valour, has arrived, with his brother Lakshmana. For Rama, truth is his valour. Rama is Dasharatha's son and has been born in the lineage of the Ikshvakus. He is devoted to dharma and therefore acts in accordance with his father's instructions. That is the reason the great-souled one controls himself and resides in the forest. A rakshasa has abducted his wife and he has come here, seeking refuge with you. There was one[34] who performed royal and horse sacrifices and offered oblations into the fire, donating hundreds and thousands of cows as *dakshina*.[35] He performed austerities and was truthful in speech, ruling the world. Rama is his son. Because of a woman,[36] he now solicits refuge with you. The two brothers, Rama and Lakshmana, desire your friendship. You should receive them and honour them, because they deserve to be worshipped.'

Hearing Hanumat's words, Sugriva was delighted in his mind. He lost his anxiety and gave up his terrible fear of Raghava. Sugriva, the lord of the apes, adopted a human form. Assuming a form that could be seen, he cheerfully spoke to Raghava. 'You follow dharma and are humble. You are brave and are kind to everyone. Vayu's son has told me the truth about your qualities. O lord! It is a great gain for me that you desire to strike a friendship with an ape like me. You have shown me honour. If you desire my friendship, I am stretching out my hand. Accept my hand in your hand and let your bond of friendship be firm.' Hearing the excellent words spoken by Sugriva, he[37] was cheerful in his mind and accepted his hand in his

[33] Clearly, Rishyamuka and Malaya were two adjacent mountains. Hanumat seems to have left Rama and Lakshmana on Rishyamuka and gone to Malaya, where Sugriva was. In that event, Hanumat must have returned to Rishyamuka and taken Rama and Lakshmana to Malaya.

[34] Dasharatha.

[35] Sacrificial fee. These were donated symbolically.

[36] Kaikeyee.

[37] Rama.

own hand. Delighted at the friendship, he grasped him and embraced him. At this, Hanumat, the destroyer of enemies, abandoned his form of a mendicant. In his own form, he used wood to kindle a fire. When the fire was blazing properly, he worshipped it with flowers. Extremely happy and controlling himself, he placed it between the two of them.[38] The two of them circumambulated the blazing fire. Sugriva and Raghava thus had a pact of friendship. Both the ape and Raghava were extremely delighted in their minds. Though they kept glancing at each other, they were not content. Rama, Dasharatha's son, knew about everything. The energetic Sugriva addressed him in these words, telling him what was in his mind.

Chapter 4(6)

'O Rama! Hanumat, my adviser and supreme among ministers, has told me about the reason why you have come to this desolate forest, about why you are residing in this forest with your brother Lakshmana and about Maithilee, Janaka's daughter, being abducted by a rakshasa. Separated from you and the intelligent Lakshmana, she was weeping. Looking for an opportunity, he[39] slew the eagle Jatayu. Without waiting for a long period of time, you will be freed from the misery that has occurred on account of you being separated from your wife. I will bring her here, like the sacred texts of the Vedas when they were lost.[40] O scorcher of enemies! Whether your wife is in the nether regions or in a world in the firmament, I will fetch her and hand her over to you. O Raghava! Know that these words of mine are true. O mighty-armed one! Abandon your grief. I will bring your beloved back. I imagine I know about Maithilee. There is no doubt. I saw her when she was being abducted by the rakshasa of the cruel deeds. O Rama!

[38] Rama and Sugriva, the pledge of friendship was taken with the fire as a witness.

[39] Ravana. Sugriva is saying that Hanumat has told him all this.

[40] This is a reference to the Vedas having been stolen by the demons Madhu and Kaitabha and Vishnu saving them in his fish (*matsya*) incarnation.

She piteously shrieked, "Alas, Rama! Alas, Lakshmana!" She was writhing along Ravana's flank, like the wife of an Indra among serpents. While I was the fifth person stationed on the slope of the mountain, she saw me and cast aside her upper garment and her auspicious ornaments.[41] O Raghava! We collected them and kept them. I will bring them. You should try to identify them.'

Sugriva spoke these pleasant words and Rama told him, 'O friend! Bring them. Why are you delaying?' Thus addressed, wishing to do what would bring Raghava pleasure, Sugriva quickly entered that deep cave. The ape took the upper garment and the ornaments, showed them to Rama and said, 'Look at these.' When he accepted the garment and the auspicious ornaments, tears arose, like the moon being filled with mist. The tears were tainted[42] because of his affection for Sita. He wept, 'Alas, beloved!' Abandoning all patience, he fell down on the ground. Several times, he pressed those supreme ornaments against his breast. He sighed gravely, like an angry snake in its hole. A continuous torrent of tears was released and standing by his side, Soumitri looked on distressed. Like Rama, he too lamented. 'O Lakshmana! Behold. When Vaidehi was being abducted, she cast aside this upper garment and these ornaments from her body on to the ground. When Sita was being abducted, she must certainly have flung them on some grass on the ground. The forms of the ornaments can be seen to be exactly as they were. O Sugriva! Tell me. What did you notice? In which direction did the rakshasa, terrible in form, abduct the beloved whom I love more than my own life? Where does the rakshasa who caused this great hardship to me reside, as a result of whom I will destroy all the rakshasas? He has abducted Maithilee and has certainly generated a great rage in me. He has brought an end to his own life and has opened up the doors to death. My beloved was abducted from the forest by a roamer in the night who oppressed her. O lord of the apes! Who is the enemy whom I have to convey to Yama's presence today?'

[41] More explicitly, though there were four other apes there, Sugriva is the only one Sita saw.

[42] They weren't tears of joy.

Chapter 4(7)

Rama was afflicted. Thus addressed, the ape Sugriva joined his hands in salutation. With his face full of tears, and tears choking his voice, he said, 'I do not know the residence or anything else about that wicked rakshasa—his capacity, valour and the wickedness of his lineage. However, I tell you truthfully that I will find out. O scorcher of enemies! Cast aside your grief. I will make every effort so that you get Maithilee back. You will slay Ravana and his followers and satisfy your own manliness. I will act so that this happens quickly and you become happy. Enough of this despairing. Remember your own patience and resort to it. It is not appropriate for someone like you to have this fickleness in intelligence. Because my wife was abducted, I too face a great calamity. I did not sorrow in this way. Nor do I abandon patience. Though I am an ordinary ape, I did not grieve. A great-souled and learned person like you should resort to his great perseverance. You should use your patience to control the tears you are shedding. That is the pledge of those who are spirited and you should not abandon perseverance. A persevering person does not forget his own intelligence and does not despair in the midst of hardship, loss of fortune, fear or an end to life. A man who always resorts to lassitude is foolish. He is helplessly submerged in grief, like a burdened boat in the water. In affection, I am joining my hands in salutation and seeking your favours. Resort to your manliness. You should not be consumed by this internal grief. Those who are immersed in sorrow do not obtain happiness. Their energy diminishes. You should not grieve. I am saying this because I have your welfare in mind. I am not instructing you. Considering my friendship, you should not grieve.'

Raghava was comforted by Sugriva in this gentle way. His face was overflowing with tears and he wiped it with the end of his garment. Having regained his normal state, the lord Kakutstha addressed Sugriva in these words. 'This is what a friend should do, gently and with one's welfare in mind. O Sugriva! You have done what is appropriate. O friend! Entreated by you, I have regained my normal state. Such a friend is extremely rare, especially at a time like this. You must make efforts to find out where that terrible and evil-souled rakshasa, Ravana, has taken Maithilee. It is proper that I believe you will succeed in this, like seeds sown in a well-prepared field during the monsoon. I have not spoken these words out of excessive confidence. O tiger among apes! They should be taken as my belief in your being able to do this. I have never uttered a falsehood earlier, nor will I ever do it. I know this to be the truth and I am taking a pledge on it.' At this, Sugriva, with the apes who were his advisers, was delighted, especially on having heard Raghava's words and his pledge. The lord of the apes and the immensely fortunate and intelligent lord of men heard each other's words. The foremost among the brave apes thought that his objective would be accomplished.

Chapter 4(8)

The ape Sugriva was satisfied at these words. He spoke these words to Rama, Lakshmana's elder brother. 'You possess all the qualities and you have become my friend. Therefore, there is no doubt that the gods have also shown me their favours in every possible way. O Rama! O unblemished one! O lord! With your help, I am capable of obtaining the kingdom of the gods, not to speak of regaining my own kingdom. With the fire as a witness, I have obtained a friend from the lineage of Raghava! O Raghava! You have become my revered friend and well-wisher. You will slowly get to know that I am a deserving friend. I am incapable of telling you about my own qualities. O supreme among those who have controlled their souls! The affection and patience of great-souled ones like you are steadfast, particularly when they have taken a pledge. When virtuous people meet other virtuous ones, gold, silver and sparkling ornaments do not have to be shared between them. Whether one is rich or poor, happy or unhappy, guilty or innocent, a friend is the supreme recourse. Even if riches have to be given up, even if happiness has to be discarded, even if life has to be given up, friendship born out of affection is seen to continue in the same way.' Sugriva was pleasant in appearance. The prosperous Lakshmana, as intelligent as Vasava, was in front. Rama agreed that it was indeed this way.

Sugriva saw that Rama was stationed there, with the immensely strong Lakshmana. He quickly cast his glance around everywhere in the forest. Not very far away, the lord of the apes saw a sala tree. It was covered with many flowers and leaves and ornamented with bees. Sugriva broke down a branch of that sala tree, filled with many flowers and leaves, and spread it out. He and Raghava seated themselves on it. On seeing that they were seated, Hanumat also broke a branch from the sala tree and Lakshmana humbly seated himself on it. Sugriva was delighted. In soft and auspicious words that were filled with affection, in syllables that were filled with joy, he addressed Rama in these words. 'I have been banished by my brother and am roaming around here, on Rishyamuka, best among mountains, afflicted by fear. I am extremely miserable, because my wife has been seized. I am terrified and shattered by fear. Bereft of my senses, I reside in this forest. O Raghava! Because of enmity, my brother Vali has exiled me in this way. O one who grants all the worlds freedom from fear! Because of Vali, I am afflicted by fear. You should show your favours to someone like me, who is without a protector.'

Kakutstha was energetic and knowledgeable about dharma. He was devoted to dharma. Thus addressed, he seemed to laugh when he replied. 'Doing a good deed is the sign of a friend. Doing a bad deed is the sign of an enemy. I will slay the one who abducted your wife today. These extremely forceful arrows are fierce in their energy. They have been crafted with reeds from Kartikeya's forest and are embellished with gold.[43] The shafts have feathers from herons and they are like the great Indra's vajra. The joints are well constructed and they are extremely sharp. They are like angry serpents. Behold. Any enemy like your brother, named Vali, who has sinned, will be slain by these arrows and shattered like a mountain.'

[43] Kartikeya was born in a clump of reeds.

Sugriva was the leader of armies. Hearing Raghava's words, he was extremely happy and uttered words of praise. 'O Rama! I am overwhelmed by grief. For those who are afflicted, you are the refuge. Since we have a pact of friendship, I will tell you about my lamentations. With the fire as a witness, you have extended your hand and have become my friend. I have taken a pledge of truth and you are more dear to me than my own life.[44] Since you are my friend, I can trust you and tell you about the misery that constantly consumes the inner recesses of my heart.' As he spoke these words, his eyes were full of tears. His voice choked with tears and he was incapable of saying anything. The flood of tears was like the turbulent force of a river. In Rama's presence, Sugriva resorted to his patience and controlled himself. He controlled his tears and wiped his auspicious eyes. The energetic one sighed and again addressed Raghava. 'O Rama! On an earlier occasion, Vali forcibly evicted me from my own kingdom. He was stronger and made me listen to harsh words when he exiled me. He abducted my wife, who was dearer to me than my own life.[45] Those who were my well-wishers were tied up in bondage. O Raghava! The extremely evil-souled one made efforts to destroy me. I have slain many apes who were thus engaged by him. O Raghava! I suspected this when I saw you too. Since I was scared, I did not come near you. A frightened person sees fear everywhere. My only recourse is foremost aides like Hanumat. Despite confronting a hardship, I am sustaining my life because of them. These gentle apes protect me from every direction. They go everywhere with me. They stay where I stay. O Rama! I have briefly told you this. What is the need to narrate it in detail? My elder brother is my enemy and Vali is famous for his manliness. My misery will end when he is destroyed. After his death and destruction, I will live happily for whatever is left of my life. O Rama! Afflicted by grief, I have told you how my misery can come to an end. Whether in happiness or in misery, a friend is always a friend's refuge.'

[44] The text has life in the plural, lives.

[45] Lives again.

Hearing what Sugriva had said, Rama addressed him in these words. 'I wish to hear the truth about what caused this enmity. O ape! On knowing about the reason for the enmity, I will be able to weigh the strengths and the weaknesses and easily ascertain how the necessary course of action can be undertaken. On hearing that you have been shown disrespect, my intolerance has become stronger. The trembling of my heart has increased, like the force of water during the rainy season. Be happy and trust me when I say that before I have strung my arrow, before I have released my arrow, your enemy has been restrained.' Sugriva was thus addressed by the great-souled Kakutstha. With the four other apes, he obtained unmatched joy. With a cheerful face, Sugriva started to tell Lakshmana's elder brother the truth about the reason for the enmity.

Chapter 4(9)

'O slayer of enemies! My elder brother, named Vali, was always greatly loved by our father, and initially, I loved him too. After our father died, the ministers showed a great deal of respect to the eldest and instated him in the kingdom, as the lord of the apes. He ruled over the great kingdom of our fathers and grandfathers and all the time, I stationed myself and bowed before him, like a servant. There was a spirited one named Mayavi and he was Dundubhi's elder brother and son.[46] On an earlier occasion, due to a woman, there was a great enmity between him and Vali.[47] When people were sleeping in the night, he appeared at the gates of Kishkindha. He roared loudly and challenged Vali to a duel. My brother was asleep. However, when he heard that terrible roar, he could not tolerate it. He quickly emerged. I and the women prostrated ourselves and

[46] He couldn't have been both, but this is what the text says. Mayavi was Maya's son and Maya and Rambha had sons named Mayavi, Dundubhi and Mahisha. Mandodari was their sister.

[47] The reason for this enmity is not clear and is not mentioned in any other text either.

tried to restrain him. However, because of his rage, he emerged to kill that supreme asura. The immensely strong one ignored all of us and emerged. Because I wished him well, I also emerged with Vali. From a distance, on seeing me and my brother stationed there, fear was generated in the asura and he quickly ran away. When he fled in fear, we also swiftly followed him, along a path that was lit up by the beams of the rising moon. The asura quickly entered a great and impenetrable hole in the ground, covered by grass. We reached and stood there. On seeing that the enemy had entered the hole, with his senses agitated and overcome by rage, Vali addressed me in these words. "O Sugriva! Steady yourself and stay here now, at the entrance to the hole, until I enter and slay the enemy in an encounter." O scorcher of enemies! In those words, he sought this from me. He made me take a pledge on his feet and entered the hole. After he had entered that hole, more than a year passed. During all that time, I stood at the entrance. I did not see my brother and was worried that something evil might have befallen him. Because of my affection, I was concerned that he might have been killed. After a long period of time, I saw red blood mixed with foam emerge from the hole and was extremely miserable. The sound of the roaring asura entered my ears. However, there were no sounds of my senior shouting as he engaged in the encounter. From the signs, I came to the conclusion that my brother had been killed. I covered the entrance to the hole with a boulder that was as large as a mountain. O friend! In distress, I performed the water rites and returned to Kishkindha. Though I tried to hide the truth, the ministers made efforts and learnt what had occurred. I was summoned by the assembly and consecrated. O Raghava! While I duly ruled over the kingdom, Vali returned, having slain that supreme asura. On seeing that I had been consecrated, his eyes turned red with rage. He bound up all my ministers and spoke harsh words. O Raghava! Though I was capable of restraining that wicked one, I did not feel inclined to do that, on account of respect towards my brother. I honoured the great-souled one and greeted him, as was proper. However, his inner thoughts were not satisfied and he did not pronounce benedictions.'

Chapter 4(10)

'He was suffused with anger and intolerance. Desiring his pleasure, I approached him and sought to placate him. "It is good fortune that you are well and that you have slain your enemy and have returned. O one who delights those who don't have a protector! I am without a protector and you alone are my protector. This umbrella has many ribs and is like a moon that has arisen. It also has whisks made out of hair. Let me hold this above your head. You are the king and deserve honours. I will remain as I used to be earlier. This kingdom was with me in trust and am returning it to you. O amiable one! O slayer of enemies! Do not be angry with me. O king! With my head bowed and my hands joined in salutation, I am beseeching you. Desiring to ensure that the kingdom wasn't empty, the ministers and the residents of the city assembled together and forcibly thrust the task of being a king on me." Though I spoke gently, the ape censured me. He repeatedly told me, "Shame! Shame!" He summoned the respected ministers and ordinary people and in their midst, abused me and my well-wishers in words full of great condemnation. "You know that earlier, in the night, the great asura, Mayavi, wished to fight. The cruel and extremely evil-minded one challenged me. Hearing his words, I emerged from the royal residence. This extremely terrible brother of mine quickly followed me. On seeing a second extremely strong one next to me, he fled in fear. Seeing that we were following, he speedily ran away and entered a great hole. Knowing that he had entered that extremely terrible and extremely large hole, I told this cruel-looking brother of mine, 'Without killing him, I am incapable of leaving this place and returning to the city. Until I have slain him, wait for me at the entrance to the hole.' Thinking that he would be stationed there, I entered that extremely impenetrable place. While I searched for him,[48] a year passed. Eventually, I found that fearful enemy and without any effort, killed the asura and all his relatives. As he lay down on the ground and shrieked, torrents of blood completely filled

[48] Mayavi.

the hole and it was impossible to pass. After having slain the valiant enemy, Dundubhi's son, I could not find a way of emerging from the hole, since the mouth was covered. I repeatedly shouted, 'Sugriva! Sugriva!' However, there was no reply and I was extremely sad. With several kicks from my feet, I shattered it.[49] Emerging, I have returned again. This cruel Sugriva forgot all affection for his brother. Seeking a way to obtain the kingdom for himself, he confined me there." Having said this, the ape Vali, forgetting all virtue, banished me in a single garment. O Raghava! Having cast me away, he seized my wife. Out of fear for him, I am roaming around this entire earth, with its forests and oceans. Miserable because my wife has been abducted, I have entered Rishyamuka, supreme among mountains. Because of a different reason, Vali cannot penetrate it.[50] I have told you everything about the great reason for the enmity. O Raghava! Behold the hardship I face, despite being innocent. O one who dispels the fear of all the worlds! O brave one! You should show me your favours and save me from fear of Vali, by restraining him.'

The energetic one, knowledgeable about dharma and full of dharma, was thus addressed. As if laughing, he started to address Sugriva in these words. 'These arrows of mine are sharp. They are invincible and are like the sun. Imbibed with my rage, they will bring down Vali, the one who is wicked in conduct. The evil-souled Vali, wicked in conduct and the abductor of your wife, remains alive only until I cast my eyes on him. I can myself see the ocean of grief you are immersed in. I will save you and you will obtain everything that you desire.'

Chapter 4(11)

Rama's words were designed to increase delight and manliness. Hearing them, Sugriva praised Raghava and worshipped him.

[49] The boulder.

[50] The reason will be told later.

'There is no doubt that when you are angry, your sharp, blazing and straight-flying arrows can consume the worlds, like the sun at the end of a yuga. Single-mindedly, hear from me about Vali's manliness, valour and perseverance, so that you can decide on what should be done next. When the sun rises, without any effort, Vali strides from the western ocean to the eastern and from the southern to the northern to offer oblations of water.[51] He climbs the summits of mountains and the greatest of peaks. The valiant one uproots them, tosses them up and catches them again.[52] To demonstrate his strength, Vali quickly shatters many sturdy trees in diverse forests. There was a buffalo named Dundubhi and his complexion was like the summit of Kailasa.[53] The valiant one bore the strength of one thousand elephants. The evil-souled one was excited because of his valour and confused because he had obtained a boon. The extremely gigantic one went to the ocean, the lord of the rivers. He sighted the ocean, full of waves and the store of jewels. He told the great ocean, "Fight with me." With dharma in his soul, the extremely strong ocean arose. O king! He addressed the asura, who had been goaded by his destiny, in these words. "O one who is accomplished in fighting! I am not capable of fighting with you. But listen. I will tell you about the one who can fight with you. In the great forest, there is a king of the mountains and he is the supreme refuge for ascetics. He is Shankara's father-in-law[54] and he is famous by the name Himalayas. He is decorated with many caves and waterfalls. There are caverns and streams. He is capable of granting you unmatched delight in a battle." The supreme among asuras realized that the ocean was frightened. Like an arrow released from a bow, he went to the forests around the Himalayas. On the white mountain there, there were large boulders that were like gigantic elephants. Dundubhi hurled many of these on the ground

[51] The average person offers oblations to the rising sun at the nearest waterbody.

[52] Like playing with a ball.

[53] Dundubhi assumed the form of a buffalo. *Mahisha* means buffalo. This can also be interpreted as Dundubhi having assumed the form of the demon Mahisha. But we have already explained that Mahisha and Dundubhi were brothers and therefore, distinct.

[54] Parvati was the daughter of the Himalayas.

and roared loudly. Himalayas had the form of a white cloud and was pleasant and agreeable in appearance. Stationed on his summit, he spoke these words. "O Dundubhi! O one devoted to dharma! You should not cause a difficulty for me. I am unskilled in the task of fighting. I am a refuge for ascetics." On hearing the words of the intelligent king of the mountains, Dundubhi's eyes turned red with rage and he spoke these words. "Whether you are unskilled in fighting or whether you are disinterested because of your fear of me, tell me about the person who can grant me a good fight in an encounter." Himalayas, accomplished in the use of words, heard this. With dharma in his soul, he had never uttered words of rage. However, he now did this and told the supreme among asuras, "There is an immensely wise one named Vali and he is like Shakra in his valour. The prosperous ape is in Kishkindha, matchless and infinite in splendour. He is immensely wise and skilled in fighting. He is capable of granting you a duel, like Namuchi did to Vasava.[55] If you desire an encounter, quickly go to him. He is always brave in all deeds in an encounter and cannot be assailed." Hearing what the Himalayas said, Dundubhi was filled with anger. He went to Vali, in the city of Kishkindha. He assumed the fearful form of a buffalo with sharp horns. He was like a giant cloud in the sky, filled with water during the rainy season. The immensely strong one arrived at Kishkindha's gate and roared like a war drum, making the earth tremble.[56] He uprooted trees that were nearby and shattered the ground with his hooves. Like an elephant, he insolently used his horns to gouge the gate. Vali had gone to his inner quarters. Hearing the sound, he became intolerant. He emerged with the women, like the moon with the stars. Vali was the lord of the apes and all those who roam around in the forest. He briefly spoke to Dundubhi, with limited syllables and sentences.[57] "Why are you roaring in this way in front of a city gate that has been barred? O Dundubhi! O immensely strong one! I know of you. Therefore, save your life."

[55] Indra killed a demon named Namuchi.

[56] There is a pun, *dundubhi* means war drum.

[57] Loosely, *akshara* is syllable and *pada* is sentence. He used these sparingly and therefore, spoke briefly.

Hearing the words of the intelligent Indra among apes, Dundubhi's eyes turned red with rage and he spoke these words. "O brave one! Since you are in the presence of women, you should not speak words like these. Grant me a battle today, so that I can get to know your strength. Or let me restrain my rage until this night is over. O ape! Accept the time till dawn to indulge in gratifying your desires with sensual objects. If one kills a person who is mad, intoxicated, sleeping, without weapons or suffering, in this world, one becomes guilty of foeticide. You are now intoxicated and confused in that way." Only slightly angered, he[58] laughed and let all the women, Tara[59] and the others, go. He told the supreme among asuras, "If you are not scared of a clash, do not take me to be intoxicated. Take this intoxication to be an indication of my capacity to drink like a hero before a skirmish." Having said this, he angrily cast aside the golden garland, given to him by his father, the great Indra. He readied himself for battle. Dundubhi was like a mountain and he seized him by the horns. Vali roared loudly as he whirled him around and flung him down. Dundubhi was crushed in a battle that robbed him of his life. When he fell down, blood began to ooze out of his ears. Having lost his life, the one who was gigantic in form fell down on the ground. He was unconscious and lost his life. Using his arms, Vali raised up the dead body and powerfully hurled it one yojana away.[60] Hurled with force, some drops of blood oozed out from the mouth and, borne by the wind, descended on Matanga's hermitage. On seeing the drops of blood fall down, the sage inflicted a great curse on Vali, the one who had done the hurling. "If he enters this place, he will die as soon as he enters." He[61] approached the maharshi, joined his hands in salutation and beseeched him. O lord of men! Scared and terrified of the curse, the ape does not wish to enter the giant mountain of Rishyamuka, or even look at it. O Rama! Knowing that he was incapable of entering

[58] Vali.

[59] Tara was Vali's wife.

[60] There are interpretations that a yojana in this context means the length of one hundred bows, that is, 600 feet.

[61] Vali.

this great forest, I gave up my distress and roam around here, with my advisers. A giant mass of bones can be seen, like the radiant summit of a mountain. These belong to Dundubhi, hurled by the valiant one.[62] These are seven large sala trees, laden with branches. Using his energy, one by one, Vali is capable of rendering them leafless.[63] O Rama! I have thus recounted to you his valour. O king! How will you be able to slay Vali in a battle? O mighty-armed one! If you can pierce these sala trees with a single arrow, I will know that you are capable of slaying Vali.'

Hearing the words of the great-souled Sugriva, Raghava playfully raised Dundubhi's skeleton with his big toe. Raising it, the mighty-armed one flung it ten yojanas away. Seeing that the skeleton had been flung away, with Lakshmana standing in front, Sugriva again spoke words that were full of import. 'O friend! When he had hurled the body away earlier, it was wet,[64] full of flesh and fresh. O Raghava! Without flesh, it is light now, in a state like that of grass. I am not yet capable of knowing whether your strength is superior to his.'

Chapter 4(12)

Hearing the words spoken by Sugriva, to instil confidence in him, the immensely energetic Rama picked up his bow. The one who bestows honours seized his bow and a terrible arrow. He shot it in the direction of the sala trees and the twang of the bowstring made the directions reverberate. The arrow, polished with gold, was released powerfully. It penetrated the seven sala trees, the slope of the mountain and then entered the ground. In an instant, the extremely swift arrow penetrated the nether regions, quickly emerged again and returned to its own quiver. On seeing that it had pierced through the seven sala trees, the bull among

[62] Vali.

[63] He shook the trees and rendered them leafless.

[64] With blood.

apes was supremely astounded at the force of Rama's arrow. With his ornaments dangling, he lowered his head down on the ground. Sugriva was extremely delighted and joined his hands in salutation before Raghava. Rejoicing, he spoke these words to Rama, who knew about dharma, was learned in all the weapons and was the best among brave ones, standing right in front of him. 'O bull among men! O lord! Using your arrows, in a battle, you are capable of slaying all the gods, with Indra, not to speak of Vali. O Kakutstha! You are the one who has shattered the seven giant sala trees, the mountain and the earth with a single arrow. Who is capable of standing before you in a battle? My sorrow has been dispelled now and I am filled with great joy. I have gained a well-wisher who is the great Indra and Varuna's equal. O Kakutstha! I am joining my hands in supplication. I have an enemy in the form of a brother. To bring pleasure to me today, please kill Vali.'

At this, Rama embraced Sugriva, who was pleasant in appearance. The immensely wise one replied in words that had Lakshmana's approval. 'With you in front, let us quickly go to Kishkindha. O Sugriva! Having gone there, challenge Vali, who is a brother only in name.' All of them swiftly went to Kishkindha, Vali's city. They remained in the dense forest and hid themselves behind the trees. Sugriva girded his loins and roared terribly, challenging Vali. The force of his roar seemed to shatter the sky. Hearing his brother's roar, the immensely strong Vali was enraged. He angrily emerged, like a sun that was about to set.[65]

There was a tumultuous clash between Vali and Sugriva. It was like an encounter in the sky between two terrible planets, Mercury and Mars. Senseless with anger, the two brothers struck each other in the encounter, using palms and fists that were like the vajra. With a bow in his hand, Rama looked at both of them. Both the brave ones were like the gods, the two Ashvins, and were exactly like each other in appearance.[66] Until Raghava could distinguish Sugriva from Vali, he could not make up his mind to release an arrow that would

[65] Alternatively, like a sun emerging from behind clouds.

[66] The Ashvins are twins.

bring an end to life. Meanwhile, Sugriva could not see his protector, Raghava. He was crushed by Vali and fled to Rishyamuka. He was exhausted. His limbs were smeared with blood. He was suffering from the force of the blows. Chased by an angry Vali, he entered the great forest. Vali was terrified of the curse. Therefore, on seeing him enter the forest, the immensely strong one retreated, saying, 'You have been saved.'

Raghava and his brother, with Hanumat, went to the forest, where the ape Sugriva was. On seeing Rama arrive, with Lakshmana, Sugriva was ashamed and distressed. He looked towards the ground and said, 'You showed me your valour and asked me to challenge him. What is it that you have done? I have been devastated by the enemy. O Raghava! At that time, you should have told me the truth, that you would not kill Vali. In that case, I wouldn't have come here.' This is what the great-souled Sugriva said, distressed and in a pitiable state. Raghava again addressed him in these words. 'O Sugriva! O son![67] Listen. Do not yield to anger. There is a reason why I could not release this arrow. O Sugriva! You and Vali were identical to each other in ornaments, garments, size and movements. O ape! I could not find any evident difference in voice, radiance, sight, valour or words. O supreme among apes! I was confused at the similarity of your appearances and could not release this immensely forceful arrow that slays enemies. As soon as I am able to identify Vali in an encounter, I will restrain him with a single arrow and he will writhe on the ground. O lord of the apes! Think of a sign to identify yourself, so that I can recognize you when you are fighting in the duel. O Lakshmana! Uproot this blossoming *gajapushpi* creeper. O Lakshmana! Hang it around the great-souled Sugriva's neck. O Lakshmana! The gajapushpi creeper has flowers and is growing on the slope of the mountain. Uproot it and hang it around his neck.' With that beautiful creeper around his neck, he was radiant. He looked like a rain cloud, garlanded with cranes. His form was resplendent. Assured by Rama's words, he again went to Kishkindha, ruled by Vali, with Rama.

[67] The word used is tata.

Chapter 4(13)

With Sugriva, Lakshmana's elder brother, with dharma in his soul, went to Kishkindha, ruled valiantly by Vali. Rama wielded a giant bow decorated with gold. He grasped arrows that were like the sun, which ensured success in a battle. Ahead of the great-souled Raghava, there were the firm-necked Sugriva and immensely strong Lakshmana. Behind them were the brave Hanumat, Nala, the valiant Nila and the immensely energetic Tara[68]—the leaders of herds of apes. They glanced at the trees that were bending down because of the burden of flowers and at rivers full of sparkling water, heading towards the ocean. There were caverns, waterfalls and caves in the mountains, the best of summits and valleys that were pleasant to see. There was water that sparkled like lapis lazuli, filled with lotuses, with leaves, buds and stamens. Along the road, they saw beautiful lakes. There were karandavas, herons, swans, vanjulakas, waterfowl, chakravakas and other kinds of birds that were calling. Without any fear from those who roamed around in the forest, they fed on the soft grass and sprouts. Everywhere, they saw deer grazing or standing on the ground. There were terrible wild elephants roaming around alone.[69] Decorated with white tusks, they were the enemies of the lakes, because they destroyed the banks. There were many others wandering around in the forest and birds flying in the sky. As they looked at these, they swiftly advanced, following Sugriva's lead.

While they were quickly proceeding, the descendant of the Raghu lineage saw a grove with a clump of trees. Rama told Sugriva, 'This clump of trees looks like a cloud in the sky. Indeed, it is like a large mass of clouds in the sky and is circled by plantain trees on the outside. O friend! What is this? My curiosity is great and I wish to know about this. I wish that you should act so as to satisfy my curiosity.' As they advanced, Sugriva heard the great-

[68] Not to be confused with Taaraa, Vali's wife. This is Taara, one of the four apes who were with Sugriva.

[69] Solitary male tuskers.

souled Raghava's words. Sugriva told him about the great forest. 'O Raghava! This extensive hermitage removes all exhaustion. There are gardens and groves, filled with succulent roots and fruits and tasty water. There were sages named *saptajana*s and they were rigid in their vows. There were seven of them.[70] They controlled themselves, with their heads downwards, or lay down in the water. Residing in the forest, they survived only on air, having that only once in seven nights. After one hundred years had passed, those seven went to heaven in their own physical bodies. It is because of their powers that there is a wall of trees all around this place. This hermitage cannot be assailed, even by Indra, the gods and the asuras. The birds avoid this place and so do the others who roam around in the forest. In their confusion, if they enter, they do not return again. The sounds of ornaments can be heard from there, with rhythm and syllables. O Raghava! There are the sounds of singing and the playing of musical instruments. There is a divine fragrance too. The three fires are lit there and the smoke can be seen.[71] It circles up around the tops of the trees, thick and red, like the body of a pigeon. O Raghava! Bow down towards them, with dharma in their souls. With your brother, Lakshmana, control yourself and join your hands in salutation. O Rama! If people bow down to the rishis who had cleansed their souls, nothing inauspicious is ever seen to occur in their bodies.' At this, with his brother, Lakshmana, Rama joined his hands in salutation in the direction of the great-souled rishis and honoured them. With dharma in his soul, having honoured them, with his brother Lakshmana, Rama proceeded with the ape Sugriva, cheerful in his mind. They proceeded a long distance from the hermitage of the saptajanas and saw the unassailable Kishkindha, ruled over by Vali.

[70] Saptajana means seven (*sapta*) people (*jana*). They are also known as *punyajanas* and were originally rakshasas.

[71] The three sacrificial fires are *ahavaniya, garhapatya* and *dakshinatya* (the fire that burns in a southern direction). Garhapatya is the fire that burns in households. Ahavaniya has various meanings, the simplest being the monthly sacrificial rites offered to the ancestors on the day of the new moon.

Chapter 4(14)

All of them quickly hurried and reached Kishkindha, ruled over by Vali. They remained in the dense forest, hiding themselves behind the trees. The large-necked Sugriva loved forests. He cast his glance around everywhere in the forest and was filled with great rage. He roared loudly, issuing a challenge for a duel. Surrounded by his friends, he roared like a cloud. He was like a rising sun and his proud stride was like that of a lion. On seeing Rama, who was accomplished in his tasks, Sugriva addressed him in these words. 'We have reached Kishkindha, Vali's city. The gates are made out of molten gold and the firm flags are rising up. This extensive place is inhabited by many apes. O brave one! Fulfil the pledge you made earlier about killing Vali. Quickly make it successful, like a creeper whose time has come.'[72]

Raghava, with dharma in his soul, was thus addressed by Sugriva. The slayer of enemies replied to Sugriva in these words. 'This gajapushpi is now a sign that you can be identified with. The sun in the sky and the garland of nakshatras are seen to traverse in a contrary direction.[73] O ape! Do not be scared. Vali and the enmity will be uprooted today. I will free you with a single arrow that is released in the course of the encounter. O Sugriva! Show me the enemy who is in the form of a brother. Vali will be slain and will writhe around in the dust of the forest. If he returns with his life even after he has come into my line of vision, I will be guilty of a crime and you can then censure me. You have seen how I shattered seven sala trees with an arrow. Know that with that strength, Vali will be killed by me today. O brave one! Even though I have faced hardship, I have never uttered a falsehood earlier. Nor will I ever utter it. I am tied down by my love for dharma. Conquer your fear.

[72] The image of a creeper requires explanation. A growing creeper needs a tree for support. Sugriva is being compared to a creeper and Rama to a tree that offers support.

[73] This has been subjected to many interpretations, the obvious one being an evil portent for Vali. Alternatively, Sugriva is being compared to the sun. But the sun is not surrounded by nakshatras during the day. Thus, this means no more than an extraordinary combination of events.

I will make the pledge come true, the way Shatakratu uses showers for budding seedlings in a field. Therefore, summon Vali, the wearer of the golden garland. O Sugriva! Make a sound so that the ape emerges. He desires victory. He prides himself on his victories. He has never suffered at your hands. Since he loves fighting, Vali will emerge alone. When he hears brave enemies challenge him to an encounter, he cannot tolerate it, especially in the presence of women. He knows about his own valour.'

Sugriva was golden and tawny in complexion. Hearing Rama's words, he roared loudly and cruelly, as if he was shattering the sky. The cows were frightened at this sound and lost their radiance. The noble ladies were anxious, as if they were suffering from the sins of a king. Like horses routed in a war, the deer quickly fled. The birds fell down on the ground, like planets that had exhausted their merits. Surya's son[74] thus enhanced his valour and his energy, roaring like the thunder of a mass of clouds. He quickly emitted the roar he was known for. He was like the lord of the rivers, when a wind makes the waves turbulent.

Chapter 4(15)

The intolerant Vali was in his inner quarters and heard the roar of his brother, the great-souled Sugriva. He heard the roar that made all the creatures tremble. On hearing this, in an instant, his intoxication was disturbed, because a great rage intruded on it. With rage all over his limbs, Vali assumed the hue of the evening, when the sun has just lost its radiance and is tinged with red. Vali gnashed his teeth and because of his rage, his complexion assumed that of the fire. He looked like a lake where red lotuses had been uprooted, together with their stalks. Hearing that intolerable sound, the ape leapt up and the force of his steps seemed to shatter the earth.

[74] Sugriva.

Tara, the well-wisher, showed her affection by embracing him. Terrified and scared, she uttered words that were for his benefit. 'O brave one! At a time when you have just woken up, it is best to cast aside this anger, like a garland that has been enjoyed. It has arrived like a flood in a river. I do not like this idea of your emerging suddenly. You should hear the reason why I am asking you to restrain yourself. Earlier, he descended in rage and challenged you to a duel. Though he descended, he was contained and crushed, and fled in various directions. He was contained and especially crushed by you. Since he has come here and is challenging you again, a suspicion has been generated in my mind. There cannot be a minor reason behind his insolence, conduct, this kind of roaring and the rage in the roaring. I do not think that Sugriva has come to you without any help. There must be a foundation of help and he is roaring on the basis of that. That ape is naturally skilled and intelligent. He does not enter into a friendship without testing the other person's valour. O brave one! I have earlier heard the account spoken about by Prince Angada. I will tell you about those beneficial words. Rama is one who crushes the armies of others and he has arisen, like the fire of destruction at the end of a yuga. The famous one is harsh in fighting and he has become your brother's aide. He is the supreme refuge for the distressed and is like a tree virtuous ones seek out for a residence under. He is the refuge for the afflicted and is the only abode for fame. He possesses knowledge and learning and is engaged in following his father's commands. He is the great store of all qualities, and like an Indra among mountains possessing minerals. There should be peace, not dissension, with that great-souled one. In deeds connected with war, he is immeasurable and is impossible to vanquish. O brave one! I am telling you a little bit about this, because I do not wish you to be malicious. I have told you what is beneficial. You should act in accordance with what you have heard. It is best to quickly instate Sugriva as the heir apparent. O brave one! O king! Why should one unnecessarily have a conflict with a younger brother? I think that peace and fraternal relations with Rama and great affection for Sugriva, casting this enmity a long distance away, are best. The ape who is your younger brother should be nurtured. Whether he is there or close at hand here, he always remains your relative. If you wish to do something that brings pleasure to me, if you wish to ensure my welfare, I am lovingly beseeching you to act in accordance with my virtuous words.'

Chapter 4(16)

With a face like that of the lord of the stars, Tara said this.[75] However, Vali reprimanded her and addressed her in these words. 'This extremely angry brother of mine is roaring and he is also an enemy. O one with the beautiful face! What is the reason for me to tolerate him? O timid one! To brave ones who cannot be assailed and do not retreat from a battle, the tolerance of a challenge is said to be worse than death. I cannot tolerate this and I am capable of fighting against those who desire a clash. Sugriva is angry, but it is the roar of a *hinagriva*.[76] You should not be distressed at the prospect of Raghava doing anything against me. He knows about dharma. He is grateful. Why should he commit a wicked act like that? Return with all the women. Why are you following me again? You have shown me your affection. You have acted faithfully towards me. Conquer your fear. I will go and fight against Sugriva. I will destroy his insolence, but I will let him escape with his life. For the sake of victory, I am taking an oath on my lives for you to return. In the encounter against my brother, I will easily be victorious and will return.' At this, Tara, agreeable in speech, embraced Vali. Weeping gently, she circumambulated him, keeping him to her right.[77] Desiring victory, she pronounced mantras of

[75] The word *tara* means star, so there is a play on words.

[76] Sugriva means someone with an excellent neck. Hinagriva means someone with an inferior neck.

[77] *Pradakshina* means to circumambulate clockwise, keeping what is being circumambulated to the right (dakshina). This is auspicious. An anticlockwise circumambulation is inauspicious.

benediction. Confused and miserable, she entered the inner quarters with the women. With the women, Tara entered her own residence.

He emerged from the city, sighing like an enraged and large snake. Filled with supreme rage, the immensely powerful Vali sighed. Wishing to see the enemy, he glanced around on all sides. He then saw the handsome Sugriva, golden and tawny in complexion. With his loins girded, he was ready, blazing like a fire. The mighty-armed one saw Sugriva stationed there. Filled with supreme rage, Vali also tied up his girdle firmly. The valiant Vali firmly girded his loins and raised his fists. Having ascertained the right time to attack, he rushed in Sugriva's direction. Vali was adorned in a golden garland and was advancing in rage. Sugriva also raised his clenched fists in his direction. Sugriva, accomplished in fighting, descended with great force. With eyes coppery red in rage, Vali addressed him in these words. 'This fist of mine is tightly clenched and the fingers are tucked away inside. I will strike you with force, so that I can take away your life.' Thus addressed, Sugriva angrily told Vali, 'My fists will descend on your head and rob you of your life.' He[78] approached him and struck him with great rage and force. Thereby, blood began to flow from the blows and he[79] looked like a mountain. Though alone, Sugriva used his energy to uproot a sala tree. He struck Vali on the body, like a bolt of thunder descending on a large mountain. Struck by the uprooted sala tree and confused, Vali trembled. He was like a boat with helmsmen, but suffering on the ocean because of its heavy burden. Both of them were valiant and terrible in strength. Their speed was like that of Suparna.[80] The fearfulness of their forms was enhanced, like the moon and the sun in the sky. However, Sugriva was milder in valour and his insolence was shattered by Vali. Exhibiting his dexterity, he sought to avoid Vali.

Raghava affixed a large arrow that was like a virulent serpent and struck Vali in the chest with this. Struck with force, Vali fell down on the ground. He was wet with streams of blood and

[78] Vali.

[79] Sugriva. He was like a mountain, exuding minerals.

[80] Garuda.

sweat. He was like a blossoming ashoka tree, uprooted by the wind. Vasava's son became unconscious in the encounter. He was like Indra's standard, when it is shattered and falls down on the ground.[81]

Chapter 4(17)

Vali was harsh in battle, but he was struck by Rama's arrow. He suddenly fell down, like a tree that has been severed. His limbs, decorated in ornaments made out of molten gold, sprawled out on the ground. He fell down, like the standard of the king of the gods when it has been freed from the ropes. The lord of large numbers of apes and bears fell down on the ground. He was like the moon, when it has been dislodged from the sky and no longer illuminates the earth. The great-souled one's body fell down on the ground. However, his prosperity, his life, his energy and his valour hadn't yet disappeared. Shakra had given him an excellent golden garland, decorated with jewels. The foremost among ape's life, energy and prosperity were sustained by this. The brave leader of the apes was wearing that garland and he looked like a rain cloud, tinged at the extremities with the hue of the evening. Though he had fallen down because his inner organs had been struck, the garland, his body and the arrow dazzled, as if Lakshmi had been divided into three. That weapon had the power to convey the brave one along the road to heaven. Released from Rama's bow, it would convey him to his supreme destination. Fallen down in the battle, he was like a fire without its rays. It was as if Yayati had been dislodged from the world of the gods after his store of merit was over. Though he was as unassailable as the great Indra, though he was impossible to withstand, like the great Indra, he was like the sun fallen down on the ground, when the time arrives for the end of a yuga. Vali, the

[81] At the time of a festival dedicated to Indra, Indra's standard is raised on a pole. However, when the festival is over, it is neglected and falls down on the ground.

great Indra's son, wearing that golden garland, was brought down. The mighty-armed one's chest was like that of a lion. With tawny eyes, his mouth blazed. He saw Rama approach him, followed by Lakshmana.

On seeing Raghava and the immensely strong Lakshmana, Vali politely uttered harsh words that were full of dharma. 'What qualities have you achieved by slaying someone who was not facing you? I was engaged in fighting and have met my death because of you. You have been born in a noble lineage. You possess spirit. You are energetic and observe vows. "Rama knows about compassion and is engaged in the welfare of subjects. He is kind and great in endeavour. He knows about time and is firm in following his vows." In this way, all the creatures speak about your fame on earth. Considering those qualities and knowing about your great lineage, despite being restrained by Tara, I faced Sugriva. When I did not see you, I arrived at the conclusion, "He should not hurt me when I am distracted and am fighting against someone else." I did not know that you have destroyed your soul and that you have raised the banner of dharma, but follow adharma. I now know that you are wicked in conduct, like a well hidden in grass. You are wicked, in the disguise of a virtuous person, like a hidden fire. I did not know that you were deceitfully enveloped in dharma. In my kingdom, or in my city, I have not committed a wicked act towards you. I do not know of any violent deed that I have done towards you. I am innocent. An ape always roams around in the forest and subsists on fruits and roots. You acted against me when I was engaged with someone else. You are the son of a lord of men. It is evident that you are pleasant to see. O king! All the signs show that you are full of dharma. Which learned person, who does not have any doubts[82] and has been born in a noble lineage, will hide himself in the signs of dharma and perpetrate such a cruel deed? You have been born in a royal lineage and are renowned as someone who follows dharma. While donning the garb of morality, why are you running after what is immoral? O king! Conciliation, donations,

[82] About right and wrong.

forgiveness, dharma, perseverance, valour and punishing those who cause injury—these are the qualities of kings. O Rama! We are animals who roam around in the forest, surviving on roots and fruits. O lord of men! This is our nature and you are a man.[83] Land, gold and silver—these are the reasons for acting against a person. What has tempted you into this forest? Which of my fruits are you after? Good policy, humility, punishing and showing favours—these represent the broad conduct of kings. Kings do not act according to their own caprices. For you, desire has been the most important. You are unsteady and prone to anger. Since you are devoted to a bow, your conduct as a king has been narrow.[84] You are not devoted to dharma. Your intelligence is not based on artha. O lord of men! You are dragged along by your senses and a conduct based on caprice. O Kakutstha! I am innocent and you have slain me with an arrow. Having performed this reprehensible deed, what will you say in an assembly of the virtuous? One who kills a king, one who kills a brahmana, one who kills a cow, one who is a thief, one who is devoted to killing creatures, one who is a non-believer[85] and one who marries before the marriage of his elder brother—all these go to hell. My skin cannot be worn. The virtuous shun my body hair and bones. My flesh cannot be eaten by those like you who follow dharma. O Raghava! Brahmanas and kshatriyas can eat five kinds of animals with five nails—a porcupine, a *shvavidha*,[86] a lizard, a hare and a turtle as the fifth. O king! Learned ones do not desire my skin and bones. I possess five nails and have been killed, though my flesh cannot be eaten. O Kakutstha! If you are the protector, the earth does not have a protector. This is like a woman with good conduct possessing a cunning husband. You are deceitful, inferior, wicked and false, though your mind seems to be generous. You violate agreements. How could you have been born to the great-souled Dasharatha? You have destroyed the harness of good conduct and transgressed the dharma of the virtuous. I have been

[83] Implying that Rama has not acted like a man.
[84] Only focusing on punishing, ignoring the others.
[85] A *nastika*. A nastika is not an atheist.
[86] Also a porcupine, though literally, something that pierces dogs.

slain by an elephant named Rama, who has abandoned the goad of dharma. O son of a king! Had you fought with me in an encounter when I could see you, you would have been killed by me today and would have seen the god Vaivasvata.[87] I am unassailable and was slain by you in an encounter when I could not see you. You were like a serpent, attacking when a man is intoxicated with liquor and is asleep. Had you not killed me in a desire to bring Sugriva pleasure, I would have captured Ravana alive in a battle, bound him by the neck and delivered him to you. Whether Maithilee has been kept in the waters of the ocean or in the nether regions, on your command, I would have brought her, like the white mare.[88] When I have gone to heaven, Sugriva's obtaining the kingdom is proper. However, your following adharma and slaying me in a battle is not proper. When a person is urged by destiny, such an addiction to desire occurs. But pardon me. Think about virtue and give me a reply.' The great-souled one was suffering, having been struck by the arrow. He said this, with his mouth dry. He glanced at Rama, who was like the sun. The son of the king of the immortals then fell silent.

Chapter 4(18)

Vali was slain by Rama and was senseless. He humbly spoke these beneficial and harsh words, which were in conformity with dharma and artha. He was like the sun when it has lost its radiance. He was like a cloud that has released its water. Like a fire that has been pacified, the best of the apes uttered these words. The lord of the apes spoke these supreme words, full of the qualities of dharma and artha.

After being addressed in this way, Rama spoke to Vali. 'Without knowing about dharma, artha, kama and the contracts that people follow, why are you now reprimanding me in this childish way?

[87] Yama.

[88] The white mare was stolen by the demons Madhu and Kaitabha and retrieved by Vishnu in his form of Hayagriva.

O amiable one! O ape! You desire to speak to me in your folly, without having asked those who possess intelligence, those who are aged and those who are revered preceptors. This land, with its mountains, forests and groves, belongs to the Ikshvakus,[89] granting the right to punish and reward animals, birds and humans there. Bharata, truthful and upright, with dharma in his soul, rules over this. He knows the essence of dharma, kama and artha and is engaged in punishing and rewarding. He possesses both good policy and humility and truth is well established in him. He is the king and he knows about the time and the place, and his valour has been seen. All of us, the other kings, act according to his instructions, which are based on dharma. As we wish, we roam around this entire earth, establishing dharma. Bharata, tiger among kings, is devoted to dharma. While he protects this entire earth, who can act contrary to dharma? We are supremely established in our own dharma. Placing Bharata's instructions at the forefront, as is proper, we chastise those who deviate from the path. Through your reprehensible deeds, you have tainted dharma. You have not based yourself on the path meant for kings, but have made kama the most important. Those who tread along the path of dharma know that there are three fathers—the elder brother, the father[90] and the one who grants knowledge. It is because of reasons of dharma that three have been thought to be like sons—a younger brother, one's own son[91] and a disciple who possesses the qualities. O ape! The dharma followed by the virtuous is subtle and extremely difficult to understand. One can differentiate between right and wrong through the soul that exists in the heart of all creatures. Like the fickle consulting the fickle, or those who are born blind consulting those who are born blind, how will you understand if you consult apes who have not cleansed their souls? I will explain to you what I have said. However, you should not censure me only because of your rage. Behold. This is the reason why I have killed

[89] Unless interpreted metaphorically, this is not quite correct, since Kishkindha wasn't part of the Ikshvaku kingdom.

[90] The biological father.

[91] The biological son.

you. Abandoning eternal dharma, you had intercourse with your brother's wife. The great-souled Sugriva is still alive. Ruma[92] is like your daughter-in-law. Falling prey to desire, you have committed a wicked act by having intercourse with her. O ape! You followed kama and transgressed dharma. You have touched your brother's wife and I have accordingly punished you. O lord of the apes! If a person acts contrary to worldly conventions, I do not think an act of punishing him is contrary to dharma. It has been said in the sacred texts that if a man follows kama and engages in intercourse with his biological sister or his younger brother's wife, he should be punished with death. Bharata is the lord of the earth and we follow his commands. You have transgressed dharma. How could that have been overlooked? Following dharma, Bharata protects the wise and punishes those who are addicted to kama and transgress this major dharma. O lord of the apes! We have only acted in accordance with Bharata's commands. According to his principles, we have punished those who violate ethical agreements. I have a friendship with Sugriva and it is just like that with Lakshmana. I will give him his wife and kingdom and he will do what is best for me. In the presence of the apes, I gave him this pledge. How can someone like me ignore a pledge that I have made? You can now comprehend all the various reasons why I have followed great dharma when I have chastised you. In every way, your chastisement is seen to be in accordance with dharma. Dharma can be seen in the act of helping a friend. Kings who wield the rod of chastisement against wicked men are unblemished and go to heaven, like virtuous ones who perform good deeds. When a mendicant performed a wicked act, like the wicked act you have performed, my noble ancestor Mandhata ensured the terrible hardship that he desired for himself.[93] If kings are distracted and ignore the sins committed by others, they perform atonement by smearing themselves in the dust of those sins. O tiger among apes! Therefore, enough of this lamentation. We are

[92] Sugriva's wife.

[93] That is, Mandhata punished the mendicant. Mandhata was from the Ikshvaku lineage and was the son of Yuvanashva. There are no details of this story about Mandhata and the mendicant, not just in the Valmiki Ramayana, but in other texts too.

subject to our own norms and have thought of dharma when killing you. Hiding themselves, men are seen to capture a large number of animals with snares, nooses and various other hidden means. This is irrespective of whether they are running away, terrified, roaming around without fear, distracted, undistracted or retreating. Men who desire flesh will certainly kill them and there is no sin in this. Therefore, royal sages who know about dharma engage in hunting. O ape! Accordingly, using an arrow, I have slain you in an encounter. Whether you are fighting or you are not fighting, you are no more than an ape. O best among apes! There is no doubt that kings are the ones who grant dharma, which is extremely difficult to obtain, and auspicious lives. On earth, they are gods in the form of men and must not be harmed, condemned, slighted, or addressed through disagreeable speech. You only base yourself on anger and do not know about dharma. Know that I am based on the dharma of my fathers and grandfathers.'

Vali was grievously hurt and was addressed by Rama in this way. Joining his hands in salutation, the lord of the apes replied to Rama. 'O best among men! There is no doubt that it is exactly as you have said. I am incapable of replying to you about what is right and what is wrong. Because I did not realize this earlier, in my confusion, I have spoken disagreeable words. O Raghava! Indeed, you should not find fault with me on that account. You are engaged in the welfare of subjects and know the truth about objectives. You are skilled in determining cause and effect. Your intelligence is unblemished. I now know how I have transgressed the most important dharma. O one who knows about dharma! Your words are in conformity with dharma. Protect me.' Vali's voice choked with tears and there was deep affliction in his tone. Like an elephant stuck in mire, he glanced towards Rama and said, 'I am not sorrowing as much over myself, Tara or my relatives, as I am over Angada. He wears golden armlets[94] and possesses the best qualities. He has been reared by me since childhood and unable to see me, he will be miserable. He will be like a lake that has gone dry

[94] Angada means armlet and there is a play on words.

because all the water has been drunk. Use your excellent intelligence and treat Sugriva and Angada in the same way. You are the chastiser and the protector. You know about what should be done and what should not be done. O lord of men! O king! Your conduct towards Angada should be the same as that towards Bharata, Lakshmana and Sugriva. You should ensure that Sugriva does not disrespect the ascetic Tara and punish her because of the crime I committed. When you show your favours, a person is capable of ruling over a kingdom. Let him follow your instructions and follow your inclinations.'

Rama, whose foresight was evident, assured Vali. 'O supreme among apes! You need not trouble yourself about what we will do. We will especially bear in mind dharma when we act towards you. The punished who is brought down through punishment and the punisher who performs the act of punishing—both of them attain the ends of cause and effect and do not suffer. Having faced the punishment, you have been cleansed of all sin. Following dharma, you have obtained your true nature and are on the path indicated by dharma.' The great-souled one's words were sweet. They were controlled and followed the path of dharma. Rama was the one who crushed others in battle. Having heard his appropriate words, the ape said, 'Scorched by the arrow, I have lost my senses. O lord! I condemned you in my ignorance. Your terrible valour is like that of the great Indra. O lord of men! Pardon me and show me your favours.'

Chapter 4(19)

Wounded by the arrow, the great king of the apes was lying down. When he was addressed in these beneficial words, there was nothing he could say in reply. His limbs had been mangled by the rocks and he had been severely hurt by the trees.[95] Struck by Rama's arrow his life ended and he was unconscious.

[95] In the course of fighting with Sugriva.

His wife, Tara, heard that Vali, tiger among apes, had been slain through an arrow released by Rama in the course of the encounter. She heard the extremely terrible and disagreeable news that her husband had been killed. Extremely anxious, with her son, she rushed out of many caves in the mountains.[96] There were extremely strong apes who were Angada's companions. However, on seeing Rama with his bow, they fled in different directions. She saw that the terrified apes were quickly running away. They were like animals running away when the leader of the herd has been slain. All of them were terrified and miserable, as if Rama's arrow was chasing them. Though she was herself grieving, she approached them. 'O apes! O miserable ones! Your king was a lion and he is in front of you. Why are you terrified and running away, leaving him there? From a distance, Rama has struck him with arrow that can strike at a long distance. Has his terrible brother brought him down for the sake of the kingdom?'[97] The apes could assume any form at will. Having heard the words of the ape's wife, realizing that this was a chaotic time, they spoke these words to the beautiful one. 'Retreat. Your son is still alive. Protect your son Angada. The destroyer, in Rama's form, is taking away Vali, who has been killed. He flung trees and large rocks at him. However, Vali was brought down by arrows that were like the vajra, as if he was brought down by the vajra.[98] His strength is great and extensive and he has enveloped everything here with that. His radiance is like that of Shakra and he has slain the tiger among apes. We must protect the city and all the brave ones must consecrate Angada. When Vali's son has been instated, all the apes will start to serve him. O one with the beautiful face! It is not appropriate that you should remain here. Let all the apes hasten and enter an impenetrable place. There are those who roam around

[96] The many caves means that other apes also rushed out with her. Tara was in Kishkindha. Therefore, this can only mean that Kishkindha had been built around caves.

[97] Tara has still not seen Vali. She has only heard that he has been killed.

[98] There was no fight where Vali had flung trees and rocks at Rama. Nor did Rama strike him with several arrows. All this is meant to illustrate that the apes don't quite know what has happened. It is a time of chaos.

in the forest. Some have wives. Others don't have wives. Those whom we have harmed will seek to harm us and we are suffering a great fear on account of them.'

Despite hearing this, the beautiful one proceeded some distance. The one with the beautiful smile spoke words that were appropriate for her. 'When my husband, the immensely fortunate lion among apes, has been destroyed, what will I do with a son, with a kingdom, or with my own self? I will go before the feet of that great-souled one, who has been brought down by the arrow released by Rama.' Saying this, weeping and senseless with grief, she rushed forward. In misery, she slapped her head, her thighs and her arms. Having advanced, she saw her husband lying down on the ground. He never retreated from a battle and was the slayer of Indras among danavas. Like Vasava with his vajra, he could fling away the best among mountains. He was like a great storm and roared like a dense mass of large clouds. He was like Shakra in his valour. He showered down on others, like a dense cloud. He roared against those who roared at him. The brave one had been brought down by another brave one. He was like a king of deer, killed by a tiger for the sake of flesh. He was like a sacrificial altar with its banner, worshipped by all the worlds. He was like a chaitya[99] that had been uprooted by Suparna for the sake of serpents.' The auspicious one saw Rama standing there, leaning on his bow for support. Rama's younger brother was with him and so was her husband's younger brother. She passed them and approached her husband, who had been slain in the encounter. On seeing him, she was scared and distressed and fell down on the ground. When she arose, as if from sleep, she saw her husband, bound by the nooses of death. 'O noble one!' Thus lamenting, she wept. She was shrieking like a female osprey. Seeing her, and on seeing that Angada had arrived, Sugriva suffered and was miserable.

[99] The word chaitya has several meanings—sacrificial shed, temple, altar, sanctuary and a tree that grows along the road.

Chapter 4(20)

Tara, with a face like that of the lord of the stars, saw him slain and lying down on the ground, an arrow released from Rama's bow having robbed him of his life. The beautiful one approached her husband and embraced him. She saw Vali, who was like an elephant, killed by the arrow. The Indra among apes possessed a complexion that was like that of the great Indra. He was like a tree that had been uprooted. She was tormented and miserable in her mind. She sorrowed and lamented. 'O one who was terrible in battle! O supreme among brave ones! O best among apes! I am in front of you. Why are you not speaking to me now? O tiger among apes! Arise. We will serve you with the best of beds. Supreme kings do not lie down on the ground in this way. O lord of the earth! It is evident that you love the earth greatly. Even though you have lost your life, you have cast me aside and are embracing her.[100] O brave one! It is evident that you followed dharma and constructed this beautiful city of Kishkindha on the road to heaven. There are those of us who were with you in the sweet and fragrant forests at the time of finding pleasure. You have ended that. I am without joy. I am without hope. I am immersed in an ocean of grief. O leader of the leaders of herds! You are now dead.[101] When Sugriva was banished, why did you seize his wife? O lord of the apes! That is the reason you have come to this state. O Indra among apes! I desired your welfare and spoke beneficial words to you. But you reprimanded me. Overcome by great confusion, you did what was not beneficial. There is no doubt that the power of destiny has brought an end to your life. Thereby, though you could not be subjugated, you have

[100] The earth.

[101] The word used is *panchatva*. Reaching a stage of panchatva, when dead, can have two possible interpretations. First, one has returned to the five (*pancha*) elements. Second, there are three normal states—being awake, sleeping (with dreams) and deep sleep (without dreams and without distractions). There is a fourth stage beyond this, known as *turiya*. This transcends consciousness and one experiences union with the brahman. The fifth stage (panchatva) is beyond this too.

come under Sugriva's subjugation. I have never faced unhappiness or misery earlier. I have not been pitied. However, I am without a protector now and tormented by grief because I have become a widow, am in a pitiable state. The brave and delicate Angada has been reared such that he is used to happiness. When his uncle becomes senseless with rage, what state will he be in? O son! Behold your father, who was devoted to dharma, well and do what needs to be done. O child! It will be extremely difficult to catch sight of him in the future. Comfort your son and instruct him about your commands. Before you leave on your journey, inhale the fragrance of his head. Rama performed a great deed when he brought you down. He has repaid the debt he made to Sugriva through his pledge. O Sugriva! When you get Ruma back, may your wishes be satisfied. Without any anxiety, enjoy the kingdom. The brother who was your enemy has been chastised. I am lamenting in this way. Why are you not speaking to me lovingly? O lord of the apes! Behold all these beautiful wives of yours.' On hearing her lamentations, all the female apes were distressed and miserable. They embraced Angada and shrieked in affliction. 'O one with the brave arms, wearing armlets! Leaving Angada behind, why are you leaving on a long journey?[102] You are leaving, abandoning us and your beloved son, who possesses the best of qualities. O beloved! O one attired in beautiful garments! O protector! Have I or your son done anything unpleasant? O brave one! I am your companion. However, abandoning me, you are going to Yama's eternal and insolent abode. O long-armed one! O lord of the lineage of the apes! Without thinking about it, if I have done anything unpleasant towards you, please forgive me. O brave one! I have come before you, with my head lowered at your feet.' Tara wept in this piteous way near her husband, with all the female apes. The one with the unblemished complexion sat down on the ground near Vali, resolving to commit *praya*.[103]

[102] This is Tara speaking again.

[103] The practice in question is *prayopavesa*. While this means voluntary fasting to death, it is adopted by someone who has no worldly desires left.

Chapter 4(21)

Tara fell down, like a star dislodged from the sky.[104] Hanumat, the leader of the apes, gently comforted her. 'Creatures perform good and bad, inauspicious and auspicious. Because of their own good deeds and misdeeds, they reap all the fruits after death. You should be grieved over. Why are you grieving? Whom are you grieving about? You are yourself distressed. Which miserable one are you taking compassion on? Who are you? Whom do you belong to? Why are you sorrowing over a body that is just like foam?[105] Prince Angada, your son, is alive and needs to be considered. You should think about what needs to be done next and about what he is capable of doing. You know that living beings are temporary. They come and go. The learned know that this is the nature of this world and, therefore, do everything auspicious that can be done. There are thousands, millions and hundreds of millions of apes.[106] Having acted so as to satisfy their hopes, he[107] has met his destiny. He looked towards artha and followed good policy. He was engaged in conciliation, gifts and forgiveness. After following dharma and conquering the earth, he has departed. One should not grieve over this. O unblemished one! You are the protector of all these tigers among apes, your son Angada, the lords among the apes and the bears and this kingdom. O beautiful one! These two[108] are tormented by grief. Gently inspire them. When you support him, Angada will rule over the earth. There are funeral rites that an offspring must now perform for the king. Determining the right time, let all those be done. Let the funeral rites be performed for the king of the apes and let Angada be consecrated. When you see that your son has obtained the throne, you will find peace.' She was oppressed by the hardship her husband had faced and Hanumat was standing near her. On hearing his words, Tara replied, 'Though

[104] The word tara means star.

[105] These shlokas are very reminiscent of the Bhagavadgita.

[106] *Prayuta* is million and *arbuda* is a hundred million.

[107] Vali.

[108] Sugriva and Angada.

there can be one hundred sons like Angada, it is best for me to embrace the body of the brave one who has died.[109] I do not seek the power of the kingdom of the apes, not even for Angada. For everything that needs to be done next, his uncle, Sugriva, is here. O Hanumat! O supreme among the apes! On your thoughts about Angada,[110] a father is a son's true relative, not the mother. There is no refuge that is better for me, in this world and in the next, than the king of the apes.[111] I will serve the brave one whose face is turned away. I am only capable of lying down with him and serving him.'

Chapter 4(22)

His[112] life was gently ebbing away and he sighed gently. He glanced around in every direction. However, he first saw Sugriva standing in front of him. Vali saw Sugriva, who was now victorious and the lord of the apes. He clearly addressed him in words that were full of affection. 'O Sugriva! Do not judge me by my crimes. Because of my sins and my destiny, my intelligence was confounded by force and I was dragged into it. O son![113] I don't think both of us are destined to enjoy happiness simultaneously. Therefore, though brothers are united by fraternal affection, it has been otherwise for us. Accept this dominion over the residents of the forest. Know that I will now go to Vaivasvata's eternal abode. While I am still alive, I am quickly giving up this kingdom, this extensive prosperity and this great and untainted glory. O brave one! O king! Given my present state, you should act in accordance with my words, although it is not easy to do. This child, Angada, is sensible. He deserves happiness and has been reared in happiness.

[109] That is, it is best for her to kill herself.

[110] About Angada being crowned.

[111] Vali.

[112] Vali's.

[113] The word used is tata.

Look at him, fallen down on the ground, tears flowing down his face. He is my biological son and I love this son more than my lives.[114] Without me, he will be without riches. Protect him in every way. In every way, you are the one who will give to him and save him. O lord of the apes! You are the one who will grant him freedom from fear. Tara's son is handsome and is like you in valour. In slaying the rakshasas, he will be with you, at the forefront. The powerful one will perform similar deeds of valour in a battle. Tara's son, Angada, is spirited and young. This daughter of Sushena's[115] can determine the subtleties of artha and is accomplished in all the different types of omens. One should have no doubt that whatever task she talks about is virtuous. Nothing happens that is contrary to Tara's point of view. Without any doubt, you must accomplish Raghava's task. It will be adharma if you don't do this.[116] Otherwise, he will disrespect you and cause you injury. O Sugriva! There is a pendant on this divine and golden necklace. The generous Shri is established in this, but will abandon it when I am dead.[117] Accept it.' Because of fraternal affection, Vali spoke to Sugriva in this way. He[118] was initially happy, and subsequently miserable, like the lord of the stars during an eclipse. However, pacified by Vali's words, he controlled himself and accepted the golden necklace that had been indicated.

Having given the golden necklace away, Vali saw that his son was standing in front of him. Preparing himself for death, he affectionately told Angada, 'From now on, serve Sugriva and remain under his control and with him at all times, tolerating the agreeable and the disagreeable, happiness and unhappiness, always, and at all places. O mighty-armed one! I have always reared you, but it is not going to be like that.[119] Show a great deal of respect for Sugriva. O scorcher of enemies! Do not go to those who are not

[114] In the plural.

[115] Meaning Tara.

[116] Because there was a pledge.

[117] Because Shri will not remain in a dead body.

[118] Sugriva.

[119] Because I am your father, I tolerated your behaviour. Sugriva will not necessarily be tolerant.

his friends. Do not go to his enemies. Sugriva is your master. Be restrained. Remain under his control and achieve his ends. Do not show excessive affection. Nor should you show lack of affection. There is great sin attached to either extreme and you must look towards what is in between.' Suffering greatly from the arrow, with his eyes rolling, this is what he said. In his open mouth, his teeth looked terrible. He gave up his life. When the brave lord of the apes died, the apes there could not find any peace. They were like cows wandering out in a forest, when there is a lion in that great forest and the lord of the cows[120] has been slain. Tara suffered in an ocean of affliction. She glanced towards her dead husband's face. She was like a creeper when the great tree it was clinging to has been severed. She sank on to the ground and embraced Vali.

Chapter 4(23)

She inhaled the fragrance from the face of the lord of the apes, her husband who was famous in the worlds. Tara addressed the dead one in these words. 'O brave one! Not having paid attention to my words, you are miserably lying down on this rough ground with pebbles on it, suffering a great hardship. O Indra among the apes! It is clear that you love the earth more than you love me. You are lying down, embracing her, and do not give me a reply. O brave one! Sugriva, who loves rash acts, has shown himself to be valiant. The foremost among the bears and apes are worshipping you, Vali. Hearing their miserable lamentations, Angada's grieving and my words, why are not waking up? O brave one! On earlier occasions, your enemies were killed and lay down here. Having been slain in an encounter, is this the bed you are going to lie down on now? O my beloved! O pure and spirited one! O one born in a noble lineage! O one who loved to fight! O one who conferred honours! You have left me alone, without a protector. Indeed, learned ones

[120] The bull.

should never bestow their daughters on brave ones. Behold! I was the wife of a valiant one. With him slain, I have just become a widow. My pride has been shattered. My eternal objective has been shattered. I have been immersed in a fathomless and great ocean of grief. There is no doubt that this firm heart of mine has an essence made out of stone. Despite seeing my husband slain, it has not been shattered into a hundred fragments. You were my husband and naturally affectionate. You were my beloved. You were valiant in battle and brave. You have now met your death.[121] Even if a woman has satisfied desire and obtained sons and even if she is prosperous with wealth and grain, if she is devoid of a husband, people speak of her as a widow. O brave one! You are now lying down on a circle of blood that is oozing out of your own body. Your bedspread has the complexion of an insect[122] and you have made your own bed. O bull among apes! I am unable to embrace you in my arms. Your body is covered with dust and blood everywhere.[123] In this extremely terrible enmity, Sugriva has become successful today. With a single arrow released by Rama, he has been freed from his fear. With you having obtained death,[124] I am looking at you. When I touch you, this arrow stuck to your heart acts as a barrier.'

Then Nila took out the arrow from the body, like taking out a flaming serpent that has hidden inside a mountainous cavern. When the arrow was extracted, its radiance was like the rays of the sun, when it is setting atop Asta.[125] Like copper-coloured and ochre-coloured[126] water flowing from a mountain, blood started to flow out from all the wounds. The brave one had been struck by the weapon. With tears flowing from her eyes, she[127] wiped the dust of battle from all over his body. On seeing that all the limbs of her

[121] Panchatva again.

[122] The *indragopa* insect, which is red in colour.

[123] This doesn't mean that she is reluctant to embrace Vali's dead body because of the dust and blood. It means that when she embraces his dead body, the dust and the blood create a barrier in between.

[124] Panchatva.

[125] The sun is believed to set behind Mount Asta.

[126] Because of minerals.

[127] Tara.

dead husband were covered with blood, the beautiful Tara spoke to the coppery-eyed Angada. 'O son! Behold the extremely terrible western state of your father.[128] He has attained this end because of his attachment to enmity and his wicked deeds. His body was like that of the young and rising sun, but he has left for Yama's abode. O son! Show your respect to the king, your father, the one who granted honours.' Thus addressed, he arose and seized his father's feet with his thick and round arms and said, 'I am Angada.' 'Angada is greeting you, as on earlier occasions.[129] Why are you not replying and saying, "O son! May you live for a long time?" I am seated near you, with my son as my aide, senseless. I am like a cow with a calf, when a lion has just killed the bull. With Rama's weapons as the water, you have performed the rituals in a sacrifice of fighting. Having accomplished it, how can you have a bath without me, your wife?[130] Satisfied with your conduct in battles, the king of the gods gave you a necklace made out of molten gold. Why can't I see it here now? O granter of honours! Even though you have lost your life, royal prosperity has not deserted you. Your radiance is like that of the sun, as it circles the king of the mountains.[131] I was not able to restrain you with my words, which were like medication. With you having been slain in the encounter, I have been killed, with my son. Prosperity is deserting not just you, but me too.'

Chapter 4(24)

Thereafter, on seeing that Vali was dead, Raghava, the scorcher of enemies, addressed Sugriva in these comforting words.

[128] The imagery is that of the setting sun.

[129] This is Tara speaking again.

[130] *Avabhritha* is the most important final component of a sacrifice, characterized by the taking of a bath. As the last bath of life, avabhritha also signifies death. The battle is thus being compared to a sacrifice and the text uses the word avabhritha. Any sacrifice, and the subsequent bath, has to be taken with the wife.

[131] The sun is believed to circle around Mount Meru.

'A person who is dead does not gain anything from grieving and lamentations. One should undertake whatever task needs to be done next. This shedding of tears is in conformity with whatever is done in the worlds.[132] However, after some time, there are other tasks that need to be undertaken. In the worlds, destiny is the cause. Destiny is behind all acts that are undertaken. Destiny is the cause that makes all creatures undertake action. No one is ever the doer. No one is the master in engaging someone else to act. The world acts according to its nature and is driven by destiny. Time cannot transcend destiny and destiny is never weakened. It[133] acts according to its own nature and never exceeds it. Destiny does not recognize a relative, a cause, valour, a friend, a kin, a relationship, or a reason. It is its own master. Those who are virtuous in their insight can see the consequences of destiny. Dharma, artha and kama are encompassed by the progress of destiny. The lord of the apes pursued the auspicious objectives of dharma, artha and kama. Having reaped the consequences of his deeds, Vali has attained his own nature.[134] The great-souled one was not concerned about protecting his own life. Having been engaged in his own dharma, he has obtained heaven. The destiny obtained by the lord of the apes is the best. Therefore, there has been enough of lamenting. It is time to show him respect.'

When Rama finished speaking, Lakshmana, the slayer of enemy heroes, addressed the senseless Sugriva in words of reassurance. 'O Sugriva! Now perform the funeral rites for him. With Tara and Angada, cremate Vali. Instruct that a lot of dry wood, sandalwood and other divine wood, should be collected for Vali's cremation. Comfort Angada, whose senses are suffering. Do not be childish in your view that this city belongs to you alone now. Let Angada fetch garlands, many kinds of garments, ghee, oil, fragrances and everything else that will be required next. Showing due respect, let

[132] In these shlokas, there is scope for interpretation and therefore, there is subjectivity in the translation.

[133] Destiny.

[134] Such as, his atman.

Tara[135] go and quickly bring a palanquin. It should possess all the qualities required for a special occasion like this. Let apes who are appropriate for bearing the palanquin be prepared. They should be capable and strong enough to carry Vali.' The extender of Sumitra's delight spoke to Sugriva in this way. Lakshmana, the destroyer of enemy heroes, then stood next to his brother.

On hearing Lakshmana's words, Tara, respectful in his mind, quickly entered the cave, wishing to find a palanquin. Having found an appropriate palanquin, Tara next found brave apes who were capable of bearing the palanquin. Grieving, Sugriva, with Angada, raised Vali on to the palanquin. The dead Vali was raised on to the palanquin. He was decorated with many kinds of ornaments, garlands and garments. King Sugriva, the lord of the apes, commanded, 'Let the appropriate funeral rites be observed for the noble one. Let apes proceed ahead of the palanquin now, scattering many kinds of jewels along the path. On earth, the funeral rites of kings can be seen, especially of those who are prosperous. Let the apes follow exactly identical practices.' Angada, Tara[136] and all the other apes milled around, lamenting the death of their relative. With their leader slain, Tara[137] and all the female apes followed their husband, lamenting in piteous tones. At the sound of the female apes lamenting inside the forest, all the forests and mountains also started to weep. In a deserted spot on the sandbank of a mountain stream, many apes, who roamed around in the forest, prepared the funeral pyre. The best of bearers lowered the palanquin from their shoulders and placed it there. Filled with sorrow, all of them stood to one side.

Tara saw that her husband was lying down on the floor of the palanquin. Extremely miserable, she raised his head on to her lap and began to lament. 'Why do you not see these people who are suffering from grief? O granter of honours! Though you have lost your life, your face is happy. Your complexion is like that of the setting sun, just as it was seen to be while you were alive. O ape! In

[135] This is not Taaraa, Vali's wife, but the male ape, Taara.

[136] The male ape.

[137] Vali's wife.

Rama's form, destiny is dragging you away. Using a single arrow in the battle, he has made all of us widows. O Indra among kings! These female apes have always been wives to you. Grasping your feet, they came along this path. Why are you not understanding that? Don't you desire these wives, whose faces are like the moon? Why are you not seeing Sugriva, now the lord of the apes? O king! These are the advisers, Tara and the others. O unblemished one! The residents of the city have surrounded you. O slayer of enemies! Take your leave of the advisers, so that all of us can sport in the forest, intoxicated with liquor.' Enveloped by sorrow on account of her husband, Tara lamented in this way. The female apes, also afflicted by grief, raised her and took her away.

Weeping, and with his senses numbed by sorrow, with Sugriva, Angada placed his father's body on the pyre.[138] As his father left on the long journey, his senses were distracted. In the proper way, he applied the fire and performed an *apasavya* circumambulation.[139] After having cremated Vali in the proper way, the bulls among apes went to an auspicious river and performed the water rites with its cool water. They kept Angada at the front and with Sugriva and Tara,[140] the apes sprinkled themselves with water. With a misery that was just as great as that of Sugriva, the immensely strong Kakutstha arranged for the funeral rites to be undertaken.

Chapter 4(25)

Sugriva was tormented by grief and his garments were wet.[141] The apes who were great advisers surrounded him. They approached the mighty-armed Rama, the performer of unsullied deeds. All of

[138] They raised it from the palanquin and placed it on the pyre.

[139] This is circumambulation in anticlockwise fashion, the exact opposite of pradakshina. In pradakshina, one keeps the person/object being circumambulated on the right. In apasavya, the person/object being circumambulated is kept on the left.

[140] Vali's wife.

[141] From the water rites.

them stood there, with their hands joined in salutation, like the rishis before the grandfather.[142] Hanumat's complexion was like that of the golden mountain.[143] His complexion was like that of the rising sun. Joining his hands in salutation, the son of the wind god spoke these words. 'O lord! It is because of your favours that Sugriva has obtained this great kingdom of the apes that belonged to his fathers and grandfathers. It was extremely difficult to obtain. With your permission, he will enter this auspicious city. With all his well-wishers, he will perform the appropriate tasks. Having bathed, following the proper rites, he will be anointed with many kinds of fragrances. In particular, he will worship you with garlands and gems. You should go to this beautiful cave in the mountains. O lord! Establish this alliance with the delighted apes.' Raghava, the destroyer of enemy heroes, was addressed by Hanumat in this way. The intelligent one, accomplished in the use of words, replied to Hanumat. 'O Hanumat! O amiable one! Following the instructions of my father, I cannot enter a village or a city for fourteen years. When the brave Sugriva, bull among the apes, enters this divine and extremely prosperous cave, let him swiftly be instated in the kingdom in the proper way.' Having told Hanumat this, Rama told Sugriva, 'Let the brave Angada be instated as the heir apparent. O amiable one! The four months that are known as the monsoon season have commenced.[144] The month of Shravana, which brings rain, is in front of us. This is not the time for me to make the effort.[145] However, you should enter the city. O amiable one! I will reside on this mountain with Lakshmana. A wind blows through this large and beautiful cave in the mountain.[146] O amiable one! There is plenty of water and many red and blue lotuses. When

[142] Brahma.

[143] Meru.

[144] This deviates from the six-season format. In the six-season format, the seasons (*ritu*) are Vasanta or spring (Chaitra, Vaishakha), Grishma or summer (Jyaishtha, Ashadha), Varsha or monsoon (Shravana, Bhadrapada), Sharada or autumn (Ashvina, Kartika), Hemanta or cold season (Margashirsha, Pousha) and Shishira or winter (Magha, Phalguna). Shravana is the July–August period.

[145] Enter the city.

[146] Not to be confused with Kishkindha.

it is the month of Kartika,[147] you will make efforts for Ravana's destruction. That is our agreement. Now enter your own abode. With your delighted well-wishers, be anointed in the kingdom.'

Having thus obtained Rama's permission, Sugriva, bull among the apes, entered the beautiful city of Kishkindha, which had been ruled over by Vali. When the lord of the apes entered, thousands of delighted apes greeted him and surrounded him from all sides. On seeing the lord of the apes, all the ordinary ones controlled themselves and with their heads lowered, prostrated themselves on the ground before him. The valiant Sugriva raised all the ordinary ones and spoke to them. The amiable and extremely strong one then entered his brother's inner quarters.

When Sugriva, bull among apes, emerged again, after entering there, all the well-wishers consecrated him, like the immortals do to the one with the thousand eyes. A white umbrella, embellished with gold, was brought. There were white whisks made out of hair and a golden staff that would enhance fame. There were all the jewels and every kind of seed and herb. There were trees that exuded milky white sap and blooming creepers. There were white garments and white unguents. There were fragrant garlands and lotuses that blossom on land and in water. There was sandalwood paste and many kinds of other divine fragrances. There was *akshata*,[148] molten gold, *priyangu*,[149] honey, ghee, curds and sandals made out of the hides of tigers and boars. Pastes used before bathing were brought—made from yellow arsenic and red arsenic. Sixteen supreme and cheerful maidens were brought there. The bulls among brahmanas were satisfied with gems, garments and food. At the right time, following the right rites, the best among apes was anointed. Kusha grass was spread around the fire that had been lit with kindling. Those who knew about the mantras offered oblations sanctified with mantras into the fire. A golden throne was covered with an excellent spread. It was beautiful and colourful, decorated

[147] October–November.

[148] This can mean grain of any kind. But it is specifically used for threshed and winnowed rice that has not been dehusked.

[149] Creeper believed to blossom at a woman's touch.

with flowers and was at the top of the palace. To the chanting of mantras, he was made to sit on that excellent seat, with his face facing the east. All the bulls among the apes invited the male and female rivers and tirthas from every direction. From every direction, they invited the oceans. This sparkling and auspicious water was filled in golden vessels. Following the ordinances laid down by the maharshis in the sacred texts, the water from the golden pots was then poured into auspicious vessels that were made out of the horns of cows.[150] Gaja, Gavaksha, Gavaya, Sharabha, Gandhamadana, Mainda, Dvivida, Hanumat, Jambavat consecrated Sugriva with those pleasant and fragrant waters, like the Vasus do to Vasava. Sugriva was consecrated by all the bulls among apes. Delighted, hundreds and thousands of the great-souled ones roared. Following Rama's words, Sugriva, bull among apes, embraced Angada and instated him as the heir apparent. Roaring, the apes anointed Angada. They praised and worshipped the great-souled Sugriva. The beautiful city of Kishkindha, inside the cave in the mountain, was filled with joyous and healthy people and decorated with flags and pennants. The ape,[151] the leader of the army, then informed the great-souled Rama about the great consecration. The valiant one obtained his wife Ruma back and like the lord of the gods, obtained his kingdom back.

Chapter 4(26)

When the ape Sugriva had been consecrated and had entered his cave,[152] with his brother, Rama went to Mount Prasravana. It was full of tigers and other animals, enveloped by the terrible roars of lions. It was dense with many kinds of shrubs and creepers. There were many kinds of trees. Bears, apes, golangulas and wild cats resided there. The mountain was always sacred and purifying,

[150] Using these, the water was sprinkled over his head.
[151] Sugriva.
[152] Kishkindha.

like a thick mass of clouds. There was a large and extensive cave on the summit of the mountain. With Soumitri, Rama accepted that as a place to dwell in. With Lakshmana, Raghava, with dharma in his soul, resided there, on Mount Prasravana, with many caverns and groves that were fit to be seen. That mountain had many objects that were extremely pleasant. However, though he resided there, Rama did not find the slightest bit of pleasure. He remembered the abduction of his wife, whom he loved more than his own life. This was particularly the case when he saw the moon rise. In the night, when he lay down and had gone to sleep, he would awaken, his senses afflicted by tears of sorrow. Thus Kakutstha grieved, always overcome by sorrow. His brother Lakshmana, who was just as miserable as him, entreated him in these words. 'O brave one! There has been enough of this grieving. You should not sorrow. It is known to you that if people sorrow, all their objectives are destroyed. On earth, you are the one who has to perform tasks[153] and you are devoted to the gods. O Raghava! You are a believer,[154] devoted to dharma, and enterprising. If you give up your enterprise, an enemy, especially a rakshasa who is valiant and deceitful in conduct, can be capable of killing you in a battle. You must uproot your misery and be steady in your enterprise. You will then be able to uproot the rakshasa, with all his relatives. O Kakutstha! You are capable of reversing the order of the earth, with its oceans, forests and mountains, not to speak of Ravana. I am only seeking to wake up your valour, which is sleeping. It is like a fire hidden beneath ashes and will blaze when the time arrives to offer oblations.'

Raghava honoured those words of Lakshmana, which were beneficial and auspicious. He addressed his well-wisher in these gentle words. 'O Lakshmana! You have spoken beneficial words of devotion and affection. They are indicative of the truthfulness of your valour. This sorrow must be abandoned. It makes all tasks suffer. I will invoke my invincible valour, energy and enterprise. I will await the autumn season, the monsoon season has arrived. At

[153] The word used is *kriyapara*. This is interpreted as being devoted to rituals, but is not necessary.

[154] The word used is *astika,* which can also be translated as theist.

that time, I will destroy the large number of rakshasas and their kingdom.' Hearing Rama's words, Lakshmana was delighted. Sumitra's descendant again addressed him in these words. 'O destroyer of enemies! These are words that are worthy of you. O Kakutstha! You have now returned to your true nature. Knowing your own valour, you must adhere to its truth. These words are worthy of a noble and learned person. O tiger among men! O Raghava! We must therefore think about restraining the enemy, while we spend these rainy nights here. Until autumn is here, you must control your rage. With me, these four months have to be spent in patience. Let us reside on this mountain, frequented by the kings of animals.[155] You are capable of slaying the enemy, even one with enhanced powers.'

Chapter 4(27)

After Vali was killed and Sugriva was consecrated, Rama resided on the slopes of Malyavat.[156] He spoke to Lakshmana. 'The season has arrived. It is time for the rain to shower down. Behold. The sky is covered with clouds that have the complexion of mountains. For nine months, the sun in the sky uses its rays to suck up the juices from the oceans and bears them in its womb. It then gives birth to juices that sustain life.[157] Using the row of stairs provided by the clouds, it is now possible to climb up into the sky and ornament the sun with garlands made out of wild jasmine and arjuna flowers. Those clouds in the sky are coloured with the coppery red hue of advancing evening and are white at the edges. It is as if the clouds are a soft bandage, tied around a wound in the sky. The sky seems to be yearning with desire. The gentle wind is like its sigh. It is tinged with the red sandalwood paste of the evening. The white clouds are like its radiant face. This earth was suffering from the summer and

[155] Lions.

[156] This means that Mount Malyavat and Mount Prasravana were identical.

[157] This equates the monsoon season to three months, mid-July to mid-October.

is now flowing with the new water. Like Sita, who is tormented by grief, it is shedding tears.[158] Like using a cup made out of the leaf of a white waterlily, one can cup one's hands and drink the cool and pleasant water that has been released from the stomachs of the clouds. The wind bears the fragrance of the ketaka flower. This mountain has flowering arjuna trees and is fragrant with ketaka flowers. It is as if this downpour is anointing Sugriva, when his enemy has been pacified. The clouds are like black antelope skin that these mountains have donned. The downpour is like sacrificial threads that they are wearing. The caves are filled with a wind that blows through them. The sky seems to be suffering, as it is struck by the lightning, which is like a golden whip. Therefore, in pain internally, it seems to be crying out. It seems to be that the lightning is struggling inside that blue cloud, just as the ascetic Vaidehi must have writhed in Ravana's lap. Since the directions cannot be clearly seen, those who are with their beloveds must find it to be beneficial. The planets and the moon have disappeared, marred by the clouds. O Soumitri! Look at the flowering wild jasmine on the slope of the mountain. Having held back their tears, they are now eager at the advent of the monsoon.[159] I am overcome by sorrow and they seem to be there to ignite my desire.[160]

'The dust has been pacified. The breeze is cool now. The extreme taints of the summer have been quietened. The expeditions of the kings have ceased. Men who were in other places have returned to their own countries. The chakravakas, followed by their beloveds, have now left, desiring to reside in Lake Manasa. However, on seeing that the rainwaters have disrupted the roads, vehicles are not travelling. The sky is radiant. But with clouds scattered everywhere, it can sometimes be seen and sometimes, it cannot be seen. It looks

[158] The first rain leads to vapour rising up from a heated earth.

[159] The flowers are covered with water resembling tears. But there is another image too, that of women who have held back their tears because their husbands have been away on work. The monsoon is usually the time when the husbands return to their wives.

[160] The subsequent shlokas have a beautiful description of the monsoon and there are shlokas that are reminiscent of Kalidasa's *Meghadutam*. However, there is also an inconsistency. The metre changes. Normally, throughout a great epic, the same metre has to be used. Therefore, speculatively, these shlokas could be a later interpolation.

like the giant ocean when it is quiet, obstructed here and there by mountains. Descending from the mountains, the new water is flowing faster along the streams, bearing copper and other ores from the mountains and flowers from sala and kadamba trees, followed by the calling of peacocks. Jambu fruit is desired and eaten. It is full of juices and resembles a bee.[161] However, struck by the wind, mango fruit of many colours is falling down on the ground, even though it is not yet ripe. The clouds are thundering in high-pitched tones. They are garlanded with cranes and the lightning is like flags. They look like the summits of mountains and like large and crazy elephants that are fighting. Arrays of cranes desire the clouds and are flying all around them. It is as if a beautiful and long garland made out of white lotuses has been raised up by the wind and is spread across the sky. Sleep gradually approaches Keshava.[162] Rivers swiftly approach the ocean. Delighted cranes approach the clouds. Filled with desire, beautiful women approach their beloveds. The extremities of the forest are full of peacocks that are dancing beautifully. There are kadamba flowers on the branches of kadamba trees. Bulls approach cows that are also equally filled with desire. The earth is full of crops and the forests are lovely. The surging rivers are bearing along water from the rains. The peacocks are dancing beautifully. The apes are comforting themselves. Crazy elephants are trumpeting at the extremities of the forest. Those separated from their beloveds are thinking about them. Inhaling the fragrant scent from the ketaka flowers, elephants are both glad and maddened. With the crazy peacocks, they are also trumpeting. But hearing the sound of the waterfalls in the mountains, they are bewildered. Bees are hanging from the kadamba flowers on the branches, but are brought down by the downpour of rain in an instant. However, they again immerse themselves in the honey in the flowers and are maddened. The branches of the jambu trees are

[161] Implicitly, these are falling down when they are ripe.

[162] This is interpreted as Keshava in the sense of Vishnu, it being believed that Vishnu sleeps from Ashadha to Kartika. However, Keshava is also another name for the month of Margashirsha (November–December). Perhaps all it means is that one is approaching that month.

radiant with large numbers of fruits with succulent juices, making them look like heaps of coal powder, or droves of bees feasting on them. The clouds are ornamented with flags made out of lightning. They are thundering in deep and loud tones. In their dazzling forms, they look like elephants that are eager to fight. In the forest, that large and maddened elephant was proceeding along a path in the mountains. It heard the cloud thundering, and suspecting that it was another elephant desiring to fight, decided to retreat. The water is falling down, sparkling like pearls. The extremely clean water is clinging to the leaves. Though their feathers have become discoloured because of the rain, the thirsty birds are delighted and are drinking it, a gift from Indra of the gods. Resplendent blue clouds filled with new water are dashing against other blue clouds. They look like a forest consumed by a conflagration dashing against another forest consumed by a conflagration, both moored at their roots to mountains. The Indras among elephants are maddened. The Indras among bulls are delighted. The Indras among animals[163] are resting even more in the forests. The Indras among mountains are beautiful. The Indras among men[164] have withdrawn from their campaigns. The Indra among gods is playing around with the clouds. Enveloped with water, the roads have become like enemies and the soldiers cannot proceed along the roads. Therefore, kings have stopped their campaigns. For brahmanas who wish to learn about the brahman and the singing of the Sama Veda, the time for studying, the month of Proshthapada,[165] has arrived. Having completed the task of accumulating riches, Bharata, the lord of Kosala, must have started the vow for Ashadha.[166] The Sarayu must certainly be swirling with water now. It must be making a roar like the one Ayodhya used to make when it saw me return. This

[163] Lions.

[164] Kings.

[165] Proshthapada is a nakshatra. More accurately, it is a collective name for two nakshatras, Purva Bhadrapada and Uttara Bhadrapada. The month of Bhadrapada, or Bhadra, is the August–September period.

[166] A *chaturmasya* sacrifice is a sacrifice performed once every four (*chatur*) months (*masa*) and is performed at the beginnings of the months of Kartika, Phalguna and Ashadha. This reference is to the one that starts on the full moon day of Ashadha.

monsoon season is prosperous with many qualities and Sugriva must be enjoying the objects of pleasure. Having conquered the enemy, he has his wife and kingdom and has established himself on earth. But my wife has been abducted and I have been dislodged from a great kingdom. O Lakshmana! I am suffering and have been devastated, like the bank of a river. Since the monsoon has made everything extremely impassable, my grief has been enhanced. It seems to me that the journey to Ravana, my great enemy, is impassable. The path is extremely difficult to traverse and I can see that one can't travel now. Sugriva is also devoted to me. However, I have not told him anything. After all, he has suffered a great deal and has met his wife after a long time. Given the heavy nature of my task, I do not desire to speak to the ape now. After resting, he will himself know when the time has arrived. There is no doubt that Sugriva will repay the favour. O auspicious Lakshmana! I will remain here, waiting for that time and waiting for the favours of Sugriva and the rivers.[167] A valiant one always repays debts resulting from something having been done for him. Those who are virtuous in their mind are not ungrateful, forgetting what has to be done in repayment.'

Having heard what had been said, Lakshmana joined his hands in salutation and honoured the words that had been spoken. Displaying the auspicious aspect of his own nature, he spoke to Rama, who was agreeable to see. 'O Indra among men! Without any delay, the lord of the apes will do everything that you have said and desired. You must resort to patience and wait for autumn. When the rains have stopped, the enemy will be chastised.'

Chapter 4(28)

The sky was clear and the lightning and clouds disappeared, as did the flock of bustling cranes. The sky was smeared with beautiful moonlight. Though Sugriva was prosperous in artha, he

[167] Because the rivers have to be crossed.

was not as swift in the pursuit of accumulating dharma. There was only a single destination in his mind and he excessively pursued only that objective. Now that his desired task had been accomplished, he always sought pleasure with women. Having obtained what he wanted, it was as if all his wishes had been satisfied. He desired his own wife and he also desired Tara. Having accomplished his objective and devoid of anxiety, day and night, he found pleasure with them. He was like the lord of the gods, sporting in Nandana with a large number of apsaras. He passed on all the tasks to the ministers and did not supervise the ministers. Basing himself on conduct that was full of desire, he paid no heed to news about the kingdom.

Marut's son was clear about objectives. He knew about the essence of artha. In particular, he knew about the dharma to be followed at different times. He was accomplished in speech and knew about how to use words. He sought the favours of the lord of the apes and addressed him in beautiful and sweet words that were full of reason. They were beneficial and truthful, like medication. They were conciliatory, but represented good policy and were full of dharma and artha. They were filled with love and affection and it was certain that they would be heard. Hanumat went to the lord of the apes and addressed him in these words. 'The kingdom and fame have been obtained. The prosperity of the lineage has also been enhanced. However, the task of accumulating friends still remains to be done. A person who knows when it is time to make friends conducts himself according to virtue. His kingdom, fame and power are also enhanced. O lord of the earth! If a person has treasure, a rod of chastisement, friends and his own self all working together, then he obtains a great kingdom. Therefore, with good conduct, be established on a path that has no dangers. You should do what your friends approached you for. If a person does not perform a task for a friend at the right time, then he does not accomplish the friend's objective and brings a great calamity on to himself. O scorcher of enemies! The time for accomplishing a task for our friend has passed. Let us search out Vaidehi and perform Raghava's task. He knows about time. O king! Though the time has passed, the wise one remains subservient to you and is not hastening you. Raghava is like a flag for the lineage and prosperity. He is a friend who lasts for a long time. He is immeasurable in his own powers. No one, except he himself, can match his qualities. He has already accomplished the task that was to be done for you. Therefore, do the task for him now. O lord of apes! You should command the best among the apes. Until he actually urges us, the time has not quite passed. Once he urges us, the time for accomplishing the task will be reckoned to have been over. O lord of the apes! You have undertaken tasks for those who have done nothing for you. Why are you then not paying back someone who has given you the kingdom and riches? You are strong and valiant. You are the lord of a large number of apes and bears. Do what will bring pleasure to Dasharatha's son. Why are you not issuing the command? Indeed, if he so desires, Dasharatha's son can use his arrows to subjugate the gods, the asuras and the giant serpents. However, he wants you to fulfil the pledge. Without being scared of losing his own life, he accomplished something agreeable for you. Let us search out Vaidehi, on earth, or in the sky. The gods, the gandharvas, the asuras, the large numbers of Maruts and the yakshas can cause him no fear. What can the rakshasas do? He possesses strength, and earlier, used it to do what was agreeable to you. O lord of the tawny ones! You should do everything to bring pleasure to Rama. O lord of apes! If you command us, who will be able to obstruct our passage in the nether regions, the water, or the sky? Therefore, command us about who will exert himself to go where and for what purpose. O unblemished one! There are more than one crore of invincible apes.'

These virtuous words were appropriate for the occasion. Sugriva was full of spirit. On hearing them, he took an excellent decision. He commanded Nila, who was always full of enterprise, to gather all the soldiers from all the different directions. 'Act so that all the soldiers and all the leaders of the groups assemble quickly, with the best of armies. Swiftly follow my command. Let all the apes who are fleet and enterprising be stationed as guards at the perimeters. Summon all of them swiftly. You should yourself be at the centre of the army. If any ape comes here after fifteen nights, without even thinking about it, he will be punished by taking away his life. With Angada, approach the aged apes. Tell them that I have made up my mind about these instructions.' Arranging for all this, the valiant one entered his residence.

Chapter 4(29)

When the sky was free of clouds, Sugriva entered his cave. Overcome by desire and sorrow, Rama had spent the monsoon nights there. He saw the clear sky and the sparkling lunar disc. He saw the autumn night, smeared by the moonlight. Sugriva was engaged in acts of desire, though Janaka's daughter had been lost. He saw that the time had passed. He was severely afflicted and senseless.[168] The intelligent one regained his senses in a short while. Vaidehi was in Raghava's heart and he started to think about her. He was seated on the summit of the mountain, decorated with gold and other ores. When he saw the autumn sky, in his mind, the thoughts of his beloved came to his mind. 'The beautiful one found delight in the calling of these cranes and her voice was like the calling of a crane. The child used to find delight in the hermitage. How can she find delight now? On seeing the sparkling, blossoming and golden *asana* trees, how can the child find pleasure, when she cannot see me? Earlier, the one who is beautiful in her limbs, who speaks in a melodious voice, used to wake up to the melodious sounds of geese calling. How will she wake up now? She used to hear the sounds of the chakravakas, which roam around in couples. How is the one with eyes like a white lotus now? Without the doe-eyed one, I find no pleasure in roaming around the lakes, rivers, wells, groves and forests. Because of separation from me, Kama[169] will severely and incessantly afflict the delicate and beautiful one, when the qualities

[168] The time for honouring the pledge had passed. The point is that Sugriva had not told Rama about his instructions to Nila and neither Nila, nor Hanumat, could directly inform Rama. That was Sugriva's call.

[169] The god of love.

of the autumn have manifested themselves.' The son of a king, best among men, lamented in this way, like a *saranga* bird[170] that craves water from the lord of the gods.

The prosperous Lakshmana had wandered around the beautiful summit of the mountain, searching for fruits. On his return, he saw his elder brother. He was immersed in these intolerable thoughts. The spirited one was alone, deprived of his senses. On witnessing his brother's grief and lamentations, he was filled with sorrow. Soumitri addressed Rama. 'O noble one! What is the point in becoming subjugated to desire? What is achieved by your own manliness being defeated and taken away? What is the point of losing control and retreating from our path? Quieten your mind and do what needs to be done. The time has come to meditate on what needs to be done. Without a distressed spirit, depending on the capability of your aides, you should perform your own task. O protector of human lineages! With you as a protector, Janakee cannot be easily obtained by anyone else. O brave one! O one who deserves to be supreme! No one can approach the crest of a blazing fire and not be burnt.' The unassailable Lakshmana, who possessed all the natural qualities, spoke these comforting words, as beneficial as medicament, filled with good policy and immersed in dharma and artha.

Rama replied, 'We must certainly look towards what needs to be done and follow the specific courses of action. O prince! Without thinking about the fruits of valour and the act, we must engage in the task, even if it is extremely difficult.' After this, he thought about Maithilee, the lotus-eyed one. With his mouth dry, Rama spoke to Lakshmana. 'The one with the thousand eyes has satisfied the earth with water. Having performed the task of making the crops sprout, he has withdrawn. O son of a king! Thundering gently and with a deep voice from the tops of mountains and trees, the clouds have released their water and are now exhausted. They are as dark as clumps of blue lotuses. Having made the ten directions dark, the force of the clouds has now been quietened, like elephants no

170 Chataka.

longer intoxicated with desire. O amiable one! The rain resulted in an extremely forceful storm, that bore the fragrance of *kutaja* and arjuna flowers and was filled with water. Having rushed around, it has withdrawn now. O Lakshmana! The sound of clouds, elephants, peacocks and waterfalls has suddenly been pacified. After the great clouds showered down on them, the summits of the mountains are clear and sparkling. They seem to have been smeared with radiance from the moon's beams. In the autumn, the river is revealing its banks very slowly, like a woman is ashamed when she gently reveals her hips, after having just indulged in an act of sexual intercourse. O amiable one! Curlews are calling in the sparkling water. Filled with large numbers of chakravakas, the waterbodies are radiant. O son of a king! O amiable one! For kings who bear enmity and desire to triumph over each other, the time for endeavour has presented itself. O son of a king! This is when kings set out on their first expeditions. However, I do not see any enterprise on Sugriva's part and he is not acting accordingly. The four months of the rainy season have passed and it has been like one hundred years.[171] O amiable one! On not being able to see Sita, I am tormented by grief. Since I have been separated from my beloved, I am afflicted by misery. I have been banished and have been deprived of my kingdom. O Lakshmana! King Sugriva is not exhibiting any compassion towards me. I have lost my kingdom and am without a protector. I have been oppressed by Ravana. I am distressed and am far from home. I am suffering from desire. He knows I have sought refuge with him. O amiable one! O scorcher of enemies! Perhaps the evil-souled king of the apes thinks of these reasons and takes me to have been subjugated. He computed the time required to search Sita out. The evil-minded one does not understand that he has contracted an agreement with me. Go and enter Kishkindha. Tell Sugriva, bull among the apes, my words. He is stupid and is addicted to carnal pleasures. "When someone who has performed a good act earlier arrives in search of some objective, a person who destroys hopes and the pledge, is the

[171] Since four months have passed since Sugriva's coronation, this must be the end of Kartika.

worst among the men of this world. If a person adheres to good or bad words spoken at the time of a pledge, such a supreme person is best among men. Whether successful or unsuccessful, those who do not act like friends, when they are dead, even predatory beasts do not eat the flesh from their carcasses. There is no doubt that you wish to see me stretch my bow, with a golden back, in battle. That bow's form is like flashes of lightning. When I am enraged in a battle, the sound of the bowstring slapping against my palm is terrible. You again wish to hear the rumble of that thunder."[172] O son of a king! However, he knows about my valour and must have fallen prey to desire. O brave one! As long as I have you as my aide, I am not worried. O vanquisher of enemy cities! The lord of the apes thinks he has accomplished his objective and does not remember the pledge, nor the reason why we started on this course of action.[173] The lord of the apes took a pledge about acting after the monsoon period was over. However, he is amusing himself and does not understand that the four months have passed. He is drinking liquor and sporting with his advisers and companions. Sugriva does not show any compassion towards us, who are miserable and distressed. O child! O immensely strong one! It is appropriate that you should go to Sugriva and tell him about the form my rage is taking. Also tell him these words. "The path along which the slain Vali advanced has not withered away. O Sugriva! Adhere to your pledge. Do not follow Vali's path. With a single of my arrows, Vali was slain in the battle. However, if you transgress truth, I will slay you with your relatives." O bull among men! Our beneficial task is being obstructed. O best among men! Therefore, without any delay, quickly speak to him accordingly. "O lord of the apes! Look towards eternal dharma and the pledge given and act truthfully. Otherwise, you will now be goaded by my arrows and follow Vali towards death and Yama's eternal abode."' He[174] saw his distressed elder brother lamenting, with his rage increasing.

[172] Though the text does not clearly indicate this, the part within quotes is obviously the message to be delivered by Lakshmana to Sugriva.

[173] The slaying of Vali.

[174] Lakshmana.

Therefore, the extender of the human lineage,[175] fierce in his energy, had harsh thoughts about the lord of the apes.

Chapter 4(30)

The son of the Indra among men,[176] the son of the god among men, was miserable and distressed in his spirit, overwhelmed by desire. Enveloped by grief, his rage increased. Rama's younger brother addressed his older brother. 'The ape will not adhere to the conduct of virtuous people. He will not think of the fruits that are consequent to actions. He will not enjoy the prosperity of the kingdom of the apes. That is the reason his intelligence does not look forward. Because of his addiction to carnal pleasures, his intelligence has been destroyed. His intelligence does not turn towards repaying what he has obtained through your favours. Let him see how his elder brother, Vali, was slain and realize that kingdoms should not be given to those who are devoid of qualities. I cannot control this anger, as its force is increasing. I will slay the false Sugriva today. After that, with the best of the apes and with Vali's son, I will search out the daughter of the king.'[177] Angry and ferocious, wishing to fight, he spoke these purposeful words. He leapt up from his seat and seized his arrows. Rama, the slayer of enemy heroes, looked towards him and spoke these words of persuasion. 'A person like you should not act in this wicked way. A noble person who slays his anger is brave and supreme among men. O Lakshmana! Following the affection we bore towards him earlier and the friendly conduct, a person like you, virtuous in conduct, should not act in this ordinary way now. Abandon harsh words and speak to him in conciliatory tones. You should tell Sugriva that the stipulated time period has passed.'

Instructed by his elder brother about what would be better, the bull among men acted exactly in that way. Lakshmana, the

[175] This is a reference to Lakshmana.

[176] Rama.

[177] Sita.

brave slayer of enemy heroes, entered the city. He was auspicious in his intelligence and wise, engaged in ensuring what would be agreeable and beneficial for his brother. Controlling his anger, Lakshmana went to the ape's residence. He wielded a bow that was like Shakra's bow. When he held it up, he looked like Mount Mandara, with one of its peaks jutting up, and like the Destroyer. Rama's younger brother was like Brihaspati[178] in his intelligence. Obeying what he had been told, he thought about the order in which he should organize his words. He was enveloped in a fire of rage, resulting from the anger and desire[179] in his brother. Lakshmana proceeded, as turbulent as a storm. He advanced with force, bringing down sala, tala, ashvakarna and other trees and shattering the tops of the mountain with his speed and strength. As he proceeded like a swift elephant, he splintered boulders with his steps. Since he wished to advance quickly on his designated task, there was a long distance between one stride and the next. He saw the great city of the king of the apes, surrounded by an army. The tiger of the Ikshvaku lineage saw the impenetrable Kishkindha, nestling in the mountain. With lips that were quivering because of his rage against Sugriva, Lakshmana saw terrible apes patrolling around Kishkindha's boundary. He was like an elephant and on seeing him, the apes in that mountain seized hundreds of mountain peaks and large trees. Seeing that they had seized weapons, Lakshmana's rage was doubled, like a fire into which kindling has been fed. Seeing him arrive, like Destiny or Death at the end of a *yuga*, there were hundreds of apes whose limbs became suffused with fear. They fled in different directions. Those bulls among apes entered Sugriva's residence and told him that Lakshmana was arriving in rage.

However, that bull among apes was busy satisfying his desire with Tara and did not listen to what those brave apes said. The advisers instructed some apes, whose complexions were like mountains, elephants or clouds, and who therefore, made the body

[178] The preceptor of the gods.
[179] For Sita.

hair stand up. All those brave ones were terrible and malformed. With nails and teeth as weapons, they emerged from the city. All of them were like tigers in their insolence. All of them possessed disfigured faces. Some of them possessed the strength of ten elephants, others strength that was ten times more. There were some whose valour was equal to that of one thousand elephants. The angry Lakshmana saw the unassailable Kishkindha, covered with extremely strong apes who held trees in their hands. All those apes emerged from inside the walls and the moats. They were suddenly seen there, fierce in their spirit. On seeing them, the brave and controlled one remembered Sugriva's transgression and his elder brother's objective and was again suffused with rage. His sighs were warm and long. His eyes turned red with rage. The tiger among men was like a fire with smoke. Because of his energy, he was like a five-hooded serpent filled with poison. His bow was like the serpent's hood and the arrows were like flickering tongues. He blazed like the fire of destruction. He was as enraged as an Indra among serpents. When he approached, Angada was terrified and filled with great sorrow. His eyes coppery red with rage, the immensely illustrious one instructed Angada, 'Let Sugriva be informed about my arrival. Tell him that Rama's younger brother, the destroyer of enemies, has come to see him. Tormented by his brother's hardship, Lakshmana is waiting at the gate.'

Hearing Lakshmana's words, Angada was filled with sorrow. He went to his father[180] and said, 'Lakshmana has come here.' On seeing Lakshmana nearby, like a gigantic storm, they roared like lions,[181] in a tone that was like that of lightning and thunder. Because of that great noise, the ape[182] woke up. His garlands and ornaments were scattered around and his eyes were coppery red, intoxicated with liquor. Hearing Angada's words, two respected advisers who were broad in their outlook also approached the Indra among the apes. These two, the advisers Plaksha and Prabhava, also

[180] Sugriva.

[181] The Critical Edition excises some shlokas and that breaks the continuity. The apes roared, on seeing Lakshmana.

[182] Sugriva.

told him about Lakshmana's arrival, using words that were full of dharma and artha. They placated Sugriva in words of conciliation, while he was seated like Shakra, the lord of the Maruts. 'The two immensely fortunate brothers, Rama and Lakshmana, have truth as their objective. They have come to you as friends. Though they deserved the kingdom, they bestowed the kingdom on you. One of them, Lakshmana, is at the door, with a bow in his hand. Since they are terrified of him and are trembling, the apes are emitting this roar. Raghava's brother, Lakshmana, is on a chariot made out of words. He has come here on Rama's instructions, using a chariot that is the objective. With your son and your relatives, bow your head down at his feet. O king! You should adhere to the truth and the pledge that you yourself took.'

Chapter 4(31)

Hearing Angada's words and those of his ministers and learning that Lakshmana was angry, the controlled Sugriva arose from his seat. He was established in good advice, knew about counsels and was accomplished in following proper policy. He told them, 'I have not shown any misconduct towards them, nor have I done them any harm. I am wondering why Lakshmana, Raghava's brother, should be angry with me. My ill-wishers and enemies are always seeking out blemishes in me. They must have told Raghava's younger brother about my sins that aren't real. That being the case, all of you accomplished ones use your intelligence and all your techniques to gently determine what his sentiments are. On account of Lakshmana or Raghava, I do not suffer from any fear. However, if a friend is unnecessarily angry, that does lead me to worry. It is always extremely easy to make a friend, but satisfying that friendship is very difficult. The mind is fickle and a trifle is enough to shatter affection. That is the reason I am scared of the great-souled Rama. I am incapable of repaying the good deed that he has done to me.'

When Sugriva said this, in the midst of the apes who were advisers, Hanumat, bull among the apes, voiced his own arguments. 'O lord of a large number of apes! It is not at all surprising that you should never forget the auspicious and extremely gentle deed that has been done towards you. The brave Raghava flung his fear far away. To accomplish a desirable objective for you, he slew Vali, who was like Shakra in his valour. Raghava is always affectionate towards you, but there is no doubt that he is angry. That is the reason he urged his brother Lakshmana, the extender of prosperity. O one who is supreme among those who know about time! Since you were intoxicated, you did not know that time had passed. The auspicious autumn has presented itself and is pervaded by dark and blossoming seven-leaves.[183] The planets and nakshatras are in a clear sky and the clouds have been dispelled. All the directions, the rivers and the lakes are pleasant. O bull among the apes! The time for action has arrived, but you did not realize this. It is evident that you were intoxicated and that is the reason Lakshmana has come here. With his wife abducted, the great-souled Raghava is afflicted. His harsh words, sent through another person,[184] should be tolerated. You have committed a crime. I do not see a way other than that of joining your hands in salutation and seeking Lakshmana's favours and forgiveness. The appointed ministers must certainly speak words that are for the king's benefit. That is the reason I have cast aside my fear and have addressed you in these steadfast words. If Raghava is enraged, he is capable of raising his bow and bringing the entire world, with the gods, the asuras and the gandharvas, under his subjugation. If one can seek his favours, one should not anger him. In particular, you should be grateful and remember the good deed he has done towards you earlier. With your son and your well-wishers, bow your head down and prostrate yourself before him. O king! Like a wife who is obedient towards her husband, adhere to the pledge you have yourself made. O Indra among the apes! You should cast aside any thoughts you might have of not

[183] Plantain trees have seven leaves.
[184] Lakshmana.

sticking to Rama's and Rama's younger brother's instructions. In your mind, you know about the human strength of Raghava, who is like Indra of the gods in his radiance.'

Chapter 4(32)

Following Rama's instructions and invited in this way, Lakshmana, the destroyer of enemy heroes, entered the beautiful cave of Kishkindha.[185] There were immensely strong apes at the gate, gigantic in size. On seeing Lakshmana, they joined their hands in salutation and stood there. The apes saw that Dasharatha's son was angry and was sighing. Therefore, they were terrified and did not surround him. He saw that huge cave, divinely beautiful and filled with jewels and flowering groves. It was handsome, strewn with gems. There were mansions, palaces and walls, adorned with many kinds of wares. It was ornamented with flowering trees, laden with fruits that yielded every object of desire. The apes were the sons of gods and gandharvas and could assume any form at will. They were handsome and pleasant in appearance, wearing celestial garlands and garments. There were beautiful fragrances from sandalwood, aloe and lotuses. The large roads seemed to be intoxicated with *maireya* and *madhu* trees.[186] There were multi-story palaces that were like the mountains Vindhya and Meru. Raghava saw sparkling mountain streams there. Along the royal road, Lakshmana saw the expansive and handsome houses of the best among the apes—Angada, Mainda, Dvivida, Gavaya, Gavaksha, Gaja, Sharabha, Vidyunmali, Subahu, the great-souled Nala, Kumuda, Sushena, Tara, Jambavat, Dadhivaktra, Nila, Supatala and Sunetra. They looked like white clouds and were decorated with divine garlands. They were ornamented with large quantities of riches and grain and

[185] Kishkindha is often referred to as a cave (*guha*). However, as this chapter makes clearer, Kishkindha was much more than an ordinary cave.

[186] Maireya is made from molasses or grain. A maireya tree probably means sugar cane. Madhu is the madhuka tree, used to make liquor.

with gems among women. The handsome house of the Indra among the apes was like the great Indra's residence. It was extremely difficult to approach and a white mountain offered protection all around it. The white summit of the palace was like the summit of Kailasa. There were flowering trees, with fruits that yielded all the objects of desire. It was prosperous and had been bestowed by the great Indra. It was like a dark blue cloud. There were trees with divine flowers and fruits, offering cool and pleasant shade. Powerful apes protected the entrance, with weapons in their hands. The sparkling gates were made out of molten gold and were covered with celestial garlands.

The immensely strong Soumitri entered Sugriva's beautiful residence, like a sun that cannot be impeded entering a giant cloud. The one with dharma in his soul passed through seven chambers that were filled with vehicles and seats. He entered an extremely protected area and saw the gigantic inner quarters. There were many couches made out of gold and silver and with supreme seats. They were resplendent there, covered with extremely expensive spreads. As soon as he entered, he heard the continuous sound of sweet music. There was the sound of singing and the quatrains and syllables of the songs were even.[187] In Sugriva's residence, the immensely strong one saw many women of diverse types, proud of their youth and beauty. Those noble ladies were fashioning garlands made out of flowers. Adorned in excellent garments, they were eagerly fashioning these excellent garlands. They were all content and were not anxious. All of them were attired in wonderful garments. Lakshmana noticed the female servants who waited upon Sugriva. Sugriva was seated on a golden and excellent throne that was covered with an extremely expensive spread. He saw him, looking like the sun. There were colourful and divine ornaments on his limbs and the illustrious one had a divine form. With divine ornaments and garments, he was as invincible as the great Indra. He was surrounded by women, wearing divine ornaments and garlands. The brave one, with a complexion like that of excellent gold, was seated on that excellent

[187] That is, not discordant.

throne, closely embracing Ruma. Not distressed in spirit, the large-eyed one looked at the large-eyed Soumitri.

Chapter 4(33)

Lakshmana, bull among men, angrily entered, unobstructed. On seeing him, Sugriva's senses were afflicted. He saw Dasharatha's son, tormented because of his brother's hardship, blazing in his energy and sighing angrily. The best among apes left his golden throne and leapt up, as if a large and ornamented standard of the great Indra was being raised up. When he leapt up, so did Ruma and the other women. It was as if Sugriva was the full moon in the sky, surrounded by a large number of stars. His eyes red,[188] the handsome one joined his hands in salutation and lurched forward. He stood there, like a giant *kalpavriksha*.[189] As Sugriva stood amidst the women, like the moon among stars, Ruma was the second one who stood there.

Lakshmana spoke to him. 'A king who is spirited, noble in birth, compassionate, grateful, truthful in speech and one who has conquered his senses is said to be great in this world. But who can be more cruel than a king who is established in adharma, harms his friends and takes false pledges? Falsehood is tantamount to killing one hundred horses.[190] Falsehood is tantamount to killing one thousand cows. A man who indulges in falsehood kills himself and his relatives for several generations. O lord of the apes! If a person does not repay the good deeds friends have formerly done to make him attain his objectives, he is an ingrate. Among all creatures, he is the one who deserves to be killed. On seeing an ungrateful person, Brahma, worshipped by all the worlds, was enraged and chanted a shloka. O ape! Hear it. "The virtuous have laid down means of atonement for the sins of killing a cow, drinking liquor, theft and

[188] Because of liquor.

[189] Tree that yields all the objects of desire.

[190] The sin of killing one hundred horses.

breaking a vow. But there is no salvation for an ingrate." O ape! You are ignoble and ungrateful. You are also false in speech. Rama performed a good deed for you earlier, but you are not paying him back. O ape! Through Rama, you have indeed accomplished your task. He desired that you should make efforts to search out Sita. You took a false pledge and are engaged in carnal pursuits. Rama did not recognize you as a snake, though you croak like a frog. You are wicked and evil-souled. Driven by compassion, the immensely fortunate and great-souled Rama conferred the kingdom of the apes on you. You are not recognizing what Rama, unblemished in his deeds, has done for you. You will instantly be slain with sharp arrows and will see Vali. The slain Vali proceeded along a path that has still not been withdrawn. O Sugriva! Stick to your pledge and do not follow Vali's path. It is certain that you have not seen arrows, which are like the vajra, being shot from the bow of one who is best among those of the Ikshvaku lineage. That is the reason your mind has not looked towards Rama's task and you are happy in your pursuit of a pleasure that goes by the name of happiness.'

Chapter 4(34)

Blazing in his energy, Soumitri said this. Tara, whose face was like the lord of the stars, spoke to Lakshmana.[191] 'O Lakshmana! The lord of the apes does not deserve to hear the harsh words that he has just heard, especially from the lips of someone like you. Sugriva is not ungrateful, deceitful or terrible. O brave one! The lord of the apes has not indulged in duplicity, or uttered a falsehood. O brave one! The ape has not forgotten the good deed that was done to him. O brave one! In an encounter, Rama did for Sugriva what anyone else would find extremely difficult to accomplish. O scorcher of enemies! It is because of Rama's favours and deeds that the ape Sugriva has obtained this eternal kingdom, Ruma and

[191] The moon is the lord of the stars (tara) and there is a play on the word Tara.

me. He used to lie down in extreme hardship earlier and has now obtained this supreme delight. Like the sage Vishvamitra, he did not realize that the appointed time had arrived. O Lakshmana! Attached to Ghritachee,[192] Vishvamitra, the great sage, with dharma in his soul, spent ten years and thought that only a single day had elapsed. The immensely energetic Vishvamitra is supreme among those who know about time. But even he did not realize that the appointed time had arrived, not to speak of ordinary people. O Lakshmana! Satisfying the dharma of the body, he was exhausted. His desire was not satiated. Rama should pardon him. O father![193] O Lakshmana! You should not suddenly succumb to anger, like an ordinary person, without ascertaining and knowing the details. O bull among men! Spirited men like you do not rashly and suddenly succumb to rage. O one who knows about dharma! For Sugriva's sake, I am controlling myself and seeking your favours. Cast aside this intolerance and great rage that has arisen. To bring pleasure to Rama, Sugriva will fling away Ruma and me, and this kingdom of the apes with its wealth, grain and riches. That is my view. Having slain Ravana in a battle, Sugriva will bring Sita and unite her with Raghava, like the moon god with Rohini.[194] Indeed, there are one trillion, three hundred and sixty thousand, one hundred thousand and one thousand rakshasas in Lanka.[195] Without slaying those invincible rakshasas, who can assume any form at will, one will not be capable of killing Ravana, Maithilee's abductor. Ravana is cruel in his deeds. O Lakshmana! Without an aide, someone like Sugriva will not be able to kill him.[196]

[192] An apsara. Usually, Vishvamitra is associated with the apsara Menaka.

[193] The word used is tata. Lakshmana is senior, though not in age. Therefore, 'father' is more likely than 'son'.

[194] The nakshatras are the wives of the moon, but the moon loves Rohini (Aldebaran) more than the others.

[195] Because of the way the numbers are written in the shloka, anything other than the one trillion can be interpreted in more than one way. Suffice to say that there were a large number of rakshasas. How could Tara possibly know this? The story goes that Vali told Angada and Tara overheard the conversation.

[196] Sugriva will not be able to kill Ravana without Rama's help. This is sometimes interpreted as Rama not being able to kill Ravana without Sugriva's help, but that interpretation seems forced.

Vali, the learned lord of the apes, said this. It is not evident to me how all of them assembled there.[197] I have only told you what I have heard. It is to help you that all the bulls among apes have been sent. A large number of apes, bulls among apes, are being summoned for the battle. That is the reason the lord of the apes has not ventured out to accomplish Raghava's objective. He is awaiting the arrival of those valiant and extremely strong ones. O Soumitri! Because of the good arrangements Sugriva had made earlier, all those extremely strong apes will arrive here today.[198] Crores and thousands of bears and hundreds of golangulas will present themselves before you today. O scorcher of enemies! Conquer your anger. O Kakutstha! There will be crores of apes who will blaze in their energy. On looking at your face, full of rage, and at your eyes, which seem to be wounded,[199] the wives of the best among the apes can find no peace. All of them are disturbed because of the first signs of fear.'[200]

Chapter 4(35)

Soumitri was gentle in nature. He heard these words spoken by Tara, full of dharma, and accepted the statement. When he accepted those words, the lord of the large number of apes cast aside his great fear of Lakshmana, like casting aside a wet garment. There was a large and colourful garland, with many qualities, around his neck. Sugriva, the lord of the apes, shredded this and forgot his intoxication. Sugriva, supreme among all the apes, delighted Lakshmana, whose strength was terrible, with these words. 'My prosperity, deeds and this eternal kingdom of the apes were destroyed. O Soumitri! It is because of Rama's favours that I got them back again. That god is famous because of his own deeds. O brave one! O destroyer of

[197] How so many rakshasas came to be in Lanka.

[198] We are subsequently told, in Chapter 4 (36), that a time limit of ten days has been set.

[199] As red as a wound.

[200] Or, former signs of fear, such as when Vali was destroyed.

enemies! With the valour that he possesses, who is capable of paying him back? Raghava, with dharma in his soul, will use his own energy to get Sita back and slay Ravana. I can only be an aide. Indeed, why does he need an aide? With a single arrow, he penetrated seven large trees and shattered a mountain and the earth. O Lakshmana! From the sound of his twanging the bow, the mountains and the earth tremble. Why does he need help? O bull among men! I will follow that Indra among men when he leads and advances to slay his enemy, Ravana. If I have transgressed in any way, out of trust and affection, a messenger must always pardon. I have committed no crime.'

When the great-souled Sugriva said this, Lakshmana spoke these words, full of love and affection. 'O lord of the apes! My brother always has a protector. O Sugriva! You are the protector, especially since you are humble. O Sugriva! Your powers and supreme purity are such that you deserve to enjoy this excellent prosperity of the kingdom of the apes. O Sugriva! There is no doubt that with you as an aide, the powerful Rama will soon slay the enemy in a battle. You know about dharma. You are grateful. You do not retreat from the field of battle. O Sugriva! What you have spoken is full of logic. O supreme among apes! With the exception of my elder brother and you, who else is capable of recognizing one's own taints and speaking in this way? In valour and strength, you are Rama's equal. O bull among apes! After a long time, destiny has supplied you as an aide. O brave one! Quickly leave this place with me. Go and comfort your friend, who is miserable because his wife has been abducted. I heard the words spoken by Rama, when he was overwhelmed with grief. O friend! Therefore, I addressed you in harsh words. Please pardon me.'

Chapter 4(36)

When the great-souled Lakshmana spoke to Sugriva in this way, he[201] spoke to his adviser, Hanumat, who was standing

[201] Sugriva.

next to him. 'Swiftly summon the apes who are there on the five mountains of Mahendra, Himalayas, Vindhya, the summit of Kailasa and the white summit of Mandara; those who are there in the mountain that is always radiant, with a complexion like that of the rising sun;[202] those who are there in the western direction, in the mountain that is always radiant beyond the ocean, the sun's abode, with the hue of evening clouds;[203] the terrible bulls among apes who reside in groves of lotuses and palm trees; the apes who reside in Mount Anjana, like elephants in their energy and with the complexion of dark clouds; the apes who are golden in complexion and reside in the cave known as Manahshila; those who reside on the slopes of Meru and Mount Dhumra; those apes, terrible in force, who reside on Mount Maharuna, which is like the rising sun in hue, and drink maireya liquor there; and those who dwell in large and extremely fragrant groves and everywhere in the beautiful extremities of the forests where there are ascetics. Quickly summon all the apes from all over the earth. Quickly send messengers to those apes and summon them with gifts and conciliation. First, sent my messengers, those who are extremely fast. After that, to make them hasten, send other apes. There are apes who procrastinate, addicted to desire. On my instructions, swiftly fetch all of them here. Those who do not follow my command and do not assemble within ten days, will be regarded as those who defile the king's command. Those evil-souled ones should be killed. On my instructions, let hundreds, thousands and crores of lions among apes depart. Let all those in the different directions follow my command. Let the best among apes, terrible in form, and like mountains and clouds, follow my command and leave for this place. Let them shroud the firmament. There are apes who know about the routes. Let all of them follow the paths to everywhere on earth. Let them swiftly follow my command and fetch all the apes here.'

Hearing the words of the king of the apes, Vayu's son[204] dispatched valiant apes in all the directions. In an instant, sent by

[202] Mount Udaya, the sun rises from behind this.

[203] Mount Asta, the sun sets behind this.

[204] Hanumat.

the king, the apes departed. They leapt up,[205] like birds and stellar bodies. They followed the footsteps of the valiant Vishnu.[206] To accomplish Rama's objective, those apes urged all the apes who were in the oceans, mountains, forests and lakes. The king of the apes was like Death, Destiny, or Kubera. Hearing Sugriva's command, they arrived. They were scared of Sugriva. Raghava was on a mountain[207] that had the complexion of a dark cloud. Three crores of extremely swift apes left from that place. There were those who were in that supreme mountain, with a complexion like heated gold, behind which, the sun sets.[208] Ten crores left from there. The summit of Kailasa is as radiant as a lion's mane. One thousand crores of apes arrived from there. There were those who resided in the Himalayas, surviving on fruits and roots. Ten trillion assembled from there. There were apes from Vindhya, terrible in their deeds and as terrible as Angaraka.[209] One thousand crores swiftly arrived from there. There were those who had homes on the shores of the milky ocean, dwelling in tamala groves. They survived on coconut fruit. Their numbers were unknown.[210] An extremely large army of extremely swift apes arrived from forests, caves and rivers. They seemed to drink up the rays of the sun.[211] Among all the apes, there were some brave apes who had swiftly gone to the Himalaya mountains. They saw a giant tree there. On that beautiful and supreme mountain, Maheshvara had performed a sacrifice in ancient times and that divine and lovely sacrifice had satisfied the minds of all the gods. From the resultant food,[212] fruits and roots were generated and the apes saw those there, as succulent as amrita. From the food, divine and agreeable fruits and roots were created. If one eats these, one is satisfied for a

[205] Into the sky.

[206] This is a reference to Vishnu's vamana (dwarf) incarnation, where Vishnu covered heaven, the earth and the nether regions in three steps.

[207] Prasravana.

[208] Mount Asta.

[209] Mars.

[210] That is, there were a large number, innumerable.

[211] They covered the sky and blanked out the sun.

[212] Offered at the sacrifice.

month.[213] The leaders of the apes, those who survived on fruit, collected those divine roots and fruits and the divine herbs. The apes went to the place where the sacrifice had been held and to bring pleasure to Sugriva, collected the fragrant flowers. All the apes urged the supreme among apes on earth to hurry and returned, ahead of the herds. The herds were extremely swift and in an instant, hastened and reached Kishkindha, where the ape Sugriva was. There were apes who had collected all the herbs, fruits and roots. They made him accept these and spoke these words. 'Following your command, all the apes on earth, all those who dwell in mountains, oceans and forests, are coming here to you.' Hearing these words, Sugriva, the lord of the apes, was delighted. Delighted, he accepted everything that they had brought.

Chapter 4(37)

He accepted everything that they had collected and brought. He comforted all the apes and gave them leave to go. He granted permission to all the brave apes who had accomplished their task. He thought that the immensely strong Raghava, and he himself, had become successful. He was supreme among all the apes and was terrible in his strength. Lakshmana spoke reassuring words to him and delighted Sugriva. 'O amiable one! If it pleases you, let us leave Kishkindha.' He heard the excellent words spoken by Lakshmana. Sugriva was extremely happy and replied in these words. 'I will abide by your instructions. Let us go then.' Sugriva said this to Lakshmana, who was auspicious in his signs. He took his leave of Tara and the other women. Sugriva addressed the best among the apes, 'Come here.' Hearing his words, the apes arrived quickly. All those who were allowed to see the women came there and joined their hands in salutation.[214] When they arrived, the king, whose

[213] One does not have to eat for a month.

[214] Everyone was not allowed in the presence of the royal women in the inner quarters.

radiance was like that of the sun, addressed them. 'O apes! Quickly ready my palanquin.' Hearing his words, the apes, swift in their valour, readied and brought a handsome palanquin. The lord of the apes saw that the palanquin had been brought. He told Soumitri, 'O Lakshmana! Quickly mount it.' Saying this, Sugriva, whose complexion was like that of the sun, ascended that golden vehicle with Lakshmana. It was carried by many apes. A white umbrella was held above his head. In every direction, he was fanned with white whisks. The bards greeted him with the sounds of conch shells and drums. Sugriva, the possessor of supreme royal prosperity, departed. He was surrounded by hundreds of apes, wielding sharp weapons in their hands. He left for the spot where Rama was.

Having reached that excellent region, frequented by Rama, with Lakshmana, the immensely energetic one descended from the palanquin. He approached Rama and stood there, his hands joined in salutation. The other apes also stood there, their hands joined in salutation. Rama saw Sugriva and that large army of apes, resembling a lake filled with lotuses and lilies.[215] He was delighted. The lord of the apes was prostrate at his feet, his head lowered. Raghava raised him up. Showing him a lot of respect and affection, he embraced him. Having raised him up, the one with dharma in his soul asked him to be seated. When he saw that he had seated himself on the ground, Rama addressed him in these words. 'O brave one! O supreme among apes! A true king is a person who apportions time out for indulging in dharma, artha and kama. If someone abandons dharma and artha and only indulges in kama, he is like a person who sleeps on the top of a tree and only wakes up when he falls down. A king who bases himself in dharma, is engaged in slaying enemies and is also engaged in collecting friends, enjoys the fruits of all the three objectives.[216] O slayer of enemies! The time for exertion has presented itself. O lord of the tawny ones! With the apes who are your ministers, think about what needs to be done.'

[215] They raised their hands up, joined in salutation, and those looked like lotuses and lilies.

[216] *Trivarga* (three objectives of life)—dharma, artha and kama.

Thus addressed by Rama, Sugriva replied in these words. 'O mighty-armed one! Prosperity, deeds and the eternal kingdom of the apes were destroyed. It is through your favours that I have got them back again. O god! O supreme among victorious ones! It is through your favours and those of your brother that I have got them back. Among men, a person who does not pay back a good deed is reviled. O slayer of enemies! There are hundreds of supreme apes. They have returned after collecting all the strong apes on earth. O Raghava! There are bears, apes and brave golangulas. They are terrible to behold. They know about desolate regions and impenetrable forests. These apes are the sons of gods and gandharvas and can assume any form at will. O Raghava! Surrounded by their own respective soldiers, they are advancing along the paths. O scorcher of enemies! There are hundreds, hundreds of thousands, crores, *ayuta*s and *shanku*s of brave apes.[217] There are arbudas[218] of apes in the centre and hundreds of arbudas at the extremities. The apes and the leaders of herds of apes are arriving from the other shores of the oceans. O king! They are arriving, like the great Indra in their valour. Their form is like the Meru and Mandara. They have made their homes in the Vindhya and Meru. They are arriving so as to slay the rakshasas and their relatives in the battle. After Ravana has been slain in the battle, they will bring Maithilee back.'

Following the instructions of the intelligent lord of the apes, the arrangements had been made. On seeing this, the son of the king[219] rejoiced. His eyes, which looked like blue lotuses, dilated.

Chapter 4(38)

Sugriva spoke to Rama, supreme among those who uphold dharma, in this way, joining his hands in salutation. He embraced

[217] An ayuta is ten thousand. Shanku is the same as *shamkha* and means one hundred billion.

[218] One hundred million.

[219] Rama.

him in his arms and replied, 'O scorcher of enemies! As long as Indra showers down during the monsoon and does not make the earth bereft of colours, as long as the sun, with the one thousand rays, removes the darkness from the sky, as long as the moon makes the earth amiable and sparkling with its amiable beams, till such time, let friends like you repay their debts. O amiable one! O handsome one! O Sugriva! But this is not extraordinary in someone like you. I know you as someone who is always pleasant in speech. O friend! With you as a protector, I will triumph over all enemies. A well-wisher and friend like you deserves to help me. By abducting Vaidehi, the worst of the rakshasas has brought about his own destruction, just as Anuhlada did with Shachi, Puloma's daughter.[220] I will soon slay Ravana with sharp arrows, just as Shatakratu, the destroyer of enemies, killed Poulami's insolent father.'

At this time, a dust arose and spread over the sky, enveloping the hot and fierce radiance of the one with the thousand rays. Because of that dust, the directions seemed to be anxious and senseless. The earth, with all its mountains, forests and groves, started to quake. The entire earth was covered with apes. They were like giant mountains, extremely strong and with sharp teeth. Those leaders of the apes could assume any form at will. In an instant, hundreds of crores of them covered everything. There were extremely strong apes from rivers, mountains and oceans. There were others who roamed around in the forest. They thundered like clouds. There were those who were like the rising sun in complexion. There were others who were as fair as the moon and still others with the complexion of lotus stamens. There were those who had made residences on the Shveta and Meru. Surrounded by crores and tens of thousands of handsome apes, a brave ape named Shatabali[221] was seen. Tara's valiant father[222] was seen, with a complexion like that of a golden mountain, and surrounded by many crores and tens of thousands.

[220] Anuhlada (or Anuhrada) was Hiranyakashipu's son and Prahlada's (or Prahrada) brother. Shachi, married to Indra, was Puloma's (a demon) daughter. She was known as Poulami. With Puloma's consent, Anuhlada abducted Shachi. Indra killed Puloma.

[221] Literally, one with the strength of one hundred.

[222] Sushena.

Hanumat's handsome father, Keshari was seen. His complexion was like that of lotus fibres, his face had the complexion of the sun. This intelligent and supreme ape was foremost among all the apes. He was surrounded by an army that consisted of thousands of apes. There was Gavaksha, the great king of golangulas and terrible in his valour. He was seen, surrounded by thousands of crores of apes. From among the bears, there was Dhumra, terrible in his speed and the slayer of enemies. He arrived, surrounded by two thousand crores. There was a leader of the herds named Panasa. The immensely valorous one arrived, surrounded by three crore of terrible ones who had complexions like giant mountains. There was a leader of the herds named Nila, with a form and complexion like that of a mass of black collyrium. That immensely gigantic one was seen, surrounded by ten crores. There was a powerful leader of the herds named Darimukha. Surrounded by one thousand crore, he presented himself before Sugriva. Mainda and Dvivida, the two immensely strong sons of the two Ashvins, were seen. Each was surrounded by one crore of apes. Gandhamadana arrived and thousands of crores and hundreds of thousands of apes followed him at the rear. Prince Angada arrived and he was like his father in valour. He was surrounded by one thousand *padma*s[223] and one hundred shamkhas. The ape Tara[224] was terrible in valour and was like the stars in his radiance. He was seen from a distance, with five crore of apes. The brave ape Indrajanu, leader of herds, was seen. The lord was surrounded by eleven crore. Rambha, with a complexion like that of the rising sun, arrived. He was surrounded by hundreds of thousands of ayutas. There was the brave ape named Durmukha, the leader of herds. The powerful one was seen, surrounded by two crore. Hanumat was seen surrounded by a thousand crore of apes who were terrible in valour and like the summit of Kailasa in form. The immensely valorous Nala arrived. He was surrounded by a hundred crore and a hundred thousand of those who dwelt on trees. There were Sharabha, Kumuda and the ape Vahni. These and many

[223] One thousand billion.

[224] Not to be confused with Taaraa.

other apes could assume any form at will. They enveloped the entire earth, with its mountains and forests. The apes roared, leapt up and jumped down. They approached Sugriva, like a large mass of clouds around the sun. Supreme in their strength, they uttered many kinds of sounds. The Indras among apes lowered their heads and presented themselves before Sugriva. Other supreme apes arrived, as was proper. They approached Sugriva and stood with their hands joined in salutation.

Sugriva, the one who knew about dharma, stood with his hands joined in salutation. He quickly presented all those bulls among apes to Rama and said, 'O Indras among apes! Dwell happily in the mountainous waterfalls and all the forests. Once you have settled down properly, the one who knows about armies[225] desires to inspect the strength of the army.'

Chapter 4(39)

Sugriva, the lord of the apes, now possessed all the means to accomplish the objective. He spoke to Rama, tiger among men and the one who afflicted enemy armies. 'The powerful ones, who can assume any form at will, have come and have settled down. These Indras among apes, those who have the complexion of the great Indra, are the ones who reside in my kingdom. There are many thousands of apes who are terrible in their valour. These terrible apes have arrived and they are like the daityas and the danavas. These powerful ones have conquered all exhaustion and are renowned for accomplishing extremely difficult tasks. They are excellent in their enterprise and are famous for their valour. O Rama! They roam around the earth, in the water and on land. They are the residents of many mountains. Waves of crores of apes have come here and they are your servants. All of them are awaiting their commands. All of them are engaged in the welfare of their

[225] Rama.

seniors. O scorcher of enemies! They are capable of accomplishing whatever you desire. O tiger among men! The time has come to tell them what you think. These soldiers are under your command and you should instruct them. I know the truth about the task that you wish for. Even then, it will be appropriate for you to command them about the truth.'

When he was addressed by Sugriva in this way, Rama, Dasharatha's son, embraced him in his arms and spoke these words to him. 'O amiable one! O immensely wise one! We must find out whether Vaidehi is alive or not and about the place where Ravana resides. After we get to know about Vaidehi and Ravana's residence, when the right time arrives, in consultation with you, I will issue my commands then. O lord of the apes. For the task at hand, neither I, nor Lakshmana, is the master. O lord of the apes! You are the master of the task that needs to be accomplished now. O lord! Determining the nature of my task, you must issue the instructions. O brave one! There is no doubt that you know about my objective. You are brave and you are my second well-wisher.[226] You are especially wise about the time. You are engaged in our welfare. You are good in accomplishing the objective and you know the purpose well.'

When he was thus addressed, in Rama's presence and that of the intelligent Lakshmana, Sugriva spoke to the leader of the herd named Vinata. This energetic lord of the apes had the complexion of a mountain and thundered like the clouds. 'O supreme among apes! Go with the apes who are sons of Soma and Surya. You know about the time, the place and good policy. You know about what should be done and what should not be done. Surround yourself with one hundred thousand spirited apes. Go towards the eastern direction,[227] with its mountains, forests and groves. Follow the routes in impenetrable mountains, forests and rivers, to search out Sita Vaidehi and Ravana's residence. Explore the beautiful rivers Bhageerathee, Sarayu, Koushiki, Kalindi, Yamuna, the giant and

[226] Lakshmana being the first.

[227] This means the east of Jambudvipa and not the east of Kishkindha.

dark mountain,[228] Sarasvati, Sindhu,[229] Shona, with water that shines like jewels, Mahi,[230] Kalamahi, adorned with mountains and groves, Brahmamala, Videha, Malavat,[231] Kashi, Kosala, Magadha, with large villages, Pundra, Vanga, the habitations of the *koshakaras*[232] and the land where there are silversmiths. Search out everything everywhere. Look for Rama's beloved wife Sita, Dasharatha's daughter-in-law, in fathomless oceans, mountains and habitations. There are large places secreted in the valleys of the Mandara. Some have squashed ears there. Others have pierced lips and ears. There are terrible ones who seem to have faces made out of iron. Others are swift, though they only possess a single foot. There are men who have inexhaustible strength. Others eat the flesh of men. There are *kiratas*[233] who decorate their ears. Some have golden complexions and are pleasant to see. The kiratas who reside in the islands eat raw fish. It has been said that there are terrible tigers among men who reside inside the waters. Search out the residences of all these and the habitations of those who dwell in groves. Leap from one place to another and ascend the mountains. There is the island of Yava,[234] full of jewels and adorned with seven kingdoms. It is full of silver and gold. Once you pass beyond it, there will be the mountain named Shishira. It is populated by gods and danavas and the summit touches the sky. There are impenetrable mountains, waterfalls and forests there. Here and there, search out the route of Ravana and Vaidehi. You should see the extremely terrible island in the ocean. There are extremely gigantic asuras there and they always seize people by their shadows. Brahma ordained that they should remain hungry for a long period of time. Go to the tirtha in the

[228] Known as Kalinda or dark.

[229] Sarasvati does not belong on the eastern side. Neither does Sindhu, unless this refers to some other river Sindhu. The geographical sections in this and the next three chapters also occur in the Matsya Purana.

[230] River Mahi is also towards the west.

[231] If this is Malava, it does not belong here.

[232] The likeliest meaning is those who earn a living from silk. But it could also mean those who make scabbards for swords.

[233] Hunters.

[234] Identified as Java.

great ocean. It is populated by giant serpents that roar loudly. Their forms are like clouds of destruction. After this, there is the terrible ocean named Lohita, with water like blood.[235] Having gone there, you should see the giant silk-cotton trees.[236] Vainateya's[237] abode is there, decorated by many kinds of jewels. It is like Kailasa and was constructed by Vishvakarma. There are terrible rakshasas named Mandeha there and their complexion is like that of mountains. They have diverse fearful forms and hang downwards from the peaks of mountains. When the time for sunrise comes, they always fall down in the water. They are scorched by the sun and repeatedly hang downwards again.[238] There is the ocean named Kshiroda, with a complexion like that of a white cloud. O invincible ones! Having gone there, you must see the waves that are like necklaces made out of pearls. In the midst of this, there is the gigantic mountain named Rishabha, white in complexion. It is surrounded by silvery and blossoming trees with divine fragrances. There is the lake named Sudarshana, full of swans. There are silver-coloured lotuses there, with dazzling golden fibres. To cheerfully sport in that lake full of lotuses, gods, charanas, kinnaras and large numbers of apsaras go there. O apes! After passing beyond Kshiroda, you should see Jaloda. This is best among oceans and is fearful to all creatures. The great *hayamukha* fire is there, created from the energy of rage.[239] It is said to possess great force and devours all mobile and immobile objects. The loud shrieks of creatures who dwell in the ocean can be heard there, when they are rendered incapacitated on seeing the *vadavamukha* fire. There is a region that is thirteen yojanas to the north of those tasty waters. The extremely large mountain with a golden peak, named Jatarupa, is there. The thousand-hooded god,

[235] Lohita means red.

[236] Silk cotton is shalmali and this *dvipa* is named Shalmali dvipa.

[237] Vinata's son, Garuda.

[238] When the sun rises, the Mandehas try to obstruct the sun's path. When oblations of water are offered at the time of sunrise, the Mandehas are scorched by the sun and fall down in the water.

[239] This is the subterranean fire, known as hayamukha (horse's head/mouth) or vadavamukha (mare's head/mouth). It emerges at the time of the final destruction and devours everything. The fire was created from the anger and rage of the sage Urva.

Ananta, attired in blue garments and worshipped by all creatures, is seated on the summit of that mountain.[240] The great-souled one's standard is a three-headed palm tree. It has been established, with its foundation, on the summit of that mountain and is radiant. The gods have created this as a mark of the eastern direction.[241] After this, there is the supremely wonderful Mount Udaya, made out of gold. It is one hundred yojanas high and its peak touches the firmament. With its foundation, it dazzles. It is divine and is made out of molten gold. There are blossoming sala, tala, tamala and karnikara trees. These are divine and are made out of molten gold. They dazzle and are like the sun. There is a peak[242] that is one yojana wide and ten yojanas high. This is firm and is named Soumanasa. It is made out of molten gold. In ancient times, Vishnu Trivikrama[243] placed his first foot there. Purushottama placed his second foot on Mount Meru. The sun is repeatedly seen atop this giant peak.[244] It then circles Jambudvipa from the north. The radiant maharshis, named vaikhanasas and valakhilyas are seen there. Those ascetics have the complexion of the sun. The dvipa known as Sudarshana is ahead of that.[245] He[246] illuminates with his energy and provides eyesight to all those who are living. On the slopes of that mountain and in caverns and forests, here and there, search for the route taken by Ravana and Vaidehi. The golden mountain is suffused by the great-souled sun's energy and is seen to assume a reddish tinge at the time of sandhya. Beyond this, the eastern direction is barred by the gods and is impossible to penetrate. With the sun and the moon missing, it is enveloped in darkness. Janakee should be searched out in all the mountains, caves and forests I have mentioned, and even in the places I have not mentioned. O bulls among the apes! Apes are only capable of going up to this spot. We do not know about what is

[240] Vishnu lies down on the serpent named Ananta.

[241] The eastern direction ends beyond this.

[242] One of Mount Udaya's peaks.

[243] In his dwarf incarnation.

[244] Soumanasa.

[245] This is where the sun resides.

[246] The sun.

beyond. That is without the sun and beyond the boundaries. Having reached Mount Udaya, you will search for Vaidehi and Ravana's residence for a month and return after that. No one will stay for more than a month. If anyone does that, he will be bound up in my residence. Go and find Maithilee. Return after accomplishing your objective. O apes! Use your skills to search that direction, loved by the great Indra and adorned with forests and groves. Get back Sita, loved by the descendant of the Raghu lineage. Return after that. May you be happy.'

Chapter 4(40)

After sending that great army of apes, Sugriva, the brave leader of large numbers of apes, desired to send apes to the southern direction. He summoned Agni's son Nila, the ape Hanumat, the great ape named Jambavat who was the grandfather's son, Suhotra, Sharari, Sharagulma, Gaja, Gavaksha, Sushena,[247] Vrishabha, Mainda, Dvivida, Vijaya, Gandhamadana, the two sons of Agni named Ulkamukha and Ananga, Angada and other brave ones. They possessed speed and valour and knew about the directions. He made Angada the leader of that large force. He then instructed the brave apes about searching the southern direction. The lord of the apes told the best among the apes about some extremely impenetrable regions in that direction. 'There is the Vindhya, with one thousand peaks. It is covered with many trees and creepers. There is the impassable river Narmada, populated by giant serpents. There is the beautiful Godavari and the great river Krishnaveni. There is the immensely fortunate Varada,[248] populated by giant serpents. There is the region of Mekhala,[249] Utkala[250] and the city of Dasharna.

[247] This is a different Sushena, not the one who was Tara's father.

[248] Identified as Wardha.

[249] Amarakantaka, where the Narmada originates.

[250] This deviates from the geography, as do subsequent references to Vanga and Kalinga.

Search everywhere in Avanti and Abhravanti, Vidarbha, Rishika and the beautiful region of Mahishaka. Search everywhere in Vanga, Kalinga and Koushika. Search all the mountains, rivers and caves in Dandakaranya. Look everywhere around the river Godavari. Go to Andhra, Pundra, Chola, Pandya, Kerala and Mount Ayomukha,[251] which is decorated with minerals. It has a beautiful peak, colourful with blossoming trees. Search out the routes on that giant mountain, with its forests full of sandalwood trees. Beyond this, you will see the river Kaveri. It has divine, auspicious and sparkling water and large numbers of apsaras sport there. Seated on the summit of Malaya, you will see the immensely energetic and supreme rishi Agastya, who is like the sun. When the great-souled one is pleased and grants you permission, cross the great river Tampraparni, full of a large number of crocodiles. It has many dense islands, which have groves of divine sandalwood trees. It is like a beautiful young woman, going to meet the beloved ocean. O apes! You must go and see Pandya. It has gates made out of gold, decorated with divine pearls and jewels. To accomplish your objective, you will then approach the ocean, with the handsome Mount Mahendra, supreme among mountains. It has a beautiful summit, made out of gold. Agastya had placed the base of this mountain inside the ocean and the peak can be seen above the great ocean. The mountain is decorated with many kinds of flowering trees and creepers. It is visited by gods, rishis, the best of yakshas and apsaras. It is extremely pleasant and is full of large numbers of siddhas and charanas. On every auspicious day, the one with the thousand eyes always goes there. There is an island on the other side of this and it is one hundred yojanas in expanse. It blazes and humans cannot penetrate it. You must search this out, everywhere. Search this place in particular for Sita's whereabouts, using every means at your disposal. This is the region of the evil-souled Ravana, who deserves to be killed.[252] The

[251] This is Mount Malaya. Literally, with iron at its mouth.

[252] This causes all kinds of problems. How did Sugriva know Ravana lived there? If he knew, why did he tell Rama he did not know where Ravana dwelt? Why did he send the apes off to other directions? Since the instructions were given in Rama's presence, why didn't Rama react?

lord of the rakshasas resides there and he is like the one with the one thousand eyes in his radiance. There is a rakshasi who resides in the middle of the southern ocean. She is famous as Angaraka and devours shadows.[253] After you cross that prosperous place, at a distance of one hundred yojanas, there is a mountain named Pushpitaka in the ocean. It is populated by siddhas and charanas. Its radiance is like that of the sun and the moon and on all sides, it is surrounded by the waters of the ocean. The large and dazzling summit seems to be writing in the sky. One peak is golden and is loved by the sun. Another peak is silvery and is loved by the moon. An ungrateful person cannot see it. Nor can a cruel person, or a non-believer. O apes! Bow your heads down and search out that mountain. After passing beyond this, at a distance of fourteen yojanas, there is the impenetrable mountain named Suryavat. This is a path that is extremely difficult to traverse. Once one has passed beyond, there is Mount Vaidyuta. It has trees with fruits that yield all the objects of desire, pleasant in all seasons. Those best of roots and fruits deserve to be eaten. O apes! Eat them. Drink the excellent honey and proceed beyond. There is the mountain named Kunjara, desired by the eyes and the mind. Vishvakarma constructed this as Agastya's residence. This extends for one yojana and rises up ten yojanas. This divine and golden resort is decorated with many kinds of jewels. The city named Bhogavati, the abode of the snakes, is there. The broad roads are impenetrable and are protected on all sides. They are protected by terrible serpents, who have sharp fangs that are full of great poison. Vasuki, the extremely terrible king of the snakes, resides there. Search the city of Bhogavati. On emerging, pass over the region where there is the great Rishabha. The mountain named Rishabha is full of every kind of jewel. Divine sandalwood trees grow there—*goshirshaka*, *padmaka*, *harishyama* and *agnisamaprabha*.[254] See those sandalwood trees, but never touch them. A terrible gandharva named Rohita guards that grove. There are five lords of the gandharvas who are like the sun in their

[253] Also known as Simhika. She seizes the shadow and thereby devours the prey.

[254] These are four species of sandalwood, respectively, ochre yellow, leafy green, sky blue and fiery red.

radiance. They are Shailusha, Gramani, Bhikshu, Shubhra and Babhru. This is the impenetrable end of the earth and those who have conquered heaven reside there. After this, there is the extremely terrible world of the ancestors and we should not go there. This is the capital of Yama, full of hardships and enveloped in darkness. O brave bulls among apes! We are only capable of searching up to this point. We have no means of proceeding beyond this. Search all this and every other place that you can see. You must find out about Vaidehi's route and return. If a person returns within a month and tells me that he has seen Sita, he will enjoy affluence and pleasures that are like mine and will sport in joy. There will be no one who will be more loved by me, more than my own life. Even if he has committed many kinds of crimes, he will be my friend. You possess infinite strength and valour. You have extensive qualities and have been born in noble lineages. In addition, you have the qualities of your own manliness. Obtain the daughter of the king of men.'

Chapter 4(41)

When the apes had left for the southern direction, Sugriva summoned the extremely energetic leader of the herds named Sushena. He possessed intelligence and valour and was like Vayu in his speed. He was terrible in his valour. He was Tara's father and the king's father-in-law. He[255] prostrated himself, joined his hands in salutation and spoke the following words. 'Please help Rama. The time has come to repay him. Surround yourself with one hundred thousand spirited apes. O amiable one! O lord! Go to Varuna's western direction, to Surashtra, Bahlika, Shura[256] and Abhira. There are prosperous habitations and large and beautiful cities. The inner groves are full of punnagas, bakulas and uddalakas.[257] O bulls among apes! Search out the routes amidst

[255] Sugriva.
[256] The region around Mathura.
[257] Uddalaka means honey. So this is a tree from which honey can be obtained.

the dense growth of ketakas. Every river bears flows of cool and auspicious water. There are forests frequented by ascetics and desolate mountains. The western direction has unapproachable routes that are encompassed by walls of mountains. You should then reach and see the western ocean. O apes! The water there is agitated by many whales and crocodiles. There are clumps of ketakas and dense growths of tamalas. The apes can sport in the groves of coconut trees. Search out Sita and Ravana's residence there. There is the habitation of Marichi and the beautiful city of Jati. There are Avanti[258] and Angalopa and the forest of Alakshita. Here and there, there are large kingdoms and habitations. There is a mountain at the confluence of the Sindhu with the ocean. There is a giant mountain named Hemagiri, with hundreds of peaks and large trees. On the beautiful slopes there, lions that can fly with their wings can be found. Whales, fish and seals make their nests there. The lions make their lairs on the summit of that mountain. Proud and satisfied elephants are there, trumpeting like clouds. They roam around in that extensive place, surrounded by water everywhere. The summit is golden, with colourful trees, and seems to touch the sky. The apes, which can assume any form at will, must search all this quickly. Near the ocean, there is a golden peak that is one hundred yojanas high. This is Pariyatra and it is extremely difficult to see.[259] O apes! Go and see it. Twenty-four crores of spirited gandharvas reside on that summit. They are terrible, as radiant as the fire, and they can assume any form at will. Apes, even if they are terrible in their valour, must not approach them. The apes must not pluck any fruit from that region. Those brave and spirited ones[260] are extremely strong and impossible to assail. Terrible in their valour, they protect the fruits and the roots there. Your task is to search out Janakee everywhere there. O apes! As long as you do not follow them,[261] you have nothing to fear from them. In the fourth part of the ocean, there is Mount Chakravat.

[258] This is not the Avanti mentioned earlier.

[259] Because it dazzles.

[260] The gandharvas.

[261] The gandharvas.

Vishvakarma constructed a chakra with a thousand spokes there. Purushottama slew Panchajana and the danava Hayagriva and obtained the chakra and the conch shell.[262] Here and there on that colourful summit and in the large caves, search for Ravana and Vaidehi. After sixty-four yojanas, there is the mountain named Varaha. It has an extremely large and golden summit. Varuna's fathomless abode is there. There is the city named Pragjyotisha there, made out of molten gold.[263] The evil-souled danava named Naraka used to dwell there. Here and there on that colourful mountain, and in the large caves, search for Ravana and Vaidehi. Once you pass beyond, there is an Indra among mountains. The inside of that mountain is made out of gold. The mountain is golden everywhere and there are innumerable waterfalls. There are elephants, boars, lions and tigers everywhere. They insolently roar all the time and the mountain itself seems to roar. That mountain is named Megha. The great and prosperous Indra, the chastiser of Paka and the possessor of tawny steeds, was crowned as the king of the gods there. This Indra among mountains is protected by the great Indra. Passing beyond, reach sixty thousand golden mountains. They have the complexion of the rising sun and are radiant everywhere. There are beautiful blossoming trees that are made out of molten gold. In their midst, there is the excellent Mount Meru, the king. In ancient times, Aditya[264] was pleased and granted the mountain a boon. He told the Indra among mountains, 'Because of my favours, everything that finds refuge in you will be golden, during the day and at night. The gods, gandharvas and danavas who reside in you will always have a reddish tinge and a golden complexion.' At the time of the western sandhya, the Adityas, the Vasus, the Rudras, the Maruts and the residents of heaven come to that excellent mountain, Meru. They worship the sun. Worshipped by them, the sun goes behind Mount Asta and can no longer be seen by any creature. The sun quickly

[262] Vishnu slew these two demons on Chakravat. He thus obtained the conch shell from Panchajana and the chakra from Hayagriva.

[263] Since Pragjyotisha is in the east, in Assam, this does not fit.

[264] The sun god.

traverses the distance of ten thousand yojanas[265] in one-and-a-half muhurtas[266] and approaches that tall peak. On the summit of that great peak,[267] there is a divine residence that is like the sun in complexion. This palace has many layers of storeys and was constructed by Vishvakarma. It is adorned with many colourful trees, full of diverse kinds of birds. This is the residence of the great-souled Varuna, with a noose in his hand. Between Meru and Asta, there is a large palm tree, with ten heads. It is handsome, made out of molten gold, and has a glittering and wonderful base. Here and there, everywhere in the impenetrable places, lakes and rivers, search for Ravana and Vaidehi. Meru Savarni is famous as being Brahma's equal. He knows about dharma and has cleansed himself through his austerities. He resides there. The maharshi Meru Savarni has a complexion like that of the sun. After you have bowed your head down on the ground in front of him, he can be asked about Maithilee's welfare and her whereabouts. When the night is over, the sun dispels darkness from the world of the living. But thereafter, he goes beyond Mount Asta. O bulls among apes! This is the point up to which apes are capable of going. We do not know about what lies beyond. That is without the sun and without boundaries. Having reached Mount Asta, you will find out about Vaidehi and Ravana's residence and return before an entire month is over. No one will stay for more than a month. If anyone stays for more, he will be bound in my residence. My brave father-in-law will go with you. You will listen to everything that he instructs and act accordingly. The mighty-armed one is a senior. The immensely strong one is my father-in-law. All of you are valiant and that is evident in all your deeds. Make him your leader and search the western direction. If we can find the wife of the infinitely energetic Indra among men, we will be able to repay the good deed that he has done for us. After this task has been accomplished, if there is any other task that can bring about his benefit, considering the time, the place and the objective, we will

265 From Mount Meru to Mount Asta.

266 One hour and twelve minutes.

267 Mount Asta.

undertake later.' Sushena and the other foremost apes heard the accomplished words spoken by Sugriva. They took their leave of the lord of the apes and left for the western direction, protected by Varuna.

Chapter 4(42)

Sugriva sent his father-in-law to the western direction. The lord of the apes then summoned the brave ape named Shatabali. The king, supreme among all the apes and the one who knew everything, addressed him in these words, for his own welfare and for Rama's welfare. 'Surround yourself with one hundred residents of the forest who are like you. Go with your ministers and with Vaivasvata's[268] sons. O valiant one! Go to the northern direction, with the Himalayas as its crest. Search everywhere for Rama's unblemished wife. When we have accomplished this task, we will do something that will bring Dasharatha's son pleasure. O supreme among those who know the objectives! We will accomplish our task and be freed from our debt. The great-souled Raghava has performed an agreeable task for us. If we are able to pay him back, our being alive will have served its purpose. Use your intelligence to determine how Janakee can be found. That is your task and our pleasure and benefit lie in this. This supreme among men is revered by all creatures. Rama is the one who triumphs over the cities of enemies and this will bring us and him pleasure. You possess intelligence and valour. There are many forests, impenetrable areas and rivers inside the mountains. Search them. There are habitations of *mlechchhas*,[269] Pulindas, Shurasenas, Prasthalas, Bharatas, Kurus, Madrakas, Kambojas, Yavanas, Shakas, Bahlikas, Rishikas, Pouravas, Tankanas, Chinas, Paramachinas, Niharas and Daradas. Search them repeatedly and search the Himalayas. Search here and

[268] Yama's.

[269] A mlechchha is a barbarian, meaning that mlechchhas do not speak Sanskrit and are not *aryas*.

there in the clumps of *lodhra*[270] and padmaka trees and in the *devadaru*[271] forests for Ravana and Vaidehi. Go to Soma's hermitage, frequented by the gods and the gandharvas. Then go to the large mountain named Mount Kala. Search the giant peaks, caves and caverns for Rama's immensely fortunate and illustrious wife. Pass beyond that large mountain, with gold in its womb. Passing beyond that Indra among mountains, you should go to the mountain named Sudarshana. Here and there, in the groves, clumps, caves and caverns, search for Ravana and Vaidehi. When you pass beyond this, there is an expanse that extends for one hundred yojanas in every direction. There is nothing but the sky there. There are no mountains, rivers or trees. All living creatures avoid it. Swiftly pass over this desolate plain that makes the body hair stand up. You will then reach the white Mount Kailasa and will be delighted. This has the complexion of white clouds and is embellished with molten gold. Kubera's beautiful palace was constructed by Vishvakarma there. There is a large lake there and it is full of lotuses and lilies. It is full of swans and karandavas and is frequented by a large number of apsaras. The prosperous King Vaishravana,[272] the king of the yakshas, the granter of riches and worshipped by all creatures, is there, sporting with the guhyakas. Here and there, in the mountain caverns that are as radiant as the moon, search for Ravana and Vaidehi. Reach Mount Krouncha and its extremely impenetrable tunnel. Enter it carefully, because it is said to be extremely difficult to enter. Welcomed by the gods, the great-souled maharshis reside there. They are themselves like the gods in form and are like the sun in their resplendence. Here and there, search the other caves of Krouncha, the summits, the peaks, the caverns and the flanks. Here and there, search Krouncha's summit too. Search Mount Kama, which is without any trees, and Manasa, the abode of birds. Creatures cannot go there. Nor can gods or rakshasas. Search every place there, the summits, the slopes and the plains. After you pass beyond Mount Krouncha, there is the mountain named Mainaka.

[270] The lotus bark tree.

[271] Species of pine. Devadaru literally means tree of the gods.

[272] Kubera.

The danava Maya's residence is there and he constructed it himself. Search Mainaka, its peaks, slopes and caves. Here and there, there are the abodes of women who have faces like mares.[273] After passing over that region, there is a hermitage frequented by the siddhas. Siddhas, vaikhanasas and the ascetic valakhilyas are there. Worship the ascetic siddhas, who have used austerities to cleanse themselves of all sins. Humbly, you can ask them about Sita's welfare and whereabouts. There is lake Vaikhanasa, covered with golden lotuses. Sparkling swans that are like the rising sun roam around there. Kubera's mount is known as Sarvabhouma. That elephant always goes to that place, accompanied by she-elephants. When you cross that lake, the sun or the moon can no longer be seen. The sky will be bereft of the large number of nakshatras. There will be no clouds. Nor will there be any sound. However, that region will be illuminated by rays that are like those of the sun. Siddhas full of austerities rest there and they are like the gods. They illuminate with their own radiance. Once you cross that region, there is the river named Shailoda. Along both its banks, there are bamboos named *kichaka*. The siddhas use these to cross over to the other bank and return. The land of Uttara Kuru is for those who have earned merits. There are thousands of rivers there. The water is full of lotuses and the lotuses are golden in complexion. The leaves of the lotuses are as blue as lapis lazuli. The forests are full of red lotuses with golden hues. There are waterbodies that are as radiant as the rising sun. The leaves are made out of expensive gems and the filaments are golden in complexion. That region is surrounded everywhere by colourful groves of blue lotuses. The banks of the river are made out of molten gold, fashioned with extremely expensive jewels and pearls that cannot be weighed. The valleys in those supreme mountains are wonderful, with jewels everywhere. There is molten gold that is like the fire in its radiance. The trees there are always laden with flowers and fruits and are thick with birds. They[274] are divine to the smell, taste and touch and satiate all the objects of

[273] Kinnaras, the feminine of the species.

[274] The flowers and fruit.

desire. The fruits of other excellent trees yield many forms of clothing. They yield colourful pearls, lapis lazuli and ornaments suitable for both men and women. In all seasons, they happily savour the fruits of other excellent trees. During the winter, there are other excellent trees that yield extremely expensive beds and wonderful spreads of different types. Other trees yield garlands that are loved by the heart and many kinds of expensive drinks and diverse types of fruit. The women possess all the qualities and are seen to possess beauty and youth. Gandharvas, kinnaras, siddhas, nagas and *vidyadharas*[275] sport with women who dazzle in their resplendence. All of them have performed good deeds. All of them are engaged in carnal pursuits. To pursue kama and artha, all of them reside with women. There are the sounds of singing and the playing of musical instruments. Wonderful sounds of laughter are heard there at all times and these are agreeable to all creatures. There is no one there who is not happy. There is no one there who loves falsehood. From one day to the next day, the agreeable qualities of that place increase. When one passes beyond Uttara Kuru, there is a body of water. In its middle, there is the giant Mount Soma, made out of gold. Those who have gone to Indra's world, those who have gone to Brahma's world, those who have gone to heaven, and the gods can see this king of mountains from up there. Though that region is without the sun, a radiance illuminates it.[276] Though the radiance of the sun cannot be seen, it is as if the sun is radiating heat. The illustrious one who is the soul of the universe,[277] Shambhu, who is the soul of the eleven,[278] and Brahma, the lord of the gods, reside there, surrounded by brahmana rishis. You should never go to the region that is beyond Uttara Kuru. Other creatures are also not permitted to travel there. Even the gods find it extremely difficult to travel to the mountain named Soma. Having seen it, you should quickly return. O bulls among apes! That is the point up to which apes are capable of travelling.

[275] Vidyadharas are semi-divine, occupying the region between heaven and earth.
[276] From the radiance of Mount Soma.
[277] Vishnu.
[278] Shiva, eleven being a reference to the eleven Rudras.

There is no sun beyond that. There are no boundaries beyond that. We do not know about what is beyond. Search everything that I have mentioned and use your intelligence to search everything that I have not mentioned. Thereby, perform a greatly desired task for Dasharatha's son and it will be a task that will be even more agreeable for me. O those who are like the wind and the fire! Perform the task of seeing Videha's daughter. When you are successful with your relatives, I will honour you with all the agreeable qualities.[279] O apes! With your enemies pacified, you will roam all over the earth. With your beloveds, you will have offspring.'

Chapter 4(43)

To accomplish the objective, Sugriva specifically spoke to Hanumat. He had decided that in accomplishing the objective, he was the best among the apes. 'O bull among the apes! I do not see who can bar your entry on earth, the firmament, the sky, the abode of the gods, or in water. You know about all the worlds, the oceans and the mountains, the asuras, the gandharvas, the serpents and the gods. O great ape! O brave one! Your speed, force, energy and dexterity is like that of your father, the extremely energetic wind god. There is no creature on earth who is your equal in energy. Therefore, you should think about how Sita can be got back. O Hanumat! You possess strength, intelligence and valour. You conduct yourself in accordance with the time and the place and good policy. You are learned about good policy.'

Hanumat was about to leave on the task. Knowing this, Raghava thought about Hanumat. 'The lord of the apes has determined that Hanumat will certainly be able to accomplish the objective. It has been decided that in accomplishing the task, Hanumat is superior to the others. That determination must be based on his former deeds. In ensuring the fruits of the action, he has been clearly chosen by

[279] With objects that possess those qualities.

his master.' On considering the conduct of the extremely energetic ape, he[280] was delighted and thought that his task had already been accomplished. His senses and heart became cheerful. Delighted, the scorcher of enemies gave him his ring, with his name inscribed on it, so that the princess[281] would accept it as a sign of recognition.[282] 'O best among the apes! Through this sign, Janaka's daughter will recognize that you have come from me and will not look upon you with anxiety. O brave one! Your conduct, your spirit, your valour and Sugriva's instruction to you are conveying to me that you will be successful.' The best among the apes joined his hands in salutation. He accepted it and placed it on his head. Having worshipped at his feet, the supreme among apes departed. As if dragging that large army of the apes, the brave ape who was the son of the wind god leapt up into the sky. He was like the sparkling lunar disc, when the clouds have disappeared, adorned with a large number of nakshatras. 'O ape! O one who is supreme in valour! O one who is not limited in valour! O extremely strong one! I am depending on your strength. O son of the wind god! O Hanumat! Act so that you go wherever Janaka's daughter happens to be.'[283]

Chapter 4(44)

Understanding the fierce command of their master, the bulls among the apes enveloped the earth, like a swarm of locusts. With Lakshmana, Rama continued to dwell in Prasravana. He waited for the one month designated for Sita to be found. The king of the mountains[284] was spread across the beautiful northern

[280] Rama.

[281] Sita.

[282] This is not a very convincing reason. No such signs were given to the apes who headed towards the north, the east or the west, reinforcing the hypothesis that it was known that Ravana was towards the south, in Lanka. Nor is the reason for giving the ring to Hanumat, as opposed to Angada, very clear.

[283] This is Rama addressing Hanumat as he left.

[284] The Himalayas.

direction. With great force, the brave ape Shatabali headed there. Vinata, the leader of the apes, left for the eastern direction. With Tara, Angada and the other apes, the son of the wind god and the leader of the apes left for the southern direction, where Agastya once travelled. Sushena, the lord of the apes and tiger among the apes, left for the terrible western direction, harshly protected by Varuna. The king had respectively urged them in all the directions. Having dispatched them in this way, the brave commander of the army of the apes was delighted, happy and cheerful. The king thus urged all the leaders of the apes and they swiftly left towards their own respective directions. The apes shouted, screamed and roared. As those supreme among apes proceeded, they bellowed, 'We will kill Ravana and bring Sita back. If I come across him, I will single-handedly slay Ravana in the battle. I will violently agitate the one who abducted Janaka's daughter. Even if I tremble because of exhaustion, I will now remain steady. I will single-handedly bring Janakee back, even if it happens to be from the nether regions. I will shatter these trees. I will splinter these mountains. I will cleave the earth. I will agitate the oceans. There is no doubt that I will leap over one yojana. I will leap over one hundred yojanas. I will do more than one hundred. No one can obstruct my path on the surface of the ground, in the ocean, in mountains, in forests and even in the middle of the nether regions.' In the presence of the king of the apes, each of those apes, intoxicated with valour, spoke these and other words.

Chapter 4(45)

When the Indras among apes had left, Rama asked Sugriva, 'How do you know everything about the globe that is the earth?'[285] Sugriva bowed down and replied to Rama. 'Listen to my words. I will tell you everything in detail. There was a danava

[285] The word used is *mandala* and this means round, circular, globe.

named Dundubhi, in the form of a buffalo. In the region near Mount Malaya, Vali fought against him. The buffalo entered a cave inside Malaya and desiring to kill him, Vali also entered Malaya.[286] I was asked to humbly wait at the entrance to the cave. But though one year had passed, Vali did not emerge. That cave was then filled with a flood of blood. On seeing this, I was astounded and the poisonous sorrow on account of my brother afflicted me. I deduced it was evident that my senior had been killed. I covered the entrance to the cave with a boulder that was like a mountain, so that the buffalo would find it impossible to emerge and would be destroyed. I had no hopes of his remaining alive and came to Kishkindha. I obtained the extremely large kingdom, with Tara and Ruma. I resided there with my friends, devoid of all anxiety. However, after having killed the bull among danavas, Vali returned. Honouring him and driven by fear, I returned the kingdom to him. But Vali's senses were distressed. The evil-souled one wished to cause me injury. As I fled with my advisers, in his rage, he pursued me. As I was chased by him, I fled over many kinds of rivers and saw forests and cities. I saw the earth, like a reflection on the surface of a mirror. I saw some places that were like a circle of fire, and others that were like the hoof print of a cow. I first went to the eastern direction and then sought refuge in the southern direction. Scared, I next went to the western direction. Thereafter, I went to the northern direction. Then Hanumat addressed me in these words. "O king! I have just remembered how Vali, the lord of the apes, was cursed by Matanga. If Vali enters the circle of his[287] hermitage, his head will be shattered into one hundred fragments. We can dwell there happily and will not suffer from any anxiety." O son of a king! That is the reason why, though he reached Mount Rishyamuka, Vali was terrified of Matanga and did not enter. O king! I have thus directly experienced everything in the earth's globe. After that, I went to the cave.'[288]

[286] There is an inconsistency. We have earlier been told that Vali killed Dundubhi in Kishkindha, whereas a cave in Mount Malaya is being mentioned now.

[287] Matanga's.

[288] In Rishyamuka.

Chapter 4(46)

Commanded by the king of the apes, all the elephants among the apes did as they had been asked and energetically departed, searching for Vaidehi. They searched everywhere, in lakes, rivers, slopes, the sky, cities, impenetrable fortifications in the rivers and mountains. All the leaders of the apes had been commanded by Sugriva. They searched the regions, with the mountains, forests and groves. Determined to find Sita, they searched throughout the day. At night, the apes assembled together on the ground. Irrespective of the season and the place, every day, when it was nightfall, the apes would find trees with fruit and make those their beds. The first day of the stipulated month was the day they left Prasravana. When the month was over, the elephants among the apes despaired and returned to the king of the apes. As had been asked to, with his advisers, the immensely strong Vinata had searched the eastern direction and returned without seeing Sita. The brave and great ape, Shatabali, searched everywhere in the northern direction and returned with his soldiers. With the other apes, Sushena hopefully searched the western direction. However, when the month was over, he returned to Sugriva. With Rama, Sugriva was seated on the slope of Prasravana. They approached him, greeted him and said, 'We have searched all the mountains, forests, cities, rivers, the extremities of the ocean and habitations. We have searched all the caves that you had mentioned. We have searched the giant thickets and creepers that spread around everywhere. We have repeatedly searched impenetrable, impassable and uneven regions and desolate spots. We have sought out extremely large creatures in the course of the search and have killed them. The great-souled one[289] is noble in birth and broad in spirit. That Indra among the apes will see Maithilee. Sita has certainly gone to the southern direction and that is where Hanumat, Vayu's son, went.'

[289] Hanumat.

Chapter 4(47)

With Tara and Angada, the ape proceeded towards the region that had been indicated by Sugriva. All those supreme among apes reached that distant spot. They searched the caves and desolate spots in the Vindhyas,[290] the summits of the mountains, the rivers, the impenetrable areas, the lakes, the large trees, the thickets of trees, the many mountains and the forests of trees. All the apes searched in all the directions. But those brave ones could not see Maithilee, Janaka's daughter. They ate the many kinds of roots and fruits. Those invincible ones dwelt there and searched here and there. But that region was difficult to search. There were large and deep caves. All those leaders of apes then abandoned that region. Without any fear, they entered another impenetrable region. The trees were sterile there and did not yield any fruit. There were no flowers, nor any leaves. The rivers had no water and roots were extremely difficult to obtain. There were no buffaloes there, nor any deer or elephants. There were no tigers and birds, nor others that can be seen in forests. There were flowering lotuses and lilies that grew in lakes and on the ground. With gentle leaves, these were worth seeing and were fragrant. However, the bees shunned them. The immensely fortunate Kandu was truthful in speech and was a store of austerities. This maharshi adhered to rituals. But he was also supremely intolerant and was impossible to control. His son was a child when he was lost in that forest. He was only ten years old and lost his life there. Thereupon, the great sage was angered. The great-souled one cursed that entire large forest. The forest would become impenetrable and would be shunned by animals and birds. However, controlling themselves, they did search the extremities of the forests, the mountains, the caverns, the waterfalls and the rivers. But those great-souled ones, wishing to bring pleasure to Sugriva, did not see Janaka's daughter there, or her abductor, Ravana.

They entered another terrible forest, covered with creepers and shrubs. There, they saw an asura who had no fear of the gods and was cruel in his deeds. The apes saw that terrible one standing

[290] This establishes that the Vindhyas were to the south of Rishyamuka.

in the forest, resembling a mountain. On seeing the one who was like a mountain, all of them girded their loins. The powerful one shouted at the apes, 'Remain there. All of you will be destroyed.' He angrily rushed towards them, doubling up his fists. When Angada, Vali's son, saw that he was descending violently, he took him to be Ravana and slew him with a slap of his palm. Struck by Vali's soon, he started to vomit blood from his mouth. Like a mountain that had been overturned, the asura fell down on the ground. When he ceased breathing, the apes, desiring success, entered and searched all the caves in the mountain. They next searched all the forests and entered another terrible cave in a mountain. Having searched again, they were saddened. They emerged and assembled together, seating themselves at a lonely spot under a tree, miserable in their minds.

Chapter 4(48)

Angada, the immensely wise one, was exhausted. But he comforted all the apes and addressed them in these words, speaking slowly. 'We have searched everywhere in the forests, mountains, rivers, impenetrable and desolate places and caverns and caves in the mountains. But nowhere have we been able to see Janakee. Nor have we seen the rakshasa who has abducted Sita, who is like the daughter of a god. A long period of time has elapsed and Sugriva is fierce in his rule. Therefore, together, let all of us search again. Let us abandon our lassitude and sorrow. Let us wake up from our sleep. Let us search for Sita, so that we can see Janaka's daughter. Persistence, skills and a mind that refuses to give up are said to be the reasons behind success in any course of action. That is the reason I am speaking to you in this way. O residents of the forest! Let us search this impenetrable forest yet again. Let us cast aside our exhaustion. Let all of us search this forest again. The fruits of this action will certainly be seen to materialize. Enough of this dejection that has come upon us. This lassitude of ours cannot be pardoned. O apes! In his anger, King Sugriva will chastise us severely. We should always be frightened of him and the great-souled Rama. I have said this for our welfare. If it pleases you, act in accordance with it. O apes! This is proper and appropriate for all of us.'

Gandhamadana was suffering from thirst, exhaustion and dejection. Hearing Angada's words, he uttered these indistinct words. 'What Angada has spoken is indeed worthy of him. These words are beneficial and appropriate. Let us act accordingly. Let us collectively again search out the route in the mountains, caves, boulders, desolate groves and the mountainous waterfalls, every such place. This is what the great-souled Sugriva instructed, to search all the forests and the impenetrable parts of the mountains.' At this, the extremely strong apes raised themselves again. They searched the southern direction, full of forests everywhere in the Vindhyas. The apes ascended a handsome silvery mountain that was like autumn clouds, with peaks and caverns. There was a beautiful grove of lodhra trees[291] there. There were groves of saptaparna trees too. Desiring to see Sita, the supreme apes searched all these spots. Though extensive in their valour, when they ascended the peak, they were exhausted. However, they could not see Vaidehi, Rama's beloved queen. The apes looked around everywhere. As they descended, they cast their eyes on the many caves on that mountain, as far as the eye could see. Exhausted and senseless, they descended on the flat ground. For a while, they stayed there, near the root of a tree. For a while, they suspended their exertions and comforted themselves. Then they rose up again and searched all the routes in the southern direction. With Hanumat as the foremost, the bulls among the apes started again. Beginning with the Vindhyas, they searched in all the directions.

Chapter 4(49)

With Tara and Angada, the ape Hanumat searched the caves and the desolate spots of the Vindhyas. In every direction,

[291] The lotus bark tree.

there were caves full of lions and tigers. There were uneven places on that king of the mountains and giant waterfalls. While they resided there, the time elapsed.[292] With large caves and impenetrable spots, that region was extremely difficult to search. However, Vayu's son[293] searched everywhere on that mountain. Gaja, Gavaksha, Gavaya, Sharabha, Gandhamadana, Mainda, Dvivida, Hanumat, Jambavat, Prince Angada and Tara, who roamed around in the forests, were not together. But they were not far from each other either. The routes along that spot in the southern direction were covered with a range of mountains. Hungry, thirsty and exhausted, they wished for some water. Then they saw a large cave that was shrouded with creepers and trees. Curlews, swans and cranes emerged from inside this. There were chakravaka birds, wet with water, their limbs red with pollen from lotuses. They approached that fragrant cave, which was extremely difficult to reach. The bulls among apes were amazed, but also anxious in their minds. Though those excellent, immensely strong and energetic apes were delighted,[294] they were also suspicious of drawing near that cave. Hanumat, the son of the wind god, possessed the complexion of a mountain peak. He was accomplished about caves and desolate plains. He told the terrible apes, 'The routes in this region of the southern direction are covered with a range of mountains. All of us are exhausted and we have not been able to see Maithilee. From every direction, swans, curlews, cranes and chakravakas wet with water are emerging. There is undoubtedly water here, from a well or from a lake. That is the reason there are gentle trees at the entrance to this cave.'

Thus addressed, all of them entered that cave, which was covered in darkness. The apes saw that there was no moon or sun there and this made their body hair stand up. That impenetrable cave was full of many kinds of trees. Holding on to each other, they entered one yojana inside. Their senses were disturbed. They were thirsty and frightened, craving water. Attentive, for some time, they leapt around inside that cave. The faces of the apes were lean and distressed. They were exhausted. As those brave ones lost hope of remaining alive,

[292] The time set by Sugriva for the search.

[293] Hanumat.

[294] Because there was water inside the cave.

they saw a light. The amiable ones approached that region, where the forest was devoid of darkness. They saw some golden trees that blazed like a flaming fire. There were sala, tala, punnaga, vanjula, dhava, champaka, nagavriksha and flowering karnikara trees. They seemed to be like sacrificial altars made out of lapis lazuli, resembling the rising sun. There were lakes full of lotuses that had the complexion of blue lapis lazuli, teeming with birds. The place was surrounded by large golden trees that were like the rising sun in complexion. There were fish and large turtles that were made of molten gold. They saw lakes full of lotuses, with sparkling water. There were mansions made out of gold and silver. These had windows fashioned out of molten gold, covered with nets of pearls. There were many storeys made out of gold and silver, decorated with lapis lazuli and gems. Everywhere there, the apes saw the best of residences. The trees were covered with flowers and fruits that had the complexion of coral and jewels. There was honey in every direction, with golden bees. There were colourful and large couches and seats made out of gems and gold. In every direction, they saw extremely expensive vehicles. There were heaps of vessels, made out of gold, silver and brass. There were heaps of divine aloe and sandalwood. There was auspicious food, roots and fruits. There were extremely expensive drinks and succulent honey. There were piles of extremely expensive and divine garments. There were colourful carpets and piles of deerskin. They searched here and there in that extremely radiant cave. Not very far away, the brave apes saw a woman. On seeing her, clad in bark and black antelope skin, they were extremely terrified. The ascetic lady was restrained in her diet and blazed because of her energy. Hanumat, with a complexion like that of a mountain, joined his hands in salutation and honoured the aged one. He asked, 'Who are you? Whom do these residences, the cave and the jewels belong to? Tell us.'

Chapter 4(50)

The immensely fortunate ascetic, clad in black antelope skin, was one who acted in accordance with dharma. Having spoken,

Hanumat spoke to her again. 'We suddenly entered this cave, enveloped in darkness. We were hungry, tired and exhausted and suffering in every possible way. Thirsty, we entered this gigantic hole in the ground. There are many kinds of attributes here and many kinds of wonderful signs. On seeing these, we are distressed and scared, deprived of our senses. Whom do these golden trees, which are like the rising sun in complexion, belong to? There is auspicious food, roots and fruits. There are golden vimanas and houses made out of silver. The windows are made out of molten gold and are covered with nets of jewels. Whose energy has led to these trees that are fashioned out of molten gold? They are sacred, with excellent fragrances. They bear flowers and fruit. Golden lotuses have been generated in the sparkling waters. How did it happen that golden fish and turtles are seen to roam around? Whose strength of austerities has resulted in this? Is it your own? We do not know anything about this. You should tell us everything.'

The ascetic lady who followed dharma was addressed by Hanumat in this way. Engaged in the welfare of all creatures, she replied to Hanumat. 'There is an immensely energetic bull among danavas named Maya.[295] He is accomplished in maya. He used his maya to construct everything in this golden forest. Earlier, this foremost among danavas was like Vishvakarma. He is the one who has fashioned these golden, divine and excellent mansions. In the great forest, he tormented himself through austerities for one thousand years. He obtained a boon from the grandfather that he would obtain all the riches of Ushanas.[296] Using all his strength, the lord[297] then arranged for all the objects of desire. For some time, he dwelt happily in this great forest. When that bull among danavas was engaged with an apsara named Hema, the lord Purandara used the valour of his vajra to slay him. Brahma then bestowed this excellent forest, with its eternal objects of desire and pleasure and these golden residences, on Hema. I am Svayamprabha and I

[295] The architect of the demons, just as Vishvakarma is of the gods.

[296] The grandfather is Brahma. Ushanas is Shukracharya, the preceptor of the demons. Thus, Brahma gave Maya the boon that we would be able to take away the riches of the preceptor of the demons.

[297] Maya.

am the daughter of Meru Savarni. O excellent ape! I guard Hema's residence. Hema is my beloved friend and is accomplished in singing and dancing. She granted me a boon that I should protect her great residence.[298] What is your task? What is the reason why you have come to this desolate region? How did you notice this impenetrable forest? Eat this auspicious food, the roots and the fruits. Drink. Thereafter, you should tell me everything.'

Chapter 4(51)

When all the leaders of the apes had rested, the ascetic lady, who single-mindedly followed dharma, addressed them in these words. 'O apes! If your exhaustion has been destroyed after eating these fruits, if you think I am capable of listening to it, I wish to hear about your account.'

Hearing her words, Hanumat, the son of the wind god, started to honestly tell her about the truth. 'Rama is the king of all the worlds and he is like the great Indra and Varuna. He is handsome and is Dasharatha's son. With his brother, Lakshmana, and his wife, Vaidehi, he entered Dandaka forest. Using his strength, Ravana abducted his wife from Janasthana. His[299] friend is the ape, King Sugriva. He is foremost among the apes and that king has sent us here, towards the southern direction, traversed by Agastya and protected by Yama. There are other foremost apes with us, Angada and the others. Ravana and all the rakshasas can assume any form at will. He[300] instructed all of us to collectively find out the route that Sita has taken. We have searched everything in the southern direction. Since all of us were hungry and exhausted, we sought refuge near the root of a tree. With pale faces, all of us started to meditate. Despite being thus immersed, we could not reach the other shore in this great ocean

[298] Though not stated clearly, Hema must have gone away to heaven after this. Indeed, she may have been sent by Indra to seduce Maya.

[299] Rama's.

[300] Sugriva.

of our thoughts. As we cast our eyes around, we saw this great cave. It was shrouded in creepers and trees and was enveloped in darkness. Swans, kingfishers, cranes and other birds were emerging from it. They were wet and their feathers were covered with drops of water. I told all the apes, "Let us enter." All of them had also deduced that this was a right course of action. Having decided to enter, we speedily set about our task. Clutching to each other's hands, we descended into the deep cave. We suddenly entered this cave, enveloped in darkness. In accomplishing our task, this is how we have managed to come here. Extremely distressed and hungry, that is how we arrived before you. Following the dharma towards a guest, you gave us roots and fruits. Suffering from hunger, we have devoured all of this. We were about to die from hunger and you have saved all of us. Tell us. What can we apes do in return to possibly pay you back?'

Svayamprabha knew everything and was thus addressed by the apes. She replied to all the leaders among the apes. 'I have followed my dharma and there is nothing that needs to be done for me. I am content that the spirited apes have been satisfied.'

Chapter 4(52)

The ascetic lady, full of dharma, addressed them in these auspicious words. Thereupon, Hanumat spoke to the one with the unblemished sight in these words. 'O one who follows dharma! All of us are seeking refuge with you. The great-souled Sugriva set a time period for us. While we have been roaming around inside this cave, that period has passed. You should rescue us from this cave. Even otherwise, since we have transgressed Sugriva's words, our lifespans are over. We are suffering from fear on account of Sugriva and you should save us. O one who follows dharma! There is a great task that we have to perform. We will not be able to perform that task if we are constrained to reside here.'

Addressed by Hanumat, the ascetic lady replied in these words. 'I think that a person who has entered cannot possibly return alive.

However, I have earned great powers because of my austerities and rituals. Using these, I am capable of saving all the apes from this cave. O bulls among apes! Close your eyes. I am incapable of saving you as long as your eyes are open.' All of them closed their eyes and covered them with their delicate fingers and hands. Desiring to leave, they cheerfully closed their eyes instantly. The great-souled apes had covered their faces with their hands. In the twinkling of an eye, they were raised out of the cave. The ascetic lady, the one who followed dharma, spoke to all of them and comforted them, after they had been taken out of that uneven region. 'This is the handsome Vindhya mountain, covered with many trees and creepers. There is the great Mount Prasravana and there is the great ocean.[301] O bulls among apes! May you be fortunate. I will return to my residence.' Saying this, the beautiful Svayamprabha entered the cave.

They saw the terrible ocean, Varuna's abode. Full of terrible and turbulent waves, it raged and the other shore could not be seen. The king had set a time period of one month. But in searching in the mountainous caves and the cave constructed through Maya's maya, this period had elapsed. At the foot of Mount Vindhya, there was a flowering tree. The great-souled ones sat down there and were immersed in their thoughts. They saw trees that were typical of the spring season and were filled with fear and dread. They were laden with flowers and the tops were covered with hundreds of creepers. They told each other that the spring season had arrived.[302] Realizing that the time for conveying the news was over, they fell down on the ground. The prince, the ape Angada, was immensely wise, with thick and long arms and shoulders like that of a lion or a bull. He spoke these words. 'All of us followed the instructions of the king of the apes and left. O apes! Do you not realize that we spent an entire month inside the cave? Meanwhile, the time that Sugriva had himself set has elapsed. All of us, who reside in the forest, should now undertake

[301] Both could be seen from the spot where they emerged.

[302] Deductions are possible about the timeline. Sugriva summoned the armies in Margashirsha, November–December. The month of Pushya, December–January, was fixed for their return. They spent around one month, January–February in the cave. Hence, the spring season is near.

an act of praya. Sugriva's nature is innately fierce and he has now obtained the status of our lord. Since we have committed a crime, he will not pardon all of us. Since we have not brought back tidings of Sita, he will certainly commit this injury. Therefore, it is better that we now engage in praya. Before we return and the king kills all of us, let us abandon our sons, our wives, our riches and our residences. This death is like being killed and is superior to that act. I have not been consecrated as the heir apparent by Sugriva. Rama, Indra among men and the performer of unblemished deeds, has consecrated me. The king is already tied to me with bonds of enmity. On seeing that I have transgressed, he will make up his mind to fiercely chastise me and kill me. When my life comes to an end, what is the point of my well-wishers witnessing my hardships? I will resort to praya on the shores of this auspicious ocean.' The prince, the heir apparent, spoke these words. Hearing this, all the best among apes addressed him in these piteous words. 'Sugriva is fierce in nature and Raghava is devoted to his beloved. We have been unable to see Vaidehi and the time set for seeing her has elapsed. Since we have been unable to accomplish what would have brought Raghava pleasure, there is no doubt that we will be killed. When we reach the side of our master, our crime will not be pardoned.' The apes were afflicted by fear. On hearing their words, Tara said, 'Enough of this misery. If it appeals to all of you, let us enter the cave and reside there. This has been constructed by Maya and is extremely difficult to penetrate. There are many trees and there is a lot of water. There is plenty to eat and drink. There is no fear here, not even from Purandara, nor from Raghava and the king of the apes.' Hearing these words, which were similar to what Angada had said, all the apes accepted this and said, 'This is a means whereby we will not be killed. Let us act in this way now.'

Chapter 4(53)

When Tara spoke in this way, Hanumat thought that this was tantamount to Angada robbing the kingdom of Tara's radiant lord.[303] Hanumat thought that Vali's son possessed the eight kinds of intelligence, the four kinds of forces and the fourteen qualities.[304] He was always full of energy, strength and valour. His prosperity waxed, like that of the moon from the first day of shukla paksha. He was Brihaspati's equal in intelligence and his father's equal in valour. He was now listening to Tara, like Purandara had once done to Shukra.[305] Though he was accomplished in all the sacred texts, he was now exhausted in an attempt to accomplish his master's objective. Therefore, Hanumat started to placate him. Using his wealth in the use of words, from among the four modes, he used the third one of bheda to wean away all the other apes.[306] When all the others were weaned away, he used the fourth mode to scare Angada. He addressed him in many terrible words that were filled with rage. 'O Tara's son! You can bear burdens and you are more capable than your father in fighting. You are certainly capable of firmly bearing the burden of the kingdom of the apes, just as your father was. O bull among apes! Apes are always fickle in their understanding. Separated from their sons and their wives, they will not tolerate your commands for a long time. They will not follow you and I am telling you what is evident. That is what will happen with Jambavat, Nila and the great ape, Suhotra. Nor will I follow you. Using the qualities of sama, dana and qualities like danda, you will not be able to wean us away from Sugriva. It is said that a

[303] Taaraa's radiant lord, that is, Sugriva. Hanumat thought that this was tantamount to Angada challenging Sugriva's authority as a king.

[304] The eight kinds of intelligence are attentiveness, capacity to listen, capacity to grasp, capacity to remember, ability to discriminate, ability to ascertain the truth, deep understanding and a capacity to distinguish between good action and bad action. The four kinds of forces are usually infantry, cavalry, elephants and chariots. But here, it probably means the capacity to selectively use *sama, dana, bheda* and danda. The fourteen qualities are knowing about time and place, fortitude, endurance, capacity to think of all the consequences, skill, self-defence, an ability to keep one's counsel secret, avoidance of pointless debates, courage, a capacity to identify the strengths and weaknesses, faith, an ability to shelter those who seek refuge, the ability to show anger at the right time and a capacity to steadfastly pursue a course of action.

[305] The preceptor of the demons.

[306] He used dissension to wean away all the other apes from Angada's decision. He then used the fourth one of danda to frighten Angada.

person who is weak should not take on someone who is stronger. Protect yourself and do not listen to these weak ones. You think and you have been told that this cave in the ground is safe. Lakshmana's arrows are easily capable of shattering it. In ancient times, it was created when Indra lightly hurled his vajra at it. Lakshmana's sharp arrows will shatter it, like a cup made out of leaves. Lakshmana possesses many kinds of sharp and iron arrows. O scorcher of enemies! If you decide to settle down here, all the apes will make up their minds to desert you. They will always remember their sons and their wives and will be anxious and hungry. They will regret it and sleep in misery. They will turn their backs on you. You will then be deprived of your well-wishers and the friends who desire what is beneficial for you. You will be extremely anxious and will tremble, even at the sight of a blade of grass. A person whom Lakshmana's terrible arrows cannot injure hasn't been born. They are extremely forceful and impossible to withstand. When they seek to kill, one cannot step aside. If you return with us and present yourself humbly and tell Sugriva everything that has happened, from the beginning, he will establish you in the kingdom. Your uncle loves dharma. He is firm in his vows and desires to be affectionate. He is pure and truthful to his pledges. He will let you live and will not kill you. He is affectionate towards your mother and wishes to do what is agreeable to her. He is alive only for her sake. He has no offspring other than you. O Angada! Therefore, let us go to him.'

Chapter 4(54)

He heard Hanumat's polite words, which were in conformity with dharma and were full of respect towards their lord.[307] However, Angada spoke these words. 'Stability in every respect of one's being, purity, non-violence, uprightness, valour and patience are not discernible in Sugriva. When his elder brother was still

[307] Sugriva.

alive, his beloved queen and wife, following dharma, was like a mother to him. But he desired her and seized her as his own. When his brother was fighting inside the hole and instated him at the entrance, he abandoned him. How can such an evil-souled one know dharma? Grasping his hand in a pledge of truth, the immensely illustrious Raghava performed a good deed for him. He forgot that. What other good deed will he remember? The coward has not been scared of adharma. He has commanded us to seek out Sita's path because he was terrified of Lakshmana. How will he follow dharma? He is wicked and ungrateful. He and his memory are both fickle. Which person, born in a noble lineage, who wishes to remain alive, will trust him as one who is noble? A son must be established in the kingdom, whether he possesses qualities or does not possess qualities. Therefore, how can Sugriva permit someone like me, born from his enemy, to remain alive? My advisers have been weaned away.[308] I have committed a crime. Who is as inferior in strength as I am? Even if I reach Kishkindha and remain alive, I will be weak and without a protector. He may punish me in secret ways. He may bind me up. For the sake of the kingdom, Sugriva can be deceitful, cruel and violent. Resorting to praya is superior to bondage and suffering. O apes! All of you have my permission to return to your houses. I am informing all of you that I will not return to the city. I will resort to praya here. That kind of death is superior for me. First greet the king and ask about his welfare. Then speak to my younger father, Sugriva, the lord of the apes. Speak words to my mother, Ruma, and first ask her if she is well. You should then ask about my mother, Tara, and reassure her. That ascetic lady naturally loves her son and will not be angry. On hearing that I have been destroyed, it is evident that she will also not remain alive.' He spoke these words to the aged ones and greeted them. Distressed in his mind, Angada lay down on the darbha grass that was spread around there. When he lay down there, the bulls among the apes started to weep. Since they were miserable, warm tears started to flow from their eyes. They

[308] From the idea of living in the cave.

censured Sugriva and praised Vali. All of them surrounded Angada and decided to engage in praya. The bulls among the apes got to know the words that Vali's son had spoken. All of them touched water and sat down, facing the eastern direction. The tips of the darbha faced the southern direction and they were on the shores of the water. Those apes, who were like the peaks of mountains, lay down there, having traversed many mountains and stepped through many caverns inside them. The salty ocean roared, like terrible thunder clouds.

Chapter 4(55)

On the slope of the mountain, all the apes sat down in an act of praya. At that time, a king of the eagles arrived at the spot. His name was Sampati and he was a bird who lived for a long time.[309] He was handsome and renowned because of his strength and manliness. He was Jatayu's elder brother. He emerged from a cave in the great mountain of Vindhya. He saw the apes seated there. Cheerful in his heart, he spoke to them. 'Destiny decides and all men in this world have to follow destiny. I have been waiting for food for a long time and destiny has presented itself before me. I will eat these apes one after another, as they progressively die.'[310] Having spoken these words, the bird glanced at the apes. The bird desired food and on hearing his words, Angada became supremely anxious. He spoke to Hanumat. 'Behold. As if on Sita's command, Vaivasvata Yama seems to have presented himself before us. He has arrived at this spot to cause a calamity to the apes. We have not accomplished Rama's task. We have not followed the king's instructions. While we did not know it, this calamity for the apes has suddenly presented itself before us. Jatayu, the king of the eagles, performed a good deed in a desire to bring pleasure

[309] Alternatively, lived for ever.

[310] Alternatively, kill them one after another, as opposed to their dying naturally.

to Vaidehi. We heard the complete details about it there. All creatures, even those born as inferior species, are doing what brings pleasure to Rama and are giving up their lives, just as we are about to. We have abandoned all thought of our lives and are exhausted, trying to accomplish Raghava's objective. We traversed through all the desolate areas, but did not see Maithilee. The king of the eagles who was slain by Ravana in the battle is happy. Freed from all fear of Sugriva, he has attained the supreme destination. After the destruction of Jatayu and King Dasharatha, and Vaidehi's abduction, all the apes face an uncertain situation.[311] Rama and Lakshmana resided in the forest with Sita. Raghava killed Vali with an arrow. All the rakshasas were slain because of Rama's rage.[312] Because of the boon given to Kaikeyee, all these catastrophes have come about.'

Hearing the words that had emerged out of Angada's mouth, the eagle with the sharp beak uttered these words in a loud and rumbling voice. 'Who has spoken these words, making my mind tremble? I love my brother, Jatayu, more than my own life. Who has announced his death? How did this encounter between the rakshasa and the eagle happen in Janasthana? I have heard my brother's name mentioned today, after a long period of time. He is younger to me and possesses all the qualities. His valour is praiseworthy. O bulls among the apes! That is the reason I wish to hear about his destruction. My brother, Jatayu, was a resident of Janasthana. How is Dasharatha, my brother's friend? His eldest son, Rama, loves his seniors and the people, and is loved by him.[313] Since my wings have been scorched by the rays of the sun, I am incapable of stretching them.[314] O destroyers of enemies! Therefore, I wish that you should lower me from this mountain.'

[311] There are several implicit statements in the argument. Had Dasharatha not died, Rama might have been recalled from the exile. Had Jatayu not died, he might have been able to prevent Ravana, or at least tell the apes about where Ravana had taken Sita. Had Sita not been abducted, none of this would have happened.

[312] In Dandakaranya.

[313] Dasharatha.

[314] The story follows later.

Chapter 4(56)

The leaders of the apes heard his words, which wavered because of his sorrow.[315] Though they honoured his words, they were unsure about their course of action.[316] Seated in the act of praya, the apes saw the eagle. They then decided, 'This terrible one will not devour all of us. In any event, if he eats us, we are seated in praya in every possible way. What is going to occur will happen and we will speedily obtain success.' Having made up their minds in this way, all the bulls among the apes lowered the eagle from the peak of the mountain.

Angada spoke to him. 'There was a powerful Indra among the apes and his name was Riksharaja.[317] O bird! The noble king had two sons who were devoted to dharma. These sons were Sugriva and Vali and they possessed intelligence and strength. King Vali, famous in the worlds because of his deeds, was my father. There is a maharatha in the lineage of the Ikshvakus and he is the king of the entire earth. This is the handsome Rama, Dasharatha's son, and he entered the forest of Dandaka, with his brother, Lakshmana, and his wife, Vaidehi. He did this because of his father's command and because he always resorts to the path of dharma. His wife was forcibly abducted from Janasthana by Ravana. The king of the eagles, named Jatayu, was the friend of Rama's father. He saw that Sita Vaidehi was being abducted through the sky. He deprived Ravana of his chariot and rescued Maithilee. However, he was exhausted and aged and was slain in the battle by Ravana. This is the way the eagle was killed by a stronger Ravana. After Rama performed his funeral rites, he reached the supreme destination. After this, Raghava contracted an act of friendship with my uncle, the great-souled Sugriva, and killed my father. Since he had acted against my father, he had bound up Sugriva and his advisers. However, having slain Vali, Rama consecrated him as the king. Sugriva was

[315] At the news of Jatayu's death.

[316] In case the eagle ate them.

[317] Here, the text uses the word Raksharaja.

instated in the kingdom, as the lord of the apes. The king, foremost among the apes, dispatched all of us. Having been thus engaged by Rama, we thus searched the routes here and there. But we could not find Vaidehi, just as the radiance of the sun is unreachable during the night. Controlling ourselves, we searched everywhere in Dandakaranya. In our ignorance, we entered a cave that extended inside the ground. We searched in that cave, constructed by Maya through his use of maya. The month that the king had decreed for us passed in that way. All of us are engaged in acting in accordance with the commands of the king of the apes. Since the contracted period was over, we were terrified and have resolved to fast and undertake praya. Kakutstha, Sugriva and Lakshmana will be angry with us if we return there. Therefore, no purpose is served by us remaining alive.'

Chapter 4(57)

The apes, who were ready to give up their lives, spoke these piteous words. The voices of the apes choked with tears. The eagle replied in a loud voice. 'O apes! My brother, named Jatayu, is younger to me. He is the one who has been spoken about, as having been killed by a stronger Ravana in the encounter. Though I cannot tolerate what I have heard, I am aged and do not possess any wings. I do not possess the strength now to save my brother from his enemy. Earlier, when Vritra was killed, the two of us wished to rival each other.[318] We approached the sun, blazing in its garland of rays. With a terrible speed, we travelled through the sky and covered it, reaching the sun at midday. Jatayu began to suffer. I saw that my brother was suffering because of the rays of the sun and became extremely anxious. Out of affection, I covered him with my wings. O bulls among the apes! When my wings were burnt, I fell down on the Vindhyas. While I resided here, I

[318] Sampati and Jatayu had a friendly contest about who could fly closer to the sun.

no longer noticed what my brother was up to.' Sampati, Jatayu's brother, said this.

The immensely wise Prince Angada replied. 'If Jatayu was your brother, you have heard what I have said. If you know about the residence of that rakshasa, tell us about it. Ravana, the lord of the rakshasas, does not possess foresight. Whether he lives nearby, or far away, if you know, tell us.'

Jatayu's elder brother was immensely energetic. Thus addressed, he spoke words that were worthy of him and delighted the apes. 'O apes! I am an eagle whose wings have been burnt. My valour has been lost. But even then, through my words, I will render excellent help to Rama. I know the world of Varuna and that of Vishnu of the three strides.[319] I know about the clash between the gods and the asuras and the churning of amrita.[320] I am the first one who will perform a task in accomplishing this objective of Rama's. However, I am aged and am robbed of my energy. My breath of life is ebbing away. I saw a young lady being abducted by the evil-souled Ravana. She was beautiful and was adorned in all the ornaments. The beautiful one shrieked, "Alas, Rama! Rama! Alas, Lakshmana!" As she writhed, she flung away the ornaments from her limbs. Her excellent silken garment was like the dazzle of the sun on the summit of a mountain. On that dark rakshasa, she was as radiant as lightning on a cloud. Since she spoke of Rama, I think that she must have been Sita. Listen, as I tell you where the residence of that rakshasa is. He is the son of Vishravasa himself and Vaishravana's[321] brother. The rakshasa named Ravana rules over the city of Lanka. This island[322] is in the ocean and is a full one hundred yojanas from here. The beautiful city of Lanka was constructed by Vishvakarma. The miserable Vaidehi, attired in

319 A reference to the dwarf incarnation. Vishnu's third stride was in the nether regions.

320 Amrita was obtained through the churning of the ocean, and the gods and the demons fought over it.

321 Kubera's.

322 The word used is dvipa. While dvipa does mean island, it is also a term that can be used for any geographical region.

silken garments, resides there. She is confined to Ravana's inner quarters and is guarded well by rakshasis. You will see Maithilee, King Janaka's daughter, there. On all sides, Lanka is protected by the ocean. When you reach the shores of the ocean, it is a full one hundred yojanas from there. When you reach the other side of the southern shore, you will see Ravana. O apes! You should hurry and quickly exhibit your valour. Through my knowledge, I can see that you will return. The first path is for *kulinga*s and others who live on grain.[323] The second is for those who survive on leftovers of sacrifices[324] and those who eat the fruits of trees.[325] The third is travelled by predatory birds, curlews and ospreys. Hawks reach the fourth level and eagles travel along the fifth. The sixth path is for swans that possess strength and valour and also have youth and beauty. However, the descendants of Vinata can go beyond this. O bulls among apes! All of us have been born from Vinata. The one who survives on flesh has perpetrated a reprehensible deed. From here, I can see Ravana and Janakee. Golden ones like us possess the divine power of eyesight. O apes! Therefore, because of our food, valour and lineage, we can always see anything up to one hundred yojanas, as if it is right in front of us. For those born in our lineage, it has been ordained that our subsistence should be through what is far away. For those who fight with their feet,[326] it has been ordained that their subsistence will be found near their feet. Think of a means so that you can leap over the salty waters. You will then reach Vaidehi and be successful in accomplishing your objective. I desire that you should convey me to the ocean, Varuna's abode. I wish to offer the water rites to my great-souled brother who has gone to heaven.'

At this, the extremely energetic apes took Sampati, whose wings had been burnt, to a spot near the shore of the lord of the male and female rivers. After this, they again brought the lord of the birds

[323] The first level of flight, lower down. Kulingas are sparrows and shrikes.

[324] Specifically, leftovers of meat offerings, such as crows.

[325] Like parrots.

[326] Like cocks.

back to the original spot. The apes were delighted on realizing that they might be successful.

Chapter 4(58)

The words of the king of the eagles were like a taste of amrita. On hearing his words, the bulls among the apes were delighted and rejoiced. With Jambavat, foremost among the apes, all the apes quickly arose from the ground and spoke to the king of the eagles. 'Where is Sita? Who saw her? Who abducted Maithilee? Tell us everything and thereby offer an indication to us, those who reside in the forest. Who will be brought down by the arrows of Dasharatha's son, which possess the force of the vajra? Who will be singled out by the valour of Lakshmana's own releases?' The apes had collectively composed themselves, wishing to hear about Sita.

He was delighted at this and again reassuring them, he addressed them in these words. 'Listen to how I heard about Vaidehi's abduction and about who told me where the large-eyed one is. For a long time, I have been on this impenetrable mountainous region that extends for many yojanas. I fell down. I am aged. My valour and breath of life have decayed. When I attained this state, my son named Suparshva, supreme among birds, sustained me by providing me food at the right time. Gandharvas are fiercely addicted to desire. Serpents are fiercely addicted to rage. Deer are fiercely addicted to fear. Like that, we are fiercely addicted to hunger. On one occasion, I was afflicted by hunger and desired some food. The day was over and the sun had set. But my son did not bring me any flesh. Because of sentiments associated with age, I censured him in my rage. I was overwhelmed by hunger and thirst. I was deprived of food and suffering. But my son, supreme among birds and the extender of my delight, entreated me. He told me the truth and addressed me in these words. "O father! In search of flesh, at the right time, I did fly up into the sky. I stationed myself properly at the entry to Mount Mahendra. There are thousands of creatures there, roaming around the shore of the ocean. With my glance lowered, I stationed myself there, obstructing one of those paths. At that time, I saw something that was like the radiance of the sun when it rises. Seizing a woman, he was advancing, like a mass of broken collyrium.[327] On seeing the two of them, I made up my mind that they could be food. However, using conciliation and humility, he pleaded that I should provide a path for them. There is no one on earth who strikes those who resort to conciliation, not even those who are inferior people. How could someone with limbs like mine not have yielded? With his energy and force, he departed, as if flinging the sky aside. At this, the creatures who roam around in the sky and on earth approached me and praised me. O father! The maharshis told me, 'It is through good fortune that Sita is alive. The wife has been taken away in some way. But there is no doubt that she will be safe.' The siddhas, supremely handsome, addressed me in this way. They also told me about Ravana, the king of the rakshasas. They showed me the ornaments that Janaka's daughter, the wife of Rama, Dasharatha's son, had flung away, with her dishevelled silken garments. She had been vanquished by the force of her grief. With her hair loose, she had wailed, mentioning the names of Rama and Lakshmana. O father! That is the reason the time passed." Suparshva, supreme among those who are eloquent in the use of words, told me everything about all this. Even after I heard this, my mind did not turn to thoughts of exhibiting valour. How can a bird like me, without any wings, undertake any such endeavour? Possessing the qualities of speech and intelligence, I have done all that I am capable of doing. Having heard what I have told you, you must now resort to your virility. With my speech and my intelligence, I have done what should bring you pleasure. You have a task to perform for Dasharatha's son and there is no doubt that it is mine too. You are supreme in intelligence. You are strong and spirited. That is the reason the king of the apes has sent you.

[327] We have earlier been told that it was Sampati himself who saw Ravana and Sita. This chapter makes it a second-hand account, through Suparshva. There are other inconsistencies too.

Even the gods will find it impossible to withstand you. Rama and Lakshmana's sharp arrows are shafted with the feathers of herons. They are sufficient to save, or chastise, the three worlds. Dashagriva is indeed addicted to desire and he possesses energy and strength. However, you are capable and there is nothing that you will find difficult to accomplish. We have spent enough time together. Now make up your minds about what is to be done. Intelligent people like you should not delay in accomplishing the task.'

Chapter 4(59)

The eagle offered the water rites and bathed. On that beautiful mountain, the leaders of the apes surrounded him from every direction and seated themselves. Angada was seated, with all the apes surrounding him. Delighted that he had won their trust, Sampati spoke again. 'O apes! Be silent and listen attentively to me. I will recount the truth about how I came to know about Maithilee. O unblemished one![328] Earlier I fell down on the summit of Vindhya. My limbs suffered because of the heat of the sun and I was burnt by the rays of the sun. Though I regained my senses after six nights, I was unconscious and senseless. I glanced in all the directions, but could not identify anything. On looking at the oceans, mountains, all the rivers and lakes and the regions in the forests, I got my intelligence back. The caves inside the mountain were filled with a large number of cheerful birds. I made up my mind that this was Vindhya, on the shores of the southern ocean. There was a sacred hermitage there, extremely revered by even the gods. It belonged to the rishi named Nishakara, who was fierce in his austerities. Nishakara, who knew about dharma, went to heaven. But even without the rishi, I resided there for eight thousand years. Through that uneven terrain, I slowly descended from the summit of Vindhya with difficulty. I found my way through the

[328] In the singular, therefore, specifically addressed to Angada.

sharp darbha grass with hardship and again reached the ground. I desired to see the rishi and was therefore full of great misery. Jatayu and I had gone to him on several occasions. Many kinds of fragrant breezes blow through the spot where his hermitage is located. Trees without flowers are never seen there, nor those without fruits. I reached the sacred hermitage and found refuge at the foot of a tree. I waited there, desiring to see the illustrious Nishakara. From a distance, I saw the rishi, blazing in his energy. After performing his ablutions, the unassailable one was returning, his face turned towards the north. Bears, antelopes, tigers, lions and many kinds of reptiles surrounded him and followed him, like living beings follow the granter of life.[329] On knowing that the rishi had returned, all the creatures followed him, just as all the ministers and soldiers follow when a king returns. On seeing me, the rishi was content and entered his hermitage again. However, he emerged in an instant and asked me the reason why I was there. "O amiable one! I can see that you are disabled and your body hair cannot be seen. Your wings have been burnt by the fire. There are wounds on your skin. I have seen two eagles earlier and they were like the wind god in their speed. Those two brothers could assume any form at will and were kings among the eagles. O Sampati! You were the elder and Jatayu was your younger brother. You used to assume the form of men and touch my feet. What disease has come over you? How did your wings fall off? Who has punished you in this way? Tell me everything that I have asked you about."'

Chapter 4(60)

'At this, I told the sage about the extremely terrible act, extremely difficult to accomplish, that I had done in my rashness, about the attempt to follow the sun. "O illustrious one! I am wounded. I am ashamed and my senses are distracted. I

[329] Brahma.

am exhausted and am incapable of addressing you in words. I and Jatayu were confounded and insolent, seeking to compete against each other. Wishing to test our valour, we flew a long distance up into the sky. In front of the sages who were there on the summit of Kailasa, we had staked a bet. We would follow the sun, until it set behind the giant Mount Asta. Together, we flew up and could see the surface of the earth below, with separate cities that looked as large as the wheels of chariots. We could hear musical instruments being sounded in some places, chants of the brahman in others. We heard women singing. They looked like fires in their red garments. We rose quickly up into the sky and stationed ourselves in the path of the sun. We could see the forest, as if it was just a patch of grass. The earth, with its tall mountains, was seen to be covered, as if with pebbles. The earth was covered with rivers, as if threaded with strings. The Himalayas, Vindhya and the extremely gigantic mountain of Meru could be seen on the surface of the earth, resembling serpents inside a waterbody. We sweated profusely and were filled with repentance and fear. We were overwhelmed with confusion and suffered from terrible unconsciousness. We could not make out the Yamya, Agneya or Varuni directions.[330] We seemed to be consumed by the fire, like the worlds being destroyed at the end of a yuga. After I made a great deal of effort, I could make out the radiance of the sun again. The sun appeared before us, with a size that was like that of the earth. Without taking my leave, Jatayu fell down on the ground. On seeing him do this, I too quickly freed myself from the sky. Since I protected him with my wings, Jatayu was not burnt. However, due to my carelessness, I was burnt and fell down, following the path of the wind. I suspected that Jatayu had fallen down in Janasthana. I was numbed and my wings were burnt. I fell down on the Vindhyas. I was deprived of my kingdom, my brother, my wings and my valour. I desired death through every means and flung myself down from the summit of the mountain."'

[330] Yamya is the south, Yama's direction. Agneya is the south-east, Agni's direction. Varuni is the west, Varuna's direction.

Chapter 4(61)[331]

'Weeping and extremely miserable, I told the best among sages this. Having reflected for a while, the illustrious one spoke to me. "You will again have small wings to replace your wings. You will also possess eyesight, the breath of life, valour and strength. In ancient times, I have heard about an extremely important task that must be accomplished. I have witnessed this through my austerities. I have heard about this and know about this. There is a king named Dasharatha and he is the extender of the lineage of the Ikshvakus. He will have an extremely energetic son named Rama. With his brother, Lakshmana, he will go to the forest. With truth as his valour, he will be appointed by his father to do this. The *nairitta*[332] named Ravana will abduct his wife from Janasthana. That Indra among rakshasas cannot be killed by gods or danavas. He will tempt Maithilee with objects of pleasure, food and succulent meals. However, immersed in her grief, the illustrious and extremely fortunate one will not enjoy any of this. Knowing this, Vasava will give Vaidehi supreme food. That food will be like amrita and even the gods find it extremely difficult to obtain this. On obtaining this food and on knowing that it has come from Indra, Maithilee will first place a little bit of it down on the ground, as an offering to Rama. 'If my husband is alive, with the lord Lakshmana, and even if he has attained divinity, let this food be rendered to them.' The apes, Rama's messengers, will be dispatched here. O bird! You must then tell them about Rama's queen. In any event, you must not leave this place. In this state, where will you go? If you wait for the right time and place, you will get your wings back. If I am so inclined, I can get you your wings back even now. However, you should remain here, to accomplish a task that will bring benefit to the worlds. You will indeed perform that task for those two princes, for the brahmanas, the gods, the sages and Vasava. I too wish to see the brothers,

[331] This entire chapter doesn't quite belong.

[332] Demon.

Rama and Lakshmana. However, I do not wish to remain alive for a long time and will give up my body."'[333]

Chapter 4(62)

'The one who was eloquent in the use of words spoke many other words. Encouraging me and instructing me, he entered his own hermitage. Extremely slowly, I crept down the caves on the mountain. I ascended Vindhya and waited for you to arrive. From then to now, a full one hundred years have passed.[334] Imbibing the sage's words in my heart, I have waited for the right time and place. After Nishakara went to heaven on his great journey, I have been tormented by remorse and have debated many kinds of things. My mind turned to killing myself, but the sage's words restrained me. The intelligence that he granted me made me preserve my life. That dispelled the grief, like a blazing flame of fire dispels darkness. I know about the valour of the evil-souled Ravana. That is the reason I did not use words to censure my son about not having saved Maithilee, when Sita was separated and he heard her lamenting. He did not do this, despite knowing about my affection for Dasharatha and about the beloved sons that had been born to him.'

As he spoke to the apes who were assembled around him, while those who roamed around in the forest looked on, his wings sprouted. He looked at the new wings sprouting on his body, with red feathers and obtained unmatched delight. He told the apes, 'This is because of the powers of maharshi Nishakara, immeasurable in his soul. The wings that were burnt down by the rays of the sun have reappeared again. I possessed valour in my youth. I can feel that strength and virility now. Make every kind of effort to search out Sita. The gain of my wings convinces me that you will also be successful in your objective.' Sampati, supreme among birds,

[333] Though not stated explicitly, Nishakara gave up his life.

[334] This is inconsistent with the one thousand years mentioned earlier.

said this to all the apes. He then flew up from the summit of that mountain, as if to test whether he could still fly up into the sky. Hearing his words, the tigers among the apes were delighted in their minds. They became eager to test their valour. The supreme among apes, with valour like that of the wind god, got their virility back. They were eager to search out the route travelled by Janaka's daughter. Desiring to head in that direction, they waited for the right moment.

Chapter 4(63)

Having been told by the king of the eagles, the apes leapt around. Like lions in their valour, they were filled with joy and roared. The apes had heard those undecaying words about Ravana from Sampati. Desiring to see Sita, they joyfully arrived at the ocean. Terrible in their valour, they travelled and arrived at that spot. It[335] was stationed there, like a giant mirror of the entire world. They approached the southern ocean from the northern direction. Together, the supreme among apes settled down there. There were many kinds of gigantic and malformed creatures that were sporting in the water. They were extremely large in form, with gaping mouths. It was turbulent with waves. It seemed to be asleep in parts, while other parts seemed to be sporting. In some places, there were masses of water that were as large as mountains. It was full of Indras among the danavas and those who resided in the nether regions. It made the body hair stand up and on seeing this, the elephants among the apes were distressed. The apes saw that the ocean was like the sky and was impossible to cross. All of them were instantly filled with grief and spoke about what could be done. Beholding the ocean, the army was miserable. Seeing that the apes were afflicted by fear, the supreme among apes[336] reassured them. 'Our task is not to grieve

[335] The ocean.
[336] Angada.

in our minds. Sorrowing is a grave sin. Grief destroys a man, just as an angry serpent destroys a child. If valour presents itself before a person, he cannot tolerate despair. A man who is inferior in his energy will not be able to accomplish his objective.'

With the apes, Angada spent the night there. Having met the aged apes, he again held consultations with all of them. The radiant standards of the apes surrounded Angada. It was as if an army of Maruts had surrounded Vasava. Who in that army of apes was capable of achieving the task, other than Vali's son, or Hanumat? Showing his respect to the aged apes and the soldiers, the handsome Angada, scorcher of enemies, spoke words that were full of meaning. 'Which immensely strong one can leap over the ocean now? Who will accomplish the task for Sugriva, the scorcher of enemies who does not deviate from his objective? O apes! Which brave one can leap across one hundred yojanas? Among all the leaders here, who is capable of freeing us from this great fear? Through whose favours will we accomplish our objective and return happily, seeing our wives, sons and homes again? Through whose favours will we cheerfully approach Rama, the immensely strong Lakshmana and the immensely strong Sugriva? If there is any ape who is capable of leaping across the ocean, let him quickly grant us the sacred dakshina of freedom from fear.' Hearing Angada's words, no one said anything. Everywhere, that army of apes seemed to be numbed. Angada, supreme among apes, again spoke to the apes. 'All of you are best among those who are strong. You are firm in your valour. You have been born in faultless lineages and have been repeatedly worshipped. No one has ever been able to restrain you from going anywhere. O bulls among apes! You should tell me. Who possesses the strength to travel there?'

Chapter 4(64)

All the supreme apes heard Angada's words. One by one, each of them spoke about the respective distances that they were capable of travelling—Gaja, Gavaksha, Gavaya, Sharabha, Gandhamadana, Mainda, Dvivida, Sushena and Jambavat. Gaja said, 'I can leap across ten yojanas.' Gavaksha said, 'I can leap across twenty yojanas.' The ape Gavaya told the apes who were there, 'O apes! I can travel thirty yojanas.' The ape Sharabha told the apes who were there, 'There is no doubt that I can travel forty yojanas.' The immensely energetic Gandhamadana told the apes, 'There is no doubt that I can travel fifty yojanas.' The ape Mainda told the apes who were there, 'I am capable of leaping across sixty yojanas.' The immensely energetic Dvivida replied, 'There is no doubt that I can travel seventy yojanas.' Sushena, supreme among apes, told the supreme among the apes, 'O bulls among apes! I can leap across eighty yojanas.' As they conversed, the eldest, Jambavat, showed all of them his respect and replied, 'Earlier, I possessed the valour required to travel. However, I have now reached the other shore of my age. Why should we be unable to go and ignore the task at hand? That is the task for which the king of the apes and Rama have made up their minds. Listen to the distance that I am capable of travelling now. There is no doubt that I can travel ninety yojanas.' Jambavat again spoke to the best among the apes. 'Indeed, I no longer possess the valour to travel beyond this point. Earlier, at the sacrifice of the great Bali, when the eternal Lord Vishnu was in his Trivikrama form, I once circumambulated him. But I am now aged and the valour of my leaps has been weakened. In my youth, my supreme strength was unmatched. Right now, there can be no dispute that I do not possess the capability to go beyond this point. Therefore, I am incapable of accomplishing the task beyond this point.'

Angada paid his respects to the immensely wise and great ape, Jambavat. He replied in words that were great in their import. 'I can travel this great distance of one hundred yojanas. However, I am not certain that I will possess the strength to return.' Jambavat, best among apes and accomplished in the use of words, told him, 'O supreme among apes and bears! Your strength in travelling is known. Why one hundred? If you so desire, it has been said that you are destined and capable of travelling one thousand yojanas and returning. O son![337] But the master must always send and never go himself. O supreme among apes! We are the ones who should be sent by you. You are instated as our master and we are the ones who must be protected by you. O scorcher of enemies! The roles of the master, those who have to be protected and the soldiers have been earmarked. O son! You must always protect those who have to be protected. O scorcher of enemies! You are the foundation for the task that has to be accomplished. The foundation of any task must be protected. That is good policy. When the foundation is tended to and possesses the qualities, flowers and fruits result. O one for whom truth is valour! You are the means to accomplish the task. O scorcher of enemies! You are the source. You possess intelligence and valour. O supreme among apes! You are my senior and are also the son of my senior. Seeking refuge in you, we are capable of accomplishing the objective.' The immensely wise and giant ape, Jambavat, spoke these words.

Vali's son, Angada, replied in these words. 'If I do not go and nor does any other bull among the apes, we will again have to undertake the task of praya. We cannot return to the intelligent lord of the apes with the message that we have been unsuccessful. In that event, I do not see any means of protecting our lives. The lord of the apes is excessive in his favours and his rage. If we go with the message that we have failed, we will head towards our destruction. There is no means other than to accomplish the task that is at hand. You should therefore think of a means whereby success can be brought about.' The brave bull among apes was addressed by Angada in this way. In reply, Jambavat spoke these excellent words to Angada. 'O brave one! This task of yours will not suffer in any way. I will urge the one through whom success can be ensured.' The best among the apes saw that Hanumat, supreme among the apes, was happily seated alone. The best among the apes urged him.

[337] The word used is tata.

Chapter 4(65)

The many hundreds and thousands of soldiers in the army of the apes were distressed. Jambavat saw this and spoke to Hanumat. 'O brave one! In the world of the apes, you are supreme in your knowledge of all the sacred texts. O Hanumat! Why are you seated alone, silent? Why are you not saying anything? O Hanumat! You are the equal of Sugriva, king of the apes. You are Rama and Lakshmana's equal in energy and strength. The immensely strong Garuda is the son of Arishtanemi and Vinata. He is famous and is supreme among all the birds. The immensely illustrious bird is immensely forceful. On several occasions, I have seen the immensely strong one pluck serpents out of the ocean. The strength of your arms is like the strength of his wings. You are not his inferior in valour and force. O supreme among apes! Among all creatures, you are special in your strength, intelligence, energy and spirit. Why are you not understanding this? The apsara Punjikasthala is famous and is best among all the apsaras. She is famous as Anjana, the wife of the ape Kesari. O son![338] She could assume any form at will.[339] But she was cursed that she would be born as a female ape. She was born as the daughter of the great-souled Kunjara, Indra among apes. As a female ape, she was beautiful in all her limbs. On one occasion, capable of assuming any form at will, she adopted the form of a woman, excellent in her youth. She roamed around on the summit of a mountain, like a streak of lightning in a cloud. She was adorned in wonderful garlands and ornaments, attired in extremely expensive silken garments. The large-eyed one's garments were yellow and sparkling, tinged with red. While she was located on the summit of the mountain, the wind god gently robbed her of those. The wind god saw her uncovered thighs, which were well formed. Her round breasts clung close to each other. Her face was beautiful and fashioned well. The illustrious one was slender at the waist, with wide hips. On seeing all her auspicious limbs, the

[338] The word used is tata.

[339] Punjikasthala was cursed that she would be born as Anjana.

wind god was confounded by desire and used force. The wind god embraced her with his long arms. Overcome by desire, he immersed himself in the limbs of that unblemished one. Terrified at this, the one who was excellent in conduct spoke these words. "Who wishes to destroy my vow of being the wife of a single husband?" Hearing Anjana's words, the wind god replied, "O one with the beautiful hips! I will not injure you. O immensely fortunate one! Do not be scared. O illustrious one! I have entered you and embraced you with my mind. You will have a son who is valiant and is full of intelligence." Later, when you were a child, you saw the rising sun in the great forest. Desiring to seize what you took to be a fruit, you leapt up into the sky. O great ape! You travelled for three hundred yojanas. But its[340] energy hurled you down and you were full of sorrow. O great ape! On seeing that you were swiftly reaching the sky, the intelligent Indra was filled with rage and hurled the vajra at you. When you fell down on the summit of the mountain, your left cheekbone was shattered. Because of this, you have been known by the name of Hanumat.[341] On seeing that you had been struck, Vayu, the bearer of scents, was himself extremely enraged and the wind ceased to blow in the three worlds. All the gods were terrified and the three worlds were agitated. The lords of the worlds sought the favours of the enraged wind god. When the wind god was placated, Brahma granted you a boon. O one who has truth as your valour! O son! Through the use of a weapon, you cannot be killed in a battle. The one with the one thousand eyes saw that though you had been brought down by the vajra, you were not wounded. Therefore, delighted in his mind, he had granted you an excellent boon. O lord! Your death will occur only when you wish for it. Kesari is terrible in his valour and you have been born in his field. You are the biological son of the wind god and you are his equal in your energy. O child! You are Vayu's son and are his equal in leaping. We now no longer possess any breath of life left. Among us, you are the one who possesses skill and valour. You are like another king of the birds.

[340] The sun's.

[341] One with a cheekbone (*hanu*), that is, one with a broken cheekbone.

O son! At the time of Trivikrama, I have circumambulated the entire earth, with its mountains, forests and groves, twenty-one times. On the instructions of the gods, we[342] have gathered the herbs that were crushed for the sake of amrita and that conferred great strength on us. However, I am aged now and my valour has decayed. At the present time, among all of us, you are the one who possesses all the qualities. O valiant one! You are excellent in leaping. Therefore, prepare yourself. All these soldiers in the army of the apes desire to witness your valour. O tiger among apes! Arise and leap across the great ocean. O Hanumat! Your capacity to travel is greater than that of all creatures. All the apes are distressed. O Hanumat! Why are you ignoring this? In your valour and great force, you are like Vishnu Trivikrama.' He was urged by Jambavat in this way. The ape who was the son of the wind god realized his own force. The army of the brave apes rejoiced when he[343] assumed a gigantic form.

Chapter 4(66)

Praised, the immensely strong Hanumat extended his size. Filled with joy and strength, he lashed his tail. All the bulls among apes praised him. Filled with energy, he assumed a supreme form. He was like a strident lion yawning in a mountain cave. Like that, Marut's biological son started to yawn. As he yawned, the intelligent one's face was radiant. He was like a blazing frying pan, or like a smoke without fire.

From the midst of the apes, he raised up his joyful body. Hanumat greeted the aged apes and spoke to them. 'The wind, the friend of the fire, breaks down the summits of mountains. Vayu's strength is immeasurable and he travels through the sky. I am Marut's biological son and the great-souled one is swift in speed. I am also swift in speed and am his equal in leaping across. The

[342] Though 'we' is used, this really means 'I'.

[343] Hanumat.

extensive Mount Meru is like a picture engraved in the sky. I am interested in circling around it one thousand times. With the force of my arms, I am interested in penetrating the ocean and raising the waters to flood the worlds, with the mountains, rivers and lakes. Such a great force will arise from my thighs and calves that the giant crocodiles will be raised up from the ocean that is Varuna's abode. I am capable of circling around Vinata's son[344] one thousand times, while he flies through the sky, populated by birds, in search of serpents to eat. The sun, with its garland of blazing rays, leaves from Mount Udaya and returns to Mount Asta. O bulls among apes! With my great and terrible force, I am interested in following him and returning, without having touched the ground in the process. I am interested in overtaking all those who course through the sky. I will agitate the ocean and shatter the earth. O apes! I will leap on the mountains and make them tremble. As I leap, the force of my thighs will rob the great ocean of its waters. When I now leap through the sky, all the creepers, herbs, flowers and trees will follow my trail. My path will be like Svati's[345] path through the sky. My leap up into the sky will be terrible and as I descend, all the creatures and all the apes will witness it. O apes! You will see me extend, like the great Meru. I will envelop the firmament and proceed, as if I am swallowing the sky. I will dispel the clouds and make the mountains tremble. As I control myself and leap, I will agitate the ocean. My strength is like that of Vinata's son or the wind god. With the exception of the king of the birds[346] or the immensely strong wind god, no creature will be able to see or follow me as I leap. In a twinkling, I will pass through the sky, which needs no support. I will descend suddenly, like lightning arising inside a cloud. When I leap across the ocean, my form will be like that of the striding Vishnu in the course of the valour of his three strides. O apes! Rejoice. Through my intelligence, thoughts and efforts, I can see that I will be able to see Vaidehi. My force is like that of

[344] Garuda.

[345] The nakshatra Svati, Arcturus. When Svati is in the ascendant, it rains and there is a harvest of crops. Hence, there is an image of the effort yielding fruit.

[346] Garuda.

the wind god. My speed is like that of Garuda. It is my view that I can travel ten thousand yojanas. Through my sudden valour, I will bring the vajra from Vasava's hand and amrita from the hand of Svayambhu Brahma. It is my view that I can go and bring back Lanka itself.' Infinitely energetic, the best among apes roared in this way.

Jambavat, supreme among apes, was extremely delighted. He said, 'O brave one! O son of Kesari! O forceful one! O son of the wind god! O son! You have destroyed the great misery of your relatives. The foremost among the apes have assembled, desiring your welfare. They will control themselves and perform all the auspicious rites required to bring about success in the objective. Through the favours of the rishis, the support of the aged apes and the favours of your seniors, you will leap across the great ocean. Each one of us will stand on one foot until you return. The lives of all the residents of the forest are dependent on your journey.'

The tiger among apes spoke to the residents of the forest in words of assent. 'Who in this world is capable of bearing the force of my leap? The summit of Mount Mahendra is stable and large. This mountain is full of boulders and cliffs. The best among birds place their feet here. If I place my feet there, it will be able to bear me when I leap across one hundred yojanas.' The ape was like the wind god. He was the son of the wind god. The scorcher of enemies climbed Mahendra, supreme among mountains. It was covered with many kinds of trees and grass that deer grazed on. There were obstructions of creepers and flowers. There were trees that were always laden with flowers and fruits. Lions and tigers roamed around there. The place was frequented by crazy elephants. The turbulent waters were full of flocks of maddened birds. The gigantic summit of Mahendra rose up. The immensely strong one, best among apes, like the great Indra in his valour, climbed up. The giant mountain was crushed by the great-souled one's feet and shrieked, like a giant elephant that has been injured by a lion. Waterbodies and heaps of boulders were dislodged, disturbed and hurled away. The animals and deer were terrified. The large trees trembled. There were many gandharva couples, intoxicated after having indulged in bouts of drinking. The birds flew up, as did large numbers of vidyadharas. Giant serpents that had hidden inside the great mountain slithered away. Hills, peaks and boulders were uprooted on that great mountain. Hissing, serpents stretched out their hoods as they emerged partially from their holes, and it seemed as if the mountain was radiant with flags. The rishis were terrified and abandoned all those peaks. The mountain seemed to suffer, like a traveller abandoned by his companions on a desolate plain. The forceful one, supreme among apes and the slayer of enemy heroes, invoked the force in himself. The extremely great one controlled his mind. The spirited one made up his mind to go to Lanka.

This ends Kishkindha Kanda.

CHAPTER FIVE

Sundara Kanda

Sarga (1): 190 shlokas
Sarga (2): 55 shlokas
Sarga (3): 37 shlokas
Sarga (4): 24 shlokas
Sarga (5): 42 shlokas
Sarga (6): 17 shlokas
Sarga (7): 69 shlokas
Sarga (8): 50 shlokas
Sarga (9): 44 shlokas
Sarga (10): 25 shlokas
Sarga (11): 69 shlokas
Sarga (12): 51 shlokas
Sarga (13): 52 shlokas
Sarga (14): 32 shlokas
Sarga (15): 32 shlokas
Sarga (16): 28 shlokas
Sarga (17): 21 shlokas
Sarga (18): 35 shlokas
Sarga (19): 30 shlokas
Sarga (20): 41 shlokas
Sarga (21): 19 shlokas
Sarga (22): 42 shlokas
Sarga (23): 20 shlokas
Sarga (24): 49 shlokas
Sarga (25): 38 shlokas
Sarga (26): 20 shlokas
Sarga (27): 8 shlokas
Sarga (28): 44 shlokas
Sarga (29): 12 shlokas
Sarga (30): 8 shlokas
Sarga (31): 27 shlokas
Sarga (32): 39 shlokas
Sarga (33): 80 shlokas
Sarga (34): 45 shlokas
Sarga (35): 68 shlokas
Sarga (36): 56 shlokas
Sarga (37): 53 shlokas
Sarga (38): 24 shlokas
Sarga (39): 17 shlokas
Sarga (40): 36 shlokas
Sarga (41): 18 shlokas
Sarga (42): 19 shlokas
Sarga (43): 16 shlokas
Sarga (44): 39 shlokas
Sarga (45): 39 shlokas
Sarga (46): 59 shlokas
Sarga (47): 20 shlokas
Sarga (48): 16 shlokas
Sarga (49): 36 shlokas
Sarga (50): 17 shlokas

Sarga (51): 39 shlokas
Sarga (52): 17 shlokas
Sarga (53): 28 shlokas
Sarga (54): 26 shlokas
Sarga (55): 38 shlokas
Sarga (56): 140 shlokas
Sarga (57): 17 shlokas
Sarga (58): 22 shlokas
Sarga (59): 22 shlokas
Sarga (60): 37 shlokas
Sarga (61): 27 shlokas
Sarga (62): 40 shlokas
Sarga (63): 26 shlokas
Sarga (64): 15 shlokas
Sarga (65): 36 shlokas
Sarga (66): 29 shlokas

Chapter 5(1)

Sita had been taken away by Ravana along a path that the charanas travelled on. The afflicter of enemies[1] sought to search her trail along these. There were pastures of grass, with the complexion of lapis lazuli and these looked like still bodies of water. Happily, the immensely strong one travelled along these. The intelligent one frightened the birds and uprooted trees with his chest. Like a striding lion, he also killed many deer. Like an elephant, the ape stood in a lake there. This was decorated with colourful and natural minerals on the rocks—blue, red, yellow, green like leaves, black and white. With their companions, there were yakshas, kinnaras, gandharvas who were like the gods and serpents there, capable of assuming any form at will. There were tens of thousands of elephants on the slope of that supreme mountain. Making up his mind to leave, he joined his hands in salutation before Surya, the great Indra, the wind god, Svayambhu and the elements. Facing the east, he joined his hands in salutation before the wind god, from whom, he had been born. He then turned towards the south, increasing his size and ready to travel towards the southern direction. Watched by the best among the apes, he had made up his mind to leap. To enhance the prospect of Rama's success, he increased his size, like the ocean on days of the full moon. Desirous of leaping across the ocean, his body

[1] Hanumat.

became immeasurably large. He pressed against the mountain with his arms and his feet. Suffering from the ape's action, for a while, the beautiful and immobile mountain wavered. All the flowers showered down from the tops of the young and blossoming trees. Showers of extremely fragrant flowers were dislodged from the trees. The mountain was covered with this everywhere and dazzled, as if it was made out of flowers. His supreme valour crushed the mountain and water started to ooze out, as if from a crazy elephant in musth. The strong one made Mount Mahendra suffer. Streaks of gold, silver and collyrium appeared. Boulders were dislodged. There were large rocks and rocks that were filled with sulphur. The mountain suffered and in turn, caused suffering to everything. Creatures hidden inside caves howled in hideous voices. Because of the suffering caused to the mountain, screams arose from the large creatures. This filled the earth, the directions and the groves. There were snakes with large hoods, the mark of the *svastika* identifiable on them. They vomited terrible fires and bit the rocks with their fangs. Stung by the poison filled with rage, the great rocks blazed like flaming fires and shattered into thousands of fragments. Clumps of herbs were generated on that mountain. However, even these were incapable of countering the poison released from the venom of the serpents.[2] The ascetics on the mountain thought that it was being shattered by demons. With large numbers of their women, the terrified vidyadharas flew away. They left behind liquor in golden vessels meant for storing liquor, extremely expensive vessels and golden pots. There were superior and inferior kinds of *lehya* and *bhakshya*.[3] There were many kinds of meat. There were shields made out of oxhide and swords with golden handles. They[4] were intoxicated, with garlands around their necks. They wore red garlands and were smeared with red paste. Their eyes were red. Their eyes were like red lotuses and they took to the sky. The women wore necklaces, anklets, armlets and bangles. Surprised, they stood in the sky with their loved ones and smiled. The vidyadharas and

[2] These were medicinal herbs.

[3] Respectively, food that is licked and eaten.

[4] The vidyadharas.

maharshis exhibited their great skills. Together, they stood in the sky and looked towards the mountain.

At that time, the rishis, cleansed in their souls, heard a sound, uttered by the charanas and siddhas who were located in the sparkling sky. 'This Hanumat is the son of the wind god and is like a mountain. Using his great force, he wishes to cross the ocean, the abode of *makaras*.[5] For Rama's sake and for the sake of the apes, he desires to perform this extremely difficult task. He wishes to reach the other shore of the ocean, which is extremely difficult to reach.'

He[6] shook his body hair. The one who was like a mountain, shook himself. He roared extremely loudly, like an extremely large cloud. His tail, covered with hair, was completely rolled up. Ready to leap, he raised it, like the king of the birds[7] raises a serpent. His tail was curled around at the back and because of the force, looked as though a large serpent was being carried away by Garuda. His arms were like gigantic clubs and he used these to support himself. The ape bent at the waist and contracted his feet. The handsome one drew in his arms and his head. The valiant one immersed himself in his energy, spirit and prowess. Concentrating his sight, he glanced at the path and the distance he would have to travel. He looked at the sky and held the breath in his heart. The elephant among apes planted his feet firmly. The immensely strong Hanumat drew in his ears. The supreme among apes addressed the apes in these words. 'Like an arrow released by Raghava, with the valour of the wind, I will go to Lanka, ruled over by Ravana. If I do not see Janaka's daughter in Lanka, with the same speed, I will go to the abode of the gods. Despite making these efforts, if I do not see Sita in heaven, I will bind Ravana, the king of the rakshasas, and bring him here. I will be successful in every way, with Sita, or I will uproot Lanka and bring it here, with Ravana.'

Hanumat, supreme among apes, spoke to the apes in this way. He leapt up with force and started to travel with great force. Because

[5] A mythical aquatic creature, which can be loosely translated as shark or crocodile.
[6] Hanumat.
[7] Garuda.

of the force of his leap, all the trees that grew on the mountain were drawn in and uprooted in every direction. There were blossoming trees with plump lapwing birds hanging on to them. Because of the force of his thighs, these were uprooted and trailed him as he proceeded through the sky. Uprooted by the force of his thighs, the trees followed the ape for some time, like relatives and kin follow someone who is leaving on a long journey. Uprooted by the force of his thighs, sala and other excellent trees followed Hanumat, like soldiers behind a lord of the earth. The ape Hanumat, who was like a mountain, was extraordinary to behold, with those many flowering trees. As if terrified of Mount Mahendra, those solid trees then sank into the salty waters of the ocean, Varuna's abode. The ape was himself covered with many kinds of flowers, shoots and buds. Like a mountain, he was as radiant as a mountain illuminated with fireflies. Because of the force, the trees shed their flowers. When their well-wisher departed, they then fell down into the water. Trees with many kinds of flowers were lightly raised because of the gust the ape created and fell down into the ocean. It was wonderful. Flowers of many kinds of hues stuck to the ape's body and he was as radiant as a cloud in the sky, tinged with flashes of lightning. The flowers raised up by that force could be seen and the water looked resplendent, like the firmament with stars in it. When he took to the sky, his arms were seen to stretch out and looked like five-headed serpents that had emerged from the summit of a mountain. The great ape was seen, as if he was drinking up the great ocean and its waves, as if he was drinking up the sky. As he followed the path of the wind, his eyes dazzled like lightning, or like two fires on a mountain. He was foremost among those with tawny eyes and the circles of his tawny eyes were large. The two eyes shone, fixed like the sun and the moon. His mouth and nose were copper coloured. His face looked like the solar disc when it is touched by the evening. As he leapt, the dazzling tail of Vayu's son was raised up in the sky, like Shakra's standard when it has been raised. The wind god's son had teeth that were white and the tail formed a huge circle. The immensely wise one was as radiant as the sun with its disc. The great ape's copper-coloured behind was radiant and looked like a large and shattered mountain, exuding ochre-hued minerals. As the lion among apes leapt across the ocean, the wind seemed to be roaring inside his armpits. The elephant among apes looked like a trailing meteor that has been dislodged from the northern sky. The large and radiant ape stretched out, like a bird that has covered the sky. He increased his size, like an elephant when it has been tied with a rope. Though his body was above, the ape cast a shadow, immersed in the ocean, and this looked like a boat being driven along by the wind. Whichever spot in the ocean the great ape advanced along, that part seemed to be maddened because of the force of his thighs. The net of waves in the ocean were like mountains and the great ape struck them with his chest, as he leapt across them with great force. There was the gust raised by the powerful ape. There was the gust released from the clouds. The ocean trembled severely and roared terribly. In his great force, he crossed over the waves, as if dragging along the net of large waves in that salty ocean. The serpents who had abodes in the ocean saw the tiger among apes leap through the sky and thought that he was Suparna.[8] The shadow of the lion among apes was beautiful in the water, ten yojanas wide and thirty yojanas long. The resplendent shadow was stretched across the salty water and it seemed as if a mass of white clouds were following Vayu's son. They saw him leap. As he swiftly leapt, the gods, the gandharvas and the danavas showered down flowers. As the lord among the apes leapt, the sun did not scorch him. To accomplish Rama's objective, the wind wafted gently. As he leapt through the sky, the rishis praised him. The gods and the gandharvas chanted praises to the immensely energetic one. On seeing that the supreme among apes suddenly lost all exhaustion, all the nagas, the yakshas, the rakshasas, the gods and the birds praised him.

When Hanumat, tiger among apes, was leaping in this way, to show respect to the Ikshvaku lineage, the ocean thought, 'If I do not act to help Hanumat, Indra among the apes, all those who wish to speak ill of me will find reason. I was extended by Sagara,

[8] Garuda.

the protector of the Ikshvaku lineage. This adviser of the Ikshvaku lineage should not suffer from exhaustion. Therefore, I must find a means so that the ape can rest. After having rested on me, he can happily take the remaining part of the leap.' Having had this virtuous thought, the ocean, the store of water, spoke to Mainaka, with a navel made out of gold and supreme among mountains. 'O best among mountains! The king of the gods has set you up here, as a barricade against the large number of asuras who reside in the nether regions.[9] You are stationed here, enveloping the immeasurable gate to *patala*[10] and preventing those who are born valiant[11] from rising up again. O supreme among mountains! O mountain! You have the capacity to increase your size, upwards, downwards and diagonally. Therefore, I am urging you to rise up. This valiant tiger among apes, Hanumat, is performing a terrible deed to accomplish Rama's objective and is leaping through the sky, above you. I should aid in the task of someone who follows the Ikshvaku lineage. Those of the Ikshvaku lineage are worshipped by me and they are worshipped even more by you. Therefore, help us, so that our task is not unsuccessful. If a task that should be performed is not performed, the virtuous become angry. Rise up above the water, so that the ape can rest on you. The supreme among apes is our guest and must be worshipped by us. O one with the large and golden navel, frequented by gods and gandharvas! Having rested on you, Hanumat can then travel the rest of the distance. On witnessing Kakutstha's non-violence, Maithilee's exile and the exertion of the Indra among the apes, you should raise yourself up.' Mainaka, with the golden navel, heard the words of the salty waters. With innumerable large trees and creepers, he swiftly arose from the water. He arose, piercing the waters of the ocean, just as the blazing rays of the sun pierce through a cloud. There were peaks made out of molten gold, full of kinnaras and large serpents. Like the rising sun, they arose and seemed to write in the sky. When the

[9] Patala, a general term for the nether regions. More specifically, there are actually seven nether regions—*atala, vitala, sutala, rasatala, talatala, mahatala* and patala.

[10] One of the seven nether regions.

[11] The asuras.

mountain arose, there were summits made out of molten gold. With the golden radiance, the sky looked like a weapon.[12] Made out of molten gold, the peaks were radiant with their own resplendence. The supreme mountain looked like one hundred suns.

Hanumat saw it rise suddenly, in front of him and in the midst of the salty waters. He decided that this was an obstruction. Having decided this, with great force, the great ape used his chest to bring down what had risen, like the wind god brings down a cloud. The supreme among mountains was thus brought down by the ape. Realizing the ape's force, he was delighted and rejoiced. He assumed the form of a man and stood on his own peak, presenting himself before the brave one who was travelling through the sky. Delighted and happy in his mind, the mountain addressed the ape in these words. 'O supreme among apes! You have performed an act that is extremely difficult to accomplish. Descend on my peaks and happily rest. The ocean was born in Raghava's lineage and extended by them.[13] That is the reason the ocean is worshipping you, as someone who is engaged in Rama's welfare. It is eternal dharma that one must pay back someone who has done a good deed. It truly wants to pay back. Therefore, you must respect it. With a great deal of respect, I have been urged by it. "When the ape has leapt over one hundred yojanas, before he travels the rest of the distance, let him rest on your peaks."[14] O tiger among apes! Rest on me and then travel. There are many fragrant and tasty tubers, roots and fruits here. O best among apes! Taste them. Rest and then travel. O best among apes! That apart, there is a relationship between you and me. It is famous in the three worlds and is accepted by those who possess the great qualities. O son of the wind god! O elephant among apes! I think you are foremost among the apes who are forceful and can leap. Indeed, even ordinary people, who seek to practise dharma, know that a guest must be honoured, not to speak of one who is as great as you. O elephant among apes!

[12] The image is of a sword, with the blue of the sky as the blade and the golden peaks as the handle.

[13] This is a reference to King Sagara.

[14] The ocean speaking to Mainaka.

The great-souled wind god is best among the gods and you are his son, his equal in force. O one who knows about dharma! If you are worshipped, the wind god is also worshipped. That is the reason you must be worshipped. But listen to another reason too. O son![15] Earlier, in *krita yuga*, mountains possessed wings. With the speed of Garuda and the wind, they travelled in all the directions. When they travelled around in this way, the large number of gods, with rishis and the creatures, were scared that they might fall down. At this, the thousand-eyed Shatakratu became angry and used his vajra to instantly sever the wings of thousands of mountains. Angry, the king of the gods also approached me, with his vajra raised. But the great-souled wind god violently flung me aside. O supreme among apes! I was thus flung into the salty waters. I was protected by your father and all my wings were preserved. That is the reason I revere the wind god and revere you. O foremost among the apes! This relationship between you and me possesses great qualities. O great ape! This being the case, it is your task to please me and the ocean and make our minds rejoice. O supreme among apes! Free yourself of your exhaustion and accept our worship. Accept our great respect cheerfully. I am delighted that I have been able to see you.'

Thus addressed, the best among apes spoke to the excellent mountain. 'I am delighted that you have shown me hospitality. Let there be no anger between us. It is time to make haste. The day is passing. I have given my pledge that I will not stop in between.' Saying this, the bull among apes embraced the mountain with his hands. As if smiling, the valiant one went up into the sky and continued to travel. The mountain and the ocean glanced at him with a great deal of respect. They worshipped the son of the wind god and showered him with blessings. Having taken his leave of the mountain and the great ocean, he rose far up. Resorting to the path followed by his father, he travelled through the sparkling sky. He went still further up and glanced down at the mountain. Without any support, the son of the wind god travelled through the sparkling sky. All the gods, the siddhas and the supreme rishis

[15] The word used is tata.

saw the extremely difficult task that Hanumat was performing and praised him. The gods and the thousand-eyed Vasava were delighted at the act performed by the one with the golden and excellent navel.[16] Shachi's intelligent consort himself spoke to the best among mountains, the one with the excellent navel, in words that were indistinct because he was so satisfied. 'O one with the golden navel! O Indra among mountains! I am greatly satisfied with you. I am granting you freedom from fear! O amiable one! Remain at ease. You have helped Hanumat, who is fearlessly performing this extremely great task of travelling one hundred yojanas, though there is reason to be afraid. He is going as the messenger of Rama Hari, Dasharatha's son. I am content that you have firmly performed this good deed.' On seeing that Shatakratu, the lord of the gods, was content, the supreme among mountains obtained unmatched delight. The mountain was granted a supreme boon[17] and remained there.

In an instant, Hanumat travelled over the ocean. At this, the gods, the gandharvas, the siddhas and the supreme rishis spoke to Surasa, the mother of the nagas and like the sun in resplendence.[18] 'The handsome son of the wind god is leaping over the ocean. For a while, become an obstruction before Hanumat. Assume the form of an extremely terrible rakshasa that is like a mountain, with horrible fangs and coppery eyes. Assume a face that rises up into the firmament. We wish to ascertain his strength and valour and know whether he can overcome you, or will be overcome by sorrow.' The goddess was thus addressed by the gods and honoured by them. In the midst of the ocean, Surasa assumed the fearful form of a rakshasa. It was disfigured, malformed and fearful everywhere. She obstructed the leaping Hanumat and said, 'O bull among the apes! The gods have said that you are my food. I will devour you. Enter my mouth.' Thus addressed by Surasa, the bull among apes joined his hands in salutation. With a cheerful face, the handsome one replied, 'Dashratha's son, named Rama, entered Dandaka

[16] Mainaka.

[17] By Indra.

[18] This attempt to test Hanumat through Surasa is strange.

forest with his brother, Lakshmana, and his wife, Vaidehi. Tied with his enmity towards the rakshasas, when he was engaged in another task, his illustrious wife, Sita, was abducted by Ravana. On Rama's instructions, I am going to him as his messenger. O one who resides in his dominion![19] You should help Rama. Listen to my truthful pledge. Otherwise, for the sake of Rama, the performer of unblemished deeds, after I have seen Maithilee, I will come and enter your mouth.' Surasa, who could assume any form at will, was thus addressed by Hanumat and said, 'My boon is that no one can transgress me.' Thus addressed by Surasa, the bull among apes became angry and said, 'Make your mouth so that you can obstruct me.' Surasa became enraged at being addressed in this way. She appeared before Hanumat with a mouth that was ten yojanas wide and twenty yojanas long. Surasa's mouth was like a cloud, ten yojanas wide and twenty yojanas long. On seeing this, Hanumat became wrathful and became thirty yojanas long. Surasa made her mouth forty yojanas high. The brave Hanumat became fifty yojanas high. Surasa made her mouth sixty yojanas wide. At this, the brave Hanumat became seventy yojanas high. Surasa made her mouth eighty yojanas long. Like a foremost mountain, Hanumat rose up ninety yojanas. Surasa made her mouth one hundred yojanas long. Vayu's intelligent son saw that gaping mouth, with Surasa's extremely terrible and long tongue resembling hell. Maruti[20] was like a cloud, but contracted his form. In an instant, Hanumat became as small as a thumb. With great speed, he swiftly descended into the mouth. Emerging and stationed in the sky, the handsome one spoke these words. 'O Dakshayani![21] I bow down before you. I have entered your mouth. I will now go where Vaidehi is. Your words have also come true.' She saw that he had been freed from her mouth, like the moon from Rahu's mouth. Assuming her own form, the goddess Surasa spoke to the ape. 'O best among apes! O amiable one! Go cheerfully and accomplish the desired objective. Bring Vaidehi before the great-souled Raghava.' Witnessing

[19] Rama's dominion.
[20] Hanumat.
[21] Daksha's daughter, Surasa being one of Daksha's daughters.

Hanumat's deed, which was extremely difficult to accomplish, all the creatures praised the ape.

Like Garuda in his force, he passed through the unassailable ocean, Varuna's abode. He then entered the sky and proceeded through it. There were clouds there and it was populated by birds. Those who were skilled in music and dancing[22] travelled there and it was frequented by Airavata.[23] Sparkling and ornamented vimanas were swiftly moving there, with lions, elephants, tigers and serpents as mounts. Their[24] forms were like the fire and they clashed like thunder and lightning. They were meant for immensely fortunate ones who had performed auspicious deeds and were decorated by those who had conquered heaven. Frequented by the fire god, many kinds of oblations were carried along. It was decorated by planets, nakshatras, the moon, the sun and a large number of stars. The place was full of a large number of maharshis, gandharvas, serpents and yakshas. It sparkled and was empty.[25] It was frequented by Vishvavasu.[26] This was the path travelled by the elephants of the king of the gods. This was the auspicious path of the moon and the sun. It was like a canopy spread over the world of the living, constructed by Brahma. There were many groups of excellent and brave vidyadharas there. Without any difficulty, the ape proceeded through the large clouds. He entered the net of clouds and repeatedly emerged again. He entered and emerged repeatedly, like the radiance of the moon amidst monsoon clouds.

There was a rakshasi named Simhika who could assume any form at will.[27] On seeing him leap, in her mind, she thought that she would extend her size. 'After a long period of time, my food has come before me. After a long period of time, this great being has come under my control.' Thinking this in her mind, she seized the

[22] Gandharvas.

[23] Indra's elephant.

[24] That of the vimanas.

[25] Not populated by humans.

[26] The king of the gandharvas.

[27] Sometimes, Simhika is also referred to as Angaraka.

shadow.[28] When his shadow was seized, the ape started to think. 'I am being violently seized and my valour has been disabled. It is as if a giant boat in the ocean is being pulled back by a contrary wind.' The ape looked around, up, down and diagonally. He saw a great spirit arising from the salty waters. He thought, 'This is the spirit, extraordinary to behold, that the king of the apes spoke about. There is no doubt that this is the extremely valorous one that seizes shadows.' The intelligent ape arrived at the right conclusion, that this was Simhika. Like a cloud during the monsoon season, he extended his gigantic form. On seeing that the giant ape was increasing his size, she extended her mouth, until it looked like patala stretched across the sky. The intelligent and great ape saw her extend her extremely large mouth, until her mouth was as large as his form. He also saw her inner organs. The immensely strong one repeatedly contracted himself and descended. The siddhas and the charanas saw him descend into her mouth. It was like the moon being swallowed on the night of the full moon by Rahu. With his sharp nails, the ape tore into her inner organs. After that, with a speed like that of thought, the valiant one flew up. On seeing that Simhika had quickly been brought down by the ape, the creatures who roam around in the sky spoke to the supreme among the apes. 'By slaying this great creature today, you have performed an extremely terrible deed. O supreme among apes! An extremely desired objective has met with success. O Indra among apes! If a person possesses four traits, perseverance, foresight, intelligence and skill, like you do, he will never falter in any task.' The revered ape was thus honoured by them. Determined to accomplish his objective, he entered and travelled through the sky, like the one who feeds on serpents.[29]

Having reached the other shore, he looked around in all the directions. At the end of the one hundred yojanas, he saw a clump of groves. He descended and saw many kinds of ornamented trees. The best among apes saw the dvipa and groves around Malaya. There was a bay near the ocean and in that bay, there were trees.

[28] Simhika devoured her prey by seizing their shadows.

[29] Garuda.

He saw the best among the wives of the ocean.[30] The one in control of himself looked at his own self, like a giant cloud that was obstructing the sky. The intelligent one thought, 'The rakshasas will see my enlarged form and my force.' The great ape thought, 'They will become curious about me.' Therefore, he contracted his body, which was like a large mountain. Like one who has been freed from a delusion, the one in control of his soul again assumed his natural form. He was capable of assuming many beautiful forms that others would find it impossible to replicate. He reached the other shore of the ocean and considering the objective, looked at his own self. In the ocean, there was a mountain named Lamba, with many wonderful peaks. The great-souled one, who was like a mass of clouds, alighted on a peak. There were many ketaka, uddalaka and coconut trees there. The ocean was full of innumerable danavas and serpents and was full of garlands of gigantic waves. He crossed the great ocean with his strength and valour and descended on the shore. He saw Lanka, which was like Amaravati.[31]

Chapter 5(2)

The immensely strong one safely crossed the insurmountable ocean. He saw Lanka, located on the summit of Trikuta. As he stood there, the valiant one was radiant and seemed to be made of flowers, since the trees released showers of flowers over him. The handsome ape, excellent in his valour, had crossed one hundred yojanas without taking a breath or suffering from any exhaustion. 'I can progressively cross many hundreds of yojanas. What is there in travelling one hundred yojanas and coming to the end of the ocean?' Thus, the best among valiant ones and supreme among the apes powerfully crossed the great ocean and went to Lanka. There was blue grassland and fragrant groves. He passed through

[30] That is, rivers.

[31] Indra's capital, the city of the immortals.

boulders and mountains. There were mountains covered with trees and blossoming forests. Hanumat, the spirited bull among apes, travelled. He stood on the mountain. From the summit of the mountain, the son of the wind god saw forests, groves and Lanka. There were *sarala*s, karnikaras, flowering kharjuras, priyalas, *muchulinda*s, kutajas, ketakas, fragrant nipas, saptaparnas, asanas and blossoming karaviras.[32] They were bent down by the weight of flowers and buds. The trees were full of birds, with the tops bent down because of the wind. There were lotuses and lilies in the waterbodies, with swans and karandavas. These were surrounded by many kinds of trees, filled everywhere with blossoming flowers. The elephant among apes saw beautiful groves.

He reached prosperous Lanka, ruled over by Ravana. It was adorned with moats that were full of lotuses and lilies. Because Sita had been abducted, it was protected well by Ravana. On every side, rakshasas with fierce bows roamed around it. The great city was surrounded by golden and beautiful ramparts. There were hundreds of mansions decorated with garlands of flags and pennants. The gates were golden and divine, decorated with the marks of creepers. Hanumat saw Lanka and it was like a city of the gods in heaven. With its white residences, Lanka was located on the summit of the mountain. It was like a handsome city in the sky and the best among apes saw it. It had been constructed by Vishvakarma and was protected by the Indra among the rakshasas. The ape saw the beautiful city, which seemed to be situated in the sky. It was full of terrible rakshasas, resembling serpents in Bhogavati. Something as clear as this was unthinkable. In earlier times, it used to be ruled over by Kubera. It was protected by terrible rakshasas who were like venomous serpents inside a cave. They were brave and possessed many fangs, with spears and lances in their hands. The large body of water[33] was like a garment and the walls were like hips. The *shataghni*s[34] and spears were like the tips of the hair. The mansions were like earrings. Having reached the northern gate, the ape started

[32] Muchulinda is a lemon tree.

[33] In the moats and in the ocean.

[34] A shataghni is a weapon that can kill one hundred at one stroke.

to think. It was like the summit of Kailasa, like a painting etched out in the sky. With the excellent mansions rising up, it seemed to be held up in the sky. He saw that the great city was protected by the ocean. The ape thought about the terrible enemy, Ravana. 'Even if the apes come here, they will not be successful. Even the gods will find it impossible to conquer Lanka in a battle. Protected by Ravana, Lanka is impenetrable and fortified. Even if the mighty-armed Raghava reaches it, what will he do? There seems to be no prospect of approaching the rakshasas and using conciliation,[35] dana, bheda or fighting.[36] There are only four great-souled apes who can come here—Vali's son, Nila, I and the intelligent king.[37] I will think about this after I have found out whether Vaidehi is alive or not. Let me first see Janaka's daughter.'

For a while, the elephant among apes thought. Engaged in ensuring Rama's objective, he stood on the summit of the mountain. 'I am incapable of entering the city of the rakshasas in this form of mine. It is protected by cruel and powerful rakshasas. The rakshasas are fierce in their energy, immensely brave and powerful. In searching out Janakee, I must deceive all of them. I must enter the city of Lanka in the night, in a tiny form that can just about be seen. To accomplish the great objective, that is what I must do, enter at the right time.' He saw that city, which is impossible for even the gods or the asuras to assail. Hanumat thought about this repeatedly and arrived at this conclusion. 'What means can I use to see Maithilee, Janaka's daughter, so that I am not seen by the evil-souled Ravana, Indra among the rakshasas? How can the task of Rama, who knows about his soul, be accomplished? How can I manage to see Janaka's daughter alone? Even if a messenger is ready to accomplish the objective, he can be harmed and rendered incapacitated if he acts against the time and the place, like darkness dispelled by the rising sun. An intelligence that cannot distinguish between gain and loss is worthless. Messengers who are insolent about their learning can defeat the objective. How can the task be

[35] Sama.

[36] Danda.

[37] Sugriva.

accomplished? How will there be no suffering? How will leaping across the ocean not be rendered futile? Rama, who knows about his soul, desires to bring an end to Ravana. However, if I am seen by the rakshasas, that task will fail. Undetected by the rakshasas, I am incapable of going there, even in the form of a rakshasa, not to speak of any other form. It is my view that even the wind cannot go there undetected. There is nothing that is unknown to the strong rakshasas. If I remain here, shrouding myself in my own form, I will be destroyed. My master's task will also suffer. That being the case, when it is night, I will diminish my size. To accomplish Raghava's objective, I will thus enter Lanka. Ravana's city is extremely difficult to approach and I will enter it at night. I will search everywhere in the mansions and seek out Janaka's daughter.' The ape Hanumat thought in this way and waited for the sun to set. Anxious to see Vaidehi, the brave one thought in this way.

When it was evening, the valiant Hanumat quickly assumed an extraordinary form that was only the size of a gnat.[38] He entered the beautiful city, laid out and divided well through large roads. The mansions were like garlands, with pillars made out of gold and silver. With lattice work that was made out of molten gold, it was like a city of the gandharvas. In that great city, he saw seven-storeyed and eight-storeyed buildings. The floors were made out of crystal and were decorated with gold. There were nets made out of pearls and there was wonderful work of lapis lazuli and jewels. The floors of the mansions of the rakshasas were dazzling. There were colourful and golden gates protected by rakshasas. Everything in Lanka was decorated and illuminated. The great ape saw Lanka. It was extraordinary in form and impossible to think of. Anxious to see Vaidehi, he was both happy and distressed simultaneously. The place was surrounded by garlands of pale mansions. There were extremely expensive gates, made out of nets of molten gold. It was illustrious and was protected by Ravana's arms. It was full

[38] The Critical Edition uses the term *prishadamshaka,* something that bites or stings an antelope. Non-Critical versions use the term *vrishadamshaka,* something that bites or stings a bull. While a gnat or similar insect is possible, something like a cat or a dog is also not ruled out.

of demons who were terrible in their strength. As if to help him, the moon rose and was radiant amidst a large number of stars. The entire world was pervaded by this canopy of moonlight. The one with many thousands of beams arose. Its complexion was like that of a conch shell, as white as milk or the stalk of a white lotus. As it arose, it illuminated everything. The brave ape saw the moon, which looked like a swan swimming in a lake.

Chapter 5(3)

He stood on the summit of Lamba, which was like an elongated cloud.[39] The intelligent Hanumat, the son of the wind god, resorted to his own spirit. The greatly spirited one, elephant among apes, entered Lanka at night. The city was protected by Ravana and was full of beautiful groves and waterbodies. It was adorned with the best of mansions, resembling autumn clouds. A sound arose, as if from the ocean. A breeze that arose from the ocean blew through it. It was protected by extremely well-nurtured soldiers, like Vitapavati.[40] There were beautiful protected gates, with white gates and turrets. The auspicious place was protected, like Bhogavati is by serpents who roam around. The paths were illuminated by the light of stellar bodies and looked like clouds tinged with lightning. A gust of wind blew, as if in Indra's Amaravati. There were giant ramparts that were made out of molten gold. The place was adorned with flags and there was the sound of tinkling from nets of bells. Cheerfully, he quickly climbed up a rampart. As he looked everywhere in the city, his heart was filled with wonder. The gates were made of molten gold and the platforms were of lapis lazuli. There were jewels, crystals and pearls and the floors were encrusted with gems. There were decorations made out of molten gold, embellished with sparkling white silver. The floors and stairs

[39] The word *lamba* means long and there is a play on words.

[40] Another name for Alakapuri, Kubera's capital.

were of lapis lazuli, with sparkling and clear work of crystal inside. There were auspicious and beautiful assembly halls that seemed to be flying through the sky. There were the sounds of curlews and peacocks. The place was populated by swans. The sounds of trumpets and ornaments echoed everywhere. He saw the city, which seemed to have been fashioned only out of riches. Lanka seemed to be flying through the sky and the ape Hanumat was delighted. He saw the auspicious city of Lanka, which belonged to the lord of the rakshasas.

Its prosperity was supreme and the valiant one started to think. 'It is impossible for anyone to attack this city with force. Ravana's soldiers protect it, wielding upraised weapons. Kumuda, Angada, the great ape Sushena, Mainda and Dvivida may be able to penetrate this region. So can the son of the sun god,[41] the ape Kushaparva, the bear Ketumala and I.' Thinking about the mighty-armed Raghava's valour and the prowess of Lakshmana, the ape became delighted.

The city was like a beautiful and ornamented woman attired in red garments. The treasure houses were like earrings. The large stores of machines were like her breasts. The large houses were illuminated by radiant lamps that dispelled the darkness. The giant ape saw the city of the Indra among the rakshasas. The spirited one, the son of the wind god, entered the city at night. He travelled along the great road, decorated with pearls and flowers. In front of him, there were the sounds of laughter and the blare of trumpets. The beautiful city possessed houses that were as firm as the vajra, strong like clubs and ornamented with diamonds. The city looked like the sky, decorated with clouds. Lanka blazed, with the beautiful houses of large numbers of rakshasas. There were colourful and white houses of the *padma*, svastika and *vardhamana* types.[42] All of these were decorated well. Wishing to perform a good deed for the king of the apes and to accomplish Raghava's objective, the handsome one roamed around, looking at the wonderful garlands

[41] Sugriva.

[42] These are different types of houses and refer to forms of architecture.

and ornaments and delighted. He heard sweet songs, chanted in the three kinds of tones[43] by women intoxicated with liquor, sounding like apsaras in heaven. The great-souled one heard the tinkling of girdles and the sound of anklets on the stairs of the houses. Here and there, there were the sounds of roaring and the slapping of arms. He saw yatudhanas engaged in studying. He saw rakshasas assemble, roaring their praise of Ravana. There were large numbers of rakshasa soldiers along the royal roads. He saw many rakshasa spies in the midst of the contingents. There were those who had been initiated into studying. There were those with matted hair or shaved heads, attired in garments made out of cowhide. Darbha grass in their hands were like weapons. Their weapons were sacrificial altars to the fire. There were others with mallets and clubs in their hands. Others wielded rods as weapons. Some possessed one eye. Others possessed many ears. There were those whose stomachs and breasts hung low. Some had cruel and malformed mouths. Others were disfigured and dwarves. Some wielded bows, swords, shataghnis and clubs as weapons. Others had excellent bludgeons in their arms, with colourful and blazing armour. Some were not very fat, others were not very lean. Some were not tall, nor were they short. Some were malformed, others had many forms. Some were excellent in form and extremely radiant. Some had lances and trees as weapons. Others wielded javelins and vajras. The giant ape saw some of them wield nooses that could be flung. Some were garlanded and smeared with pastes. Others were adorned in the best of ornaments. There were immensely strong ones, wielding sharp spears and vajras. The ape saw a hundred thousand rakshasas attentively protecting the centre. The giant ape saw the extremities, surrounded by ramparts. It was like divine heaven and there were celestial sounds. There were the sounds of horses neighing and the tinkle of ornaments. There were chariots, vehicles and vimanas and auspicious elephants and horses. There were elephants with four tusks, resembling a mass of white clouds. The ornamented and beautiful gates were full of maddened animals

[43] Slow, medium and fast.

and birds. The ape entered the protected residence that belonged to the lord of the rakshasas.

Chapter 5(4)

The moon reached the midpoint in the sky.[44] The giant cascade of moonlight spread everywhere. The intelligent one looked at the radiant body in the sky,[45] resembling a crazy bull roaming around amidst a herd of cows. This was the one who destroyed the sins of the worlds and made the great ocean wax. It was the one who illuminated all creatures. He saw the one with the cool rays rise up. The prosperity that is there on earth in Mandara, in the ocean during the evening and in the water in Pushkara—all that radiant beauty existed in the moon. The radiant moon illuminated the sky like a swan inside a cage made out of silver, like a lion in a cavern in Mandara and like a brave and proud elephant. The radiant moon was full, without any horns.[46] It was stationed there, with the sharp-horned one with humps.[47] It was like a giant white mountain with tall peaks. It was like an elephant with tusks made out of molten gold. When the moon appeared, all the sins disappeared, including the sins caused by rakshasas who flourished by surviving on flesh. All the taints vanished from the minds of women.[48] The illustrious one illuminated the evening with a radiance that was like that of heaven. Sounds that were pleasant to hear started from stringed musical instruments. Women who possessed good characters slept with their husbands. The ones who wander around in the night, creatures who are terrible in their conduct, started to roam around.

[44] This entire chapter has a metre that is somewhat different. It is full of imagery and descriptions, with the metaphors sometimes sounding forced and artificial.

[45] The moon.

[46] Meaning that there were no crescents.

[47] A reference to the mark on the moon, in the shape of a bull.

[48] This is a reference to playful quarrels between women and their lovers, which now vanished.

The intelligent ape saw houses that were full of maddened and intoxicated people and places where chariots, horses and excellent seats were kept. There were brave and prosperous people. They[49] lunged excessively at each other, nudging each other with their thick arms. They were intoxicated and spoke excessively to each other. Since they were intoxicated, they abused each other. The rakshasas beat their chests and hurled themselves on the bodies of women. He saw beautiful women smear themselves with unguents before sleeping. Large elephants trumpeted. The virtuous ones were honoured properly. The radiant and brave ones sighed, like serpents hissing in a lake. There were those who were intelligent, indulging in beautiful speech. There were faithful ones, foremost in the world. There were those who possessed many kinds of beautiful names. He also saw such yatudhanas in the city. He rejoiced when he saw the ones with beautiful forms. They possessed many qualities, qualities that were worthy of them. They were radiant in those forms. However, he also saw some who were malformed. Among them, there were extremely generous women, extremely pure in their sentiments and best among beautiful ones. They were devoted to their loved ones and addicted by nature to drinking. He saw some extremely radiant ones who were like stars. There were prosperous women, blazing in their ornaments. In the middle of the night, they were engaged in intercourse. He saw some women who clung to their loved ones, like birds cling to flowers. There were yet others who were seated on the floors of the mansions, happily lying down in the laps of their beloveds. They loved their husbands and were devoted to dharma. The intelligent one saw some who were in the throes of love. There were naked women with golden complexions. There were some with complexions of refined gold, meant for others.[50] There were also those who were like the moon in complexion. Some with beautiful complexions in their limbs were separated from their beloveds. He saw women who obtained their handsome beloveds and were filled with great

[49] The rakshasas.

[50] This probably means courtesans.

delight. The best among apes saw such extremely beautiful women, happy in their homes. There were garlands of faces that were like the moon. There were garlands of beautiful eyebrows and curved eyelashes. He saw garlands of ornaments and beautiful garlands that were like lightning. However, the extremely noble Sita, based on a virtuous path and born in a royal lineage, wasn't there. Born in a virtuous lineage, she was like a blossoming creeper. But he did not see the slender one, born through mental powers.[51] She was established on the eternal path of looking towards Rama, filled with desire for him. The beautiful one was always established in her husband's mind. She was supreme among women and special. She was afflicted by the heat[52] and her throat was choked with tears. Earlier, she wore extremely expensive and excellent jewels around her throat. She was born with beautiful eyelashes and a sweet voice. She was like a female peacock[53] that was no longer dancing in the forest. It was as if the marks on the moon were indistinct marks. It was as if a mark made with gold was covered with dust. It was like the mark left by an arrow in a deep wound. It was as if the lines made by clouds had been dispelled by the wind. He did not see Sita, the wife of Rama, lord of men and supreme among eloquent ones. For some time, the ape was therefore filled with distress and for some time, he was numbed.

Chapter 5(5)

The one who could assume any form at will roamed around the mansions, but did not find what he desired. Full of dexterity, the ape wandered around Lanka. He approached the prosperous residence of the Indra among the rakshasas. It was surrounded by radiant ramparts that possessed the complexion of the sun. It was

[51] Through Brahma's mental powers.

[52] Of separation from Rama.

[53] The text uses the word *nilakantha*. This means a peacock/peahen with a blue neck.

protected by terrible rakshasas, the way a great forest is protected by a lion. Having looked at the residence, the elephant among apes climbed up. It was decorated with silver and the colourful gates were adorned with gold. There were wonderful chambers, surrounded by beautiful gates. There were brave elephant riders on elephants, devoid of exhaustion. There were horses with attendants and chariots with drivers. There was armour for the body, made out of the skins of lions and tigers and decorated with ivory, gold and silver. Chariots always roamed around, making wonderful sounds. There were many jewels there and excellent seats and vessels. There were maharathas there, giant chariots and large seats. Here and there, extremely beautiful animals and birds could be seen. In every direction, the place was full of many thousands of these. It was protected well by rakshasas and the guards for the inner quarters were humble. In every direction, the place was full of foremost and excellent women. There were happy gems among women in the residence of the Indra among the rakshasas. The sound made by excellent jewellery was like the sound that arose in the ocean. There was excellent and supreme sandalwood, possessing qualities that could be used by a king. There were the sounds of tambourines and drums. The noise of conch shells resounded. The rakshasas always worshipped it[54] on every auspicious day of festivities, offering oblations. It was as deep as the ocean and made a sound like that of the ocean. The great-souled one possessed a great residence. It was full of great jewels and garments. The great ape saw that it was filled with great people. Full of elephants, horses and chariots, its form was radiant. The great ape thought that this was like Lanka's jewel. The ape roamed around from one house to another house and in the groves of the rakshasas. Without any fear, he wandered around everywhere in that palace. With great force, he leapt on to Prahasta's residence. With another leap, he went to the residence of the valiant Mahaparshva. Thereafter, the great ape leapt to Kumbhakarna's residence, which was like a cloud, and from there to Vibhishana's. He went to the houses of Mahodara, Virupaksha,

[54] Ravana's residence.

Vidyutjihva and Vidyunmali. The great ape then leapt to that of Vajradamshtra. With great force, the intelligent leader of the apes then went to the houses of Shuka, Sarana and Indrajit. The leader of the apes went to the houses of Jambumali, Sumali, Rashmiketu and Suryashatru. Hanumat, the son of the wind god went to the houses of Dhumraksha, Sampati, Vidyutrupa, Bhima, Ghana, Vighana, Shukanabha, Vakra, Shatha, Vikata, Hrasvakarna, Damshtra, the rakshasa Romasha, Yuddhanmatta, Matta, Dvajagriva, Nadina, Vidyutjihva, Indrajihva, Hastimukha, Karala, Pishacha, Shonita, Kramamana and Krama. In those extremely expensive houses, the great ape, the son of the wind god, saw their prosperity and wealth. In every direction, he passed through all their houses and approached the prosperous residence of the Indra among the rakshasas.

As he wandered around, the supreme among apes, tiger among apes, saw rakshasis with malformed eyes sleeping near Ravana. They held spears and clubs in their hands. They wielded javelins and spikes. He saw many contingents of soldiers in the house of the lord of the rakshasas.[55] There were extremely swift horses that were red, white and black. There were handsome elephants born in noble lineages, capable of taking on elephants of the enemy. These elephants were skilled and trained, Airavata's equal in a battle. They were capable of slaying the soldiers of the enemy and he saw them in that house. Like clouds, they exuded musth. They exuded minerals like mountains. They roared like clouds and the enemy found them unassailable in a battle. There were thousands of *vahini*s[56] there, decorated in molten gold. They were covered in nets of gold and looked like the rising sun. He saw these in the residence of Ravana, Indra among rakshasas. The ape who was the wind god's son saw palanquins of different shapes. There were collections of colourful creepers and chambers where paintings were kept. There were other chambers for sporting, with mountains made out of wood. There was a beautiful chamber for satisfying sexual desires and another

[55] The word used is *gulma*. The basic unit was a *patti*, with 250 men. Three pattis constituted a gulma. Ten gulmas constituted a *gana*.

[56] A *sena* consisted of five hundred elephants and the same number of chariots. Ten senas constituted a *pritana* and ten pritanas constituted a vahini.

chamber for the day. He saw these in the residence of Ravana, Indra among the rakshasas. There was an excellent spot that was like the plains of Mandara and it was full of pens for peacocks. He saw an excellent house that was filled with standards and staffs. There was an infinite quantity of jewels and everywhere, heaps of riches. Patient and attentive supervisors tended to these, like in the residence of the lord of the *bhutas*.[57] The rays of these jewels indicated Ravana's energy. Because of this, that residence was radiant, like the rays of the one with the rays.[58] There were couches and seats made out of molten gold. The leader of the apes saw sparkling vessels. The bejewelled vessels were moist with madhu and *asava*.[59] Delightful and without obstructions, it was like Kubera's residence. There was the tinkling of anklets and the sound of girdles. There was the noise of drums and the clapping of hands. The many chambers in the palace were filled with hundreds of jewels among women. Hanumat entered that large residence, with many extensive chambers.

Chapter 5(6)

The powerful one saw that network of houses.[60] They had windows that were decorated with lapis lazuli. It looked like a giant net of clouds during the monsoon, penetrated with lightning and mixed with a net of birds. There were many kinds of houses and halls. There were major ones for storing conch shells and weapons, halls for bows. He again saw pleasant and large chambers above those houses, like attics. There were many kinds of riches in those houses, extremely revered by gods and asuras. They were devoid of all kinds of taints. The ape saw the strength

[57] Meaning Kubera.

[58] Meaning the sun.

[59] Both are forms of liquor, asava probably made through a process of distillation.

[60] In this chapter, as well as in some others, the beauty is in the cleverness of the poetry and the play on words. Translated, the content sometimes sounds artificial and forced. The similes and metaphors are impossible to capture in a translation.

they had accumulated for themselves. He saw the houses of the lord of Lanka, constructed with a great deal of care and effort, as if by Maya himself.[61] It possessed all the excellent qualities on earth. He then saw an excellent house that had no comparison. It rose up loftily, like a cloud. It was pleasant to see, with a beautiful form made out of gold. This belonged to the lord of the rakshasas and was similar to his own strength. It was spread out like a heaven on earth. It blazed in prosperity and was filled with many kinds of jewels. It was covered with flowers from many trees and was like the summit of a mountain, covered with pollen. It dazzled, like an excellent woman. It was like a cloud, being worshipped by the lightning. It blazed with prosperity, like a vimana in the sky meant for the performers of good deeds, being borne along by excellent swans. It was like the summit of a mountain, colourful with many minerals. It was like the firmament, coloured with planets and the moon. He saw it and it was like a colourful cloud. He saw the jewel among vimanas, coloured with many gems.[62] The earth was created so that it could be full of mountain ranges. The mountains were created so that they could be full of arrays of trees. The trees were created so that they could be full of arrays of flowers. The flowers were created so that they could be full of filaments and petals. The white houses were also created and so were the lakes, full of excellent flowers. There were also lotuses with filaments and colourful and superb groves. The great ape saw a great vimana there, radiant and named Pushpaka. It was large and radiant with jewels. It was taller than the excellent houses. Birds made of lapis lazuli were in it and also birds made of silver and coral. There were colourful serpents made out of many kinds of riches. There were steeds from noble breeds, auspicious in their limbs. The wings of the birds were of coral, molten gold and flowers. Without any water, the wings were curved. The wings were as radiant as Kama[63] himself. These birds, with excellent faces and excellent wings, were

[61] Lanka was built by Vishvakarma, but as if by Maya.

[62] Descriptions of the residence are interspersed with descriptions of Pushpaka vimana.

[63] The god of love.

constructed. The goddess Lakshmi was fashioned,[64] seated on a lotus, with excellent hands and with a lotus in her hand. She was worshipped by elephants with excellent trunks, holding lotuses with filaments in their trunks. The house was beautiful in this way. He wondered at its beauty, which was like that of a beautiful mountain. He again looked at it, extremely fragrant and extremely beautiful, like a mountain with beautiful caverns during the spring. The ape approached and wandered around that revered city, protected by the one with ten faces and arms.[65] However, he did not see Janaka's extremely revered daughter, vanquished by the force of the qualities her husband possessed, and became extremely miserable because of this. Therefore, the one with the cleansed soul thought in many ways. He had made up his mind to search out Janaka's daughter. Unable to see her, his mind became extremely miserable. The great-souled one roamed around, casting his glance here and there.

Chapter 5(7)

In the midst of those best among houses, Hanumat, the son of the wind god, saw an extremely large and excellent residence. It was half a yojana long and one yojana wide. This was the residence of the Indra among the rakshasas and had many mansions inside it. He was searching for the whereabouts of the large-eyed Vaidehi Sita. Hanumat, the slayer of enemies, wandered around everywhere. There were elephants with four tusks and with three tusks. It was extensive, without obstructions, and was protected by rakshasas wielding weapons. This was the residence of Ravana and his rakshasi wives. It was full of princesses whom he had abducted, using his force. It was like an ocean, turbulent because of the force of the wind and filled with crocodiles, makaras, fish and serpents. The prosperity that existed with Vaishravana[66] and with Indra with

[64] That is, an image of the goddess.

[65] In the text, 'ten' is an adjective for faces, not arms.

[66] Kubera.

the tawny steeds, all that always existed in Ravana's house, without any diminishing. Whatever prosperity existed with King Kubera, Yama or Varuna, such prosperity and more existed in the rakshasa's house. In the midst of those mansions, there was a residence that was constructed very well. The son of the wind god saw this, filled with many chambers. It was divinely constructed, fashioned in heaven by Vishvakarma for Brahma. This was the vimana named Pushpaka and it was decorated with every jewel. After performing supreme austerities, Kubera obtained this from the grandfather. Through his energy, the lord of the rakshasas defeated Kubera and obtained it. There were images of wolves, fashioned out of silver and gold. The pillars were constructed extremely well and blazed in their prosperity. It was like Meru or Mandara, etched out in the sky. It was decorated everywhere and was full of secret chambers that were auspicious in form. Vishvakarma had fashioned it well and it blazed like the fire and the sun. The stairs were made out of gold and the altars were beautiful and excellent. There were windows and ventilators made out of gold and crystal. The best of platforms were made out of jewels like blue sapphire and emeralds. The great ape climbed on to the divine vimana, Pushpaka. Fragrances arose from the drinks, food and rice stored there. A divine and beautiful fragrance could be smelt, blown along by the wind. Like a friend speaking to an excellent friend, that fragrance seemed to tell the great spirit,[67] 'Come here', summoning him to the spot where Ravana was. Hanumat left in that direction and saw a large and auspicious gallery, loved by Ravana's mind, like an excellent woman who is loved. The stairs were made out of jewels, embellished with golden nets. The floor was made out of crystal and there were images made out of ivory inside. There were a large number of pillars, decorated with pearls, coral, silver, gold and gems. These were even, upright and extremely tall, ornamented all over. Using those tall pillars, like a bird, it seemed to take off and leave for the sky. It was covered with a huge carpet, marked with all the signs of the earth.[68] The

[67] Hanumat.

[68] Rivers, oceans, mountains and forests were painted on the carpet.

residence of the lord of the rakshasas was marked by the calling of crazy birds, the scent of divine fragrances and the spreading out of supreme carpets. It was thick with the smoke and incense of aloe. It was as sparkling white as a swan. Colourfully decorated with flowers, it was as greatly radiant as the celestial cow. The agreeable colour generated delight in the heart. It destroyed sorrow and seemed to generate divine prosperity. Protected by Ravana, it satisfied like a mother, using excellent objectives of the five senses to cater to the five senses. The son of the wind god thought, 'This is perhaps heaven, the world of the gods. This is perhaps Indra's city. This is perhaps the supreme objective.' While thinking in this way, he saw golden lamps. He thought, 'There is the radiance of the lamps, Ravana's energy and the brilliance of the ornaments. It is as if in an act of gambling, a skilled gambler is being defeated by a gambler who possesses greater skills.'

He saw thousands of beautiful women, attired in many kinds of garments. With garments and garlands of many shades, they were seated on many kinds of seats. Midnight was over. They had fallen prey to drinking and sleep. After having sported, in the second half of the night, they were sleeping even more deeply. As they slept, their inner ornaments were radiant, but silent. It was like a great grove full of lilies, where the swans and the bees were quiet. The son of the wind god saw that their eyes were closed and their teeth were covered by their lips. He saw the faces of those excellent women, covered with the fragrance of lotuses. The faces were like lotuses that had bloomed during the day, but now that it was night and day was over, the petals of the lotuses had closed. It seemed as if crazy bees were incessantly hovering around those faces, which were like lotuses, as if seeking out blooming lotuses. The handsome and great ape reasoned it out in this way. He thought, 'In qualities, these faces are the equal of lotuses that bloom in the water.' With the radiance of those women, that pavilion was like the clear sky during the autumn, decorated by stars. The lord of the rakshasas was surrounded by those radiant ones and was like the handsome lord of the stars, surrounded by the stars. The ape thought, 'When their merit is exhausted, stars are dislodged from the sky. All these assembled ones are like that.' From the radiance of the women, there was an auspicious complexion in the palace. They clearly seemed to be like large stars with auspicious rays. Their excellent garlands and garments were scattered around and their heavy breasts were revealed. After drinking and exertions, sleep had taken away their senses. For some, the marks on the foreheads were smudged. For some, the anklets had fallen off. For some other supreme women, the necklaces had been placed to one side. Some wore necklaces made of pearls. For some, the garments were displaced. Like young female horses, for some, the noose of the girdle had been loosened. There were some with excellent earrings, but their garlands were torn. They were like creepers in a great forest, crushed by an Indra among elephants. Some women slept like swans and between their breasts, there were prominent necklaces, with a hue like that of the moon's beams. Others had necklaces made of lapis lazuli and these looked like kadamba birds. The golden threads of others looked like chakravakas. Their radiant hips were like the banks of a river, decorated by flocks of swans, karandavas and chakravakas. They slept like the banks of an illustrious river, full of crocodiles, with the large nets of gold like radiant lotuses. On some, the auspicious marks left by the ornaments were themselves like ornaments on their delicate limbs and on their nipples. The inhalation of breath by some disturbed the ends of the garments of others and they repeatedly breathed on each other's faces. There were many kinds of dazzling and golden ornaments around the necks of those wives, and radiant in form, they rose up like flags. As if with rays that are auspicious, the earrings of some moved around, because of the breath that was gently exhaled by those excellent women. The breath was pleasant and fragrant because of the scent of liquor made from molasses.[69] The breath from their faces seemed to serve Ravana. Some of Ravana's women repeatedly inhaled the fragrance from the mouths of their co-wives, mistakenly taking those to be Ravana's face. The minds of those supreme women were excessively attached to Ravana. They were not completely

[69] More literally, sugar.

independent, and therefore, acted agreeably towards their co-wives. Some were ornamented and slept using their own arms as pillows. Those beautiful women were decorated with garments and bracelets. Some slept on the bosom of another, some in the arms of another. Some slept in the lap of another, some on the thighs of another. They embraced the thighs, flanks, waists and backs of others. Others were intoxicated and overcome by affection, clung to each other. Some slender-waisted ones were delighted at being able to touch the limb of another. The women slept with their arms entwined with each other. It was as if a garland of women had been fashioned out of each other's arms. It was as radiant as a garland, with crazy bees hovering around it. Clinging to each other, they were like a garland made out of flowers adhering to each other, or like a blossoming creeper during a spring month, tended to by the breeze. As their shoulders clung to each other, they were like a grove, frequented by bees. Ravana's women were like a grove. Even if one tried, the ornaments, limbs, garments and garlands of those women couldn't clearly be distinguished from those of others. With many kinds of complexions, Ravana's women slept happily. When one looks without blinking, they were like blazing golden lamps. Those women were the daughters of royal sages, daityas and gandharvas, forced to surrender to the rakshasa's desire. There was no woman who had not been abducted, obtained through the qualities of valour. There was no one who had desired another man, or had indulged in intercourse with another. The only exception was the supreme lady, Janaka's daughter. There was no one who was not of noble birth. There was no one who was ugly. There was no one who was unaccomplished. There was no one who did not know how to serve. None of his wives was weak in spirit. There was no one who was not desired and loved. The lord of the apes thought, 'Just as the rakshasa king's wives are with their husband, it would have been good had Raghava's noble-born wife by dharma been with her husband.' Greatly distressed, he again thought, 'It is certain that Sita is superior to them in qualities. Though the lord of Lanka is great-souled, he has performed an extremely ignoble act.'

Chapter 5(8)

Hanumat looked around and saw excellent couches that were like divine ones, decorated with crystal and jewels. In one spot, he saw a white umbrella that was like the lord of the stars, decorated with garlands at the top. In every direction, there were whisks made of hair in their hands.[70] There were many kinds of fragrances and the scent of excellent incense. It[71] was covered with an excellent spread and the best of sheep hide was spread over it. In every direction, it was embellished with ropes that were made out of garlands. On that, he[72] was like a cloud, with blazing and excellent earrings. The mighty-armed one's eyes were red and his garments were made out of gold. His limbs were smeared with fragrant red sandalwood paste. He was like a cloud in the sky, with the qualities of lightning and as red as the evening. He wore divine jewellery and he was extremely handsome, capable of assuming any form at will. He was asleep and was like Mandara, with its trees and creepers. Having sported in the night, he was adorned in supreme ornaments. He was loved by the rakshasa maidens and brought happiness to the rakshasas. The great ape saw him lying down there, after a bout of drinking. The brave lord of the rakshasas was asleep on a radiant couch. Ravana was sighing like a serpent. The supreme among apes approached him, and then, anxious and scared, retreated. He ascended and resorted to another platform and from there, the great ape looked at the tiger among rakshasas, who was asleep. Lying down on that excellent couch, the Indra among the rakshasas was resplendent. He was like a giant waterfall, with a fragrant elephant inside it. The great-souled one saw that the Indra among rakshasas had spread out his arms, with golden armlets on them. They looked like Indra's standard. There were wounds from the tips of the tusks, created when Airavat had attacked him. His thick shoulders bore marks of being struck with

[70] Of the women attendants.
[71] A specific couch.
[72] Ravana.

the vajra and Vishnu's chakra. The shoulders were appropriate for such a strong one, thick and developed well. It was seen that the nails, thumbs, fingers and palms bore excellent marks. The arms were round, like the trunks of elephants. They were round, like clubs, with well-formed joints. As he slept on that sparkling couch, they were spread around, like five-headed serpents. The upper part of his body was smeared with sandalwood paste that was extremely cool and extremely fragrant, with a hue like that of a hare's blood.[73] He was the one who made yakshas, serpents, gandharvas, gods and danavas scream. Excellent women had massaged him and smeared those excellent unguents on him. The ape saw him lying there on that couch, with his arms spread out. He was like a giant and angry serpent, asleep inside Mandara. The full arms of the lord of the rakshasas were as radiant as a mountain, or like Mandara with its peaks. As the lion among the rakshasas lay down and exhaled, the excellent fragrance of mangoes, punnagas and supreme bakula emerged from his large mouth and filled that house. However, the scent of liquor dominated all this, mixed with juices from sweet rice. He had taken off his golden and radiant crown, dazzling with many kinds of pearls and jewels. Because of the earrings, his face blazed. He was ornamented by a necklace smeared with red sandalwood paste. It dazzled on his thick, broad and large chest. He was attired in a white silk garment and his eyes were like wounds.[74] An extremely expensive and yellow garment was tied well around him.[75] He was like a pile of black beans and sighed like a serpent. He was like an elephant sleeping in the great waters of the Ganga. He was illuminated from the four directions with four golden and blazing lamps. Thereby, all his limbs were like clouds tinged with lightning.

In the house of the lord of the rakshasas, at his feet, the extremely great-souled one saw his wives and his beloved wife. Their faces were like the moon and they were ornamented with the best of earrings. The leader of the apes saw that they were adorned

[73] The sandalwood was red.

[74] They were red.

[75] The yellow garment was tied on top of the white one.

with garlands and ornaments that did not fade. They wore excellent ornaments and were accomplished in dancing and the playing of musical instruments. The ape saw them sleeping, on the arms and lap of the Indra among the rakshasas. The tips of the ears of those women were embedded with diamonds. He saw their earrings and armlets, made out of molten gold. Their faces were like the moon and the delicate earrings sparkled. The mansion was resplendent, like the sky with a large number of stars. The women of that Indra among the rakshasas were exhausted and tired from drinking and exertions.[76] As soon as they found a chance, those slender-waisted ones fell asleep. One could be seen to be asleep, embracing her veena. She was like a lotus floating away on a great river and clutching to a boat. Like an affectionate mother attached to her infant child, another black-eyed and beautiful one slept embracing a drum. Another lovely one who was beautiful in all her limbs and possessed beautiful breasts embraced a war drum, as if she had got back her lover after a long time. Another lotus-eyed one slept while embracing a flute, as if a beautiful lady was embracing her lover and had been overcome by sleep. Another one possessed soft, thick and beautiful golden breasts. With intoxicated eyes, she slept while embracing a drum.[77] There was another unblemished one, with a flat stomach. Exhausted from lust, she slept while clutching a cymbal next to her arms and sides. Another embraced a small drum, as if she was attached to that small drum. The beautiful one slept, as if embracing her young child. Another lotus-eyed woman, intoxicated by desire, slept while clutching on to a drum with her arms, as if in the throes of passion. Another radiant and beautiful lady fell down in her sleep, while clutching a pot. She looked like a sparkling and speckled garland made out of flowers during the spring. Another clutched her own breasts, which were like golden pots, with her hands. Vanquished by the power of sleep, that weak one slept while embracing herself. There was another one with eyes like lotus petals, with a face that was like the full moon. The one

[76] Sexual exertions.

[77] Different types of drums have been named and we have translated all of them as drum.

with the beautiful hips was senseless with desire and slept while embracing another one. Those supreme women embraced different kinds of unknown musical instruments. While they slept, they crushed them with their breasts, like women full of desire embrace men full of desire.

Among all those women, asleep and spread out on a beautiful bed and alone, the ape saw another lady who was full of beauty. She was excellently adorned in ornaments made out of pearls and jewels. She seemed to be adorning that excellent residence with her own beauty. She was the desired one, with a golden complexion and fair. She was the mistress of the inner quarters. The ape saw Mandodari, beautiful in form, lying down on that bed. The mighty-armed son of the wind god saw that ornamented one and reasoned that this one, full of the wealth of beauty and youth, could be Sita. The leader of the apes was filled with great delight and rejoiced. He slapped his arms and kissed his tail. In his joy, he played, sang and walked around. He climbed pillars and fell down on the ground. He exhibited the nature of apes.

Chapter 5(9)

While he was there, the great ape dismissed such thoughts.[78] Thinking about Sita, he thought of something else. 'Separated from Rama, the beautiful one should not be able to sleep. She will not eat, decorate herself with ornaments or drink. If another man approaches, even if that happens to be the lord of the gods, she will not approach him. Even among the gods, there is no one who is Rama's equal.' He decided that the person who was there in that drinking hall must be someone else. Some were exhausted from sporting, others from singing. Others were exhausted from dancing and intoxicated with liquor. Some were resting on tambourines, drums and seats. There were other women who were lying down

[78] That the lady who was sleeping was Sita.

on the best of spreads. There were thousands of women who were adorned in ornaments. They possessed good conduct and could speak about beauty. They could converse about the meanings behind the songs. They were accomplished about the time and the place. They knew how to speak appropriate words. The leader of the apes saw them sleeping, after their sexual pursuits. Amidst them, the lord of the rakshasas was radiant. He was like a bull amidst a large herd of cattle. The Indra among the rakshasas was dazzling, himself surrounded by all of them. He was like a giant male elephant in the forest, surrounded by female elephants. In the residence of the lord of the rakshasas, the great-souled tiger among the apes saw a hall for drinking, filled with all the objects of desire. In that hall for drinking, he saw pieces of flesh from deer, buffaloes and wild boar, laid out. In large golden vessels, the tiger among the apes saw half-eaten bits of peacocks and cocks. Hanumat saw the meat of wild boar, *vardhanasaka*s,[79] porcupines, deer and peacocks, preserved in curds and salt. Many kinds of *krikara*s[80] had been cooked. There were half-devoured *chakora* birds. The flesh of buffaloes, porcupines and goats had been prepared. There were many kinds of superior and inferior lehya, *peya* and *bhojya*.[81] There were sour and salty sauces and many kinds of sweetmeats.[82] Extremely expensive necklaces, anklets, armlets, vessels for drinking and eating, diverse types of fruits and garlands made of flowers were strewn around, making the place look even more prosperous. Here and there, couches and seats were laid out properly. Even without a fire, the drinking hall was seen to blaze. Meat had been prepared exceedingly well, seasoned properly and was separately laid out in that drinking hall. There were many kinds of divine and sparkling *sura*,[83] as if they had been prepared by the gods. There was liquor made from sugar, asava,

[79] This can mean goat, a kind of bird, or a kind of deer.

[80] Partridges.

[81] The four types of food are those that are chewed (*charvya*), sucked (*choshya* or *chushya*), licked (lehya) and drunk (peya). Bhakshya is the same as charvya and bhojya is the same as choshya.

[82] A specific type of sweetmeat known as *ragashadava*, made from the juices of grapes, pomegranates and black gram.

[83] Sura is a general term for liquor.

liquor made from honey, liquor made from flowers and liquor made from fruits. They had separately been flavoured with many kinds of powders. The floor was covered with many kinds of garlands and these made it radiant. The vessels and smaller pans were made out of gold and crystal. There were other smaller vessels that were made out of molten gold. The ape saw pots made out of silver and molten gold there and these were filled with copious quantities of excellent liquor. He saw golden pots that were encrusted with gems. The great ape saw silver vessels that were full. He saw some vessels from which the drinks had been half drunk, others from which the drinks had been completely drunk. There were some from which nothing had been drunk. In some places, there were many kinds of food. In other distinct places, there were many kinds of drink. As he roamed around, in some places, he saw half-eaten food. The smaller vessels had been shattered in some places. In others, the pots had been agitated. In some places, garlands, water and fruits were together. In some places, the couches were empty. In others, many women, supreme in beauty, were asleep, embracing each other. Some women were asleep, overcome by the strength of sleep. As they slept, they stole the garments of others and covered themselves with these. The wind from their breaths gently made the colourful garments and garlands on their bodies quiver, as if a gentle breeze was blowing. The wind blew in different directions, bearing along many kinds of scents—from the cool sandalwood, liquor, honey, juices and different kinds of flowers. Many kinds of fragrant scents blew everywhere in Pushpaka vimana then, from accompaniments used in baths, sandalwood and incense fumes. Some extremely beautiful women were not dark, others were dark. In that residence of the rakshasa, others were golden in complexion. They were senseless from acts of desire and had come under the subjugation of sleep. As they slept, their forms were like those of lotuses.

In this way, the extremely energetic ape searched everywhere in Ravana's inner quarters, but did not see Janakee. The great ape looked at all the women. However, a great thought came over him, about what was virtue and dharma. 'In the inner quarters, I have looked at the wives of someone else, while they were asleep. This will indeed make my dharma suffer severely. In this kingdom, I have looked at the wives of someone else. I have thus seen someone else's wives.' After this the spirited one again had a different thought. He was clear about what needed to be done and was single-mindedly devoted to that task. He decided, 'All of Ravana's wives were trusting and I could have looked at them with eyes of desire. However, there was not the slightest bit of agitation in my mind. The mind is the reason behind what all the senses do, be it in a fortunate situation or an unfortunate one. I am extremely well controlled. I am incapable of searching out Vaidehi somewhere else. When one searches for women, they are always found amidst other women. A creature can only be found among those who are similar in birth. One is capable of finding a lost woman amidst female deer. With a pure mind, I have searched everywhere in Ravana's inner quarters for Janakee, but have not found her.' The valiant Hanumat searched among the maidens of the gods, the gandharvas and the serpents, but did not see Janakee. The ape did not see her there, but saw the other beautiful women. The valiant one seriously thought about going elsewhere.

Chapter 5(10)

That residence was full of colourful chambers covered with creepers and chambers for sleeping. Anxious to see Sita, he wandered around inside it. However, he did not see the one who was beautiful to behold. Unable to see the one who was loved by the descendant of the Raghu lineage, the great ape thought, 'Wishing to see Maithilee, I have searched, but not seen her. It is certain that Sita is dead. The child, supremely interested in protecting herself and her good conduct, has remained on the noble path. There is no doubt that the foremost among the rakshasas, extremely evil in conduct, has killed her. The women of the king of the rakshasas are malformed. They are disfigured and are without radiance. They possess large faces and long and malformed eyes. On seeing them, the daughter of King Janaka has been destroyed from fright. I have spent a long period of time with the apes, but have not been able to see Sita, or establish my manliness. There is no way I can go to Sugriva. That powerful ape will chastise me with sharp punishment. I have searched everywhere in the inner quarters. I have seen all of Ravana's women. However, I have not seen the virtuous Sita. My exertions have been in vain. When I return and approach all the other apes, what will they say? "O brave one! Having gone there, what did you do? Tell us." Having not seen Janaka's daughter, what will I say? The time has passed. It is certain that they will ask me to resort to praya. I have come to the other shore of the ocean. When I return and meet the other apes, what will the aged Jambavat and Angada say? However, being indifferent[84] is the source of prosperity. Indifference is supreme happiness. Therefore, I must again search where I have not searched before. Indifference always accomplishes the objective in every possible way. A creature who acts ensures success from that action. Therefore, resorting to indifference, I will again make supreme efforts. In this region, protected by Ravana, I will search places I have not seen earlier. The drinking hall has been searched and the chamber full of flowers. The chambers with paintings have been searched and so have the chambers for sporting. All the paths in gardens and all the vimanas have been searched.'

Having thought this, he started to search again, in houses that were underground, in houses that were in sanctuaries and in houses that were far away from the main houses. He again started to leap up and leap down, stay and proceed. He opened doors and opened windows. He entered and emerged, climbed up and climbed down. The great ape roamed around in all the spaces. The ape went everywhere in Ravana's inner quarters and did not leave out any space that was more than four fingers in width. He searched the paths between the ramparts and went to the platforms and sanctuaries. He looked in all the wells. Hanumat saw many kinds of rakshasas there, malformed and disfigured. But he did not see Janaka's daughter. He saw excellent women from among the

[84] Indifferent to joy or unhappiness. Therefore, not yielding to despondency.

vidyadharas. Their beauty was unmatched in the world. However, Hanumat did not see the one who brought delight to Raghava. There were beautiful women from among the nagas. Their faces were like the full moon. Hanumat saw them there, but he did not see the slender-waisted Sita. The Indra among rakshasas had crushed naga maidens and forcibly abducted them. Hanumat saw them there, but did not see Janaka's daughter. The mighty-armed one saw those other excellent women there, but did not see her. The mighty-armed Hanumat, the son of the wind god, became depressed. The Indra among the apes, the son of the wind god, saw that his act of leaping across the ocean had become unsuccessful and was again immersed in thoughts. Hanumat, the son of the wind god, descended from the mansion. His senses afflicted by grief, he was immersed in thoughts.

Chapter 5(11)

The leader of the apes crossed the mansion and the ramparts. Hanumat resorted to a force that was like that of lightning in the clouds. Hanumat went beyond Ravana's residence. However, unable to see Janakee Sita, the ape spoke these words. 'Looking for Rama's beloved, I have again wandered around Lanka. However, I have not seen Vaidehi Sita, who is unblemished in all her limbs. I have searched everywhere on earth—pools, ponds, lakes, rivers, groves, marshes, impenetrable spots and mountains. But I have not seen Janakee. Sampati said that Sita is here, in Ravana's residence. That is what the king of the eagles said, but I have been unable to see her. How can Sita, Vaidehi, Maithilee, Janaka's daughter, even though she has been incapacitated, serve Ravana, evil in conduct? I think that the rakshasa must have been scared of Rama's arrows. When he abducted Sita and was flying swiftly, he must have dropped her down somewhere. Or perhaps, as she was being abducted along the path followed by the siddhas, I think the noble one must have seen the ocean and fallen down inside it. Her arms were crushed by the force of Ravana's thighs. Therefore, I think that the large-eyed and noble one has given up her life. As she was being progressively carried across the ocean, Janaka's daughter must have struggled and fell down in the ocean. Alas! While the ascetic Sita was trying to protect her chastity without a relative, has the inferior Ravana devoured her? The dark-eyed one is without any taints. Has she been eaten by the wives of the Indra among the rakshasas, who are wicked in their intent? She is like the full moon. Her eyes are like lotus petals. While she was meditating on Rama's face, she may have been distressed and has died. "Alas, Rama! Alas, Lakshmana! Alas, Ayodhya!" Lamenting in this way, Vaidehi Maithilee may have cast aside her body. Otherwise, in Ravana's residence, lamenting like a *sharika* bird that has been caged, she must certainly have died. Rama's slender-waisted wife has been born in Janaka's lineage. How can the one with eyes like lotus petals remain in Ravana's subjugation? Janaka's daughter has been destroyed or killed and is dead. How can one inform Rama about his beloved wife? What is better? There is a sin in informing him. There is a sin in not informing him. What should indeed be done? This seems to me to be a difficult choice. The time for performing the task is over. What is a better course of action?' In this way, Hanumat started to think again. 'If I go to the city of the Indra among the apes without having seen Sita, how will my manliness have been established? My feat of leaping across the ocean will be in vain. And so will the act of entering Lanka and seeing the rakshasas. When the apes return to Kishkindha, what will Sugriva and the two sons of Dasharatha say? If I go to Kakutstha and give him this extremely disagreeable news that I have not been able to see Sita, he will immediately give up his life. These will be harsh, terrible, cruel, sharp and extremely intolerable words about Sita. They will scorch the senses. Having heard them, he will no longer exist. On seeing him face this great hardship and making up his mind to die, the intelligent Lakshmana, who is extremely devoted to him, will also no longer exist. Hearing that the two brothers have been destroyed, Bharata will also die. On seeing that Bharata is dead, Shatrughna will no longer exist. There is no doubt that on seeing their sons dead, the mothers, Kousalya, Sumitra and Kaikeyee, will no longer exist. Sugriva, the lord of the apes, is grateful and fixed on the objective of truth. On seeing Rama face this state, he will give up his life. The ascetic Ruma will be distressed in her mind and will grieve. She will be miserable and unhappy. On account of sorrow over her husband, she will be afflicted and will give up her life. Afflicted by sorrow on account of Vali and afflicted by grief on account of the king[85] having died, Tara will also no longer exist. When his mother and father have been destroyed, and on account of hardship over Sugriva, how will Prince Angada be able to sustain his life? The residents of the forest[86] will be overcome by sorrow on account of their master. They will strike their heads with their palms and their fists. The apes have been comforted, favoured and respected by the illustrious king of the apes. They will give up their lives. The elephants among the apes will no longer assemble and sport in the forests, the mountains and the canopied areas. They will suffer hardship on account of their master. With their sons, wives and advisers, they will assemble on the summits of mountains and fall down on uneven terrain.[87] The apes will resort to poison, hanging, entering the fire, fasting and weapons.[88] Because of the destruction of the Ikshvaku lineage and because of the destruction of the residents of the forest, I think that there will be terrible lamentations. Therefore, I will not leave this place and go to the city of Kishkindha. Without Maithilee, I am incapable of meeting Sugriva. As long as I do not leave this place, the two great-souled maharathas and the spirited apes will sustain their lives on hope. As long as I am unable to see Janaka's daughter, I will reside in this region near the ocean. There are roots, fruits and water here. I will control myself and live near the root of a tree. I will resort to vanaprastha. I will generate a fire through the use of kindling sticks and enter that pyre. I will sit down and accomplish the task of fasting to death. My body will be eaten by crows and predatory beasts. It is my view that this kind of departure is approved of by the rishis. If I do not see Janakee, I will enter deep water. I have been born from a noble foundation. I am extremely fortunate. I am illustrious and possess a

[85] Sugriva.
[86] Meaning the apes.
[87] Killing themselves.
[88] Again, to kill themselves.

garland of deeds. If I do not see Sita, all these will be destroyed and it will be like a night that lasts for a long period of time. Perhaps I will become an ascetic, controlling myself and resorting to the foot of a tree. Without having seen the dark-eyed one, I will not leave this place. If I leave this place without knowing about Sita, Angada and all the other apes will no longer exist. However, there are many kinds of taints associated with dying. A person who is alive may be fortunate. Therefore, I should sustain my life. If one is alive, it is certain that a meeting may take place.' In this way, he repeatedly bore many kinds of sorrows in his mind. The elephant among the apes was not able to cross over to the other shore of this ocean of grief. 'I will kill the immensely strong Ravana Dashagriva. He abducted Sita because of his desire and this will be some kind of revenge. Perhaps I will seize him and progressively drag him across the ocean, presenting him to Rama, like an animal rendered to Pashupati.'[89] Having been unable to see Sita, he was filled with these kinds of thoughts. With his soul overcome by sorrow, the ape reflected. 'As long as I do not see Sita, Rama's illustrious wife, I will continue to repeatedly search the city of Lanka. If I convey Sampati's words to Rama, and Raghava does not see his wife, he will burn down all the apes. I will reside here, controlling my food and controlling my senses. Because of what I have done, all the men and all the apes should not be destroyed. There is the large grove of Ashoka, filled with giant trees. I will go to that. That has not been searched by me. I will bow to the Vasus, the Rudras, the Adityas, the Ashvins and the Maruts and go there, increasing the sorrow of the rakshasas. I will vanquish the rakshasas and give the queen, the delight of the Ikshvaku lineage, to Rama, like the fruits of asceticism.' With his senses afflicted, Hanumat thought in this way for some time.

After this, the mighty-armed son of the wind god arose. 'I bow down before Rama, together with Lakshmana. I bow down before the queen who is Janaka's daughter. I bow down before Rudra, Indra, Yama and Vayu. I bow down before the moon, the sun and the large number of Maruts.' The son of the wind god bowed

[89] The lord of the animals, Shiva.

down to them and to Sugriva. He glanced in all the directions and headed towards Ashokavana.[90] He first made up his mind to go to the auspicious Ashokavana. The ape, the son of the wind god, later thought about what was to be done. 'It is certain that the grove will be full of many rakshasas. Many kinds of excellent arrangements for Ashokavana will have been thought of. There is no doubt that guards have been earmarked and they will protect the trees. The illustrious one who is inside all creatures[91] will not blow very strongly there. For the sake of Rama and Ravana, I have contracted my size. The gods and the large number of rishis will bring me success here. The illustrious Svayambhu Brahma, the gods of all the directions, Agni, Vayu, Puruhuta,[92] the wielder of the vajra, Varuna, with the noose in his hand, Soma, Aditya, the great-souled Ashvins and all the Maruts will grant me success. The illustrious lord of all beings who ensures success for all creatures will grant me success. The others, who are unseen along the path,[93] will also grant me that. She has a high nose. She has white teeth. She is without any injuries. She has a beautiful smile and possesses eyes like lotus petals. She has a pleasing appearance and is like the lord of the stars[94] to behold. When will I see her? He is inferior and wicked, cruel in his deeds. He adorns himself with ornaments and garments that are extremely terrible. He abducted the ascetic lady with force. When will she come within my range of vision?'

Chapter 5(12)

The immensely energetic one thought for an instant. Making up his mind, he then leapt on to the wall of that residence.[95] With

[90] The Ashoka grove.
[91] The wind.
[92] Indra.
[93] Other minor divinities.
[94] The moon.
[95] Towards Ashokavana, which was outside the residence.

joy writ all over his limbs, the great ape based himself on the wall and looked at all the different kinds of blossoming trees at the advent of spring—salas, ashokas, beautiful blooming champakas, uddalakas, nagavrikshas and mangoes that had the colour of a monkey's face. Like an iron arrow shot from a bowstring, he then leapt into that grove of trees, which was full of mango trees and enveloped by hundreds of creepers. He entered that wonderful place, surrounded everywhere with silver and gold trees and resounding with the calls of birds. The grove was colourful because of the many kinds of birds and herds of animals. Hanumat, the ape, saw that it was like the rising sun. It was surrounded by many kinds of trees that yielded flowers and fruits. It was always populated by maddened cuckoos and bhringarajas. There were these animals and birds and it was also full of happy men. There were flocks of maddened peacocks and many other birds of diverse kinds. While the ape searched for the beautiful and unblemished princess, he woke up birds that were happily asleep. As the many birds flew up, the trees were struck by their wings and released showers of flowers of many different hues. Hanumat, the son of the wind god, was himself radiant, covered with flowers. In the middle of Ashokavana, he looked like a mountain made out of flowers. The ape rushed around in all the directions, having advanced amidst the trees. On seeing him, all the creatures thought that spring[96] had arrived. The earth was resplendent, separately covered by flowers that had showered down from the trees, and looked like an ornamented woman. The trees trembled because of the force of that spirited one. Thus, the ape lead to the showering down of many kinds of flowers. The tops of the trees were bare, shorn of flowers, fruits and leaves. They looked like defeated gamblers, who had flung away their garments and ornaments. The best of trees trembled because of Hanumat's force. Full of flowers, they swiftly shed their flowers, leaves and fruits. The birds on the trees were left with only the branches as refuge. It was as if all the trees had been stirred by the wind. The trees looked like a young maiden with her hair dishevelled and her sandalwood

[96] In its personified form.

paste smudged. It was as if someone had drunk from her lips, leaving teeth marks, as if she had been injured from nails and teeth. Crushed by his tail, hands and feet, Ashokavana itself looked like an excellent tree that had been shattered. With his force, the ape tore at the large creepers that were like bonds. He was like the wind during the monsoon, dispelling masses of clouds over the Vindhyas. As he roamed around there, the ape saw beautiful floors encrusted with jewels and silver. There were golden floors too. There were many kinds of ponds filled with excellent water. Here and there, there were flights of stairs, embedded with extremely expensive gems. There were golden trees along the colourful banks—the sand was made out of pearls and coral and the bottoms were made out of crystal and precious stones. There were clumps of blooming lotuses and lilies, with the sound of chakravakas. Flocks of aquatic birds, swans and cranes, called. In every direction, the river had tall trees alongside it. The canals were tended to properly, with auspicious water like amrita in them. There were hundreds of creepers and the region was shrouded with *santanaka* trees. The grove was enveloped with many kinds of shrubs and the interior had karavira trees. He saw a mountain with a lofty peak and it was like a cloud. In every direction, it was surrounded by peaks. There were caves in the mountain and it was enveloped with many kinds of trees. The tiger among apes saw one of the earth's beautiful mountains. The ape saw the mountain, with the river descending from it, like a beloved one arising from her beloved's lap and leaping down. Descending into the water, the tops of the trees were beautiful. They looked like an angry woman, being restrained by her beloved relatives. The great ape looked at the water in the river again. It was like a beloved who was happy, having reached her beloved again. Not very far from this,[97] Hanumat, tiger among apes, the son of the wind god, saw ponds filled with lotuses and with flocks of many kinds of birds. Though artificial, the pond was full of cool water. The steps were embedded with the best of gems and the beautiful sand was made out of pearls. There was a colourful grove, filled

[97] The mountain.

with many kinds of wonderful herds of animals. With the extremely large mansions, Vishvakarma had constructed this. Though the grove was artificial, it was ornamented everywhere. All the trees there yielded flowers and fruits. There were umbrellas and large platforms. All the smaller platforms were made out of gold. The great ape saw a single golden *shimshupa* tree.[98] It was covered with many kinds of creepers and shrouded in a large number of leaves. In every direction, it was surrounded by platforms made out of gold. He saw parts of the ground where fountains welled out from holes and many other golden trees that blazed like the fire. The brave and great ape thought, 'The radiance of these trees is like that of Meru. Though an ape, I have become golden in complexion.' Those large number of golden trees were fanned by the wind and there was the sound of hundreds of bells. On seeing this, he was overcome by wonder. With great force, he climbed up the shimshapa tree, which was full of leaves. The top was covered with beautiful young shoots and leaves.

He thought, 'From here, I will be able to see Vaidehi, who desires to see Rama. Afflicted by grief, she will roam here and there and come here, as she wills. The Ashokavana of the evil-souled one is firm and beautiful. It is ornamented with champaka, sandalwood and bakula trees. This beautiful pond is frequented by flocks of birds. It is certain that Janakee, Rama's wife, will come here. For Raghava, Rama's beautiful queen is always beloved. Skilled in roaming around in the forest, Janakee will certainly come here. She is the one with eyes like a fawn and is knowledgeable about this forest. Afflicted by thinking of Rama, she will come to this grove. Because of Rama, the beautiful-eyed queen is tormented by grief. She has always been attached to residing in the forest. The one who wanders around in the forest will come here. In earlier times, Rama's beloved wife, Janaka's daughter, always desired those who roamed around in the forest. The young Janakee, who is attached to the performance of sandhya rites, will certainly come here. The one

[98] Alternatively, shimshapa, the Indian rosewood. Indeed, the spelling should be shimshapa. Also used for the ashoka tree, which is what is probably meant here.

with the beautiful complexion will want the auspicious waters of the river for the sake of sandhya rites. This auspicious Ashokavana is worthy of her. Everything that is auspicious is revered by the one who is the wife of Rama, Indra among kings. If the queen, whose face is like the lord of the stars, is alive, she will certainly come here for the sake of the auspicious waters of the river.' This was the view of the great-souled Hanumat. He waited for the wife of the Indra among men. He hid himself in the leaves, thick with blossoming flowers, and looked at everything there.

Chapter 5(13)

Searching for Maithilee, he looked around. He looked at everything that was on the ground. The trees were beautifully adorned with santanaka creepers. They adorned everything there and were full of divine fragrances and juices. Enveloped with animals and birds, it was like Nandana. The ponds were decorated with golden lotuses and lilies. There were many seats and carpets and many underground houses. The trees were full of flowers from all the seasons and beautiful fruit. The radiance of the blossoming ashokas was like the shine of the rising sun. Maruti saw that everything there seemed to be ablaze. Denuded of leaves, the branches were unprepared for the birds that repeatedly descended and perched there. However, the trees were covered with hundreds of colourful flowers. All the way down to the roots, the ashokas, the destroyers of sorrow,[99] were covered with flowers. The great burden of flowers made the trees bend down, as if to touch the ground. There were flowering karnikaras and kimshukas in bloom. Because of their radiance, everything in that region seemed to be ablaze. There were punnagas, saptaparnas, champakas and uddalakas. These had many large and extended roots and were radiant with flowers. Some possessed the complexion of molten gold. Some were

[99] There is a play on words, *a* + shoka, without sorrow.

like the flames of fires. Some were like blue collyrium. There were thousands of ashoka trees there. It was like many colourful groves—Nandana and Chaitraratha. It was superior to all of them and was unthinkable. It was divine and beautiful, surrounded by prosperity. It was like a second sky, with the flowers like a large number of stellar bodies. With hundreds of colourful flowers and jewels, it was like the fifth ocean.[100] The trees were full of flowers from all the seasons, with sweet and fragrant scents. In that beautiful grove, sounds arose from many kinds of animals and flocks of birds. Many kinds of auspicious scents were borne along and these fragrances were pleasant. There was a heap of fragrances that was like an Indra among mountains, like a second Gandhamadana. Not very far from there, in Ashokavana, the bull among apes saw a lofty place of worship.[101] It was as white as Kailasa and thousands of pillars stood in its centre. The stairs were made out of coral and the sacrificial altars were made out of molten gold. It blazed in its prosperity and its end could not be seen with the eyes. Sparkling and tall, it seemed to etch out a painting in the sky.

He then saw her, like the trace of the pure crescent moon at the beginning of shukla paksha. She was attired in a soiled garment and was surrounded by rakshasis. She was distressed and lean from fasting. She was sighing repeatedly. Her beautiful form and radiance could only be discerned slightly. She was like the flame of the fire when it has been enveloped in a net of smoke. She was attired in a single and excellent garment that was yellow in colour. She was without ornaments. She was like a lotus pond, covered in mud and without lotuses in it. The ascetic one was faded and ashamed, tormented by grief. She was like Rohini, afflicted by the planet Mangala. Her miserable face was full of tears. The fasting had made her emaciated. She was immersed in her thoughts. She was extremely miserable and always full of sorrow. She was unable

[100] The text uses the word *panchama,* meaning fifth. This could be a typo and perhaps *dvitiya,* meaning second, is intended. A second ocean makes perfect sense. There are seven oceans and in standard lists, the fifth is an ocean made out of sugar cane juice (*ikshu sagara*). This too makes sense, but less so.

[101] *Chaityaprasada.*

to see her dear ones and only saw the large number of rakshasis. She was like a doe separated from her own kin and surrounded by a pack of dogs. A single braid of hair, with a hue like that of a dark serpent, hung down, up to her hips. She deserved happiness, but was tormented by grief. She was not accomplished in handling hardships. He saw the large-eyed one, more faded and lean than normal. Because of various logical reasons, he decided that this must be Sita.

Her form, when she had been seen being abducted by the rakshasa who could assume any form at will, had been described and this woman's form was like that. Her face was like the full moon and her eyebrows were excellent. Her beautiful breasts were round. Through her radiance, the queen dispelled darkness from all the directions. Her hair was dark. Her lips were like *bimba* fruit.[102] She possessed a firm and slender waist. With eyes like lotus petals, Sita was like Manmatha's Rati.[103] She was desired by the entire world, like the radiance of the full moon. With her excellent body, she was seated on the ground, controlling herself like an ascetic. The timid one sighed a lot, like the terrified wife of an Indra among serpents. Since she was immersed in an extensive and large mass of grief, she was no longer radiant. She was like the flame of a fire, when it has been enveloped in a mass of smoke. She was like a memory that has been lost, or a prosperity that has been thrown away. She was like faith that has been shattered, like a hope that has been frustrated. She was like obstructions in the path of success, like an intelligence that has been tainted. She was like deeds that have suffered through calumny, though the act has not been done.[104] She was suffering because of the obstruction caused to Rama and was afflicted at having been abducted by a rakshasa. With eyes like those of a helpless fawn, she glanced around here and there. Her face was cheerless and her eyelashes, with sidelong glances, were filled with tears. With a miserable face, she sighed repeatedly. She was distressed and was covered in filth and dust. Though she deserved

[102] The fruit of *Momordica monadelpha*.

[103] Manmatha, also known as Madana or Kama, is the god of love and Rati is his wife.

[104] The calumny is false. The act of censure has not actually been done.

to be ornamented, she was without ornaments. She was like the radiance of the king of the nakshatras[105] at a time when it is covered by dark clouds. After having repeatedly glanced at Sita, his mind was unsure about the course of action. She was like learning that has turned lax because it has not been studied and used. With great sorrow, Hanumat accepted that this person without ornaments, like words that have meaning but are without polish, was indeed Sita. He looked at the large-eyed and unblemished princess. Because of various reasons, he debated and determined that this was Sita. Rama had described Vaidehi's limbs and hers were like that. The ornaments that should have enhanced the beauty of her body could not be seen. There used to be well-crafted earrings, in the shape of a dog's teeth, on her ears. There used to be colourful ornaments, made out of jewels and corals, on her hands. However, because she had worn these for a long time, there were dark marks where these used to be. He thought, 'I think these are the ones Rama described. I cannot discern the ones that are missing. But there is no doubt that the ones that are not missing are the ones that were described. She had flung aside her auspicious upper garment, with a yellow complexion like that of a golden plate. It had adhered to a tree and the apes had seen it there. Her excellent ornaments had been dropped on the ground. There were others that had been dropped, making a great sound. Having been worn for a long time, this garment has faded a lot. Even then, it is clear that this one's complexion and radiance are identical to those of the other one. This one with the golden complexion is Rama's beloved queen. She has not been destroyed. Nor has she been destroyed in his mind. She is the one because of whom Rama has been tormented in four ways—compassion, non-violence, sorrow and desire. The compassion was because his wife had disappeared,[106] the non-violence because she was one who sought refuge,[107] the sorrow because a wife had disappeared and desire because of a beloved. This dark-eyed queen's form and the elegance of her major and minor limbs are exactly like Rama's. This

[105] The moon.

[106] This is irrespective of whether the person was a wife or not, hence, compassion.

[107] And violence was caused to her.

queen's mind is vested in him and his is vested in her. It is because of her that the one with dharma in his soul is able to sustain his life even for an instant. Rama is mad with desire for her and has performed an extremely difficult task. Without Sita, the mighty-armed one has been able to remain alive for more than an instant.' Thus, seeing Sita, the son of the wind god was delighted. Mentally, he praised Lord Rama.

Chapter 5(14)

Sita deserved to be praised and the bull among apes praised her. He also praised Rama's delightful qualities and started to think again. For a short while, the spirited Hanumat reflected on Sita. He lamented and his eyes filled with tears. 'She is revered by Lakshmana. She is humble towards her seniors. She loves her seniors. If Sita is afflicted by grief, destiny is indeed very difficult to cross. However, like the Ganga at the onset of the monsoon, because of the efforts of Rama and the intelligent Lakshmana, the queen is not excessively agitated. She is his equal in good conduct, age and character. She is his equal in nobility of birth and signs. Raghava deserves the dark-eyed Vaidehi and she deserves him.' He saw her, golden in complexion, like Shri,[108] loved by the worlds. In his mind, he went to Rama and addressed him in these words.[109] 'It is for the sake of this large-eyed one that the immensely strong Vali has been slain, and Kabandha, who was Ravana's equal in valour, has been brought down. In the forest, Rama used his valour to slay the rakshasa Viradha, terrible in his valour, in a battle, like the great Indra bringing down Shambara. There were fourteen thousand rakshasas who were terrible in their deeds. With arrows that were like the flames of the fire, they were killed in Janasthana. Khara was killed in the battle and Trishira was brought down. Rama,

[108] Lakshmi.

[109] The subsequent sentences are more like Hanumat thinking aloud, rather than words addressed to Rama.

who knows about his soul, killed the greatly energetic Dushana. The wealth of the apes is extremely difficult to obtain and was protected by Vali. It is for her sake that Sugriva obtained it and is honoured by the world. It is for the sake of the large-eyed one that I have crossed the handsome ocean, the lord of the male and female rivers, and have examined this city. For her sake, if Rama whirls around this earth, with its frontiers in the ocean, and even does it to the entire universe, it is my view that this would be proper. If there is a comparison between the dominion of the three worlds and Sita, Janaka's daughter, all the *kala*s of the dominion of the three worlds falls short of one kala of Sita.[110] She is the daughter of the great-souled Janaka, the king of Mithila who follows dharma in his conduct. Sita is firm in her vows towards her husband. When the field was being ploughed, she split the earth and rose up, from the mouth of the plough. She was then covered by the auspicious dust from the field and these were like the pollen from lotuses. Dasharatha was valiant and noble in conduct. He never retreated from a battle. This illustrious queen is his eldest daughter-in-law. Rama knows his soul. He knows about dharma and is grateful. This is his beloved wife, who has now come under the subjugation of the rakshasis. Because of the strength of affection towards her husband, she gave up all the objects of pleasure and not thinking about the miseries, entered the desolate forest. She was attentive towards serving her husband and content with fruits and roots. She obtained great happiness in the forest, as if she was in her own residence. Her limbs are golden in complexion and she always smiles when she talks. This unfortunate one has to undergo this intolerable misery. She is good in conduct and Raghava desires to see her. Ravana is crushing her, like a thirsty person does to a store of water. Through getting her back again, Raghava will certainly find joy. That will be like a king, who has been dislodged from the kingdom, getting the earth back again. She has given up desire and the objects of pleasure. She has been separated from her relatives.

[110] There are sixteen kalas (parts) of the moon and this is extended to everything, the whole consisting of sixteen parts. All the sixteen parts of the three worlds fall short of one-sixteenth part of Sita.

She is sustaining her body only because she desires to meet him. She does not see the rakshasis, or these trees with their flowers and fruits. It is certain that single-mindedly, she only sees Rama. Among all ornaments, the husband is the greatest ornament for a woman. This one is separated from him. Though she deserves to be adorned, she is not adorned. Separated from her, Lord Rama is performing an extremely difficult task. He is sustaining his own body and is not sinking down in sorrow. The tips of her hair are black. Her eyes are like lotuses. She deserves happiness, but is miserable. Knowing this, my mind is also distressed. She is like the earth in her forgiveness. Her eyes are like lotuses. She used to be protected by Raghava and Lakshmana. At the foot of the tree, she is now being guarded by rakshasis with malformed eyes. She is like a lotus whose beauty has been destroyed by ice. One after another, she has suffered from hardships. She is like a female chakravaka, separated from her companion. Janaka's daughter has faced this calamity and is miserable. The ashoka trees are bending down under the burden of flowers on the tips of their branches and are generating sorrow in her. The winter is over and the one with thousands of cool beams[111] has arisen.' The ape looked at all this, considered and made up his mind that this was indeed Sita. The spirited one, strong among the apes and the bears, was seated on that tree.

Chapter 5(15)

The sparkling moon arose in the sparkling sky, with a complexion like that of a clump of lotuses, as if a swan was entering the blue water. The radiance of the one whose radiance is sparkling seemed to help him. The cool rays of the moon seemed to sprinkle the son of the wind god. He saw Sita, with a face resembling the full moon. She was immersed in a burden of sorrow, like a heavily laden boat submerged in water. Hanumat, the son of the wind god, wished to

[111] The moon.

see Vaidehi. Not very far from her, he noticed rakshasis who were terrible to behold. There were those with one eye, many ears, with ears covering the body, without ears, with ears like cones and with high noses that stretched up to the head. There were those whose heads were gigantic, others whose necks were long and thin. There were those with dishevelled hair, without hair and hair that was like blankets. There were those with elongated ears and foreheads and with breasts that hung down. There were those with long lips and with lips that began at the chin. There were those whose faces hung down and those whose knees hung down. They were short, tall, hunchbacked, malformed and dwarfs. The teeth jutted out and the mouths were malformed. There were those with green eyes and disfigured faces. They were malformed and dark in complexion. They were black, angry and quarrelsome. They wielded giant spears, spikes and clubs made out of black iron. There were those with faces like wild boar, deer, tigers, buffaloes and jackals. There were those with feet like elephants, camels and horses and others with heads that were drawn in. There were those with a single hand or foot and those whose ears were like those of donkeys and horses. Some others possessed ears like cows, elephants and monkeys. Some had no nose, others had large noses. Some had horizontal noses, others were with malformed noses. Some had noses like elephants. For others, the nose was affixed to the forehead. Some had feet like elephants, others possessed gigantic feet. Some possessed feet like cows, others had hair on their feet. Some possessed large heads and necks, others large breasts and stomachs. Some possessed large mouths and eyes, others long tongues and nails. There were those with faces like goats, elephants, cows and pigs. There were those with faces like horses, camels and donkeys. The rakshasis, terrible to behold, wielded spears and clubs in their hands. They were angry and quarrelsome. Their teeth jutted out and their hair was the colour of smoke. The rakshasis possessed malformed faces. They were always drinking. They always loved flesh and drink. Their limbs were smeared with flesh and blood. They subsisted on flesh and blood. The best among apes saw them. Their sight was such that it made the body hair stand up.

They were seated around a large tree with a large trunk. The prosperous Hanumat noticed the unblemished queen and princess, Janaka's daughter, seated under the tree. She was tormented by grief and her radiance had faded. Her hair was covered in filth. She was like a star that had fallen down on the ground after its merit had been exhausted. The greatness of her character made her prosperous, but she was unable to see her husband and was in the midst of a calamity. She was without her excellent ornament, the ornament of her husband's love. Seized by the lord of the rakshasas, she was without her relatives. She was like the wife of an elephant, separated from her herd and captured by a lion. She was like the marks of the moon at the end of the monsoon, when it is covered by autumn clouds. Her form was suffering, like that of a veena that is not touched. She should be with her husband, but was separated from him and was under the subjugation of the rakshasas. In the midst of Ashokavana, she was immersed in an ocean of grief. She was surrounded by them, like Rohini by the planets. The queen was like a creeper without flowers and Hanumat saw her there. Her limbs were smeared in filth and her body was devoid of ornaments. She was like a lotus in mud. She shone, but did not shine. The beautiful one was attired in a wrinkled and dirty garment. The ape Hanumat saw the one with eyes like those of a fawn. There were marks of distress on the queen's face. Without her husband's energy, she was faded. Sita, the dark-eyed one, protected herself through her own good conduct. Hanumat saw Sita, with eyes like those of a fawn. As terrified as a fawn, she glanced around in different directions. The trees, bearing shoots, seemed to be burnt down by her sighs. She was in a tide of sorrow, with a fresh wave of sorrow rising up. The son of the wind god obtained unsurpassed delight on seeing Maithilee. She was radiant even without her ornaments. Her well-proportioned limbs were full of forgiveness. On seeing the one with the maddening eyes, delight was generated in him. However, having bowed to Raghava, Hanumat also shed tears. The valiant one bowed down to Rama and Lakshmana. Delighted at having seen Sita, Hanumat composed himself.

Chapter 5(16)

While he was searching for Vaidehi in that grove full of trees in blossom, a little bit of the night was still left. Towards the end of the night, he heard chants of the brahman being uttered by the *brahmarakshasas*[112] who were excellent as officiating priests at sacrifices, knowledgeable in the six Vedangas.[113] The mighty-armed and immensely strong Dashagriva was woken up by the auspicious sounds of musical instruments that were pleasant to hear. The powerful Indra among the rakshasas was woken up at the right time. With his garlands and garments dishevelled, he thought of Vaidehi. Intoxicated by desire, he was severely afflicted by his desire for her. The rakshasa was not capable of suppressing this desire in himself. He adorned himself in all kinds of excellent ornaments and went to the spot where there were many trees filled with all kinds of flowers and fruits. It was surrounded by lakes and adorned with many kinds of flowers. It was supremely extraordinary and was always full of colourful and maddened birds. He saw the avenues, with gates made out of gold and gems. It was pleasant to the eye and was full of many kinds of deer.[114] There were many kinds of deer and fruit that had fallen down. Ashokavana was always full of trees and he entered it. As he proceeded, only one hundred women followed Pulastya's descendant, like the women of the gods and the gandharvas following the great Indra. Some of those women held lamps made out of gold. Others held whisks and fans made out of hair and palm leaves in their hands. Some walked ahead, with golden vessels filled with water. Others proceeded at the rear, holding round cushions. To the right walked a beautiful woman with a golden and bejewelled plate full of drink in her right hand. Another one proceeded at the rear, holding a

[112] A brahmarakshasa is a brahmana who has become a rakshasa.

[113] The six Vedangas are *shiksha* (articulation and pronunciation), *chhanda* (prosody), *vyakarana* (grammar), *nirukta* (etymology), *jyotisha* (astronomy) and *kalpa* (rituals).

[114] The text uses the word of *ihamriga,* so this is something other than ordinary deer (*mriga*). The word ihamriga means wolf. Interpretations take this word to mean artificial deer.

golden staff with an umbrella that was like a swan and as radiant as the full moon. The eyes of Ravana's excellent women were still full of sleep. But they followed their brave husband, like lightning follows a cloud. The ape who was the son of the wind god heard the sound from the girdles and anklets of these excellent women.

The ape Hanumat saw the one who was unthinkable in his strength and manliness, the performer of unmatched deeds, approach the area around the entrance. All the directions were illuminated by the many lamps that were carried. These were being carried ahead of him and were wet with fragrant oil. He was full of desire and insolence and his large eyes were slanted. He was like Kandarpa,[115] without a bow being carried. His excellent upper garment dazzled with the froth from crushed amrita.[116] When it got attached to his armlet, he playfully freed it. He[117] was hidden in the thick mass of leaves, surrounded by flowers. It was as if he[118] was approaching him. The elephant among apes looked everywhere and saw Ravana's excellent women, full of youth and beauty. The extremely handsome and extremely illustrious king was surrounded by them. With these women, he entered the grove that was full of the sounds of animals and birds. The immensely strong one was intoxicated. His ears were like cones and his ornaments were colourful. He saw Vishravasa's son, the lord of the rakshasas. He was surrounded by those excellent women, like the moon by the stars. The great and spirited ape saw the immensely energetic one. The ape thought, 'This is the mighty-armed Ravana.' The immensely energetic Hanumat, the son of the wind god, leapt down. Though he was fierce in his energy, he was surpassed by the other one's energy.[119] Hanumat hid himself behind the leaves.[120] Ravana desired to see the one whose limbs were fair, with excellent hips and well-formed breasts, with hair that was dark at the tips.

[115] Madana or Kama, the god of love.

[116] Amrita is being used here as a term for liquor.

[117] Hanumat.

[118] Ravana.

[119] Ravana's energy was greater than that of Hanumat.

[120] Despite having jumped down from the tree.

Chapter 5(17)

At that time, the unblemished princess, Vaidehi, saw Ravana, the lord of the rakshasas. He was full of youth and beauty and was adorned with excellent ornaments. The beautiful one trembled, like a plantain tree in a storm. The large-eyed one, beautiful in complexion, covered her stomach, thighs and breasts with her hands. She sat down and wept. Dashagriva saw Vaidehi, protected by a large number of rakshasis. She was miserable and afflicted by grief, like a boat submerged in the ocean. Firm in her vows, she was seated on the bare ground. She was like the branch of a tree, severed and fallen down on the ground. Her beautiful limbs were adorned with filth. Though she deserved to be ornamented, there were no ornaments on her. In her wishes and with horses that were her own resolution, she seemed to be going towards Rama, the lion among kings who knew about his soul. Full of her thoughts and sorrow, she was weeping alone, as if dried up. Devoted to Rama, the beautiful one did not see an end to her miseries. Seated there, she seemed to writhe like the wife of an Indra among the serpents. She was like Rohini, invaded by the smoke of the planet that is like a comet.[121] She possessed good conduct and was born in a noble lineage. Her conduct was in conformity with dharma. In addition, she was full of good conduct. However, she seemed to have been born in a wicked lineage.[122] She was like great deeds that were now suffering, like respect suffering from dishonour. She was like wisdom that had decayed and hopes that had been dashed. She was like expectations that had been belied, like commands that had been countered. She was like a direction that blazes at the time of destruction, like worship that has been taken away. She was like a devastated lotus, like an army with the brave warriors killed. She was like the radiance of austerities when it has been destroyed, like

[121] The text uses the word *dhumaketu,* which means something that has smoke as its standard. The word usually means a comet or a meteor. However, the image is of Rohini being attacked by the evil planet Ketu. Therefore, dhumaketu can simply mean the smoking Ketu.

[122] Because of her present state.

a river that has withered away. She was like a sacrificial altar that has been greatly desecrated, like the flame of a fire that has been pacified. She was like the night of a full moon when the lunar disc has been devoured by Rahu. She was like a lotus pond when it has suffered severely from an elephant's trunk, with the petals of the lotuses destroyed and with the birds frightened away. Afflicted by sorrow on account of her husband, she was like a river where the flow of water has dried up. She seemed to be devoid of good cleansing, like a night in krishna paksha. She was extremely delicate. She was born with excellent limbs. She deserved a house that was full of stores of jewels. But like the stalk of a lotus that has just been uprooted, she was being scorched by the heat. She was like the wife of a king among elephants, separated from the herd, seized and tied to a pillar, sighing in her great grief. She wore a single long braid in her hair. But though she took no care, she was still radiant. She was like the earth covered with a wealth of trees, blue at the end of the rainy season. Because of fasting, sorrow, thoughts and fear, she was emaciated and lean. The store of austerities ate little and was miserable. Miserable with grief, she joined her hands in salutation, as if before a god, and sought Dashagriva's defeat at the hands of the foremost among the Raghu lineage. He[123] saw that the unblemished one, with white eyes with excellent lashes that were coppery red at the ends, was weeping, for the sake of his death. Maithilee was extremely devoted to Rama. Ravana tempted her.

Chapter 5(18)

The joyless and miserable ascetic lady was surrounded by them.[124] On seeing this, Ravana addressed her in sweet words that were full of meaning. 'O one with thighs like the trunk of an elephant! On seeing me, you have hidden your breasts and stomach. Because

[123] Ravana.

[124] The rakshasis.

of your fear, you desire that you might yourself disappear. O large-eyed one! I desire you. O beloved one! Show me great respect. You possess qualities in all your limbs. All the worlds find you to be pleasant. O Sita! No men, or rakshasas who can assume any form at will, can harm you. Dispel the fear that has arisen on account of me. O timid one! There is no doubt that when rakshasas use force to abduct and have intercourse with the wives of others, in every way, this is their own dharma.[125] O Maithilee! There is desire in my body and with that desire coursing through, I desire you. But despite this, if you do not desire it, I will not touch you. O queen! O beloved one! Trust me. You have nothing to fear on this account. I truly love you. You should not become addicted to this sorrow. Your hair is in a single braid. You are sleeping on the ground. You are thinking and your garment is faded. You are fasting at the wrong times. These will bring no benefit to you. O Maithilee! When you get me, you will obtain wonderful garlands, sandalwood, aloe, many kinds of garments, divine and other ornaments, extremely expensive drinks, beds and seats, songs, dances and musical instruments. You are a jewel among women. Do not behave in this way. Have ornaments on your body. O one who is excellent in form! On obtaining me, how can you not become beautiful to behold? This birth is beautiful and your youth is ebbing away. It is like the swift flow of water. Once it has passed, it does not return again. O one who is auspicious to behold! I think that after creating you, the one who has created all forms, the creator of the universe,[126] did not create any other form like you. O Vaidehi! You possess beauty and youth. On approaching you, which man, even if it is the grandfather himself,[127] is capable of withdrawing? O one whose face is like the one with the cool beams! O wide-hipped one! Whichever part of your body I look at, my eyes become affixed to that. O Maithilee! Give up this confusion and become my wife. Among the many excellent women here, become my chief queen. O timid one! All the jewels that have been forcibly seized from the worlds, this kingdom and I myself belong

[125] This is sanctioned for rakshasas.

[126] Brahma.

[127] Brahma.

to you. O beautiful one! For your sake, I will conquer the entire earth with its garland of many cities and give it to Janaka. I do not see anyone else on earth who can counter me in strength. Behold my great energy in a battle, when I engage in a duel. The armies of adversaries, gods and asuras, were incapable of withstanding me. They were unsuccessful in encounters and were scattered by me. Their standards were routed. Desire me today and I will perform an excellent good deed for you in return. Let your limbs be extremely radiant with ornaments. I will do this good deed for you and behold your excellent form. O one with the beautiful face! In return for my generosity, do a good deed for me. As you desire, enjoy these objects of pleasure. O timid one! Drink and sport. Give away all the riches on earth, as you wish. You can confidently do whatever you want. You can command without any fear. Because of my favours, you can sport and your relatives can also sport. O fortunate one! Behold my prosperity. That prosperity and fame will become yours. O extremely fortunate one! Rama's garments consist of tattered rags. What will you do with him? Rama will be defeated. Bereft of prosperity, he will roam around in the forest. He will resort to the vow of sleeping on the bare ground. There will be a doubt about whether he will remain alive or not. O Vaidehi! Even if he so wishes, Rama will not be able to see you. You will be like the moonlight when it is covered by dark clouds with flocks of cranes in the front. From my hands, Raghava does not deserve to get you. That would be like Hiranyakashipu's deeds passing into Indra's hands. O one with the beautiful smiles! O one with the beautiful teeth! O one with the beautiful eyes! O charming one! O timid one! Like Suparna takes away a serpent, you are stealing my mind. Your silken garments have faded. You are lean and without ornaments. On seeing you, I am no longer interested in desiring my own wives. All my other women who are in the inner quarters possess all the qualities. O Janakee! Rule over all of them. O one whose hair is black at the tips! These women are supreme in the three worlds. They will serve you, like the apsaras serve Shri. O one with the excellent eyebrows! O one with the beautiful hips! As it pleases you, enjoy me and all the riches and wealth in the worlds, those that belong to Vaishravana.[128] O queen! Rama is not my equal in austerities, strength, valour, riches, energy or fame. Drink. Sport. Pleasure. Enjoy the objects of the senses. There are stores of riches from the directions. There is the entire earth. O one who should play! As you wish, sport with me. Let your relatives meet you and sport too. O timid one! Along the shores of the ocean, there are always nets of flowering trees. Sport with me in those groves. Adorn your limbs with golden and sparkling necklaces.'

Chapter 5(19)

Sita heard the words of the terrible rakshasa. Her tone was miserable and afflicted. She replied slowly, in a miserable voice. Sita was afflicted by grief and weeping. The ascetic lady was trembling. The beautiful one, devoted in vows to her husband, thought about her husband. The one with the beautiful smiles placed a blade of grass between them and replied.[129] 'Withdraw your crazy mind from me. Turn your mind towards those who are your own. You should not crave me, like those who are the performers of wicked deeds should not aspire for success. My duty is to have a single husband. I will not perform the reprehensible task of deviating from this. I have been born in a great and auspicious lineage and have also got a noble lineage.'[130] Having said this, the illustrious Vaidehi turned her back towards Ravana. Then she again spoke these words. 'I am the wife of another person and it is inappropriate that I should be your wife. It is virtuous to have an eye towards dharma. O virtuous one! Follow the vows of the virtuous. O one who roams around in the night! The wives of others should be protected, just as you protect your own ones. Treat others like your own self and find pleasure in your own

[128] Kubera.

[129] When one was speaking to an unworthy person, there was a custom of placing a blade of grass in between.

[130] The one she married into.

wives. A person who is not satisfied with his own wives is fickle. His senses are fickle. For someone whose wisdom is inferior in this way, the wives of others will convey him to his defeat. Are there no virtuous people here? Or do you not follow those virtuous ones! That is the reason your words and mind have turned towards what is false and do not accept the medication prescribed by the discriminating. After having obtained a king who is not cleansed in soul and is addicted to bad policy, prosperous kingdoms and cities are destroyed. In that way, Lanka, full of heaps of jewels, has obtained you. Because of the crimes of a single person, it will soon be destroyed. O Ravana! O one who lacks foresight! The creatures will rejoice at the destruction of a perpetrator of wicked deeds who has brought about his destruction because of what he himself has done. People who have been slighted by your wicked deeds will be delighted and will say, "It is good fortune that this terrible one has faced this calamity." I am incapable of being tempted through prosperity or wealth. Like radiance cannot be separated from the sun, I cannot be separated from Raghava. He is the greatly revered protector of the worlds. After having used his arm as a pillow, how can I use the arm of another one as a pillow? I am an appropriate wife for that lord of the earth. I am his, like learning and bathing at the end of a vow belong to a brahmana who knows about his soul. O Ravana! I am miserable and it is best that you should take me to Rama, like a female elephant that lives in the forest meets with a lord of elephants. It is appropriate that you should wish to have Rama, bull among men, as your friend. That is unless you desire a terrible death for yourself. The wielder of the vajra may let you go. The Destroyer may let you go for a long time. However, when he is enraged, Raghava, the lord of the worlds, will not let someone like you escape. You will hear a great roar from the sound of Rama's bow. It is like the thunder of the vajra, when released by Shatakratu. Marked with the signs of Rama and Lakshmana, those well-jointed and swift arrows, shafted with the feathers of herons, will soon descend here, like flaming serpents. They will slay the rakshasas and envelop everything everywhere, without leaving any space anywhere. Like

Vinata's son[131] plucking out a serpent with force, Rama will be the great Garuda and the Indra among the rakshasas will be a great serpent. My husband is the destroyer of enemies and will quickly take me away from you. Like Vishnu with the three strides, he will take away the blazing prosperity from the asuras. Because of the wicked deeds you performed, the army of the rakshasas was slain in Janasthana and it became a killing field. You were incapable of protecting them. You entered the lonely hermitage when the two lions among men weren't there. O inferior one! You abducted me when the two brothers had gone out. Like a dog smells out the scent and is incapable of remaining in a spot when there is a tiger present, you smelt out Rama and Lakshmana. In a conflict with them, you will be unable to withstand both of them together, just as in the conflict, one of Vritra's arms was incapacitated by Indra's arms. Swiftly, with Soumitri, the protector Rama will take away your life with his arrows, just as the sun dries up a little bit of water. Whether you go to Kubera's mountain or his residence, or whether you go to King Varuna's assembly hall, there is no doubt that Dasharatha's son will free you,[132] just like a great tree is uprooted by a bolt of thunder that is its destiny.'

Chapter 5(20)

The lord of the rakshasas heard Sita's harsh words. He replied to Sita in words that were disagreeable, though they seemed to be agreeable. 'In whatever form women are sought to be assured, that is exactly the way a person becomes subservient. A person who speaks pleasantly is rebuffed in exactly the same way.[133] Because my desire for you has been awakened, I have controlled my rage. This is like an excellent charioteer controlling the horses, even when they

[131] Garuda.

[132] Of your life.

[133] If a man is conciliatory, he has to yield to women. If he speaks sweetly, he is rebuffed.

are striding along a smooth road. Among men, desire is undesirable, since it binds them down. Among people, compassion indeed leads to affection. O one with the beautiful face! That is the reason I have not killed you. Since you are addicted to someone who is on a false exile,[134] you should be slain and should not be shown respect. O Maithilee! Because of the harsh and terrible words you have spoken to me, you deserve to be killed.' Ravana, the lord of the rakshasas, spoke to Vaidehi in this way. Thereafter, full of rage and fury, he again spoke to Sita. 'I will protect you for two months. After that, you will be killed by me. O one who is beautiful in complexion! By then, you must climb on to my bed. After those two months, if you do not desire me as your husband, you will be cooked in the great kitchen as my breakfast.' On seeing that the Indra among the rakshasas was thus censuring Janakee, the large-eyed maidens of the gods and the gandharvas grieved. When she was censured by the rakshasa, some used their lips and others used their faces and eyes to somehow comfort her.

Reassured by them, Sita, encased in the pride and strength of her good conduct, spoke these beneficial words to Ravana, the lord of the rakshasas. 'Your deeds are reprehensible and it is certain that there is no one who is able to restrain you from adhering to something that is not beneficial. Like Shachi is to Shachi's lord, I am the wife of the one with dharma in his soul. In the three worlds, who other than you will desire me in his mind? O worst among rakshasas! I am the wife of the infinitely energetic Rama. Having spoken these wicked words, who will free you from your destination? This is like a proud elephant and a hare who are together in the forest. Rama is said to be the elephant and you are said to be the inferior hare. You have abused the protector of the Ikshvaku lineage and are not ashamed. You will not be able to approach his dominion, not even with your eyes. O ignoble one! These eyes of yours are cruel, malformed and black and tawny. Since you have looked at me with these, why have they not fallen down on the ground? I am the wife of the one with dharma in his soul and Dasharatha's

[134] Meaning Rama.

daughter-in-law. Since you spoke about me, why has your tongue not shrivelled away? You ought not to speak about the austerities Rama has observed. O Dashagriva! You deserve to be burnt down. Yet, I am not burning you down with my energy. I belong to the intelligent Rama and you are incapable of abducting me. There is no doubt that this has been ordained by destiny for the sake of you being killed. You used your bravery against your brother, the lord of riches,[135] who possessed strength. However, for Rama, why did you resort to stealing his wife?'[136]

Ravana, the lord of the rakshasas, heard Sita's words. He dilated his cruel eyes and looked towards Janakee. He was like a blue cloud. His arms and head were huge. His stride possessed the spirit of a lion. He was handsome and the tips of his tongue and eyes blazed. He was attired in red garlands and garments. The ornaments on his body were made out of molten gold. With colourful garlands and pastes, he looked like a mountain covered with dust that was moving. A long dark blue *shronisutra*[137] extended around his body. It looked like the serpent around Mandara, at the time of extracting amrita.[138] He was adorned with earrings that had the complexion of the rising sun. He was like a mountain with ashoka trees that were full of red blossoms and shoots. His eyes red with rage, he looked at Vaidehi. Like a serpent that was sighing, Ravana spoke to Sita. 'You are pointlessly following someone who follows bad policy.[139] I will destroy you today, like the sun destroys sandhya with its energy.'[140]

Having told Maithilee this, King Ravana, who made his enemies scream, commanded all the rakshasis, who were terrible to behold. Some had a single eye, others had a single ear. For some, the ear covered the body. There were those with ears like cows and

[135] Kubera.

[136] Without using your strength.

[137] Usually, a string tied around the loins. But sometimes, also used for the belt to which a sword was tied.

[138] When amrita was produced by churning the ocean, Mandara was the base and Vasuki was the rope used for churning.

[139] Meaning Rama.

[140] The morning sandhya, dispelled by the light of the rising sun.

elephants, others with long ears or no ears. There were those with feet like elephants, horses or cows, others with hair on the feet. There were those with a single eye, or a single foot. There were those with thick feet, or no feet. Some possessed gigantic heads and necks, others possessed gigantic breasts and stomachs. There were those with gigantic faces and eyes, long tongues, or no tongues. There were those without noses. There were those with mouths like those of lions, cows or pigs. 'O rakshasis! All of you collectively act so that Sita Janakee swiftly comes under my subjugation. Act favourably and unfavourably, use sama, dana and bheda. Raise the prospect of danda and make Vaidehi comply.' The Indra among the rakshasas repeatedly instructed his rakshasis. Overcome by desire and anger, he censured Janakee.

A rakshasi named Dhanyamalini quickly approached Dashagriva. She embraced him and spoke these words. 'O great king! Sport with me. What use will this Sita be to you? As a vehicle for desire, if someone uses a person who is not interested in desire, that only torments his body. A greater pleasure is obtained from a person who wishes to use herself as a vehicle of desire.' Thus addressed, the powerful one flung that rakshasi away. With a complexion like that of the blazing sun, he entered his residence. The maidens of the gods, the gandharvas and the nagas were all around him, surrounding Dashagriva as he entered that excellent house. Maithilee based herself on supreme dharma and trembled because of her fear for Ravana. Confounded by desire, he abandoned Sita and entered his own radiant residence.

Chapter 5(21)

King Ravana, who made his enemies scream, spoke to Maithilee in this way. Having instructed all the rakshasis, he departed. The Indra among the rakshasas left and went to his inner quarters again. The rakshasis, terrible in form, rushed towards Sita. The rakshasis, senseless with rage, reached Sita. They addressed Vaidehi in these extremely harsh words. 'The great-souled Ravana is the excellent descendant of Pulastya. O Sita! However, you are showing great disrespect to the idea of being Dashagriva's wife.'

After this, a rakshasi named Ekajata spoke these words to Sita, addressing her as one whose waist could be clasped in the hands.[141] Her eyes were coppery red in anger. 'Among the six Prajapatis, the fourth Prajapati is a son born through Brahma's mental powers.[142] He is renowned as Pulastya. Through his mental powers, the energetic maharshi Pulastya had a son. His name was Vishravasa and he was like Prajapati in his radiance. O large-eyed one! His son is Ravana, the one who makes his enemies scream. You should become the wife of that Indra among rakshasas. O one who is beautiful in her limbs! Why are you not showing due respect to the words I have spoken?' At this, a rakshasi named Harijata spoke these words. Her eyes were like those of a cat and she widened them in her anger. 'The thirty-three gods[143] and the king of the gods have been vanquished by him. You should become the wife of that Indra among rakshasas. He is immersed in valour. He is brave. He does not retreat from the field of battle. He is strong and brave. Why don't you wish to become his wife? The immensely strong king will give up his wives, the ones he respects the most. Ignoring all those immensely fortunate ones, Ravana will serve you. In the prosperous inner quarters, full of many kinds of jewels, there are one thousand women. Abandoning all of them, Ravana will serve you. In battles, he has disarmed the gods, the serpents, the gandharvas and the danavas. The one who has defeated them in battles has come to your side. The great-souled Ravana possesses all the riches. O wicked one! Why don't you want to become the wife of that Indra among rakshasas? The sun does not scorch him. The wind god is terrified of him and does not blow. O long-eyed one! Why aren't you by his side? Scared of him, the trees shower down flowers. O

[141] The waist was slender enough to be cupped by the two hands. But a slender waist was not a sign of beauty among the rakshasas.

[142] The number of Prajapatis varies from text to text and eleven or fourteen is a more common number. Therefore, it is difficult to determine which six are meant.

[143] Eight Vasus, eleven Rudras, twelve Adityas and two Ashvins.

one with the excellent eyebrows! The mountains and clouds yield the water that he desires. O beautiful one! He is king of kings in the kingdom of the nairittas. Why don't your thoughts turn towards becoming Ravana's wife? O queen! O beautiful one! This is the truth and I have spoken beneficial words to you. O one with the beautiful smiles! Accept them. Otherwise, you will no longer exist.'

Chapter 5(22)

The rakshasi women, with disfigured faces, approached Sita. Harshly, those women addressed her in these disagreeable and harsh words. 'O Sita! The inner quarters are pleasing to all creatures. It is full of expensive couches. Why don't you show due respect to the idea of residing there? You are a human and you should not show a great deal of respect to the idea of being a human's wife. Withdraw your mind from Rama. Otherwise, you will no longer exist. O unblemished one! He has been dislodged from his kingdom. He has failed in his objective. He is impotent.'

Sita, whose eyes were like lotuses, heard the words of the rakshasis. Her eyes overflowing with tears, she spoke these words. 'All of you have come together and have spoken words that are condemned by the worlds. In your minds, why aren't these words regarded as sin? A human lady should not become the wife of a rakshasa. If you want, all of you can eat me. But I will not act in accordance with your words. He may be distressed and he may have been separated from his kingdom. But he is my husband and my preceptor.'

Hearing Sita's words, the rakshasis became senseless with rage. Goaded by Ravana, they censured her in harsh words. Hanumat was silent, hidden in the shimshapa tree. The ape heard the rakshasis censure Sita. As she trembled, they angrily surrounded her from all directions. They licked their blazing lips in a horrible way and bit their elongated teeth. Extremely angry, they quickly grabbed their battleaxes and said, 'This one does not deserve to be the wife of Ravana, the lord of the rakshasas.' The one with the beautiful face was censured in this terrible way by the rakshasis. Shedding tears, she approached the shimshapa tree. Near the shimshapa tree, Sita was surrounded by the rakshasis. The large-eyed one reached the spot and was overwhelmed by sorrow. She was wan and her face was distressed. The garment that she wore was faded. In every direction, those terrible rakshasis censured her.

There was a rakshasi named Vinata and she was terrible to behold. Her teeth and stomach jutted out. Assuming an angry form, she said, 'O Sita! You have displayed enough affection towards your husband. O fortunate one! In everything, it is thought that anything in excess leads to hardship. O fortunate one! I am satisfied with you. You have followed the norms created by humans. O Maithilee! However, I speak words to you that are in the nature of medication. Act accordingly. Serve Ravana as your husband. He is the lord of all the rakshasas. He is brave and handsome. He is like Vasava, the lord of the gods. He is accomplished and is ready to renounce. He speaks pleasantly to everyone. Rama is a miserable human. Abandon him and seek refuge with Ravana. O Vaidehi! You will have celestial unguents on your limbs. You will be adorned in celestial ornaments. From today, become the mistress of all the worlds. O queen! O beautiful one! Be like Svaha[144] to Agni, or Shachi to Indra. O Vaidehi! Rama is miserable and has lost his lifespan. What do you have to do with him? If you do not act in accordance with these words, in this very instant, all of us will eat you up.'

There was another one and her name was Vikata. Her breasts hung down. She roared, raised her fists and angrily spoke to Sita. 'O extremely evil-minded one! You have uttered many words that are disagreeable in form. O Maithilee! Because of our mildness and our compassion towards you, we have tolerated them. But you are not acting according to our beneficial words, which are appropriate for the time. You have been brought to this shore of the ocean, which is extremely difficult to reach. O Maithilee! You have entered Ravana's terrible inner quarters. You are imprisoned

[144] Agni's wife.

in Ravana's house and are protected exceedingly well by us. Even Purandara himself will find it impossible to save you. O Maithilee! Act in accordance with my beneficial words. There has been enough of shedding tears. Cast aside this futile grief. Serve affection and delight. Abandon this incessant misery. O Sita! As you wish, sport happily with the king of the rakshasas. O timid one! You know that the youth of women is not permanent. Until it is over, enjoy the happiness. O one with the maddening eyes! With the king of the rakshasas, roam in the beautiful gardens, mountains and groves. O beautiful one! Seven thousand women will remain under your control. Serve Ravana as your husband. He is the lord of all the rakshasas. O Maithilee! If you do not act in accordance with the words I have spoken, I will pluck out your heart and eat it.'

There was a rakshasi named Chandodari and she was cruel to behold. She twirled around a giant spear and spoke these words. 'The eyes of this one are as agitated as that of a deer. Because of her fear, her breasts are trembling. On seeing her, abducted by Ravana, a great desire arises in me. It is my view that I will eat her liver, spleen, the flesh above the heart, the heart and its muscles, the entrails and the head.'

At this, a rakshasi named Praghasa spoke these words. 'Let us crush this cruel one's neck. Why are we delaying? Let us then inform the king that the woman has died. There is no doubt that he will then tell us to eat her up.'

At this, a rakshasi named Ajamukhi spoke these words. 'Let us kill her, chop her up into equal pieces and divide those amongst us. We will divide her among ourselves. I do not like quarrels. Let drinks be brought quickly and many kinds of garlands.'

At this, a rakshasi named Shurpanakha spoke these words. 'I like what Ajamukhi has said. Liquor destroys all kinds of sorrow. Let it be brought quickly. After we have tasted human flesh, we will dance in Nikumbhila.'[145]

Sita, who was like the daughter of a god, was censured in this fashion by the extremely terrible rakshasis. She let go of her fortitude and wept.

[145] In front of the goddess named Nikumbhila.

Chapter 5(23)

The cruel rakshasis uttered many harsh and terrible words. Janaka's daughter wept. She was greatly terrified and her voice was indistinct because of her tears. Thus addressed, the spirited Vaidehi told the rakshasis, 'A woman should not become the wife of a rakshasa. I will not act in accordance with your words. If all of you so wish, you can eat me up.' Sita was like the daughter of a god and was in the midst of the rakshasis. She had been censured by Ravana. Afflicted by grief, she could not find any peace. She trembled a lot and seemed to sink into her own body. She was like a doe in the forest, separated from her herd and oppressed by wolves. Because of her great sorrow, she clung on to a blossoming branch. Grieving and with her mind shattered, she thought about her husband. Her large breasts became wet from the tears that were flowing from her eyes. She reflected, but could not see an end to her miseries. She trembled and fell down, like a plantain tree in a storm. Because she was frightened and scared of the rakshasis, her face turned pale. Sita's long braid of hair was also seen to tremble, as if it was a wriggling snake. She sighed, afflicted by grief. The sorrow robbed her of her senses. Afflicted, Maithilee shed tears and lamented. Afflicted by grief, she exclaimed, 'Alas, Rama!' The beautiful one again said, 'Alas, Lakshmana! Alas, my mother-in-law Kousalya! Alas, Sumitra! The aphorism that learned people cite is indeed true. "If it is the wrong time, for a woman or a man, it is extremely difficult to come by death." I am being oppressed by these cruel rakshasis. I am miserable and without Rama. But even then, I am alive, for more than an instant. I am miserable and have a limited store of merit. I will perish, like one without a protector. I am like a laden boat tossed around in the ocean, struck by the force of the wind. I am unable to see my husband and am under the control of the rakshasis. I am indeed suffering because of my sorrow, like a bank deluged by the water. His eyes are like lotus petals and his brave stride is like that of a lion. He is grateful and pleasant in speech. Those who are able to see my lord are fortunate. Rama knows about his soul and I have been separated from him in every way. It is as if I have tasted a fierce poison. It is extremely rare that I should still be alive. Earlier, what kind of great sin have I committed in a different life? That is the reason I have obtained this extremely terrible and dreadful misery. Surrounded by this great sorrow, I wish to give up my life. When I am protected by these rakshasis, I cannot reach Rama. Indeed, shame on being a human. Shame on being under someone else's control. I am incapable of giving up this uneasy life.'

Chapter 5(24)

Her lowered face was overflowing with tears. The child, Janaka's daughter, lamented and started to speak. She seemed to be mad and crazy. She grieved and her senses were in a whirl. Like a young mare, she writhed and rolled around on the ground. 'When Raghava was distracted, the rakshasa Ravana, who can assume any form at will, crushed me and brought me here by force, though I was crying. I am under the control of the rakshasis and I am being censured in an extremely terrible way. Suffering from great grief, I am thinking. I am not interested in remaining alive. There is no point to my remaining alive. There is no point to ornaments. Without maharatha Rama, I am residing amidst these rakshasis. Since I have been separated from him, shame on an ignoble person like me. Since I am able to sustain my life for more than an instant, my life must be a wicked one. Without the beloved one, what respect do I have for life? What is the point to happiness? He is the lord of the earth, up to the frontier of the ocean. He is pleasant in speech. I will cast aside my body. Let it be sliced up and eaten. Abandoned by my beloved, I cannot withstand this sorrow for a long time. I will not touch Ravana, the roamer in the night, with my left foot. Where is the question of doing something reprehensible, like desiring him? He does not know a refusal. He does not know me. He does not know my lineage. His nature is cruel and he wishes to obtain me. I will be cut, sliced, divided and burnt in a blazing fire, but I will not serve Ravana. What is the point behind this long prattling? Raghava is famous, wise, grateful and compassionate. He is good in conduct. I suspect that because of my misfortune, I may suffer and he may turn hard-hearted. He single-handedly disabled fourteen thousand rakshasas in Janasthana. Why should he not be able to reach me? I have been imprisoned by the rakshasa Ravana, who is limited in valour. Indeed, my husband is capable of slaying Ravana in a battle. In a battle in Dandakaranya, Rama slew Viradha, bull among rakshasas. Why should he not be able to reach me? Lanka is in the middle of the ocean and is extremely difficult to assail. However, should he so desire, there will be no obstruction in the path of Raghava's arrows. His beloved wife has been abducted by a rakshasa. What is the reason why Rama, firm in his valour, has still not reached her? I suspect that Lakshmana's elder brother does not know that I am here. Had he known it, the spirited one would have shown his intolerance towards the oppressor. The king of the eagles would have gone to Raghava and told him about the abduction. But he was brought down by Ravana in an encounter. Though he was aged, Jatayu performed a great deed in protecting me. In a duel, he stood before Ravana. If Raghava knows that I am here now, he will use his arrows and angrily remove rakshasas from all the worlds. He will blow away the city of Lanka. He will dry up the great ocean. He will destroy Ravana's name and his inferior deeds. The protectors of the rakshasis will be slain in house after house and they will weep, just as I am now. There is no doubt about this. Rama and Lakshmana will search out the Lanka of the rakshasas. When the two of them see an enemy, he will not be able to remain alive even for an instant. Lanka will soon become like a cremation ground, with the roads filled with the smoke from funeral pyres. There will be flocks of vultures everywhere. In a short while, my wish will be fructified. This evil course of action is telling me about the destruction that all of you will face. Inauspicious portents are being seen in Lanka. In a short while, it will be robbed of its lustre. There is no doubt that Ravana, worst among the rakshasas, will be slain and the invincible Lanka will be destroyed and dried up, like a woman who has become a widow. It is auspicious and prosperous now. But its lord and the rakshasas will be destroyed. The city of Lanka will become like a woman whose husband has been destroyed. There is no doubt that rakshasa maidens will weep in house after house. In a short while, I will hear the sounds of those who are afflicted by grief. It will be dark and the radiance will be destroyed. The bulls among the rakshasas will be killed. The city of Lanka will be burnt down by Rama's arrows. When the brave Rama knows that I am now in Ravana's residence, the ends of his eyes will turn red. The cruel and wicked Ravana has set a time period for me. But it is actually his time that is over. The nairittas perform wicked deeds and do not know what should not be done. Because of their adharma, a great catastrophe now presents itself. The rakshasas who eat flesh do not know about dharma. It is certain that the rakshasa is thinking of me as breakfast. What will I do without Rama? He is pleasant to behold. His eyes are red at the ends. Unable to see him, I am extremely miserable. If there is someone here who can give me some poison now, without my husband, I wish to quickly see the god Vaivasvata.[146] Rama, Lakshmana's elder brother, does not know that I am alive. Had they known this, they would have searched out my route above.[147] There is no doubt that on account of sorrow over me, Lakshmana's brave elder brother has gone to the world of the gods. He has given up his life on earth. The gods, the gandharvas, the siddhas and the supreme rishis are blessed. They are able to see Rama, my lotus-eyed protector. Perhaps the intelligent one is observing dharma and kama for their sake. I am the wife of the royal sage Rama. He is the *paramatman*.[148] There is affection towards someone who can be seen. There is no affection towards someone who cannot be seen.[149] But those who are ungrateful destroy affection and Rama will not destroy it. Do I not possess any qualities? Why am I suffering misfortune in this way? I am the beautiful Sita who deserves the best.

[146] Yama.

[147] Meaning, on earth and above it.

[148] The supreme soul.

[149] This shows some doubt about Rama no longer being affectionate towards her, because he cannot see her.

But I am without Rama. Without the great-souled one, it is better to be dead than alive. Rama is unblemished in his character. He is brave and is the destroyer of enemies. Or perhaps the two brothers, best among men, are roaming around, having taken to the forest. They may have cast aside their weapons and are surviving on roots and fruits in the forest. Perhaps the evil-souled Ravana, Indra among rakshasas, has deceitfully killed the two brave brothers, Rama and Lakshmana. I have come to a point in time where, in every possible way, I desire to die. But even when I face this hardship, death has not been ordained for me. The great-souled sages who revere truth are indeed blessed. Those immensely fortunate ones have conquered their souls. Therefore, they have no likes or dislikes. Misery results from likes. Affection leads to greater fear. Those great-souled ones have separated themselves from either. I bow down before them. I have been abandoned by my beloved Rama, who knows about his soul. Having come under the subjugation of the wicked Ravana, I will cast aside my life.'

Chapter 5(25)

When Sita said this, the terrible rakshasis became senseless with rage. Some of them went to the spirited Ravana to tell him about this. The rakshasis, terrible to behold, approached Sita. They again addressed her in harsh words, the purport of which was a single objective. 'O ignoble one! O Sita! O one who has made up his mind to be wicked! The rakshasis will happily devour your flesh now.' Sita was thus censured by those ignoble ones.

An aged rakshasi named Trijata was lying down. On seeing this, she spoke these words. 'O ignoble ones! Eat your own selves. Do not devour Sita. This is Janaka's beloved daughter. She is Dasharatha's daughter-in-law. Today, I have seen a terrible dream that makes the body hair stand up. This is about her husband's existence and the destruction of the rakshasas.' When Trijata said this, the rakshasis became senseless with rage. All of them were terrified and addressed

Trijata in these words. 'What kind of night was it and what dream have you seen? Tell us.'

Hearing the words that emerged from the mouths of the rakshasis, at that time, Trijata addressed them in words that described what she had seen in the dream. 'There was a divine palanquin made out of ivory and it was in the sky. It was yoked to one thousand horses and Raghava was himself in it. In my sleep, I saw Sita, attired in white garments. I can see her now, on Mount Shveta, surrounded by the ocean. Sita joined Rama, like the radiance attached to the sun.[150] I also saw Raghava astride a gigantic elephant with four tusks. It was as large as a mountain and with Lakshmana, he[151] wandered around on it. Those two tigers among men blazed in their own energy. Wearing white garlands and garments, they presented themselves before Janakee. Janakee was on the summit of the mountain. Her husband grasped her and placed her on the shoulder of the tusker in the sky. After this, the lotus-eyed one arose from her husband's lap. I saw that she used her hands to wipe the moon and the sun. Thereafter, those two princes were on that excellent elephant. With the large-eyed Sita, they stationed themselves above Lanka. Kakutstha came here himself, with his wife, Sita. He was on a chariot that was yoked to eight white bulls. Wearing white garments, Lakshmana approached. He was with his brother, Lakshmana, and his wife, Sita. From the Pushpaka vimana, Ravana fell down on the ground. He was seen to be dragged along by a woman, with his head shaven and attired in black garments. He was on a chariot that was yoked to donkeys. His garlands and unguents were red. He headed in the southern direction and entered a lake full of mud. A woman dressed in red garments tied Dashagriva by the throat. She was dark and her limbs were covered with mud. She dragged him in the southern direction. Dashagriva rode a wild boar, Indrajit rode a porpoise and Kumbhakarna rode a camel. They left for the southern direction. I saw an assembly hall that was filled with

[150] Sita joined Rama on the palanquin.
[151] Rama.

the sounds of singing and the playing of musical instruments. Rakshasas attired in red garlands and red garments were drinking there. The beautiful city of Lanka, filled with horses, chariots and elephants, was seen to be plunged in the ocean, with its arches and gates shattered. In Lanka, all the rakshasa women were smeared with ashes. They were drinking oil and dancing, laughing in loud voices. All the bulls among rakshasas, Kumbhakarna and the others, grasped a red garment and entered a lake filled with cowdung. Go away.[152] You will be destroyed. Raghava will obtain Sita. With the rakshasas, he will kill you in his great rage. His beloved and extremely revered wife followed him on his exile to the forest. Raghava will not condone the act of her being terrified and censured. Therefore, enough of these cruel words. One must resort to reassurances. The idea of requesting Vaidehi appeals to me. In the midst of miseries, if a woman sees this kind of a dream, she will be freed from all her varied miseries and obtain supreme pleasure. O rakshasis! Why do you want to address her in words of censure? A terrible fear for the rakshasas has presented itself from Raghava. Bow down and please Maithilee, Janaka's daughter. She will certainly save the rakshasis from this great fear. The signs on this large-eyed one's limbs are such that nothing contrary, however subtle, can be seen. There is only the shadow of a bad quality, arising out of dread and misery.[153] She does not deserve unhappiness. This is the queen who presented herself in the sky. I can see that the prospect of Vaidehi accomplishing her objective has presented itself. Raghava will be victorious and the Indra among the rakshasas will be destroyed. I can see that her eyes, which are as large as lotus petals, are throbbing. There is a reason for this and hear from me about this great joy. Suddenly, one of Vaidehi's arms is trembling. The left arm of this accomplished one has become a trifle erect. Her excellent left thigh is like an elephant's trunk. It is trembling, indicating that Raghava will stand before her. A bird is entering its nest on a branch and

[152] This is Trijata speaking, after recounting the dream.
[153] The only discernible bad quality is the grief.

repeatedly uttering words of comfort, that happiness will arrive. It is calling repeatedly, as if cheerfully urging her.'

Chapter 5(26)

Sita heard the unpleasant words spoken by Ravana, Indra among the rakshasas. Afflicted by these disagreeable tidings, she was terrified, like the daughter of a king of elephants attacked by a lion along the extremities of a forest. The timid one was amidst the rakshasis and was severely censured by Ravana's words. Sita was like a young girl released in the middle of a desolate forest and lamented. 'In this world, the learned do speak the truth. Death does not come before the appointed time. With my merits exhausted, I am being threatened here and am able to sustain life for more than an instant. I am joyless and am filled with many kinds of misery. Since it has not been shattered into one thousand fragments, like the summit of a mountain struck by a bolt of thunder, my heart must indeed be extremely hard. However, not the slightest bit of sin can be attributed to me. The one who is disagreeable to behold[154] can kill me. I am not inclined to give myself to him, any more than a brahmana can give a mantra to someone who is not a brahmana. Before long, the ignoble Indra among the rakshasas will certainly use sharp weapons to sever my limbs, like a scalpel is used to slice a foetus, unless the lord of the worlds[155] comes here. For a miserable person like me, these two months of misery will seem to be like a long time. I will be like a thief who has committed a crime against the king, and at the end of the night, has been bound up before being killed. Alas, Rama! Alas, Lakshmana! Alas, Sumitra! Alas, Rama's mother and my mother! I am limited in fortune and face this calamity, like a boat in the great ocean, tossed around in a strong storm. Those two spirited sons of the king sought to capture

[154] Ravana.
[155] Rama.

the creature that was in the form of a deer. They will certainly be killed because of me, like two bulls among lions struck by a bolt of lightning. I am limited in fortune and it is certain that Destiny tempted me then, in the form of a deer. Thus, the son of a noble one abandoned a stupid person like me and Rama's younger brother abandoned Lakshmana's elder brother. Alas, Rama! O one who is truthful in his vows and long-armed! O one whose face is like the full moon! Alas! O one who loves to bring benefit to the world of the living! Alas! You do not know that I will be killed by the rakshasas. I have had no divinity other than you. My forgiveness, sleeping on the ground, control, dharma and vows towards my husband have proved to be futile, like an act done for men who are ungrateful. The dharma that I followed has been unsuccessful. The devotion towards a single husband is futile. Lean and pale, I am unable to see you. I am without you and have no hope of meeting you. You obeyed the rule of following your father's command. Having followed this vow, you will return from the forest. You will be without fear and will have accomplished your objective. I think that you will find pleasure with large-eyed women. O Rama! There is desire in me for you. I am tied to my affection for you. However, before long, I will be destroyed. My austerities and vows have been futile and I abandon them. I am limited in fortune. Shame on this life. Someone like me must quickly give up life, through poison or sharp weapons. But in this house of the rakshasa, there is no one here who will give me poison or a weapon.' Tormented by thought, she thought a lot. She seized her braid of hair and thought, 'I will hang myself with this braid and quickly go to Yama's abode.' In this way, Sita lamented a lot. She remembered Rama in all her soul. She trembled, with her mouth dry, and approached that excellent tree which was full of flowers. Delicate in all her limbs, she approached it and seized a branch of that tree. The one with the auspicious limbs thought of Rama, Rama's younger brother and her own lineage. Many kinds of portents presented themselves before her—many that did not indicate sorrow, indicating that perseverance ensures victory in this world. Those are portents that had earlier been seen, as signifying success.

Chapter 5(27)

The unblemished one was there, distressed. Her hair was beautiful. Her joy had vanished and her mind was suffering. But auspicious omens presented themselves before the auspicious one, like dependents cluster around a man who is prosperous. Her auspicious left eye had long eyelashes. It was bright, large and dark, set in a white disc. That single eye started to throb, like a red lotus when it is struck by a fish. Her beautiful left arm was round and thick. It deserved to be smeared with excellent aloe and sandalwood paste. For a long time, her beloved had used it as an excellent pillow. That started to quickly quiver. She had been born with two excellent thighs. They were close together and plump, like the trunk of an Indra among elephants. The left one started to tremble, as if indicating that Rama was standing in front of her. Her excellent complexion was like that of gold, but was slightly soiled because of dust. Her eyes sparkled. Her limbs were excellent and the tips of her teeth were sharp. Her garment was slightly dislodged.[156] Her eyebrows were excellent. These and other signs seemed to speak and tell her that her objective would be successful, just as a seed is devastated and destroyed by the wind and the sun, but is rejuvenated with delight when it rains. Her lips were like the bimba fruit. Her eyes, eyebrows and the tips of her hair were excellent. Her eyelashes were curved. Beautiful white teeth could be seen inside her mouth. She was like the moon, freed from Rahu's mouth. Her sorrow was dispelled. Her exhaustion vanished. Her fever was quietened. She was like a creature who wakes up in delight. The noble one's fair face was radiant. It was as if the one with the cool beams has arisen in the night.

Chapter 5(28)

The brave Hanumat heard the truth about everything—Sita, Trijata and the censure of the rakshasis. He looked at the

[156] Another good omen.

queen, who was like a god in Nandana. After this, the ape had many different kinds of thought. 'Many thousands and tens of thousands of apes have searched for her route in all the directions and I have found her. I am a well-appointed spy who is capable of remaining unnoticed by the enemy. I have wandered around in secret and have not been detected by them. In particular, I have examined this city of the rakshasas and the power of Ravana, the lord of the rakshasas. I should comfort the wife of the one who is immeasurable and is compassionate towards all beings. She desires to see her husband. I will comfort the one whose face is like the full moon. She confronts a hardship that she has not faced earlier and sees no signs of it coming to an end. The senses of this queen are overcome by grief. If I return without reassuring her, a taint will be attached to that act of departure. If I leave, this illustrious princess will be unaware about her salvation. Janakee will give up her life. The mighty-armed one's face is like the full moon and he is eager to see Sita. He deserves to be comforted by me. However, in the presence of the ones who roam around in the night, I am incapable of speaking to her. Indeed, how should I set about my task? That is the reason I face a difficulty. If I do not comfort her during whatever is left of the night, there is no doubt that, in every way, she will give up her life. If I do not speak to this slender-waisted one, when Rama asks me what words did Sita utter about him, what will I say in reply? If I quickly leave this place, without Sita's message, with his angry and fierce eyes, Kakutstha will burn me down. For Rama's sake, even if I urge my master[157] to come here, his arrival with his soldiers will be unsuccessful. I will remain among the rakshasis who are here and watch out for an opportunity. She is in a great deal of torment and I will slowly comfort her. I am extremely small in stature. In particular, I am an ape. I can speak the language of humans, such as Sanskrit.[158] But if I speak the language of humans, such as Sanskrit, Sita will think that I am Ravana and will be frightened. I must certainly speak in the language of humans, in words that are

[157] Sugriva.

[158] The word used is *samskrita,* which means cultured and polished. Instead of Sanskrit as we know it today, this may simply mean the polished language of humans.

full of meaning. Without that, this unblemished one is incapable of being comforted by me. Because of the rakshasas, she is already scared. If she sees my form and I speak to Janakee, she will again be overcome by terror. When that fear is engendered, this spirited one will make a sound. The large-eyed one knows that Ravana can assume any form at will. When Sita suddenly makes a sound, the large number of rakshasis, who are like the Destroyer, will wield many kinds of terrible weapons and assemble. The ones with the disfigured faces will then surround me from all sides. They will use their strength to try and kill me and capture me. They will see me run around on the branches, the trunks and twigs of these excellent trees. Consequently, they will be filled with fear and suspicion. They will see my giant form wandering around in the grove. The rakshasis with the disfigured faces will be filled with dread and fear. The rakshasis will summon the rakshasas whom the Indra among rakshasas has appointed in the residence of the Indra among rakshasas. Causing anxiety, they will descend here with force to crush me, wielding many weapons like spears, arrows and swords in their hands. They will angrily surround me. Even if I destroy that army of rakshasas, I will not be able to reach the other shore of the great ocean. Many swift-acting ones will envelop me and capture me. This one[159] will not know whether I have been captured or have not been captured. Wishing to harm, these violent ones may cause injury to Janaka's daughter. Rama and Sugriva's task will face a danger. She is surrounded by rakshasas and signs of her trail have vanished. Janakee resides here, surrounded and protected by the ocean. If I am killed or captured by the rakshasas in the encounter, I do not see anyone else who can help in accomplishing Rama's task. When I am killed, even when I think about it, I do not see any other ape who can leap one hundred yojanas across this large and extensive ocean. If I so wish, I am capable of killing thousands of rakshasas. But then, I will not be able to reach the other shore of the great ocean. The outcome of a battle is uncertain and in doubt. The idea does not appeal to me. Which wise person will embark on

[159] Sita.

an uncertain act, when he is himself unsure? There is a great sin in my speaking to Sita. However, if I do not speak to her, Vaidehi will give up her life. Accomplished objectives are lost if one acts against the time and the place, like darkness is dispelled at the rising of the sun, especially if the messenger is confused. Even if the intelligence has distinguished what must be done from what must not be done, if the messenger prides himself on being learned, the task may be destroyed and is not successful. How can the task not be destroyed? How can I avoid confusion? How can my leaping across the ocean not be rendered unsuccessful? How can she hear my words and not be agitated?' Intelligent among intelligent ones, Hanumat thought in this way. 'Rama is unblemished in his deeds and is my friend. If I think about him in my mind and recount those exploits, there will be no agitation. Rama is supreme among the Ikshvaku lineage and knows about his soul. I will offer words about him, auspicious words that are in conformity with dharma. I will make her hear all those sweet words that I speak. I will make everything intelligible, so that she trusts me.' Hidden among the branches of the tree and glancing towards the lady, the greatly fortunate one spoke many sweet words about the lord of the world.

Chapter 5(29)

The great ape reflected thus, in many kinds of ways. He spoke sweet words and made Vaidehi hear those. 'There was a king named Dasharatha and he possessed chariots, elephants and horses. He was auspicious in conduct and performed great deeds. He was upright and immensely illustrious. He was born in a lineage of emperors and was like Purandara in his strength. He was devoted to non-violence. He was not inferior. He was compassionate and truth was his valour. He was foremost among those of the Ikshvaku lineage. He was prosperous and extended his prosperity. He possessed all the qualities of a king. He was extensive in prosperity and was a bull among kings. He was famous in the four corners of earth. He was happy and conferred happiness. He loved his eldest son, whose face was like the lord of the stars. His name was Rama and he was especially best among all archers. He protected his own conduct and protected his people. He protected the world of the living. Dharma represented supreme austerities for him. The brave one did not waver from the truth. Following his aged father's command, with his wife and his brother, he went on an exile to the forest. In the great forest there, while on hunts, he killed Khara and Dushana. On hearing that they had been slain in Janasthana, Ravana was angry and abducted Janakee. I have heard about her from Raghava and have found her, with the beauty, complexion and prosperous signs that were described.' After saying this, the bull among apes stopped for a while. Hearing this, Janakee was filled with great wonder. Her excellent hair curved at the tips. The timid one's face was covered with her hair. But she raised it and looked at the shimshapa tree. Not knowing what to think, she looked diagonally, up and down. She then saw the adviser of the lord of the apes. The son of the wind god resembled the rising sun.

Chapter 5(30)

Her mind awhirl, she saw the ape, humble and pleasant in speech, hidden inside the branches. Seeing the best among apes present himself humbly, the beautiful Maithilee thought that this was a dream. Seeing him, she was struck severely and lost her senses, as if she had lost her life. In a short while, the large-eyed one regained her senses and started to think. 'Today, I have seen a malformed ape in my dream and this is prohibited by the sacred texts. I hope that Rama, Lakshmana and my father, King Janaka, are well. This is not a dream. Afflicted by sorrow and grief, there is no sleep for me. Since I am without the one whose face is like the full moon, there is no happiness for me. In all my sentiments, I am tormented by his thoughts. I have felt my desire for him today. Since I am always thinking about him and seeing him, I must have heard this. Perhaps I have been thinking about my wishes and debating them with my intelligence. What is the reason why he possesses this kind of form? The form is clearly manifest and it is speaking to me. I bow down before the lord of speech, the wielder of the vajra, Svayambhu and the fire god. This resident of the forest is in front of me. Let what he has spoken come true and let there be no violation of this.'

Chapter 5(31)

The immensely energetic Hanumat, the son of the wind god, joined his hands in salutation, holding them above his head. He addressed Sita in sweet words. 'Your eyes are like lotus petals. You are attired in a silken garment that is faded. Who are you? O unblemished one! You are standing, holding on to a branch of the tree for support. Why are tears of sorrow flowing from your eyes? This looks like water that is spreading along the petals of two lotus flowers. O beautiful one! Who are you? Have you been born among the gods, the asuras, the serpents, the gandharvas, the rakshasas, the yakshas or the kinnaras? O one with the beautiful face. Who are you? Have you been born among the Rudras, the Maruts, or the Vasus? O beautiful one! To me, you seem to be a divinity. Are you Rohini, best among stellar bodies and best among those who possess all the qualities? Abandoned by the moon, have you fallen down from the abode of the gods? O dark-eyed one! Are you the fortunate Arundhati and have you angered your husband, Vasishtha, through some confusion?[160] O extremely slender-waisted one! Are you grieving because your son, father, brother or husband has left this world and gone to that world?[161] Marks can be discerned on your body and it is my view that you must be the queen of a king or a princess. If it pleases you, tell me what I am

[160] Thus leading to a curse.
[161] The world hereafter.

asking. Are you the Sita who has been forcibly abducted by Ravana from Janasthana?'

Vaidehi spoke these words to Hanumat, who was still in his refuge on the tree. 'I am the daughter of the great-souled Janaka of Videha. My name is Sita and I am the intelligent Rama's wife. I spent twelve years in Raghava's residence, a place that can satisfy all the objects of desire. I enjoyed all human objects of pleasure. In the thirteenth year, the king and his preceptor prepared to instate the descendant of the Ikshvaku lineage in the kingdom. When arrangements were being made for Raghava's consecration, the queen named Kaikeyee spoke these words to her husband. "From today, I will not consume the daily drink and eat the daily food. If Rama is consecrated, that will be an end to my life. O supreme among kings! You had gladly given me your word earlier. If that is not going to be rendered false, let Raghava go to the forest." The king was truthful in speech. Hearing Kaikeyee's cruel and disagreeable words, he was confused. He remembered the boon he had granted to the queen. The aged king was established in the dharma of truth. Weeping, he sought the kingdom from his illustrious eldest son. In his mind, the handsome one thought that his father's words were dearer than the consecration. He accepted those words. He does not receive without giving. He never speaks anything disagreeable. Rama has truth as his valour and he does these even at the expense of his life. The immensely illustrious one cast aside his immensely expensive upper garment. He mentally gave up the kingdom and entrusted me with his mother. Without him, the thought of residing in heaven does not appeal to me. I was quickly ready to leave for the forest, ahead of him. The immensely fortunate Soumitri, the delight of his friends, was ahead of us. Adorning himself in the bark of trees, he followed his elder brother. We were firm in our vows and showed a great deal of respect to the command of our lord.[162] We had not seen the forest, severe to behold, earlier. But we entered it. The infinitely energetic one resided in Dandakaranya and I, his wife, was abducted by the rakshasa, the evil-souled Ravana. He has

[162] Dasharatha.

shown me the favour of letting me live for two months. When that period of two months is exceeded, I will give up my life.'

Chapter 5(32)

Hearing her words, Hanumat, the leader of the apes, transited from one kind of sorrow to another kind of sorrow. Comforting her, he replied, 'O queen! I am Rama's messenger and have come to you with his message. O Vaidehi! Rama is well and has asked about your welfare. He knows about the *brahmastra* weapon.[163] He is supreme among those who know the learning of the Vedas. O queen! He is Rama, Dasharatha's son, and he has asked about your welfare. The immensely energetic Lakshmana is loved by him and follows his master. He is tormented by grief and greets you, with his head bowed down.'

The queen heard about the welfare of those two lions among men. Delight and joy pervaded through all her limbs and she told Hanumat, 'This is a fortunate account and seems to me like a common aphorism. "Even if it is one hundred years, as long as a man is alive, joy comes to him."' Meeting each other, they were greatly affectionate towards each other. They confidently started to converse with each other. Sita was miserable with grief. Hearing her words, Hanumat, the leader of the apes, attempted to approach her. But as soon as Hanumat sought to inch closer to her, Sita suspected that he might be Ravana. 'Alas! Shame. Shame on what I have done. Why have I told him this? Having assumed a different form, it is Ravana who has come to me.' Afflicted by grief, she let go of the branch of the ashoka tree. The one with the unblemished limbs sat down on the ground. The mighty-armed one spoke to Janaka's daughter. However, scared and terrified, she did not look at him again.

Sita, with a face like the moon, saw that he was worshipping her. With a long sigh, she addressed the ape in a sweet tone. 'O

[163] Brahma's weapon.

one who uses maya! Even if you are Ravana himself and have immersed yourself in maya, you have again given rise to torment in me. This is not right. You are indeed the Ravana who abandoned his own form and assumed the form of a mendicant. I have seen that in Janasthana. O roamer in the night! O one who can assume any form at will! I am miserable and emaciated because of fasting. You are again giving rise to torment in me. This is not right. If you have indeed come here as Rama's messenger, may you be fortunate. O best among the apes! I love accounts about Rama and I am asking you about them. O ape! Tell me about Rama's qualities. I love them. O amiable one! Steel my mind, just as water erodes the bank of a river. I was abducted a long time ago. O resident of the forest! Sleeping happily, I am seeing this dream where Raghava has sent someone. Even if I see the brave Raghava and Lakshmana in a dream now, I will not suffer. But even the dream is censuring me. I do not think that I have seen this ape in my dream, because prosperity is incapable of arising from that.[164] I am now in the midst of prosperity. How have my senses been confused in this way? Is this because of the movement of the wind?[165] Has this perverse condition arisen from madness? Is this a mirage? Perhaps I am mad and confused and this is a sign of madness. I must ascertain the nature of my own self and about this resident of the forest.' Thus, in many kinds of ways, Sita debated the pros and the cons. Since rakshasas can assume any form at will, she then thought that this must be the lord of the rakshasas. Having decided this, the slender-waisted Sita, Janaka's daughter, did not reply to the ape.

Hanumat, the son of the wind god, understood what Sita was thinking. He spoke words that were pleasant to the ear and delighted her. 'He is as energetic as the sun. Like the moon, he is loved by the world. Like the god Vaishravana, he is the king of all the worlds. He is full of valour, like the immensely illustrious Vishnu. He is

[164] A dream.

[165] In Ayurveda, wind (*vata*), bile (*pitta*) and phlegm (*kapha*) are the three *doshas* or humours in the body and they are always striving against each other. This is a reference to vata.

truthful and pleasant in speech, like the god Vachaspati.[166] He is handsome, extremely fortunate and beautiful, like the embodied form of Kandarpa. He is angry and strikes at the right place. He is the best maharatha in the world. The world rests on the arms of the great-souled one. The form of a deer drew Raghava away from the hermitage and you were abducted from that deserted spot. You will witness the consequences of that. Before a long period of time, the valiant one will slay Ravana in a battle. He will angrily release arrows that blaze like the fire. I am a messenger sent by him and I have come here before you. Because he has been separated from you, he is afflicted by grief and has asked about your welfare. The immensely energetic Lakshmana is one who extends Sumitra's delight. The mighty-armed one has greeted you and has asked about your welfare. O queen! The ape named Sugriva is Rama's friend. He is the king of the foremost among the apes and he has asked about your welfare. Rama, Sugriva and Lakshmana always remember you. O Vaidehi! Despite being under the control of the rakshasis, it is good fortune that you are still alive. You will soon see Rama, maharatha Lakshmana and the infinitely energetic Sugriva, amidst crores of apes. I am Sugriva's adviser and I am an ape named Hanumat. Leaping across the great ocean, I entered the city to come here to see you. O queen! I am not the one you take me to be.[167] Abandon your suspicion. Trust my words.'

Chapter 5(33)

Vaidehi heard that account of Rama from the bull among the apes. She replied in words that were gentle and sweet. 'How did you come into contact with Rama? How did you get to know Lakshmana? How did this meeting between apes and men take place? O ape! What are the signs on Rama and Lakshmana? If you

[166] The lord of speech, Brihaspati.

[167] That is, Ravana.

again tell me these, I will not be immersed in sorrow. Where was he? What is Rama's form like? How were his thighs? How were his arms? Tell me about Lakshmana.'

Hanumat, the son of the wind god, was addressed by Vaidehi in this way. At this, he started to recount the truth about Rama. 'O Vaidehi! O lotus-eyed one! You know this. But it is good fortune that you are asking me about your husband's appearance and that of Lakshmana. O large-eyed one! I will tell you about the marks and signs Rama and Lakshmana possess. Listen. Rama's eyes are like the petals of a lotus. All creatures find him to be pleasant. O Janaka's daughter! He was born with beauty and accomplishments. He is like the sun in energy, like the earth in forgiveness, like Brihaspati in his intelligence and like Vasava in his fame. He protects the world of the living. He protects his own people. The scorcher of enemies protects his own conduct and dharma. O beautiful one! In the world, Rama is the protector of the four varnas. He is the one who ensures that ordinances are observed in this world. He is radiant. He is worshipped. He is exceedingly devoted to the vow of brahmacharya. He does good deeds for the virtuous. He knows how to implement tasks. He knows about royal skills. He is humble. He is revered by the brahmanas. He is learned and possesses good conduct. The scorcher of enemies is modest. He knows about the Yajur Veda. He is humble. He knows the rites of the Vedas. He is greatly worshipped. He is knowledgeable about *dhanurveda*, the Vedas and the Vedangas. The mighty-armed one possesses broad shoulders. His neck is like a conch shell and his face is auspicious. His collarbone is hidden. His eyes are coppery red. O queen! Rama is famous among people. His voice is like the sound of a kettledrum. The powerful one's complexion is soothing. His limbs are symmetric and well proportioned. His complexion is dark. He is firm in three places.[168] He is long in three places.[169] He is even in three places.[170] He is tall in three places.[171] He has three

[168] Breast, wrist and feet.

[169] Eyebrows, arms and soles.

[170] Hair, testicles and knees.

[171] Breast, navel and lower abdomen.

lines.[172] There are three spots that are depressed.[173] There are four parts that aren't too long.[174] There are three twirls in his hair. He has four lines.[175] He has four lines.[176] He is four cubits tall.[177] He is symmetric in four parts.[178] There are fourteen parts that are symmetric.[179] He possesses four teeth.[180] He possesses four kinds of gait.[181] His lips, cheekbones and nose are large. He is smooth in five parts.[182] He has excellent joints in eight places.[183] He has ten lotuses.[184] Ten parts are large.[185] He is extensive in three ways.[186] He is pure in two ways.[187] Six parts of the body are high. He is fine in nine places.[188] Raghava obtains three things.[189] He is devoted to the dharma of truth. He is prosperous. He accumulates and dispenses favours. He knows about the time and the place. He speaks pleasantly to everyone. His stepbrother, Soumitri, cannot be defeated. He is like him in affection, form and qualities. Those two roamed around the earth, searching for your trail. They saw the lord of the animals,[190] who had been dislodged by his elder

[172] On the belly and in the neck.

[173] The middle of the soles, the lines on the soles and the nipples.

[174] The neck, the penis, the back and the shanks.

[175] At the root of the thumb, indicating knowledge of the four Vedas.

[176] On the forehead, indicating longevity.

[177] The word used is *kishku*. Kishku is the length of a forearm, that is, one cubit. If a cubit is taken as 18 inches, this gives a height of 72 inches, or 6 feet.

[178] Cheeks, arms, shanks and knees.

[179] Eyebrows, nostrils, eyes, ears, lips, nipples, elbows, wrists, knees, testicles, loins, hands, feet, thighs.

[180] This is not to be taken literally. All it means is that the four teeth, at the ends of the upper and lower jaws, were large.

[181] Lion, tiger, elephant and bull.

[182] Hair, eyes, teeth, skin and soles.

[183] Arms, fingers, toes, eyes, ears, thighs, calves and knees.

[184] Ten parts of the body that are like lotuses—face, mouth, eyes, tongue, lips, palate, breasts, nails, hands and feet.

[185] Chest, head, forehead, neck, arms, heart, mouth, feet, back and ears.

[186] Radiance, fame and deeds.

[187] The father's side and the mother's side.

[188] Hair, moustache, beard, nails, body hair, skin, joints in the fingers, penis and perception.

[189] Dharma, artha and kama.

[190] Meaning Sugriva.

brother. He was on the slope of Rishyamuka, in a region that was full of many trees. Sugriva, pleasant to behold, was seated there, terrified of his brother. We are the ones who serve Sugriva, the king of the apes who is devoted to the truth. His elder brother had dislodged him from the kingdom. Those two, supreme among those who wield bows and attired in bark, came to the beautiful region in Mount Rishyamuka. The bull among apes saw the two tigers among men, wielding bows. His fear confused him and he leapt down from the summit of the mountain. Stationed on the summit, the Indra among the apes soon sent me to those two. Because of the command of the lord Sugriva, I went to those two tigers among men, who possess beauty and the signs. I joined my hands in salutation and stood there. Ascertaining the nature of the truth, those two were delighted with me. Taking those two tigers among men on my back, I went to that spot.[191] I told the great-souled Sugriva the truth. They spoke to each other and a great affection resulted. Those two lords among men, accomplished in their deeds, and the lord of the apes comforted each other and recounted what had happened earlier. At this, Lakshmana's elder brother assured Sugriva, who had been restrained by his brother, Vali, fierce in his energy, because of a woman. Lakshmana told Sugriva, the Indra among the apes, about the sorrow that Rama, the performer of unblemished deeds, was suffering from, because of your disappearance. Hearing the words that Lakshmana had spoken, the Indra among the apes sat down. He lost his radiance, like the sun when it has been grasped by a planet.[192] There were ornaments that had adorned your body. When you were being abducted by the rakshasa, the mass of ornaments had fallen down on the ground. The leaders of the apes brought all those to Rama. Cheerfully, they showed him these. But they had no idea about your route. I gave Rama the jingling ornaments that I had collected and he lost his consciousness. He was like a god. He displayed those ornaments on his lap and lamented like a god. He looked at

[191] Where Sugriva was.

[192] An eclipse, the planet being Rahu.

them and wept repeatedly. They ignited a fire of grief in Dasharatha's son. Afflicted by grief, the great-souled one lay down for a long time. Using many kinds of words, with a great deal of difficulty, I made him get up again. With Soumitri, Raghava repeatedly looked at those extremely expensive ornaments and then showed them to Sugriva. O noble one! Because he could not see you, Raghava was tormented. He was incessantly consumed by a fire, like the fire that rages inside a mountain.[193] Because of you, Raghava suffered from lack of sleep, grief and worries. They tormented the great-souled one, like a fire to a house in flames. Because of the sorrow at not being able to see you, Raghava trembled. It was like a large pile of boulders trembling because of a huge earthquake. O daughter of a king! Though he roamed around in extremely beautiful groves, rivers and waterfalls, because he could not see you, he found no pleasure in these. O Janaka's daughter! Raghava, tiger among men, will soon kill Ravana, with his friends and relatives, and get you back. Rama and Sugriva contracted an agreement with each other, about the slaying of Vali and about searching you out. The spirited Rama killed Vali in an encounter. In an assembly of all the bears and the apes, he made Sugriva their lord. O queen! The unity between Rama and Sugriva was generated in this way. Know me as Hanumat and I have come here as their messenger. When he got his kingdom back, Sugriva summoned the great apes. For your sake, he despatched those extremely strong ones in the ten directions. They were commanded by Sugriva, the extremely energetic Indra among the apes. Resembling the king of the mountains, they left towards different parts of the earth. The prosperous and extremely strong Angada is Vali's son. Surrounded by one-third of the forces, this tiger among apes left. We lost our way in Vindhya, supreme among mountains. We were overcome by great grief and many days and nights passed. The designated time passed and we lost all hope of accomplishing our task. Terrified of the king of the apes, we were ready to give up our lives. O queen! We searched forests, impenetrable areas in the mountains and mountainous waterfalls.

[193] A volcano.

But we could not find you and were ready to give up our lives. O Vaidehi! We were immersed in a severe ocean of grief and lamented with Angada about your loss, Vali's death, our engaging in praya and Jatayu's death. We had not been able to follow the command of our master. We had lost hope and were about to die. As if to accomplish the task, a large and valiant bird arrived there. This was the brother of the king of the eagles.[194] His name was Sampati and he was a king of the eagles. Hearing about his brother's death, he angrily spoke these words. "Why has my younger brother been killed? Who has destroyed him? O supreme among the apes! I wish to hear this from you." Angada told him the exact truth about the great destruction in Janasthana, wrought by the rakshasa who was terrible in form. Hearing about Jatayu's death, Aruna's son was saddened. O beautiful one! He informed us about your residing in Ravana's abode. We heard Sampati's words, which enhanced our delight. With Angada at the forefront, all of us left that spot. The bulls among the apes were content and happy. They were anxious to see you. When the army of the apes saw the ocean, they were depressed. However, I dispelled their terrible fear and leapt across the one hundred yojanas. I entered Lanka, filled with rakshasas, in the night. I saw Ravana, and you suffering from grief. O unblemished one! I have told you everything, just as it occurred. O queen! I am the messenger of Dasharatha's son. Speak to me. Rama made the effort because of you and I have come here because of you. O queen! Know me to be the son of the wind god, Sugriva's adviser. Kakutstha, supreme among those who wield all kinds of weapons, is well. Lakshmana, who possesses all the excellent signs, is engaged in serving his senior. O queen! I am engaged in ensuring the welfare of your valiant husband. Following Sugriva's words, I am the only one who has come here. I have come without any help. I can roam around, assuming any form at will. Desiring to search out your trail, I have crossed over the southern direction. I will dispel the grief of the army of the apes. I will remove their torment. I will tell them that, through good fortune, I have been able to meet

[194] Jatayu.

you. O queen! It is through good fortune that my leaping across the ocean has not been futile. It is through good fortune that I have come here. Catching sight of you will bring me fame. The immensely valorous Raghava will soon kill Ravana, the lord of the rakshasas, with his friends and relatives, and get you back. O Vaidehi! There is an excellent mountain named Kouraja.[195] From there, the ape Kesari went to Gokarna. My father, the great ape, was commanded by the gods and the rishis. At the sacred tirtha that was near the lord of the rivers, he killed Shambasadana.[196] O Maithilee! Hence, I was born in the ape's field, through the wind god. Because of my own deeds, I am famous in the worlds as Hanumat. O Vaidehi! So that you trust me, I have recounted your husband's qualities.'

Sita was afflicted because of her grief. However, because of the indications he had given, she trusted him and accepted him as a messenger. Janakee obtained great joy and delight. From her eyes, with those curved eyelashes, tears of joy started to flow. Her face was beautiful and her large eyes were coppery red and white. The large-eyed one became as radiant as the lord of the stars, when it is freed from Rahu. She thought it obvious that Hanumat was an ape and nothing else. After this, Hanumat spoke to the one who was beautiful to behold. 'Urged by the maharshis, the foremost among the apes killed the asura Shambasadana in a battle. O Maithilee! I have been born from Vayu and in my power, I am the equal of that ape.'[197]

Chapter 5(34)

To inspire confidence in Sita, the immensely energetic Hanumat, the son of the wind god, again spoke these words of assurance. 'O immensely fortunate one! I am an ape who is the intelligent

[195] Across different versions of the text, the name of this mountain varies widely. The Critical Edition uses Kouraja.

[196] The demon named Shambasadana and the tirtha named Gokarna were on the shores of the ocean. Kesari was thereafter granted the boon of a son.

[197] Kesari.

Rama's messenger. O queen! Look at this ring. It bears the mark of Rama's name. O fortunate one! Because of this, your grief should be diminished. Take it and look at it. It used to be an ornament on your husband's hand. O Janakee! I got it from your husband. You should be delighted.'

Her face was beautiful. Her large eyes were coppery red and white. She was filled with great joy, like the lord of the stars when freed from Rahu. The young one was delighted at news of her husband and also felt shy. Content at news about her beloved, she praised the great ape. 'O supreme ape. You are valiant. You are capable. You are wise. Single-handedly, you have penetrated this spot, full of rakshasas. The ocean extends for one hundred yojanas and is the abode of makaras. Using your praiseworthy valour, you have crossed it, as if it was a puddle.[198] O bull among the apes! I do not think that you are an ordinary ape. You have no fear and respect for Ravana. O best among the apes! If you have been sent by Rama, who knows about his soul, you are worthy of being addressed by me. The invincible Rama sent you without testing you, in particular, to me. He did not know about your valour. It is good fortune that the accomplished Rama has dharma in his soul and is devoted to dharma, just as the immensely energetic Lakshmana, the extender of Sumitra's delight, is. If Kakutstha is well, why is he not igniting his great rage, like the fire that arises at the end of a yuga, and burning up the girdle of the ocean? Those two are capable of restraining even the gods. But I think I must suffer this misery and calamity. Is Rama not distressed? Is he not tormented? Is Purushottama engaged in the task that must be undertaken next? Is he miserable and scared? Is the task confusing him? Is the son of the king engaged in the tasks that a man must undertake? Is he resorting to the two or three modes?[199] Has the scorcher of enemies won over well-wishers and friends? Has he obtained friends and have friends approached him? Does he have

[198] The text uses the word *goshpada*. This literally means the mark of a cow's foot in the soil and the small puddle of water that fills up such a mark, that is, a trifle.

[199] This refers to sama, dana, danda and bheda. Dana does not fit the context. Therefore, two modes probably refers to danda and bheda, while three modes refers to sama, danda and bheda.

good friends? Do the friends show him respect? Does the son of the king hope for the favours of the gods? Will he obtain manliness and good fortune? With me away, I hope Raghava has not lost his affection for me. O ape! Will he free me from this hardship? He always deserves happiness. He does not deserve unhappiness. Having faced this great misery, I hope that Rama is not despondent. How are Kousalya and Sumitra? Have you heard anything about whether Bharata is well? Raghava deserves respect. Is he grieving because of me? Is Rama distracted because of something else? Will he save me? Bharata is devoted to his brother. For my sake, will he send a terrible *akshouhini*,[200] protected by standards and ministers? For my sake, will the handsome Sugriva, the lord of the apes, give him brave apes who use teeth and nails as weapons? Will the brave Lakshmana who knows about weapons, the extender of Sumitra's delight, use his net of arrows to devastate the rakshasas? In a short while, will I see Ravana and his well-wishers destroyed in a battle by Rama, using his terrible weapons? His face has the complexion of gold. His face is as fragrant as a lotus. Without me, has it dried up and become sorrowful and miserable, like a lotus bereft of water and scorched by the sun? He gave up his kingdom because of his devotion to dharma and took me to the forest on foot. He was not distressed, nor scared. He did not grieve. Does he still bear that kind of fortitude in his heart? In his affection, he does not differentiate between his mother, his father, or anyone else. I am as equal as anyone else. O messenger! I wish to remain alive only as long as I am inclined to hear about my beloved.' The queen spoke these words, full of deep meaning and full of sweet meaning, to the Indra among the apes. The beautiful one ceased, wishing to hear those beautiful words, full of Rama, again.

Hearing Sita's words, the son of the wind god, terrible in valour, joined his hands in salutation above his head. He again spoke these words in reply. 'O lotus-eyed one! Rama does not know that you are here. Hearing my words, Raghava will swiftly arrive here. He will bring a large army consisting of large numbers of apes and bears. He

[200] An akshouhini is an army consisting of 21,870 chariots, 21,870 elephants, 65,610 horse riders and 109,350 foot soldiers.

will stupefy and agitate Varuna's abode with his torrent of arrows. Kakutstha will pacify the rakshasas in the city of Lanka. If the goddess of death is stationed in his path, with gods and asuras, Rama will kill them too. Because he cannot see you, the noble one is overcome by sorrow. Like an elephant afflicted by a lion, Rama cannot find any peace. O queen! I swear to you on the mountains Dardara,[201] Malaya, Vindhya, Meru, Mandara and roots and fruits. You will see Rama's handsome face, with excellent eyes, lips like the bimba fruit and with beautiful earrings, like the full moon when it rises. O Vaidehi! You will soon see Rama seated on the top of Mount Prasravana, like Shatakratu in the vault of heaven. Raghava does not consume any flesh. He does not partake of any liquor. He does not eat the well-prepared forest fare every day, but only on every fifth day. His inner soul is completely immersed in you. Therefore, Raghava does not drive away the gnats, mosquitoes, insects and reptiles from his body. Rama is always thinking. Rama is always overcome by sorrow. He is overcome by desire for you and does not think of anyone else. In general, Rama does not sleep. Even if that excellent man sleeps, he speaks the sweet words, "This is Sita", and awakens. If he sees a fruit or a flower or anything else that pleases the mind of a woman, he sighs several times and addresses you, "Alas, beloved!" O queen! He is ever tormented. He addresses you, "O, Sita!" The great-souled son of the king is firm in his vows. He is making efforts to get you back.'

She was grieving just as much as Rama was grieving. On hearing this account of Rama, her sorrow was dispelled. Videha's daughter was like the moon on a night at the beginning of autumn, when the clouds have gone away.

Chapter 5(35)

Sita, with a face like the full moon, heard his words. She spoke these words, which were full of dharma and artha, to Hanumat.

[201] This mountain is also called Dardura.

'O ape! Rama's mind is not on anyone else and he is overcome by sorrow—the words uttered by you are like amrita mixed with poison. Death[202] seems to tie up a man with a noose and drag him towards prosperity or extremely pervasive and extremely terrible adversity. O supreme among apes! Indeed, living creatures cannot resist destiny. Look at Soumitri, Rama and me being confused by this adversity. How will Raghava reach the other shore of this ocean of grief? He is like an exhausted person swimming in the ocean when the boat has been destroyed. Having destroyed the rakshasas, slain Ravana and uprooted Lanka, when will my husband see me? He should be told to hurry, before this year is over. I will only remain alive till the end of this year. O ape! This is the tenth month of the year and two months remain. That is the time the cruel Ravana has earmarked for me. Even when his brother, Vibhishana, has entreated with him not to oppress me, his mind is not inclined to do so. The idea of returning me does not appeal to Ravana. Ravana has come under the subjugation of destiny and death stands in his path. O ape! Vibhishana's eldest daughter is a maiden named Anala. Her mother sent her to me and she is the one who herself told me about this. There is an intelligent bull among the rakshasas named Avindhya. He is patient, good in conduct, aged and extremely revered by Ravana. For the sake of being saved from Rama, he also told the rakshasa this. But the evil-souled one did not listen to his beneficial words.[203] O best among the apes! I hope that my husband will soon get me back. After all, my inner soul is pure and he possesses many qualities. O ape! Enterprise, manliness, spirit, non-violence, gratitude, valour and power exist in Raghava. Without his brother, he slew fourteen thousand rakshasas in Janasthana. Which enemy will not be terrified of him? Hardship is incapable of disturbing that bull among men. I know about him, just as Puloma's daughter[204] knows about Shakra. O ape! The brave Rama's net of arrows is like the rays of the sun. The rakshasa's enemies are like water and will be dried up, just as the water is dried

[202] In the sense of destiny.

[203] This bit about Anala and Avindhya doesn't quite belong.

[204] Shachi.

up.' Afflicted by grief, she conversed about Rama in this fashion. Her face was full of tears.

The ape Hanumat told her, 'Hearing my words, Raghava will swiftly arrive here. He will bring a large army with him, full of large numbers of apes and bears. O unblemished one! Alternatively, I can free you from the rakshasas right now and from the misery here. Climb on to my back. With you on my back, I will cross the ocean. I even bear the strength to carry Lanka, with Ravana. O Maithilee! I will establish you on Prasravana now, with Raghava, like oblations offered to Shakra through the fire. O Vaidehi! With Lakshmana, you will see Raghava today, while he is engaged in his task, like Vishnu for the death of the daityas. The immensely strong one is in his hermitage. On seeing you, he will be energized. He will be like Purandara seated on the head of the king of the elephants.[205] O queen! O beautiful one! Do not hesitate. Ascend my back. Like Rohini with the moon, wish to be united with Rama. Ascend my back and swim across the sky that is like the great ocean, conversing with the wonderfully rayed moon and the sun. O beautiful one! When I take you away from here, none of the residents of Lanka possesses the strength to follow in my path. There is no doubt that I will leave just as I came here, leaping through the sky. O Vaidehi! Behold my enterprise.'

Maithilee heard the extraordinary words spoken by the best among the apes. She was astonished and all her limbs were filled with delight. She told Hanumat, 'O Hanumat! How can you wish to carry me over such a long distance? O leader of the apes! I think this is nothing more than the nature of an ape. You possess a small body. O bull among the apes! Yet, you wish to take me away from here, to the presence of my husband, who is an Indra among men.'

Hearing Sita's words, Hanumat, the handsome son of the wind god, thought that this was a new kind of insult directed towards him. 'This dark-eyed one does not know about my spirit and my power. Therefore, let Vaidehi see that I can assume any form at will.' Hanumat, supreme among apes, thought this. The destroyer

[205] Airavata.

of enemies showed Vaidehi his own form. The intelligent bull among the apes leapt down from the tree. To instil confidence in Sita, he started to increase his size. He became as large as Mount Mandara and blazed like the lord who was the fire god. The bull among the apes stood in front of Sita. The extremely strong ape was like a mountain and his face was coppery red. His terrible teeth and nails were like the vajra. He told Vaidehi, 'I possess the strength to carry Lanka from here, with its mountains, forest regions, palaces, turrets, gates and its lord.[206] O queen! That being the case, remove all hesitation from your mind. O Vaidehi! Dispel all the grief in Raghava, together with Lakshmana.'

Seeing him, standing like a mountain, Janaka's daughter, with large eyes like lotus petals, replied to the son of the wind god, 'O great ape! I know about your spirit and your strength. Your extraordinary speed is like Vayu and your energy is like Agni. O bull among the apes! How can any ordinary person come to this place, reaching the other shore of the immeasurable ocean? I know that you possess the strength to go and carry me too. We must certainly turn our minds to the best means of quickly achieving success in the objective. O best among the apes! But it is not desirable that I should go with you. Your great speed is like Vayu's speed and that speed may confound me. I will be in the sky, progressively crossing over the ocean. As you proceed, because of fear and the force, I will fall down from your back. I will fall down in the ocean, full of whales, crocodiles and fish. I will be disabled by my fear and will quickly become excellent food for them. O destroyer of enemies! There is no doubt that it is not possible for me to go with you. I am doubtful because you will also have my burden to bear. The rakshasas, terrible in their valour, will see that I am being carried away. The evil-souled Ravana will command them to follow. Those brave ones will surround you, with spears and clubs in their hands. O brave one! Because of me being a burden, you will face a danger. You are without a weapon and many rakshasas with weapons will attack you from the sky. With me to protect, how will you possess

[206] Ravana.

the strength to engage with them? You will have to fight with the rakshasas, who are cruel in their deeds. O supreme among apes! Afflicted by fear, I will fall down from your back. The rakshasas are terrible and possess great strength. O excellent ape! How will you counter them? They may triumph over you. If you ignore me and fight, I may fall down. When I fall down, the wicked rakshasas will seize me and take me away. They may take me away from your hands and even kill me. In any battle, victory and defeat are seen to be uncertain. Censured by the rakshasas, I may face a calamity. O best among the apes! All your efforts will then be rendered futile. If you wish, you are sufficient to kill all the rakshasas. However, if you kill the rakshasas, Raghava's fame will be diminished. Alternatively, the rakshasas may seize and hide me in a place that the apes and Raghava do not know about. Then every effort that you have made on my account will be futile. That is the reason there is great merit in Rama coming here with you. O mighty-armed one! The great-souled Raghava, his brother, you and the lineage of your own king are dependent on my remaining alive. If those two[207] lose hope and are tormented by grief, all the bears and apes will give up their lives. O ape! O supreme among apes! Since my devotion to my husband is of utmost importance, I cannot touch another person's body and ascend your back. I do not wish to. I did have to touch Ravana's body, but that was because he used force against me. I was helpless and disabled, without a protector. What could I have done? It is appropriate that Rama kills Dashagriva, with the rakshasas, and takes me away from here. I have seen and heard about the great-souled one's valour. He can crush in battles. The gods, the gandharvas, the serpents, the rakshasas—no one is Rama's equal in a battle. The extremely strong one is like Vasava in valour. On witnessing the work of his wonderful bow, who will be able to stand before Raghava, with Lakshmana? He blazes like the fire, when that fire is fanned by the wind. With Lakshmana, Raghava is a destroyer in a battle. He is like a maddened dishagaja. Aided in a battle by the best among the apes, he will be like the sun

[207] Rama and Lakshmana.

at the end of a yuga, with his arrows like its rays. O best among the apes! Quickly bring my husband here, with Lakshmana and the other leaders. I have suffered from grieving about Rama for a long time. O foremost among the apes! Act so that you can give me delight.'

Chapter 5(36)

The tiger among apes was delighted at hearing these words from Sita. The one who was eloquent in the use of words replied, 'O queen! O one who is auspicious to behold! The words that you have spoken are worthy of you. This is in conformity with the nature of virtuous women who are humble. The large ocean extends for one hundred yojanas. It is not appropriate for a woman to ascend my back and cross it. O humble one! O Janakee! You have spoken about a second reason—no one other than Rama should touch you. O queen! This is worthy of the great-souled one's wife. O queen! Other than you, who else is capable of uttering such words? O queen! I will tell Kakutstha everything accurately, all that you have said in my presence. O queen! I said what I did because of many reasons. I wished to ensure pleasure to Rama. My mind was full of affection towards him. Lanka is difficult to penetrate and the great ocean is extremely difficult to cross. I possess the strength. That is the reason I mentioned it. I wish to take you right now, because of my friendship for Raghu. I am filled with affection and devotion for my senior. There was no other reason for my mentioning it. O unblemished one! If you are not interested in going with me, give me a sign that Raghava can recognize.' Hanumat spoke to her in this way.

Sita, who was like the daughter of a god, gently spoke the following words, with the syllables punctuated by tears. 'As the best sign, tell my beloved the following. "There is a spot at the foot of Mount Chitrakuta, towards the north-east. Ascetics reside in hermitages there. There is plenty of roots, fruits and water.

Mandakinee is not very far from that sacred hermitage. The clumps of groves there are full of many kinds of fragrant flowers. While we were strolling, we became wet and I lay down on your lap. After some time, Bharata's elder brother lay down on my lap.[208] A crow desired flesh and pecked me with its beak. At this, I picked up a stone and restrained the crow. But the crow hid itself and continued to peck at me. The crow did not refrain from its desire to obtain flesh. When I was angry at the bird, my garment was dislodged and I sought to tighten the string. You saw me in that state. You laughed at me and I was both angry and ashamed. Suffering from the crow that was seeking food, I sought refuge with you. Exhausted, I sat down and again clung to you. I was both angry and happy and was comforted by you. My face and eyes were full of tears and you gently wiped them away. O lord! Enraged by the crow, I was then seen by you. Sighing like a virulent serpent, he spoke these words.[209] 'O one with thighs like an elephant's trunk! Who has pierced you between the breasts? Who has shown this anger towards a five-hooded serpent and played in this way?' He looked around and saw the crow. Its sharp talons bore traces of blood and it was stationed there, facing my direction. 'Is this crow, supreme among birds, Shakra's son? It is roaming around on earth and seems to possess a speed like that of the wind.' After this, the mighty-armed one's eyes whirled around in rage. The supreme among intelligent ones made up his mind about the cruel crow. He picked up a blade of grass and invoked it with brahmastra. It blazed like the fire of destruction and he hurled the flaming blade in the bird's direction. He hurled the blazing blade of grass towards the crow. Followed by it, the crow adopted many different modes of flight. Wishing to save itself, it roamed around all the worlds. It was abandoned by its father[210] and by all the gods and the maharshis. Having circled the worlds, it came and sought refuge with you. It fell down on the ground and sought refuge with the one who grants refuge.

[208] Sita sometimes addresses Rama directly and sometimes indirectly.

[209] There is a break in continuity because the Critical Edition excises some shlokas. The crow had pecked at Sita between her breasts and hurt her.

[210] Indra.

Though it deserved to be killed, Kakutstha protected it because of his compassion. Having not been able to find peace anywhere in the worlds, it had come to you as refuge. It had returned, tired and distressed. He told it, 'It is impossible for brahmastra to fail. What should be done?' It replied, 'Let it destroy my right eye.' It bowed down before Rama and King Dasharatha. Having been released by the brave one, it returned to its own abode. O lord of the earth! For my sake, you released a brahmastra at a crow. How can you pardon someone who has abducted me? O bull among men! Therefore, out of compassion towards me, undertake great efforts. I have heard that non-violence is supreme dharma. I also know about your great valour, great enterprise and great strength. You cannot be agitated. You are like the deep ocean that cannot be crossed to the other shore. You are like Vasava and are the lord of the earth, right up to the ocean. You are supreme among those who know about weapons. You are spirited and strong. O Raghava! What is the reason that you are not releasing your weapons towards the rakshasas? The serpents, the gandharvas, the asuras and large numbers of Maruts are incapable of withstanding Rama's force in a battle. If the valiant one has any respect for me, why does he not use his sharp arrows to destroy the rakshasas and take me away? Why does Lakshmana, the scorcher of enemies, not follow his brother's command? Why does the brave and extremely strong one not save me? Those two tigers among men are like Vayu and Indra in their energy. Even the gods find them to be unassailable. Why are they ignoring me? There is no doubt that I have committed a great crime. Though they are capable, those two scorchers of enemies are ignoring me." For my sake, bow down your head and greet the lord of the world.[211] The spirited Kousalya gave birth to this excellent son. Ask about his welfare. Ask about the excellent one Sumitra gave birth to, the one who followed Rama. He gave up all the garlands and jewels, beloved and beautiful women and the great riches from the world that are extremely difficult to obtain. He did this to honour and please his father and his mother. Because he was devoted, the one

[211] Sita is now speaking to Hanumat.

with dharma in his soul gave up supreme happiness. He followed his brother Kakutstha and protected him in the forest. The mighty-armed one has shoulders like a lion. He is spirited and is pleasant to behold. His behaviour towards Rama is like that towards a father and towards me like that towards a mother. The brave Lakshmana did not know that I was being abducted. The handsome one serves his seniors. He is capable and does not speak much. For my father-in-law, this prince was most loved and the best. I have always loved Lakshmana more than his brother, Rama. The valiant one carries whatever burden is imposed on him. On seeing him, Raghava no longer remembers the aged and noble one.[212] For my sake, convey these words to him[213] and ask about his welfare. Lakshmana is loved by Rama. He is always mild, pure and accomplished. Repeatedly, tell my brave lord, Rama, this. "O Dasharatha's son! I will only sustain my life for a month. If it is more than a month, I will no longer remain alive. I am stating this truthfully. You must save me from Ravana. The evil-acting one has defiled me. O brave one! Like Koushiki, you must save me, even from patala."'"[214]

After this, Sita removed the auspicious and divine *chudamani*[215] and tied it up in her garment. She gave it to Hanumat, so that it could be given to Raghava. The brave one received the excellent jewel. His arm could not pass through it, so he fixed it to his finger.[216] The supreme among apes accepted the excellent jewel and greeted her. He circumambulated Sita, bowed down and stood by her side. At having been able to see Sita, he was filled with great delight. Though his body was still there, his mind went out to Rama. He accepted that extremely expensive and supreme jewel.

[212] Dasharatha.

[213] Lakshmana.

[214] This is interpreted in two ways. When Indra killed Vritra, Lakshmi entered the earth and Vishnu saved her and returned her to Indra. According to this interpretation, Koushiki means Lakshmi, since Koushika is one of Indra's names. Alternatively, Koushiki is the sage Utathya's wife. Varuna carried her away to patala, but Utathya saved her.

[215] Jewel worn on the top of the head.

[216] There was a small hole (bore) in the chudamani for a thread or strand of hair to pass through it. Hanumat's size was greatly reduced. Even then, his arm could not pass through that bore. His finger did.

It was powerful and had been worn by Janaka's daughter. He was like an excellent mountain that had been freed from a storm. With a delighted mind, he readied himself for his return.

Chapter 5(37)

After having given Hanumat the jewel, Sita told him, 'From this token, Rama will ascertain the truth. Seeing this, the brave Rama will remember three things—me, my mother and King Dasharatha. O supreme among apes! Urge your enterprise again and think about what needs to be done next to accomplish the objective. O supreme among apes! You are worthy of setting about this task. Think about making efforts so that misery comes to an end.' The son of the wind god, terrible in his valour, pledged to do what she had said. He bowed his head down before Vaidehi and prepared to leave. The queen got to know that the ape who was the son of the wind god was ready to go. With her voice choking with tears, Maithilee addressed him in these words. 'O Hanumat! Ask about the welfare of both Rama and Lakshmana and about that of all the aged apes, Sugriva and his advisers. You must think of a means whereby the mighty-armed Raghava can help me to cross this ocean of grief. The illustrious Rama must accomplish this while I am still alive. O Hanumat! Speak such words to him and you will accomplish dharma. On constantly hearing the words of encouragement that I have spoken, the manliness of Dasharatha's son will be enhanced and he will get me back. Hearing the message and the words that I have spoken, the brave one will properly resort to his valour and accomplish the objective.'

Hearing Sita's words, Hanumat, the son of the wind god, joined his hands in salutation above his head. He spoke these words in reply. 'Kakutstha will swiftly arrive, surrounded by apes and bears. He will vanquish the enemies in the battle and dispel your grief. I do not see any mortals, immortals or asuras who are interested in standing before him when he volleys out his arrows. The sun god,

Parjanya and Vaivasvata Yama are not capable of standing before him in a battle, especially when you are the reason. He is worthy of ruling over the entire world, right up to the frontiers of the ocean. O Janaka's daughter! Rama's victory will be for your sake.' His words were spoken well, appropriate and were full of the truth. Hearing them, Janakee showed him a lot of respect and spoke to him. As he was leaving, Sita glanced at him repeatedly.

Filled with affection towards her husband, she entreated him in friendly words. 'O brave one! O scorcher of enemies! If you so think, reside here for one day. Hide yourself in some place. Rest and then leave tomorrow. Someone like me is unfortunate. O brave one! However, your presence will save me from this great sorrow for at least a short while. O tiger among apes! After you leave, until you return, there is no doubt that were will be an uncertainty about my remaining alive. The sorrow about not being able to see you will also torment me. O ape! It will be like another kind of sorrow igniting the present sorrow and increasing it. O brave one! O lord of the apes! There is still a great doubt before me and that concerns your companions, the apes and the bears. This great ocean is extremely difficult to cross. How will they be able to manage it? How will the soldiers, the apes and the bears, and the two best of men manage that? There are only three creatures who possess the strength to cross this ocean—Vinata's son,[217] you and the wind god. O brave one! This is extremely difficult to cross and that is the task you must devote yourself to. O one who is supreme in accomplishing tasks! Do you see any solution to this? If you wish, you alone are capable of accomplishing this objective. O slayer of enemy heroes! You possess sufficient fame and can generate strength. With all his soldiers, if Rama vanquishes Ravana in the battle and with me, returns in victory to his own city, this will enhance his fame. If Kakutstha, the destroyer of enemy forces fills Lanka with his arrows and takes me away, that will be worthy of him. You are like the great-souled one in your valour. Act so that he can exhibit his valour in the battle.'

[217] Garuda.

Those words were full of meaning and were full of reasons. Hearing them, Hanumat spoke his final words in reply. 'O queen! Sugriva, the lord of the apes and the leader of the soldiers of the apes and the bears, is full of spirit. For your sake, he has made up his mind. He is surrounded by thousands and crores of apes. O Vaidehi! To destroy the rakshasas, he will come here swiftly. The apes are there. They are full of valour. They are spirited and extremely strong. They have made up their minds and follow his command. They are great and infinitely energetic. They do not weaken in their tasks. Nothing can bar their progress, above, below and diagonally. Using their great enterprise, they have circumambulated the earth, with its oceans and mountains, several times, following the path resorted to by the wind. There are many residents of the forest who are my equal and superior to me. There is no one in Sugriva's presence who is inferior to me. If I can reach this place, why can't those extremely strong ones? The best ones are sent. The ordinary ones are not sent. O queen! Therefore enough of this lamentation. Set aside your sorrow. The leaders of the apes will arrive here in a single leap. Those two extremely spirited ones, lions among men, will arrive here before you on my back, like the rising moon and the sun. Those two brave ones, Rama and Lakshmana, supreme among men, will come to the city of Lanka and destroy it with their arrows. Raghava, the descendant of the Raghu lineage, will kill Ravana and his companions. O beautiful one! Having obtained you, he will return to his own city. O fortunate one! Therefore, comfort yourself. Wait for the time and you will see Rama, blazing like the fire. The Indra among the rakshasas will be slain, with his sons, advisers and relatives. You will be united with Rama, like Rohini with the moon. O queen! O Maithilee! You will quickly reach the other shore of this ocean of grief. You will soon see Ravana being killed by Rama.' Having comforted Vaidehi in this way, Hanumat, the son of the wind god, made up his mind to leave. He spoke to Vaidehi again. 'You will soon see Raghava. He has made up his mind to slay your enemies. With a bow in his hand, Lakshmana will present himself at the gate of Lanka. You will soon see the apes assemble, with complexions like Indras among elephants. They are brave. They are like lions and tigers in their valour and use nails and teeth as weapons. O noble one! There will be many leaders of foremost apes dancing around in Lanka, on the summit of Malaya. They will be like mountains and clouds. Rama cannot obtain peace. He is like an elephant afflicted by a lion. His inner organs are oppressed by the terrible arrows of Manmatha. O queen! Do not weep and grieve. Do not have anything disagreeable in your mind. You have a husband and a protector who is like Shakra, Shachi's husband. Does anyone exist who is superior to Rama? Is there anyone who is Soumitri's equal? Those two brothers, who are like the fire god and the wind god, are your support. O queen! You will not reside in this place for a long time, inhabited by the extremely terrible hordes of rakshasas. Your beloved will arrive in a short while. Permit me. It will be only a short while before we meet again.'

Chapter 5(38)

On hearing the words of Vayu's great-souled son, Sita, who was like the daughter of a god, spoke words that were beneficial for her own self. 'O ape! On seeing you and hearing these pleasant words, I am delighted. I am like seeds that have half-sprouted, when the earth obtains rain. My limbs are afflicted by grief and I wish to touch the body of that tiger among men. Therefore, act compassionately towards me. O one who is supreme among all the apes! Give this sign to Rama. Tell him how he angrily flung the blade of grass towards the crow and destroyed one of its eyes.[218] You should remember. "The *tilaka* mark on my forehead had once got effaced and you had drawn a tilaka mark on the side of my cheek. How can the valiant one, who is the equal of the great Indra and Varuna, condone this abduction of Sita? She is residing amidst the rakshasas. I have protected this divine chudamani extremely well.

[218] The word now used is *ishika*. This means blade of grass, but also means arrow. Since we have earlier been told that Rama invoked a blade of grass with brahmastra, we will continue to stick to blade of grass.

O unblemished one! On seeing it, I have rejoiced in my hardship, as if I had seen you. This beautiful piece was produced from the water. Immersed in sorrow, I will not be able to survive after this. I am bearing this intolerable misery for your sake. The extremely terrible rakshasis censure me in words that shatter the heart. O destroyer of enemies! I will only sustain my life for one month. O son of a king! If it is more than a month, without you, I will not remain alive. The king of the rakshasas is terrible and the sight of him does not bring me happiness. If I hear that you are not coming, I will not remain alive even for an instant."'

Hearing Vaidehi's piteous words, Hanumat, the extremely energetic son of the wind god, spoke to her in a voice that was choking with tears. 'O queen! I am truthfully swearing before you. Because he grieves over you, Rama has withdrawn from everything. Since Rama is overwhelmed with sorrow, Lakshmana is tormented. Tolerate this in some way. This is not the time to grieve. O beautiful one! In a short while, you will see an end to your sorrows. For the sake of seeing you, those two unblemished princes will undertake efforts to burn down Lanka. O large-eyed one! Having slain the cruel Ravana and his relatives in the battle, the two Raghavas will get you and their own city back. O unblemished one! Give me another sign so that Rama knows. To generate delight in him, you should again give me something else.'

Thus addressed, she said, 'This is an excellent token. Rama will see this, the ornament from my hair. O Hanumat! O brave one! This is sufficient for him to trust your words.' The supreme among apes accepted that beautiful and excellent gem. He bowed his head down before the queen and prepared to leave. Making up his mind to leap and exert himself, the bull among the apes used his great force to increase his size. On seeing this, the face of Janaka's daughter filled with tears. Distressed and in a voice choking with tears, she said, 'O Hanumat! The two brothers, Rama and Lakshmana, are like lions. Ask about their welfare and about that of Sugriva and all his advisers. You must think of a means whereby the mighty-armed Raghava can save me from this ocean of grief. This force of sorrow is fierce. I am also censured by the guards. When you reach Rama, tell him about this. O supreme among apes! May your journey be auspicious.' The princess spoke these meaningful words. Having accomplished his objective, the ape was delighted in his mind. He could see that only a little bit of the task remained to be accomplished. He made up his mind to leave for the northern direction.

Chapter 5(39)

He was ready to leave and she honoured and praised him with her words. Having left that spot, the ape started to think. 'I have seen the dark-eyed one and only a little bit of the task remains to be accomplished. I will ignore the three modes and check out the fourth.[219] For rakshasas, the quality of sama has not been thought of. Nor does dana work for those who possess plenty of riches. For people who are insolent about their strength, bheda will not be successful. Therefore, the idea of valour appeals to me. With the exception of valour, nothing can accomplish the objective. It is determined that nothing else will achieve the purpose. If the best of their heroes are killed in an encounter now, subsequently the rakshasas may behave in a milder way. After having accomplished the indicated task, if a person accomplishes many other tasks without having contravened the primary task, he is the one who has truly accomplished the objective. Even if a task is light, there is more than one means to accomplish it. He who knows that there are many means of achieving it is a person who truly knows and is capable of accomplishing the objective. If I leave this place and go to the residence of the lord of the apes after having ascertained the truth about the superiority and inferiority of them versus us, I will then have indeed followed my master's command. Indeed, how can I now be at ease and withstand the rakshasas in a battle? Indeed,

[219] Ignore sama, dana and bheda and test danda. The intention is to test Ravana's strength.

how can I use the essence of my own strength? How will Dashanana show respect to me in a battle? I will face Dashanana in a battle. This grove belongs to the cruel one and is like Nandana. It is full of many kinds of trees and creepers and is pleasing to the eye and the mind. I will destroy it, like a fire in a forest that is dry. When this is devastated, Ravana will show his anger towards me. At this, the lord of the rakshasas will summon a large army that consists of horses, maharathas and elephants. They will use tridents made out black iron and spears as weapons and a great battle will follow. Using my invincible valour, I will engage with those who are terrible in their valour. I will slay the soldiers who have been urged on by Ravana. After that, I will happily go to the residence of the lord of the apes.'

After this, the son of the wind god, terrible in his valour, used the great force of his thighs to uproot and fling away the trees. The brave Hanumat shattered the grove meant for pleasure and the many trees and creepers that were full of maddened birds. The grove was crushed. The trees were shattered and so were the waterbodies. The summits of the mountains were crushed and became disagreeable to see. Chambers made of creepers and chambers filled with pictures were destroyed. Giant serpents, predatory beasts and deer were whirled around. Chambers made out of stone were devastated and so were other residences. That great grove assumed a devastated form. The great-souled and great ape thus generated great displeasure and accomplished his objective. The ape wished to fight single-handedly against many extremely strong ones. He assumed a blazing form and remained at one of the gates.

Chapter 5(40)

All the residents of Lanka were scared and terrified at the sounds of the birds shrieking and noise of the trees being shattered. Afraid and terrified, the animals and the birds screamed and fled. Cruel portents presented themselves before the rakshasas. The rakshasas, with disfigured faces, woke up from their sleep. They saw that the grove had been destroyed and saw the brave and great ape. The mighty-armed, greatly spirited and immensely strong one saw the rakshasis. To instil fear in them, he assumed an extremely gigantic form. The immensely strong one was gigantic in size and was like a mountain. On seeing the ape, the rakshasis asked Janaka's daughter, 'Who is he? Whom does he belong to? Where has he come from? Why has he come here? Why did he have a conversation with you? O large-eyed one! Tell us. O immensely fortunate one! Do not be afraid. O dark-eyed one! What did he talk to you about?' At this, the virtuous Sita, beautiful in all her limbs, said, 'How can I know about rakshasas who can assume any form at will? You are the ones who know about who he is and what he is doing. There is no doubt that only a snake knows about the trail of another snake. I am also scared of him. I do not know who he is. I only know him as a rakshasa who has come here, assuming any form at will.' Hearing Vaidehi's words, the rakshasis fled swiftly. Some remained, while others left, to inform Ravana about this.

The rakshasis, with disfigured faces, went to Ravana. They started to tell him about the malformed and terrible ape. 'O king! There is an ape with a terrible form in the middle of Ashokavana. Having conversed with Sita, the infinitely valorous one remains there. We have asked Sita Janakee, with eyes like a deer, about the ape. But though we have asked several times, she does not wish to tell us. He may be Vasava's messenger, or he may be Vaishravana's messenger. Or Rama, desiring to search out Sita, may have sent him. He possesses a terrible form. Your pleasure grove is full of many kinds of diverse animals and is beautiful. He has destroyed it. There is nothing in that region which has not been destroyed. However, he has not destroyed the place where Sita Janakee was. It is not obvious whether this was to protect Janakee or whether he was exhausted. But how can he have exhaustion? She must have been protected by him. There is a well-grown shimshapa tree that Sita herself had resorted to. It has beautiful and thick branches and leaves. That has been spared by him. His form is terrible. You should command that terrible chastisement be wreaked on him. He is the one who has conversed with Sita and has destroyed the grove. O lord of large numbers of rakshasas! You have accepted her in your mind. Other than someone who wants to give up his life, who will dare to converse with Sita?'

Hearing the words of the rakshasis, Ravana, the lord of the rakshasas, blazed like a fire into which oblations had been offered. Because of his anger, his eyes whirled around. There were brave rakshasas who were exactly like him and they were named *kimkaras*.[220] The immensely energetic one commanded them to seize Hanumat. There were eighty thousand spirited kimkaras. They emerged from his residence, with iron clubs in their hands. They possessed huge stomachs and large teeth. They were immensely strong and terrible in form. All of them wished to fight and were eager to seize Hanumat. They approached the ape, who was stationed at the entrance. They attacked with great force, like insects towards a fire. They attacked the best among apes with colourful clubs, bludgeons that were decorated with gold plating and arrows that were like the sun. However, the spirited and handsome Hanumat was like a mountain. He lashed his tail on the ground and roared loudly. At the sound of that roar, they became uncertain and were filled with fear. They saw Hanumat, as tall as a cloud in the evening. But because of the command of their master, the rakshasas attacked the ape without hesitation. Here and there, they attacked him with colourful and terrible weapons. From every side, the immensely strong one was surrounded by those brave ones. He remained at the gate and seized a terrible iron club. Seizing that club, he slew the ones who roamed around in the night. Seizing that, the son of the wind god roamed around in the sky, like Vinata's son moving around, having seized a serpent. The brave son of the wind god killed the kimkara rakshasas. Desiring to fight again, he remained at the gate. There were some rakshasas who managed to escape from that great fear. They went and told Ravana that all the kimkaras had been killed. Hearing that the immensely strong rakshasas had been killed, the king rolled his eyes. He commanded

[220] The word means servant.

Prahasta's son,[221] who was unmatched in valour and extremely difficult to vanquish in a battle.

Chapter 5(41)

Having killed the kimkaras, Hanumat started to think. 'I have shattered the grove, but the palace in the sanctuary[222] has not been destroyed. Therefore, I must also destroy the palace.' Having thought this, Hanumat made up his mind to exhibit his strength. The palace in the chaitya was as tall as the summit of Meru. Hanumat, best among apes and the son of the wind god, took a leap and climbed up on it. The invincible one attacked the tall palace in the sanctuary. Hanumat blazed in his prosperity and was like Pariyatra mountain. Hanumat, the son of the wind god, assumed an extremely gigantic form. He slapped his arms and filled Lanka with that sound. That sound of slapping struck the ears with a great clap. As a result of that sound, the birds fell down from the sky. 'The extremely strong Rama and the immensely strong Lakshmana will be victorious. King Sugriva, protected by Raghava, will be victorious. I am the servant of Rama, the Indra of Kosala and the performer of unblemished deeds. I am Hanumat, the son of the wind god and I have killed the enemy soldiers. In a battle, thousands of Ravanas are not capable of standing before me. I will strike with thousands of boulders and trees. I will shatter the city of Lanka and pay my respects to Maithilee. While all the rakshasas look on, I will accomplish my objective and leave.' Stationed atop the palace in the sanctuary, the bull among apes roared in a terrible way and that roar generated fear among the rakshasas.

Attracted by the great sound, hundreds of guards of the sanctuary advanced. They seized many kinds of weapons—spikes, swords and battleaxes. Gigantic in size, they surrounded the son of

[221] Named Jambumali.

[222] The word used is chaitya.

the wind god and released these. Surrounded by large numbers of rakshasas, the best among apes was resplendent. He was like a large whirlpool in the extensive waters of the Ganga. Enraged, the son of the wind god assumed a terrible form. The palace possessed a large pillar that was embellished with gold and had one hundred sharp edges. Using force, Hanumat, the son of the wind god, uprooted this. The immensely strong one whirled this around. Like the wielder of the vajra against the asuras, he killed hundreds of rakshasas. Stationed in the sky, the handsome one spoke these words. 'There are thousands of great-souled and strong apes who are just like me. They follow the orders of Sugriva and have been sent by him. There are hundreds, tens of thousands, hundreds of thousands and crores. Sugriva and they will come and destroy all of you. This city of Lanka will no longer exist, nor you, nor Ravana. You are tied in a bond of enmity with the great-souled lord of Ikshvaku.'

Chapter 5(42)

The Indra among rakshasas commanded Prahasta's powerful son. This was Jambumali, who possessed large teeth. He left, wielding a bow. He was attired in red garlands and garments. He wore a wreath and beautiful earrings. His eyes were large and wide. He was fierce and impossible to vanquish in a battle. His excellent bow was like Shakra's bow and he had large and beautiful arrows. He extended it[223] with force and it made a sound like the vajra and a bolt of thunder. The loud roar of him twanging the bow filled the directions. It suddenly penetrated the sub-directions and the sky and filled them up. He arrived on a chariot that was yoked to donkeys. On seeing this, Hanumat, filled with force, roared in delight. Hanumat, the large ape, was standing on the arch of the gate. The mighty-armed Jambumali pierced him with sharp arrows. He struck him on the face with an arrow that was in the shape of a crescent and on the head

[223] The bow.

with an arrow with a single tuft. He pierced the lord of the apes in the arms with ten iron arrows. His coppery red face was struck by an arrow and looked resplendent. It looked like a blooming lotus in the autumn, pierced by the rays of the sun.

Struck by the rakshasa's arrow, the great ape was enraged. Next to him, he saw a large and extremely huge boulder. The powerful one used his strength to uproot it and hurled it with force. Angrily, the rakshasa struck him back with ten arrows. Hanumat, fierce in his valour, saw that his attempt had been futile. The valiant one uprooted a giant sala tree and whirled it around. The immensely strong ape was whirling around that sala tree. On seeing this, the extremely strong Jambumali shot many arrows at him. He severed the sala tree with four arrows and struck the ape's arms with five. He pierced him with one arrow in the chest and ten between the breasts. His body covered in arrows, he was filled with great rage. He seized a club and whirled it around with force. Endowed with immense strength, he whirled it around with great force and even greater force. He flung down the club on Jambumali's broad chest. He[224] no longer possessed a head, arms or thighs. His bow, chariot, horses and arrows could no longer be seen. Using force, he killed maharatha Jambumali. With his limbs and ornaments shattered, he was killed and fell down on the ground. Jambumali was killed and so were the extremely strong kimkaras. Hearing this, Ravana was angry and his eyes turned red with rage. His coppery red eyes rolled around in anger. Prahasta's immensely strong son had been killed. The lord of those who roam around in the night quickly commanded the extremely brave and valiant sons of his advisers.

Chapter 5(43)

At this, the Indra among rakshasas urged the sons of his ministers. Seven of them emerged from the residence, as radiant as the

[224] Jambumali.

one with the seven rays.[225] They were extremely strong and were surrounded by extremely strong archers. They were accomplished in the use of weapons. They were best among those who knew about weapons and in their rivalry, sought to outdo each other. Their large chariots were embellished with nets made out of gold and had pennants and flags. These were yoked to horses and thundered like clouds. The infinitely valorous ones had colourful bows that were plated with molten gold. They twanged them cheerfully, like lightning amidst the clouds. On knowing that the kimkaras had been killed, their mothers, relatives and well-wishers were filled with grief and scared. Rivalling each other, adorned in ornaments made out of molten gold, they[226] rushed to fight Hanumat, who was stationed near the gate. They released showers of arrows and their chariots thundered and roared. The bulls among the nairittas roamed around and showered down like clouds filled with rain. Hanumat was enveloped by that shower of arrows. His form became invisible, like that of a king of mountains because of the rain. Swift in his movements, the ape, roaming around in the sparkling sky, evaded those arrows and the speedy chariots of those brave ones. The brave one could be seen in the sky, toying with those archers. He was like the wind god in the sky and the archers were like clouds. He roared in a terrible voice and terrified that large army. Hanumat roamed around and attacked the valiant rakshasas with force. The scorcher of enemies killed some with slaps and some with his feet. He killed some with his fists and tore some others with his nails. The ape crushed some with his chest and some others with his thighs. Because of his roars, some others fell down on the ground. Some were killed. Others fell down on the ground. Seeing this, all the soldiers were afflicted by fear and fled in the ten directions. Elephants shrieked in broken voices. Horses fell down on the ground. The seats, standards and umbrellas fell down on the ground, which was strewn with shattered chariots. He killed those prosperous rakshasas. The ape was extremely strong and fierce in

[225] Meaning the sun.

[226] The sons of the ministers.

his valour. He again wished to fight against some other rakshasas. Therefore, the brave one again went to the gate.

Chapter 5(44)

Having got to know that the sons of the ministers had been killed by the great-souled ape, Ravana concealed his thoughts and thought of an excellent means. There were five foremost leaders of the soldiers—Virupaksha, Yupaksha, the rakshasa Durdhara, Praghasa and Bhasakarna. These brave ones were skilled in good policy and Dashagriva commanded them. He was eager to seize Hanumat, who possessed Vayu's speed in battle. 'All of you advance in front of the army. Take a large army with you, with horses, chariots and elephants. Chastise the ape. When you approach the one whose residence is in the forest, you must be attentive. The action that you undertake must not be contrary to the time and the place. Debating about his deeds, I do not think that he is an ape. He possesses great strength. In every way, he must be a great creature. Using the strength of his austerities, perhaps Indra has created him for some objective of his. With all of you, I have vanquished the serpents, the yakshas, the gandharvas, the gods, the asuras and the maharshis. To invade us in some way, they must have created him. There is no doubt about this and he must be seized. The ape is cruel in his valour and you must not disrespect him. I have seen apes earlier, who were quick and extensive in their valour—Vali, Sugriva, the immensely strong Jambavat, the commander Nila and others like Dvivida. But their terrible speed, energy, prowess, intelligence, strength, enterprise and capacity to change form was not like his. It is thus known that this is a great creature in the form of an ape. Resort to great efforts and seek to capture him. You are sufficient in the field of battle. If they so wish, the three worlds, with Indra, the gods, the asuras and humans are incapable of standing before you. Nevertheless, someone who desires victory in a battle must know about good policy. Make efforts to protect yourselves. Success in a battle is fickle.' All those greatly energetic ones accepted the words spoken by their master.

Like the fire in their energy, they attacked with great force. There were chariots, crazy elephants and extremely swift steeds. There were many kinds of sharp weapons. All of them had every kind of force. The giant ape saw those brave and radiant ones. Garlanded by the rays of his own energy, he was like the rising sun. Near the gate, he possessed great force, great spirit and great strength. He was immensely intelligent, immense in his enterprise, gigantic in size and immense in strength. Stationed in all the directions, all of them looked at him. Here and there, they used terrible weapons to strike at him. Durdhara used five sharp and sparkling arrows, yellow at the tip and with the complexion of lotuses, to strike him in the chest. The ape was pierced in the chest with those five arrows. He leapt up into the sky and roared, the sound echoing in the ten directions. On his chariot, the brave Durdhara readied his bow. The immensely strong one showered him with many hundreds of arrows. From the sky, the ape countered these showers of arrows, like the wind dispels a cloud filled with rain at the end of the rainy season. The son of the wind god was oppressed by Durdhara. The powerful one roared loudly and again extended his size. From a distance, the ape violently descended on Durdhara's chariot. He descended with great force, like a mass of lightning on a mountain. The eight horses were crushed. The chariot, the wheel and the kubara[227] were shattered. Giving up his life, Durdhara fell down on the ground. Virupaksha and Yupaksha saw that he had fallen down on the ground. Filled with rage, those two invincible scorchers of enemies leapt up. When they suddenly leapt up, stationed in the sparkling sky, the mighty-armed ape struck them in the chests with two clubs. The forceful and immensely strong one struck them with force. He was like Suparna in his valour and they fell down on the ground again. The ape uprooted a sala tree. Using this, the son of the wind god slew those two brave rakshasas. Knowing that those three had been killed by the spirited ape, Praghasa attacked with

[227] Kubara is the pole for attaching the yoke to the chariot.

great force and struck the ape powerfully. The valiant Bhasakarna angrily seized a spear in his hand. The illustrious tiger among apes was alone and there were two of them. Praghasa pierced him with a spear that was sharp at the tip. The rakshasa Bhasakarna struck that supreme ape with a javelin. Pierced by those two on the body, his body hair became smeared with blood. Angry, the ape assumed a radiance that was like that of the rising sun. He uprooted the summit of a mountain, with the animals, serpents and the trees. With that, Hanumat, elephant among apes, killed those two brave rakshasas. When those five leaders had been killed, the soldiers were disheartened and the ape destroyed what remained of the army. Like the one with the thousand eyes against the asuras, the ape struck horses with horses, elephants with elephants, warriors with warriors and chariots with chariots, destroying them. Elephants and horses were killed. Wheels and giant chariots were shattered. Rakshasas were slain. Everywhere on the ground, the paths were obstructed with these. In the battle, he killed the brave ones with their soldiers, standards, leaders and mounts. After this, the brave ape again stood by the gate. He was like Death, having made up his mind about the destruction of the subjects.

Chapter 5(45)

Hanumat crushed the five commanders, with their followers and their mounts. At this, the king[228] looked at Prince Aksha, who was not wounded and was ready and eager to fight in the battle. He urged him with his eyes and the powerful one[229] picked up a colourful and golden bow and leapt up, like a sacrificial fire when oblations have been offered into it by the best of brahmanas. The valiant one ascended a gigantic chariot that was like the rising sun in complexion and was armoured with a plate made out of

[228] Ravana.
[229] Aksha.

molten gold. The bull among the nairittas ventured forth against the large ape. It[230] was fashioned out of the store of austerities he had accumulated and won for himself. It was decorated with armour that was made out of molten gold. The flag and the standard were decorated with jewels. It was yoked properly to eight excellent horses that possessed the speed of thought. It moved without obstructions and gods and asuras could not assail it. With a complexion like that of the sun, it could be controlled and could move around in the sky. A quiver, eight swords and bells were fixed to it. In due order, spears and javelins were arranged in the designated places. He ascended the chariot, which was like the sun in complexion. Filled with all the required objects, it was resplendent. There were ropes that dazzled like the sun and the moon. He emerged, like an immortal in his valour. The noise of horses, elephants and large chariots filled the sky and the earth, with its mountains. With the army, he approached the gate. The capable ape was standing there, waiting.

Having reached the ape, Aksha, the one with the tawny eyes, saw him standing there, like the fire of destruction at the end of a yuga, ready to destroy subjects. He was astonished and was filled with respect. He looked at him, with a lot of respect in his eyes. The immensely strong son of the king[231] weighed the force and valour of the enemy, the great-souled ape, and his own strength and increased his own size, like the sun at the end of the winter. Having considered the valour, stability and invincibility of Hanumat, though he was filled with rage in the battle, he controlled himself and provoked him[232] with three sharp arrows. He saw that the ape was proud and had conquered his exhaustion, having defeated the enemy. Aksha looked at him with an agitated mind and picked up a bow and arrow in his hand. His necklace and armlets were made out of gold and his earrings were beautiful. Swift in his valour, he approached the ape. Their unmatched encounter generated respect even among the gods and the asuras. Witnessing the battle between the ape and

[230] The chariot.

[231] Aksha.

[232] Hanumat.

the prince, the earth shrieked. The sun did not radiate heat. The wind did not blow and the mountain quaked. The sky screamed and the ocean was agitated. The brave one who knew the truth about affixing, aiming and releasing, struck the ape on the head with three arrows that were excellent at the tips and with golden tufts. These were like venomous serpents. When those arrows struck him on the head, blood started to flow from the wounds and he dilated his eyes. With the arrows like rays, he was like the sun when it has just arisen. He was as radiant as the sun, with its garland of rays. In the battle, the supreme adviser of the lord of the apes glanced at the excellent and eager son of the king, with his wonderful weapon and his wonderful bow. He was filled with delight and was keen to fight in the battle. Filled with strength and energy, his rage increased, like the one with the rays in front of Mandara. Using his eyesight, which were like the flames of a fire, he burnt down Prince Aksha's soldiers and mounts. The rakshasa's bow was like Shakra's bow.[233] In the encounter, he showered down arrows like a cloud. The lord of the apes was like a mountain and he swiftly showered down arrows on him, like a cloud showering down on an excellent mountain. The ape saw him in the battle, terrible in his valour and with increasing energy, strength, valour and arrows. On seeing Prince Aksha in the encounter, like a cloud in his valour, he roared in joy. Because of his childish nature, he[234] was brave and insolent in the battle. His anger increased, with his eyes like wounds. He approached the ape, who was unmatched in fights, like an elephant approaches a giant pit that is covered with grass. When those forceful arrows descended on him, he roared like the thundering of a cloud. The son of the wind god, terrible to behold, swiftly leapt up into the sky, extending his arms and his thighs. The supreme and powerful one among the rakshasas was supreme among all charioteers. When the powerful one leapt up, he too leapt up and enveloped him with arrows, like a cloud raining down hail on a mountain. The brave ape followed Vayu's path and like the wind, sought out gaps in between the

[233] A rainbow.

[234] Aksha.

arrows that were released. Terrible in his valour, he moved around, with the speed of thought. Using his eyes, he glanced at Aksha with a great deal of respect. With the bow and arrows, he was eager in the battle and shrouded the sky with many kinds of excellent arrows. The son of the wind god thought. The arrows pierced the ape between the arms. Struck by the noble prince, the great-souled one roared. The mighty-armed one knew the truth about what should be done in specific situations.

He thought about his adversary's prowess in the encounter. 'He is not acting like a child and his radiance is like that of the young sun. The extremely strong one is accomplishing this great deed. He is one who displays deeds in all kinds of encounters. But the idea of killing him does not appeal to me. This great-souled one is great and brave. He is controlled and can withstand a lot in an encounter. Because of the deeds and qualities he has exhibited, there is no doubt that he is revered by the serpents, the yakshas and the sages. He is stationed in front of me and is looking at me, with enhanced valour, enterprise and will. The valour of the one who acts fast will make the minds of even the gods and asuras tremble. If he is ignored, he will certainly overpower me. In this encounter, his valour is increasing. The idea of killing him appeals to me, because if an expanding fire is ignored, that cannot be tolerated.' He thus debated the enemy's force. Accordingly, the valiant one determined his own course of action. The immensely strong one, the great ape, made up his mind to kill him. Using slaps from his palms, the brave ape who was the son of the wind god and was following Vayu's path, slew the eight extremely swift horses. The great chariot was struck by the palm of the minister of the lord of the apes and destroyed. The seat was shattered and the kubara broke. Slain, the eight horses fell down from the sky on to the ground. The maharatha abandoned his chariot. Wielding a bow and a sword, he leapt up from the ground into the sky. His body took to the air, like the wind in its own abode. The ape also wandered around in the sky, frequented by the king of the birds,[235]

[235] Garuda.

the wind and the siddhas. The son of the wind god, forceful and valiant, used his austerities, like a brave and fierce rishi. He seized him by the feet, slowly and firmly. The ape whirled him around one thousand times, like the lord of the birds does to a large serpent. Though he was like his father[236] in valour, the excellent ape hurled him down on the ground with great force. His arms, thighs, waist and head were shattered. Blood started to flow from his wounds. His bones and eyes were crushed. His joints were fragmented and his entrails strewn around. The rakshasa was slain and Vayu's son felled him on the ground. The great ape crushed him down on the ground and generated a great fear in the lord of the rakshasas. On seeing that the prince had been killed by the ape, the maharshis who are great in their vows and move around unimpeded, the assembled creatures, the yakshas, the serpents and the gods, with Indra, were filled with wonder. Prince Aksha, with eyes like wounds, was as resplendent as the son of the wielder of the vajra. Having killed him, the brave one[237] again went to the gate. He was like Death, when the time arrives for the destruction of subjects.

Chapter 5(46)

When Prince Aksha was killed by Hanumat, the great-souled lord of the rakshasas was enraged. However, he controlled himself and commanded Indrajit, who was like a god. 'You are supreme among those who know about weapons and can cause grief to gods and asuras. The gods, with Indra, have witnessed your deeds. Having worshipped the grandfather,[238] you have obtained weapons. When you resort to that strength of weapons, the asuras, the large number of Maruts and all those in the three worlds are unable to overcome their exhaustion against you in

236 Ravana.

237 Hanumat.

238 Brahma.

a battle. You are protected by the valour in your arms. You are also protected by your austerities. You know about the time and the place. You are supreme among intelligent ones. In a battle, there is nothing that you cannot accomplish. If you make up your mind and think about it, there is no deed you cannot accomplish. There is no one in the three worlds who does not know about the strength of your weapons and about your own strength. Your austerities and strength and the valour and power of your weapons in a battle are like mine. There is no one who can withstand you in the field of battle. Having thought about this, I am certain that I need suffer no exhaustion in my mind. All the kimkaras and the rakshasa Jambumali have been killed. So have the five brave commanders who were the sons of the advisers. Your beloved brother, Prince Aksha, has been killed. O destroyer of enemies! They did not possess the essence that you and I have. O intelligent one! I have witnessed the great strength, power and valour of this ape. Therefore, look towards your own essence and powerfully do something that is worthy of your own strength. Act so that the affliction of our soldiers can end and so that they find peace, when the enemy has been quietened. Consider your own strength and that of the enemy. O supreme among those who know about weapons! Prepare. Sending someone like you will not be recommended by the best among intelligent ones. But it is my view that this is what a kshatriya should do and is also in accordance with the dharma of kings. O destroyer of enemies! You will know how to use many kinds of weapons in the encounter. You will certainly know how to bring about the desired victory in the battle.'

Having heard his father's words, the accomplished one, with a power like that of the son of a god, circumambulated his lord with an undistressed mind. The brave one made up his mind to fight. Indrajit was worshipped by his own people. Eager to fight, he enthusiastically prepared himself for the battle. The son of the lord of the rakshasas was handsome, with eyes like the petals of lotuses. The immensely energetic one emerged, like the ocean on the day of the full moon. Indrajit, who was like Indra, ascended a chariot whose speed could not be checked. It was yoked to four *vyalas*[239] who were like the king of the birds in their speed, with sharp and pointed teeth. The supreme among archers was on that chariot. He knew about weapons and was supreme among those who knew about weapons. On that chariot, he swiftly advanced towards the spot where Hanumat was.

There was the clatter of the chariot. There was the sound from the twanging of the bow. Hearing this, the brave ape was even more delighted. Accomplished in fighting, he[240] picked up his gigantic bow and sharp arrows that were like darts. He advanced towards Hanumat. Filled with delight, with the bow in his hand, he too advanced towards the encounter. All the directions paled. The animals howled in hideous tones. The serpents and the yakshas assembled, as did the maharshis and the siddhas. Large flocks of birds covered the sky and extremely happy, started to call. The ape saw that Indrajit's chariot was advancing. The forceful one roared loudly and extended his size. Indrajit was on that divine chariot, with his colourful bow. He twanged his bow and created a sound that was like the clap of thunder. Both of them were extremely forceful. Both of them were extremely strong and were not scared of fighting. The ape and the son of the lord of the rakshasas were bound in enmity, like the Indra of the gods against the Indra of the asuras. He[241] was immeasurable and moved around along the path followed by his father, extending his size. As the brave one advanced on his great chariot and released his torrent of arrows, he avoided them. The brave one, the destroyer of enemy heroes, shot arrows that were long and sharp, with excellent shafts and colourful tufts that were made out of gold. They were aimed well and as they descended, they possessed the force of the vajra. There was the clatter of the chariot. There was the sound of drums, tambourines and kettledrums. There was the sound from the twanging of the

[239] Vyalas in Indrajit's chariot are usually taken to be tigers. However, a vyala is any vicious beast and can be a tiger, a lion, a leopard, an elephant, or even some kind of reptile.

[240] Indrajit.

[241] Hanumat.

bow. Hearing this, he[242] leapt up again. The great ape quickly moved around in the space left by the arrows. Though he[243] was accomplished in striking the target, the ape rendered this aim futile. Hanumat, the son of the wind god, remained ahead of the arrows and again stretched out his arms. Both of them were full of speed. Both of them were accomplished in modes of fighting. An excellent encounter ensued, agreeable to the minds of all creatures. Hanumat did not know the rakshasa's weak spot. The son of the wind god did not know the great-souled one's weak spot. They were like gods in their valour. As they clashed, it was as if they rendered each other's poisons futile.

The great-souled one saw that he was missing his aim. His arrows were failing and were falling down. He had a great thought. Accomplished in his soul, he controlled himself. The son of the king of the rakshasas made up his mind about the brave and foremost ape. Having noticed that the ape could not be killed, he thought of capturing him. The brave one was supreme among those who knew about weapons. He affixed the grandfather's extremely energetic weapon and aimed it towards the supreme ape. The one who knew the truth about weapons knew that he could not be killed. Therefore, Indrajit captured the mighty-armed son of the wind god. The ape was bound by the rakshasa's weapon. He could not move and fell down on the ground. The foremost ape realized that his force was constrained and that he had been tied down by the power of the weapon of the powerful one.[244] He thought that this was a favour being shown to him by the grandfather. This was Svayambhu's mantra and the brahmastra had been invoked with that mantra. Hanumat thought that this was a boon bestowed by the grandfather. 'I do not possess the strength to free myself from the bondage of this weapon, because of the powers of the preceptor of the worlds. I have thus determined that I must remain in the bonds of this weapon. Therefore, I must follow whatever ensues.' The ape thought about the energy of the weapon and about the

[242] Hanumat.

[243] Indrajit.

[244] Meaning Brahma.

favour the grandfather had shown towards him. He thought about his strength of freeing himself from it[245] and decided to follow the grandfather. 'Though I have been bound by the weapon, there is no fear in me. I am protected by the grandfather, Indra and the wind god. Even if I am captured by the rakshasas, there is a great quality associated with that. I will have a conversation with the Indra among the rakshasas. Therefore, let the enemy capture me.' The slayer of enemy heroes decided this. Having considered it, he made no attempt to move. The enemy captured him. Having been captured by them, he roared and censured them.

The rakshasas saw that the scorcher of enemies was motionless. They tied him up with ropes made out of hemp and barks from trees. The idea of being captured by the enemy appealed to him. He tolerated being seized by those brave ones. He was certain that the Indra among the rakshasas would be curious to see him. Once he was bound in bark, the valiant one was freed from the bondage of the weapon. When there is another kind of bondage, the bondage of a weapon ceases to exist. When the supreme among apes was tied up in bonds made out of bark from trees, the brave Indrajit started to think. 'He has been freed from the weapon. Once a person is tied up in some other way, there cannot be the bonds from a weapon. Alas! My great deed has been rendered futile. The rakshasas have ignored the rules of a mantra. Yet another mantra cannot be used on a weapon. Therefore, all of us face a danger.' Bound up, Hanumat was dragged along by the rakshasas. But he had not yet realized that he had been freed from the bondage of the weapon. The cruel rakshasas beat Hanumat with sticks and their fists. They dragged the ape to the presence of the Indra among the rakshasas. Indrajit saw that because of the bondage of ropes and barks from trees, he had been freed from the bondage of the weapon. He exhibited the immensely strong and foremost ape to the king and all his companions.

The excellent ape was bound, like a crazy elephant. The rakshasas conveyed him to Ravana, Indra among the rakshasas.

[245] Which would occur in due course.

'Who is this? Whom does he belong to? Where has he come from? What is his task? Where is his refuge?' The brave rakshasas conversed in this way. Other rakshasas present were angry and said, 'Kill him. Burn him. Eat him.' After passing through those paths, the great-souled one suddenly found himself in the presence of the king of the rakshasas. He saw him, adorned by expensive jewels and surrounded by companions who were seated at his feet. The immensely energetic Ravana saw that supreme ape. He was being dragged here and there by the rakshasas with disfigured forms. The supreme among apes also saw the lord among the rakshasas. He was full of energy and strength and seemed to scorch like the sun. Dashanana looked at the ape, his eyes rolling around in anger. The best among his ministers were there, skilled and aged and good in conduct. He commanded them to ask the ape, in due order, about the reason why he had come here and his intention. The lord of the apes said, 'I have come to you as a messenger.'

Chapter 5(47)

Terrible in his valour, Hanumat was astounded at his[246] deed. Eyes coppery red with anger, he looked at the lord of the rakshasas. He was radiant and resplendent, on an extremely expensive golden throne. His immensely radiant crown was adorned with a net of pearls. There were colourful golden ornaments, as if they had been fashioned with the mind. They were embedded with diamonds and embellished with extremely expensive jewels. There was a sacred thread that was made out of expensive silk and he was smeared with red sandalwood paste. He was smeared with many colourful unguents, with diverse auspicious marks. His large heads were a sight to behold. With red eyes, he was terrible in form. His large and sharp teeth blazed and his lips hung down. With ten heads, the brave and extremely expensive one was dazzling. He was like the

[246] Indrajit's.

summit of Mandara, surrounded by many predatory beasts. There was a radiant necklace on his chest, resembling a mass of excellent and black collyrium. His face had the complexion of the full moon and he was like a cloud garlanded with cranes. There were armlets on his arms, which were smeared with excellent sandalwood paste. The armlets shone, the thick arms resembling five-hooded serpents. He was seated on a large and excellent throne made out of crystal, decorated with gems, and a superb spread was laid over this. There were women on every side, ornamented exceedingly well. They served him, standing close to him, with whisks made of hair in their hands.

Four ministers, insolent because of their strength, were seated there. These were the rakshasas Durdhara, Prahasta, the rakshasa Mahaparshva and the minister, Nikumbha. These ministers were skilled in all the techniques of counselling. They were like the four oceans that surround the entire world. These ministers were skilled in all the techniques of counselling and there were others with auspicious intelligence. They were like the advisers of the gods, comforting the lord of the gods.

Hanumat saw the infinitely energetic lord of the rakshasas. He was seated, like a cloud full of water atop the summit of Meru. He[247] had been oppressed by the rakshasas who were terrible in valour. Filled with great wonder, he looked at the lord of the rakshasas. Hanumat saw the radiant lord of the rakshasas. Confounded by his energy, in his mind, he thought the following. 'What a form. What patience. What spirit. What resplendence. Marked with all the signs, the king of the rakshasas is wonderful. Had adharma not become stronger, this lord of the rakshasas might have become the protector of the world of the gods, and even of Shakra. All the immortals and the danavas are indeed terrified of him. If he seeks to become angry, he will reduce the entire world to a single ocean.'[248] The intelligent ape thought this and many other things when he saw the infinitely energetic power of the king of the rakshasas.

[247] Hanumat.

[248] This is what happens at the time of the universal destruction.

Chapter 5(48)

Ravana, who made the worlds shriek, was suffused with great rage. The mighty-armed one looked at the coppery eyed one who was standing in front of him. The king's eyes were coppery red with rage. He spoke words full of great meaning, appropriate at the time, to Prahasta, his excellent adviser. 'Ask the evil-souled one where he has come from. What is the reason why he has come here? Why did he destroy the grove and oppress the rakshasis?' Hearing Ravana's words, Prahasta spoke these words. 'O fortunate one! Be reassured. O ape! You have no reason to be terrified. Even if you have been sent by Indra to Ravana's residence, tell me the truth. O ape! Do not be scared. You will be released. You have assumed a beautiful form and have entered this city. Do you belong to Vaishravana, Yama or Varuna? Are you a messenger sent by Vishnu, who desires victory? Though you possess the form of an ape, your energy does not show you to be an ape. O ape! If you tell us the truth now, you will be released. If you do not speak the truth, it will be extremely difficult for you to remain alive. State the reason why you have entered Ravana's residence.'

The supreme ape was thus addressed by the lord of large numbers of rakshasas. He said, 'I do not belong to Shakra, Yama or Varuna. I have no friendship with the lord of riches[249] and Vishnu has not urged me. Since birth, I have been an ape and I have come here in that form. It is extremely difficult to see the Indra among the rakshasas and I have now seen him. I destroyed the grove of the king of the rakshasas so that I might be able to see him. At this, those strong rakshasas arrived, wishing to fight with me. Wishing to protect my own body, I fought against them in the battle. Even the gods and the asuras are incapable of tying me down in a bond made of weapons. I have that privilege because of a boon that was conferred on me by the grandfather. I surrendered to the weapon because I wished to desire the king. Though I have been freed from that weapon, I have been greatly oppressed by the rakshasas. Know

[249] Kubera.

that I am the messenger of the infinitely energetic Raghava. O lord! Listen to my words. They are like medication.'

Chapter 5(49)

The supreme among apes was spirited. He saw the greatly spirited Dashanana. Without any anxiety, he addressed him in words that were full of meaning. 'I have come to your residence because of Sugriva's command. O Indra among the rakshasas. Your brother,[250] the lord of the apes, has asked about your welfare. Listen to the instruction of the great-souled Sugriva, your brother. These words are full of dharma and artha and will be beneficial in this world and in the next. There was a king named Dasharatha and he had chariots, elephants and horses. He was like a father and friend to people and was like the lord of the gods in his radiance. The lord, his mighty-armed eldest son, always did what brought his father pleasure. Following his father's command, he left and entered the forest of Dandaka. He was with his brother, Lakshmana, and his wife, Sita. The immensely energetic one is named Rama and he resorts to the path of dharma. His wife, devoted to her husband, got lost in the forest. She is the daughter of the great-souled King Janaka of Videha. With his younger brother, the prince searched for the queen's trail. Having reached Rishyamuka, he met Sugriva, who pledged that he would help search for Sita. Rama bestowed the kingdom of the apes on Sugriva. Having slain Vali in an encounter, the prince established Sugriva as the lord in the kingdom of large numbers of apes and bears. Sugriva, devoted to the truth, was eager to search for Sita's trail. The lord of the apes sent the apes in all the directions. Hundreds, thousands and tens of thousands of apes left to search in all the directions, above, below and in the sky. Some of them are equal to Vinata's son.[251] Some of them are like

[250] The word brother is only meant to underline affection.

[251] Garuda.

the wind god. Those immensely strong and brave apes are swift and nothing can obstruct their path. My name is Hanumat and I am the biological son of the wind god. For Sita's sake, I have quickly crossed one hundred yojanas. Wishing to see her, I crossed the ocean and came here. You know about dharma and artha. You have obtained the results of your austerities. O immensely wise one! You should not confine someone else's wife. This is against dharma and there are many kinds of dangers associated with such an act. It destroys the foundation of someone who does it and intelligent people like you should not do it. If Rama and Lakshmana resort to their rage, who—not even the gods and the asuras—is capable of standing before their arrows and escaping? O king! There is no one in the three worlds who can cause harm to Raghava, and having done that, enjoys happiness. Therefore, these beneficial words are in conformity with dharma and artha in the three periods of time.[252] Listen to them and return Janakee to the god among men. It is extremely difficult to see the queen and it is through good fortune that I accomplished that. The remaining and subsequent part of the task will be undertaken by Raghava. I have noticed that Sita is overcome by sorrow. You have seized her, without knowing that she is like a five-hooded serpent. Her energy is such that she is like swallowed food that is exceedingly mixed with poison. Even the asuras and the immortals are incapable of digesting her. You have obtained dharma and the fruits of your austerities. By seizing her, you will destroy good policy, your own life and whatever you have received. Because of your austerities, you see that you cannot be killed by asuras and gods. Therefore, you consider yourself to be great. Sugriva is not a god. Nor is he an asura, or human. He is not a rakshasa, a gandharva, a yaksha or a serpent. O king! Raghava is human and Sugriva is lord of the apes. O king! Therefore, how will you be able to save your life? The fruits of dharma do not coexist with the fruits of adharma. Since dharma destroys adharma, search for that kind of fruit. There is no doubt that, so far, you have obtained the fruits of dharma. You will soon reap the fruits

[252] Past, present and future.

of this adharma. Comprehend the slaying in Janasthana.[253] Also comprehend the slaying of Vali. For your own welfare, comprehend the friendship between Rama and Sugriva. If I so wish, I can single-handedly destroy Lanka, with its horses, chariots and elephants. But that is not what has been decided. In the presence of large numbers of apes and bears, Rama pledged that he would destroy the enemies who had oppressed Sita. Even if Purandara himself causes an injury to Rama, he cannot obtain happiness, not to speak of people like you. Know that the one who is under your subjugation, the one you know as Sita, is your night of destruction. She will destroy all of Lanka. In the form and image of Sita, this is a noose of destiny. You have yourself strung it around your neck. Think of how you can be safe. You will see this city, with its mansions and streets, burnt down, consumed by Sita's energy and suffering from Rama's rage.'

Without any distress and speaking skilfully, the unmatched ape made him hear these disagreeable words. Dashanana's eyes widened in anger. He commanded that the great ape should be killed.

Chapter 5(50)

Hearing the words of the great-souled ape, Ravana was senseless with anger and commanded that he should be killed. When the evil-souled Ravana ordered his death, Vibhishana suggested that this was not recommended for a messenger. Since the lord of the rakshasas was angry, he thought about the task that was at hand. Having determined what should be done, the victor over enemies pacified and worshipped his elder brother. The one who was excellent in the use of words spoke these exceedingly beneficial words. 'O king! This is contrary to dharma and is condemned as being against the conduct of the worlds. For someone brave like you, this is tantamount to murdering the ape. There is no doubt that this enemy is insolent and has done something disagreeable

[253] Of the rakshasas.

that can't be measured. However, the learned do not speak about killing a messenger. There are many kinds of punishments indicated for a messenger. Disfiguring the limbs, striking with a whip, shaving the head and engraving marks on the body—these are said to be the punishments for a messenger. But we have not heard about a messenger being killed. Your intelligence is refined in dharma and artha. You can certainly make up your mind about what is superior and what is inferior. How can someone like you be immersed in anger? Spirited people control their rage. You are supreme among all the gods and the asuras. In what is said to be dharma, in the conduct of people, in the sacred texts, in using one's intelligence and for someone who is as brave as you, this should not be done. I do not see any qualities associated with the killing of this ape. That kind of punishment should be inflicted on those who have sent this ape. Whether he is virtuous or wicked, others have sent him here. He is dependent on others and has spoken the words of others. One should not kill a messenger. O king! If he is killed, I do not see anyone else who can travel through the sky and then return here again, after crossing to the other shore of this great ocean. O vanquisher of the cities of enemies! Therefore, do not make attempts to kill him. You should not resort to attempts that facilitate the work of the gods and Indra.[254] Those two sons of the king are insolent. They love fighting. If he is killed, I do not see any other messenger who can travel over this long distance unobstructed and goad those two into battle. You are valiant, enterprising and spirited. The gods and the asuras find you impossible to vanquish. You delight the minds of the nairittas. When there is the prospect of a war, you should not destroy that opportunity. There are brave and controlled ones engaged in your welfare. They are born in noble lineages and possess great qualities. They are spirited and supreme among those who wield weapons. There are crores of well-armed warriors ahead of you. You must make the enemy realize your power. Let someone follow your command, take one part of your army and capture those two foolish princes.'

[254] Who seek to eliminate Ravana.

Chapter 5(51)

The immensely strong Dashagriva heard the beneficial words spoken by his excellent brother, appropriate for the time and the place. He said, 'You have spoken well. The killing of a messenger is condemned. Certainly, it is someone else who should be killed. Let him be chastised. Indeed, the tail is the beloved ornament for apes. Let it be burnt swiftly and let him leave with a burnt tail. Let all his kin and well-wishers, friends and allies, see him in a distressed and afflicted state, with his limb disfigured.' The Indra among the rakshasas commanded the rakshasas to ignite his tail and carry him everywhere around the city, including the crossroads.

Harsh in their anger, the rakshasas heard his words. They bound up his tail in tattered cotton garments. As his tail was being bound, the great ape increased his size, like a fire in the forest when it has obtained some dry kindling. The rakshasas sprinkled his tail with oil and applied fire, igniting it. But his soul was filled with rage and intolerance and his face was like the rising sun. He flung them down. The cruel rakshasas assembled together and tied up the supreme among apes again. Having been tied up, the brave one made up his mind about what was appropriate at the time. 'Even if I am bound, these rakshasas are incapable of doing what they wish against me. I can again tear up the bonds, leap up and kill them. I am alone sufficient to fight against all the rakshasas in a battle. However, for the sake of pleasing Rama, I will tolerate this. I must again roam around Lanka. When I looked over Lanka during the night, I did not properly see the fortifications that have been laid out. Now that night is over, I must certainly examine these. If they wish, let them tie me up again and ignite my tail. Even if the rakshasas oppress me, I will not suffer from any mental exhaustion.' Therefore, the spirited and great ape reduced his size. Delighted, the rakshasas advanced and seized the elephant among the apes. With the sound of conch shells and drums, they announced their own deeds. The rakshasas, cruel in their deeds, roamed around the city with him. Hanumat wandered around the great city of the rakshasas. The great ape saw wonderful palaces. The grounds were laid out well and neatly divided by crossroads. The ape saw paths thick with houses, points at which roads met, crossroads, quadrangles and royal roads. Everywhere, the rakshasas announced that the ape was a spy.

When the tip of Hanumat's tail was being set on fire, the rakshasis, with malformed eyes, went and told the queen this disagreeable news. 'O Sita! The ape with a coppery red face had a conversation with you. His tail has been set on fire and he is being conveyed around.' She heard these words, which were as cruel as she herself being abducted. Vaidehi was tormented by grief and prayed to the fire god. She desired the welfare of the great ape. The large-eyed one controlled herself and worshipped the bearer of oblations. 'If I have served my husband, if I have observed austerities, if I have been devoted to a single husband, may you be cool to Hanumat. If the intelligent one[255] has any compassion towards me, if there is a little bit of good fortune left for me, may you be cool to Hanumat. If I possess good conduct, if the one with dharma in his soul[256] knows that I am eager to meet him, may you be cool to Hanumat. If the mighty-armed and noble Sugriva, devoted to the truth, can save me from this misery, may you be cool to Hanumat.' The one with eyes like those of a fawn circumambulated the flames of the fire, fierce in its rays. The fire flamed up, as if telling her that all would be well with the ape.

When the tail was on fire, the ape started to think. 'Why is this blazing fire not burning me down everywhere? It can be seen that the flames are large, but no pain is being caused to me. It is as if a ball of snow has been placed on the tip of my tail. When I leapt, I saw the extraordinary powers of Rama over the mountain[257] and the lord of the rivers. It is evident that this is something like that. For the intelligent Rama's sake, the ocean and Mainaka showed him respect. Why should the fire not act in a similar way? Because of Sita's non-violence, Raghava's energy and the friendship with

[255] An indirect reference to Rama.

[256] Rama.

[257] Mainaka.

my father,[258] the fire is not burning me.' The ape among elephants again thought for an instant. The great ape leapt up with force and roared. As tall as the summit of a mountain, the handsome one went to the city's gate. The son of the wind god stood away from the arrays of rakshasas. In an instant, he again became as large as a mountain. Immediately, he assumed an extremely tiny form and freed himself from the bonds. Having freed himself, the handsome one again assumed the form of a mountain. He looked around and found a club near the gate. It was polished with black iron and the mighty-armed one seized it. Using this, the son of the wind god killed all the guards. Valiant and terrible in battle, he slew them. He then looked around Lanka again. His tail was on fire, with a garland of flames. He was as radiant as the sun, with its garland of rays.

Chapter 5(52)

Having accomplished his desire, the ape looked around Lanka. His enthusiasm increased and he thought about the part of the task that remained to be accomplished. 'What remains to be done? What should I do now? How can the rakshasas be tormented again? I have destroyed the grove. I have afflicted and slain the rakshasas. I have destroyed part of the army. However, the fortification remains to be destroyed. When the fortification is destroyed, the task will easily be accomplished.[259] Even if a little bit of effort is made, the effort will be successful. The bearer of oblations is blazing on my tail. It is appropriate that I should offer these excellent houses to it as kindling and satisfy it.' Thus, the great ape roamed around the tops of the houses in Lanka. His tail was on fire, like a cloud tinged with lightning. Hanumat released a fire that possessed flames like those of the fire of destruction. United with the wind, it became extremely

[258] The wind god.
[259] Of invading Lanka.

strong and greatly powerful. The fire spread, blazing like the fire of destruction. Borne along by the wind, the ignited fire spread from one house to another one. There were nets made out of gold, pearls and jewels. The houses were full of extremely expensive gems and all these were destroyed. Like the abodes of the siddhas when they have exhausted their store of merit, those mansions were shattered and fell down on the ground. He saw colourful minerals oozing out from all the houses, mixed with diamonds, coral, lapis lazuli, pearls and silver. A fire is never satisfied with wood and grass that can be found here and there. Like that, Hanumat was not content with the destruction of the Indras among the rakshasas. Lanka seemed to have been struck by a curse. It was enveloped in blazing flames. It was like warriors retreating, when their foremost leaders have been killed. It was overcome by the strength of Hanumat's rage. The rakshasas were scared and distressed. They were terrified because of the blazing flames of the fire. The great-minded Hanumat saw Lanka in this state, as if it had been struck by Svayambhu's rage.[260] He had killed a large number of rakshasas. He had destroyed the grove and many trees. He had released the fire in the abodes of the rakshasas. In his mind, the great-souled one reached out to Rama. The great ape, supreme among apes, ignited all of Lanka with the fire from his tail and then put that out in the ocean.[261]

Chapter 5(53)

The city was on fire and destroyed. The large numbers of rakshasas were terrified. On seeing Lanka in this state, the ape Hanumat started to think. 'A great fear has arisen here, and there is a sense of self-loathing in me. Having performed the task of burning Lanka down, have I done something that should not have been done? The best among men who use their intelligence to restrain the

[260] This is probably an oblique reference to the destruction that comes at the end of one of Brahma's days.

[261] The fire on the tail.

anger that has arisen, like water is used to quench a fire, are blessed and great-souled. If the noble Janakee was consumed in the process of burning down Lanka, in my ignorance, I will have destroyed the task of my lord. The reason why this task was started will have become unsuccessful. By burning down Lanka, I have not been able to save Sita. There is no doubt that I have accomplished a desired task. However, having been overcome by rage, I have destroyed the foundation. It is evident that Janakee has been destroyed. Nothing that can be seen has not been burnt. Everything in the city of Lanka has been burnt and nothing remains. The task has been rendered futile because of a confusion in my intelligence. Therefore, the idea of giving up my life here appeals to me. Shall I leap into the fire now, or shall I use the fire with the mare's head?[262] Shall I offer my body up to the creatures who reside in the ocean? If I remain alive, how can I possibly see the lord of the apes? Having destroyed all aspects of the task, how can I meet those two tigers among men? Indeed, I have exhibited the taint that arises from anger. In the three worlds, apes are known for their fickleness. Shame on the sentiments of *rajas*.[263] That has led to this helplessness and instability. Though my lord had asked me to, because of my passion, I have not been able to protect Sita. When Sita is destroyed, both of them[264] will be destroyed. When they are destroyed, Sugriva and his relatives will also be destroyed. Bharata has dharma in his soul and is affectionate towards his brother. When he hears this, with Shatrughna, will he be able to remain alive? The lineage of the Ikshvakus is devoted to dharma. When it is destroyed, there is no doubt that all the subjects will be afflicted and tormented by grief. Therefore, I am unfortunate and have destroyed the accumulation of dharma and artha. With my soul overcome by the taint of anger, it is evident that I have destroyed the world.' While he was thinking this, some omens presented themselves before him. Having himself experienced these earlier, he started to think again. 'Perhaps the fortunate one who

[262] Vadavamukha, the subterranean fire in the ocean.

[263] There are three qualities (*guna*)—*sattva* (goodness), rajas (passion and energy) and *tamas* (inactivity and darkness). This refers to the quality of passion and energy.

[264] Rama and Lakshmana.

is beautiful in all her limbs has been protected by her own energy. A fire does not destroy another fire. She is the wife of the infinitely energetic one, with dharma in his soul. She is also protected by her own good conduct and the fire will not touch her. When I engaged in my task of burning everything down, because of Rama's powers and Vaidehi's good deeds, the fire will not have consumed her. He is like a god to his three brothers, Bharata and the others. Rama's mind is devoted to her. How could she have been destroyed? The unmanifest lord[265] is the one who spreads everywhere and burns. But it did not burn my tail. How could it have burnt the noble one? Because of her austerities, truthfulness in speech and single-minded devotion towards her husband, the fire cannot burn her. The fire has not consumed her.'

He was thinking there, about the queen's devotion to dharma. At that time, Hanumat heard the words of the great-souled charanas. 'Indeed, Hanumat has performed a task that is extremely difficult to withstand. He has unleashed a fire in the residence of the terrible rakshasa. He has burnt this city of Lanka, with its mansions, ramparts and gates. However, Janakee was not burnt and we are astounded at this extraordinary event.' On seeing the auspicious omens, which were full of great qualities, and also because he heard the words of the rishis, Hanumat was delighted in his mind. The ape accomplished the desire in his mind. He got to know that the princess was unharmed. He made up his mind that he would return only after he had seen her once again.

Chapter 5(54)

Janakee was at the foot of the shimshapa tree. He presented himself before her, greeted her and said, 'It is good fortune that I see you here, unharmed.' As he prepared to leave, Sita looked at him repeatedly. Filled with affection towards her husband, she

[265] The fire.

addressed Hanumat in these words. 'If you so wish, you can single-handedly accomplish this task. O destroyer of enemy heroes! You are sufficient. This increase in your strength is laudable. However, if Kakutstha attacks Lanka and takes me away, that will be worthy of him. Therefore, tell him the truth so that the great-souled one is urged to exhibit a valour in the battle that is worthy of him.' Hanumat heard these humble words, full of reason. He replied in these words. 'Surrounded by the brave ones among the apes and the bears, Kakutstha will swiftly come here. He will vanquish the enemy in the battle and dispel your grief.' Hanumat, the son of the wind god, assured Vaidehi in this way. Having made up his mind to leave, he worshipped Vaidehi.

The tiger among the apes was eager to see his lord. The crusher of enemies climbed up Arishta, supreme among mountains. There were herds of elephants on the summit. There were dark blue forests. It was surrounded by many sala, tala, ashvakarna trees and bamboos. It was ornamented with flowering creepers. It was full of many kinds of animals. It was decorated with streaks of minerals. There were many waterfalls. There were piles of boulders. It was frequented by maharshis, yakshas, gandharvas, kinnaras and serpents. There was a dense growth of creepers and trees. The caves were populated by lions. There were large numbers of tigers. The trees had succulent roots and fruits. The extremely strong one, supreme among apes, climbed that mountain. He was goaded by the joy of soon being able to see Rama. The beautiful peaks of the mountain were crushed by his steps. Making a loud noise, the boulders were shattered. Having ascended the Indra among mountains, the great ape increased his size. He wished to cross from the southern shore to the northern shore of the salty ocean. The brave son of the wind god climbed the mountain. He then saw the terrible ocean, frequented by fish and serpents. Like the wind, the son of the wind god took to the sky. From the southern direction, the tiger among apes headed for the northern direction. The ape pressed down on that excellent mountain and it entered the ground, with all the creatures inhabiting it shrieking. The peaks trembled and the trees fell down. The flowering trees were crushed by the force of his thighs. Destroyed, they fell down on the ground, as if they had been struck by Shakra's weapon. There were extremely energetic lions inhabiting the caverns and these were afflicted. They roared in terrible voices and the sound was like that of the sky being shattered. The vidyadhara women leapt up suddenly from the mountain, terrified, their garments dishevelled and their ornaments flung away. There were extremely large and powerful serpents, with flaming tongues and filled with great poison. When their hoods and necks were crushed, they writhed. The kinnaras, the gandharvas, the yakshas and the vidyadharas suffered. They abandoned that supreme mountain and took to the sky. The beautiful mountain was afflicted by that powerful one. With its trees and tall peaks, it entered rasatala. The mountain was ten yojanas wide and thirty yojanas tall. It became level with the earth.

Chapter 5(55)

Without any exhaustion, he leapt across the sky, which was like an ocean. The moon was like a beautiful water lily. The sun was like an auspicious karandava. The Tishya[266] and Shravana nakshatras were like swans. The clouds were like moss and lichen. The nakshatra Punarvasu was like a giant fish. The red-limbed one[267] was like a giant crocodile. Airavata was like a large island. Svati nakshatra was like a graceful swan. The wind was like turbulent waves. The beams of the moon were like cool water. The serpents, yakshas and gandharvas were like full-blown lotuses and lilies. As he traversed through the extensive sky, the abode of the wind, the handsome ape seemed to devour the sky and etch a painting on the lord of the stars.[268] It was as if he was about to steal the sky, with its nakshatras and the solar disc. As he proceeded, Hanumat seemed to fling away the nets of clouds. There were large and dense

[266] Also known as Pushya.

[267] Mars.

[268] The moon.

clouds in the sky, possessing many hues—white, red, blue, yellow, green and pink. He repeatedly entered these nets of clouds and emerged again. He seemed to be like the moon, sometimes hidden and sometimes visible. He roared loudly, in a tone like that of a large cloud. The immensely energetic one again proceeded through the middle of the ocean. The valiant one touched the Indra among mountains[269] that possessed an excellent nave. With great force, like an iron arrow released from a bowstring, he approached it. After some time, he saw the great mountain Mahendra. It was like a cloud and the bull among apes roared.

In every direction, the apes heard the sound of this roar. All of them were eager, desiring to see their well-wisher. Jambavat, supreme among apes, was delighted in his mind. He summoned all the apes and addressed them in these words. 'There is no doubt that, in every way, Hanumat has been successful in his objective. Had he not been successful, he would not have roared in this way.' The apes heard the force of his arms and thighs and the great-souled one's roar. They rejoiced. Here and there, they started to jump around. Delighted, they leapt around from the summit of one mountain to the summit of another mountain. They wished to see Hanumat. Rejoicing, they seized flowering branches from the tops of the trees. The apes waved these around, as if they were garments. The great ape descended, like a giant cloud. On seeing him, all the apes stood there, their hands joined in salutation. The summit of Mount Mahendra was dense with trees. With great force, the ape, who was like a mountain himself, descended there. All the bulls among apes were delighted in their minds. They surrounded the great-souled Hanumat. Filled with great delight, all of them surrounded him. Since he had returned safe, their faces were full of joy. They brought gifts, roots and fruits, and offered these to him. The apes honoured the best among apes, the son of the wind god. They were happy. Some started to cackle. Rejoicing, some other bulls among apes brought the branches of trees.

[269] Mainaka.

Hanumat, the great ape, worshipped the seniors and the aged, Jambavat and the others, and Prince Angada. He was worshipped by the two of them[270] and honoured by the other apes. The brave one briefly stated, 'I have seen the queen.' He grasped the hand of Vali's son and sat down in a beautiful spot in a spot on Mahendra. Happy, Hanumat told the bulls among the apes, 'I have seen Janaka's daughter in Ashokavana. The unblemished one is protected by extremely terrible rakshasis. Desiring to see Rama, the child has her hair in a single braid. She is tired because of her fasting. Her garments are soiled. Her hair is matted. She is emaciated.' Maruti spoke these words, which were full of great meaning and like amrita. On hearing this, all the apes were delighted. Some whooped. Others yelled. Other extremely strong ones roared. Some cackled, Others roared back in response. Delighted, some other elephants among apes lashed their tails. Some raised their long and curved tails and waved them around. There were other apes who were like elephants. In their joy, they leapt down from the summit of the mountain and touched Hanumat. In the midst of the brave ones among the apes, when Hanumat spoke those words, Angada spoke these excellent words. 'There is no ape who is your equal in spirit and valour. You have leapt across the extensive ocean and returned again. It is through good fortune that you have seen the illustrious queen who is Rama's wife. It is through good fortune that Kakutstha will now abandon the grief that has resulted from his separation with Sita.' Delighted, the apes sat down on large boulders and surrounded Angada, Hanumat and Jambavat. Those excellent apes wished to hear about the leaping across the ocean and the sight of Lanka, Sita and Ravana. All of them joined their hands in salutation and looked towards Hanumat's face. The handsome Angada was surrounded by many apes. He was worshipped by them, like the lord of the gods surrounded by the gods in heaven. There was the illustrious and famous Hanumat. There was Angada, with armlets on his arms. Filled with those delighted ones, the large and tall summit of the mountain blazed in its prosperity.

[270] Jambavat and Angada.

Chapter 5(56)

On the summit of Mount Mahendra, with Hanumat at the forefront, the supremely strong apes were filled with great delight. Jambavat, rejoicing, asked the delighted great ape, the son of the wind god, about the details of the task he had undertaken. 'How did you see the queen? What happened there? What is the conduct of Dashanana, cruel in his deeds, towards her? O great ape! I am asking you the truth about everything. After having heard, we will again decide about what course of action should be taken next. When we go to the one who has control over his soul[271] and speak to him, tell us what we can reveal to him and what must be kept a secret.'

Thus addressed, his body hair stood up. He bowed his head down in the direction of Queen Sita and replied, 'In your presence, I came to the summit of Mahendra and leapt up into the sky. I controlled myself, desiring to reach the southern shore of the ocean. While I proceeded, a terrible impediment presented itself before me. A saw an extremely charming, golden and divine mountain. It obstructed my path and I thought the mountain was an impediment. I approached that divine, golden and supreme mountain. I made up my mind that I would have to shatter it. I struck that great mountain with my tail. The summit was like the sun and it shattered into one thousand fragments. Knowing what was my intention, the great mountain addressed me as a "son" and those sweet words delighted my mind.[272] "Know me to be your father's brother. I am the friend of the wind god. I am famous as Mainaka and I reside in the great ocean. O son! All the supreme mountains used to possess wings earlier. They freely roamed around the earth, causing obstructions everywhere. Hearing about the conduct of the mountains, the illustrious and great Indra, the chastiser of Paka, used his vajra to shatter their wings into thousands of fragments. O child! I was saved because your great-souled father, the wind god, hurled me

[271] Rama.

[272] In different places, the sequence of meeting Mainaka, Surasa and Simhika varies.

into the great ocean. O scorcher of enemies! I must seek to help Rama. Rama is supreme among those who uphold dharma and he is like the great Indra in his valour." I heard this from the great-souled Mainaka. I told the mountain about the task that was in my mind. Then, the great-souled Mainaka granted me permission. Resorting to excellent speed, I proceeded along the rest of the journey. For a very long period of time, I speedily proceeded along the path. I then saw the goddess Surasa, the mother of the serpents. In the midst of the ocean, the goddess addressed me in these words. "O supreme among apes! The immortals have indicated that I can devour you. Therefore, I must eat you. You have come to me after a long time." When Surasa told me this, I joined my hands in salutation and stood before her. With my face pale, I addressed her in these words. "The prosperous Rama, Dasharatha's son and the scorcher of enemies, has entered the forest of Dandaka with his brother, Lakshmana, and Sita. The evil-souled Ravana has abducted his wife, Sita. Following Rama's command, I am going to him as a messenger. O one who resides in his dominion! You should seek to help Rama. Otherwise, after seeing Maithilee and Rama, unblemished in his deeds, I will present myself before your mouth. I am truthfully pledging this. Listen to me." Surasa can assume any form at will and she was thus addressed by me. She said, "No one can transgress the boon that I received." Surasa was ten yojanas wide and said this. In an instant, I extended myself to a size of fifteen yojanas. She extended her mouth to make it as large as my size. On seeing her extended mouth, I reduced my form. In an instant, I again assumed the size of a thumb. I quickly descended into her mouth and in an instant, emerged again. Assuming her own form, the goddess Surasa again spoke to me. "O supreme among apes! O amiable one! May you accomplish your objective. Go happily. Bring Vaidehi back to the great-souled Raghava. O mighty-armed one! O ape! May you be happy. I am pleased with you." At this, all the creatures uttered words of praise to me. After this, like Garuda, I leapt up into the extensive sky. My shadow was seized, but I could not see anything. Having lost my speed, I looked around in the ten directions. I could not see anything that could have robbed me of my speed. I thought,

"Who has caused this obstruction in my path? This kind of impediment has arisen, but no form can be seen." While I was thinking, I cast my glance in a downward direction and I saw a terrible rakshasi lying down in the water. The terrible one laughed and roared loudly. Without the slightest bit of fear, the horrible one addressed me in these words. "O large one! Who are you and where are you going? I am hungry and you have been desired by me. Be my food and please my body. I have been without food for a long time." I agreed to her words. I increased my size so that it became larger than what her mouth could hold. Desiring to devour me, the terrible one also started to increase the size of her large mouth. She did not understand me, nor the changes I brought about in my form. In an instant, I reduced my large size. Having seized her heart, I leapt up into the sky again. I extracted her heart, which was like a mountain. Extending her arms, the terrible one fell down in the salty waters. I heard the siddhas and charanas who were in the sky. "The terrible rakshasi, Simhika, has been quickly slain by Hanumat." Having killed her, I again remembered what remained to be done. After having travelled a long distance, I saw the southern shore of the ocean, decorated by trees. The city of Lanka is there. I reached the city that was the abode of the rakshasas when the sun was about to set. Undetected by the guards, terrible in their valour, I entered. There, I searched throughout the night for Janaka's daughter. Though I went to Ravana's inner quarters, I did not see the slender-waisted one there. Finally, I saw Sita in Ravana's abode. She could not see how she would reach the other shore of her ocean of grief. I saw her grieving, in a spot surrounded by walls. There was an excellent grove and a house constructed out of gold. Leaping over the wall, I saw many trees. In the midst of Ashokavana, there was a large shimshapa tree. Ascending that, I saw a grove of golden plantain trees. I saw the supremely beautiful one, not very far from the shimshapa tree. She was young and her eyes were like the petals of lotuses. Because of fasting, her face was emaciated. She was surrounded by cruel and disfigured rakshasis, who devour flesh and blood, like a deer by tigresses. I saw the lady, Rama's unblemished wife. I saw her, near that shimshapa tree. Then I heard an uproar, mixed with the sounds of girdles and anklets, in Ravana's residence and it increased in volume. Extremely anxious, I reduced my own size. Like a bird, I hid myself in the dense growth of the shimshapa tree. After this, the immensely strong Ravana and Ravana's wives reached the spot where Sita was. The beautiful Sita saw the lord of large numbers of rakshasas. She compressed her thighs and her thick breasts and covered them with her arms. Sita was supremely miserable and Dashagriva spoke to her. She did not say anything. He bowed his head down and said, "Treat me with a great deal of respect. O proud one! O Sita! Because of your insolence, if you do not welcome me, after two months, I will drink your blood." She heard the words of the evil-souled Ravana. Extremely angry, Sita spoke these excellent words. "O worst among rakshasas! I am the wife of the infinitely energetic Rama. I am the daughter-in-law of Dasharatha, the protector of the lineage of the Ikshvakus. Having spoken something that should not have been said, how has your tongue not fallen down? O ignoble one! Where is your valour? You came to abduct me when my husband was not present. You committed that crime when you were not seen by the great-souled one. You are not Rama's equal, not in serving, nor in fighting. Raghava performs sacrifices. He is truthful in speech. He prides himself in fighting." When Janakee spoke these harsh words, Dashanana suddenly blazed with anger, like a fire on a funeral pyre. The cruel one dilated his eyes and raised his right fist. When he was about to kill Maithilee, the women present started to wail. From among those women, one of the evil-souled one's wives rose up.[273] This beautiful one was named Mandodari and she restrained him. He was afflicted by desire and she addressed him in sweet words. "What do you have to do with Sita? You are like the great Indra in your valour. O lord! Find pleasure with the daughters of the gods, the gandharvas and the yakshas. What will you do with Sita?" Together, the assembled women quickly raised the immensely strong roamer in the night and took his away to his own residence.

[273] Earlier, we were told that Dhanyamalini restrained Ravana, Mandodari not having been mentioned.

When Dashagriva left, the rakshasis, with disfigured faces, censured Sita in cruel and extremely terrible words. Janakee reckoned that their words were like blades of grass. Though they censured Sita, they were unsuccessful in their attempts. After a while, those rakshasis, the devourers of flesh, refrained from their futile censure and roaring. They went and informed Ravana about Sita's great resolution. All of them assembled together, having lost their hopes and enterprise. They surrounded her from all directions and came under the subjugation of sleep. When they fell asleep, Sita remained engaged in the welfare of her husband. She lamented in piteous and distressed tones and extremely miserable, grieved. I saw Sita in that extremely terrible state. Though I had rested, because I thought about it, my mind was not at peace. Thinking about a means to start a conversation with Janakee, I started to praise the lineage of the Ikshvakus, worshipped by large numbers of royal sages. Having heard the words I had spoken, the queen replied to me, her eyes overflowing with tears. "O bull among the apes! Who are you? Whom do you belong to? Why have you come here? Why are you affectionate towards Rama? You should tell me this." Hearing her words, I uttered the following words. "O queen! Your husband, Rama, has an aide who is terrible in his valour. The brave one's name is Sugriva and the immensely strong one is the Indra among the apes. Know that I am his servant. I am Hanumat and I have come here. Your husband, Rama, unblemished in his deeds, has sent me here. O illustrious one! The prosperous tiger among men, Dasharatha's son, himself gave me this ring to give you, as a sign. Therefore, I wish that you should command me. O queen! What should I do now? Shall I convey you to Rama and Lakshmana's side? What is your reply?" Sita, Janaka's daughter, heard my words and understood. She said, "Let Raghava destroy Ravana and take me back." I bowed my head down before the noble and unblemished queen. I sought a sign that would bring pleasure to Raghava's heart. Thus addressed, the beautiful one gave me an excellent and supreme jewel. Having given it to me, she was extremely anxious and also gave me a message to convey in words. I controlled myself and bowed down before the princess. I circumambulated her and made up my mind to return here. However, having made up her mind, she again replied. She said, "O Hanumat! You must tell Raghava about what is happening to me here. Hearing that, the brave Rama and Lakshmana, with Sugriva, must quickly come here. Act accordingly. If that does not happen, two months of my life are left. Kakutstha will not be able to see me. I will die like one without a protector." Hearing her piteous words, I was filled with rage. Thereafter, I thought about what remained to be accomplished of the task. I increased my size, so that it became like a mountain. Desiring to fight, I started to destroy that grove. The clumps in the grove were destroyed and the terrified animals and birds started to flee. Having woken up, the rakshasis, with disfigured faces, started to look around. Seeing me in that grove, they assembled from here and there. Having assembled, they quickly went and told Ravana about this. "O king! An evil-souled one has destroyed your impenetrable grove. O immensely strong one! The ape does not know about your valour. O Indra among kings! Because of his wicked intelligence, he has done this disagreeable act towards you. Quickly command that he should be killed, so that he can head towards his destruction." Hearing this, the Indra among the rakshasas unleashed rakshasas named kimkaras. They were extremely difficult to defeat and they followed Ravana's inclinations. There were eighty thousand of them, with spears and clubs in their hands. With a club, I killed them in that part of the grove. When these were killed, the remaining ones lost their valour. They went and told Ravana that I had killed his soldiers. I then thought of attacking the chaitya and mansion there. With a pillar, I again killed one hundred rakshasas who were there. This was like an ornament of Lanka and it was destroyed by me. He then commanded Prahasta, Jambumali's son. He was with many rakshasas. They were fearful and terrible in form. That rakshasa possessed strength and was accomplished in fighting. However, with an extremely terrible club, I killed him and his followers. Hearing this, the Indra among the rakshasas sent an extremely strong son of one of his ministers. Ravana sent him, with a large army of foot soldiers. With the club, I conveyed all of them to Yama's abode. Hearing that the son of the minister had been killed, Ravana sent four brave commanders, who were dexterous in exhibiting their valour in a battle. I killed all of them, with their soldiers. Dashagriva again sent his extremely strong son, Aksha. Ravana sent him to fight, with a large number of rakshasas. The prince, who was Mandodari's son, was learned about fighting. He suddenly leapt up into the sky, with a sword and a shield. However, I seized him by the feet. Whirling him around one hundred times, I flung him down and crushed him. Dashanana heard that Aksha had been killed. Ravana's second son is named Indrajit. Extremely angry, he commanded this powerful one, who is invincible in battle. In the encounter, I destroyed the energy of all those soldiers and that of the bull among rakshasas. Having done this, I was filled with great delight. However, the mighty-armed and immensely strong one made great and renewed efforts. He had been sent by Ravana with other brave ones, who were crazy and intoxicated. The extremely swift one bound me down with a brahmastra. The rakshasas bound me with ropes. Having seized me, they dragged me to Ravana's presence. On seeing me, the evil-souled Ravana asked, "Why have you come to Lanka? Why have you killed the rakshasas?" I told him, "I have done everything for Sita's sake. O lord! Desiring to see her, I came to your residence. I am the biological son of the wind god. I am the ape Hanumat. Know me to be the ape who is Rama's messenger and Sugriva's adviser. I have come here before you with Rama's message. Listen to the message that I am conveying to you. It is full of dharma and artha. It is beneficial and is like medication. 'While I dwelt in the mountain Rishyamuka, filled with large trees, I contracted a friendship with Raghava, who is valiant in battle.[274] O king! He told me that his wife had been abducted by a rakshasa. I undertook a pledge that I would help him. The lord Sugriva had been deprived of his kingdom by Vali.[275] With the fire as a witness, Raghava and Lakshmana contracted a pledge of friendship with him. In the encounter, using a single arrow, he destroyed Vali. He made the lord of the apes the great king over all

[274] This message is being delivered by Sugriva, which is odd.

[275] Though this is Sugriva's message, Sugriva is being mentioned in the third person.

the apes. With all our souls, we must now endeavour to help him. That is the reason, following dharma, he[276] is being sent to your presence. Swiftly bring Sita and hand her over to Raghava. Otherwise, the brave apes will destroy your army. From earlier times, who does not know about the power of the apes? They are invited to go, even to the presence of the gods.' I have told you what the king of the apes told me to tell you." When I said this, he looked at me with anger in his eyes, as if he was going to burn me down. He commanded the rakshasas, terrible in their deeds, to kill me. He has a brother named Vibhishana, who is extremely intelligent. For my sake, he beseeched the king of the rakshasas. "O tiger among the rakshasas. This should not be done. Abandon this thought. O rakshasa! The texts on royal policy have said that a messenger must not be killed. Instead, those who speak beneficial words say that the true message must be extracted from a messenger. O one who is unmatched in valour! Even if a messenger commits a grave crime, he can be disfigured. The sacred texts say that he must not be killed." Having heard Vibhishasana's words, Ravana instructed the rakshasas who were present to immediately set my tail on fire. Hearing his words, from every side, they bound up my tail in straw, bark and cotton cloth. Terrible in their valour, the rakshasas roared like lions. They struck me with staffs and fists and set my tail on fire. Tied up by the rakshasas with many ropes, I was like a puppet. However, I did not suffer at all and looked at the city during the day. The brave rakshasas bound me up and applied fire to me. They announced this along the royal roads and arrived at the city's gate. After this, I assumed an extremely gigantic form and again contracted myself. I freed myself from those bonds and assumed my natural form. Seizing an iron club, I killed those rakshasas. After that, with great force, I leapt on to the city's gate. With my tail, I set fire to the city and its mansions and turrets. Without any fear, I burnt down everything, like the fire of destruction does to subjects. Having burnt Lanka down, I again had a doubt. Having burnt Lanka down, I was unsure whether I had burnt Sita down in the

[276] Hanumat.

process. Then I heard words spoken by the charanas, uttered in auspicious syllables. They said, "It is amazing that Janakee has not been burnt down." Hearing those extraordinary words, I again had another thought. I went and saw Vaidehi again and took leave from her yet again. It is because of Raghava's powers, your energy and to accomplish Sugriva's objective that I have done all this. I have done all this there, properly. Now let us do all that which remains to be done.'

Chapter 5(57)

Hanumat, the son of the wind god, told them everything. He then again started to speak these excellent words. 'Because of Raghava's enterprise, Sugriva's efforts and Sita's good conduct, I was able to perform that great leap. O bull among the apes! The noble Sita's conduct is worthy of her. Ravana can burn down the worlds because of his austerities. If he is angry, he can burn them down. The lord of the rakshasas is powerful in every way. Though he touched her body, he has not been destroyed because of his austerities. It is like touching a flame with one's hand. That is the reason she has not behaved like a flame of fire. If she is enraged, Janaka's daughter is capable of removing all sins. In the midst of the evil-souled Ravana's Ashokavana, the virtuous one is in that pitiable state, under the shimshapa tree. She is tormented by grief and is surrounded by the rakshasis. She is like the marks on the moon, losing all resplendence at having been surrounded by the marks of clouds. Vaidehi does not think of Ravana, who is insolent because of his strength. Though Janakee has been confined, the one with the excellent hips is devoted to her husband. In all her soul, the auspicious Vaidehi is devoted to Rama. She is single-mindedly devoted to Rama, like Puloma's daughter to Purandara. She is attired in a single piece of garment, though it is soiled and covered with dust. She is tormented by griefs. Her limbs are miserable. Sita is engaged in her husband's welfare. In the midst of the rakshasis, she is repeatedly censured. I saw her in that pleasure garden, amidst malformed rakshasis. She is distressed and wears her hair in a single braid. She is devoted to thinking about her husband. She lies down on the ground. Her limbs are faded, like a lotus at the onset of the winter. In her attempt to refuse Ravana, she has made up her mind to die. Somehow, I managed to instil confidence in the one with eyes like those of a fawn. Thereafter, I spoke to her and told her everything. Hearing about the friendship between Rama and Sugriva, she was filled with joy. She is controlled and full of good conduct. She is excellent in devotion to her husband. That is the reason she has not killed the great-souled Dashagriva Dashanana. Rama will only be the instrument in bringing about his death.[277] Full of grief, the immensely fortunate Sita is like this. Everything that must now be done should be undertaken.'

Chapter 5(58)

Hearing his words, Vali's son took the permission of all the great apes, with Jambavat at the forefront. 'In this situation, let me tell you what I think we should do. It is proper that we should see those two princes when we have Vaidehi with us. I am alone sufficient to go to the city that is full of large numbers of rakshasas. I will quickly destroy Lanka and the immensely strong Ravana and bring her back, not to speak of a situation where I have these brave and powerful ones, who have cleansed their souls, with me. The apes are accomplished in the use of weapons. They are capable of ensuring victory. In the battle, I will destroy Ravana, with his soldiers, his vanguard, his sons and his brothers. Shakrajit's[278] weapons may be impossible to countenance in a battle—they are Brahma, Aindra, Roudra, Vayavya and Varuna weapons.[279] But

[277] That is, the real cause is Sita.

[278] Indrajit's.

[279] Divine weapons respectively associated with Brahma, Indra, Rudra, Vayu and Varuna.

I will destroy them and kill the rakshasas. I seek your permission to restrain them with my valour. I will incessantly shower down a continuous downpour of boulders. I can kill even the gods in an encounter, not to speak of the roamers in the night. The ocean may cross the shoreline, Mandara may tremble, but the army of soldiers cannot make Jambavat quake in a battle. The brave ape who is Vayu's son is sufficient to destroy all the numerous rakshasas and the rakshasas who are their ancestors. From the force of the thighs of Panasa and that of the great-souled Nila, Mandara can be shattered, not to speak of rakshasas in the battle. Among the gods, the asuras, the yakshas, the gandharvas, the serpents and the birds, tell me who can fight against Mainda and Dvivida. These two supreme among apes are extremely forceful and are the sons of the two Ashvins. These two are proud that they have received excellent boons from the grandfather. They are supremely haughty. In earlier times, to show respect to the two Ashvins, the grandfather of all the worlds gave them the unmatched boon that no one would be able to kill them. Haughty and intoxicated because of the boon, these two brave apes crushed a large army of the gods and drank amrita. All the other apes can stand and watch. When they are enraged, these two brave apes are alone capable of destroying Lanka, with its horses, chariots and elephants. Even though the queen has been seen, it is not proper for the apes to go to the great-souled Raghava's presence without her. It is not appropriate for you,[280] famous for your valour, to report that you have seen the queen, but have not brought her back. O supreme among apes! Even in the world of the immortals and the daityas, there is no one who is our equal in leaping and valour. Hanumat has killed the brave ones among the rakshasas. What should we do now? We should get Janakee?'

He had thus made up his mind. However, Jambavat, supreme among apes and one who understood the objective, though extremely delighted, spoke these words that were full of meaning. 'O prince! It is as you perceive it. We are not incapable of doing what you

[280] This is directed at Hanumat.

have made up your mind about. But you must consider what Rama intends and then determine the best means of accomplishing the objective.'

Chapter 5(59)[281]

The residents of the forest, the brave ones with Angada at the forefront, and the great ape, Hanumat, accepted the words that Jambavat had spoken. With Vayu's son at the forefront, all of them were delighted. The bulls among the apes abandoned the summit of Mahendra and started to leap away. They were like Meru and Mandara and like maddened elephants. Those immensely strong ones, gigantic in size, shrouded the sky. Hanumat was in control of his soul and greatly strong. He was worshipped by all creatures. His force was great, as if he was being borne along by the power of sight. His purpose was to accomplish his lord, Raghava's, objective, and to obtain great fame. All the foremost ones wished to tell their loved ones what had happened. All of them were delighted at the prospect of war. All the spirited ones had made up their minds about ensuring Rama's revenge. Those residents of the forest leapt. They leapt up into the sky. They reached a forest that was like Nandana, filled with trees and creepers. There was a grove named Madhuvana there and it was protected by Sugriva. It could not be approached by any creature and it pleased the hearts of all beings. An immensely brave ape named Dadhimukha always protected it. This foremost among apes was the great-souled Sugriva's maternal uncle. Having approached the large and beautiful grove that belonged to the Indra among the apes, the apes became extremely ferocious. Delighted, the apes saw the gigantic Madhuvana. Tawny, with the complexion of honey,[282]

[281] This entire incident of Madhuvana is irrelevant to the main line of the story and may well have been inserted later.

[282] Madhu is honey, so *madhuvana* means a grove filled with honey. Madhu also means liquor and the apes clearly became intoxicated.

the apes asked the prince[283] for some honey. After taking the permission of the aged apes, with Jambavat at the forefront, the prince gave them permission to taste some honey. The residents of the forest were delighted at having obtained the permission. Filled with joy, they began to dance around, here and there. Some sang, others bowed down. Some danced, others laughed. Some fell down, others wandered around. Some leapt, others spoke incoherently. Some leaned against each other. Some spoke excessively to each other. Some leapt from one tree to another tree. Some leapt down from trees on to the ground. With great force, some sprang down from the tops of large trees on to the ground. Some sang, others laughed and approached others. Some laughed, others laughed at others. Some wept, others made others weep. Some roared, others made others roar. The soldiers in the army of the apes were excited. Having drunk the honey, they were haughty and intoxicated. There was no one there who was not drunk. There was no one there who was not satiated. The ape named Dadhivaktra[284] saw that the grove was being destroyed and the trees, full of leaves and flowers, were also being destroyed. He was filled with anger and tried to restrain the apes. While they raged, the aged ape, the protector of the grove, reprimanded them. The immensely fierce and energetic one thought of means to protect the grove from those apes. He addressed some in harsh words. He approached others and struck them with his palms. He approached others and made them quarrel with each other. He approached others and tried conciliation. However, they were intoxicated and forcibly countered him. He couldn't restrain them by force. They got together and fearlessly attacked him. They saw nothing wrong in dragging him along in this way. They struck him with their nails. They bit him with their teeth. All the assembled apes struck the ape with their palms and feet. In their intoxication, they robbed the great forest of all its possessions.[285]

[283] Angada.

[284] Dadhivaktra is the same as Dadhimukha.

[285] Flowers, fruits and trees.

Chapter 5(60)

Hanumat, best among apes and bull among the apes, told them, 'O apes! Without any anxiety in your minds, drink the honey.' Hearing Hanumat's words, the supreme one among the apes, Angada, was delighted in his mind and told the apes to drink the honey. 'I must certainly make Hanumat's words come true and do what he says, even if it is a task that should not be performed, not to speak of at a time like this.'[286] Hearing the words that emerged from Angada's mouth, the bulls among apes were delighted and praised him. The apes honoured him. All the apes worshipped Angada, bull among the apes. Like the flow of a swift river, they headed towards Madhuvana. Delighted, they used their valour to attack the grove's guards. Those accomplished ones saw that they had been granted permission and they had heard about Maithilee. Together, they leapt on all the hundreds of guards of the grove of Madhuvana who approached and struck them. They seized many *drona*s of honey.[287] They got together and struck.[288] Others devoured the honey, brown in complexion, some drank honey and flung away the vessels thereafter. Still holding the leftover honey, others got intoxicated and struck others. Some resorted to the roots of trees. Others clung to branches. Some were extremely drunk. They spread out leaves and lay down on these. Because of the honey, the apes became mad. Though intoxicated, they seemed to be cheerful. They playfully struck each other. Others addressed others in slurred voices. Some roared. Others cheerfully whistled. Some apes were intoxicated by the honey and slept on the ground.

Dadhimukha sent those who were meant to protect the honey. However, attacked by those terrible apes, they fled in different directions. They were dragged by their thighs and were seen to be flung up into the sky. Extremely anxious, they went and addressed Dadhimukha in these words. 'Because of the boon granted by

[286] An occasion for celebration at having found Sita.

[287] A drona is a wooden vessel, as well as an unit of measurement. The wooden vessel holds as much as a drona.

[288] The guards.

Hanumat, they are destroying Madhuvana with their force. We have been dragged by our thighs and are seen to have been flung up into the sky.' The ape Dadhimukha, the guardian of the grove, became angry. Hearing that Madhuvana had been destroyed, he comforted those apes. 'Come here. Let us go to those extremely insolent apes. We will use our strength to restrain those who are devouring the honey.' Hearing Dadhimukha's words, the brave bulls among apes assembled together and again went to Madhuvana. Having seized a giant tree, Dadhimukha was in their midst. All those apes attacked with force. The apes picked up boulders, trees and rocks. Having seized these, they angrily went to where those elephants among apes were. The brave ones had imbibed the words of their master in their hearts. With salas, talas and rocks as weapons, they attacked swiftly. Thousands of brave guards attacked the insolent and strong apes who were on trees or under the trees. The bulls among apes saw the angry Dadhimukha. With Hanumat at the forefront, they attacked with force. Angada angrily used his arms to strike the immensely strong and mighty-armed *aryaka*,[289] who was wielding a tree. Intoxicated and blind, he did not realize that this was his maternal uncle. Using force, he swiftly crushed him down on the ground. In an instant, the ape among elephants suddenly lost his senses. His arms were shattered. He was distracted and blood began to flow. He could no longer fight. Somehow, the bull among apes managed to extricate himself from those apes. He went to a solitary spot and told the assembled servants. 'Let the others remain here. Let us go to where the master of the apes, the thick-necked Sugriva, is with Rama. I will make the king hear all the sins Angada has committed. On hearing my words, he will become intolerant and will slay these apes. Madhuvana is desired by the great-souled Sugriva. It is divine and belonged to his fathers and grandfathers. Even the gods find it impossible to approach it. Greedy for honey, all these apes have lost their lifespans. Sugriva will chastise and kill them and their well-wishers. These evil-souled ones have disregarded the

[289] Aryaka means noble one. More specifically, it means maternal uncle. Here, it means Dadhimukha, Angada's maternal uncle.

command of the king and deserve to be killed. Our intolerance, power and anger will certainly be successful.' The immensely strong Dadhimukha said this to the guardians of the grove. Surrounded by all the guardians of the grove, he quickly got up. In a short while, he reached the residence in the forest where the intelligent ape, Sugriva, the son of the sun, was. On seeing Rama, Lakshmana and Sugriva, he descended from the sky on to the flat ground. Surrounded by all the guards, the immensely valiant one, Dadhimukha, the supreme lord of the guardians, descended. His face was distressed. He joined his hands in salutation above his head. He lowered his head at Sugriva's auspicious feet.

Chapter 5(61)

The ape fell down, with his head lowered. On seeing this, the bull among apes became anxious in his mind and addressed him in these words. 'Arise! Why have you fallen down at my feet? Arise! O brave one! Do not be scared. Tell me the truth about what has happened.' Thus assured by the great-souled Sugriva, the immensely wise Dadhimukha arose and spoke these words. O king! Riksharaja, you, or Vali had never allowed unrestricted access to the grove and those apes have consumed it. When they were restrained by the guards of the grove, they oppressed them. Without any heed, they devoured and drank the honey. While some are devouring, others are flinging away what is left of the honey. When they are restrained, they are showing their eyebrows.[290] When they[291] angrily restrained them, they were oppressed. Those enraged bulls among apes prevented them[292] from entering the grove. They have many brave apes, bulls among apes. Eyes red with rage, they have driven away those other apes.[293] Some have been struck with the hands.

[290] In anger.
[291] The guards.
[292] The guards.
[293] The guards.

Some have been struck with the thighs. As they wished, they have dragged some and flung them up into the sky. While you are here as their master, those brave apes have been struck. As they wish, they are devouring all of Madhuvana.'

While he was reporting this to Sugriva, bull among apes, the immensely wise Lakshmana, the destroyer of enemy heroes, asked, 'O king! This ape[294] resides in the grove. Why has he come here? He is addressing you in grieving words. What is he drawing your attention towards?' Hearing the words spoken by the great-souled Lakshmana, Sugriva, eloquent in the use of words, replied to Lakshmana. 'O noble Lakshmana! This brave ape, Dadhimukha, has told me that the brave apes, Angada and other foremost ones, have devoured the honey. They should not have acted in this way and done what should not have been done. When they have overpowered the grove, those apes must have accomplished their task. There is no doubt that Hanumat, and no one else, has seen the queen. No one other than Hanumat could have accomplished the task. Hanumat, bull among apes, possesses the intelligence to accomplish the objective. He is established in conduct, valour and learning. With Jambavat as the leader, Angada as the lord of the force and Hanumat as the supervisor of the work, there cannot have been any other outcome. Indeed, Angada and the other foremost ones have destroyed Madhuvana. Those bulls among apes have returned after searching the southern direction. They returned and entered Madhuvana. Having arrived there, those apes destroyed the entire grove. When they were restrained by the guards, they collectively struck them with their thighs. This is the reason he has come here, to tell us about it in sweet words. This ape is named Dadhimukha and he is famous for his valour. O mighty-armed one! O Soumitri! Behold the truth. Sita has been seen. That is the reason all those apes have come and are drinking the honey. O bull among men! This famous grove has been bestowed as a divine boon. Had they not seen Vaidehi, those residents of the forest would not have destroyed it.'

[294] Dadhimukha.

At this, with Raghava, Lakshmana, with dharma in his soul, was delighted. They heard the words, pleasant to hear, that emerged from Sugriva's mouth. The immensely illustrious Rama and Lakshmana were extremely delighted. Hearing what Dadhimukha had said, Sugriva also rejoiced. Sugriva again addressed the guardian of the grove[295] in these words. 'O amiable one! Since they have accomplished their task, I am glad that they have devoured the grove. Since they were successful in their task, they can be pardoned and I forgive them. Since those apes, as insolent as the lord of animals,[296] with Hanumat as the foremost, have been successful in their task, with the two Raghavas, I wish to quickly see them and hear about the efforts they made to reach Sita.'

Chapter 5(62)

Hearing the words spoken by Sugriva, the ape Dadhimukha was delighted. He paid his respects to Raghava, Lakshmana and Sugriva. He bowed down before Sugriva and the two immensely strong Raghavas. With the other brave apes, he leapt up into the sky. As was the case earlier, he left with great speed. He descended from the sky on to the ground and entered that grove. He entered Madhuvana and saw those leaders of the apes. Having passed out the honey as water, all of them were still excited, but sober and chastened now. The brave one joined his hands in salutation and approached them. Delighted, he gently spoke these words to Angada. 'O amiable one! You should not be angry that the guards were enraged and tried to restrain and obstruct you. They did it in their ignorance. O immensely strong one! You are the prince and the lord of this grove. We have earlier committed a crime because of our folly. Therefore, you should pardon us. O supreme among apes! You are just like your father, the former lord of the

[295] Dadhimukha.
[296] A lion.

apes, and just like Sugriva. It is not otherwise. O unblemished one! I went to your paternal uncle and told him about all the residents of the forest arriving here. Hearing that you have come here, with all the leaders of the apes, he is not angry, but rejoiced, even on hearing that this grove has been destroyed. Sugriva, your paternal uncle and the lord of the apes, rejoiced. The king said, "Quickly send those apes here."' Hearing the words spoken gently by Dadhimukha, Angada, eloquent in the use of words, addressed the best among apes in these words. 'O leaders of the apes! I suspect that Rama has heard the account about our arriving here. O scorchers of enemies! Therefore, having accomplished our objective, it is not proper that we should remain here. As they wished, those who roam in the forest have drunk honey. They have rested. What is left to be done, except go to the place where Sugriva, my senior, is? I will do whatever the assembled leaders of the apes tell me. I am obedient to whatever task all of you indicate. Though I am the prince, I am not a lord who ought to command you. You have been successful in your objective and it is inappropriate for me to instruct you.' Angada said this and hearing these undecaying words, the residents of the forest were delighted in their minds and replied in these words. 'O king! O lord of the apes! Who but a lord can speak in this way? Every person who is prosperous is intoxicated and intolerant and thinks of himself as "I". These words are extremely worthy of you and no one else could have spoken them. This humility is telling us about your future good fortune. All of us have come here and are waiting for the right time to go where Sugriva, the undecaying lord of the brave apes, is. O best among the apes! Without you saying so, the apes are not able to step forward anywhere. We are telling you this, truthfully.'

When they said this, Angada replied, 'Fine. Let us go.' Having said this, he leapt up from the ground. All the leaders of the apes followed him and leapt up. They rose up into the sky and didn't leave any empty spaces, like the fire that arises from a sacrifice. Those apes rose up into the sky, powerfully and suddenly. They roared in loud voices, like clouds urged along by the wind.

Even before Angada reached, Sugriva, lord of the apes, spoke to the lotus-eyed Rama, who was senseless with grief. 'O fortunate one! Be comforted. There is no doubt that the queen has been seen. Otherwise, after the time indicated by us was over, they would not have come here. The mighty-armed Prince Angada, supreme among the apes, would not have come into my presence had the objective not been accomplished. Had he not been successful, he would not have made such an attempt. His face would have been distressed. He would have been distracted and his mind would have been cheerless. Had the lord of the apes been miserable, he would not have destroyed Madhuvana, protected formerly by his fathers and grandfathers. O Rama! O excellent offspring of Kousalya! O one who is good in his vows! Be comforted. There is no doubt that the queen has been seen and by no one other than Hanumat. There is no one else who could have accomplished the task. He has been the instrument. O supreme among intelligent ones! Hanumat certainly possesses intelligence, enterprise, valour and the energy of the sun—required for success. When Jambavat is the leader, Angada is the leader of the army and Hanumat is the supervisor, it cannot but be otherwise. O infinitely valiant one! You should no longer be overcome by thoughts.'

A cackling sound was then heard to approach from the direction of the sky. The residents of the forest were proudly roaring about Hanumat's deeds. As they approached Kishkindha, they seemed to be conversing about that success. The supreme among apes[297] heard the sound of the apes roaring. Cheerful in his mind, he stretched and curled up his tail. Desiring to see Rama, with Angada and the ape Hanumat at the forefront, the apes approached. With Angada and other foremost ones, those brave ones were filled with joy. They descended near the king of the apes and Raghava. The mighty-armed Hanumat bowed his head down. He told Raghava that the queen was unharmed and in control of herself. Having ascertained what was being said, Lakshmana was delighted and looked at Sugriva and the son of the wind god with affection and a great deal

[297] Sugriva.

of respect. Raghava, the destroyer of enemy heroes, was delighted and happy. He looked at Hanumat with a great deal of respect.

Chapter 5(63)

They went to Mount Prasravana, with its colourful groves. They bowed their heads down before Rama and the immensely strong Lakshmana. With the prince at the forefront, they greeted Sugriva. They then started to recount about Sita. In Rama's presence, all the apes told them everything about her being imprisoned in Ravana's inner quarters, the censuring by the rakshasis, her affection towards Rama and the time that had been given.[298] Hearing that Vaidehi was unharmed, Rama replied, 'How is Queen Sita? What is her attitude towards me? O apes! Tell me everything about Vaidehi.' Hearing Rama's words, in Rama's presence, the apes urged Hanumat, who was skilled in telling, to recount everything about Sita.

Hearing their words, Hanumat, the son of the wind god and eloquent in the use of words, spoke about how Sita had been seen in the following words. 'The ocean stretches for one hundred yojanas and I leapt across it. Having reached, I searched around for Janakee Sita's trail. The evil-souled Ravana's city, Lanka, is there. It is located on the southern shore of the ocean. I saw Sita there, in Ravana's inner quarters. O Rama! The beautiful one, your heart's desire, is sustaining her life in you. I saw her in the midst of the rakshasis, being censured repeatedly. In that pleasure garden, she is guarded by rakshasis with disfigured forms. Though she deserves to be happy with you, the queen faces this misery. She is confined to Ravana's inner quarters, guarded well by the rakshasis. She wears her hair in a single braid. She is distressed and is thinking about you. She lies down on the ground and her limbs are faded, like a lotus at the onset of the winter. Having refused Ravana, she has made up her mind to die. O Kakutstha! With her mind following you, the queen is

[298] The period of two months set by Ravana.

sustaining herself somehow. O unblemished one! I slowly mentioned the fame of the Ikshvaku lineage. O tiger among men! That instilled her confidence in me.[299] After this, I told the queen everything about why I had gone there. Hearing about the friendship between Rama and Sugriva, she was filled with joy. She is controlled and full of good conduct, faithful to you. Thus I saw Janaka's immensely fortunate daughter. O bull among men! She is fierce in her austerities and devoted to you. O immensely wise one! O Raghava! As a sign, she told me about what had occurred in secret, about the incident of the crow in Chitrakuta. Janakee told me, "O Vayu's son! Tell Rama, tiger among men, about everything that you have seen here. When you speak to him and Sugriva is listening, give him what I have protected with great care. This is the beautiful chudamani and I have protected it carefully. You should remember the tilaka you drew with a piece of stone. I am sending you this beautiful piece,[300] produced from the water. O unblemished one! Looking at this, I used to find joy in my hardship, as if I was looking at you. O Dasharatha's son! I will sustain my life for one more month. Having come under the subjugation of the rakshasa, I cannot sustain my life for more than one month." Sita, emaciated in her limbs and following dharma, addressed me in this way. With large eyes like those of a doe, she is confined to Ravana's inner quarters. O Raghava! I have told you everything, exactly as it occurred. Every means possible should be used to cross over the ocean.' Realizing that the two princes were reassured, he gave Raghava the token of recognition. Vayu's son told him everything about the queen's account, as it happened.

Chapter 5(64)

Hanumat spoke in this way to Rama, Dasharatha's son. With Lakshmana, he clutched that jewel to his heart and wept.

[299] For whatever reason, Hanumat does not mention Rama's ring, which he had carried with him, to win Sita's confidence.

[300] The jewel.

On seeing that excellent jewel, Raghava was afflicted with grief. With his eyes overflowing with tears, he spoke to Sugriva. 'A cow is affectionate towards her calf and her affection oozes out.[301] On seeing this jewel, that is what is happening with my heart. My father-in-law gave this excellent jewel to Vaidehi, when she became a bride. When it was fixed to her head, it became even more beautiful. This jewel was produced from the water and was worshipped by his ancestors. Extremely satisfied at a sacrifice, the intelligent Shakra had bestowed it as a gift. O amiable one! On seeing this excellent jewel, right now, I feel as if I am seeing my father and the lord of Videha.[302] This is the jewel that used to look beautiful on my beloved's head. On seeing it, I think that I have met her. O amiable one![303] Tell me again and again what Sita Vaidehi said. Your words are like water, like water sprinkled on a senseless person. O Soumitri! What can be more painful than this? Without Vaidehi having returned, I am seeing this jewel that has been produced from the water. If Vaidehi can sustain herself for a month, she will remain alive for a long time. O amiable one! Without that dark-eyed one, I cannot remain alive even for an instant. Take me to the spot where my beloved was seen. After getting to know where she is, I cannot remain here even for an instant. She is most timid among the timid. How can the one with excellent hips remain in the midst of terrible rakshasas who generate fear? Her face is like the autumn moon, when it has freed itself from the darkness, but is enveloped by clouds. Therefore, among those rakshasas, it is not radiant. O Hanumat! Tell me truthfully. What did Sita say? This is the way I will remain alive, like a diseased person is with medicine. She is sweet and her conversation is sweet. What did my beautiful one say? Without me, how is the beautiful one? O Hanumat! Tell me. Facing a greater and greater misery, how has Janakee remained alive?'

[301] In the form of milk.

[302] Janaka.

[303] This is addressed to Hanumat.

Chapter 5(65)

Hanumat was thus addressed by the great-souled Raghava. He told Raghava everything that Sita had said. 'O bull among men! This is what Queen Janakee said. As a sign, she spoke about something that had occurred earlier in Chitrakuta. Janakee was happily asleep with you, but awoke before you. A crow suddenly descended and pecked at her, between her breasts. O Bharata's elder brother! Taking your turn, you were asleep on the queen's lap. However, that bird again caused pain to the queen. It repeatedly tore at her, severely. When she was wet with blood, she awoke you. O scorcher of enemies! You were happily asleep. However, repeatedly suffering from the crow, the queen awoke you. O mighty-armed one! You saw that she had been injured between the breasts. Sighing like an angry serpent, you spoke to her. "O timid one! Who has lacerated you between the breasts with his talons? Who is sporting with an enraged five-hooded serpent?" Looking around, she suddenly pointed to the crow. "There it is, stationed in front of me, with blood on its sharp talons. Does this crow, supreme among birds, indeed belong to Shakra? It swiftly roams around on earth, with a speed like that of the wind. O mighty-armed one![304] At this, your eyes rolled around in rage. O supreme among intelligent ones! You decided to act cruelly towards that crow. You picked up a blade of darbha grass and invoked brahmastra on it. It blazed like the flaming fire of destruction and headed in the direction of the bird. You flung the blazing darbha towards the crow. The blazing darbha followed the crow. It was abandoned by its father[305] and by all the gods and the maharshis. It circled around the three worlds, but could not find a protector. O one who is a refuge! It fell down on the ground and sought refuge with you. O Kakutstha! Though it deserved to be killed, because of your compassion, you saved it. O Raghava! It was not possible to render the weapon futile. Therefore, it robbed the crow of its right eye. O Rama! Having

[304] These are Sita's words, being quoted by Hanumat.

[305] Indra.

bowed down to you and to King Dasharatha, the crow then took leave of you and returned to its own abode. In this way, you are supreme among those who know about weapons. You are spirited and good in conduct. O Raghava! Why are you not using your weapons against the rakshasas? The serpents, the gandharvas, the asuras and all the large numbers of Maruts are incapable of standing before Rama in a battle. If that valiant one has the slightest bit of respect for me, let him swiftly use his extremely sharp arrows to kill Ravana in a battle. Why is Lakshmana, scorcher of enemies, not following his brother's command? Why is that Raghava, supreme among men, not protecting me? Those two capable tigers among men are like Vayu and Agni in their energy. Even the gods find them to be invincible. Why are they ignoring me? There is no doubt that I have committed an extremely grave crime. Though they are capable, this is the reason those two scorchers of enemies are ignoring me." I heard Vaidehi's piteous words, spoken amidst tears. I again addressed the noble one in these words. "O queen! I swear truthfully that Rama has become indifferent because of his grief over you. Rama is overcome by sorrow and Lakshmana is tormented. Sustain yourself in some fashion and you will no longer confront a period of sorrow. O beautiful one! In a short while, you will see an end to your misery. Those two princes, tigers among men, are the destroyers of enemies. In their eagerness to see you, they will reduce Lanka to ashes. In a battle, Raghava will slay the terrible Ravana and his relatives. The mighty-armed one will certainly take you back to his own city. O unblemished one! Give me a sign so that Rama can recognize it. You should give something that will generate joy in him." She looked in all the directions and unbraided her excellent braid. O immensely wise one! She freed this jewel and gave it to me in this piece of cloth. O supreme among the Raghu lineage! For your sake, I accepted the divine jewel. Desiring to return here quickly, I bowed my head down before her. On seeing that I was preparing to leave and had expanded my body, Janaka's daughter, the one with the beautiful complexion, spoke to me. Her face overflowing with tears, in a distressed and choking voice, she said, "O Hanumat! Rama and Lakshmana are like lions. When you reach them, ask about their welfare and that of Sugriva and all his advisers. You must act so that the mighty-armed Raghava can make me cross over this ocean of grief. This flood of sorrow is fierce. The guards are censuring me. O supreme among apes! When you reach Rama, tell him this. May your journey be auspicious." O king! O lion among kings! Full of sorrow, these are the words spoken by the noble Sita. Accept the words uttered by me and believe that Sita is safe in every possible way.'

Chapter 5(66)

'O tiger among men! Out of affection, love and respect for you, though she had respectfully replied to me, the queen spoke again. "You must speak many such words to Rama, Dasharatha's son, so that he quickly gets me back, after having killed Ravana in a battle. O brave one! O destroyer of enemies! If you so think, reside here for one day. Hide yourself in some spot. Having rested, leave tomorrow. O ape! I am limited in fortune. However, because of your presence, my sorrow and hardship will be dispelled for an instant. O valiant one! Between your going and your return, there is no doubt that there will be a threat to my life. The sorrow of not being able to see you will also torment me. On top of the present misery, I will be overcome by another misery. From this state of hardship, I will suffer a greater unhappiness. O brave one! A doubt presents itself before me. There is no doubt that you possess a large number of apes and bears as aides. How will they cross the great ocean, which is extremely difficult to cross? How will the soldiers of the apes and the bears do this? How will those two supreme men? O unblemished one! There are only three creatures who have the capacity to cross the ocean—Vinata's son,[306] Vayu and you. O brave one! This is extremely difficult to cross. Therefore, engage yourself in this task. O supreme among those who can accomplish tasks!

[306] Garuda.

What solution do you perceive? If you wish, you alone are capable of accomplishing this task. O slayer of enemies! Your fame and ability to enhance your strength is sufficient. If Rama kills Ravana and all his soldiers in a battle and having become victorious, takes me back to his own city, this would bring him fame. I belong to the brave one and was secretly abducted from the forest. Out of fear of the rakshasas, Raghava should not do that.[307] Lanka is full of soldiers. If Kakutstha, the afflicter of enemy soldiers, takes me away in this way, this will be worthy of him. You must act so that the valiant and great-souled one behaves in this way and exhibits his valour in battle." I heard the words spoken by her and they were full of meaning and reason. Having heard what she said, I spoke my final words of reply. "O queen! The ape and the bear soldiers and Sugriva, the lord of the apes who is full of spirit, have made up their minds for your sake. They are full of valour. They are spirited and immensely strong. The apes have made up their minds and are waiting for the command. There is nothing that can obstruct their path, above, below and diagonally. They are great and infinitely energetic and do not suffer in any task. Those immensely fortunate apes are full of strength and resorting to the path followed by the wind, have circumambulated the earth several times. Those residents of the forest are equal to me and superior. There is no one in Sugriva's presence who is inferior to me. I came from there to here. Why can't those extremely strong ones? Usually, the better ones are not sent. It is the ordinary ones who are sent.[308] O queen! Therefore, enough of this lamentation and grieving. The leaders of the apes will arrive here in a single leap. Those two immensely fortunate ones, lions among men, will arrive before you riding on my back, like the rising moon and the sun. You will soon see Raghava, who is like a lion and is the slayer of enemies. With a bow in his hand, Lakshmana will present himself at the gate of Lanka. You will soon see the apes assemble, with complexions like Indras among elephants. Those brave ones are like lions and tigers

[307] Take me away in secret.

[308] That is, the others are superior to me.

in their valour and use their nails and teeth as weapons. They are like mountains and clouds. You will soon hear the sound of the best among apes roaring in Lanka, on the summit of Malaya. With the destroyer of enemies, you will return from exile in the forest. You will soon see Raghava consecrated in Ayodhya." At these words spoken by me, her voice was no longer distressed. I comforted her with these auspicious and beneficial words. The daughter of the king of Mithila obtained peace, though she was still suffering on account of you. I left.'

This ends Sundara Kanda.

PENGUIN BOOKS

THE VALMIKI RAMAYANA VOLUME 3

Bibek Debroy is a renowned economist, scholar and translator. He has worked in universities, research institutes, industry and for the government. He has widely published books, papers and articles on economics. As a translator, he is best known for his magnificent rendition of the Mahabharata in ten volumes, and additionally the *Harivamsha*, published to wide acclaim by Penguin Classics. He is also the author of *Sarama and Her Children*, which splices his interest in Hinduism with his love for dogs.

PRAISE FOR *THE MAHABHARATA*

'The modernization of language is visible, it's easier on the mind, through expressions that are somewhat familiar. The detailing of the story is intact, the varying tempo maintained, with no deviations from the original. The short introduction reflects a brilliant mind. For those who passionately love the Mahabharata and want to explore it to its depths, Debroy's translation offers great promise . . .'—*Hindustan Times*

'[Debroy] has really carved out a niche for himself in crafting and presenting a translation of the Mahabharata . . . The book takes us on a great journey with admirable ease'—*Indian Express*

'The first thing that appeals to one is the simplicity with which Debroy has been able to express himself and infuse the right kind of meanings . . . Considering that Sanskrit is not the simplest of languages to translate a text from, Debroy exhibits his deep understanding and appreciation of the medium'—*The Hindu*

'Debroy's lucid and nuanced retelling of the original makes the masterpiece even more enjoyably accessible'—*Open*

'The quality of translation is excellent. The lucid language makes it a pleasure to read the various stories, digressions and parables'—*Tribune*

'Extremely well-organized, and has a substantial and helpful Introduction, plot summaries and notes. The volume is a beautiful example of a well thought-out layout which makes for much easier reading'—*Book Review*

'The dispassionate vision [Debroy] brings to this endeavour will surely earn him merit in the three worlds'—*Mail Today*

'Debroy's is not the only English translation available in the market, but where he scores and others fail is that his is the closest rendering of the original text in modern English without unduly complicating the readers' understanding of the epic'—*Business Standard*

'The brilliance of Ved Vyasa comes through, ably translated by Bibek Debroy'—*Hindustan Times*

THE VALMIKI RAMAYANA 3

Translated by Bibek Debroy

PENGUIN BOOKS
An imprint of Penguin Random House

PENGUIN BOOKS

USA | Canada | UK | Ireland | Australia
New Zealand | India | South Africa | China

Penguin Books is part of the Penguin Random House group of companies whose addresses can be found at global.penguinrandomhouse.com

Published by Penguin Random House India Pvt. Ltd
7th Floor, Infinity Tower C, DLF Cyber City,
Gurgaon 122 002, Haryana, India

First published in Penguin Books by Penguin Random House India 2017

10 9 8 7 6 5

ISBN 9780143428060

Typeset in Sabon by Manipal Digital Systems, Manipal
Printed at Replika Press Pvt. Ltd, India

www.penguin.co.in

For Professor Shailendra Raj Mehta

Contents

Acknowledgements

This journey, with Penguin, started more than a decade ago. It is a journey of translating Sanskrit texts into English, in unabridged form. It commenced with the Bhagavad Gita in 2006, followed by the Mahabharata (2010 to 2014) and the Harivamsha (2016). It continues with the Valmiki Ramayana and will be followed by the Puranas. To the best of my knowledge, the great translator, Manmatha Nath Dutt (1855–1912), is the only other person who has accomplished the 'double' of unabridged translations of both the Valmiki Ramayana and the Mahabharata in English. In this journey with Penguin, special thanks to Meru Gokhale, Ambar Sahil Chatterjee and Paloma Dutta. All three have made this journey easier to traverse.

My wife, Suparna Banerjee (Debroy), has not only been *patni*, she has been *grihini* and *sahadharmini* too. Had she not provided an enabling and conducive environment, juggling professional commitments and carving out the time required for translating would have been impossible. यः तया सह स स्वर्गो निरयो यस्त्वया विना (2.27.16).

This translation is based on the Critical Edition brought out (between 1951 and 1975) by the Oriental Institute, now part of Maharaja Sayajirao University, Baroda. When I started work on translating the Mahabharata in 2009, there was a thought, however hazy, of attempting the Valmiki Ramayana too. Therefore, one had to acquire the seven published volumes of the Critical Edition. Those who have tried this acquisition will testify this is no mean task. Multiple channels and multiple efforts failed. The Oriental Institute is not known for its marketing and distribution successes.

The context changed in 2015, because I joined the government. By then, I had still not been able to get copies of the Critical Edition. What with joining the government, which made finding time difficult, and an inability to get the text, I remarked to my wife that destiny willed otherwise. A few months later, on a flight, I found myself seated next to Shailendra Mehta, economist, scholar, friend, and currently president, director and distinguished professor at MICA, Ahmedabad. 'What next, after the Mahabharata?' asked Shailendra and I described my frustration. A few weeks down the line, Shailendra Mehta walked into my office, lugging a trolley bag, with all seven volumes in them. 'All yours,' he said. What destiny willed was clear enough. The dedication of this three volume set to Shailendra is a paltry attempt to say thank you.

'What next, after the Valmiki Ramayana?' Life moves on to the Puranas, beginning with the Bhagavata Purana. At one point, the Mahabharata translation seemed like a mammoth task, stretching to infinity. With the major Puranas collectively amounting to four times the size of the Mahabharata, they are more monumental than the mammoth. But as always, if it so wills, destiny finds a way.

Introduction

The Ramayana and the Mahabharata are known as *itihasa*s. The word itihasa means 'it was indeed like that'. Therefore, the word is best rendered as legend or history, and not as myth. This does not mean everything occurred exactly as described. In a process of telling and retelling and oral transmission, embellishments are inevitable. However, the use of the word itihasa suggests a core element of truth. There were two great dynasties—*surya vamsha* and *chandra vamsha*.[1] The first proper king of the surya vamsha was Ikshvaku and the Ramayana is a chronicle of the solar dynasty, or at least a part of its history. Similarly, the first king of the chandra vamsha was Ila and the Mahabharata is a chronicle of the lunar dynasty. The Puranas also describe the histories of the solar and lunar dynasties. Though there are some inconsistencies across genealogies given in different Puranas, the surya vamsha timeline has three broad segments: (1) from Ikshvaku to Rama; (2) from Kusha to Brihadbala; and (3) from Brihadbala to Sumitra. In that stretch from Ikshvaku to Rama, there were famous kings like Bharata (not to be confused with Rama's brother), Kakutstha, Prithu, Yuvanashva, Mandhata, Trishanku, Harishchandra, Sagara, Dilipa, Bhagiratha, Ambarisha, Raghu, Aja and Dasharatha. These ancestors explain why Rama is referred to as Kakutstha, Raghava or Dasharathi.

Rama had two sons—Lava and Kusha. Ikshvaku and his descendants ruled over the kingdom of Kosala, part of today's Uttar Pradesh. The Kosala kingdom lasted for a long time, with

[1] The solar and the lunar dynasty, respectively.

the capital sometimes in Ayodhya and sometimes in Shravasti. When Rama ruled, the capital was in Ayodhya. After Rama, Lava ruled over south Kosala and Kusha ruled over north Kosala. Lava's capital was in Shravasti, while Kusha's capital was in Kushavati. We don't know what happened to Lava thereafter, though he is believed to have established Lavapuri, today's Lahore. The second segment of the surya vamsha timeline, from Kusha to Brihadbala, doesn't have any famous kings. Brihadbala was the last Kosala king. In the Kurukshetra War, he fought on the side of the Kouravas and was killed by Abhimanyu. The third segment of the surya vamsha timeline, from Brihadbala to Sumitra, seems contrived and concocted. Sumitra is described as the last king of the Ikshvaku lineage, defeated by Mahapadma Nanda in 362 BCE. Sumitra wasn't killed. He fled to Rohtas, in today's Bihar.

The Ramayana isn't about these subsequent segments of the timeline. Though there are references to other kings from that Ikshvaku to Rama stretch, it isn't about all of that segment either. Its focus is on Rama. It is difficult to date the poet Kalidasa. It could be anytime from the first century CE to the fifth century CE. Kalidasa wrote a *mahakavya*[2] known as *Raghuvamsha*. As the name of this mahakavya suggests, it is about Raghu's lineage, from Dilipa to Agnivarna, and includes Rama. But it isn't exclusively about Rama. Ramayana is almost exclusively about Rama. That's the reason it is known as रामायण = राम + अयण. अयन means travel or progress. Thus, Ramayana means Rama's progress. There is a minor catch though. अयन means travel or progress and अयण is a meaningless word. The word used in Ramayana is अयण, not अयन. This transformation occurs because of a rule of Sanskrit grammar known as internal *sandhi*. That is the reason रामायन becomes रामायण.

Who is Rama? The word राम means someone who is lovely, charming and delightful. There are Jain and Buddhist versions (*Dasharatha Jataka*) of the Rama account and they differ in significant details from the Ramayana story. For instance, in Jain accounts, Ravana is killed by Lakshmana. In *Dasharatha Jataka*,

[2] Epic.

Sita is Rama's sister. In Ramayana and Purana accounts, Rama is Vishnu's seventh *avatara*.[3] Usually, ten avataras are named for Vishnu, though sometimes, a larger number is also given. When the figure is ten, the avataras are *matsya*,[4] *kurma*,[5] *varaha*,[6] *narasimha*,[7] *vamana*,[8] Parashurama, Rama, Krishna, Buddha and Kalki (Kalki is yet to come). In the cycle of creation and destruction, *yugas*[9] follow each other and one progressively goes down *krita yuga* (alternatively *satya yuga*), *treta yuga*, *dvapara yuga* and *kali yuga*, before the cycle starts again. In the list of ten avataras, matysa, kurma, varaha and narasimha are from the present krita yuga; Vamana, Parashurama and Rama are from the present treta yuga; Krishna is from dvapara yuga; and Buddha and Kalki are from kali yuga. Rama was towards the end of treta yuga. (In the 'Uttara Kanda', dvapara yuga has started.) Just as Krishna's departure marked the transition from dvapara yuga to kali yuga, Rama's departure marked the transition from treta yuga to dvapara yuga.

When did these events occur? It is impossible to answer this question satisfactorily, despite continuous efforts being made to find an answer. At one level, it is an irrelevant question too. There is a difference between an incident happening and it being recorded. In that day and age, recording meant composition and oral transmission, with embellishments added. There was noise associated with transmission and distribution. It is impossible to unbundle the various layers in the text, composed at different points in time. Valmiki is described as Rama's contemporary, just as Vedavyasa was a contemporary of the Kouravas and the Pandavas. But that doesn't mean today's Valmiki Ramayana text is exactly what Valmiki composed, or that today's Mahabharata text

[3] Incarnation, or descent.
[4] Fish.
[5] Turtle.
[6] Boar.
[7] Half-man, half-lion.
[8] Dwarf.
[9] Eras.

is exactly what Krishna Dvaipayana Vedavyasa composed. Therein lies the problem with several approaches to dating.

The first and favoured method of dating is undoubtedly the astronomical one, based on positions of *nakshatra*s and *graha*s,[10] or using information about events like eclipses. However, because layers of the text were composed at different points in time, compounded by precession of the equinoxes, this leads to widely divergent dates for an event like Rama's birth, ranging from 7323 BCE to 1331 BCE. Second, one can work with genealogies, notwithstanding problems of inconsistencies across them. One will then obtain a range of something like 2350 BCE to 1500 BCE. Third, one can work with linguistics and the evolution of language, comparing that of the Ramayana to other texts. Fourth, one can work with the archaeological evidence, such as the pottery discovered in sites known to be associated with the Ramayana. Even then, there will be a wide range of dates, from something like 2600 BCE to 1100 BCE. Fifth, one can consider geography, geology, changes in the course of rivers. Finally, there are traditional views about the length of a *manvantara*[11] or yuga. Given the present state of knowledge, it is impossible to impart precision to any dating of the incidents in the Ramayana. Scholars have grappled with the problem in the past and will continue to do so in the future. This may be an important question. But from the point of view of the present translation, it is an irrelevant one.

The present translation is about the Ramayana text. But what is the Ramayana text? After a famous essay written by A.K. Ramanujan in 1987 (published in 1991), people often mention 300 Ramayanas. It is impossible to fix the number, 300 or otherwise, since it is not possible to count satisfactorily—or even define—what is a new rendering of the Ramayana story, as opposed to a simple retelling, with or without reinterpretation. Contemporary versions, not always in written form, are continuously being rendered. There are versions of the Ramayana story in East Asia (China, Japan),

[10] Constellations/stars and planets.

[11] Lifespan of a Manu.

South-East Asia (many countries like Thailand, Indonesia and Malaysia), South Asia (Nepal, Sri Lanka) and West Asia (Iran). As mentioned earlier, there are Buddhist and Jain versions. Every state and every language in India seems to have some version of the Rama story. Our impressions about the Rama story are often based on such regional versions, such as, the sixteenth-century *Ramcharitmanas* by Goswami Tulsidas. (Many of these were written between the twelfth and seventeenth centuries CE.) Those depictions can, and will, vary with what is in this translation. This translation is about the Sanskrit Ramayana. But even there, more than one text of the Sanskrit Ramayana exists—Valmiki Ramayana, Yoga Vasishtha Ramayana, Ananda Ramayana and Adbhuta Ramayana. In addition, there are versions of the Ramayana story in the Mahabharata and in the Puranas. With the exception of the Ramayana story in the Mahabharata, the Valmiki Ramayana is clearly the oldest among these. This is a translation of the Valmiki Ramayana and yes, there are differences between depictions in the Valmiki Ramayana and other Sanskrit renderings of the Rama story.

If one cannot date the incidents of the Ramayana, can one at least conclusively date when the Valmiki Ramayana was written? Because of the many layers and subsequent interpolations, there is no satisfactory resolution to this problem either. The Valmiki Ramayana has around 24,000 *shloka*s, a shloka being a verse. The Mahabharata is believed to have 100,000 shlokas, so the Valmiki Ramayana is about one-fourth the size of the Mahabharata. These 24,000 shlokas are distributed across seven *kanda*s—'Bala Kanda' (Book about Youth), 'Ayodhya Kanda' (Book about Ayodhya), 'Aranya Kanda' (Book of the Forest), Kishkindha Kanda (Book about Kishkindha), 'Sundara Kanda' (Book of Beauty), 'Yuddha Kanda' (Book about the War) and 'Uttara Kanda' (Book about the Sequel). Kanda refers to a major section or segment and is sometimes translated into English as Canto. 'Canto' sounds archaic, 'Book' is so much better. This does not mean the kanda-wise classification always existed. For all one knows, initially, there were simply chapters. In this text itself, there is a reference to the Valmiki Ramayana possessing 500 *sarga*s. The

word sarga also means Book, but given the number 500, is more like a chapter. (For the record, the text has more than 600 chapters.) Most scholars agree 'Uttara Kanda' was written much later. If one reads the 'Uttara Kanda', that belief is instantly endorsed. The 'Uttara Kanda' doesn't belong. This isn't only because of the content, which is invariably mentioned. It is also because of the texture of the text, the quality of the poetry. It is vastly inferior. To a lesser extent, one can also advance similar arguments for the 'Bala Kanda'. Therefore, the earlier portions were probably composed around 500 BCE. The later sections, like the 'Uttara Kanda', and parts of the 'Bala Kanda', were probably composed around 500 CE. It isn't the case that all later sections are in 'Uttara Kanda'.

There is a mix of earlier and later sections across all kandas. The word kanda also means trunk or branch of a tree. The Mahabharata is also classified into such major sections or Books. However, in the Mahabharata, these major sections are known as *parvas*. The word parva also means branch. However, parva suggests a smaller branch, one that is more flexible. Kanda suggests one that is more solid, less flexible. There may have been slight variations in shlokas across different versions of the Sanskrit Mahabharata, but fundamentally the Sanskrit Mahabharata is a single text. The original text expanded, like a holdall, to include everything. Those different versions have been 'unified' in a Critical Edition published by the Bhandarkar Oriental Research Institute, Poona (Pune). In the case of the Valmiki Ramayana, with its kanda-kind of classification, the evolution seems to have been different. If someone was unhappy with what Valmiki had depicted, he simply composed another Ramayana. In Sanskrit, mention has already been made of the Yoga Vasishtha Ramayana, Ananda Ramayana and Adbhuta Ramayana. This continued to happen with vernacular versions.

This translation is of the Valmiki Ramayana. It is necessary to stress this point. Both the Ramayana and the Mahabharata are so popular that one is familiar with people, stories and incidents. That doesn't necessarily mean those people, stories and incidents occur in the Valmiki Ramayana in the way we are familiar with them. Just as the Bhandarkar Oriental Research Institute produced a Critical

Edition of the Mahabharata, between 1951 and 1975, the Oriental Institute, Baroda, produced a Critical Edition of the Valmiki Ramayana. This translation is based on that Critical Edition, published sequentially between 1958 and 1975. Producing a Critical Edition meant sifting through a large number of manuscripts of the Valmiki Ramayana. The editors had around 2000 manuscripts to work with. Not all of these were equally reliable. Therefore, in practice, they worked with fifty to hundred manuscripts, the specific number depending on the kanda in question. It is not that there were significant differences across the manuscripts and broadly, there was a Southern Recension (version) and a Northern one, the latter sub-divided into a North-Western and a North-Eastern one. The earliest of these written manuscripts dates to the eleventh century CE. In passing, the language may have been Sanskrit, but the script wasn't always Devanagari. There were scripts like Sharada, Mewari, Maithili, Bengali, Telugu, Kannada, Nandinagari, Grantha and Malayalam. Since this translation is based on the Baroda Critical Edition, it is necessary to make another obvious point. Even within the Sanskrit Valmiki Ramayana, not everything we are familiar with is included in the Critical text. For instance, the configuration of nakshatras and planets at the time of Rama's birth is not part of the Critical text. Nor is the bulk of one of the most beautiful sections of the Valmiki Ramayana, Mandodari's lamentation. Those are shlokas that have been excised. That's also the case with a shloka that's often quoted as an illustration of Lakshmana's conduct. नाहं जानामि केयूरं नाहं जानामि कुण्डलं। नूपुरं तु अभिजानामि नित्यं पादाभिवन्दनात॥ This is a statement by Lakshmana to the effect that he cannot recognize the ornament on Sita's head or her earrings. Since he has always served at her feet, he can only recognize her anklets. This too has been excised. There are instances where such excision has led to a break in continuity and inconsistency and we have pointed them out in the footnotes.

There are two numbers associated with every chapter. The first number refers to the kanda, while the second number, within brackets, refers to the number of the chapter (sarga) within that kanda. Thus, Chapter 1(33) will mean the thirty-third chapter in

'Bala Kanda'. The table below shows the number of chapters and shlokas we have in the Critical Edition. The Critical text has 606 chapters, 106 more than the 500 sargas mentioned in the text itself. And there are 18,670 shlokas. If one considers chapters and shlokas from non-Critical versions, irrespective of which version it is, there are almost 650 chapters and just over 24,000 shlokas. Compared to such non-Critical versions, very few chapters have been excised from 'Bala', 'Ayodhya', 'Aranya', 'Kishkindha' or 'Sundara' kandas. The excision is primarily from 'Yuddha' and 'Uttara' kandas. The excision of shlokas is uniformly spread throughout the kandas, though most excision, relatively speaking, is from the 'Ayodhya', 'Yuddha' and 'Uttara' kandas.

Name of kanda	*Number of chapters*	*Number of shlokas*
Bala Kanda	76	1941
Ayodhya Kanda	111	3160
Aranya Kanda	71	2060
Kishkindha Kanda	66	1898
Sundara Kanda	66	2487
Yuddha Kanda	116	4435
Uttara Kanda	100	2689
Total	606	18,670

Valmiki is the first poet, *adi kavi*. By the time of classical Sanskrit literature, some prerequisites were defined for a work to attain the status of mahakavya. Kalidasa, Bharavi, Magha, Shri Harsha and Bhatti composed such works. Though these notions and definitions came later, the Valmiki Ramayana displays every characteristic of a mahakavya and is longer than any of these subsequent works. The story of how it came about is known to most people who are familiar with the Ramayana. The sage Valmiki had gone, with his disciple Bharadvaja, to bathe in the waters of the River Tamasa. There was a couple of *krouncha*[12] birds there, in the act of making

[12] Curlew.

love. Along came a hunter[13] and killed the male bird. As the female bird grieved, Valmiki was driven by compassion and the first shloka emerged from his lips. Since it was composed in an act of sorrow—*shoka*—this kind of composition came to be known as shloka. So the Ramayana tells us. Incidentally, this first shloka doesn't occur in the first chapter. It isn't the first shloka of the Valmiki Ramayana. The incident and the shloka occur in the second chapter. More specifically, it is the fourteenth shloka in the second chapter and is as follows. मा निषाद प्रतिष्ठां त्वमगमः शाश्वतीः समाः। यत्क्रौंचमिथुनादेकमवधी काममोहितम् ॥ 'O nishada! This couple of curlews was in the throes of passion and you killed one of them. Therefore, you will possess ill repute for an eternal number of years.'

Till a certain period of history, all Sanskrit works were in poetry or verse, not in prose. The Vedangas are limbs or auxiliaries and the six Vedangas are *shiksha*,[14] *chhanda*,[15] *vyakarana*,[16] *nirukta*,[17] *jyotisha*[18] and *kalpa*.[19] These are needed to understand not just the Vedas, but also Sanskrit works. Chhanda is one of these. Chhanda can be translated as metre and means something that is pleasing and delightful. Chhanda *shastra* is the study of metres or prosody. Sanskrit poetry wasn't about what we tend to identify as poetry today, the act of rhyming. Chhanda begins with the concept of *akshara*, akin to, but not exactly identical with, the English concept of syllable, that is, part of a word with a single vowel sound. Other than possessing a single vowel sound, an akshara must not begin with a vowel. Aksharas can be *hrasva* or *laghu*—light or L—and *guru*—heavy or G. Simply stated, with a short vowel, the akshara is L and with a long vowel, the akshara is G. There are some additional conditions, but we needn't get into those. Every verse consists of four *pada*s, the word pada meaning one quarter. Depending on how

[13] *Nishada*.
[14] Articulation and pronunciation.
[15] Prosody.
[16] Grammar.
[17] Etymology.
[18] Astronomy.
[19] Rituals.

many aksharas there are in a pada and the distribution of those aksharas into L and G, there were a variety of metres. Depending on the subject and the mood, the poet consciously chose a metre. Analysing in this way, there were more than 1300 different metres. One of the most popular was *anushtubh*. This figures prominently in the Valmiki Ramayana, the Mahabharata and the Puranas. The anushtubh structure meant eight aksharas in each pada, with a total of thirty-two aksharas. In addition, for anushtubh, in every pada, the fifth akshara would have to be L and the sixth akshara would have to be G. In classical Sanskrit literature, conditions were also applied to the seventh akshara, but such refinements came later. For that first verse, the decomposition runs as follows: (1) L L L G L G L G; (2) L G L G L G L G; (3) L L G G L G G L; (4) G G L L L G G L. (1) *ma ni sha da pra tish tham*; (2) *tva ma ga mah shash vati sa mah*; (3) *yat kroun cha mi thu na de ka*; (4) *ma va dhi ka ma mo hi tam*. It is not that Valmiki only used anushtubh. There are actually sixteen different metres in the Valmiki Ramayana.

It is impossible to capture the beauty of chhanda in an English translation. One can attempt to do a translation in verse, but it will fail to convey the beauty. If the original text is poetry, one starts with an initial question. Should one attempt a translation in verse or in prose? This translation is based on the premise that the translation should be as close as possible to the original Sanskrit text. One should not take liberties with the text. This translation is therefore almost a word-to-word rendering. If one sits down with the original Sanskrit, there will be almost a perfect match. In the process, deliberately so, the English is not as smooth as it might have been, had one taken more liberties, and this is a conscious decision. Had one attempted a translation in verse, one would perforce have had to take more liberties. Hence, the choice of prose is also a deliberate decision. As composers, there is quite a contrast between Valmiki and Vedavyasa. Vedavyasa focuses on people and incidents. Rarely does the Mahabharata attempt to describe nature, even if those sections are on geography. In contrast, Valmiki's descriptions of nature are lyrical and superlative, similar to Kalidasa. A translation can never hope to transmit that flavour. There is no substitute to

reading the original Sanskrit, more so for the Valmiki Ramayana than for the Mahabharata.

Which occurred earlier, the incidents of the Ramayana or the Mahabharata? Which was composed earlier, the Ramayana or the Mahabharata? The Ramayana incidents occurred in treta yuga, the Mahabharata incidents in dvapara yuga. Rama was an earlier avatara, Krishna a later one. Hence, the obvious deduction is that the Ramayana incidents predated those of the Mahabharata—an inference also bolstered by the genealogy and astrological arguments mentioned earlier. However, and not just for the sake of being perverse, consider the following. Geographically, the incidents of the Mahabharata mostly occur along an east–west axis, along either side of what used to be called Uttarapath, the northern road, more familiar as Grand Trunk Road or National Highway (NH) 1 and 2. The incidents of the Ramayana often occur along a north–south axis, along what used to be called Dakshinapath, the southern road. Sanjeev Sanyal[20] has made the point that while Uttarapath remained stable over time, the Dakshinapath during Rama's time was different from the subsequent Dakshinapath, with the latter more like today's NH 44. To return to the point, the geographical terrain of the Mahabharata was restricted to the northern parts of the country, with the south rarely mentioned. The Aryan invasion theory has been discredited because of a multitude of reasons, but myths and perceptions that have lasted for decades are difficult to dispel. However, regardless of the Aryan invasion theory, the Ramayana reveals a familiarity with the geography of the southern parts of the country that the Mahabharata does not. The fighting in the Mahabharata, in the Kurukshetra War, is cruder and less refined. In the Ramayana, bears and apes may have fought using trees and boulders, but humans did not. A human did not tear apart another human's chest and drink blood. The urbanization depicted in the Ramayana is rarely found in the Mahabharata. We have cited these counter-arguments to make a simple point. Which incident

[20] *Land of the Seven Rivers: A Brief History of India's Geography*, Sanjeev Sanyal, Penguin, 2012.

occurred earlier and which text was composed earlier are distinct questions. They should not be confused. Even if the Ramayana incidents occurred before the incidents of the Mahabharata, that doesn't automatically mean the Ramayana was composed before the Mahabharata. The Rama story occurs in the Mahabharata, known as the 'Ramopakhyana' section. There is no such reference to the Mahabharata incidents in the Ramayana. This is the main reason for arguing that the Ramayana was composed before the Mahabharata.

The relationship between the 'Ramopakhyana' and the Valmiki Ramayana is also of scholarly interest. Which was earlier? Did one borrow from the other, or did both have a common origin? That need not concern us. What should be stressed is the obvious—the Valmiki Ramayana wasn't composed at a single point in time and there is a difference between the original composition and the present text, as given to us say in the Critical Edition. If bears and apes fought with the help of trees and boulders, and Angada suddenly kills someone with a weapon, that part is probably a later composition, with the composer having deviated from the original template. If a verse is in anushtubh, but deviates from the L–G pattern, this may have been a conscious decision, but in all probability, reflects the inferior skills of a subsequent poet. If we take the Critical text as it stands, while there are no direct references to the incidents of the Mahabharata, there are plenty of indirect allusions. There are shlokas reminiscent of the Bhagavatgita. When Bharata comes to Rama to inform him about Dasharatha's death, Rama asks him about the welfare of the kingdom, reminiscent of similar questions asked by Narada to Yudhishthira. In the Valmiki Ramayana, there are references to kings of the lunar dynasty (Yayati) and incidents (Ilvala and Vatapi) that are only described in the Mahabharata. The evidence may be circumstantial and speculative, but it is the following. It is as if the later composers knew about the Mahabharata incidents and the text, but consciously avoided any direct references.

Why is another translation of the Valmiki Ramayana needed? Surely, there are plenty floating around. That's not quite true. Indeed, there are several translations of the Valmiki Ramayana,

including some recent ones, but they are abridged. In any act of abridgement, some sections are omitted or summarized. Abridged translations, no matter how good they are, are not quite a substitute for unabridged translations, which bring in the nuances too. To the best of my knowledge, the list of unabridged translations of the Valmiki Ramayana is the following: (1) Ralph T.H. Griffith;[21] (2) Manmatha Nath Dutt;[22] (3) Hari Prasad Shastri;[23] (4) Desiraju Hanumanta Rao and K.M.K. Murthy;[24] and (5) Robert P. Goldman.[25] Given the timelines, the Goldman translation is the only one based on the Critical Edition. Having translated the Mahabharata,[26] it was natural to translate the Valmiki Ramayana. The intention was to do a translation that was popular in style. That meant a conscious decision to avoid the use of diacritical marks, as would have been the case had one used IAST (International Alphabet of Sanskrit Transliteration). If diacritical marks are not going to be used, there may be problems rendering names, proper and geographic. We have sought to make the English renderings as phonetic as is possible. Thus, we use 'Goutama' to refer to the sage of that name—although others have often referred to him elsewhere as 'Gautama'. We have chosen Goutama on the logic that if Gomati is not Gamati, why should Goutama be rendered as Gautama? There remains the question of what one does with vowel sounds. How does one differentiate the short sound from the long? Should Rama be written as Raama and Sita as Seeta? That seemed to be too artificial and contrary to popular usage. On rare occasions, this does

[21] *The Ramayana of Valmiki, translated into English verse,* Ralph T.H. Griffith, E.Z. Lazarus and Company, London, 1895.

[22] *Valmiki Ramayana,* Manmatha Nath Dutt, R.K. Bhatia, Calcutta, 1891–92. Manmatha Nath Dutt (Shastri) was one of India's greatest translators (in English). He also translated the Mahabharata and several Puranas.

[23] *The Ramayana of Valmiki,* Hari Prasad Shastri, Shanti Sadan, London, 1952.

[24] This is net based, on the site http://www.valmikiramayan.net/ and leaves out 'Uttara Kanda'.

[25] *The Ramayana of Valmiki: An Epic of Ancient India,* Robert P. Goldman, Princeton University Press, 1984 to 2016.

[26] *The Mahabharata,* Bibek Debroy, Penguin (India), 10 volumes, 2010–2014, boxed set 2015.

cause a problem, with a danger of confusion between the ape Taara and his daughter Taaraa, Vali's wife. Such occasions are however rare and we have explained them. However, there are also instances where we have deviated from popular usage. Hanumat is a case in point, where Hanuman seemed to be too contrary to grammatical principles. There are some words that defy translation, *dharma* is an example. Hence, we have not even tried to translate such words. The Goldman translation is academic in style. This translation's style is more popular. Therefore, there is no attempt to overburden the reader with extensive notes. However, a straight translation may not be self-explanatory. Hence, we have put in footnotes, just enough to explain, without stretching the translation.

As with the Mahabharata, the Valmiki Ramayana is a text about dharma. Dharma means several different things—the dharma of the four *varna*s and the four *ashrama*s, the classes and stages of life; the governance template of *raja dharma*, the duty of kings; principles of good conduct, *sadachara*; and the pursuit of objectives of human existence, *purushartha*—dharma, *artha* and *kama*. As with the Mahabharata, the Valmiki Ramayana is a *smriti* text. It has a human origin and composer, it is not a *shruti* text. Smriti texts are society and context specific. We should not try to judge and evaluate individuals and actions on the basis of today's value judgements. In addition, if the span of composition was one thousand years, from 500 BCE to 500 CE, those value judgements also change. The later composers and interpreters may have had problems with what the earlier composers authored. A case in point is when Sita is being abducted by Ravana. At a certain point in time, men and women universally wore an upper garment and a lower one. When she is being abducted through the sky, Sita casts aside and throws down not just her ornaments, but her upper garment too. As this translation will illustrate, this caused problems for subsequent composers and interpreters.

To return to the notion of dharma—transcending all those collective templates of dharma—there is one that is individual in nature. Regardless of those collective templates, an individual has to decide what the right course of action is and there is no universal answer as to what is right and what is wrong. There are always

contrary pulls of dharma, with two notions of dharma pulling in different directions. It is not immediately obvious which is superior. Given the trade-offs, an individual makes a choice and suffers the consequences. Why is there an impression that these individual conflicts of dharma are more manifest in the Mahabharata than in the Ramayana?

The answer probably lies in the nature of these two texts. What is the difference between a novel and a long story, even when both have multiple protagonists? The difference between a novel and a long story is probably not one of length. A novel seeks to present the views of all protagonists. Thus, the Mahabharata is a bit like a novel, in so far as that trait is concerned. A long story does not seek to look at incidents and actions from the point of view of every protagonist. It is concerned with the perspective of one primary character, to the exclusion of others.

If this distinction is accepted, the Valmiki Ramayana has the characteristics of a long story. It is Ramayana. Therefore, it is primarily from Rama's point of view. We aren't told what Bharata or Lakshmana thought, or for that matter, Urmila, Mandavi or Shrutakirti. There is little that is from Sita's point of view too. That leads to the impression that the Mahabharata contains more about individual conflicts of dharma. For the Valmiki Ramayana, from Rama's point of view, the conflicts of dharma aren't innumerable. On that exile to the forest, why did he take Sita and Lakshmana along with him? Was Shurpanakha's disfigurement warranted? Why did he unfairly kill Vali? Why did he make Sita go through tests of purity, not once, but twice? Why did he unfairly kill Shambuka? Why did he banish Lakshmana? At one level, one can argue these are decisions by a personified divinity and therefore, mere humans cannot comprehend and judge the motives. At another level, the unhappiness with Rama's decisions led to the composition of alternative versions of the Ramayana. Note that Sita's questions about dharma remained unanswered. If you are going to the forest as an ascetic, why have you got weapons with you? If the *rakshasas*[27]

[27] Demons.

are causing injuries to hermits, punishing the rakshasas is Bharata's job, now that he is the king. Why are you dabbling in this? Note also Rama's justification at the time of Sita's first test. It wasn't about what others would think, that justification came later. The initial harsh words reflected his own questions about Sita's purity. Thus, Rama's conflicts over dharma also exist. It is just that in the Valmiki Ramayana, it is about one individual alone.

In conclusion, this translation is an attempt to get readers interested in reading the unabridged Valmiki Ramayana. Having read abridged versions, and there is no competition with those, to appreciate the nuances better, one should read the unabridged. And, to appreciate the beauty of the poetry, one should then be motivated to read the text in Sanskrit. A translation is only a bridge and an unsatisfactory one at that.

CHAPTER SIX

Yuddha Kanda

Sarga (1): 16 shlokas
Sarga (2): 21 shlokas
Sarga (3): 32 shlokas
Sarga (4): 88 shlokas
Sarga (5): 22 shlokas
Sarga (6): 18 shlokas
Sarga (7): 16 shlokas
Sarga (8): 16 shlokas
Sarga (9): 22 shlokas
Sarga (10): 21 shlokas
Sarga (11): 59 shlokas
Sarga (12): 22 shlokas
Sarga (13): 23 shlokas
Sarga (14): 21 shlokas
Sarga (15): 33 shlokas
Sarga (16): 29 shlokas
Sarga (17): 40 shlokas
Sarga (18): 42 shlokas
Sarga (19): 34 shlokas
Sarga (20): 24 shlokas
Sarga (21): 35 shlokas
Sarga (22): 43 shlokas
Sarga (23): 42 shlokas
Sarga (24): 36 shlokas
Sarga (25): 28 shlokas
Sarga (26): 33 shlokas
Sarga (27): 22 shlokas
Sarga (28): 36 shlokas
Sarga (29): 18 shlokas
Sarga (30): 26 shlokas
Sarga (31): 86 shlokas
Sarga (32): 32 shlokas
Sarga (33): 46 shlokas
Sarga (34): 30 shlokas
Sarga (35): 26 shlokas
Sarga (36): 43 shlokas
Sarga (37): 21 shlokas
Sarga (38): 37 shlokas
Sarga (39): 32 shlokas
Sarga (40): 64 shlokas
Sarga (41): 35 shlokas
Sarga (42): 37 shlokas
Sarga (43): 27 shlokas
Sarga (44): 38 shlokas
Sarga (45): 42 shlokas
Sarga (46): 51 shlokas
Sarga (47): 135 shlokas
Sarga (48): 87 shlokas

Sarga (49): 37 shlokas
Sarga (50): 19 shlokas
Sarga (51): 47 shlokas
Sarga (52): 35 shlokas
Sarga (53): 50 shlokas
Sarga (54): 29 shlokas
Sarga (55): 129 shlokas
Sarga (56): 19 shlokas
Sarga (57): 90 shlokas
Sarga (58): 54 shlokas
Sarga (59): 106 shlokas
Sarga (60): 49 shlokas
Sarga (61): 68 shlokas
Sarga (62): 52 shlokas
Sarga (63): 53 shlokas
Sarga (64): 24 shlokas
Sarga (65): 21 shlokas
Sarga (66): 38 shlokas
Sarga (67): 42 shlokas
Sarga (68): 33 shlokas
Sarga (69): 26 shlokas
Sarga (70): 42 shlokas
Sarga (71): 22 shlokas
Sarga (72): 33 shlokas
Sarga (73): 34 shlokas
Sarga (74): 27 shlokas
Sarga (75): 33 shlokas
Sarga (76): 34 shlokas
Sarga (77): 38 shlokas
Sarga (78): 54 shlokas
Sarga (79): 18 shlokas
Sarga (80): 57 shlokas
Sarga (81): 35 shlokas
Sarga (82): 39 shlokas
Sarga (83): 42 shlokas
Sarga (84): 33 shlokas
Sarga (85): 29 shlokas
Sarga (86): 23 shlokas
Sarga (87): 47 shlokas
Sarga (88): 59 shlokas
Sarga (89): 34 shlokas
Sarga (90): 33 shlokas
Sarga (91): 30 shlokas
Sarga (92): 30 shlokas
Sarga (93): 27 shlokas
Sarga (94): 29 shlokas
Sarga (95): 26 shlokas
Sarga (96): 31 shlokas
Sarga (97): 33 shlokas
Sarga (98): 26 shlokas
Sarga (99): 44 shlokas
Sarga (100): 22 shlokas
Sarga (101): 43 shlokas
Sarga (102): 36 shlokas
Sarga (103): 25 shlokas
Sarga (104): 27 shlokas
Sarga (105): 28 shlokas
Sarga (106): 20 shlokas
Sarga (107): 36 shlokas
Sarga (108): 19 shlokas
Sarga (109): 27 shlokas
Sarga (110): 23 shlokas
Sarga (111): 31 shlokas
Sarga (112): 18 shlokas
Sarga (113): 43 shlokas
Sarga (114): 46 shlokas
Sarga (115): 51 shlokas
Sarga (116): 90 shlokas

Chapter 6(1)

Hanumat spoke those words in a proper way. Hearing them, Rama was filled with delight and replied in the following words. 'O Hanumat! You have performed a great task that is extremely difficult to accomplish. There is no other person on earth who is capable of doing this, not even in his mind. I do not see anyone other than Garuda, Vayu and Hanumat who can cross the great ocean. The city of Lanka is protected extremely well by Ravana, and the gods, the *danava*s,[1] the *yaksha*s,[2] the *gandharva*s,[3] the serpents and the *rakshasas*[4] find it impossible to penetrate it. Even if someone enters, how can he emerge with his own life? It is unassailable and is protected extremely well by the rakshasas. Other than someone who possesses a valour and strength that is equal to Hanumat's, who is capable of doing this? Hanumat has performed a great act of service for Sugriva. He has exhibited a strength and valour that is worthy of him. A person who is engaged as a servant and lovingly performs an extremely difficult task for his master, is said to be superior among men. If a capable person is engaged in a royal task and does not perform it attentively, he is said to be worst among men. Hanumat has accomplished the task he was appointed to do. He has satisfied Sugriva and has not diminished his own self. Through obtaining sight of Vaidehi, I, the lineage of Raghu, and the immensely strong Lakshmana have been protected, in accordance with *dharma*. However, my mind is still distressed and I am suffering. He has performed a good deed for me and I am unable to perform an equally good deed in return. But let me embrace Hanumat, who is everything to me. At the present time, that is all I can do for the great-souled one. The task of searching out Sita's trail has been accomplished in every possible way. But when I think of the ocean, my mind is distressed yet again. How can

[1] Demons.

[2] Yakshas are semi-divine species, described as companions of Kubera, the lord of riches.

[3] Semi-divine species, companions of Kubera, celestial musicians.

[4] Demons.

one cross to the other shore of this ocean, the great store of water? How will these attentive apes cross over to the southern shore? I have heard the account about Vaidehi. How will the apes now cross over to the other shore of the ocean?' Apprehensive and grieving, the mighty-armed Rama, the destroyer of enemies, told Hanumat this and became immersed in thought.

Chapter 6(2)

Rama, Dasharatha's handsome son, was filled with grief. To dispel his sorrow, Sugriva addressed him in these words. 'O brave one! Why are you tormented, like an ordinary person? Like an ungrateful person abandons friendship, give up this torment. O Raghava! I do not see any reason for this torment now. After all, we have got to know where the enemy resides. O Raghava! You are persevering, knowledgeable about the sacred texts, wise and learned. Discard this ordinary sentiment, like a person with a cleansed soul gives up what destroys the objective. We will cross the ocean, populated by large crocodiles. We will invade Lanka and slay your enemy. If a person is distressed and without enterprise, with his soul enveloped in sorrow, all his objectives suffer and he faces a hardship. In every way, all these leaders of the apes are brave and capable. They are full of enterprise. For your sake, they will even enter a fire. I can discern this through their delight, and reasoning adds firm conviction to this. You must use your valour to get Sita back and slay the enemy. We will construct a bridge and see that city. O Raghava! You must act in this way towards the king of the rakshasas. You will see the city of Lanka, located on the summit of Trikuta. When you see him, you must certainly kill Ravana in the encounter. When a bridge is constructed over the ocean and all our soldiers reach Lanka, it is certain that they will be victorious. In a battle, these brave apes can assume any form at will. O king! Therefore, get rid of this confused intelligence that destroys all objectives. In this world of men, sorrow destroys all valour. If a man valiantly engages in a task, capability will follow. O immensely wise one! At this time, resort to spirit and energy. Even for brave and great-souled people like you, sorrow over something lost or destroyed renders all objectives unsuccessful. You are best among intelligent ones. You are skilled in the teachings of all the sacred texts. With advisers like me, you are certain to vanquish the enemy. O Raghava! When you wield your bow, I do not see anyone in the three worlds who can stand before you in a battle. The task that you have entrusted to the apes will not suffer. You will soon cross over the eternal ocean and see Sita. O lord of the earth! Therefore, enough of resorting to grief. Resort to anger. *Kshatriya*s who do not make efforts are wicked. All of them are terrified of terrible ones. Use your subtle intelligence and, together with us, think about how the terrible ocean, the lord of the rivers, can be crossed. These apes are brave in battle and can assume any form at will. They will shower down rocks and trees and destroy their enemies. Through some means, we will cross over Varuna's abode. What is the need to speak a lot? In every possible way, you will be victorious.'

Chapter 6(3)

Sugriva's words were full of great meaning and reasoning. Kakutstha accepted them and told Hanumat, 'In every possible way, I am extremely competent to cross over the ocean, quickly building a bridge over the ocean, or drying it up. How many impenetrable forts exist in Lanka? Tell me that. O ape! I wish to know everything about them, as if I have seen them myself. You have comfortably seen, exactly as it exists, the size of the army, the gates, forts and arrangements, the preparations made for guarding and the residences of the rakshasas in Lanka. Tell me the truth about all this. You are accomplished in every possible way.'

Hanumat, the son of the wind god, was best among those who were accomplished in the use of words. Hearing Rama's words, he again addressed him in these words. 'Listen to everything—the forts, the preparations, the arrangements, the manner in which the city of Lanka is guarded and the soldiers. Lanka is supremely prosperous and the ocean is terrible. The large number of soldiers are divided into formations and the mounts have been instructed. Lanka is happy and full of joy. It is full of crazy elephants. It is full of large chariots and large numbers of rakshasas. The firm gates are closed and sealed with large beams. There are large gates and four extremely large ones. There are large and extremely strong machines.[5] When enemy soldiers arrive, they are rebuffed by these. Large numbers of brave rakshasas have fashioned hundreds of terrible *shataghnis*[6] and the gates are protected exceedingly well with these. They are sharp and made out of black iron. There is a giant rampart made out of gold and it is extremely difficult to penetrate. At intervals, this is decorated with gems, coral, lapis lazuli and pearls. There are extremely terrible moats everywhere. These are fathomless and are filled with extremely auspicious and cool water. They are also filled with crocodiles and fish. Along the gates, there are four extensive drawbridges. These have firm fortifications and many machines are placed atop these. In every direction, the moats are covered with machines. When invading enemy soldiers escape, these are used to fling them away. One of these drawbridges is strong and cannot be shaken. It is extremely firm. It is decorated with many golden pillars and platforms. O Rama! Ravana is naturally inclined to fight. He is ready and not distracted. He is powerful and ready to command. The city of Lanka is like a fort of the gods and is impregnable. It generates fear. It has four kinds of fortifications—water, mountains, forests and artificial ones. O Raghava! It is located on the distant other shore of the ocean. There is no approach in any direction and it cannot be reached by a boat either. The fortification has been constructed on the summit of a mountain and it is like a fortification of the gods. Lanka is extremely difficult to conquer and is full of horses and elephants. There are trenches, shataghnis and many kinds of machines. The city of Lanka, which belongs to the evil-

[5] Like catapults.

[6] A shataghni is a weapon that can kill one hundred at one stroke.

souled Ravana, is radiant. There are ten thousand rakshasas along the western gate. All those unassailable ones wield spears in their hands. They are the best among warriors who fight with swords. There are one hundred thousand rakshasas along the southern gate. Those excellent warriors possess four kinds of forces.[7] There are one million[8] rakshasas along the eastern gate. All of them are skilled in the use of all weapons and wield swords and shields. There are one hundred million rakshasas along the northern gate. They are extremely revered and are the sons of noble lineages. They are on chariots, or have horses as their mounts. There are hundreds of thousands in battle formations in the middle. There are more than one crore rakshasas, *yatudhanas*[9] who are invincible. I shattered the drawbridges and filled up the moats. I burnt the city of Lanka and demolished the ramparts. Through whatever means possible, we must cross Varuna's abode. Once that is done, it is certain that the apes will destroy the city of Lanka. With Angada, Dvivida, Mainda, Jambavat, Panasa, Nala and the commander Nila, why will you need the rest of the army? We will leap and go to Ravana's great city. We will destroy the ramparts and residences and bring Maithilee back. Therefore, quickly command all the forces to be gathered. We will be delighted to leave in a short while.'

Chapter 6(4)

In due order, Hanumat described it, exactly as it was. Hearing his words, the immensely energetic Rama, with truth as his valour, said, 'You have described the city of Lanka, belonging to the terrible rakshasas. I am telling you truthfully that I will quickly destroy it. O Sugriva! The idea of leaving immediately appeals to me. The sun has reached midday and this is an auspicious moment for victory. The

[7] Chariots, horses, elephants and foot soldiers.

[8] *Ayuta* is ten thousand, *niyuta* is one hundred thousand, *prayuta* is one million and *arbuda* is one hundred million.

[9] A yatudhana is an evil spirit or demon.

nakshatra[10] is Uttara Phalguni today and tomorrow, there will be a conjunction with Hasta. O Sugriva! Surrounded by all the soldiers, let us leave. Auspicious portents are manifesting themselves before me. I will slay Ravana and bring back Sita Janakee. This upper eyelid of mine is twitching. It seems to be telling me that my desire of obtaining victory will be fulfilled. Examining the path, let Nila proceed ahead of the army. Let him be surrounded by one hundred thousand spirited apes. O Nila! O commander! Quickly lead the army along a path that is full of honey, with roots, fruits, cool groves and water. You must always be ready to protect yourself against the rakshasas. Along the path, those evil-souled ones will seek to destroy the roots, fruits and water. Let the residents of the forest leap into low grounds, fortifications in the forests, and forests to check if the soldiers of the enemy are hidden there. Let immensely strong ones be ahead of the terrible army, which will have the complexion of waves in the ocean. Let it be led by hundreds and thousands of lions among apes. Gaja is like a mountain. Gavaya is immensely strong. Let them and Gavaksha proceed in front, like proud bulls in front of a herd of cows. As the army of apes advances, let the ape Rishabha, bull among apes and a lord of the apes, protect the right flank. Gandhamadana is as spirited and invincible as an elephant in musth. As the army of the apes advances, let him be stationed along the left flank. I will proceed in the middle of the army, delighting the flood of soldiers. I will be astride Hanumat, like the lord[11] on Airavata. Let Lakshmana, who is like Death, be astride Angada, like the lord of creatures and the lord of riches astride Sarvabhouma.[12] Jambavat, the great spirited lord of the bears, Sushena and the ape named Vegadarshi—let these three protect the rear.' Hearing Raghava's words, Sugriva, the lord of the army and the immensely brave bull among apes, commanded the apes.

Desiring to fight, all the large numbers of apes leapt up. They quickly jumped from the caves and the summits. Rama, with dharma in his soul, and Lakshmana were worshipped by the king of the apes

[10] There are twenty-seven nakshatras, which are stars/constellations.

[11] Indra.

[12] The comparison is with Kubera, Kubera's elephant being named Sarvabhouma.

and proceeded in a southern direction, with the soldiers. As they proceeded, they were surrounded by hundreds, tens of thousands, hundreds of thousands and crores of apes that possessed the complexion of elephants. The large army of apes followed them. All of them were protected by Sugriva and were delighted and happy. Those apes jumped, leapt and roared. They sported and played on musical instruments, proceeding southwards. They devoured extremely fragrant honey and fruits. They carried large trees that were full of many clusters of flowers and buds. Proud, they suddenly carried each other and flung each other down. They leapt down and leapt up. Others flung down others. In Raghava's presence, the apes roared, 'Ravana and all the roamers in the night deserve to be killed by us.' With many apes, Rishabha, the brave Nila and Kumuda cleared the path in front. King Sugriva, Rama and Lakshmana were in the middle. Those destroyers of enemies were surrounded by many strong and terrible ones. The brave ape, Shatabali, was surrounded by tens of crores. Single-handedly, he protected the entire army of apes. Surrounded by one hundred crores, Kesari, Panasa, Gaja and the extremely strong Arka protected one flank. With Sugriva in the front, Sushena and Jambavat, surrounded by many bears, protected the rear. The brave Nila, the commander, was a bull among apes. He was best among those who could leap, and protected the army. Darimukha, Prajangha, Jambha and the ape Rabhasa proceeded, urging the brave apes on all sides to hurry. In this way, proud of their strength, the tigers among apes proceeded. They saw Sahya, best among mountains and full of trees and creepers. That large and terrible army of apes was like waves in the ocean. They marched with a great roar, like the terrible force of the ocean. Those brave elephants among apes were alongside Dasharatha's son. Swiftly, all of them leapt forward, like well-trained horses when they are goaded. Borne aloft by those two apes,[13] those two bulls among men were radiant. They were like the moon and the sun, when they touch the two large planets.[14]

[13] Hanumat and Angada.

[14] Jupiter and Venus.

The learned and talented Lakshmana, astride Angada, addressed Rama in auspicious words that were full of meaning. 'We will swiftly kill Ravana and get back Vaidehi, who has been abducted. Successful in your objective, you will return to Ayodhya, which is full of prosperity. O Raghava! I can see great portents in the sky and on the ground. I see all these auspicious omens, indicating success in your objective. An auspicious and favourable wind is blowing, gentle, beneficial and pleasing to the soldiers. The animals and birds are speaking in full and gentle tones. All the directions are clear and the sun is sparkling. Ushanas,[15] descended from Bhrigu, is following you, with a pleasing light. The sacred and supreme *rishi*s, born in a pure way from Brahma, are all circling around Dhruva, manifesting their rays.[16] The royal sage Trishanku, our supreme and great-souled grandfather from the lineage of the Ikshvakus is radiant and sparkling, with his priest.[17] The nakshatra Vishakha is sparkling, without anything to mar it. This is the supreme nakshatra for the great-souled Ikshvakus. The terrible nakshatra of the *nairitta*s[18] is suffering. This is Mula and its foundation has been touched and is suffering from a comet. All this has presented itself for the destruction of the rakshasas. It is time and, suffering from the planet,[19] it is as if their nakshatra has been seized by death. The tasty waters are pleasant and the forests are full of fruit. An extremely fragrant breeze is blowing. There are seasonal flowers on the trees. O lord! Arrayed in battle formations, the soldiers of the apes seem to be even more resplendent. They are like the soldiers of the gods at the time of

[15] Meaning Shukra (Venus).

[16] The *saptarshi*s are the seven great sages. The list varies, but the standard one is Marichi, Atri, Angira, Pulastya, Pulaha, Kratu and Vasishtha. In the sky, the saptarshis are identified with the constellation of Ursa Major (Great Bear). The saptarshis were Brahma's mental sons. Dhruva is the Pole Star.

[17] Trishanku was born in the solar dynasty and his priest (Vishvamitra) gave him the boon that he would be in the sky, after Trishanku started to fall down from heaven. Astronomically, Trishanku is identified as the Southern Cross. Depending on the location in India, this can usually be seen on the southern horizon between April and June.

[18] Demons.

[19] This means the comet.

the *tarakamaya* battle.[20] O noble one! Look at all this. You should be delighted.' Happy, Soumitri spoke to his brother, comforting him in this way.

The giant army proceeded, covering the entire earth. It was full of tigers among bears and apes, using nails and teeth as weapons. With the tips of their hands and the tips of their feet, the apes raised a terrible dust that entered inside the world and took away the sun's radiance. Through night and day, the great army of apes marched. Protected by Sugriva, the soldiers were happy and cheerful. All the spirited apes marched, delighted at the prospect of war. Desiring to free Sita, they did not tarry even for an instant. They reached Mount Sahya and Mount Malaya, full of trees and populated by many animals. There were wonderful groves, rivers and waterfalls. Rama also went and saw Sahya and Malaya. The apes enjoyed themselves, among the *champaka*, *tilaka*, mango, *ashoka*, *sinduvaraka*,[21] *karavira* and *timisha* trees. Intoxicated in their strength, the apes enjoyed fruits that tasted like *amrita*, roots and flowers from the trees. Cheerfully, honey-brown in complexion, they drank honey from long honeycombs that were one *drona*[22] in size and proceeded. They broke the trees and pulled out the creepers. As they proceeded, the bulls among apes flung away excellent boulders. Insolent because of the honey, some apes roared among the trees. Some reached out to the trees. Others leapt down. The entire earth was full with those bulls among apes, just as when the earth is full of ripened paddy.

The lotus-eyed Rama reached Mahendra. The mighty-armed one ascended the summit, which was ornamented with trees. Having ascended the summit, Rama, Dasharatha's son, saw the abode of the waters, filled with turtles and fish. They progressively crossed over the giant mountain of Malaya and reached the ocean, which roared terribly. Rama, supreme among those who cause pleasure, with Sugriva and Lakshmana, descended quickly to the excellent forest along the shore. There were rocks underneath and it was

[20] Famous battle between the gods and the demons. It took place after Chandra, the moon, abducted Tara, Brihaspati's wife.

[21] The five-leaved chaste tree (*Vitex negunda*), but this should read *sindhuvaraka*.

[22] A drona is a wooden vessel, as well as an unit of measurement.

washed with waves of water that suddenly arose. Having reached the extensive shoreline, Rama spoke these words. 'O Sugriva! We have reached Varuna's abode. We must now think about what we pondered earlier.[23] The other shore of the ocean, the lord of the rivers, cannot be discerned. Without a proper means, we are incapable of crossing this ocean. Therefore, let us reside here while we have consultations about how this army of apes can cross over to the other shore.' The mighty-armed one was afflicted because of Sita's abduction. Having reached the ocean, Rama instructed that they should camp there. 'The time for consultations about how we should cross the ocean has arrived. Let no one leave his battalion and go off anywhere else. However, let the brave apes proceed and ascertain whether there is any danger for us.'

Hearing Rama's words, Sugriva and Lakshmana made the soldiers set up camp on the extensive shore of the ocean, filled with trees. Near the ocean, that army was radiant. It looked like a beautiful second ocean, filled with water that had a honey-brown complexion. The bulls among apes reached the forest along the shore. They settled down there, desiring to cross over to the other shore of the great ocean. Having reached the great ocean, the army of the apes was delighted. They looked at the great ocean, turbulent because of the force of the wind. The distant other shore was populated by large numbers of rakshasas. The leaders among the apes sat down and looked at Varuna's abode. At the end of the day and the beginning of the night, it was terrible, filled with horrible crocodiles and alligators. When the moon arose, it turned turbulent and reflected the moon's image. There were giant crocodiles that were as terrible as the wind. It was populated with whales and *timingila*s.[24] Varuna's abode was filled with blazing serpents and snakes. There were gigantic creatures and many kinds of mountains in the deep. It was extremely difficult to cross. It was impenetrable. It was impassable. It was fathomless and was the abode of asuras. The impenetrable depths was agitated by the wind and were filled

[23] A means of crossing the ocean.

[24] Timingila is a fish that devours whales (*timi*).

with *makaras*,[25] serpents and snakes. Large torrents of water rose and fell. There were radiant and large serpents in the water, speckled with dots that seemed to be made out of fire. The ocean reached down to the region of *patala*,[26] the dominion of the enemies of the gods. The ocean was like the sky. The sky was like the ocean. No distinction could be seen between the ocean and the sky. The water mixed with the sky and the sky mixed with the water. With stars in the sky and jewels in the water, both seemed to be the same. One was filled with rising clouds and the other was filled with rising waves. There was no particular distinction between the two, the ocean and the sky. Each making its own terrible noise, they seemed to clash against each other. The waves of the king of the rivers and the great clouds seemed to be engaged in a battle. In the grip of the wind, the jewels and waves in the water roared. Filled with a large number of creatures, it seemed to angrily rise up. The great-souled ones saw the abode of the waters, lashed by the wind. A wind arose in the sky and the waves seemed to be conversing with it. Waves roared and whirled around in the water, as if the ocean was intoxicated.

Chapter 6(5)

Self-controlled, Nila protected the virtuous army in the proper way and it camped itself on the northern shore of the ocean. Mainda and Dvivida, bulls among apes, roamed around in all the directions, protecting the soldiers.

When the army had settled down along the shore of the lord of the male and female rivers, Rama saw that Lakshmana was by his side and addressed him in these words. 'Indeed, as time passes, my sorrow is becoming less. However, the grief at not being able to see my beloved is increasing from one day to the next day. I am not

[25] Mythical aquatic creatures, which can be loosely translated as sharks or crocodiles.
[26] One of the seven nether regions.

distressed that my beloved is far away. Nor am I distressed that she has been abducted. I am grieving that her age is passing. O wind! Blow where my beloved is. Touch her and touch me. It is through you that I can touch her body. It is through the moon that our eyes meet. As she was being abducted, my beloved must have spoken to me. "Alas, lord!" That thought is scorching my body, as if I have imbibed some poison. Night and day, the fire of desire is consuming my body. It is acting as kindling to the great flames of my thoughts. O Soumitri! Without you, I will immerse myself in the ocean and sleep. When I sleep in this way, perhaps the water will somehow quench my blazing desire. Burnt by this desire, I am capable of remaining alive only because I and the one with the beautiful thighs are located on the same earth. A paddy field without water survives by imbibing water from an adjacent paddy field that is full of water. In that way, I am alive by being sprinkled, having heard that she is alive. When will I defeat the enemies and see the beautiful-hipped and lotus-eyed Sita, extensive in her prosperity? Her beautiful lips are like the *bimba* fruit. Her face is like a lotus. When will she raise it slightly and I drink from it, like a diseased person drinking medicine? Her thick breasts are close together, they are like palm fruit. They are delightful. When will they tremble and press against me? The dark-eyed one has left and is in the midst of the rakshasas. I am her protector. But she is without a protector and cannot find anyone to save her. In the autumn, the moon's outline drives away dark clouds. Like that, when will she appear, driving away and agitating the rakshasas? Sita is naturally slender. Because of sorrow, fasting and the adversity faced from the time and the place, she has become even more slender. When will I strike the Indra among rakshasas with arrows in his chest and bring Sita back, thereby dispelling the sorrow in my heart? When will the virtuous and anxious Sita, who is like a daughter of the immortals, cling to my neck and release tears of joy? When will I suddenly free myself from this terrible sorrow that has resulted from the separation with Maithilee, like one casts away a soiled garment?' In this way, the intelligent Rama lamented there. At the end of the day, the sun's form diminished and sunset arrived. Remembering the lotus-eyed one, he was overwhelmed with grief. However, comforted by Lakshmana, Rama worshipped the *sandhya*.[27]

Chapter 6(6)

The Indra among rakshasas was like the great-souled Shakra. Having seen the terrible deeds, which caused fear, wrought by Hanumat in Lanka, he lowered his face and a bit ashamed, spoke to all the rakshasas. 'The city of Lanka is impossible to assail. But he entered and destroyed it, despite being only an ape. He saw Sita Janakee. He destroyed the palace and the *chaitya*.[28] The best among rakshasas were killed. Hanumat agitated the entire city of Lanka. O fortunate ones! What should be done? What is our subsequent task? Speak about what we are capable of doing, so that we can take appropriate action. Spirited and noble ones have said that consultations are the foundation of victory. O immensely strong ones! Therefore, the idea of consulting about Rama appeals to me. There are three types of people in the world—superior, inferior and mediocre. Let me tell you about the qualities and bad traits they possess. A supreme man is said to be one who consults capable ministers and undertakes beneficial acts after the advice, doing the same with friends who have a similar objective and relatives who are favourably inclined. He performs an act after such collective consultations, paying due attention to destiny. A man is said to be mediocre if he determines an objective alone, uses only his mind to decide what constitutes dharma and undertakes the task alone. If a man does not distinguish between the good and the bad, depending on destiny alone, and decides that he will undertake an act, such a man is said to be inferior. Just as men are always classified into superior, inferior and mediocre, advice is also known to be superior, inferior and mediocre. Superior advice is said to be

[27] Sandhya is any conjunction of day and night. Hence, it is dawn, as well as dusk.

[28] The word chaitya has several meanings—sacrificial shed, temple, altar, sanctuary and a tree that grows along the road.

that discussed and arrived at by ministers through unanimity, in conformity with the foresight of the sacred texts. When seeking the objective, the ministers have many kinds of views and one finally has to be chosen through consensus, this is said to be mediocre advice. When they debate with each other and discuss different points of view, without being able to arrive at a consensus, that advice is said to be inferior. O supreme among ministers! You are virtuous. Consult well and decide on the course of action. I will undertake that. Rama is surrounded by thousands of brave apes. He is approaching the city of Lanka and will lay siege to us. It is evident that the spirited Raghava will easily cross the ocean, with his younger brother, his soldiers and his followers. Our enmity with the apes has commenced. Therefore, consult and tell me what is beneficial for the city and the soldiers.'

Chapter 6(7)

The Indra among rakshasas said this to the immensely strong rakshasas. Having heard this, all of them joined their hands in salutation to Ravana, the lord of the rakshasas, and said, 'O king! Our extremely large army is full of clubs, spears, swords, javelins and spikes. Why are you distressed? The lord of wealth[29] resides on the summit of Kailasa and is surrounded by many yakshas. You created a great carnage and brought him under your subjugation. O lord! He boasted of his friendship with Maheshvara. He is extremely strong and is a guardian of the world. However, you angrily defeated him in a battle. You killed, agitated and oppressed large numbers of yakshas. From the summit of Kailasa, you seized the *vimana*[30] and brought it here. Out of fright, Maya, Indra among the danavas, desired your friendship. O bull among the rakshasas! He bestowed his daughter[31] on you as a wife. There was an Indra

[29] Kubera.
[30] Pushpaka.
[31] Mandodari.

among danavas. His name was Madhu and he brought pleasure to Kumbhinasa.[32] He was insolent about his valour and invincible. However, you subjugated him and brought him under control. O mighty-armed one! You went to *rasatala*[33] and subjugated and seized the *nagas*[34] Vasuki, Takshaka, Shankha and Jati. O lord! There were brave danavas who were infinitely strong. In addition, they had also obtained a boon. In an encounter, you fought against them for an entire year. O scorcher of enemies! Using your own strength, you brought them under subjugation. O lord of rakshasas! There are many kinds of *maya* you learnt there. Varuna's sons were brave and valiant in battle. Their followers possessed the four kinds of forces. O mighty-armed one! You defeated them. O king! You immersed yourself in the ocean of Yama's army. The staff of death was like a giant crocodile there and the region was full of silk-cotton trees. You countered Death and obtained a great victory. Through that great battle, you made all the worlds extremely content. The earth was full of many brave kshatriyas, as if with large trees, who were like Shakra in their valour. In a battle, Raghava is not equal to them in valour, qualities or enterprise. They were extremely difficult to vanquish. O king! However, you overcame them and killed them. O king! The calamity that has arisen is due to an ordinary person. You should not take this to heart. You will kill Raghava.'

Chapter 6(8)

There was a rakshasa named Prahasta and he possessed the complexion of a dark cloud. He was a brave commander. He joined his hands in salutation and spoke these words. 'There are

[32] Kumbhinasa was Ravana's sister, married to Madhu.

[33] One of the seven nether regions.

[34] Throughout the translation, we have generally used serpents for nagas and snakes for *sarpas*. Nagas are not quite snakes. They are semi-divine, can assume human forms and live in specific regions.

no gods, danavas, gandharvas, *pishachas*,[35] birds or serpents whom you are incapable of afflicting in a battle, not to speak of apes. All of us were distracted and trusting and were thus deceived by Hanumat. Otherwise, that dweller in the forest would not have left with his life. Command me and I will remove apes from the entire earth, its mountains, forests and groves, right up to the frontiers of the ocean. O roamer in the night! I will arrange for your protection from the apes. Because of the crime you have committed,[36] there will not be the slightest bit of misery for you.'

There was a rakshasa named Durmukha. Extremely angry, he said, 'He[37] oppressed all of us and that cannot be forgiven. This is an additional attack unleashed on the prosperous Indra among the rakshasas, his city and his inner quarters, by the Indra among the apes. From this instant, I will single-handedly repulse and kill the apes, whether they enter the terrible ocean, the sky or rasatala.'

Seizing a terrible club that was smeared with flesh and blood, extremely angry, the immensely strong Vajradamshtra said, 'What do we have to do with the pitiable ascetic Hanumat? The invincible Rama, Sugriva and Lakshmana exist. I will single-handedly agitate the army of the apes, approach Rama, Sugriva and Lakshmana and kill them with this club.'

The brave and valiant Nikumbha was Kumbhakarna's son. Extremely enraged, he spoke to Ravana, the one who made the worlds shriek. 'All of you remain here with the great king. I will single-handedly slay Raghava and Lakshmana.'

There was a rakshasa named Vajrahanu and he was like a mountain. He angrily licked his lips with his tongue and spoke these words. 'All of you get rid of your anxiety and perform your own tasks. I will single-handedly devour all the leaders of the apes. Rest assured and sport. Be at ease and drink *madhu* and *varuni*.[38] I will single-handedly slay Sugriva, Lakshmana, Angada, Hanumat, Rama and all the elephants in the battle.'

[35] Malevolent beings.

[36] Sita's abduction.

[37] Hanumat.

[38] Forms of liquor.

Chapter 6(9)

Nikumbha, Rabhasa, the immensely strong Suryashatru, Suptaghna, Yajnakopa, Mahaparshva, Mahodara, the invincible rakshasas Agniketu and Rashmiketu, Indrajit, Ravana's extremely energetic and strong son, Prahasta, Virupaksha, the immensely strong Vajradamshtra, Dhumraksha, Atikaya and the rakshasa Durmukha became angry and seized clubs, spears, javelins, spikes, tridents, battleaxes, bows, arrows and large and sharp swords. All of them blazed in their energy. Those rakshasas stood up and told Ravana, 'Today we will slay Rama, Sugriva, Lakshmana and the pitiable Hanumat who attacked Lanka.'

Vibhishana restrained all those who had seized weapons. He joined his hands in salutation, made them sit down again and spoke these words. 'O father![39] The learned ones have said that if the objective cannot be attained through the three modes, only then is it the time to display valour.[40] O father! Following the tested methods, valour is only successful against those who are distracted, engaged with someone else, or those who are suffering on account of misfortune. How can you resort to strength and defeat someone who is attentive? How can you wish to attack him in that way? He has conquered his rage and is invincible. Hanumat has performed the extremely difficult deed of crossing the terrible ocean, the lord of the male and female rivers. Who can dispute that? O those who roam around in the night! The valour and strength of the enemy is immeasurable. One should never be rash and take them lightly. The illustrious Rama's wife was abducted. Earlier, what did he do to the king of the rakshasas in Janasthana? Khara crossed his limits and was killed by Rama in a battle. Depending on one's strength, one must certainly protect the lives of creatures. That is the reason an extremely great fear has arisen on account of Vaidehi. She was abducted and must be abandoned. What is the purpose in provoking

[39] The word used is *tata*, which can be translated as either father or son, depending on whom Vibhishana is addressing. Since words are primarily addressed to Ravana, we have translated it as father.

[40] That is, use *danda* only if *sama, dana* and *bheda* do not work.

a quarrel? He is full of valour and follows dharma. A pointless enmity with him is futile. Let Maithilee be given to him. Maithilee should be given to him before he uses his arrows to shatter this city, with its elephants, horses and many kinds of jewels. Let Sita be given before the extremely terrible and large army of invincible apes attacks Lanka. If Rama's beloved wife is not voluntarily returned, the city of Lanka and all the brave rakshasas will be destroyed. As a relative, I am seeking to pacify you. Act in accordance with my words. I am speaking about a beneficial medication. Let Maithilee be given back. The son of the king will release invincible arrows with new heads and tufts. They will be like the rays of the autumn sun. Before Dasharatha's son does that, let Maithilee be given to him. Abandon rage. It destroys the dharma of happiness. Serve the dharma that extends pleasure and deeds. Be pacified, so that our sons and relatives remain alive. Give Maithilee back to Dasharatha's son.'

Chapter 6(10)

Vibhishana uttered those extremely well-articulated and beneficial words. However, goaded by destiny, Ravana replied in harsh words. 'One can reside with an enemy or an angry and virulent serpent, but one cannot dwell with an enemy who states himself to be a friend. O rakshasa! I know about the conduct of relatives in all the worlds. Relatives are always delighted at the hardships their relatives face. O rakshasa! They disrespect and seek to bring down relatives who are important, successful, learned, devoted to dharma in their conduct and brave. They are like assassins and are always delighted at each other's hardships. They conceal their terrible thoughts and therefore bring fear to relatives. In earlier times, in a pond full of lotuses, some elephants were heard to chant a shloka when they saw men with nooses in their hands. Hear my words. "Fire, other weapons and nooses aren't as fearful to us as terrible relatives who are engaged in their own selfish pursuits and bring us fear. There is no doubt that they will speak about the means whereby we can be captured. Out of all kinds of fear, we know that the hardship which results from relatives is the most fearful. It is evident there is wealth in cows. It is evident there is self-control in *brahmana*s. It is evident there is fickleness in women. It is evident there is reason for fear in relatives."[41] O amiable one! You do not desire that I should be honoured by the world, nor my prosperity, nobility of birth and the fact that I stand on the heads of enemies. O roamer in the night! Had anyone else spoken such words, this very instant, he would have ceased to exist. O worst of the lineage! Shame on you.'

Vibhishana spoke about good policy. Being addressed in these harsh words, he rose up into the sky with a club in his hand, along with four rakshasas. The handsome Vibhishana was in the sky. Having conquered his rage, he spoke to his brother, the lord of the rakshasas. 'O king! Since you are my brother, you can tell me whatever you wish. However, I cannot pardon these harsh and false words that you have spoken. O Dashanana! Those who have not cleansed their souls and have come under the subjugation of destiny do not accept well-articulated and beneficial words addressed to them. O king! Men who always speak what is pleasant are easy to get. But for disagreeable words that are like medication, a speaker and a listener are both extremely rare. You are bound in the noose of destiny, which takes away all creatures. This destruction could not be ignored, just as a burning house cannot be. I do not wish to see you slain by Rama's sharp arrows, decorated with gold and like a blazing fire. In the field of battle, brave and strong people who are accomplished in the use of weapons sink down when destiny comes upon them, like a bridge made with sand. Using whatever means, protect yourself, the city and these rakshasas. May you be fortunate. I am leaving. Without me, be happy. Desiring your welfare, I tried to restrain you. O roamer in the night! But my words were not to your liking. When their time and lifespan is over, men do not accept the beneficial words spoken by their well-wishers.'

[41] It is not clear from the text where the elephant quote ends. This seems to be the right place. Wild elephants are referring to domesticated elephants being used to trap and capture them.

Chapter 6(11)

Ravana's younger brother spoke these harsh words to Ravana. Having said them, in an instant, he reached the spot where Rama and Lakshmana were. His form was like the summit of Meru and he blazed like a flash of lightning. From the ground, the lords of the apes saw him standing in the sky. With the apes, the invincible Sugriva, lord of the apes, saw this fifth person.[42] With the other apes, the intelligent one started to think. Having thought for a while, he addressed all the apes, with Hanumat at the forefront, in these excellent words. 'He possesses all the weapons and he is with four rakshasas. Behold. There is no doubt that the rakshasas are advancing so as to kill us.' Hearing Sugriva's words, all those excellent apes raised *sala* trees and boulders and spoke these words. 'O king! Quickly command us, so that we can kill these evil-souled ones. They have limited lifespans. Let us bring them down on the ground and kill them.' While they were conversing in this way, Vibhishana reached the northern shore and stationed himself in the sky. The immensely wise and great Vibhishana stationed himself in the sky. On seeing them, he addressed them in a loud voice. 'The rakshasa named Ravana is wicked in conduct and is the lord of the rakshasas. I am his younger brother and am known by the name of Vibhishana. Having slain Jatayu, he abducted Sita from Janasthana. Incapacitated and distressed, she has been imprisoned and is exceedingly well-protected by the *rakshasi*s.[43] I repeatedly entreated him in many kinds of virtuous words filled with reason that Sita should be returned to Rama. But he did not heed them. Goaded by destiny, Ravana did not accept them. Though those beneficial words that were spoken were like medication, he acted in a contrary way. He spoke harshly to me and disrespected me, as if I was a servant. Abandoning my sons and my wife, I am seeking refuge with Raghava. Quickly inform the great-souled Raghava, the refuge of all the worlds, about Vibhishana presenting himself.'

[42] There were four other rakshasas.

[43] Rakshasa lady.

Sugriva was dexterous in his valour. Hearing these words, he swiftly went to the presence of Rama and Lakshmana and said, 'Ravana's younger brother is known by the name of Vibhishana. With four other rakshasas, he is seeking refuge with you. Know that Vibhishana has been sent by Ravana. O supreme among those who know what is proper! I think it proper that he should be captured. This rakshasa is deceitful in intelligence and has come here because he has been instructed. O Raghava! When you trust him, he will hide himself and strike you with maya. Using severe chastisement, he and his advisers should be killed. This Vibhishana is the cruel Ravana's brother.' Wrathful, the leader of the army told Rama this. He was accomplished in the use of words and skilled in speech. Having said this, he was silent. The immensely strong Rama heard Sugriva's words. He spoke to Hanumat and the foremost apes who were near him. 'You have heard what the king of the apes has said about Ravana's younger brother. These words are full of deep meaning and reasoning. In a time of hardship, a capable well-wisher who desires eternal prosperity must use purposeful and intelligent words of advice. What do you think?' Asked in this way, they attentively articulated their own views. Desiring Rama's welfare, they addressed him politely. 'O Raghava! There is nothing in the three worlds that is unknown to you. O Rama! You are asking us as well-wishers and showing us honour. You possess the vow of truth. You are brave and follow dharma. You are firm in your valour. You take action after due examination. You can remember. You have devoted your soul to well-wishers. Therefore, one by one, your advisers will speak to you. They are capable and full of intelligence. One by one, they will give you their reasons.'

After this, the intelligent Angada spoke first to Raghava. The ape's words were that Vibhishana should first be tested about his intentions. 'Since he has come from the enemy, there is every reason to be suspicious of him. One should not hastily believe that Vibhishana is a trustworthy person. Those who are deceitful in intelligence roam around, hiding their own sentiments. They strike at a weakness and can lead to an extremely great calamity. One must decide on one's conduct after judging the pros and the cons. If there is an accumulation of qualities, one must follow that course. If there are evils, one must discard it. If there are extremely great evils, without any hesitation, one must discard it. O king! If one knows that there is a great accumulation of qualities, one must act accordingly.'

Sharabha spoke determined words that were full of meaning. 'O tiger among men! As a counter, let us quickly send spies after him. Let a spy who is subtle in intelligence ascertain the exact nature of the truth. After examining the different courses of action, if it is proper, he can be accepted.'

Jambavat was accomplished in intelligence and knew about the sacred texts. Considering the objective, he proclaimed the following words, which were full of qualities and devoid of demerits. 'Vibhishana has come from the wicked Indra among rakshasas, who is bound in enmity towards you. He has come at the wrong time and place. He must be suspected in every possible way.'

Mainda was accomplished in distinguishing between good and bad policy. He was skilled in speaking and spoke words that were full of excellent reasons. 'O lord of the supreme among men! Vibhishana has said that he is Ravana's younger brother. Let him be questioned, sweetly and slowly. Let his true sentiments be ascertained. Act thereafter. O bull among men! Use your intelligence to decide whether he is evil or not evil.'

Hanumat was supreme among advisers and full of purity. Slowly, sweetly and briefly, he spoke these words. 'You are best in intelligence. You are capable and supreme among eloquent ones. When speaking, even Brihaspati is incapable of surpassing you. O king! O Rama! I am not speaking so as to rival the others, nor do I desire superiority over the others. I am speaking these words because it is an important matter. Your advisers have spoken about determining the pros and the cons. I see a problem in this and that kind of action cannot be pursued. Short of engaging someone, it is not possible to determine his capability. To me, there seems to be a problem in suddenly engaging someone. Your advisers have spoken about employing a spy. This is impossible to achieve and I do not see how that can be brought about. This Vibhishana has arrived at the wrong time and place. I will tell you what my thoughts are about this. Listen to me. For him, this is the right time and place and that is the reason he has come here. He has come from one person to another person,[44] having judged their respective qualities and sins. He has seen the wickedness in Ravana and the valour in you. This is according to his intelligence and that is the reason he has come here. O king! It has been suggested that he should be questioned by men who are in disguise. Having considered it, here is my view on that. If an intelligent person is suddenly questioned, he will be suspicious. Thus, a person who has come happily may be falsely questioned and the friendship may be destroyed. O king! It is impossible to suddenly ascertain the inclinations of someone else. Without possessing a great deal of skill, it is impossible to determine what there is in someone's inner mind. I do not detect any evil sentiments in what he has spoken. His face is also pleasant. Therefore, I do not doubt him. A deceitful person does not approach in such a self-assured way, unsuspecting in his mind. His words are not evil. Therefore, I do not doubt him. Even if one hides it, it is impossible not to reveal something in one's form. Even if men try forcibly, the inner sentiments are revealed. O supreme among those who know what must be done! You know what must be done. If appropriate to the time and the place, a task that should be undertaken must be done quickly, so that it is successful. Considering your enterprise and Ravana's false conduct and hearing about the slaying of Vali and Sugriva's consecration, he must have first turned his mind to seeking the kingdom[45] and has come here. With this consideration at the forefront, he should be added to our side. To the best of my ability, I have spoken about this rakshasa's uprightness. O supreme among intelligent ones! Having heard, you must finally decide on what is proper.'

[44] From Ravana to Rama.

[45] Of the rakshasas.

Chapter 6(12)

Hearing what Vayu's son had said, Rama was pleased in his mind. The invincible and learned one replied, stating what he had decided. 'I also wish to speak about my attitude towards Vibhishana. All of you are interested in our welfare and therefore, I wish that all of you should hear this. Someone who has arrived as a friend must never be discarded, even if there are taints in him. The virtuous ones condemn that.'

Hearing Rama's words, Sugriva, the lord of the apes, was goaded by his affection and replied to Kakutstha. 'O one who knows about dharma! O lord of the worlds! O one who is like the jewel on a crest! How wonderful. You have spoken like a spirited and noble one, established along the path of virtue. My inner thoughts are also that this Vibhishana is pure. On the basis of his inclinations, this is my surmise and I have examined it in every possible way. O Raghava! Therefore, let him quickly become one of our equals. We will then obtain the friendship of the immensely wise Vibhishana.'

Rama examined the words that had been spoken by Sugriva. He then addressed the bull among apes in words that were even more auspicious. 'How does it matter whether this roamer in the night is extremely wicked or not wicked? He is incapable of causing the slightest bit of injury to me. O lord of large numbers of apes! If I so wish, I can kill pishachas, danavas, yakshas and all the rakshasas on earth with the tips of my fingers. It has been heard that an enemy arrived and sought refuge. As is proper, a dove honoured and invited him and offered him his own flesh. He received someone who had come to kill his wife. O best among apes! If a dove did that, what about a person like me?[46] The rishi Kanva's son was Kandu and he was a supreme sage. He was full of dharma and spoke the truth. Listen to the chant he had recited in ancient times. "O scorcher

[46] This is a story from the Mahabharata. A fowler captured a she-pigeon or she-dove. Since the fowler was hungry and a guest, the he-pigeon or he-dove offered his body to the fowler as food.

of enemies! Even if an enemy wishing to cause injury arrives in a distressed state, with his hands cupped, and seeks refuge, he should not be killed. Even if an enemy is insolent, if he seeks refuge in a distressed state, a person who has cleansed his soul should protect that enemy, even at the cost of his own life. Because of fear, confusion or desire, if he does not protect, despite possessing the capacity and the spirit, he commits a sin and is condemned by the worlds. If a potential protector sees someone who seeks refuge being destroyed, when the person who should have been protected departs, he takes away all the good deeds of the potential protector. There is a great sin in not protecting someone who seeks refuge. It destroys heaven and fame. It destroys strength and valour." I will truly follow the meaning of Kandu's excellent words. It leads to the following of dharma. It leads to fame. It leads to the fruit of heaven being obtained. If a person seeks refuge and says, "I am yours", against all creatures, I will grant him freedom from fear. That is my vow. O best among the apes! Bring him here. Whether it is Vibhishana or whether it is Ravana himself, I will grant him freedom from fear.' After hearing Sugriva's words, the lord of men addressed the lord of the apes in this way. Vibhishana quickly arrived to meet him, like the king of the birds meeting Purandara.

Chapter 6(13)

When Raghava granted him freedom from fear, Ravana's younger brother, lowered himself, and with his faithful companions, descended on to the ground. Vibhishana, with dharma in his soul, descended and sought refuge at Rama's feet, with the four rakshasas. Vibhishana addressed Rama in these words. They were appropriate and full of dharma, causing delight. 'I am Ravana's younger brother and I have been humiliated by him. You are the refuge of all creatures and I am seeking refuge with you. I have abandoned Lanka, my friends and my riches. My kingdom, my life and my happiness are now vested in you. I will help you in killing the rakshasas and attacking Lanka. As long as I am alive, I will attack and penetrate that army.'

Thus addressed, Rama embraced Vibhishana. Rejoicing, he told Lakshmana, 'Fetch water from the ocean. O one who shows honours! Using that, quickly consecrate the immensely wise Vibhishana as the king of the rakshasas, so that I am pleased.' Thus addressed, following Rama's instruction, in the midst of the foremost apes, Soumitri consecrated Vibhishana as the king. Seeing that Rama was pleased, the apes immediately emitted a loud roar and uttered words praising him.[47]

Hanumat and Sugriva spoke to Vibhishana. 'The ocean cannot be agitated. How can we cross Varuna's abode? We must swiftly find a means so that all the soldiers can cross over Varuna's abode, the lord of the male and female rivers.' Addressed in this way, Vibhishana, who knew about dharma, replied, 'To proceed, King Raghava should seek refuge with the ocean. The immeasurable and great ocean was dug by Sagara. Knowing that Rama is a relative, the great ocean should perform this task.'[48] The learned rakshasa, Vibhishana, spoke in this way. Raghava was naturally devoted to dharma and this appealed to him, since it was a good deed to accomplish the purpose. He first smiled and then spoke to the immensely energetic Lakshmana and Sugriva, the lord of the apes. 'O Lakshmana! Vibhishana's advice appeals to me. With Sugriva, tell me if the idea appeals to you. Sugriva is always learned and you are skilled in offering counsel. Both of you decide whether what has been said appeals to you.' Thus addressed, both those brave ones, Sugriva and Lakshmana, spoke these words with humility. 'O tiger among men! O Raghava! Why will it not appeal to us? At this time, what Vibhishana has spoken will bring us joy. Varuna's abode is terrible. Without building a bridge across the ocean, not even Indra, with the gods and the *asuras*, is capable of reaching Lanka. Let us act exactly in accordance with the brave Vibhishana's words. We have spent an excessive amount of time already. Let us engage with

[47] Praising Rama.

[48] Sagara was Rama's ancestor.

the ocean.' Thus addressed, Rama spread out *kusha* grass on the shores of the lord of the male and female rivers, like a sacrificial altar laid out for a fire.

Chapter 6(14)

Having spread out kusha grass on the ground, Rama controlled himself and attentively lay down there, spending three nights. But the careless ocean did not show himself to Rama,[49] despite Rama making every effort to show him the honour that he deserved and worshipping him. At this, Rama became angry at the ocean and the corners of his eyes turned red.

Lakshmana, with the auspicious marks, was near him and he said, 'O Lakshmana! Behold. An ignoble one has been worshipped. The ocean has not shown himself. This is arrogance. The qualities of virtuous ones—tranquility, forgiveness, uprightness and pleasantness in speech, are incapable of yielding fruits when directed at those devoid of qualities. The world regards a man who praises himself, is wicked and shameless, proceeds in a contrary direction and raises the rod of chastisement everywhere as someone who is virtuous. Conciliation is not capable of ensuring deeds. Conciliation is not capable of ensuring fame. O Lakshmana! Nor, in this world, can one obtain victory in the field of battle through that. Today, the makaras in this abode of makaras will be mangled with my arrows. O Soumitri! Behold. Everywhere, I will obstruct the flow of the water. O Lakshmana! Behold. I will mangle the giant snakes, the fish, the trunks of elephants[50] and the serpents. In the great encounter today, I will use my arrows to dry up the ocean, with its conch shells, nets of oysters, fish and makaras. This abode of makaras takes me to be someone who is forgiving. He considers me to be incapable. Shame on those who are forgiving towards such

[49] In personified form.

[50] Elephants in the water.

people. O Soumitri! Bring me my bow and the arrows that are like virulent serpents. Even if he cannot be agitated, I am angry and will agitate the ocean. The turbulent waves do not cross the shoreline. However, with my arrows, I will make Varuna's abode cross all boundaries.'

Saying this, with the bow in his hand, he dilated his eyes in rage. The invincible Rama looked like the blazing fire of destruction at the end of a *yuga*. He stretched his bow and made the world tremble with a terrible arrow. He released the fierce arrow, like Shatakratu does with the *vajra*. That excellent arrow blazed in its energy and was immensely forceful. It entered the waters of the ocean and terrified the serpents. With the large crocodiles and makaras and an extremely terrible wind, there was great turbulence in the ocean. A large garland of waves, filled with conch shells and oysters, spread out in every direction. Everywhere in the great ocean, there were violent waves full of smoke. With mouths flaming and eyes blazing, the serpents suffered. So did the immensely valiant danavas who resided in patala. Thousands of waves, like Vindhya and Mandara, leapt up in the king of the waters, filled with crocodiles and makaras. The torrent of waves whirled around, terrifying the serpents and the rakshasas. Giant crocodiles leapt up from the abode of the waters.

Chapter 6(15)

After this, from the middle of the ocean, Sagara[51] himself arose, like the sun arising atop the great mountain of Meru. The ocean was seen, together with serpents with flaming mouths. He was dressed in red garlands and garments and his eyes were like the petals of lotuses. He was adorned with molten gold and his complexion was like that of mild lapis lazuli. After having taken the valiant one's permission first, Sagara approached Raghava, with the bow and arrow in his hand. He joined his hands in salutation

[51] The personified form of the ocean.

and spoke these words. 'O Raghava! O amiable one! The earth, the wind, the sky, water and light are stationed in their natural states, following their eternal paths. I am also in my natural state. I am fathomless and cannot be leapt across. I am telling you that it will be unnatural for me not to be fathomless. O son of a king! My water is full of crocodiles and sharks and out of desire, avarice or fear, it is impossible for me to stupefy it. O Rama! I will arrange it so that you can cross over me. While the soldiers are crossing, the crocodiles will not strike. O amiable one! This one, named Nala, is Vishvakarma's son. Thanks to the boon bestowed on him by his father, he is Vishvakarma's equal. This ape, great in endeavour, will build a bridge over me and I will bear it. He is just like his father.' Having said this, the ocean vanished.

The immensely strong Nala, supreme among apes, arose and addressed Rama in these words. 'I will construct an extensive bridge over Varuna's abode. The great ocean has spoken the truth. I can resort to my father's capability. On Mandara, Vishvakarma granted my mother a boon. Vishvakarma said, "The son born through you will be my equal." Since I had not been asked, I had not spoken to you about my qualities. Therefore, let the bulls among the apes now fashion the bridge.'

Given their leave by Rama, hundreds of thousands of delighted leaders of the apes left in every direction and went to the great forest. The bulls among the apes resembled boulders and dragged boulders. The apes shattered these and started to drag them towards the ocean. The apes filled the ocean with salas, *ashvakarna*s, *dhava*s, bamboos, *kutaja*s, *arjuna*s, *tala*s, tilakas, timishas, *bilva*s, *saptaparna*s, blossoming *karnikara*s, mangos and ashoka trees. The supreme among apes brought some trees with roots, others without roots. Like Indra's standard, the apes raised up and dragged trees. Large boulders were violently hurled in and the waters surged up, touching the sky and then falling back again. In the middle of the lord of the male and female rivers, Nala constructed a gigantic bridge that was ten *yojana*s wide and one hundred yojanas long. Boulders were flung in. Boulders were thrown in there. At that time, a tumultuous sound arose within that great ocean. Thus, Nala constructed a beautiful and handsome bridge across the abode of the makaras. It was as radiant as Svati's path in the firmament.[52] Wishing to see this extraordinary sight, the gods, the gandharvas, the *siddhas*[53] and the supreme rishis arrived and stood there, in the sky. The apes roared. They leapt up and leapt down. This was unthinkable. This was impossible to believe. This was extraordinary and made the body hair stand up. All the creatures witnessed the bridge being built over the ocean. There were thousands of crores of greatly energetic apes. Having constructed the bridge across the ocean, they crossed over to the other shore of the great ocean. It was beautiful, large and constructed well. It was planned well and the path was smooth. The radiant and grand bridge could be seen like a line drawn through the ocean.

With a club in his hand, Vibhishana stood on the shore of the ocean. He stood there with his advisers, waiting to attack the enemy. The handsome Rama and Lakshmana were in front of the soldiers. With dharma in their souls, the archers were with Sugriva. Some apes passed along the middle, others passed through the sides. Others did not use that path, but leapt into the water. Some resorted to the sky and leapt across, like Suparna. The giant roar of the ocean was surpassed by their loud roars. The terrible army of the apes crossed over the terrible ocean. Using the bridge built by Nala, the army of the apes crossed. The king[54] made them camp at a spot on the shore where there were many roots and fruits and a lot of water. Raghava performed an extraordinary task that was very difficult to accomplish. On seeing this, the gods, together with the siddhas, the *charanas*[55] and the *maharshis*, approached Rama and separately sprinkled him with auspicious water. 'O god among men on earth! Defeat the enemy. Rule up to the frontiers of the ocean for an eternal number of years.' Thus was Rama, god among men, honoured and worshipped with many kinds of auspicious words.

[52] Meaning, not just the path of Svati nakshatra, but the entire Milky Way.
[53] Successful sages.
[54] Sugriva.
[55] Celestial bards.

Chapter 6(16)

Rama, Dasharatha's son, crossed the ocean with the army. The prosperous Ravana spoke to his two advisers, Shuka and Sarana. 'The entire army of the apes has crossed over the ocean, which is extremely difficult to cross. Rama's act of constructing a bridge across the ocean is unprecedented. I would never have been able to believe that a bridge could be constructed across the ocean. I must certainly pay attention to this army of the apes. Without being detected, the two of you penetrate the army of the apes and ascertain the number and valour of the foremost among the apes. Which advisers of Rama and Sugriva have assembled? Which brave apes are striding around in front? How was a bridge constructed over the ocean, full of water? Where have the great-souled apes camped? You must ascertain the truth about Rama's conduct, valour and weapons and those of the brave Lakshmana. Who are the commanders of the immensely energetic apes? To find the truth out about all this, the two of you must swiftly depart and return.' The two rakshasas, Shuka and Sarana, were commanded in this way. Those two brave ones adopted the forms of apes and entered the army of the apes. They found that army of apes to be unthinkable and their body hair stood up. Shuka and Sarana were unable to count their number. Everywhere, there were some who had crossed, some who were crossing and some who wished to cross. Some had camped, others were setting up camp. There was a terrible roar from that loud army.

Though those two immensely energetic ones, Shuka and Sarana, were disguised, Vibhishana detected and captured them and spoke to Rama. 'O destroyer of enemy cities! These two are spies and have come here from Lanka.' Seeing Rama, those two were distressed and lost all hopes of remaining alive. Terrified, they joined their hands in salutation and spoke these words. 'O amiable one! Sent by Ravaṇa, the two of us have come here. O descendant of the Raghu lineage! We were to find out everything about your army.'

Hearing their words, Rama, Dasharatha's son, engaged in the welfare of all beings, laughed and said, 'Have you seen the entire army? Have you examined us well? Have you accomplished the task you were told to? If you have, return at ease. When you enter the city of Lanka, exactly recount the words I speak to the king of the rakshasas, the younger brother of the lord of riches. "When you abducted Sita, you resorted to your strength. As you wish, display that, with your soldiers and your relatives. When it is tomorrow, you will see me use my arrows to destroy the city of Lanka, with its gates and ramparts, and the army of the rakshasas. O Ravana! Use all your strength to free yourself from my rage. When it is tomorrow, I will be like Vasava with his vajra, unleashing his vajra on the danavas."'

Having been thus commanded, the two rakshasas, Shuka and Sarana, praised Raghava for being devoted to dharma and said, 'May you be victorious.' They went to the city of Lanka and spoke to the lord of the rakshasas. 'O lord of the rakshasas! We were captured by Vibhishana and deserved to be killed. However, on seeing us, the infinitely energetic Rama, with dharma in his soul, freed us. The four bulls among men are in the same place. They are brave, like the guardians of the world. They are accomplished in the use of weapons and are firm in their valour. They are Rama, Dasharatha's son, the handsome Lakshmana, Vibhishana and the greatly energetic Sugriva, who is like the great Indra in his prowess. Even if all the other apes remain standing, these are capable of uprooting and flinging away the city of Lanka, with its gates and its ramparts. Rama's weapons are just as his form is. Even if the other three remain standing, he can single-handedly destroy the city of Lanka. The army is protected by Rama, Lakshmana and Sugriva. All of them are invincible, even to the gods and the asuras. The forms of the residents of the forest are joyous and they have standards. The residents of the forest have arrived, desiring to fight. Enough of this enmity. Peace is indicated. Give Maithilee back to Dasharatha's son.'

Chapter 6(17)

Not scared, Sarana spoke these words, which were like medication. King Ravana heard them and replied to Sarana.

'Even if the gods, the gandharvas and the danavas attack me, even if there is fear from all the worlds, I will not give Sita away. O amiable one! You have been severely oppressed by the apes and are terrified. That is the reason you now think that returning Sita will be a virtuous deed. What is the name of the enemy who is capable of defeating me in a battle?' Ravana, the lord of the rakshasas, spoke these harsh words. Having spoken them, he ascended to the top of his palace, as white as snow in complexion. It was as tall as many palm trees put together. Ravana wished to see for himself. Ravana was senseless with rage and he was with the two spies. He looked at the ocean, the mountains and the forests. He saw that the entire ground was filled with apes. He saw that the end of that large army of innumerable apes could not be seen.

Beholding this, King Ravana asked Sarana, 'Among the foremost of apes, who are the brave and extremely strong ones? In every direction, which ones, great in enterprise, will advance in front? Whom will Sugriva listen to? Who are leaders among the leaders? O Sarana! Tell me everything. Who are the chiefs among the apes?'

Using these words, the Indra among the rakshasas asked Sarana. Among the residents of the forest, he[56] told him about the ones who were foremost among the foremost. 'There is an ape standing there, facing Lanka. He seems to be dancing. He is surrounded by hundreds and thousands of leaders. Everything in Lanka, the walls and the ramparts, the mountains, the forests and the groves, are trembling because of his loud roar. He is stationed in front of all the Indras among the apes in Sugriva's army. This brave and great-souled leader is named Nila. There is another valiant one whose arms are raised upwards. He is stamping on the ground with his feet. He is yawning and is looking towards Lanka with rage. He is like the summit of a mountain and his complexion is like the filament of a lotus. In great anger, he is repeatedly lashing his tail. The ten directions are resounding with the sound of his tail. Sugriva has instated him as the heir apparent in the kingdom of the apes. His name is Angada and he is challenging you in the encounter.

[56] Sarana.

There are some apes who are tightening their bodies and slapping them. They are roaring. These bulls among apes have got up and are yawning in anger. They are terrible and impossible to withstand. They are fierce and awesome in valour. There are ten billion and one million of these brave ones, camped in that sandalwood grove. They are following one who wishes to attack Lanka and crush it with his own army. He possesses the complexion of silver and he is Shveta. He has his army and he is terrible in valour. This intelligent and brave ape is famous in the three worlds. He is the one who swiftly approached Sugriva and has gone back again, dividing his army into many separate battalions and delighting them. In front of the banks of the Gomatee, there is Mount Ramya. It is also named Samkochana and that mountain is full of many kinds of trees. A leader named Kumuda used to rule over that kingdom. He is the one who is followed by one lakh of apes. He possesses a long tail and his extensive body hair is extremely long, coppery brown, yellow, black and white. He is the performer of terrible deeds. He is spirited, angry and terrible and desires to fight. He hopes that he will crush Lanka with his own army alone. There is one who is like a lion, with a long and tawny mane. Standing alone, he is looking at Lanka, as if he will burn it down with his eyes. O king! This handsome one always dwells on Vindhya, the dark mountain, and Mount Sahya. This is the leader named Rambha. There is one whom four hundred thousand leaders among apes have surrounded and are following, as the energetic one advances to crush Lanka. He is shaking his ears and repeatedly yawning. He does not abandon his herd and death cannot defeat him. He is immensely strong and without fear. O king! He always dwells on the beautiful Salvyeya mountain. He is the leader named Sharabha. O king! All these powerful leaders are known as *vihara*s.[57] There are one lakh and forty thousand of them. They are stationed there, like giant clouds that have covered the sky. The great sound of drums can be heard in the midst of those brave apes. Those foremost and terrible apes desire to fight. In their midst, like Indra among the gods, there is the

[57] Those who wander around.

leader named Panasa, who is impossible to withstand in a battle. He always resides on the supreme mountain of Pariyatra. He is foremost among all leaders and in different formations, there are one lakh and fifty thousand who serve him. He is in the midst of that terrible and radiant army that is marching along, looking like a second ocean along the shores of the ocean. This is the leader named Vinata, who is like Dardara.[58] He roams around, drinking the waters of the river Parnasha, supreme among rivers.[59] The leader named Krathana is summoning six lakh ape soldiers to come and do battle. That ape nourishes a body that is ochre in complexion. This is the energetic Gavaya and he is angrily advancing against you. There are seven lakh and seventy thousand who serve him. He is saying that he will crush Lanka with his army alone. These are the foremost leaders among leaders. They are terrible and impossible to withstand. They are strong and can assume any form at will. They cannot be numbered.'

Chapter 6(18)

'I[60] will tell you about the brave leaders you are looking at. For Raghava's sake, they are ready to give up their lives. There is one who has a lot of thick and soft hair on his tail—coppery, yellow, black and white. He is terrible in his deeds. This is a leader named Hara, who seems to be dragging the earth and seizing the radiant rays of the sun. There are one hundred thousand following him at the rear, holding up trees and eager to climb into Lanka. O destroyer of enemy cities! There are thousands of crores of greatly energetic apes. They wish to fight against you and be victorious. You can see the ones who are stationed there, like dark and large clouds. They are like masses of black collyrium. They possess the valour of truth

[58] The mountain, also known as Dardura.

[59] Parnasha is identified with the river Banas, in Rajasthan. That is, Vinata used to reside in that region earlier.

[60] This is a continuation of Sarana speaking.

in an encounter. Those brave ones use nails and teeth as weapons. They are fierce in their anger and lead to fear. They are innumerable and cannot be discerned, like another shore to the distant shore of the ocean. O king! There is one who is in the midst of extremely terrible bears who reside in mountains, uneven regions and rivers. O king! He is like Parjanya, surrounded in every direction by clouds. He is the one who resides in the supreme mountain known as Rikshavanta, drinking the waters of the Narmada. He is the lord of all the bears and he is the leader named Dhumra. Behold his younger brother, who is like a mountain. He is like his brother in beauty and superior to him in valour. He is the great leader of the forces, named Jambavat. He may be truculent towards his seniors, but he is intolerant in striking. When the gods and the asuras fought, Jambavat helped and performed an extremely great deed for the intelligent Shakra. Consequently, he obtained many boons. Having ascended the summits of mountains, they[61] hurl down gigantic boulders that are huge in size, resembling large clouds. They are not scared of dying. They possess hair and are like rakshasas and pishachas. A large number of his soldiers are wandering around, as energetic as the fire. That wrathful one is stationed amidst the apes. Stationed there, all the apes are looking towards this leader among leaders. O king! This lord of apes worships the one with the one thousand eyes. With an army of strong soldiers, he is the leader named Rambha. There is the one who has advanced for one yojana along that mountain and has hauled his body up the mountain for one yojana. He is supreme in his beauty and his four feet can be seen. He is known by the name of Samnadana and he is the grandfather of the apes. In a battle, he fought against the intelligent Shakra, but was not defeated in that encounter. He is a leader among leaders. His valour is like Shakra's prowess. In former times, to help the residents of heaven in the battle between the gods and the asuras, this one, with a black tail, was born from a gandharva maiden. O lord of the rakshasas! King Vaishravana,[62] your brother, always sports

[61] Jambavat's soldiers.

[62] Kubera.

happily on an Indra among mountains, frequented by *kinnaras*.[63] This handsome and bull among apes resides there, seated under a *jambu* tree. He never indulges in boasting in an encounter and he is the leader named Krathana. He is stationed there, surrounded by one thousand crore apes. He hopes that he will crush Lanka with his own army. There is the one who wanders around the Ganga, terrifying the leaders of elephants and remembering the old enmity between elephants and apes. This leader and commander of a herd is advancing, uprooting trees. He is the one who resides in caves in mountains. This foremost leader in the army of the apes resides on Mount Ushirabija, along the river Haimavati, and is like Mandara. This best among apes finds pleasure, like Shakra himself in heaven. O king! There is the extremely intolerant leader named Pramathi and one hundred thousand follow him. You can see him, like a cloud that has been raised by the wind. As he circles around, a large quantity of dust is raised. There are extremely strong and terrible *golangulas*[64] with black faces. You can see that one crore of them have crossed the bridge. The extremely swift Gavaksha is the leader of the golangulas. Surrounding him, those energetic ones are advancing towards Lanka, to crush it. There is a place where trees yield all the fruits that one desires and are worshipped by the bees. He resides on that mountain, which has a complexion like the hue of the sun. Its[65] radiance always dazzles and thus lends its hue to the birds and the animals. The great-souled maharshis never forsake its slopes. O king! He finds pleasure on that beautiful Mount Kanchana. He is foremost among the foremost apes and he is the leader named Kesari. There are sixty thousand peaks in the beautiful Mount Kanchana. O unblemished one! Like you among the rakshasas, there is an excellent peak among them. Tawny brown, white and copper-coloured, with honey-brown faces, they reside on that excellent peak, with teeth and nails as weapons. They possess four teeth, like lions. They are as invincible as tigers. All

[63] Kinnara, also known as *kimpurusha*, is a semi-divine species, described as Kubera's companions.

[64] With a tail like that of a cow, langur.

[65] The mountain's.

of them blaze like the fire and are like virulent poison. Like crazy elephants, they raise their extremely long tails. They are like giant mountains and their roar is like that of large clouds. There is a valiant leader who is stationed amidst them. O king! He is famous on earth by the name of Shatabali. He hopes to crush Lanka with his army alone. Gaja, Gavaksha, Gavaya, Nala and the ape Nila—each one of these leaders is surrounded by ten crores. That apart, there are other foremost apes who reside on Mount Vindhya. They are dexterous in their valour and it is impossible to enumerate their large numbers. O great king! All of them are extremely powerful. All of them have bodies that are like large mountains. In an instant, all of them are capable of hurling down boulders and shattering the earth.'

Chapter 6(19)

Hearing Sarana's words, Ravana, the lord of the rakshasas, looked at the entire army. Shuka then addressed him in these words. 'You can see them stationed there, like large and crazy elephants. O king! They are like *nyagrodha* trees[66] along the Ganga or sala trees in the Himalayas. They are extremely difficult to counter. They are strong and can assume any form at will. They are like *daitya*s and danavas. In a battle, their valour is like that of the gods. There are twenty one thousand crores, one thousand *shanku*s and one hundred *vrinda*s of them.[67] These are Sugriva's advisers and they always make their homes in Kishkindha. These apes have been born from gods and gandharvas and they can assume any form at will. You can see two young ones stationed there and they are like the gods in their forms. These two are Mainda and Dvivida and no one can equal them in battle. With Brahma's permission, these two have partaken of amrita. In the battle, they hope to crush

[66] The Indian fig tree.

[67] These numbers are explained later.

Lanka with their energy alone. You can see an angry ape stationed there, like an elephant with a shattered temple.[68] He can agitate the ocean with his strength. O lord! He is the one who came to Lanka and met Vaidehi and you. This is the ape you saw earlier and he has come again. He is the eldest son of Kesari and is known to be the son of the wind god. He is famous as Hanumat and he is the one who leapt across the ocean. This best among apes can assume any form at will and he is full of strength and beauty. Everywhere, his progress is always unimpeded, like that of the lord.[69] When he was a child, he saw the rising sun and wished to drink it up. He leapt up three thousand yojanas and descended again. "I will seize the sun and thus satisfy my hunger." Intoxicated by his strength, this was his thought in earlier times. The sun god, rising above Mount Udaya, cannot be touched by the gods, the rishis and the danavas. Unable to reach it, he fell down. When the ape fell down, his jaw was broken on a slope of the mountain. Since his jaw was firm, it was broken only a little. That is the reason he is Hanumat. I know the truth about the ape through *yoga* and *agama*.[70] I am incapable of describing his strength, beauty and power. Using his energy, he hopes to single-handedly crush Lanka. After him, there is the brave and dark one, with eyes like the petals of lotuses. He is an *atiratha*[71] of the Ikshvaku lineage, famous in the world because of his manliness. He never deviates from dharma and never crosses dharma. He knows about *brahmastra*[72] and he is supreme among those who possess knowledge about the Vedas. He shatters the sky with his arrows and even shatters mountains. His anger is like that of Death and his valour is like that of Shakra. From Janasthana, you abducted his wife, Sita. O king! He is Rama and he has come to fight against you in the encounter. There is one on his right, with a complexion like that of pure molten gold. His chest is broad and his eyes are coppery red. His hair is black and curled. This is his

[68] An elephant in musth.

[69] Vayu.

[70] Keeping it simple, agama is a class of sacred texts that are outside the mainstream.

[71] An atiratha is a great warrior, greater than a *maharatha*.

[72] Brahma's weapon.

brother Lakshmana and he loves him more than his own life. He is accomplished in good policy and fighting and he is learned in all the sacred texts. He is intolerant, impossible to defeat, victorious, valiant, intelligent and strong. He has always been like Rama's right arm, as if his[73] breath of life is coursing outside his body. For Raghava's sake, he does not bother about preserving his own life. He hopes that in the battle, he will slay all the rakshasas. There is one who is standing on Rama's left flank. He is protected by rakshasas and he is King Vibhishana. This prosperous one was consecrated as a king of kings in Lanka.[74] He is angry with you and is advancing in the battle. You can see someone stationed in the middle, like an immobile mountain. He is the unvanquished master of all the foremost apes, possessing energy, fame, intelligence, learning and noble birth. This ape is as radiant as the Himalaya mountains. He resides in Kishkindha, with its impenetrable caves and trees. He dwells there, with the foremost apes, in a fortification in the mountains that is impossible to penetrate. He wears a golden and radiant garland, with one hundred lotuses. Lakshmi, loved by gods and humans, is established in him. After slaying Vali, Rama gave this Sugriva this garland, Tara and the eternal kingdom of the apes. One hundred thousand crores is said to be a shanku and such numbers are advancing to fight in the cause of Sugriva, Indra among the apes.[75] O great king! Look at this army, which has presented itself, like a flaming planet. Therefore, great efforts are recommended, so that we are victorious and the enemy is defeated.'

Chapter 6(20)

Ravana saw the leaders of the apes who were indicated by Shuka, his own brother Vibhishana, stationed near Rama,

[73] Rama's.

[74] By Rama.

[75] The Critical Edition excises shlokas where one hundred thousand shankus are said to be a *mahashanku* and one hundred thousand mahashankus are said to be a vrinda.

the immensely valorous Lakshmana who was like Rama's right arm and Sugriva, the king of the apes, terrible in his valour. Somewhat anxious in his mind, he became angry. After the end of the conversation, he reprimanded the two brave ones, Shuka and Sarana. In an angry voice that was full of intolerance, he addressed them in these harsh words. 'Those like you should not earn a living as advisers. You have spoken disagreeable words to the king, the lord who can reward and punish you. The enemy is acting against us and has invaded, seeking a battle. Both of you have uttered words of praise about those who should not be applauded. Your service to your preceptors, seniors and the aged has been futile. Though you earn a living from the sacred texts on royal policy, you have not grasped the essence. Even if you have grasped, you have not understood. Or the burden of knowledge has confused you. With such foolish advisers, it is fortunate that I am still here. Are you not scared of death that you have addressed me in these harsh words? This is the tongue that commands you and confers good and bad on you. Even if they are touched by a fire, trees may remain in a forest. However, if one is touched by a crime committed against the king, the criminal no longer remains. These two wicked ones have praised the side of the enemy and I should kill them. However, the former good deeds done by them have made my anger mild. Go far away from here and do not be seen near me. Remembering the good deeds you have done to me, I do not wish to kill you. Though you are ungrateful and have turned your faces away from me, because of my affection, I am going to treat you as if you are already dead.' Thus addressed, Shuka and Sarana were ashamed. Saying, 'May you be victorious,' they withdrew from Ravana's presence.

Mahodara was near him and Dashagriva spoke to him. 'Quickly bring spies, who are accomplished in good policy, here.' Following the command of the king, spies were swiftly summoned. They joined their hands in salutation and presented themselves, pronouncing benedictions of prosperity and victory. Those spies were faithful, brave, devoted and bereft of fear. Ravana, the lord of the rakshasas, addressed them in these words. 'Leave this place. Go and test Rama's behaviour towards his close ministers and among those who have assembled, the ones who are pleased with him. When does he sleep? When is he awake? What else does he do? Use your skills to ascertain everything completely and then return. If kings get to know about the enemy through learned spies, in the course of the encounter, the enemy can be restrained with only a little bit of effort.' The spies were delighted and agreed. Placing Shardula at the forefront, they circumambulated the lord of the rakshasas. They then left for the spot where Rama and Lakshmana were.

Disguising themselves, they approached Mount Suvela and saw Rama, Lakshmana, Sugriva and Vibhishana. However, those rakshasas were detected by Vibhishana, the Indra among rakshasas, with dharma in his soul. He had them easily captured. They were afflicted by the brave ones who were dexterous in their valour and lost their senses.[76] Sighing, they reached Lanka again. These spies roamed around in the night and always wandered around outside.[77] They presented themselves before Dashagriva and told him that an extremely large body of soldiers were camped near Mount Suvela.

Chapter 6(21)

The spies informed the lord of Lanka that an army that could not be agitated was camped near Mount Suvela. They also told him about Raghava. Ravana heard from the spies that the immensely strong Rama had arrived. Somewhat anxious, he addressed Shardula in these words. 'O one who roams around in the night! Your complexion is distressed and not what it should be. I hope you did not come under the subjugation of the wrathful enemy.'

Thus asked, Shardula became senseless with fear. He softly addressed the tiger among rakshasas. 'O king! I was incapable of

[76] The dexterity in valour refers to the apes. The Critical Edition excises shlokas where Rama orders for the release of the spies.

[77] That is, outside the city.

spying on those bulls among apes. They are valiant and strong and are protected by Raghava. I was incapable of conversing with them or questioning them. The apes, resembling mountains, protected the path in every direction. In disguise, no sooner had I penetrated that army, than I was forcibly captured by many and they oppressed me in diverse ways. I was severely struck with thighs, fists, teeth and palms. Those powerful and intolerant apes paraded me around. Conveyed all over the place, I was taken to Rama's presence. All my limbs were covered in blood. I was distracted and my senses were in a whirl. When the apes sought to kill me, I joined my hands in salutation and beseeched them. Raghava saved me and gave me scope to live as I chose. Rama has filled the great ocean with rocks and boulders. With his weapons, he has reached Lanka's gate and is stationed there. Everywhere, he is surrounded by the apes, who are arranged in the form of a Garuda *vyuha*.[78] Having released me, the immensely energetic one is advancing towards Lanka. Before he reaches the ramparts of the city, quickly do something. Either swiftly give him Sita, or grant him an excellent fight.' Hearing this, the lord of the rakshasas was tormented in his mind. Ravana addressed Shardula in these great words. 'Even if the gods and the gandharvas fight against me and even if there is fear from all the worlds, I will not return Sita.'

Having said this, the immensely energetic Ravana spoke again. 'When you spied on the army, who were the brave apes who were present there? What kind of power do those invincible apes possess? Whose sons and grandsons are they? O rakshasa! Tell me the truth about this. One should certainly decide to fight after knowing about their strengths and weaknesses and about the size of the army.' Shardula, the excellent spy, was addressed by Ravana in this way. In Ravana's presence, he started to speak these words. 'O king! Riksharaja's son[79] is extremely difficult to vanquish in a battle. Gadgada's son is known by the name of Jambavat. There is another one of Gadgada's sons. There

[78] A vyuha is a battle formation, this one shaped in the form of Garuda.

[79] Sugriva.

is another one who is the son of Shatakratu's preceptor.[80] It is his son who single-handedly created the carnage among the rakshasas. Sushena, with dharma in his soul, is the valiant son of Dharma.[81] O king! The amiable ape, Dadhimukha, is Soma's son. Sumukha, Durmukha and the ape Vegadarshi are like Death in the form of apes. Indeed, they were created by Svayambhu himself. Nila, the commander, is the son of the fire god himself. The son of the wind god is famous by the name of Hanumat. The young, invincible and strong Angada is Shakra's grandson. The powerful Mainda and Dvivida have been born from the two Ashvins. Vaivasvata[82] has five sons there and they are like Death, the destroyer—Gaja, Gavaksha, Gavaya, Sharabha and Gandhamadana. Shveta and Jyotirmukha have been born from the sun god. The ape Hemakuta is Varuna's son. The brave Nala, supreme among apes, is Vishvakarma's son. The brave and swift Sudurdhara is the son of the Vasus. There are ten crore apes who desire to fight. I am incapable of recounting the other handsome sons of the gods. Dasharatha's young son can withstand a lion. He is the one who killed Dushana, Khara and Trishira. There is no one on earth who is Rama's equal in valour. He is the one who killed Viradha and Kabandha, who was like Death. There is no man on earth who can narrate Rama's qualities. The rakshasas who went to Janasthana were slain by him. Lakshmana, with dharma in his soul, is a bull among elephants. Someone who comes in the path of his arrows, even if it is Vasava, will not remain alive. Your brother, Vibhishana, is supreme among the rakshasas. Having accepted the city of Lanka,[83] he is engaged in ensuring Raghava's welfare. I have thus told you everything about the army of the apes. They have camped on Mount Suvela. You should decide what needs to be done next.'

[80] Shatakratu's preceptor is Brihasapati and Brihaspati's son is Kesari. Hanumat is Kesari's son.

[81] Meaning Yama.

[82] Yama.

[83] As a gift from Rama, when Rama consecrated Vibhishana as the king of Lanka.

Chapter 6(22)

The spies told the king of Lanka that Raghava and an army that could not be agitated was camped on Mount Suvela. Through the spies, Ravana heard that the immensely strong Rama had arrived. He was somewhat anxious and spoke to his advisers. 'O advisers! All of you control yourselves and come quickly. O rakshasas! The time for consultations has arrived.' Hearing his words, the ministers swiftly arrived. He consulted with his rakshasa advisers. The invincible one consulted about what should be done next. Then, having granted permission to the advisers to leave, he entered his own residence.

He summoned the immensely strong rakshasa, Vidyujjihva.[84] With the one who was skilled in maya, the one who was great in the use of maya[85] entered the spot where Maithilee was. The lord of the rakshasas told Vidyujjihva, who knew about maya. 'Use your maya to confound Sita, Janaka's daughter. O one who roams around in the night! Use your maya to create Raghava's head. Fashion a great bow and arrows and present yourself before me.' Thus instructed, Vidyujjihva, who roamed around in the night, agreed. He used his maya well and showed Ravana the result. The king was satisfied at this and gave him some ornaments.

The immensely strong one entered Ashokavana. The younger brother of the lord of riches saw the one who was in distress, though she did not deserve to be distressed. Overwhelmed by grief, she was seated on the ground, with her face lowered down. She sorrowed in Ashokavana, thinking about her husband. Near her, terrible rakshasis tended to her. Having approached Sita, he happily pronounced his name. He spoke these insolent words to Janaka's daughter. 'O fortunate one! You comforted yourself by thinking about your husband Raghava, the slayer of Khara. However, he has been killed in the battle. I have killed him and the foundation of your pride has been severed in every possible way. O Sita!

[84] Vidyut-Jihva.

[85] Respectively Vidyujjihva and Ravana.

Because of the calamity you face, you will now become my wife. O foolish one! You pride yourself on being learned. Withdraw from something that has little merit. O Sita! Hear the account of your husband being killed, as terrible as Vritra's death. Indeed, Raghava crossed the ocean and attacked, so as to kill me. He was surrounded by a large army that had been brought together by the Indra among the apes. This reached and camped on the southern shore of the ocean. Rama arrived with this large army when the sun was about to set. They were exhausted at the end of the journey. The army was stationed there, happily asleep. In the middle of the night, the first spies approached it. My large army was led by Prahasta and reached the spot where Rama and Lakshmana were. His large army was destroyed at night. The attacking rakshasas repeatedly raised their weapons—spears, clubs, swords, *chakra*s, large iron staffs, nets of arrows, javelins, radiant and spiked maces, daggers, lances, spikes, chakras[86] and bludgeons to bring down the apes. While Rama was asleep, Prahasta struck him. Without anyone restraining his hand, he used a large sword to sever his head. Vibhishana was attacked and captured easily. It is through good fortune that Lakshmana and all the soldiers of the apes fled in different directions. O Sita! Sugriva, the lord of the apes, had his neck broken. With his jawbone shattered, Hanumat was slain by the rakshasas and is lying down. Just as Jambavat rose up on his knees, he was killed in the battle. He was severed with many javelins, just as a tree is cut down. Mainda and Dvivida, the bulls among the apes, have been killed. They sighed and wept and were covered in blood. Struck in the middle, those slayers of enemies were killed with the sword. Lying down on the ground, Panasa screamed. Mangled by many iron arrows, Darimukha is lying down in a pit. While he was shrieking, the greatly energetic Kumuda was killed by arrows. The rakshasas struck Angada's body with many arrows. With blood flowing from his body, Angada fell down on the ground. Some apes were crushed, caught in the nets of elephants and chariots. Lying down, they were dispersed, like clouds by the

[86] The word chakra is mentioned twice.

force of the wind. Others were terrified and fled, but were pursued and killed by the rakshasas while they fled, like large elephants by lions. Some fell down in the ocean. Some resorted to the sky. The bears, mingling with the apes, climbed trees. There were many with tawny eyes and disfigured eyes who were killed by the rakshasas along the shores of the ocean, in mountains and in forests. Thus, my soldiers killed your husband and his soldiers. This head, wet with blood and smeared with dust, has been seized.'

After this, the extremely unassailable Ravana, lord of the rakshasas, spoke to the rakshasis in Sita's hearing. 'Fetch the rakshasa Vidyujjihva, the performer of cruel deeds. He is the one who himself collected Raghava's head from the field of battle.' Vidyujjihva brought the head and the bow and arrows. He bowed his head down and stood in front of Ravana. King Ravana spoke to the rakshasa Vidyujjihva, the one with a large tongue, who was stationed there, asking him to come closer. 'Quickly place the head of Dasharatha's son in front of Sita. It is best that the pitiable one sees the final state of her husband.' Thus addressed, the rakshasa flung down the beloved head before Sita and quickly vanished. Ravana flung down the large and radiant bow and said, 'This is Rama's, famous in the three worlds. This is truly Rama's bow, which makes a sound when it is twanged. After having killed the human in the night, Prahasta brought it here.' With the head flung down by Vidyujjihva, Ravana flung the bow down on the ground. He told the illustrious daughter of the king of Videha, 'Submit yourself to me.'

Chapter 6(23)

Sita saw the head and the excellent bow. She heard about the destruction of Sugriva and Hanumat. The eyes and the complexion of the face were just like her husband's face. So were the tips of the hair, the forehead and the auspicious *chudamani*.[87]

[87] Jewel worn on the top of the head.

She was convinced because of all these signs and became extremely miserable. She shrieked like a female curlew and condemned Kaikeyee. 'O Kaikeyee! May your wishes come true. The delight of the lineage has been killed. O one who is devoted to dissensions! You have destroyed the entire lineage. O Kaikeyee! What harm did the noble Rama do to you? Why did you exile him to the forest, with bark as garb?' Trembling, the ascetic Vaidehi said this. Like a severed plantain tree, the young one fell down on the ground. In a short while, she regained her senses and comforted herself. The large-eyed one inhaled the fragrance of the head and lamented. 'Alas! O mighty-armed one! I have been destroyed. I have followed one who was brave in his vows. This is your final state and I have become a widow. It is said that if a husband dies first, that is a bad quality in a woman. However, since you are good and virtuous in your conduct, you have departed before me. From one sorrow, I have moved to another sorrow. I am immersed in an ocean of grief. The one who stirred himself to save me has himself been brought down. O Raghava! You are the son of my mother-in-law, Kousalya. You were like a calf and she was like a cow. She is like a cow without her calf. O one whose valour is unthinkable! There are those who said that you would live for a long time. They uttered a lie. O Raghava! Your lifespan has been limited. Perhaps your wisdom was destroyed. Perhaps, despite your wisdom, your virtue was destroyed.[88] Perhaps this is the power of destiny, which cooks creatures. You knew about the sacred texts of good policy. How could your death not have been foreseen? You were skilled in discerning hardships and accomplished in avoiding them. Thus, you have been embraced by the terrible and extremely violent night of destruction. O lotus-eyed one! You have been killed and have been taken away from me. O mighty-armed one! Abandoning me, the ascetic one, you are lying down. O bull among men! Like a beloved woman, you are embracing the auspicious earth. I have always worshipped your beloved bow carefully, with fragrances and garlands. O brave one! This is it, decorated with

[88] Thus the destruction.

gold. O unblemished one! In heaven, it is certain that you have met your father and my father-in-law, Dasharatha, together with the earlier ancestors. Having performed great and beloved deeds, you have become a nakshatra in the sky. But in the process, you have neglected your own auspicious lineage of royal sages.[89] O king! Why are you not looking at me? Why are you not replying to me? I am your wife and have been your companion, since the time you were a boy and obtained me, as a girl. You accepted my hand and took a pledge, "I will travel with you." O Kakutstha! Remember that. I am extremely miserable. Take me with you. O supreme among those who reach their destinations! Why have you departed, leaving me? I am extremely miserable. I have been left in this world and you have gone to that world. This body was embraced by me and deserves to be adorned with fortunate objects. It is certainly being dragged by predatory beasts now. Why have you not obtained *agnishtoma*, *agnihotra* and other sacrifices and rites, with plenty of *dakshina*,[90] and not been honoured properly?[91] In her grief, Kousalya wishes to see us. Three of us left on the exile and she will only see Lakshmana return. When she asks him, he will certainly tell her how the army of your friends and you were killed by the rakshasas in the night. She will hear that you have been killed while asleep and that I am in the residence of the rakshasas. O Raghava! Her heart will be shattered. O Ravana! It is best that you bring me down on top of Rama. Perform this excellent and fortunate deed and unite the husband with the wife. Join my head with his head and my body with his body. O Ravana! I will follow and reach the destination obtained by my great-souled husband. I do not wish to remain alive even for an instant, because that would be a wicked life. In my father's house, I have heard brahmanas who are learned in the Vedas speak about this. Those women who love their husbands obtain great worlds. He possessed forgiveness, self-control, truthfulness, dharma, gratefulness and non-violence towards all beings. When he is dead, what will happen to me?' Tormented by grief, thus did the

[89] Presumably, by not leaving a descendant.
[90] Sacrificial fee. These were donated symbolically.
[91] As funeral rites.

large-eyed one lament, as Janaka's daughter beheld her husband's head and the bow there.

While Sita was lamenting there, a rakshasa joined his hands in salutation and approached his master. He said, 'O son of a noble one! May you be victorious.' He greeted him, obtained his favours and informed him that Prahasta, the commander of the army, had arrived. 'O lord! All the advisers are well and Prahasta has come with them. Please see them. There is some urgent task that needs to be undertaken.' Hearing what the rakshasa had said, Dashagriva left Ashokavana to go and see the ministers. He entered the assembly hall. Knowing about Rama's valour, he consulted with all his capable ministers about what he should himself do next. Within a short while after Ravana's departure, the head and the excellent bow vanished. The Indra among rakshasas held consultations with his capable ministers, who were terrible in their valour. He determined what he should do about Rama. Ravana, the lord of the rakshasas, was like Death. Wishing his welfare, the commanders of the battalions were stationed near him. He told them, 'Quickly beat a drum with a stick. Make the sound be heard and summon the soldiers. Do not tell them the reason.' The commanders of the battalions followed his instructions and swiftly assembled a large army. They informed their master, who desired to fight, that the forces had been summoned.

Chapter 6(24)

On seeing that Sita was confounded, her beloved friend, a rakshasi named Sarama,[92] quickly approached her beloved Vaidehi. Ravana had asked her to protect Sita and contract her friendship. However, she was compassionate and was firm in her vows and actually protected her. Sarama saw that her friend, Sita,

[92] Sarama is believed to have been Vibhishana's wife, although nothing like that is clearly stated.

had lost her senses. Having rolled around on the ground like a mare, she had just arisen and was covered with dust. Affectionately, the one who was good in her vows comforted her friend. 'O timid one! Because of my affection towards you as a friend, I have myself overheard everything that Ravana told you and what you said in reply. I abandoned all fear of Ravana and hid myself in the desolate sky. O large-eyed one! That was because of you and I do not care for my own life. There is a reason why the lord of the rakshasas was scared and left. O Maithilee! I know everything about the reason for his departure. Rama knows about his soul. It is not possible to approach the tiger among men when he is asleep and kill him. The apes fight with trees and it is not possible to kill them, even by the gods. They are extremely well protected by Rama and the bull among the gods.[93] The handsome one has long and rounded arms. He is powerful and his chest is broad. He is an archer who can withstand everything. He possesses dharma in his soul and is famous on earth. He is valiant and always protects himself and others. He is with his accomplished brother, Lakshmana, who knows the sacred texts about good policy. He is the one who slays large tides of enemy soldiers. His strength and manliness are unthinkable. O Sita! It is not possible for the handsome Raghava, the slayer of enemies, to be killed. The one who acts against all creatures has done this with his perverted intelligence. The one who knows about maya has invoked a terrible maya on you. All your miseries have now gone and your good fortune has presented itself. It is certain that prosperity will now serve you. Hear the most pleasant tidings of all. With the army of the apes, Rama has crossed the ocean. Having reached the southern shore of the ocean, they have camped there. I have seen Kakutstha, with Lakshmana, accomplish this objective. Protected by the army, the two of them are stationed there, near the ocean. He[94] sent some rakshasas who were dexterous in their valour. They have brought the news here, that Raghava has crossed the ocean. O large-eyed one! Having heard this, Ravana, the lord

[93] Indra.

[94] Ravana.

of the rakshasas, is consulting all his advisers about what should be done.'

While the rakshasi Sarama was telling Sita this, a terrible sound was heard, signifying that the soldiers were making all kinds of efforts. The sound of sticks struck against musical instruments was heard and the loud sound of drums. Sweet in speech, Sarama told Sita, 'O timid one! The terrible sound of drums is indicative of a war starting. Listen to the deep rumbling of drums, like the sound of clouds. Crazy elephants are being readied. Horses are being yoked to chariots. Here and there, foot soldiers are arming and preparing themselves. The royal roads are full of soldiers who are extraordinary to behold. The forceful ones are roaring, like waves of water in the ocean. There are sparkling weapons, armour and shields. The chariots, horses, elephants and the rakshasas have been ornamented. Behold the many kinds of radiance, of different hues, that have been created. It has the form of the fire, when it burns down a forest during the summer. Hear the sound of the bells. Hear the clatter of the chariots. Hear the horses neighing. Hear the blaring of the trumpets. A tumultuous sound has been created by the rakshasas preparing themselves and it makes the body hair stand up. Shri, the destroyer of sorrow, serves you. A fear has arisen for the rakshasas from the lotus-eyed Rama, like for the daityas from Vasava. He has conquered his rage and his valour is unthinkable. Having defeated and killed Ravana in the battle, your husband will come before you. With Lakshmana, your husband will exhibit his valour against the rakshasas. Among the enemy, he will be like Vishnu, the slayer of enemies, accompanied by Vasava. Rama will quickly arrive and you will be on his lap. With the enemy brought down, I will see you accomplish your objective. O beautiful one! When the one with the broad chest approaches you and embraces you against his chest, you will shed tears of joy. O queen! You have sported this single braid for a long time and it has reached your hips. O Sita! The immensely strong Rama will soon loosen it for you. O queen! You will see his face, resembling a full moon that has arisen. You will be freed from these tears of misery, like a female snake that sheds its skin. O Maithilee! Ravana will soon be slain in the battle. You deserve all the happiness that you love. You will obtain that happiness. United with the great-souled Rama, you will be delighted, like the earth, full of crops, rejoices when it has excellent rains. O queen! He is like the fearless sun that circles around the excellent mountain,[95] driving its steeds swiftly along its path and exhibiting its powers to all creatures. You will soon find refuge with him.'

Chapter 6(25)

She had been confounded by his[96] words and tormented. Sarama brought her delight, like the water from the sky does to the earth. She[97] desired to ensure the welfare of her friend and knew about the right time. At the right time, she smiled first and then addressed her friend in these words. 'O dark-eyed one! I am capable of conveying your words to Rama and telling him that you are well. I can return, hiding myself. When I course through the sky, without any support, no one is capable of following my path, not even the wind god or Garuda.'

Addressed yet again, Sita spoke to Sarama in sweet and gentle words, her former sorrow having been dispelled. 'You are capable of coursing through the sky and even going to rasatala. But understand what must not be done and what must be done now. If you wish to do what is agreeable to me and if your mind is made up about this, I desire that you should go and find out what Ravana is doing now. I wish to know that. Ravana is cruel and possesses the strength of maya. He makes the enemy scream. The one with evil soul confounded me, like someone is instantly affected by drinking varuni. He used the rakshasis, who always guard me, to constantly censure me and reprimand and slight me. I am anxious and scared. My mind is not at peace. In Ashokavana, I am anxious

[95] Meru.

[96] Ravana's.

[97] Sarama.

because of my fear. If I get to know everything that he has decided and if you report all that to me, it will be a great favour to me.' As Sita said this, Sarama, gentle in her speech, replied to her in these words, wiping away the tears of sorrow. 'O Janakee! If that is your intention, I will go. I will go and see what the enemy's intention is and return.'

Having said this, she approached that rakshasa. She heard what Ravana was telling his ministers. Accomplished in discerning, she heard what the evil-souled one had decided. She then quickly returned to Ashokavana. Having entered the place again, she saw Janaka's daughter. She was waiting for her, like a lotus that is faded and has lost its beauty.[98] Sarama, soft in her speech, returned again and Sita embraced her extremely gently, offering her own seat to her. 'Be seated here comfortably. Tell me the truth. What has the cruel and evil-souled Ravana decided to do?' Sarama was thus addressed by the trembling Sita. She told her everything about the conversation between Ravana and his ministers. 'O Vaidehi! The mother of the Indra of the rakshasas[99] and the aged and understanding minister, Aviddha, spoke great words, urging for your release. "Let Maithilee be honoured and given to the Indra among men. The extraordinary event that transpired in Janasthana[100] should be sufficient. Which man on earth could have performed the crossing of the ocean, the sighting by Hanumat[101] and the slaying of the rakshasas in an encounter?" The aged ministers addressed him in many kinds of ways. However, he is not interested in freeing you, like a person who is excessively addicted to riches. O Maithilee! Before he dies in the battle, he is not interested in freeing you. With his advisers, that is what the cruel one has decided. Because of his addiction to death and his greed, his mind is quite made up. He is incapable of freeing you out of fear, not until he is restrained in a battle. He

[98] It is possible to interpret and translate this as Shri separated from the lotus on which she is seated.

[99] Ravana's mother was Kaikasi.

[100] The destruction of the rakshasas.

[101] Of Lanka and Sita.

will destroy himself and all the rakshasas. O dark-eyed one! In the battle, Rama will slay Ravana with his arrows and use every possible means to take you back to Ayodhya.'

At this time, the sound of drums and conch shells was heard. All the soldiers heard the ground tremble. The servants of the king of the rakshasas in Lanka heard the sound created by the soldiers of the apes. They lost their energy and their enterprise and were filled with distress. Because of the sins of their king, they could no longer see what was beneficial for them.

Chapter 6(26)

To the sound of conch shells mixed with that of drums, the mighty-armed Rama Raghava, the conqueror of enemy cities, advanced. Ravana, the lord of the rakshasas, heard the sound. He thought for a while and glanced at the advisers. In the assembly hall, the immensely strong Ravana spoke to all the advisers in a voice that echoed. 'I have heard what you have said about Rama crossing the ocean, his valour and his collection of forces. I also know that you possess the valour of truth in a battle.'

There was a rakshasa named Malyavat and he was extremely wise. He was Ravana's maternal grandfather and hearing his words, he said, 'O king! A king who is learned, humble and a follower of good policy obtains prosperity for a long time and keeps his enemies under his subjugation. At the right time, if he contracts peace with the enemy, or fights against them, or extends his own alliances, he obtains great prosperity. A king who is inferior or equal must seek peace. An enemy must not be underestimated and there must be war only if one is superior. O Ravana! That is the reason an agreement of peace with Rama appeals to me. Give Sita, the reason for the conflict, back to him. All the divine rishis and the gandharvas desire his victory. Do not engage in a conflict with him. An alliance with him is preferable. The illustrious grandfather created two parties—gods and asuras, and they resort to dharma and *adharma*. O Ravana! It has been heard that dharma is on the side of the great-souled gods and adharma is on the side of the rakshasas and the asuras. When dharma devours adharma, *krita yuga* results.[102] When adharma devours dharma, there is the onset of *tishya*. While you roamed around the worlds, you caused great damage to dharma and accepted adharma. That is the reason the enemies are stronger than us. Indeed, it is because of your distractions that adharma is devouring us. The side of the gods and those who seek to enhance the gods is prospering. You are addicted to material pursuits and do whatever you like. This has engendered great anxiety among the rishis, who are like the fire. Their invisible powers are blazing like the fire. They have cleansed their souls through austerities and are devoted to propagating dharma. Those brahmanas always officiate at the principal sacrifices. They follow the rituals and offer oblations into the fire, loudly reciting the Vedas. Through chanting the name of the *brahman*, they overcome the rakshasas and like clouds during the summer, all of them are forced to flee in different directions. The rishis are like the fire and a smoke arises from their agnihotras, dispelling the energy of the rakshasas in the ten directions. In diverse sacred regions, firm in their vows, they observe fierce austerities and scorch the rakshasas. Having seen many ominous signs and diverse terrible portents, I can discern the terrible destruction of all the rakshasas. Clouds are thundering in terrible tones in the sky, giving rise to fear. Everywhere in Lanka, they are showering down warm blood. The mounts are weeping and shedding drops of tears. The standards are pale and faded and no longer shine as they used to. Predatory beasts, jackals and vultures are shrieking in extremely hideous voices. They are incessantly entering Lanka and gathering in droves. In dreams, dark women with white teeth are laughing, stationed in front of the houses and robbing them. Dogs are eating the sacrificial offerings in houses. Cows are giving birth to donkeys and mongooses are giving birth to rats. Cats are

[102] There are four yugas—krita (*satya*), *treta*, *dvapara* and *kali*. As one progressively moves from krita yuga to kali yuga, dharma declines. Tishya yuga is another name for kali yuga.

having intercourse with leopards and pigs with dogs. Kinnaras are having intercourse with rakshasas and humans. There are pigeons and other birds, pale and with red feet. Urged by destiny, they are roaming around, for the destruction of the rakshasas. There are *sharikas*[103] in houses, chirping away. They are fighting in groups and those which are defeated, are falling down. On several occasions, in the form of a dark brown and monstrous man with a shaved head, Death is looking at the houses. There are other evil portents that are manifesting themselves. I think that Rama is Vishnu, who has adopted a human body. This Raghava, firm in his valour, is not a mere man. He has performed the supremely wonderful act of building a bridge across the ocean. O Ravana! Have a treaty of peace with Rama, king of men.' Malyavat, supreme among the supreme in manliness and strength, spoke these words there. Wishing to again test what was in the mind of the lord of the rakshasas, he became silent and looked at Ravana.

Chapter 6(27)

Malyavat spoke these beneficial words. However, the evil-souled Dashanana was under the subjugation of time and could not tolerate them. He was under the subjugation of rage and he furrowed his forehead. His eyes rolled around and he spoke to Malyavat, 'With benefit in your mind, you have uttered harsh and injurious words. You have spoken in favour of the enemy and the words have not penetrated my ears. Rama is a pitiable human. He is alone and has sought refuge with apes. He has been abandoned by his father and has made a home in the forest. Why do you take him to be capable? I am the lord of the rakshasas and cause fear to the gods. I am not inferior in all kinds of valour. Why do you think that I am inferior? I think that you spoke these harsh words because you detest my valour, because you are partial

[103] The bird *Turdus salica*.

towards the enemy, or because you have been urged by the enemy. I am powerful and I am instated in my position. Which learned person, who knows about the truth of the sacred texts, will speak harsh words against such a person, unless he has been urged by the enemy? I have brought Sita from the forest. She is like Shri, without her lotus. Why will I be scared and return her to Raghava? Wait for a few days. You will see Raghava, with Sugriva and Lakshmana and surrounded by crores of apes, killed by me. In a battle, the gods cannot stand before me in a duel. Why should such a Ravana bear the burden of fear in an encounter? I will never bend down. I would rather be sliced into two. This is my innate nature. By nature, I am impossible to cross. If Rama has easily been able to build a bridge across the ocean, what is the marvel in that? Why should that give rise to fear? With his army of apes, Rama has crossed the ocean. I truthfully pledge before you that he will not return with his life.' Angry and agitated, Ravana spoke those words. Realizing this, Malyavat was ashamed and did not utter any words in reply. As is proper, he pronounced benedictions so that the king's victories might increase. Having taken his permission, Malyavat left for his own residence.

To decide what should be done, Ravana had consultations with his advisers. The rakshasa made arrangements so that Lanka could be protected in an unmatched way. He assigned the eastern gate to the rakshasa Prahasta, the southern to Mahavirya, Mahaparshva and Mahodara and the western gate to his son, Indrajit, who was well versed in maya and was surrounded by many rakshasas. He assigned the city's northern gate to Shuka and Sarana and told his ministers that he would also be there himself. The rakshasa Virupaksha, greatly valiant and brave, was placed at the centre of the army, together with many rakshasas. In this way, the bull among rakshasas made arrangements for Lanka and, under the subjugation of destiny, thought that he had succeeded. Having instructed the preparations for the entire city, he then gave his ministers permission to leave. He was worshipped by large numbers of ministers, who pronounced benedictions for victory. He then entered his great and prosperous inner quarters.

Chapter 6(28)

The king of men, the king of apes, the ape who was Vayu's son, Jambavat, the king of bears, the rakshasa Vibhishana, Angada, Vali's son, Soumitri, the ape Sharabha, Sushena, with his sons Mainda and Dvivida, Gaja, Gavaksha, Kumuda, Nala and Panasa reached. They assembled and discussed what should be done about the enemy. 'It can be seen that this city of Lanka is protected by Ravana. It is extremely difficult for even the asuras, the serpents, the gandharvas and the immortals to vanquish it. Placing the objective at the forefront, we must consult and decide. Ravana, the lord of the rakshasas, is always inside it.'

While they were conversing in this way, Ravana's younger brother, Vibhishana, uttered the best of words, articulated properly and full of meaning. 'My advisers, Anala, Sharabha, Sampati and Praghasa, went to the city of Lanka and have returned here again. All of them assumed the forms of birds and penetrated the enemy's forces. They controlled themselves and observed the arrangements that have been made. I have been precisely told about the arrangements made by the evil-souled Ravana. O Rama! I will tell you everything exactly. Listen. With his forces, Prahasta has reached the eastern gate and is stationed there. Mahavirya, Mahaparshva and Mahodara are towards the south. Surrounded by many rakshasas, Indrajit is at the western gate. They wield spears, swords, bows, javelins and clubs in their hands. Ravana's son is protected by brave ones armed with many kinds of weapons. There are many thousands of rakshasas, with weapons in their hands. Extremely anxious and surrounded by many rakshasas, Ravana is himself stationed at the northern gate. With a large army of rakshasas, Virupaksha, with a large spear, sword and bow, is stationed at the centre of the army. They saw many kinds of battalions thus arranged in Lanka. After that, all my advisers quickly returned here again. There are thousands of elephants and tens of thousands of chariots in the city. There are twenty thousand horses and more than one crore of rakshasas. They are brave and strong, like assassins in a battle. These roamers in the night are always engaged in ensuring the welfare of the king of the rakshasas. O lord of the earth![104] For each rakshasa who is going to fight, there are one hundred thousand to tend and support him.' The ministers had spoken about these arrangements in Lanka and Vibhishana repeated them to the lotus-eyed Rama. He again said, 'O Rama! When Ravana fought against Kubera, six hundred thousand rakshasas advanced with him. They were like the evil-souled Ravana in valour, bravery, energy, spirit, pride and insolence. There is no reason to be intolerant. I am trying to anger you, not frighten you. In your valour, you are capable of restraining even the gods. You are surrounded by a large army with the four kinds of forces. With the vyuhas of this army of the apes, you will crush Ravana.'

After Ravana's younger brother had spoken these words, so that the enemy could be countered, Raghava spoke these words. 'Surrounded by many apes, Nila, bull among apes, should be at Lanka's eastern gate, so that he can fight against Prahasta. Surrounded by a large army, Angada, Vali's son, should cause obstructions to Mahaparshva and Mahodara, at the southern gate. Surrounded by many apes, Hanumat, the son of the wind god, immeasurable in his soul, should attack the western gate and penetrate there. The inferior Ravana, is full of strength because he has obtained a boon. He loves to do unpleasant things to large numbers of daityas, danavas and great-souled rishis. He roams around all the worlds, scorching the subjects. I will myself try to kill that Indra among rakshasas at the northern gate, accompanied by Soumitri. I will enter and crush Ravana and his forces there. Let the powerful Indra among apes, Jambavat, the king of the bears, and the younger brother of the Indra among the rakshasas be at the centre of the army. In the battle, the apes should not assume the form of men. That way, in the midst of the army and the battle, we will be able to make out the apes. Among our people too, that will be means of identifying the apes. There are only seven of us humans who will fight against the enemy—I, my greatly energetic brother, Lakshmana, my friend, Vibhishana, and with him, his four advisers.' Desiring to accomplish

[104] Rama.

success in the objective, Rama spoke these words to Vibhishana. He saw the beautiful slopes of Mount Suvela. The intelligent one made up his mind to ascend Suvela. The great-souled Rama covered the entire earth with his large army. Rejoicing, he advanced towards Lanka. The great-souled one made up his mind to slay the enemy.

Chapter 6(29)

Having made up his mind to ascend Suvela and with Lakshmana following him, Rama addressed Sugriva in these gentle and supreme words. Vibhishana, the roamer in the night, knew about dharma, counsels and rites, and was devoted to him. He also spoke to him. 'Suvela, the virtuous Indra among mountains, is colourful with hundreds of minerals. Let all of us climb it and spend the night there. From there, we will see the residence of that evil-souled rakshasa, who abducted my wife for the sake of ensuring his own death. He doesn't know about dharma. He doesn't possess good conduct or lineage. The rakshasa is inferior in intelligence and that is the reason he has performed that reprehensible deed. When the worst among rakshasas is mentioned, my rage increases. Because of the crime committed by that inferior one, I will see the destruction of all the rakshasas. Having come under the noose of destiny, one commits a sin. Because of the crime committed by a person who is inferior in his soul, his lineage is destroyed.' Extremely angry with Ravana, he spoke in this way. To dwell there, Rama then started to climb Suvela's colourful summit. Controlling himself, Lakshmana followed him at the rear. He was addicted to performing great acts of valour and held up his bow and arrows. Sugriva and his advisers and Vibhishana followed him. So did Hanumat, Angada, Nila, Mainda, Dvivida, Gaja, Gavaksha, Gavaya, Sharabha, Gandhamadana, Panasa, Kumuda, Rambha, the leader of the herd, and many other apes who were swift in their speed. They[105]

[105] The apes.

roamed around in mountains and with Raghava, hundreds of them ascended that mountain with a speed like that of the wind. From every direction, they climbed the mountain within a short while.

From the summit, they saw the city, as if it was suspended in the air. It was auspicious, with the best of gates and adorned with supreme ramparts. The leaders among the apes saw that Lanka was full of rakshasas. The best among apes saw the dark roamers in the night also stationed there, adding to the collection of ramparts, since they seemed to form another rampart. The apes saw that all the rakshasas desired to fight and while Rama looked on, they emitted a loud roar. The evening was red and the sun set. There was the radiance of the full moon and night arrived. Rama, the lord of the army of the apes, was welcomed and honoured by Vibhishana, together with Lakshmana, the leader of the herds[106] and the herds. They happily resided on the slopes of Suvela.

Chapter 6(30)

The bulls among the apes spent the night on Suvela. The brave ones saw Lanka, with its forests and groves. These were flat, peaceful and beautiful, extremely large in size. Witnessing the beauty, they were filled with wonder. It was full of champakas, ashokas, *punnaga*s, salas and talas. It was shrouded with *tamala* groves and dense with *nagakeshara* trees.[107] There were flowering *hintala*s,[108] arjunas, *neepa*s and saptaparnas. There were tilakas, karnikaras and *patalas*[109] in every direction. It was beautiful, with creepers, with flowers at the tips, enveloping the many kinds of divine trees, making Lanka resemble Indra's Amaravati. There were wonderful blossoms and red and delicate leaves. There were blue grasslands and colourful groves and forests. The lovely trees

[106] Sugriva.

[107] Flowering tree, the text uses the word *nagamala*.

[108] Variety of palm.

[109] *Bignonia suaveolens*.

were bedecked with fragrant flowers and fruits, just as men wear ornaments. Like Chaitratha and like Nandana, it was pleasing to the mind. The forests were beautiful in all the seasons and were radiant with bees. Gallinules and lapwings called, peacocks danced. Cuckoos could be heard in the waterfalls in the forests. The birds were always excited and bees buzzed around. There were clumps that were full of birds like cuckoos. Large bees sang and smaller bees swarmed. There was the chirping of wagtails and the calling of cranes.

Delighted and happy, the brave apes, who could assume any form at will, entered those forests and groves.[110] The extremely energetic apes entered there and an extremely pleasant and fragrant breeze began to blow, mixed with the fragrance of flowers. Some other brave apes, leaders of their herds, took Sugriva's permission and emerging from their herds, advanced towards Lanka, which was adorned with flags. As those supreme among those who roar roared in loud voices, the birds were scared and animals and birds terrified. Lanka trembled. They crushed the ground with their feet and created a great force. A dust was created by their feet and suddenly rose up. Frightened by that sound, bears, lions, boars, buffaloes, elephants and deer fled in the ten directions. The single tall peak of Trikuta rose up and touched the sky. It was enveloped with flowers everywhere and seemed to be made out of gold. It sparkled and was beautiful to see, extending for one hundred yojanas. It was lovely, handsome and gigantic and even the birds found it difficult to approach. It was impossible to climb, even in one's thoughts, not to speak of people who sought to ascend. Protected by Ravana, Lanka nestled on that peak. The city had towering gates that were like white clouds. These were made out of gold and there were beautiful silver ramparts. Lanka was supremely adorned with palaces and storeyed mansions. Nestled in between,[111] it was like the sky, Vishnu's region, at the end of the summer. There was a palace ornamented with one thousand pillars there. It resembled the peak of Kailasa and could

[110] Clearly having descended from Suvela.

[111] Between heaven and earth.

be seen, as if it was an etching in the sky. This sanctuary of the Indra among the rakshasas was a supreme ornament for the city. One hundred rakshasas always protected all of it. With the apes, Rama, Lakshmana's prosperous elder brother, saw the prosperous city, which had accomplished its objective of being wealthy. It was full of jewels and possessed diverse arrangements. It was decorated with garlands of palaces. There were large machines and huge doors in the city. With his great force, Rama saw it.

Chapter 6(31)

Having seen various signs, Lakshmana's elder brother addressed Lakshmana, who possessed all the auspicious signs, in these words. 'O Lakshmana! Let us gather cool water and groves full of fruits. Let us divide this army into vyuhas and wait. We can see that a terrible fear has presented itself and that it will cause a destruction of creatures. There will be death for the best of bears, apes and rakshasas. A harsh wind is blowing and the earth is trembling. The summits of mountains are quivering and falling down on the ground. Like harsh and cruel predatory beasts, the clouds are rumbling in harsh tones. They are showering down cruel drops of water mixed with blood. The evening is extremely terrible and resembles red sandalwood. A blazing ball of fire is falling down from the sun. Birds and animals are miserable. In their distress, they are facing the sun and calling in terrible tones. This is ominous and generates great fear. Though its radiance cannot be seen in the night, the moon is scorching us. Its beams are black and red, just as it is at the time of the destruction of the world. O Lakshmana! Behold. A blue mark can be seen in the sun's disc. It is small, harsh and ominous and the extremities are extremely red. The nakshatras can no longer be seen to be circling as they used to. O Lakshmana! Behold. All this seems to be telling us that the end of the yuga and the world has arrived. Crows, hawks and vultures are circling below. Jackals are also howling in loud and inauspicious voices. This invincible city is protected by Ravana. Surrounded by the apes on all sides, let us swiftly attack with force.' Lakshmana's brave elder brother spoke to Lakshmana in this way. The immensely strong one quickly descended from the summit of the mountain.

Raghava, with dharma in his soul, descended from the mountain. He looked at his own army, which was extremely difficult for the enemy to assail. Raghava knew about the right time. With Sugriva, since the time was right, he urged the great army of the king of the apes. Surrounded by the large army and leading from the front, with a bow in his hand, the mighty-armed one advanced towards the city of Lanka. Vibhishana, Sugriva, Hanumat, Jambavat, the king of the bears, Nala, Nila and Lakshmana followed him. The extremely large army of bears and residents of the forest was at the rear. As they followed Raghava, they covered the entire ground on earth. The apes, the restrainers of the enemy, were like excellent elephants. They seized hundreds of peaks from the mountains and gigantic trees. After an extremely long period of time, the two brothers who were scorchers of enemies, Rama and Lakshmana, approached Ravana's city of Lanka. It had garlands of flags, with beautiful gardens. It was decorated with groves. There was a wonderful rampart that was very difficult to breach. There were tall gates and turrets. It was extremely difficult for even the gods to attack. Commanded and urged by Rama's words, the residents of the forest attacked it.

Lanka's northern gate was as tall as a mountain peak. Ravana and his younger brother, the archer, laid siege to it and stationed themselves there. Rama, Dasharatha's son, with the brave Lakshmana as his companion, stationed himself there, at the city of Lanka, protected by Ravana. Ravana himself was stationed at the northern gate. Protected by him, no one other than Rama was capable of attacking that gate. Ravana was stationed there, like Varuna is in the terrible ocean. In every direction, it was protected by terrible rakshasas wielding weapons, like the danavas in patala. Inferior ones would have been scared away. He[112] saw many kinds of warriors spread around and masses of weapons and armour.

[112] Rama.

Nila, the commander of the army reached the eastern gate and with Mainda and the valiant Dvivida, remained there. With Rishabha, Gavaksha, Gaja and Gavaya, the extremely strong Angada assumed control over the southern gate. Hanumat, the strong ape, protected the western gate. He was with Pramathi, Praghasa and other brave ones. Sugriva was himself stationed in the centre of the army. He sighed like Suparna and was with all the best among the apes. Thirty-six crores of famous leaders of the apes were where the ape Sugriva was, crushing the enemy present there. On Rama's command, Lakshmana, with Vibhishana, placed one crore of apes at every gate. Towards Rama's rear and not far from him, were Sugriva and Jambavat, in the centre of the army and with many soldiers following. Those tigers among apes possessed teeth like those of tigers. Seizing trees and peaks of mountains, they were happy, waiting to fight. All of them stretched and lashed their tails. All of them used teeth and nails as weapons. All of them quivered in their colourful limbs. All of them had grim visages. Some possessed the strength of ten elephants, others that of one hundred. Some possessed valour that was equal to that of one thousand elephants. There were those with the strength of a multitude of elephants, others with ten times that. There were others whose strength could not be measured. All the leaders among the apes were there. Their gathering together was wonderful and extraordinary. The soldiers of the apes were like a swarm of locusts. They seemed to cover the sky and envelop the earth. There were apes who had reached and settled down in front of Lanka. There were one hundred thousand separate divisions of bears and residents of the forest. Some reached Lanka's gates. Others spread around, to fight on every side. In every direction, the apes covered all the mountains. One crore of them advanced towards the city. The forces of the apes wielded trees in their hands. Even the wind found it extremely difficult to penetrate Lanka and they surrounded it from every side. Suddenly besieged in this way, the rakshasas were surprised. The apes resembled clouds and were like Shakra in their valour. As the waves of soldiers advanced, a tumultuous sound arose. It was like the sound of the water when the ocean is agitated. As a consequence of that great sound, Lanka, with all its ramparts, gates, mountains, forests and groves, started to tremble. The army was protected by Rama, Lakshmana and Sugriva. It was more invincible than all the gods and the asuras put together.

Having himself arranged the soldiers in this way, with a view to slaying the rakshasas, he repeatedly consulted with his ministers and decided what should be done. He knew about the truth and was eager to undertake what should be done next. With Vibhishana's sanction, he remembered the dharma of kings. He summoned Angada, Vali's son, and spoke to him. 'O amiable one! O ape! Go to Dashagriva and convey my words to him. Without any fear or distress, enter the city of Lanka. Go to the one who has lost his prosperity and wealth. Bereft of his senses, he is about to die. "O one who roams around in the night! O rakshasa! Because of your delusion and insolence, you have committed crimes against rishis, gods, gandharvas, *apsara*s, serpents, yakshas and kings. The insolence you derived from a boon granted by Svayambhu, the one who uses the rod of chastisement, will certainly be dispelled today. I am afflicted because you abducted my wife. I am stationed at the gates of Lanka, wielding the rod of chastisement. O rakshasa! Slain by me, you will obtain the destinations meant for gods, maharshis and all the royal sages and go there. O worst among rakshasas! In abducting Sita, you used your strength and maya. Exhibit those now and surpass me. I will use my sharp arrows to destroy all rakshasas on earth, unless you seek refuge with me and return Maithilee. Vibhishana, with dharma in his soul and supreme among rakshasas, has come here. Without any thorns, the handsome one will certainly obtain the prosperity of Lanka. Resorting to adharma, you do not have the capacity to enjoy the kingdom even for an instant. You have not cleansed your soul and have foolish and wicked aides. O rakshasa! Resort to your fortitude and valour and fight. In the battle, I will pacify and purify you with my arrows. Even if you assume the form of a bird and course through the three worlds with the speed of thought, when you come within the range of my vision, you will not be able to retain your life. I am speaking these beneficial words to you.

Prepare for your funeral rites. Make the proper arrangements in Lanka. Your life depends on me."'

Rama was unblemished in his deeds. Having been thus addressed by him, Tara's son took to the sky, like the lord of oblations.[113] In a short instant, the handsome one descended within Ravana's residence. He saw Ravana seated there with his advisers, without any anxiety. The bull among apes descended close to him. Angada, with golden bracelets, looked like the fire. In the hearing of the advisers, he made himself known and reported all of Rama's words, without adding or taking anything away. 'I am the messenger of Rama, the Indra of Kosala who is unblemished in his deeds. I am Angada, Vali's son. You may have heard of me. Raghava Rama is the extender of Kousalya's delight. He tells you, "O worst of beings! O cruel one! Come and fight against me. With your advisers, sons, kin and relatives, I will kill you. After I have killed you, there will no longer be any fear in the three worlds. Today, I will uproot the enemy and the thorn of the gods, the danavas, the yakshas, the gandharvas, the rakshasas and the rishis. Once you are killed, Vibhishana will obtain the prosperity, unless you bow down before me and respectfully return Vaidehi."'

The bull among apes addressed him in these harsh words. Hearing them, the lord of large numbers of those who roam around in the night was filled with intolerance. His eyes turned copper-red with rage and he commanded his aides, 'Seize this one, inferior in intelligence. Dishonour him and kill him.' He[114] blazed in his energy, like the fire. Hearing Ravana's words, four terrible roamers in the night seized him. Knowing his own nature, Tara's son allowed himself to be captured. The brave one wished to exhibit his strength to the large numbers of yatudhanas. Like a bird, Angada seized the ones who clung on to his arms and leapt on to the palace that resembled a mountain. While the Indra among rakshasas looked on, all those rakshasas were whirled around by the force of the leap and fell down on the ground. The top of the palace was as tall as

[113] The fire god.

[114] Angada.

the peak of a mountain. While Dashagriva looked on, he attacked it. Having destroyed the top of the palace, he announced his own name. He uttered a loud roar and leapt into the sky.

When the palace was destroyed, Ravana was filled with great rage. Able to see his own destruction, he sighed deeply.

Rama was surrounded by many delighted apes. Desiring to slay the enemy, he advanced to fight. The ape Sushena was very brave and was like the summit of a mountain. He was there, surrounded by many apes who could assume any form at will. On Sugriva's instructions, this invincible ape progressively marched around all the gates, like the moon amidst the nakshatras.

There were hundreds of *akshouhinis*[115] of the residents of the forest. Having crossed the ocean, they were camped in Lanka. On seeing them, some rakshasas marvelled. Others were terrified. There were others who were delighted at the prospect of a battle and leapt up. The apes covered the entire area between the ramparts and the moat. The apes were like a second rampart. On seeing this, the rakshasas were distressed. At this great and terrible occurrence, there was an uproar in the capital of the rakshasas. The rakshasas seized large weapons and advanced, like winds that blow at the end of a yuga.

Chapter 6(32)

After this, the rakshasas went to Ravana's residence and reported that Rama, with the apes, had laid siege to the city. On hearing that the city had been besieged, the roamer in the night was filled with anger. He doubled the arrangements and ascended to the top of the palace. He saw that in every direction, Lanka, with its mountains, forests and groves, had been surrounded by innumerable bands of apes who wished to fight. He saw that

[115] An akshouhini is an army, consisting of 21,870 chariots, 21,870 elephants, 65,610 horse riders and 109,350 foot soldiers.

because of the apes, the entire earth was brown. He began to think, 'How can they be destroyed?' Having thought for a long period of time, Ravana resorted to his fortitude. With dilated eyes, he looked at Raghava and the leaders among the apes.

While the Indra among rakshasas looked on, wishing to bring pleasure to Raghava, the different parts of the army began to climb into Lanka. Their faces were coppery. Their complexions were golden. For Rama's sake, they were ready to give up their lives. With salas, talas and boulders as weapons, they attacked Lanka. The apes used trees, the peaks of mountains and fists as their weapons. Using these, they broke down the tops of the palaces and the turrets. The moats were filled with clear water. The apes filled these up with earth, the tops of mountains, grass and wood. Other leaders of herds climbed into Lanka with herds of thousand, herds of crores and herds of hundreds of crores. The apes shattered the golden gates. They destroyed the arches that possessed the hue of the summit of Kailasa. The apes leapt up, leapt down and roared. With complexions like those of gigantic elephants, they attacked Lanka. The apes could assume any form at will and attacked Lanka's ramparts. They shouted, 'Victory to the extremely strong Rama and the immensely strong Lakshmana. Victory to King Sugriva, protected by Raghava.' They shouted and roared in this way. The leaders of the apes—Virabahu, Subahu and Nala—the residents of the forest, stationed themselves at the ramparts and crushed them. Looking for an opportunity, they stationed their formations there.

Kumuda was at the eastern gate, surrounded by ten crore of strong apes who desired victory. The brave ape, Shatabali, attacked the southern gate, surrounded by twenty crore of strong ones. The ape Sushena, Tara's father, was at the western gate. He was surrounded by sixty crore of strong ones. With Soumitri, Rama attacked the northern gate and barricaded it. He was with the strong Sugriva, the lord of the apes. Surrounded by one crore of immensely brave ones, the gigantic Golangula and Gavaksha, terrible to behold were by Rama's side. Dhumra, the destroyer of enemies, was surrounded by one crore of immensely brave and extremely forceful bears and was by Rama's side. The immensely brave Vibhishana was armoured and had a mace in his hand. He was surrounded by his advisers and was also where the immensely strong one[116] was. Gaja, Gavaksha, Gavaya, Sharabha and Gandhamadana rushed around on all sides, protecting the army of the apes.

Ravana, the lord of the rakshasas, was filled with rage. He instructed all the soldiers to quickly emerge. Urged by Ravana, those soldiers cheerfully attacked. They were like the force of the great ocean at a time when it is full. A terrible engagement took place between the rakshasas and the apes, like that between the gods and the asuras in ancient times. Proclaiming their own valour, those terrible ones[117] used blazing clubs, spears, javelins and battleaxes to slay the apes. The forceful apes used gigantic trees, the peaks of mountains and nails and teeth to slay the rakshasas. Some terrible rakshasas were stationed on the ramparts and used spears and javelins to strike at the apes who were on the ground. The apes became angry and leapt on to the ramparts. The apes attacked the rakshasas and brought them down. As a result of that tumultuous engagement, mud was created from the flesh and the blood of the rakshasas and the apes. It was extraordinary.

Chapter 6(33)

The great-souled apes fought with the rakshasas. Both sides were strong and enraged and it was extremely terrible. The rakshasas, terrible in their valour, desired Ravana's victory. They were on horses with golden harnesses, with standards that were like the flames of the fire. They were on chariots that were like the sun, adorned in beautiful armour. The tigers among rakshasas emerged and roared in the ten directions. The large army of the apes, who could assume any form at will, also desired victory. They attacked

[116] Rama.

[117] The rakshasas.

the rakshasa soldiers. At that time, when they attacked each other, there were duels between the rakshasas and the apes.

The immensely energetic rakshasa, Indrajit, fought against Angada, Vali's son, like Andhaka against Tryambaka.[118] Sampati, always intolerant in a battle, fought against Prajangha. The ape Hanumat angrily attacked Jambumali. Extremely angry, Vibhishana, the rakshasa who was Ravana's younger brother, clashed against Mitraghna,[119] who possessed a fierce force in an encounter. Gaja fought against the extremely strong rakshasa, Tapana. The greatly energetic Nila fought against Nikumbha. Sugriva, Indra among apes, clashed against Praghasa. In the encounter, the handsome Lakshmana fought against Virupaksha. The invincible Agniketu, the rakshasa Rashmiketu, Suptaghna and Yajnakopa clashed against Rama. Vajramushti fought against Mainda and Ashaniprabha against Dvivida. The two foremost apes clashed with those two extremely terrible rakshasas. The brave and terrible rakshasa, Pratapana, could bear great burdens in battles. He fought against Nala, who had a fierce force in battle. The powerful Sushena was famous as Dharma's[120] son. That great ape fought against Vidyunmali. Other terrible apes fought against other rakshasas. Many duels took place and there were many kinds of fights. There was a great and tumultuous engagement and it made the body hair stand up. Desiring victory, the brave rakshasas and apes fought. Blood flowed from the bodies of the apes and the rakshasas and a river was created from this, with the bodies like dams and the hair like moss. Like Shatakratu with his vajra, Indrajit angrily struck Angada, who could shatter the soldiers of the enemy, with a club. In the battle, the handsome and forceful ape, Angada, shattered his gold-embellished chariot and killed his horses and charioteer. In the field of battle, Sampati was struck by Prajangha with three arrows, but used an ashvakarna tree to kill Prajangha. In the encounter, the enraged and immensely strong Jambumali was

[118] Shiva.

[119] Also known as Shatrughna. Indeed, Shatrughna is a more appropriate name. One slays the enemy (*shatru*), not one's friends (*mitra*).

[120] Yama's.

on his chariot and used a javelin to strike Hanumat between the breasts. Hanumat, the wind god's son, climbed on to the chariot and used the palm of his hand to swiftly crush that rakshasa. The rakshasa Tapana was swift in the use of his hands and used sharp arrows to strike Gaja and mangle his limbs. However, Gaja used the summit of a mountain and his fists to slay him. Praghasa seemed to be devouring the soldiers. But Sugriva, the lord of apes, used a saptaparna tree to pierce and kill him. Lakshmana oppressed the rakshasa Virupaksha, who was terrible to behold, with a shower of arrows and then used a single arrow to kill him. The invincible Agniketu, the rakshasa Rashmiketu, Suptaghna[121] and Yajnakopa pierced Rama with arrows. Enraged in the battle, Rama used four terrible arrows that were like the flames of a fire to sever their four heads. In the encounter, Mainda struck Vajramushti with his fist and killed him. Like a city turret that falls down, with his chariot and his horses, he fell down on the ground. While all the rakshasas looked on, Dvivida used the summit of a mountain, which was like the vajra to the touch, to strike Ashaniprabha. In the battle, Dvivida, Indra among apes, used a tree as a weapon and Ashaniprabha struck him with arrows that were like the vajra. With his body deeply pierced by the arrows, Dvivida became senseless with rage. Using a sala tree, he killed Ashaniprabha, together with his charioteer and his horses. Nila had the complexion of a mass of blue collyrium and in the battle, Nikumbha pierced him with sharp arrows that were like lightning in the clouds. Nikumbha, the roamer in the night, was swift in the use of his hands. In the encounter, he laughed and again struck Nila with one hundred arrows. In the battle, Nila was like Vishnu. In the encounter, he used the wheel of a chariot to sever the heads of Nikumbha and his charioteer. Vidyunmali was on his chariot. He used arrows that were ornamented with gold to strike Sushena. He then roared repeatedly. Sushena, supreme among apes, saw that he was on his chariot. He used the summit of a mountain to quickly bring down the chariot. Vidyunmali, the roamer in the night, was dexterous. He swiftly descended from the chariot and

[121] This should probably be Shatrughna.

stood on the ground, with a club in his hand. At this, Sushena, bull among apes, was filled with rage. He seized an extremely large boulder and rushed towards the roamer in the night. Vidyunmali, the roamer in the night, saw that he was descending. He swiftly used the club to strike Sushena, supreme among apes, in the chest. Struck by that terrible club in the great battle, the supreme among apes, did the unthinkable. He struck him in the chest with the boulder and brought him down. Vidyunmali, the roamer in the night, was severely struck by the boulder. With his heart shattered, he lost his life and fell down on the ground. Thus, the brave apes fought against the brave roamers in the night. They crushed each other in the duels, like the daityas against the residents of heaven.

The place was littered with shattered and fragmented javelins, swords, clubs, spears, spikes and darts and chariots and warhorses. Crazy elephants, apes and rakshasas were killed. Wheels, axles, yokes and poles were shattered and fell down on the ground. There was a terrible fight and large numbers of jackals gathered. In different directions, there were headless torsos of apes and rakshasas. It was a tumultuous engagement, like a battle between the gods and the asuras. Crushed by the bulls among the apes, the bodies of the roamers in the night oozed out blood. However, they resorted to their spirits and fought again, desiring for the time when the sun would set.[122]

Chapter 6(34)

While the apes and the rakshasas fought in this way, the sun set. Night, which would take away lives, arrived. They were bound in terrible enmity towards each other and fought, desiring victory. A nocturnal fight ensued between the apes and the rakshasas. 'You are a rakshasa,' said the apes. 'You are an ape,' said the rakshasas. In the battle that took place in that

[122] The powers of rakshasas increase at night.

terrible night, they fought against each other and killed each other. 'Kill.' 'Shatter.' 'Come here.' 'Why are you running away?' These extremely tumultuous sounds were heard in the darkness. In the darkness, the dark rakshasas were clad in golden armour and could be seen, like blazing herbs in an Indra among mountains. That darkness was extremely difficult to cross and the rakshasas were senseless with anger. They descended on the apes with great force and devoured them. The terrible apes used their sharp teeth, leaping on to the horses with golden harnesses and standards that were like the flames of the fire and crushing them in their rage. They used elephants to climb on to other elephants. They brought down the standards and flags from their chariots. Senseless with anger, they shattered them with their teeth. Rama and Lakshmana used arrows that were like venomous serpents to kill the best among rakshasas, those who could be seen and those who could not be seen. The earth was enveloped in a dust that arose from the hooves of horses and the rims of chariots. As they fought, this blocked the ears and the eyes. A terrible encounter raged and it made the body hair stand up. The blood created a river of blood that was extremely swift in its flow. There was the sound of drums, smaller drums, tambourines, conch shells and flutes and it was wonderful. There was the sound of slain and injured rakshasas and that of apes being struck by weapons. It was extremely terrible. Because of the fighting, the earth was offered gifts of weapons instead of flowers. There was mud created by the blood. It was impossible to penetrate and impossible to discern. The terrible night brought destruction to the apes and the rakshasas. It was like the night of destruction that all creatures find extremely difficult to cross.

In the terrible darkness, the delighted rakshasas attacked Rama and showered down arrows on him. They descended angrily, roaring and creating a noise that resembled the rumble created by the seven oceans. In the twinkling of an eye, Rama used six arrows that were like the flames of a fire to strike six roamers in the night—the invincible Yajnashatru, Mahaparshva, Mahodara, Vajradamshtra and the gigantic Shuka and Sarana. They were struck in their inner organs by the torrent of Rama's arrows. Saving their lives, they withdrew from the battle. The immensely strong one used arrows that were like the flames of the fire, with golden and colourful shafts, to make the directions and the sub-directions clear again. There were other brave rakshasas who were stationed in front of Rama. When they approached, like insects before a fire, they were also destroyed. Thousands of gold-shafted arrows descended and the night became colourful, like the autumn sky with fireflies.

There was the shouting of rakshasas and the roaring of apes. This made the terrible night become even more terrible. That loud sound spread in every direction and Mount Trikuta, filled with caverns, seemed to become distressed. There were golangulas large in size, with a radiance like that of the darkness. They crushed the roamers in the night with their arms and devoured them.

In the battle, Angada was stationed, ready to slay the enemy. He swiftly killed the charioteer and horses of Ravana's son. A horrible and extremely terrible encounter ensued. With his horses and chariot slain by Angada, Indrajit abandoned his chariot. He used his great maya and vanished. Ravana's wicked son vanished, but was harsh in fighting. Ravana's brave son became senseless with rage and used the boon given to him by Brahma. Though he was invisible, he released sharp arrows that were as radiant as the vajra. Against Rama and Lakshmana, he used arrows that became terrible serpents. In the battle, he angrily used these to pierce the two Raghavas all over their bodies.

Chapter 6(35)

Rama, the powerful prince, commanded ten extremely strong leaders of the apes to search for his[123] trail. The scorcher of enemies instructed Sushena's two sons, Nila, bull among apes, Angada, Vali's son, the spirited Sharabha, Vinata, Jambavat, the immensely strong Sanuprastha, Rishabha and the bull

[123] Indrajit's.

Rishabhaskandha. Delighted, those terrible apes seized trees and all of them leapt up into the sky, searching the ten directions. However, Ravana's son knew about weapons and was supreme in the use of weapons. Though they were swift, his arrows were swifter and he used those to restrain their speed. Those apes, terrible in their force, were deeply mangled by iron arrows. Because of the darkness, they could not see him, just as the sun is shrouded in clouds.

Ravana's son, the one who was victorious in assemblies, pierced all the inner organs of Rama and Lakshmana with arrows. They were severely struck. The brave and angry Indrajit incessantly pierced the bodies of the two brother, Rama and Lakshmana, with arrows that were in the form of serpents. Copious quantities of blood flowed out from their wounds. Both of them assumed the appearance of flowering *kimshuka*s.[124] Ravana's son was like a mass of collyrium mixed with oil and his eyes were red. Though he was invisible, he spoke to the two brothers. 'When I render myself invisible and fight, not even Shakra, the lord of the gods, is capable of seeing and approaching me, not to speak of those like you. O descendants of the Raghu lineage! I have covered you in this net of arrows shafted with heron feathers. Overcome with rage, I will now convey you to Yama's abode.' He spoke in this way to the two brothers, Rama and Lakshmana, who knew about dharma. He pierced them with sharp arrows and roared in delight. He was dark, like a mass of black collyrium mixed with oil. In that great encounter, he stretched his large bow and repeatedly struck them with terrible arrows. He knew about inner organs and those sharp arrows struck deep into the inner organs of the brave Rama and Lakshmana. He roared repeatedly. In the field of battle, both of them were bound by nets of arrows. In the twinkling of an eye, they were not even capable of looking. They looked like the great Indra's standard, when it is loosened from its ropes and is quivering. Afflicted by their inner organs being mangled, those two brave ones trembled. The lords of the earth cast aside their large bows and fell down on the ground. Exuding blood, those two brave ones lay down on beds meant for

[124] Tree with red blossoms.

heroes. All their limbs were entwined by those arrows and they were severely afflicted. On their bodies, there was not even the space of a single finger that was not pierced, mangled and wounded by arrows, from the fingers to the feet. They were cruelly struck by the rakshasa who could assume any form at will. Fearful streams of blood started to flow, like water from springs. Pierced in his inner organs by the arrows, Rama fell down first. This was the result of Indrajit's rage, who had vanquished Shakra earlier. He was pierced by *naracha*s,[125] half-narachas, *bhalla*s,[126] *anjalika*s,[127] *vatsadanta*s,[128] *simhadashtras*[129] and *kshura*s.[130] He lay down on that bed meant for heroes, flinging away from his hand his stringed bow, which was bent in three places and was decorated with gold. Rama, bull among men, fell down at a distance that was the range of one arrow away from him. On seeing this, Lakshmana lost all hope of remaining alive. Those two brave ones were bound and lay down, having fallen down. With Vayu's son at the forefront, the apes assembled and surrounded them. They were afflicted and suffered from great misery.

Chapter 6(36)

The residents of the forest looked everywhere on earth and in the sky and saw the two brothers, Rama and Lakshmana, covered with arrows. The rakshasa had accomplished his task and withdrew, like the god with the rains.[131] With Hanumat, Sugriva, Vibhishana, Nila, Dvivida, Mainda, Sushena, Sumukha and Angada quickly came to that spot and started to grieve for the two

[125] A naracha is an iron arrow.
[126] Arrows with broad heads.
[127] Arrows with heads shaped like crescents.
[128] Arrows with heads shaped like a calf's tooth.
[129] Arrows with heads shaped like a lion's tooth.
[130] Kshura or *kshurapra* is an arrow with a sharp edge.
[131] The image is of Indra withdrawing after showering down.

Raghavas. They were not moving and breathed faintly. They were covered in streams of blood. They were pierced with nets of arrows and were immobile. They were lying down on beds of arrows. They were sighing like snakes that couldn't make any efforts, their valour exhausted. Blood flowed from their limbs and they looked like two golden standards. Those two brave ones were lying down on beds meant for heroes. They were lying down and not making any efforts. The leaders surrounded them, their eyes filled with tears. They saw that the two Raghavas had fallen down, enveloped in the nets of arrows. All the apes, with Vibhishana, were distressed. The apes searched in all the directions of the sky. But because he was enveloped in his maya, they could not see Ravana's son in the battle. Vibhishana used his own maya to cut through the maya and looking around, saw his brother's son stationed there. He[132] was unmatched in his deeds and could not be countered in an encounter. Vibhishana saw the brave one, invisible because of the boon he had obtained.

Indrajit saw that the two were lying down because of the deed he had performed. Extremely delighted and happy, he told all the nairittas, 'These two extremely strong ones are the slayers of Dushana and Khara. The two brothers, Rama and Lakshmana, have been killed by my arrows. Even if all the large numbers of rishis, gods and asuras come together, they are incapable of freeing these two from the bonds of arrows. It was because of what they did that my father was afflicted by grief and was immersed in thoughts. He was incapable of laying his body down on a bed and the three *yama*s of the night passed.[133] It is because of them that the city of Lanka is as turbulent as a river during the monsoon. I have taken the foundation of the calamity away and have destroyed it in every possible way. Like clouds during the autumn,[134] all the valour of Rama, Lakshmana and all the residents of the forest will be fruitless.' He said this to all the rakshasas who were by

[132] Indrajit.

[133] A yama is a period of three hours. Since it is made up of three yamas, the night is known as *triyama*.

[134] Because clouds don't rain during the autumn.

his side. Ravana's son then struck all the leaders of the herds. He afflicted them with torrents of arrows and terrified the apes. The mighty-armed one laughed and spoke these words. 'O rakshasas! In front of the army, I have bound them down with terrible bonds of arrows. All of you look at those two brothers.' The one who fought in mysterious ways said this to all the rakshasas. They were filled with great wonder and satisfied at his deed. Like clouds, all of them emitted a loud roar. They said, 'Rama has been killed,' and worshipped Ravana's son. Seeing that those two, Rama and Lakshmana, were not moving and were lying down on the ground and not breathing, he also thought that they had been killed. Filled with delight, Indrajit, the conqueror of assemblies, entered the city of Lanka and caused happiness to all the nairittas.

The bodies of Rama and Lakshmana were pierced with arrows, in all the limbs and smaller limbs. On seeing this, Sugriva was filled with fear. Vibhishana spoke to the terrified Indra among apes, whose face was distressed and full of tears and whose eyes were also overflowing with tears. 'O Sugriva! Enough of this scare. Control this flow of tears. This is usually what happens in battles. Victory is uncertain. O brave one! Even if there is a bit of good fortune left with us, the two brothers, Rama and Lakshmana, will fling aside this unconsciousness. O ape! I am without a protector. Therefore, steady yourself. For those who are devoted to truth and dharma, death cannot give rise to fear.' Saying this, Vibhishana wet his hand with water and wiped Sugriva's auspicious eyes. The intelligent one wiped the face of the king of the apes. Without any fear, he spoke these words. 'The time has come. O Indra among kings of apes! This is not the time to indulge in lassitude. This is not the time to indulge in excessive affection. That can give rise to death. Therefore, cast aside this lassitude. It destroys all tasks. Think of the welfare of the soldiers who have had Rama at their forefront. As long as Rama suffers from the catastrophe of losing consciousness, they have to be protected. When the two Kakutsthas regain their senses, they will drive away our fear. This is nothing for Rama. Nor will Rama die. This will not diminish his prosperity. The lifespan, extremely difficult to obtain, has not deserted him. Therefore, comfort yourself and resort to your own strength, until I place all the soldiers back in their ranks. O bull among the apes! They are scared and have dilated their eyes in fear. The apes are speaking into each other's ears. On seeing me run around, instilling happiness in the army, let the apes give up their terror, just as one casts aside a garland that has been enjoyed.' Vibhishana, Indra among the rakshasas, reassured Sugriva. Thereafter, he comforted the soldiers of the apes, who were running away.

Indrajit, great in his use of maya, was surrounded by all the soldiers. He entered the city of Lanka and went before his father. Ravana was seated. He joined his hands in salutation and greeted him, telling his beloved father that Rama and Lakshmana had been killed. In the midst of the rakshasas, Ravana heard that the enemy had been brought down. Delighted, he leapt up and embraced his son. He inhaled the fragrance of his head. Happy in his mind, he asked questions. Asked, he told his father everything, just as it had occurred. On hearing the maharatha's[135] words, his heart was filled with floods of joy. The fever caused by Dasharatha's son passed. He praised his son in joyous words.

Chapter 6(37)

Having accomplished his objective, Ravana's son entered Lanka. Distressed, the bulls among the apes surrounded Raghava and protected him. Hanumat, Angada, Nila, Sushena, Kumuda, Nala, Gaja, Gavaksha, Gavaya, Sharabha, Gandhamadana, Jambavat, Rishabha, Sunda, Rambha, Shatabali and Prithu collected trees and constructed vyuhas in every direction. The apes glanced in all the directions, upwards and diagonally. Even if a blade of grass moved, they thought that it might be a rakshasa.

[135] Great warrior, more specifically, a maharatha is someone who can single-handedly fight ten thousand warriors.

Ravana was delighted and gave his son, Indrajit, permission to leave. He summoned the rakshasis who were entrusted with the task of protecting Sita. Commanded by him, the rakshasis presented themselves, including Trijata. Delighted, the lord of the rakshasas spoke to the rakshasis. 'Tell Vaidehi that Rama and Lakshmana have been killed by Indrajit. Make her ascend Pushpaka and show her that they have been killed in the battle. She was insolent because she sought refuge with her husband. She did not serve me. In the field of battle, he and his brother have been restrained. Maithilee need not be uncertain now. She need not be anxious. She has no hope. Adorned in all the ornaments, Sita can present herself before me. In the battle today, Rama and Lakshmana have come under the subjugation of death. Having seen this, with her hopes destroyed, she will find no other recourse.' Having heard the words of the evil-souled Ravana, the rakshasis agreed and went to where Pushpaka was. Following Ravana's commands, the rakshasis brought Pushpaka and conveyed it to Ashokavana, where Maithilee was. On account of her husband, she was overcome by sorrow. The rakshasis seized Sita and made her ascend Pushpaka vimana. With Trijata, Sita ascended Pushpaka. Ravana caused Lanka to be decorated with flags, standards and garlands. Delighted, the lord of the rakshasas arranged for it to be proclaimed in Lanka that Raghava and Lakshmana had been killed by Indrajit in the battle.

With Trijata, Sita left on the vimana and saw all the soldiers of the apes who had been brought down. Her mind was happy to see the devourers of flesh.[136] However, she was miserable and grieved to see the apes standing by the side of Rama and Lakshmana. Sita saw that both of them were lying down on beds of arrows and that, afflicted by arrows, Rama and Lakshmana were unconscious. Their armour was cast away. The two brave ones had flung away their bows. Pierced by arrows in all their limbs, they were lying down on the ground, on beds of arrows. She saw the two brave brothers, bulls among men. Extremely miserable with grief, Sita started to lament piteously. Looking at them, the two brothers, whose power

[136] The rakshasas who had been killed.

was like that of the gods, she sorrowed and her eyes filled with tears. She believed that they had been killed and filled with sorrow, she spoke these words.

Chapter 6(38)

On seeing that her husband and the extremely strong Lakshmana had been killed, Sita was overcome with great sorrow. She lamented piteously. 'Those who can read signs[137] said that I would have sons and would not be a widow. They did not know. Since Rama has been killed today, all of them have uttered a falsehood. They said that I would be the queen at a great sacrifice and that I would be the wife supporting such a sacrifice. They did not know. Since Rama has been killed today, all of them have uttered a falsehood. Those learned ones told me that I was blessed. I would be the wife of a brave king. They did not know. Since Rama has been killed today, all of them have uttered a falsehood. In my hearing, those brahmanas spoke the auspicious words that I would be close to my husband. They did not know. Since Rama has been killed today, all of them have uttered a falsehood. Indeed, I have marks of the lotus on the soles of my feet. Because of that, women are consecrated on a throne, with their husbands, who are Indras among men. The inauspicious signs on women who become widows and are limited in fortune are missing. As I look at myself, those signs cannot be discerned. The signs of the lotus on women convey a truth. Since Rama has been slain today, that has been rendered false. My hair is extremely fine, black and smooth. My eyebrows do not touch each other. My hips are round and possess no hair. There are no gaps between my teeth. My temples, eyes, hands, feet, ankles and thighs are perfect in proportion. My fingers are smooth and my nails are delicate and well rounded. My breasts are plump and there is no gap between them. My nipples are depressed. My navel is turned inwards.

[137] Astrologers, soothsayers.

My flanks and breasts are smooth. My complexion is like that of a jewel. My body hair is soft. It is said that I possess the auspicious signs and stand on twelve limbs.[138] Those who are learned about the signs of maidens have spoken of me as one who has the complexion of barley, with no gaps in the hands and the feet,[139] and as one who smiles gently. The brahmanas who are skilled and know about what will happen said that I would be consecrated on the throne with my husband. Everything has been rendered false. Having got to know what had happened, those two brothers searched in Janasthana and crossed the ocean that cannot be agitated. Thereafter, they have been slain in a puddle.[140] Indeed, the two Raghavas knew about the use of Varuna, Agneya, Aindra, Vayavya and Brahmashira weapons. They were like Vasava. Rama and Lakshmana have been killed by someone who used maya to remain invisible in the battle. They were my protectors and I have no protector now. Having come within the range of vision of Raghava in an encounter, no enemy could return with his life, even if he possessed the speed of thought. The burden of destiny is extremely heavy. Death is extremely difficult to vanquish. That is the reason Rama and his brother are lying down, having been brought down in the battle. I am not grieving over the death of my husband and Lakshmana or for myself or my mother, as I am over my ascetic mother-in-law. She incessantly thinks about the time when the vow will be over and about when she will be able to see Sita, Rama and Lakshmana return.'

While she was lamenting, the rakshasi Trijata spoke. 'O queen! Do not grieve unnecessarily. Your husband is alive. O queen! Let me tell you about the great signs whereby one knows that these two brothers, Rama and Lakshmana, are alive. When leaders are killed in a battle, the faces of the warriors do not show any rage. Nor are they filled with joy.[141] O Vaidehi! This vimana has the name of Pushpaka.

[138] Ten toes and two soles.

[139] No space between the fingers and the toes.

[140] The text uses the word *goshpada*. This literally means the mark of a cow's foot in the soil and the small puddle of water that fills up such a mark, that is, a trifle.

[141] This is not very clear. It probably means that the other warriors do not stand around, but do something instead.

Had they been killed, it would not have brought you here, through the sky. When the foremost and valiant warrior has been killed, the soldiers lose all eagerness and enterprise. They wander around in the battle, like a boat in the water that has lost its rudder. O spirited ones! These ones are without fear and show no anxiety. The soldiers are protecting the two Kakutsthas, who have been vanquished in the battle through the use of maya. These signs should give rise to joy and you should be devoid of your anxiety. You will see that the two Kakutsthas have not been killed. Out of my affection, I am telling you this. I have never uttered a falsehood in the past, nor will I ever speak it. Because of your character and good conduct, you have found a place in my heart. Indra, with the gods and the asuras, is incapable of defeating these two in a battle. Having looked at their faces, this is what I can tell you. O Maithilee! Gently look at the great signs. They are still breathing and their beauty has not deserted them. In general, when men lose their breath of life and their lives, their faces are seen to be greatly distorted. O Janaka's daughter! Give up your misery, grief and confusion. It is impossible for Rama and Lakshmana not to remain alive.' Hearing her words, Sita Maithilee, who was like a daughter of the gods, joined her hands in salutation and said, 'May it be that way.' With the speed of thought, Pushpaka vimana returned. The distressed Trijata and Sita entered Lanka. With Trijata, she got down from Pushpaka and the rakshasis made her enter Ashokavana. Sita entered the pleasure ground of the Indra among the rakshasas, filled with many clumps of trees. Having seen the two princes, she thought about them and was filled with great sorrow.

Chapter 6(39)

Dasharatha's two sons were tied down in the terrible bonds of arrows. They were lying down, covered with blood and sighing like serpents. All the foremost and immensely strong apes, with Sugriva, were filled with sorrow and surrounded the great-souled ones.

At this time, the valiant Rama regained his senses. Despite being bound down by the arrows, he used yoga to steady his spirit. He saw his brother, covered in blood and severely unconscious, lying down on the ground. Suffering and with a distressed face, he lamented. 'What will I do with Sita? What is the point of remaining alive? Today, I can see my brother vanquished in a battle, lying down. If I search the world, I am capable of finding a woman like Sita. But one cannot find a brother, adviser and companion like Lakshmana. If he, the extender of Sumitra's delight, returns to the five elements,[142] while these apes look on, I will give up my life. What will I tell my mother, Kousalya? What will I tell Kaikeyee? What will I tell the mother, Sumitra, who desires to see her son? If I return without you, how will I comfort her? Without her calf, she will tremble and shriek like a female osprey. What will I tell Shatrughna and the illustrious Bharata? He went to the forest with me, but I will return without him. Sumitra is firm in her vows and I will not be able to approach her. I will give up my body here. I am not interested in remaining alive. Shame on me. Shame on my evil and ignoble deeds, since this has happened. Lakshmana has fallen down and is lying on a bed of arrows, as if he has lost his life. O Lakshmana! When I was greatly distressed, you always comforted me. Now that you have lost your life, when I am distressed, you will be incapable of speaking to me. In the battle today, he killed many rakshasas who are lying down on the ground. Slain by the enemy, the brave one is now lying down on the ground. He is lying down on this bed of arrows, covered in his own blood. He is radiant in this net of arrows, like the sun when it is about to set. Your inner organs have been pierced by arrows and you are incapable of seeing. Though you are not speaking, the dust and red tinge in your eyes are eloquent. When I went to the forest, the immensely radiant one followed me. In that way, I will follow him to Yama's abode. He was always devoted to the welfare of his relatives. He always followed me. He has been reduced to this state because of my ignoble and evil policy. I do not remember any words the brave Lakshmana spoke

[142] The text uses the word *panchatva*. This simply means death, that is, when the body is separated into the five elements.

in rage. I have never heard any harsh or disagreeable words. With one shot, he was capable of releasing five hundred arrows. In the use of weapons, Lakshmana was thus superior to Kartavirya.[143] With his weapons, the great-souled one could destroy Shakra's weapons. He deserved to lie down on an extremely expensive bed, but is lying down on the ground. There is no doubt that the false words I have uttered will destroy me. I have not made Vibhishana the king of the rakshasas. O Sugriva! You should return this instant. O king! Without me, the powerful Ravana will overwhelm you. O Sugriva! Use the bridge across the ocean again and with Angada at the forefront and with your soldiers and well-wishers, return. I am content with the extremely difficult tasks that have been accomplished in the battle by Hanumat and the others, the king of the bears and the lord of the golangulas. Deeds have been done by Angada, Mainda and Dvivida. Kesari and Sampati fought fiercely in the battle. For my sake, Gavaya, Gavaksha, Sharabha, Gaja and other apes were ready to give up their lives in the battle. O Sugriva! It is impossible for humans to cross their destiny. O scorcher of enemies! As a friend and a well-wisher, you have done everything you could. O Sugriva! O one scared of adharma! You have done everything you could. O bulls among the apes! You have performed the acts of friends. With my permission, all of you should now go where you wish.'

All the apes heard his lamentations. Tears flowed from their dark-rimmed eyes. Vibhishana steadied all the formations. With a club in his hand, he quickly went to the spot where Raghava was. He resembled a mass of dark collyrium. Seeing him advance swiftly, all the apes took him to be Ravana's son and fled.

Chapter 6(40)

The immensely energetic and immensely strong king of the apes asked, 'Why is this army distressed, like a boat in the water

[143] Kartavirya Arjuna.

that has been rendered immobile because of the wind?' Hearing Sugriva's words, Angada, Vali's son, replied, 'Do you not see the immensely strong Rama and Lakshmana? Those two brave sons of Dasharatha are tied down in nets of arrows. Covered in blood, those two great-souled ones are lying down on the ground on beds of arrows.' At this, Sugriva, Indra among the apes, told his son[144] Angada, 'I do not think that is the reason why there are scared. Their faces are distressed. They are fleeing in different directions, abandoning their weapons. The apes have dilated their eyes in terror and are rambling incoherently. They are not ashamed of each other and are not glancing back. They are jostling against each other and are jumping over the ones who have fallen down.'

At this time, holding a club in his hand, the brave Vibhishana approached Sugriva, looked at him and said, 'May Raghava be prosperous.' Sugriva saw that Vibhishana had caused terror among the apes.[145] He told Jambavat, the king of the bears, who was near him, 'Vibhishana has come here. On seeing him, the bulls among the apes are running away in fear, suspecting him to be Ravana's son. They are terrified and are fleeing in many directions. Quickly steady them and tell them that it is Vibhishana who has come.' Thus addressed by Sugriva, Jambavat, the king of the bears, assured the apes and made the ones who were fleeing return. Abandoning their fear, all the apes returned, after hearing the words of the king of the bears and seeing Vibhishana.

Vibhishana, with dharma in his soul, saw that Rama's body was pierced with arrows and so was that of Lakshmana. His senses were afflicted. He dipped his hands in water and wiped his eyes. His mind suffered from grief and he wept and lamented. 'These two brave and spirited ones loved to fight. They have been brought to this state by rakshasas who fight in mysterious ways. My brother's son is a wicked son and is evil in his soul. That rakshasa is deceitful in his intelligence and has dislodged two who are upright in their valour. They have been pierced a lot

[144] Son by extension.

[145] Because they took him to be Indrajit.

with arrows and blood is flowing. They can be seen, sleeping on the ground like porcupines. Depending on their valour, I desired a status for myself. However, these two bulls among men are asleep, waiting for their bodies to be destroyed. With their lives under threat now, my desire for the kingdom will be destroyed. My enemy, Ravana, will accomplish his pledge and his wishes will be satisfied.' When Vibhishana lamented in this way, the spirited Sugriva embraced him. The king of the apes spoke these words. 'O one who knows about dharma! There is no doubt that you will obtain the kingdom of Lanka. Ravana and his son will not obtain this kingdom. These two, Raghava and Lakshmana, are not badly wounded. Once they get out of their confusion, they will slay Ravana and his companions in the battle.' He comforted and assured the rakshasa in this way.

His father-in-law, Sushena, was by his side and Sugriva addressed him. 'With the large numbers of brave apes go to Kishkindha. Take these two brothers, Rama and Lakshmana, the scorchers of enemies, with you. Until they have regained their senses, remain there. I will kill Ravana, together with his sons and his relatives. Like Shakra got his lost prosperity back, I will bring back Maithilee.' Hearing the words of the Indra among the apes, Sushena spoke these words. 'There was a great and extremely terrible battle between the gods and the asuras. The danavas were skilled in avoiding the touch of the arrows. Despite the gods knowing about the use of weapons, they repeatedly struck them. They were afflicted and destroyed. They lost their senses and almost lost their lives. Brihasapti used his knowledge of mantras and herbs to treat them. Let apes who are swift in their speed, Sampati, Panasa and the others, quickly go to the ocean with milky waters and fetch those herbs. The apes know about the great herbs in the mountains— *sanjivakarani* and the divine *vishalya*, created by the gods.[146] In the excellent ocean, there are two mountains named Chandra and Drona. Amrita was churned there and the supreme herbs are there. The gods placed

[146] Sanjivakarani means something that imparts life, vishalya means something that removes stakes.

the supreme herbs in the mountains there. O king! Let Hanumat, Vayu's son, go there.'

At this time, a wind arose, accompanied by clouds tinged with lightning. This agitated the water in the ocean and seemed to make the mountains tremble. As a result of the strong wind resulting from the wings, all the large trees on the island fell down. Their branches and roots were shattered and flung into the salty waters. The snakes and serpents that resided there[147] were terrified. All of them quickly submerged, deep into the salty ocean. In a short while, all the apes saw Garuda, Vinata's immensely strong son, blazing like a fire. In the form of arrows, snakes had tied down the two immensely strong men.[148] On seeing him arrive, these fled. Seeing the two Kakutsthas, Suparna honoured them. He touched their faces, which possessed the radiance of the moon, with his hands. Their wounds were healed by the touch of Vinata's son. Their bodies quickly became smooth and excellent in complexion. The great qualities of their energy, valour, strength, endurance and enterprise, as well as their foresight, intelligence and memory were doubled. Garuda raised those two extremely valiant ones, who were Vasava's equal. He cheerfully embraced them.

Rama said, 'It is through your favours that we have been able to overcome the great calamity caused through the powers of Ravana's son. We have swiftly become strong. My heart is as pleased at meeting you as with meeting my father Dasharatha and my grandfather, Aja. O handsome one! Who are you, adorned with divine garlands and pastes? Your garments sparkle and you are adorned with divine ornaments.'

The immensely radiant and immensely strong king of the birds was pleased in his heart. With delight in his eyes, Vinata's son replied, 'O Kakutstha! I am your friend, as loved by you outside your body as your breath of life is inside. I am Garuda and I have come here to help the two of you. The asuras are immensely valiant and the danavas are immensely strong. But they, and all the gods

[147] In the ocean.

[148] Rama and Lakshmana.

and gandharvas, even if they placed Shatakratu at the forefront, were incapable of freeing you from this extremely terrible bondage of arrows fashioned through the strength of maya by Indrajit, cruel in deeds. These nagas are Kadru's offspring. Their fangs are sharp and filled with virulent poison. Because of the strength of maya of the rakshasa, they assumed this form of arrows. O one who knows about dharma! O Rama! O one who has truth as his valour! With your brother, Lakshmana, the slayer of enemies in the battle, you are fortunate. Having heard what happened, out of affection for the two of you and observing my friendship, I quickly came here. The two of you have now been freed from the extremely terrible bondage of arrows. However, you must always remain vigilant. In all encounters, the rakshasas naturally fight in deceitful ways. But for brave ones like you, pure in sentiments, uprightness constitutes your strength. In the field of battle, you must never trust the rakshasas. He is an example to show that the rakshasas are always deceitful.' Having told Rama this, the extremely strong Suparna affectionately embraced him and prepared to leave. 'O friend! O Raghava! O one who knows about dharma! O one who is affectionate even towards his enemies! I desire your leave, to return where I came from. With arrows that are like waves, you will only leave the young and the aged in Lanka, killing your enemy, Ravana. You will get Sita back.' Having said this, Suparna, swift in his valour, removed the wounds from Rama. In the midst of those residents of the forest, he circumambulated and embraced the valiant one. Like the wind, Suparna then penetrated the sky.

The leaders of the apes saw that the wounds on the two Raghavas had healed. They roared like lions and lashed their tails. Kettledrums and drums were sounded. Delighted, they blew on conch shells. As was the case earlier, they started to jump around. Some brave apes, who fought with trees, boasted. Hundreds and thousands of them uprooted trees and stood there. They emitted loud roars and scared the roamers in the night. Desiring to fight, the apes assembled before Lanka's gates. A terrible and tumultuous roar arose among the herds of apes, like the extremely terrible roar of the clouds in the night, when summer is over.

Chapter 6(41)

The spirited apes created an extremely tumultuous sound. Ravana, together with the rakshasas, heard the sounds of their roaring. They heard that terrible, deep and rumbling sound. In the midst of his advisers, he spoke these words. 'It is evident that the apes are delighted. An extremely loud roar, like the thunder of the clouds, has arisen amidst them. There is no doubt that there is a reason for their great joy. That is the reason this loud roar is agitating Varuna's abode. The two brothers, Rama and Lakshmana, were bound down with sharp arrows. Because of this extremely loud roar, a doubt has arisen in me.' Having said this to his ministers, the lord of the rakshasas spoke to the nairittas who were near him. 'Go and quickly find out everything about the roamers in the forest. At this time of grieving, how has a reason for delight arisen?' Thus addressed, they swiftly climbed up the ramparts and saw the army protected by the great-souled Sugriva. They saw that the two Raghavas had been freed from the extremely terrible bondage of arrows and that the two immensely fortunate ones had got up. The rakshasas were distressed. With their hearts full of fear, they descended from the ramparts. With pale faces, all of them presented themselves before the Indra among the rakshasas. With distress in their faces, the roamers in the night, accomplished in the use of words, told Ravana everything about that disagreeable and unpleasant news. 'In the battle, Indrajit had bound down the two brothers, Rama and Lakshmana, in bonds of arrows and had disabled their arms. They can be seen in the field of battle, freed from the bondage of arrows. In their valour, they are like Indras among elephants and, like elephants, have severed their bonds.'

Hearing their words, the immensely strong Indra among the rakshasas was overcome by thoughts and sorrow. With a distressed face, he said, 'Indrajit was granted a terrible boon and tied them down with arrows, invincible and like the sun, in the form of virulent serpents. He crushed them in the encounter. Despite the bondage of that weapon, if my enemies have freed themselves, I can see a great danger presenting itself before all my soldiers. They were shrouded in arrows that possessed Vasuki's energy. However, that has been rendered unsuccessful. Despite having faced that in the battle, my enemies are still alive.' Having said this, he sighed like an enraged serpent. In the midst of the rakshasas, he spoke to the rakshasa named Dhumraksha. This rakshasa was filled with great strength and was terrible in his deeds. 'Leave and kill Rama and the apes.' Thus addressed by the intelligent Indra among the rakshasas, Dhumraksha prostrated himself. Delighted, he emerged from the king's residence.

Emerging through the gate, he told the commander of the forces, 'Ask the forces to hurry. Why delay in fighting?' Following Ravana's command and hearing Dhumraksha's words, the commander of the forces told the soldiers who followed him to quickly ready the army. Those roamers in the night were terrible in form and bells were tied to their bodies. They roared happily and surrounded Dhumraksha. They wielded many kinds of weapons in their hands. There were spears and clubs in their hands. There were bludgeons, lances, staffs and extremely terrible iron maces. There were clubs, *bhindipalas*,[149] javelins, spikes and battleaxes. The terrible rakshasas emerged, roaring like clouds. Some were on chariots. Others carried decorated standards and readied nets made out of gold. These[150] were yoked to mules with many kinds of faces, extremely swift steeds and excellent elephants that were crazy and excited. As unassailable as tigers, the tigers among rakshasas emerged. Dhumraksha ascended a divine chariot that roared like a mule. It was decorated with gold and yoked to mules that had faces like wolves and lions. Surrounded by rakshasas, the immensely valorous Dhumraksha emerged laughingly through the western gate, where Hanumat, the leader of the herd, was stationed.

The extremely terrible rakshasa left and he was terrible to behold. From the sky, terrible birds tried to restrain him.[151] An extremely terrible vulture descended on the top of his chariot and

[149] Catapults or javelins that are like blowpipes, with arrows shot through them.

[150] The chariots.

[151] These were ominous portents.

seated itself on the top of his flag. Others that fed on corpses also descended. A giant torso, wet with blood, fell down on the ground near Dhumraksha and emitted a harsh roar. A god showered down blood and the earth trembled. The wind blew in a contrary direction, with a sound like that of a storm. The directions were enveloped in waves of darkness and could not be discerned. The rakshasas saw these ominous signs, the harbingers of fear. These extremely terrible portents manifested themselves and Dhumraksha was distressed. However, the strong one was eager to fight and emerged. He was surrounded by many extremely terrible roamers in the night. He saw the army of several apes. It was like the ocean and was protected by Raghava's arms.

Chapter 6(42)

With a terrible roar, the rakshasa Dhumraksha emerged. All the apes desired to fight. On seeing this, they were delighted and roared. A terrible fight ensued between the apes and the rakshasas. They fought against each other and slew each other with terrible trees and spears and clubs. In every direction, the apes were struck down by the terrible rakshasas. Using trees, the apes also felled the rakshasas down on the ground. Enraged, the rakshasas pierced the apes with sharp and terrible arrows that were shafted with the feathers of herons. They used clubs, terrible spears, heavy bludgeons, terrible maces and colourful tridents. The immensely strong apes also routed the rakshasas. They were excited because of their intolerance and fearlessly performed these deeds. Their bodies were mangled by arrows. Their bodies were struck by spears. However, the leaders among the apes seized trees and boulders. Terrible in their force, the apes roared here and there. They announced their names and crushed the terrible rakshasas. An extraordinary and terrible battle ensued between the apes and the rakshasas. Many boulders and trees with many branches were used. Some rakshasas were crushed by apes who wished for victory. Some who subsisted on blood[152] vomited blood from their mouths. Some were struck along the flanks. There were piles of those who had been struck by trees. Some were shattered with boulders and some were torn apart with teeth. Standards were crushed and shattered. Mules were brought down. Chariots were fragmented. The roamers in the night were brought down. The apes, terrible in their valour, repeatedly flung themselves on the rakshasas, tearing their faces apart with the sharp nails on their hands. Their faces turned pale, their hair was torn out.[153] Senseless because of the smell of blood, they fell down on the ground. This made the rakshasas, terrible in their valour, extremely angry. In the battle, they rushed against the apes with palms that possessed the touch of the vajra. When they were attacked with force, the apes retaliated with greater force. They brought the enemy down with fists, feet, teeth and trees.

Dhumraksha, bull among the rakshasas, saw that the soldiers were being made to flee. In his anger, he fought and created carnage among the apes. Some were crushed with lances, other apes began to ooze out blood. Some others were struck with clubs and fell down on the ground. Some were struck with maces, others shattered with bhindipalas. Others were struck with spears and, senseless, lost their lives. Some residents of the forest were killed and, wet with blood, fell down on the ground. Some were driven away and destroyed, as the angry rakshasas fought. The hearts of some were shattered and they lay down on one side. Some were struck with tridents and their entrails came out. That encounter between the apes and the rakshasas was great and extremely terrible. Many kinds of weapons were used and so were boulders and trees. There was the sweet sound of bowstrings being twanged. Other sounds seemed to possess a rhythm. It was as if a song was gently being sung by the gandharvas. In the field of battle, Dhumraksha laughed. With a bow in his hand, he drove away the apes in all the directions, showering arrows over them. Maruti saw that the soldiers were distressed and afflicted because of Dhumraksha. He seized a gigantic boulder and

[152] Rakshasas.

[153] A description of the rakshasas.

angrily attacked. His eyes were coppery red. He was like his father in valour and his anger doubled the strength. He flung that boulder towards Dhumraksha's chariot. On seeing that boulder descend, he quickly raised a club, leapt down with great force from the chariot and stood on the ground. Having crushed the chariot, its wheels, *kubara*,[154] horses, standard and the bows, the boulder fell down on the ground. Hanumat, the wind god's son, destroyed the chariot. He then used trees with trunks and branches to create carnage among the rakshasas. The rakshasas were covered with blood, their heads crushed. Others were mangled by the trees and fell down on the ground. Hanumat, the son of the wind god, drove away the rakshasa soldiers. He seized the summit of a mountain and rushed towards Dhumraksha. As he descended, the valiant Dhumraksha raised his club. Roaring, he violently attacked Hanumat. The club was studded with many spikes. With force and anger, Dhumraksha brought it down on Hanumat's head. But the ape possessed the strength of the wind god. Though he was struck by a club that was terrible in form, he paid no heed to the blow. Instead, he brought down the summit of the mountain on Dhumraksha's head. Struck by the summit of the mountain, all his limbs were shattered. He suddenly fell down on the ground, like a mountain that has been fragmented. Seeing that Dhumraksha had been killed, the remaining roamers in the night were frightened. Slain by the apes, they entered Lanka. The son of the wind god killed the enemy. From their wounds, a river of blood started to flow. Exhausted from having slain the enemy, the great-souled one was delighted and was worshipped by the apes.

Chapter 6(43)

Ravana, the lord of the rakshasas, heard that Dhumraksha had been killed. The commander of the forces was present there, his hands joined in salutation. He told him, 'Let invincible rakshasas,

[154] Kubara is the pole for attaching the yoke to the chariot.

terrible in their valour, quickly emerge. Let them place Akampana, skilled in the use of all weapons, at the forefront.'

Terrible in appearance, with horrible eyes, the best among rakshasas seized many kinds of weapons. Urged by the commander of the forces, they attacked. Akampana left, surrounded by terrible rakshasas. He was astride a large chariot that had the complexion of a cloud and made a loud clatter, like the rumbling of a cloud. He himself possessed the complexion of a cloud and was adorned with ornaments made out of molten gold. In a great battle, even the gods were incapable of making him quake. Among the others, Akampana's energy was like that of the sun. He rushed forward angrily, wishing to fight. But suddenly, the horses that bore his chariot along seemed to be struck with lassitude.[155] Though he took joy in fighting, his left eye started to twitch. The complexion of his face paled and his voice became tremulous. Though it was an excellent day, it turned into a bad day and a harsh wind started to blow. All the animals and birds shrieked in cruel tones and this signified fear. However, his shoulders were like those of a lion and he was like a tiger in his valour. Without thinking about these omens, he rushed forward into the field of battle. As the rakshasa emerged with the other rakshasas, there was an extremely loud roar that seemed to agitate the ocean. The large army of the apes was terrified by this sound. With trees and boulders as weapons, they stationed themselves for the battle. An extremely fierce battle ensued between the apes and the rakshasas. For the sake of Rama and Ravana, they were ready to give up their lives. All of them were extremely strong and brave. All of them were like mountains. The apes and the rakshasas desired to slay each other. There was the sound of those extremely spirited ones roaring as they clashed. One could hear them roaring at each other in great rage. As the apes and the rakshasas fought, an extremely terrible dust that was red in hue arose and spread in the ten directions. Like a white silken garment waving in the wind, this dust covered all creatures and they could no longer distinguish each other on the field of battle.

[155] Ominous portents.

Because of the dust, standards, flags, armour, horses, weapons and chariots could not be seen. There was only the extremely loud and tumultuous sound of roaring and clashing. This could be heard in the battle, but nothing could be seen. Exceedingly angry, apes killed other apes in the battle. Because of the darkness, rakshasas also killed other rakshasas. The apes and the rakshasas killed the enemy and also those from their own side. Wet with blood, the earth smeared itself with mire. The dust was sprinkled with waves of blood and settled down. The earth was seen to be strewn with dead bodies. The energetic apes and rakshasas quickly struck each other with trees, spears, boulders, lances, clubs, bludgeons and javelins. The apes were like mountains and terrible in their deeds. With arms like clubs, they fought against the rakshasas and killed them in the battle. The rakshasas were also angry and had spears and javelins in their hands. With those extremely terrible weapons, they slew the apes who were there. The apes used large trees and large rocks to attack and rout the rakshasas, using their valour to counter those weapons.

At this time, the brave apes, Kumuda, Nala and Mainda became supremely angry and displayed excellent force. In the field of battle, those extremely swift leaders among the herds of apes seemed to be sporting as they created great carnage, using trees against the rakshasas.

Chapter 6(44)

Witnessing the extremely great deeds performed by those excellent apes in the battle, Akampana was filled with fierce rage. His form became senseless with rage and he seized his supreme bow. Witnessing the deeds performed by the enemy, he addressed his charioteer in these words. 'O charioteer! Quickly drive the chariot there, where a large number of rakshasas are being slain in the battle. The strong apes, terrible in form, are there. With trees and boulders as weapons, they will stand before me there. They pride themselves on fighting and I wish to slay them. It can be seen that they are crushing all the rakshasa soldiers.' The chariot of the supreme among warriors was drawn by swift horses. In his anger, Akampana attacked the apes and enveloped them in nets of arrows. The apes were incapable of standing there, not to speak of fighting in the battle. They were routed by Akampana's arrows and all of them ran away.

The immensely strong Hanumat saw that his relatives had come under the subjugation of death and were being subdued by Akampana. He attacked and all the leaders among the apes saw that great ape. All those brave apes assembled in the battle and surrounded him. The leaders among the apes saw that Hanumat was stationed there. Because he was strong, the strong ones also sought succour in him. Hanumat was stationed there, with a complexion like that of a mountain. Akampana showered down arrows on him, like the great Indra pouring down rain. Torrents of sharp arrows descended on his body, but he paid no heed to them. The immensely strong one had made up his mind to slay Akampana. The immensely energetic Hanumat, the son of the wind god, laughed. He made the earth quake and attacked the rakshasa. He roared and blazed in his energy. His invincible and radiant form was like that of the fire. The bull among the apes knew that he possessed no weapons. Filled with anger, he used his force to uproot a mountain. Maruti seized that great mountain in one of his hands. The valiant one emitted an extremely loud roar and whirled it around. With that, he attacked Akampana, Indra among the rakshasas, the way Purandara had used his vajra to attack Namuchi in a battle. Akampana saw that the summit of the mountain had been raised up. From a distance, he used arrows that were in the shape of a half-crescent to shatter it. In the sky, the summit of the mountain was shattered by the rakshasa's arrows and, fragmented, fell down. On seeing this, Hanumat became senseless with rage. Full of anger and intolerance, the ape approached an ashvakarna tree. He swiftly uprooted it and like a great mountain, held it up. The immensely radiant one seized the ashvakarna tree, which possessed a gigantic trunk. Greatly happy, he seized it and whirled it around in the battle. Full of great rage, he rushed forward with it. The trees were quickly shattered from the force of his thighs. The earth was shattered from the force of his footsteps. Elephants climbed atop elephants and chariots atop chariots. The intelligent Hanumat slew rakshasa foot soldiers with this. In the battle, he was as angry as Death and destroyed lives. Hanumat saw that the rakshasas were running away. He descended angrily and caused fear to the rakshasas.

Seeing this, the brave Akampana became angry and roared. He used fourteen sharp arrows that could tear the body apart. Using these, the immensely valiant Akampana pierced Hanumat. He was pierced with many showers of arrows. The brave Hanumat could be seen, like a tall mountain. Using supreme speed, he uprooted another tree and used this to quickly strike Akampana, Indra among rakshasas, on the head. In rage, the great-souled Indra among apes struck the rakshasa and he died and fell down in the battle. Akampana, Indra among rakshasas, was slain and lay down on the ground. On seeing this, all the rakshasas were pained, like trees during an earthquake. All the rakshasas were defeated and cast aside their weapons. Terrified and pursued by the apes, they fled towards Lanka. Their hair was dishevelled and they were scared. They were defeated and their pride was destroyed. Sweat dripped from their limbs. As they fled, they sighed. As they entered the city in their fright, they trampled over each other. Confounded, they repeatedly looked back towards the rear. Those immensely strong rakshasas entered Lanka. All the apes assembled together and worshipped Hanumat. He was also delighted and worshipped all the apes back, as they respectively deserved. Hanumat was spirited and kindly disposed towards them. Desiring victory, according to their capabilities, the apes roared. They again dragged away the rakshasas who were still alive.

Maruti killed the assembled rakshasas. The great ape dazzled in his valour. In the field of battle, he was like the powerful Vishnu, when he destroyed the terrible enemy that was in the form of the great asuras. The large number of gods worshipped the god. So did Rama himself and the extremely strong Lakshmana. So did Sugriva, foremost among the apes, and the immensely strong Vibhishana.

Chapter 6(45)

Hearing that Akampana had been killed, the Indra among the rakshasas became angry. With a slightly crestfallen face, he glanced towards his advisers. He thought for a while and consulted with his ministers. He went all around Lanka and inspected all the battalions. He saw the city of Lanka, with garlands of flags and standards. It was protected by large numbers of rakshasas and many battalions covered it. Ravana, the lord of the rakshasas, saw that the city was barricaded. At that time, intolerant, he spoke to Prahasta, who was skilled in fighting. 'O one who is accomplished in fighting! The city will be suddenly besieged and attacked. I do not see any other means of escaping from a battle. With the exception of I, Kumbhakarna, you, my general, Indrajit and Nikumbha, there is no one else who can bear a burden like this. Therefore, quickly collect some forces and gather them together. For the sake of victory, advance to the spot where the residents of the forest are. When you advance, it is certain that the army of the apes will prove to be fickle. Hearing the roars of the Indras among the rakshasas, they will run away. Apes are fickle and insolent, their minds waver. They will not be able to tolerate the roar, like elephants can't stand the sound of lions roaring. O Prahasta! When those soldiers run away, Rama and Lakshmana will be helpless and without a support, easily subjugated. It is better to make certain a danger that is uncertain.[156] Whether favourable or unfavourable, what do you think is a better course of action for us?' Thus addressed by Ravana, the general, Prahasta, replied to the Indra among the rakshasas, the way Ushanas spoke to the Indra among the asuras. 'O king! Earlier, we have held consultations with the skilled ministers on this. After consulting with each other, there was a dispute among us about what should be done. I think that the best course of action is to return Sita. If she was not returned, we foresaw that there would be a battle. I have always been honoured by you, with gifts, respect

[156] The sense seems to be the following. If the rakshasas wait for the attack, the danger is uncertain. If the rakshasas attack, the danger is certain.

and many kinds of conciliation. When the time arrives, why will I not do what is agreeable to you? I will not protect my life, sons, wives or riches. For your sake, behold. I will give up my life in the battle and offer it as an oblation.' The general spoke in this way to Ravana, his master.

Having said this, Prahasta spoke to the commanders who were standing in front of him. 'Quickly assemble a large army of rakshasas. In the field of battle, I will use arrows that possess the force of the vajra to kill the residents of the forest and satisfy birds with their flesh.' In the rakshasa's[157] residence, the immensely strong commanders heard his words. They swiftly readied an army. In a short while, there were brave rakshasas, armed with various kinds of sharp weapons, and elephants in Lanka. Some satisfied the fire with oblations. Others bowed down before brahmanas. A fragrant breeze started to blow, carrying the smell of clarified butter. There were many kinds of garlands. With mantras, oblations were offered. Cheerfully, the rakshasas prepared many kinds of equipment required for the battle. Speedily, the rakshasas brought bows and armour. While King Ravana looked on, they surrounded Prahasta. With the king's permission, terrible battledrums were sounded. Prahasta ascended a divine chariot that had been prepared. It was yoked to swift horses and there was a well-trained charioteer. It roared like a large cloud and was as radiant as the sun and the moon. There was an invincible standard with the mark of a serpent. There were excellent bumpers and excellent wheels. There were nets of gold and it seemed to smile in its prosperity. Commanded by Ravana, he ascended this chariot. Surrounded by a large army, he quickly emerged from Lanka. Battledrums were sounded, with a sound like that of clouds. As the commanders of the army departed, the sounds of conch shells could be heard. With the sound of these terrible roars, the rakshasas advanced towards the front. They were terrible in form and gigantic in size. Prahasta was at the front. Arrayed in an extremely terrible formation, he emerged through the eastern gate, surrounded by a large army that was like a herd

[157] Ravana's.

of elephants. He was surrounded by an army that resembled waves in the ocean. Like an enraged Death, Prahasta quickly emerged. There was the sound of his departure and the rakshasas roared. All the creatures in Lanka howled in hideous voices. In a sky that was devoid of clouds, birds that fed on flesh and blood circled the chariot in a counterclockwise direction.[158] Horrible jackals vomited fires with flames. Meteors descended from the sky. Harsh winds started to blow. The planets seemed to clash against each other and lost their lustre. Blood showered down and sprinkled those who were towards the front. A vulture descended on the standard and faced the southern direction. The charioteer had taken part in several clashes. However, when he was urging the horses, the goad fell down from the *suta*'s[159] hand. As he emerged, there was a radiance and prosperity that was extremely difficult to obtain. However, this vanished in an instant and though the ground was even, the horses lost their footing.

Prahasta, famous for his strength and manliness, emerged. With many kinds of weapons, the soldiers of the apes countered him in the battle. An extremely tumultuous sound arose among the apes. They uprooted heavy trees and seized boulders. The soldiers on both sides, large numbers of rakshasas and residents of the forest, rejoiced. They were forceful and capable and desired to slay each other. A large sound of their challenging each other was heard. For the sake of victory, the evil-minded Prahasta headed in the direction of the army of the king of the apes. He entered that army with great force, like an insect that is about to die heads towards the fire.

Chapter 6(46)

The terrible Prahasta, terrible in his valour, emerged. He was surrounded by extremely large rakshasas who roared. The

[158] Regarded as inauspicious.

[159] The sutas were charioteers and bards.

large army of the apes saw him and, filled with anger, roared back at Prahasta. The rakshasas, desiring victory, seized glittering weapons—swords, spikes, daggers, spears, clubs, maces, bludgeons, javelins, many kinds of battleaxes and different kinds of bows—and rushed against the apes. Desiring to fight, the bulls among the apes seized flowering trees and long and large boulders. As they rushed against each other, there was an extremely great encounter. There were many showers of rocks, and showers of arrows also rained down. In the battle, many rakshasas killed many leaders among the apes. Many apes also killed many rakshasas. Some were crushed through spears, some through supreme weapons. Some were struck with clubs, some were severed with battleaxes. Some lost all enterprise and fell down on the ground. The hearts of some were shattered, pierced by arrows aimed at them. Some were sliced into two with swords and, writhing, fell down on the ground. The rakshasas used spears to rip apart the sides of the apes. Angry, hordes of apes surrounded the rakshasas from all directions. Using trees and the summits of mountains, they crushed them down on the ground. They severely struck them with palms, hands and fists that were like the vajra to the touch. They[160] vomited blood from their mouths and their teeth and eyes were smashed. As the apes and the rakshasas fought in the battle, there was a tumultuous sound. There was the sound of those in distress and roars, like the roaring of lions. Enraged, apes and rakshasas followed the path meant for heroes. They dilated their eyes and fearlessly performed these cruel deeds.

Narantaka, Kumbhahanu, Mahanada and Samunnata—these advisers of Prahasta killed the residents of the forest. They descended swiftly and killed the apes. With a single strike of the summit of a mountain, Dvivida killed Narantaka. Swift in the use of his hands, the ape Durmukha uprooted a large tree and brought down the rakshasa Samunnata. The wrathful Jambavat seized a large boulder and used this to strike the energetic Mahanada on the chest and bring him down. Tara clashed against the valiant

[160] Rakshasas.

Kumbhahanu and struck him on the head with a tree. The rakshasa lost his life. Prahasta was astride his chariot and could not tolerate these deeds. With a bow in his hand, he created terrible carnage among the residents of the forest. There was turbulence in both the armies. They roared like the immeasurable ocean, when it is agitated. Prahasta was skilled in fighting. In that great battle, he wrathfully used a great flood of arrows to afflict the apes. The earth was covered with the bodies of apes and rakshasas, like terrible mountains that had fallen down. The earth was seen to be covered with floods of blood, as if it was covered with flowering *palasha* trees in the month of Madhava.[161] The bodies of slain warriors were like banks. The shattered weapons were like large trees.[162] There was a large river with waves of blood that headed for the ocean that was Yama. Livers and spleens were its great mire. The scattered entrails were the moss. The severed heads and torsos were the fish, the flesh was the lichen. The vultures were like large numbers of swans. The herons were like geese. The fat was the foam, the shrieks of the afflicted were its roar. There was such a river in the field of battle and it was impossible for cowards to cross. It was like a river at the end of the summer, frequented by swans and cranes. The best among the rakshasas and apes found that river extremely difficult to cross. They were like devastated lotuses in a lotus pond when a herd of elephants has crossed over it.

Stationed on his chariot, Prahasta shot floods of arrows. Nila saw that the spirited one was slaying the apes. As Prahasta, the extremely invincible one, descended, the great and valiant ape uprooted a tree and struck him with this. Struck by this, the enraged bull among the rakshasas roared. He rained down showers of arrows on the commanders of the apes. He[163] was unable to counter these and received them with closed eyes, like a bull receives a sudden and swift autumn downpour. In that way, Nila closed his eyes and received the extremely terrible shower of Prahasta's

[161] Madhava is a name for the month of Magha (January–February). Palasha trees have red flowers.

[162] Along the banks.

[163] Nila.

arrows, which were very difficult to resist. But this shower of arrows enraged him. The great Nila seized an extremely large sala tree and slew Prahasta's horses, which were as swift as thought, with this. Prahasta, the commander of the army, found that his bow had been shattered. He seized a terrible club and leapt down from his chariot. Those two leaders of the respective armies were spirited and angry. Though there were wounds on all their limbs, they stood there, like elephants with shattered temples. They tore at each other like a lion and a tiger attacking each other with their extremely sharp teeth. They were like a lion and a tiger in their efforts. Those two brave and valiant ones desired victory and did not retreat from the field of battle. Desiring fame, they were like Vritra and Vasava. With supreme ease, Prahasta struck Nila on the forehead with the club and blood started to flow from this blow. Blood covered the great ape's limbs. He seized an extremely large tree and angrily hurled it towards Prahasta's chest. This blow was unthinkable. However, the strong one seized the giant club and rushed towards Nila, the strong ape. He descended with great force and anger. On seeing this, the great ape, extremely swift, seized a large boulder. Prahasta desired to fight and in the encounter, was ready to fight with the club. However, Nila quickly brought the boulder down on his head. Nila, the foremost ape, released this giant boulder and it shattered the terrible Prahasta's head into many fragments. He lost his life. He lost his beauty. He lost his spirits. He lost his senses. He suddenly fell down on the ground, like a tree severed at the roots. With his head shattered, a lot of blood started to flow and ooze out from his body, like a waterfall from a mountain.

When Prahasta was killed by Nila, that large army of rakshasas was distressed and wavered. It left for Lanka. With the leader killed, they were incapable of remaining there, like water is driven back on confronting a dam. With the leader of the army killed, the rakshasas lost their enterprise. They were benumbed and went to the residence of the lord of the rakshasas. The immensely strong Nila was victorious. He met Rama and Lakshmana and was praised for his own deeds. The leader of the herd was delighted.

Chapter 6(47)

In the battle, the protector of the rakshasa soldiers was slain by the bull among the apes. Armed with terrible weapons, the army of the king of the rakshasas was like the ocean in its force. But they ran away. They went to the lord of the rakshasas and told him that the commander had been killed by the son of the fire god.[164] Hearing their words, the lord of the rakshasas was filled with rage. He heard that Prahasta had been killed in the battle. He was afflicted by grief and his senses were overcome by anger. Like Indra speaking to the foremost warriors of the immortals, he spoke to the foremost warriors among the nairittas. 'My commander[165] has killed Indra's forces. However, he, with his companions and his elephants, has been killed. This enemy should not be taken lightly. I will not hesitate. For the sake of victory and to destroy the enemy, I will myself go to the wonderful field of battle. With a flood of arrows, I will burn down that army of apes, together with Rama and Lakshmana, like a blazing fire burns down a forest.'

Having said this, the enemy of the king of the immortals, with a dazzling and shining form, ascended a radiant and blazing chariot which was yoked to excellent steeds. Conch shells, drums and cymbals were sounded. Palms were slapped and there were leonine roars. The foremost king of the rakshasas departed, worshipped with auspicious benedictions. The foremost king of the rakshasas was surrounded, like the Rudra, the lord of the immortals, by demons.[166] They were like dark clouds in their forms. They subsisted on flesh and their eyes blazed like the fire. The immensely energetic one suddenly emerged from the city and saw that the army of the apes was stationed in front. He saw that it was roaring like the giant ocean or like a cloud. There were upraised trees and boulders in their hands.

[164] Nila.
[165] Prahasta.
[166] *Bhutas*.

The army of the rakshasas was extremely terrible. Seeing this, Rama, followed by the soldiers and extensive in his prosperity, with arms resembling an Indra among serpents, spoke to Vibhishana, supreme among those who knew how to use weapons. 'There are many flags, standards and weapons. There are spikes, swords, spears, chakras and other weapons. The army possesses elephants that are as large as mountains. It cannot be agitated and is full of fearless ones. Whom does it belong to?' Vibhishana was Shakra's equal in valour. Hearing the words Rama had spoken, he told him about this excellent army, which consisted of great-souled bulls among the rakshasas. 'There is a great-souled one astride that elephant. He is like a sun that has just arisen and his face is coppery red in complexion. His being astride it is making the elephant's head tremble. O king! Know him to be Akampana.[167] There is one on a chariot, with a standard bearing a lion on it. He is stretching a bow that is as radiant as Shakra's bow. He is as radiant as a fierce elephant with extended tusks. He is named Indrajit, supreme among excellent ones.[168] There is an archer astride that chariot. He is like Vindhya, Asta or Mahendra. He is the atiratha Atikaya. He is drawing a bow that is unmatched in size. He is name Atikaya because his body is exceedingly large.[169] There is one whose eyes are coppery red and he resembles the newly risen sun. Astride an elephant with jangling bells, that great-souled one is roaring harshly. He is the brave one named Mahodara. He is astride a chariot with a colourful and golden harness. He resembles an evening cloud or a mountain. He has raised a spear that is blazing in its rays. This is Pishacha and he is like the lightning in his speed. That one has seized a sharp spear. He is astride an Indra among bulls that is like a mountain. This *kimkara*[170] is like thunder in his speed and his radiance is like that of lightning. That one who is advancing

[167] Unless there was more than one Akampana, there is a consistency problem. Akampana has already been killed by Hanumat.

[168] Alternatively, one who has obtained an excellent boon.

[169] *Kaya* means body and *ati* means exceedingly.

[170] As in, Ravana's servant.

is the illustrious Trishira.[171] That one has the form of a cloud. His chest is broad, firm and formed well. His standard has the king of the serpents. Controlled, he is twanging his bow. He is Kumbha. That one has seized a blazing and smoking club encrusted with molten gold and diamonds. He is advancing with the standard of the army of the rakshasas. That is Nikumbha, the performer of terrible and extraordinary deeds. That one is on a chariot that is shining brightly, as dazzling in form as the fire. There are bows, swords, masses of arrows and flags on the chariot. That one is Narantaka and he fights with the summits of mountains.[172] That one can assume many kinds of terrible forms. He is surrounded by large-eyed and radiant demons[173] with faces like tigers, camels, large serpents and lions. He is the one who destroyed the pride of even the gods. His lustre is like that of the moon. A white umbrella with slender spokes is held above his head. This is the great-souled lord of the rakshasas. He is advancing like Rudra surrounded by bhutas. He wears a diadem and his earrings are moving. His terrible form is like that of Vindhya, Indra among mountains. He is the one who destroyed the pride of the great Indra and of Vaivasvata. As radiant as the sun, the lord of the rakshasas is advancing.'

Rama replied to Vibhishana, the scorcher of enemies. 'The dazzling and great energy of Ravana, the lord of the rakshasas, is amazing. Ravana is blazing like the sun and like the sun's rays, he is extremely difficult to look at. From the signs on his form it is evident that he is full of energy. The bodies of the brave gods and danavas are not like this. They do not dazzle as much as the body of the Indra among the rakshasas. All of them resemble mountains. All of them fight with mountains. All of them are wielding lustrous weapons. All the warriors are extremely energetic. The king of the rakshasas is radiant. He shines in his terrible valour. He is surrounded by fierce ones, like Death is by embodied bhutas.' Saying this, the

[171] Since Rama killed Trishira in Janasthana, there may be another consistency problem.

[172] Narantaka has already been killed by Dvivida.

[173] Bhutas.

valiant Rama seized his bow and picked up an excellent arrow, with Lakshmana following him.

The great-souled lord of the rakshasas spoke to those immensely strong rakshasas. 'Have no fear. Station yourselves properly and tend to the gates, the houses and turrets.' He swiftly gave them permission to leave and the rakshasas went to their appointed places. He then shattered the apes, which were like waves in the ocean, filled with large fish. The Indra among rakshasas was ready to fight and descended violently with his blazing bow and arrows. On seeing this, the lord of the apes[174] uprooted the summit of a large mountain and attacked the lord of the rakshasas with this. The summit of the mountain was full of many trees and peaks and seizing it, he hurled it towards the roamer in the night. On seeing it violently descend, he pierced it with arrows with golden tufts. The excellent and large summit of the mountain was full of trees. With the summit shattered, it fell down on the ground. The protector of the world of the rakshasas then picked up an arrow that was like a gigantic snake, with a hue like that of Death. He seized it and it was like the fire in its force. With sparks flying, it possessed a flaming form. That arrow was like the great Indra's vajra in its speed. To kill Sugriva, he angrily released it. The arrow was released from Ravana's arm. It was sharp at the tip and had an excellent form, like Shakra's vajra. It approached Sugriva and pierced him with force, like Guha's fierce spear shattering the Krouncha mountain.[175] Afflicted by the arrow, he lost his senses. Shrieking, the brave one fell down on the ground. Seeing that he had lost his senses and had fallen down on the ground, the yatudhanas who were fighting roared in delight.

Gavaksha, Gavaya, Sudamshtra, Rishabha, Jyotimukha and Nala raised boulders that were gigantic in size and rushed towards the Indra among the rakshasas. The lord of the rakhasas used innumerable arrows that were sharp at the tips to rend this attack fruitless. With nets of arrows that were made out of gold and were

[174] Sugriva.

[175] Kartikeya shattered Mount Krouncha with his spear.

colourfully tufted, he pierced the Indras among the apes. Pierced by the arrows of the enemy of the gods, the Indras among the apes, terrible in form, fell down on the ground. He then enveloped the army of the apes with nets of fierce arrows. Those foremost among brave ones were struck. Pierced by the arrows, they were scared and shrieked. They ran away and sought refuge with Rama.

The great-souled Rama seized his bow and, with his bow, started to swiftly leave. However, Lakshmana approached him, joined his hands in salution, and spoke words that were full of great meaning. 'O noble one! If I wish, I am capable of killing this evil-souled one. I will destroy this inferior one. O lord! Grant me permission.' For Rama, truth was valour and the immensely energetic one said, 'O Lakshmana! Go. Take care against the enemy in the encounter. Ravana is extremely brave. In an encounter, his valour is extraordinary. If he is enraged, there is no doubt that the three worlds are incapable of standing before him. Seek out his weak spots. Hide your own weak spots. Control yourself and make efforts, using your eyes and your bow to protect yourself.' Hearing Raghava's words, he embraced and worshipped him. Honouring Rama, Soumitri set out to do battle. He saw Ravana, with arms that were like the trunks of elephants. He blazed as he held aloft his terrible bow. He enveloped the apes, showering them with nets of arrows and mangling and scattering their bodies.

The immensely energetic Hanumat, son of the wind god, saw this. He sought to counter this net of arrows and attacked Ravana. To scare Ravana, the intelligent Hanumat approached his chariot, raised his right hand and uttered these words. 'You cannot be routed by gods, danavas, gandharvas, yakshas and rakshasas. But you face fear from apes. I have raised my right hand and this has five branches. I will destroy the life that has been in your body for a very long time.' Hearing Hanumat's words, the eyes of Ravana, terrible in his valour, turned red with anger and he spoke these words. 'Without any hesitation, strike me quickly. Be steady and obtain fame. O ape! After ascertaining your valour, I will destroy you.' Hearing Ravana's words, the son of the wind god spoke these words. 'Remember that I have already killed your son Aksha.'

Thus addressed, the immensely energetic Ravana, the lord of the rakshasas, struck the valiant son of the wind god on the chest with his palm. Struck by the palm, he wavered repeatedly. However, enraged, he struck the enemy of the immortals with his palm instead. Struck by the palm of the great-souled ape, Dashagriva was whirled around, like the earth during an earthquake. Seeing that Ravana had suffered in the battle because of the blow from the palm, the rishis, the apes, the siddhas, the gods and the asuras roared. After this, the immensely energetic Ravana regained his composure and spoke these words. 'O ape! Excellent. Though you are my enemy, your valour is praiseworthy.' Thus addressed by Ravana, Maruti replied in these words. 'O Ravana! Since you are still alive, shame on my valour. Those with good deeds speak through their blows. O one evil in intelligence! Why are you boasting? In truth, my fist will convey you to Yama's abode.' At Maruti's words, he blazed in rage. With reddened eyes, the valiant one carefully raised his right fist and brought it down with force on the ape's chest. Struck severely on the chest, Hanumat reeled again.

Seeing that the immensely strong Hanumat was distracted, the atiratha quickly steered his chariot and advanced towards Nila. The lord of the rakshasas used terrible arrows that were like serpents and could penetrate extremely deep into the inner organs. He used these blazing arrows against Nila, the commander of the army of the apes. Nila, the commander of the army of the apes, was struck by this flood of arrows. He picked up the summit of a mountain with one hand and hurled it towards the lord of the rakshasas. The great-souled and energetic Hanumat also regained his composure. Seeing this and wanting to fight, he spoke these angry words to Ravana, the lord of the rakshasas, who was engaged in fighting with Nila. 'When you are fighting with someone, it is not proper to attack someone else.' The immensely strong Ravana struck the summit with seven arrows that were extremely sharp. Struck in this way, the summit shattered and fell down. The commander of the army of the apes saw that the summit of the mountain had been fragmented. The slayer of enemy heroes blazed in anger, like the fire of destruction. In the battle, Nila hurled ashvakarna, dhava, sala, flowering *chutas*[176] and many other kinds of trees. Ravana severed all the trees that were hurled at him. He rained down extremely terrible showers of arrows on the son of the fire god.[177] He was showered by these torrents of arrows, like a cloud raining down on a large mountain. He made his form extremely small and leapt on to the top of the standard.[178] The son of the fire god stationed himself on the top of the standard. Seeing this, Ravana blazed in anger, while Nila roared. The ape leapt from the top of his standard to the top of his bow and then to the top of his diadem. Witnessing this, Lakshmana, Hanumat and Rama were astounded. The immensely energetic Ravana was also amazed at the ape's dexterity. He picked up the blazing and wonderful Agneya weapon. The apes rejoiced and shouted at Nila having fearlessly countered Ravana in the battle and on seeing that he had accomplished his objective. Ravana was provoked by the roar of the apes. His heart was disturbed and he wasn't sure about what he should do. Ravana thus picked up and affixed the Agneya arrow. The roamer in the night aimed in the direction of Nila, who was stationed atop the standard. The immensely energetic Ravana, the lord of the rakshasas said, 'O ape! You are dexterous and supreme in the use of maya. O ape! But if you are capable, protect your life. Create numerous forms that are exactly like you. Even then, you will not be able to escape from the arrow that I have affixed. Protect your life. Even if you are alive, you will be destroyed.' Saying this, the mighty-armed Ravana, the lord of the rakshasas, aimed the arrow and struck the commander of the army. In the form of the arrow, the weapon struck Nila on his chest. Violently scorched, he fell down on the ground. However, because of his father's greatness and because of his own energy, he did not lose his life. He sank down on his knees on the ground.

Dashagriva saw that the ape was unconscious. But he was eager to fight. On a chariot that roared like the clouds, he attacked Soumitri. When he brandished his immeasurable bow, with an undistressed spirit, Soumitri spoke to him. 'O Indra of the roamers

[176] Mango trees.

[177] Nila.

[178] Ravana's standard.

in the night! Advance against me. You should not fight against apes.' The king heard these loudly proclaimed words and the fierce twanging of his bow. He approached the spot where Soumitri was stationed. The rakshasa spoke words that were filled with anger. 'O Raghava! It is good fortune that you have come within the range of my vision. O one perverse in intelligence! You will now meet your end. You will proceed to the land of the dead this very instant. My net of arrows will envelop you.' Though he roared with his white-tipped teeth, Soumitri wasn't disturbed. He replied, 'O king! Those who are great in their powers do not roar. O supreme among those who are wicked in their deeds! Why are you indulging in self-praise? O Indra among the rakshasas! I know your valour, strength, power and prowess. Come. I am stationed here, with a bow and arrows in my hand. Why indulge in pointless self-praise?' When he said this, the lord of the rakshasas became angry and shot seven well-tufted arrows. However, Lakshmana severed these with gold-tufted and colourful arrows that were sharp at the tips and edges. The arrows of the lord of Lanka were violently countered, like serpents repulsed by Indras among serpents. Seeing this, he became angry and shot other sharp arrows. He rained down showers of terrible arrows. However, Rama's younger brother was not agitated. He affixed excellent kshura, *ardhachandra*, *karni* and bhalla arrows[179] and severed those. Lakshmana swiftly affixed arrows that were sharp at the tips. They were like the great Indra's vajra in their force and were blazing in form. To slay the lord of the rakshasas, he released them. The Indra among the rakshasas countered and severed them. He then struck Lakshmana on the forehead with an arrow that was like the fire of destruction in its powers and had been given to him by Svayambhu. Lakshmana was afflicted by Ravana's arrow and wavered. As he trembled, he leaned on his bow. He regained his senses with difficulty and severed the bow of the enemy of the Indra among the gods. When his bow was severed, Dasharatha's son struck him with three arrows that were sharp at

[179] Kshurapras (kshuras) are arrows with sharp edges, ardhachandras are in the shape of a half-moon, karnis are barbed and bhallas have broad heads.

the tips. Afflicted by those arrows, the king wavered, but regained his senses with difficulty. His bow was severed and he suffered from those arrows. He was wet with sweat and there was blood on his body. In the battle, summoning up all his fierce energy, the enemy of the gods seized a spear that had been given to him by Svayambhu. It was like the fire and emitted smoke. It terrified the army of the apes. The protector of the kingdom of the rakshasas quickly hurled this blazing spear towards Soumitri. As that weapon descended, Bharata's younger brother struck it with his arrows, like oblations being offered into the fire. Despite this, the spear penetrated into the broad chest of Dasharatha's son. Brahma's spear struck Soumitri between the breasts. However, he remembered whose portion he himself was and thought of Vishnu. Thus, the thorn of the gods was unable to oppress and raise the lord who destroyed the insolence of the danavas with his arms.[180] In a battle, Bharata's younger brother was like the Himalayas, Mandara or Meru, and the three worlds, together with the immortals, were incapable of afflicting him with their arms. He was born from Vishnu's portion, although he had resorted to a human body. On seeing the state of the unconscious Lakshmana, Ravana was amazed.

The son of the wind god was enraged and attacked Ravana. With a fist that was like the vajra, he angrily struck him on the chest. As a result of that blow with the fist, Ravana, the lord of the rakshasas, trembled and fell down. He sank down on his knees on the ground. Seeing that Ravana, terrible in his valour, was unconscious in the battle, the rishis, the apes and the gods, with Vasava, roared. Lakshmana had been afflicted by Ravana. The energetic Hanumat raised him up with his arms and took him to Raghava. The son of the wind god was a well-wisher and supremely devoted. The ape was light in his stride and the enemies were unable to make him quake. Soumitri was extremely difficult to vanquish in a battle. The spear left him and returned to its place in Ravana's chariot. In the great battle, the immensely energetic Ravana also regained his

[180] The Critical Edition excises a few shlokas where Ravana tries to pick up the unconscious Lakshmana with his arms.

senses. He picked up sharp arrows and seized his great bow. The stake was removed from Lakshmana, the slayer of enemies, and he regained his composure. He remembered his own self and that he had been born from Vishnu's portion.

Brave warriors from the great army of the apes had been brought down. In the battle, seeing this, Raghava attacked Ravana. At this, Hanumat approached him and spoke these words. 'If you ascend my back, you will be able to chastise the rakshasa.' Rama heard the words spoken by the son of the wind god. The brave one quickly climbed on to the great ape, Hanumat. In the encounter, the lord of men saw that Ravana was astride his chariot. Seeing this, the immensely energetic one rushed against Ravana, just as an angry Vishnu raised his weapon against Virochana's son.[181] He twanged his bow fiercely, with a sound that was like the clap of thunder. In a deep voice, Rama spoke these words to the Indra among the rakshasas. 'Stay. O tiger among the rakshasas! Stay. Having performed such a disagreeable act towards me, how can you possibly escape? Even if you go to the worlds of Indra, Vaivasvata, the sun god, Svayambhu, the fire god, Shankara or the different directions, you will not be able to escape from me today. You struck down someone with your spear today, but he overcame his distress and quickly arose. O king of large numbers of rakshasas! In the battle today, death will come to you and to your sons and wives.'[182] Hearing Raghava's words, the Indra among the rakshasas used sharp arrows that were like the flames of the fire of destruction to strike the great ape. In the battle, he was struck by the rakshasa's arrows. However, because of his natural energy, his energy increased in consequence. The greatly energetic Rama saw that the tiger among apes had been wounded by Ravana and was overcome with rage. Rama approached and used arrows that were sharp at the tips to sever his chariot, its wheels, the horses, the standard, the umbrella, the large flag, the charioteer, the javelins, the spears and the swords. He then used an arrow that was like the thunder and the vajra to swiftly strike Indra's enemy in his

[181] Bali.

[182] The use of the word wives is odd. Non-Critical versions say grandsons instead.

broad and beautiful chest, like the illustrious Indra striking Meru with his vajra. The king was incapable of being agitated or made to waver by the thunder or the vajra. However, struck by Rama's arrow he was severely afflicted. The brave one wavered and let go of his bow. Rama saw that he was reeling and picked up a blazing ardhachandra arrow that had the complexion of the sun. The great-souled one swiftly severed the diadem of the lord of the rakshasas. The setting on the diadem lost its lustre. It was as resplendent as the sun, but seemed to lose its rays. It was like a venomous serpent that had lost its poison. In the battle, Rama spoke to the Indra among the rakshasas. 'You have accomplished great and terrible deeds. You have killed brave ones on my side. Therefore, it is evident that you are exhausted. In this state, I will not use my arrows to convey you to the land of the dead.' He was addressed in this way and lost his pride and his joy. He lost his bow, and his horses and charioteer were slain. He was afflicted by the arrows and his great diadem was shattered. The king swiftly entered Lanka.

When the immensely strong Indra among the roamers of the night, the enemy of the gods and the danavas, had left, in the field of that great battle, Rama, with Lakshmana, arranged for the stakes to be removed from the apes. The Indra of the enemies of the gods was routed in this way. The gods, the asuras, the large number of bhutas, the directions, the oceans, the rishis, and all creatures on land and in the water rejoiced.

Chapter 6(48)

Frightened and afflicted by Rama's arrows, the king lost his pride and his senses suffered. He entered the city of Lanka. Like an elephant by a lion or a serpent by Garuda, the king had been overcome by the great-souled Raghava. Raghava's arrows were like Brahma's staff and as radiant as lightning. The lord of the rakshasas suffered because of these and remembered them. He seated himself on a supreme and divine throne made out of gold. Ravana looked at the rakshasas and spoke these words. 'All the supreme austerities I have performed have become useless. I am like the great Indra, but I have been vanquished by a human. Brahma spoke terrible words to me. "Know that you will face fear from humans." That has now come to be true. I asked that I could not be killed by gods, danavas, gandharvas, yakshas, rakshasas and serpents, but I did not ask the same about humans. Since this is evident, all of you should make the best efforts. Let the rakshasas station themselves on the tops of the turrets and patrol there. Awake Kumbhakarna, who suffers because of Brahma's curse. He is unmatched in his gravity and is one who removes the insolence of the gods and the danavas.' Knowing that he had been defeated and that Prahasta had been killed, the immensely strong one commanded the terrible army of the rakshasas. 'Take care at the gates and climb atop the walls. Awake Kumbhakarna, who is deep in slumber. That rakshasa sleeps for nine, six, seven or eight months. Quickly wake up the immensely strong Kumbhakarna. In a battle, the mighty-armed one is the support of all the rakshasas. He will swiftly slay the apes and the two princes. The foolish Kumbhakarna sleeps all the time, he is devoted to ordinary pleasures.[183] He will engage in an extremely terrible clash against Rama. If he wakes up, there will no longer be any sorrow for me. If he cannot help me in this terrible catastrophe I now face, what is the point of his possessing a strength that is like that of Shakra?'

Hearing the words of the Indra among the rakshasas, the rakshasas, in great fear, went to Kumbhakarna's residence. The devourers of flesh and blood were commanded by Ravana. Taking fragrances, garlands and food with them, they quickly went. They entered through the great gate into an area that was one yojana wide on all sides. This was Kumbhakarna's cave and all kinds of scents wafted in all directions. Those immensely strong ones entered the cave and could only remain there with a great deal of difficulty, because of Kumbhakarna's breathing. They entered that beautiful and auspicious cave, encrusted with gold and jewels. They saw the

[183] Literally, the pleasures of villagers.

tiger among nairittas lying down and he was terrible to behold. His sleeping and disfigured form was spread out like a mountain.

Kumbhakarna was deep in slumber and together, they tried to wake him up. The hair on his body stood up upright and he sighed like a serpent. He was terrible to behold. As he slept, his great breaths terrified them. His nostrils were horrible and his mouth was as large as patala. They saw the immensely strong Kumbhakarna, tiger among the nairittas. As a supreme offering, they placed a pile of flesh that was as large as Meru in front of the great-souled Kumbhakarna. Those tigers among nairittas had gathered an extraordinary heap from the meat of deer, buffaloes and boars. There were many pots filled with blood and liquor. They placed these in front of Kumbhakarna, the enemy of the gods. They smeared the scorcher of enemies with excellent unguents and sandalwood paste. They covered him with divine garlands, fragrances and perfumes. They ignited fragrant incense and praised the scorcher of enemies. Thousands of yatudhanas roared like thundering clouds. They blew on conch shells that were as radiant as the moon. Together, those intolerant ones roared and made a tumultuous sound. The roamers in the night roared and clapped their hands. Seeking to wake Kumbhakarna up, they created this tumultuous sound. There were conch shells, drums, kettledrums and gongs. They clapped and slapped and roared like lions. The sound spread in the directions and up into the sky. Hearing this sudden sound, flying birds fell down. But despite this terrible noise the great-souled Kumbhakarna did not wake up from his slumber. Therefore, all the large numbers of rakshasas seized catapults, clubs, maces, summits of mountains, pestles and bludgeons. Kumbhakarna was sleeping happily, lying down on the ground. The fierce rakshasas used these and their fists to strike him on the chest. The rakshasa Kumbhakarna's breathing was like a gale. Despite being strong, the rakshasas were incapable of standing before him. Those rakshasas, terrible in their valour, stationed themselves there. Together, ten thousand rakshasas started to make a sound with drums, smaller drums, kettledrums, conch shells and trumpets. He was like a mass of dark collyrium and did not awake. Though they created a noise and struck him, he did not realize any of this. Using these means, they were incapable of waking him up. They then started to make greater and extremely terrible efforts. They struck horses, camels, donkeys and elephants with rods and goads.[184] They applied all their strength to drums, conch shells and kettledrums. They struck his body with large pieces of wood that had spikes on them. They applied all their strength to clubs and maces. Lanka was filled with that great sound, with all its mountains and its forests. Even then, he did not awake. One thousand drums were sounded simultaneously in every direction, using sticks fashioned out of refined gold. However, he continued to sleep on and did not wake up, because he was controlled by the curse. The roamers of the night became angry. All of them, terrible in their valour, were suffused with great rage. The rakshasas used all their valour to wake him up. Some beat on drums. Others emitted loud roars. Some pulled out his hair. Others bit his ears with their teeth. But Kumbhakarna was deep in slumber. He did not move. They struck him on the head, the chest and all over the body with solid clubs. Everywhere, they tied him up with ropes and shataghnis. But though he was struck, the rakshasa, gigantic in size, did not wake up. Thousands of elephants were made to run around all over his body. At this touch, Kumbhakarna awoke from his deep slumber.

Summits of mountains and trees had been brought down on his body. He had been subjected to great blows. Having awoken from his sleep, he sprang up. Suffering from hunger, he yawned. His arms were like the hoods of coiled serpents, as firm in essence as the summits of mountains. He flung these around. His disfigured mouth gaped like the subterranean fire. The roamer in the night opened this and yawned. When he yawned, his mouth was like patala. It was seen to be like the sun arising atop Meru's peak. Having woken up, the extremely strong roamer in the night yawned. When he woke up, his breathing was like a storm raging in a mountain. When Kumbhakarna stood up, his form was like that of a cloud with cranes, raining down at the end of summer. His large eyes

[184] So that they would make a noise.

blazed like giant planets. They were as radiant as the fire, dazzling like the glitter of lightning. Hungry, he ate the flesh and thirsty, drank the blood. Shakra's enemy drank from the pots filled with fat and liquor. Knowing that he was satisfied, all the roamers in the night approached him. They bowed their heads down in prostration and surrounded him from all directions.

The bull among the nairittas comforted all the nairittas. Surprised at having been woken up, he spoke to all the rakshasas. 'Why have you suddenly woken me up? Is the king well? Has some kind of fear arisen? I think it is clear that some kind of grave danger has presented itself. Why else would you have suddenly woken me up? Today, I will uproot the fear that the king of the rakshasas faces. I will shatter the great Indra and pacify the fire god. I would not have thus been woken up from my sleep because of a trifling reason. Therefore, tell me the truth about why I have been woken up.'

The enraged Kumbhakarna, the scorcher of enemies, spoke in this way. Yupaksha, the king's adviser, joined his hands in salutation and said, 'There is not the slightest bit of fear that has arisen for us on account of the gods. Nor is there any kind of fear from the daityas or the danavas. O king! The fear that has presented itself is due to a human. Apes who are like mountains have surrounded Lanka. Since Rama is tormented on account of Sita's abduction, there is a tremendous fear that has arisen from him. Earlier, a single ape burnt down the great city and killed Prince Aksha, his companions and his elephant. The lord of the rakshasas, Poulastya, the thorn of the gods, himself went out to fight and escaped from Rama, who is like the sun in his energy. The king has never suffered from gods, daityas or danavas. However, that act has been done by Rama. His life was in danger, but he managed to escape.' He heard Yupaksha's words to the effect that his brother had been defeated in the battle. Kumbhakarna widened his eyes and told Yupaksha, 'O Yupaksha! Today, in the battle, I will vanquish all the soldiers of the apes, together with Lakshmana and Raghava. I will only see Ravana after that. I will satisfy the rakshasas with the flesh and the blood of the apes. I will myself drink Rama and Lakshmana's blood.' His proud words were laced with his enhanced rage.

Hearing his words, Mahodara, the foremost among the nairitta warriors, joined his hands in salutation and spoke these words. 'First hear Ravana's words and the pros and cons. O mighty-armed one! After that, defeat the enemy in the battle.' Hearing Mahodara's words, the immensely energetic and immensely strong Kumbhakarna departed, surrounded by the rakshasas. His eyes were horrible and he was terrible in appearance and valour. Having woken him up, the rakshasas swiftly headed for Dashagriva's residence. They went to Dashagriva, seated on his supreme throne. Joining their hands in salutation, all the roamers in the night said, 'O bull among rakshasas! Your brother, Kumbhakarna, has woken up. Will he leave? He has come here to meet you.' Rejoicing, Ravana spoke to the rakshasas who had presented themselves. 'I wish to see him. After showing him the due honours, bring him here.'

Thus addressed, all the rakshasas returned to Kumbhakarna and reported the words uttered by Ravana. 'The king, the bull among all the rakshasas, desires to see you. You should make up your mind to go and delight your brother.' The invincible Kumbhakarna agreed to the command issued by his brother. The immensely valiant one leapt up from his bed. He washed his face. He bathed and happily adorned himself in excellent ornaments. Thirsty, he quickly had a drink that would enhance his strength. Following Ravana's command, the rakshasas quickly brought him liquor and many kinds of food, so that they might take him back swiftly. He drank from two thousand pots and prepared to leave. He was slightly intoxicated and maddened with his energy and strength. Kumbhakarna was cheerful and resembled Death. Surrounded by the army of rakshasas, he went to his brother's residence. At Kumbhakarna's footsteps, the earth trembled. His form illuminated the royal road, like the radiance of the one with one thousand rays lights up the earth. He left, surrounded by those who joined their hands in salutation, like Shatakratu going to Svayambhu's residence. Some sought refuge with Rama, the one who grants refuge.[185] Some walked with him, or were distressed and

[185] This refers to those along the road. Presumably, there were apes among them too, not just rakshasas.

fell down. Some were distressed and ran away. Some were terrified and lay down on the ground. He was diademed, like the summit of a mountain. In his energy, he seemed to touch the sun. On seeing this extraordinary sight, the residents of the forest were afflicted by fear and fled here and there.

Chapter 6(49)

On seeing the diademed Kumbhakarna, gigantic in size, the valiant and immensely energetic Rama picked up his bow. He saw the best among rakshasas, who looked like a mountain. The lord[186] himself looked like Narayana in ancient times, ready to stride. He looked like a cloud full of rain, adorned in armlets made out of gold. On seeing him, the great army of apes ran away. The army fled and the rakshasa increased his size. Witnessing this, Rama was astounded and spoke to Vibhishana. 'Who is this? He resembles a cloud. He wears a diadem and his eyes are tawny. He is like a cloud tinged with lightning. Who is this brave one, who can be seen in Lanka? Who is the one who has suddenly surfaced on earth like a meteor? His giant and solitary form can be seen. On seeing him, all the apes are running away, here and there. Tell me. Who is this extremely large person? Is he a rakshasa or an asura? I have never seen such a creature earlier.'

Vibhishana was asked by the prince who was unblemished in his deeds. The immensely wise one replied to Kakutstha in these words. 'He is the powerful Kumbhakarna and he is the son of Vishravasa. He is the one who defeated Vaivasvata[187] and Indra in a battle. O Raghava! In encounters, he has routed thousands of gods, danavas, yakshas, serpents, those who survive on flesh, gandharvas, *vidyadharas*[188] and snakes. The immensely strong Kumbhakarna wielded a spear in his hand and his eyes were

[186] Rama. The allusion is to Vishnu's *vamana* (dwarf) incarnation.

[187] Yama.

[188] Vidyadharas are semi-divine, occupying the region between heaven and earth.

distorted. The confused gods thought that he was Death and were incapable of killing him. The immensely strong Kumbhakarna is naturally energetic. The other Indras among rakshasas obtain their strength because of boons. As soon as he was born, the great-souled one was afflicted by hunger and ate up many thousand creatures. Seeing that they were being devoured, the suffering creatures were terrified. They went and told Shakra this and sought refuge with him. The great Indra was enraged. The wielder of the vajra struck Kumbhakarna with his sharp vajra. Struck by Shakra's vajra, the great-souled one wavered and roared loudly in rage. Hearing the intelligent Kumbhakarna's roar, the terrified creatures on earth were scared again. The immensely strong Kumbhakarna became angry at the great Indra. He uprooted one of Airavata's tusks and struck Vasava on the chest with this. Struck by Kumbhakarna and afflicted, Vasava trembled. All the gods, the rishis and the danavas were suddenly distressed. With Shakra, the subjects went to the spot where Svayambhu was. They told Prajapati about Kumbhakarna's depredations, about how he had devoured the subjects and oppressed the gods. "If he continues to incessantly devour subjects in this fashion, within a short space of time, the world will be empty." Hearing Vasava's words, the grandfather of all the worlds summoned all the rakshasas and also saw Kumbhakarna. Seeing Kumbhakarna, Prajapati was also terrified. Visualizing the emptiness, Svayambhu said, "Poulastya[189] has certainly created you for the destruction of the worlds. Therefore, from now on, you will lie down, as if you are dead." Succumbing to Brahma's curse, he fell down before the lord.[190] Extremely frightened, Ravana spoke these words. "O Prajapati! You are cutting down a grown and golden tree at the time when it will yield fruit. It is not proper for you to curse your own great-grandson. There is no doubt that your words cannot be false. Let him sleep. But designate a time for him to be awake and for him to lie down." Hearing Ravana's words, Svayambhu again said, "Let him sleep for six months and let him

[189] That is, Vishravasa.

[190] Brahma.

remain awake for a single day. On that single day, this brave one will be hungry and will roam around the earth. His mouth will be open and he will angrily devour the worlds, like a fire." Faced with a calamity and dreading your valour, King Ravana has now woken up Kumbhakarna. The brave one, terrible in his valour, has emerged from his camp. Extremely angry, he is rushing towards us, devouring the apes. Seeing Kumbhakarna, the apes have fled. When he is angry in a battle, how can the apes counter him? Let all the apes be told that this is a mechanical contrivance that has turned up. Once the apes know this, they will not be scared.'

The words that emerged from Vibhishana's mouth were full of reasoning. Hearing them, Raghava spoke these words to Nila, the commander. 'O son of the fire god! Go and station all the soldiers in vyuhas. Seize the gates, roads and passages to Lanka. Gather the summits of mountains, trees and boulders. Let all the apes be stationed with their weapons, with boulders in their hands.' Nila, the commander of the army of the apes, was instructed by Raghava. The elephant among the apes issued the appropriate instructions to the army of the apes. Seizing the summits of mountains and with the complexion of mountains themselves, Gavaksha, Sharabha, Hanumat and Angada advanced towards the gates. With boulders and trees raised up in their hands, that fierce army of the apes was resplendent. It looked like a great mass of gigantic and fierce clouds, filled with water, approaching a mountain.

Chapter 6(50)

The tiger among rakshasas was intoxicated and still drowsy. Handsome and pervasive in his valour, he proceeded along the royal road. The extremely invincible one was surrounded by thousands of rakshasas. As he proceeded, from the houses, flowers were showered down on him. He saw the large and beautiful residence of the Indra among the rakshasas. It was as radiant as the sun to behold and it was decorated with nets of gold. Like the sun penetrates a mass of clouds, he entered the residence of the lord of the rakshasas. From a distance, like Shakra seeing the seated Svayambhu, he saw his brother seated on his throne. He went to his brother's residence and then entered his chamber. He saw his anxious brother seated, inside Pushpaka vimana. Dashagriva saw that Kumbhakarna had presented himself. Delighted, he quickly arose and brought him close to him. His brother was seated on the couch. The immensely strong Kumbhakarna worshipped his feet and asked, 'What is to be done?' Delighted, Ravana arose and embraced him. He was embraced by his brother and duly honoured. Kumbhakarna then seated himself on an auspicious, divine and supreme seat. The immensely strong Kumbhakarna sat down on that seat. With eyes red with anger, he addressed Ravana in these words. 'O king! Why did you make efforts to wake me up? Tell me. Who has caused you fear? Who should now become a dead person?' His angry brother, Kumbhakarna, was there.

With his eyes rolling around in rage, Ravana addressed him in these words. 'O immensely strong one! You have been asleep for an extremely long period of time. Since you have been asleep, you do not know about the fear that Rama has caused to me. Rama, Dasharatha's son, is strong and he is with Sugriva. He has crossed the ocean with his army and has attacked our foundation. Alas! Look at Lanka, with its forests and groves. Having crossed easily by means of a bridge, it is now covered with an ocean of apes. In the battle, the apes have killed the foremost among the rakshasas. I do not see any way of destroying the apes in the battle. My treasury is completely exhausted and you must save me and this terrified city of Lanka, which only has children and old ones left. O mighty-armed one! For the sake of your brother, perform this extremely difficult deed. O brother! O scorcher of enemies! I have never had to utter such words earlier. I have affection and supreme respect for you. O bull among rakshasas! In many battles with the gods and the asuras, you have countered the battle formations of the gods and vanquished the asuras in encounters. Among all creatures, no one who is your equal in strength can be seen. Therefore, perform this supremely agreeable task for me. O one who loves to fight! O one who loves his relatives! This will appeal to you. Use your energy to shatter the enemy's army, like a strong wind drives away a cloud during the autumn.'

Chapter 6(51)

Kumbhakarna heard the lamentations of the king of the rakshasas. He laughed and spoke these words. 'We had foreseen this evil earlier, when we had held consultations about what we should do. However, you did not accept the beneficial words that were spoken to you. Indeed, you have quickly reaped the consequences of your evil deeds, just as the perpetrators of wicked acts descend into hell. O great king! At first, you acted without thinking. Because of your valour and insolence, you did not reflect on the consequences. If a person bases himself on his prosperity and does what should be done later, earlier, and what should be done earlier, later, he does not know the difference between good policy and bad policy. If an act is undertaken that is contrary to the time and the place, those acts become tainted, like oblations that haven't been prepared properly. After having an agreement with his advisers, if a person does three kinds of acts and follows five kinds of modes, he is the one who is along the right path.[191] A king is on the right path if he adheres to agreements, uses his intelligence and the intelligence of his advisers and looks towards his well-wishers. O lord of the rakshasas! At the right time, a man must pursue all three of dharma, *artha* and *kama*, or any two of these.[192] If a king or a prince hears which of

[191] The three kinds of acts are seeking peace through an alliance, surrendering and swearing allegiance and fighting. The five kinds of modes are starting an act, ensuring the means to accomplish it, deciding on the time and place for the action, guarding against failure and ensuring the chances of success.

[192] Either one pursues dharma, artha and kama together, or dharma and artha, dharma and kama, or artha and kama. The idea is not to pursue one to the exclusion of the other two.

the three is best, but nevertheless, does not comprehend, even if he is extremely learned, he is a failure. O best among the rakshasas! At the right time, if a person uses gifts, conciliation, bheda and valour,[193] he knows both good policy and bad policy. If one consults with advisers and follows dharma, artha and kama at the right time, such a person does not face any hardships in the world. If a king considers the beneficial consequences that will follow and what is good and bad for himself, he knows the true nature of objectives and lives, together with his advisers. Men who do not know the purport of the sacred texts are like animals in their intelligence. Because of their insolence, they do not desire consultations, nor do they internalize them. The task of those who do not know about the sacred texts is to speak words that are not beneficial. Despite desiring great prosperity, they are ignorant about the sacred texts on wealth.[194] There are audacious and eloquent men who converse about what is not beneficial, pretending that it is beneficial. Even if they outwardly consider consultations, in practice, they perform evil acts. Some learned ones are in connivance with the enemy and ensure the destruction of their master. Such ministers ensure the performance of perverse deeds. The master must be able to identify those who pretend to be friends, but are actually enemies when it comes to offering advice. Through their conduct, he must be able to discern advisers who speak of what is harmful. Fickle deeds enable the swift finding out of those who are perverse. Their weaknesses can be detected, just as birds find out holes in Mount Krouncha. If a person ignores the enemy and does not protect himself, he faces a calamity and is dislodged from his own position.'

Dashagriva heard what Kumbhakarna had to say. He knit his eyebrows in rage and spoke these words. 'Do you take yourself to be my senior preceptor that you are instructing me in this way? Why are you exhausting yourself through words? This is the time for appropriate action. What is the point of repeating now what has already been done because of confusion, delusion, strength, energy

[193] Respectively, dana, sama, bheda and danda.

[194] The text uses the word *arthashastra*.

or prosperity? This is the time to think about what is appropriate now. Use your valour to dispel my present misery. If you indeed feel any affection for me because I am your brother, if your heart feels it should be done and if your intelligence also agrees on the act, this is what you should do. If a person helps someone who faces a hardship and removes that distress, he is a true well-wisher. If he helps when the need arises, he is a true relative.' Though spoken patiently, these were extremely terrible words.

Kumbhakarna noticed that his brother's senses were excessively agitated. He also realized that he was angry. Therefore, softly and gently, he uttered these kind words of assurance. 'O king! O destroyer of enemies! Listen to my words. O Indra among rakshasas! Enough of this torment. Abandon this rage. You should return to your normal state. O king! As long as I am alive, you should not think about such things. I will destroy the person because of whose deeds you are being tormented. Whatever be your state, I must speak beneficial words to you. O king! I spoke those words as a relative and because of brotherly affection. This is the time for a relative to act gently. Behold. Therefore, in the battle, I will create carnage amidst the enemy. O mighty-armed one! Behold me today in the field of battle. Rama and his brother will be slain and the army of the apes will be driven away. In the battle today, you will see me bring back Rama's head. O mighty-armed one! Be happy. May Sita be miserable. Behold the extremely desired objective today, of Rama being killed. He is the one who killed all the relatives of the rakshasas in Lanka. They are overcome by sorrow because they are grieving over their relatives having been killed. Today, after the enemy is destroyed in the battle, I will wipe away their tears. Sugriva, the lord of the apes, is like a mountain. Behold. In the battle today, I will disperse him, like the sun scatters away a cloud. O one whose valour in battle is unmatched! You do not have to look for anyone else to send. I will uproot your extremely strong enemies. I will even fight against Shakra, Yama, the wind god, Kubera and Varuna. My body is as large as a mountain. When I roar with my pointed teeth and wield a sharp spear, even Purandara is terrified. Otherwise, the enemy can quickly turn mild and throw the weapons away. As long as someone faces me, he is incapable of remaining alive. I do not need a spear, a club, a sword or sharp arrows. If I am angry, with my bare hands, I can slay the wielder of the vajra. Today, if Raghava can withstand the force of my fists, I will bring him down with my torrents of arrows and drink Raghava's blood. O king! Why are you tormented by thoughts? I am standing in front of you. I am here to destroy your enemies. I am ready to leave. Give up this fear of Rama. O king! I will kill him in the battle and also Raghava Lakshmana and the immensely strong Sugriva. I wish to give you great and extraordinary fame. I will bring you happiness by slaying Dasharatha's son. I am leaving, so that I can bring you something pleasant. After killing Rama and Lakshmana, I will eat all the chief leaders among the apes. O king! Sport as you will and drink the best of varuni. Cast away your fever and do all that you must. Today, after I have sent Rama to Yama's abode, Sita will come under your subjugation, for a long period of time.'

Chapter 6(52)

Kumbhakarna, the powerful one with strong arms, spoke in this way. Hearing his words, Mahodara said, 'O Kumbhakarna! Though you have been born in a noble lineage, you are audacious and your perspective is ordinary.[195] Because you are insolent, you are incapable of knowing what should be done at all times. O Kumbhakarna! It is not that the king cannot differentiate between good policy and bad policy. Because of childish folly and audacity, you only desire to speak. The bull among rakshasas does know about enhancing and diminishing,[196] he knows how the apportionment of time and place needs to be done and he can distinguish between those on one's own side and the enemy's. A strong person who is ordinary in intelligence and does not respect

[195] Mahodara's arguments are difficult to understand and we have taken some liberties.

[196] Of alliances and relationships.

his seniors is capable of undertaking acts. Why should a learned person act in that way? You have spoken as if dharma, artha and kama are separate objectives. Their nature is such that there are no signs to distinguish between them. Whatever be the consequences, action must always be undertaken. It is better to undertake even wicked deeds. Those also have consequences. It is not necessary that the fruits of dharma and artha are superior. Adharma and *anartha*[197] can also give rise to unintended consequences. Even if a man indulges in acts of kama, in this world and in the next, he obtains the fruits of those deeds. The king set his heart on this act[198] and our views coincided with his. If one displays bravery against an enemy, what is there to condemn in that? Because of your ordinary nature, you have cited reasons for advancing alone. I will tell you why that is inappropriate and not virtuous policy. Earlier, in Janasthana, Raghava killed many extremely strong rakshasas. How will you defeat him alone? Look at all the immensely energetic rakshasas in the city. They are terrified because they have been vanquished earlier. Rama, Dasharatha's son, is like an enraged lion. He is like a snake that is asleep. Ignorantly, you wish to wake him up. He always blazes in his energy and anger and is impossible to assail. He is as intolerable as Death. Who wants to approach him? When one faces an enemy, the outcome is always in doubt. The idea of your advancing alone does not appeal to me. Whether one is superior or inferior and even if the enemy is ordinary, who wishes to take a chance that the life may be given up and one may come under subjugation? O supreme among rakshasas! There is no man who is his equal. He is like Indra and the sun god. How can you speak of fighting against him?'

Having thus angrily spoken to Kumbhakarna, in the midst of the rakshasas, Mahodara spoke to Ravana, the one who made the worlds scream. 'After having already obtained Vaidehi, why are you conversing? If you so desire, Sita will come under your

[197] The reverse of artha.

[198] Of kama.

subjugation. O lord of the rakshasas! I have thought of a means whereby Sita might be persuaded. If it appeals to your intelligence, listen to this. Announce that five of us—I, Dvijihva, Samhradi, Kumbhakarna and Vitardana—are setting out to kill Rama. Having gone, we will make efforts and fight against him. If we defeat the enemy, you need not think of any other devices. However, even after we have fought, if the enemy survives, let us implement the strategy that has come to my mind. We will return from the battle with blood all over and our bodies pierced by sharp arrows that have Rama's name inscribed on them. We will fall at your feet and say, "Raghava and Lakshmana have been devoured by us. Fulfil our wishes." O king! Astride elephants, get it proclaimed everywhere in the city that Rama, his brother and his soldiers have been killed. O destroyer of enemies! Being pleased, bestow on your servants objects of pleasure, servants, objects of desire and riches. Give many warriors garlands, garments and unguents meant for heroes. Rejoicing, you yourself indulge in drinking. This rumour will spread thick and fast and reach everywhere. Then go to Sita alone and comfort her. Tempt her with riches, grain, objects of desire and jewels. O king! Using this means, generate fear and grief. Even if she does not desire it, with her protector destroyed, Sita will come under your subjugation. She will believe that her beloved husband has been killed. Because of her hopelessness and the fickleness of feminine nature, she will come under your subjugation. Earlier, she has been reared in happiness. She deserves happiness, but is afflicted by misery. Knowing that she will obtain happiness with you, she will go to you in every possible way. This is the good policy I have thought of. If you see Rama, a calamity may befall you.[199] Remain here and do not suffer from anxiety. You will obtain great gains without taking part in a fight. O lord of the earth! If a king defeats the enemy without fighting, without the soldiers being destroyed and without facing any uncertainty, he obtains great fame, merits, prosperity and deeds for a long period of time.'

[199] In a battle.

Chapter 6(53)

Thus addressed, Kumbhakarna rebuked Mahodara. He spoke to his brother, Ravana, best among rakshasas. 'I will slay the evil-souled one who has caused you this terrible fear. Today, I will wipe Rama away. Without any enemies, you will be happy. Like clouds without water, brave ones do not unnecessarily roar. Behold. As I obtain my objective, my deeds in the battle will roar. Brave ones demonstrate by performing extremely difficult deeds. They do not praise themselves, nor do they think highly of themselves. O Mahodara! When they hear words spoken by the likes of you, only kings who pride themselves on their learning, but are actually feeble in intelligence, find them to be appealing. Those who are cowards in a battle are always pleasant in speech. They always seek to follow the king and thereby, ensure destruction. Possessing access to the king, well-wishers behave like enemies. The treasury is exhausted, the soldiers have been killed. The king is the only one left in Lanka. I am leaving. I am ready for battle, to defeat the enemy. In the great battle today, I will rectify your bad policy.'

When the intelligent Kumbhakarna spoke these words, the lord of the rakshasas laughed and replied in these words. 'There is no doubt that Mahodara is terrified of Rama. O son![200] O one who is accomplished in fighting! The idea of fighting does not appeal to him. As a well-wisher and in strength, there is no one who is equal to you. O Kumbhakarna! For the sake of slaying the enemy and for victory, depart.'

The destroyer of enemies[201] quickly picked up a sharp spear. It was made entirely out of iron. It blazed and was embellished with molten gold. It was as terrible as Indra's vajra. It was as heavy as the vajra and could devastate gods, danavas, gandharvas, yakshas and kinnaras. It was bound with giant ropes and adorned with red garlands. It naturally emitted sparks of flame and was coloured with the blood of enemies. Having seized this sharp spear, the immensely

[200] The word used is tata,

[201] Kumbhakarna.

energetic Kumbhakarna addressed Ravana in these words. 'I am going alone. Let this large army remain here. I am hungry and angry now. I will devour the apes.' Hearing Kumbhakarna's words, Ravana addressed him in these words. 'Depart, but surround yourself with soldiers with spears and clubs in their hands. The great-souled apes are swift in their conduct. They are crazy and will destroy anyone who is alone, distracted or inattentive. Therefore, go, but surround yourself with an extremely invincible army. Destroy the party of the enemy, which has caused injury to us rakshasas.' The immensely energetic Ravana arose from his seat. He slung a necklace studded with gems at the ends around Kumbhakarna's neck. The great-souled one also fixed armlets, rings, other excellent ornaments and a chain that resembled the moon. Ravana also arranged that his body would be smeared with divine perfumes and garlands, with beautiful earrings on his ears. The large-eared Kumbhakarna was adorned with golden armlets, braclets and breastplates. He was like a fire that had been fed with excellent oblations. A large and black thread adorned his loins. He looked like Mandara at the time when amrita was obtained, coiled around by the serpent.[202] Capable of bearing a great burden, he bore the burden of the golden armour. He resembled the brilliant lightning, radiant in its own illuminations. After fixing the armour, he was resplendent. He looked like a king of mountains, enveloped by clouds in the evening. The rakshasa had ornaments on all his limbs and a spear in his hand. He was as resplendent as Narayana, exerting himself while taking his three strides.[203]

He embraced his brother and circumambulated him. Bowing his head down before him, the immensely strong one departed. To the sound of praises and benedictions, Ravana sent him off. Conch shells and drums were sounded. There were soldiers with excellent weapons. The sound of elephants, horses and chariots was like the thunder of clouds. The great-souled one, supreme among charioteers, was followed by charioteers. The immensely strong Kumbhakarna was followed by terrible ones who were mounted on snakes, camels,

[202] A reference to the churning of the ocean.

[203] A reference to Vishnu's vamana incarnation.

donkeys, horses, lions, wolves, other animals and birds. He held a sharp spear in his hand and flowers were showered down. An umbrella was held above his head. He was intoxicated by his pride and maddened by the smell of blood. The enemy of the danavas and the gods departed. There were many immensely strong foot soldiers and they roared loudly. These terrible rakshasas followed him. Their eyes were horrible and they held weapons in their hands. Their eyes were red and their forms were extremely gigantic. They were like masses of dark collyrium. They held aloft spears, swords and sharp battleaxes. There were many clubs, maces and bludgeons. They bore extremely invincible and large palm trees on their shoulders. These were meant to be hurled. Thus, the immensely energetic and immensely strong Kumbhakarna descended. He emerged from the city in this terrible form and it made the body hair stand up. His breadth was that of one hundred bows and his height was that of six hundred bows. He was fierce. His eyes were like the wheels of a cart. He resembled a large mountain. Resembling a giant mountain that has been burnt, he approached the rakshasas. Kumbhakarna, with the gigantic mouth, laughed and spoke these words. 'Today, I will angrily burn down the foremost apes and their different herds, like insects before a fire. Those apes reside in the forest as they will and have not committed a crime. For those like us, that species is like an ornament in the city's groves. Raghava, together with Lakshmana, are the foundation for this siege of the city. When he is killed, all of them will be killed. I will slay him in the battle.' When Kumbhakarna spoke in this way, the rakshasas emitted an extremely terrible roar and this seemed to make the ocean tremble.

As the intelligent Kumbhakarna swiftly descended, in every direction, many terrible portents manifested themselves. Clouds, filled with meteors and lightning, thundered in extremely terrible tones. The earth, with its oceans and forests, trembled. With blazing pieces of flesh in their mouths, hideous jackals howled. Birds flew around in an anticlockwise direction.[204] As he[205] proceeded along

[204] The anticlockwise direction is inauspicious.

[205] Kumbhakarna.

the road, a vulture descended on the top of his spear. His left eye twitched and his left arm throbbed. A blazing meteor fell down with a terrible sound. The sun lost its lustre. The pleasant breeze stopped to blow. These great omens made the body hair stand up. However, Kumbhakarna was urged by the strength of Death. He did not think about these and departed.

Resembling a mountain, he used his feet to scale over the rampart. He saw the extraordinary army of the apes, resembling a mass of clouds. The apes saw the best among the rakshasas, who was like a mountain. Like clouds dispelled by the wind, they fled in all the directions. Like a net of clouds that has been dispersed, that extremely fierce army of the apes fled in all directions. On seeing this, Kumbhakarna was delighted. He roared like the thunder of the clouds in the sky. On hearing his terrible roar, like sala trees severed at the roots, many apes fell down on the ground. For the sake of slaying the enemy, the great-souled Kumbhakarna emerged with his large club. The large number of apes were filled with a great dread, as if the lord[206] had arrived with the staff of chastisement at the end of a yuga.

Chapter 6(54)

He roared loudly and it resounded in the ocean. He seemed to generate a storm and seemed to shatter the mountains. The apes saw the one with the terrible eyes advance. Maghavan, Yama and Varuna were incapable of killing him. On seeing him, they fled in different directions. On seeing that they were fleeing, Vali's son, Angada, spoke to Nala, Nila, Gavaksha and the immensely strong Kumuda. 'Terrified because of your fear, where are you running away, behaving like ordinary apes? You have forgotten yourselves, your valour and the nobility of your births. O amiable ones! It is best to return. Why are you protecting your lives? This rakshasa is a

[206] Yama.

great terror, but he cannot fight.[207] This great terror has arisen and has been fashioned by the rakshasas. O apes! Return and we will destroy him with our valour.'

Here and there, the apes reassured themselves with difficulty and assembled. In the field of battle, they picked up trees and the summits of mountains in their hands. Having returned, the residents of the forest were angry. In great rage, like maddened elephants, they struck him. The immensely strong ones used lofty summits of mountains, boulders and trees that flowered at the top. However, he did not tremble. Descending on his body, boulders shattered into one hundred fragments. Trees that flowered at the top were shattered and fell down on the ground. Extremely angry, like a fire that has arisen in the forest, he made supreme efforts and crushed the immensely energetic soldiers of the apes. Wet with blood, many bulls among apes lay down. They were restrained and fell down on the ground, like trees with coppery red blossoms. Some apes leapt and ran away, without looking back. Some fell into the ocean and some sought refuge in the sky. Superior in strength, the rakshasa slew those brave ones. Some fled along the path they had used to cross the ocean. In fear, their faces turned pale and some resorted to low ground. Bears climbed up trees and some sought refuge in mountains. Some were submerged in the ocean. Some sought refuge in caves. Some apes were distressed, while some helplessly stood there.

On seeing that the apes were routed, Angada said, 'O apes! Return. Let us stay and fight. If you are routed and go to any place on earth, I do not see a spot for all of you. Return. Why are you protecting your lives? You are running away, casting aside your weapons. This does not befit your manliness. Your wives will laugh at you and even if you live, it is as good as being dead. All of us have been born in noble lineages and are great and pervasive. This act of being scared is indeed ignoble. Why are you giving up your valour and running away? At that time, you boasted in assemblies

[207] The suggestion is that the terror is an imagined one and even that Kumbhakarna is a mechanical contrivance.

of people. You said that you were fierce and great. Where have those words gone? If you hear aspersions of being cowards, shame on your lives. Tread the path followed by virtuous people and cast aside this fear. If there is a short lifespan on earth, let us lie down after being killed. It is difficult for those who suffer from lassitude in the field of battle to obtain Brahma's world. Alternatively, obtain fame by killing the enemy in the battle. Once Kumbhakarna sees Kakutstha, he will not return with his life intact. He will be like an insect that approaches a blazing fire. If we have this urge to run away and protect our lives and a single person routs all of us, our fame will be destroyed.' The brave Angada, wearing golden armlets, spoke these words. Those who were running away replied in words that are condemned by brave ones. 'The rakshasa Kumbhakarna is creating great carnage. This is not the time or the place. We love our lives and are leaving.' Speaking these words, all of them fled in different directions. The leaders of the apes had seen the terrible one, with terrible eyes, approach. At the head of the army, the brave ones who were running away were comforted and assured a lot by Angada. Then, all of them returned. Rishabha, Sharabha, Mainda, Dhumra, Nila, Kumuda, Sushena, Gavaksha, Rambha, Tara, Dvivida and Panasa, with the son of the wind god leading the way, quickly advanced in the direction of the fighting.

Chapter 6(55)

On hearing Angada's words, gigantic in form, they returned. All of them made up their minds and desired to fight. Their valour was invoked and their bravery was enhanced. Because of Angada's words, they stationed themselves at the head of the army. They advanced happily, making up their minds to die. The apes, ready to give up their lives, engaged in a tumultuous battle. They used extremely large trees and huge mountains. The apes quickly raised these and rushed towards Kumbhakarna. The valiant Kumbhakarna was enraged and raised a club. In every direction, gigantic in size, he oppressed and dispersed the foe. Uprooted by Kumbhakarna, fifteen hundred and thousands of apes were strewn around and lay down on the ground. He used his hands to pick up sixteen, eight, ten, twenty and thirty apes at a time, fling them into his mouth and eat them. Extremely angry, he devoured them, like Garuda does to serpents.

Stationed in the sky, Hanumat showered down summits of mountains and many kinds of trees on Kumbhakarna's head. He shattered those summits of mountains with his spear. The immensely strong Kumbhakarna shattered that shower of trees. Seizing the sharp spear, he rushed towards the fierce army of the apes. As he advanced, Hanumat seized a giant mountain and stood in front of him. He angrily struck Kumbhakarna, terrible in form, with force, using that excellent mountain. Thus attacked, he was agitated. His body became wet with fat, sprinkled with blood. The spear was like a flash of lightning and was like a mountain that blazed at the summit. Using this, he struck Maruti in the chest, just as Guha struck Mount Krouncha with the tip of his spear. When he was struck in the chest with this spear, his senses were afflicted and he vomited blood from his mouth. In that great battle, Hanumat roared terribly, like the thunder of the clouds at the end of a yuga. Seeing that he[208] was distressed, the large number of rakshasas rejoiced and suddenly roared. The apes were distressed and afflicted by fear. They ran away from Kumbhakarna.

Nila hurled the summit of a mountain towards the intelligent Kumbhakarna. On seeing that it was descending, he struck it with his fist. Struck by the fist, the summit of the mountain was shattered. Blazing with sparks, it fell down on the ground. Rishabha, Sharabha, Nila, Gavaksha and Gandhamadana—these five tigers among apes attacked Kumbhakarna. Those immensely strong ones struck Kumbhakarna, gigantic in size, everywhere with boulders, trees, palms, feet and fists. These blows were like a gentle touch and he did not feel any pain. He embraced the immensely swift Rishabha in his arms. The bull among apes suffered from being squeezed in

[208] Hanumat.

Kumbhakarna's arms. The terrible bull fell down, vomiting blood from his mouth. In the battle, Indra's enemy struck Sharabha with his fist, Nila with his knee and Gavaksha with his palm.[209] Suffering from the blows they had received, they repeatedly oozed out blood. They fell down on the ground, like kimshuka trees that had been cut down. Those great-souled and foremost apes fell down. Thousands of apes attacked Kumbhakarna. He was like a mountain and all those bulls among apes possessed the complexion of mountains. Those immensely strong ones leapt on him, climbed up his body and bit him. Those bulls among apes, struck Kumbhakarna, gigantic in form, with their nails, teeth, fists and thighs. He was like a mountain and was covered with thousands of apes. The tiger among rakshasas was as radiant as an overgrown mountain.[210] The immensely strong one seized all the apes with his hands. He angrily devoured them, like Garuda does to serpents. They were flung into Kumbhakarna's mouth, which resembled patala. However, the apes emerged through his nostrils and his ears. Angry and resembling a mountain, he devoured the apes. Enraged, the supreme among rakshasas mangled all the apes. Because of the flesh and the blood, the rakshasa created a mire on the ground. He roamed around amidst the army of the apes, like the raging fire of destruction. With the spear in his hand, the immensely strong Kumbhakarna was like Shakra with the vajra in his hand, or Yama with the noose in his hand. Just as the fire consumes a dry forest during the summer, like that, Kumbhakarna scorched the soldiers of the apes. Without leaders, the herds were slain. The apes were terrified and anxious and wailed in extremely piteous tones. Kumbhakarna killed many apes. Distressed and with their senses afflicted, they sought refuge with Raghava.

Seeing that the immensely strong Kumbhakarna was descending, the brave Sugriva, lord of the apes, leapt up. The giant ape raised the summit of a mountain and attacked him. With great force, he rushed towards the immensely strong Kumbhakarna. Kumbhakarna

[209] Inexplicably, the Critical Edition excises a shloka where he struck Gandhamadana with his feet.

[210] Overgrown with trees.

saw that the ape was descending. He tightened his limbs and faced the Indra among the apes. He was devouring giant apes and his body was covered with the blood of apes. On seeing that Kumbhakarna was stationed there, Sugriva addressed him in these words. 'You have struck down brave ones and have performed an extremely difficult deed. You have devoured the soldiers and obtained supreme fame. Abandon this army of apes. What will you do with ordinary ones? O rakshasa! Withstand this mountain that I am hurling towards you.' Full of spirit and patience, the king of the apes spoke these words. Hearing them, Kumbhakarna, tiger among rakshasas, spoke these words. 'You are Prajapati's grandson and the son of Riksharaja. You possess fortitude and manliness. O ape! Why are you roaring?' Hearing Kumbhakarna's words, he suddenly released the mountain and struck Kumbhakarna in the chest with it. That mountain was like the vajra or thunder. The summit of the mountain smacked against his broad chest and was violently shattered. The apes were suddenly distressed and the large number of rakshasas roared, rejoicing. Struck by the summit of the mountain, he was enraged. He opened his mouth and roared in anger. To kill the lord of the apes, he hurled that spear that glittered like lightning.

The sharp spear was bound with golden ropes and was hurled from Kumbhakarna's hand. With the speed of the wind, the son of the wind god swiftly leapt up, seized it in his hands and broke it. The giant spear was made out of iron and weighed one thousand *sahasras*.[211] The bull among apes broke it on his thighs and was delighted. On seeing that the spear had been broken, the great-souled lord of the rakshasas became angry. Malaya was near Lanka. He uprooted its peak and struck Sugriva with this. In the battle, struck by the summit of the mountain, the Indra among apes lost his senses and fell down on the ground. On seeing that he had lost his senses and had fallen down, all the yatudhanas who were fighting were delighted and roared. Kumbhakarna displayed a terrible and extraordinary valour in the battle. He seized Sugriva and raised him up, just as a terrible wind disperses a cloud. His form was like that

[211] A sahasra is a measure of weight.

of a giant cloud. In the battle, Kumbhakarna raised him up and roamed around. He was radiant, resembling Meru in his beauty. He looked like Meru, with its tall and terrible peak raised up. In the battle, the brave one raised him up and walked away, being praised by the Indras among the rakshasas. When the king of the apes was seized, the residents of heaven were astounded and a roar was heard in their residences. Indra's enemy was like Indra and resembled Indra in valour. Having seized the king of the apes, he thought, 'If this one is killed, Raghava and all the soldiers will be killed.' Hanumat saw that, here and there, the army of the apes was running away. Kumbhakarna had seized the ape Sugriva. The intelligent son of the wind god thought, 'Now that Sugriva has been seized, what should I do? In every situation, I should do what is proper. I can assume the size of a mountain and destroy this rakshasa. I can advance against the immensely strong Kumbhakarna and shatter his body with a blow of my fists. The king of the apes will be freed and on seeing this, all the apes will be delighted. Alternatively, the king can also free himself, even though he has been seized by the residents of heaven, the asuras and the serpents. Since Kumbhakarna has struck him with a mountain in the battle, I think that the lord of the apes has still not gained consciousness. The instant Sugriva regains his consciousness in this great battle, he will do what is best for himself and for the apes. If the great-souled Sugriva is freed by me, his eternal fame will be destroyed and he will find this unpleasant and suffer from it. Therefore, I will wait for some time, so that the king can exhibit his valour. My task is to reassure the army of the apes that has been routed.' Having thought in this way, Hanumat, the son of the wind god, steadied the great army of the apes. The great ape[212] was writhing and Kumbhakarna entered Lanka with him. Those who were in the mansions, houses and turrets worshipped him and showered down flowers in front of him. The great-souled one[213] regained his consciousness with difficulty. He was still stuck between his[214] arms. He looked at the city and the royal road and

[212] Sugriva.

[213] Sugriva.

[214] Kumbhakarna's.

thought repeatedly. 'Having been seized by him, what should I do now? Right now, I am capable of undertaking an act that can bring the desired benefit to the apes.' Thinking this, the king of the apes violently used his hands. He used his nails to rip apart the ears of Kumbhakarna, the enemy of the Indra of the immortals. He used his teeth to bite his nose and struck his sides with his feet. Kumbhakarna's ears and nose were torn apart, bruised and mangled. There was blood from the wounds and he became full of rage. He flung Sugriva down and crushed him on the ground. He was crushed on the ground with that terrible force and struck by the enemy of the gods. However, he leapt up into the sky with force and went to Rama's presence again. The immensely strong Kumbhakarna was deprived of his ears and nose. Wet with blood, he was radiant, like a mountain with waterfalls. From the city, the great-souled one violently emerged in front of the army of the apes. In the battle, the rakshasa Kumbhakarna devoured them, like the blazing fire of destruction does to the subjects. He was hungry and desired flesh and blood. He entered the vanguard of that army of the apes. Because he was confused in the battle, Kumbhakarna ate up rakshasas, apes, pishachas and bears.[215] In a single hand, he angrily held one, two, three and many apes and rakshasas at the same time and hurled them into his mouth. As the immensely strong one devoured the apes, they struck him back with the summits of mountains and his body was covered with fat and blood.

As they were being devoured, the apes sought refuge with Rama. At that time, Lakshmana, Sumitra's son, the afflicter of enemy armies and the conqueror of enemy cities, angrily started to fight. He pierced the valiant Kumbhakarna's body with seven arrows. Lakshmana affixed and shot some other arrows too.

However, the immensely strong Kumbhakarna passed over Lakshmana. As if causing an earthquake, he rushed towards Rama. Rama, Dasharatha's son, invoked the *roudra* weapon and shot sharp arrows towards Kumbhakarna's chest. As he violently rushed towards Rama, he was pierced by him. He became so angry that

[215] He also ate up those who were on his own side.

flames mixed with coal started to emerge from his mouth. Arrows tufted with the feathers of peacocks were embedded in his chest. The giant club was dislodged from his hand and fell down on the ground. The immensely strong one thought that he had been deprived of all his weapons.[216] He created great carnage with his fists and his feet. His limbs were struck by arrows and blood started to flow. He oozed out blood, like waterfalls in a mountain. Because of his terrible anger and because of the blood, he became senseless. He rushed around, devouring apes, rakshasas and bears.

At that time, Lakshmana, with dharma in his soul, spoke to Rama, after having reflected on many techniques that could be used to kill Kumbhakarna. 'He cannot distinguish the apes from the rakshasas. Crazy with the smell of blood, he is devouring those on his own side, as well as those on the enemy's side. Let bulls among apes climb on to his body from all directions and properly cover it. Let the leaders of the herds lead their herds and surround him from every direction. Through this means, the evil-minded one will suffer from a heavy burden. The rakshasa will fall down on the ground and will not be able to kill the apes.' Hearing the words of the intelligent prince, the apes were delighted and started to climb up Kumbhakarna. Kumbhakarna was angry at these apes climbing up. He shook himself with great force, like a wicked elephant tries to shake off an elephant rider. Seeing that he was shaking himself, Rama realized that the rakshasa was enraged. He grasped an excellent bow and rushed towards him with great force. He grasped a bow that was like a serpent. It was strung firmly and fiercely and was colourful with gold. Rama comforted the apes and descended, with a quiver full of arrows fixed. A large number of apes surrounded the one who was extremely difficult to vanquish. The immensely strong Rama advanced, followed by Lakshmana. He saw the great-souled and extremely strong Kumbhakarna. The slayer of enemies was diademed and all his limbs were covered with blood. Like an angry *dishagaja*,[217] he was rushing around in all the directions. Surrounded

[216] The Critical Edition excises a shloka where his other weapons also fell down.

[217] Four (sometimes eight) elephants are believed to hold up the four (or eight) directions.

by rakshasas, he was angrily searching for apes. He was like Vindhya and Mandara and was decorated with golden armlets. Blood flowed from his mouth and he was like a cloud that had arisen during the monsoon. He licked the blood along the corners of his mouth. Like Yama the Destroyer, he trampled the army of the apes. The best among rakshasas blazed like the flames of the fire.

On seeing him, the bull among men stretched his bow. The bull among nairittas became enraged at the twanging of the bow. He couldn't tolerate the sound and rushed towards Raghava. He was like a storm or a cloud. His arms were like the coils of the supreme king of serpents. His complexion was like that of a mountain. Seeing him descend in the battle, Rama spoke to Kumbhakarna. 'O lord of the rakshasas! Come. Do not be distressed. Having grasped the bow, I am standing before you. O Shakra's enemy! Know me to be Rama. In a short while, you will lose your senses.' Knowing that this was Rama, he laughed in a distorted voice, as if he was shattering the hearts of all the residents of the forest with that sound. The terrible one laughed in that distorted tone, resembling the thunder of the clouds. The immensely energetic Kumbhakarna addressed Raghava in these words. 'Know that I am not Viradha, Kabandha or Khara. Nor am I Vali or Maricha. It is Kumbhakarna who has arrived. Behold my large and terrible club that is completely made out of iron. In earlier times, I have used this to vanquish the gods and the danavas. Just because I do not possess ears and a nose, you should not take me lightly. I do not feel the slightest bit of pain at my ears and nose having been severed. O tiger among the Ikshvakus! Display your valour and dexterity on my body. After having witnessed your manliness and valour, I will devour you.'

Hearing Kumbhakarna's words, Rama released tufted arrows. They were like the vajra in their force. However, even after being struck by them, the enemy of the gods was not agitated or distressed. Those arrows had cut down the best of sala trees and had slain Vali, bull among the apes. But Kumbhakarna's body was like the vajra and they could not pain him. The shower of arrows rained down on his body. However, the enemy of the great Indra seemed to drink them up. He countered the force of Rama's arrows and struck back with the fierce force of his club. The club was smeared with blood and could terrify the large army of the gods. The rakshasa used the fierce force of the club to strike and drive away the army of the apes. Rama then released the supreme vayavya weapon towards the roamer in the night. It severed his arm, which was still holding on to the club. With his arm severed, he roared loudly. The arm was like the summit of a mountain and was severed by Raghava's arrow, while still holding on to the club. It fell down on the army of the king of the apes and killed many apes who were in that army. The apes who had not been maimed or killed were distressed and sought refuge in the extremities of the army. Suffering in all their limbs, they witnessed an extremely terrible encounter between the lord of the rakshasas and the Indra among men. Kumbhakarna's arm had been severed by the weapon, like the summit of an excellent mountain severed by a large sword. He used his other arm to uproot a tree and in the battle, attacked the Indra among men with this. With the sala tree that had been violently uprooted, this arm looked like the coils of a serpent. Using an arrow that was colourful with molten gold, Rama invoked the *aindrastra* and severed this. Kumbhakarna's arm was like a mountain. Severed, it fell down on the ground. Writhing there, it shattered trees, boulders, rocks, apes and rakshasas. In the battle, Rama saw that his arms had been severed and had fallen down and roared loudly. He seized two sharp ardhachandra arrows and severed the rakshasa's feet. His arms had been severed. His feet had been severed. With a gaping mouth that resembled the mouth of the subterranean fire, he roared violently and rushed towards Rama, like Rahu advancing towards the moon in the sky.[218] Rama used arrows that were sharp at the tips and were tufted with gold to fill up his mouth. His mouth filled with these, he was unable to speak. Because of this great misery, he lost his senses. Rama picked up an arrow that was like the wind in its speed. It was like the rays of the sun and was like the staff of Brahma or Yama. He invoked aindrastra on his sharp and well-tufted arrow. Encrusted colourfully with tufts of diamonds and molten gold, it blazed like the

[218] The foot had been severed, he still possessed his thighs.

radiant sun. Its force was like that of the great Indra's vajra. Rama shot this towards the roamer in the night. The arrow was released from Raghava's arm and illuminated the ten directions with its radiance. It could be seen to blaze, like a fire without smoke. Like Shakra's vajra in its powers, it advanced. The head of the lord of the rakshasas resembled the summit of a huge mountain. The teeth were excellently formed and the beautiful earrings were moving. Like Vritra's head severed by Purandara in earlier times, this head was severed. The rakshasa's head was like a mountain. Struck by Rama's arrow, it fell down. As it fell down, it shattered the arches, houses, turrets and ramparts. Gigantic in size, the rakshasa was like the Himalayas and fell into the ocean, crushing the crocodiles, giant fish and serpents and then submerging into the ground there.[219]

The extremely strong Kumbhakarna, the enemy of brahmanas and gods, was killed in the battle. The earth and all the mountains trembled. Delighted, the gods roared loudly. The *devarshi*s,[220] the maharshis, the serpents, the gods, the creatures, the birds, the *guhyaka*s,[221] the yakshas and the large number of gandharvas who were in the sky rejoiced at Rama's valour. The several apes were delighted, their faces resembling blooming lotuses. Raghava had slain the enemy, who was terrible in valour and impossible to be assailed. The beloved one was worshipped. Kumbhakarna had crushed the soldiers of the gods. He was never exhausted and had never been defeated in great battles. Having slain him in the encounter, Bharata's elder brother rejoiced, just as the lord of the immortals did when the great asura, Vritra, had been killed.

Chapter 6(56)

The rakshasas saw that Kumbhakarna had been killed by the great-souled Raghava. They went and reported this to Ravana,

[219] The torso fell into the ocean.

[220] Divine sages.

[221] Semi-divine species, companions of Kubera.

Indra among the rakshasas. Hearing that the immensely strong Kumbhakarna had been killed in the battle, Ravana was tormented by grief. He lost his senses and fell down on the ground. Hearing that their paternal uncle had been killed, Devantaka and Narantaka, and Trishira and Atikaya,[222] were oppressed by grief and wept. Hearing that their brother had been slain by Rama, the performer of unblemished deeds, Mahodara and Mahaparshva were filled with sorrow. Ravana, bull among the rakshasas, regained his senses with difficulty. Distressed because Kumbhakarna had been killed, he lamented. 'Alas! O brave one! O destroyer of the insolence of enemies! O Kumbhakarna! O immensely strong one! Having tormented the soldiers of the enemy, why have you left me and departed? You were my right arm and depending on that, I was not scared of gods and asuras. With that fallen down, I can no longer exist now. How could this have happened! The brave one robbed the gods and the danavas of their insolence. He was like the fire of destruction. He has now been slain by Raghava in the battle. The strike of the vajra could never cause him any suffering. He is sleeping on the ground. How could he have been afflicted by Rama's arrows? These large numbers of gods, stationed in the sky with the rishis, are roaring in delight on seeing you killed in the battle. Having accomplished their objective, it is certain that the apes will rejoice today. From all directions, they will clamber up the fortifications and gates of Lanka. What will I do with the kingdom? What will I do with Sita? Without Kumbhakarna, I have no attachment towards remaining alive. Raghava killed my brother today. If I do not kill him in an encounter, it is better for me to be dead. My life will be fruitless. Today, I will go to the region where my younger brother is. Without my brother, I am not interested in remaining alive, not even for an instant. Considering the injury I have caused to them in the past, the gods will laugh at me. O Kumbhakarna! With you killed, how will I triumph over Indra? The great-souled Vibhishana came to me and spoke auspicious words. Because of my ignorance, I did not accept them then. A terrible shame

[222] All four were Ravana's sons. Mahodara and Mahaparshva were Ravana's brothers.

has come over me because of Vibhishana's words and the death of Kumbhakarna and Prahasta. The handsome Vibhishana followed dharma and was banished by me. The wicked deed that I did has brought this sorrow on to me.' His soul was greatly disturbed and extremely piteously, he lamented over Kumbhakarna in many kinds of ways. Knowing that Indra's enemy had been killed, Dashanana fell down, severely afflicted.

Chapter 6(57)

The evil-souled Ravana lamented in this way, tormented by grief. Hearing this, Trishira spoke these words. 'O king! The immensely valiant one, my uncle in the middle,[223] has been killed in this way. Virtuous people do not lament in the way you are doing. O lord! You are alone sufficient to take care of the three worlds. Therefore, why are you sorrowing in this fashion, like an ordinary person? You possess a spear given to you by Brahma, armour, a bow and arrows and a chariot that is yoked to one hundred donkeys, clattering like the thunder of a cloud. With your weapons, you have chastised the gods and the danavas. You possess all the weapons and are in a position to chastise Raghava. O great king! It is best that you remain. I will go out and fight. Like Garuda against the serpents, I will destroy the enemies. Just as the king of the gods did to Shambara and Vishnu did to Naraka, today, brought down by me in the battle, Rama will lie down.' Hearing Trishira's words, Ravana, the lord of the rakshasas, goaded by destiny, regarded this as if he had been born again. Hearing Trishira's words, Devantaka, Narantaka and the energetic Atikaya were delighted at the prospect of fighting. Ravana's brave sons were like Shakra in their valour. Those bulls among nairittas roared, 'I', 'I'. All of them roamed around in the sky. All of them were accomplished in the use of maya. All of them had robbed the gods of their insolence. All of them were unassailable in

[223] The text uses the word tata. Literally, my father in the middle.

the field of battle. All of them possessed the strength of weapons. All of them were extensive in their deeds. It had never been heard that any of them had been defeated in a battle. All those brave ones knew about the use of weapons. All of them were accomplished in fighting. All of them were superior in knowledge. All of them had obtained boons. They were the equal of the sun in radiance. Surrounded by these sons, who could crush the army of an enemy in a battle, the king was as radiant as Maghavan, surrounded by immortals who could crush the insolence of great danavas. He embraced his sons and adorned them in ornaments. He pronounced benedictions over them and sent them out to fight. Ravana also sent the two brothers, Mahodara and Mahaparshva, to protect the princes in the battle. They honoured the great-souled Ravana, who made his enemies shriek. Having circumambulated him, those gigantic ones departed.

Those immensely strong ones smeared themselves with fragrances from all the herbs. Those six supreme nairittas emerged, desiring to fight. There was an elephant named Sudarshana and it was like a dark cloud. It had been born in Airavata's lineage. Mahodara ascended this. He had all the weapons with him and was also adorned with quivers. He was radiant astride the elephant, like the sun atop Mount Asta. Trishira, Ravana's son, ascended an excellent chariot that was yoked to excellent horses and stocked with all the weapons. Wielding a bow, Trishira was radiant astride the chariot. He looked like a rainbow amidst the clouds, tinged with lightning and blazing meteors. With three diadems, Trishira was radiant on that excellent chariot.[224] He looked like the Himalayas, Indra among mountains, with its three golden peaks. The energetic Atikaya was the son of the Indra among rakshasas. He was supreme among all archers and ascended a supreme chariot. It possessed excellent wheels and axles, was yoked well and possessed an excellent seat and pole. It blazed with quivers, arrows, seats, spears, swords and clubs. He was radiant because of his colourful and golden diadem. Because of his ornaments, he dazzled like the

[224] Literally, Trishira means one with three heads. The three diadems make it clear that he did possess three heads.

illumination of Meru. The extremely strong son of the king was radiant astride the chariot. He was surrounded by tigers among the nairittas, like the wielder of the vajra by the immortals. Narantaka was astride an excellent white horse that was like Uchchaishrava. It was gigantic in size and possessed the speed of thought. It had a golden harness. Grasping a spear that had the complexion of a meteor, Narantaka dazzled. Like the energetic Guha, he seized a spear, for using it against the enemy in the battle. Devantaka seized a club that was encrusted with diamonds. He resembled Vishnu's form, when he had held up a mountain in his arms.[225] The immensely energetic and valiant Mahaparshva seized a club. With the club in his hand, he was as radiant as Kubera in a battle. Surrounded by an unmatched army, those great-souled ones set out. They were like the gods leaving Amaravati, surrounded by an unmatched army. The elephants, horses and chariots rumbled like thunder. Rakshasas, the best of warriors, followed the great-souled ones. Like the rays of the sun, those great-souled princes were radiant. They blazed because of their diadems, like shining planets in the firmament. An array of white umbrellas was held aloft their heads. They resembled an autumn cloud in the sky, adorned with an array of swans. They had made up their minds to defeat the enemy or die. The brave ones departed, resolving to fight.

They roared and shouted, shooting arrows. Indomitable in battle, those great-souled ones departed, desiring victory. The earth seemed to tremble because of the slapping[226] and clapping. The leonine roars of the rakshasas seemed to penetrate the sky. Those immensely strong Indras among the rakshasas rejoiced as they emerged. They saw the army of the apes, holding aloft boulders and trees. The great-souled apes also saw the army of the nairittas. There were arrays of elephants, horses and chariots and hundreds of bells tinkled. With great weapons raised, it looked like a dark cloud. Surrounded by nairittas in every direction, it looked like a blazing fire or the sun. The apes saw that army advance, fixed in its aim.

[225] This is probably a reference to Mount Mandara.
[226] Of chests.

They raised giant boulders and roared repeatedly. The large number of rakshasas could not tolerate the roar emitted by the leaders of the apes. They could not tolerate this fierce and supreme delight. Therefore, those immensely strong ones roared back in more terrible tones. The leaders of the apes penetrated that terrible army of the rakshasas. They raised the summits of mountains and trees and roamed around. Some apes took to the sky, others remained on the ground. With trees and boulders as weapons, they angrily roamed around amidst the soldiers of the rakshasas. The apes, terrible in their valour, were countered with torrents of arrows. However, they produced an excellent shower of trees, mountains and boulders. In the battle, the rakshasas and the apes roared like lions. The apes used boulders to crush the yatudhanas. In the encounter, some angrily killed those who were covered with armour. Some climbed on to chariots, elephants and horses and killed those brave ones. The yatudhanas were violently attacked by the apes. They were brought down with the summits of mountains. Their eyes were gouged out with fists. Those bulls among rakshasas wavered, were brought down and roared. The apes and the rakshasas released boulders and swords. In an instant, the earth was covered with these and flooded with blood. There were piles of dead bodies of rakshasas who could crush their enemies. With their spears shattered, they had been flung down, or were being flung down, by the apes. The roamers in the night killed the apes with the dead bodies of apes. The apes also killed the rakshasas with the dead bodies of rakshasas. The rakshasas seized the boulders and killed the apes with these. The apes also seized the weapons and killed the rakshasas with these. They attacked and killed each other with rocks, spears and other weapons. In the battle, the apes and the rakshasas roared like lions. With their armour and bodyguards shattered, the rakshasas were killed by the apes. Blood began to flow there, like sap from trees. In the battle, some apes destroyed chariots with chariots, elephants with elephants and horses with horses. Using kshurapras, ardhachandras, bhallas and sharp arrows, the rakshasas fragmented the trees and the boulders of the Indras among the apes. In the encounter, the earth was strewn with shattered summits of mountains, severed trees and slain apes and rakshasas. It became impossible to traverse. There was a tumultuous clash and in the forefront of the armies, the rakshasas were brought down. The maharshis and large numbers of gods rejoiced and roared at this.

Narantaka was astride a horse that was like the wind in its speed. He seized a sharp spear and penetrated the army of the king of the apes, the way a fish enters the great ocean. With that blazing spear, the brave and great-souled enemy of Indra killed seven hundred apes in an instant. He slew the soldiers and the bulls among the apes. The vidyadharas and maharshis saw the great-souled one astride the back of the horse, roaming around amidst the army of the apes. They saw that there was a mire of flesh and blood in his path. There were bodies of apes who had fallen down, resembling mountains. Whenever the bulls among apes thought of showing their valour, Narantaka overcame and pierced them. At all ends of the battlefield, Narantaka raised his blazing spear and burnt the soldiers of the apes, the way a fire consumes a forest. By the time the residents of the forest raised trees and boulders, they were struck and brought down, like the vajra shattering mountains. The powerful Narantaka roamed around in all directions. Like the wind during the monsoon, he extensively covered all parts of the battlefield. Among all the brave ones whom the valiant one pierced, not a single one was capable of running away, remaining in one place, moving, rising up or leaving. Though he was alone, with the spear that was as energetic as the sun, he seemed to be like many. He routed the soldiers of the apes and brought them down on the ground. When the spear descended on them, it was like being crushed by the vajra. The apes were incapable of withstanding it and shrieked in loud voices. As the brave apes fell down, they assumed the forms of mountains, with their peaks shattered by the vajra. The best among the apes were reduced to the state they were in when they were brought down by the great-souled Kumbhakarna. They presented themselves before Sugriva.

Sugriva saw that, terrified by their fear of Narantaka, the army of the apes was running away, here and there. He saw the soldiers running away. He also saw Narantaka advancing, astride the back of the horse and holding the spear. Having seen him, Sugriva, lord of the apes, spoke to the brave Prince Angada, who was Shakra's equal in valour. 'O brave one! This rakshasa is astride a horse and is agitating the army of the apes. Go and take away his life.' Hearing his master's words, Angada descended. The army[227] was like a mass of clouds and it was as if a cloud with rays had emerged from that army. Angada, supreme among the apes, was like a mass of rocks. He was radiant with his armlets and looked like a mountain with minerals. The immensely strong one possessed no weapons, only his nails and teeth. Approaching Narantaka, Vali's son spoke these words. 'Stay. What are you doing to these ordinary apes? This spear has the touch of the vajra. Hurl it towards my chest.' Hearing Angada's words, Narantaka became angry. He bit his lips with his teeth and sighed like a serpent. He suddenly hurled the blazing spear and pierced Angada. But striking the chest of Vali's son, which was as firm as the vajra, it shattered and fell down on the ground. He[228] saw that the spear had been shattered, as if the coils of a serpent had been severed by Garuda. Vali's son raised his palm and struck the horse on the head. The horse's head was shattered by the slap of the palm and it fell down on the ground. Its feet were broken and its pupils were gouged out. Though it was like a mountain, its tongue stuck out. On seeing that the horse had been killed and had fallen down, Naranataka was overcome with rage. In the battle, the immensely powerful one raised his fist and struck Vali's son on the head. Angada's head was smashed by the fierce fist and he oozed out blood that was extremely warm. For an instant, there was a blazing loss of consciousness. When he regained consciousness, he was astounded. Angada's fist was like the summit of a mountain and his force was like that of the vajra. Vali's great-souled son brought it down on Narantaka's chest. Crushed by the fist, his chest was shattered. He seemed to be in flames. He vomited blood and blood covered his body. Narantaka fell down on the ground, as if a mountain had been shattered by the vajra and had been brought

[227] Of the apes.
[228] Angada.

down. In the forefront of the field of battle, Narantaka, supreme among brave ones, was slain by Vali's son. The supreme gods in the sky and the residents of the forest roared loudly. Angada performed an extremely difficult act of valour and this delighted Rama's heart. He was himself surprised at this extremely brave and valiant act and, rejoicing, started to fight again.

Chapter 6(58)

Seeing that Narantaka had been killed, the bulls among the nairittas, Devantaka, Trimurdha,[229] Poulastya[230] and Mahodara, shrieked. Mahodara mounted an Indra among elephants that was like a cloud. The immensely brave one attacked Vali's valiant son. The powerful Devantaka was tormented, suffering hardship on account of his brother. He seized a blazing club and attacked Angada. The brave Trishira was astride a chariot that was like the sun, yoked to excellent horses. He rushed towards Vali's son. Those three Indras among the nairittas were the destroyers of the pride of the gods and attacked. Angada uprooted a giant tree with branches. The brave Angada violently hurled it towards Devantaka. The giant tree, with the giant branches, blazed like Shakra's vajra. Trishira shattered it with arrows that were like virulent serpents. Seeing that the tree had been severed, Angada leapt up. The elephant among apes showered down trees and boulders. Angrily, Trishira used sharp arrows to shatter these. Surantaka[231] shattered the trees with the tip of his club. Trishira attacked the brave Angada with arrows. Mahodara rushed towards Vali's son on an elephant and struck him on the chest with javelins that were like the vajra. Devantaka angrily approached and struck Angada with a club. However, having done this, he swiftly retreated some distance away. He was simultaneously attacked by those three foremost nairittas.

[229] The same as Trishira.

[230] Meaning Mahaparshva.

[231] The same as Devantaka.

However, despite this, Vali's powerful and immensely energetic son wasn't distressed. He raised his palm and struck that great elephant severely.[232] With its eyes jutting out, the elephant shrieked and fell down.[233] In the battle, Vali's immensely strong son plucked out a tusk and attacked and struck Devantaka. Like a tree in the wind, all his limbs trembled. With the complexion of the sap of lac, copious quantities of blood emerged from his mouth. With difficulty, the powerful and greatly energetic Devantaka got a grip on himself. He firmly struck Angada with that terrible club. Struck by the club, the son of the Indra among the apes sank to his knees on the ground. However, he leapt up again. As he was jumping up, Trishira struck him with three arrows that were like venomous serpents. Those terrible arrows struck the son of the king of the apes on his forehead.

Angada was attacked by three bulls among nairittas. Discerning this, Hanumat and Nila went there. Nila hurled the summit of a mountain towards Trishira, but the intelligent son of Ravana shattered this with sharp arrows. That flat rock was fragmented with hundreds of arrows and emitting sparks and flaming, the summit of the mountain fell down. Seeing this, Devantaka was delighted. In the encounter, he seized a club and advanced and attacked the son of the wind god. Seeing that he was descending, Hanumat, the son of the wind god, leapt up. With a fist that was as forceful as the vajra, he struck him on his head. His head was crushed and shattered by the blow of the fist. His teeth fell out. His eyes jutted out. His tongue hung down. Devantaka, the son of the king of the rakshasas, lost his life and suddenly fell down on the ground.

When he was killed, the immensely strong Trimurdha, the foremost among rakshasa warriors and the enemy of the gods, was angry and attacked. He showered down arrows, fierce and sharp at the tips, on Nila's chest. When torrents of arrows were rained down, the body of the commander of the ape army was mangled. But Nila increased the size of his body and repulsed this with his great strength. When Nila regained his senses, he uprooted

[232] The context makes it clear that this was Devantaka's elephant, not Mahodara's.
[233] It died.

a mountain that had clumps of trees. Having uprooted it, with a terrible and fierce force, he used it to strike Mahodara on the head. The mountain descended and shattered Mahodara and the elephant. He was uprooted and, losing his life, fell down on the ground. He fell down, like a mountain struck by the vajra.

Seeing that his paternal uncle had been slain, Trishira became angry. He seized a bow and pierced Hanumat with sharp arrows. Hanumat uprooted Trishira's horse and angrily tore it apart with his nails, like the king of deer against an Indra among elephants. Trishira, Ravana's son, seized a javelin that was like Death on the night of destruction and hurled it towards the son of the wind god. It sped through the sky like a meteor. However, the tiger among apes seized it as it descended, broke it and roared. The terrible javelin was shattered by Hanumat. On seeing this, the large number of apes rejoiced and roared like clouds. Trishira, supreme among rakshasas, raised a sword and in anger, thrust this down into the chest of the Indra among apes. Hanumat, the son of the wind god, was struck by the blow of the sword. He struck the valiant Trishira on the chest with his palm. Struck by the palm, the immensely energetic Trishira lost his senses. The weapon was dislodged from his hands and he fell down on the ground. As the sword was falling down, the great ape seized it. Like a mountain in size, he roared and terrified all the nairittas. The roamer in the night was unable to tolerate this roar. He leapt up and struck Hanumat with his fist. Because of that blow of the fist, the great ape became wrathful. He seized the bull among rakshasas by his diadem. Angry, the son of the wind god used that sharp sword to sever his heads,[234] with the diadems and earrings, just as Shakra severed the head of Tvashta's son.[235] Like stellar bodies dislodged from the sun's path, the heads of Indra's enemy, with eyes that were as large as mountains and as fiery as the fire, fell down on the ground. Trishira, the enemy of the gods, was like Shakra in his valour and was killed by Hanumat. The apes roared and made the earth tremble. The rakshasas fled in different directions.

[234] Trishira possessed three heads.

[235] Indra killed Trishira (a different Trishira) or Vishvarupa, the son of Tvashtri/Tvashtra/Tvashta.

Trishira and Mahodara had been killed and so had the invincible Devantaka and Narantaka. On seeing this, the immensely strong Mahaparshva became extremely intolerant and angry. He seized an auspicious club that emitted sparks and was completely made out of iron. It was bound in a golden garment and was smeared with flesh and blood. Its form was radiant, decorated with the blood of enemies. He wore red garlands and was fiery and blazed in his energy. He was as terrifying as Airavata, Mahapadma and Sarvabhouma.[236] The immensely strong Mahaparshva became greatly enraged and seized a club. Like the blazing fire that arises at the end of a yuga, he attacked the apes. The ape Rishabha leapt up. The powerful one approached and stood in front of Mahaparshva, Ravana's younger brother. Seeing the ape standing in front, resembling a mountain, he angrily struck him on the chest with the club that was like the vajra. The bull among apes was struck by the club. His chest was mangled and copious quantities of blood oozed out. After a long period of time, Rishabha, bull among apes, regained his senses. He bit his lips in rage and glanced towards Mahaparshva. In the field of battle, he seized the terrible club and repeatedly struck Mahaparshva, the crazy leader of the army. He was mangled by the club and his eyes and teeth fell off. Like a mountain shattered by the vajra, Mahaparshva fell down. Thus, Ravana's brother was killed. The army of nairittas resembled the ocean. Wishing to only protect their lives, they abandoned their weapons and ran away, like the ocean when it crosses the shoreline.

Chapter 6(59)

Atikaya was like a mountain and was one who robbed the gods and the danavas of their pride. He saw the tumultuous sight of

[236] There are eight elephants who guard the eight directions—Airavata, Pundareeka, Vamana, Kumuda, Anjana, Pushpadanta, Sarvabhouma and Suprateeka. Airavata is also regarded as the king of elephants and is Indra's mount. Mahapadma is another name for Pundareeka.

his own army being distressed and it made the body hair stand up. He saw that his brothers, who possessed a valour that was equal to that of Shakra's, had been killed. He saw that his paternal uncles, the brothers Mahodara and Mahaparshva, bulls among rakshasas, had also been killed in the battle. In the encounter, the immensely energetic one, the beneficiary of a boon from Brahma, became angry. Shakra's enemy mounted a chariot that was as radiant as an array of one thousand suns and attacked the apes. Adorned in a diadem and polished earrings, he twanged his giant bow. He announced his name and roared loudly. There was the terrible sound of his roaring like a lion, announcing his name and twanging his bow. The apes were terrified. They saw his form, which was like that of Vishnu engaging in his three strides. Afflicted by fear, all the apes fled in the ten directions. Seeing that Atikaya was attacking, the apes lost their senses. In the battle, they sought refuge with the one who grants refuge, Lakshmana's elder brother. From a distance, Kakutstha saw Atikaya astride a chariot that was like a mountain. He was brandishing a bow and was roaring like a cloud of destruction.

On seeing the great-souled one, Raghava was extremely surprised. He assured the apes and spoke to Vibhishana. 'Who is this? He is like a mountain. He wields a bow and his eyes are tawny. He is mounted on a giant chariot that is yoked to one thousand horses. He possesses sharp spears and exceedingly sharp javelins and spikes. With the rays of the weapons, he looks like Maheshvara, surrounded by the bhutas. He is radiant and dazzling, like the tongue of Death. Surrounded by javelins, he is like a cloud tinged with lightning.[237] On his excellent chariot, all the bows that have been arranged have golden backs, resembling Shakra's bow[238] in the sky. Who is this tiger among rakshasas who is roaming around in the field of battle? This best among charioteers is advancing on a chariot that is as energetic as the sun. The radiant top of his standard has a mark of Rahu on it. His arrows are shining like the rays of

[237] Javelin is only partly correct. The text uses the word *rathashakti*. While *shakti* is a javelin, rathashakti is the pole that holds up the standard in a chariot. Hence, these were special kinds of javelins.

[238] The rainbow.

the sun and are illuminating the ten directions. His bow is curved in three places and roars like a cloud. It is ornamented with a golden back. His bow is as dazzling as Shatakratu's excellent bow. His giant chariot has a standard, flags and a seat. With four drivers, it is roaring like thunder. There are thirty-eight quivers on his chariot. There are bows with terrible bowstrings, golden and brown. Two swords are slung from the sides of the chariot, illuminating the sides. Each of them is beautiful and clearly ten cubits long, with handles that are four cubits.[239] The patient one is like a giant mountain and wears a red garland around his neck. He is like Death. He possesses a large mouth, like Death. He is like the sun, inside a cloud. Golden armlets adorn both his arms. He is as radiant as the excellent mountain of the Himalayas, with its two peaks. With two earrings, his face is shining and possesses auspicious eyes. He is like the full moon between the two stars in Punarvasu.[240] O mighty-armed one! Tell me. Who is this supreme rakshasa? On seeing him, all the apes are afflicted by grief and are running away in different directions.

Vibhishana was asked by Prince Rama, infinite in his energy. The greatly energetic one replied to Raghava. 'The immensely energetic Dashagriva is the younger brother of King Vaishravana.[241] Ravana, terrible in his deeds and great in his enterprise, is the lord of the rakshasas. He has a valiant son who is Ravana's equal in battles. He serves the aged and is learned. He is supreme among those who are accomplished in the use of all weapons. He is skilled in mounting the backs of horses, elephants and chariots, in wielding the bow and the sword, in bheda, conciliation, dana and good policy. Resorting to the strength of his arms, Lanka is free from fear. He is the son of Dhanyamali and he is known by the name of Atikaya.[242] Cleansing his soul, he worshipped Brahma and performed austerities. He obtained weapons and defeated the

[239] The text doesn't clearly state what is four cubits long, the handle or the scabbard.

[240] A nakshatra is not a star, but can be a constellation too. Punarvasu is the constellation of Gemini (Mithuna), with the two stars, Gemini and Pollux.

[241] Kubera.

[242] Dhanyamali/Dhanyamalini has been mentioned before. At that time, we weren't told that she was Ravana's wife.

enemies. Svayambhu granted him the boon that he cannot be killed by the gods and the asuras. He obtained this divine armour and this chariot that is as radiant as the sun. Hundreds of gods and danavas have been defeated by him. He has protected the rakshasas and slain yakshas. The intelligent one used his arrows to stupefy Indra's vajra. In a battle, he countered the noose of the king of the waters.[243] This powerful Atikaya is a bull among the rakshasas. He is Ravana's intelligent son and has destroyed the pride of the gods and the danavas. O bull among men! Therefore, let us act quickly, before he uses his arrows to destroy the soldiers of the apes.

The powerful Atikaya entered the army of the apes. He stretched his bow and roared repeatedly. He saw the supreme among charioteers, terrible in his form, stationed on the chariot. The foremost among the apes attacked the great-souled one. Kumuda, Dvivida, Mainda, Nila and Sharabha used trees and the summits of mountains and simultaneously attacked him. The immensely energetic Atikaya, supreme among those who knew about all weapons, used his gold-tufted arrows to sever those trees and mountains. In the forefront of the battle, the powerful roamer in the night, terrible in his form, used arrows that were completely made out of iron to pierce those apes. Those apes were afflicted by those showers of arrows and their bodies were mangled. In that great battle, they were incapable of countering Atikaya. The rakshasas terrified the soldiers and the brave ones among the apes, just as a young and angry lion drives away herds of deer. In the midst of the ape soldiers, the Indra among the rakshasas did not kill anyone who was not fighting.

Wielding the bow, he went up to Rama and proudly spoke these words. 'I am stationed on my chariot, with a bow and arrow in my hands. I never fight with an ordinary person. Let anyone who possesses strength and enterprise swiftly grant me a duel now.' Hearing his words, Soumitri, the slayer of enemies, became angry and intolerant and attacked. He smiled and seized his bow. In front of Atikaya, he stretched his great bow. Having angrily attacked, Soumitri picked up an arrow from his quiver. The twang

[243] Varuna.

of Lakshmana's fierce weapon terrified the roamers in the night and filled the earth, the mountains, the sky, the ocean and the directions. Hearing the terrible roar of Soumitri's bow, the powerful and immensely energetic son of the Indra among the rakshasas was astounded. Seeing that Lakshmana had presented himself before him, Atikaya was angry. He picked up a sharp arrow and spoke these words. 'O Soumitri! You are a child. You are not accomplished in fighting. Go away. I am like Death. Why do you wish to fight with me? The Himalayas, the sky or the earth are unable to withstand the force of weapons released from my arm. You desire to awake a fire of destruction that is happily asleep. Cast aside your bow and return. If you fight against me, you will lose your life. Or perhaps your obstinacy doesn't allow you to retreat. In that case, remain and give up your life. Go to Yama's abode. Behold my sharp arrows. They destroy the pride of enemies. They are embellished with molten gold and are like Ishvara's[244] weapons. This arrow is like a serpent and will drink blood, just as an enraged king of deer drinks the blood of a king of elephants.' Hearing Atikaya's proud and angry words in the battle, the extremely strong prince and prosperous one was also enraged. He spoke words that were full of great import. 'One doesn't become powerful only through the use of words. One doesn't become a virtuous person only through self-praise. I am stationed here, with a bow and arrow in my hands. O evil-souled one! Show me your valour. Demonstrate it through your deeds. You should not indulge in self-praise. Only a person who possesses manliness is said to be brave. You are an archer and are astride a chariot that has all the weapons. Demonstrate your valour through arrows or other weapons. Thereafter, I will use sharp arrows to bring down your head, just as at the right time, the wind brings down a palm fruit from its stem. My arrows are embellished with molten gold. Today, they will drink the blood that oozes out from the wounds created in your body by these stakes. Taking me to be a child, you should not take me lightly. Whether I am a child or whether I am aged, in the encounter you will know me as Death.'

[244] Probably meaning Shiva.

He heard Lakshmana's words, full of great meaning. Enraged, Atikaya picked up a supreme arrow. The vidyadharas, bhutas, gods, daityas, maharshis, guhyakas and great-souled ones witnessed that encounter. Angry, Atikaya affixed the arrow to his bow. As if eating up the sky that was in between them, he shot this at Lakshmana. The sharp arrow descended, like a venomous serpent. Lakshmana, the slayer of enemy heroes, severed this with an ardhachandra arrow. That arrow was like the hood of a serpent and was splintered. Seeing this, Atikaya became extremely angry and affixed five arrows. The roamer in the night shot these towards Lakshmana. However, Bharata's younger brother severed them with his sharp arrows. Lakshmana, the slayer of enemy heroes, severed these with his sharp arrows. He then picked up a sharp arrow that blazed in its energy. Lakshmana affixed this to his excellent bow. He stretched it with force and released the arrow. He drew the bow all the way back and released the arrow with drooping tufts. It struck the forehead of the brave and supreme rakshasa. The arrow penetrated the forehead of the terrible rakshasa. In the battle, with blood streaming from him, he looked like an Indra among the serpents. The rakshasa trembled, just like the turrets of Tripura when they were struck by Rudra's terrible arrow. Lakshmana made him tremble. Having reassured himself and regained his breath, the immensely strong one thought. 'This was an excellent strike with the arrow. My enemy deserves praise.' As he lowered himself on his arms, he thought in this way.[245] He mounted his chariot and roamed around on that chariot. The bull among rakshasas fixed one, three, five and seven arrows to his bow, stretched it and released them. Those arrows were like death and were shot from the bow of the Indra among rakshasas. They were tufted with gold and dazzled like the sun. They made the sky blaze. The rakshasa shot a flood of arrows. However, Raghava's younger brother wasn't scared. He severed these with many sharp arrows. Ravana's son saw that his arrows had been countered in the battle. The enemy of Indra of the gods angrily seized a sharp arrow. The immensely energetic one affixed and violently released

[245] The blow made him bend down and he probably got off the chariot.

this arrow. It approached Soumitri and struck him between the breasts. In the battle, Atikaya struck Soumitri in the chest. Like musth from a crazy elephant, a copious quantity of blood began to flow. The lord violently freed himself from that stake. He picked up a sharp arrow and affixed a weapon to it. When the great-souled one invoked agneyastra on that arrow, the bow and the arrow blazed. The extremely energetic Atikaya affixed the *sourastra*.[246] He affixed a gold-tufted arrow that resembled a serpent. Lakshmana shot that terrible and blazing arrow towards Atikaya and it was like the deadly staff of the Destroyer.[247] The roamer in the night saw that the arrow had been invoked with agneyastra. He shot a blazing arrow that had been invoked with suryastra. Those two arrows struck each other in the sky, blazing in their energy, like two wrathful serpents. They consumed each other and fell down on the ground. Their rays were reduced to ashes and those two excellent arrows were no longer radiant. Angry, Atikaya released the *aishika* weapon.[248] The valiant Soumitri severed this with aindrastra. On seeing that the aishika had been destroyed, the prince who was Ravana's son angrily invoked *yamyastra*[249] on an arrow. The roamer in the night shot this weapon towards Lakshmana and Lakshmana destroyed this with *vayavyastra*.[250] Angry, Lakshmana showered down arrows on Ravana's son, like rain pouring down from a cloud. They struck Atikaya and severed his armour, which was encrusted with diamonds. Shattered violently by the arrows, it fell down on the ground. Lakshmana, the slayer of enemy heroes, saw that the arrows had been rendered unsuccessful. The immensely illustrious one showered down thousands of arrows. Torrents of arrows were showered down on the immensely strong Atikaya and he was devoid of his armour. However, the rakshasa was not pained in the encounter. Moreover, the supreme among men was incapable of wounding him in the battle. At this, Vayu approached

[246] Divine weapon named after the sun god. Suryastra is a synonym.
[247] Yama.
[248] Another divine weapon, invoked on a blade of grass and associated with Tvashta.
[249] Named after Yama.
[250] Named after Vayu.

and spoke these words. 'He has obtained a boon from Brahma and is clad in armour that makes it impossible to kill him. He has to be splintered with brahmastra. There is no other means to kill him.' Soumitri's valour was like that of Indra and he heard Vayu's words. He affixed an arrow that was irresistible in its force and suddenly invoked brahmastra. Soumitri invoked that supreme weapon on an excellent arrow that was sharp at the tips. The directions, the moon, the sun, the giant planets, the sky and the earth were terrified and agitated. That well-tufted arrow was like Yama's messenger and brahmastra was affixed to the bow. That arrow was like the vajra. In the battle, Soumitri shot this towards the son of Indra's enemy. It was shot by Lakshmana and was irresistible in its force. It descended, blazing away, on an arrow that was colourfully tufted, embellished with excellent gold and diamonds. In the battle, Atikaya saw it approach. On seeing it, Atikaya violently struck it with many sharp arrows. However, that arrow possessed Suparna's force and with great speed, approached him. Atikaya saw that blazing arrow approach, resembling Death. He made vain efforts to strike it with spears, swords, clubs, battleaxes, javelins, ploughs[251] and bows. However, blazing like the fire, that arrow rendered all these extraordinary weapons futile. It struck and severed Atikaya's head, decorated with the diadem. The head, with the helmet on the head, was struck by Lakshmana's arrow and fell down violently on the ground, like one of Himalayas' peaks. With their faces resembling blooming lotuses, the many apes were delighted. They worshipped Lakshmana, who had accomplished his objective. The invincible enemy, terrible in his strength, had been killed.

Chapter 6(60)

The large number of rakshasas who had not been killed quickly went to Ravana and told him that the bulls among the

[251] Plough (*hala*) is probably a typo and should be arrow.

rakshasas, Devantaka, Trishira, Atikaya and the others had been slain. Hearing that they had been violently killed, the king lost his senses and tears flowed from his eyes. Because of the terrible news of his sons being killed and the news that his brothers had been killed, the king thought for a long time. The king was distressed and was deeply submerged in an ocean of grief. Seeing this, Indrajit, the son of the king of the rakshasas, addressed him in these words. 'O father! O Indra among the rakshasas! You should not lose your senses, not as long as Indrajit is alive. In a battle, a person who has been struck by the arrows of Indra's enemy will find it impossible to protect his life. Today, you will see the bodies of Rama and Lakshmana mangled and pierced by my arrows. They will lose their lives and lie down on the ground. Their bodies will be completely pierced by arrows. Listen to the pledge taken by Shakra's enemy. This is properly based on manliness and has fortune to back it up. Today, I will torment Rama and Lakshmana with a flood of arrows. Today, in the sacrificial ground used by Bali, Vishnu's fierce enemy, Indra, Vaivasvata, Vishnu, Mitra, the Sadhyas, the Ashvins, Vaishvanara,[252] the sun god and the moon god will witness my immeasurable valour.' The enemy of Indra of the gods said this. Without his spirit being distressed, he sought the king's permission. He mounted an excellent chariot that was like the wind in speed, yoked to excellent donkeys.

The immensely energetic one mounted a chariot that was like Indra's chariot. The scorcher of enemies swiftly went to the place where the fighting was taking place. As the great-souled one proceeded, many extremely strong ones followed him. They were cheerful and wielded the best of bows in their hands. Some were mounted on the backs of elephants and some were astride excellent horses. They wielded spears, clubs, swords, battleaxes and maces. There were the blaring of conch shells and the terrible and loud noise of drums. Worshipped by the roamers in the night, the enemy of Indra of the gods departed. The slayer of enemies had a white umbrella, with the complexion of a conch shell or the moon. He was as radiant

[252] Agni.

as the full moon in the sky. The brave one was fanned with golden whisks that were also decorated with gold. He was handsome and foremost among all archers, fanned by the best of whisks. Indrajit left Lanka, like the sun in his energy. In his valour, as radiant as the shining sun in the sky, he illuminated the city. He left, surrounded by that large army. Seeing this, Ravana, lord of the rakshasas, spoke to his handsome son. 'O son! You have defeated Vasava and there is no charioteer who can stand before you, not to speak of a mortal human. You will slay Raghava.' Having said this, the Indra among the rakshasas pronounced great benedictions over him.

The greatly energetic one, the destroyer of enemies, reached the field of battle. He stationed the rakshasas all around his chariot. His complexion was like the one who devours oblations.[253] With the proper mantras, the best among rakshasas offered oblations into the fire. He prepared the oblations, with parched grain and clarified butter, and placed garlands and fragrances in front. The powerful Indra among rakshasas rendered these oblations into the fire. The weapons were used in place of reeds. *Vibhitaka*[254] was used as kindling. There were red garments and ladles made out of iron. He spread out javelins like a bed of reeds and lit a fire. He grasped the neck of a live goat that was completely black. With the kindling that was offered, a fire without smoke resulted. From the signs, it was seen that victory would be obtained. The fire itself arose in personified form and, with flames that were like molten gold in complexion, circumambulated and accepted the oblations. He was supreme among all those who possessed knowledge of the brahmastra. He invited all the weapons to remain on his bow and his chariot. The weapons were invited and oblations were offered into the fire. The sun, the planets, the moon, the nakshatras and the firmament were terrified. Blazing in energy like the fire and like the great Indra in his powers, he offered oblations into the fire. With his bow, arrows, sword, chariot, horses and charioteer, he assumed the unthinkable form of remaining invisible.

[253] The fire.

[254] A kind of myrobalan.

In the great battle, he left his soldiers behind and quickly attacked the army of the apes. Remaining invisible, he shot nets of fierce arrows. These rained down, like water from dark clouds. Their bodies were mangled by Shakrajit's[255] arrows. They were struck by maya and screamed in hideous tones. In the battle, the apes were like mountains. However, they were brought down, like excellent mountains shattered by Indra's vajra. In the battle, they could only see arrows that were sharp at the tips penetrate the soldiers of the apes. The rakshasa, the enemy of Indra of the gods, was deep in his use of maya and they were unable to see him. The great-souled lord of the rakshasas covered all the directions with innumerable arrows sharp at the tips. He shrouded the radiance of the sun and caused distress to the Indras among the apes. Spears, swords and battleaxes, resembling a blazing fire, pierced them. They were like raging fires, emitting sparks. This fierce shower rained down on the soldiers of the king of the apes. The leaders of the apes were struck by these blazing and sharp arrows. Afflicted by Shakrajit's arrows, they were like blossoming kimshukas. They clung to each other and roared in hideous tones. The weapons of the Indra among the rakshasas mangled the bulls among the apes and made them fall down. Struck and with their eyes torn out, some looked up into the sky. Some leaned on each other and fell down on the ground. Hanumat, Sugriva, Angada, Gandhamadana, Jambavat, Sushena, Vegadarshina, Mainda, Dvivida, Nila, Gavaksha, Gaja, Gomukha, Kesari, Hariloma, the ape Vidyuddamshtra, Suryanana, Jyotimukha, the ape Dadhimukha, Pavakaksha, Nala and the ape Kumuda—all of them were struck with spears, javelins and sharp arrows, all invoked with Indrajit's mantras. The supreme rakshasa pierced all those tigers among apes. The foremost leaders among the apes were mangled with clubs and pierced with arrows that were gold-tufted.

He next rained down arrows that are as radiant as the rays of the sun on Rama and Lakshmana. Rama's beauty was supreme and he did not think about this shower of arrows, regarding it as

[255] Shakrajit is the same as Indrajit.

no more than a shower of rain. However, looking at it, he spoke to Lakshmana. 'O Lakshmana! This Indra among rakshasas, the enemy of Indra of the gods, is resorting to the brahmastra again. He is fiercely bringing down the soldiers of the apes. He is engaging with us and afflicting us with these arrows. The great-souled one has obtained a boon from Svayambhu. He is in the sky and has made his terrible form invisible. How can one fight against someone who doesn't possess a body? How can one raise a weapon and kill Indrajit? I think that the illustrious Svayambhu cannot be thought of and this shows the power of his weapon. O intelligent one! Remain here with me and tolerate this shower of arrows now. This Indra among rakshasas has concealed himself and is enveloping all the directions with his nets of arrows. All the best among the valiant ones have fallen down and the army of the king of the apes is no longer resplendent. Let us fall down, unconscious. Let us abandon all anger and joy and withdraw from the battle. On seeing this, it is certain that this enemy of the immortals will return, having obtained success in the field of battle.' At this, they allowed themselves to be struck by Indrajit's nets of weapons. Having caused them distress in the field of battle, the Indra among rakshasas roared in delight. With Rama and Lakshmana, the soldiers of the king of the apes were suddenly immersed in misery in that encounter. He[256] returned to the city protected by Dashagriva's arms.

Chapter 6(61)

In the forefront of the field of battle, the soldiers and the leaders of the apes lost their senses. Sugriva, Nila, Angada and Jambavat did not know what they should do. Vibhishana was supreme among those who were intelligent and he saw that the soldiers were distressed. He spoke these unmatched words of assurance to the brave king of the apes. 'Do not be frightened. This is not the time

[256] Indrajit.

for despondency. The two noble ones are disabled and suffering because of the words uttered by Svayambhu.[257] That is the reason they have succumbed to the net of Indrajit's weapons. This supreme weapon was given by Svayambhu Brahma and its force is irresistible. The two princes have shown it respect and have fallen down. This is not the time for despondency.'

Hearing Vibhishana's words, the intelligent Maruti showed his respects to Brahma's weapon. Hanumat said, 'These spirited soldiers of the apes have been struck down. We must comfort those who are still alive.' In the night, those two brave ones, Hanumat and the supreme among the rakshasas,[258] roamed around in the field of battle, with torches in their hands. They had fallen down in every direction, with blood oozing from the wounds in their bodies. Their tails, hands, thighs, feet, fingers and heads had been mangled. The earth was strewn with fallen apes who were like mountains. Blazing weapons could also be seen, fallen down on the ground. Vibhishana and Hanumat also saw Sugriva, Angada, Nila, Sharabha, Gandhamadana, Jambavat, Sushena, Vegadarshina, Ahuka, Mainda, Nala, Jyotimukha, Dvivida and Panasa—brought down in the battle. Sixty-seven crores of spirited apes had been brought down by Svayambhu's beloved weapon in the fifth part of the day.[259]

Hanumat and Vibhishana searched for Jambavat and looked at the army that had been afflicted by the arrows, resembling the terrible waves of the ocean. He was naturally old and aged and had been pierced with hundreds of arrows. Prajapati's brave son[260] was like a fire that had been pacified. Having seen and met him, Poulastya[261] spoke these words. 'You have been shattered by these sharp arrows. Are you still alive?' Having heard Vibhishana's words, Jambavat, bull among the bears, managed to utter these

[257] The boon granted by Brahma.

[258] Vibhishana.

[259] A day of twelve hours was divided into five parts, each consisting of 144 minutes. This incident occurred in the fifth segment, the last part of the day.

[260] Jambavat.

[261] Vibhishana.

words with difficulty. 'O Indra among the nairittas! O immensely brave one! I have recognized you through your voice. My body has been pierced with sharp arrows and I am unable to see you with my eyes. O nairitta! Anjana had an excellent son through the wind god. He is Hanumat, supreme among the apes. Is he still alive?' Hearing Jambavat's words, Vibhishana asked, 'Ignoring the two noble ones,[262] why are you asking about Maruti? O noble one! The supreme affection you have displayed towards the son of the wind god is not shown towards King Sugriva, Angada or Raghava.' Hearing Vibhishana's words, Jambavat replied in these words. 'O tiger among nairittas! Listen to the reason why I asked about Maruti. If that brave one is alive, even if this army has been destroyed, we will be alive. If Hanumat has lost his life, even if we are alive, we will be as good as dead. O son![263] Maruti is like the wind. He is like the fire in his valour. As long as he is alive, there is still hope.'

At this, Hanumat, the son of the wind god, humbly approached the aged Jambavat and grasped his feet. The senses of the bull among bears were afflicted. However, on hearing Hanumat's words, he thought that he had got back his life again. The immensely energetic Jambavat spoke to Hanumat. 'O tiger among the apes! Come here. You must save the apes. There is no one else who possesses sufficient valour to be a supreme friend to them. This is the time to show that valour. I do not see anyone else. Bring joy to the brave armies of the bears and the apes. Free Rama and Lakshmana from their wounds and the stakes. O Hanumat! You must progressively travel beyond the ocean and go to the supreme spot, the Himalayas, best among mountains. O slayer of enemies! You will see the golden Mount Rishabha there, supreme among mountains, and also see Mount Kailasa. O brave one! In between those two summits, you will see a mountain that is full of herbs. It blazes and is unmatched in its radiance. It has all the herbs. O tiger among apes! You will see four herbs on the summit there. They

262 Rama and Lakshmana.

263 The word used is tata.

blaze and illuminate the ten directions. These are the great herbs—*mritasanjivani*, *vishalyakarani*, *souvarnakarani* and *sandhani*.[264] O Hanumat! You must get all of these and return swiftly. O son of the one who conveys fragrances![265] You will thereby comfort them and bring life back to the apes.'

Hearing Jambavat's words, Hanumat, bull among the apes, was filled with strength, the way the ocean is filled with the force of the waters. He stood on the summit of the mountain[266] and pressed down on that excellent mountain.[267] The brave Hanumat was seen to resemble a second mountain. The mountain was shattered and suffered from the pressure of the ape's feet. It suffered from that great burden and was incapable of bearing it. Suffering from the force exerted by the ape, the mountain blazed and fell down on the ground. Because of what Hanumat did, the peaks were shattered. As that supreme among mountains was whirled around, the apes were incapable of remaining there. The trees and the slopes of the mountain were crushed and shattered. In the night, Lanka was terrified. The large gates were whirled around and the houses and the turrets were shattered. It was as if the city was dancing. He was himself like a mountain on earth and crushed the earth. The son of the wind god agitated the earth, with all its oceans. As he pressed down on the mountain with his feet, his mouth resembled the mouth of the subterranean fire. He opened it wide and roared fiercely, terrifying the rakshasas. All the rakshasas in Lanka heard the extraordinary sound of his roar and because of their fear, were unable to move. Terrible in his valour, Maruti bowed down before Rama. For Raghava's sake, the scorcher of enemies resolved to undertake this supreme task. He raised up his tail, which resembled a serpent. He bent his back and contracted his ears. He opened his mouth, like the mouth of the subterranean fire. With terrible

[264] Mritasanjivani brings the dead back to life, vishalyakarani removes stakes and heals wounds, souvarnakarani restores the original complexion of the body and sandhani repairs broken bones.

[265] That is, the wind.

[266] Trikuta.

[267] Pressed down with his feet.

force, he leapt up into the sky. As he leapt up, because of the force and speed of his arms and his thighs, clumps of trees, boulders, rocks and ordinary apes were lifted up, and when the momentum was lost, these fell down into the water. He stretched out his arms, which looked like the coils of serpents. With a valour that resembled that of the enemy of the serpents,[268] the son of the wind god left for Meru, the excellent king of the mountains, seemingly dragging the directions away with his force. The garlands of waves in the ocean were agitated and all the creatures that dwelt there were severely hurled around. He was like the chakra released from Vishnu's arm and as he swiftly departed, he looked at all this. Without any exhaustion, he traversed the path followed by the sun.

The best among apes suddenly saw the Himalayas, supreme among mountains. There were diverse kinds of waterfalls there. There were many caverns and springs. The beautiful peaks were like masses of white clouds. He reached the great Indra among mountains. There were tall and terrible peaks that rose up. He saw the great and sacred hermitages, populated by supreme and divine rishis. He saw Brahma's treasure,[269] the abode of silver,[270] Shakra's abode, the place where Rudra released his bow, Hayanana,[271] the blazing Brahmashira,[272] the servants of Vaivasvata,[273] the abode of the vajra, the abode of Vaishravana,[274] Suryanibandhana, which blazes like the sun,[275] Brahma's abode, Shankara's bow and the navel of the earth.[276] In the Himalayas, there was the excellent and lofty Mount Kailasa and the excellent, lofty and golden Mount

[268] Garuda.

[269] Alternatively, Brahma's abode.

[270] Interpreted as Kailasa, Shiva's abode.

[271] Horse-faced, place where Vishnu is worshipped in his form of Hayagriva (horse-necked).

[272] There are stories about Rudra having severed Brahma's fifth head (shira).

[273] Probably meaning Yama.

[274] Kubera.

[275] Surya (the sun god) was excessively brilliant and Vishvakarma shaved off a part of this brilliance. The place where Surya was bound down, for this task to be done, is known as Suryanibandhana.

[276] This is the spot through where one enters the nether regions.

Rishabha. He saw the Indra among mountains that had all the herbs. It blazed and was illuminated because of all the herbs. The son of Vasava's messenger[277] was amazed to see this, blazing like the rays of the fire. That Indra among mountains was filled with herbs and he started to search for the right herbs. The great ape had travelled across thousands of yojanas. The son of the wind god roamed around the mountain that was full of divine herbs. However, knowing that someone had come, all the great herbs on that excellent mountain made themselves invisible. Unable to see them, the great-souled Hanumat became enraged and roared loudly. He was intolerant and his eyes turned as red as the fire.

He addressed the Indra among mountains in these words. 'O god! It is extremely evident that you do not have the least bit of compassion for Raghava. Behold the great strength of my arms today. O Indra among mountains! You will find yourself shattered.' There were peaks, summits and trees on that mountain. There were thousands of minerals, including gold. He seized it with force and leapt up. The summit of the mountain was dislodged and the peaks fragmented. He uprooted it and leapt up into the sky, scaring the worlds and the Indras among the gods and the asuras. With a speed and force that surpassed that of Garuda, he proceeded, praised by many creatures who resided in the sky. He seized the summit, which was as radiant as the sun and resorted to the path followed by the sun. He was himself as radiant as the sun and approached the sun, resembling a second sun. That mountain was extremely radiant and the son of the one who bears fragrances[278] was himself like a mountain. He resembled the chakra, with one thousand edges, hurled with a great gust by Vishnu into the sky.

The apes saw him and roared. On seeing them, he also roared back in delight. Hearing the roars that they let out, the residents of Lanka roared in even more terrible voices. The great-souled one descended on that excellent mountain,[279] amidst the soldiers of the apes. He lowered his head down and greeted the best among the

[277] Vayu is Indra's messenger.

[278] Vayu.

[279] Trikuta.

apes and embraced Vibhishana. The two human princes inhaled the fragrance of the great herbs and were freed from all their wounds. The brave apes also stood up. The ape who was the son of the bearer of fragrances used his fierce valour to carry back the mountain with herbs.[280] Using his force, he returned again to Rama.

Chapter 6(62)

Sugriva, the immensely energetic lord of the apes, addressed the immensely strong Hanumat, indicating the subsequent course of action. 'Kumbhakarna and the four princes have been killed. Therefore, it is not possible for Ravana to undertake any action now. There are apes who are extremely strong and dexterous. Let those bulls among apes swiftly take torches and attack Lanka.'

The sun had set and it was the start of a terrible night. The bulls among apes headed for Lanka, with torches in their hands. With torches in their hands, large numbers of apes attacked it from all sides. The guards, with malformed eyes, suddenly ran away. Cheerfully, they set fire to the turrets, floors of mansions, many roads and palaces. The fire burnt down and consumed thousands of houses and all the residences of rakshasas, who loved their homes. There was armour decorated with gold and vessels full of garlands and garments. Because they had been drinking, their eyes were unsteady and they lurched as they walked. Their garments were entwined with those of their lovers, though they were filled with intolerance because of the enemy. They had maces and spears in their hands, but they were eating and drinking. With their beloveds, they were lying down on extremely expensive beds. They swiftly grabbed their sons and fled in different directions. Thousands of houses of the residents of Lanka were burnt by the fire and blazed repeatedly. There were extremely firm and extremely expensive houses, with deep qualities. They were made out of gold, in shapes

[280] He returned it to the Himalayas.

of the moon and the half-moon. They were excellent and with many floors, shining like the moon. There were colourful windows and couches everywhere. Decorated with jewels and coral, they seemed to touch the sun. There was the sound of herons and peacocks and the jingling of ornaments. Those houses that were like mountains were burnt by the fire. Surrounded by the fire, the turrets looked like masses of clouds tinged by lightning, when summer is over. Beautiful women who were asleep in mansions were burnt. Throwing aside all their ornaments, they lamented, 'Alas!' Surrounded by the fire, the houses fell down. They were like the shattered summits of mountains, struck by the vajra of the wielder of the vajra. From a distance, as they were burnt, the houses resembled the summits of the Himalayas, blazing with groves of herbs. The tops of the mansions were burnt and blazed, engulfed in flames. In the night, Lanka seemed to be full of flowering kimshukas. The keepers of elephants set the elephants free. The keepers of horses set the horses free. Lanka was like the turbulent ocean at the time of the end of the worlds. On seeing a freed horse, an elephant was scared and retreated. On seeing a frightened elephant, a horse was scared and retreated. In a short while, the city was burnt by the apes. It seemed as if the earth was ablaze at the time of the terrible destruction of the worlds. From ten yojanas away, one could hear the sounds of the women screaming, as they were burnt and scorched and enveloped in smoke.

With their bodies burnt by the fire, the enemy rakshasas emerged. Desiring to fight, the apes attacked them violently. The sound emitted by the apes and the rakshasas resounded in the ten directions, the ocean and the earth. The great-souled Rama and Lakshmana had been freed of their wounds. With excellent bows in their hands, they fearlessly advanced. Rama twanged his excellent bow and this created a tumultuous sound that caused fear to the rakshasas. Stretching his giant bow, Rama was as radiant as the illustrious and enraged Bhava,[281] stretching a bow made out of the Vedas. The sound created by the apes, the roar of the rakshasas and

[281] Shiva.

the sound of Rama twanging his bow —these three pervaded the ten directions. Because of the arrows released from his bow, the main turrent of the city, resembling Kailasa's peak, was shattered and fell down on the ground. On witnessing Rama's arrows, in mansions and houses, the Indras among the rakshasas armoured themselves and created a tumult. As they prepared for battle, they roared like lions. To the Indras among the rakshasas, that night was terrible. The great-souled Sugriva, Indra among the apes, commanded, 'O apes! Approach the gates and fight. If someone is present there, but acts in a contrary way, he will slight the command of the king and should be killed.'

The foremost among the apes held blazing torches in their hands and were stationed at the gates. Ravana was filled with intolerance. The ten directions were agitated because of his yawning and stomping around. He was seen to resemble Rudra, with rage permeating his body. Angry, with many rakshasas, he sent Kumbha and Nikumbha, the two sons of Kumbhakarna. The lord of the rakshasas commanded all the rakshasas, 'O rakshasas! Roar like lions and advance.' Thus urged, the brave rakshasas emerged from Lanka, with blazing weapons and roaring repeatedly. There were terrible horses, chariots and elephants, with innumerable foot soldiers. They had blazing spears, clubs, swords, javelins, spikes and bows. That army of rakshasas was terrible and was filled with terrible valour and manliness. There were nets of golden armour on the arms and they brandished battleaxes. They whirled around great weapons and affixed arrows to their bows. The air was filled with the intoxicating scent of perfumes, garlands and liquor. With so many terrible and brave ones, the roar resembled that of a thundering cloud.

On seeing the invincible army of the rakshasas advance, the army of the apes stirred itself and roared. The army of the rakshasas also attacked the army of the enemy with great force, like insects heading towards a fire. There were iron clubs in their hands and bludgeons in their fists. That excellent army of the rakshasas was supremely radiant. The roamers in the night were terrible in form and their brave warriors used swords and sharp arrows to sever the heads of the enemy apes. A warrior who was striking someone else was killed.[282] A warrior who was bringing someone else down was brought down. A warrior who was censuring someone else was censured. A warrior who was biting someone else was bitten. Some said, 'Strike me.' Others said, 'You are being struck.' Someone else said, 'I will strike you.' Someone spoke to another and said, 'Why are you suffering this hardship by remaining here?' They raised giant spears, javelins, swords and fists. There was a great and tumultuous battle between the apes and the rakshasas. In the battle, the rakshasas killed apes in tens and sevens. The apes brought down rakshasas in tens and sevens. Hair and garments were dishevelled. Armour and standards were cast aside. The apes attacked and surrounded the army of the rakshasas.

Chapter 6(63)

There was a tumultuous battle that led to the slaughter of brave warriors. Desiring to fight, Angada approached the brave Kampana. Challenging Angada, the angry Kampana first struck him with the great force of a club. Severely struck, he reeled. When he regained his senses, the energetic one hurled the summit of a mountain. Afflicted by the blow, Kampana fell down on the ground. With the brave ones killed, the army of the Indra among the rakshasas was distressed. It retreated towards the spot where Kumbhakarna's son[283] was. Kumbha reassured the army and attacked with force. Controlling himself, the supreme among archers seized his bow. He shot excellent arrows that were like virulent serpents, capable of tearing the body apart. With excellent arrows affixed, his excellent bow was like a second bow of Indra, tinged with lightning, astride the radiant Airavata.[284]

[282] Signifying the violation of the rules of war and the chaos.
[283] Kumbha.
[284] There is a double image of Indra astride Airavata, wielding his bow, and of the rainbow as Indra's bow.

He drew his bow all the way back to his ears and using an arrow with a golden shaft, tufted with the feathers of birds, struck Dvivida. The excellent ape possessed the complexion of the summit of Trikuta. However, suddenly struck, his feet tottered. He was agitated and fell down, writhing. Mainda saw that his brother had been routed in the great encounter. He seized a giant boulder and attacked with force. The immensely strong one flung the boulder towards the rakshasas. However, Kumbha shattered the boulder with five sparkling arrows. He affixed another arrow with an excellent tip, resembling a virulent serpent. The immensely energetic one struck Dvivida's elder brother in the chest. The blow pierced Mainda, the leader of the apes, in his inner organs. Senseless, he fell down on the ground. Angada saw that his immensely strong maternal uncles had been brought down. He attacked Kumbha, who had his bow upraised, with force. As he descended, Kumbha pierced him with five iron arrows and three other sharp arrows, the way one strikes an elephant with a goad. Kumbha pierced the valiant Angada with many kinds of arrows, which were extremely sharp, pointed and keen, decorated with gold. Though he was pierced in his limbs, Angada, Vali's son, did not tremble. He rained down showers of boulders and trees on his head. Kumbhakarna's son sliced down all of them and all the boulders hurled by Vali's handsome son. Seeing that the leader of the apes was descending on him, Kumbha pierced him between the eyebrows with arrows, the way one strikes an elephant with a flaming torch. He was covered with blood, flowing from his eyes. Angada covered these with one hand and used the other hand to seize a sala tree. That tree was like Indra's standard, like Mandara. While all the rakshasas looked on, he hurled it with force. However, he shot it down with seven arrows that were capable of mangling the body. On seeing this, Angada was distressed. He lost his senses and sank down. The invincible Angada was distressed, as if he was submerged in an ocean. Witnessing this, the best among the apes went and informed Raghava.

Hearing that Vali's son was suffering in the great battle, Rama commanded the best among the apes, with Jambavat at the forefront. The tigers among the apes heard Rama's command. Extremely enraged, they attacked Kumbha, who was brandishing his bow. Their eyes red with rage, they held trees and boulders in their hands. The bulls among the apes desired to protect Angada. Jambavat and the apes Sushena and Vegadarshi angrily attacked Kumbhakarna's brave son. Seeing those extremely strong apes advance, he countered them with torrents of arrows, the way one dams a store of water with rocks. The great-souled Indras among the apes were unable to breach his storm of arrows, just as the great ocean cannot cross the shoreline. The large number of apes were afflicted by these arrows. On seeing this, the lord of the apes kept his brother's son, Angada, in the background. In the battle, Sugriva attacked Kumbha with force, just as a powerful lion attacks an elephant that is roaming around on the slope of a mountain. He uprooted giant boulders and many ashvakarna and dhava trees. The immensely strong one hurled many other trees. Kumbhakarna's invincible son used his sharp arrows to sever that invincible downpour of trees that enveloped the sky. Kumbha aimed his fierce and sharp arrows at these trees. Shattered by them, they were as radiant as terrible shataghnis. That shower of trees was severed by the valiant Kumbha. On seeing this, the handsome and great-spirited lord of the apes was not distressed. Though he was himself pierced by those arrows, he tolerated it. He violently seized Kumbha's bow, which was as resplendent as Indra's bow, and broke it. He swiftly attacked and performed this extremely difficult deed. Kumbha was like an elephant with its tusks broken and he angrily spoke to him. 'O Nikumbha's elder brother! Your valour and the force of your arrows are extraordinary. Both you and Ravana possess good intentions[285] and powers. You are the equal of Prahlada, Bali, Vritra's destroyer,[286] Kubera and Varuna. You have been born in the likeness of your father, who was supreme in strength. O mighty-armed one! O slayer of enemies! If you wield the spear in your hand, the gods cannot cross you, just as someone who has conquered his senses cannot be agitated. Because of the boon he received, your paternal uncle[287] can withstand the gods and the danavas. However, Kumbhakarna could withstand the gods and the

[285] Towards rakshasas.
[286] Indra.
[287] Ravana.

asuras because of his valour. You are Indrajit's equal in the wielding of the bow and Ravana's equal in powers. Because of your strength and valour, you are now the best in the world of the rakshasas. Today, let all the creatures witness the great and extraordinary encounter between you and me, like that between Shakra and Shambara. You have performed unmatched tasks and have shown your skill in the use of weapons. You have brought down brave apes who were terrible in their valour. O brave one! If I do not kill you, I am scared of being censured. However, you are exhausted because of what you have done. Rest and then behold my strength.' Sugriva's words sounded like respect, but actually indicated disrespect. Like oblations rendered into a fire, they served to enhance his energy. Kumbha leapt up and attacked Sugriva. He angrily struck him on the chest with a fist that had the force of the vajra. His skin was splintered and blood started to flow out. With the great force of his fist, he struck him again on the chest. It was as if the blazing vajra had struck Mount Meru. However, the force of the blow ignited his energy again. Thus struck, the immensely strong Sugriva, bull among apes, countered with his own fist, which was like the vajra. His fist was as radiant as the solar disc, emitting one thousand rays. He brought that clenched fist down on the valiant Kumbha's chest. Struck by the fist, the rakshasa swiftly fell down. His limbs were red,[288] like the sky when its radiance has dissipated. Kumbha fell down, his chest shattered by the fist. His form was like that of the earth when it is afflicted by Rudra. He was terrible in his valour, but was killed in the battle by the bull among the apes. The earth, with its mountains and forests, trembled. The rakshasas were filled with greater fear.

Chapter 6(64)

Nikumbha saw that his brother had been brought down by Sugriva. He glanced at the Indra among the apes, as

[288] Because of the blood, with an implicit comparison with the evening sky.

if he would burn him down in rage. The brave one grasped his club, which was like the peak of an excellent mountain. It was auspicious, decorated and plated and was five fingers in width. It was bound in a golden piece of cloth and studded with diamonds and rubies. It was as terrible as Yama's staff and dispelled the fear of the rakshasas. It was like Shakra's standard. In the battle, the immensely energetic Nikumbha, terrible in his valour, seized it and opening his mouth wide, roared. There was golden armour on his chest and armlets on his arms. He was adorned with earrings and decorated with a colourful garland. Because of the radiance of his ornaments and his club, Nikumbha was as resplendent as a cloud, tinged with lightning and a radiant rainbow. The tip of his club thundered like the gust of a storm. It blazed and roared, like a fire without smoke. As the great-souled one whirled his club, it was as if the city with the excellent residences of the gandharvas[289] was whirled around, or Amaravati with all its residences was whirled around. As Nikumbha whirled his club around, it was as if the firmament, with the stars, the planets, the nakshatras, the moon and the giant planets, was also whirled around. As he dazzled and whirled his club around, he became impossible to approach. Nikumbha was blind with rage, like the fire of destruction that arises at the end of a yuga. Because of their fear, the rakshasas and the apes were incapable of moving. However, with his chest bared, the strong Hanumat stood in front of him. His[290] arms were like clubs and his shining club dazzled. The strong one used his strength to bring it down on his chest. The club struck his steady and broad chest and shattered into one hundred fragments. Shattered, it fell down, like hundreds of meteors dislodged from the sky. Struck by the blow of the club, the great ape wavered a little. But he was like a mountain during an earthquake. Struck in this way, Hanumat, supreme among apes and immensely strong, used his strength to clench his fist. The immensely energetic one, like Vayu in valour,

[289] Meaning Alakapuri, Kubera's capital.
[290] Nikumbha's.

raised it and with force and strength, brought it down on the valiant Nikumbha's chest. At this, his skin splintered and blood started to flow. The fist seemed to blaze, like lightning in the sky. Nikumbha trembled because of the blow. However, he recovered and seized the immensely strong Hanumat. In that terrible battle, seeing that Nikumbha had raised the immensely strong Hanumat, the residents of Lanka roared. The son of the wind god was being carried off by Kumbhakarna's son. But he struck him with a fist that possessed the force of the vajra. Hanumat, the son of the wind god, quickly freed himself and flung Nikumbha down on the ground. Making great efforts, he flung Nikumbha down and crushed him. He flung him down with force and leapt on to the valiant one's chest. He seized him with his arms and twisted his head around. He tore off his head and emitted a loud and terrible roar. Suffering, Nikumbha roared in the encounter with the son of the wind god. An extremely terrible battle commenced between Dasharatha's son and the army of the Indra among the rakshasas and it was devastating.

Chapter 6(65)

Hearing that Nikumbha had been killed and Kumbha brought down, Ravana was greatly enraged and blazed like a fire. Because of both anger and sorrow, the nairitta became senseless. He commanded the large-eyed Makaraksha, Khara's son. 'O son! I am instructing you. Take an army with you and go. Slay Raghava and Lakshmana, together with the residents of the forest.' Hearing Ravana's words, Makaraksha, the roamer in the night who was Khara's son, prided himself on his bravery and signified his assent. He greeted Dashagriva and circumambulated him. Obeying Ravana's instructions, the strong one emerged from the auspicious house. The commander of the army was near him and Khara's son addressed him in these words. 'Swiftly bring a chariot and quickly summon the soldiers.' Hearing his words, the roamer in the night who was the commander of the army brought and presented the chariot and the army. The roamer in the night[291] circumambulated the chariot and ascended it. He instructed the charioteer to quickly drive the chariot away. Makaraksha spoke to all the rakshasas. 'O rakshasas! All of you remain in front of me and fight. The great-souled Ravana, the king of the rakshasas, has commanded me to kill Rama and Lakshmana in the battle. O roamers in the night! I will slay Rama and Lakshmana with my excellent arrows today and also the ape Sugriva and the other apes. Today, I will use my spear to bring down the large army of the apes. I will burn down those who approach, like a fire consuming dry kindling.' Hearing Makaraksha's words, the strong roamers in the night controlled themselves and armed themselves with many kinds of weapons. They were cruel and could assume any form at will. They were tawny eyed and armoured. They roared like elephants. With their dishevelled hair, they were fearful. Gigantic in form, they surrounded Khara's son, who was huge in size. They cheerfully attacked and made the earth tremble. Thousands of conch shells and drums were sounded in every direction. A great sound of beating and clapping arose.

The rakshasa's standard fell down violently. The whip was also dislodged from the charioteer's hand. The horses yoked to the chariot lost all their valour. Their feet wavered. They were distressed and there were tears in their eyes. A harsh and extremely terrible wind, mixed with dust, started to blow. This is what happened when the terrible and evil-minded Makaraksha marched out. The rakshasas were terrible in their valour. Despite witnessing these ominous portents, they paid no heed to them. All of them emerged and went to where Rama and Lakshmana were. Their complexions were like dense clouds, elephants and buffaloes. In the forefront of the battle, they had formerly been mangled by clubs and swords. They were accomplished in fighting and exclaimed, 'I', 'I'. As they roamed around, the roamers in the night roared.

[291] Makaraksha.

Chapter 6(66)

The bulls among the apes saw Makaraksha emerge. Desiring to fight, all of them leapt up and stood ready. An extremely great encounter commenced between the roamers in the night and the apes, like that between the gods and the danavas. It made the body hair stand up. They were brought down with trees and spears. They were brought down with clubs and maces. The apes and the roamers in the night crushed each other. In every direction, the roamers in the night used spears, javelins, clubs, swords, spikes, darts, bhindipalas and showers of arrows. With nooses, maces, staffs and other kinds of weapons, the roamers in the night caused carnage amidst the lions among the apes. The apes were afflicted by the torrents of arrows shot by Khara's son. All of them were scared and suffered from fear, resulting in flight. The rakshasas saw that all the residents of the forest were running away. Proud as lions and desiring victory, the rakshasas roared. In every direction, the apes fled. Rama comforted them and countered the rakshasas with a shower of arrows.

On seeing that the rakshasas had been restrained, Makaraksha, the roamer in the night, blazed in anger, like a fire. He spoke these words. 'O Rama! Wait. There will be a duel with me. The sharp arrows shot from my bow will take your life away. You slew my father in Dandakaranya. I remember your deed. On seeing you in front of me, my rage has increased. O evil-souled Raghava! My limbs are on fire, since at that time, I did not see you in the great forest. O Rama! It is good fortune that I am able to see you approach me now. Like a hungry lion that sees a deer, I have been craving for this. Today, the force of my arrows will dispatch you to the kingdom of the dead. You will then meet the brave ones you have killed earlier. O Rama! What is the need to speak much? Listen to my words. In the field of battle, all the worlds will behold me. O Rama! This great battle will use weapons, clubs, arms, or whatever that you are used to fighting with.' Hearing Makaraksha's words, Rama, Dasharatha's son, laughed. He replied in these words, though the other one continued to speak. 'In Dandaka, I killed fourteen thousand rakshasas, your father, Trishira and Dushana. O wicked one! Vultures, jackals and crows will use their sharp beaks, nails and goads[292] today and satisfy themselves with your flesh.'

Khara's son, the roamer in the night, was thus addressed by Rama. In the field of battle, he shot torrents of arrows towards Raghava. Rama severed that shower of arrows with many arrows. Severed, thousands of gold-tufted arrows fell down on the ground. As those two energetic ones clashed against each other, an encounter commenced between the rakshasa who was Khara's son and Dasharatha's son. The sound of bowstrings slapping against palms was like the roar of clouds in the sky. The sound emitted by twanging bows was heard in the field of battle. To witness the extraordinary encounter, all the gods, danavas, gandharvas, kinnaras and giant serpents assembled in the firmament. Though their bodies were pierced, their strength was doubled. In the field of battle, they sought to counter each other's deeds. In the battle, the rakshasa sliced down torrents of arrows that Rama shot. Using innumerable arrows, Rama also severed the arrows the rakshasa shot. All the directions and the sub-directions were covered with arrows. The earth was covered everywhere and nothing could be seen. The mighty-armed Raghava became angry and severed the rakshasa's bow. He used eight iron arrows to pierce his charioteer. Rama used his arrows to shatter his chariot and brought down the horses yoked to the chariot. Deprived of his chariot, Makaraksha, the roamer in the night, stationed himself on the ground. Stationed on the ground, the rakshasa seized a spear in his hand. With a radiance like that of the fire of destruction at the end of a yuga, he terrified all creatures. The roamer in the night whirled that blazing and great spear. In the great battle, he angrily hurled it towards Raghava. Released from the hand of Khara's son, it blazed as it descended. However, with four arrows, Raghava severed the spear in the sky. Decorated with divine gold, that spear was splintered into many parts. Struck by Rama's arrows, it was shattered and fell down on the ground, like a giant meteor. The spear was destroyed

[292] That is, claws like goads.

by Rama, the performer of extraordinary deeds. On seeing this, all the beings who were in the firmament uttered words of praise. Makaraksha, the roamer in the night, saw that the spear had been destroyed. He raised his fist and told Kakutstha, 'Wait. Wait.' On seeing him descend, the descendant of the Raghu lineage laughed. He affixed *pavakastra*[293] to his bow. In the battle, Kakutstha killed the rakshasa with this weapon. With his heart shattered, he fell down and died. All the rakshasas saw that Makaraksha had been brought down. Afflicted by their fear of Rama's arrows, they fled to Lanka. Using the force of his arrows, the son of King Dasharatha killed the roamer in the night who was Khara's son. It was as if a mountain had been struck by the vajra and had been shattered. On seeing this, the gods rejoiced.

Chapter 6(67)

Hearing that Makaraksha had been killed, Ravana, the victor in assemblies, was enraged. He instructed his son, Indrajit, to fight. 'O brave one! Slay those two extremely valiant brothers, Rama and Lakshmana. While they can be seen, you will remain invisible. Therefore, you are stronger in every way. You have performed the unrivalled deed of having defeated Indra in a battle. When you see two ordinary humans, how can you not slay them in a battle?' Thus addressed by the Indra among the rakshasas, he accepted his father's words. Following the prescribed rites, Indrajit offered oblations to the fire in the sacrificial ground. As he offered oblations into the fire, rakshasa women respectfully arrived at the spot where Ravana's son was, carrying red headdresses. The weapons were used as beds of reeds. Vibhitaka was offered as kindling. There were red garments and ladles made out of iron. All around the fire, beds of reeds were spread out. He seized a goat that

[293] Divine weapon named after Pavaka, the fire god. Therefore, pavakastra is a synonym for agneyastra.

was completely black and alive by the throat.[294] When the kindling was properly offered, the flames arose, without any smoke. The signs that manifested themselves indicated victory. Having accepted the oblations, the fire god himself arose.[295] The flames, which had the complexion of molten gold, circumambulated him. He offered oblations into the fire and satisfied the gods, the danavas and the rakshasas. He ascended the auspicious and excellent chariot that was capable of vanishing. The excellent chariot was yoked to four horses and stocked with sharp arrows. A great bow was placed in it and it was resplendent. With its golden embellishments, its form dazzled. The chariot was decorated with the marks of deer, full moons and half-moons. Indrajit's blazing form was like that of the fire, adorned with a giant necklace that was made out of molten gold. His standard was decorated with lapis lazuli. He was protected by Brahma's weapon, which was like the sun. Ravana's extremely strong son was extremely invincible.

Indrajit, the victor in assemblies, emerged from the city. He had offered oblations into the fire. He had uttered the rakshasa mantras that enabled him to become invisible. He said, 'Today, in the battle, I will kill the two who are false mendicants in the forest.[296] In the supreme encounter, I will give my father, Ravana, victory. I will destroy all apes on earth and kill Rama and Lakshmana. I will cause great delight.' Having said this, he vanished. He angrily descended, urged by Dashagriva's words. Indra's enemy came to the battle with a fierce bow and sharp iron arrows. In the midst of the apes, he saw those two extremely brave ones, like two three-hooded serpents. Those two brave ones were shooting nets of arrows. He thought, 'These are the ones.' He strung his bow and showered down arrows on them, enveloping them, like a cloud showering down rain. With his chariot, he reached the sky and could not be seen with the eyes. Remaining there, he pierced Rama and Lakshmana with sharp arrows. All around, Rama and Lakshmana were enveloped by the force of his arrows. They sought

[294] Indrajit seems to have offered the live goat as an offering into the fire.
[295] In personified form.
[296] In the sense that a true mendicant has no use for weapons.

to invoke divine weapons on the arrows on their bows. Those two immensely strong ones covered the sky with their nets of arrows. However, though those arrows were like weapons used by the gods, they could not touch him. He covered the firmament with a darkness that was like smoke. The handsome one enveloped the directions with a dark mist and rendered them invisible. The slap of his bowstring against his palm could not be heard. There was no sound from the axle of his chariot or the hooves of his horses. His movement could not be heard and his form could not be seen. Through that dark and dense cloud, there was the extraordinary downpour of his arrows. The mighty-armed one showered down iron arrows and rained down other arrows. Because of the boon he had obtained, he possessed arrows that were like the sun. Angrily, in the battle, Ravana's son used these to severely pierce Rama everywhere on his body. Like rain showering down on two mountains, those two were struck by floods of iron arrows. Those two tigers among men shot sharp arrows that were gold-tufted. Ravana's son was in the firmament and those arrows, tufted with the feathers of herons, reached and pierced him there. Covered with blood, they fell down on the ground. Those two supreme men were severely afflicted by these floods of arrows. As these descended, they severed them with many broad-headed arrows. Dasharatha's two sons shot their excellent weapons in whatever direction those sharp arrows were seen to descend from. However, Ravana's atiratha son roamed around in all the directions. Skilled in striking the objective, he used his sharp arrows to pierce Dasharatha's two sons. Those two brave ones were severely pierced with gold-tufted arrows that had been crafted well. Dasharatha's two sons looked like blossoming kimshukas. No one knew where he was. No one could see his bow or arrows. Like the sun when it is shrouded in clouds, no one could make out where he was. Pierced by him, the apes were killed and lost their lives. Hundreds of them fell down on the ground.

Extremely angry, Lakshmana addressed his brother in these words. 'To destroy all the rakshasas, I am going to invoke brahmastra.' Rama spoke to Lakshmana, the bearer of auspicious signs. 'For the sake of one, you should not destroy all the rakshasas on earth. You should not kill someone who is not fighting, is hiding, has joined his hands in salutation and is seeking refuge, is running away or is distracted. O immensely strong one! We must make efforts to kill this one alone. We will use immensely forceful weapons that are like venomous serpents. This inferior one uses maya. He is powerful because he is invisible. While all the leaders of the apes look on, this rakshasa will be killed. Whether he enters the ground or the sky, whether he is in the nether regions or in the firmament, irrespective of whether he hides himself, he will be scorched by my weapons. He will lose his life and fall down on the ground.' Surrounded by the bulls among the apes, the great-souled and brave descendant of the Raghu lineage spoke these words. The great-souled one swiftly searched for a means whereby the performer of terrible and cruel deeds might be killed.

Chapter 6(68)

He[297] discerned what was in the great-souled Raghava's mind. He withdrew from the battle and entered his own city. He remembered the deaths of the spirited rakshasas. His eyes coppery red in rage, the brave and immensely radiant one emerged. Surrounded by rakshasas, the immensely valiant Poulastya Indrajit, the thorn of the gods, emerged through the western gate. Indrajit saw those two brothers, Rama and Lakshmana. Those two brave ones were ready to fight. He resolved to use his maya. On his chariot, Indrajit placed an image of Sita that was made out of maya. Surrounded by a large army, he desired to kill her. The extremely evil-minded one made up his mind to confound everyone. In an attempt to kill Sita, he proceeded in the direction of the apes. The residents of the forest saw him emerge from the city. Enraged and desiring to fight, they attacked him, with boulders in their hands. Hanumat, tiger

[297] Indrajit.

among apes, was in the lead. He seized an extremely large peak of a mountain, impossible for others to grasp.

He saw the miserable Sita on Indrajit's chariot. Her hair was in a single braid. She was distressed and because of fasting, her face was emaciated. Raghava's beloved was without ornaments. She was clad in a single faded garment. Though she was the best among women, she was covered in filth and dust all over her body. For a while, he glanced towards her and thought that she was Maithilee. Her face was overflowing with tears. Hanumat was dejected. She did not say anything. She was afflicted by grief. The ascetic lady was devoid of any joy. He saw Sita in the chariot used by the son of the Indra among the rakshasas. The great ape thought, 'What is this?' With the best among the apes, he rushed towards Ravana's son. Seeing the army of the apes, Ravana's son became senseless with rage. He unsheathed his sword and seized Sita by the hair on her head. They saw that woman being oppressed by Ravana's son on the chariot. Because of the maya, she was shrieking, 'Rama! Alas, Rama!' Seeing that she had been seized by the hair, Hanumat was filled with misery. Tears of sorrow flowed from the eyes of the son of the wind god. In his rage, he spoke these harsh words to the son of the lord of the rakshasas. 'O evil-souled one! It is for your own destruction that you have touched a lock of her hair. You have been born in a lineage of *brahmarshi*s,[298] but have resorted to the womb of a rakshasi.[299] Shame on you. Since you possess such an inclination, you are wicked in conduct. You are cruel and ignoble. You are evil in conduct and inferior. Your valour is evil. Such an act is ignoble. You are cruel and there is no compassion in you. Maithilee has been dislodged from her home and her kingdom. She has been dislodged from Rama's arms. O cruel one! What crime has she committed that you wish to slay her? If you kill Sita, you will not remain alive for a long period of time. Because of this deed, you deserve to be killed and you have come into my hands. In this world, those who kill women are condemned and deserve to be

[298] A sage with knowledge of the supreme being (brahman).

[299] A reference to Ravana's parentage.

killed by people. You will give up your life in this world and not obtain any fruits after death.' Surrounded by apes with upraised weapons, Hanumat said this. He angrily rushed towards the son of the Indra among the rakshasas.

The immensely valiant army of the residents of the forest descended. Terrible in force, the army of the rakshasas countered them. Agitating the army of the apes with thousands of arrows, Indrajit replied to Hanumat, best among the apes. 'Sugriva, Rama and you came here for her. While you look on, I will kill that Vaidehi today. O ape! After killing her, I will take care of Rama, Lakshmana and you. I will slay Sugriva and the ignoble Vibhishana. O ape! You have said that women should not be killed. However, anything that causes misery to the enemy is a task that should be undertaken.' The Sita made out of maya was weeping. Having said this, Indrajit used his sharp-edged sword to kill her. That ascetic lady was sliced along the trail followed by the sacred thread.[300] The wide-hipped one, beautiful to see, fell down on the ground. Having killed the lady, Indrajit spoke to Hanumat. 'Behold. She was Rama's and I have killed her in my rage.' Indrajit himself killed her with his large sword. He sat cheerfully in his chariot and roared loudly. The apes who were nearby heard this sound. He was impossible to approach. He opened his mouth wide and roared. Thus, the evil-minded one killed Sita. Ravana's son was delighted in his mind. The apes saw his rejoicing form. With miserable appearances, they ran away.

Chapter 6(69)

They heard that terrible roar, which was like the sound of Shakra's vajra. Looking towards him, the bulls among the apes fled in all the directions. Hanumat, the son of the wind god, spoke to all of them. Their faces were dejected. They were miserable

[300] The sacred thread slopes down from the left shoulder towards the right. Hence, Sita was diagonally sliced from left to right.

and were separately running away. 'O apes! Why are you running away with dejected faces? Why have you lost all interest in fighting? Where has your bravery gone? I am marching to battle, ahead of you. Follow me at the rear. For brave ones who have been born in noble families, it is not proper to retreat.' Thus addressed by Vayu's intelligent son, they became angry. Delighted in their minds, they seized the summits of mountains and trees. The bulls among the apes roared and descended on the rakshasas. In the great battle, they surrounded and followed Hanumat. In every direction, Hanumat was surrounded by the foremost among the apes. Like a fire with flames, he began to consume the army of the enemy. The extremely large ape created carnage among the rakshasas. Surrounded by the soldiers of the apes, he was like Yama, the Destroyer. The great ape was filled with grief and rage. Hanumat hurled a large boulder towards the chariot of Ravana's son. On seeing it descend towards the chariot, the charioteer urged the well-trained horses and conveyed the chariot far away. The boulder was rendered unsuccessful and penetrated the earth. It could not reach Indrajit, his chariot, or his charioteer. The army of the rakshasas suffered because of the descending rocks. Hundreds of residents of the forest roared and attacked. They held aloft trees and summits of mountains that were gigantic in size. Terrible in their valour, the apes hurled these in the midst of the enemy. The apes were immensely valiant and struck them bravely with trees. The roamers in the night, terrible in form, were injured in the battle. Indrajit saw that his soldiers were afflicted by the apes. He angrily seized his weapons and advanced towards the enemy. Surrounded by his soldiers, he shot torrents of arrows. Firm in his valour, he slew many tigers among the apes. In the battle, his followers used spears, vajras, swords, javelins and heavy clubs to kill apes. The immensely strong Hanumat, terrible in his valour, caused carnage among the rakshasas, using sala trees with trunks and branches and boulders. Repulsing the army of the enemy, Hanumat said, 'O residents of the forest! Let us retreat. We need not strive against this army any more. We fought for the sake of Janaka's daughter. We strove and were ready to give up our lives because we sought to do what would bring Rama pleasure. But she has been killed. We must inform Rama and Sugriva about this. We will do what they ask us to do in retaliation.' The best among the apes spoke to all the apes and restrained them in this way. Gently, but fearlessly, he returned with his army.

Seeing that Hanumat was headed towards the spot where Raghava was, Indrajit went to Nikumbhila,[301] to offer oblations into the fire. Following the prescribed rites, the rakshasa lit the fire in the sacrificial ground. On devouring the oblations of blood, the fire blazed up. The flames were seen to be dense, satisfied by the offerings of blood. Like the sun in the evening, fierce flames arose. Indrajit knew about the rites. To ensure the prosperity of the rakshasas, he followed the rites and offered oblations. The rakshasas knew about what should be done, and what should not be done, at sacrifices. They watched and stood around in large numbers.

Chapter 6(70)

Hearing the great sound of the battle between the rakshasas and the residents of the forest, Raghava spoke to Jambavat. 'O amiable one! There is no doubt that Hanumat has performed an extremely difficult deed. The terrible and extremely loud sound of fighting can be heard. Therefore, surround yourself with your own army. Go and help him. Go and quickly help the best among the apes while he is fighting.' The king of the bears agreed and surrounded himself with his own army. He approached the western gate, where the ape Hanumat was. As he was advancing, the lord of the bears saw Hanumat along the path. He was surrounded by apes who had fought and were now sighing. Along the path, Hanumat saw that ready army of bears. It was terrible and was like a dark cloud. He met it and made it return.

With that army of the apes, the immensely illustrious one swiftly went to Rama's presence. Miserable, he spoke these words. 'We

[301] The sacrificial ground.

were fighting in the battle and saw Indrajit, Ravana's son, kill the weeping Sita. O slayer of enemies! On seeing this, I was distressed and my senses were in a whirl. Therefore, I have come to you, to tell you about what has occurred.' Hearing his words, Raghava became senseless with grief. He fell down on the ground, like a tree severed at the roots. Raghava was like a god and he fell down on the ground. On seeing this, all the excellent apes leapt up and approached from all directions. They sprinkled him with water that was fragrant with the scent of lotuses and lilies, just as one sprinkles an intolerable and consuming fire that has suddenly arisen.

Extremely miserable, Lakshmana engulfed the ailing Rama in his arms and spoke words that were full of meaning. 'O noble one! You have remained established on an auspicious path. You have conquered your senses. But dharma is futile. It cannot save you from adversities. Dharma is not like mobile and immobile objects that can be seen. Therefore, it is my view that it does not exist. Immobile objects are evident and mobile objects are also like that. Artha is not like that. Otherwise, someone like you would not have faced this catastrophe. Had adharma led to consequences, Ravana would have gone to hell. Nor would someone like you, devoted to dharma, have confronted this adversity. There is no hardship for him and you have faced this hardship. The fruits of adharma have become those of dharma and the fruits of dharma have become those of adharma. If people are not attached to adharma and unite themselves with dharma, if they follow dharma, they should obtain the fruits of dharma. For those in whom dharma is established, artha must be enhanced. But those who follow dharma are suffering. Therefore, both of them[302] must be futile. O Raghava! Those who are wicked in their deeds must be killed because of their adharma. Who will slay the one who has killed dharma because of his deeds? Perhaps someone follows the recommended rituals and is killed, or kills someone else instead. Perhaps this is ascribed to destiny and the person is not affected by the wicked deed. O afflicter of enemies! How does one counter

[302] Dharma and adharma.

destiny? How can one be attached to what is not manifest? How is one capable of attaining supreme dharma? O foremost among those who are virtuous! If there is virtue, why are you suffering from this vice? Why has someone like you faced this calamity? Perhaps those who are weak in strength and suffer from lack of virility follow dharma. It is my view that it[303] is weak in strength and robbed of honour. It should not be served. If dharma is for the strong, its qualities should manifest themselves in valour. Abandon dharma and follow the principle that dharma exists where there is strength. O scorcher of enemies! If dharma is indeed based on speaking the truth, why did our cruel father bind you down to a falsehood?[304] O scorcher of enemies! Had dharma or adharma existed, Shatakratu, the wielder of the vajra, would not have killed a sage and performed a sacrifice thereafter.[305] O Raghava! Those who resort to adharma can destroy dharma. O Kakutstha! In everything, a man does as he wishes. O father![306] O Raghava! It is my view that dharma lies in this.[307] When you were deprived of the kingdom, that was the time when dharma was severed at the roots. Here and there, artha must be accumulated and made to prosper. All the rites flow from this, like rivers from mountains. A man who is deprived of artha is limited in energy. All his rites are destroyed, like a small stream during the summer. A person used to happiness may desire happiness and abandon artha. However, he then indulges in evil acts and sins result. A person with artha has friends. A person with artha has relatives. A person with artha is a true man in this world. A person with artha is learned. A person with artha is brave. A person with artha is intelligent. A person with artha is immensely fortunate. A person with artha possesses great qualities. I have told you about the great taints that come about through the abandoning of artha. O brave one! By making

[303] Dharma.

[304] By not instating Rama as the heir apparent.

[305] Indra killed a sage named Vishvarupa. This was adharma, but he atoned for it by performing a sacrifice.

[306] The word used is tata.

[307] In strength.

up your mind to abandon the kingdom, that is what you have done. A person who possesses artha is encircled by dharma, kama and artha. A person without riches cannot desire artha. He is incapable of searching out artha. O lord of men! Everything flows from artha—delight, desire, pride, dharma, anger, tranquility and self-control. If a person follows dharma in this world, but his artha is destroyed, as in you, all those are missing in him, like planets on a bad day. O brave one! Established in the words of your senior, you proceeded on an exile. Your wife, more loved than your own life, was abducted by a rakshasa. O brave one! Thus, today, Indrajit has brought about this great misery on you. O Raghava! Arise. I will dispel it with my deeds. O unblemished one! I will arise for the sake of your beloved. I am enraged at witnessing the death of Janaka's daughter. I will use my terrible arrows to bring down Lanka, with its horses, elephants, chariots and the Indras among the rakshasas.'

Chapter 6(71)

Lakshmana, devoted to his brother, comforted Rama. Instructing the divisions to remain in their places, Vibhishana arrived at the spot. He was surrounded by his four brave advisers, who were wielding many kinds of weapons. They looked like masses of dark collyrium, like a herd of elephants. He approached the great-souled Raghava, who was immersed in his grief. He also saw the apes, with tears streaming from their eyes. He saw the great-souled Raghava, the delight of the Ikshvaku lineage. He was senseless and was lying down on Lakshmana's lap. Vibhishana saw Rama, ashamed and tormented by grief. Distressed in his soul and suffering internally, he asked, 'What is this?' Lakshmana glanced at Vibhishana's face and at Sugriva and the apes. His voice choking with tears, he spoke these words. 'Raghava has heard that Indrajit has killed Sita. O amiable one! Having heard Hanumat's words, he has lost his senses.' As Soumitri was speaking, Vibhishana stopped him. Rama was senseless, but he addressed him in words that were full of meaning. 'O Indra among men! In an afflicted state, Hanumat told you that. But I think that what he said is like the ocean drying up. I know the intention of the evil-souled Ravana. O mighty-armed one! He will never kill Sita. Desiring his welfare, I beseeched him several times that he should give up Vaidehi. But he never heeded those words. It is impossible to see her through sama, bheda, dana, not to speak of fighting. How could it be possible through any other means?[308] That rakshasa departed after confounding the apes. He is offering oblations in the sanctuary named Nikumbhila. On returning, he will offer oblations and Ravana's son will become unassailable in battle, even to the gods, with Vasava. That is indeed the reason why he has used maya and caused confusion. O father![309] He did not desire an obstruction caused through the valour of the apes. Before it is completed, we should go there, with our soldiers. O tiger among men! Cast aside this futile torment that has come over you. On seeing you afflicted by sorrow, all the forces are suffering. Be assured. Steady your heart and remain here. Resort to your spirit. Send Lakshmana with the soldiers who will be summoned. Once he abandons his task,[310] this tiger among men will slay him with his sharp arrows. His arrows are sharp and fierce, with a speed like that in the wings of birds. The arrows of this amiable one are like birds and will drink his blood. O mighty-armed one! Instruct Lakshmana for the destruction of the rakshasa, like the wielder of the vajra using his vajra. He possesses the auspicious signs. O best among men! There is no time to waste. One must now do whatever is necessary to slay the enemy. Therefore, tell him that he should kill the enemy. Release him, like the great Indra crushing the city of the asuras. If he finishes his sacrifice, the Indra among rakshasas will be invisible to gods and asuras. If he fights after completing his sacrifice, there will be a great danger to even the gods.'

[308] The sense seems to be that it would have been impossible for Indrajit to bring Sita out in public.

[309] The word used is tata.

[310] The sacrifice.

Chapter 6(72)

Afflicted by grief, Raghava heard these words. He was unable to clearly comprehend what the rakshasa had said. Rama, the victor of enemy cities, then resorted to his fortitude. He spoke to Vibhishana, who was seated near the apes. 'O lord of the nairittas! O Vibhishana! I wish to again hear the words that you have spoken. Tell me what you want.' Hearing Raghava's words, Vibhishana, eloquent in the use of words, carefully repeated the words again. 'O mighty-armed one! As you had instructed, I arranged the forces in different divisions. O brave one! I followed your words and progressively stationed them. In every direction, the entire army was apportioned out. The leaders and the others were properly laid out in separate parts. O immensely illustrious one! Listen to something else that I have to report. Because you are needlessly tormented, our hearts are also tormented. O king! Abandon this grief and the false torment that has come upon you. Abandon the worries that only enhance the delight of the enemy. O brave one! Be cheerful and exert yourself if you wish to obtain Sita and slay the roamers in the night. O descendant of the Raghu lineage! I am speaking to you. Listen to my beneficial words. It is best that Soumitri should surround himself with a large army and go there. He should reach Nikumbhila and kill Ravana's son in a battle, using arrows that are like venomous serpents, released from the circle of his bow. The great archer, the victor in assemblies, will kill Ravana's son with his arrows. Because of his austerities, that brave one has obtained a boon from Svayambhu. He has obtained the Brahmashira weapon and horses that can go wherever they want. "O Indra's enemy! If an enemy strikes you before you have reached Nikumbhila and before you have offered oblations into the fire, the person who strikes you will be the cause of your death."[311] O king! This is what the intelligent one ordained as a means of his death. O Rama! For the sake of killing Indrajit, command a large army. When he has been killed, know that Ravana and the large number of his well-wishers will also have been killed.'

[311] This is what Brahma told Indrajit.

Hearing Vibhishana's words, Rama spoke these words. 'O one who has truth as his valour! I know about his terrible maya. He is wise and knows about the use of brahmastra. He is immensely strong and great in his use of maya. In a battle, he can render the gods, together with Varuna, unconscious. On his chariot, the immensely illustrious one roams around in the firmament, invisible. O brave one! One cannot discern his movement, like the sun when it is enveloped in clouds.' Knowing about the valour and maya of the evil-souled enemy, Raghava addressed Lakshmana, who was accomplished in his deeds, in the following words. 'Surround yourself with the entire army of the Indra among the apes. O Lakshmana! Be with the leaders of the herds, with Hanumat at the forefront. Surround yourself with the soldiers of Jambavat, the lord of the bears. The son of the rakshasa possesses the strength of maya. Kill him. This great-souled roamer in the night knows about his maya. With his advisers, he will follow you at the rear.'

Hearing Raghava's words, Lakshmana, terrible in his valour, seized his excellent bow, accompanied by Vibhishana. He bound his armour, wielding a sword. He held arrows and a golden bow. Touching Rama's feet, Soumitri cheerfully said, 'Today, arrows will be released from my bow and piercing Ravana's son, will descend into Lanka, the way swans enter a pond. Today, my arrows will be released from the string of this great bow and pierce his terrible body, devastating him.' He spoke these words before his radiant elder brother. Having worshipped at his senior's feet, he circumambulated him. He then left for the Nikumbhila sanctuary, protected by Ravana's son. Having heard the benedictions from his brother, Lakshmana, the powerful prince, quickly left, together with Vibhishana. Hanumat was surrounded by many thousands of apes and with Vibhishana's advisers, followed Lakshmana. He[312] left with speed, surrounded by a large army of soldiers of the apes. Along the path, he saw that the army of the king of the bears was also stationed. Soumitri, the delight of his friends, travelled a long distance. From a distance, he saw the army of the Indra among the

[312] Lakshmana.

rakshasas, arrayed in the form of a vyuha. The scorcher of enemies reached, with the bow in his hand. Following Brahma's dictum, the descendant of the Raghu lineage was ready to defeat the one who invoked maya. The army of the enemy possessed many kinds of sparkling and radiant weapons. It was thick with standards and dense with large chariots. It was immeasurable in force and caused fear. It was like darkness, but he penetrated it.

Chapter 6(73)

In that situation, Ravana's younger brother[313] addressed Lakshmana in meaningful words that would ensure his success and cause injury to the enemy. 'O Lakshmana! Make efforts to break this large army. When it is shattered, the son of the Indra among the rakshasas will become visible. Shower down excellent arrows that are like Indra's vajra on the enemy. Quickly attack, before he accomplishes the sacrifice. O brave one! Slay the evil-souled one. Ravana's son is cruel in his deeds and causes fear to all the worlds.'

Hearing Vibhishana's words, Lakshmana, the possessor of the auspicious signs, showered down arrows in the direction of the son of the Indra among the rakshasas. Bears and apes, fighting with trees and excellent boulders, collectively attacked that army. Desiring to kill the soldiers of the apes, the rakshasas countered and attacked with sharp arrows, swords, spears and javelins. There was a tumultuous engagement between the apes and the rakshasas. A large sound was heard everywhere around Lanka. Enveloped with many kinds of weapons, sharp arrows, trees and raised summits of mountains, the sky looked terrible. In the encounter, the rakshasas, with malformed faces, hurled down weapons and created an extremely great fear among the apes. In a similar way, all the apes used trees and the summits of mountains to strike and kill the bulls

[313] Vibhishana.

among the rakshasas in the encounter. The foremost among the bears and the apes were gigantic in size and extremely strong. The rakshasas were slaughtered by them and a great fear was instilled in them.

Hearing that his own army was distressed and afflicted by the enemy, the invincible one[314] arose, without completing the sacrifice. With rage generated in him, Ravana's son emerged from amidst the trees and the darkness. The rakshasa mounted the chariot that had already been yoked and kept ready. He was like a mass of black collyrium and his bow and arrows were terrible. He was cruel and his mouth and eyes were red. He was like Death, the destroyer. On seeing him astride the chariot, the army of rakshasas, terrible in their force, returned, to fight with Lakshmana. Hanumat was like a mountain and extremely unassailable. At that time, the slayer of enemies seized a gigantic tree. He burnt down the soldiers of the rakshasas, like the fire of destruction. In the battle, the ape rendered many unconscious with that tree. The rakshasas saw that the spirited son of the wind god was destroying them. Thousands of them obstructed Hanumat. They wielded sharp spears and had javelins and swords in their hands. There were swords. Those with spears in their hands fought with spears. Those with javelins in their hands fought with javelins. There were maces, clubs and spikes that were auspicious to behold. There were hundreds of shataghnis and bludgeons that were made out of iron. The rakshasas used terrible battleaxes and bhindipalas. The force of the fists was like that of the vajra. The palms were like the vajra. From every direction, they advanced and attacked the one who was like a mountain, while he angrily created great carnage among them.

Indrajit saw that the best among the apes was like a mountain. The son of the wind god, the slayer of enemies, was killing the enemy. He told the charioteer, 'Take me to the spot where the ape is. If he is ignored, he will cause destruction to the rakshasas.' Thus addressed, the charioteer went to the spot where Maruti was. On the chariot,

[314] Indrajit.

he bore along the extremely invincible Indrajit. Approaching, the rakshasa showered down arrows, swords, javelins, cutlasses and battleaxes on the ape's head. Maruti received all those terrible weapons. Overcome by great rage, he spoke these words. 'O evil-minded son of Ravana! If you are brave, fight. If you approach the son of the wind god, you will not return with your life. O evil-minded one! In this battle, if you wish to have a duel with me, fight with your arms and withstand me. You will then be supreme among the rakshasas.' In a desire to slay Hanumat, Ravana's son raised his bow and arrow. Vibhishana told Lakshmana, 'This is Ravana's son and he has vanquished Vasava. He is now stationed on his chariot and desires to kill Hanumat. Your arrows are unmatched and are capable of shattering the enemy. O Soumitri! They are terrible and can bring an end to life. Slay Ravana's son with these.' The great-souled Vibhishana, who caused fright to the enemy, said this. He saw that the invincible one, resembling a mountain and terrible in his strength, was mounted on his chariot.

Chapter 6(74)

When Vibhishana said this, Soumitri was filled with delight. He grasped a bow in his hand and quickly left. Having gone a short distance away, he entered a large forest. Vibhishana showed Lakshmana the ongoing sacrifice. Ravana's energetic brother showed Lakshmana an extremely terrible nyagrodha that was like a dark cloud. 'This is the spot where Ravana's strong son renders offerings to creatures. After they have accepted these, he goes out to fight. Thereafter, the rakshasa becomes invisible to all creatures. He uses his excellent arrows to bind enemies down in the battle and kill them. Ravana's strong son has not yet entered the nyagrodha. Use your sharp arrows to destroy him, his charioteer, his horses and his chariot.' The immensely energetic Soumitri, the delight of his friends, agreed. He stood there, stretching his colourful bow. Ravana's strong son was on a chariot that had the complexion of the fire. Indrajit was armoured, with a sword and a standard. He showed himself.

The immensely energetic one spoke to the unvanquished Poulastya. 'In this encounter, I am challenging you. Give me a good fight.' Ravana's spirited and extremely energetic son was addressed in this way. On seeing Vibhishana there, he spoke these harsh words. 'You were born and reared here. You are my father's brother. O rakshasa! You are my paternal uncle. How can you cause injury to a son? O one with evil intelligence! Kinship, affection and relationships do not exist in you. There is no sign of fraternal affection. O defiler of dharma! There is no dharma in you. O one with evil intelligence! You are a person to be grieved over. You should be condemned by the virtuous. You have abandoned your own relatives and have become a servant to the enemy. This is not good behaviour or intelligence. You do not comprehend the great difference. How can one compare residence with one's relatives to the inferior state of seeking refuge with the enemy? Others may possess qualities and one's own relatives may be devoid of qualities. But relatives who are devoid of qualities are superior. An enemy is always an enemy. O roamer in the night! O Ravana's younger brother! Only a harsh person like you is capable of showing this ruthlessness towards your own relatives.' Thus addressed by his brother's son, Vibhishana replied, 'O rakshasa! Why are you indulging in self-praise? You do not seem to be aware of my good conduct. O son of the Indra among the rakshasas! O wicked one! Abandon the harshness that comes from insolence. I have been born in the lineage of rakshasas, the perpetrators of cruel deeds. However, the qualities and conduct that exist in me are primarily those of humans, not those of rakshasas. I find no pleasure in being terrible. I do not take delight in adharma. If a brother indulges in wicked conduct, how can such a brother be restrained? If a person indulges in stealing another person's possessions, if a person touches another person's wife and if a person does not trust his well-wishers—these three sins can bring about destruction. The terrible slaying of maharshis, the conflict with all the gods, arrogance, anger, enmity and perversity—these sins will destroy my brother's life and prosperity. They envelop and shroud his qualities, like clouds do to mountains. Because of these taints, my brother, your father, has been abandoned by me. The city of Lanka, you, and your father, will no longer exist. You are extremely insolent. You are childish. You are arrogant. O rakshasa! You are bound in the noose of destiny. Tell me whatever you wish. You are now facing a catastrophe here. Why are you speaking to me? O worst of rakshasas! You are incapable of entering the nyagrodha. The two Kakutsthas will oppress you and you are incapable of remaining alive. In this encounter, fight with Lakshmana, god among men. When you have been killed, you will perform the work of the gods in Yama's eternal abode. Raise yourself and exhibit your own strength. Use all the weapons and the inexhaustible arrows. Having come within the reach of Lakshmana's arrows today, you and your army will no longer remain alive.'

Chapter 6(75)

Hearing Vibhishana's words, Ravana's son became senseless with rage. He spoke harsh words and attacked forcefully. On the well-ornamented and giant chariot, yoked to black horses, he held up his weapons and sword. He was stationed, like Death. He was lofty and giant in size. His force was extensive and firm. He touched his terrible bow and the arrows that destroyed enemies. Extremely angry, he spoke to Soumitri, Vibhishana and the tigers among the apes, 'Behold my valour. Today, showers of invincible arrows will be released from my bow. Released, they will pour down in the encounter, like water from the sky. Today, arrows will be released from my large bow. They will destroy bodies, like fire does a mass of cotton. Sharp arrows, spears, javelins, swords and spikes will mangle you. Today, all of you will leave for Yama's eternal abode. In the battle, the dexterity of my hands will shoot torrents of arrows. I will roar like a cloud. Who will stand before me?'

Lakshmana heard the Indra among rakshasas roaring. With a fearless face, he angrily addressed Ravana's son in these words. 'O rakshasa! You have spoken about accomplishing the task of crossing over to the unapproachable distant shore. But the intelligent person is one who accomplishes the task of crossing over to the distant shore. O evil-minded one! You think you have accomplished the objective. But you have not accomplished it and the objective is extremely difficult to reach. Know that it cannot be accomplished through words alone. Be successful first. At that time, you followed the path of becoming invisible. But that is a path resorted to by thieves. It is not something that is patronized by brave people. O rakshasa! I have come and am stationed within range of your arrows. Demonstrate your energy today. Why are you indulging in words of self-praise?'

Having been thus addressed, the immensely strong Indrajit, the victor in assemblies, touched his terrible bow and shot sharp arrows. He released extremely forceful arrows that were like venomous serpents. They reached Lakshmana and fell down, sighing like serpents. In the battle, Indrajit, Ravana's son, pierced Lakshmana, who possessed the auspicious signs, with extremely swift and forceful arrows. His limbs were severely pierced by the arrows and blood started to flow. The handsome Lakshmana was resplendent, like a fire without smoke. Indrajit reflected on the deed he had achieved. He approached, roared loudly and spoke these words. 'O Soumitri! These arrows are sharp at the edges and have been shot from my bow. They can take lives away. They will now take away your life. O Lakshmana! When you lose your life and are killed by me today, herds of jackals and flocks of hawks and vultures will descend on you. The extremely evil-minded Rama is always a friend to kshatriyas, but is always ignoble. You are his devoted brother and he will see that you have been slain by me today. Your armour will be shattered and will fall down on the ground. Your bow will be fragmented. O Soumitri! Your head will be severed. You will be slain by me today.'

Angry, Ravana's son spoke these harsh words. Lakshmana, who knew about the meanings behind words, replied in words that were full of reasoning. 'O rakshasa! Why are you praising a deed you have not yet accomplished? Perform an act so that I can have faith in your self-praise. I will not speak any harsh words, nor will I abuse you in any way. O worst among beings! Behold. Without indulging in self-praise, I will kill you.' Having said this, Lakshmana affixed five iron arrows and drawing the bow back all the way up to his ear, struck the rakshasa on the chest with great force. Struck by those arrows, Ravana's son became angry. He aimed three arrows properly and pierced Lakshmana back. As they sought to slay each other, there ensued an extremely terrible and tumultuous clash in the battle between the lion among men and the lion among rakshasas. Both of them were full of strength. Both of them were valiant. Both of them were extremely brave. Both of them were accomplished in the use of all weapons. Both of them were extremely difficult to vanquish. Both of them were equal in strength and energy. Those two extremely brave ones fought, like two planets engaging in the firmament. Those two were impossible to assail and they fought like Bala and Vritra.[315] Those two great-souled ones fought like maned lions. Stationed there, those two shot arrows along many paths. The lion among men and the lion among rakshasas fought cheerfully. The supreme man and the supreme rakshasa were exceedingly happy. They wielded their bows and arrows, desiring victory. They severely showered down floods of arrows on each other, like clouds pouring down rain.

Chapter 6(76)

Dasharatha's son, the slayer of enemies, affixed an arrow and angrily shot it towards the Indra among rakshasas, sighing like a serpent. Ravana's son heard the noise of the palm slap against the bowstring. With his face pale, he glanced towards Lakshmana. Vibhishana saw that the face of the rakshasa who was Ravana's

[315] That is, Indra and Vritra.

son had turned pale. Soumitri was engaged in fighting and he spoke to him. 'I can see the signs in Ravana's son. O mighty-armed one! There is no doubt that he will be broken quickly.' At this, Soumitri affixed arrows that were like the flames of the fire. He shot these sharp arrows, like snakes emerging from their holes. Lakshmana's arrows were like Shakra's vajra to the touch. Struck by these, he was benumbed for a while and his senses were agitated. He regained consciousness after some time and his senses recovered. The brave one saw that Dasharatha's brave son was stationed there.

His eyes red with rage, he approached Soumitri. Having approached, he again addressed him in harsh words. 'Do you not remember my valour in the first encounter? In the encounter, you and your brother were bound down and were writhing. My arrows were like Shakra's vajra. In that first great battle, with all your companions, you were lying down on the ground, unconscious. I think that you do not retain any memory of that, or perhaps you desire to go to Yama's abode. That is the reason you wish to attack me. If you have not witnessed my valour in that first encounter, I will show it to you today. Steady yourself now.' Saying this, he pierced Lakshmana with seven arrows and used ten sharp-edged and excellent arrows to strike Hanumat. With his rage doubled, he angrily used one hundred well-aimed arrows to pierce the valiant Vibhishana. On seeing what Indrajit had done, Rama's younger brother paid no heed to it. He laughed and said, 'This is a trifle.' The bull among men affixed and released terrible arrows. In the battle, with no fear on his face, Lakshmana angrily shot these at Ravana's son. 'O roamer in the night! Brave ones who come to fight do not strike like this. These arrows of yours are light, limited in valour and pleasant. In a battle, brave ones who seek victory do not fight like this.' Saying this, he showered down arrows. Shattered by the arrows, a gold-embellished armour was fragmented and fell down on the floor of the chariot, like a net of stars dislodged from the sky. In the battle, the brave Indrajit's armour was shattered by iron arrows and he was wounded. But he was as firm as a mountain. As they engaged in that tumultuous battle, they sighed and glanced at each other. All their limbs were pierced by arrows and blood started to flow. They repeatedly exhibited their excellence in use and knowledge of weapons. The high and low trajectories of their arrows traced patterns in the sky. They shot arrows with dexterity, aimed well and colourfully, without any blemishes. Both of them, the man and the rakshasa, were terrible and fierce. The terrible sounds of their palms slapping could be separately heard. It was like the extremely terrible sound of thunderous clouds in the sky. In the battle, gold-tufted arrows descended on their bodies. Smeared with blood, they emerged again and penetrated the ground. There were other extremely sharp weapons that clashed against each other in the sky. Thousands of their arrows clashed and severed each other. Piles of arrows accumulated in that terrible battle. They resembled piles of blazing kusha grass at a sacrifice dedicated to the fire. With wounds in their bodies, those two great-souled ones were resplendent. They looked like blossoming *shalmali* and kimshuka trees in the forest, devoid of leaves. Terrible and tumultuous clashes repeatedly took place as Indrajit and Lakshmana sought to triumph over each other. In the battle, Lakshmana struck Ravana's son and Ravana's son struck Lakshmana. They struck each other and neither suffered from exhaustion. Nets of arrows deeply pierced the bodies of those two spirited ones. Those two immensely brave ones were as radiant as mountains with emanating peaks. Severely wounded by the arrows, they were smeared with blood. They dazzled in all their limbs and were like blazing fires. As they fought against each other, a long period of time elapsed. However, in the forefront of that encounter, neither of them suffered from exhaustion.

Lakshmana had never been defeated in the field of battle. To dispel any exhaustion he might suffer in the encounter, Vibhishana arrived at the spot where the clash was taking place. The immensely energetic one spoke agreeable and beneficial words.

Chapter 6(77)

On seeing that the man and the rakshasa were engaged with each other and fighting, Ravana's brave brother presented himself in the field of battle. He stood there and stretched his giant bow, shooting large arrows, sharp at the tips, towards the rakshasas. Well-aimed, those arrows, which were like flames to the touch, descended. They shattered the rakshasas, like the vajra shatters a large mountain. Vibhishana's companions, supreme among rakshasas, used spears, javelins and swords to sever brave rakshasas in the battle. Vibhishana was surrounded by those rakshasas and looked like an elephant amidst proud young tuskers. The apes loved to fight with the rakshasas. At that time, the supreme among rakshasas, who knew about time, urged them with these words. 'Stationed here is the only refuge for the Indra among rakshasas. This is all that remains of his army. O lords among the apes! Why are you waiting? When this wicked rakshasa is killed in the forefront of the battle, with the exception of Ravana, all the rest of his army will be destroyed. The brave Prahasta has been killed and so has the immensely strong Nikumbha. So have Kumbhakarna, Kumbha and Dhumraksha, the roamer in the night. So have Akampana, Suparshva, the rakshasa Chakramali, Kampana, Sattvavanta, Devantaka and Narantaka. These extremely strong ones, many supreme rakshasas, have been killed. When one has used one's arms to swim across the ocean and cross it, this puddle[316] is a trifle. O apes! Only this much remains to be defeated. All the rakshasas who approached, insolent of their strength, have been killed. For Rama's sake, I will cast aside all compassion and kill my brother's son. However, it is not proper to kill a son one has given birth to.[317] Even if I desire to kill him, the tears in my eyes will be an impediment. That is the reason the mighty-armed Lakshmana must pacify him. O apes! Slay all those of his servants who dare to approach.' They were thus urged by that illustrious rakshasa. The Indras among apes were delighted and lashed their tails. The tigers among apes roared repeatedly. They uttered many kinds of sounds, like peacocks when they catch sight of clouds.

[316] Goshpada.

[317] Though Indrajit is his brother's son, he is like a son.

Jambavat was surrounded by all of his own herds. They attacked the rakshasas with rocks, nails and teeth. The lord of the bears struck them and abandoning their fear, the immensely strong rakshasas surrounded him, with many kinds of weapons. In the battle, Jambavat was slaying the soldiers of the rakshasas and they attacked him with arrows, sharp battleaxes, javelins, staffs and spears. There was a tumultuous clash between the apes and the rakshasas, like the angry battle between the gods and the asuras. There was a loud and terrible noise. Enraged, Hanumat uprooted a sala tree from the mountain. He clashed against thousands of rakshasas and created carnage. In the battle, Indrajit had a tumultuous duel with his paternal uncle. The slayer of brave enemies then attacked Lakshmana again.

Those two brave ones, Lakshmana and the rakshasa, fought in the battle. Desiring to kill each other, they showered down floods of arrows. Those two extremely strong ones glanced at each other and covered each other with nets of arrows, just as swift clouds envelop the moon and the sun at the end of the summer. Because of their dexterity in the use of their hands, the acts of picking up the bow, affixing an arrow, aiming it, releasing it, stretching the bow, shooting the arrow, adjusting the hold or striking the target could not be seen. In every direction, there were nets of arrows, shot powerfully from the bows. The sky was covered and nothing could be seen. Everything was covered in great darkness and it seemed to be even more terrible. The wind did not blow then and the fire did not blaze. The maharshis exclaimed, 'May all be well with the worlds.' The gandharvas and the charanas came and assembled there.

The lion among rakshasas possessed four black horses adorned with gold. Soumitri used four arrows to pierce these four horses. As his charioteer was driving around, the dexterous Raghava used another broad-headed arrow to sever his handsome head from his body. Ravana's son saw that his charioteer had been slain in the battle. He was distressed and lost his cheer in the battle. The leaders of the apes saw that the rakshasa had distress written on his face. They were extremely delighted and worshipped Lakshmana. Four lords of the apes—Pramathi, Sharabha, Rabhasa and Gandhamadana, became intolerant and attacked powerfully. Those apes quickly leapt on to his excellent horses. Those four extremely brave ones, terrible in their valour, descended there. The apes, resembling mountains, stood on the backs of the horses and because of the pressure, blood started to flow from their mouths. The maharatha's horses were crushed and killed. With force, they[318] then leapt up and came to Lakshmana's side. His horses had been killed. His chariot had been crushed. His charioteer had been killed. However, Ravana's son showered down arrows and attacked Soumitri. Lakshmana was like the great Indra. He shot sharp and excellent arrows at the one who was on foot. He[319] also shot sharp and excellent arrows and he[320] countered them with his fierce storm of arrows.

Chapter 6(78)

With his horses slain, the immensely energetic roamer in the night was stationed on the ground. Indrajit became extremely angry and blazed in his energy. Those two archers wished to kill each other and shot fierce arrows. They were like two bull elephants in the forest, emerging in search of victory over each other. The rakshasas and the residents of the forest devastated each other. Here and there, they attacked each other, but did not forsake their masters in the battle. He resorted to his great dexterity and aiming towards Lakshmana, showered down arrows, like Purandara showering down rain. Indrajit shot these showers of arrows that were extremely difficult to repulse. However, Lakshmana, the slayer of enemies, fearlessly countered them. Ravana's son formed the view that Lakshmana was clad in impenetrable armour. Extremely angry, and displaying his dexterity in using weapons, Indrajit therefore pierced Lakshmana in the forehead with three well-tufted

[318] The four apes.
[319] Indrajit.
[320] Lakshmana.

arrows. With those arrows adhering to his forehead, the descendant of the Raghu lineage was resplendent. He took pride in fighting and in the forefront of the battle, he looked like a mountain with three peaks. In the great battle, he was afflicted by the rakshasa's arrows. Swiftly, Lakshmana struck him back with five arrows. Lakshmana and Indrajit were brave and possessed extremely strong bows. Terrible in their valour, they struck each other with sharp arrows. Those two archers clashed against each other, and desiring victory over each other, pierced each other's bodies with arrows everywhere.

Vibhishana became extremely angry and killed his horses.[321] He struck him in the chest with five arrows that were like the vajra to the touch. Those gold-tufted arrows reached their target and penetrated his body. They were smeared with blood and looked like giant red serpents. The immensely strong Indrajit became angry with his paternal uncle and attacked him in the midst of the excellent rakshasas, using an arrow given by Yama. The immensely energetic Lakshmana saw that he had picked up that great arrow and, terrible in his valour, picked up another arrow. In a dream, Kubera, immeasurable in his soul, had himself given him this. It was impossible to vanquish and impossible to withstand, even for Indra, the gods and the asuras. At the same time, those two excellent arrows were affixed to the excellent bows. As those two brave ones stretched them, they blazed in their great radiance. As those two arrows were released from their bows, they illuminated the sky. With great energy, the points struck each other and fell down. They crashed against each other like giant planets and fell down. In the battle, they shattered into a hundred fragments and fell down on the ground. Both of them saw that their arrows had been repulsed in the field of battle. Both Lakshmana and Indrajit were ashamed, but anger was generated in them. Angry, Soumitri affixed Varuna's weapon. In the battle, Indrajit stationed himself and released

[321] By excising shlokas, the Critical Edition breaks continuity. Indrajit's horses have already been killed. In the excised shlokas, Indrajit returns to Lanka and comes back with another chariot and horses. While fighting against Lakshmana, he then attacks Vibhishana. Those shlokas have also been excised.

Rudra's great weapon. There was an extremely tumultuous and wonderful clash. The beings who were in the firmament surrounded Lakshmana. A fearful and terrible engagement continued between the apes and the rakshasas. The many beings who were in the sky were astounded and gathered around. In the battle, the rishis, the ancestors, the gods, the gandharvas, Garuda and the serpents, with Shatakratu at the forefront, protected Lakshmana.

Raghava's brave younger brother affixed another excellent arrow that was like fire to the touch and would prove to be extremely terrible for Ravana's son. It was well tufted, with a rounded frame and excellent joints. It had been crafted well. The arrow was decorated with gold and would bring an end to the body. It was impossible to counter and impossible to withstand. It caused great fear to rakshasas. It was excellent, like venomous poison. It was worshipped in assemblies of the gods. In ancient times, in the battle between the gods and the asuras, the immensely energetic lord Shakra, borne by tawny steeds, had used this for victory over the danavas. In the battle, Soumitri invoked the unvanquished aindrastra. The best among men affixed this excellent arrow to the excellent bow. He affixed the arrow that could crush the enemy to the bow. The invincible one readied himself, like the Destroyer at the time of the destruction of the worlds. Lakshmana possessed the auspicious qualities. He affixed it to his excellent bow, drew it back and spoke meaningful words that were meant to accomplish his objective. 'If Rama has dharma in his soul, if he is devoted to the truth, if he is Dasharatha's son and if he is unmatched in his manliness, then slay Ravana's son.'[322] In the battle, the brave Lakshmana drew the bow all the way back up to his ear and released the arrow towards Indrajit. Lakshmana, the slayer of enemy heroes, invoked aindrastra. Indrajit's handsome head was clad in a helmet and was adorned with earrings. The head was severed from the body and fell down on the ground. The rakshasa's giant head was severed from his shoulders. It was seen on the ground, shining like gold and covered in blood. Slain, Ravana's son swiftly fell down on

[322] This is addressed to the arrow.

the ground. His armour and helmet were shattered and his bow was fragmented.

With Vibhishana, all the apes roared in joy at his death, just as the gods had when Vritra had been killed. In the firmament, the gods, the great-souled rishis and the gandharvas and the apsaras pronounced chants of victory. The large army of the rakshasas saw that he had fallen down. They were slaughtered by the apes who desired victory and fled in different directions. The rakshasas were slaughtered by the apes and cast aside their weapons. Deprived of their senses, all of them rushed towards Lanka. Terrified, many hundreds of rakshasas fled in different directions. All of them abandoned their weapons, the spears and the battleaxes. Afflicted by the apes, some were frightened and entered Lanka. Some fell down in the ocean and some sought refuge in the mountain. They saw that Indrajit was lying down, having been killed in the battle. Among the thousands of rakshasas, none could be seen. When the sun sets, its rays no longer remain. Like that, when he fell down, the rakshasas set in different directions. The rays of the sun had been pacified. The fire had been put out. The immensely energetic one had departed and his life had set. When the son of the Indra among the rakshasas fell down, many sufferings of the world were pacified and enemies who had been destroyed rejoiced. With the illustrious Shakra, all the bulls among the gods were delighted. The rakshasa, the perpetrator of wicked deeds, had been killed. The sky and the water were purified and the daityas and danavas rejoiced. Someone who had caused fear to all the worlds had fallen down.

Together, all the gods, the gandharvas and the danavas said, 'May the brahmanas roam around, devoid of anxiety and with all the sins cleansed.' The bull among the nairittas was supreme in his strength. On seeing that he had been slain in the battle, the leaders of the apes were delighted and applauded this. Vibhishana, Hanumat and Jambavat, the leader of herds of bears, were delighted at the victory and praised Lakshmana. The bulls among the apes leapt, shouted and roared. With the objective having been attained, they surrounded the descendant of the Raghu lineage. The apes lashed their tails and slapped themselves. They exclaimed, 'Lakshmana has been victorious.' Delighted in their minds, the apes embraced each other. They conversed with each other about Raghava's many qualities. The gods saw and heard that their beloved well-wisher, Lakshmana, had accomplished an extremely difficult task in the battle. They were happy and their minds were filled with great delight, on hearing that Indra's enemy had been killed.

Chapter 6(79)

Lakshmana, the possessor of auspicious qualities, was covered with blood all over his body. But he was delighted at having been able to kill Shakrajit in the battle. The immensely energetic one returned with Jambavat, the valiant Hanumat and all the residents of the forest. Lakshmana leant on Vibhishana and Hanumat and quickly reached the spot where Sugriva and Raghava were. Soumitri greeted Rama and approached him. He drew near his brother, just as Indra's younger brother[323] approaches Shakra. The brave one told him that the terrible Indrajit had been killed. Delighted, Vibhishana informed Rama that the great-souled Lakshmana had severed the head of Ravana's son. He made him sit down on his lap and embraced the injured one. He inhaled the fragrance of his head and repeatedly touched him. The bull among men spoke these words of assurance to Lakshmana. 'You have performed a supremely beneficial deed, one that is extremely difficult to accomplish. Since Ravana will emerge, I will be freed of my enemies today. On hearing that his son has been brought down, he will come with a large army with battle formations. The lord of the rakshasas will be tormented by grief because his son has been killed and will emerge. He will surround himself with a large army and will be difficult to vanquish. But I will kill him. You have killed Shakrajit in the battle today. O Lakshmana! With you as my protector, and of Sita

[323] Vishnu.

and this earth, nothing is very difficult for me to obtain.' Raghava comforted his brother and embraced him.

Happy, Rama addressed Sushena in these words. 'O immensely wise one! Soumitri is devoted to his friends and he is suffering from these wounds. Act so that he can be happy and well soon. Act quickly, so that Soumitri and Vibhishana are cured of their wounds. The brave soldiers of the bears and the apes fight with trees. There are others who have fought and are suffering from wounds and stakes. Make all the efforts so that they can be happy and well soon.' The leader of the apes was thus addressed by the great-souled Rama. Through the nose, Sushena gave Lakshmana a supreme medicine. Once he had inhaled its fragrance, all his wounds were healed. His pain was gone and all his injuries were cured. Following Raghava's command, he[324] also treated Vibhishana, best among the well-wishers, and all the other foremost apes. Soumitri attained his natural state. His wounds were healed and his pain was gone. In a short while, his fever disappeared and he was happy. Rama saw that the lord of the apes, Vibhishana, Jambavat, the lord of the bears, and Soumitri were hale and had got up, freed from injuries. With the soldiers, he rejoiced for a long period of time. Dasharatha's great-souled son worshipped the extremely difficult task that had been accomplished by Lakshmana. On hearing that Shakrajit had been brought down in the battle, the Indras among the herds rejoiced.

Chapter 6(80)

Poulastya's advisers heard that Indrajit had been killed. Distressed, they went and told Dashagriva the news. 'O great king! O immensely radiant one! In the battle, your son has been killed by Lakshmana, with Vibhishana's help, while all of us looked on. When he engaged in fighting, the brave one was invincible in encounters. Indrajit, your brave son, defeated the gods. But he

[324] Sushena.

has been slain by Lakshmana.' Hearing that fearful, dreadful and terrible news about his son's death in the battle, he lost his senses for a long period of time. After some time, the king, the bull among the rakshasas, regained his senses. He was afflicted by grief on account of his son and miserable. With his senses in a whirl, he lamented. 'O foremost in the army of the rakshasas! Alas! My child! O maharatha! Having defeated Indra, how could you have come under Lakshmana's subjugation today? Indeed, when you were angry in a battle, your arrows could have even penetrated Death and the peaks of Mandara, not to speak of Lakshmana. Today, I hold a great deal of respect for King Vaivasvata.[325] O mighty-armed one! It is because of him that you have been subjected to the dharma of time. This is the path followed by excellent warriors and large numbers of immortals too. If a man desires heaven, he should be killed for the sake of his lord. On seeing that Indrajit has been killed, the large number of gods, all the guardians of the world and the rishis will sleep happily today, freed from fear. Without Indrajit, all the three worlds and the earth with its groves seems lonely and empty to me today. Today, I will hear the screams of the nairitta maidens in the inner quarters, like the roars of herds of female elephants in mountain caverns. O scorcher of enemies! You were the heir apparent over the rakshasas in Lanka. Abandoning them, your mother and your wife, where have you gone? O brave one! When I had left for Yama's abode, you should have performed the funeral rites for me. But the opposite has happened. Sugriva, Lakshmana and Raghava are alive. Without uprooting my stakes, why have you abandoned us and left?' Ravana, the lord of the rakshasas, lamented in this and other ways. Because of the calamity over his son, he was immersed in great rage.

He was naturally terrible and the rage of his fire made him senseless. His form was like that of the angry and unassailable Rudra. Tears dropped from his enraged eyes, like drops of oil from the flames of blazing lamps. The loud sound of his gnashing his teeth could be heard, as if the danavas were dragging around

[325] Yama.

a mechanical contrivance. He was like the fire of destruction. In whichever direction he looked, the rakshasas were scared and terrified and hid themselves. As he looked at the directions, he was like an enraged Death, desiring to devour all mobile and immobile objects. All the rakshasas could not approach him. Ravana, the lord of the rakshasas, became extremely angry. Desiring to assign rakshasas to the field of battle, he spoke to them in their midst. 'I have performed supreme austerities for one thousand years and when these were over, Svayambhu was pleased with me. As a consequence of those austerities and because of Svayambhu's favours, I have never suffered any fear from asuras and gods. Brahma gave me armour that dazzles like the sun. When I crushed the gods and the asuras, the strength of the vajra could not shatter it. I will now wear that, astride my chariot in the battle. Even Purandara himself will be unable to act against me today. When he was pleased with me, Svayambhu gave me a great bow and arrows. I used those when I crushed the gods and the asuras. To the terrible sound of hundreds of trumpets, let that bow of mine be taken out for the great battle in which Rama and Lakshmana will be killed.'

The brave one was tormented because his son had been killed and fell prey to rage. Ravana thought about it in his mind and resolved to kill Sita. His eyes were coppery red and extremely terrible. He was horrible to behold. He was miserable and in a distressed voice, he glanced towards all the roamers in the night and addressed them. 'My child used maya to deceive the residents of the forest. He showed them the sight of Sita being killed. I will make that come true. This is pleasing to me. Vaidehi is devoted to the friend of the kshatriyas[326] and I will destroy her.' Having told his advisers this, he swiftly touched his sword and drew it out. It possessed all the qualities and was as radiant as a clear sky. Surrounded by his advisers, he left the assembly hall with great force. Ravana was afflicted by sorrow on account of his son and his eyes were full of grief. Having angrily seized the sword, he violently went to the spot where Maithilee was. On seeing the angry

[326] Rama.

rakshasa leave, the rakshasas roared like lions. They embraced each other and said, 'Today, those two brothers will see him and be agitated. When angry, he has vanquished the four guardians of the world. In battles, he has brought down many other enemies.' While they were conversing, he went to Ashokavana. Senseless with rage, Ravana rushed towards Vaidehi. He was extremely angry. His well-wishers, those who thought about his welfare, sought to restrain him. But he rushed forward angrily, like a planet in the sky heading towards Rohini. The unblemished Maithilee was guarded by the rakshasis. She saw the enraged rakshasa, holding the excellent sword. On seeing him with the sword, Janaka's daughter was distressed, though many well-wishers tried to restrain him and make him withdraw.

'This one is angry and is himself rushing towards me.[327] Though I have a protector, this evil-minded one will render me without a protector. I have been devoted to my husband and he has urged me many times. He has asked me to be his wife and seek pleasure. But he has been rebuffed by me. That is the reason he has come here. It is evident that he has lost hope. It is evident that he is full of anger and confusion and is ready to kill me. Or, for my sake, this ignoble one might have brought down the two brothers, Rama and Lakshmana, tigers among men, in the battle today. If the two princes were destroyed because of me, that would be a shame. I was inferior and did not act in accordance with Hanumat's words. I could have easily left on his back. Though I would have been censured, I would have been on my husband's lap and would not have had to grieve today. I think that Kousalya's heart will be shattered when she hears that her son has been destroyed in the battle. She has only a single son. When she remembers the great-souled one and weeps, she will think about his birth, his childhood, his youth and all the acts of dharma he has performed. On hearing about her son being killed, she will lose all hope. Though she will perform the funeral rites, she will be unconscious. It is certain that she will enter a fire or enter water. Shame on Kubja Manthara, the

[327] These are Sita's thoughts.

one with evil inclinations. It is because of her that Kousalya will suffer from this hardship.'

The ascetic Maithilee lamented in this way. She was like Rohini separated from the moon and under the subjugation of a planet. The lord of the rakshasas, had an intelligent adviser named Suparshva. He saw her. Though he was restrained by the other advisers, he spoke these words to Ravana. 'You are Dashagriva and you are the younger brother of Vaishravana himself. How can you forget dharma in your rage and desire to kill Vaidehi? You have studied the knowledge of the Vedas and have bathed thereafter.[328] You have always been devoted to your own dharma. O brave one! O lord of the rakshasas! How can you think of killing a woman? O king! Look at Maithilee. She possesses beauty. Therefore, with us, release your anger towards Raghava. You should arise now. It is the fourteenth day of *krishna paksha*. Surround yourself with an army and emerge on *amavasya*[329] for the sake of victory. You are brave and intelligent. You have a chariot and a sword. Station yourself on an excellent chariot. Kill Rama, Dasharatha's son, and you will obtain Maithilee.' The generous-souled well-wisher said this and Ravana accepted the words that were in conformity with dharma. The valiant one went to his residence. Then, surrounded by the well-wishers, he again went to the assembly hall.

Chapter 6(81)

Distressed and extremely miserable, the king entered the assembly hall. He sat down on his excellent seat and sighed like an angry lion. The extremely strong one spoke to all the commanders of the force. He was afflicted by hardship on account of his son. Ravana joined his hands in salutation and spoke these words. 'All of you surround yourselves with all the elephants and

[328] Bathing is an act of purification, performed after concluding a period of studies.

[329] The day of the new moon is amavasya, that is, the next day.

the horses. Emerge with hordes of chariots and surround yourselves with foot soldiers. In the battle, you should only surround Rama and kill him. Like clouds during the monsoon, cheerfully shower down arrows. Otherwise, in the great battle tomorrow, while all the worlds look on, I will pierce Rama's body with sharp arrows and kill him.' The Indra among rakshasas said this and the rakshasas accepted his words. They quickly emerged on chariots, surrounded by armies of elephants.

There was an extremely terrible battle just before sunrise. There was a tumultuous clash between the rakshasas and the apes. In the battle, the apes and the rakshasas struck each other with colourful clubs, spears, swords and battleaxes. Rivers of blood started to flow. The elephants and chariots were the banks, the horses were the fish and the standards were the trees. Large number of bodies were borne along. In the battle, the Indras among the apes leapt up and leapt down. They shattered the standards, armour, chariots, horses and many kinds of weapons. With their sharp teeth and nails, the apes tore out the hair, ears, foreheads and noses of the rakshasas. In the encounter, one hundred bulls among apes rushed towards a single rakshasa, like birds rush towards a tree with fruits. The terrible rakshasas were like mountains and slew the apes with heavy clubs, spears, swords and battleaxes. The large army of apes was slaughtered by the rakshasas and sought succour with Rama, Dasharatha's son, the one who provides refuge.

At this, the immensely energetic and valiant Rama seized his bow. He entered the army of the rakshasas and showered down floods of arrows. When the extremely terrible Rama entered, he was like the sun in the sky. He burnt them down with the flames of his arrows and they could not approach him. To the roamers in the night, the extremely terrible Rama was like Death. In the battle, they saw Rama perform deeds that were extremely difficult to achieve. He drove away that large army and shattered the giant chariots. They could not see Rama, just as one cannot see the wind in the forest. Rama was swift in his deeds. He severed, mangled and routed the army, afflicting them with his weapons and scorching them with his arrows. But they could not see him. Though they were struck in their bodies, they could not see Raghava, just as creatures are unable to see the inner soul that is established in the senses. 'This is he, he is slaying the army of elephants. This is he, he is destroying the giant chariots. This is he, he is devastating the foot soldiers and horses with his sharp arrows.' In the encounter, all the rakshasas saw Rama's likeness everywhere. Finding Raghava's resemblance in each other, they angrily slew each other. The great-souled one had confounded them with the supreme *gandharvastra*[330] and scorched the army of the enemy. That is the reason they saw Rama everywhere. In the battle, the rakshasas saw thousands of Ramas. And, in the great battle, they next saw a single Kakutstha. The great-souled one was roaming around with a bow with a golden handle. He brandished it like a circle of fire and they could not see Raghava. The bow was like the rim of a wheel, with the arrows as spokes. The body was like a navel and emitted sparks as the breath of life. There was the roar of the palm slapping against the bowstring. The plucking of the bowstring was full of energy and intelligence. Applying divine weapons to the bowstring, he slaughtered the rakshasas in the encounter. They saw Rama's wheel, like the subjects see the wheel of time. There was an army of ten thousand chariots that were as fleet as the wind. There were eighteen thousand spirited elephants. There were fourteen thousand horses with riders. There was a complete complement of two hundred thousand rakshasa foot soldiers. The rakshasas could assume any form at will. Using arrows that were like the flames of the fire, within the eighth part of a day,[331] Rama destroyed all these. The horses were killed. The chariots were destroyed. They were exhausted and their standards were shattered. The remaining roamers in the night returned to the city of Lanka. The field of battle was full of slain elephants, foot soldiers and horses. It looked like a pleasure ground for the enraged Rudra, the wielder of the Pinaka. The gods, the gandharvas, the siddhas and the supreme rishis praised Rama's deeds and worshipped him.

[330] Divine weapon named after gandharvas.

[331] Three hours.

Rama spoke to Sugriva, who was near him. 'The strength of such divine weapons exists in me, or in Tryambaka.' The great-souled Rama, who was Shakra's equal and had cleansed all sins, slaughtered the army of the rakshasas, using his *astra*s and his *shastra*s.[332] He was praised by the large numbers of delighted gods.

Chapter 6(82)

There were thousands of elephants and horses with riders. There were chariots with the complexion of the fire. There were thousands of standards. There were thousands of rakshasas who fought with clubs and maces. There were golden and colourful standards. There were brave ones who could assume any form at will. They were slain with sharp arrows decorated with gold. Rama, the performer of unblemished deeds, did this to the army sent by Ravana. The remaining roamers in the night heard about, and saw, this devastation. They were distressed and overcome by thoughts.

The rakshasis had become widows. Their sons had been killed. They shrieked because their relatives had been killed. They met the rakshasas and lamented in their sorrow. 'Shurpanakha is aged and ugly. Her stomach hangs down. Rama is like Kandarpa[333] in his beauty. How could she have approached him in the forest? He is delicate and great in spirit. He is engaged in the welfare of all creatures. She should be killed by people. She is inferior in beauty. But she saw him and was smitten with desire. She is devoid of all the qualities. He possesses the qualities and is greatly energetic. His face is beautiful, her face is ugly. How could the rakshasi have desired Rama? These people are limited in their fortune. She is

[332] The text uses both the words astra and shastra. Both mean weapons. Broadly, an astra is hurled, while a shastra is held in the hand. Shastra is typically used for a human weapon, while astra is a term also used for a divine weapon, such as one invoked on an arrow.

[333] The god of love.

wrinkled and has grey hair. She committed a ridiculous misdeed, condemned by all the worlds. That led to the destruction of the rakshasas and Khara and Dushana. That ugly woman oppressed Raghava. Ravana contracted this great enmity because of her. The rakshasa Dashagriva brought Sita for his own destruction. Dashagriva will not get Sita, Janaka's daughter. However, he has been bound in an eternal enmity with the powerful Raghava. Rama single-handedly killed the rakshasa Viradha, who craved for Vaidehi. That spectacle is sufficient proof.[334] There were fourteen thousand rakshasas who were terrible in their deeds. He killed them in Janasthana, using arrows that were like the flames of fire. In the encounter, he used arrows that were like the sun to kill Khara, Dushana and Trishira. That is sufficient proof. Kabandha fed on blood and his arms were one yojana long. He was killed, while he was roaring in anger and suffering. That is sufficient proof. Vali was like a cloud and he was the son of the one with one thousand eyes. Rama killed Vali. That is sufficient proof. With his wishes destroyed, the distressed Sugriva resided on Mount Rishyamuka and he was established in the kingdom. That is sufficient proof. For the welfare of all the rakshasas, Vibhishana spoke words that were full of dharma and artha. However, because of his confusion, those did not appeal to him. Had the younger brother of the lord of treasure acted in accordance with Vibhishana's words, this city of Lanka wouldn't have become afflicted with grief and wouldn't have become a cremation ground. Despite hearing that Kumbhakarna had been killed by the immensely strong Raghava and about his beloved son, Indrajit, Ravana did not understand. Wails can be heard in family after family of the rakshasas. 'My son, my brother, my husband, has been killed in the battle.' Hundreds and thousands of chariots, horses and elephants have been killed and destroyed by the brave Rama in the battle, and so have rakshasa foot soldiers. Assuming Rama's form, Rudra, Vishnu, the great Indra Shatakratu, or Death himself is killing us. With the best among brave ones killed

[334] Of Rama's powers.

by Rama, there is no hope of our remaining alive. We do not see an end to our fears. Therefore, we are lamenting. The brave Dashagriva has obtained boons for the field of battle. Therefore, he does not comprehend this extremely terrible fear that has arisen from Rama's hands. When he engages in a battle against Rama and is attacked, the gods, the gandharvas, the pishachas and the rakshasas will not be able to save him. In every battle that Ravana engages in, evil portents are seen. They are telling us about Rama destroying Ravana. Pleased, the grandfather granted Ravana freedom from fear through gods, danavas and rakshasas. However, he did not ask about humans. Therefore, we[335] are certain that there is a fear from humans. A terrible destruction of life will occur for the rakshasa Ravana. Powerful because of the boon he had obtained, the rakshasa caused oppression. Blazing in their austerities, the gods worshipped the grandfather. Satisfied, for the welfare of the gods, the great-souled grandfather addressed all the gods in these great words. "From today, in the three worlds, the danavas and the rakshasas will always be full of fear and will wander around till eternity." All the gods, with Indra at the forefront, went and propitiated Mahadeva, the one with the bull on his banner, the destroyer of the city of Tripura. Mahadeva was pleased and addressed the gods in these words. "For your welfare, a woman will be born and she will ensure the destruction of the rakshasas." Earlier, hunger consumed the danavas. Like that, Sita has been engaged by the gods. She is the slayer of rakshasas and will devour us, together with Ravana. The evil-minded and insolent Ravana has brought this about through his misdeeds. This terrible misfortune has occurred and we are immersed in grief. We do not see anyone in the world who can offer us protection from what Raghava has unleashed, like Death at the time of the destruction of a yuga.' All the women of the roamers in the night said this and embraced each other in their arms. They sorrowed and grieved, afflicted by fear. They shrieked in these extremely terrible voices.

[335] The text actually uses the singular, since the women are lamenting individually.

Chapter 6(83)

In every family in Lanka, there were the screams of the rakshasis. Ravana heard the piteous sounds of these lamentations. He sighed deeply and thought for a while. Ravana, terrible to behold, was extremely angry. He bit his lips with his teeth and his eyes were red with rage. He was like the fire of destruction. Even the rakshasas found him difficult to look at and lost their senses. The lord of the rakshasas spoke to the rakshasas who were near him. He seemed to burn them down with his eyes and because of their fear, they could not clearly make out what he said. 'Tell Mahodara, Mahaparshva and the rakshasa Virupaksha to obey my commands and ask the soldiers to swiftly depart.'[336] Hearing his words, the rakshasas were afflicted by fear. Following the king's orders, they urged the rakshasas who were still not agitated. All the rakshasas, terrible to behold, agreed to what he had said. All of them performed acts of benediction and advanced towards Ravana. As is proper, all the maharathas worshipped Ravana. They joined their hands in salutation and stood there, wishing for the victory of their master. Ravana was senseless with rage.

He laughed and spoke to Mahodara, Mahaparshva and the rakshasa Virupaksha. 'From my bow, I will today shoot arrows that are like the sun at the time of the destruction of a yuga. I will convey Raghava and Lakshmana to Yama's abode. By slaying the enemy, I will extract revenge for Khara, Kumbhakarna, Prahasta and Indrajit. The net of my arrows will go and cover everything and the firmament, the directions, the rivers and the ocean will no longer be seen. My arrows will be waves that arise from the bow that is the ocean. I will use these to crush the herds of apes, in their respective divisions and subdivisions. Their faces are like blooming lotuses and their complexions are like the filaments of lotuses. Those herds are like lotus ponds and I will crush them like an elephant. In the

[336] Mahodara and Mahaparshva have already been killed. However, Ravana may have been confused. There is also the hedge that the rakshasas couldn't clearly make out what he said. But since Mahodara and Mahaparshva are killed again, there is a clear case of inconsistency.

encounter, the leaders of the herds will have arrows embedded in their faces today. They will be strewn around the earth, like lotuses with stalks. Today, there will be a terrible fight against the apes who use trees as weapons. Shooting a single arrow in the battle, I will pierce hundreds. Husbands have been killed. Brothers have been killed. Sons have been killed. By slaying their enemies today, I will perform the act of wiping away their tears. They will be mangled by my arrows today. They will be scattered around, senseless. In the battle today, I will make efforts to cover the earth with apes, so that the ground cannot be seen. Today, I will use my arrows to cause affliction. I will satisfy jackals, vultures and all the others that survive on flesh with the flesh of the enemy. Swiftly prepare my chariot. Swiftly bring me my bow. Let the roamers in the night who remain follow me into the battle.'

Hearing his words, Mahaparshva spoke to the commanders who were present there. 'Let all the forces be readied.' The angry commanders went around, from one house of a rakshasa to another house. Light in their valour, they went all around Lanka and urged the soldiers. In a short while, the rakshasas, terrible in their valour, emerged. With horrible faces, they roared. They wielded many kinds of weapons in their arms. There were swords, spears, javelins, clubs, maces, ploughs, sharp-edged spikes and large and heavy bludgeons. There were staffs, sparkling chakras, sharp battleaxes, bhindipalas, shataghnis and many other excellent weapons. Following Ravana's command, the commanders quickly brought a chariot. They urged the charioteer to hurry and yoke eight horses to this chariot. Blazing in his own energy, he ascended this divine chariot. Ravana's spirit was deep and he seemed to shatter the earth. Obtaining Ravana's permission, Mahaparshva, Mahodara and the invincible Virupaksha climbed on to their chariots. They roared cheerfully and seemed to shatter the earth. Desiring victory, they emitted terrible roars and emerged. The energetic one[337] was like Yama, the Destroyer. Advancing into battle, he held aloft his bow and emerged, surrounded by an army of large numbers of

[337] Ravana.

rakshasas. The maharatha's chariot was yoked to swift horses. He emerged through the gate where Rama and Lakshmana were.

The sun lost its radiance. The directions were covered in darkness. Birds shrieked in terrible tones. The earth trembled. Blood showered down from the sky. The horses stumbled. A vulture descended on the top of the standard. Jackals howled in inauspicious tones. His left eye throbbed. His left arm twitched. His face turned pale. His voice was slightly distorted. The rakshasa Dashagriva proceeded to fight and these evil portents, signifying his death in the battle, manifested themselves. A meteor fell down from the sky, with a sound like that of a storm. Vultures called out in hideous tones. Crows cawed. These terrible portents manifested themselves, but he paid no heed to them. Ravana was confounded. He was urged by destiny, for the sake of his own destruction. He emerged.

Hearing the clatter of the chariots of the great-souled rakshasas, the apes returned and a clash commenced between the two armies. There was a tumultuous battle between the apes and the rakshasas. Desiring victory, they angrily slaughtered each other. Dashagriva was angry. He used arrows decorated in gold to cause great carnage in the army of the apes. Ravana sliced off the heads of the foremost ones in the army. Some were breathless and were killed. Some were shattered along the flanks. The heads of some were severed. Some lost their eyes. Dashanana dilated his eyes in rage. On his chariot, he wandered around here and there in the battle. Wherever he went, the leaders of the apes were unable to withstand the force of his arrows.

Chapter 6(84)

The earth was strewn with apes whose bodies had been mangled by Dashagriva's arrows. They were incapable of tolerating the descent of Ravana's arrows, just as insects are incapable of tolerating a blazing fire. They were afflicted by those sharp arrows. They screamed and fled in different directions. They were like elephants, consumed and surrounded by the flames of a fire. As

Ravana advanced in the battle and pierced them with his arrows, he drove away the army of the apes, like the wind dispelling large clouds. The Indra among the rakshasas created carnage among the residents of the forest. In the battle, he then swiftly approached Raghava. Sugriva saw that the apes were routed in the encounter and were running away. He quickly urged Sushena to take care of the divisions and made up his mind to fight. The brave ape[338] was just like him and he put him in charge. Using a tree as a weapon, Sugriva himself then marched in the direction of the enemy. With large boulders and many kinds of large trees, all the leaders of the herds followed him, staying by his side or at the rear. In the encounter, Sugriva roared in a loud voice. He brought down and killed many excellent rakshasas. Gigantic in size, the lord of the apes crushed the rakshasas. He was like the wind at the time of the destruction of a yuga, devastating large trees. He showered down innumerable boulders on the rakshasa army, just as a cloud showers down hail stones on a flock of birds in a grove. Showers of boulders were hurled by the king of the apes. The heads of the rakshasas were crushed. Mangled, they fell down like mountains. In every direction, the rakshasas were devastated and brought down. Shattering them, Sugriva roared.

The archer rakshasa, Virupaksha, announced his name. The invincible one leapt down from his chariot and climbed astride an elephant. The maharatha Virupaksha mounted that elephant. He uttered a terrible roar and rushed towards the apes. At the head of the army, he shot terrible arrows towards Sugriva. He cheered up the anxious rakshasas and urged and assured them. The Indra among the apes was severely pierced by the rakshasa's sharp arrow. He was angry. In great rage, he made up his mind to kill him. The brave ape held aloft a tree. He advanced in front of that large elephant and struck it. Sugriva's blow struck that giant elephant. It retreated the distance of a bow and trumpeted loudly. The valiant rakshasa descended from the injured elephant. He quickly advanced towards his enemy, the ape. Dextrous in his valour, he seized a shield made of oxhide and a sword.

[338] Sushena.

He approached Sugriva, who stood there, censuring him. Sugriva was angry. He seized a giant boulder that was like a cloud and hurled it towards Virupaksha. The bull among the rakshasas saw that the boulder was descending. Extremely brave, he struck him back with the sword. In front of the army, he angrily struck Sugriva with the sword. Struck by the sword, his armour was shattered and it fell down. The ape let go of what had fallen down. He leapt up and slapped him with his palm, making a terrible sound that was like that of thunder. Using his skills, the rakshasa freed himself from the blows Sugriva was ready with. He raised his fist and struck him in the chest. At this, Sugriva, lord of the apes, became angrier. He saw that the rakshasa had freed himself from his blows. The ape discerned an opportunity to strike Virupaksha. With his huge palm, he angrily struck him on the region around his temple. That blow of the palm was like the force of the great Indra's vajra and he fell down on the ground. He fell down, covered in blood, and vomited blood. His angry eyes were dilated and he was covered in froth and blood. Virupaksha was seen to have become even more disfigured.[339] He writhed and trembled, his sides were covered with blood. The apes saw that their enemy was roaring piteously. The spirited apes and the rakshasas engaged with each other properly. The two terrible armies were like two thundering oceans. They were like two oceans that had crossed their shorelines. They saw that the immensely strong one, with the disfigured eyes, had been killed by the king of the apes. All the soldiers of the apes and the rakshasas became as turbulent as the Ganga.

Chapter 6(85)

In the great battle, they swiftly killed each other's soldiers. Both the armies were diminished, like lakes during a strong summer. At the destruction of his army and at Virupaksha's death, Ravana,

[339] There is a pun. The word *virupaksha* means one with malformed or disfigured eyes. Virupaksha's eyes became more malformed.

the lord of the rakshasas, became twice as angry. In front of the two armies, he saw that his soldiers were being slaughtered and destroyed. He was distressed to see this reversal of fate in the battle. Mahodara, the destroyer of enemies, was near him and he told him, 'O mighty-armed one! At at time like this, my hope of victory is established in you. O brave one! Exhibit your valour now. Slay the forces of the enemy. This is the time to repay the debt to your master. Fight well.'

Thus addressed by the Indra among the rakshasas, Mahodara signified his assent. Like an insect heading towards a fire, he entered the forces of the enemy. The immensely strong one created carnage among the apes. The energetic one was goaded by his master's words and by his own valour. Sugriva saw that the large army of the apes was routed in the battle. He immediately attacked Mahodara. The immensely energetic one, the lord of the apes, seized a large and terrible boulder that was like a mountain. He hurled this, so as to kill him. Mahodara saw that the boulder was suddenly descending. Though it was difficult to approach, he fearlessly pierced it with his arrows. The rakshasa countered it with his storm of arrows. The boulder was shattered into a thousand fragments and fell down on the ground, like a flock of anxious vultures. Seeing that the boulder had been fragmented, Sugriva became senseless with rage. In the field of battle, he uprooted a sala tree and hurled it towards the rakshasa. The brave one, the victor over enemy cities, shattered it with his arrows. Angry, he[340] saw a club that had fallen down on the ground. He whirled around that blazing club and brandished it. Striking with force, he used the tip of the club to slay his excellent horses. With his horses slain, the brave one leapt down from his large chariot. The rakshasa Mahodara angrily seized a mace. In the battle, those two brave ones faced each other with a club and a mace. They roared like two excellent bulls, like clouds tinged with lightning. The roamer in the night angrily hurled his mace. The lord of the apes struck his mace with his club. The mace and the club were shattered and

[340] Sugriva. Apes using weapons is rare, suggesting that this incident about Mahodara doesn't belong, Mahodara having already been killed.

fell down on the ground. From the ground, the energetic Sugriva picked up a terrible iron bludgeon that was decorated with gold. He raised it and hurled it. But his adversary also flung a mace. These two crashed against each other, were shattered and fell down on the ground. With their weapons shattered, they used their fists to engage with each other. They were full of energy and strength and were like blazing fires. They struck each other and roared repeatedly. They struck each other with their palms and fell down on the ground. They quickly leapt up again and struck each other. The brave and unvanquished ones used their arms to fling each other down. A sword was lying not far away and so was a shield. The rakshasa Mahodara was swift in his force and he seized these. There was another giant sword and shield that had fallen down. Sugriva, best among the apes, was quicker and he seized these. Their limbs were full of rage and they roared as they attacked each other. They were accomplished in the use of weapons. In the encounter, they cheerfully held up their swords. They swiftly circled and executed motions from the right. They both focused on being victorious and angrily attacked each other. The brave Mahodara was immensely swift and prided himself on his bravery. The evil-minded one brought his sword down on that giant shield. As he tried to extricate the sword, which was stuck, the elephant among apes used his own sword to sever his head, adorned with a helmet and with earrings. With his head severed, he fell down on the ground. On seeing this, the army of the Indra among the rakshasas did not remain there any longer. Having killed him, with the other apes, the ape[341] roared. Dashagriva was angry, while Raghava rejoiced.

Chapter 6(86)

When Mahodara was killed, the immensely strong Mahaparshva agitated Angada's army with his terrible arrows. He severed

[341] Sugriva.

the heads of all the foremost apes from their bodies and brought them down, like the wind severing fruits from their stems. The rakshasa used arrows to sever the arms of some and severed the shoulders of others. He angrily shattered the flanks of other apes. The apes were afflicted by the shower of Mahaparshva's arrows. All their faces were filled with distress and they lost their senses. Angada saw that his army was anxious and was afflicted by the rakshasa. The mighty-armed one resorted to his force, like the ocean on a day of the full moon. He seized an iron club that was as dazzling as the rays of the sun.[342] In the battle, the best among the apes attacked Mahaparshva. Mahaparshva lost his senses because of that blow. Senseless, with his charioteer, he fell down on the ground from the chariot. The energetic king of the bears was like a mass of black collyrium and his forces were like a mass of clouds. He angrily seized a giant boulder that was like the summit of a mountain. The extremely valiant one used this to swiftly slay his horses and shatter his chariot. In a short while, the immensely strong Mahaparshva regained his senses. He pierced Angada repeatedly with many arrows. He pierced Jambavat, the king of the bears, between the breasts with three arrows and struck Gavaksha with many arrows. Gavaksha and Jambavat were afflicted by these arrows. On seeing this, Angada became senseless with rage and seized a terrible club. The club was as radiant as the rays of the sun and was made out of iron. Standing at a distance, Angada angrily hurled the club towards the rakshasa. The powerful one seized the club in both his hands and whirled it around. To slay Mahaparshva, Vali's son hurled it towards him. The club was powerfully flung towards the rakshasa. It knocked off the bow and arrow from his hand and also brought down his helmet. Vali's powerful son attacked him with force. He angrily struck him on the temple with his palm, just below the earring. The immensely swift and immensely radiant Mahaparshva became angry. He seized an extremely large battleaxe in one hand. It was firm and had been washed in oil. It sparkled and its essence was

[342] The use of a weapon suggests the same interpolation about the Mahaparshva incident.

as hard as stone. Extremely angry, the rakshasa brought this down on Vali's son. It had been severely struck towards his left shoulder. However, the enraged Angada freed himself from the battleaxe. The brave Angada was his father's equal in valour. Enraged, he tightened his own fist, which was like the vajra. He knew about inner organs and aimed it towards the rakshasa's chest and his heart. He brought down the fist, which was like Indra's vajra to the touch. In the great battle, he brought this down on the rakshasa. His heart was quickly crushed. Slain, he fell down on the ground. When he fell down on the ground, his soldiers were agitated. In the encounter, Ravana became extremely angry.

Chapter 6(87)

In the great battle, Ravana saw that the two rakshasas, Mahodara and Mahaparshva, had been killed and that the immensely strong and brave Virupaksha had also been killed. He was filled with great rage. He urged his charioteer and spoke to him in these words. 'My advisers have been killed and the city has been barricaded. Slaying Rama and Lakshmana, I will destroy this misery. Rama is the tree and Sita is the flowers and fruits that result. I will kill him in the battle. Sugriva, Jambavat, Kumuda and Nala are his branches.' The atiratha was astride a giant chariot and its clatter sounded in the ten directions. Roaring, he advanced and quickly attacked Raghava. The rivers, mountains and forests were filled with that sound. The earth, with all its boars, animals and elephants, quaked. He used an extremely terrible and extremely fearful weapon known as *tamasa*.[343] This scorched all the apes. In every direction, they fell down. Hundreds of divisions in the army were shattered by Ravana's excellent arrows. On seeing this, Raghava stationed himself.

He saw that the unvanquished Rama was stationed there. He was with his brother, Lakshmana, like Vasava with Vishnu. He

[343] Meaning darkness.

seemed to be etching on the sky with his giant bow. His eyes were like the petals of lotuses and the scorcher of enemies was long-armed. The apes had been routed in the battle and had been brought down by Ravana. On seeing this, Raghava cheerfully grasped his bow at the middle. He started to stretch that excellent bow with great force. It emitted a loud noise and seemed to shatter the earth. Ravana came within the range of the arrows of the two princes. It was as if Rahu had come near the moon and the sun. The sound of the torrent of Ravana's arrows and of Rama stretching the bow made the rakshasas fall down in their hundreds. Lakshmana wished to fight with him first. He shot sharp arrows from his bow and these arrows were like the flames of a fire. No sooner had the archer Lakshmana shot these into the sky, than the immensely energetic Ravana countered these arrows with his own arrows. Displaying the dexterity of his hands, he severed one of Lakshmana's arrows with one arrow, three arrows with three arrows and ten arrows with ten arrows. Ravana, the victor in assemblies, passed over Lakshmana. He approached Rama, who was stationed like an immobile mountain.

His eyes red with rage, he approached him in that battle. Ravana showered down arrows on Raghava. There was a downpour of arrows, released from Ravana's bow. On seeing that these were falling down, Rama swiftly seized a broad-headed arrow. The flood of arrows blazed and were immensely forceful. They were like venomous serpents. Raghava severed these with sharp and broad-headed arrows. Raghava swiftly attacked Ravana and Ravana attacked Raghava. They showered down many kinds of sharp arrows on each other. Colourful circles of arrows zoomed around, to the left and to the right. Undefeated in battle, they countered each other's arrows. As they simultaneously fought with each other, all the creatures were terrified. It was as if Rudra and Yama were shooting arrows at each other. The air became thick with many kinds of arrows zooming around. It was as if it was dense with clouds, tinged with garlands of lightning, at the end of the summer. In the midst of these showers of arrows, the sky seemed to possess windows. Those arrows were swift in speed and exceedingly sharp.

They were speedy and tufted with the feathers of vultures. Because of the arrows, there was a terrible and supreme darkness. It was as if large clouds had arisen after the sun had set. As they desired to slay each other, the battle was tumultuous. It was unapproachable and unthinkable, like that between Vritra and Vasava. Both of them were supreme archers and accomplished in the use of weapons. Both of them were foremost among those who knew about weapons, and they roamed around in the battle. Wherever both of them went, the place became full of arrows. They were like waves in the ocean, struck by the wind. Ravana, the one who made the worlds shriek, was skilful in the use of his hands. He shot a garland of iron arrows towards Rama's forehead. They were shot from a terrible bow and possessed the complexion of dark lotuses. However, Rama bore it on his head and was not pained. Rama was filled with anger. He affixed an arrow, chanted mantras on it and invoked *roudrastra* on it. The immensely energetic and valiant one shot this from his bow. Severing the arrows of the Indra among the rakshasas, he shot more arrows. Those arrows descended on his armour, which was like a giant cloud. However, because the Indra among rakshasas could not be killed,[344] these did not lead to any pain in him. Rama was accomplished in the use of all weapons. The lord of the rakshasas was mounted on his chariot and he struck him on the forehead with a supreme weapon. However, Ravana countered these arrows. Like five-hooded serpents that were in the form of arrows, these hissed and penetrated the ground. Having destroyed Raghava's weapons, Ravana became senseless with rage. He affixed the extremely terrible asura weapon. This released sharp arrows. Some had the faces of lions and tigers, others had the faces of herons and crows. Some had the faces of vultures and hawks, others had the faces of jackals. Some had the faces of wolves, others had gaping mouths and were extremely fearful. Some had five heads with flickering tongues. Some arrows had the faces of donkeys, others had faces that were like those of boars. Some had faces like dogs and cocks, some had faces like venomous makaras. The immensely energetic one used his

[344] Because of his invincible armour.

maya to shoot these towards Rama and they sighed like serpents. The descendant of the Raghu lineage confronted the asura weapon. Great in his endeavour, he released *pavakastra*, which was like the fire. There were arrows with faces like blazing fires, others with faces that resembled the sun. There were faces like the moon and the half-moon, other faces like comets. There were faces that possessed the complexions of planets and nakshatras, other faces resembling giant meteors. There were some with tongues like lightning. He shot these sharp arrows. Ravana's terrible arrows were repulsed by Raghava's weapon. They were destroyed in the sky and shattered into thousands of fragments. Rama, the performer of unblemished deeds, destroyed that weapon. On seeing this, all the apes, who could assume any form at will, roared.

Chapter 6(88)

When that weapon was countered, the rage of Ravana, the lord of the rakshasas, was doubled. Thereafter, he resorted to another weapon. The immensely radiant one resorted to another terrible weapon that had been fashioned by Maya.[345] Ravana released this terrible weapon towards Raghava. From the bow, blazing spears, clubs and maces, with essence as hard as the vajra, emerged in all the directions. There were bludgeons and deceptive nooses, blazing like thunder. Many kinds of sharp weapons descended, like the wind at the end of a yuga. The prosperous Raghava was supreme among those who knew about weapons. The immensely radiant one destroyed that weapon with the supreme gandharva weapon. When that weapon was countered by the great-souled Raghava, Ravana's eyes turned coppery red with rage and he invoked sourastra. From the intelligent Dashagriva's bow, which was terrible in force, large and radiant chakras descended. As these descended, the sky blazed everywhere. As these descended,

[345] The architect of the demons.

the directions were illuminated, as if by the moon, the sun and the planets. In the field of battle, Raghava countered Ravana's chakras with torrents of arrows and other diverse weapons. Ravana, the lord of the rakshasas, saw that the weapon had been destroyed. He pierced Rama in all the inner organs with ten arrows. He was pierced by ten arrows that emerged from Ravana's large bow. However, the immensely energetic Raghava did not tremble. Raghava, the victor in assemblies, became angry. He pierced Ravana, all over his body, with many arrows.

At this time, Raghava's powerful younger brother became angry. Lakshmana, the slayer of enemy heroes, seized seven arrows. Ravana's standard had the figure of a man atop it. The immensely radiant one used these extremely forceful arrows to sever that into many fragments. The nairitta's charioteer's head was handsome, with blazing earrings. The immensely strong Lakshmana used an arrow to sever this. Lakshmana used five sharp arrows to shatter the bow, which was like an elephant's trunk, of the Indra among the rakshasas.

Ravana's horses were like dark clouds. They were well trained and were like mountains. Vibhishana leapt up and killed them with his club. With the horses slain, Ravana leapt down with great force from that large chariot, filled with a terrible rage towards his brother. He picked up a javelin. That giant javelin blazed, it flamed like the vajra. The powerful Indra among the rakshasas hurled this towards Vibhishana. Lakshmana severed it with three arrows before it could reach Vibhishana, and the apes who were fighting roared. Shattered into three pieces, that javelin, with golden garlands, fell down, emitting sparks. It blazed like a giant meteor that has been dislodged from the firmament. The accomplished one then picked up a giant javelin that was as unassailable as Death. It blazed in its own energy. The evil-souled and strong Ravana prepared to hurl this blazing and extremely terrible javelin with force and its radiance was like that of Shakra's vajra. Vibhishana's life was in danger. The brave Lakshmana advanced quickly. To free him, the brave Lakshmana grasped his bow and showered down arrows on Ravana, with the javelin still held in his hand. The great-souled one shot torrents of arrows. Having been neutralized in his act of valour, he[346] made up his mind not to strike. Ravana saw that his brother had been freed by Lakshmana. He turned his face towards Lakshmana and spoke these words. 'Priding yourself on your valour, you have freed this rakshasa Vibhishana. Now escape from this javelin that will descend on you. This javelin is smeared with blood and will pierce your heart. It will be hurled from my arm, which is like a club. It will depart after robbing you of your life.' That javelin was adorned with eight bells that made a loud noise. It had been constructed by Maya. It was invincible and killed the enemy. It seemed to blaze in its energy. Having said this, extremely angry, Ravana hurled this towards Lakshmana and roared. It was hurled with terrible force and made a sound like that of Shakra's vajra. In the field of battle, the javelin descended on Lakshmana with force. As the javelin descended through the sky, Raghava entreated it, 'May all be well with Lakshmana. May you fail. May your efforts be futile.' It descended with great force on Lakshmana's broad chest. It blazed and was immensely radiant, like the tongue of the king of the serpents.[347] Because of the force with which Ravana had hurled it, the javelin penetrated extremely deep into Lakshmana's heart and he fell down on the ground.

Raghava was nearby and saw the state Lakshmana was in. Because of affection towards his brother, the immensely energetic one was distressed in his heart. His eyes full of tears, he thought for a while. He became greatly angry, like the fire at the end of a yuga. Raghava thought that this was not the time to be despondent. For the sake of killing Ravana, he continued in that extremely tumultuous battle. In the great battle, Rama saw that Lakshmana had been mangled by the javelin. His body was covered with blood and he resembled a serpent in a mountain. The javelin had been hurled by the powerful Ravana. The best among the apes made efforts to pluck it out. However, they were unable to do so. The rakshasa was dexterous in the use of his hands and he afflicted

[346] Ravana decided not to throw the javelin at Vibhishana.

[347] Vasuki.

and oppressed them with his floods of arrows. Having pierced Soumitri, the javelin had penetrated the ground. Rama grasped that fearful javelin in his arms and drew it out. Enraged in the battle, the powerful one broke it. While he was drawing out the javelin, the powerful Ravana showered down arrows, which penetrated the inner organs, all over his body. Not thinking about these arrows, he embraced Lakshmana.

Raghava spoke to Hanumat and Sugriva. 'O supreme among the apes! Remain standing around Lakshmana. This is the time for valour and I have desired this for a very long time. The evil-souled Dashagriva, evil in his intentions, must be killed. Like a *chataka* bird that wishes to see a cloud at the end of the summer, I have waited for this. O apes! At this time, hear the truthful pledge that I am taking. Before long, the world will be without Ravana or without Rama. I have lost my kingdom, I have dwelt in the forest, I have roamed around in Dandaka and the rakshasas have approached and have oppressed Vaidehi. I have faced great hardships and the misery has been like hell. Slaying Ravana in the battle today, I will free myself from all of these. That is the reason why I have summoned this army of the apes, killed Vali in the battle and instated Sugriva in the kingdom. That is the reason a bridge was built across the ocean and the ocean was crossed. In this battle today, the wicked one has come within the range of my vision. Now that he has come within the range of my vision, he does not deserve to remain alive. The sight of Ravana is like the sight of a poisonous snake to me. O invincible ones! O bulls among the apes! Be reassured and watch this battle between me and Ravana. Seat yourselves on the peaks of mountains. In my battle today, let the three worlds, the gandharvas, the gods, the rishis and the charanas see Rama and witness what it means to be Rama. Today, I will perform deeds that the worlds, with their mobile and immobile objects, will always talk about, as long as the earth exists.'

Having said this, Rama controlled himself. In the battle, he struck Dashagriva with sharp arrows that were decorated in gold. Ravana showered down blazing iron arrows and clubs on Rama, the way a cloud pours down showers. Desiring to kill each other,

Rama and Ravana shot arrows at each other and these arrows created a tumultuous noise. Rama and Ravana's arrows were shattered and scattered. Their tips blazed in the sky and they then fell down on the ground. There was the great sound of Rama and Ravana slapping their palms against bowstrings. It was wonderful and all the creatures were terrified. The great-souled one[348] created a net through his showers of arrows and they issued from his bow, blazing. Afflicted by these and frightened, Ravana fled from the encounter, just as the wind drives away clouds.

Chapter 6(89)

He fought this tumultuous battle with the evil-souled Ravana. Shooting torrents of arrows, he addressed Sushena in these words. 'Because of Ravana's force, Lakshmana has fallen down on the ground. He is writhing like a serpent. O brave one! This is causing grief in me. This brave one is wet with blood and I love him more than my own life. Behold. My mind is so distressed that I am incapable of fighting. This brother of mine took pride in fighting and he possesses auspicious qualities. If he dies,[349] what happiness is there in my remaining alive? I am ashamed of my valour. The bow is falling down from my hand. My arrows are falling down. My sight is dimmed with tears. My terrible thoughts are increasing and I wish to die. I have seen my brother brought down by the evil-souled Ravana. I am overcome by great grief. I am lamenting and my senses are distracted. I have nothing to do with fighting. There is no purpose to my life and no use for Sita. I have seen my brother, Lakshmana, brought down in the battle, covered with dust. What will I do with the kingdom? What will I do with my life? I have nothing to do with this fight. In the field of battle, Lakshmana has been brought down and is lying down.'

[348] Rama.

[349] The text uses the expression 'attains panchatva'.

The brave Sushena comforted Rama and addressed him in these words. 'O mighty-armed one! Lakshmana, the extender of prosperity, is not dead. His mouth is not distorted. His face has not turned dark and dull. It can be seen that his face is extremely radiant and clear. The palms of his hands are like lotuses and his eyes are extremely clear. O lord of the earth! These are not the signs of someone who has lost his life. O brave one! O slayer of enemies! Do not grieve in vain. He is alive. Though he is lying down on the ground, with his body loose, these signs tell us that it is as if he is sleeping. O brave one! His heart is breathing and he is trembling repeatedly.' The one who knew about the use of words, Sushena, addressed Raghava in these words. Hanumat was near him and he then quickly addressed him in these words. 'O amiable one! Swiftly go to the mountain that has all the herbs. O brave one! The auspicious Jambavat has spoken to you about this earlier. Bring the herb that grows on its southern peak. There is the auspicious one named vishalyakarani, which cures all wounds. There are souvarnakarani, sanjivani and *sandhanakarani*.[350] Quickly go and bring these back. These are required to bring life back to the brave and great-souled Lakshmana.'

Thus addressed, Hanumat went to the mountain with the herbs with the speed of thought. However, the handsome one could not identify those great herbs. The infinitely energetic son of the wind god had a thought. 'Let me take the entire summit of the mountain and leave this place. If I go without taking vishalyakarani and waste time, there will be a sin. There may be a great calamity.' The immensely strong Hanumat thought in this way. Hanumat quickly seized and uprooted the summit of the mountain. 'O bull among the apes![351] I could not identify the herbs. Therefore, I have brought back the entire summit of the mountain.' Thus addressed, Sushena, the best among the apes, praised the son of the wind god. He pulled out the herbs. The supreme among apes crushed those herbs. Sushena, the extremely radiant one, applied these to Lakshmana,

[350] Referred to earlier as sandhani.

[351] On return, Hanumat is addressing Sushena. Because the Critical Edition has excised some shlokas, there is a break in continuity.

through the nose. Lakshmana, the slayer of enemy heroes, had been wounded. Inhaling these, he was cured of his wounds and relieved of his pain. He quickly arose from the ground. The apes saw that Lakshmana had stood up from the ground. Extremely delighted, they praised and worshipped Sushena.

Rama, the slayer of enemy heroes, told Lakshmana, 'Come. Come to me.' With tears flowing from his eyes, he embraced him, deep in his affection. Raghava embraced Soumitri and said, 'O brave one! It is good fortune that I see you again, having returned after dying. There would have been no purpose to my remaining alive, or to Sita, or to victory. Had you died, what would have been the purpose of remaining alive?' The great-souled Raghava told him this. With a weak and feeble voice, Lakshmana replied to him in these words. 'O one who has truth as his valour! You have taken a pledge earlier.[352] Having taken that pledge, you ought not to speak like someone who lacks spirit. O unblemished one! Virtuous ones do not take pledges that are falsified. The sign of greatness is to fulfil a pledge. O unblemished one! On my account, your army has faced a loss in hope. Fulfil your pledge now, by killing Ravana. If an enemy comes within the range of your arrows, he cannot remain alive, just as a giant elephant cannot escape from a roaring lion that has sharp teeth. I wish to quickly see the death of that evil-souled one. Before the sun has set, that task must be accomplished.'

Chapter 6(90)

Raghava heard the words that Lakshmana spoke. In front of the army, he shot terrible arrows towards Ravana. Dashagriva was astride his chariot and struck Rama with extremely terrible arrows that were like the vajra, like rain pouring down from a cloud. Rama controlled himself and used arrows that were like blazing fires, embellished with gold, to pierce Dashagriva in the encounter.

[352] Of killing Ravana.

Rama was on the ground, while the rakshasa was mounted on a chariot. The gods, the gandharvas and the danavas said that this was a fight among unequals. With the handsome and excellent chariot of the king of the gods, he descended from heaven, in front of Kakutstha.[353] The chariot was colourfully made out of gold and was decorated with hundreds of bells. It was like the rising sun and the kubara was made out of lapis lazuli. There were well-trained horses with golden harnesses and the whips were white. The horses were decorated in nets of gold that resembled the sun. There was a golden standard on a pole. Stationed on a chariot, with the goad in his hand, Matali, the charioteer of the one with one thousand eyes, joined his hands in salutation and addressed Rama in these words. 'O Kakutstha! For your victory, the one with the one thousand eyes has sent this chariot. O great-spirited one! O prosperous one! O destroyer of enemies! He has given it to you. This is Indra's great bow and this armour is like the fire. These arrows are like the sun and this javelin is sparkling and sharp. O brave one! Mount this chariot and slay the rakshasa Ravana, like the great Indra did to the danavas. O Rama! I will be your charioteer.' Thus addressed, Rama greeted him and circumambulated the chariot. He mounted it and was radiant, pervading the worlds with his prosperity.

There was an extraordinary battle between the mighty-armed Rama and the rakshasa Ravana, a duel that made the body hair stand up. Raghava was supreme in the knowledge of weapons. He destroyed the gandharvastra of the king of the rakshasas with his gandharvastra, divine weapons with his divine weapons. The roamer in the night, the lord of the rakshasas, became greatly angry and again shot the extremely terrible rakshasa weapon. Arrows embellished in gold were released from Ravana's bow. They turned into extremely virulent serpents and approached Kakutstha. Their mouths blazed. They vomited blazing fires from their mouths. Terrible and with mouths gaping, they approached Rama. They were like Vasuki to the touch. They were blazing serpents, extremely

[353] Because of excision of shlokas, the Critical Edition breaks the continuity. The 'he' is Matali, Indra's charioteer, who has been asked by Indra to bring Indra's chariot to Rama and act as Rama's charioteer.

poisonous. They covered all the directions and the sub-directions. In the battle, Rama saw that those serpents were descending. He applied the extremely terrible Garuda weapon. Gold-tufted and as resplendent as the fire, it was released from Raghava's bow. It turned into golden eagles, the enemies of serpents, and roamed around. They destroyed all those arrows that were in the form of extremely swift serpents. The arrows used by Rama were like eagles, but could assume any form at will. When his weapon was countered, Ravana, the lord of the rakshasas, became angry. He showered down extremely terrible torrents of arrows on Rama. He afflicted Rama, the performer of unblemished deeds, with thousands of arrows and used storms of arrows to pierce Matali. Ravana brought down the seat on the chariot and the chariot's standard. He also struck Indra's horses with nets of arrows. On seeing Rama afflicted, the gods, the gandharvas, the danavas, the charanas, the siddhas and the supreme rishis were distressed. The Indras among the apes and Vibhishana were also pained, on seeing that the moon that was Rama being devoured by the Rahu that was Ravana. The *prajapatya* nakshatra Rohini is loved by the moon.[354] It was as if it had been attacked by Budha,[355] signifying danger to all subjects. The ocean seemed to be on fire and its waves were circled in smoke. It seemed to angrily leap up and touch the sky. The rays of the sun were dimmed and an excellent man, with the complexion of a weapon, could be seen there, holding a headless torso on his lap and touched by a comet. The nakshatra Vishakha, presided over by the divinities Indra and Agni and the nakshatra of the Kosalas, could be seen in the sky, attacked by Angaraka.[356] The one with ten heads and twenty arms seized his bow and arrow. Dashagriva could be seen, resembling Mount Mainaka. Rama was restrained by the rakshasa Dashagriva and could not affix his arrows in the field of battle. He angrily knit his brows and his eyes turned red. He was filled with great rage, as if he would burn down with his eyes.

[354] The older name for Rohini used to be Prajapati. As such, Rohini is presided over by Prajapati.

[355] Mercury.

[356] Angaraka is Mangala (Mars).

Chapter 6(91)

Seeing that the intelligent Rama was enraged, all the beings were terrified and the earth trembled. The mountains, with their lions and tigers, quaked. The trees swayed. The ocean, the lord of the rivers, was agitated. Dense clouds thundered in the sky in harsh tones. Evil portents roared and manifested themselves in all the directions. On seeing that Rama was greatly angry, there were terrible omens. All the beings were terrified and Ravana was scared. The gods astride their vimanas, the gandharvas, the giant serpents, the rishis, the danavas, the daityas and the eagles roaming around in the sky witnessed the battle, which was like that of the world getting destroyed. Using many kinds of terrible weapons, those two brave ones fought against each other. All the gods and the asuras assembled in personified forms to witness the great encounter. Delighted, they spoke the following words. The asuras present said, 'Victory to Dashagriva.' The gods repeatedly said, 'Victory to Rama.'

At that time, Ravana was filled with rage. Desiring to strike Raghava, the evil-souled one picked up a great weapon. Its essence was as hard as the vajra. It emitted a loud roar and was capable of scorching all enemies. It was as heavy as the summit of a mountain and it was extremely terrible to behold. Its sharp tip was filled with smoke and it was like the fire that engulfs at the end of a yuga. He seized this extremely terrible weapon, which even Death found difficult to approach. In its capacity to tear and shatter, it caused fear to all creatures. In his anger, Ravana seized this blazing spear. Extremely angry, the valiant one seized the spear in the middle. In the battle, he was surrounded by an army of brave rakshasas. Raising it in the battle, the one who was gigantic in size roared horribly, delighting his own soldiers. He was angry and his eyes were red. The earth, the sky, the directions and the sub-directions trembled at the terrible noise emitted by the Indra among the rakshasas. The evil-souled one emitted an extremely loud roar. All the creatures were terrified and the ocean was agitated. The extremely valiant Ravana seized that giant spear. He emitted an extremely loud roar and addressed Rama in these harsh words. 'O Rama! This spear has an essence like that of the vajra. I have angrily raised it up. It will now take away your life, since you sought to help your brother. In front of the armies, you have slain brave rakshasas. You pride yourself in fighting. Today, I will swiftly kill you and balance affairs. O Raghava! Stay there now. I will kill you with this spear.' Having said this, the lord of the rakshasas hurled the spear. As it descended, Raghava countered it with a storm of arrows, just as Vasava counters a fire of destruction that has arisen with a flood of water. Ravana's giant spear was scorched by the arrows that emerged from Rama's bow, just as insects are by a fire. However, in the sky, those arrows touched the spear and were shattered and reduced to ashes. At this, Raghava was filled with rage. Matali had brought a javelin constructed by Vasava. Extremely angry, Raghava, the descendant of the Raghu lineage, seized this. The powerful one raised it up and the javelin resounded to the sound of bells. It blazed in the sky, like a dazzling meteor at the end of a yuga. He flung this and the spear of the Indra among the rakshasas fell down. The giant spear was shattered by the javelin and fell down, robbed of its brilliance. Rama then used sharp arrows that were extremely forceful, like the vajra, to pierce his extremely swift steeds. He pierced Ravana in the chest with sharp arrows. Raghava also struck him in the forehead with three excellent arrows. The Indra among the rakshasas was mangled all over his limbs with these arrows and blood started to flow from his body. He was like a blossoming ashoka amidst other trees. His body was pierced by Rama's arrows. The Indra among the roamers in the night was wet with blood all over his body. In the midst of that assembly, he was filled with regret. He was filled with extremely great rage.

Chapter 6(92)

Ravana prided himself on fighting. But he was angry that he had been worsted by Kakutstha in the battle. He was filled with great rage. With his eyes blazing, the valiant one angrily seized his bow. In the great battle, he angrily attacked Raghava. Like a cloud showering down from the sky, Ravana rained down hundreds of torrents of arrows on Raghava, like a pond being filled up. In the battle, Kakutstha was covered with nets of arrows released from the bow. However, like an immobile large mountain, he did not tremble. Stationed in the battle, he used his arrows to counter those nets of arrows. The valiant one received them, as if they were the rays of the sun. The great-souled roamer in the night used the dexterity of his hands and angrily struck Raghava in the chest with thousands of arrows. In the battle, Lakshmana's elder brother was covered with blood. He was seen to be like a giant and blossoming kimshuka tree in the forest. The extremely energetic Kakutstha was angry at having been struck by these arrows. As radiant as the sun that arises at the end of a yuga, he grasped arrows. Both Rama and Ravana were extremely angry. In the battle, they were unable to see each other, because it was dark with arrows.

The brave Rama, Dasharatha's son, was filled with rage. He laughed and addressed Ravana in these harsh words. 'O worst among the rakshasas! When I did not know, you abducted my helpless wife from Janasthana. Therefore, you are hardly brave. In the great forest, she was without me and was miserable. You abducted her forcibly. Yet, you consider yourself to be brave. O brave one![357] You oppressed a woman, someone else's wife, when she was without a protector. You committed the deed of a coward. Yet, you consider yourself to be brave. You broke rules. You are shameless. You possess no character. In your insolence, you invited death. Yet, you consider yourself to be brave. As the brother of the lord of treasures, you are indeed full of bravery and strength. The deed that you committed is indeed praiseworthy. It is full of fame and greatness. Your insolent act was contemptible and vile. Because of what you did, you will now reap the great fruits. O evil-minded one! You consider yourself to be brave. Despite having abducted Sita like a thief, you have no shame. Had you used your strength

[357] In sarcasm.

to oppress Sita in my presence, you would have been slain with my arrows at that very instant and seen your brother, Khara. O evil-souled one! It is good fortune that you have now come within the range of my vision. Today, I will use sharp arrows to convey you to Yama's abode. Today, my arrows will sever your head, with those radiant earrings. It will lie down in the dust of the battle field, dragged around by predatory creatures. O Ravana! Your chest will be flung down on the ground and vultures will descend on it. They will drink the blood that flows out from the wounds that my arrows will create. My arrows will mangle you today. You will lose your life and fall down. Like Garuda against serpents, birds will drag out your entrails.' The brave Rama, the slayer of enemies, said this. The Indra among rakshasas was near him and he showered down arrows on him. Rama desired to slay his enemy in the battle and his valour, strength, delight and strength of weapons doubled. All kinds of weapons manifested themselves before him. The immensely energetic one was delighted and the dexterity of his hands increased. He recognized these auspicious signs that manifested themselves before him. Rama struck the rakshasa Ravana yet again.

Dashagriva was struck by a storm of boulders from the apes and the shower of Raghava's arrows. His heart was in a whirl. He could not use his weapons, stretch his bow or use his valour to counter this. His inner soul was suffering. He did hurl arrows and many kinds of weapons. However, because the time of his death had arrived, these did not serve any purpose in the battle. His charioteer saw that his leader was in such a state on the chariot. He wasn't scared, but gently withdrew the chariot from the battle.

Chapter 6(93)

Urged by the strength of Death, he was confused and angry. His eyes red with rage, Ravana spoke to the charioteer. 'O one with evil intelligence! Am I inferior in valour? Am I incapable? Am I bereft of manliness? Am I a coward? Am I light in spirit?

Am I devoid of energy? Has maya deserted me? Have my weapons been cast away? You are resorting to your own intelligence and are showing me disrespect. Why are you slighting me? Why are you ignoring what I desire? In the sight of the enemy, you have brought my chariot away. O ignoble one! Over a long period of time, I have earned fame, valour, energy and trust. Because of you, these have now been destroyed. My enemy is famous for his valour and his valour causes delight. He saw that I had come to fight with him. However, you have made me a coward. O evil-minded one! In your confusion, you withdrew this chariot. This truth is beyond debate, you have been bribed by the enemy. A well-wisher who desires to ensure what is beneficial does not act in this way. What you have done is just like what an enemy would do. Swiftly take this chariot back, before my enemy withdraws. If you have been with me and if you remember my qualities, do that.'

The charioteer had his welfare in mind, though he had been harshly addressed by a foolish person. He entreated Ravana in these beneficial words. 'I am not a coward. I am not stupid. Nor have I been bribed by the enemy. I am not mad. I am not without affection. Nor have I forgotten the good deeds you have done to me. I desired your welfare and sought to protect your fame. My mind was full of affection towards you. That is why I did something agreeable in the guise of the disagreeable. O great king! I am devoted to ensuring your pleasure. Therefore, you should not reprimand my faults, as if by someone who is light and ignoble. Listen to the reason why I withdrew the chariot from the battle, as one would from the force of water in a river. Having performed great deeds in the battle, I could understand that you were exhausted. O brave one! I take no delight in preventing you from taking on a confrontation. These steeds yoked to the chariot were tired from bearing the chariot along. They were suffering, like cows during the summer when they are lashed by rain. Many kinds of portents presented themselves before us. As I circled around, I noticed all these different signs of danger. One must know about the time and the place, the good and the bad signs and the misery, delight, exhaustion, strengths and weaknesses of the warrior on the chariot. One must know about the nature of the ground—low, plain or uneven. One must know about the time of battle and the signs of weakness in the enemy. A person who wishes well for the warrior in the chariot must know about driving forward, remaining in one place and withdrawing and also everything about the warrior in the chariot. I did that so that you could rest and so could the horses yoked to the chariot and so that your terrible exhaustion might be reduced. O brave one! I did not withdraw the chariot on my own volition. O lord! Everything that I did is because I am full of affection towards my master. O slayer of enemies! Command me properly and tell me. O brave one! With a relieved mind, I will act accordingly.'

Ravana was satisfied at the words of the charioteer. He praised him in many ways. Since he loved fighting, he said, 'O charioteer! Swiftly drive my chariot in Raghava's direction. Ravana does not retreat without killing the enemy in the battle.' Ravana, the lord of the rakshasas, said this. Satisfied, he gave him an auspicious and excellent ornament for the hand. Urged by Ravana's words, the charioteer quickly goaded the horses. In a short while, the great chariot of the Indra among the rakshasas was stationed in front of Rama.

Chapter 6(94)

The king of men saw the chariot of the king of the rakshasas return suddenly. It possessed a huge standard and roared. It was yoked to black horses and was terrible in its radiance. It was like Indra's weapon[358] in the clouds, with flags of lightning, and was stocked with weapons. He[359] showered down arrows, like a cloud pouring down rain. He[360] saw his enemy descend on a chariot that was like a cloud. It possessed a clatter like that of the vajra shattering a mountain. Rama spoke to Matali, the charioteer of the

[358] The rainbow.

[359] Ravana.

[360] Rama.

one with the thousand eyes. 'O Matali! Look at the enraged enemy descending on his chariot. He is again descending with great force, from left to right.[361] It is my view that he has made up his mind to kill himself in the battle. Therefore, be attentive and proceed in the direction of the enemy's chariot. I wish to destroy it, just as a wind drives away clouds that have arisen. Do not be distracted. Do not be frightened. Let your grasp and sight be firm. Control the reins and the goad and drive the chariot quickly. You are used to driving Purandara's chariot and it is not desired that I should instruct you. I wish to fight single-mindedly. Therefore, I am reminding you, not teaching you.' Matali was satisfied with Rama's words. The excellent charioteer of the gods drove the chariot. He kept Ravana's great chariot on the left. The dust raised from the wheels of the chariot made Ravana quaver.

Dashagriva was angry and his coppery red eyes dilated. Rama was facing his chariot and he showered him with arrows. Rama tolerated this oppression, using his patience to overcome the rage. In the battle, he grasped Indra's bow, which possessed an extremely great force. In the great battle, they wished to kill each other. Those two extremely energetic ones used arrows that were as resplendent as the sun's rays and oppressed each other. Facing each other, they were like two proud lions. Desiring Ravana's destruction, the gods, the gandharvas, the siddhas and the supreme rishis gathered to witness the duel. Terrible portents that made the body hair rise up arose. They signified Ravana's destruction and Raghava's victory. The gods showered down blood on Ravana's chariot. Fierce winds circled around in a counterclockwise direction. A large flock of vultures roamed around in the sky. Wherever the chariot[362] proceeded, they accompanied it. Resembling a red hibiscus flower,[363] evening shrouded Lanka. But the ground was seen to blaze, as if it was day. Accompanied by storms, giant meteors fell down, with a loud noise. Since this signified harm to Ravana, the rakshasas were distressed. Wherever Ravana was, the earth trembled. The

[361] Counterclockwise, therefore, inauspicious.

[362] Ravana's chariot.

[363] The *japa* flower.

arms of rakshasas who tried to strike were seized.[364] Coppery, yellow, dark and white rays were seen to descend from the sun on Ravana's limbs, like minerals flowing from a mountain. Vultures followed him and vomited flames from their mouths. Facing him and looking towards him, terrified jackals howled in inauspicious tones. In the battle, a perverse wind started to blow and raised dust, so that the sight of the king of the rakshasas became unclear. Though there were no sounds from the clouds, in every direction, Indra's thunder descended on the soldiers, making a terrible noise that was impossible to tolerate. All the directions and sub-directions were enveloped in darkness. There was a shower of dust and it became extremely difficult to see the sky. Hundreds of sarika birds[365] quarrelled horribly with one another and fell down on his chariot, making a hideous sound and shrieking in terrible voices. The horses showered sparks from their loins and incessant drops of water from their eyes. In this way, there were many kinds of fearful portents, signifying Ravana's terrible destruction. For Rama, in every direction, pleasant and auspicious omens manifested themselves, indicating his victory. Raghava knew about the nature of portents. He saw the portents that manifested themselves in the field of battle and was filled with delight. In the battle, he exhibited greater valour and supreme conduct.

Chapter 6(95)

There was an extremely cruel and extremely great duel in the battle between Rama and Ravana then and it was fearful to all creatures. The soldiers of the rakshasas and the large army of the apes seized weapons. But they stationed themselves and did not move.[366] As they watched the powerful man and rakshasa engage with each other, all their hearts were filled with great wonder. They

[364] That is, they were rendered immobile.

[365] A sarika bird is a kind of thrush, *Turdus salica*.

[366] They were spectators to the duel.

anxiously held many weapons in their hands. But as they witnessed the battle, their minds were filled with amazement and they did not strike each other. The eyes of Ravana's rakshasas and Raghava's apes were filled with amazement. The soldiers were like paintings. Raghava and Ravana saw those portents. They were firm in their intolerance and made up their minds to fight fearlessly. Kakutstha was sure he would win. Ravana was certain he would die. They displayed their fortitude and all their spirit in that battle.

The valiant Dashagriva was filled with rage. Raghava was on his chariot and he shot his arrows in the direction of his standard. Those arrows failed to reach the standard on Purandara's chariot. They touched the pole of the chariot and fell down on the ground. The valiant Rama drew his bow angrily. He made up his mind to strike back at every strike. He shot a sharp arrow in the direction of Ravana's standard. It was like a huge serpent and blazed in its own energy. The arrow pierced Dashagriva's standard and penetrated the ground. It severed the standard on Ravana's chariot and brought it down on the ground. The extremely strong Ravana saw that his standard had been destroyed. In the battle, because of the fire of his rage, he seemed to blaze. Overcome with anger, he seemed to vomit out large showers of arrows. Ravana pierced Rama's divine horses with arrows. Though pierced, the horses did not lose their feet. They were firm in their hearts and it was as if they had been struck with the stalks of lotuses. Ravana saw that the horses were not frightened. Extremely angry, he showered down arrows again. Using his maya, he brought down showers of arrows that were in the form of clubs, maces, chakras, bludgeons, summits of mountains, trees, spears and battleaxes. With no exhaustion in his heart, he shot thousands of arrows. It was terrible and tumultuous and generated fear. There was a horrible echo. In that battle, there were many great weapons that were invincible. Letting Raghava's chariot be, in every direction, Dashagriva, whose mind had been made up about his destruction, quickly shot continuous arrows on the army of the apes. Kakutstha saw that in the battle, his enemy, Ravana, was covering everything. Laughingly, he affixed sharp arrows. In the encounter, he shot hundreds and thousands of arrows. On seeing this, Ravana incessantly covered the sky with his own arrows. Both of them showered down radiant arrows. Consequently, there seemed to be a second dazzling sky that was made out of arrows alone. No arrow missed the target. Having pierced, no arrow failed in its purpose. In that battle, Rama and Ravana shot arrows. They incessantly fought against each other, to the left and to the right. They shot torrents of arrows and no space was left in the sky. Rama struck Ravana's horses. Ravana struck Rama's horses. They struck each other and countered what the other one had done.

Chapter 6(96)

In that battle, Rama and Ravana fought. On witnessing this, all the creatures were astounded in their hearts. They were engaged in killing each other and were terrible in form. In the encounter, they afflicted each other from their excellent chariots. The chariots moved in different modes—circular, straight, advancing and retreating. The charioteers, who knew about the techniques charioteers should follow, exhibited many kinds of movements. Rama wounded Ravana and Ravana wounded Rama. They used speed in forward movements and also used speed in rearward movements. From those two excellent chariots, they showered down nets of arrows. They roamed around in that battle, like clouds showering down rain on earth. They exhibited many kinds of movements in that encounter. They stood there again, facing each other. The carriage of one chariot met the carriage of the other. The mouth of one horse faced the mouth of another.[367] As they stood there, flags faced flags. With four sharp and blazing arrows shot from his bow, Rama made Ravana's four horses retreat. When his horses were forced to retreat, the roamer in the night was filled with rage and shot sharp arrows towards Raghava. Raghava was severely pierced by the strong Dashagriva. But there was no discomfiture in him, nor

[367] That is, the adversary's horse.

was he pained. The roamer in the night again shot arrows towards the charioteer of the one who holds the vajra in his hand and these made a noise like the clap of thunder. Those immensely forceful arrows descended on Matali's body. However, they did not cause the slightest bit of confusion or pain. Raghava was angry at this oppression of Matali, as if he himself had suffered. He shot a net of arrows and his enemy retreated. His enemy was on his chariot and the brave Raghava shot twenty, thirty, sixty, hundreds and thousands of arrows. The seven oceans were agitated by the sound of clubs, maces and bludgeons and the wind created by the tufts of the arrows. The residents of the ocean, in the nether regions of patala, were agitated. All the thousands of danavas and serpents were distressed. The entire earth, with its mountains, forests and groves, trembled. The sun lost its radiance and the wind did not blow.

All the gods, the gandharvas, the siddhas, the supreme rishis, the kinnaras and the giant serpents were worried. They said, 'May there be safety to cattle and brahmanas. May the worlds remain till eternity. In this battle, may Raghava be victorious over Ravana, the lord of the rakshasas.' The mighty-armed extender of the deeds of the Raghu lineage became angry. Rama affixed a kshura arrow, that was like virulent poison, to his bow. Ravana's handsome head blazed, with its earrings. While the three worlds looked on, he severed the head and it fell down on the ground. However, Ravana sprouted another head that was exactly similar. Rama, who was swift in action, became angry. Acting with a quick hand, he affixed an arrow and severed this second head of Ravana's. However, no sooner was this head severed, than another one was seen. Rama used arrows that were like the vajra to sever this too. In this way, one hundred heads that were equally radiant were severed. No signs were seen about Ravana's end, or his life being over. The brave extender of Kousalya's delight was accomplished in all weapons. Having used many arrows, Raghava started to think. 'All these arrows have killed Maricha, Khara, Dushana, Viradha in the Krouncha forest and Kabandha in the Dandaka forest. In this encounter, what is the reason for their being countered by Ravana, evil in his intelligence?'

While remaining attentive in the encounter, Raghava thought in this way and showered down floods of arrows on Ravana's chest. On his chariot, Ravana, the lord of the rakshasas, was also angry. In the battle, he struck Rama back, showering down maces and clubs. The gods, the danavas, the yakshas, the pishachas, the serpents and the rakshasas witnessed this great encounter that continued through the night. During night, day, *muhurta* or *kshana*,[368] there was no break in the battle between Rama and Ravana.

Chapter 6(97)

At this, Matali reminded Raghava. 'O brave one! Why are you acting towards him as if you don't know what is to be done? O lord! To kill him, use the grandfather's weapon. The time for his destruction, which the gods spoke about, has come now.' Rama was reminded by Matali's words. He seized a blazing arrow that sighed like a serpent. In the battle, the valiant one used an invincible and great arrow given by Brahma, and which had been given to him earlier by the illustrious rishi Agastya. For Indra's sake, the infinitely energetic Brahma had fashioned this earlier. Earlier, he had given it to the lord of the gods, when he had desired to conquer the three worlds. The wind was in its feathers, the fire and the sun were in its points. Its body was made out of space. It was as heavy as Meru and Mandara. Its form blazed. It was well tufted and decorated with gold. Its energy had been fashioned out of all the elements and it was like the sun in its radiance. It was like the smoking fire of destruction. It was as radiant as a venomous serpent. It was swift in action and could shatter hordes of men, elephants and horses. It could shatter gates, barricades and mountains. Many kinds of blood were smeared on its limbs. Extremely terrible, it was smeared with fat. Its essence was as firm as the vajra. It emitted a loud

[368] Kshana is a measurement of time, with differing interpretations. A second or an instant is accurate enough. Muhurta is forty-eight minutes.

roar. It could shatter many assemblies. It was terrible and terrified everyone. It sighed like a serpent. It was fearful, with Yama's form. In a battle, it always provided food to herons, vultures, cranes, herds of jackals and rakshasas. It brought delight to the Indras among the apes and led to lassitude among the rakshasas. It was colourful and had many kinds of swift feathers, including those of Garuda. This was an excellent arrow that could destroy the fear of the worlds and of the Ikshvakus. It robbed the enemy of his deeds and caused delight to one's own self.

The immensely strong Rama chanted mantras over this great arrow, following the rites mentioned in the Vedas. The powerful one affixed it to his bow. Extremely angry, he stretched his terrible bow and attentively, shot this arrow, which could shatter the inner organs, towards Ravana. It was as invincible as the vajra and was released from an arm that was as strong as the vajra. It was as irresistible as Death and descended on Ravana's chest. The arrow, which could bring an end to the body, was released with great force. It shattered the evil-souled Ravana's heart. The forceful arrow could bring an end to life. It took away Ravana's life, and smeared with blood, penetrated the ground. Having killed Ravana, the arrow had a form that was wet with blood. Having performed its task, it quietly returned to the quiver. His breath of life was separated from his body and he fell down. The bow and arrows also fell down from his hand. The immensely radiant Indra among the nairittas, whose force was terrible, lost his life. He fell down on the ground from his chariot, like Vritra when he was slain by the vajra.

On seeing that he had fallen down on the ground, the remaining roamers in the night were terrified by fear. With their protector killed, they fled in different directions. On seeing that Dashagriva had been killed and that Raghava was victorious, the apes, who fought with trees, roared and attacked them. They were afflicted and routed by the apes. In their fear, they rushed towards Lanka. Their refuge had been killed. They were in a pitiable state and their faces were full of tears. Delighted and desiring victory, the apes roared. They proclaimed Raghava's victory and Ravana's death.

In the firmament, the pleasant drums of the gods were sounded. A wind that was extremely pleasant, with the scent of divine fragrances, started to blow. Lovely flowers were showered down from the sky and descended on the ground. Since he had performed an extremely difficult deed, they were showered down on Raghava's chariot. Praises of Raghava were heard in the sky. The great-souled gods uttered words of acclaim. At the terrible Ravana, who caused fear to all the worlds, being killed, the gods and the charanas were filled with great joy. Raghava was delighted at having been able to kill the bull among the rakshasas and having accomplished the desires of Sugriva and the immensely strong Angada. The storm was pacified. The directions were peaceful and the sky sparkled. The earth did not tremble and there was no strong wind. The sun's radiance became steady. Delighted at Raghava's victory, Sugriva, Vibhishana, the other well-wishers and Lakshmana surrounded the charming one. Following the rites, they worshipped him. The one who was steadfast in his pledge had killed the enemy. Surrounded by his own forces, he dazzled in the field of battle. The immensely energetic delight of the king of the Raghu lineage[369] was surrounded by them, like Indra by large numbers of gods.

Chapter 6(98)

On seeing that Ravana had been killed by the great-souled Raghava, the rakshasis who were in the inner quarters were afflicted by grief and rushed out.[370] Though they were restrained by many, they writhed around in the dust on the ground. Afflicted by sorrow, their hair was dishevelled. They were like cows, when the calves had been killed. With the rakshasas, they emerged from the northern gate. They entered the terrible field of battle and searched for their slain husbands. They lamented everywhere, 'Alas, noble

[369] Meaning Dasharatha.

[370] There were Ravana's wives and there were the wives of other rakshasas too.

one! Alas, protector!' They roamed amidst the headless torsos, on the ground that was a mire of blood. They were crushed with sorrow because of their husbands. Tears flowed from their eyes. They shrieked and screamed like female elephants, when the leaders of the herd had been killed.

They saw the immensely radiant Ravana lying down on the ground. He was gigantic in size and great in bravery. He was like a mass of dark collyrium. They suddenly saw their husband lying down on the ground, in the dust of the battle. Like severed forest creepers, they fell down on his body. One embraced him with a great deal of respect, another wept. One embraced his feet, another clung to his neck. Another raised her hands up and writhed around on the ground. On seeing the face of the slain one, another was filled with confusion. One took up his head on her lap, another looked at his face and cried. Like dew on a lotus flower, another wiped his face with her tears. They suffered on seeing their husband, Ravana, slain and lying down on the ground. They shrieked in many ways. Overcome by grief, they lamented repeatedly. 'He terrified Shakra. He terrified Yama. He took Pushpaka away from King Vaishravana. In battles, he created great fear for gandharvas, rishis and the great-souled gods. Such a person is lying down, killed in the battle. He knew no fear from asuras, gods or serpents. But he faced fear from a human. He could not be killed by the gods, the danavas or the rakshasas. But he is lying down, slain in the battle by a human on foot. The gods, the yakshas and the asuras were incapable of killing him. How could he have obtained his death at the hands of a mortal, limited in spirit?' In this way, the women wept and lamented. Afflicted by sorrow, they lamented again and again. 'You did not listen to the well-wishers, who always spoke about what was beneficial for you. With you killed, we have also been brought down. Your brother, Vibhishana, spoke desirable and beneficial words to you. However, because of your confusion and because you desired your own death, you reprimanded him in harsh words. Had you returned Sita Maithilee to Rama, this terrible catastrophe wouldn't have occurred today. Our great foundation has been struck down. Had you followed your brother's wishes, Rama would have been one of our friends. All of us wouldn't have become widows and the desires of the enemy wouldn't have been fulfilled. You were repeatedly cruel towards Sita and used force to imprison her. The rakshasas, you and we—all three have been brought down in the same way. O bull among rakshasas! You acted out of your own desire, but that wasn't desirable. Everything is driven by destiny. Destiny decides the killer and the killed. O mighty-armed one! In the battle, the destruction of the apes, of the rakshasas and of you has been brought about because of the forces of destiny. In this world, when the results of destiny arise, artha, kama, valour or commands are incapable of resisting them.' Miserable, the wives of the lord of the rakshasas lamented in this way. With tears flowing from their eyes, they were as grief-stricken as female curlews.

Chapter 6(99)

The wives of the rakshasa lamented in this way. The eldest and beloved wife looked miserably at her husband. She saw that Dashagriva had been killed by Rama, whose deeds were unthinkable. Mandodari piteously lamented about her husband. 'O mighty-armed one! You were known as Vaishravana's younger brother. When you were angry, even Purandara was scared of standing before you. Anxious at hearing your name, the rishis, the gods of the earth, the illustrious gandharvas and the charanas fled in different directions. O king! O bull among rakshasas! Rama, a mere human, has vanquished you in the battle. Why are you not ashamed at this? Full of prosperity and valour, you invaded the three worlds. You could not be resisted. Yet, you have been slain by a man wandering around in the forest. Assuming any form at will, you roamed around in the dominion of men. In a battle, you should not have come about your destruction at the hands of Rama. In the field of battle, I do not believe that Rama performed this act. Nor do I think he attacked and invaded you in every possible way. In earlier times, you conquered your senses and vanquished the three worlds. As remembrance of that, the senses have defeated you now. In Rama's form, Vasava himself may have come to destroy your maya beyond any possible doubt. As soon as your brother Khara, surrounded by many rakshasas, was killed in Janasthana, it was evident that he was no mere human. Even the gods find it extremely difficult to penetrate the city of Lanka. As soon as Hanumat used his valour to enter, we were distressed. I told you not to engage in an enmity with Raghava. But since you did not heed that, this evil has come upon us. O bull among the rakshasas! For the destruction of your prosperity, your body and your own relatives, a sudden desire for Sita came upon you. O evil-minded one! She is superior to Arundhati[371] and Rohini. You oppressed the respected one. This was not an act that was worthy of you. Maithilee is no match for me in nobility of birth, beauty or gentleness. But because of your confusion, you did not comprehend whether she was superior to me or equal to me. In every way, among all beings, there is a reason for death. As for you, Maithilee is the reason for your death. Maithilee will find pleasure with Rama, freed from grief. I am limited in fortune. That is the reason I am immersed in this terrible ocean of grief. I have sported with you in Kailasa, Mandara, Meru and the grove of Chaitraratha, in beautiful vimanas that were unmatched in their prosperity. Clad in colourful garlands and garments, I have seen many regions. O brave one! With your death, I am now deprived of all those objects of pleasure. O immensely fortunate one! My brother-in-law[372] speaks the truth and what he said was true. "This one[373] has presented herself for the destruction of the foremost among the rakshasas. Desire and anger have arisen and addiction to them will bring about hardship." You have brought about all this. The lineage of the rakshasas is without a protector. You were famous for your strength and manliness and I should not grieve over you. But because of my feminine nature, my mind is whirling around in pity. You have accepted your good deeds and bad deeds and have attained your own destination. Since I am

[371] Vasishtha's wife.

[372] Vibhishana.

[373] Sita.

miserable at being separated from you, I am grieving about myself. You possess the complexion of a dark cloud. You are attired in yellow garments. You wear auspicious armlets. Why are you lying down, covered in blood, with your entire body stretched out? I am afflicted by grief. You seem to be asleep. Why are you not replying to me? You were immensely valiant and accomplished. You did not run away from an encounter. I am the granddaughter of a yatudhana.[374] Why are you not replying to me? Your club is as radiant as the sun and you used it to oppress enemies in battles. It is like the vajra of the wielder of the vajra and you always revered it. It is polished with nets of gold and in battles, you have struck enemies with this. Arrows have shattered it into a thousand fragments and they are scattered around. Shame on my heart. It is not shattering into a thousand fragments. You are dead and the consequence is that I am afflicted by grief.'

At this time, Rama spoke to Vibhishana. 'Restrain the women and perform funeral rites for your brother.' Having comforted them, Vibhishana addressed Rama in the following words. He knew about dharma and he used his intelligence to think about it. His beneficial words were full of dharma and artha. Following what Rama had said, he replied in these words. 'He abandoned the vows of dharma. He was cruel. He was violent and followed falsehood. He was attracted to the wives of others. I should not perform funeral rites for him. He was an enemy in the form of a brother. He was always engaged in what was injurious. Though the respect due to a senior deserves worship, Ravana does not deserve to be worshipped. O Rama! Men on earth will refer to me as someone cruel. However, on hearing about all his qualities, they will subsequently say that I performed a good deed.' On hearing this, Rama, supreme among the upholders of dharma, was greatly delighted. The one who knew about words and was eloquent in the use of words addressed Vibhishana in these words. 'I have obtained victory because of your powers. Therefore, I must do what is agreeable to you. O lord of the rakshasas! You must certainly pardon the words that I use.

[374] Mandodari's grandfather was Sumali.

The roamer in the night followed adharma and falsehood. He was attached to desire. However, he was always energetic, strong and brave in battles. It has been heard that he could not be defeated by the gods, with Shatakratu at the forefront. The great-souled Ravana was full of strength and he made the worlds scream. With death, enmity ends and we no longer have any need for that. Therefore, let his funeral rites be performed. He belongs to me, just as he does to you. O mighty-armed one! Following the prescribed ordinances, his funeral rites should be performed by you. You will then obtain great dharma and fame.'

Hearing Raghava's words, Vibhishana hurried. He arranged for the proper funeral rites for Ravana. Following the ordinances, Vibhishana applied fire. He repeatedly entreated the women and comforted them. With all the rakshasis, Vibhishana entered.[375] He then approached Rama's presence and stood there humbly. With his soldiers and Sugriva and Lakshmana, Rama was delighted that his enemy had been killed, just as Vritra had been by Shatakratu.

Chapter 6(100)

On witnessing Ravana's death, the gods, the gandharvas and the danavas conversed about this auspicious account and left on their respective vimanas. Conversing about the terrible Ravana's death, Raghava's valour, the excellent fight put by the apes, Sugriva's counsel and the love and valour of Soumitri Lakshmana, those immensely fortunate ones happily returned to wherever they had come from. Raghava's divine chariot had been given by Indra and was as radiant as the fire. The mighty-armed one worshipped Matali and gave him leave to return with that. Having obtained Raghava's permission, Matali, Shakra's charioteer, ascended that divine chariot and ascended to heaven. When he ascended to heaven on that chariot, Raghava, supreme among warriors, was extremely

[375] The city of Lanka.

delighted and embraced Sugriva. He embraced Sugriva and was greeted by Lakshmana. Worshipped by the best among the apes, he went to the place where the forces were camped.

Soumitri Lakshmana, full of spirit and blazing in energy, was near him. Rama spoke to him. 'O amiable one! Vibhishana must be consecrated in Lanka. He is devoted and faithful and has done good deeds for me. Though he is Ravana's younger brother, this is my supreme desire. O amiable one! Let us see Vibhishana consecrated in Lanka.' Soumitri was thus addressed by the great-souled Raghava. He happily agreed and brought a golden pot. In the midst of the rakshasas in Lanka, following Rama's command, Soumitri used that golden pot to consecrate Vibhishana. The one with dharma in his soul consecrated Vibhishana, who was pure in his soul. On seeing that Vibhishana, Indra among rakshasas, had been consecrated in Lanka, the advisers[376] and the rakshasas who were devoted to him rejoiced. With Lakshmana, Raghava was filled with great delight. Granted by Rama, Vibhishana obtained that great kingdom. Having comforted the ordinary people, he came to Rama. Happy in their minds and content, the roamers in the night who were residents of the city brought and offered him[377] unbroken grain,[378] sweetmeats[379] and divine parched grain.[380] The invincible and valiant one accepted all these auspicious objects and offered them to Raghava and Lakshmana. Rama saw that Vibhishana had accomplished his objective and was now prosperous. Therefore, wishing to do what would bring him pleasure, he accepted everything.

The brave ape Hanumat, who was like a mountain, was standing near him, with his hands joined in salutation and his head bowed down. Rama addressed him in these words. 'Take the permission of this amiable and great king, Vibhishana. Resort to humility and enter Ravana's residence. Tell Vaidehi that I, Sugriva and Lakshmana are well. O supreme among victorious ones! Tell

[376] Vibhishana's four advisers.

[377] Brought Vibhishana.

[378] *Akshata,* unhusked grain.

[379] *Modaka.*

[380] *Laja.*

her that I have killed Ravana. O lord of the apes! Convey this agreeable news to Vaidehi. Ascertain her message and return.'

Chapter 6(101)

Hanumat, the son of the wind god, was instructed in this way. Worshipped by the roamers in the night, he entered the city of Lanka. The immensely energetic one entered Ravana's residence and saw her, terrified like Rohini separated from the moon. He approached her in secret, bowed his head down and greeted her. He started to tell her everything that Rama had said. 'O Vaidehi! Rama, Sugriva and Lakshmana are well. With the help of Vibhishana, Lakshmana and the apes, Rama, the destroyer of enemies, has accomplished his objective and has killed the enemy. He has said that he is well. O queen! The valiant Ravana has been made to die. The brave Rama, the descendant of the Raghu lineage, has asked about your welfare. Having accomplished his inner desires, extremely happy, he has told you this. "O queen![381] I am conveying this agreeable news and am also praising you. O one who knows about dharma! It is my good fortune that you are still alive after my victory in the battle. O Sita! We have obtained victory. Be at ease. Dispel your anxiety. The enemy, Ravana, has been killed and Lanka has been brought under subjugation. I have not slept. My resolution was firm that I would win you back. A bridge was built across the great ocean and the pledge has been accomplished. As long as you are in Ravana's residence, you need not have any fear. Everything in this prosperous Lanka is now under Vibhishana's control. Therefore, be comforted and at ease. It is as if you are in your own house. This one is going to you.[382] He is happy and eager to see you."'

[381] These are Rama's words, being stated by Hanumat. Hence, we have put them within quotes.

[382] This is probably a reference to Hanumat. But since the subject isn't mentioned, it is conceivable that Rama meant Vibhishana.

Thus addressed, with a face like the moon, Sita leapt up. Her joy constricted her and she was unable to say anything. Since Sita did not reply, the best among the apes spoke to her. 'O queen! What are you thinking? Why are you not replying to me?' Sita based herself on dharma and was thus addressed by Hanumat. Extremely delighted, and in a voice choking with tears, she replied. 'I have heard this pleasant news that my husband has obtained victory. I was overwhelmed with joy and, for a while, was unable to speak. O ape! You have brought me this agreeable news. However, though I have thought about it, I do not see anything here that I can give you and honour you with. O amiable one! O ape! You have brought me this agreeable news. However, I do not see anything on earth that can be given to someone like you. Gold, silver, many riches, a kingdom or the three worlds are not sufficient for someone who brings this news.' When Vaidehi Sita spoke in this way, stationed in front of her, the ape joined his hands in salutation and heard her words.

He replied, 'You are engaged in doing what brings your husband pleasure. You desire your husband's victory. It is only someone like you who can speak such gentle words. O amiable one! Your words are gentle and profound. They are superior to heaps of jewels and the kingdom of the gods. I have obtained my objective. I have seen Rama victorious, having slain the enemy. In qualities, that is superior to the kingdom of the gods and everything else. Earlier, all these rakshasis have censured you. If you permit it, I wish to kill them. They are terrible in form and conduct. They are cruel and their eyes are crueller. You are devoted to your husband and when you were in Ashokavana, they oppressed you. These rakshasis are extremely terrible and they are horrible in speech. Grant me this boon. I wish to kill them, using different kinds of blows. O beautiful one! I will strike them and bring them down with fists, hands, feet, teeth and terrible blows with the thighs. I will eat up their noses and ears. I will pull out their hair. When I strike, kill and make them suffer, their mouths will turn extremely dry. O illustrious one! In this way, I wish to strike them in many different ways. O queen! They have committed crimes towards you and I want to kill them.' Vaidehi, Janaka's daughter, was addressed by Hanumat in this way. The illustrious one replied to Hanumat in words that were full of dharma. 'O supreme among apes! They were dependent on the king and under his control. They acted in accordance with someone else's command. It is not proper to be angry with servant maids. Because of my former wicked deeds, this misfortune has come upon me. That is the reason I obtained all this. In this world, one reaps the consequences of one's own deeds. Destiny determined that this kind of misfortune had to be suffered. Ravana's servant maids are weak in strength and I am pardoning them. The rakshasis censured me because they were commanded by Ravana. O supreme among apes! Since he has been killed, they will no longer roar. In this connection, there is an ancient shloka that was chanted by a bear in a tiger's presence. It is full of dharma. O ape! Hear it. "The wicked acts committed by others are evil committed by others. They do not touch you. A pledge must be honoured. For virtuous people, good conduct constitutes ornaments."[383] O ape! The wicked do not deserve to be killed. Since there is no one who does not commit a crime, it is better and noble to show them compassion. The rakshasas can assume any form at will and roam around the world, causing injury. But though they act wickedly, one should not act inappropriately towards them.' Hanumat, accomplished in the use of words, was thus addressed by Sita. He replied to Sita, Rama's illustrious wife. 'You are indeed an illustrious and appropriate wife for Rama. O queen! Give me your message of reply, so that I can go to the spot where Raghava is.'

Thus addressed by Hanumat, Vaidehi, Janaka's daughter, replied, 'O supreme among apes! I wish to see my husband.' Hearing her words, Hanumat, the immensely radiant son of the

[383] The story is as follows. A tiger pursued a hunter. The hunter climbed a tree on which a bear was perched. The hunter and the bear agreed that they would not push each other down. The tiger asked the bear to push the hunter down, but he refused. When the tiger asked the hunter to push down the bear, he tried, but wasn't successful. The tiger repeated the request to the bear, citing violation of the pledge. However, the bear refused and chanted the shloka.

wind god, delighted Maithilee and addressed her in these words. 'O noble one! You will see Rama, whose face is like the full moon, and Lakshmana, like Shachi sees the lord of the gods. His friends stand firm and his enemy has been killed.' He addressed Sita, who was as radiant as Shri herself. With great speed, Hanumat went to the spot where Raghava was.

Chapter 6(102)

Rama was supreme among all wielders of the bow. Having gone there, the immensely wise ape, who knew about the meanings of words, addressed him. 'This task was started because of her and it has led to fruits. The queen, Maithilee, is tormented by grief. You should see her. She is immersed in grief and her eyes are overflowing with tears. Having heard about your victory, she has been filled with joy. She trusted me because of the earlier occasion.[384] Because of her trust in you, she said, "My husband has been successful in his objective. I wish to see him, together with Lakshmana." Hanumat told the one who was supreme among the upholders of dharma this. With his eyes full of tears, Rama suddenly started to think. He emitted deep and warm sighs. He looked at the ground. Vibhishana was like a cloud and was nearby. He told him, 'Let Vaidehi be adorned in divine ornaments and let her be smeared with celestial pastes. After she has bathed her head, let her be brought here quickly.'

Thus addressed by Rama, Vibhishana hurried. Urged by his master and accompanied by women, he entered the inner quarters, where Sita was. 'O Vaidehi![385] Adorn yourself in divine ornaments and smear yourself with celestial pastes. O fortunate one! Mount a vehicle. Your husband desires to see you.' Thus addressed, Vaidehi replied to Vibhishana, 'O lord of the rakshasas! I wish to see my

[384] When Hanumat visited her in Ashokavana.

[385] The Critical Edition excises a shloka where we are told that Vibhishana tells Sita this, after greeting her.

husband without having had a bath.' Hearing her words, Vibhishana said, 'Rama is your husband and you should act in accordance with what he has said.' The virtuous Maithilee was faithful and devoted to her husband and treated her husband like a divinity. Hearing his words, she consented. Sita bathed her hair and young maidens ornamented her. She was adorned in extremely expensive ornaments. She was attired in extremely expensive garments. She ascended a dazzling palanquin that was covered with an extremely expensive spread. Protected by many rakshasas, Vibhishana took her there. He went there and made it known to the great-souled one that he had arrived. He bowed down and happily informed that Sita had arrived.

She had resided in the residence of a rakshasa for a long time. On hearing that she had arrived, Raghava was filled with all three of joy, misery and rage. He saw that Vibhishana was near him. He reflected and thought deeply. Raghava addressed him in these cheerless words. 'O lord of the rakshasas! O amiable one! You have always been engaged in ensuring my victory. Let Vaidehi be quickly brought into my presence.' Vibhishana heard Raghava's words of command. He endeavoured to ensure that everyone was swiftly cleared from that place. Men with cloaks[386] and headdresses, with staffs made of cane in their hands, roamed around everywhere, dispersing people. Everywhere, hordes of bears, apes and rakshasas were made to withdraw some distance away. When all of them were being withdrawn, a roar arose. It was like the sound of the ocean, when it is agitated by a storm. In every direction, the terrified people were being dispersed away. On seeing this, because of resentment and compassion, Raghava prevented this. Rama was angry and seemed to burn down with his sight. He addressed the immensely wise Vibhishana in words of censure. 'Ignoring me, why are you making these people suffer? Cease this attempt to disperse people. They are my own people. Women do not need houses, garments, walls, condemnation and this kind of royal treatment. Their covering is good conduct. There is no sin to women being

[386] *Kanchuka,* this can also be translated as jacket, upper garment, or armour.

seen at time of adversity, hardship, war, *svayamvara*,[387] sacrifice or marriage. She has simultaneously suffered from war and great hardship. There is no sin to her being seen, especially because this is in my presence. O Vibhishana! Let her be brought quickly before me. Let Sita see me stationed here, surrounded by all the large numbers of my well-wishers.'

Thus addressed by Rama, the distressed Vibhishana humbly brought Sita to Rama's presence. Hearing Rama's words, Lakshmana, Sugriva and the ape Hanumat were also extremely unhappy. They detected terrible signs in the way he was looking towards his wife. They debated[388] that Raghava was unpleasant towards his wife. Because of her shame, Maithilee seemed to shrink into her own body. Following Vibhishana, she approached her husband. In that assembly of people, because of her shame, she covered her face with her garment. As she approached her husband, she wept and exclaimed, 'O noble one!' Regarding her husband as a divinity, she was filled with amazement, delight and affection. With a face that was even more amiable, she glanced towards her husband's amiable face. She looked for a long time at her beloved's face, which was as handsome as the full moon when it has arisen. All her mental fatigue was dispelled. Her own face sparkled like the moon.

Chapter 6(103)

Rama glanced at Maithilee, who was bowed down, next to him. He started to express the anger that raged in his heart. 'O fortunate one! Having defeated the enemy in a battle, you have been won back by me. I have thus achieved what could be accomplished through manliness. My great intolerance has been quenched and I have cleansed the oppression. At the same time, I have removed

[387] When a maiden chooses her own husband.

[388] Within themselves, not publicly.

the disrespect that the enemy exhibited towards me. Today, my manliness has been seen. My efforts have been successful. Through my own powers, I have accomplished the pledge today. When you were alone, you were taken away by a fickle rakshasa. That was a taint brought about by destiny. As a human, I have vanquished it. If a man does not use his energy to cleanse the disrespect that has been shown to him, what is the point of his manliness? He is limited in his energy. In leaping over the ocean and crushing Lanka, Hanumat performed praiseworthy deeds that have been rendered successful today. Sugriva and his soldiers exhibited valour in the field of battle and provide beneficial counsel. Today, their exertions have met with success. The devoted Vibhishana abandoned his brother, who was devoid of qualities, and presented himself before me. His exertions have met with success.' Hearing such words, uttered by Rama, Sita's eyes widened, like those of a doe, and became full of tears.

Seeing her, Rama was again filled with rage. He blazed, like a fire into which an excessive quantity of clarified butter had been sprinkled. He knit his eyebrows in a frown. With his eyes, he glanced sideways at her. In the midst of the apes and the rakshasas, he addressed Sita in these harsh words. 'A man must act so as to cleanse any oppression caused to him. O Sita! I have been successful in that, cleansing the oppression at the hands of the enemy. Despite his austerities and despite cleansing his soul, the sage Agastya found the southern direction to be unassailable. I have conquered that world of the living. O fortunate one! Let it be known to you that this exertion in the field of battle, accomplished well because of the valour of my well-wishers, was not undertaken for your sake. My conduct has always been such as to ward off bad reputation in every possible way. I have cleansed the blemish that was associated with my famous lineage. You are standing in front of me and there is a doubt about your character. I am firm in my antipathy towards you, just as a person suffering in the eyes detests a lamp. O Janaka's daughter! Therefore, you have my permission to go wherever you want. O fortunate one! These ten directions exist. I have nothing to do with you. If a woman has resided in the house of another, which energetic man, who has been born in a noble lineage, will take her back again, in a happy frame of mind? You were on Ravana's lap.[389] He has looked at you with wicked eyes. When I mention my great lineage, how can I take you back again? I won you back for a reason and I have got that fame back. I have no attachment for you. You can go wherever you desire. O fortunate one! I have spoken to you in this way after making up my mind. If it makes you happy, you can turn your mind towards Lakshmana or Bharata, Sugriva, Indra among apes, or Vibhishana, Indra among rakshasas. O Sita! Turn your mind towards them, or whatever else makes you happy. Ravana saw your divine and lovely beauty. O Sita! When you were roaming around in his house for such a long time, he must have molested you.' Maithilee deserved to hear pleasant words, but heard these unpleasant ones spoken by her beloved. She released floods of tears and trembled severely for a very long time. She was like a creeper struck by the trunk of a gigantic elephant.

Chapter 6(104)

Vaidehi was thus addressed in harsh words by the enraged Raghava and they made the body hair stand up. She was gravely pained. Earlier, Maithilee had never heard such words in an assembly of people. Hearing her husband's harsh words, she was ashamed and mortified. Because of the stakes in those words, Janaka's daughter was like a dog impaled by spikes.[390] She shed copious tears. She wiped her face, which was overflowing with tears. Speaking in a slow and low voice, she addressed her husband in these words. 'Such words are extremely terrible to the ear. O brave one! Like an ordinary man speaking to an ordinary woman, why are you making me hear such harsh words? O mighty-armed one! I am not what you take me to be. You should have trust in me. I swear on my own character. Because

[389] While Sita was being abducted.

[390] Perhaps from the quills of a porcupine, though that is not necessary.

of the conduct of ordinary women, you are casting doubts on the entire species. If I have been tested by you, you should cast aside all doubt. O lord! I did not go to him. When he touched my body, I was incapacitated. I did not commit the crime out of my own desire. It was destiny. My heart was under my control and it was devoted to you. When one does not have a protector, what can one do with a body that comes under someone else's control? O one who grants honours! We have grown up in proximity. If you have not understood my sentiments from that, I have been destroyed for an eternity. O brave one! You sent Hanumat to look for me. I was in Lanka then. O brave one! Why did you not abandon me then? O brave one! In the presence of the Indra among the apes, had you abandoned me then, I would have given up my life. There would have been no need for the exertion, or the need to set lives at risk. There would have been no need for this pointless suffering borne by your well-wishers. O tiger among men! However, you only followed your rage. You were like a feeble man, placing importance on a feminine sentiment. I was not really born from Janaka. I was born from the earth. O one who knows about conduct! You did not set great score to my conduct. Though you accepted my hand in marriage when both of us were children, this was not sufficient proof. You have turned your back towards my devotion, good conduct and everything else.' Her voice choking with tears, she said this and wept.

Distressed and immersed in thought, Sita then spoke to Lakshmana. 'O Soumitri! Prepare a funeral pyre for me. That is the medication for a calamity. Having suffered from a false accusation, I am not interested in remaining alive. My husband is displeased with my qualities and has abandoned me in an assembly of people. It is better that I should enter a fire, the destination for those who do not have a destination.' Vaidehi told Lakshmana, the slayer of enemy heroes, this. Filled with great intolerance, she glanced towards Raghava. From the indicated signs, Soumitri understood what was in Rama's mind. Given the valiant Rama's inclination, Soumitri prepared a funeral pyre. With her face lowered, Vaidehi slowly circumambulated Rama and approached the blazing fire. Maithilee bowed down to the gods and the brahmanas. She joined her hands in salutation and approached the fire. 'If my heart has always been with Raghava and never wavered, let the fire, which is a witness to the world, save me in every possible way.' Having said this, Vaidehi circumambulated the fire. Without the slightest bit of hesitation in her mind, she entered the blazing flames.

There was an extremely large gathering of the young and the aged there and they saw Maithilee enter the fire. As she entered the fire, loud and extraordinary sounds of lamentation arose from the rakshasas and the apes.

Chapter 6(105)

King Vaishravana, Yama, with the ancestors, the thousand-eyed great Indra, Varuna, the scorcher of enemies, the handsome three-eyed Mahadeva, with the bull as his banner, and Brahma, the creator of all the worlds and supreme among those who know about the brahman—all of them arrived in vimanas that were as radiant as the sun. They arrived in the city of Lanka and approached Raghava. The best among the gods raised their large arms, their hands full of ornaments, and spoke to Raghava, while he stood there, his hands joined in salutation. 'You are the lord of all the worlds. You are supreme and best among those who know. How can you ignore Sita when she descends into the fire? Why don't you comprehend your nature as the best among all the gods? Among the Vasus, you are the foremost Vasu, Ritadhama, who was a Prajapati.[391] He was Svayambhu, the original creator of the three worlds. Among the Rudras, you are the eighth Rudra.[392] Among the Sadhyas, you are the fifth.[393] The two Ashvins are your ears and the sun and the moon

[391] There are eight Vasus. The names vary, though Ritadhama is not a name in the standard lists. Ritadhama means one whose abode is the truth.

[392] There are eleven Rudras. Since the names vary in different lists, the eighth Rudra cannot be given a specific name.

[393] There is no unambiguous number of Sadhyas, but a number of twelve is sometimes given.

are your eyes. O scorcher of enemies! You are seen at the beginning and the end of the worlds. Like an ordinary human, you are ignoring Vaidehi.' The guardians of the worlds addressed Raghava, the lord of the worlds, in this way. Rama, supreme among the upholders of dharma, replied to the best among the gods. 'I think of myself as human. I am Rama, Dasharatha's son. You illustrious ones should tell me who I am and what I am.'

When Kakutstha said this, Brahma, supreme among those who know about the brahman, responded. 'O Rama! O one for whom valour is the truth! Hear the truth. You are the god Narayana. You are the handsome lord who has the chakra as a weapon. You are the single-tusked boar. You are the one who has vanquished his enemies in the past and will in the future. You are without decay. You are the brahman. O Raghava! You are the truth in the middle and at the end.[394] You are supreme dharma in the worlds. You are Vishvaksena.[395] You are the four-armed one. You are the wielder of the Sharnga bow. You are Hrishikesha. You are Purusha.[396] You are Purushottama.[397] You have not been vanquished. You are the Vishnu who wields the sword. You are the immensely strong Krishna. You are the leader of armies and villages. You are intelligence. You are the spirit. You are forgiveness. You are self-control. You are the origin. You are the destruction. You are Upendra. You are Madhusudana. You perform deeds for Indra. You are the great Indra. You are Padmanabha.[398] You are the one who ends battles. You are the one who grants refuge. You are the refuge. The maharshis have spoken of you as the divine one. You are the one with one thousand horns. You are the soul of the Vedas. You are the one with one hundred tongues. You are the great bull. You are the sacrifice. O scorcher of enemies! You are *vashatkara*.[399] You are *omkara*.[400] No one knows about

[394] Of the universe.
[395] Vishnu's name, meaning one whose soldiers can go everywhere.
[396] The supreme being.
[397] The excellent being.
[398] One with a lotus in his navel.
[399] Vashatkara is the exclamation '*vashat*' made at the time of offering an oblation.
[400] The sound of '*om*'/'*aum*'.

your origin or your end. You are seen in all creatures, in cattle and in brahmanas. You are in all the directions, the sky, the mountains and the rivers. You possess a thousand feet. You are the one with Shri. You possess a hundred heads. You possess a thousand eyes. You bear the earth, with all its creatures and the mountains. You are the giant serpent,[401] seen in the water at the bottom of the earth. O Rama! You sustain the three worlds, with the gods, the gandharvas and the danavas. O Rama! I am your heart. The goddess Sarasvati is your tongue. O lord! The gods, created by Brahma, are your body hair. Night has been said to be the closing of your eyes and day the opening of your eyes. You are the pure speech of the Vedas. There is nothing without you. Everything in the universe is your body. The earth is your patience. The fire is your anger. Your equanimity is Soma.[402] You bear the *srivatsa* mark.[403] In ancient times, with three valorous strides, you traversed the three worlds. Having bound the great asura, Bali, you made the great Indra the king. Sita is Lakshmi and you are the god Vishnu. You are Krishna. You are Prajapati. You entered a human body in this world for the sake of killing Ravana. O supreme among the upholders of dharma! You have performed the task for us. O Rama! Now that Ravana has been killed, we can cheerfully return to heaven. Your strength and valour are invincible. Your power never fails. Men who are devoted to you never fail. O god! If men faithfully chant about you as the ancient Purushottama, it is certain that they will never be vanquished.'

Chapter 6(106)

Hearing the auspicious words spoken by the grandfather, the fire god arose, holding Vaidehi in his lap. She was like the rising sun, adorned in ornaments made out of molten gold. The young

[401] Shesha.

[402] The moon.

[403] Vishnu bears the srivatsa mark (or curl) on his chest. This is the place where Lakshmi resides.

one was attired in red garments. Her dark hair was curled. She was wearing garlands that did not fade and ornaments. That was the form of the spirited one. Holding Vaidehi in his lap, the fire god gave her to Rama. The fire, the witness of the world, told Rama, 'O Rama! This is Vaidehi and there is no sin in her. She possesses good conduct and her conduct is firm. In words, thoughts, intelligence and sight, she has always followed you. She was distressed, incapacitated and separated from you in the lonely forest. At that time, the rakshasa Ravana, full of valour, abducted her. Though she was protected and confined in the inner quarters, her mind was always devoted to you. She was guarded by terrible rakshasis who were terrible in their intelligence. They tempted and censured Maithilee in many ways. But her inner thoughts were always in you and she did not even think about that rakshasa. Her sentiments are pure. She is faultless. O Raghava! Accept her. She should not suffer in any way. I am commanding you.' The immensely energetic one, patient and firm in his valour, was addressed in this way.

Rama, supreme among the upholders of dharma, replied to the best of the gods. 'Before the three worlds, Sita certainly needed to be purified. The auspicious one has dwelt for a long period of time in Ravana's inner quarters. Had Janakee not been purified, virtuous people would have told me that Rama, Dasharatha's son, is foolish and is driven by desire. I know that Maithilee, Janaka's daughter, is single-mindedly devoted to me and that her mind is only on me. However, I am devoted to the truth. For the sake of persuading the three worlds, I ignored Vaidehi when she entered the fire. This large-eyed one was protected through her own energy and Ravana could not violate her, just as the great ocean does not cross the shoreline. The extremely evil-souled one was unable to approach Maithilee even in his thoughts. She was like the blazing flames of the fire and there was no question of his approaching and oppressing her. The auspicious one did not consider the prosperity in Ravana's inner quarters. Just as the sun is not separate from its radiance, Sita is not separate from me. Maithilee, Janaka's daughter, has been purified before the three worlds. No one is capable of sullying her deeds. I must certainly act in accordance with all the beneficial words you have spoken. The gentle guardians of the world have also spoken about what is beneficial.' When he spoke these words, because of his deeds, he was praised by the extremely strong ones. The immensely strong Rama was united with his beloved. Raghava, who deserved happiness, was happy.

Chapter 6(107)

Hearing the auspicious words spoken by Raghava, Maheshvara spoke words that were even more auspicious. 'O lotus-eyed one! O mighty-armed one! O broad-chested one! O scorcher of enemies! O supreme among those who wield weapons! It is good fortune that you have accomplished this task. On account of the fear of Ravana, a terrible darkness had spread over all the worlds. It is good fortune that you have dispelled this in the battle. You must see and comfort the distressed Bharata, the illustrious Kousalya, Kaikeyee and Sumitra, Lakshmana's mother. You must obtain the kingdom of Ayodhya and delight the well-wishers. O immensely strong one! You must establish the noble lineage of the Ikshvakus. You must perform a horse sacrifice and obtain excellent fame. You must donate riches to the brahmanas and go to heaven. Your father, King Dasharatha, is on this vimana. O Kakutstha! Your immensely illustrious senior has come to the world of men. Having been saved by you, his son, he went to Indra's handsome world. With your brother, Lakshmana, greet him.'

Their father was seated on the top of the vimana. Hearing Mahadeva's words, Kakutstha, with Lakshmana, bowed down before him. Their father blazed in his own prosperity. He was attired in dazzling garments. With his brother, Lakshmana, the lord saw his father. Astride the vimana, on seeing his son, whom he loved more than his own lives,[404] King Dasharatha was filled with great joy. When the lord approached that excellent seat, the mighty-

[404] Used in the plural.

armed one took him up on his lap. Embracing him in his arms, he commended him in these words. 'In heaven, I receive a great deal of respect from the gods and the rishis. O Rama! However, I am telling you truthfully. Listen to me. Without you, this is nothing. O supreme among eloquent ones! The words that Kaikeyee spoke, for the sake of exiling you, are still impaled in my heart. I see that you are well with Lakshmana and I have embraced you. Today, I have been freed from my misery, like the sun from mist. O son! I have been saved by you, my great-souled and excellent son, just as the sage Ashtavakra, with dharma in his soul, saved a brahmana.[405] O amiable one! O Purushottama! I now know that the lords of the gods had ordained it that you would kill Ravana in this world. O Rama! Kousalya will indeed attain her objective. She will see you return home. O slayer of enemies! When she sees you return from the forest, she will be happy. O Rama! The men who see you return to the city will indeed be successful in their objectives. They will see you consecrated as the king, sprinkled with water. The strong Bharata is pure. He follows dharma and is devoted to you. I desire to see you and he unite. O amiable one! You have spent fourteen years in the forest, residing there with Sita and the intelligent Lakshmana. The period of your exile in the forest is over. You have been successful in accomplishing your pledge. You have also killed Ravana in the battle and have satisfied the gods. O slayer of enemies! You have performed a praiseworthy deed and have obtained fame. Instated in the kingdom, may you have a long life, with your brothers.'

When the king said this, Rama joined his hands in salutation and said, 'O one who knows about dharma! Show your favours towards Kaikeyee and Bharata. You told Kaikeyee, "I am disowning you and your son." O lord! That terrible curse should not touch Kaikeyee or her son.' When Rama joined his hands in salutation and said this, the great king agreed. He embraced Lakshmana and again spoke these words.[406] 'Devotedly serve Rama and Vaidehi Sita. You will then make me extremely happy and obtain the fruits of dharma.

[405] Ashtavakra's story is told in the Mahabharata. The brahmana in question is Kahoda, Ashtavakra's father. Kahoda had been imprisoned, but Ashtavakra saved him.

[406] These are addressed to Lakshmana.

O one who knows about dharma! You will obtain dharma and great fame on earth. When Rama is pleased, you will also obtain greatness in heaven. O fortunate one! O extender of Sumitra's delight! Serve Rama. Rama is always engaged in ensuring what is auspicious for all the worlds. Indra, the three worlds, the siddhas and the supreme rishis approach the great-souled one and worship him as Purushottama. He has been spoken of as the unmanifest one, the one without decay. O amiable one! He is the heart of the gods, who were created by Brahma. Rama is the scorcher of enemies and is subtle. Having served at his feet, you will obtain dharma and great fame. Serve him and Vaidehi Sita with devotion.' The mighty-armed Lakshmana was standing there, his hands joined in salutation, and he was addressed in this way.

The king, with dharma in his soul, then addressed Vaidehi in these auspicious words. 'O Vaidehi! You should not harbour any anger towards him. Rama had your welfare in mind and wished to purify you. O one with the excellent brows! Though I must certainly mention it in my words, you need not be instructed about serving your husband. He is a supreme divinity to you.' He thus instructed his two sons and Sita, his daughter-in-law. In a blazing vimana, Dasharatha then went to Indra's world.

Chapter 6(108)

After Kakutstha[407] left, the great Indra, the chastiser of Paka, spoke in an extremely happy voice to Raghava, who was standing there, his hands joined in salutation. 'O Rama! O scorcher of enemies! Your seeing us should not be fruitless. I am full of affection for you. Tell me what you desire.' Kakutstha was addressed in this way. With his brother, Lakshmana, and his wife, Sita, he joined his hands in salutation and said, 'O lord of all the gods! O supreme among eloquent ones! If you are full of affection for me,

[407] Meaning Dasharatha.

I will tell you. Please act accordingly and make my words come true. There are valiant ones who have gone to Yama's abode on my account. Let all those apes regain their lives and stand up. Devoted to me and seeking to ensure my pleasure, they did not think about death. Through your favours, let them be united again. This is the boon I ask for. Let them be free of their pains. Let them be free of their wounds. Let them be full of strength and manliness. O one who grants honours! I desire to see the golangulas and the Indras among the bears. Wherever the apes are, let there be sparkling rivers and the best of roots and fruits, irrespective of the season.'

Hearing the words of the great-souled Raghava, the great Indra replied in words that bore signs of affection. 'O son![408] O descendant of the Raghu lineage! You have asked for a great boon. The apes will arise, as if they have awoken after being asleep. They will be filled with great delight and will meet their well-wishers, relatives, kin and near ones. O great archer! Even if the season isn't right, the trees will be colourful with flowers and laden with fruit. The rivers will be full of water.'

Earlier, their bodies had been covered with wounds. They were now hale, without any wounds. All the apes were astounded and exclaimed, 'What is this?' All the supreme gods saw that Kakutstha had completely attained his objective. They first praised him, who deserved praise, together with Lakshmana. 'O brave one! Take your leave of the apes and go to Ayodhya. Comfort the devoted and ascetic Maithilee. Meet your brother, Bharata. Grieving over you, he is observing vows. Go and consecrate yourself and delight the residents of the city.' Saying this, the gods took their leave of Rama and Soumitri. They cheerfully went to heaven in vimanas that were like the sun. Kakutstha honoured all the excellent gods. With his brother, Lakshmana, he instructed that the camps should be set up. Protected by Lakshmana, that illustrious and large army was full of joy. In every direction, it blazed and dazzled in its prosperity. Night set in, illuminated by cool beams.[409]

[408] The word used is tata.

[409] Of the moon.

Chapter 6(109)

Having slept during the night, Rama, the slayer of enemies, awoke happily. After having proclaimed his victory, Vibhishana joined his hands in salutation and addressed him in these words. 'O Raghava! Many objects for bathing, unguents for the body, garments, ornaments, sandalwood paste, diverse kinds of divine garlands and lotus-eyed women who know about ornaments have all been kept ready, so that you can bathe.' Thus addressed, Kakutstha replied to Vibhishana, 'Invite Sugriva and the best among the apes to have a bath. The mighty-armed and delicate prince is devoted to the truth. He is used to happiness. However, on my account, the one with dharma in his soul is suffering. With Bharata, Kaikeyee's son who follows dharma, I will now have a bath with extremely expensive garments and ornaments. See how we can swiftly return to that city. This route to return to Ayodhya is extremely difficult to travel on.'

Thus addressed by Kakutstha, Vibhishana replied, 'O son of a king! I will convey you to the city in a single day. O fortunate one! There is a vimana named Pushpaka and it is like the sun. This belonged to my brother, Kubera, but Ravana used his force to seize it. That vimana is like a cloud and it is here. Using that vehicle, without any anxiety, you can go to Ayodhya. O wise one! However, if you are favourably inclined towards me, if you remember my qualities and if you have any affection for me, reside here for some more time. With your brother, Lakshmana, and your wife, Vaidehi, you will be worshipped with all the objects of desire. O Rama! Leave after that. I am full of affection for you. My soldiers and the large number of my well-wishers have made arrangements so that you can be honoured properly. Accept everything that I have prepared. O Raghava! I am your well-wisher and am affectionately entreating you. I am your servant. Show me your favours. I am certainly not trying to order you.' While all the rakshasas and the apes heard this, thus addressed, Rama replied to Vibhishana. 'O brave one! O scorcher of enemies! I have been worshipped by you and your advisers. With supreme affection, you have made every effort that you can. O lord of the rakshasas! Indeed, it is not that I don't want to act in accordance with your words. However, my mind is urging me to hurry, so that I can see my brother, Bharata. He came to Chitrakuta to make me return. He bowed his head down and beseeched me. But I did not act in accordance with his words. Kousalya, Sumitra, the illustrious Kaikeyee, the seniors, the well-wishers and the residents of the city are there, with their sons. O lord of the rakshasas! Quickly present that vimana before me. With my task accomplished, it is not proper that I should reside here. O amiable one! O Vibhishana! I have been worshipped. Grant me permission. You should not be angry with me. Bring it swiftly.'

It had gold all over its body and its platform was made out of lapis lazuli and jewels. There were deep chambers everywhere, with the complexion of silver. It was ornamented with white flags and standards. It was decorated with golden mansions that were ornamented with golden lotuses. Nets of bells were strewn around. The windows were embellished with pearls and jewels. Lattice work with bells was everywhere and it made a pleasant sound. It was like the summit of Meru and had been created by Vishvakarma. It was decorated with many mansions, with hues of silver and gold. The floors were made out of colourful crystal. Colourful in all its parts, there were excellent seats made out of lapis lazuli. There were extremely expensive and extremely thick and handsome spreads. The invincible vimana, as swift as thought, was presented. Vibhishana came and informed Rama that it was ready.

Chapter 6(110)

Rama saw that Vibhishana had presented Pushpaka and had decorated it with flowers. He was standing nearby and spoke to him.[410] Humbly, with his hands joined in salutation, the lord among the rakshasas hurriedly asked, 'O Raghava! What will I do?' Having

[410] Vibhishana spoke to Rama.

thought a little, while Lakshmana heard, Raghava addressed him in words that were great in affection. 'O Vibhishana! Make careful efforts so that all these residents of the forest are honoured with gems, chariots and all kinds of ornaments. O lord of the rakshasas! It is with their help that Lanka has been attacked and won. They have been cheerful and have given up all fear of losing their lives. They did not retreat from the battle. O one who shows honours! They deserve honours. If these leaders of the apes are shown respect, they will be grateful and happy. Listen to me. All of them will come near you because you are generous, collect friends, are compassionate and are famous.' Thus addressed by Rama, Vibhishana divided up jewels and wealth and honoured all the apes. The leaders of the herds were worshipped with jewels and wealth.

Having seen this, Rama ascended that excellent vimana. He took the illustrious and ashamed Vaidehi on his lap. His valiant brother, the archer Lakshmana, was with him. From the vimana, Kakutstha spoke to all the apes, the immensely valorous Sugriva and the rakshasa Vibhishana. 'O supreme among apes! You have performed the task of friends. With my leave, all of you return wherever you wish. O scorcher of enemies! O Sugriva! You have always been scared of offending dharma. You have done everything that a friend and a well-wisher should do. Surrounded by all your soldiers, return quickly to Kishkindha. O Vibhishana! Reside in your own kingdom of Lanka, bestowed by me on you. Even the gods, with Indra, are incapable of assailing you. I will return to Ayodhya, my father's capital. I desire to take the permission and leave from all of you.'

Thus addressed by Rama, all the apes, the Indra among the apes, Vibhishana and all the rakshasas joined their hands in salutation and said, 'We wish to go to Ayodhya. Take all of us with you. O son of a king! After seeing you sprinkled in the course of the consecration and greeting Kousalya, we will quickly return to our own houses.' The one with dharma in his soul was thus addressed by the apes and Vibhishana. The handsome Raghava spoke to Sugriva and Vibhishana. 'This will bring me delight. I will obtain the greatest of joys if I go to the city with large numbers of my well-wishers. O

Sugriva! With the apes, swiftly ascend the vimana. O Vibhishana! O Indra among the rakshasas! You also ascend, with your advisers.' Delighted, Sugriva and his soldiers and Vibhishana and his advisers swiftly ascended the divine Pushpaka. This was Kubera's supreme resort. When all of them had ascended, with Raghava's permission, it leapt up into the sky. The radiant vimana proceeded, yoked to swans. Rama was delighted and resembled Kubera.

Chapter 6(111)

With Rama's permission, the excellent vimana leapt up. It was like a giant cloud that seemed to be breathing. The descendant of the Raghu lineage cast his eye around everywhere. Rama spoke to Maithilee Sita, whose face was like the moon. 'O Vaidehi! Look at Lanka, constructed by Vishvakarma. It is placed atop the summit of Trikuta and is like the summit of Kailasa. Behold the field of battle, covered with a mire made out of flesh and blood. O Sita! There was a great destruction of apes and rakshasas. O large-eyed one! On your account, this is where I killed Ravana. Kumbhakarna and Prahasta, roamer in the night, were killed there. That is where Lakshmana killed Indrajit, Ravana's son, in the battle. Other powerful rakshasas were killed—Virupaksha, who was impossible to look at, Mahaparshva, Mahodara, Akampana, Trishira, Atikaya, Devantaka and Narantaka. His wife is named Mandodari. She is lamenting there, surrounded by thousands and thousands of her co-wives. O one with the beautiful face! Look at the *tirtha* on the ocean there.[411] That is where we crossed over the ocean and spent the night. O large-eyed one! That is the bridge I constructed over the ocean, the abode of the waters. It was extremely difficult to build and it was done for your sake. This is Nala Setu.[412] O Vaidehi! Behold the ocean that cannot be agitated. It is Varuna's abode. It is roaring

[411] Tirtha means a place of pilgrimage. But etymologically, it means a place where one descends into the water. In this context, the latter meaning is appropriate.

[412] *Setu* means bridge, the bridge being named after Nala.

and the distant shore cannot be seen. It is full of conch shells and oysters. O Maithilee! Behold that golden Indra among mountains.[413] It seems to possess a golden navel. When Hanumat leapt across the ocean, this is where he rested. That is where Vibhishana, the king of the rakshasas, arrived. O Sita! Kishkindha, with its beautiful groves, can be seen there. That is Sugriva's beautiful city, where I killed Vali. O Sita! Rishyamuka, the supreme and large mountain can be seen, as if it is a cloud tinged with lightning. It is covered with gold and other minerals. Sugriva, Indra among the apes, came and met me here. O Sita! I contracted a pledge for the sake of Vali's destruction. The lake of Pampa, with its colourful groves, can be seen there. Separated from you and extremely miserable, I lamented there. I met Shabaree, who followed dharma, along its shore. That is where I killed Kabandha. His arms were one yojana long. O Sita! Janasthana can be seen there, with the beautiful tree. O one who loves pleasure! On your account, that is where a great encounter raged between the cruel Ravana and the great-souled Jatayu. That is where I used my swift arrows to kill and bring down Khara, Dushana and the immensely valiant Trishira in a battle. O one who is beautiful to behold! The colourful cottage of leaves can be seen there. Ravana, Indra among the rakshasas, forcibly abducted you from there. That is the beautiful Godavari, with its sparkling and auspicious waters. O Maithilee! Behold. Agastya's hermitage can be seen. O Vaidehi! Sharabhanga's great hermitage can be seen there. That is where Shakra Purandara, with the one thousand eyes, arrived. O slender-waisted one! A residence of ascetics can be seen there. Atri, the leader of the group and like the sun and the fire in his splendour, was there. O Sita! That is where you met the ascetic lady who followed dharma.[414] That is the region where I killed Viradha, who was gigantic in size. O one with the excellent body! Chitrakuta has shown itself there. To seek my favours, Kaikeyee's son had come there. From a distance, Yamuna, with its colourful groves, can be seen. O Maithilee! Bharadvaja's beautiful hermitage

[413] Mainaka.
[414] Atri's wife, Anasuya.

has revealed itself. O one with the beautiful complexion! Ganga, with the three flows, can be seen. That is Shringaverapura, where Guha arrived. Ayodhya, my father's capital, can be seen there. O Vaidehi! We have returned to Ayodhya. Bow down before it.'

At this, all the apes, the rakshasas and Vibhishana leapt up, to see the city that was beautiful to behold. It was garlanded with white mansions. There were large roads, full of elephants and horses. The apes saw the city of Ayodhya. It was like Amaravati, the city of the great Indra.

Chapter 6(112)

After a full fourteen years were over, it was the fifth lunar day.[415] Lakshmana's elder brother reached Bharadvaja's hermitage. He controlled himself and worshipped the sage. After greeting him, he asked Bharadvaja, the store of austerities, 'O illustrious one! Have you heard that all is well with the city, that there is no disease and there are plenty of alms?[416] Is Bharata conducting himself well? Are my mothers alive?'

The great sage, Bharadvaja, was asked by Rama in this way. He smiled first. Cheerfully, he replied to the best among the Raghu lineage. 'Bharata has smeared himself with mud and is awaiting you with matted hair. He has your sandals in front of him. All is well in your house. A long time ago, attired in bark, you entered the great forest. You were dislodged from the kingdom and were only interested in undertaking tasks of dharma. Your wife was the third.[417] You followed the words of your father. You gave up everything and proceeded on foot. Like an immortal dislodged from heaven, you gave up all the objects of desire. O victor in assemblies! On seeing you, I was initially filled with compassion. You followed Kaikeyee's words and survived on wild roots and fruits. You

[415] *Panchami* in *shukla paksha*.

[416] If the city is prosperous, there will be plenty of alms to be distributed.

[417] Lakshmana was the second.

have now returned, having accomplished your objective. You are prosperous, with large numbers of friends and well-wishers. On seeing you, having triumphed over the enemy, my heart is filled with great delight. O Raghava! I know everything about your joy and misery. You obtained a great deal of this. For the sake of the brahmanas and to protect all the ascetics, you undertook that great slaughter in Janasthana. I know about the sighting of Maricha, Sita's oppression, the sighting of Kabandha, the arrival in Pampa, the friendship with Sugriva and that you killed Vali because of that. I know about searching for Vaidehi, the deed performed by the son of the wind god, the building of Nala Setu for Vaidehi's sake and about the delighted leaders of the apes setting Lanka on fire. In a battle, you killed Ravana, the thorn of the gods, with his sons, relatives, advisers, soldiers and mounts. The gods came before you and granted you a boon. O one who is devoted to dharma! Through my austerities, I know all this. O supreme among those who wield weapons! I will also grant you a boon. I will offer you *arghya*.[418] Accept it and go to Ayodhya tomorrow.'

The son of the king bowed his head down and accepted these words. Having cheerfully agreed, the handsome one asked for a boon. 'O illustrious one! As I proceed towards Ayodhya, may all the trees along the road overflow with honey. May they yield unseasonal fruits.' Trees without fruit became full of fruit. Trees without flowers became full of flowers. All the trees with dry leaves started to flow with honey.

Chapter 6(113)

Looking towards Ayodhya, Raghava was thoughtful. While he was thinking, he saw the apes. Rama was swift in his valour and sought to do what brought pleasure. He wished to do something

[418] Objects always offered to a guest—*padya* (water to wash the feet), *achamaniya* (water to wash the mouth/face), arghya (a gift) and *asana* (a seat).

pleasant.[419] The intelligent and energetic one spoke to the ape Hanumat. 'O supreme among the apes! Swiftly and quickly, go to Ayodhya. Find out if all is well with the people and in the king's palace. Go to Guha in Shringaverapura. It is in an impenetrable part of the forest. Convey my words and news about my welfare to the lord of the *nishada*s.[420] On hearing that I am well, without disease and free from anxiety, Guha will be happy. He is a friend who is like my own self. Happy, Guha, the lord of the nishadas, will tell you about the road towards Ayodhya and about Bharata's conduct. Convey my words and news about my welfare to Bharata too. Tell him that I, with my wife and Lakshmana, have been successful in our objective. Tell him about Vaidehi's abduction by the powerful Ravana, the conversation with Sugriva and Vali's death in the battle, the search for Maithilee and you finding her after leaping over the great and inexhaustible waters of the ocean, our reaching the ocean and seeing the ocean, the construction of the bridge, Ravana's death, the boons granted by the great Indra, Brahma and Varuna and my meeting with my father because of Mahadeva's favours. Tell him that I have vanquished a great number of enemies and have obtained supreme fame and that I have returned successful in my objective, with immensely strong friends. On hearing all this, the expression Bharata wears on his face will reveal to you his inclinations towards me. Everything will be known through Bharata's limbs. The truth will be discerned through the complexion of his face and what he says. If one is prosperous with all the objects of desire in a kingdom, full of elephants, horses and chariots, obtained from the father and grandfathers, which person's mind will not change? Having been associated with this prosperous kingdom, if Bharata desires it for himself, let that descendant of the Raghu lineage rule over the entire earth. O ape! Get to know his inclination and conduct. You must return swiftly, before we proceed too far.'[421] Hanumat, the son of the wind god, was commanded in this way. He assumed a human form and hurried towards Ayodhya.

[419] Conveying the news that day, instead of waiting for the next day.

[420] The nishadas were hunters who dwelt in mountains and forests.

[421] Towards Ayodhya.

He leapt across his father's path,[422] the auspicious residence of the Indras among the serpents. He crossed the terrible confluence of the Ganga and the Yamuna and descended. The valiant one reached Shringaverapura and approached Guha. Hanumat cheerfully addressed him in these auspicious words. 'Kakutstha Rama, with truth as his valour, is your friend. With Sita and Soumitri, he has asked about your welfare. After obtaining Bharadvaja's permission, he followed the words of the sage and has spent the night of the fifth lunar day there. You will see Raghava today.' The immensely energetic one, his body hair standing up in delight, said this. The powerful one leapt up with great force and without even thinking about it, departed. He saw Rama's[423] tirtha, the rivers Valukini and Gomatee and the extremely terrible forest of sala trees. The tiger among elephants swiftly traversed a long distance.

He approached the flowering trees near Nandigrama. When he was one *krosha*[424] away from Ayodhya, he saw the miserable Bharata, attired in bark and black antelope skin. From having resided in the hermitage, he was emaciated. He had filth on his limbs and wore matted hair. He was grieving because of the hardship his brother had suffered. He was controlled, surviving on roots and fruits. He was following the dharma of ascetics. Matted hair was coiled high on his head. His garments were of bark and deerskin. He was controlled and had cleansed his soul. His energy was like that of a brahmana rishi. With the sandals in front, he ruled over the earth. In the world, he protected the four varnas from all kinds of fear. Pure advisers and priests were present with him. There were also commanders of the forces, attired in ochre garments. The citizens were devoted to dharma. Since the prince was attired in rags and black antelope skin, they had also given up objects of pleasure. He[425] knew about dharma and was like a second Dharma in embodied form. Hanumat, the son of the wind god, joined his hands in salutation and addressed him in these words. 'Kakutstha

[422] The sky, the path followed by Vayu.

[423] Parashurama's.

[424] One krosha is two miles, however, the definition was not standardized.

[425] Bharata.

resided in Dandakaranya, attired in bark and sporting matted hair. You are grieving over him. He has asked about your welfare. O lord! I am conveying pleasant news. Abandon this terrible sorrow. You will be united with your brother, Rama, this very instant. Having slain Ravana, Rama has got Maithilee back. Having been successful in his objective, he has arrived, with his immensely strong friends. The immensely energetic Lakshmana has also come and so has the illustrious Sita of Videha, like Shachi with the great Indra.'

Bharata, Kaikeyee's son, was thus addressed by Hanumat. He was delighted. But that joy also led to confusion and he suddenly fell down. In a short while, Raghava[426] reassured himself and arose. Bharata spoke to Hanumat, who had brought the pleasant news. Freed from sorrow and full of joy, he respectfully embraced the ape. The handsome Bharata made him wet with large drops of tears. 'Out of compassion, you have come here. Are you a god or a man? O amiable one! You have brought me pleasant tidings and I will give you what is agreeable—one hundred thousand cows, one hundred excellent villages and sixteen maidens who are auspicious in conduct as your wives. They wear earrings and are golden in complexion. These women are as amiable as the moon. They are decorated in all the ornaments. They are accomplished and have been born in noble families.' From the supreme among the apes, the prince heard the extraordinary news about Rama's arrival. He was delighted at the prospect of seeing Rama. Rejoicing, he again spoke these words.

Chapter 6(114)

'It has indeed been several years since he left for the great forest. I have now heard delightful news about my lord being recounted. The popular saying occurs to me. "If a man is alive, there will be fortune, even after one hundred years." How did the meeting

[426] Bharata.

between Raghava and the apes take place? Where did it happen? What was the reason? I am asking you. Tell me the truth.'

Asked by the prince, he sat down on a mat and told him everything about Rama's conduct in the forest. 'Because of the boon granted to your mother, Rama left on an exile. Grieving over his son, King Dasharatha died. O lord! Messengers quickly brought you to the royal residence. You entered Ayodhya, but did not desire the kingdom. You went to Mount Chitrakuta and invited your brother, the afflicter of enemies, to accept the kingdom. But he followed the path of dharma and virtue. He stuck to the king's words and refused the kingdom. You accepted the noble one's sandals and returned. O mighty-armed one! Everything about what occurred till then is known to you. Hear from me about what happened after you returned. You returned and he entered the desolate and extremely large forest of Dandaka, full of animals and birds and extending all the way up to the ocean. As they proceeded through that desolate forest, the powerful Viradha was seen and he roared extremely loudly. He raised his hands up high and emitted an extremely loud roar. However, while he was trumpeting like an elephant, they flung him down into a pit, with his face hanging downwards. Those brothers, Rama and Lakshmana, performed this extremely difficult deed. In the evening, they went to Sharabhanga's beautiful hermitage. After greeting Rama, for whom truth is valour, the sage, Sharabhanga went to heaven. All of them reached Janasthana. There were fourteen thousand rakshasas who were terrible in their deeds. While he was residing there, the great-souled Raghava killed them.[427] After this, Shurpanakha arrived in Rama's presence. Commanded by Rama, Lakshmana suddenly arose. The immensely strong one seized his sword and sliced off her nose and ears. The suffering child approached Ravana. The terrible rakshasa named Maricha was Ravana's follower. Assuming the form of a bejewelled deer, he tempted Vaidehi. Seeing this, Vaidehi told Rama, "Seize it. This handsome and beautiful one should be in our hermitage." Wielding

[427] The Critical Edition has the wrong sequence of events. Non-Critical versions preserve the right sequence.

a bow and arrows, Rama rushed after it. Rushing after it, he slew it with arrows with drooping tufts. O amiable one! When Raghava rushed after the deer and Lakshmana had also left, Dashagriva entered the hermitage. He quickly seized Sita, like a planet seizes Rohini in the sky. In an encounter, he killed the eagle Jatayu, who desired to save her. Violently seizing Sita, the rakshasa departed quickly. Apes who were like mountains were based on the summit of a mountain and they witnessed the extraordinary sight of Sita being seized. They were amazed to see Ravana, the lord of the rakshasas, rush away. Ravana, the one who made the worlds shriek, entered Lanka. He entered his large and auspicious residence, embellished all around with gold. Having entered, Ravana sought to comfort Maithilee with his words. When Kakutstha returned, he saw the eagle and was distressed. When the eagle was killed, Rama cremated his father's beloved friend. They wandered in the region around the Godavari, filled with blossoms. In the great forest, the rakshasa named Kabandha approached. Following Kabandha's words, Rama, for whom truth is his valour, went to Mount Rishyamuka and met Sugriva. Even before they met, affection had been generated in their hearts.[428] When they met and conversed, a great love was generated between them. With the valour of his own arms, Rama killed the immensely large and immensely strong Vali in a battle and returned his own kingdom to him.[429] With all the apes, Sugriva was instated in the kingdom. He gave a pledge to prince Rama that he would search out the trail. The Indras among the apes were commanded by the great-souled Sugriva. Ten crores of apes were sent in all the directions. Among them, we got lost in Vindhya, supreme among mountains. We were tormented by great grief and a long period of time elapsed. The valiant brother of the king of the eagles is named Sampati. He informed us that Sita was dwelling in Ravana's abode. My relatives were overcome by sorrow, but I overcame the misery that was engulfing me. I resorted to my own valour and leapt across one hundred yojanas. I went to the rakshasa's Ashokavana and saw

[428] Hanumat had been used as a messenger before Rama and Sugriva actually met. That must be the explanation for this statement.

[429] To Sugriva.

her alone there. She was clad in a faded silken garment. She was miserable, but was firm in her vows. I met the unblemished one in the proper way and asked her everything. I obtained the jewel as a sign. Successful in the objective, I returned. I went to Rama, who is unblemished in his deeds. I gave him the token, the giant jewel that radiated rays. Hearing about Maithilee, he rejoiced and like an afflicted person who drinks amrita and regains his life, he too recovered his hopes of remaining alive. He arose and made arrangements for victory, making up his mind to destroy Lanka. Like the fire that destroys all the worlds, he wished to destroy the world. Reaching the ocean, Nala constructed a bridge. Using that bridge, the army of brave apes crossed. Nila killed Prahasta and Raghava killed Kumbhakarna. Lakshmana killed Ravana's son and Rama himself killed Ravana. Kakutstha, the scorcher of enemies, met Shakra, Yama, Varuna and the divine sages and received boons. Having obtained the boons, he was delighted and met the apes.[430] Astride the Pushpaka vimana, he went to Kishkindha.[431] Having reached the Ganga again, he is residing in the presence of the sages. Tomorrow, when it is the conjunction of the nakshatra Pushya, without any impediments, you will see Rama.'

Hearing about the great and truthful words from Hanumat, Bharata was delighted and joined his hands in salutation. With his mind rejoicing, he spoke these words. 'What I have desired for a long time has indeed become completely fulfilled.'

Chapter 6(115)

On hearing this, Bharata, for whom truth was valour, was supremely delighted. Rejoicing, the slayer of enemy heroes

[430] Who had been revived.

[431] As they were returning from Lanka to Ayodhya in the Pushpaka vimana, the Critical Edition excises some shlokas. In those excised shlokas, they stopped in Kishkindha to pick up the wives of the apes, who also came to Ayodhya to join in the festivities. With those shlokas excised, this reference to Kishkindha is unnecessary.

commanded Shatrughna. 'To the sound of musical instruments, let pure men offer worship of extremely fragrant flowers at all the temples[432] and chaityas of the city. Let the wives of the king,[433] the advisers, the soldiers and the wives of the soldiers emerge, so that they can see Rama, whose face is like the moon.' Hearing Bharata's words, the valiant Shatrughna, the slayer of enemy heroes, divided artisans into groups of thousands and urged them. 'Let the entire stretch up to Nandigrama be levelled. Level the low spots. Level the uneven spots. Sprinkle the entire ground with water that is as cool as ice. Let others spread parched grain and flowers everywhere. Let flags be raised along the roads of this supreme and excellent city. Before the sun rises, let all the houses be decorated. Let garlands of extremely fragrant flowers, in the five colours,[434] be strewn around. Let hundreds of men sprinkle the walls along the royal road.'

There were thousands of crazy elephants and these were decorated with gold. There were other elephants and female elephants with golden harnesses. Yoking their chariots, excellent maharathas quickly emerged. All of Dasharatha's wives mounted vehicles. With Kousalya and Sumitra at the forefront, they emerged. The earth seemed to tremble from the sound of the hooves of the horses, the clatter of the wheels of the chariots and the noise of conch shells and drums. The entire city reached Nandigrama. There were the best among brahmanas, with dharma in their souls. There were the chiefs of the *shrenis*,[435] with all their divisions. There were ministers, with garlands and sweetmeats in their hands. In addition to the sound of conch shell and drums, there were the sounds of bards singing panegyrics. He[436] was surrounded by all these. The one who knew about dharma placed the noble one's sandals on his head. He took a white umbrella that was decorated with white

[432] The word 'temple' should not convey the wrong impression. A better translation is 'houses of the gods'. In all probability, these were in individual residences and were not collective places of worship.

[433] Dasharatha's wives.

[434] Since these are flowers, this probably means red, blue, white, yellow and pink.

[435] A shreni is like a guild, it is an association of traders or artisans who follow the same line of business. The word means a rank or line.

[436] Bharata.

garlands. He also took white whisks made out of hair, decorated with gold, and appropriate for a king. He was lean and emaciated because of his fasting. He was attired in bark and black antelope skin. Having already heard about his brother's arrival, he was filled with joy. With his advisers, the great-souled one advanced to receive Rama.

Looking towards the son of the wind god, Bharata addressed him in these words. 'I hope the fickleness that characterizes monkeys has not taken hold of you. I cannot see the noble Kakutstha Rama, the scorcher of enemies.' Hearing the words spoken, Hanumat replied to Bharata, for whom truth was his valour, in words that were indicative of deep meaning. 'Because of Bharadvaja's favours, trees that always yield fruits and flowers and flow with honey have been obtained. The sound of crazy humming bees can be heard. O scorcher of enemies! That was the boon conferred by Vasava. That is how hospitality, with all the qualities, was offered to the soldiers. The terrible and joyous sound of the residents of the forest can be heard. I think that the army of the apes is crossing the river Gomatee. Behold. A lot of dust has arisen in the direction of the Valukini. I think the apes are shaking the beautiful forest of sala trees. From a distance, the divine Pushpaka vimana can be seen. It sparkles like the moon. Using his mental powers, Brahma constructed it. Having slain Ravana and his relatives, the great-souled one obtained it through the favours of the lord of treasure. It is divine and possesses the speed of thought. The two brave Raghavas, with Vaidehi, the immensely energetic Sugriva and Vibhishana, Indra among the rakshasas, are in it.'

A great sound of rejoicing arose and seemed to touch the sky. Women, children, the young and the aged shouted, 'Rama is coming.' They descended from their chariots, elephants and horses and took to the ground. Like the moon in the sky, the men saw the vimana. Delighted, they joined their hands in salutation in Raghava's direction. They welcomed him in the proper way and worshipped Rama. Lakshmana's elder brother was on a vimana that had been constructed by Brahma with his mental powers. With long and large eyes, he was radiant, like a second wielder of the vajra. His brother, Rama, was in the front of the vimana, like the sun atop Meru. Bharata lowered his head down and worshipped him.

When the vimana touched down, Bharata, for whom truth was his valour, happily approached Rama and greeted him again. Kakutstha had seen him after a long time. Full of joy, he made Bharata rise, embraced him and placed him on his lap. The scorcher of enemies, Bharata, then happily approached Lakshmana and Vaidehi, greeted them and announced his name. Kaikeyee's son also embraced Sugriva, Jambavat, Angada, Mainda, Dvivida, Nila and Rishabha. The apes, who could assume any form at will, assumed human forms. Cheerfully, they asked Bharata about his welfare. Bharata addressed Vibhishana in words of conciliation. 'It is good fortune that this extremely difficult task has been accomplished with your help.' Shatrughna greeted Rama and Lakshmana. Full of humility, he subsequently worshipped at Sita's feet.

Rama approached his miserable mother, who was afflicted by grief. He bowed and seized her feet, delighting his mother's mind. He greeted Sumitra and the illustrious Kaikeyee. With all his mothers, he then approached the priest.[437]

Joining their hands in salutation, all the residents told Rama, 'O mighty-armed one! O extender of Kousalya's delight! Welcome.' When the citizens joined their hands in salutation, Bharata's elder brother saw that it was like an array of blooming lotuses.

Bharata, who knew about dharma, himself took Rama's sandals and inserted the feet of the Indra among men into these. Joining his hands in salutation, Bharata told Rama, 'I have protected this kingdom in trust and I am returning it to you. My birth has become successful today and my wishes have also been fulfilled. I have seen the king of Ayodhya return. I have taken care of your treasury, stores of grain, the city and the army. Because of your energy, everything is ten times what it used to be.' The apes and the rakshasa Vibhishana witnessed Bharata's devotion to his brother and heard him. They shed tears. Delighted, Raghava placed Bharata on his lap.

[437] Vasishtha.

With the soldiers, they used that vimana to go to Bharata's hermitage. With the soldiers, Raghava reached Bharata's hermitage. They got down from the vimana and stood on the ground, before it. Rama told the excellent vimana, 'I give you permission to go to the god Vaishravana.' Having obtained Rama's permission, the excellent vimana headed in a northward direction and went to the residence of the lord of treasures.

Like Shakra, the lord of the immortals, approaching Brihaspati, Raghava approached his own priest.[438] He pressed his feet. The valiant one sat down with him, but on a separate auspicious seat.

Chapter 6(116)

Bharata, the extender of Kaikeyee's delight, placed his hands in salutation above his head. He spoke to his elder brother Rama, for whom truth was his valour. 'Honouring my mother's words, you gave me the kingdom. I have given it back to you, just as you had given it to me. I cannot bear this burden alone, which has been imposed on me by a stronger bull. I am like one who is young and am not interested in bearing this heavy load. I think that this prosperous kingdom is similar to a dam being shattered by a great flood of water. It is difficult to bridge. This is like a donkey trying to follow the footsteps of a horse, or a crow that of a swan. O lord! O scorcher of enemies! I am not interested in following in your footsteps. A tree that has been planted inside one's house may grow up and become large, extremely difficult to climb, with a large trunk and branches. Its flowers may dry up and it may not show any flowers. Nothing may indeed be obtained by the person who planted it. O mighty-armed one! I wish to make this analogy known to you.[439] O Indra among men! I am devoted to you and am your servant. Instruct me. Let the universe, all around, see you

[438] Vasishtha.

[439] The analogy probably means that Bharata has planted the tree. But now that the tree has grown up, it requires Rama to look after it.

consecrated today. Blazing in your energy, scorch like the midday sun. After sleeping, awake to the sounds of many trumpets blaring, the sounds of girdles and anklets and the sweet sounds of singing. As long as the wheel revolves[440] and as long as the earth is here, may you be the lord of everything on this extensive earth.'

Hearing Bharata's words, Rama, the victor over enemy cities, accepted these words and sat down on an auspicious seat. Following Shatrughna's words, accomplished tenders of the beard,[441] who were pleasant in the use of their hands, swiftly surrounded Raghava. Bharata, the immensely strong Lakshmana, Sugriva, Indra among the apes, and Vibhishana, Indra of the rakshasas, bathed first. The matted hair was cleaned. He bathed and wore colourful garlands, with unguents smeared. Donning extremely expensive garments, he blazed in his prosperity. The valiant extender of the lineage of the Ikshvakus[442] arranged for the personal care of Rama and the prosperous Lakshmana. All of Dasharatha's wives arranged for Sita's personal care. Those spirited ones also made themselves look beautiful. Kousalya, delighted and affectionate towards her son, also took care to make all the other wives of the Raghavas[443] look beautiful.

On Shatrughna's words, the charioteer named Sumantra yoked a chariot that was beautiful in all its parts. The chariot was like the divine solar disc. On seeing it, the mighty-armed Rama, for whom truth was valour, mounted it. Placing the priest at the forefront, King Dasharatha's advisers prepared everything properly in Ayodhya. They consulted about the conduct, so that the city might become prosperous. 'Arrange everything for the consecration so that the great-souled one becomes worthy of victory. For Rama's sake, you should perform everything in an auspicious manner.' In this way, all the ministers requested the priest. Making up their minds to see Rama, they then quickly emerged from the city. Like the one with the thousand eyes on a chariot yoked to tawny

[440] The wheel of time.

[441] Barbers.

[442] Presumably meaning Shatrughna.

[443] The wives of the other three brothers.

horses, the unblemished Rama mounted the chariot and left for the supreme city. Bharata seized the reins and Shatrughna grasped the umbrella. Lakshmana fanned the whisk atop his head. Sugriva, lord of the apes, held a whisk that was made out of white hair. Vibhishana, Indra among the rakshasas, held another one that was like the moon. Large numbers of rishis, the gods and large numbers of Maruts praised Rama from the sky and the sweet sounds of these were heard. There was an elephant named Shatrunjaya and it was like a mountain. The immensely energetic Sugriva, lord of the apes, mounted this. The apes proceeded on nine thousand elephants. They assumed the forms of humans and adorned themselves in all the ornaments. There was the sound of conch shells being blown and drums were sounded.

The tigers among men went to the city that was garlanded with mansions. They[444] saw the atiratha Raghava arrive, radiant in form, on a chariot, with attendants in front. They honoured Kakutstha and were greeted back by Rama. As he was surrounded by his brothers, they followed the great-souled one. Surrounded by advisers, brahmanas and ordinary people, like the moon by nakshatras, Rama blazed in his prosperity. Minstrels proceeded in front, with *svastikas*[445] in their hands. Trumpets were sounded rhythmically. They surrounded him and proceeded, chanting auspicious songs. Maidens and brahmanas proceeded in front, with gold-hued unhusked grain in their hands. There were also men holding sweetmeats. Rama told the ministers about his friendship with Sugriva, the powers of the son of the wind god and the deeds of the apes. On hearing this, the residents of the city of Ayodhya were astounded. Having told them this, Rama entered Ayodhya, full of happy and healthy people, surrounded by the apes. In every house, the residents of the city raised auspicious flags.

He entered the beautiful palace, his father's residence and the abode of the Ikshvakus. The great-souled one reached and entered his father's residence. He greeted Kousalya, Sumitra and Kaikeyee.

[444] The citizens.

[445] A svastika is a kind of musical instrument.

The prince, the descendant of the Raghu lineage, spoke to Bharata, supreme among those who followed dharma, in sweet words full of meaning. 'This excellent residence has a large Ashokavana. It is full of pearls and lapis lazuli. Make Sugriva stay here.' Hearing his words, Bharata, for whom truth was his valour, took Sugriva by the hands and entered that residence. They entered and urged by Shatrughna, oil lamps, couches and spreads were quickly brought. Raghava's immensely energetic younger brother spoke to Sugriva, 'O lord! Command the messengers about Rama's consecration.' Sugriva quickly gave four Indras among apes four pots that were decorated with all kinds of jewels. 'O apes! In the morning, go to the four oceans and collect water and fill these pots. Act according to my command.' The great-souled apes, who resembled elephants, were addressed in this way. As swift as Garuda, they quickly leapt up into the sky. Jambavat, Hanumat, the ape Vegadarshi and Rishabha filled and brought four pots of water. They brought a fifth pot, filled with water from one hundred rivers. Sushena,[446] full of spirit, brought a pot, decorated with all kinds of jewels, filled with water from the eastern ocean. Rishabha swiftly brought water from the southern ocean. Gavaya brought water from the great western ocean and covered the water in the golden pot with red sandalwood powder and *karpura*.[447] The one who was like the wind god in valour, the one who was like Garuda and the wind in valour[448] quickly brought cool water from the northern ocean in a large pot that was decorated with jewels.

For the sake of Rama's consecration, with the advisers, Shatrughna reported this to the supreme priest and his well-wishers. With the brahmanas, the aged Vasishtha proceeded. With Sita, he asked Rama to sit down on a seat encrusted with gems. Vasishtha, Vamadeva, Jabali, Kashyapa, Katyayana, Suyajna, Goutama and Vijaya sprinkled the tiger among men with water, just as the Vasus did to Vasava, the one with the thousand eyes.

[446] There is an obvious inconsistency in the names of the four apes who went to the four oceans.

[447] Camphor.

[448] That is, Hanumat.

The officiating priests who were brahmanas did this first. They were then followed by maidens, ministers, warriors and merchants, who cheerfully consecrated him too, with the juices of all the herbs, while the gods were stationed in the sky. The four guardians of the world were there, with all the gods. Shatrughna held a white and auspicious umbrella. Sugriva, lord of the apes, held a whisk made out of white hair, while Vibhishana, Indra among the rakshasas, held another one that was like the moon. Urged by Vasava, Vayu gave Raghava a golden garland that blazed in form and was made out of one hundred lotuses. Urged by Shakra, he also gave the Indra among men a necklace made out of pearls. It was encrusted with all the jewels and was decorated with gems and jewels. At the well-deserved consecration of the intelligent Rama, divine gandharvas sang and large numbers of apsaras danced. The earth was full of succulent grain. The trees were full of fruits and fragrant flowers. This is what happened at the festivities for Raghava. The bull among men first gave brahmanas one hundred bulls and followed it up with one hundred thousand horses and also cows with calves. Raghava also gave brahmanas thirty crores of gold,[449] many kinds of ornaments and extremely expensive garments. The bull among men gave Sugriva a divine garland. It was golden, studded with gems and resembled the rays of the sun. He gave the patient Angada, Vali's son, a bracelet that was colourful with lapis lazuli and gems and was decorated with diamonds and jewels. Rama gave Sita an excellent necklace made out of pearls. It was decorated with the best of jewels and was like the beams of the moon. While Vaidehi looked on, he gave Vayu's son a radiant and divine garment and auspicious ornaments. While all the apes and her husband repeatedly looked on, Janaka's daughter took off her necklace.[450] Since he[451] knew about signs, he looked at Janaka's daughter and spoke to her. 'O immensely fortunate one! O beautiful one! Give this necklace to whoever you are satisfied with. He has always possessed manliness, valour, intelligence and other qualities. Give it to Vayu's son.'

[449] Golden coins.

[450] Probably not the one Rama had just given her.

[451] Rama.

The dark-eyed one gave the necklace to Vayu's son. Wearing that necklace, Hanumat, bull among apes, was radiant. It was as white and pure as the moon and he looked like a mountain with white clouds. Glancing towards Mainda, Dvivida and Nila, the scorcher of enemies, the lord of the earth, gave them all the objects of desire. He honoured all the aged apes and all the other bulls among the apes, as they deserved, and gave them garments and ornaments. All of them were worshipped, as they deserved, with all the desired ornaments. Delighted, all of them returned to wherever they had come from.

Full of great joy, the extremely generous Raghava ruled. Rama knew about dharma and was devoted to dharma. He told Lakshmana, 'O one who knows about dharma! Remain here with me. This earth has been powerfully ruled by former kings and the burden has been borne by our forefathers. You are like me. Be the heir apparent and bear this burden with me.' Though he repeatedly entreated Soumitri with all his soul, Soumitri did not accept this assignment. At this, the great-souled one instated Bharata as the heir apparent. Raghava, with dharma in his soul, obtained that excellent kingdom. With his well-wishers, brothers and relatives, he performed many kinds of rites and sacrifices. The bull among kings performed *poundarika, ashvamedha, vajapeya* and many other sacrifices. Raghava ruled the kingdom for ten thousand years. He sacrificed excellent horses at one hundred ashvamedha sacrifices and gave away copious quantities of dakshina. The powerful one possessed arms that stretched all the way down to his thighs. He had broad shoulders. With Lakshmana as his follower, Rama ruled the earth. As long as Rama ruled the kingdom, no widows lamented. There was no fear from predatory beasts. There was no fear on account of disease. There were no bandits in the world. No one suffered from lack of riches. The aged did not have to perform funeral rites for the young.[452] Everyone was cheerful. Everyone was devoted to dharma. They looked towards Rama and did not cause violence towards each other. As long as Rama ruled the kingdom,

[452] That is, the young did not die before the old.

people were without disease and devoid of sorrow. They lived for one thousand years and had one thousand sons. The trees extended their trunks and always had flowers. They always had fruit. The rain showered down at the right time. The breeze had a pleasant touch. People were satisfied with their own tasks and performed their own duties. As long as Rama ruled, there was no falsehood in the subjects and they were devoted to dharma. All of them possessed the qualities and all of them were devoted to dharma. Rama ruled the kingdom for ten thousand years.

This ends Yuddha Kanda.

CHAPTER SEVEN

Uttara Kanda

Sarga (1): 27 *shlokas*
Sarga (2): 29 *shlokas*
Sarga (3): 31 *shlokas*
Sarga (4): 31 *shlokas*
Sarga (5): 41 *shlokas*
Sarga (6): 55 *shlokas*
Sarga (7): 50 *shlokas*
Sarga (8): 25 *shlokas*
Sarga (9): 37 *shlokas*
Sarga (10): 42 *shlokas*
Sarga (11): 41 *shlokas*
Sarga (12): 29 *shlokas*
Sarga (13): 39 *shlokas*
Sarga (14): 25 *shlokas*
Sarga (15): 31 *shlokas*
Sarga (16): 31 *shlokas*
Sarga (17): 31 *shlokas*
Sarga (18): 33 *shlokas*
Sarga (19): 26 *shlokas*
Sarga (20): 25 *shlokas*
Sarga (21): 29 *shlokas*
Sarga (22): 43 *shlokas*
Sarga (23): 46 *shlokas*
Sarga (24): 35 *shlokas*
Sarga (25): 50 *shlokas*
Sarga (26): 47 *shlokas*
Sarga (27): 42 *shlokas*
Sarga (28): 46 *shlokas*
Sarga (29): 40 *shlokas*
Sarga (30): 42 *shlokas*
Sarga (31): 40 *shlokas*
Sarga (32): 72 *shlokas*
Sarga (33): 23 *shlokas*
Sarga (34): 44 *shlokas*
Sarga (35): 65 *shlokas*
Sarga (36): 46 *shlokas*
Sarga (37): 14 *shlokas*
Sarga (38): 17 *shlokas*
Sarga (39): 24 *shlokas*
Sarga (40): 18 *shlokas*
Sarga (41): 27 *shlokas*
Sarga (42): 23 *shlokas*
Sarga (43): 19 *shlokas*
Sarga (44): 22 *shlokas*
Sarga (45): 28 *shlokas*
Sarga (46): 18 *shlokas*
Sarga (47): 18 *shlokas*
Sarga (48): 20 *shlokas*
Sarga (49): 18 *shlokas*
Sarga (50): 20 *shlokas*

Sarga (51): 16 *shloka*s
Sarga (52): 16 *shloka*s
Sarga (53): 23 *shloka*s
Sarga (54): 21 *shloka*s
Sarga (55): 20 *shloka*s
Sarga (56): 17 *shloka*s
Sarga (57): 35 *shloka*s
Sarga (58): 14 *shloka*s
Sarga (59): 23 *shloka*s
Sarga (60): 19 *shloka*s
Sarga (61): 38 *shloka*s
Sarga (62): 14 *shloka*s
Sarga (63): 17 *shloka*s
Sarga (64): 15 *shloka*s
Sarga (65): 26 *shloka*s
Sarga (66): 17 *shloka*s
Sarga (67): 18 *shloka*s
Sarga (68): 17 *shloka*s
Sarga (69): 27 *shloka*s
Sarga (70): 19 *shloka*s
Sarga (71): 17 *shloka*s
Sarga (72): 21 *shloka*s
Sarga (73): 19 *shloka*s
Sarga (74): 19 *shloka*s
Sarga (75): 18 *shloka*s
Sarga (76): 22 *shloka*s
Sarga (77): 19 *shloka*s
Sarga (78): 29 *shloka*s
Sarga (79): 24 *shloka*s
Sarga (80): 25 *shloka*s
Sarga (81): 24 *shloka*s
Sarga (82): 19 *shloka*s
Sarga (83): 16 *shloka*s
Sarga (84): 16 *shloka*s
Sarga (85): 23 *shloka*s
Sarga (86): 16 *shloka*s
Sarga (87): 20 *shloka*s
Sarga (88): 20 *shloka*s
Sarga (89): 15 *shloka*s
Sarga (90): 25 *shloka*s
Sarga (91): 16 *shloka*s
Sarga (92): 17 *shloka*s
Sarga (93): 17 *shloka*s
Sarga (94): 19 *shloka*s
Sarga (95): 18 *shloka*s
Sarga (96): 18 *shloka*s
Sarga (97): 20 *shloka*s
Sarga (98): 26 *shloka*s
Sarga (99): 18 *shloka*s
Sarga (100): 26 *shloka*s

Chapter 7(1)

When the rakshasas had been slain and Rama had obtained the kingdom, all the rishis came to congratulate Raghava. Koushika, Yavakrita, Raibha, Chyavana, and Medhatithi's son, Kanva—these were the ones who resided in the eastern direction. Svastyatreya, the illustrious Namuchi, Pramuchi and Agastya were the ones who came from the southern direction. Prishadgu,

Kavasha, Dhoumya and the great rishi, Roudreya, were the ones who came with their disciples, from the western direction. Vasishtha, Kashyapa, Atri, Vishvamitra, Goutama, Jamadagni and Bharadvaja—there were these seven maharshis.[453] Those great-souled ones reached Raghava's residence, radiant as the fire, and waited for the *pratihara*.[454] Following their words, the great-souled pratihara quickly went. He swiftly entered and approached Raghava. He suddenly saw Rama, who was like the full moon when it has arisen, and told him that Agastya and the other rishis had arrived. The king was like the rising sun in his radiance. Hearing that the sages had come, he told the gatekeeper to ensure they were comfortable and to make them enter. On seeing the sages arrive, Rama stood up and joined his hands in salutation. He controlled himself, greeted them and offered them seats. Those bulls among rishis sat down, as they deserved, on comfortable seats with golden and colourful spreads. Rama asked them about their welfare, together with that of their disciples and their companions.

The maharshis, who knew about the Vedas, addressed Rama in these words. 'O descendant of the Raghu lineage! We are well in every possible way. It is good fortune that we see you are well, having slain your enemies. O Rama! We no longer suffer from the burden of Ravana, lord of the rakshasas. There is no doubt that you can conquer the three worlds with your bow. O Rama! It is good fortune that you killed Ravana, with his sons and grandsons. It is good fortune that we see you victorious today, with your wife. It is good fortune that Prahasta, Vikata, Virupaksha, Mahodara and the invincible Akampana, the roamers in the night, have been killed by you. O Rama! Kumbhakarna was gigantic in size and there was no one as large as him in this world. It is good fortune that you brought him down in the battle. It is good fortune that the Indra among rakshasas turned up to have a duel with you. The gods could not kill him, but you were victorious over him. However, Ravana's defeat in the encounter was hardly surprising. After all, it is good fortune

[453] By implication, from the northern direction.

[454] The pratihara is the gatekeeper or doorkeeper. They waited for the gatekeeper to announce their arrival to Rama.

that you killed Ravana's son, when he turned up to have a duel with you. O mighty-armed one! O brave one! It is good fortune that you could free yourself from the enemy of the gods, who was like Death. You were victorious. O amiable one! On hearing that Indrajit had been killed, we were amazed. All the creatures found it impossible to kill him. He could invoke great maya in a battle. O brave one! O amiable one! You gave us something sacred. As dakshina, you gave us freedom from fear. O Kakutstha! O afflicter of enemies! It is good fortune that you are prospering in your victory.'

Rama was greatly astounded. He joined his hands in salutation and said, 'Passing over the two immensely valiant Kumbhakarna and Ravana, the roamer in the night, why are you praising Ravana's son? Passing over the immensely valiant Mahodara, Prahasta and the rakshasa Virupaksha, why are you praising Ravana's son? What were his powers? What was his strength and his valour? What was the reason for his being superior to Ravana? If I am capable of hearing it, if you are indeed capable of telling me and if this is not a secret account, I wish to hear the story. How did he defeat Shakra and how did he obtain a boon?'

Chapter 7(2)

Hearing the words of the great-souled Raghava, the immensely energetic Kumbhayoni[455] spoke these words. 'O king! Hear about his conduct and about his great energy and strength, about how he killed enemies in battle, though enemies couldn't kill him. O Raghava! However, I will start by telling you about Ravana's lineage and birth. I will tell you about how a boon was bestowed on him. O Rama! Earlier, in krita yuga, the lord Prajapati[456] had a son. He was a brahmana rishi named Pulastya and he was like the grandfather himself. It is impossible to recount the qualities about his conduct in following dharma. One can only say that he

[455] Agastya's name.
[456] Brahma.

was Prajapati's son and mention his name. To observe dharma, he went to the slopes of the large mountain, Meru. The bull among sages went to Trinavindu's hermitage and resided there. The one with dharma in his soul performed austerities there. He studied and controlled his senses. But maidens went to that hermitage and created obstructions. They were the maidens of gods and serpents, daughters of royal sages and apsaras. They went to that region and sported there. The objects of desire of all the seasons were present there and the grove was beautiful. Those maidens always went to that region and sported. The immensely energetic and great sage became angry and said, "Anyone who comes within my range of vision will become pregnant." They returned after hearing the great-souled one's words. Scared of the brahmana's curse, they did not go to that region again. However, the daughter of the royal sage, Trinavindu, had not heard this. Not scared at all, she went to that hermitage and began to roam around. At that time, the great rishi who was Prajapati's son was studying there. Because of his austerities, he was radiant and blazed. She heard the sounds of the Vedas being chanted and she saw the store of austerities. Her body turned pale and the signs of her being pregnant were clearly visible. On seeing her form, she became greatly anxious. "How did this happen?" Finding out her state, she went and stood before her father. Seeing her in that state, Trinavindu asked, "How have you come to assume a form like this?" The maiden was distressed. She joined her hands in salutation and spoke to the store of austerities.[457] "O father! I do not know the reason why my form has become like this. However, earlier, I was searching for my friends and went alone to maharshi Pulastya's hermitage. But when I went to the hermitage of the one with the cleansed soul, I did not see any of my friends there. Seeing my distorted form, I came here." The royal sage, Trinavindu, dazzled in radiance because of his austerities. Meditating, the rishi perceived the act which led to this consequence. He got to know about the curse that the maharshi with the cleansed soul had imposed. Taking his daughter with him, he went to Pulastya and addressed him thus. "O illustrious one! My daughter is adorned

[457] Meaning Trinavindu.

with her own qualities. O maharshi! I am myself offering her to you as alms. Accept her. When you engage in austerities, your senses will become exhausted. There is no doubt that she will always serve you devotedly." Hearing the words of the royal sage who followed dharma, the brahmana agreed and accepted the maiden. Having given her away, the king went to his own hermitage. Since then, the maiden resided there and satisfied her husband with her qualities. The immensely energetic one was pleased and addressed her in these words. "O fortunate one! You possess an abundance of qualities and I am pleased with you. Therefore, I will now grant you a son who will be like me in qualities. He will extend both lineages and will be famous as Poulastya. You heard me chanting the Vedas. Therefore, there is no doubt that his name will be Vishrava."[458] Thus addressed, the maiden was delighted in her inner soul. Within a short period of time, that daughter had a son named Vishrava.[459] He was full of purity and dharma and was famous in the three worlds. Vishrava, bull among sages, observed austerities, just like his father.'

Chapter 7(3)

Within a short period of time, Vishrava, Pulastya's son and bull among sages, started to perform austerities, just like his father. He was truthful, accomplished, devoted to studying, pure, always devoted to dharma, unattached to all objects of pleasure and possessed good conduct. On knowing about his good conduct, the great rishi, Bharadvaja, bestowed his own daughter, Devavarnini, on Vishrava as a wife. Vishrava, bull among sages, was filled with great delight. Following dharma, he accepted Bharadvaja's daughter. The one with dharma in his soul had an energetic son who was extraordinary, possessing all the qualities of a brahmana.

[458] From *vishruta* (heard). The son's name was Vishrava. Poulastya means Pulastya's son. Therefore, he was also Poulastya.

[459] The same as Vishravasa.

When he was born, his paternal grandfather[460] was extremely happy. With the other celestial rishis, he happily gave him a name. "Since he is Vishrava's son and is like Vishrava himself, he will therefore be known by the name of Vaishravana." The immensely energetic Vaishravana began to grow up in that hermitage, like a fire into which oblations have been offered. While he was in that hermitage, the great-souled one arrived at the determination, "Since dharma is the supreme objective, I will also control myself and follow dharma." In the great forest, he tormented himself through austerities for one thousand years. He followed the rituals for a full one thousand years. He lived only on water, he survived only on air, or he ate nothing. In this way, he passed one thousand years as if it was only one year. With large numbers of extremely energetic gods and with Indra, Brahma went to the hermitage and spoke these words. "O child! O one who is good in vows! I am pleased with your deeds. Ask for a boon. It is my view that you are fortunate and deserve to be granted a boon." The grandfather was in front of him and Vaishravana replied, "O illustrious one! I wish to be a guardian of the world and look after all treasures." Content in his mind and happy, with the large number of gods, Brahma told Vaishravana that he agreed to this. "After Yama, Indra and Varuna, I was about to create a fourth guardian of the world. That is the status you have asked for. O one who knows about dharma! Therefore, go and become Dhanesha.[461] From now, you will become a fourth, after Yama, Indra and Varuna. This Pushpaka vimana is like the sun. Accept this as a vehicle you can move around in, so that you can travel just as the gods do. May you be fortunate. All of us will return to wherever we came from. O son! Having granted you a great boon, we have also become successful."

'With Brahma at the forefront, all the gods left through the sky. Dhanesha went to his father and bowed down in humility, addressing him in these words. "O illustrious one! I have obtained a boon from the one who was generated from a lotus.[462] O lord!

[460] Pulastya.

[461] The lord of riches, *dhana* + *isha*, Kubera.

[462] Brahma.

However, Prajapati has not indicated a place for me to live in. O illustrious one! O lord! Therefore, search out and indicate a residence for me, so that no suffering of any type is caused to any being there." Thus addressed by his son, Vishrava, bull among sages, replied in these words. "O one who knows about dharma! O one who is learned about dharma! Listen. Vishvakarma constructed a beautiful city named Lanka for the rakshasas to reside in. It is like Indra's Amaravati. It is a beautiful city, with turrets made out of gold and lapis lazuli. In earlier times, because they were afflicted by fear of Vishnu, the rakshasas abandoned it and it is empty. All the large number of rakshasas have gone to the nether regions of rasatala. Make your mind agreeable to the prospect of dwelling there. There will be no taint associated with your residing there and no one will be obstructed in any way." The one who had dharma in his soul heard the words of his father, who abided by dharma. He dwelt in Lanka, on the summit of a mountain. Within a short period of time, thousands of happy and delighted nairittas gathered around and filled the place up, under his rule. Vishrava's son, the lord of the nairittas, happily resided there, in Lanka, with the ocean as the frontier. From time to time, the lord of treasures, humble in his soul, used Pushpaka to happily go and visit his father and his mother. He would be praised by gods, large numbers of gandharvas, siddhas and charanas. Prosperous and surrounded by them, like the sun with the energy of its rays, he would travel to his father's presence.'

Chapter 7(4)

Hearing Agastya's words, Rama was filled with surprise. He repeatedly looked towards Agastya, whose form was like that of *tretagni*.[463] How was it possible for the rakshasas to have resided in Lanka earlier? He shook his head, smiled and said, 'O illustrious one! The devourers of flesh used to live in Lanka earlier. Hearing

[463] The three fires, *garhapatya, ahavaniya* and *dakshinagni*.

you say this, I am filled with wonder. We have heard that the rakshasas were born from Pulastya's lineage. However, on the basis of what you have recounted, I now think their origins lie elsewhere. Were they stronger than Ravana, Kumbhakarna, Prahasta, Vikata and Ravana's sons? O brahmana! Who was their ancestor? What was his name? What was the strength of his austerities? What were the crimes they committed that they were driven away by Vishnu earlier? O unblemished one! You should tell me everything about this. You have generated a curiosity in me. Dispel it, the way the sun drives away darkness.'

Hearing Raghava's words, embellished with cleansed speech, Agastya seemed a little surprised and spoke to him. 'In ancient times, Brahma was born from the lotus in the waters.[464] He first created the waters and to protect them, created various creatures. Those creatures humbly presented themselves before the one who had created the creatures.[465] They were scared and afflicted because of hunger and thirst and asked, "What shall we do?" Prajapati smiled at all of them. The one who confers honours said, "Take care and protect." Among those hungry creatures, there were some who said, "We shall protect." There were some, who despite being devoured, said, "We shall be swift." "Those of you who said we shall protect shall be rakshasas. Those of you who said we shall be swift shall be yakshas."[466] There were two brothers who were bulls among rakshasas and they were Heti and Praheti. Those two scorchers of enemies were like Madhu and Kaitabha.[467] Praheti was devoted to dharma and did not desire a wife. However, for the sake of obtaining a wife, Heti undertook supreme efforts. There was a maiden named Bhaya and she caused great fear. She was Kala's[468] sister. The immensely intelligent one, immeasurable in his soul, himself went and sought to marry her. Through her, Heti, bull among rakshasas, had a son. He was best among sons and

[464] The lotus in Vishnu's navel, Vishnu resting in the waters.

[465] That is, Brahma.

[466] These are Brahma's words. 'We shall protect' is *rakshama*. Hence, rakshasas. 'We shall be swift' is *yakshama*. Hence, yakshas.

[467] Demons killed by Vishnu.

[468] Kala means time, destiny, death.

he was known as Vidyutkesha. Heti's son, Vidyutkesha, was as radiant as a blazing fire. The immensely energetic one started to grow up, like a lotus in the water. When the fortunate roamer in the night became a youth, his father sought to get him married off. Sandhya's daughter was like Sandhya herself in powers. For his son, Heti, the bull among rakshasas, sought her. O Raghava! Sandhya thought, "She will certainly have to be given to someone else." Therefore, she bestowed her on Vidyutkesha. Vidyutkesha, the roamer in the night, obtained Sandhya's daughter. Like Maghavan with Poulami, he pleasured with her. O Rama! Within a short time, through Vidyutkesha, Salakantakata[469] was conceived, just as dense clouds are conceived from the waters of the ocean. The foetus in the rakshasi's womb was as radiant as a cloud. She went to Mandara and delivered, like Ganga delivering Agni's son.[470] Having delivered, she desired Vidyutkesha again. Forgetting her own son, she found pleasure with her husband. The child she delivered was like the autumn sun in his radiance. He covered his face in his hands and wept as loudly as a cloud. For a beneficial purpose, the lord Hara was proceeding on his bull. With Uma, he saw the weeping son of the rakshasa. Parvati was overcome by compassion. Therefore, the destroyer of Tripura[471] made the son of the rakshasa as old as his mother. Mahadeva is without decay and without change. He also made the child immortal. To cause pleasure to Parvati, he also gave him a city[472] that could travel through the sky. O son of a king! Uma also gave boons to rakshasis. They would deliver as soon as they conceived and the infant would instantly acquire the same age as that of the mother. Sukesha[473] became insolent because of the boons he received. Thanks to that proximity with the lord Hara, he obtained prosperity. Having obtained the city that travelled through the sky, like Purandara, the immensely intelligent one travelled everywhere in the sky.'

[469] Sandhya's daughter.

[470] Agni's son means Skanda. There are different stories about the birth of Skanda, Kartikeya or Kumara. In some of these, Ganga figures.

[471] Shiva.

[472] A vimana that was like a city.

[473] Vidyutkesha's son.

Chapter 7(5)

'There was a gandharva named Gramani and he was like Vishvavasu[474] in his resplendence.[475] He had a daughter named Devavati and she was like a second Shri. He saw that the rakshasa Sukesha followed dharma and had obtained boons. Following dharma, he bestowed her on Sukesha, like Daksha bestowing Shri.[476] She obtained a beloved husband who was prosperous because he had obtained boons. Devavati was content, like a poor person who has got riches. United with her, the roamer in the night was also resplendent. He was like a giant elephant born from Anjana,[477] in the company of a female elephant. O Raghava! Through Devavati, Sukesha, lord of the rakshasas, had three sons who were like three eyes to the rakshasa. They were Malyavat, Sumali and Mali—supreme among strong ones. Like the three worlds, they were without any anxiety. They were as stable as the three fires. They were as sharp as the three mantras.[478] They were as terrible as the three that cause disease.[479] Sukesha's three sons dazzled like the three fires. They grew up without any impediments, just as a disease that is ignored does. They realized that their father had obtained great prosperity because of his boons. Therefore, the brothers made up their minds to go to Meru and torment themselves through austerities. O supreme among kings! The rakshasas resorted to terrible rituals. They observed terrible austerities that terrified all creatures. Resorting to truth, uprightness and self-control, they performed austerities that are extremely difficult to undertake on earth. The three worlds, with the gods, the asuras and humans, were tormented. The lord with the four faces[480] was on a supreme

[474] The king of the gandharvas.

[475] This is still Agastya speaking.

[476] There is an allusion to Daksha marrying off his daughters to Dharma. Though the names of the daughters married to Dharma varies, Shri/Lakshmi typically figures in the list.

[477] One of the dishagajas.

[478] Mantras associated with the Rig Veda, Sama Veda and Yajur Veda.

[479] *Vata, pitta* and *kapha*. These can be loosely translated as wind, bile and phlegm. In Ayurveda, these are the three *doshas* or humours in the body and they are always striving against each other.

[480] Brahma.

vimana. He came before Sukesha's sons and invited them, "I will grant boons."[481] Knowing that Brahma was about to grant boons, with all the large number of gods, together with Indra, surrounding him, they trembled like trees. They joined their hands in salutation and said, "O god! If we have worshipped you, if you wish to grant us boons, let us be invincible. Let us slay our enemies and let us live forever. Through the powers of Vishnu, let us be devoted to each other." The lord Brahma, devoted to brahmanas, told Sukesha's sons that it would indeed be that way. He then went to Brahma's world. O Rama! All those roamers in the night obtained the boon. Because they had obtained the boon, they became fearless and started to oppress the gods and the asuras. The gods, the large number of rishis and the charanas were slaughtered by them. Like men in hell, they could not find a protector. O supreme among the Raghu lineage! The undecaying Vishvakarma was an excellent artisan. Happy, the rakshasas went to him and said, "You are the one who builds residences for the gods, according to what they want. O immensely wise one! Build a similar residence for us too, on the Himalayas, Meru or Mandara. Create a great residence for us that is like Maheshvara's residence." The mighty-armed Vishvakarma told them about a residence for the rakshasas that would be like Shakra's Amaravati. "There is a mountain named Trikuta on the shores of the southern ocean. There is a peak in the middle of that mountain and it is like a cloud. Even the birds find it extremely difficult to approach, since there are ragged slopes on four sides. It[482] extends for thirty yojanas and has golden ramparts and gates. Following Shakra's command, I will construct the city of Lanka. O excellent rakshasas! You will reside in that impenetrable city, just as Indra and the gods dwell in Amaravati. O slayers of enemies! When you reach the fortified city of Lanka and are surrounded by many rakshasas, enemies will find it impossible to assail you." O Rama! Hearing Vishvakarma's words, the rakshasas went to Lanka with one thousand followers and started to reside there. There were firm walls and moats. The place was full of hundreds of golden

[481] Invited them to ask for boons.

[482] The residence, that is, the city.

houses. Having reached Lanka, those cheerful roamers in the night found pleasure there. There was a *gandharvi*[483] named Narmada and she followed all kinds of dharma. She had three daughters who were as radiant as Hri, Shri and Kirti.[484] The rakshasi[485] followed the order, eldest downwards, and bestowed them on the rakshasas. The daughters possessed faces that were like the full moon and having bestowed them, she was delighted. The three Indras among the rakshasas obtained the three daughters of the gandharvi. The immensely fortunate mother bestowed them in the nakshatra when Bhaga is the divinity.[486] O Rama! O lord! Thus, Sukesha's sons obtained wives. They sported with those wives, like the immortals do with apsaras. Malyavat's wife was the beautiful Sundari.[487] O Rama! Hear about the offspring Sundari had. The sons were Vajramushti, Virupaksha, the rakshasa Durmukha, Suptaghna, Yajnakopa, Matta and Unmatta, and there was a beautiful daughter, Anala. Sumali's wife had a face that was like the full moon. Her name was Ketumati and he loved her more than his own life. O great king! In due order, hear about the offspring that Sumali, roamer in the night, had through Ketumati—Prahasta, Kampana, Vikata, Kalakarmuka, Dhumraksha, Danda, the immensely strong Suparshva, Sahladi, Praghasa and the rakshasa Bhasakarna. Sumali's daughters were Raka, Pushpotkata, the sweet-smiling Kaikasi and Kumbhinasi. Mali's wife was the gandharvi Vasuda and she was beautiful in form. Her eyes were like the petals of lotuses and these eyes made her resemble an excellent *yakshi*.[488] O Raghava! Hear about the offspring Sumali's younger brother had through her. I will recount them. Mali's sons were Anala, Anila, Hara and Sampati and they are Vibhishana's advisers.[489] Thus, those three roamers in the night, bulls among rakshasas, were surrounded by hundreds of sons.

[483] Gandharva lady.

[484] Hri is the personification of modesty and Kirti is the personification of deeds.

[485] The gandharvi is being described as a rakshasi.

[486] Each nakshatra has an associated divinity, which is often the original Vedic name of the nakshatra. Bhaga is the divinity for Uttara Phalguni nakshatra and Bhaga is also the god for marital prosperity.

[487] Since *sundari* means beautiful, there is a pun.

[488] Yaksha lady.

[489] Earlier, these names have been given as Anala, Sharabha, Sampati and Praghasa.

Insolent because of their strength and valour, they oppressed the gods, together with Indra, the rishis, the serpents and the danavas. Like the wind, they roamed around the entire universe. They were controlled and in battles, they were like Death. They were extremely insolent because of the boons they had received. They destroyed all the sacrifices and rituals.'

Chapter 7(6)

'The gods and the rishis, the stores of austerities, were slaughtered by them. Afflicted by grief, they went and sought refuge with Maheshvara, the god of the gods. They approached Kamari,[490] Tripurari,[491] the one with the three eyes. The gods joined their hands in salutation. Suffering from fear, they stuttered in their words. "O illustrious one! O one who causes an impediment to enemies! Sukesha's sons, having obtained a boon from the grandfather, face no hurdles. O lord of subjects! They are oppressing all the subjects. O one who provides a refuge! They have destroyed our refuges and our hermitages. They have driven Shakra away from heaven and are sporting in heaven, like Shakra. O god! The rakshasas are insolent because of the boon and say, 'I am Vishnu.' 'I am Rudra.' 'I am Brahma.' 'I am the king of the gods.' 'I am Yama.' 'I am Varuna.' 'I am the moon god.' 'I am the sun god.' Invincible in battle, they obstruct all those who advance in front of them. O god! That is the reason we are afflicted by fear. You should grant us freedom from fear. Assume an inauspicious form[492] and slay the thorns of the gods." Thus addressed by all the gods, Kapardi Nilalohita,[493] the lord of large numbers of gods, took Sukesha's side and said, "I will not slay them. Those asuras cannot be killed by me. However,

[490] The enemy (*ari*) of Kama (the god of love). Since Shiva burnt down Kama, this means Shiva.

[491] The enemy (ari) of Tripura, meaning Shiva.

[492] There is a reason for the use of this expression. *Shiva* means auspicious and the word used for inauspicious is *ashiva*.

[493] Kapardi and Nilalohita are Shiva's names.

I will counsel you about how they can be killed. O bulls among the gods! Place the following kind of effort at the forefront. Go and seek refuge with Vishnu. That lord will slay them." At this, they praised Maheshvara, uttering sounds of victory. Afflicted by fear on account of those who roamed around in the night, they approached Vishnu. With a great deal of respect, they bowed down before the god who holds the conch shell and the chakra. Scared and suffering from Sukesha's sons, they spoke these words. "O god! Sukesha's three sons are like the three fires. Because of the boon they obtained, they attacked us and took away our positions. There is an impenetrable city named Lanka and it is located on the summit of Trikuta. Based there, those roamers in the night oppress all of us. O Madhusudana! Therefore, for bringing us pleasure, slay them. Their faces are like lotuses. Use your chakra to sever them and offer them to Yama. We are scared and there is no one who can dispel our fear like you. O god! Destroy our fear, the way the sun destroys mist." Janardana, the god of the gods, was addressed by the gods in this way. The one who grants freedom from fear, the one who offers fear to the enemy, replied to the gods. "I know the rakshasa Sukesha. He is insolent because of the boon he has received from Ishana.[494] I know Malyavat, the eldest among the sons. I will slay the worst among the rakshasas. They have transgressed all agreements. O gods! I will kill them in a battle. Be without anxiety." All the gods were addressed in this way by Vishnu. They praised Janardana, the lord Vishnu. Happy, they returned to their residences.

'Malyavat, the roamer in the night, heard about the efforts made by the gods. He addressed his two brave brothers in these words. "The immortals and the rishis assembled and went to Shankara. Desiring our deaths, they addressed the one with the three eyes in these words. 'O god! Sukesha's sons have become strong because they obtained a boon. At every step, they assume terrible forms and are engaged in obstructing us. O Uma's lord! We have been overcome by those rakshasas and are incapacitated. Because of those evil-souled ones, we are scared of remaining in our own residences. O three-eyed one! Therefore, for our benefit, slay

[494] Mahadeva.

them. O supreme among those who strike! Burn those rakshasas down with your *humkara*.'[495] The slayer of Andhaka[496] heard the words spoken by the gods. He touched his head with his hand and addressed them in these words. 'O gods! Sukesha's sons cannot be slain by me in a battle. However, I will counsel you about how they can be killed. Janardana holds the chakra and the conch shell in his hand. He is attired in a yellow garment. He will slay them in a battle. Resort to that refuge.' They heard what they desired from Hara and greeted Kamari. They went to Narayana's residence and told him everything. At this, Narayana spoke to the gods, with Indra at the forefront. 'O gods! Do not suffer from anxiety. I will slay the enemies of the gods.' O bulls among rakshasas! The gods are afflicted by fear and Hari has pledged to kill us. Therefore, think about what is best. Narayana has caused misery by vanquishing Hiranyakashipu, Mrityu and other enemies of the gods. He desires to kill us." Hearing Malyavat's words, Mali and Sumali replied to their elder brother, like the two Ashvins[497] speaking to Vasava. "We have studied, donated at sacrifices and protected our prosperity. We have obtained health and long lifespans. We are established in our own dharma. The ocean that is the gods cannot be agitated, but with innumerable weapons, we have immersed ourselves in that. We have always vanquished the gods in battles. Death has no fear for us. Narayana, Rudra, Shakra and Yama are always scared of standing in front of us. O lord of the rakshasas! There is no crime we have committed towards Vishnu. Vishnu's mind is disturbed because of the crimes we have committed towards the gods. Therefore, let us arise and surround ourselves with all the soldiers. Let us kill the gods. This taint has arisen because of them." Mali and Sumali said this to the lord Malyavat, their elder brother.

'All the rakshasas announced the preparations. They angrily emerged to fight, like Jambha,[498] Vritra and Bala. They were astride

[495] Humkara means to utter the sound *'hum'*, a sound believed to possess special powers.

[496] Shiva killed a demon named Andhaka.

[497] The word used in the text translates as the two sons of the sun god. The Ashvins are sons of the sun god.

[498] Alternatively, Jrimbha. These are names of famous demons.

chariots, Indras among elephants and horses that were as large as mountains. Their mounts were donkeys, bulls, camels, dolphins, serpents, makaras, tortoises, fish, birds that were like Garuda, lions, tigers, boars, *srimaras* and *chamaras*.[499] Proud of their valour, all the rakshasas left Lanka. To fight, the enemies of the gods left for the world of the gods. All the other residents of Lanka saw that Lanka's destruction was imminent. All the creatures saw reason for fear and were mentally disturbed. Fearful and ominous portents manifested themselves on earth and in the sky, signifying the swift destruction of the Indras among the rakshasas. Clouds showered down bones and warm blood. The ocean crossed its shoreline and mountains moved. Thousands of bhutas were tormented and danced, laughing out aloud in voices like the thundering of clouds. Large flocks of vultures, emitting flames from their mouths, circled among the rakshasas, like the wheel of time. The rakshasas were proud of their strength and paid no attention to these great portents. Entangled in the noose of death, they did not retreat from their journey. The roamers in the night, blazing like sacrificial fires, placed Malyavat, Mali and Sumali at their forefront. Like embodied creatures seeking refuge with the Creator, all of them sought refuge with Malyavat, who was like Mount Malyavat. The army of Indras among the rakshasas roared like a large and dense cloud. Desiring victory and commanded by Mali, they went to the world of the gods. Through messengers of the gods, the lord Narayana heard about the preparations made by the rakshasas and made up his mind to fight. Wielding a chakra, a sword and excellent weapons, he advanced towards the soldiers of the enemies of the gods. Gods, siddhas, rishis, giant serpents, best among gandharvas and apsaras sung his praises. The wind generated from Suparna's wings whirled around and shattered the weapons in that army of the king of the rakshasas. It resembled a dark and large mountain and it stared to quake. Thousands of roamers in the night surrounded Madhava and pierced him with supreme weapons that were sharp and smeared with flesh and blood. Their forms were like the fire of destruction that comes at the end of a yuga.'

[499] A srimara is a kind of animal that is found in marshy places, similar to deer. A chamara is a yak.

Chapter 7(7)

'The rakshasas roared like clouds and approached the mountain that was Narayana. They showered down torrents of arrows, like clouds pouring down on mountains. Vishnu was dark blue and those excellent roamers in the night were also dark blue. It seemed as if clouds were showering down on a mountain made out of dark collyrium. The arrows released from the rakshasa bows penetrated Hari, like locusts on a field, gnats on a mountain, makaras in the ocean and creatures around a pot of amrita. They were as swift as the vajra and the wind. It was as if the destruction of the worlds had arrived. Chariot riders were on chariots. Elephant riders were mounted on the tops of elephants. Horse riders used excellent horses. Others were on foot or in the sky. Those Indras among rakshasas were like mountains and used hundreds of arrows, swords and spears. Like a brahmana undertaking *pranayama*,[500] Hari seemed to lose his breath. In that great battle, like a giant whale attacked by fish, he was struck all over his body by the roamers in the night. He used the Sharnga bow against the rakshasas. He stretched the bow all the way back and shot arrows that were as swift as thought, with faces like the vajra. Vishnu shattered hundreds and thousands into fragments as small as sesamum seeds. Like a rising wind drives away clouds, that shower of arrows drove them away. Purushottama then blew on his giant conch shell, Panchajanya. This king of conch shells was born from the water and Hari blew on it with all his strength. There was a terrible roar, like a cloud thundering at the end of a yuga. The sound of that king of conch shells terrified the rakshasas, like elephants in musth are scared by a lion in the forest. The horses were incapable of remaining there. The elephants lost their musth. Because of the blare of the conch shell, the warriors became weak and were dislodged from their chariots. The arrows released from Sharnga bow had faces that were like the vajra and possessed excellent tufts. They shattered

[500] Yoga has eight elements—*yama* (restraint), *niyama* (rituals), *asana* (posture), pranayama (control of the breath), *pratyahara* (withdrawal), *dharana* (retention), *dhyana* (meditation) and *samadhi* (liberation).

the rakshasas and penetrated the ground. Other terrible rakshasas were mangled by arrows released from Narayana's bow and fell down, like mountains struck by the vajra. They were wounded by Adhokshaja's[501] arrows. Blood began to exude from these wounds, like golden ore oozing out in mountains. The rakshasas were roaring, but this was surpassed by the blare of the king of conch shells, the sound created by Sharnga bow and Vishnu's roaring. The arrows released from Narayana's Sharnga were as terrible as the rays of the sun, the waves of the ocean and storms from clouds battering large mountains. Hundreds and thousands of arrows were shot swiftly. *Sharabha*s drive away lions.[502] Lions drive away elephants. Elephants drive away tigers. Tigers drive away leopards. Leopards drive away dogs. Dogs drive away cats. Cats drive away snakes. Snakes drive away mice. Like that, in that battle, Vishnu's powers drove the rakshasas away. Vishnu drove them away and they lay down on the ground. Madhusudana killed thousands of rakshasas. He made the conch shell roar, like the king of the gods makes clouds roar. They were devoured by Narayana's arrows. Because of the blaring of the conch shell, they lost their senses. Routed, the army of the rakshasas fled towards Lanka. The army of the rakshasas was shattered by Narayana's arrows and routed.

'In the encounter, Sumali sought to counter Hari with his shower of arrows. His arms were decorated with golden ornaments and he raised them, like an elephant raising its trunk. Like a cloud tinged with lightning, the rakshasa roared in delight. His charioteer's head blazed with earrings. While Sumali was roaring, he[503] severed it and without the charioteer, the horses dragged the rakshasa around, here and there. A man without control is whirled around by his senses, which are like horses. In that way, those distracted horses dragged around Sumali, lord of the rakshasas. In the battle, Mali seized his bow and arrows and attacked. Mali's arrows were decorated with gold. Released from his bow, they penetrated Hari the way *krouncha* birds enter the water. He was struck by thousands of

[501] One of Vishnu's names.

[502] A sharabha is a mythical animal and the concept has evolved over time. A sharabha has eight legs, lives in the mountains, slays lions and lives on raw flesh.

[503] Vishnu.

arrows shot by Mali in the encounter. However, just as a person who has conquered his senses is not agitated, Vishnu was not disturbed. The illustrious one, the creator of all beings, twanged his bow. The wielder of the mace shot torrents of arrows in Mali's direction. Those arrows were as radiant as lightning and like the vajra, penetrated Mali's body. They drank his blood, like serpents drinking amrita in ancient times. Having countered Mali, Hari used his force to bring down Mali's diadem, chariot, standard, bow and horses. Having been deprived of his chariot, Mali, supreme among those who roam around in the night, seized a club. With the club in his hand, he leapt up, like a lion springing on a mountain. He was like Indra striking a mountain with his vajra, or like Yama striking Ishana.[504] In the battle, he struck Garuda on the forehead with this. Garuda was severely struck by Mali's club. Suffering from the pain, he bore the god away from the fight. When the god was thus withdrawn because of what Mali had done, a giant clamour arose, because the rakshasas roared. The younger brother of the one with tawny horses[505] heard the sound of the rakshasas roaring. Having been made to withdraw,[506] he wished to kill Mali and released his chakra. It was as radiant as the solar disc and illuminated everything with its own radiance. The chakra was like the wheel of time and brought down Mali's head. The terrible head of the Indra among the rakshasas was severed by the chakra. It fell down, covered with blood, like Rahu's head in ancient times. The gods were extremely delighted. With all their strength, they roared like lions and uttered words of praise for the god.[507] Seeing that Mali had been killed, Sumali and Malyavat were tormented by grief. With all their soldiers, they rushed towards Lanka. Having gained his composure, the great-minded Garuda returned. Enraged, he used the force of his wings to drive away the rakshasas. Narayana's arrows were like the vajra and were released from his bow. With dishevelled hair, the roamers in the night were driven away by these, as if struck by the great Indra's vajra. Their arrows were shattered, their weapons fell

[504] Shiva.

[505] Indra is the one with tawny horses and Vishnu is Indra's younger brother.

[506] The Critical Edition excises a shloka where Vishnu looks angrily at Garuda.

[507] Vishnu.

down. Their bodies were struck and mangled by the arrows. Their eyes rolled around in fear and their entrails emerged. The army seemed to have gone mad. They were like elephants afflicted by lions. With their elephants, the roamers in the night screamed loudly. It was just as they had been crushed by a lion in ancient times.[508] Routed by the net of Hari's arrows, they flung aside the nets of their own arrows. Resembling clouds of destruction, those roamers in the night fled, just as dark clouds are dispelled by the wind. Their heads were severed by blows from the chakra. Their limbs were crushed by blows from the mace. Many were sliced down by blows from the sword. The Indras among the rakshasas fell down, like mountains. Their faces were severed by the chakra. Their chests were crushed by the club. Their necks were broken by the plough.[509] Their heads were shattered by the club. Some were sliced down with the sword. Others suffered because of the arrows. From the sky, the rakshasas were swiftly brought down into the waters of the ocean. Their garments were dislodged. Their necklaces and earrings were strewn around. The roamers in the night, resembling dark clouds, were seen to be continuously brought down. They were like dark mountains that were being brought down.'

Chapter 7(8)

'They were slaughtered by Padmanabha[510] and turned their backs. Malyavat retreated, like the ocean when it confronts the shoreline. His eyes red with rage, the roamer in the night shook his head. He addressed Padmanabha in these harsh words. "O Narayana! You do not know about the eternal dharma of kshatriyas. We do not wish to fight. There are others who have been routed. Even then, as you please, you are killing us. O lord of the gods! You have committed the sin of killing those who have

[508] This is a reference to Vishnu's *narasimha* (half-man, half-lion) incarnation. In that form, Vishnu killed Hiranyakashipu.

[509] A plough is typically Balarama's weapon.

[510] Vishnu, the one with the lotus in his navel.

retreated. A person who kills in this way does not attain heaven and does not reap the fruits of his good deeds. O wielder of the conch shell and the chakra! If you love the idea of fighting, I am stationed in front of you. Exhibit your strength. I will see it." The powerful younger brother of the king of the gods replied to the Indra among the rakshasas. "The gods were terrified on account of their fear of you and I have granted them freedom from fear. By destroying the rakshasas, I am fulfilling my pledge. I have always preferred doing something agreeable for the gods to my own lives.[511] Even if you go to rasatala, I will kill you." The god said this, his eyes as red as lotuses. Enraged, the Indra among the rakshasas pierced him with a javelin and roared. Adorned with bells, the javelin roared and was released from Malyavat's hand. It was radiant on Hari's chest, like lightning inside a cloud. The one who is loved by the wielder of the spear plucked out the javelin.[512] The lotus-eyed one then flung it towards Malyavat. Released from Govinda's hand, that javelin was like one hurled by Skanda, desiring to kill the rakshasa. It was like a giant meteor unleashed on a mountain of collyrium. His broad chest was radiant because of a sparkling necklace. It shattered it and brought down the Indra among the rakshasas, like the summit of a mountain by the vajra. It shattered his armour and he was immersed in great darkness.[513] However, like an immobile mountain, Malyavat regained his composure again. He picked up a spear that was completely made out of iron, embellished with many spikes. Seizing this, he firmly struck the god between the breasts. Engaged in the battle, the roamer in the night next struck Vasava's younger brother with his fist and retreated a bow length away. At this, loud sounds of praise were heard in the sky. Having struck Vishnu, the rakshasa struck Garuda. Vinata's son angrily struck the rakshasa with the force of his wings, the way a powerful wind scatters away a heap of dry leaves. Sumali saw that his elder brother had been driven away by the force of the wings of the Indra among birds. With all his forces, he left for Lanka. The rakshasa Malyavat was routed by the

[511] The text uses the plural.

[512] The wielder of the spear is Kartikeya. That is, Vishnu is loved by Kartikeya.

[513] That is, he lost his senses.

force of the wings. Ashamed, he collected his own force and also left for Lanka. O Rama! In this way, the lotus-eyed Hari killed many rakshasas in the battle and routed the best among their leaders. Afflicted by fear, they were incapable of fighting back against Vishnu. With their wives, they left Lanka. They went to patala and started to reside there. O descendant of the Raghu lineage! All the rakshasas approached Sumali, who was famous for his valour and had been born in Salakantakata's lineage, and resorted to him.[514] You slew the rakshasas named Poulastya. Sumali, Malyavat and Mali were their ancestors. O immensely strong one! All of them were stronger than Ravana. O victor over enemy cities! No one other than the lord of the gods, the god Narayana, the wielder of the conch shell, chakra and mace, could have slain those rakshasas. You are the eternal four-armed god, Narayana. O unvanquished one! O lord! O one without decay! You have been born to slay the rakshasas.'

Chapter 7(9)

'After some time, the rakshasa named Sumali emerged from rasatala and started to wander around everywhere in the world of the mortals. He was like a dark cloud and his earrings were made out molten gold. He had his daughter with him and this maiden was like Shri without the lotus. He saw the lord of treasures, proceeding on Pushpaka. He saw him proceeding through the sky, resembling a fire. The rakshasa spoke to his daughter, who was known by the name of Kaikasi. "O daughter! This is the time to give you away. Your youth is passing. O daughter! You are like Shri with the lotus and possess all the qualities. With dharma in our minds, all of us are like puppets in your cause.[515] Scared of being refused, you have not approached any grooms so far. All those who

[514] There is no indication that Malyavat had been killed.

[515] Searching for an appropriate groom. According to dharma, the daughter has to be given away to someone in marriage.

desire respect are always miserable on account of their daughters. O daughter! They do not know who will be a groom for their daughter. A maiden always places three families in uncertainty—the mother's lineage, the father's lineage and the lineage into which she is bestowed. O daughter! Therefore, you should yourself go and accept Vishrava, born in the Poulastya lineage, as your husband. He is best among the supreme sages and has been born in Prajapati's lineage. In this way, there is no doubt that sons and daughters will be born who are like the sun in their energy, just as this lord of treasures is." O Rama! At that time, the brahmana who was Pulastya's son was engaged in agnihotra, looking like a fourth fire. It was a terrible time of the day.[516] However, out of respect for her father, she did not think about this. She approached him and stood there, her eyes cast downwards, towards her feet. He saw the one with the excellent hips, with a face like the full moon. The extremely generous one, who blazed in his energy, asked, "O fortunate one! Whose daughter are you? Where have you come from and what is the reason why you have come here? O beautiful one! Tell me the truth about this." Thus addressed, the maiden joined her hands in salutation and replied, "O sage! Through your own powers, you are capable of knowing what is in my mind. O brahmana! Know that I have come here because I have been commanded by my father. My name is Kaikasi. The remaining bit is only known to you." At this, the sage meditated and determined the reason. He addressed her in these words. "O fortunate one! I have got to know the reason that is in your mind. You have come to me at a terrible time of the day. O fortunate one! Therefore, listen to the kind of sons you will give birth to. They will be terrible. They will perform terrible deeds. They will love terrible people. O one with excellent hips! You will give birth to rakshasas who are cruel in their deeds." Hearing his words, she bowed down before him and replied in these words. "O illustrious one! You are descended from Brahma and such sons should not be born from someone like you." At this, the sage said, "The son who will be born after this will be appropriate for my lineage. He will have dharma in his soul."

[516] The evening.

'O Rama! The maiden was addressed in this way. After some time, she gave birth to a horrible and extremely terrible son in the form of a rakshasa. He had ten heads and large teeth. He was like a mass of black collyrium. His lips were coppery red and he had twenty arms. His mouth was large and his hair blazed. As soon as he was born, jackals spouted out flames from their mouths. Predatory creatures started to circle in a counterclockwise direction. The gods showered down blood. Clouds thundered harshly. In the sky, the sun's lustre faded. Giant meteors fell down on the ground. His father, who was like the grandfather, gave him a name. "Since he has been born with ten heads, he will be known as Dashagriva." After this, the immensely strong Kumbhakarna was born. There was no one else who was as gigantic as him in size. After this, the one with the malformed face was born and she was named Shurpanakha. Vibhishana, with dharma in his soul, was a son who was born to Kaikasi later. Those extremely energetic ones grew up in that great forest. Among them, the cruel Dashagriva was the one who caused anxiety to the worlds. The maharshis were engaged in pursuits of dharma. Without thinking about it, the crazy and wicked Kumbhakarna devoured them and terrified the three worlds. Vibhishana possessed dharma in his soul and always remained on the path of dharma. He studied, was controlled in his diet, fasted and controlled his senses.

'On some occasion, the immensely energetic god who was the lord of treasures came to see his father, mounted on Pushpaka. Kaikasi saw him, blazing in his energy. Because of the rakshasi nature of her intelligence, she told Dashagriva, "O son! Look at your brother, Vaishravana. He is enveloped in energy. You are brothers and should be similar. But look at yourself and look at him. O Dashagriva! O one who is infinitely brave! O son! Act so that you can quickly become Vaishravana's equal." Hearing his mother's words, the powerful Dashagriva was filled with unlimited intolerance and took a pledge. "Know that this is my true pledge. I will become like my brother or superior to him. O mother! I will soon be like that. Abandon the torment in your heart." Angry with his younger brother, Dashagriva resolved, "I have decided that I will perform austerities to obtain what I desire." To accomplish the objective, he went to the auspicious hermitage of Gokarna.'

Chapter 7(10)

Rama asked the brahmana, 'What did the brothers do in the forest? O brahmana! Great in their vows, what kind of austerities did they undertake?'

Controlled in his mind, Agastya replied to Rama. He told him about the rites of dharma the brothers observed. 'Kumbhakarna was always devoted to dharma. In the heat of the summer, he tormented himself amidst the five fires.[517] During the monsoon, despite being drenched by rain, he was in *virasana*.[518] During the winter, he was always submerged in water. Ten thousand years passed in this way. He was controlled in his pursuit of dharma and always based himself on the path of virtue. Vibhishana, with dharma in his soul, was always pure and devoted to dharma. For five thousand years, he stood on one foot. When the rites were over, large numbers of apsaras danced. Flowers showered down and the gods were agitated. For another five thousand years, he raised his hands up. He studied and controlled his mind. With his head raised, he looked at the sun. In this way, Vibhishana spent ten thousand years, controlled in his mind, as if he was in Nandana, in heaven. For ten thousand years, Dashanana ate nothing. At the end of every thousand years, he offered one of his heads as an oblation into the fire. Nine thousand years passed in this way. Nine heads were offered into the fire. At the end of ten thousand years, the one with dharma in his soul wished to sever his tenth head. However, the grandfather arrived there. Extremely happy, the grandfather arrived, with the other gods. He said, "O son! O Dashagriva! O son! I am pleased with you. O one who knows about dharma! Quickly seek the boon that you desire. What do you wish for? What can I do for you now, so that your efforts are not in vain?" Delighted in his soul, Dashagriva replied. He bowed his head down before the god and his voice choked in joy. "O illustrious one! For creatures, there never is a fear that is as great as that of death. There is no enemy like death. I desire to be immortal. O supervisor of creatures! Till eternity, let birds, serpents, yakshas, daityas, danavas, rakshasas and gods be unable

[517] Four fires in four directions and the sun overhead.

[518] Literally, posture of a hero. A seated position used by ascetics.

to kill me. O one who is worshipped by the immortals! There is no other creature I need to think about. All other creatures, humans and others, are like grass." The rakshasa Dashagriva, with dharma in his soul, said this. O Rama! With the gods, the grandfather replied in these words. "O bull among rakshasas! It shall be as you say. I am pleased with you. Therefore, listen to my auspicious words. O unblemished one! O rakshasa! You have already offered your heads into the fire and they will again be restored, as they used to be." The grandfather said this to the rakshasa Dashagriva and the heads that had been offered as oblations into the fire sprouted again. O Rama! After having said this to Dashagriva, Prajapati, the grandfather of the worlds, addressed Vibhishana in these words. "O Vibhishana! O child! Your intelligence is in conformity with dharma. O one who knows about dharma! O one who is excellent in vows! I am pleased with you. Ask for a boon." Vibhishana, with dharma in his soul, joined his hands in salutation and replied in these words. "May I always be surrounded by all the qualities, just as the moon is by its beams. O one who is excellent in vows! Since the preceptor of the worlds is satisfied with me and has offered to grant me a boon, I am successful. Let my intelligence be in accordance with the *ashrama* I am in.[519] Let me be devoted to that kind of dharma and let me observe that kind of dharma. O extremely generous one! This is the only supreme boon that I have in mind. In this world, if a person is devoted to dharma, there is nothing that he cannot obtain." Prajapati was delighted and told Vibhishana, "O child! You already follow dharma and it will be as you say. O one who afflicts enemies! Though you have been born in the lineage of rakshasas, there will be no adharma in your intelligence. I grant you immortality." O scorcher of enemies! After this, he prepared to confer a boon on Kumbhakarna. At this, all the gods joined their hands in salutation and addressed Prajapati in these words. "You should not grant a boon to Kumbhakarna. You know that the evil-minded one will terrify the worlds. O Brahma! He has already devoured seven apsaras from Nandana, ten of the great Indra's followers, rishis and humans. O one who is infinite in radiance! Give him a boon that will confuse him. Let the worlds be

[519] The four ashramas of *brahmacharya*, *garhasthya*, *vanaprastha* and *sannyasa*.

secure and let him also be satisfied." Addressed in this way by the gods, Brahma, born from the lotus, started to think. As he thought of her, the goddess Sarasvati presented herself by his side. Standing next to him, Sarasvati joined her hands in salutation and spoke to him in these words. "O god! I have come here. What shall I do?" When she arrived, Prajapati addressed Sarasvati in these words. "For that Indra among rakshasas, become the speech that the gods desire." Thus addressed by Prajapati, she agreed and entered.[520] "O Kumbhakarna![521] O mighty-armed one! Ask for the boon that is in your mind." Hearing these words, Kumbhakarna replied in these words. "O god of the gods! I desire that I may be able to sleep for many years." With the gods, the grandfather said that it would indeed be like that. Having got him to say this, the goddess Sarasvati left for heaven. The evil-souled Kumbhakarna was miserable and thought, "What are these words that emerged from my mouth now?" Thus, the brothers, blazing in their energy, received boons. They went to a *shleshmataka*[522] forest and happily resided there.'

Chapter 7(11)

'Sumali got to know that the roamers in the night had obtained boons. Abandoning his fear, with his companions, he emerged from rasatala. The rakshasa's advisers were Maricha, Prahasta, Virupaksha and Mahodara. Extremely angry, they emerged. Sumali was surrounded by these bulls among the rakshasas. He went to Dashagriva, embraced him and said, "O son! It is good fortune that the wish we thought about has materialized. You have obtained a boon like this. It is the best in the three worlds. O mighty-armed one! We suffered from great fear on account of Vishnu. Because of that, we abandoned Lanka and went to rasatala. We were routed and slighted and had to abandon our own residences. All

[520] Entered Kumbhakarna's tongue.

[521] This is Brahma speaking.

[522] The Assyrian plum, *Cordia myxa*.

of us collectively fled and entered rasatala. This city of Lanka is ours and is desired by the rakshasas. However, your brother, the intelligent lord of treasures, resides there. O mighty-armed one! If you are capable of swiftly obtaining it back, using sama or dana, that should be done. O son! There is no doubt that you should be the lord of Lanka. O immensely strong one! You will be the lord of all of us." Dashagriva spoke to his maternal grandfather, who had presented himself. "The lord of treasures is our senior and one should not speak about him in this way." Dashagriva, the roamer in the night, spoke these words. At this, Prahasta humbly replied, citing reasons. "O Dashagriva! O mighty-armed one! You should not speak in this way. There is no fraternal relationship for brave ones. Listen to my words. Aditi and Diti were sisters and they were together. Those two extremely beautiful ones were the wives of Kashyapa Prajapati. Aditi gave birth to the gods, the lords of the three worlds. Diti gave birth to the daityas and they were born from Kashyapa himself. O one who knows about dharma! O brave one! Before Vishnu exhibited his powers, everything, the forests, the oceans and the earth, with all its mountains, used to belong to the daityas. However, exhibiting his powers, Vishnu killed them in a battle and brought the undecaying three worlds under the subjugation of the gods. You are not the only one who will cause such a transgression.[523] The gods have done this earlier. Therefore, act in accordance with my words." Dashagriva was thus addressed by the evil-souled Prahasta. Having thought for a while, he signified his assent. Full of delight, that very night, with those roamers in the night, the valiant Dashagriva went to the forest. Dashagriva, the roamer in the night, based himself in Trikuta. He sent Prahasta, accomplished in the use of words, as an emissary. "O Prahasta! O bull among nairittas![524] Go quickly and convey my words to the lord of riches. First speak words that are in conformity with sama. 'O king! This city of Lanka belongs to the great-souled rakshasas. O amiable one! O unblemished one! It is not proper for

[523] Of enmity with a brother.

[524] There seems to be a typo in the Critical Edition. Kubera is referred to as a bull among the nairittas.

you to reside here. O infinitely brave one! Therefore, you should follow my words, uttered in conformity with sama, and return it. You will then show affection and also follow dharma.'" Having gone there, Prahasta, accomplished in the use of words, said this. He conveyed all of Dashagriva's words to the lord of treasures. The god Vaishravana heard Prahasta's words. The one who was accomplished in the use of words replied to Prahasta in these words. "Go and tell Dashagriva this. 'O mighty-armed one! The city and kingdom that are with me belong to you. Enjoy them, bereft of thorns. O fortunate one! I will soon act completely in accordance with the rakshasa's words. But can you wait until this has been reported to our father?'" Having said this, the lord of riches went to his father's presence. He greeted his senior and told him what Dashagriva desired. "O father! Dashagriva has sent a messenger to me. He wants me to give him the city of Lanka, which was formerly populated by large numbers of rakshasas. O one who is good in vows! Instruct me about what I should do in this situation." Thus addressed, the brahmana rishi Vishrava, bull among sages, addressed the lord of treasures in these words. "O son! Listen to my words. The mighty-armed Dashagriva has also said this in my presence. However, I have reprimanded that extremely evil-minded one several times. In anger, I have repeatedly told him that he will be destroyed. O son! Listen to my beneficial words, which are full of dharma. That extremely evil-minded one is confused because he obtained a boon. He cannot distinguish between who should be respected and who should not be respected. Having succumbed to his terrible nature, he did not comprehend my curse. O mighty-armed one! Therefore, go to Mount Kailasa and construct your residence there. With your followers, abandon Lanka. There is the beautiful river Mandakinee there, supreme among rivers. The waters are covered with golden lotuses that are like the sun. O lord of treasures! Without this, you will not obtain peace from this enmity with the rakshasas. You know that he has obtained a supreme boon." Thus addressed, he showed respect towards his father and accepted these words. He left with his wives, the citizens, his advisers, the mounts and the riches. Prahasta went to Dashagriva and told him everything. "The city of Lanka is empty and it is thirty yojanas in expanse. With us, enter it and follow your own dharma." The rakshasa Prahasta addressed Ravana in this way and with his brothers, his forces and his followers, he entered the city of Lanka. The roamers in the night consecrated him and Dashanana started to live in that city. The roamers in the night, who resembled dark clouds, obtained their objects of desire in that city. The lord of treasures showed respect to his father's words. On that mountain, he resided in a city that sparkled like the moon. There were the best of ornamented and decorated residences. It was like Purandara's Amaravati.'

Chapter 7(12)

'Once the Indra among rakshasas had been consecrated, with his brothers, he thought about whom to bestow his rakshasi sister on. He gave the rakshasi, his sister Shurpanakha, to the Indra among danavas named Vidyujjihva,[525] from the Kalakeya lineage. O Rama! Having bestowed his sister, the king was roaming around on a hunt and saw Maya, Diti's son. Dashagriva, roamer in the night, saw that he was with a maiden. "Why are you wandering around alone in this forest, where there are no humans to hunt?" Thus addressed, Maya told the roamer in the night, "I will tell you everything that has occurred. Listen to my words. O son![526] Earlier, you may have heard about the apsara named Hema. Just as Poulami was given to Shatakratu, the gods bestowed her on me. O son! I was attached to her for five hundred years. After that, to accomplish some task of the gods, she has been away for fourteen years. For Hema's sake, I have constructed a city made out of gold. I have fashioned it out of maya and it is colourful with diamonds and lapis lazuli. However, separated from her and extremely miserable, I did not find the slightest bit of attachment to that place. Therefore, I abandoned the city. Taking my daughter with me, I

[525] Vidyut-jihva.
[526] The word used is tata.

have come to this forest. O king! This is my daughter and she has been reared by her.[527] With her, I am looking around for a groom for her. For all respectable men who are fathers, a daughter is the source of unhappiness. A daughter always causes uncertainty in two families.[528] O son! Through my wife, two sons have been born to me. Mayavi is the first and Dundubhi followed later. I have told you the truth about everything that you asked. O son! Having said this, who are you? Let me know who you are." Thus addressed, the Indra among rakshasas humbly replied. "I am the son of Poulastya and my name is Dashagriva." Hearing that he was the son of a brahmana rishi, Maya was filled with joy. The idea of bestowing his daughter on him appealed to him. Smiling, the Indra among daityas addressed the Indra among rakshasas in these words. "O king! This daughter of mine has been born from the apsara Hema. This maiden's name is Mandodari. Accept her as your wife." O Rama! Dashagriva replied, signifying his agreement. He lit a fire there and accepted her hand. O Rama! Maya did not know about the curse imposed by the store of austerities.[529] Even if he had, he would have bestowed her on someone born in the grandfather's lineage. He also gave an invincible and extremely wonderful javelin, obtained through supreme austerities. This was the one he struck Lakshmana with. In this way, the lord and master of Lanka obtained a wife. He went to the city with his wife and got his two brothers married off. Vairochana's granddaughter was named Vajrajvala.[530] Ravana wedded her to Kumbhakarna, as his wife. Shailusha, the great-souled king of the gandharvas had a daughter. Her name was Sarama. Vibhishana, who knew about dharma, obtained her as a wife. She was born along the shores of Lake Manasa. O son! At the time of the moon, the water in Lake Manasa started to overflow. Out of affection towards her daughter, the mother shouted out these words. "O lake! Do not extend further." That is the reason she became Sarama.[531] In this way, the rakshasas obtained wives

[527] By Hema.

[528] Probably meaning the father's and the mother's.

[529] On Ravana, by Vishrava.

[530] Vairochana is Bali. Vajrajvala was Bali's daughter's daughter.

[531] Derived from *sara/sarasa* (lake) and *ma* (do not).

and found pleasure with their respective wives, like the gandharvas in Nandana. Mandodari gave birth to a son named Meghanada. All of you know him by the name of Indrajit. In earlier times, as soon as he was born, this son of a rakshasa wept in a loud voice. This sounded like the thunder of a cloud. All of Lanka seemed to be stupefied by the sound. Thus, his father himself named him Meghanada.[532] O Rama! He grew up in Ravana's auspicious inner quarters. He was protected by excellent women, like fire hidden inside wood.'

Chapter 7(13)

'After some time, the fierce sleep created by the creator of the worlds manifested itself before Kumbhakarna. His brother was seated nearby and Kumbhakarna addressed him in these words. "O king! I am suffering from sleep. Get a residence created for me." The king engaged artisans who were like Vishvakarma and they constructed a residence for Kumbhakarna that was like Kailasa. It was white and one yojana wide. Its length was double that. It was a sight to be seen and was constructed for Kumbhakarna, freed of all obstructions. Everywhere, it was decorated with pillars, made out of crystal and colourful with gold. It was made beautiful with lapis lazuli and there were nets of bells. The gates were encrusted with ivory and the platforms were made out of diamonds and crystal. It was always pleasant everywhere, like a sacred cave inside Meru. Kumbhakarna, roamer in the night, went to sleep there. He slept for many thousands of years and did not wake. When Kumbhakarna was overcome by sleep, Dashanana continuously obstructed the gods, the rishis, the yakshas and the gandharvas. Extremely enraged, Dashanana went to the wonderful groves, Nandana and the others, and devastated them. He sported like an elephant in the river, like the wind flinging away trees and like the vajra shattering mountains. He always caused devastation.

[532] One whose roar (*nada*) is like that of a cloud (*megha*).

'The lord of treasures got to know about Dashagriva's conduct. Displaying his fraternal affection, Vaishravana, who knew about dharma, reminded him about his own lineage, sending a messenger to Lanka for Dashagriva's benefit. He[533] went to the city of Lanka and met Vibhishana, who followed dharma, showed him respect and asked about the reason for his arrival. He asked about the king's[534] welfare and that of his kin and relatives. He then showed him the assembly hall where Dashanana was seated. He saw the king there, blazing in his own energy. He uttered pronouncements of victory and worshipped him. Thereafter, he was silent for a while. He then approached Dashagriva, who was seated on a couch covered with excellent spreads. The messenger addressed him in these words. "O king! O amiable one! I will tell you everything that your brother has said, relevant and appropriate for both your conduct and your lineage. 'Everything that you have done so far is sufficient. Be virtuous, so that it adds to your character. If you are capable, be established in virtue and act in accordance with dharma. I have seen Nandana destroyed. I have heard that the rishis have been killed. O king! I have heard about the gods making preparations against you. O lord of the rakshasas! You have shown me disrespect in many ways. However, if crimes are committed by children, they must be protected by their own relatives. I have gone to the slopes of the Himalayas and am engaged in following dharma. I have controlled myself and have resorted to fierce vows. I have controlled my senses. I have seen the lord god[535] there, together with the goddess Uma. There, my left eye was brought down by the goddess.[536] Parvati was sporting there, assuming an unmatched form. I only wanted to find out who this auspicious one was. There was no other fraudulent reason. However, because of the powers of the goddess, my left eye was burnt down. Like a stellar body covered

[533] The messenger.

[534] Kubera's.

[535] Mahadeva.

[536] Since Kubera looked at Shiva and Parvati with envy, his eye was destroyed. Subsequently, this lost eye was replaced with a yellow eye. This is the standard story, with a slight variation given here.

in mist, my eye turned yellow. Thereafter, I went to that extensive slope on the mountain. I observed a great vow for a full eight hundred years. When the rituals were over, the god Maheshvara was pleased with me. Happy in his mind, the lord addressed me in these words. "O one who knows about dharma! O one who is good in vows! O lord of treasures! I am pleased with your austerities, since you have undertaken this vow and have completed it. There is no third person who can accomplish a vow like this. This vow is extremely difficult to observe and I accomplished it in ancient times. O lord of treasures! Therefore, the idea of a friendship with me should appeal to you. O unblemished one! You have won me over with your austerities. Be my friend. Your left eye was burnt down because of the powers of the goddess. Your name as the one with a single yellow eye will remain for eternity." Through Shankara's permission, I thus obtained his friendship. Having returned, I have heard about your wicked resolutions. O defiler of the lineage! Withdraw from this association with those who follow adharma. With large numbers of rishis, the gods are thinking about a means to get you killed.'" Thus addressed, Dashagriva's eyes turned red with rage. He wrung his hands, bit his lips and spoke these words. "O messenger! I have understood what you are trying to say through these words. You and my brother, who sent you, will no longer exist and nor will your residences. What the protector of riches has spoken about will bring no benefit to me. That foolish one has told me about a friendship with Maheshvara. I think that a senior and an elder brother must not be killed. Therefore, having heard his words, this is what I have decided. Resorting to the valour in my arms, I will conquer the three worlds. Because of what he[537] has done, right this instant, I will convey the four guardians of the world to Yama's eternal abode." Having said this, the lord of Lanka killed the messenger with his sword and gave the body to the evil-souled rakshasas to devour. Performing the auspicious rites, Ravana ascended his chariot. Desiring to conquer the three worlds, he went to the place where the lord of treasures was.'

[537] Kubera.

Chapter 7(14)

'He was with six advisers who were always insolent because of their strength—Mahodara, Prahasta, Maricha, Shuka, Sarana and the brave Dhumraksha. They always loved to fight. Surrounded by them, the prosperous one proceeded to burn down the worlds in his rage. He crossed cities, rivers, mountains, forests and groves and reached Mount Kailasa in an instant. Those who were in the mountain[538] heard the Indra among rakshasas announce, "I am the king's brother." They went to where the lord of treasures was. They went and told him everything about what his brother had decided to do. Dhanada[539] gave them permission to go and fight. The army of the king of the nairittas was turbulent, like a waxing ocean. It seemed to make the mountain quake. A battle ensued between the yakshas and the rakshasas. Soon, the yakshas' advisers were distressed. On seeing that the soldiers were in this state, Dashagriva, the roamer in the night, uttered roars of delight and angrily attacked. The Indra among rakshasas possessed advisers who were terrible in valour. Each one of them fought against one thousand. Dashagriva immersed himself in the soldiers, killing them with clubs, maces, swords, spears and javelins. Without pausing to breathe, Dashanana slaughtered them. He showered down like a dense cloud and countered the Indra among the yakshas. The evil-souled one raised a club that was like the staff of Death. He penetrated the yaksha soldiers and conveyed them to Yama's eternal abode. Those soldiers were like an extensive mass of dry kindling. In extremely terrible fashion, he consumed them, like a fire fanned by the wind. The advisers, Mahodara, Shuka and the others, were in the middle. They drove away the few remaining yakshas, like the wind dispelling clouds. The limbs of some were mangled in the clash. In the battle, others fell down on the ground. Some bit their lips with their teeth. Others were bitten with teeth and fell down on the ground. In the field of battle, they clung to each other in fear and their weapons were dislodged. The yakshas lost all enterprise, like a bank destroyed by the waters. Those who were killed went to heaven, though they had fought on

[538] The yakshas who were there.

[539] The lord of treasures, Kubera.

earth. The large number of rishis looked on and there was no space left in the firmament.[540] O Rama! At this time, the extremely great yaksha named Samyodhakantaka arrived there, with a large army and mounts. Like Vishnu striking, the yaksha struck Maricha and he fell down on the ground, like one whose merit has been exhausted falling down from the sky. In a short while, the roamer in the night regained his senses and assured himself. He fought against the yaksha and made him run away. O Rama! Doorkeepers protected the gate, which was golden all over and was embellished with lapis lazuli and silver. At this time, Dashagriva, roamer in the night, entered through there. The doorkeeper known as Suryabhanu tried to restrain him. The yaksha uprooted the gate and struck him with that. The yaksha struck him severely with the gate. O Rama! However, because of the boon he had obtained from the one who was born from the waters,[541] no harm was done to him. He then struck the yaksha with that gate. The yaksha could no longer be seen. It was as if he had consumed him. On witnessing his valour, all the yakshas fled. Afflicted by fear, they entered rivers and caves.'

Chapter 7(15)

'On seeing that hundreds and thousands of yakshas had been driven away, the lord of treasures himself emerged to fight. There was a yaksha named Manichara and he was extremely difficult to vanquish. Surrounded by thousands of yakshas with the four kinds of forces, he started to fight. In the battle, the yakshas struck the rakshasas with clubs, maces, spears, javelins, spikes and bludgeons and drove them away. Prahasta killed one thousand in the encounter. Using his club, Mahodara killed another one thousand. O Rama! The evil-souled Maricha became enraged. In the twinkling of an eye, be brought down two thousand. In that great encounter, Dhumraksha attacked Manibhadra.[542] He angrily struck him in the chest with a

[540] It was dense with spectators.

[541] Brahma.

[542] Manibhadra is the same as Manichara.

club. However, Manibhadra did not tremble. He too picked up a club and struck the rakshasa. Struck on the head, Dhumraksha lost his senses and fell down. Struck, Dhumraksha fell down, covered with blood. On seeing this, Dashanana became extremely angry and attacked Manibhadra. He was like the fire that arises at the time of the destruction of a yuga. The bull among rakshasas angrily attacked and struck him with three javelins. In the battle, the king of the rakshasas next struck him with a club. Because of that blow, his crown was dislodged to one side. Since that time, the yaksha has been known as Parshvamouli.[543] Having repulsed the great-souled yaksha, Manibhadra, in the battle, he pronounced his name with an extremely loud roar and this resounded in that mountain.

'From a distance, the lord of treasures could be seen, wielding a club. Shukra, Proshthapada, Shamkha and Padma were with him.[544] He saw his brother in the battle, dislodged from his respectability because of the curse. The intelligent one addressed him in words that were appropriate for the grandfather's lineage. "O evil-minded one! Though I try to restrain you, you do not understand. When you go to hell later, you will realize the consequences. A stupid man who is confused and drinks poison will understand the consequences of his deeds in the form of fruits. Nothing that you do is in conformity with dharma, which would have delighted the gods. You do not comprehend where your present sentiments are taking you. A person who shows disrespect to his mother, father, brother or preceptor, will see the consequences when he comes under the subjugation of the king of the dead. This body is temporary. If a foolish person does not perform austerities, he is tormented later. When he is dead, he sees the state he has reduced himself to. No one who is evil in intelligence can ever cultivate true intelligence. He reaps the consequences according to the acts he has undertaken.

[543] Meaning, one whose crown leans towards one side.

[544] Kubera is accompanied by treasures (*nidhi*) named Padma and Shamkha, in personified form. Padma emerges from a *padma* (lotus) and Shamkha emerges from a *shamkha* (conch shell). Manibhadra is usually Kubera's general. Proshthapada is a nakshatra. More accurately, it is a collective name for two nakshatras, Purva Bhadrapada and Uttara Bhadrapada. Presumably, this nakshatra and Shukra (Venus) were with Kubera, in embodied form.

Through the deeds they have themselves undertaken earlier, men obtain intelligence, beauty, strength, riches, sons, advisers and everything else. Your intelligence is such that you will go to hell. However, I will not converse with you. It is my decision that one should not do that with those who are evil in conduct." Having said this, he struck all the advisers, Maricha and the others, such that they were repulsed and forced to run away. After this, the great-souled Indra among the yakshas struck Dashagriva on the head with a club. However, he did not waver from the spot. O Rama! In that great battle, they then struck each other. They did not fall unconscious. Nor were they exhausted. Both of them became even more intolerant. In the battle, Dhanada[545] released agneyastra. Dashagriva countered the weapon with *varunastra*. The lord of the rakshasas then immersed himself in the maya of the rakshasas. He struck Dhanada on the head with his gigantic club. Thus struck, he lost his senses and blood started to flow. The lord of treasures fell down, like an ashoka tree severed at the root. Padma and the other nidhis took the lord of treasures to the grove of Nandana and revived Dhanada. O Rama! Thus, Dhanada was vanquished by the lord of the rakshasas. As a sign of his victory, he seized Pushpaka vimana. It was full of golden pillars and its doors were made of gems and lapis lazuli. There were nets of pearls and trees with fruits that yielded all the objects of desire. It could travel wherever it wished. Having won it through his valour, the king mounted it. Having defeated the god Vaishravana, he descended from Kailasa.'

Chapter 7(16)

'O Rama! The lord of rakshasas defeated his brother, Dhanada. He then went to the clump of reeds where Mahasena was born.[546] Dashagriva saw that golden clump of reeds. He saw that net of rays, resembling a second sun. O Rama! He ascended the

[545] Kubera, the lord of treasures, the one who grants treasures.

[546] Mahasena is Kartika. As a child, he was left in a clump of reeds.

mountain and in the beautiful extremity of a forest, saw that in the sky, Pushpaka's progress was impeded. On seeing that Pushpaka couldn't move, surrounded by his advisers, the rakshasa began to think. "This can go wherever it wants. How has its movement been impeded? What is the reason why Pushpaka cannot advance? This must be the act of someone who is on this mountain." The intelligent Maricha spoke to Dashagriva. "O king! There must be some reason why Pushpaka cannot advance." Bhava's follower, the powerful Nandishvara[547] arrived by his side and fearlessly addressed the Indra among the rakshasas. "O Dashagriva! Return. Shankara is sporting on this mountain. Therefore, this mountain has been made impassable for birds, serpents, yakshas, daityas, danavas, rakshasas and all creatures." His eyes turned coppery red with rage and he descended from Pushpaka. Saying, "Who is this Shankara?" he went to the bottom of the mountain. He saw the lord Nandishvara standing not far away, holding a spear and resembling a second Shankara. The rakshasa saw that he was an odd kind of human[548] and ignored him. In his foolishness, he laughed, like a cloud filled with water. The illustrious Nandi was like a second body of Shankara's and became angry. He spoke to the rakshasa Dashagriva, who had presented himself there. "O evil-minded rakshasa! You have seen my odd kind of human form and in your foolishness, have slighted me. You have laughed at me. Therefore, in the lineage of the vanaras, there will be born those who are like me in form, so as to ensure your destruction. They will be my equal in bravery and energy. O roamer in the night! Because of what you have done, I am capable of killing you right now. But I do not wish to kill you. Because of your own former deeds, you have already been killed." The roamer in the night paid no heed to Nandi's words.

'He approached the mountain and spoke these words. "O lord of the earth![549] This mountain has prevented my progress and has

[547] Often known simply as Nandi.

[548] The text uses the word *vanara*. Nandi doesn't have the face of an ape. He has the face of a bull, with a human body. Therefore, vanara should not be translated as ape. Vanara actually means a special kind of man. This explains our translation.

[549] The word used is Gopati. *Go* means cattle, as well as the earth. Gopati can therefore be translated both as lord of the earth and lord of cattle.

impeded Pushpaka's movement. I will destroy its foundation. O Bhava! What powers allow you to sport like a king? It should be known to me. I do not know why I should be scared." O king! Having said this, he inserted his arms under the mountain and tried to raise it, the way a predatory beast raises a tree with an animal on it. O Rama! At this, Mahadeva laughed at what he had done. As if he was sporting, he pressed down on the mountain with the big toe of his foot. Thus pressed, the hands that were under the mountain were crushed. The rakshasa's advisers who were present were astounded. The rakshasa became angry at his hands being crushed. He emitted an extremely loud roar that filled up the three worlds. Thinking that the worlds were about to end, humans were terrified at the sound. The gods were also agitated and were distracted from their own tasks. Mahadeva, seated on the summit of the mountain, was pleased.[550] Freeing his hands, he addressed Dashanana in these words. "O roamer in the night! I am pleased with your valour and your ferocity. You let out a roar in your pain and that one was extremely terrible. Therefore, your name should be Ravana and this will be your name. Gods, humans, yakshas and others who are on the surface of this world will address you by this name—Ravana, who makes the worlds scream.[551] O Poulastya! Confidently proceed along whichever path you want to follow. O lord of the rakshasas! I am giving you permission to leave." Ravana obtained his name from Maheshvara himself. Having greeted Mahadeva, he mounted the vimana. O Rama! After this, Ravana roamed around on earth. Here and there, he started to obstruct the extremely brave kshatriyas.'

Chapter 7(17)

'O king! After this, the mighty-armed one wandered around on earth. Ravana reached a forest in the Himalayas and

[550] The Critical Edition excises shlokas and breaks the continuity. Ravana prayed to Mahadeva. That is the reason Mahadeva was pleased.

[551] The word *rava* means shriek/yell. Hence, Ravana can be interpreted in two ways—someone who himself shrieks, or someone who makes the worlds shriek.

roamed around there. There, he saw a maiden with matted hair, clad in black antelope skin. Like a goddess, she was observing noble rituals and performing austerities. He saw the beautiful maiden who was observing that extremely great vow. His soul was confused because of desire. He smiled and asked her, "O fortunate one! Acting against your youth, why are you behaving in this way? This kind of reaction is not right for someone who possesses your beauty. O fortunate one! Whose daughter are you? O unblemished one! Who is your husband? I am asking you. Tell me. Why are you performing austerities in this secluded place?" The maiden was thus asked by the ignoble rakshasa. The store of austerities followed the due rituals of hospitality and said, "A brahmana rishi who follows dharma is my father and his name is Kushadhvaja. The prosperous one is Brihaspati's son and he is like Brihaspati in intelligence. The great-souled one always practises the Vedas. I have been born as his eloquent daughter.[552] I am known by the name of Vedavati. Desiring to accept me as a bride, gods, gandharvas, yakshas, rakshasas and serpents have gone to my father. O lord of the rakshasas! However, my father did not bestow me on them. O mighty-armed one! I will tell you the reason. Listen. My father intended that Vishnu, supreme among the gods and the lord of the three worlds, should be his son-in-law. My father did not want anyone else. There was a king of the daityas, named Shambhu, and he was insolent because of his strength. On hearing that the one with dharma in his soul wished to bestow me in this way, he was filled with rage. While my father was asleep during the night, the evil one killed him. My distressed mother embraced my father's head. With him, the immensely fortunate one entered the funeral pyre. My desire is to make my father's wish about Narayana come true. That is the virtuous intention in my heart. Even if I have to die, I will accomplish my father's wish. I have taken that pledge and am therefore undertaking these pervasive austerities. O bull among rakshasas! I have thus told you everything. Know that I have resorted to this dharma because I desire Narayana as my husband. O king! O Poulastya's descendant! I know about you. Because of

[552] Alternatively, speech has been born to him as a daughter.

my austerities, I can know everything that goes on in the three worlds." At this, Ravana spoke to the maiden who was observing this extremely great vow. Suffering from Kandarpa's arrows, he alighted from the top of the vimana. "O one with the excellent hips! Since your inclinations are like that, you are blind. O one with eyes like a fawn! It is the aged who should seek to accumulate dharma. You possess all the qualities. You should not act in this way. O timid one! You are the most beautiful in the three worlds. It is a rule that youth does not last. Who is this Vishnu that you have spoken about? O fortunate one! O beautiful one! You desire him. But he is not my equal in valour, austerities, pursuing pleasure or strength." Without any fear, the maiden replied to the roamer in the night, though the rakshasa had used his hand to seize her by the hair. Angry, Vedavati cut off the bit of hair with her hand.[553] Having lit a fire and made up her mind to die, the supreme one said, "O ignoble one! Having been oppressed by you, I no longer wish to remain alive now. O rakshasa! While you look on, I will enter this fire. I am faultless and am without a protector. Since you have oppressed me, for the sake of your destruction, I will be born again. This is especially because women are incapable of killing evil ones. If I curse you, my store of austerities will be diminished.[554] If I have performed good deeds, if I have given donations and I have rendered oblations, I will be born as the virtuous daughter of someone who follows dharma, but not through the womb." Having said this, she entered the blazing fire. From the firmament, divine flowers rained down in every direction. Using your superhuman bravery, you attacked and killed an enemy who was like a mountain. However, in her rage, she had already killed him. In this way, the immensely fortunate one was born on earth again, from the mouth of a plough in the field, like the flame of a fire from a sacrificial altar. In krita yuga, her name was Vedavati. For the destruction of that rakshasa, she was born in treta yuga. She was born from a plough and people referred to her as Sita.'

553 The Critical Edition excises a shloka that says one of her hands had turned into a sword.

554 Any act of cursing reduces the accumulated merits of austerities.

Chapter 7(18)

'When Vedavati entered the fire, Ravana ascended Pushpaka and started to roam around the earth. The rakshasa reached Ushirabijá[555] where, with the gods, King Marutta was performing a sacrifice. There was a brahmana rishi named Samvarta and he was just like his brother, Brihaspati. Surrounded by all the large numbers of brahmanas, the one who knew about dharma was officiating at the sacrifice. The gods saw that the rakshasa was invincible because of the boon he had obtained. Scared of being oppressed, they assumed the forms of other species. Indra turned into a peacock, Dharmaraja into a crow, the lord of treasures into a lizard and Varuna into a swan. Ravana, the lord of the rakshasas, approached the king and said, "Give me a fight or say that you have been vanquished by me." At this, King Marutta asked him, "Who are you?" The rakshasa laughed out aloud and addressed him in these words. "O king! I am pleased at your ignorance. You do not know about Ravana, Dhanada's younger brother. Who in the three worlds does not know about my strength? I have defeated my brother and have seized his vimana." King Marutta replied to the rakshasa, "You are indeed blessed that you have vanquished your elder brother in a battle. This is not an act that is in conformity with dharma and is condemned by the worlds. It is not something to boast about. Having performed the evil-minded act of defeating your brother, you are boasting about it. Earlier, what act of dharma have you accomplished that you obtained this boon and strength? You are praising yourself through words, but I have never heard of you before." The king seized his bow and arrow and angrily emerged to fight. However, the great rishi, Samvarta obstructed his path and addressed Marutta in words filled with affection. "If you listen to my words, this clash will not be good for you. If this sacrifice to Maheshvara is not completed, your lineage will be destroyed. How can someone who has consecrated himself for a sacrifice fight? How can someone who has consecrated himself for a sacrifice be cruel? The outcome of a battle is always uncertain and the rakshasas are

[555] This is described as a mountain and as a place where King Marutta performed a sacrifice.

extremely difficult to defeat." Hearing his preceptor's words, King Marutta desisted. He cast aside his bow and arrows. Composing himself, he stationed himself near the sacrifice. Shuka[556] decided that he had been defeated and announced, "Ravana is victorious.' He uttered a roar of delight. He[557] devoured the great rishis who had assembled for the sacrifice. Satisfying himself with their blood, he again wandered around the earth.

'When Ravana had left, Indra and the gods, the residents of heaven, assumed their own forms and spoke to the respective species. Delighted, Indra spoke to the peacock with the blue feathers. "O bird! O one who knows about dharma! O bird! I am pleased with you because of the good deed you have done. My one thousand eyes will be displayed on your feathers. When I shower down, as a mark of my affection, you will also be delighted." O lord of men! Before this, the feathers of all peacocks used to be blue. Having obtained the boon from the lord of the gods, all of them became multi-hued. O Rama! Dharmaraja spoke to the crow who was standing in front of him. "O bird! I am extremely pleased with you. Hear my words of affection. I afflict other creatures with various kinds of disease. But because of my affection towards you, they will have no powers over you. There is no doubt about this. O bird! Because of the boon I am granting you, you will have no fear of death. Until men kill you, you will not die. Men who are in my dominion will be afflicted by hunger. With their relatives, they will be satisfied whenever you eat." Varuna spoke to the swan who wanders around in the waters of the Ganga. O lord of those who use their wings to travel! Hear my words. They are full of affection. O amiable one! Your complexion will be beautiful, like that of the lunar disc. Your excellent radiance will be like that of white foam. When you approach my body,[558] your form will always be handsome. As a mark of my affection, you will always enjoy unmatched joy." O Rama! In earlier times, swans did not possess a complexion that was white all over. Their wings were blue at the tips and their breasts were smooth, but like tender grass

[556] Ravana's adviser.
[557] Ravana.
[558] Varuna's body is the water.

at the ends. Vaishravana spoke to the lizard who was seated on the mountain. "I am pleased with you and am granting you a golden complexion. Till eternity, your head will always be golden in hue. Because of my affection, you will possess this golden complexion." At the sacrifice, the gods thus bestowed these boons on them. With the king, they again returned to their own residences.'

Chapter 7(19)

'Having defeated Marutta, the lord of the rakshasas left. Dashanana wished to fight in the cities of the Indras among men. He approached all the Indras among kings who were like the great king or Varuna. The Indra among rakshasas told them, "Give me a fight. Alternatively, say that you have been defeated by me. This is my firm determination. If you do not act in this way, you will not be able to escape from me." O son! There were many wise kings who followed dharma. Knowing about the strength the enemy had obtained through the boon, they said that they had been defeated. Dushyanta, Suratha, Gadhi, Gaya, Pururava—all these kings said that they had been defeated. After this, Ravana, lord of the rakshasas, approached Ayodhya. Like Shakra protects Amaravati, it was protected extremely well by Anaranya. He approached this king and said, "Grant me a battle. Otherwise, say that you have been defeated by me. That is my command." Anaranya became extremely angry and told the Indra among the rakshasas, "O lord of the rakshasas! I will grant you a duel." The Indra among men had heard about him and had already collected an extremely large army. He emerged with this, ready to slay the rakshasa. There were thousands of elephants and tens of thousands of horses. He emerged instantly, covering the earth with his foot soldiers and chariots. Ravana's forces clashed against the king's forces. O king! Like oblations rendered into a fire, these lives were destroyed. The Indra among men saw that his large army was being destroyed, like the waters of the five rivers when they reach the great ocean. He himself brandished his bow, which was like Shakra's excellent bow.

Senseless with rage, the Indra among men attacked Ravana. The descendant of the Ikshvaku lineage brought down eight hundred arrows on the head of the king of the rakshasas. Though the arrows descended on him, they did not wound him even a bit. They were like torrents of rain pouring down from a cloud on the summit of a mountain. The king of the rakshasas became angry and struck the king on the head with his palm, bringing him down from the chariot. Suffering in his limbs and trembling, the king fell down on the ground. He was like a large sala tree, struck by a bolt of lightning in the forest and brought down. The rakshasa laughed and spoke to the king of the Ikshvaku lineage. "Having fought against me, what are the fruits you have obtained now? O lord of men! There is no one in the three worlds who can grant me a duel. I have a suspicion that you have been intoxicated by addiction to objects of pleasure and have not heard about my strength." The king's life was weakened and he uttered these words. "What can I possibly do? Destiny is difficult to cross. O rakshasa! You are praising yourself, but I have not been defeated by you. I have suffered because of destiny and you are only an instrument. What am I capable of doing now? My life is ebbing away. O rakshasa! Listen to the words that I am speaking. You have slighted the lineage of the Ikshvakus. If I have given donations, if I have offered oblations, if I have performed good deeds, if I have observed austerities and if I have protected my subjects properly, my words will come true. A great-souled one will be born in this lineage of the Ikshvakus. He will be an extremely energetic king and he will take away your life." At this, the drums of the gods were sounded from the tops of the clouds. When this curse was pronounced, flowers were showered down from the sky. O Indra among kings! The king went to his due position in heaven. O Rama! When the king went to heaven, the rakshasa returned.'

Chapter 7(20)

'The lord of the rakshasas terrified all the mortals on earth. In a dense forest, he approached Narada, supreme among sages. The immensely energetic divine rishi, Narada, was infinite in his radiance. Seated atop a cloud, he spoke to Ravana, who was astride Pushpaka. "O lord of the rakshasas! O amiable one! O Vishrava's son! Wait. I am pleased with your noble lineage, your valour and your energy. Just as I was satisfied when Vishnu killed the daityas, I am extremely content that you have afflicted and crushed eagles and serpents in battles. However, I have something to tell you. If you wish to listen, it is worth hearing. O bull among the rakshasa! After hearing, it is for you to decide on your next course of action. You cannot be killed by the gods. Why are you killing people on earth? People on earth are under the subjugation of death and have already been killed. O mighty-armed one! O lord of the rakshasas! Behold humans on earth. Because they pursue different objectives, they do not know about their destination. Some people are delighted in pursuit of musical instruments and dancing. Some others are miserable, with tears flowing down from their eyes. People are confused because of their affection towards mothers, fathers, sons, wives and other loved ones, destroying themselves. They do not even understand their own hardships. These people are already devastated because of their confusion. What is the point of causing them suffering? O amiable one! There is no doubt that you have already conquered the world of the mortals." Blazing in his energy, the lord of Lanka was thus addressed. He bowed down before Narada, smiled and said, "O maharshi! O one who sports with gods and gandharvas! O one who loves fights! Indeed, for the sake of being victorious, I will go to rasatala. Having conquered the three worlds, I will bring the serpents and the gods under my subjugation. Thereafter, I will churn the ocean, the store of juices, for the sake of amrita." The illustrious rishi Narada spoke to Dashagriva. "If that is where you want to go, why follow any other path now? This extremely difficult path goes towards the city of the king of the dead. O extremely invincible one! O afflicter of enemies! Follow this path to Yama." Dashanana was like an autumn cloud. Thus addressed, he smiled and said that he would do what he had been asked to. He said, "O great brahmana! Therefore, I will head towards the southern direction, so as to kill Vaivasvata, the king who is the son of the sun god. O illustrious one! O lord! Desiring to fight, I have already taken a pledge that I will defeat the four guardians of the world. Hence, I will proceed towards the city of the king of the dead. I will engage with Death, the one who causes suffering to all creatures." Having said this, Dashagriva greeted the sage. Cheerful, with his ministers, he left towards the southern direction. The immensely energetic Narada thought for a while. Resembling a fire without smoke, the Indra among brahmanas thought. "How can one cause injury to Death? He follows dharma and afflicts the three worlds, with Indra included, and the mobile and immobile objects, when their lifespans decay. He always drives away the three worlds and makes them suffer with fear. How can the Indra among rakshasas voluntarily go to him? He[559] is the ordainer and arranges destiny for the performers of good and bad deeds. He is the conqueror of the three worlds. How can he be conquered? And if that happens, who will be the ordainer? Full of curiosity, I will also go to Yama's abode."'

Chapter 7(21)

'The Indra among brahmanas was light in his valour. Having thought, he headed for Yama's abode, intending to tell him what had occurred. He saw Yama there, with the god Agni at the forefront. Depending on what they deserved, he was ordaining the destiny for all creatures. Yama saw that maharshi Narada had arrived. Following dharma, he welcomed him with a seat and arghya and said, "O celestial rishi! Is all well? I hope dharma is not suffering. O one who is worshipped by gods and gandharvas! Why have you come?" The illustrious rishi, Narada, addressed him in these words. "Listen to what I have to say and then determine what needs to be done. O king of the dead! There is a roamer in the night named Dashagriva. He is extremely difficult to defeat. He is coming here, intending to use his valour to subjugate you. O lord! That is the reason I have swiftly come here. You exert

[559] Yama.

the staff of chastisement. What will you do now?" At this time, the rakshasa's vimana could be seen, advancing through the sky. It could be seen from a distance, like the rays of the rising sun. The immensely strong one illuminated the spot with Pushpaka's radiance, driving away all the darkness. He approached. The mighty-armed Dashagriva cast his eye around, here and there. He saw creatures enjoying the fruits of their good deeds and suffering from their bad deeds. Those who had committed wicked deeds were being slaughtered because of what they themselves had done. Ravana, strongest among the strong, freed them. Using his superior strength, the rakshasa freed the dead. The ones who were meant to protect the dead[560] became extremely angry and attacked the Indra among the rakshasas. Those brave ones showered down hundreds and thousands of spears, clubs, javelins, bludgeons, spikes and darts on Pushpaka. Like speedy bees, they started to shatter Pushpaka's seats, mansions, platforms and gates. Pushpaka vimana possessed a divine origin. Because of Brahma's energy, it was indestructible. Though shattered in the battle, it became whole again. Together with King Dashanana, Ravana's immensely valiant advisers also freely fought, resorting to their strength. The advisers of the Indra among the rakshasas fought in that great battle. Their bodies were covered with blood and they were struck with all kinds of weapons. Yama's large forces and the rakshasa's immensely fortunate advisers fought against each other in the clash, striking with different kinds of weapons. Then they[561] abandoned the rakshasa's immensely energetic advisers and attacked Dashanana with a shower of spears. The best among rakshasas was on the vimana and was mangled with these blows, blood flowing from his body. He looked like a blossoming ashoka tree. However, he was strongest among the strong and showered down spears, maces, javelins, spikes, darts, arrows, clubs, trees, mountains and other weapons. They countered all these with their own weapons. Hundreds and thousands of them attacked the terrible rakshasa who was fighting alone. Resembling mountains and clouds, all of them surrounded him. They incessantly

[560] Yama's servants.

[561] Yama's soldiers.

showered down catapults and spears. With his armour shattered, he became angry. He became wet because of the blood that was flowing. He abandoned Pushpaka and stood on the ground. With the bow in his hand, the lord of the rakshasas stood on the ground. Having regained his senses in an instant, he was like another Death. He affixed the divine *pashupata* weapon to his bow. Saying, "Wait, wait," he stretched his bow. In the battle, that arrow was garlanded by flames and was followed by predatory beasts.[562] It was shot towards those forces, intending to burn them down like trees. Its energy consumed Vaivasvata's soldiers. They fell down in the battle, like trees burnt by a conflagration. Surrounded by his advisers, the rakshasa, terrible in his valour, emitted an extremely loud roar and seemed to make the earth tremble.'

Chapter 7(22)

'Vaivasvata Yama heard his loud roar. He thought that the enemy had been victorious and that his own forces had been destroyed. He decided that his warriors had been killed and his eyes became red and dilated with rage. He asked his charioteer to quickly ready his chariot and bring it. The charioteer brought the divine chariot, which made a loud noise. The immensely energetic one mounted that large chariot and was astride it. Death was mounted in front, with a noose and a club in his hands, just as he does when he is about to destroy the three worlds, with their mobile and immobile objects. The personified form of Kaladanda[563] was stationed next to him on the chariot. This was Yama's divine weapon and blazed in its energy. The three worlds were terrified and the residents of heaven trembled. They saw that Death was enraged and this brought fear to the three worlds. The advisers of the Indra among rakshasas saw the gruesome chariot, with Death mounted on it. It was a sight that brought fear to the three worlds.

[562] Which would eat the dead bodies.

[563] Yama's rod of chastisement.

All of them lost their spirits and their senses. They were afflicted by fear. "We are not capable of fighting." Saying this, they fled. The rakshasa also saw the chariot that brought fear to the three worlds. However, he was not agitated or distressed. Yama approached Ravana and showered down spears and javelins, angrily piercing the rakshasa in his inner organs. Ravana remained steady and released showers of arrows on Vaivasvata's chariot, like a cloud pouring down rain. He[564] brought down one hundred large javelins on his broad chest. The rakshasa was incapable of countering these and suffered from these wounds. Yama, the afflicter of enemies, struck him with many weapons. The battle raged for seven nights and neither one was routed or defeated. The battle between Yama and the rakshasa continued again. Both wished to be victorious and neither one retreated from the encounter. With Prajapati at the forefront, the gods, the gandharvas, the siddhas and the supreme rishis assembled as spectators in the field of battle. As the foremost among the rakshasas and the lord of the dead fought, it was as if the destruction of the worlds had arrived. The Indra among rakshasas became angry in the encounter. He incessantly shot arrows from his bow and enveloped the sky. He quickly struck Mrityu with four arrows and the charioteer with seven arrows.[565] He struck Yama in the inner organs with one thousand arrows.

'Yama became violently angry. Garlands of flames issued from his mouth. There were angry flames in his mouth and his breath. The gods, the danavas and the rakshasas witnessed this extraordinary sight. The blazing fire of anger was about to burn down the enemy's army. Mrityu became extremely angry and spoke to Vaivasvata. "O god! Quickly grant me permission, so that I can slay this enemy in the battle. Naraka, Shambara, Vritra, Shambhu, the powerful Kartasvara, Namuchi, Virochana, Madhu, Kaitabha and many other powerful and extremely invincible ones have become distressed on seeing me. Why worry about this roamer in the night? O one who knows about dharma! It is best to grant me

[564] Yama.

[565] Mrityu (Death) is usually a synonym for Yama, but is being described separately here.

permission, so that I can kill him now. After seeing me, no one is capable of remaining alive even for an instant. This is not because of my strength. It is because of the importance that has been given to me. If I touch anyone, that person can no longer remain alive." The powerful Dharmaraja heard his words and told Mrityu, "I will kill him." The lord Vaivasvata's eyes turned red with rage. He raised the invincible Kaladanda in his hand. Death's solid noose was right next to it and so was the personified form of the club, like fire to the touch. As soon as they saw these, the lives of creatures started to dry up, not to speak of embodied beings being struck by these and suffering from these. Surrounded by flames, it was about to consume the roamer in the night. Angry, the powerful one touched the extremely terrible Kaladanda with his hand. All the creatures fled from the field of battle. On seeing that Yama had raised his Kaladanda, the gods were agitated. As soon as he raised this Kaladanda in Ravana's direction, the grandfather showed himself and spoke these words. "O Vaivasvata! O mighty-armed one! O one who is infinite in valour! You should indeed withdraw the Kaladanda and not use it against the roamer in the night. O bull among the gods! I have granted him a boon. You should not render the words I spoke false. Placing Mrityu at the forefront, I had fashioned this Kaladanda earlier and in bringing down all creatures, it will be invincible. O amiable one! Therefore, you should not bring it down on this rakshasa's head. If it is brought down, no one is capable of remaining alive even for an instant. If it is brought down and the rakshasa does not die, or if Dashagriva dies, in either case, a falsehood will be committed. Therefore, control the Kaladanda, which you have raised to bring about the death of the Indra among the rakshasas. While all the worlds look on, make my words come true." Thus addressed, with dharma in his soul, Yama replied. "I have withdrawn the Kaladanda. You are like the lord Vishnu to us. However, now that I am engaged in this battle, what am I capable of doing? This rakshasa is insolent because of his boon and I cannot kill him. Therefore, in the eyes of this rakshasa, I should be destroyed." Having said this, he vanished with his chariot and his horses. Dashagriva announced that he had become victorious. Cheerful, he left Yama's abode on Pushpaka. With the gods and with Brahma at the forefront, Vaivasvata went to heaven. Narada, the great sage, was delighted.'

Chapter 7(23)

'Thus, Dashagriva defeated Yama, the bull among the gods. Proud at his victory, Ravana saw his own aides. Maricha and the others were emboldened by his victory.[566] Ravana comforted them and took them up on Pushpaka. He happily entered rasatala, the store of the waters. This was full of large numbers of daityas and serpents and was Varuna's well-protected dominion. He went to the city of Bhogavati,[567] protected by Vasuki. He went to the city that was full of jewels and brought the serpents under his subjugation. Daityas known as Nivatakavachas had obtained boons and resided there. The rakshasa approached them and challenged them in a battle. All those daityas were extremely brave and full of strength. Invincible in fighting, they wielded many kinds of weapons and started to fight. They fought with each other for more than a year. However, they could not defeat each other. Nor was either side destroyed. The undecaying grandfather could travel anywhere in the three worlds. Astride his excellent vimana, the god swiftly arrived there. He restrained the Nivatakavachas who were engaged in fighting. Knowing about the truth, the aged grandfather addressed them in these words. "The gods and the asuras are incapable of defeating this Ravana in a battle. Nor are the gods and the asuras, with Indra included, capable of bringing about your destruction. The idea of your friendship with this rakshasa appeals to me. There is no doubt that you should be united and should be each other's well-wishers." With the fire as a witness, Ravana contracted an alliance of friendship with the Nivatakavachas and became happy. They honoured each other and spent one year in bliss. Dashanana obtained honours that were superior to what he got in his own

[566] They had run away earlier.

[567] The capital city of the nagas.

city. From them, he learnt more than one hundred different kinds of maya. He roamed around in rasatala, the city of the Indra of the waters.

'He reached a city named Ashma,[568] protected by the Kalakeyas. He conquered it in an instant and killed four hundred daityas. The lord of the rakshasas then saw Varuna's divine abode. It possessed the complexion of a white cloud and was stationed like Kailasa. He saw the cow named Surabhee there. Milk continuously flowed from her. The milk that flows from her gives rise to the ocean named Kshiroda.[569] The powerful Chandra,[570] whose cool beams bring welfare to subjects, was generated from there and the supreme rishis, the Phenapas,[571] survive on this. Amrita was generated there and the *sura*[572] the gods subsist on. Men on earth know her by the name of Surabhee. Ravana circumambulated the supremely wonderful being. He then entered the extremely terrible city, protected by many kinds of forces. There were hundreds of different kinds of flows, with hues like those of autumn clouds. He saw Varuna's excellent house, which was always cheerful. In an encounter, he attacked and killed the commander of the forces. He said, "Go and quickly tell the king that I have come. Ravana has come here, desiring to fight. Grant him a fight. If you do not wish to be terrified, join your hands in salutation and say that you have been vanquished." At this time, the great-souled Varuna became angry. He emerged with his sons and grandsons and with Gou and Pushkara.[573] They possessed the qualities of valour and surrounded themselves with their own forces. They yoked chariots that could travel wherever they willed, as radiant as the sun, and emerged to fight. There was an extremely terrible clash that made the body hair stand up, between the sons of the Indra of the waters and the rakshasa Ravana. In a short while, the immensely brave advisers of the rakshasa Dashagriva brought down all of Varuna's forces.

[568] *Ashma* means made of stone.

[569] An ocean whose water is made out of milk.

[570] The moon, the moon god.

[571] Phenapas are sages who survive on foam.

[572] A kind of liquor.

[573] Gou and Pushkara are the names of two of Varuna's commanders.

Varuna's sons saw that the net of arrows had afflicted their own forces in the battle and withdrew from the field of battle. Ravana was on the ground, but now returned to Pushpaka. On seeing this, they[574] mounted swift chariots and advanced through the sky. They were now in comparable situations[575] and a terrible and great clash commenced in the sky, like that between the gods and the danavas. In that battle, they used arrows that were like the fire to make Ravana retreat and cheerfully emitted many kinds of roars. On seeing that his king was suffering in this way, Mahodara became angry. The brave one wished to fight and gave up all fear of death. He saw that their horses were like the wind and could go wherever they willed. Therefore, Mahodara struck them with his club and made them fall down on the ground. In the battle, he killed the horses of Varuna's sons. Having seen that they had thus been deprived of their chariots, he quickly emitted a loud roar. Destroyed and killed by Mahodara, their chariots, horses and excellent charioteers fell down on the ground. The great-souled Varuna's sons abandoned their chariots. Though they were distressed, because of their own powers, those brave ones remained stationed in the sky.[576] They strung their bows and pierced Mahodara. Enraged in the battle, they collectively attacked Ravana. Angry, Dashagriva was stationed like the fire of destruction. He showered down immensely forceful arrows and struck them in their inner organs. The invincible one brought down many kinds of clubs, hundreds of broad arrows, spears, javelins, shataghnis and spikes on them. Those brave ones were driven away and the foot soldiers were crushed. Having struck Varuna's sons, the rakshasa let out a loud roar. He showered down many terrible weapons, like floods of rain from a cloud. All of them were repulsed and fell down on the ground. Servants swiftly withdrew them from the field of battle and delivered them to their houses. The rakshasa told them to convey his message to Varuna. Varuna's minister was named Prabhasa and he told Ravana, "The immensely energetic lord of the waters has gone to Brahma's

[574] Varuna's sons.

[575] Because Varuna's sons were also on chariots travelling through the sky.

[576] They did not fall down on the ground.

world.[577] You have challenged him to a battle, but Varuna has gone there, to listen to the gandharvas.[578] O brave one! With the king gone, why are you unnecessarily exerting yourself? The brave princes assembled here, but they have been defeated." Hearing this, the Indra among rakshasas announced his name. Uttering roars of delight, he emerged from Varuna's abode. He returned along the route he had used to come. Proceeding through the sky, the rakshasa headed in the direction of Lanka.'

Chapter 7(24)

'The evil-souled Ravana returned cheerfully. Along the path, he abducted the daughters of royal sages, gods and gandharvas. If the rakshasa saw any beautiful woman or maiden, he slew her relatives and placed her in his vimana. In this way, Ravana seized the daughters of serpents, yakshas, men, rakshasas, daityas and danavas. Their hair was long. Their limbs were beautiful. Their faces were like the full moon. All of them were young. Afflicted by fear, their breasts hung down. They were like the rays of the fire. Their fear gave rise to a fire of grief. Suffering from misery, they trembled and shed warm tears. As they sighed, their breathing seemed to ignite everything. It was as if the fire of an agnihotra sacrifice had been lit inside Pushpaka. Some were afflicted by great sorrow and wondered, "When will he kill me?" Overwhelmed by sorrow and misery, the women remembered their mothers, fathers, brothers, sons and fathers-in-law and collectively lamented. "What will my son do without me? What will my mother and my brother do?" They were immersed in an ocean of grief. "Alas! What will I do without my divinity, my husband? O Death! Show me your favours and convey me to Yama's abode. In earlier times, in a different body, what evil deeds have been committed by me? That

[577] There is an inconsistency, since we have earlier been told that Varuna had emerged to fight.

[578] The gandharvas were going to sing in Brahma's presence.

is the reason I have been oppressed in this way and am submerged in an ocean of grief. Indeed, I do not see any end to my present sorrows. Since this wicked one has proved to be supreme, shame on this world of men. Ravana is powerful and is stronger than my relatives. He is like a rising sun that has destroyed the stars. Alas! This rakshasa is extremely strong. If I know about the means of his death, I will be delighted. Alas! He is evil in conduct and does not understand this himself. This evil-souled one is strong in every possible way. This act of oppressing other people's wives is an act that is worthy of him. This evil-minded one always finds delight in the wives of others. Therefore, because of what he has done to women, Ravana deserves to be killed." Because of the curses of the women, he lost his energy and his radiance was diminished. They were virtuous and devoted to their husbands. They based themselves on the path of virtue.

'While they lamented in this way, Ravana, the lord of the rakshasas, entered the city of Lanka and was worshipped by the roamers in the night. The sister of the king of the rakshasas was extremely miserable. She fell down at his feet and attempted to speak. Ravana raised his sister and comforted her. He said, "O fortunate one! What is it? Tell me quickly." Her eyes overflowing with tears, the rakshasi replied in these words. "O king! Because of your strength, I have become a widow. O king! Because of your valour, the daityas have been slain in the battle. They were known as the Kalakeyas and were immensely strong and brave. O brother! I loved my husband more than my own life. But at that time, because he was regarded as an enemy, he was killed. O king! When you killed this relation of mine, it is as if you killed me too. It is because of you that the appellation of 'widow' is being applied to me and I have been forced to suffer this. You should certainly have protected your brother-in-law in the battle. O king! However, you have slain him in the battle and are not ashamed." The rakshasa was addressed and reprimanded by his sister in this way. He comforted her and spoke to her in words of conciliation. "O child! Enough of this grieving. You should not be scared in any possible way. In particular, I will always satisfy you with honours and gifts. I was intoxicated in the battle. Desiring victory,

I shot arrows. O auspicious one! In the heat of the battle, I did not distinguish friend from foe. O sister! That is how I killed your husband in the battle. That being the case, right now, I will do whatever is beneficial for you. Go and reside with your prosperous brother, Khara. I will grant your brother the gift that he will be the lord of fourteen thousand greatly energetic rakshasas. The lord Khara is your brother. He is the son of your mother's sister. You will see that he will himself always do whatever you ask him to do. For the sake of protecting Dandaka, quickly go to that brave one. The immensely strong Dushana will be the commander of the forces. Earlier, the enraged Ushanas had cursed him that he would reside in this part of the forest, inhabited by rakshasas. There is no doubt that this will happen."[579] Having said this, Dashagriva commanded his soldiers, fourteen thousand rakshasas who could assume any form at will. Fearless, Khara surrounded himself with these rakshasas, who were terrible to behold, and quickly left for Dandaka. With all his thorns destroyed, he established a kingdom there. Happy, Shurpanakha started to live in the forest of Dandaka.'

Chapter 7(25)

'Dashagriva bestowed that terrible forest on Khara. Having comforted his sister, he was happy and also reassured himself. With his followers, the great-souled Indra among the rakshasas entered a giant grove in Lanka, known by the name of Nikumbhila. O amiable one! It was filled with hundreds of sacrificial altars and adorned with chaityas. He saw a sacrifice, blazing in prosperity, going on there. He saw his own son, Meghanada, the scorcher of enemies, there. He was attired in black antelope skin, his hair was tied in a knot on the top of his head and he held a water pot. The lord of the rakshasas approached and embraced him in his arms. He asked, "O child! What are you doing

579 More accurately, Ushanas (Shukracharya) had cursed Danda, from the lineage of the Ikshvakus, that he would be destined to live in this way.

here? Tell me." For the sake of extending the prosperity of the sacrifice, his preceptor, the great ascetic Ushanas, foremost among brahmanas, replied to Ravana, best among rakshasas. "O king! I will tell you. Listen to everything. Your son has performed seven extremely pervasive sacrifices—agnishtoma, ashvamedha sacrifice, *bahusuvarnaka*, *rajasuya* sacrifice, *gomedha*, and *vaishnava*.[580] He has now engaged in *maheshvara* sacrifice, something that any man finds extremely difficult to undertake. After this, your son has obtained a boon from Pashupati himself. He has obtained a divine chariot that can travel in the firmament at will. He has obtained the maya named *tamasi*. Through this, one can create darkness. O lord of the rakshasas! If one fights with the use of this maya, not even the gods or the asuras are capable of knowing how to fight against such a person in a battle. He has also obtained a quiver filled with inexhaustible arrows and an extremely invincible bow. O amiable one! He has also got a powerful weapon that can crush the enemy in a battle. O Dashanana! Your son has obtained all these boons. The sacrifice was completed today and I was waiting here for you." At this, Dashagriva replied, "What you have done is not good.[581] You have used various objects to worship the enemy, with Indra at the forefront. However, what has been done is done. One cannot undo it. O amiable one! Come. Let us proceed towards our own residence." With his son and with Vibhishana, Dashagriva left. He made the women, who were distressed and weeping, descend.[582] They possessed all the auspicious signs and were ornamented with jewels. They were the maidens of the gods, the danavas and the rakshasas. They were adorned in many kinds of ornaments and blazed in their own energies. Vibhishana saw that those women were overwhelmed by grief. Knowing what his[583] intentions were, the one with dharma in his soul addressed him in these words. "This kind of action destroys fame, prosperity and the lineage. You act according to your caprices and cause

[580] Ashvamedha is a horse sacrifice, rajasuya is a royal sacrifice. A cow is sacrificed in gomedha, bahusuvarnaka means that a lot of gold is donated.

[581] Dashagriva is speaking to Meghanada, not to Shukracharya.

[582] From Pushpaka.

[583] Ravana's.

oppression to beings. You oppressed their relatives and abducted these beautiful women. O king! This is exactly the way Madhu crossed you and abducted Kumbhinasi." Ravana replied in these words. "I do not understand this. What have you said? Who is the one named Madhu?" Vibhishana angrily replied in these words. "Hear about the fruits that result from wicked acts. Our maternal grandfather is Sumali and his elder brother is Malyavat. That famous roamer in the night is aged and wise. He is the elder father[584] of our mother and is thus our senior. His daughter's daughter is named Kumbhinasi. Our mother's sister is Anala and she is her daughter. Therefore, following dharma, she is a sister to us brothers. O king! The rakshasa Madhu used force to abduct her. Your son was engaged in this sacrifice then and I was performing austerities in the water. He slew the best among the rakshasas, your revered advisers. O king! She was protected in your inner quarters, but he forcibly abducted her. O great king! On hearing about this, I forgave him and did not kill him. A brother must always bestow a maiden on a groom. Know that the fruits of what one does is reaped in this world."[585] At this, Dashagriva's eyes turned red with rage. He said, "Let my chariot be readied quickly. Let the brave ones prepare. Let my brother, Kumbhakarna, and the other foremost roamers in the night ascend their mounts. Let them arm themselves with many kinds of weapons. In the battle today, I will kill Madhu, since he is not scared of Ravana. I desire to fight and, surrounded by well-wishers, I will go to Indra's world. I will conquer heaven and bring Purandara under my subjugation. I will sport on my return, adorning myself with the riches of the three worlds." Four thousand akshouhinis of rakshasas proceeded in the front. They left quickly, armed with many kinds of weapons and wishing to fight. Indrajit was at the forefront of the soldiers and the commanders were with him. Ravana was in the middle and the brave Kumbhakarna was at the rear. Vibhishana, with dharma in his soul, remained in Lanka, performing acts of dharma.

[584] Meaning father's elder brother.

[585] Vibhishana is implying that Madhu's act is the consequence of Ravana's wicked deeds.

'All those immensely fortunate ones proceeded towards Madhupura.[586] All those rakshasas left with chariots, elephants, donkeys, camels, horses and blazing and large serpents, and there was no space left in the sky. There were hundreds of daityas who were firm in their enmity towards the gods. On seeing that Ravana was proceeding, they followed him at the rear. Dashanana went to Madhupura and entered. He didn't see Madhu there, but he saw his sister. She joined her hands in salutation and bowed her head down at his feet. His sister, Kumbhinasi, was terrified of the king of the rakshasas. Ravana, the best among the rakshasas, raised her and said, "Do not be frightened. What can I do for you?" She replied, "O king! O immensely strong one! O one who grants honours! If you are pleased with me, you should not kill my husband now. O Indra among kings! I am faithful to my husband. Look towards me and make your words come true. O mighty-armed one! You have yourself told me that I should not be scared." On seeing that his sister was standing there, Ravana asked, "Who is your husband? Quickly tell me that. For the sake of conquering the world of the gods, I will take him with me. Because of compassion and affection towards you, I will refrain from the act of killing Madhu." Thus addressed, she awoke the roamer in the night,[587] who was asleep. Cheerfully, the rakshasi spoke to the extremely learned one. "My brother, Dashagriva, the roamer in the night, has come here. He desires to conquer the world of the gods and is asking for your help. O rakshasa! For the sake of helping him, go with your relatives. He has been gentle and has honoured you. You should do what he has thought of." Hearing her words, Madhu agreed. He saw the best among the rakshasas and as is proper, welcomed him. Following dharma, he worshipped Ravana, the lord of the rakshasas. The valiant Dashagriva was worshipped in Madhu's residence. Having spent the night there, he prepared to leave. He went to Mount Kailasa, Vaishravana's abode. The Indra among rakshasas, whose complexion was like that of the great Indra, made his forces camp there.'

[586] Madhu's city.

[587] Madhu.

Chapter 7(26)

'When the sun was about to set, the valiant Dashagriva reached the spot and made his soldiers set up camp there. The sparkling moon arose, as radiant as the mountain itself. Because of the radiance of the moon, he saw the many qualities of the trees there. There were groves of divine karnikaras and dense growth of *kadamba*. There were ponds with blooming lotuses and the waters of the Mandakinee. He heard the sweet sounds of bells being rung. Large numbers of apsaras sang in Dhanada's abode. Driven by the wind, the trees released showers of flowers. Residence on that mountain was intoxicating, with the scent of spring flowers. A pleasant breeze blew, mixed with the sweet fragrance and pollen from the *madhupushpa*[588] flower. This enhanced Ravana's desire. There was singing. There were many flowers. There was a cool breeze. The mountain possessed all the qualities. The night progressed, illuminated by a moon that had arisen. The extremely valiant Ravana succumbed to the arrows of desire. He sighed and sighed and looked towards the moon. At that time, Rambha, supreme among all the apsaras, was seen there. She was adorned in celestial flowers and her face was like the full moon. She was adorned in wet flowers that belonged to all the six seasons. She was covered in a blue garment that had the complexion of a cloud full of water. Her face was like the moon and her auspicious eyebrows were like bows. Her thighs were like the trunks of elephants and her hands were as delicate as petals. She passed through the midst of the soldiers and Ravana noticed her. Suffering from the arrows of desire, the Indra among rakshasas seized her. As she was passing, he seized her by the hand. He smiled and asked, "O one with the beautiful hips! Where are you going? What objective are you striving for? Who will rise[589] and enjoy pleasure with you? Your lips possess the fragrance of blooming lotuses. Who will inhale that? Who will obtain satisfaction from the amrita that is in your lips?

[588] The wild croton tree. Alternatively, this can be taken to be the honey tree, or the ashoka.

[589] The imagery is of the moon rising.

O timid one! Your auspicious and full breasts are like golden pots and there is no space between them. Whose chest will you allow them to be crushed against? Your thighs are round and golden. They are thick and ornamented with a golden girdle. Your hips are like heaven. Today, whom will you allow to mount them? There is no man who is superior to me, not even Shakra, Vishnu and the Ashvins. O timid one! Therefore, it is not proper that you should go to anyone other than me. O one with the plump hips! Come and rest on this auspicious slope of the mountain. There is no other lord in the three worlds who is my equal. Dashanana is joining his hands in salutation and is beseeching you. I am the lord and the master of the three worlds. Serve me." Thus addressed, Rambha joined her hands in salutation, trembling. She said, "Show me your favours. You should not speak to me in this way. You are my senior. Indeed, if anyone else seeks to oppress me, you should protect me. Following dharma, I am your daughter-in-law. I am telling you the truth." With her face cast downwards, she looked towards her feet and addressed Dashagriva in this way. He said, "You can be my daughter-in-law only if you are my son's wife." Agreeing, Rambha replied to Ravana in these words. "O bull among the rakshasas! Following dharma, I am your son's wife. Your brother, Vaishravana, has a son whom he loves more than his own life. He is famous in the three worlds as Nalakubara. In following dharma, he is like a brahmana. In valour, he is a kshatriya. In his anger, he is like the fire. In forgiveness, he is the equal of the earth. Because the son of the guardian of the world gave me a sign, I am going to him, adorning myself in all the ornaments. The sentiments I possess towards him are not like those I have towards anyone else. O king! O scorcher of enemies! That is the truth. Therefore, you should let me go. The one with dharma in his soul is eagerly waiting for me to reach. You should not be an impediment for your son.[590] Therefore, you should release me. O bull among rakshasas! Follow the path pursued by the virtuous. You should be respected by me. In that way, I should be protected by you." Rambha spoke these words and they were full of dharma.

[590] By extension.

'The rakshasa was reprimanded in this way. However, the strongest of the strong was overcome by confusion and seized her. He was angry and confounded by desire. He thus started to have intercourse with her. Rambha was deprived of her ornaments. Her garlands were cast aside. She was like the bank of a river, when it had been destroyed by a sporting elephant. She was trembling and ashamed. Terrified, she went to Nalakubara and joined her hands in salutation, falling down at his feet. The great-souled Nalakubara saw the state she was in. He asked, "O fortunate one! Why have you fallen down at my feet?" She sighed and trembled. Joining her hands in salutation, she started to tell him everything, exactly as it had happened. "O god! This Dashagriva had come here, headed towards heaven. His soldiers and aides were spending the night here. O scorcher of enemies! He saw me going to meet you. The rakshasa seized me and asked me who I was and whom I belonged to. I told him the entire truth. However, his soul was overwhelmed by desire and he did not listen to my words. O god! O lord! I entreated him, telling him that I was his daughter-in-law. However, he ignored all that and forcibly raped me. O one who grants honours! Thus, you should pardon me my crime. O amiable one! The strength of a woman is not the same as that of a man." Hearing this, Vaishravana's son became enraged. Hearing about this severe act of rape, he started to meditate. In this way, Vaishravana's son got to know everything about that deed. His eyes became coppery red with rage and he instantly took some water in his hand. Having touched water, he followed the rituals and flung it up into the sky.[591] He then pronounced a terrible curse on the Indra among the rakshasas. "She did not desire it, yet you forcibly raped her. Therefore, you will not be able to approach any other maiden who does not desire it. If a woman does not desire it and you rape her because of your desire, your head will shatter into seven fragments." As resplendent as a blazing fire, he pronounced this curse. The drums of the gods were sounded and flowers rained down from the sky. All the gods, with Prajapati as the foremost, were delighted. They got to know about the death of a rakshasa

[591] Flung the water up into the air as part of the ritual of invoking a curse.

who oppressed all the worlds. Dashagriva heard the curse that made the body hair stand up. The idea of having intercourse with a woman who did not desire it no longer appealed to him.'

Chapter 7(27)

'Having crossed Kailasa with the other rakshasas, the immensely energetic Dashagriva, roamer in the night, reached Indra's world. The soldiers of the rakshasas approached it from every direction. The sound that arose in the world of the gods was like that of the ocean being shattered. Hearing that Ravana had reached, Indra's throne started to wobble. He spoke to all the assembled gods. "O Adityas, Vasus, Rudras, Vishvadevas, Sadhyas and Maruts! Get ready to fight against the evil-souled Ravana." The gods, Shakra's equal in battle, were thus addressed by Shakra. Faithful to the prospect of fighting, those great-spirited ones armoured themselves. The great Indra was distressed and scared of Ravana. He approached Vishnu and addressed him in these words. "O Vishnu! O one who is great in valour and bravery! What will I do? This rakshasa is powerful and has come here, desiring to fight. He is powerful because of the boon that he has obtained. Indeed, there is no other reason.[592] O god! O Prajapati![593] Tell us the truth about what must be done. Namuchi, Vritra, Bali, Naraka and Shambara were stupefied and consumed. Do something like that. O god of the gods! O extremely strong one! There is no one other than you. You are the supreme refuge. O Purushottama! There is no one other than you. You are the prosperous Narayana. You are the eternal Padmanabha. You are the one who has established me in this eternal kingdom of the gods. O god of the gods! Therefore, you should yourself tell me the truth. Will you use a sword and a chakra to fight against this enemy in the battle?" The god and lord, Narayana, was addressed by Shakra in this way. He replied, "Do

[592] For his strength.

[593] This word is being used for Vishnu.

not be frightened. Hear from me about what must be done. No god or danava is capable of fighting against this evil-acting one, or advancing against him and slaying him in a battle. Because of the boon that has been conferred on him, he is extremely difficult to vanquish. Intoxicated because of his strength, in every possible way, he will perform great deeds. The rakshasa also has his son as his aide. I can foresee all this through my divine sight. O Shakra! You have asked whether I will fight against him in the battle. I will not fight against Ravana, the lord of the rakshasas. Vishnu does not retreat from a battle without slaying the enemy. However, this rakshasa has obtained a boon and it is extremely difficult for me to accomplish that objective now. O Indra of the gods! O Shatakratu! But I am taking a pledge before you. I will be the reason for the death of this rakshasa in a battle. In an encounter, I will slay Ravana and his son. Once I know that the time has arrived, I will satisfy the gods."

'At this time, night was over and a roar was heard. In every direction, Ravana's soldiers started to fight. A battle commenced between the gods and the rakshasas. It was terrible, with tumultuous roars. Many kinds of weapons were used in the battle. The rakshasas were cruel and were terrible to behold. Following Ravana's command, his advisers rushed out to fight. There were Maricha, Prahasta, Mahaparshva, Mahodara, Akampana, Nikumbha, Shuka, Sarana, Sahlada, Dhumaketu, Mahadamshtra, Mahamukha, Jambumali, Mahamali and the rakshasa Virupaksha. Surrounding himself with these extremely strong ones, Sumali, Ravana's senior and bull among rakshasas, entered amidst the soldiers. With those other roamers in the night, he angrily used many kinds of sharp weapons to devastate all the large numbers of gods. At this time, the eighth Vasu, the Vasu known as Savitra, entered the great field of battle.[594] A battle raged between the gods and the rakshasas. They[595] angrily tolerated the deeds of the rakshasas and did not retreat from the battle. In the encounter, the brave rakshasas also faced the

[594] The names of the eight Vasus vary from text to text. The one referred to as Savitra is more commonly known as Prabhasa.

[595] The gods.

gods. They struck each other with hundreds and thousands of many different kinds of terrible weapons. The gods were extremely brave. Using their own energies, they used many kinds of terrible weapons in the battle and conveyed the rakshasas to Yama's abode. At this time, the brave rakshasa named Sumali angrily used many kinds of weapons and attacked in the battle. He wrathfully struck all the forces of the gods with many kinds of sharp weapons and destroyed them, like the wind dispelling clouds. He oppressed all the gods with showers of large arrows, spears and terrible javelins. Though they tried to control themselves, they could not stand before him. The gods were driven away by Sumali. However, the eighth of the Vasus, the god Savitra, remained there. He surrounded himself with his own forces and struck the roamer in the night. Brave and extremely energetic, he countered him in the battle. There was an extremely crazy and extremely terrible encounter between their forces. Neither Sumali, nor the Vasu, retreated from the battle. The extremely great-souled Vasu used large arrows to instantly bring down his gigantic chariot, which was yoked to serpents. Using hundreds of sharp arrows, he destroyed his chariot in that battle. Then, to kill him, the Vasu seized a club in his hand. He swiftly seized that auspicious club, which blazed like Kaladanda. Savitra struck Sumali on the head with this and brought him down. Blazing like a meteor, it descended on his head and brought him down, just as the great vajra, released by the one with one thousand eyes, shatters a mountain. His bones, body or flesh could no longer be seen. In that encounter, the club reduced him to ashes and brought him down. On seeing that he had been killed in the battle, in every direction, all the rakshasas collectively fled, shrieking in loud tones.'

Chapter 7(28)

'Sumali was killed, reduced to ashes by the Vasu. In the battle, Ravana's son saw this and also saw that his own soldiers had been driven away, afflicted by the arrows. The powerful one became angry. Meghanada remained there and made all the rakshasas return. His chariot possessed the complexion of the fire. His giant chariot could go anywhere at will. Like a blazing conflagration in the forest, he attacked all those soldiers. He entered, wielding many kinds of weapons. On seeing him, all the gods fled in different directions. There was no one who was capable of remaining in front of him and fighting. Seeing that all of them were pierced and terrified, Shakra spoke to them. "You should not be frightened. Nor should you run away. Return to the field of battle. This son of mine has never been vanquished. He is advancing to fight." Shakra's son was the god known as Jayanta. On a chariot that had been wonderfully crafted, he advanced into the battle. All the gods surrounded Shachi's son. They remained there and clashed against Ravana's son in the battle. The great clash between the god, the son of the great Indra, and the rakshasa, the son of the Indra among the rakshasas, was one between two equals. The rakshasa's son used arrows that were embellished with gold to bring down the charioteer, Matali's son, from his seat.[596] In the field of battle, Shachi's son, Jayanta, also angrily pierced back the charioteer of Ravana's son. Enraged, the extremely energetic rakshasa dilated his eyes. Ravana's son repulsed Shakra's son with showers of arrows. Ravana's son seized and brought down large and firm weapons—shataghnis, spears, javelins, clubs, swords, battleaxes and extremely large summits of mountains. The worlds were distressed and a great darkness was generated. Ravana's son continued to strike the enemy. Shachi's son was surrounded by the forces of the gods on all sides. However, they suffered in many kinds of ways and fled. They were incapable of differentiating each other, distinguishing the enemy from the gods. Here and there, in every direction, they were routed and ran away.

'There was a brave and valiant daitya named Puloma. At this time, he seized Shachi's son and ran away. He seized his grandson and entered the great ocean. This noble Puloma was Shachi's father and his[597] maternal grandfather. The gods witnessed this extremely terrible sight of Jayanta being destroyed. They were cheerless

[596] Matali is Indra's charioteer and Matali's son is Jayanta's charioteer.

[597] Jayanta's.

and distressed and fled in different directions. Ravana's son was delighted and surrounded himself with his own forces. Emitting a loud roar, he rushed against the gods. On seeing that his son had been destroyed and witnessing the valour of Ravana's son, Indra of the gods asked Matali to bring him his chariot. Matali readied that divine, extremely terrible and large chariot. It was borne along at the speed of thought. Clouds that thundered loudly and lightning were attached to the chariot. As it proceeded, turbulent and noisy winds preceded it. As Vasava headed for the battle, many musical instruments were sounded and there were controlled sounds of praise. Large numbers of apsaras danced. The Rudras, Vasus, Adityas, Sadhyas and large numbers of Maruts armed themselves with diverse weapons, surrounded the lord of the gods and emerged. As Shakra emerged, a harsh wind started to blow. The sun lost its radiance and giant meteors started to fall down.

'At this time, the brave and powerful Dashagriva mounted a divine chariot that had been constructed by Vishvakarma. It made the body hair stand up and was yoked to extremely large serpents. The wind generated from their breathing ignited the field of battle. Brave daityas and roamers in the night surrounded the divine chariot and advanced against the great Indra in the battle. He restrained his son[598] and himself advanced into the battle. Ravana's son sat down.[599] A battle commenced between the gods and the rakshasas. Terrible weapons that resembled clouds were showered down in the battle. The evil-souled Kumbhakarna raised many kinds of weapons. However, in the encounter, he did not know whom he should fight against. He used his teeth, arms, feet, spears, javelins, arrows and anything to angrily strike the gods. The roamer in the night approached the immensely fortunate Rudras and Adityas and started to fight against them, incessantly showering down weapons. In that battle, using many kinds of sharp weapons, the gods and the large number of Maruts drove away all the rakshasa soldiers. Some were killed by weapons. Others writhed around on the

[598] Ravana asked Meghanada not to fight against Indra.

[599] He withdrew from the battle.

ground. Others remained in the battle, clinging to their mounts—chariots, donkeys, camels, serpents, horses, dolphins, boars and others with faces like pishachas. Some clung to these with their arms. Others were stupefied and uprooted. The roamers in the night were pierced by the weapons of the gods and died. The field of battle seemed to be a painting. Dead and crazy rakshasas were strewn around on the ground. A river of blood started to flow. The place was full of herons and vultures. A river began to flow in the field of battle and the weapons were like crocodiles. Meanwhile, the powerful Dashagriva became angry. He saw that his entire army had been brought down by the gods. He swiftly submerged himself in the army, which resembled a waxing ocean. He slew the gods in the encounter and approached Shakra. Shakra stretched his large bow, which emitted an extremely large sound. The sound of it being twanged resounded in the ten directions. Indra stretched that great bow and brought down arrows that were as radiant as the sun on Ravana's head. However, the mighty-armed Dashagriva remained there. He showered down arrows and dislodged Shakra's bow. They fought against each other and showered down arrows in every direction. Nothing could be discerned then. Everything was covered in darkness.'

Chapter 7(29)

'When that darkness was generated, the rakshasas and the gods, intoxicated by their strength, fought and killed each other. Out of the large armies of the gods and the rakshasas, only one-tenth remained in the battle. This is all that was left. The rest had been conveyed to Yama's abode. Submerged in that darkness, all the gods and the rakshasas could not distinguish each other, but fought against each other. However, three were not confused, despite being immersed in that net of darkness—Indra, Ravana and Ravana's immensely strong son. Ravana saw that all those forces had been slain in the battle. He was suffused with a fierce anger and emitted a loud roar. Filled with rage, the invincible one spoke to his son, who was astride his chariot.[600] "Take me to the midst of the enemy soldiers. Today, I will myself use my valour against all the gods. I will strike them with extremely firm weapons, destroy them and dislodge them from the firmament. I will slay Indra, Varuna, Dhanada and Yama. I will myself kill all the gods and establish myself above them. This is not the time for sorrow. Convey my chariot quickly. I have already told you twice. Take me right up to the end. Any place that we are in is like Nandana. Take me now to the spot where Mount Udaya is." Hearing his words, the charioteer urged the horses, which possessed the speed of thought, and took him to the midst of the enemy. Ascertaining his intention, Shakra, the lord of the gods, stationed in the battle on his chariot, addressed the gods in these words. "O gods! Listen to my words. This is what appeals to me. It is best that we seize the rakshasa Dashagriva while he is alive. Because of these soldiers, he is exceedingly strong and he is on a chariot that is as energetic as the wind. He is waxing, like the waves of the ocean during the full moon. He is fearless because of the boon he has obtained and it is impossible to kill him now. Therefore, in this battle, we must endeavour to capture him. When Bali was seized, I enjoyed the three worlds. In that way, the idea of capturing this wicked one appeals to me." After this, Shakra abandoned Ravana and went to a different spot. The immensely energetic one fought against the rakshasas and destroyed them in the battle. Dashagriva did not retreat and penetrated from the north. Shatakratu penetrated from the southern flank. The lord of the rakshasas penetrated one hundred yojanas. He showered down arrows and countered the entire army of the gods. Shakra saw that his own forces had been penetrated. He did not retreat and fearlessly approached Dashanana. At this time, on discerning that Ravana was being devoured by Shakra, the danavas and the rakshasas emitted roars of, "Alas! He will be killed." At this, senseless with rage, Ravana's son ascended his chariot. Enraged, he penetrated that extremely terrible army. He entered, using the maya that had been given to him by Gopati[601] earlier. Invisible to

[600] However, the words are directed more towards the charioteer.

[601] Lord of the earth or lord of cattle. Here, it means Shiva.

all creatures, he countered those soldiers. After this, abandoning the gods, he swiftly rushed towards Shakra. The immensely energetic and great Indra saw his enemy's son. He afflicted Matali and the horses with excellent arrows. Using the dexterity of his hands, he then countered the great Indra with showers of arrows. Shakra abandoned the chariot and Matali. Ascending Airavata, he started to look around for Ravana's son. However, because of the strength of his maya, the rakshasa could not be seen in the battle. He enveloped the infinitely energetic and great Indra with torrents of arrows. Ravana's son thought that Indra was exhausted. He used his maya to bind him up and took him amidst his own soldiers. Using the strength of his maya, he seized the great Indra in the battle. On seeing this, all the gods exclaimed, "Who has taken him away? The learned one cannot be seen. Someone has used maya to take him away." Meanwhile, all the large numbers of angry gods attacked Ravana and showered down weapons on him. In the battle, Ravana clashed against the Vasus, the Adityas and the Maruts. Afflicted by weapons, he was incapable of remaining there and fighting. He was exhausted and his form was of one suffering from those blows. Remaining invisible in the battle, Ravana's son spoke to his father. "O father! Come. Let us leave and withdraw from this fight. Our victory is evident. Assure yourself and be devoid of any anxiety. Shakra, the lord of the three worlds and of the soldiers of the gods, has been captured by me. The gods have been routed. With the energetic enemy captured, enjoy the three worlds as you wish. Why unnecessarily exert yourself in this battle? It is futile." The army of the gods also retreated from the field of battle. Hearing the words of Ravana's son, Dashanana also assured himself. The master and lord of roamers in the night thus lost anxiety in the battle and was victorious. He cheerfully left for his own residence and addressed his son in these words. "Your valour is like that of an extremely strong person and you have extended the respect towards my lineage. Your valour is like that of the immortals and you have vanquished the lord of the gods and the gods. Quickly fetch Vasava. Surrounding yourself with the soldiers, head for the city.[602] With

[602] Lanka.

the advisers following me, I will also quickly leave for that place." Thus, Ravana's son captured the lord of the gods. Surrounded by his forces and his mounts, the rakshasa reached his own residence. Thereafter, cheerful in his mind, he gave the rakshasas permission to leave.'

Chapter 7(30)

'Ravana's extremely strong son vanquished the great Indra. With Prajapati at the forefront, all the gods went to Lanka. They approached Ravana, who was surrounded by his sons and brothers. Remaining stationed in the sky, Prajapati addressed him in a conciliatory tone. "O child! O Ravana! I am pleased with your son in the battle. His valour and generosity are amazing. They are like yours, or superior to yours. With your own energy, you have conquered all the three worlds. You have made your pledge come true. I am pleased with my own son.[603] O Ravana! Your son, Ravana's son, is extremely strong. He will be famous in the world as Indrajit.[604] This rakshasa will vanquish strong enemies. O king! With his support, you have brought the gods under your subjugation. You should release the mighty-armed and great Indra, the chastiser of Paka. In return for setting him free, what should the gods give you?" At this, the immensely energetic Indrajit, the victor in assemblies, said, "O god! In return for setting him free, I desire immortality." The god who was born from the lotus replied to Ravana's son. "There is no creature on earth who can be immortal." Thereupon, Indrajit replied to the one who was born from the lotus. "Then hear about the kind of success I want for setting Shatakratu free. O god! Whenever I worship the fire and render oblations into it, prior to advancing into battle, desiring to defeat the enemy, if I fight before completing the rituals and before offering oblations into the fire, let it be possible for me to be killed only then. All men

[603] Because Ravana was descended from Brahma.

[604] Someone who has vanquished Indra.

seek the boon of immortality through austerities. Let immortality be conferred on me through my valour." The god Prajapati replied in words signifying his assent. Having been freed by Indrajit, Shakra and the gods went to heaven.

'Meanwhile, Shakra was distressed. His garments and garlands were dislodged. O Rama! He was overcome by thoughts and was immersed in deep reflection. On seeing him in that state, the god Prajapati spoke to him. "O Shatakratu! Why are you suffering from this anxiety? Remember the wicked deed you committed earlier. O Indra of the immortals! O lord! In earlier times, I created many subjects. Their complexion was identical. Their languages were the same. All of them were identical in form. There was no distinction between them, in appearance or in signs. With single-minded attention, I thought about these subjects. To create some kind of distinction between them, I fashioned a woman. From the existing subjects, I used the best of their limbs to create her. I constructed a woman without blemish, with beauty and qualities.[605] Because she was without blemish, her name became Ahalya. O Indra of the gods! O bull among the gods! Having created the woman, a thought then occurred to me. Whom would she belong to? O Shakra! O lord! O Purandara! You got to know about the woman and because of your sense of superiority, you thought that she would be your wife. However, I bestowed her on the great-souled Goutama. After she had been with him for many years, she was oppressed by you.[606] At that time, I got to know about the great sage's fortitude. Through the fruits of his austerities, he got to know that his wife had been touched by you. Even then, the great sage, with dharma in his soul, continued to find pleasure with her. When I bestowed her on Goutama, the gods lost all hope of obtaining her. However, you were angry and overcome by desire, you went to the sage's hermitage. You saw that woman, who blazed like the flame of a fire. O Shakra! You were full of desire and intolerance and oppressed her. The supreme rishi saw you in the hermitage then. Supremely energetic, he cursed

[605] The word *ahalya* means without being ploughed, without being furrowed. Therefore, it means one without blemish. That is the reason she was known as Ahalya.

[606] Adopting Goutama's appearance, Indra seduced her.

you in his rage. 'O Indra of the gods! You will face catastrophe and misfortune. O Vasava! Without any fear, you oppressed my wife. O king! Therefore, in a battle, you will be captured by the enemy's hand. O evil-minded one! There is no doubt that the sentiments you have brought into currency will also be prevalent among humans. If an extremely strong person perpetrates this great act of adharma, half of that will therefore devolve on you and half will be borne by the perpetrator. O Purandara! Since you have started this practice of adharma, your status will not be permanent. No one who becomes Indra of the gods will ever be permanent. This is the curse I pronounce.' This is what he told you. The extremely great ascetic also reprimanded his wife. 'O one who has not been modest! You will remain near my hermitage, but will be disfigured. You are the one who possesses youth and beauty. However, in this world, you will no longer be the only one who is beautiful in this way. Your beauty was extremely difficult to obtain and all the subjects approached you. This confusion resulted because it only existed in you.' Since then, all the subjects started possessing beauty. All this, including the new kind of creation, occurred because of that sage's curse. O mighty-armed one! Remember the evil deed that you committed. O Vasava! You have been seized by the enemy because of that and not because of any other reason. Control yourself and quickly perform a vaishnava sacrifice. You will go to heaven after you have purified yourself through that sacrifice. O Indra of the gods! Your son has not been destroyed in the great battle. His grandfather has taken him and hidden him inside the great ocean." Hearing this, the great Indra performed a vaishnava sacrifice. The gods again went to heaven and brought it under their control. O Rama! I have recounted the kind of strength Indrajit possessed. He defeated Indra of the gods and other creatures. What next?'

Chapter 7(31)

At this, the immensely energetic Rama was astounded. He bowed down and again addressed Agastya, supreme among sages, in these words. 'O illustrious one! O supreme among brahmanas! Was the world empty then? Was Ravana, lord of the rakshasas, not rebuffed by anyone? Or perhaps all the lords of the earth were deprived of valour. Since the kings were deprived of excellent weapons, many of them were vanquished.'

Hearing Raghava's words, the illustrious rishi, Agastya, smiled and spoke to Rama, as if the grandfather was speaking to Ishvara.[607] 'O bull among kings! In this way, he obstructed the kings. O Rama! O lord of the earth! Ravana roamed around the earth. There was a city named Mahishmati[608] and it was as resplendent as the city in heaven. He reached the place inhabited by the supreme Vasuretas.[609] In his powers, the king who was there was the equal of Vasuretas. His name was Arjuna and he was like a fire kindled on a bed of reeds. The lord Arjuna, the powerful king of the Haihayas went to the Narmada, to sport with the women. Ravana, the Indra among the rakshasas, reached the region on that very day. He asked the advisers, "Where is King Arjuna? You should quickly tell me that. I am Ravana and I have come here today to fight against the best among men. Without any hesitation, you should go and tell him about my arrival." The learned advisers were addressed by Ravana in this way. They told the lord of the rakshasas, "The king is not here." Vishrava's son heard from the citizens that Arjuna had left. He withdrew and went to the Vindhyas, the mountains that were like the Himalayas. It was covered with clouds and seemed to have sprouted out of the ground. Ravana saw the Vindhyas, etched like a painting in the sky. It possessed one thousand peaks and its caverns were full of lions. Waterfalls with cool water descended and they seemed to be laughing. The lofty peaks rose up towards heaven. Gods, danavas, gandharvas and kinnaras sported there with their wives and there were large numbers of apsaras. Unmatched sparkling water flowed along the rivers. It was as if serpents with flickering tongues were in the waters. With radiant caverns, the mountain was like the Himalayas. Having seen the Vindhyas, Ravana proceeded towards

[607] Meaning Maheshvara.

[608] The capital of the Chedi kingdom, adjacent to Avanti. In today's Madhya Pradesh.

[609] Vasuretas is the name of the fire god.

the Narmada. The river flowed downwards towards the western ocean and its sacred waters moved continuously. Buffaloes, srimaras, lions, tigers, bears and excellent elephants suffered from the heat. Becoming thirsty, they agitated that store of waters. *Chakravaka*s, *karandava*s, swans, waterfowls and cranes were always crazy and called everywhere. The river was stretched out like a woman. The flowering trees were like ornaments, the chakravakas were like her two breasts, the extensive banks were like hips and the flocks of swans were like a girdle. Her limbs were smeared with pollen from the flowers, the foam from the water was like a garment. Bathing there was like touching her and the blooming lotuses were like her auspicious eyes. Reaching the Narmada, supreme among rivers, Dashanana quickly descended from Pushpaka and bathed there, like approaching a desirable and beautiful woman. He sported along its banks, adorned with many kinds of flowers. With his advisers, the bull among the rakshasas sat down. Having reached and seen Narmada, the lord of the rakshasas was delighted.

'Ravana, the lord of the rakshasas, laughed in sport and spoke to his advisers—Maricha, Shuka and Sarana. "Behold. The one with the one thousand rays has made the world golden. The sun, whose fierce rays radiate heat, is located in the middle of the sky. However, on knowing that I am seated here, the sun is behaving like the moon.[610] The waters of the Narmada are cool and fragrant, destroying all exhaustion. Because of its fear of me, the wind is also blowing in a restrained way. The Narmada is the best among rivers and is one that enhances pleasure. With fish and birds hidden in the waters, it is stationed like a frightened woman. In encounters, you have been wounded by the weapons of kings who are Indra's equal. Blood has flowed out, like the juices from red sandalwood. All of you also bathe in Narmada, just as large and crazy elephants bathe in the Ganga, holding large lotuses in their trunks. It brings pleasure to men. Bathe in this great river and cleanse yourselves of your sins. This bank is like the autumn moon in its radiance. I will slowly put together a garland of flowers for Umapati."[611] Having been

[610] The sun's rays are cool and not hot.
[611] Shiva.

instructed by Ravana, Maricha, Shuka and Sarana, with Mahodara and Dhumraksha, immersed themselves in the Narmada. Like the giant elephants Vamana, Anjana and Padma bathing in the Ganga, the elephants of the Indra among the rakshasas also agitated the river Narmada. The rakshasas bathed in the excellent waters of the Narmada. They ascended from the waters and started to collect offerings of flowers for Ravana. Narmada's beautiful bank was as radiant as a white cloud. In a short while, those Indras among rakshasas created a pile of flowers that resembled a mountain. Ravana, the lord of the rakshasas, held those accumulated flowers and descended into the river, like a giant elephant wishing to bathe in the Ganga. Having bathed, Ravana emerged from the waters of the Narmada. He followed the rituals and chanted excellent hymns. As Ravana joined his hands in salutation and advanced, those seven rakshasas[612] followed Ravana, the lord of the rakshasas, wherever he went. They carried a golden *linga*[613] everywhere. Ravana set up that linga in the middle of an altar made out of sand and worshipped it with fragrant flowers and immortal scents. The supreme Hara removes the afflictions of all virtuous people. He is the one who grants boons. He is the one who wears the moon as an adornment. The roamer in the night worshipped him. He then stretched out his large hands and danced.'

Chapter 7(32)

'Ravana, Indra among the rakshasas, rendered that offering of flowers at a spot on the banks of the Narmada. Arjuna, best among victorious ones, was the lord and master of Mahishmati. Not very far from that spot, he was submerged in the waters of the Narmada, sporting with his women. In their midst, King Arjuna was radiant. He was like a male elephant in the midst of one

[612] Maricha, Shuka, Sarana, Mahodara and Dhumraksha are obviously five of these. The other two are probably Mahaparshva and Prahasta.

[613] Shiva linga.

thousand female elephants. He wished to test the supreme strength of his one thousand arms. Therefore, Arjuna used his arms to stem Narmada's flow. The sparkling waters reached the dam created by Kartavirya's arms. Flooding the bank, the force started to flow in the reverse direction. The flood of Narmada's waters was full of fish, crocodiles and makaras and spread over the flowers and laid out kusha grass,[614] as if it was the monsoon. The flood of waters created by Kartavirya carried away all the offerings of flowers Ravana had gathered. Ravana had only completed half of the rituals and had to abandon them. He saw that Narmada was like a beautiful and beloved woman who had turned perverse. He saw that the increasing flood of waters resembled an ocean. However, instead of heading westwards, it was flowing in an easterly direction. Ravana saw that the waters of the river were behaving like a wanton woman. The birds were also disturbed from their natural and excellent state. Making a sound, Ravana pointed with the fingers of his left hand and commanded Shuka and Sarana to determine the reason for this sudden increase in flow. The brothers, Shuka and Sarana, were commanded by Ravana. Those brave ones left through the sky, heading in the western direction. Those two roamers in the night travelled for only half a yojana and saw a man sporting in the waters with women. He resembled a giant sala tree. His loosened hair was as turbulent as the waters. His eyes were red with intoxication. His form was as resplendent as that of Madana. The scorcher of enemies had barricaded the river with his one thousand arms, as if the mountain with the one thousand feet[615] had barricaded the earth. There were one thousand young and excellent women around him. They were like one thousand maddened female elephants around a bull elephant. The rakshasas, Shuka and Sarana, saw this extraordinary sight. They returned and told Ravana what they had seen. "O lord of the rakshasas! There is a man who resembles a giant sala tree. He is sporting with women and has barricaded Narmada. The waters of the river have been obstructed with his one thousand arms. That is the reason these

[614] Prepared by Ravana.

[615] This is a reference to Mount Meru.

torrents, resembling waves in the ocean, have been created." He heard what Shuka and Sarana had to say. "That is Arjuna." Saying this, Ravana arose, desiring to fight. The lord of the rakshasas left in Arjuna's direction. He roared loudly and red rain showered down from clouds. Mahodara, Mahaparshva, Dhumraksha, Shuka and Sarana surrounded the Indra among rakshasas and went to the spot where Arjuna was.

'The terrible and powerful rakshasa dazzled like a mass of collyrium. In a short while, he reached the pool in Narmada. He saw the Indra among men, surrounded by the women, resembling a bull elephant filled with desire. King Arjuna also saw the rakshasas. Filled with strength, the eyes of the Indra among rakshasas turned red with rage. In a rumbling voice, he told his advisers, "This is Arjuna. O advisers! Quickly tell the king of the Haihayas that the one who is named Ravana has arrived to fight." Hearing Ravana's words, holding their weapons, Arjuna's ministers arose and addressed Ravana in these words. "O Ravana! You are virtuous and you have determined an opportune time to fight. You wish to fight against our king, who has been drinking and is surrounded by women. He is intoxicated and is in the midst of those who are full of desire. You are like a tiger that has approached an elephant. O Dashagriva! Pardon us now. O son![616] Sleep during the night. If you like the idea of fighting, you can fight tomorrow with Arjuna. Alternatively, if you are filled with thirst for a fight and you must do it now, slay us. You can then approach Arjuna and fight with him." At this, Ravana's advisers killed the king's advisers in the encounter. Hungry, they devoured them. As those who followed Arjuna clashed against Ravana's ministers, a tumultuous sound arose along the banks of the Narmada. With arrows, spears, javelins that were like the vajra to the touch and weapons that could drag, they roared with Ravana and powerfully attacked the warriors on the side of the lord of the Haihayas. There was an extremely terrible sound, like that made by crocodiles, fish and makaras in the ocean. With an energy that was like that of the fire, Ravana's advisers, Prahasta, Shuka and Sarana, angrily consumed Kartavirya's forces. Arjuna was still sporting. The

[616] The word used is tata.

men who were supposed to guard the gate went and told Arjuna what Ravana and his ministers had done. Arjuna told them and the women, "Do not be frightened." Like Anjana getting out of the waters of the Ganga, he arose from the water. Arjuna was like a fire and his eyes were filled with rage. He was extremely terrible and blazed like the fire that arrives at the end of a yuga. Wearing excellent and golden armlets, he quickly climbed up the bank. Seizing a club, he rushed against the rakshasas, just as the sun attacks darkness. He flung his arms around and raised that giant club. Using a force that was like that of Garuda, Arjuna descended on them. Prahasta fought with a mace and stood in his way, just as Mount Vindhya obstructs the path of the sun. He was stationed like Vindhya and did not waver. Maddened, he raised that terrible mace, which was plated with iron. Thundering like a cloud, Prahasta angrily hurled this. The tip of that mace blazed with flames, resembling a flowering ashoka. Hurled from Prahasta's hand, it seemed to burn everything down. Kartavirya Arjuna was like an elephant in his valour. As the mace headed towards him, he used his club to skilfully counter it. The lord of the Haihayas then attacked Prahasta. He whirled the heavy club around in five hundred of his arms. Prahasta was struck by the great force of that club. He fell down, like a stationary mountain struck by the vajra wielded by the wielder of the vajra. On seeing that Prahasta had fallen down, Maricha, Shuka, Sarana, Mahodara and Dhumraksha withdrew from the field of battle.

'When the advisers withdrew and Prahasta was brought down, Ravana quickly attacked Arjuna, supreme among kings. There was an extremely terrible battle between the king with one thousand arms and the rakshasa with twenty arms. It made the body hair stand up. They were like two agitated oceans, two mountains that began to move at the foundations, two suns that were full of energy and two fires that consumed everything. They were like two powerful elephants, like two bulls filled with desire. They roared like clouds and were as strong as lions. The rakshasa and Arjuna were as angry as Rudra and Death. They severely struck each other with their clubs. The man and the rakshasa tolerated those terrible blows of the clubs, just as mountains withstand the blow of the vajra. Echoes result when there is thunder. Like that, the sound of the clubs descending were heard in all the directions. When Arjuna's club descended on his chest, the sky was filled with a golden tinge, as if through a flash of lightning. In a similar way, Ravana repeatedly brought down the radiant club on Arjuna's chest, like a meteor descending on a large mountain. Arjuna did not suffer. Nor did the lord of large numbers of rakshasas. The encounter between them was between two equals, like that between Bali and Indra in earlier times. They were like two bulls fighting with their horns, or like two elephants fighting with their tusks. The man and the best among rakshasas struck each other. In the great duel, Arjuna wrathfully used all his strength and brought the club down between Ravana's breasts. However, he possessed an armour because of the boon. But the club descended on Ravana's chest and weakened him. It was shattered into two pieces and fell down on the ground, where the soldiers were. The club released by Arjuna struck Ravana. He was benumbed and roared, withdrawing only the distance of one bow length. Arjuna saw that Dashagriva was suffering. He violently seized him, the way Garuda seizes a serpent. Dashanana was forcibly seized in those one thousand arms. The powerful king bound him down, like Narayana did to Bali. On seeing that Dashagriva had thus been captured, the siddhas, charanas and gods uttered words of praise and showered down flowers on Arjuna's head. It was like a tiger seizing a deer, or a lion seizing an elephant. The king of the Haihayas repeatedly roared in delight, like a cloud. Regaining his senses, Prahasta saw that Dashanana had been bound. With the other rakshasas, he angrily rushed towards the king. The roamers in the night powerfully descended on him, just as at the end of the summer, clouds rush towards the ocean. They said, "Release him. Let him go. Wait. Wait for us." Saying this, they showered down clubs and spears on Arjuna. However, Arjuna was not scared. The slayer of enemies deftly avoided and seized the weapons of the enemy. He used extremely excellent weapons to shatter and drive away the rakshasas, just as the wind drives away clouds. Kartavirya Arjuna terrified the rakshasas. Seizing Ravana and surrounded by his well-wishers, he entered his city. He was like Puruhuta[617] and the brahmanas and citizens showered down flowers

[617] Indra.

on him. Arjuna entered the city with him, just as the one with one thousand eyes captured Bali.'

Chapter 7(33)

'This act of seizing Ravana was like that of capturing the wind. The rishi Pulastya heard the gods conversing about this in heaven. Out of affection towards his son's son, the one with great fortitude trembled. The great rishi went to see the lord of Mahishmati. The brahmana resorted to the path followed by the wind, travelling at a speed that was like that of the wind. With his valour and speed like that of thoughts, he reached the city of Mahishmati. He saw that it was like Amaravati, populated by happy and well-nourished people. Like Brahma entering Indra's Amaravati, he entered the city. It was as if the sun had descended and arrived on foot. It was a sight that was extremely difficult to behold. The news about his arrival was conveyed to Arjuna. The lord of the Haihayas heard the news about Pulastya. He joined his hands above his head in salutation and went forward to receive the best among brahmanas. Like Brihaspati before Indra, the priest advanced ahead of the king, carrying arghya and *madhuparka*.[618] The rishi arrived, like a sun that has arisen. On seeing this, Arjuna approached and worshipped him, like Indra honouring Ishvara.[619] He offered him padya, arghya and madhuparka. In a voice that was filled with delight, the Indra among kings spoke to Pulastya. "Today, you have made Mahishmati just like Amaravati. O Indra among all the Indras among brahmanas! I have seen you today. It is a sight that is extremely difficult to behold. O god! I am fortunate today. My lineage has been uplifted today. Your feet are worshipped by large numbers of gods and I have been able to worship them today. O brahmana! This kingdom, my sons, my wives and all of us belong to you. What is the task that needs to be done? Command us." Pulastya asked King Arjuna of the Haihayas about whether all was

[618] Madhuparka is a mixture comprising of honey, customarily offered to a guest.

[619] Maheshvara.

well with dharma, the fire[620] and the servants. He told the king, "O Indra among kings! O one with eyes like the petals of a lotus! O one with a face like the full moon! Since you have vanquished Dashagriva, your strength is infinite. My grandson is extremely difficult to defeat. The oceans and the winds remain immobile and stationary, out of their fear for him. But you have captured him today. O son! Your fame has been enhanced and your name has been heard everywhere. O child! However, pay heed to my words and release Dashanana." Without uttering any words to counter this, Arjuna accepted Pulastya's command. Cheerfully, the Indra among Indras among kings released the Indra among the rakshasas. Arjuna released the enemy of the gods and honoured him with divine ornaments, garlands and garments. With the fire as a witness, he contracted a pact of non-violence and friendship with him. Bowing down before Brahma's son,[621] he returned to his residence. Pulastya met the powerful Indra among the rakshasas. Though he had been embraced[622] and treated like a guest and released thereafter, he was ashamed. Having freed Dashagriva, Pulastya, supreme among sages and the grandfather's son, went to Brahma's world. Thus, Ravana was afflicted by Kartavirya. Because of Pulastya's words, he subsequently released him. O descendant of the Raghava lineage! If someone is strongest among the strong and desires his own welfare, he should never disrespect others. Thus the king with one thousand arms contracted friendship with the devourer of flesh. However, he[623] was insolent and continued to roam around the entire earth, causing carnage among men.'

Chapter 7(34)

'Ravana, the lord of the rakshasas, was freed by Arjuna. He roamed around the earth, slighting everyone. Ravana was insolent. Whenever he heard that any rakshasa or human was

[620] Meaning whether sacrifices were being properly conducted.

[621] Pulastya.

[622] By Arjuna.

[623] Ravana.

superior in strength, he approached him and challenged him to a fight. The city of Kishkindha was protected by Vali. On one occasion, he went there and challenged Vali, who wore a golden garland, to a fight. The adviser among the apes, the lord Tara, Tara's father,[624] addressed Ravana, who had arrived with a desire to fight, in these words. "O Indra among the rakshasas! Vali is your equal in strength. But he is not here. No other ape is capable of standing before you. O Ravana! Remain here for a while. Having performed sandhya[625] in the four oceans, Vali will soon return. Behold these piles of bones that are as white as conch shells. These belong to those who came here with a desire to fight against the energetic lord of the apes. O Ravana! O rakshasa! Clash against Vali only if you have drunk the juices of amrita. Otherwise, your life will be over. Alternatively, if you wish to die quickly, go to the southern ocean. You will see Vali there, bowing down before the sun." Ravana, the lord of the rakshasas, was reprimanded by Tara. He mounted Pushpaka and left for the southern ocean.

'Ravana saw Vali there, engaged in the sandhya worship. He was like a golden mountain, like the rising sun in his complexion. Resembling a mass of dark collyrium, Ravana descended from Pushpaka. Desiring to quickly seize Vali, he silently advanced on foot. However, at ease, Vali opened his eyes and saw Ravana. Though he got to know about his evil intentions, he was not scared. He was like a lion that sees a hare, like Garuḍa seeing a serpent. Ravana's intentions were wicked. Vali thought, "Evil in his intentions, he wishes to seize me now. I will grasp him by my side and go to the great oceans.[626] This enemy will be seen to dangle from my lap, like a garment dangling from my side. Dashagriva will be like a serpent seized by Garuda." Having made up his mind, Vali continued to listen.[627] He was like a king of the mountains

[624] The male ape is Tara and is the father of Taraa, Vali's wife.

[625] The evening rituals.

[626] To perform sandhya, Vali had to progressively go to the four oceans.

[627] The text of the Critical Edition causes a problem of translation here. Non-Critical editions use the word *mounam*. This simply means Vali waited silently. The Critical Edition uses the word *karnam* instead, meaning ear. We have hence interpreted it as Vali listening with his ears, since his eyes were closed. But the word also means diagonal or the diameter of a circle. It is possible that as part of the sandhya rituals, Vali had drawn auspicious signs on the ground.

and chanted mantras from the sacred texts. The king of the apes and the king of the rakshasas wished to seize each other. They were insolent and strong and exerted themselves to accomplish this task. Through the sound of the footsteps, Vali decided that Ravana was about to seize him. Without looking backwards, he extended his arms and grasped him, like the one born from the egg[628] seizes a serpent. The lord of the rakshasas desired to seize the ape, but was captured by him instead. Grasping him close to his side, the ape powerfully leapt up into the sky. He struck and pierced him repeatedly with his nails. Vali seized Ravana, like the wind seizing a cloud. The advisers of the rakshasa saw that Dashanana was being abducted. Desiring to free him, they roared in terrible voices and rushed behind them. They followed Vali, who was radiant in the middle of the sky. It was as if clouds in the sky were following the one with the rays.[629] Those excellent rakshasas tried to reach Vali. However, because of the force of his arms and his thighs, they were exhausted and fell down. Vali's trail was impossible to follow, even if Indras among mountains had attempted it. The Indra among apes was extremely swift and followed a path that even the birds couldn't follow. He progressively reached all the oceans and performed the sandhya rites there. Travelling through the sky, the ape was worshipped by all the creatures who roamed around in the sky. With Ravana, Vali went to the western ocean. The ape performed the sandhya worship there, bathed and chanted. Bearing Ravana, he then went to the northern ocean. He performed the sandhya worship in the northern ocean. Bearing Dashanana, Vali then went to the eastern ocean, the great store of waters. Vasava's son, the lord of the apes, performed the sandhya worship there. Seizing Ravana, he then returned towards Kishkindha. The ape had performed the sandhya rites in the four oceans. Exhausted at having had to bear Ravana, he descended in a grove in Kishkindha. The supreme ape freed Ravana from his flank and laughing at Ravana, asked him, "Where have you come from?" Ravana had been filled with great amazement. He was tired and his eyes rolled around. The lord of the rakshasas

[628] Garuda.
[629] The sun.

addressed the lord of the apes in these words. "O Indra among the apes! O one whose complexion is like that of the great Indra! I am Ravana, Indra among the rakshasas. I had come here, desiring to fight, but have suffered at your hands. Your strength is amazing. Your valour and depth are amazing. You seized me like an animal and travelled around the four oceans. O brave ape! I do not see any other brave one who could have borne me and travelled around like this, without suffering from exhaustion. O bull among apes! There are only three creatures who possess this kind of movement—thought, the wind and Suparna. There is no doubt about this. O bull among the apes! I have witnessed your strength. In front of the fire, I desire to contract an everlasting and affectionate pact of friendship with you. O lord of the apes! Wives, sons, the city, the kingdom, all the objects of pleasure, garments, food and everything else that I possess, will be divided and belong to both of us." After this, the ape and the rakshasa lit a fire. With fraternal sentiments, they embraced each other. The ape and the rakshasa stretched out their hands and cheerfully entered Kishkindha, like two lions entering a cave in the mountains. Like Sugriva, Ravana resided there for a month. His advisers were interested in oppressing the three worlds. They arrived and took him away. O lord! This is the former conduct of Vali towards Ravana. Having made him suffer, in the presence of the fire, he behaved towards him like a brother. O Rama! Vali's unmatched strength was extraordinary. However, he was consumed by you, like an insect by a flame.'

Chapter 7(35)

Rama humbly joined his hands in salutation before the sage who dwelt towards the south. He spoke to him in words that were full of meaning. 'Vali and Ravana were unmatched in their strength. However, it is my view that they were not Hanumat's equal in valour. Prowess, skill, strength, patience, wisdom, the attainment of good policy, valour and power—all of these found a home in Hanumat. On seeing the ocean, the army of the apes was distressed. However, comforting them, the ape leapt across one hundred yojanas. He made the city of Lanka suffer. In Ravana's inner quarters, he saw and spoke to Sita, comforting her. Single-handedly, Hanumat brought down the best of the soldiers, the sons of the ministers, the kimkaras and Ravana's son. He then freed himself from the bondage and addressed Dashanana. Like the fire does to the earth, he burnt down Lanka. The deeds that Hanumat accomplished in the battle are unheard of, even among Death, Shakra, Vishnu and the lord of treasures. It is because of the strength of his arms that I obtained Lanka, Sita, Lakshmana, victory, the kingdom, friends and relatives. Had Hanumat, lord of the apes, not been my friend, who knows what would have happened? It would not have been possible to find Janakee. In a desire to bring pleasure to Sugriva, when there was an enmity with Vali, why did he not burn him[630] down like a herb? I think Hanumat did not know about his own strength then. Though he could see the lord of the apes[631] suffering, despite being alive, he did not try. O illustrious one! O great sage! O one who is worshipped by the immortals! Tell me everything about Hanumat in detail, the complete truth.'

The rishi heard Raghava's words, which were full of reason. In Hanumat's presence, he addressed him in these words. 'O best among the Raghu lineage! What you have said about Hanumat is indeed true. There is no one else who is his equal in strength, speed and intelligence. However, in earlier times, the rishis imposed an inviolate curse on him. That is the reason this powerful one, the afflicter of enemies, did not know about his strength. O Rama! O immensely strong one! In his childhood, because of childishness, he did something. I am incapable of even describing it. O Raghava! O Rama! But if it is your intention to hear this, then listen with single-minded attention. I will tell you. There is a mountain named Sumeru. Because of a boon bestowed on it by the sun, its complexion is golden. His father, named Kesari, used to rule over the kingdom there. His beloved wife was known as Anjana. She gave birth to Vayu's excellent son. Anjana gave birth to a son whose

[630] Vali.

[631] Sugriva.

complexion was like that of a grain of paddy.[632] Desiring to collect some fruit, she then left and wandered around in that desolate region. Separated from his mother, he was afflicted by severe hunger. The child wept, like the child in a clump of reeds.[633] The sun was rising, resembling a japa flower.[634] On seeing it and desiring some fruit, he leapt up towards the sun. The child's form was like that of the rising sun and he leapt up in the direction of the rising sun. Wishing to seize the rising sun, he leapt up into the middle of the sky. Thus, overcome by childish sentiments, Hanumat leapt up. The gods, the danavas and the siddhas were struck by great wonder. "Vayu, Garuda and thought does not possess the kind of speed with which Vayu's son is travelling through the excellent sky. If this is the kind of speed and valour he possesses as a child, what will his force be when he is strong and young?" As he leapt, Vayu also leapt behind his son. He wished to protect him from the fear of being burnt down by the sun and there was a wind that was as cool as ice. Through the strength of his father, the child progressively travelled through many thousands of yojanas across the sky and easily reached the sun. The sun saw him approach, but took him to be a child who cannot commit a crime. Therefore, the sun did not burn him down. On the day he leapt up to seize the sun, on the same day, Rahu desired to seize the sun. O Rama! Astride the sun's chariot, he was severely seized by him.[635] Attacked, Rahu, the afflicter of the moon and the sun, was terrified. In rage, Simhika's son[636] went to Indra's abode. His eyebrows knit in a frown, he spoke to the god, who was surrounded by a large number of gods. "O Vasava! To satisfy my hunger, you have given me the moon and the sun. O slayer of Bala and Vritra! Why have you now given them to someone else? Today is the right time[637] and I approached the sun, to seize it. Though Rahu was approaching, someone else violently seized the sun." Hearing Rahu's words, Vasava was filled

[632] *Shalishuka,* a variety of rice.
[633] Meaning Kartikeya.
[634] The red hibiscus.
[635] Rahu was seized by Hanumat.
[636] Rahu.
[637] For an eclipse.

with fear. He leapt up from his throne, abandoning it. He cast aside his golden garland. Indra mounted the Indra among elephants.[638] Its complexion was like that of Mount Kailasa. It possessed four tusks and exuded musth. It was tall and was decorated with golden bells that seemed to laugh out aloud. With Rahu leading the way, he went to the place where the sun and Hanumat were. There, leaving the elephant and Rahu behind, he approached and saw the one whose form was like the summit of a mountain. He[639] let go of the sun and glanced towards Rahu. Desiring to seize Simhika's son, he leapt up into the sky again. O Rama! Letting go of the sun, the ape advanced. On seeing his large form, Rahu, who was only a mouth,[640] retreated. Terrified, Simhika's son sought a protector in Indra and repeatedly spoke to him. "O Indra! Save me. O Indra!" When Rahu was shrieking, Indra heard the words that he spoke and replied, "Do not be scared. I will kill him." At that time, Maruti saw the gigantic Airavata. Taking it to be some kind of fruit, he rushed towards the king of elephants. He rushed towards Airavata, wishing to seize it. In an instant, his form became terrible, as radiant as that of Indra or Agni. When he rushed forward in this way, Shachi's lord wasn't greatly enraged.[641] He released the vajra from his hand and struck him with that. Struck by Indra's vajra, he fell down on the mountain. When he fell down, his left jawbone was shattered. Struck by the vajra, the child lost his senses and fell down. Angry at Indra, Vayu wished to cause harm to the subjects. The lord is inside all creatures. Just as Vasava obstructs the rain, he obstructed the excretory organs of all creatures. Suffering from Vayu's rage, all the creatures were incapable of breathing. All the joints in their bodies became like pieces of wood. There was no *svadha*[642] and no sounds of vashatkara. There were no rites and dharma was abandoned. Because of Vayu's rage, the three worlds

[638] Airavata.

[639] Hanumat.

[640] Rahu is only a mouth, the body having been chopped off by Vishnu at the time of the churning of the ocean, when Rahu disguised himself as a god and had a bit of the amrita.

[641] That is, he struck him a mild blow.

[642] *Svadha* is an oblation offered to the ancestors.

became like hell. Afflicted by unhappiness and desiring happiness, the subjects, the gandharvas, the gods, the asuras and men rushed to Prajapati. The gods were suffering. They joined their hands in salutation and spoke to the one who had been born from the navel. "O illustrious one! You have created the four kinds of subjects.[643] Through Vayu, you have given us our lifespans. O excellent one! You have made him the lord of life. Why is he hating us now? In their misery, people are weeping, like women in the inner quarters. O lord! We are suffering because of Vayu and are seeking refuge with you. O slayer of enemies! We are oppressed and suffering because the wind has been obstructed." Prajapati, the lord of subjects, heard the subjects. Having been addressed, he spoke to the subjects. "There must be some reason. There must be a reason why Vayu is angry and has caused this obstruction. O subjects! You must listen to everything. Having heard, you must pardon him. The lord of the immortals, Indra, has brought down his son today, listening to the words that Rahu spoke. That is the reason, Vayu, your king, is angry. Vayu does not possess a body. But he roams around in bodies and nurtures them. Without Vayu, all bodies will be reduced to dust. Vayu is the breath of life and happiness. Vayu is everywhere in this world. Abandoned by Vayu, there will be no happiness in the world. Today, abandoned by Vayu, the world has lost its lifespan. There is no breath of life today and everyone is stationed like a piece of wood. All this has happened to us because of Vayu's obstruction. By causing displeasure to Aditi's son,[644] you should not head towards destruction." With the subjects, the gods, the gandharvas, the serpents and the guhyakas, Prajapati went to the spot where Vayu was, clasping his son, who had been struck by Indra of the gods. The one who perpetually moves[645] was embracing his son, whose complexion was as golden as that of the fire. With the gods, the siddhas, the rishis, the serpents and the rakshasas, the one with the four faces[646] looked compassionately towards him.'

[643] Those born from wombs, those born from eggs, plants and those born from sweat (insects and worms).

[644] Vayu.

[645] Vayu.

[646] Brahma.

Chapter 7(36)

'The grandfather saw that Vayu was afflicted because his son had been killed. Raising the child in his lap, he arose and stood in front of the creator. His earrings, diadem, garland and golden ornaments moved.[647] He prostrated himself thrice at the creator's feet. The one who knew about the Vedas stretched out his long hand that was adorned with ornaments and raised Vayu. He touched the child. As soon as he was touched by the one who was born from the waters and from the lotus, like crops that are sprinkled with water, he regained his life. On seeing that the one who had seemed to lose his life was full of life, the one who bore fragrances[648] rejoiced. As in earlier times, he started to move around in all creatures. Freed from the disease that had been brought about by Vayu, all the subjects were delighted. They were like lotuses in a pond, freed from cold winds. Brahma Triyugma, Trikaku, Tridhama, worshipped by the Tridashas, spoke to the gods, desiring to bring pleasure to Vayu.[649] "O great Indra, Agni, Varuna, lord of treasures and Maheshvara! You know everything. Even then, I will tell you what is beneficial. In future, this child will perform deeds for you. To satisfy Vayu, all of us should therefore confer boons on him." At this, the one with the one thousand eyes and auspicious face was filled with affection. He flung a garland made out waterlilies around his neck and said, "Your jawbone was shattered because of the vajra released from my hand. O tiger among apes! Your name will be Hanumat.[650] I will also grant you a supreme and excellent boon. From now, my vajra will not be able to kill you." Martanda[651] told the illustrious

[647] Because he suddenly stood up.

[648] Vayu.

[649] *Tridasha* is an expression used for the gods in general. Tridasha means thirty and refers to twelve Adityas, eleven Rudras and eight Vasus, adding up to thirty-one. *Triyugma* means three pairs, that is, one possessing the three pairs. The three pairs are *yasha* (fame) and *virya* (valour); *aishvarshya* (prosperity) and *shri* (riches); and *jnana* (knowledge) and *vairagya* (detachment). *Trikaku* means one with three peaks and is used to signify that a person possesses thrice the usual excellence. *Tridhama* means someone who is glorified in the three worlds.

[650] Literally, the one with the jaw.

[651] Surya, the sun god.

grandfather. "I will give him a hundredth part of my energy, so that he possesses the capability to study the sacred texts. I will grant him sacred texts so that he becomes eloquent in speech." Varuna granted him the boon that for a million years, he would not die from Varuna's noose or waters. Yama said that his staff would not be able to kill him and that he would never suffer from disease. "I also give him the boon that he will never be distressed and will be happy in battles." The one who grants boons[652] said, "My club will not be able to kill him, the possessor of tawny pupils, in a battle." Shankara granted him the supreme boon, "My weapons, or weapons that come from me, will not bring about his death." The great-souled Brahma spoke these words. "Under no circumstance, will Brahma's staff be able to kill him. He will have a long lifespan." Vishvakarma looked at the child, who was like the rising sun. The immensely intelligent one, supreme among artisans, spoke about the following boon. "I have fashioned all kinds of weapons for the gods. At the time of battle, these will not be able to kill him." Thus, the gods ornamented him with boons. The one with the four faces, the preceptor of the worlds, was happy and spoke to Vayu. "He will cause fear to the enemy and grant his friends freedom from fear. O Maruta![653] This son of yours, Maruti, will be invincible. In battles, to bring suffering to Ravana and to do what brings Rama pleasure, he will perform deeds that will make the body hair stand up." Saying this, with the grandfather at the forefront, all the immortals took their leave of Vayu and went away, to wherever they had come from.

'The bearer of scents clasped his son and brought him home. He told Anjana about the boons that had been conferred and left. O Rama! He obtained boons and those boons added to his strength. This was added to his own strength and he became as full as the ocean. The bull among apes was filled with strength. Without any fear, he started to cause harm to maharshis in their hermitages.

[652] The Critical Edition uses the expression Varada, one who grants boons. Non-Critical Editions say Dhanada, Kubera. In any event, this boon is being conferred by Kubera.

[653] Maruta is a specific term for Vayu, not to be confused with Marut. Maruti means Maruta's son.

He shattered and destroyed the ladles and vessels for agnihotra sacrifices and the piles of bark. What could those peaceful ones do? Because of what Brahma had done, he could not be killed by all the Brahmadandas.[654] Knowing this, the rishis always pardoned him. Even when Kesari, Vayu and Anjana tried to restrain him, the ape continued to transgress the boundaries. O best among the Raghu lineage! Moderately angry, they cursed him. "O ape! Using your strength, you are obstructing us. Therefore, confounded by our curse, you will not remember it for a long period of time." Because of the energy in the curse of the maharshis, his energy vanished. Mild in form, he roamed around in the hermitages. Vali and Sugriva's father was named Riksharaja. He was the king of all the apes and in his energy, he was like the sun. The lord of the apes ruled over the kingdom of the apes for a long time. After this, the one named Riksharaja succumbed to the dharma of time. The ministers, skilled in counselling, consecrated Vali in the ancestral kingdom and Sugriva at Vali's feet.[655] His[656] friendship with Sugriva was deep, without any blemishes, like that between Vayu and Agni. O Rama! At the time of the enmity between Vali and Sugriva, since he had succumbed to the curse, he did not know about his own strength. O Rama! Vali made Sugriva wander around. At that time, Maruti did not know about his own strength. In this world, there is no one who is superior to Hanumat in valour, enterprise, intelligence, power, good conduct, gentleness, good policy, depth, skill, bravery and patience. In earlier times, this Indra among the apes desired to learn grammar from Surya's mouth. To learn this great text, the immeasurable one followed Surya from Mount Udaya to Mount Asta. He is as fathomless as the ocean. He is like the fire in his ability to burn down the worlds. In his ability to destroy the worlds, he is like Death. Who can stand before Hanumat? There are other great Indras among the apes—Sugriva, Mainda, Dvivida, Nila, Tara, Tareya, Anala and Rambha. O Rama! The gods created them for your sake. I have told you everything that you asked

[654] Brahmadanda means Brahma's staff (*danda*). But it also means punishment and curses levied by brahmanas.

[655] Sugriva was instated as the heir apparent.

[656] Hanumat's.

about. I have recounted Hanumat's conduct as a child. O Rama! I have happily conversed with you. We will now leave.'

Having said this, all the rishis went away to wherever they had come from.

Chapter 7(37)

Taking leave of them, Rama embraced his friend Pratardana, the fearless king of Kashi, and addressed him in these words. 'O king! I have met you. You have exhibited supreme friendliness and affection. With Bharata, you have made great efforts.[657] You can now leave for the city of Varanasi, in Kashi. It is beautiful and is protected by you, possessing excellent walls and gates.' Saying this, Kakutstha arose from this excellent seat. The one with dharma in his soul embraced him close to his bosom. He took leave of his friend and greeted the other lords of the earth. Raghava smiled at them and spoke to them in words that were full of sweet syllables. 'Your affection is deep and your energy protects. You are always controlled and devoted to dharma and the truth. It is because of the powers and energy of you great-souled ones that the evil-minded and evil-souled Ravana, lord of the rakshasas, has been killed. I am only the instrument. Your energy has slain Ravana, his companions, his sons and his relatives in the battle. On hearing that the daughter of King Janaka had been abducted in the forest, the great-souled Bharata had summoned you here. All of you great-souled kings assembled to make efforts. A long period of time has elapsed and the idea of your return appeals to me.' The kings were filled with great delight and replied, 'O Rama! It is good fortune that you have been victorious and are established in this kingdom. It is good fortune that Sita has been got back. It is good fortune that the enemy has been defeated. This constitutes a great deed for us. This was our supreme desire. O Rama! We wanted to see you victorious and the enemy killed. O

[657] This hangs loose. It is not clear what Pratardana has helped Bharata about. (It is not clear from non-Critical Editions either.) The interpretation is that Pratardana had offered (Bharata) that he would help Rama fight against Ravana.

Kakutstha! You have praised us because of your generosity. It is only someone who deserves to be praised who can praise in this way. We seek your leave to depart. You will always remain in our hearts. O great king! We will always be affectionate towards you.'

Chapter 7(38)

The great-souled kings left in different directions. The earth trembled as those brave ones cheerfully left for their own cities. For Raghava's sake, many thousands of akshouhinis had come and assembled. All of them happily returned. Full of strength and pride, all the kings said, 'We were unable to remain in front and witness the encounter with Ravana. Bharata summoned us later and it was a futile exercise. Had the kings been there, there is no doubt that they would have killed the rakshasa. Protected by the strength of the arms of Rama and Lakshmana, without any anxiety, we would have happily fought on the other shore of the ocean.' Thousands of kings conversed in this and other ways. Conversing, the maharathas went to their own kingdoms. Having gone to their cities, to bring pleasure to Rama, the kings donated many kinds of jewels. There were horses, gems, garments, elephants crazy with musth, divine sandalwood and celestial garments. Bharata, Lakshmana and maharatha Shatrughna collected those treasures and returned again to Ayodhya. Those bulls among men returned to the beautiful city of Ayodhya and gave all those jewels to the great-souled Raghava. Filled with joy, Raghava accepted all those and gave all those to the great-souled Sugriva. He gave them to Vibhishana, other bears and apes, other brave ones with Hanumat as the foremost and the immensely strong rakshasas. Cheerful in their minds, they accepted everything that Rama had given them. The immensely strong ones wore them on their heads, necks and arms. They drank many kinds of extremely fragrant liquor.[658] They ate meat and extremely sweet fruit. All of them resided there for more than a month. But

[658] Madhu. Therefore, alternatively, honey.

because of their affection towards Rama, it seemed to be only an instant. Rama found pleasure with the apes who could assume any form at will, with the immensely valiant kings[659] and the extremely strong rakshasas. The pleasant and second month of Shishira[660] also passed. All the apes and rakshasas were delighted.

Chapter 7(39)

The bears, apes and rakshasas resided there. The immensely energetic Raghava spoke to Sugriva. 'O amiable one! Go to Kishkindha, which is impossible for even the gods and the asuras to assail. Without any thorns and with the advisers, rule over the kingdom. O mighty-armed one! Filled with great affection, look towards Angada, Hanumat, the immensely strong Nala, the brave Sushena, your father-in-law, Tara, supreme among strong ones, the invincible Kumuda, the extremely strong Nila, the brave Shatabali, Mainda, Dvivida, Gaja, Gavaksha, Gavaya, the immensely strong Sharabha and the immensely strong and invincible Jambavat, the king of the bears. Look towards Gandhamadana with affection. Filled with affection, look towards all the other extremely great-souled ones who were ready to give up their lives for my sake. Do not do anything disagreeable to them.' Saying this, he repeatedly praised Sugriva.

In sweet words, Rama addressed Vibhishana in these words. 'O king! You are revered. Follow dharma and rule Lanka. It is the city of the rakshasas and of your brother, Vaishravana. O king! You should never turn your mind towards adharma. Indeed, it is certainly intelligent kings who enjoy the earth. O king! Always remember me and Sugriva with great affection. Go, devoid of any anxiety.' Hearing Rama's words, the bears, the apes and the rakshasas repeatedly lauded Kakutstha in words of praise. 'O mighty-armed one! Your intelligence and valour are extraordinary. O Rama! Your sweetness has always been supreme, like that of Svayambhu.'

[659] However, the kings had already left.

[660] Shishira is winter, the months of Magha and Phalguna.

While all the apes and rakshasas were speaking in this way, Hanumat bowed down and addressed Raghava in these words. 'O king! I have always had great affection for you. O brave one! I have always been controlled in my devotion towards you. I do not feel like going elsewhere. O brave one! There is no doubt that as long as Rama's account is heard on earth, until that time, life will reside in my body.' Thus addressed, the Indra among kings arose from his seat and raising and embracing Hanumat, addressed him in these words. 'O best among apes! There is no doubt that this will happen. As long as the worlds remain, my account will also remain. As long as my account travels around in the worlds, there is no doubt that until that time, life will reside in your body.' Raghava took off the necklace from around his neck. It was made of lapis lazuli and possessed the complexion of the moon. Affectionately, he fastened it around Hanumat's neck. The great ape clasped the necklace close to his chest. He was as radiant as the Himalaya mountains, when the moon adorns the crest. Hearing Raghava's words, all the apes arose. The immensely strong ones bowed their heads down at his feet and departed. Rama embraced the mighty-armed Sugriva and clasped Vibhishana, with dharma in his soul, close to his bosom. All their voices choked with tears. There were tears in their eyes and they were almost senseless. They took their leave of Raghava with a great deal of sorrow, as if they were confounded.

Chapter 7(40)

The mighty-armed one gave leave to the bears, apes and rakshasas. Rama was happy and with his brothers, found joy in this happiness. On one afternoon, with his brothers, Raghava heard sweet speech being spoken from the sky. 'O amiable one! O Rama! Look towards my face with a peaceful glance. O lord! Know me to be Pushpaka. I have come here from Mount Kailasa. Following your command, I went to Dhanada. O best among men! However, when I presented myself before him, he told me, "Having slain the invincible Ravana, lord of the rakshasas in a battle, the great-souled Raghava, Indra among men, has won you. O amiable one! I am greatly delighted that he has killed that evil-souled one, Ravana, with his companions, sons, advisers and relatives. Rama, supreme in his soul, has conquered Lanka and you. O amiable one! I am commanding you. You should bear him. It is my supreme desire that you should belong to the descendant of the Raghava lineage. Be his vehicle and bear him to all the worlds. Without any anxiety, go there." Knowing the instructions of the great-souled Dhanada, I have again come to your presence. Therefore, accept me.' Kakutstha agreed and honoured Pushpaka with parched grain, fragrant flowers and excellent perfumes. 'Go where you wish. Come when I remember you.' Saying this, Rama released Pushpaka again. Adorned with flowers, Pushpaka left for the desired direction. Thus, knowing about its own soul, Pushpaka vanished.

Bharata joined his hands in salutation and addressed the descendant of the Raghu lineage in these words. 'When you are ruling over the kingdom, all kinds of extraordinary creatures who aren't human are repeatedly seen. A little more than a month has passed, but there is no disease among mortals. O Raghava! Even creatures who are old and decayed do not die. Women give birth to sons. The men are healthy. O king! The people who are residents of the city are filled with great joy. At the right time, Vasava showers down rain that is like amrita. The wind that blows is extremely pleasant to the touch. O lord of men! There has not been a king like this for a long time. This is what the inhabitants of the city and the countryside are talking about.' Bharata spoke these extremely sweet words. On hearing them, Rama was delighted. He was filled with pleasure, happiness and joy.

Chapter 7(41)

Having let go of Pushpaka, decorated with gold, the mighty-armed Rama entered Ashokavana.[661] The place was adorned

[661] To state the obvious, this is not the Ashokavana in Lanka.

with sandalwood, aloe, mango, *tunga*,[662] *kalayeka*[663] and *devadaru* trees in every direction. It was covered with *priyangu*s, kadambas, *kurubaka*s, jambus, patalas and *kovidara*s. There were beautiful flowers and pleasant fruits everywhere. The beautiful leaves and flowers fluttered and it was full of intoxicated bees. There were birds of many hues—cuckoos and *bhringaraja*s. Hundreds of other kinds of colourful birds resided on the branches of mango trees and decorated them. Some trees were like molten gold. Other trees were like the flames of the fire. There were other radiant trees that possessed the complexion of blue collyrium. There were many kinds of ponds and they were filled with excellent water. The extremely expensive stairs were made out of jewels, with crystal deep inside them. There were clumps of blossoming lotuses, adorned with chakravaka birds. There were many kinds of walls and the platforms made out of stone were decorated. Here and there, parts of the grove were like lapis lazuli and gems. The grass was excellent and the trees were laden with flowers. It was like Indra's Nandana, or like Brahma's Chaitraratha. In that spot, Rama's grove had a form like that. There were seats outside the houses and the houses were covered with creepers. The descendant of the Raghu lineage entered that prosperous Ashokavana. He sat down on an auspicious seat that was decorated with bouquets of flowers.

Rama sat down on a seat that was covered with a spread of kusha grass. Kakutstha clasped Sita in his arms and like Indra offering Shachi amrita, made her drink excellent *maireya* liquor. Rama asked the servants to quickly bring different kinds of meat, various types of fruit and other objects to be used. Young and beautiful women who were under the influence of drink, accomplished in singing and dancing, danced before the king. Thus, with Sita, whose face was beautiful, Rama was delighted. Like a god, he spent many days finding pleasure with Vaidehi. While the great-souled Raghava, king among men, sported himself in this way, the auspicious winter season passed. In the forenoon, following dharma, the one who knew about dharma performed all the tasks that had to be

[662] Tree with red flowers, *Mallotus phillippensis*.

[663] A kind of fragrant wood.

done for the city. In the remaining half of the day, he was in the inner quarters. In the forenoon, Sita performed the tasks meant for the gods. In particular, she joined her hands in salutation and served her mothers-in-law. Thereafter, adorned in many colourful ornaments, she went to Rama, just as in heaven Shachi goes to the one with the one thousand eyes when he is seated. On seeing that his wife was expecting, Raghava was infinitely delighted and uttered words of praise. He said, "O Vaidehi! These are signs of my getting an offspring. Tell me. What do you wish for? What should I do to satisfy your wishes?" Vaidehi smiled and addressed Rama in these words. "O Raghava! I wish to see the sacred forests where the hermitages are. The rishis, sacred in their deeds, reside along the banks of the Ganga. O brave one! I wish to survive on fruits and roots and live near their feet. O Kakutstha! This is my supreme desire, that even if it is for one night, I should reside with those sacred ones who subsist on roots and fruits." Rama, unblemished in his deeds, promised that he would act in this way. "O Vaidehi! Be assured. There is no doubt that you will go there tomorrow." Kakutstha said this to Maithilee, Janaka's daughter. With his well-wishers, Rama then left for the chambers that were in the middle.[664]

Chapter 7(42)

Learned people came and seated themselves near the king on all sides. They spoke about many kinds of things and laughed. Vijaya, Madhumatta, Kashyapa, Pingala, Kusha, Suraji, Kaliya, Bhadra, Dantavakra and Sumagadha—they conversed about many kinds of things that made them laugh. In the course of one such conversation, Raghava asked, 'O Bhadra! What is being talked about in the city? What is happening in the kingdom? What do the residents of the city and the countryside, who are dependent on me, say about me? What do the dependents say about Sita, Bharata and Lakshmana? What do the dependents say about Shatrughna

[664] He emerged from the inner quarters.

and my mother, Kaikeyee? If there are complaints about a king, the residents leave for a new kingdom.'

Thus addressed by Rama, Bhadra joined his hands in salutation and said, 'O king! The residents who are in the city speak auspicious words. O amiable one! They speak about the victory you earned after killing Dashagriva. O bull among men! In their own cities, the citizens repeatedly converse about this.' Thus addressed by Bhadra, Raghava replied in these words. 'The residents of the city may utter agreeable words and disagreeable ones too. Hearing about what they say, I will perform auspicious deeds and avoid inauspicious ones. Do not be scared. Have no fear or anxiety. Tell me what people in the city and the countryside speak about.' Hearing the words spoken by the great-souled Raghava, Bhadra joined his hands in salutation. He controlled himself and uttered these extremely beautiful words in reply. 'O king! Hear about the agreeable and disagreeable words citizens speak in the crossroads, the forests and the groves. "Rama performed the extremely difficult task of building a bridge across the ocean. No gods or danavas had ever done this earlier. He killed the invincible Ravana, with his forces and his mounts. He brought the apes, the bears and the rakshasas under his subjugation. Raghava killed Ravana in the battle and got Sita back. Turning his back on any intolerance, he again brought her back to his own house. But what kind of a heart does he possess? He finds pleasure and happiness with Sita. Though Ravana had forcibly abducted her earlier, he takes her up on his lap. She had been taken to Lanka and had been confined in Ashokavana. She had been under the subjugation of the rakshasas. Why does Rama not find this reprehensible? We will also have to tolerate this from our wives. Subjects follow whatever a king does." O king! The residents of the city say this and many other things, in all the cities and the countryside.' Hearing the words that he spoke, Raghava was greatly afflicted. He asked all the well-wishers, 'Do they say this?' All of them lowered their heads down on the ground and bowed before him. Despondent, they replied to Raghava, 'There is no doubt about this.' Kakutstha heard the words that all of them spoke. The scorcher of enemies gave all of them permission to leave.

Chapter 7(43)

Having allowed the well-wishers to go, Raghava thought and made up his mind. He spoke these words to the gatekeeper who was near him. 'Quickly fetch Soumitri Lakshmana, the one with the auspicious signs, the mighty-armed Bharata and the unvanquished Shatrughna. Hearing Rama's words, the gatekeeper joined his hands in salutation above his head. Without being barred, he went to Lakshmana's house and entered. Joining his hands in salutation again, he addressed him in these words. 'The king wishes to see you. Go there without any delay.' Hearing Raghava's command, Soumitri agreed. Mounting his chariot, he went to Raghava's residence. Seeing that Lakshmana had left, the gatekeeper went to Bharata's presence. Joining his hands in salutation, he spoke these words. 'The king desires to see you.' Bharata heard the words that the gatekeeper had spoken. He swiftly got up from his seat and went there on foot. Seeing that Bharata had left, he[665] quickly went to Shatrughna's residence. Joining his hands in salutation, he addressed him in these words. 'O best among the Raghu lineage! Come. Let us go. The king wishes to see you. Lakshmana and the immensely illustrious Bharata have already left.' Hearing his words about what Rama had commanded, Shatrughna bowed his head down on the ground and went to where Raghava was.

Hearing that the princes had come, he[666] was overcome by thoughts and his senses were distracted. He lowered his head and with a disturbed mind, addressed the gatekeeper in these words. 'Quickly make the princes enter and bring them before me. My life depends on them. They are like my breath of life outside my body.' The princes were attired in white garments. Hearing the commands of the Indra among men, they carefully controlled themselves and entered, joining their hands in salutation. They glanced at his face, which was like the moon when it is grasped by a planet. It was like the setting sun, bereft of all radiance. They saw that the intelligent Rama's eyes were full of tears. They glanced at his face,

[665] The gatekeeper.

[666] Rama.

which resembled a lotus with its lustre lost. They quickly lowered their heads at Rama's feet and greeted him. All of them controlled themselves and stood there. However, Rama's eyes were only full of tears. The mighty-armed one embraced them with his arms and raised them. Asking them to be seated, he addressed them in these words. 'You are everything to me. You are my life. O lords of men! I rule over this kingdom because of what you have done. You are accomplished in the sacred texts. You are full of intelligence. O lords of men! Therefore, for my sake, again make efforts.'

Chapter 7(44)

All of them sat down, distressed in their minds. With his mouth dry, Kakutstha addressed them in these words. 'O fortunate ones! All of you listen to what is in my mind. Do not act in a contrary way. Hear what the citizens are saying about me and Sita. There is great and terrible condemnation among the residents of the city and the countryside. It has shattered my inner organs. I have been born in the lineage of the great-souled Ikshvakus. In the city, they are conversing about Sita's evil conduct. O amiable ones! You know that Ravana abducted Sita in the desolate Dandaka forest and that he was destroyed by me. O Soumitri! You yourself saw that the bearer of oblations to the gods[667] and Vayu, who travels in the sky, declared Sita to be devoid of sin. In earlier times, in the presence of the gods and all the rishis, the moon and the sun also averred that Janaka's daughter was devoid of all sin. In the presence of the gods and the gandharvas, in the island of Lanka, the great Indra delivered the one who is pure in conduct into my hands. In my inner soul, I know that the illustrious Sita is pure. That is the reason I accepted Vaidehi and returned to Ayodhya. However, grief because of this great condemnation is shattering my heart now. This great condemnation is spoken about in the cities and in the countryside. In this world, if a person's bad deeds are spoken about, that person

[667] The fire.

is destined for the inferior worlds as long as this recital takes place. The gods condemn bad deeds. The gods honour deeds. Therefore, great-souled ones undertake all acts that lead to deeds. O bulls among men! Scared and terrified of condemnation, I am prepared to give up my life and all of you, not to speak of Janaka's daughter. That is the reason you see me immersed in this ocean of grief. I do not see any other misery that can be greater. O Soumitri! Tomorrow morning, ask Sumantra to prepare the chariot. Ascend it with Sita and leave her at the end of the kingdom. The extremely great-souled Valmiki has a hermitage on the other bank of the Ganga. It is like heaven and is located on the banks of the Tamasa. O descendant of the Raghu lineage! Leave her in that desolate region. O Soumitri! After doing this, return quickly. Act in accordance with my words. Do not at all answer me back about Sita. If you try to restrain me, I will be greatly displeased. I am urging all of you, on my arms and on my life, that after I have stopped speaking, you do not entreat me in any way. If you respect me, if you follow my commands, you will now take Sita away from here. Act in accordance with my words. She has earlier told me that she wants to see the great hermitages located on the banks of the Ganga. Her wish will also be satisfied.' With tears flowing from his eyes, Kakutstha said this. Surrounded by his brothers, the one with dharma in his soul then entered.

Chapter 7(45)

Miserable in his mind, Lakshmana spent the night. His mouth dry, he addressed Sumantra in these words. 'O charioteer! Swiftly yoke the horses to the excellent chariot. Cover the auspicious seat with spreads so that Sita can come there from the king's residence. From the king's residence, I will take Sita to the hermitage of the maharshis, the performers of sacred deeds. Quickly fetch the chariot.' Sumantra acted as he was told and yoked the excellent steeds. The extremely beautiful and excellent chariot was equipped with a pleasant couch with spreads. He brought it to Soumitri, who brought delight to his friends, and said, 'O lord!

The chariot has arrived. Do what you have to.' Thus addressed by Sumantra, Lakshmana entered the royal residence. The bull among men approached Sita and told her, 'O queen! We have been commanded by the king. I am to take you and quickly go to the auspicious hermitage of the sages on the banks of the Ganga.' Vaidehi was thus addressed by the great-souled Lakshmana. Filled with unmatched delight, the idea of going appealed to her. Taking extremely expensive garments and many kinds of jewels, Vaidehi prepared to go. 'I will give these ornaments to the wives of the sages.' Soumitri agreed to what she had said and made Maithilee mount the chariot. Remembering Rama's command, they quickly left on those horses.

At that time, Sita spoke to Lakshmana, who enhanced prosperity. 'O descendant of the Raghu lineage! I can see many inauspicious signs. My eye is twitching and there is a trembling in my body. O Soumitri! A sense of disquiet can be discerned in my heart. Though I am extremely eager, I am also suffering from a great lack of fortitude. O large-eyed one! To my eyes, the earth seems to be empty. With his brothers, I hope your brother is well. O brave one! In particular, I hope so are my mothers-in-law. I hope all the creatures in the city and the countryside are well.' Joining her hands in salutation, Sita sought this from the gods. Hearing this, Lakshmana bowed his head down and honoured Maithilee. With his heart dry, he said, 'All is well.' They reached a hermitage on the banks of the Gomatee where they could dwell.[668] Arising in the morning, Soumitri spoke to the charioteer. 'Quickly yoke the chariot. Like Tryambaka[669] in the mountain, I will today bear the waters of the Bhageerathee on my head.'[670] Without thinking about it, the charioteer swiftly yoked the horses, which possessed the speed of thought, to the chariot. He joined his hands in salutation and told Maithilee, 'Mount.' Hearing the charioteer's words, Sita ascended that excellent chariot, together with Soumitri and the intelligent Sumantra. After they had travelled for half a day, Lakshmana saw

[668] For the night.
[669] Shiva.
[670] That is, Lakshmana wants to bathe in the Ganga.

the Bhageerathee, the store of waters. Miserable, he wept loudly. Sita saw that Lakshmana was greatly afflicted and spoke these words. 'O one who knows about dharma! Why are you weeping? We have reached the banks of the Jahnavee and I have wished this for a long time. O Lakshmana! This is the time for joy. Why are you distressed? O bull among men! You have always remained at Rama's feet. Are you filled with grief because you have been away from him for two nights? O Lakshmana! I also love Rama, more than my own life. However, I am not grieving in this way. Do not be childish. Make me cross the Ganga and make me see the ascetics. I will give them these expensive garments and ornaments. I will honour the maharshis, as they deserve. After spending a night there, we will return to the city again.' Hearing her words, he wiped his auspicious eyes. Using a boat, Lakshmana crossed the sacred Ganga.

Chapter 7(46)

The nishadas prepared and brought an extremely large boat. Raghava's younger brother first made Maithilee climb on to it and then ascended it himself. Lakshmana told Sumantra, 'Stay with the chariot.' Tormented by grief, he asked the boatman to steer the boat. Lakshmana reached the other bank of the Bhageerathee. Joining his hands in salutation and with his voice choking with tears, he addressed Maithilee in these words. 'O Vaidehi! As a result of what people are saying, the noble and intelligent one has asked me to do something that is driving a great stake into my heart. It is better for me to die now. Death would be superior to this. He has engaged me in this kind of task, condemned by the world. O one who is good in vows! Show me your favours and do not be angry with me.' Joining his hands in salutation and prostrating himself on the ground, Lakshmana said this. He desired death for himself and was weeping, his hands joined in salutation. On seeing this, Maithilee became extremely anxious and addressed Lakshmana in these words. 'O Lakshmana! I do not understand this. Tell me the truth. I can see that you are not well. Is everything well with the king? I am urging you in the name of the king among men. What is the truth behind you being tormented? In my presence, you are being commanded by me. Tell me.' When Vaidehi took a pledge in this way, Lakshmana's senses were distressed. With his face and with his words choking because of the tears, he spoke these words. 'O Janaka's daughter! In the midst of the courtiers, he heard the extremely terrible condemnation being voiced about you by the residents of the city and the countryside. O queen! I cannot utter those words in front of you. I have turned my back on those intolerant words[671] that were in the king's heart. As far as I am concerned, you are innocent. But because of those words, the king has cast you aside. O queen! Scared, he has accepted the words spoken by the residents of the city and the countryside and there can be no countering of that decision. I will have to leave you at the end of this hermitage. Though you are expecting, the king has instructed me through his commands. O auspicious one! I will have to leave you here in this sacred and beautiful grove with the hermitages of the brahmana rishis. Do not grieve. King Dasharatha was my father. The brahmana Valmiki, the extremely illustrious bull among sages, was his great friend. Happily seek refuge at the feet of the great-souled one. O Janaka's daughter! Fast and with great attentiveness, reside there with him. Be devoted to your husband and always have Rama in your heart. O queen! That is the way you will obtain great benefit.'

Chapter 7(47)

Janaka's daughter heard Lakshmana's terrible words. Overcome by great sorrow, Vaidehi fell down. She regained her senses after a while, but her eyes were full of tears. With a distressed voice, Janaka's daughter addressed Lakshmana in these words. 'O Lakshmana! The creator has certainly created my body for the sake of suffering grief. Therefore, today, misery has manifested itself in embodied form

[671] I am ignoring them. I have forgotten them.

before me. What crime have I committed in an earlier life? Whom have I separated from his wife? I am pure in conduct. Nevertheless, the king has abandoned me. Earlier, I resided in a hermitage, following Rama's footsteps. O Soumitri! The misery put me into turmoil, but I controlled it.[672] O amiable one! How will I dwell alone in a hermitage? Tell me. Overcome with sorrow, how will I handle this grief? How will I tell the sage about the injury the king has done to me? What is the reason why the great-souled Raghava has abandoned me? O Soumitri! Indeed, I should not remain alive. I should give up my life in the waters of the Jahnavee. But if I do that, my husband's royal lineage will laugh at me. O Soumitri! Do what you have been commanded to. I will suffer misery. Abandon me. Follow the instructions of the king. However, listen to my words. In particular, I am joining my hands in salutation before my mothers-in-law. Ask them to accept this honour. I am bowing my head down and worshipping at their feet. Ask about their welfare and that of the king. "Always behave towards the citizens as you behave towards your brothers. This is your supreme dharma and you will obtain excellent fame because of this. O bull among men! Let the citizens benefit from the king following dharma. I am not grieving over my own body. O descendant of the Raghu lineage! Free yourself from the condemnation of the citizens."'[673] Thus addressed by Sita, Lakshmana's senses were afflicted. He bowed his head down on the ground and was incapable of saying anything. Weeping in a loud voice, he circumambulated her. Then he again mounted the boat and urged the boatman. Bearing the burden of sorrow, he reached the northern bank. Confounded by grief, he quickly ascended the chariot. Like one without a protector, he repeatedly glanced back towards Sita. As he proceeded, Lakshmana saw that she was writhing around on the other bank. From the chariot and from a distance, Lakshmana repeatedly looked back towards her. Anxious, he repeatedly looked back towards Sita, who was overwhelmed with grief. The ascetic lady was overcome by the

[672] Because I was with Rama.

[673] The text doesn't suggest any reason for this part to be put within quotes. Sita might have directed these words at Lakshmana too. But it seems as if this is a message to Rama, to be conveyed by Lakshmana. Therefore, we have put it within quotes.

burden of grief. The illustrious one could not see her protector.[674] She was filled with misery and wept in a loud voice, like a peahen in the forest.

Chapter 7(48)

The sons of the sage saw Sita weeping there. They rushed to the illustrious Valmiki, supreme in intelligence. The sons of the sage worshipped the feet of the sage, the maharshi. All of them told him about a lady weeping in a loud voice. 'O illustrious one! O great-souled one! We have never seen anything like this before. There is a wife who is like Shri. She is confounded and is shrieking in a distorted tone. O illustrious one! It is best that you come and see for yourself. She is like a goddess who has been dislodged from the sky. We do not think she is human. You should go and welcome her with proper rites.' Hearing their words, the one who knew about dharma used his intelligence to determine what should be done. He used the insight obtained through his austerities and went to the spot where Maithilee was. Walking on foot for a short while, the great sage reached the place. Taking excellent arghya, he reached the banks of the Jahnavee. He saw Raghava's beloved wife there, like one who was without a protector. Sita was overcome by the burden of grief. Valmiki, bull among sages, addressed her in sweet words, as if delighting her with his energy. 'O queen! O Dasharatha's daughter-in-law! O Rama's queen! O Janaka's daughter! O one who is devoted to her husband! Welcome. Because of the fruits of dharma, I have got to know that you have come. My heart has got to know about all the reasons. O Sita! Through the insight obtained through austerities, I know that you are devoid of sin. O Vaidehi! You are pure in sentiments and you have now come to me. My hermitage is not very far from here. Ascetics engaged in austerities are there. Reside there. They will always nurture you, like their own children. Accept this arghya. Do not be scared and have no anxiety.

[674] This could mean either Rama or Lakshmana.

Do not grieve. It is as if you are in your own home.' Sita heard the extraordinary words uttered by the sage. She bowed her head down at his feet. Joining her hands in salutation, she agreed. The sage left. Joining her hands in salutation, she followed him at the rear towards the spot where the controlled ascetics, always devoted to dharma, were. They saw the sage coming, with Vaidehi following him. Extremely happy, they came there and spoke these words. 'O best among sages! O lord! You have come after a long time.[675] All of us are greeting you. Tell us what we should do.' Hearing their words, Valmiki replied, 'Sita, the wife of the intelligent Rama, has arrived. She is Dasharatha's daughter-in-law and Janaka's daughter. Though she is innocent, she has been abandoned by her husband. She must always be protected by me. Look towards her with great affection. Pay heed to my words. In particular, honour her.' The immensely illustrious one repeatedly assured Vaidehi. Surrounded by his disciples, the greatly ascetic one returned to his own hermitage.[676]

Chapter 7(49)

After seeing that Maithilee Sita had entered the hermitage, Lakshmana was distressed in his mind. He was overcome by a terrible and severe torment. The greatly energetic one spoke to Sumantra, the charioteer who was also a counsellor. 'Because of the torment on account of Sita, you will behold the intelligent Rama's misery. What can be a greater misery for Raghava than having to give up Janaka's daughter, his wife who is pure in conduct? It is evident this is destiny. O charioteer! I think the separation of Raghava from Vaidehi is because of that. Destiny is impossible to cross. When he is angry, Raghava can kill the gods, the gandharvas, the asuras and the rakshasas. But he has to follow destiny. Earlier, because of my father's command, he had to reside for fourteen years

[675] Obviously, Valmiki had gone to meet Sita from his own hermitage. The other sages, in their respective hermitages, had not met him for some time.

[676] He left Sita with the other ascetics.

in the extremely terrible and desolate forest. On hearing the words of the citizens, this exile of Sita is a greater grief than that. It seems to me to be cruel. O charioteer! This is a deed that destroys fame. How can it be based on dharma? He acted in this way towards Maithilee only because citizens spoke injurious words.' Lakshmana said this and many other things.

Hearing these, Sumantra joined his hands in salutation and said the following words. 'O Soumitri! You should not be tormented about Maithilee. O Lakshmana! In front of your father, the brahmana had mentioned this earlier. He said that Rama's misery would be lasting and that he would have few friends. After some time, this great one, with dharma in his soul, would abandon you, Maithilee, Shatrughna and Bharata. O Soumitri! You should mention this to Bharata. When the king[677] had asked, Durvasa had told him this. O bull among men! In the presence of the great king, Vasishtha and me, the rishi had spoken these words. On hearing the rishi's words, the bull among men[678] had told me, "O charioteer! Never reveal this in front of people." O one who is amiable to behold! I controlled myself and never acted contrary to the words spoken by that guardian of the world. O amiable one! I should not have revealed it in front of you either. O descendant of the Raghu lineage! However, if you wish to hear it, listen. The Indra among men had told me about this secret earlier. Nevertheless, I can recount it before you.' Destiny is extremely difficult to transgress. Hearing these great words, filled with grave meaning, Soumitri replied in the following words. 'O charioteer! Tell me the truth.'

Chapter 7(50)

The charioteer was thus urged by the great-souled Lakshmana. He began to speak the words that had been uttered by the rishi. 'In ancient times, there was a great sage named Durvasa and he was

[677] Dasharatha.
[678] Dasharatha.

Atri's son. He resided in Vasishtha's sacred hermitage during the rainy season. To see the great-souled priest,[679] your greatly energetic and immensely illustrious father had himself gone to that hermitage. He saw the great sage[680] seated to Vasishtha's left, blazing in his energy and resembling the sun. Humbly, he greeted those two sages, best among ascetics. Thus worshipped, both of them welcomed the king. Having been offered padya, fruits and roots, he sat down with the sages. Having sat down with them, he engaged in an extremely pleasant conversation with the supreme rishis. It was midday and the sun was in the middle of the sky. After some time, in the course of the conversation, the king joined his hands in salutation and spoke to Atri's great-souled son, the store of austerities. "O illustrious one! How long will my lineage last? What will be Rama's lifespan? What will be the lifespans of my other sons? What will be the lifespan of Rama's daughter? O illustrious one! I wish to know what will happen to my lineage. Please tell me."

'Hearing the words spoken by King Dasharatha, the extremely energetic Durvasa started to speak. "Rama will be the lord of Ayodhya for a long period of time. His followers will be happy and prosperous. However, for some reason, the one with dharma in his soul, will abandon the illustrious Maithilee for a long period of time. After ruling the kingdom for eleven thousand years, Rama will go to Brahma's world. The destroyer of enemy cities will perform many prosperous horse sacrifices. Kakutstha will establish many royal lineages."[681] After telling the king about these lineages that would come, the extremely energetic and immensely radiant one became silent. When the sage became silent, King Dasharatha honoured those two great-souled ones and returned to his excellent city. I heard what the sage had said in those earlier times. Having heard, I secreted it in my heart. There can be no violation of what he said. O Raghava! That being the case, you should not be tormented. O supreme among men! For Sita's sake and for Raghava's sake, be firm.'

[679] Vasishtha.

[680] Durvasa.

[681] The Critical Edition excises a shloka where Durvasa said Rama would have two sons.

Hearing the extremely astounding words spoken by the charioteer, he[682] uttered words of praise and obtained unmatched delight. Lakshmana and the charioteer conversed with each other along the route. Since the sun had set, they spent the night near the Gomatee.

Chapter 7(51)

The descendant of the Raghu lineage spent the night near the Gomatee. Having woken in the morning, Lakshmana departed. When half of the day was over, the maharatha entered Ayodhya, full of jewels and inhabited by healthy and happy people. The extremely intelligent Soumitri was filled with great despondency. 'What will I say when I go there and approach Rama's feet?' While he was thinking this, he saw Rama's residence in front of him. It was extremely large and was like the moon. The supreme among men descended near the gate of the royal residence. He entered without being obstructed, his face hung downwards and distress in his mind. He saw the miserable Raghava, seated on his excellent seat. He saw his elder brother in front of him, his eyes full of tears. With his senses afflicted, Lakshmana grasped his feet. He controlled himself and joining his hands in salutation, spoke these miserable words. 'O noble one! Placing your command at the forefront, I have abandoned Janaka's daughter. As commanded, I have left her on the banks of the Ganga, in Valmiki's auspicious hermitage. O brave one! I have returned thereafter, to serve at your feet. O tiger among men! Do not grieve. The progress of time is like this. Therefore, someone who is spirited and learned like you should not sorrow. All stores of riches are exhausted. Everything that rises up must fall down. Any association ends in disassociation. Life ends in death. You are capable of assuring your soul yourself. You can conquer your mind and all the worlds. O Kakutstha! Why are you then sorrowing like this? Bulls among men who are like you are not confounded in this

[682] Lakshmana.

way. O king! You abandoned Maithilee because of the censure. O tiger among men! Control yourself and resort to your fortitude. Cast aside this feeble intelligence. Do not be tormented.' Kakutstha was addressed by the great-souled Lakshmana in this way. Filled with great affection, he spoke to Soumitri, who was devoted to his friends. 'O Lakshmana! O best among men! It is indeed as you have said. O brave one! I am satisfied that you have acted in accordance with my command. O amiable one! My torment has been dispelled and I have withdrawn from it. O Lakshmana! You have entreated me in extremely sweet words.'

Chapter 7(52)

Sumantra arrived and addressed Raghava in these words. 'O king! Some ascetics are waiting at the gate, having been stopped there. At the forefront of those maharshis is one who is named Bhargava Chyavana. O great king! They have urged that they wish to see you. O tiger among men! They reside along the banks of the Yamuna and seek your favours.' Hearing his words, Rama, who knew about dharma, replied, 'Let the great-souled brahmanas, with Bhargava at the forefront, enter.' Placing the king's command at the forefront, he[683] joined his hands in salutation above his head and asked the many revered ascetics who were at the gate to enter. There were more than one hundred of them, blazing in their own energies. Those great-souled ascetics entered the royal residence. Those brahmanas held pots filled with water from all the tirthas. They held many kinds of fruits and roots that they had brought for Rama. Rama accepted everything that had been offered with affection—all the water from the tirthas and the many kinds of fruit. The mighty-armed one spoke to all those great sages, 'As you deserve, please sit down on these excellent seats.' Hearing the words spoken by Rama, all those maharshis sat down on those beautiful and golden seats, spread with cushions. The destroyer of enemy

[683] Sumantra.

cities saw that the rishis had seated themselves. Controlling himself and joining his hands in salutation, Raghava addressed them in these words. 'O stores of austerities! Why have you come here? What can I do for you? All the commands of the maharshis will be cheerfully undertaken. Everything in this kingdom and the life that is in my heart is all for the sake of the brahmanas. I am stating this truthfully.' On hearing his words, loud words of praise arose from the rishis who resided along the banks of the Yamuna, fierce in their austerities. Filled with great delight, those great-souled ones said, 'O best among men! Other than you, there is no one on earth who could have said this. O king! We have been to many kings who are extremely strong. Despite hearing about the importance of the task, the idea of taking a pledge to accomplish it did not appeal to them. However, displaying the due respect to brahmanas, you have taken a pledge without ascertaining the reason. There is no doubt that you will do what you have promised to. You will certainly save the rishis from a great fear.'

Chapter 7(53)

When the rishis said this, Kakutstha addressed them in these words. 'Tell me what task must be done for you. I will destroy your fear.' When Kakutstha said this, Bhargava spoke these words. 'O lord of men! Hear the reason for our fear and it is the foundation of the country's fear too. O Rama! Earlier, in krita yuga, there was an extremely strong daitya. He was the eldest son of Lola and the great asura's name was Madhu. He was the refuge of brahmanas and possessed great intelligence. He had unmatched affection for the extremely generous gods. Madhu was full of valour, extremely controlled and devoted to dharma. Revering him a lot, Rudra gave him an extraordinary boon. Extremely delighted, the great-souled one gave the immensely valiant one an extremely radiant trident that was superior to his own trident and addressed him in these words. "You possess unmatched dharma. I am greatly delighted with you. Therefore, as a mark of my favours, I am giving you this excellent and auspicious weapon. O great asura! As long as you do not act against the gods and the brahmanas, till that time, this trident will remain with you. However, if you act in a contrary way, you will no longer possess it and it will be destroyed. As long as you possess it, you can fight without any anxiety. The trident will consume[684] and again return to your hand." Having obtained this boon from Rudra, the great asura again bowed down before Mahadeva and addressed him in these words. "O illustrious one! O god! O lord of the gods! Let this excellent trident also remain in my lineage." When Madhu said this, the god Shiva Mahadeva, the lord of all creatures, replied, "This cannot be. However, because of my auspicious favours, your words cannot be futile either. Therefore, this trident will pass on to one of your sons. As long as the trident is in the hand of that son and as long as he holds the trident in his hand, he cannot be killed by any creature." Thus, Madhu obtained this great and extraordinary boon from the god. The best among the asuras created an extremely radiant residence.[685] His immensely fortunate and beloved wife was Kumbhinasi. The immensely radiant one was the daughter of Visvavasu and Anala. Her son was the terrible and extremely valiant one named Lavana. Since childhood, he was evil in his soul and wicked in his conduct. On seeing that his son was insolent, Madhu became filled with sorrow. However, though he grieved, he did not tell him anything. Having left his world, he entered Varuna's abode. He gave Lavana the trident and told him about the boon. Thanks to the powers of the trident and his own evil-souled nature, he tormented the three worlds, especially the ascetics. These are the powers of Lavana and his trident. O Kakutstha! Having heard about it, determine what is best for us. O Rama! O brave one! Earlier, because of our fear, we have sought freedom from fear from many kings. But we have not been able to find a protector. We heard that you have killed Ravana, with his forces and mounts. We seek a protector in you. There is no other king on earth. We are afflicted by fear on account of Lavana and desire that you should save us.'

[684] The enemy.

[685] For housing the trident.

Chapter 7(54)

Thus addressed by the rishi, Rama joined his hands in salutation and replied. 'What does Lavana eat? What is his conduct? Where does he reside?' Hearing Raghava's words, all the rishis told him how Lavana had grown up. 'He eats all creatures, especially ascetics. His conduct is always terrible. He always resides in Madhuvana. Every day, he always kills and eats ten thousand lions, tigers, deer, leopards and humans. The immensely strong one eats many other creatures. They face destruction, as if they face Death with a gaping mouth.' Hearing this, Raghava addressed the great sages in these words. 'Let your fear be dispelled. I will slay that rakshasa.' He thus took a pledge before the sages, fierce in their austerities. The descendant of the Raghu lineage summoned all his brothers and asked them, 'O brave ones! Who will slay Lavana? Whose share does he belong to? Is he meant for the mighty-armed Bharata or Shatrughna?' When Raghava said this, Bharata replied in these words. 'I will kill him. He should be part of my share.' Hearing Bharata's words, Lakshmana's younger brother,[686] who was full of power and valour, got up from his golden seat. Bowing down before the lord of men, Shatrughna spoke these words. 'The mighty-armed middle one[687] among the descendants of Raghu has performed his appointed task. O noble one! Earlier, the noble one has protected the empty city of Ayodhya, despite his heart being tormented while he waited for your return. O king! He had to tolerate many kinds of hardship. In Nandigrama, the great-souled one slept on a bed of misery. He ate fruits and roots. He had matted hair and was attired in bark. The descendant of the Raghava lineage undertook such kinds of hardships. O king! If you send me, while he remains here, he will not have to face a hardship again.' Thus addressed by Shatrughna, Raghava again said, 'O Kakutstha! Then let it be that way. Act according to my instructions. O mighty-armed one! I am conferring the kingdom of the auspicious city of Madhu on you, since it is your wish that Bharata should reside here. You are brave and accomplished in learning. You are capable

[686] Shatrughna.

[687] The brother in the middle.

of establishing a prosperous city and an auspicious countryside in Madhu's dominion. When a lineage is uprooted and a king is also slain, a person who does not set up a king there goes to hell.[688] Pay heed to my words. Having killed Madhu's son, Lavana, who is wicked in his determination, follow dharma and rule over that kingdom. O brave one! You should not speak any words in reply that contradict mine. Since I am older and since you are a child, there is no doubt that you must act in this way. O Kakutstha! With Vasishtha at the forefront, and with the other brahmanas following the rituals and pronouncing mantras, it is my desire that I should make efforts to consecrate you.'[689]

Chapter 7(55)

When Rama spoke in this way, Shatrughna, who was full of valour, was filled with great shame. In a soft and gentle voice, he replied, 'O bull among men! One must certainly act in accordance with your command. O immensely fortunate one! It is impossible to cross your instructions. O king! O bull among men! I will indeed do what you desire.' When the brave and great-souled Shatrughna said this, Rama was delighted and spoke to Lakshmana and Bharata. 'Control yourselves and bring all the objects required for the consecration. I will consecrate the invincible tiger among men today. O Katkusthas![690] Convey my command and summon the priest, the priests who will offer oblations, the priests who will officiate and all the ministers.' Thus commanded by the king, the maharathas acted in that way. With the priest at the forefront, they made arrangements for the consecration and entered the royal palace, which was like Purandara's residence. After this, the great-souled Shatrughna's consecration was undertaken, delighting everyone who was in Raghava's prosperous city. Having performed the consecration,

[688] To prevent anarchy, a king is needed. Therefore, a person who kills an existing king must ensure that there is a subsequent king.

[689] As the king of Madhu's dominion.

[690] In the dual, addressing Lakshmana and Bharata.

Raghava took Shatrughna up on his lap and addressed him in these sweet words, filling him with energy. 'O destroyer of enemy cities! O amiable one! O descendant of the Raghu lineage! I am giving you this divine and invincible arrow. Kill Lavana with it. O Kakutstha! When he was lying down on the great ocean and could not be seen by the gods and the asuras, the god Svayambhu[691] created this arrow. While he was invisible to all creatures and was filled with rage in a desire to kill the evil-souled Madhu and Kaitabha, the brave one fashioned this excellent arrow. Desiring to create the three worlds, he used this excellent arrow to kill those two in the battle and created the worlds. O Shatrughna! Desiring to kill Ravana earlier, I did not shoot this arrow because there would have been great fear among creatures. The great-souled Tryambaka gave Madhu the excellent weapon of a giant trident for the sake of slaying the enemy. Keeping it in that residence and repeatedly worshipping it, he[692] looks towards all the directions, seeking to obtain food for himself. Whenever anyone wishes to challenge him to a battle, the rakshasa seizes the trident and reduces him to ashes. O tiger among men! When he is outside the city, he is without a weapon.[693] With your weapon, remain at the gate, before he has entered the city. O bull among men! O mighty-armed one! Challenge him to a fight before he has entered the residence. You will thereby slay the rakshasa. If you act in any other way, he cannot be killed. O brave one! If you do what I have said, he will be destroyed. I have told you everything about the calamity that resulted from the trident. The prosperous Shitikantha[694] gave it and it is invincible.'

Chapter 7(56)

Kakutstha said this and repeatedly praised him. The descendant of the Raghu lineage again spoke these words. 'O bull among

[691] Vishnu.

[692] Lavana.

[693] When he is hunting for food outside the city, he doesn't have the trident with him.

[694] The one with the blue throat, Shiva.

men! There are four thousand horses, two thousand chariots and one hundred elephants here. The shops along the roads have many kinds of merchandise.[695] O Shatrughna! Let dancers and actors follow you. O bull among men! Take ten thousand golden coins. O Shatrughna! Go with sufficient quantities of riches and mounts. O brave one! Take excellent, cheerful and healthy forces who are armed properly. O supreme among men! Address them, give them gifts and make them happy. O Raghava! In a place where there are no wives and relatives, large numbers of servants reside only when they are happy. Therefore, depart with a lot of happy people and a large army. However, approach Madhuvana alone, with a bow in your hand. That way, the subjects will not know that you are going there to fight. Without arising suspicion, you will be able to approach Lavana, Madhu's son. O bull among men! There is no one else who can bring about his death. As soon as he sees anyone approach, Lavana kills him. O amiable one! Lavana should be killed when summer is over and it is a night in the rainy season. That is the time for the evil-minded one's death. Let your soldiers advance with the maharshis at the forefront. When there is a little bit of summer left, the waters of the Jahnavee can be crossed. Control yourself and make all the forces camp along the banks of the river. O one who is light in valour! With your bow, advance ahead.' Rama spoke in this way to the immensely strong Shatrughna. He[696] summoned the foremost commanders and addressed them in these words. 'These are the camps earmarked for you to reside in. Dwell there, without any conflicts. But make sure there are no impediments.' Having been commanded in this way, the large army departed. He greeted Kousalya, Sumitra and Kaikeyee. Circumambulating Rama, he bowed his head down before him. Shatrughna, the scorcher of enemies, took Rama's leave. He joined his hands in salutation and bowed down before Lakshmana and Bharata. Controlling himself, Shatrughna circumambulated the priest, Vasishtha. The immensely strong one departed.

[695] Take those with you.
[696] Shatrughna.

Chapter 7(57)

After the entire army had left, it resided for one month along the path. Shatrughna left quickly, alone and speedily. After residing for two nights along the way, the brave descendant of the Raghava lineage reached Valmiki's excellent and sacred hermitage. He greeted the great-souled Valmiki, supreme among sages. He joined his hands in salutation and addressed him in these words. 'O illustrious one! I have come here, wishing to do something for my senior. Tomorrow morning, I will leave for the west, Varuna's direction.' Hearing Shatrughna's words, the bull among sages smiled and replied, 'O great-souled one! O immensely illustrious one! Welcome. O amiable one! My hermitage is for the lineage of the Raghavas. Without any hesitation, accept a seat, padya and arghya from me. Accept the honours and fruits and roots as food. O Kakutstha! Eat and be filled with great satisfaction.' After eating, the mighty-armed one asked the maharshi. 'Near the hermitage, there are signs of a former sacrifice. Whom does this belong to?'

Hearing what he said, Valmiki replied in these words. 'O Shatrughna! Listen to whom this place belonged to in earlier times. Your ancestor was the son of the great-souled King Sudasa. His son was named Mitrasaha. He was valiant and devoted to dharma. Even when he was a child, Soudasa[697] started to hunt. While he was roaming around, the brave one saw two rakshasas. They were in the form of two terrible tigers. Even when they devoured thousands of deer, they were not satisfied. It was not sufficient for them. He saw that those two rakshasas had emptied the forest of all deer. Filled with rage, he used a large arrow to kill one of them. Soudasa, bull among men, brought down one. Without anxiety and with his intolerance over, he looked towards the slain rakshasa. While he was thus looking, the rakshasa's companion was filled with great and terrible torment. He told Soudasa, "You have slain my companion, though he has committed no crime. O wicked one! Therefore, I will give you the reaction to your action." Having said this, the rakshasa vanished from the spot. When time passed,

[697] Sudasa's son, Mitrasaha.

Mitrasaha became the king. The king performed a sacrifice near that hermitage.[698] He performed a great horse sacrifice, tended to by Vasishtha. There was a great sacrifice there and it lasted for an extremely large number of years. It was extensive and greatly prosperous and was like a sacrifice of the gods. When the sacrifice was over, the rakshasa remembered the former enmity. It assumed Vasishtha's form, came before the king and said, "Now that the sacrifice is over, give me some flesh to eat. Quickly give it to me. You should not think about it." He heard the words spoken by the rakshasa who could assume any form at will. The lord of the earth spoke to those who were skilled in preparing food. "Swiftly prepare tasty oblations[699] that are mixed with meat, so that the preceptor is satisfied." Hearing the king's command, the cook was scared in his mind. But the rakshasa assumed the form of a cook and did what had been asked. It offered the flesh of a human to the king and said, "These are tasty oblations with meat, prepared by me." O tiger among men! He,[700] with his wife, Madayanti, offered the meat prepared and brought by the rakshasa and offered it to Vasishtha. The brahmana got to know that food with human flesh had been brought. He was filled with great rage and started to say the following. "O king! Since you wish to serve this kind of food to me, there is no doubt that this will be your food." The king and his wife repeatedly prostrated themselves before him. They told Vasishtha what the one in the form of a brahmana[701] had told them. Learning from the lord of men that the rakshasa had distorted everything, Vasishtha again spoke to the king, lord of men. "I spoke those words when I was overcome by rage. I am incapable of rendering them false. However, I will grant you a boon. The duration of this curse will be for twelve years. O Indra among kings! Because of my favours, you will not remember the past." Thus the king, the destroyer of enemies, was cursed in this way. He got his kingdom back and protected the subjects. O

[698] Where the rakshasa had been killed.

[699] *Havishya.*

[700] Soudasa.

[701] The rakshasa.

Raghava! This is the auspicious and extensive sacrificial ground of Kalmashapada.[702] You asked about it. His hermitage is nearby.'

Having heard the extremely terrible account about that Indra among kings, he[703] honoured the maharshi and entered the cottage made out of leaves.

Chapter 7(58)

On the night when Shatrughna entered the cottage made out of leaves, Sita gave birth to two sons that very night. In the middle of the night, the children who were sons of the sages came and gave Valmiki the agreeable news about Sita's auspicious delivery. 'O immensely energetic one! Protect her and destroy the evil demons.' Hearing their words, the sage was filled with delight. He protected her by performing the rituals that would kill demons and destroy rakshasas. The brahmana took some kusha grass in his fist and cut it.[704] To protect them and destroy demons, Valmiki gave each of the two one half. To the pronouncement of mantras, the one who was born first was named Kusha. He was cleansed with kusha grass. That is the reason he was named Kusha. The one who was born later was carefully cleansed with the cut off bit that was left. The aged one thus gave him the name of Lava. Hence, those two twin sons obtained the names of Lava and Kusha. He[705] said, 'Because of what I have done, they will be famous by these two names. They were protected in this way at the hands of the controlled sage. They were protected and were cleansed of all sin. They[706] performed the rites to protect them and gave them their *gotra*s and their names. They pronounced that these two auspicious ones were the sons of Rama and Sita.' In the middle of the night,

[702] Soudasa's name. He was thus known as Kalmashapada, because his feet (*pada*) had a blemish (*kalmasha*). The story has been recounted earlier.

[703] Shatrughna.

[704] The word *lava* means to cut off.

[705] Valmiki.

[706] The sages.

Shatrughna heard this extremely pleasant news. In the night, he went to the cottage of leaves and said, 'This is good fortune. It is fortunate.' In this way, the great-souled Shatrughna rejoiced. Swift in speed, the monsoon night in the month of Shravana passed. In the morning, the immensely valiant one performed the morning rituals in due order. He joined his hands in salutation and took the sage's permission. He then again left for the western direction. Spending seven nights along the way, he reached the banks of the Yamuna. There, he resided in the hermitage of the rishis who are auspicious in their deeds. Residing with the immensely illustrious sages, with Bhargava at the forefront, the king[707] heard many kinds of accounts.

Chapter 7(59)

When night commenced, Shatrughna asked the brahmana Chyavana, the descendant of the Bhrigu lineage, about Lavana's strengths and weaknesses. 'O brahmana! Using the strength of the trident, whom has he brought down earlier? Who are the ones who came to have a duel with the one who possesses the excellent trident?'

Hearing the words spoken by the great-souled Shatrughna, the immensely energetic Chyavana replied to the descendant of the Raghu lineage. 'O bull among men! It[708] has performed innumerable deeds. There was the conduct of the powerful one from the Ikshvaku lineage.[709] Hear about it. Earlier, in Ayodhya, there was a powerful king who was Yuvanashva's son. The valiant one was famous in the three worlds as Mandhata. That lord of the earth brought the entire earth under his rule. The king then made efforts to conquer the world of the gods. Indra and the great-souled gods suffered from terrible fear, because

[707] Shatrughna.
[708] The trident.
[709] Mandhata.

Mandhata was making efforts, wishing to conquer the world of the gods. The king took a pledge, "I will take away half of Shakra's throne and half of his kingdom. I will bind down large numbers of gods." The chastiser of Paka got to know about his wicked intention. He addressed Yuvanashva's son in these comforting words. "O bull among men! You have still not been able to become the king of the human world. Without bringing the earth under your subjugation, you desire the kingdom of the gods. O brave one! After having brought the entire earth under your subjugation, use your servants, forces and mounts to obtain the kingdom of the gods." Thus addressed by Indra, Mandhata replied in these words. "O Shakra! Where on earth is my rule countered?" The one with the one thousand eyes said, "There is the rakshasa named Lavana. O unblemished one! He is Madhu's son and in Madhuvana, he does not follow your commands." The one with the one thousand eyes spoke these disagreeable and terrible words. Hearing these, the king was unable to say anything in reply. Ashamed, he lowered his face. The lord of men was ashamed. With a lowered face, he did not say anything. Taking his leave of the one with one thousand eyes, he again returned to this prosperous world.

'His heart was filled with intolerance. With his servants, forces and mounts, the unblemished one arrived to bring Madhu's son under his subjugation. The bull among men desired to fight against Lavana. He sent a messenger to Lavana. He went to Madhu's son and spoke many disagreeable words. Consequently, the rakshasa ate up the messenger. When the messenger did not return for a long time, the king was filled with rage. From every direction, he afflicted the rakshasa with a shower of arrows. Lavana laughed and seized the trident in his hand. To slay the king and his followers, he hurled that excellent weapon. Blazing, the trident reduced the king, his servants, his forces and his mounts to ashes and returned to Lavana's hand. Thus, the extremely great king was slain with his forces and mounts. O brave one! The strength of that excellent trident is immeasurable. There is no doubt that you will kill Lavana tomorrow morning, as long as he has not taken up his weapon. If you are swift, your victory is certain.'

Chapter 7(60)

The great-souled Shatrughna desired the auspicious victory. While they were talking and conversing, the night passed quickly. The morning sparkled. Goaded by hunger and searching for food, at that time, the brave rakshasa emerged from his city. Meanwhile, the brave Shatrughna crossed the river Yamuna. With a bow in his hand, he stood at the gate of Madhupura.[710] The rakshasa was cruel in his deeds. When half the day was over, he returned with a large burden of many thousands of creatures he had killed. He saw Shatrughna stationed at the gate, holding a weapon. The rakshasa asked him, 'Why are you acting in this way? O worst among men! In my rage, I have eaten thousands who have wielded weapons like this. Do you wish for your death? O worst of men! Today, I have not collected my complete quota of food. O evil-minded one! How have you managed to enter my mouth on your own?' Having said this, he laughed repeatedly. Shatrughna was full of valour. Filled with anger, tears started to fall from his eyes. The great-souled Shatrughna was filled with anger towards him. Rays of energy began to emerge from all over his body. Extremely enraged, Shatrughna spoke to the roamer in the night. 'O one who is evil in intelligence! I wish to fight against you. There will be a duel with you. I am Dasharatha's son and the intelligent Rama's brother. My name is Shatrughna. I am the slayer of enemies.[711] I have come here wishing to kill you. Therefore, I wish to fight against you. Grant me a duel. You are the enemy of all creatures. You will not escape from me with your life.' Thus addressed, the rakshasa laughed and replied to the best of men, 'O evil-minded one! It is good fortune that you have come here. The rakshasa named Ravana was my brother through my mother's side.[712] O worst among men! On account of a woman, he was slain by the evil-minded Rama. Earlier, I have pardoned and ignored that destruction of Ravana's lineage. However, in particular, you are standing in front of me now. I have

[710] Madhu's city.

[711] Since *shatrughna* means a slayer of enemies, there is a play on words.

[712] Lavanasura's mother was Kumbhini, Madhu's wife. Kumbhini was Ravana's sister.

not only defeated all these creatures. You, and these worst among men, are like grass to me. O evil-minded one! You desire to fight. I will grant you a fight. I will give you what you want. Let me prepare my weapon.' Shatrughna told him, 'Clinging on to your life, where will you go? A person who has cleansed his soul does not let go of an enemy who has arrived, even if he happens to be weak. If a person is weak in intelligence and lets an enemy go, that foolish-minded one is killed, like a coward.'

Chapter 7(61)

He heard what the great-souled Shatrughna had spoken. Filled with fierce anger, he said, 'Wait. Wait.' He wrung one hand with another hand and gnashed his teeth. Lavana challenged the tiger of the Raghu lineage. Shatrughna, the slayer of the enemies of the gods, addressed Lavana, who was terrible in his valour, in these words. 'When you defeated the others, Shatrughna had not yet been born. Today, struck by arrows, you will go to Yama's abode. Just as the gods witnessed Ravana being killed in the battle, the rishis, the brahmanas and the learned ones will see a wicked one like you killed by me today. O roamer in the night! You will fall down today, burnt by my arrows. The city and the countryside will obtain peace. Today, an arrow that is like the vajra will be shot from my hand and will penetrate your heart, like the rays of the sun entering a lotus.' Thus addressed, Lavana became senseless with rage and hurled a giant tree at Shatrughna's chest. The brave one shattered this into one hundred fragments. The rakshasa saw that his attempt had been rendered futile. The powerful one again seized many trees and hurled them towards Shatrughna. As the large number of trees descended, the energetic Shatrughna used three and four arrows with drooping tufts to sever each of these. Shatrughna shot a shower of arrows towards the rakshasa's chest. However, the rakshasa was full of valour and was not distressed. Lavana laughed and playfully uprooted a tree. He struck him on the head with this and with his limbs affected, he lost his senses.

When the brave one fell down, great sounds of lamentation arose among the rishis, the large number of gods, the gandharvas and the apsaras.

Shatrughna had fallen down on the ground. Thinking that he had been killed, the rakshasa ignored him. He found the opportunity to enter his own residence. However, on seeing that he had fallen down on the ground, he did not seize his trident. Taking him to be dead, he raised up that burden of food. Honoured by the rishis, at the gate of the rakshasa's house, he regained his senses in an instant and again seized his weapons. He grasped the divine, invincible and excellent arrow. It was terrible, blazing in energy, and filled the ten directions. It resembled the vajra. It was like the vajra in force. It was like Meru and Mandara in its powers. It was covered everywhere with drooping tufts and was invincible in battle. The revered arrow was smeared all over with sandalwood paste. Its feathers were beautiful. It was extremely terrible to Indras among danavas, Indras among mountains and asuras. It scorched like the fire of destruction that manifests itself at the end of a yuga. On seeing it, all the creatures were filled with terror. The gods, the asuras, the gandharvas, large numbers of apsaras and the entire universe were troubled. They presented themselves before the grandfather. They spoke to the god, the lord of the gods, the one who grants boons, the great grandfather. 'O god! Has the destruction of the worlds arrived? Is this the end of the yuga? O great grandfather! We have not seen anything like this before, or heard of it. O lord! The gods are filled with fear and confusion. It is the destruction of the worlds.' Hearing their words, Brahma, the grandfather of the worlds, told them that there was no reason to fear. There was nothing for the gods to be scared about. 'Shatrughna has picked up this arrow to kill Lavana. O supreme among the gods! All of you have been confounded by its energy. O children! This arrow is full of energy and you are scared because of that. Earlier, this belonged to the eternal god who is the creator of the worlds.[713] The great-souled one created this great arrow to slay the two daityas, Madhu and Kaitabha. Only Vishnu knows

[713] Vishnu.

about this arrow, which is filled with energy. Earlier, it was the embodied form of the great-souled Vishnu himself. Go and behold how Rama's great-souled and brave younger brother uses it to slay Lavana, best among rakshasas.' They heard the pleasant words of the god of the gods. They went to the spot where Shatrughna and Lavana were fighting.

The divine arrow was held in Shatrughna's hand. All the creatures saw it, like the fire that arises at the time of the destruction of a yuga. The descendant of the Raghu lineage saw that the sky was covered with gods. He repeatedly roared like a lion and again glanced towards Lavana. The great-souled Shatrughna challenged him and filled with rage, Lavana presented himself for the encounter. The best among archers stretched his bow all the way back up to his ears and shot that large arrow towards Lavana's broad chest. Swiftly penetrating his chest, it entered rasatala. Having gone to rasatala, the celestial arrow was worshipped by the gods. It then quickly returned to the descendant of the Ikshvaku lineage. Lavana, the roamer in the night, was shattered by Shatrughna's arrow. He suddenly fell down on the ground, like a mountain struck by the vajra. When the rakshasa Lavana was killed, while all the creatures looked on, that divine and giant trident returned again to Rudra. With a single arrow, the brave one of the Raghu lineage brought down and killed the terror of the three worlds. With his bow and arrow raised, he was as dazzling as the one with the one thousand rays, when it dispels darkness.

Chapter 7(62)

When Lavana was killed, the gods, with Indra and Agni at the forefront, spoke these extremely sweet words to Shatrughna, the scorcher of enemies. 'O child! It is good fortune that you have been victorious. It is good fortune that the rakshasa Lavana has been killed. O tiger among men! O Raghava! Ask for a boon. O mighty-armed one! All of us have assembled here to confer a boon on you, desiring that you should be victorious. The sight of us cannot be futile.' Hearing the words spoken by the gods, the brave one raised his hands in salutation above his head. Controlling himself, the mighty-armed Shatrughna replied, 'This Madhupura[714] is beautiful. It is splendid and has been constructed by the gods. It is my desired boon that it should be quickly populated.' Pleased in their minds, the gods agreed to what Raghava had said. 'There is no doubt that this beautiful city will be full of Shurasenas.'[715] Having said this, the great-souled ones went to heaven. The immensely energetic Shatrughna summoned his soldiers. Hearing Shatrughna's command, the soldiers arrived quickly. Instructed by Shatrughna, they started to construct residences. In twelve years, an auspicious city that was like heaven was constructed. Without any fear, the Shurasenas started to reside in this dominion. The fields were full of crops and Vasava rained at the right time. The brave men were without disease and it was protected by Shatrughna's arms. Located on the banks of the Yamuna, it was ornamented and was in the shape of a half moon. It was adorned with the best of houses. It was adorned with quadrangles and shops. Earlier, the place had been rendered empty by Lavana. It was now beautiful, filled with those brave ones and prosperous with many kinds of merchandise. Shatrughna, Bharata's brother, did everything to make it wealthy and prosperous. Greatly delighted, he looked at it and was filled with supreme joy. After having resided in that beautiful and auspicious city for twelve years, his mind turned towards the idea of seeing Rama's feet again.

Chapter 7(63)

After twelve years had passed, followed by a few servants, forces and followers, Shatrughna went to Ayodhya, protected by Rama. He asked the ministers, the foremost commanders and the priest to return. He proceeded on an excellent chariot, yoked

[714] Identified with Mathura.

[715] Literally, *shurasenas* mean brave soldiers.

to radiant steeds. As he proceeded, the descendant of the Raghu lineage resided in seven or eight places. Anxious to see Raghava, he quickly proceeded to Ayodhya. The handsome descendant of the Ikshvaku lineage entered the beautiful city. The mighty-armed one entered the place where the immensely radiant Rama was. He greeted the great-souled one, who seemed to blaze in his energy. Joining his hands in salutation, he spoke to Rama, for whom, truth was his valour. 'O great king! I have done everything, just as you had asked me to do. I have killed the wicked Lavana and I have populated that city. O descendant of the Raghu lineage! Separated from you, twelve years have passed. O king! Separated from you, I am not interested in residing there any more. O Kakutstha! O one who is infinite in valour! Show me your favours. Without you, my residence there is like that of a calf without its mother.' When Shatrughna said this, he embraced him and said, 'O brave one! Do not grieve in this way. A kshatriya should not act in this fashion. O Raghava! Kings do not suffer when they have to live somewhere else. O Raghava! The dharma of kshatriyas is to protect the subjects. O brave one! From time to time, come to Ayodhya to see me. O best among men! Having come here, return to your own city again. There is no doubt that I love you greatly, more than my own life. However, the protection of the kingdom is a task that must certainly be undertaken. O Kakutstha! Therefore, reside here with me for five nights. After that, with your servants, forces and mounts, go to Madhura.'[716] Rama's words were full of dharma and agreeable to the mind. Though Shatrughna was distressed at these words, he uttered words of agreement. As commanded by Raghava, Kakutstha[717] resided there for five nights. After that, the great archer made arrangements to depart. He took his leave from the great-souled Rama, for whom, truth was his valour, and also from Bharata and Lakshmana. He ascended his great chariot. The great-souled Lakshmana and Bharata followed him for some distance. Thereafter, Shatrughna quickly went to the city.

[716] Madhupura or Mathura.
[717] Shatrughna.

Chapter 7(64)

After Shatrughna had left, Raghava happily sported with his brothers. Following dharma, he protected the kingdom. After some days, an aged brahmana from the countryside came to the king's gate, holding the dead body of a male child. He lamented in many kinds of words and the syllables were filled with affection. He said, 'Alas, son! Your rites have not been performed. What wicked deed did I commit in an earlier life? I have had to see you, my only son, face death. You are a child and have not attained youth. You are only five years old. O son! Causing me grief, you have faced death before your appointed time. O son! Grieving over you, there is no doubt that I, and your mother, will also die within a few days. I do not remember having spoken anything false. Nor do I remember having caused injury. What is the evil act I have committed? Today, my son, yet a child, has been conveyed to Vaivasvata's eternal abode, without having performed the rites for his father. In Rama's dominion, this has not been seen, or heard of, earlier. It is terrible to behold. Someone is dying before his appointed time. There is no doubt that Rama has committed some wicked deed. O king! Bring this child, who has come under the subjugation of death, back to life. O king! With your brothers, you will enjoy a long lifespan. O extremely strong one! Till now, we have happily slept in your kingdom. This dominion of the great-souled Ikshvakus is without a protector now. The child has had to go because we have now obtained Rama as a protector and a king. If the subjects are not protected in the proper way, the taint devolves on the king. Because of the evil deeds of a king, people die before their time. Alternatively, people in your city and the countryside are performing inappropriate tasks and you are not protecting them. That is the reason this fear has resulted before its time. It is extremely evident and certain that this has happened because of the king's transgression in the city or in the countryside. That is the reason this child has died.' Tormented by sorrow on account of his son, he repeatedly censured and reprimanded the king with many kinds of words.

Chapter 7(65)

The brahmana lamented in this piteous way, filled with misery and grief. Raghava heard everything. Sorrowing and extremely tormented, he summoned his ministers, Vasishtha, Vamadeva, his brothers and the merchants. With Vasishtha, eight brahmanas entered. They told the king, who was like a king, 'May you prosper.' Markandeya, Moudgalya, Vamadeva, Kashyapa, Katyayana, Jabali, Goutama and Narada—all these bulls among brahmanas sat down on seats. As they deserved, the ministers and the merchants were honoured. All of them sat down, blazing in their energy. After honouring the brahmanas, Raghava told them everything.

Hearing the king's miserable words, in the presence of the rishis and the king, Narada replied in these auspicious words. 'O king! Listen to the reason why this child died before his appointed time. O brave one! O descendant of the Raghu lineage! After listening, do what must be done. O Rama! Earlier, in krita yuga, only brahmanas were ascetics. O king! Someone who was not a brahmana never became an ascetic then. In that yuga, all of them openly blazed with the power of the brahman. All of them were far-sighted and no one died before his time. After that, in treta yuga, men possessed bodies.[718] Kshatriyas, who had performed austerities in their earlier lives, were born.[719] Because of valour and austerities, in treta yuga, these great-souled men were superior to those who had been born in the earlier yuga.[720] All the brahmanas and the kshatriyas were both equal in valour.[721] No particular superiority could be distinguished between the two sets. At that time, the four varnas were established everywhere. Adharma established one foot on the ground.[722] Touched by adharma, brahmanas became wicked. Because of the wicked deeds, the former lifespans became limited. However, there were also people in the world who continued to

[718] In krita yuga, there were those who did not possess bodies.

[719] By implication, there were no kshatriyas in krita yuga.

[720] The kshatriyas were superior to the brahmanas who had been born in krita yuga.

[721] The brahmanas and kshatriyas of treta yuga.

[722] Dharma declines as one goes down the cycle of four yugas. Dharma has four feet in krita yuga, three in treta yuga, two in dvapara yuga and one in kali yuga.

follow and were devoted to the true dharma. In treta yuga, there were brahmanas and kshatriyas who tormented themselves through austerities. All the other people served them. That was the supreme dharma of vaishyas and shudras. In particular, shudras worshipped all the varnas. When dvapara yuga presented itself, a second foot of adharma descended again. At the end of the present yuga, dvapara is approaching. O bull among men! Adharma and falsehood are prospering. When dvapara approached, vaishyas started to engage in austerities. O bull among men! However, shudras did not obtain the right to perform the fierce austerities of dharma. O best among men! Those inferior in varna are tormenting themselves through great austerities. However, those born in shudra wombs will only obtain the right to perform austerities in kali yuga. O Rama! O king! In dvapara, a shudra is performing a great act of adharma. Within the limits of your kingdom, he is performing great austerities. An evil-minded shudra is performing austerities. That is the reason this child has died. O tiger among kings! If an evil-minded man performs an act of adharma within a king's kingdom or city, there is no doubt that the king swiftly goes to hell. O tiger among men! Therefore, carefully search within your own dominion to find out where the evil-acting one is. This is the way dharma and lifespans will increase among men. O best among men! The child will also come back to life.'

Chapter 7(66)

It was as if Narada's words were full of amrita. Hearing them, he obtained infinite delight and addressed Lakshmana in these words. 'O amiable one! O Lakshmana! Go and comfort the best among brahmanas. Place the child's dead body in a pot filled with oil. O amiable one! Use perfumes, extremely expensive oil and fragrances to ensure that the child's body does not decay. Let the body of the child, whose deeds are unblemished, be protected. Act so that his muscles and joints do not suffer.' Kakutstha commanded Lakshmana, the one with the auspicious signs, in this way. In his mind, the immensely illustrious one thought of Pushpaka and asked it to come. Discerning the indication, in an instant, Pushpaka, decorated with gold, arrived near Raghava. It bowed down and said, 'O lord of men! O mighty-armed one! I am under your control. Your servant has arrived.' Hearing the beautiful words spoken by Pushpaka, the lord of men greeted the maharshis and mounted it. He grasped his bow, his quivers and his swords, beautiful in its resplendence. He entrusted the city to the two brave ones, Soumitri and Bharata. He headed in the western direction and searched everywhere in the desert. He went to the beautiful northern direction, covered by the Himalayas. He could not find the slightest bit of misdeed there. The lord of men searched everywhere in the eastern direction. The descendant of a royal sage then went to the southern direction. He saw a great lake on the northern slope of Shaivala.[723] Near that lake, an ascetic was tormenting himself through great austerities. Raghava saw the handsome one, hanging face downwards. He approached the one who was tormenting himself through these excellent austerities. Raghava spoke these words. 'O one who is excellent in vows! You are blessed. O one who is firm in valour! You are pervasive in austerities. Whose womb have you been born in? I am asking you out of curiosity. I am Rama, Dasharatha's son. Why do you wish to do this? Is it to obtain heaven or get a boon? Why are you tormenting yourself through these austerities? O ascetic! I wish to hear. O fortunate one! Are you a brahmana or an invincible kshatriya? Are you a vaishya or a shudra? Tell me the truth.'

Chapter 7(67)

Rama, the performer of unblemished deeds, spoke these words. Hearing them, with his face hanging downwards, he replied in these words. 'I have been born in the womb of a shudra and have resorted to these fierce austerities. O Rama! O immensely

[723] A peak in the Vindhyas.

illustrious one! I wish to go to heaven in my own physical body. O king! I do not utter a falsehood. I wish to conquer the world of the gods. O Kakutstha! Know me to be a shudra. My name is Shambuka.' Hearing the shudra's words, Raghava unsheathed his sparkling sword, extremely beautiful in its radiance, from its scabbard and severed his head. In that instant, the child came back to life. The lotus-eyed Rama went to Agastya's hermitage. Delighted and happy, he bowed down in humility and greeted the great-souled one, who seemed to be blazing in his energy. After having obtained supreme hospitality, the lord of men sat down. The immensely energetic and great sage, Kumbhayoni,[724] spoke to him. 'O best among men! O Raghava! Welcome. It is good fortune that you have come here. O Rama! I respect you a lot. You possess many excellent qualities. O king! You are a guest and should be honoured. You are always in my heart. The gods have said that you have arrived, after killing the shudra. Because you have acted in accordance with dharma, the brahmana's son has come back to life. O Raghava! Spend the night here with me. When it is morning, you can use Pushpaka to return to your own city. O amiable one! This ornament was constructed by Vishvakarma. It is divine and celestial in form. It blazes in its own energy. O Kakutstha! O Raghava! Do something that will bring me pleasure and accept it. Great fruits are obtained if one gives away what has been given to one's own self earlier. O bull among men! Therefore, I am following the rituals and giving it to you. Accept it.' The great-souled Rama accepted it from the sage. The colourful and celestial ornament blazed like the sun. Rama accepted that excellent ornament. He then asked, 'O brahmana! This divine ornament is extremely wonderful. It has an excellent form. Where did it come from? O illustrious one! How did you get it? Who brought it to you? O brahmana! O immensely illustrious one! I am asking you out of curiosity. There are many kinds of supreme and wonderful treasures with you.' When Kakutstha said this, the sage replied in these words. 'O Rama! Hear about what happened in the treta yuga that has just passed.'

[724] Agastya's name.

Chapter 7(68)

'Earlier, in treta yuga, there was an extremely large forest. It extended for one hundred yojanas in every direction. It was devoid of animals and birds. There were no men in the forest. O amiable one! Wishing to perform excellent austerities, I went to that forest. I was incapable of discerning the expanse of that forest. There were roots and many kinds of trees with pleasant fruits to eat. In the midst of the forest, there was a lake that was one yojana wide. It was full of lotuses and waterlilies and covered everywhere with lichen. The excellent water was pleasant and extremely tasty. There was no mud. It was not agitated and it was full of beautiful birds. Near that lake, there was a large and extraordinary hermitage. It was ancient and extremely sacred. However, there were no ascetics there. O bull among men! I resided there for a summer night. When it was morning, I arose and approached the lake. I saw a dead body there. It was well-nourished and without any decay. O king! It was near that store of waters, full of great beauty. O Raghava! O lord! I remained there for a while, thinking. Who was this on the shore of the lake and why? In a short while, I saw a divine and extraordinary sight. An extremely large vimana arrived, yoked to swans and possessing the speed of thought. O descendant of the Raghu lineage! There was an extremely divine being on that vimana. O brave one! A thousand apsaras, adorned in divine ornaments, were worshipping him. There were others who were singing beautiful songs and playing on musical instruments. O Rama! While I looked on, he descended from the vimana. O descendant of the Raghu lineage! The divine being started to eat the dead body. As he wished, he devoured many bits of that flesh and was satiated. After this, the divine being descended into the lake. O bull among men! As is proper, the divine being touched the water.[725] He then started to mount that supreme and excellent vimana. I saw the one, who resembled a god, ascend. O bull among men! I addressed him in these words. "You resemble a god. Who are you? Why did you eat this condemned food? O amiable one!

[725] He washed his hands and mouth.

Why did you eat it? You should tell me the reason. You are radiant and are like a revered god. Such inclinations are extraordinary. O amiable one! This food is condemned. I wish to hear the truth about this."'

Chapter 7(69)

'O Rama! He heard the words I had spoken, uttered with auspicious syllables. O descendant of the Raghu lineage! The divine being joined his hands in salutation and replied. "O brahmana! Listen to my account, as it occurred. It is full of both joy and misery. O brahmana! You have asked me about it. This is impossible for me to cross. In earlier times, my immensely illustrious father was the king of Vidarbha. He was valiant and was famous in the three worlds as Sudeva. O brahmana! He had two sons, born from two different wives. I was known as Shveta and my younger brother was Suratha. When my father went to heaven, the citizens consecrated me. Controlling myself, I followed dharma and ruled over the kingdom. O one good in vows! In this way, one thousand years passed. O brahmana! I ruled over the kingdom and following dharma, protected the subjects. O supreme among brahmanas! Through some means, I got to know about my lifespan. Taking the dharma of time to heart, I went to the forest. That forest was impenetrable and was devoid of animals and birds. I entered it near this auspicious lake and started to perform austerities. I instated my brother, Suratha, as the king over the kingdom. Having approached this lake, I performed austerities for a long time. O great sage! I performed austerities for three thousand years. After having performed these extremely difficult austerities, I obtained Brahma's excellent world. O supreme among brahmanas! While I was in heaven, I was overcome by hunger and thirst. O extremely generous one! They obstructed me and my senses were afflicted. I went to the grandfather, the best in the three worlds, and spoke to him. 'O illustrious one! In Brahma's worlds, there should not be any hunger or thirst. Since I have come under the subjugation of hunger and thirst, what deed have I committed? O god! O grandfather! Tell me. What should be my food?' The grandfather told me, 'O Sudeva's son! Your food is your own succulent flesh. You will always eat that. While you were performing those excellent austerities, you nourished your own body. O Shveta! O immensely intelligent one! Without sowing, nothing is reaped. You did not give the slightest bit to creatures who resided in the forest. O child! Therefore, despite being in heaven, you are suffering from hunger and thirst. You nourished your own excellent body through food. You will devour it, as if it is the juice of amrita. That is what will satiate you. O Shveta! When the extremely great and invincible rishi, Agastya, arrives in that forest, you will be freed from this hardship. O amiable one! O mighty-armed one! He is capable of saving large numbers of gods, not to speak of someone like you who has succumbed to hunger and thirst.' I heard the decision of the illustrious one, the god of the gods. O supreme among brahmanas! I thus eat this condemned food, my own body. O brahmana! I have been eating it and many years have passed. O brahmana rishi! It does not decay and I obtain excellent satisfaction. This is how my hardship came about. You should free me from this hardship. Who can save me, other than the brahmana Kumbhayoni? O supreme among brahmanas! O brahmana rishi! You should show me your favours. In return for saving me, accept this ornament." I heard the words of the divine being, full of grief. In return for saving him, I accepted that excellent ornament. I accepted that auspicious ornament. Immediately, the former human body of the royal sage was destroyed. When the body was destroyed, the royal sage was greatly delighted. Content and delighted, the king went to heaven again. O Kakutstha! He was like Shakra. Because of what I did, he gave me this extraordinary and divine ornament.'

Chapter 7(70)

Raghava heard Agastya's extraordinary words. Showing him respect and astounded, he again started to ask. 'O illustrious one! This forest, where Shveta, the king of Vidarbha, tormented himself through austerities, is terrible. There are no animals and birds. Why is that the case? There are no creatures in the forest that he entered to undertake austerities in. It is desolate and there are no humans here. How did this happen? I wish to hear the truth about this.'

Rama's words were full of curiosity. The immensely energetic one heard these words and started to speak. 'O Rama! In earlier times, in krita yuga, the lord Manu held the rod of chastisement. He had a great son, Ikshvaku, who was the extender of the lineage. He instated this eldest son, invincible on earth, in the kingdom and said, "Be the originator of royal lineages on earth." O Raghava! The son promised his father that he would do this. Extremely delighted, Manu again said, "O extremely generous one! I am greatly pleased with you. There is no doubt that you will be the originator. Protect the subjects using the rod. However, do not use the rod of chastisement without valid reason. If the rod is brought down on men when they commit crimes, that punishment is sanctioned and conveys the king to heaven. O mighty-armed one! O son! Therefore, be careful in using the rod. A person who acts in this way obtains supreme dharma in this world." Manu instructed his attentive son about many other things. Happy, he then proceeded to heaven, to Brahma's supreme world. When he went to heaven, the infinitely radiant Ikshvaku was filled with a serious thought. "How will I have sons?" Manu's son performed many kinds of rituals. The one with dharma in his soul then had one hundred sons who were like the sons of the gods. O son![726] O descendant of the Raghu lineage! The youngest among them was foolish and unaccomplished in learning. He did not serve his seniors. His father gave this one, who was limited in energy, the name of Danda. He knew the rod of chastisement would descend on his body.[727] O Raghava! He saw a terrible taint in his son. O scorcher of enemies! He gave him the kingdom that was between the mountains Vindhya and Shaivala. Danda became the king of the beautiful region between the slopes

[726] The word used is tata.

[727] The word danda means both rod and punishment.

of the two mountains. O Rama! He constructed an unmatched and excellent city there. O lord! He named this city Madhumanta. As his priest, he brought Ushanas, who was excellent in his vows. In this way, the king made him the priest of the kingdom, which was full of delighted people. It was like a kingdom of the gods in heaven.'

Chapter 7(71)

The maharshi who was born from the pot told Rama this. He then started to speak subsequent words to him. 'O Kakutstha! In this way, Danda, evil in his soul, ruled over that kingdom, which was bereft of thorns, for an innumerable number of years. On one occasion, in the beautiful month of Chaitra,[728] he went to Bhargava's[729] beautiful hermitage. Bhargava's daughter was unmatched on earth in her beauty. Danda saw the excellent one roaming around in the region of the forest. On seeing her, the one who was extremely evil in his intelligence, was afflicted by the arrows of Ananga.[730] Extremely eager, he approached the maiden and addressed her in these words. "O one with the beautiful hips! Where have you come from? O beautiful one! Whose daughter are you? O one with the excellent waist! I am asking you because I am suffering on account of Ananga." He was confused and crazy with desire. When he said this, Bhargava's daughter beseeched the king and replied in these words. "Know me to be the eldest daughter of Bhargava, the lord who is unblemished in his deeds. O Indra among kings! My name is Araja and I live in this hermitage. O Indra among kings! My father is your preceptor. You are the great-souled one's disciple. If the great ascetic is extremely angry, he will impose a hardship on you. O best among king! If this is your intention, you should follow the virtuous path indicated by dharma, and seek my hand from my immensely radiant father. Otherwise, you will have to reap terrible fruits. If my father

[728] March–April.

[729] Shukracharya.

[730] The god of love.

is angry, he can burn down the three worlds." Danda was suffering from the arrows of desire and was addressed by Araja in this way. Crazy with desire, he joined his hands in salutation above his head and replied, "O one with the beautiful hips! Show me your favours. You should not waste time in this way. O one with the beautiful face! Because of you, my life is being shattered. To get you, I am ready to be killed and ready to perform an extremely terrible and vile act. O timid one! I am devoted to you. Serve me. I am completely distracted by my attachment towards you." Having said this, the strongest of the strong seized the maiden with both of his hands. Though she writhed, he started to have intercourse with her, as he desired. Danda perpetrated this extremely horrible and extremely terrible and injurious act. He then quickly left for his excellent city of Madhumanta. Not far from the hermitage, Araja started to weep. Greatly terrified, she waited for her father, who was like a god.'

Chapter 7(72)

'In a short while, the divine sage, infinite in his radiance, returned to his own hermitage. He was surrounded by his disciples and was suffering from hunger. He saw the miserable Araja, smeared all over with dust. She was like the moonlight in the morning, no longer radiant because the sun was in front. Especially because he was suffering from hunger, he was filled with rage. About to burn down the three worlds, he spoke to his disciples. "Behold these perverse signs. I know that this has been done by Danda. Like the angry flames of a fire, I will bring down a terrible hardship on him. With his followers, the evil-minded and evil-souled one will head towards destruction. He is like a person who desires to touch the blazing flames of a fire. He has performed such an evil act, terrible to behold. Therefore, the evil-minded one will reap the fruits of his wicked deed. The evil-minded one has perpetrated a vile act. Within seven nights, with his servants, forces and mounts, the king will be killed. In every direction, an expanse of one hundred yojanas around the evil-minded one's dominion will be destroyed. The chastiser of Paka will bring down a great shower of dust. Everywhere, all creatures and all mobile and immobile objects will be destroyed by this great shower of dust. Within seven nights, everyone who resides within Danda's kingdom will be reduced to dust and will vanish." Blazing in his anger, he said this to the residents of the hermitage and asked the people to go to regions that were beyond the frontiers of this country. Hearing the words spoken by Ushanas, all the people who resided in the hermitage left that kingdom and started to reside in regions that were outside its limits. Having told the people this, the sage spoke to Araja. "O evil-minded one! Control yourself and dwell here, in this hermitage. There is an extremely beautiful and dazzling lake that extends for one yojana. O Araja! Do not suffer from anxiety. Enjoy it and wait for your time. During those nights, all creatures who reside near you will never be killed by that shower of dust." Having said this, Bhargava went to live somewhere else. As the one who knew about the brahman had said, within a week, everything was reduced to ashes. The area between the slopes of Vindhya and Shaivala are Danda's kingdom. Because of the act of adharma that had been done, it had been cursed by the brahmana rishi in earlier times. O Kakutstha! Since that time, it has been known as Dandakaranya.[731] Because the ascetics reside here, it is also known as Janasthana.[732] O Raghava! I have thus told you everything that you had asked me about. O brave one! The time for performing the sandhya rituals is passing. O tiger among men! In every direction, all the maharshis are holding full pots of water, to perform the water rites and worship the sun. O Rama! The sun has set. Go with the excellent brahmana rishis and perform the water rites.'

Chapter 7(73)

Following the rishi's words, Rama worshipped the sandhya, near the sacred waters of the lake, populated by apsaras. Rama

[731] Danda's/Dandaka's forest (*aranya*).

[732] Literally, place where people reside.

touched the water and worshipped the western sandhya. He then entered the hermitage of the great-souled Kumbhayoni. For food, Agastya arranged roots and fruits with many kinds of qualities, herbs and sacred green leaves. The best among men ate the food that was like amrita. Happy and content, he spent the night there. In the morning, the scorcher of enemies arose and performed the ablutions. The supreme of the Raghu lineage went to the rishi to seek permission to leave. Rama greeted the maharshi who had been born from the pot. He said, 'I seek your permission to depart. Please grant me leave. O great-souled one! I am blessed and favoured at having seen you. To purify myself, I will come here to see you again.' Kakutstha spoke these words to the one who was extraordinary to behold. With his eye towards dharma, the store of austerities was greatly delighted. He said, 'O Rama! These words of yours are extremely wonderful and are full of auspicious syllables. O descendant of the Raghu lineage! You are the one who will purify all the worlds. O Rama! Even if someone sees you for an instant, that person is purified and goes to heaven. He is worshipped in heaven by the gods. Creatures on earth who glance at you with terrible eyes are immediately slain by Yama's staff and go to hell. Without any anxiety, proceed along the path you desire, without any fear. Follow dharma and rule over the kingdom. You are the refuge of the universe.' When the sage said this, the king joined his hands in salutation. He honoured the wise and sacred sage. He greeted the best among sages and all the other stores of austerities. Without any anxiety, he mounted Pushpaka, which was decorated with gold. As he left, in every direction, large numbers of sages pronounced benedictions. With a complexion like that of the great Indra, it was as if the immortals were worshipping the one with the thousand eyes. When Rama was firmly seated in Pushpaka, decorated with gold, he was like the moon amidst clouds, at the onset of the rainy season.

After half a day, Kakutstha reached Ayodhya and was worshipped in every direction. He descended from the vimana. He allowed the beautiful Pushpaka, which could go wherever it wished, to leave. Rama went to the inner chambers and addressed the gatekeeper in these words. 'Go to Lakshmana and Bharata, who are light in their valour. Without any delay, go and tell them that I have arrived.'

Chapter 7(74)

The gatekeeper heard the words spoken by Rama, the performer of unblemished deeds. He told them what Raghava had said and brought the princes there. Raghava saw that his beloved Bharata and Lakshmana had come. Rama embraced them and addressed them in these words. 'I have performed the brahmana's excellent task exactly. O Raghavas! I again want to build a bridge for dharma.[733] With the two of you, I wish to perform an excellent rajasuya sacrifice. Eternal dharma is vested in this. Mitra, the slayer of enemies, performed a rajasuya sacrifice. Having performed that excellent sacrifice and having offered excellent oblations, he obtained the status of being Varuna. Soma, who knows about dharma, followed dharma and performed a rajasuya sacrifice. He obtained fame in all the worlds and an eternal position. Today, with me, the two of you should think about what is best and beneficial. Control yourselves and tell me about our welfare.' Raghava was accomplished in the use of words. Hearing his words, Bharata joined his hands in salutation and spoke the following words. 'O virtuous one! Supreme dharma is vested in you. O mighty-armed one! The entire earth is vested in you. O infinitely valiant one! So is fame. O great-souled one! All the kings look towards you, as the immortals do towards Prajapati. You are the protector of the world. O king! O immensely strong one! The subjects look towards you, as they do towards a father. O Raghava! You are the refuge of the earth and that of all living beings. O king! Why do you want to undertake this kind of a sacrifice? It can be seen that all the royal lineages on earth will be destroyed because of this. O king! When you are filled with rage, all the men on earth who are filled with manliness will

[733] That is, he wants to perform a sacrifice.

be destroyed because of this.[734] O tiger among men! O one who is infinite in qualities and valour! You should not destroy the earth. It is already under your subjugation.' Rama, for whom truth was his valour, heard Bharata's words, which were like amrita, and was filled with great delight. He spoke these auspicious words to the one who extended Kaikeyee's delight. 'Because of the words you have spoken today, I am delighted. I am content. These words are not the result of impotence. They are full of dharma. O tiger among men! You have spoken about how the earth can be protected. O one who knows about dharma! Because of what you have said, I am giving up my desire to undertake a rajasuya sacrifice. The dharma of a respected king is to undertake sacrifices whereby the subjects are protected. Therefore, I am listening to your words. You have controlled yourself and spoken words that are full of virtue.'

Chapter 7(75)

When Rama said this to the great-souled Bharata, Lakshmana also addressed the descendant of the Raghu lineage in these auspicious words. 'The great sacrifice of ashvamedha purifies from all sins. O invincible one! If you wish to purify yourself, you should undertake this, the best among sacrifices. The ancient account of the extremely great-souled Vasava has been heard. When he committed the act of killing a brahmana,[735] Shakra purified himself through a horse sacrifice. O mighty-armed one! In ancient times, there was a clash between the gods and the asuras. There was a great daitya named Vritra and he was revered by the worlds. He was one hundred yojanas wide and three yojanas tall. Filled with attachment towards the three worlds, he always looked towards them with affection. He knew about dharma. He was grateful and he possessed great intelligence. Extremely controlled, he followed dharma and ruled over the entire earth. When he ruled, the earth

[734] If they do not accept Rama's overlordship, they will have to fight and will be killed.

[735] Vritra was the son of a brahmana.

could be milked for all the objects of desire. It yielded succulent roots and fruits. Without being tilled, the earth yielded extremely large quantities of crops. When the great-souled one ruled, the kingdom could be enjoyed in this fashion. It was prosperous and was extraordinary to behold. The thought arose in his mind, "I will perform supreme austerities. Austerities represent the supreme benefit. Austerities represent supreme happiness." He instated his eldest son, Parameshvara, in the city. He resorted to fierce austerities and tormented all the gods. When Vritra tormented himself through these austerities, Vasava was greatly afflicted. He went to Vishnu and addressed him in these words. "O mighty-armed one! Through his austerities, Vritra has conquered all the worlds. The one with dharma in his soul is powerful and I am incapable of countering him. O lord of the gods! As long as he undertakes these austerities, he will hold sway over these worlds and they will remain under his subjugation. O immensely strong one! You are ignoring this extremely pervasive one. O lord of the gods! If you are angry with him, Vritra will be destroyed in an instant. O Vishnu! When he approaches you, as long as you look towards him with affection, till then, he will remain the protector of the worlds. It is because of the favours you have done that he obtains this extremely great fame in the worlds. It is because of what you have done that everything in the universe is peaceful and without decay. O Vishnu! All these residents of heaven are looking towards you. You should render great assistance in slaying Vritra. You have always aided these great-souled ones. No one else can withstand him. You are the refuge of all those who do not have a refuge."'

Chapter 7(76)

The slayer of enemies heard Lakshmana's words and said, 'O Lakshmana! Complete the account about Vritra being killed.' Hearing what Raghava had said, Lakshmana, the extender of Sumitra's delight, again started to speak about the divine account. 'Vishnu heard the words of the one with one thousand eyes and those of all the residents of heaven. He spoke to all the gods, with Indra at the forefront. "I am already bound in affection towards the extremely great-souled Vritra. Therefore, to bring you pleasure, I cannot slay the great asura. However, I must certainly do what will bring you great happiness. Hence, I will tell you about the means whereby you can kill Vritra. O supreme among gods! I will divide myself into three parts. O one with one thousand eyes! There is no doubt that Vritra can be killed through this means. One part will enter Vasava, the second part will be in the vajra, while the third part will be in the earth. O Shakra! Thereby, Vritra will be killed." Addressed by the lord of the gods in this way, the gods replied in these words. "O slayer of daityas! There is no doubt that what you have said will transpire. May you be fortunate. Desiring to slay the asura Vritra, we will depart now. O extremely pervasive one! Pervade Vasava with your own energy." Thereafter, with the one with one thousand eyes at the forefront, all those great-souled ones went to the forest where Vritra, the great asura, was. They saw the supreme asura tormenting himself. Full of energy, he seemed to drink up the three worlds and burn up the sky. On seeing the best among asuras, all the gods were terrified. "How can we kill him? How can we not be defeated?" While they were thinking in this way, Purandara, the one with one thousand eyes, seized the vajra in his hands and brought it down on Vritra's head. It was as terrible as the fire of destruction, blazing in its great rays. It scorched Vritra's head and the universe was terrified. The lord of the gods[736] thought that this killing of Vritra should not have been done. The immensely illustrious one went to the end of the worlds. However, wherever Indra went, the sin of killing a brahmana followed him. It entered his body and Indra was filled with misery. With the enemy dead and Indra also destroyed, the gods, with Agni at the forefront, went to Vishnu, the best in the three worlds, and repeatedly worshipped him. "O god! You are the supreme refuge. You are the lord who predated the creation of the universe. You have assumed the form of Vishnu for the sake of protecting all creatures. You have ensured that Vritra was killed. However, Vasava has been contained because

[736] Indra.

of the sin of killing a brahmana. O tiger among the gods! Instruct a way for him to be freed." Hearing their words, Vishnu spoke to the gods. "If Shakra, the wielder of the vajra, performs a sacrifice to me, he will be purified. Let the chastiser of Paka perform the sacred horse sacrifice for me. He will be freed from fear and will again become Indra of the gods." The gods were commanded by his words, which were like amrita. Praised by the gods, Vishnu, the lord of the gods, departed.'

Chapter 7(77)

Lakshmana recounted everything about Vritra being killed. The best among men then started to speak about whatever was left of the account. 'The immensely valiant Vritra, who caused fear to the gods, was thus killed. However, because he had killed Vritra and was surrounded by the sin of killing a brahmana, Shakra did not regain his senses for some time. Having lost his senses and unconscious, he sought refuge in the end of the worlds. Writhing like a serpent, he resided there for some time. When the one with one thousand eyes was destroyed, the universe became anxious. The earth was destroyed. The forests were dry and without any juices. There were no flows in the stores of waters, lakes and rivers. Because there were no rains, all living beings were agitated. When the worlds were being destroyed, the gods were scared in their minds. As they had been told by Vishnu earlier, they started to perform the sacrifice. All the large numbers of gods, with the preceptors and the rishis, collectively went to the spot where Indra was, confounded by his fear. They saw the one with the one thousand eyes, confounded by the sin of having killed a brahmana. With the lord of the gods[737] at the forefront, they commenced the horse sacrifice. O lord of men! For the sake of purifying himself from the sin of killing a brahmana, the great-souled and extremely great Indra undertook the prosperous horse sacrifice. When the sacrifice was over, the

[737] Indra.

sin of killing a brahmana emerged from the great-souled one's body and asked, "What place has been ordained for me?" The gods were satisfied. Filled with joy, they told it, "O invincible one! Divide yourself into four parts." Hearing the words spoken by the great-souled gods, in their presence, the sin of killing a brahmana, which was finding it difficult to find a place to reside in, said the following. "These are the places I have chosen. One of my parts will dwell in rivers, when they are full of water. The second part will reside in trees. I am stating this to you truthfully. Young women are full of pride. To destroy their pride, my third part will reside in them for three nights.[738] O bulls among gods! My fourth part will resort to those who kill brahmanas, without first considering whether they have been injured by them." Thus addressed, all the gods replied, "O one who is finding it difficult to find a place to dwell in! Everything shall be exactly as you have stated it. May you accomplish what you desire." Delighted, the gods worshipped the one with one thousand eyes. Vasava was cured of his fever and cleansed of his sin. The entire universe was pacified and found a refuge in the one with one thousand eyes. Shakra worshipped that extraordinary sacrifice. O descendant of the Raghu lineage! Such are the powers of the horse sacrifice. O extremely fortunate one! O king! Perform a horse sacrifice.'

Chapter 7(78)

Lakshmana, eloquent in the use of words, spoke these words. Hearing them, the immensely energetic Raghava smiled and replied in these words. "O best among men! O Lakshmana! It is indeed as you have said, the complete story of Vritra's death and the fruits of a horse sacrifice. O amiable one! I have heard that in ancient times, Kardama Prajapati's son was named Ila. He was handsome and was extremely devoted to dharma. He was the lord of Bahlika. The immensely illustrious king brought the entire

[738] During the menstrual cycle.

earth under his subjugation. O tiger among men! He protected the kingdom as if it was his own son. O amiable one! O descendant of the Raghu lineage! The gods, the extremely large daityas, the giant asuras, the serpents, the rakshasas, the gandharvas and the extremely great-souled yakshas always worshipped him. They were scared of him. The three worlds were scared of the great-souled one's rage. The king was like that, established in dharma and valour. His intelligence was extremely pervasive and the immensely illustrious one ruled over Bahlika. The mighty-armed one went on a hunt to a beautiful forest, with his servants, forces and mounts. It was the pleasant month of Chaitra. In the forest, the king killed hundreds of thousands of animals. Despite having killed them, the great-souled king was not satisfied. The great-souled one killed tens of thousands of many kinds of animals. He then reached the spot where Mahasena[739] was born. At that time, the invincible Hara, the lord of the gods, was sporting there with the daughter of the king of the mountains and with his own companions. To please the goddess, in a waterfall in the mountain there, Uma's lord, the one with the bull on his banner, had transformed himself into a woman. In that part of the forest, all the creatures which were male in nature had also got transformed into female forms. At this time, King Ila, Kardama's son, reached the place, having killed thousands of animals. O descendant of the Raghu lineage! He saw that the predatory creatures, the birds and the animals, and he and his companions, had all become feminine. On seeing what had happened to himself, he was filled with great sorrow. Knowing that this had happened because of Umapati,[740] he was terrified. With his servants, forces and mounts, the king sought refuge with the great-souled god, Shitikantha Kapardi.[741] With the goddess, the immensely illustrious granter of boons laughed. The granter of boons himself addressed Prajapati's son in these words. "Arise! O royal sage! O Kardama's son! O immensely strong one! Arise! O amiable one! O one who is good in vows! Ask for

[739] Kartikeya.

[740] Uma's lord, Uma's husband, Shiva.

[741] Shitikantha and Kapardi are Shiva's names, Kapardi meaning the one with matted hair.

any boon other than that of becoming a man." Having been thus refused by the great-souled one, the king was afflicted by sorrow. In the form of a woman, he did not ask for any other boon from that excellent god. Filled with great sorrow, the king prostrated himself before the daughter of the king of the mountains. "O great goddess! O one who is in everyone's heart! O granter of boons! O beautiful one! You are the one who grants boons to the worlds and even to Isha.[742] O goddess! O amiable one! O one who should be worshipped! Your sight cannot be futile. I am bowing down before you." She was near Hara and got to know what was in the mind of the royal sage. Honouring Rudra, the goddess replied in these auspicious words. "The god, the granter of boons, will grant you half of your boon and I will grant you the other half. As you wished, between a man and a woman, therefore accept half." He heard the excellent and extraordinary boon granted by the goddess. Delighted, the king replied in these words. "O goddess! If you are pleased with me, let me be a woman for one month, sought after because she is unmatched in beauty on earth. For the next month, I can become a man." The goddess with the extremely beautiful face got to know his desire. She replied in auspicious words. "It will be that way. O king! When you are in the form of a man, you will not remember what happened as a woman. In the next month, when you are a woman, you will not remember what happened as a man." In this way, the king who was Kardama's son remained a man for one month. In the next month, he became the woman Ila,[743] most beautiful in the three worlds.'

Chapter 7(79)

Rama recounted this account about Ila. Hearing this, Lakshmana and Bharata were greatly surprised. Wishing to know about the great-souled king in detail, they joined their hands in salutation

[742] Shiva.

[743] Ila as man and Ilaa as woman.

and asked again. 'How did the king bear the hardship of being a woman? When he was a man, how did he conduct himself?'

Their words were full of curiosity. Hearing them, Kakutstha started to recount what happened to the king. 'In the first month, she was a woman, most beautiful in the worlds. She surrounded herself with her former followers, who also became women. Most beautiful in the worlds, she quickly entered that forest, full of trees, shrubs and creepers. With eyes like a lotus, she wandered around on foot. She abandoned all the mounts that had surrounded her from all sides. Ila roamed around in the caverns in the mountains. Not very far from the mountain, in that part of the forest, there was the best of lakes, extremely beautiful. It was full of many kinds of birds. Ila saw Soma's son, Budha, there. His form was radiant, like the full moon when it rises. Difficult to approach, he was tormenting himself through fierce austerities in the midst of the water. He was famous, desirable and young. O descendant of the Raghu lineage![744] With her companions, who were formerly male but were now female, she was surprised to see him. All of them started to agitate the waters of the lake. On seeing her, Budha was also afflicted by the arrows of Kama. He was disturbed and started to advance through the water. He saw Ila, most beautiful in the three worlds. He started to think, "Who is this? She is superior to a goddess. Earlier, I have not seen such wonderful beauty in a goddess, a naga or asura lady, or an apsara. If she has not been married already, she is just right for me." Arriving at this conclusion, he arose from the waters on to the land. Having reached his hermitage, he summoned four of those women. They arrived and worshipped the one with dharma in his soul. The one with dharma in his soul asked them, "Who is she? She is the most beautiful in the worlds. Why has she come here? Without any delay, tell me the truth." His words were auspicious. They were sweet, with sweet syllables. Hearing them, all those women replied in sweet words. "The one with the beautiful hips has always been our mistress. She doesn't have a husband. With us, she roams

[744] In the singular, though it should be dual, since both Bharata and Lakshmana are being spoken to.

around in the forest and the extremities of the forest." Hearing the words spoken by those women, the brahmana recalled the sacred learning known as *avartani*.[745] He got to know everything about what had happened to the king. The bull among sages spoke to all those women. "O fortunate ones! Become kimpurushas[746] and reside on the slopes of this mountain. Construct residences wherever you can find a spot on this mountain. All kinds of roots, leaves and fruits can always be found here. As women, you will also find husbands who will be known as kimpurushas." They heard the words of Soma's son, to the effect that they had become kimpurushas. They constructed many kinds of residences on that mountain and started to reside there.'

Chapter 7(80)

Hearing about the origin of kimpurushas, Lakshmana and Bharata told Rama, the lord of men, that this was extraordinary. The immensely illustrious Rama continued to speak about the great-souled son of Prajapati. 'The supreme among rishis saw that all those kinnara ladies had left. He seemed to smile and spoke to that extremely beautiful lady. "O one with an extremely beautiful face! I am Soma's son and he loves me dearly. O beautiful one! Serve me. Glance towards me with gentle and affectionate eyes." Alone and without her friends, she heard his words. Ila, best among beautiful ones, replied to the great planet. "O amiable one! I am also driven by desire and am under your control. O Soma's son! Command me. Do whatever you want with me." Hearing her extremely wonderful words, he was filled with delight. Driven by desire, the son of the moon found his pleasure with her. While Budha found his pleasure with Ila, the one with the beautiful face, the month of Madhava[747] passed. However, he was so driven by

[745] The brahmana means Budha. Avartani means a crucible, a place where things are whirled around. Specifically, it is a kind of learning that facilitates memory retention.

[746] Also known as kinnaras, semi-divine species described as Kubera's companions.

[747] The month of Magha.

desire that it seemed to be only an instant. When the month was over, Prajapati's handsome son,[748] with a face like that of the full moon, arose from his bed. He saw Soma's son there, tormenting himself in the lake. His arms were raised up and he was without any support. The king spoke to him. "O illustrious one! With my followers, I entered this impenetrable mountain. I cannot see those soldiers. Where have my companions gone?" Having been deprived of his senses,[749] the royal sage said this. Hearing this, he[750] replied in auspicious and greatly comforting words. "Because of a great shower of hailstones, your servants have been brought down. You were scared because of the storm and the shower and slept in the hermitage. O fortunate one! Be reassured and do not fear, or have any anxiety. O brave one! Eat roots and fruits and dwell wherever you wish." The immensely illustrious king was comforted by these words, though he was distressed that his servants and companions had been destroyed. He replied in these auspicious words. "With my servants gone, I will abandon my own kingdom. O brahmana! I seek your permission to reside here for some time. O brahmana! My eldest son is immensely illustrious and is devoted to dharma. He is known by the name of Shashabindu. He will receive my kingdom. With my servants and wives gone, I am sad and cannot remain here either. O immensely energetic one! Your words are not agreeable either."[751] When the Indra among kings spoke these supremely extraordinary words, Budha first comforted him and then said, "If it pleases you, dwell here.[752] O Kardama's immensely strong son! You should not be tormented. If you reside here for a year, I will do what will be beneficial for you." Budha was unblemished in his deeds and knew about the brahman. Hearing what he had said, he made up his mind to reside there. During the months when she was a woman, the auspicious one incessantly found pleasure with him. During the months when he was a man, he turned his mind towards dharma. In the ninth month, Ila, the one with the beautiful hips,

[748] Ila, in the form of a man.
[749] Having lost his memory.
[750] Budha.
[751] Of residing there.
[752] For some time.

delivered Soma's son's son. This was Pururava, who was like his father in energy. As soon as he was born, the one with the beautiful hips handed him over to his father. Ila's son was extremely strong and was like Budha in complexion. The king had assumed the form of a man and Budha comforted him. The one with the cleansed soul delighted him by telling him accounts that were full of dharma.'

Chapter 7(81)

Rama told them about this extraordinary birth. The immensely illustrious Lakshmana and Bharata spoke to him again. 'O best among men! Beloved by Soma's son, she resided there for one year. You should tell us the truth about what she did next.' Hearing the sweet words in which he had been asked, Rama started to again recite the account of Prajapati's son. 'After one year, when the brave one had again become a man, the extremely intelligent and extremely pervasive Budha summoned the extremely illustrious Samvarta, Bhrigu's son, Chyavana, the sage Arishtanemi, Pramodana, Modakara and the sage Durvasa. He was accomplished in the use of words and knew about the truth. He summoned all these well-wishers. He controlled himself and patiently told them, "This mighty-armed king is Ila, the son of Kardama. All of you know what happened to him. Therefore, decide what is best for him." While they were conversing in this way, the extremely energetic Kardama came to the hermitage, with many great-souled brahmanas—Pulastya, Kratu, Vashatkara and the immensely energetic Omkara.[753] Those immensely energetic ones came to the hermitage. Since all of them had come, they were delighted in their minds. Desiring the welfare of the lord of Bahlika, they started to say different things. For the sake of the supreme welfare of his son, Kardama spoke these words. "O brahmanas! Listen to my words. This is what is best for the king. I do not see any medication other than the one with the bull on his banner. There is no sacrifice the

[753] Here, both Vashatkara and Omkara are proper names.

great-souled one[754] loves more than a horse sacrifice. Therefore, for the king's sake, let all of us perform this extremely difficult sacrifice." After Kardama had said this, the idea appealed to all the bulls among the brahmanas, that they should perform a sacrifice to worship Rudra. Samvarta's disciple was the royal sage, who was the destroyer of enemy cities. He was famous as Marutta and he made the arrangements for the sacrifice. Near Budha's hermitage, this great sacrifice took place. Those immensely illustrious ones sought to greatly satisfy Rudra. When the sacrifice was over, Umapati was filled with great delight. He told all the brahmanas the following about Ila. "O supreme among brahmanas! I am delighted with your devotion and this horse sacrifice. What can I do that is agreeable and auspicious for the lord of Bahlika?" When the lord of the gods said this, the brahmanas controlled themselves and replied, "Show your favours and let Ila be a man, as he used to be." Pleased, Rudra again conferred manhood on the extremely energetic Ila and having given him this, he vanished. When the horse sacrifice was over and Hara could no longer be seen, all the far-sighted brahmanas returned to wherever they had come from. The king abandoned Bahlika. In the excellent middle part of the country, he populated the city of Pratishthana,[755] which brought him fame. Shashabindu, the destroyer of enemy cities, was the king of Bahlika. Ila, Prajapati's powerful son, was the king in Pratishthana. In due course, Ila obtained Brahma's supreme world and Ila's son, Pururava, became the king in Pratishthana. O bulls among men! Such are the powers of a horse sacrifice. Someone who was a woman became a man, something that is extremely difficult to achieve.'

Chapter 7(82)

Kakutstha recounted this to his infinitely radiant brothers. He again addressed Lakshmana in words that were filled with

[754] Shiva.

[755] Identified as Jhusi, near Prayaga.

dharma. 'O Lakshmana! Vasishtha, Vamadeva, Jabali, Kashyapa and all the other foremost brahmanas—summon them, consult with them and place them at the forefront for a horse sacrifice. I will worship and release a horse that possesses qualities.' Hearing the words spoken by Raghava, the one who was swift in his valour summoned all the brahmanas and made them meet Raghava. Raghava saw those extremely invincible ones, who were like gods. He worshipped at their feet and they pronounced benedictions on him. Raghava joined his hands in salutation before those excellent brahmanas and spoke to them about the horse sacrifice, in words that were filled with dharma. Those foremost brahmanas heard those extraordinary words about the horse sacrifice and were extremely happy. Discerning their views, Rama told Lakshmana, 'O mighty-armed one! Send for the great-souled Sugriva. Let the fortunate one quickly come here with the many great apes who seek refuge with him and enjoy the excellent sacrifice. O mighty-armed one! Let Vibhishana, light in his valour, come to the horse sacrifice, surrounded by many rakshasas who can travel anywhere at will. O tiger among men! Let the kings who wish to bring me pleasure swiftly come to the sacrificial arena, with their followers. O Lakshmana! There are brahmanas, devoted to dharma, who are in the kingdom.[756] Invite all of them to the horse sacrifice. O mighty-armed one! There are rishis who are stores of austerities and maharshis who are in the kingdom. Invite them, with their wives. O mighty-armed one! Issue instructions for a large sacrificial ground being prepared on the banks of the Gomatee, in the Naimisha forest. That is an exceedingly sacred spot. O immensely strong one! In advance, let one hundred thousand vehicles with beautiful rice[757] and ten thousand vehicles with sesamum and black gram[758] be despatched. Let the immensely intelligent Bharata proceed in advance, with many crores of gold and many hundreds of silver.[759]

[756] This requires explanation. There are ascetics who have left for the forest. Technically, those are outside the kingdom. Those who are in the kingdom are thus in the householder stage (garhasthya).

[757] Beautiful in the sense of being whole and not having cracked.

[758] *Mudga.*

[759] Meaning coins.

Let there be shops along all the roads, dancers and actors, merchants, the young and the old, controlled brahmanas, skilled artisans and learned craftsmen. Let all my mothers and the princes who are in the inner quarters leave. For the sake of being consecrated in the sacrifice, let a golden image of my wife be prepared.[760] Let the immensely intelligent Bharata leave in advance.'

Chapter 7(83)

Bharata's elder brother made everyone leave in advance. He then released a black horse that possessed all the qualities. He engaged Lakshmana and the officiating priests to leave with the horse. With his soldiers, Kakutstha followed it towards Naimisha. The mighty-armed one saw the extremely wonderful sacrificial arena. The prosperous one obtained great delight and said, 'Let all the kings reside in Naimisha.' Rama was honoured and honoured back those who had assembled from all the kingdoms. The immensely radiant, best among men, instructed that all those great-souled kings and their followers should be presented with extremely expensive gifts. With Shatrughna,[761] he quickly engaged Bharata to offer food, drinks and garments to those great-souled ones and their followers. With Sugriva, the great-souled apes were engaged in bowing down to all the brahmanas and serving them. Vibhishana was surrounded by many rakshasas wearing garlands. Like a servant, he presented himself before the rishis, fierce in their austerities. In this way, the well-arranged horse sacrifice commenced. Lakshmana was engaged to protect and tend to the horse. At the great-souled one's horse sacrifice, no words other than the following were heard. 'Do not stop giving until the seekers are satisfied.' The apes and rakshasas were seen to give them everything. At the king's excellent sacrifice, there was no one who was dirty, distressed, diseased or thin. It was surrounded by happy and healthy people. There were great-souled

[760] A sacred task must always be performed with one's wife.

[761] Shatrughna naturally returned for the sacrifice.

sages who had lived for a long time. They said, 'We have not seen a sacrifice like this, with its flood of gifts. Silver, gold, jewels and garments are being incessantly given and no end can be seen to this. We have not seen anything like this, at sacrifices by Shakra, Soma, Yama or Varuna.' This is what the stores of austerities said. There were apes everywhere. There were rakshasas everywhere. They could be seen, their hands laden with garments, riches and objects of desire. The sacrifice of the lion among kings was like this, with all the qualities. Undiminished, it continued for more than a year.

Chapter 7(84)

While that extremely wonderful sacrifice was being conducted, with his disciples, Valmiki, bull among sages, swiftly arrived there. He saw that sacrifice, which was almost divine and was extraordinary to behold. He went to the secluded spot where the rishis were residing in their auspicious cottages. He told his disciples, 'Both of you[762] control yourselves and go to the place where the sacrifice is being held. Filled with great delight, chant the entire Ramayana *kavya*[763] in the sacred residences of the rishis, the abodes of the brahmanas, the paths, the royal roads, the houses of the kings and the gate of Rama's mansion, where the rituals are being held. In particular, sing it before the officiating priests. There are many kinds of succulent fruit from the best of mountains. Eat and taste them and then sing. O children! If you eat those fruit, you will not be exhausted. Eat the extremely tasty roots from the city. King Rama is seated amidst the rishis. On hearing the sound, if he summons you, sing and make him hear it too. Earlier, I have instructed you about the different segments I have measured out. Filled with joy, sing twenty *sargas*[764] every day. You must not be

[762] Lava and Kusha.

[763] A long poem.

[764] A sarga is a section. Since we are later told that the Valmiki Ramayana has 500 sargas, one can deduce that a sarga has roughly fifty shlokas. Therefore, sarga roughly corresponds to a chapter (*adhyaya*).

greedy and desire the slightest bit of riches. What use have those who live in hermitages, surviving on fruits and roots, for riches?[765] If Kakutstha asks you whose sons you are, tell the king that you are Valmiki's disciples. These strings[766] are extremely melodious and you have been instructed about the positions.[767] Without any worries, sing in extremely melodious and sweet tones. Sing right from the beginning and do not ignore the king. Following dharma, the king is the father of all creatures. Be attentive and cheerful. From tomorrow morning, sing the sweet songs, observing rhythm and metre.' The sage Prachetas[768] instructed them in these and many other ways. After this, the immensely illustrious and extremely powerful Valmiki became silent. Those two princes placed the wonderful and auspicious words uttered by the rishi in their hearts. Eager, they happily slept during the night, like the two Ashvins instructed by Bhargava's[769] polished teaching.

Chapter 7(85)

When the night was over, those two bathed in the morning and offered oblations to the fire. As the rishi had instructed them earlier, they first sung in those respective places. Kakutstha heard them sing in spots that their preceptor had instructed them about. They sung in those melodious tones and such a recital had never been heard before. It had been composed in many different segments and was full of rhythm and metre. Hearing this from the two children, Raghava was filled with curiosity. In between the tasks, the king, tiger among men, summoned the great sages, the kings, the learned ones, the merchants, the reciters of ancient accounts, those who were accomplished in the use of sounds and aged brahmanas. When all of them had assembled, he summoned

[765] Do not accept any riches as a reward for the singing.

[766] Of the musical instruments, the veena.

[767] Of the chords.

[768] Valmiki was the son of Prachetas, one of the Prajapatis.

[769] Shukracharya's.

the two singers. The large number of delighted rishis and the immensely energetic kings seemed to drink up the king and the two singers with their eyes. They told each other, 'All of them are similar. The two are like Rama and it is as if they are his mirror images. Had they not had matted hair and had they not been attired in bark, we would not have discerned any difference between the two singers and Raghava.' Hearing this conversation, which caused delight, the two sons of the sage[770] started to sing. The sweet and superhuman singing, like that of the gandharvas, commenced. The singing was so rich that none of the listeners were content. It started at the beginning, with the first sarga, about the sighting of Narada. They continued singing the other sargas, until twenty had been completed. When it was afternoon, Raghava, devoted to his brother, spoke to Bharata. 'We have heard twenty sargas. O Kakutstha! Quickly give eighteen thousand gold coins to the two great-souled ones. They are children and their efforts should not be in vain.' Kusha and Lava did not accept the gold that was given to them. Surprised, those two great-souled ones asked, 'What will we do with these? We are residents of the forest and survive on wild roots and fruits. In the forest, what will we do with gold and silver?' When they said this, all the listeners and Rama were curious and extremely surprised. Extremely eager to hear the learned recital of the kavya, Rama asked those two immensely energetic sons of a sage. 'O great-souled ones! How long is this kavya? How long has it been in existence? Who is the composer of this great kavya? Where does that bull among sages dwell?' When Raghava asked this, the sons of the sage replied, 'The illustrious Valmiki is the composer and he obtained this treasure through a sacrifice. He instructed us, so that we could recite this account to you, in its entirety. O Indra among kings! Including the beginning, it has five hundred sargas. O king! It has all the good and bad things about your birth and life. O king! O maharatha! If your thoughts are inclined towards hearing it, where there are gaps in the sacrifice, hear it from me and my younger brother.'[771] Rama agreed to this. Taking their leave

[770] Lava and Kusha.

[771] Thus, this reply is by Kusha.

of Raghava, they happily went to the spot where the bull among sages was residing. With the sages and the great-souled kings, Rama heard the sweet singing and went to the arena where the rituals were being performed.

Chapter 7(86)

With the sages, the kings and the apes, Rama heard that extremely wonderful song for several days. Through the song,[772] he got to know that Lava and Kusha were Sita's sons. In the midst of the courtiers, Rama spoke these words.[773] 'Go to the presence of the infinitely illustrious one[774] and tell him my words. If she is pure in conduct and if the great sage imagines her to be devoid of sin, then let her establish her purity. Go and ascertain whether the sage is comfortable with this and also find out Sita's wishes. After this, to assure me, return quickly and tell me. Tomorrow morning, for the sake of purifying herself and me, let Maithilee, Janaka's daughter, take a pledge in the midst of the courtiers.' Hearing Raghava's extremely extraordinary words, the messengers quickly went to the spot where the bull among sages was residing. The messengers prostrated themselves before the great-souled one, blazing in his infinite splendour. They repeated Rama's gentle and sweet words. Hearing what they said and ascertaining what was in Rama's mind, the extremely energetic sage replied in these words. 'O fortunate ones! It will be that way and Raghava will be satisfied. Sita will do that. For a woman, a husband is the divinity.' Thus addressed by the sage, all of Rama's greatly energetic messengers returned to Raghava, assured him, and told him all the sage's words. On hearing the great-souled one's words, Kakutstha was delighted. He spoke to the rishis and kings who were assembled there. 'O illustrious ones! Come with your disciples. O kings! Come

[772] The 'Uttara Kanda' part.

[773] To messengers.

[774] Valmiki.

with your followers. Let all the others who desire it also come and see Sita take the pledge.' Hearing the words of the great-souled Raghava, there were loud words of praise from all the best among rishis. The great-souled kings applauded Raghava. 'O best among men! Other than you, no one else on earth could have said this.' Having made up his mind about what would happen the next day, the slayer of enemies gave everyone permission to leave.

Chapter 7(87)

When night was over, the king, Raghava, went to the sacrificial ground and summoned all the immensely energetic rishis. Vasistha, Vamadeva, Jabali, Kashyapa, Vishvamitra, Dirghatapa, the great ascetic Durvasa, Agastya, Bhargava, Shakti, Vamana, Markandeya, the great ascetic Moudgalya, Bhargava Chyavana, Shatananda, who knew about dharma, the energetic Bharadvaja, Suprabha, Agni's son, many other sages who were firm in their vows and all the kings who were tigers among men assembled. Filled with curiosity, the extremely valiant rakshasas and the immensely strong apes—all these great-souled ones also assembled. Kshatriyas, vaishyas and thousands of shudras—all of them also assembled, to see Sita take the pledge. All of them came there and were like mountains made out of stone.

They heard the sage coming quickly, accompanied by Sita. With her face cast downwards, Sita followed the rishi at the rear. Her voice choked with tears and in her mind, she joined her hands in salutation before Rama. The beautiful one could be seen to advance, following the brahmana. Sita was behind Valmiki and loud roars of praise arose. There were sounds of uproar everywhere. On seeing her immersed in this great misery, they were overcome by grief. Some praised Rama. Others praised Sita. There were yet others who praised both of them. The bull among sages entered in the midst of that crowd of people, with Sita as his companion. Valmiki spoke to Raghava. 'O Dasharatha's son! This is Sita. She is excellent in her vows and follows dharma. Without having committed a crime, she was abandoned near my hermitage. O Rama! O one who is great in vows! That was because you were scared about people censuring you. You should grant your permission, so that Sita can establish your trust in her. These twins were born as Janakee's sons. These invincible ones are your sons. I am telling you this truthfully. O descendant of the Raghava lineage! I am the tenth son of Prachetas. I do not remember having uttered a falsehood. These are your sons. I have performed austerities for many thousands of years. If Maithilee isn't innocent, I will not reap the fruits of those. O Raghava! Had I not known Sita to be pure through my five senses and through my mind as the sixth, I would not have accepted her near that waterfall in the mountain. She is pure in conduct. She is devoid of sin. Her husband is her divinity. However, you are scared because people condemned you. She will instil confidence in you.'

Chapter 7(88)

When Valmiki said this, Raghava replied with his hands in salutation, noticing the one with the complexion of a goddess in the midst of the assembly. 'O greatly fortunate one! O one who knows about dharma! It is indeed exactly as you have stated it. O brahmana! I have confidence in your unblemished words. In the presence of the gods, Vaidehi had instilled confidence in me earlier. O brahmana! I know that she is innocent. However, scared because of the condemnation of the people, I abandoned Sita. You should pardon me. I know the twins who have been born, Lava and Kusha, are my sons. However, I will be delighted if Maithilee establishes her purity in the midst of the world.' Getting to know about Rama's intention, all the supreme gods, with the grandfather at the forefront, assembled. The Adityas, the Vasus, the Rudras, the Vishvadevas, the large number of Maruts, the Ashvins, the rishis, the gandharvas, the large number of apsaras, the Sadhyas, all the gods and all the supreme rishis arrived. An auspicious, sacred and pleasant breeze started to blow, with a divine fragrance, and delighted the hearts of all the large numbers of best among the gods. Controlled, the men from all the kingdoms saw this wonderful and unthinkable event and thought that it was like during the former krita yuga.

Sita was dressed in an ochre garment. Her face was cast downwards. On seeing that all of them had assembled, she joined her hands in salutation and said, 'If I have not thought of anyone other than Raghava in my mind, then let the goddess earth open up a chasm for me.' When Vaidehi took this pledge, something extraordinary occurred. A divine and excellent throne arose from the middle of the earth. Infinitely valiant serpents held it up on their hoods. It was divine, with a celestial form, and was ornamented with every kind of jewel. The goddess earth was seated on it and engulfed Maithilee in her arms. Welcoming and honouring her, she made her sit on that throne. Seated on that throne, without any kind of obstruction, Sita started to enter the earth and a downpour of flowers showered down from the sky. Suddenly, extremely loud words of praise arose from among the gods. 'O Sita! You are to be praised. Such is your good conduct.' Stationed in the sky, the gods uttered many such words. Cheerful in their hearts on seeing Sita enter, they said this. All the sages and the tigers among kings who were in the sacrificial ground were greatly surprised. So were all the mobile and immobile objects in the sky and on earth, the immensely gigantic danavas and the lords of the serpents who were in patala. Some roared in joy. Some were immersed in thought. Some glanced towards Rama. The minds of some were on Sita. For a while, on seeing Sita enter, all those assembled ones from the world were confounded.

Chapter 7(89)

When the sacrifice was over, Rama was extremely distressed. Unable to see Vaidehi, he thought that the universe was empty. He was overcome by great grief and could not find any peace in his mind. He gave loads of riches to all the kings, the bears, the apes, the rakshasas, the large crowds of people and the best among brahmanas and gave them leave to depart. The lotus-eyed Rama gave all of them leave. With Sita in his heart, he entered Ayodhya. The descendant of the Raghu lineage said, 'After Sita, I will not take another wife.' From one sacrifice to another sacrifice, the golden image of Janakee represented his wife. He performed vajapeya, with ten times as many qualities, and gave away a lot of gold.[775] The prosperous one performed many other great sacrifices—agnishtoma, *atiratra* and *gosava* and gave away a lot of dakshina. In this way, the great-souled Raghava ruled over the kingdom for a very long period of time, carefully ensuring dharma. The bears, apes and rakshasas always obeyed Rama's command. From one day to another day, Raghava delighted all the kings. The rain god showered down at the right time. The directions were clear and sparkled. The city and the countryside were full of large numbers of people who were happy and healthy. No one died at the wrong time. Creatures did not suffer from disease. As long as Rama ruled over the kingdom, there were no acts of adharma. After a long period of time had passed, surrounded by her sons and grandsons, Rama's illustrious mother followed the dharma of time. Sumitra and the illustrious Kaikeyee followed her. Having performed many acts of dharma, they went to heaven. All of them were established in heaven, with King Dasharatha. Those immensely fortunate ones met him and obtained the fruits of performing dharma together. Especially addressed to his mothers, from time to time, Rama gave away a lot of gifts to brahmanas and ascetics. Addressed to his ancestors, he performed many extremely difficult sacrifices. Rama, with dharma in his soul, did this to enhance the prosperity of the gods and the ancestors.

Chapter 7(90)

After some time, Yudhajit, the king of Kekaya, sent his own preceptor to the great-souled Raghava. This infinitely radiant

[775] The vajapeya sacrifice has ten times the qualities of an ashvamedha sacrifice.

brahmana rishi, Gargya, was the son of Angiras. He came with a gift of ten thousand excellent horses, offered as a token of affection. The king also sent Rama blankets, colourful jewels, excellent garments and many ornaments. Raghava heard that maharshi Gargya had come. He was the beloved messenger, of Ashvapati, his maternal uncle.[776] Kakutstha arose and with his followers, advanced one krosha to honour Gargya and accept those riches. He affectionately asked all the relevant questions about the welfare of his maternal uncle. After the immensely fortunate one had seated himself, Rama started to ask, 'O illustrious one! What are the words spoken by my maternal uncle, as a result of which, you have come here? You are the best among those who know the use of words and you have come here, like Brihaspati himself.' Hearing the words spoken by Rama, the brahmana rishi started to tell Raghava about the task at hand in detail and it was extraordinary. 'O mighty-armed one! O bull among men! Your maternal uncle, Yudhajit,[777] has spoken these words. If it appeals to you, listen to them affectionately. The kingdom of the gandharvas is adorned with roots and fruits. It is an extremely beautiful country and is located on both sides of the Sindhu. The gandharvas, armed with weapons and accomplished in fighting, protect it. There are three crores of the immensely strong ones and those brave ones are the sons of Shailusha. O Kakutstha! O mighty-armed one! If the idea appeals to you, control yourself, conquer those two auspicious gandharva cities and populate them. There is no one else who can be the refuge for those two extremely beautiful dominions. O mighty-armed one! I am not telling you a lie.'

Hearing these words, Raghava was pleased with the maharshi and with his maternal uncle. He looked towards Bharata and spoke words of agreement. Delighted, Raghava joined his hands in salutation before the brahmana and said, 'O brahmana rishi! These two princes will conquer that country. Bharata has two brave sons, Taksha and Pushkala. They will attentively follow

[776] Bharata's maternal uncle was Ashvapati, by extension, Rama's maternal uncle. Yudhajit was Ashvapati's son.

[777] Since Yudhajit is not the maternal uncle, this is a misstatement.

dharma and protect my maternal uncle well. Placing Bharata at the forefront, these two princes and their forces and followers will slay the sons of the gandharva and populate those two cities. The one who is extremely devoted to dharma[778] will instate his two sons in those two excellent cities and again return to my presence.' Having told the brahmana rishi this, he commanded Bharata, his forces and his followers, and consecrated those two princes. At the time of an agreeable nakshatra, they placed the son of Angiras at the forefront. With the soldiers and the two princes, Bharata departed. As they left the city, the soldiers seemed to be led by Shakra. They were invincible to the gods and the asuras and followed Raghava[779] at some distance. Creatures that fed on flesh and extremely large rakshasas also followed Bharata, thirsty for blood. There were many extremely terrible creatures at the front, those that subsisted on flesh. Thousands of them wished to eat the flesh of the sons of the gandharva. Many thousands of lions, tigers, jackals and birds that roamed in the sky preceded the army at the front. Not suffering from any disease, the army spent one and a half months along the route. They then reached Kekaya, full of happy and healthy people.

Chapter 7(91)

The lord of Kekaya heard that Bharata had come as the commander. With Gargya, Yudhajit was filled with great delight. With a large crowd of people, Yudhajit emerged. He swiftly advanced against the gandharvas, who were like the gods in their forms. Light in their valour, Bharata and Yudhajit met. With their forces and foot soldiers, they reached the city of the gandharvas. Hearing that Bharata had arrived, the immensely brave gandharvas assembled, desiring to fight. They roared in every direction. A tumultuous battle that made the body hair

[778] Meaning Bharata.

[779] Bharata.

stand up commenced. It was extremely terrible and continued for seven nights, but neither side could defeat the other. There was an extremely terrible weapon made out of black iron and it was named Samvarta. Enraged, Bharata, Rama's younger brother, invoked it against the gandharvas. Shattered by Samvarta, they were bound in the nooses of death. In an instant, three crores of great-souled ones were struck. The residents of heaven could not remember a strike which was this terrible. In an instant, those great-souled ones were reduced to this state. Bharata, Kaikeyee's son, slew those brave ones and populated two excellent and prosperous cities there. Taksha became the king of Takshashila and Pushkara[780] of Pushkaravata. These were two beautiful cities in the land of Gandhara, in the dominion of the gandharvas. They were full of heaps of jewels and adorned with groves. They were extensive in their qualities and sought to rival each other. Both of these were the best among beautiful places and unblemished in their conduct. There were well-laid-out shops and filled with gardens and vehicles. Both these beautiful and excellent cities were large and splendid. There were lofty, beautiful and excellent houses, similar to each other in complexion. There were large temples and these made the beautiful cities even more beautiful. Bharata, Raghava's younger brother, resided there for five years. Then Kaikeyee's mighty-armed son returned to Ayodhya again. Bharata greeted the great-souled Raghava, who was like another Dharma, just as Vasava greets the prosperous Brahma. He told him the excellent account about the gandharvas being killed and the populating of that country. Hearing this, Raghava was delighted.

Chapter 7(92)

Hearing this, with his brothers, Raghava was delighted. Raghava addressed his brother in these extraordinary words. 'O Soumitri! These two sons of yours, Angada and Chandraketu,

[780] Pushkara is the same as Pushkala.

are accomplished in dharma. They are firm in wielding bows and deserve kingdoms. I will consecrate them in virtuous and beautiful kingdoms that are appropriate, without any obstructions. Let these two archers find pleasure there. They should not suffer from any other king there. Nor should the hermitages there be destroyed. O amiable one! Search for such a country, so that we do not commit a crime.' Thus addressed by Rama, Bharata replied, 'There is the land of Karapatha. It is beautiful and without any disease. Instate the great-souled Angada in that city. Instate Chandraketu in beautiful Chandrakanta, which is also without disease.' Raghava accepted the words that Bharata had spoken. He brought that country under his subjugation and instated Angada there. The beautiful city of Angadiya was populated by Angada. It was beautiful and was protected by Rama, who was unblemished in his deeds. Chandraketu populated the Malla kingdom[781] with wrestlers. It was divine, like a city in heaven and became famous by the name of Chandrakanta. Rama, Bharata and Lakshmana were filled with great delight. They consecrated the princes and the two of them left with their forces and followers. Angada occupied the territory towards the west and Chandraketu towards the north. Soumitri followed Angada and Bharata followed Chandraketu, to help them along the flanks. Lakshmana resided in Angadiya for one year. When his invincible son was instated, he returned again to Ayodhya. Bharata resided there for more than a year. He then returned to Ayodhya, near Rama's feet. Both of them, Soumitri and Bharata, served at Rama's feet. Both of them were exceedingly devoted to dharma. Though time passed, because of their affection, they did not discern it. In this way, they spent ten thousand years, attentively pursuing dharma and always engaged in tasks meant for the citizens. Fulfilled in their minds, they spent this time, established along the path of supreme dharma and surrounded by prosperity. The three of them were prosperous and blazed in their energy. They were like three fires at virtuous sacrifices, when oblations had been offered into the fire.

[781] The Malla kingdom was in between Kosala and Videha. The word *malla* means wrestler or boxer.

Chapter 7(93)

Rama was established along the path of dharma. After some time, Time[782] arrived at the king's gate, adopting the form of an ascetic. He addressed the patient and illustrious Lakshmana in these words. 'Go and tell the king that I have come here for an important task. I am the messenger of Atibala, the infinitely energetic maharshi. O immensely strong one! Because of something that needs to be done, I have come here to see Rama.' Hearing his words, Soumitri hurried and went and told Rama what the ascetic had urged. 'O king! O immensely radiant one! Because of your pursuit of dharma, may you be triumphant in both the worlds.[783] An ascetic's messenger, like the sun in radiance, has come here to meet you.' Hearing the words that Lakshmana had uttered, Rama replied, 'O son![784] Let the immensely energetic ascetic messenger, who will convey the words, enter.' Soumitri assented and made the sage enter. He seemed to blaze in his energy and burn down with his rays. Radiant in his own energy, he approached the best among the Raghu lineage. The rishi spoke these sweet words to Raghava. 'May you prosper.' The immensely energetic one was in front of him and Rama worshipped him with arghya. Having given him that, he eagerly started to ask about his welfare. Rama, supreme among eloquent ones, asked about his welfare. The immensely illustrious one then sat down on a divine and golden seat. Rama said, 'O great sage! Welcome. Let me know about the message that has brought you here as a messenger.' Urged thus by the lion among kings, the sage spoke the following words. 'This can only be uttered between the two of us. Anyone who witnesses these words has to be killed. O Raghava! Anyone who hears or sees must be killed. It is only then that I will tell you about the words of the best among sages.' Rama pledged this and told Lakshmana, 'O mighty-armed one! Send the doorkeeper away and remain at the door. O Soumitri! Anyone who hears or sees the conversation between the two of us, me and the

[782] *Kala,* also Death or Destiny.

[783] This world and the world hereafter.

[784] The word used is tata.

rishi, will be killed.' Thus, Kakutstha engaged Lakshmana at the door. Raghava then told the sage, 'Speak. Attentively, tell me about the words spoken by the learned one. Do not worry. It will remain only in my heart.'

Chapter 7(94)

'O Rama! O mighty-armed one! Hear the reason why I have come here. O immensely strong one! I have been sent by the grandfather of the gods. O destroyer of enemy cities! O brave one! I am your eldest son, created out of your own maya. I am the Destroyer who gathers up everything. O mighty-armed one! The illustrious grandfather, the lord and master of all the worlds, has said that it is time for you to protect your own world. "In earlier times, when all the worlds were drawn in, you used your own maya to lie down on the great ocean.[785] In those ancient times, I was born from you. You used your maya to generate the handsome serpent Ananta who lies down in the water and two extremely strong creatures. They were Madhu and Kaitabha and their bones covered everything and constituted mountains. The earth was formed from their fat. I was also born from a divine lotus, as resplendent as the sun, originating in your navel. You said that creation was my task and invested everything in me. O lord of the universe! Having taken up the burden invested on me, I worshipped you. Because you are more energetic than me, I asked you to protect creatures. Since that time, for the sake of protecting all creatures, you gave given up your eternal and invincible form and assumed the form of Vishnu. Having been born as Aditya's valiant son, you delighted your brothers[786] and helped them and the worlds in every possible way. O supreme in the universe! Terrified and desiring Ravana's death, they came to you and you made up your mind to become human. You have resided here for eleven thousand years. Now destiny requires you

[785] These are Brahma's words, being repeated.

[786] The Adityas, the gods.

to return to your own ancient city. It is only because of your mental powers that you became the son of a human and have spent a full lifespan. O best among excellent men! It is time for you to return to our presence." O great king! O brave one! O fortunate one! If you still desire to rule over the subjects, reside here. I have conveyed the grandfather's words. O Raghava! Alternatively, conquer that wish and become Vishnu, the protector of the world of the gods. Let the gods be devoid of their anxiety.' He heard the words spoken by the grandfather, as repeated by Time. Raghava laughed and addressed the one who destroys everything in the following words. 'I have heard the extremely wonderful words of the god of the gods. I am greatly delighted that you have happened to come here. O fortunate one! I will go where you have come from. There is nothing to think about, since the thought had already occurred to me. I am under the control of the gods and I must do everything that they want. O one who destroys everything! What the grandfather has mentioned, will happen.'

Chapter 7(95)

While the two were conversing in this way, the illustrious rishi, Durvasa, arrived at the royal gate, desiring to see Rama. The excellent rishi approached Soumitri and said, 'Before my purpose is defeated, quickly make me see Rama.' Hearing the sage's words, Lakshmana, the slayer of enemy heroes, greeted the great-souled one and addressed him in these words. 'O illustrious one! Tell me about the task. What is the purpose? What can I do? O brahmana! Raghava will eagerly do it. Please wait for a while.' Hearing these words, the tiger among rishis became polluted with rage. As if burning him down his eyes, he addressed Lakshmana in these words. 'O Soumitri! Present me before Rama this very instant. Otherwise, I will curse the kingdom, the city, you and Raghava. O Soumitri! I will not spare Bharata's sons and yours. I am incapable of restraining the rage in my heart any longer.' The great-souled one's words were terrible. He thought about those words in his mind and determined what he should do. 'Let all creatures not be destroyed. One person's death is superior.' Having decided this, he went and told Raghava. Hearing Lakshmana's words, Rama gave Time permission to leave. The king swiftly emerged and saw Atri's son. He greeted the great-souled one, who seemed to blaze in his energy. Kakutstha joined his hands in salutation and asked, 'What needs to be done?' The lord, best among sages, heard the words Raghava had spoken. Durvasa replied, 'O Rama! O one who is devoted to dharma! Listen. O Raghava! My one thousand years are over today.[787] O unblemished one! Therefore, I wish to eat whatever has been cooked by you.' Hearing his words, Rama was filled with great delight. He offered the best among sages whatever had been cooked. The best among sages ate the food, which was like amrita. 'O Rama! This is virtuous.' Having said this, he returned to his own hermitage. When the immensely energetic one had gone, Raghava was pleased in his mind. However, remembering the words uttered by Time, he was filled with sorrow. Remembering those terrible words, he was greatly tormented by grief. He was distressed in his mind. With his face cast downwards, he was incapable of saying anything. Raghava thought about the words spoken by Time. The immensely illustrious one said, 'There is no other way', and was silent.

Chapter 7(96)

Lakshmana saw that the miserable Raghava's face was cast downwards, like the moon when it is eclipsed. He cheerfully addressed him in sweet words. 'O mighty-armed one! You should not be tormented on my account. The progress of destiny is like this and has been ordained earlier. O amiable one! Slay me without hesitation and fulfil your pledge. O Kakutstha! Men who do not keep their promises go to hell. O great king! O Raghava! If you are pleased with me and if you are favourably disposed towards

[787] Durvasa had taken a vow not to eat for one thousand years.

me, slay me without any hesitation. Make dharma flourish.' When Lakshmana said this, Rama's senses were in a whirl. He summoned his ministers and his priest. In their midst, the lord of men recounted what had happened—the pledge before the ascetic and Durvasa's arrival. Hearing this, all the ministers looked towards the preceptor. The greatly energetic Vasishtha spoke these words. 'O mighty-armed one! I had already foreseen this incident that makes the body hair stand up. O Rama! You will be separated from the immensely illustrious Lakshmana. Destiny is powerful. Do not make your pledge false. If pledges are destroyed, dharma also heads towards destruction. When dharma is destroyed, there is no doubt that everything in the three worlds, mobile and immobile objects and gods and rishis, are also destroyed. O tiger among men! For the sake of protecting the three worlds, kill Lakshmana today and make the universe safe.' In the midst of that assembly of courtiers, Rama heard these words, which were full of dharma and artha. He told Lakshmana, 'O Soumitri! Let there not be a catastrophe. Therefore, I am casting you away. Virtuous ones have decreed that killing and abandoning are both regarded as the same.' Rama spoke these words, his eyes overflowing with tears. Lakshmana quickly left and entered his own residence. He went to the Sarayu, joined his hands in salutation and touched the water. He controlled all the flows in his body and did not release his breaths. When he stopped breathing, Shakra, large numbers of apsaras, the gods and large numbers of rishis showered down flowers. Unseen by all men, Shakra seized the immensely strong Lakshmana and made him enter heaven in his physical body. The supreme among the gods were delighted that Vishnu's fourth part had arrived. Happy and full of joy, with the rishis, they worshipped him.

Chapter 7(97)

Having let Lakshmana go, Rama was overwhelmed by sorrow and grief. He told the priest, the ministers and the merchants, 'Today, I will consecrate Bharata, who is devoted to dharma, in the kingdom. Let the brave one be the lord of Ayodhya. After that, I will leave for the forest. Before time passes, let all the arrangements be made. Today, I will go to the destination that Lakshmana has gone to.' Hearing the words spoken by Raghava, all the ordinary subjects were severely afflicted. They bowed their heads down on the ground. It was as if they had lost their lives. On hearing what Rama had said, Bharata also lost his senses. He condemned the kingdom and told Raghava, 'O king! O descendant of the Raghu lineage! I am taking a pledge on the truth. Without you, I do not desire the world of heaven, or the kingdom. O king! O lord of men! Instate Kusha and Lava. Let the brave Kusha rule Kosala and Lava rule the north.[788] Let messengers who are swift in their valour go to Shatrughna. Let them tell him about our imminent departure for heaven and ask him to come here.' Hearing what Bharata had said, all the citizens were miserable and tormented. Their faces were downcast. On seeing this, Vasishtha spoke these words. 'O Rama! O child! Behold the people on earth. They are overcome by ordinary sentiments. Knowing what they desire, you should not do something that is disagreeable to them.' Hearing Vasishtha's words, he made those ordinary people rise up. Kakutstha asked all of them, 'What shall I do?' All the ordinary people addressed Rama in these words. 'O Rama! We will go wherever you go. This is our supreme delight. In our view, this is our supreme dharma. We are firm in following you. Our hearts will always be satisfied at that. O Kakutstha! If you have affection for the citizens and if you are extremely fond of them, let them proceed along the same virtuous path as you, with their sons and wives. O lord! If you do not wish to abandon us, take us with you, to the forest for asceticism, to impenetrable places, to rivers and to oceans.' Hearing their determination, he considered what should be done. Since the devotion of the citizens was firm, he told them that he agreed. Having decided this, on that very day, Raghava instated the brave Kusha in Kosala and Lava in the north. The great-souled one consecrated Kusha and Lava. He gave each of them one thousand chariots, thirty thousand elephants, ten thousand horses and riches. They were surrounded by many jewels

[788] That is, North Kosala.

and riches and happy and healthy people. Having been consecrated, those two brave ones left for their own cities. The great-souled one then sent a messenger to Shatrughna.

Chapter 7(98)

Urged by Rama's words, the messenger, light in his valour, swiftly left for Madhura and did not spend any nights during the journey.[789] He reached Madhura in three days and nights and told Shatrughna everything about what had transpired—the abandonment of Lakshmana, Raghava's pledge, the consecration of the two sons and the decision of the citizens to follow. The intelligent Rama had created a beautiful city for Kusha to the north of the Vindhya mountains and it was named Kushavati. The beautiful city that was referred to as Shravati[790] was for Lava. Leaving Ayodhya empty, Bharata intended to follow Raghava. He reported all this to the great-souled Shatrughna. The messenger stopped and added, 'O king! Hurry.' The news was terrible and the destruction of the lineage was nigh. Hearing this, the descendant of the Raghu lineage summoned the ordinary people and the priest, Kanchana, and told all of them about what had happened. He also said that with his brothers, he too would be destroyed.[791] Therefore, the valiant lord of men instated his two sons. Subahu obtained Madhura and Shatrughati obtained Vaidisha. He divided the forces in Madhura among the two sons. With riches and grain, he established these two kings. He took his leave from the king of Vaidisha, Shatrughati.[792] Alone on a chariot, Raghava left for Ayodhya.

He saw the great-souled one,[793] blazing like a fire. He was attired in a thin silken garment, with the undecaying sages. He

[789] That is, did not waste any time in resting along the way.

[790] Alternatively, Shravasti.

[791] Would die.

[792] Non-Critical versions also mention Subahu of Madhura. In the Critical version, this is left implicit.

[793] Rama.

controlled his senses, joined his hands in salutation and greeted Rama. The one who knew about dharma thought about dharma and spoke these words. 'I have instated my two sons, the warriors of the Raghava lineage. O king! Know that I have made up my mind about following you. Since your command is impossible to cross, please do not say anything contrary. O brave one! You should not abandon me, especially because I am devoted to you.' The descendant of the Raghu lineage realized that he had firmly made up his mind. Agreeing with Shatrughna, Rama spoke words of agreement. When he had finished speaking, innumerable apes, who could assume any form at will, bears and large numbers of rakshasas assembled. Knowing that Rama was about to be destroyed, all the sons of the gods, the sons of the rishis and the sons of the gandharvas also assembled. All of them assembled and greeted Rama. 'O king! O immensely illustrious one! We have come to follow you. O Rama! O bull among men! If you go without taking us, it will be as if you have raised Yama's staff and brought us down.' Hearing the words of the bears, apes and rakshasas, he spoke these sweet and gentle words to Vibhishana. 'O Vibhishana! O Indra among rakshasas! O immensely valiant one! As long as there are subjects, please hold up Lanka.[794] Follow dharma and protect the subjects. Do not say anything back in reply.' After this, Kakutstha spoke to Hanumat. 'You have already made up your mind to remain alive. Do not make that pledge of yours come false. O lord of the apes! As long as my account is spoken about in the world, till then, remain alive and follow your pledge.' Kakutstha Raghava then told all the apes and bears, 'Come with me.'

Chapter 7(99)

When night was over and it was morning, the broad-chested, immensely illustrious and lotus-eyed Rama spoke to the priest. 'Let the fires of agnihotra and vajapeya sacrifices proceed in front,

[794] That is, rule over Lanka.

with the flames blazing because of clarified butter and decorating the large road.' The energetic Vasishtha looked towards everything and ensured that all the rituals connected with the great journey[795] were properly observed. Wearing a silken garment and to the chanting of the name of the brahman, he[796] proceeded along the decorated road, holding some kusha grass in his hand. He said nothing. He did not try to avoid the difficult stretches along the path.[797] Like the blazing sun, he emerged from his house. Extremely controlled, Padma Shri[798] was on Rama's left. The large-eyed Hri[799] was to his right, stationed slightly ahead. Many kinds of arrows and the bow that was used in battles followed Kakutstha. All of these were in embodied form. The Vedas, Savitree, the protector of everything, Omkara, Vashatkara—all of these followed Rama, in the form of brahmanas. The great-souled rishis and all the brahmanas followed Kakutstha and reached the gate to heaven. All the women from the inner quarters followed them, the aged and young female servants and the servants who were eunuchs. Bharata and Shatrughna also proceeded, with those from their inner quarters. With Rama having taken that vow, they also took the same vow as Raghava. All the controlled and great-souled brahmanas were with the agnihotra fire. With their sons and wives, they followed the immensely intelligent Kakutstha. Cheerfully, all the ministers and the array of servants, with their sons and relatives, followed Raghava. All the ordinary people, happy and healthy, surrounded them. Delighted with his qualities, they followed Raghava as he proceeded. All of them were supreme in their happiness and health, and bathed. As all of them followed Rama's vow, a proud tumult arose. No one there was miserable. No one there was ashamed or sad. All of them were happy and delighted. It was extremely extraordinary. The inhabitants of the countryside wished to see the king emerge. They were tormented to see him and all of them followed him. Extremely

795 *Mahaprasthana*, death.

796 Rama.

797 He did not try to avoid stones etc. and seek out the most comfortable stretch of the path.

798 In embodied form. Padma is another name for Lakshmi/Shri, since she is on a lotus.

799 The embodied form of modesty.

controlled, the bears, the apes, the rakshasas and the residents of the city followed him at the rear, filled with great devotion.

Chapter 7(100)

Sarayu, with the sacred waters, flowed in a westward direction. After having travelled for more than half a yojana, the descendant of the Raghu lineage saw the river. At that instant, surrounded by all the gods and the great-souled rishis, Brahma, the grandfather of the worlds, arrived at the spot where Kakutstha had presented himself at the gate to heaven. All of them came to the spot where Kakutstha had presented himself before heaven. They arrived on one hundred crores of celestial vimanas. Flowers showered down. A strong wind started to blow. Hundreds of trumpets blared and gandharvas and apsaras assembled. On foot, Rama approached the waters of the Sarayu. From the sky, the grandfather spoke these words. 'O Vishnu! O fortunate one! O Raghava! Come. It is good fortune that I have met you. Enter with your brothers and with the gods, in your own bodies. Enter your own eternal and great Vaishnavi energy, which is like the sky. O god! You are the refuge of the world. O large-eyed one! With the exception of your own maya, which you have resorted to earlier, there is no one who is capable of knowing you. You cannot be thought of. You are the great being. You are without decay and accumulate everything. O immensely energetic one! As you wish, enter your own body.' Hearing the grandfather's words, the immensely intelligent one made up his mind. In his own body and with his younger brothers, he entered his Vaishnava energy. When the god assumed his form of Vishnu, the gods, the Sadhyas and the large number of Maruts, with Indra and Agni at the forefront, worshipped him. So did the large number of divine rishis, the gandharvas, the apsaras, the birds, the serpents, the yakshas, the daityas, the danavas and the rakshasas. All of them were happy and delighted. All their wishes had come true. Uttering words of praise and without any blemishes, all of them went to heaven.

The immensely energetic Vishnu spoke to the grandfather. 'O one who is good in vows! You should also grant these large numbers of people.[800] All of these spirited ones have followed me, out of affection. They are devoted and you should honour them. For my sake, they have given up their bodies.' Hearing Vishnu's words, Brahma, the lord and preceptor of the worlds, said that all the assembled people could go to the world known as Santanika. 'O Rama! If anyone born as inferior species thinks of you and gives up his life out of devotion, that person will also reside in Santanika. It possesses all the qualities and is only next to Brahma's world. The apes will return to whichever gods they had been born from and so will the bears. The rishis, the serpents and the yakshas will also regain their own portions.' When the lord of the gods said this, they reached the place from where they would leave the earth. Their eyes filled with tears of joy and without any lassitude, they went to the Sarayu. Full of joy, all those creatures submerged themselves in the water. They gave up their bodies as humans and ascended vimanas. Those born as inferior species also approached the waters of the Sarayu. Their forms became divine and celestial. They were as radiant as gods. All mobile and immobile objects also went to the waters of the Sarayu. From those unblemished waters, they went to the world of the gods. There were apes, bears and rakshasas that had been born from the portions of the gods. All of them gave up their bodies in the water and entered their own portions. The preceptor of the worlds and heaven thus ensured that all of them obtained heaven. Thereafter, with the happy and delighted gods, the immensely intelligent one also went to heaven. The Uttara Kanda account, worshipped by Brahma, ends here. It is part of the famous and excellent Ramayana composed by Valmiki.

This ends the Uttara Kanda.

This ends the Valmiki Ramayana.

[800] Entry into heaven.